BRITISH ISLES
POLITICAL MAP

MERIDIAN OF GREENWICH

SHETLAND
Lerwick

ORKNEY
Kirkwall

CAITHNESS

SUTHERLAND

Wick

ROSS AND CROMARTY

NAIRN
MORAY

Inverness

N E S S

SCOTLAND

ABERDEEN

Aberdeen

KINCARDINE

ANGUS

PERTH
KINROSS
Perth

Dundee

FIFE

Kirkcaldy

DUMBARTON
LANARK
STIRLING

Greenock

RENFREW

LOTHIAN
MIDLOTHIAN
LOTHIAN

Edinburgh

Glasgow

BERWICK

AYR
LANARK
PEEBLES

SELKIRK
ROXBURGH

DUMFRIES

Ayr

KIRKCUDBRIGHT

WIGTOWN

NORTHUMBERLAND

South Shields

Newcastle

Sunderland

Carlisle

DURHAM

Middlesbrough

CUMBERLAND

WESTMORLAND

YORKSHIRE

Bradford

York

Blackpool

Preston

Leeds

Hull

LANCASHIRE

Bolton

Huddersfield

FLINTSHIRE

Liverpool

Oldham

Grimsby

Holyhead

Birkenhead

LINCOLNSHIRE

ANGLESEY

Crewe

DENBIGHSHIRE

Manchester

Stoke-on-Trent

Sheffield

NOTTINGHAMSHIRE

Nottingham

CAERNARVON
SHIRE

MERIONETH
SHIRE

SHROPSHIRE
STAFFORDSHIRE

RUTLANDSHIRE

Derby

Leicester

Norwich

MONTGOMERY
SHIRE

Wolverhampton

Birmingham

Coventry

NORFOLK

Great Yarmouth

CARDIGANSHIRE

RADNOR

HEREFORD

Northampton

Cambridge

SUFFOLK

CARMARTHEN

BRECKNOCK
SHIRE

Ipswich

PEMBROKESHIRE

Rhondda

8

GLOUCESTER
SHIRE

9

Oxford

11

ESSEX

Harwich

Swansea

Newport

Luton

10

London

Southend-on-Sea

Cardiff

GLAMORGAN

Bristol

Reading

Croydon

Greenwich

KENT

Canterbury

Dover

Ostend

SOMERSETSHIRE

Southampton

SURREY

Folkestone

Strait of Dover

Calais

Dunkirk

DEVON
SHIRE

Exeter

Bournemouth

HAMPSHIRE

SUSSEX

Hastings

Brighton

Lille

CORNWALL

DORSETSHIRE

Portsmouth

Plymouth

Penzance

Torquay

Dieppe

Amiens

Cherbourg

Channel Islands (BR.)

Le Havre

Rouen

Caen

FRANCE

Paris

N o r t h   S e a

A t l a n t i c   O c e a n

North Channel

Irish Sea

St. George's Channel

English Channel

LONDONDERRY
Londonderry

ANTRIM

DONEGAL

NORTHERN IRELAND

TYRONE

ULSTER

Belfast

DOWN

FERMANAGH

ARMAGH

MONAGHAN

SLIGO

LEITRIM

CAVAN

LOUTH

MAYO

CONNAUGHT

ROSCOMMON

LONGFORD

WESTMEATH

MEATH

REPUBLIC

GALWAY

Galway

OFFALY

KILDARE

Dublin

DUBLIN

CLARE

SHANNON AIRPORT

TIPPERARY

IRELAND

LEINSTER

KILKENNY

CARLOW

WICKLOW

LIMERICK

Limerick

Waterford

WEXFORD

KERRY

Tralee

MUNSTER

CORK

WATERFORD

Killarney

Cork

Cobh

Key to numbered counties
1 · LEICESTERSHIRE
2 · NORTHAMPTONSHIRE
3 · HUNTINGDONSHIRE
4 · CAMBRIDGESHIRE
5 · BEDFORDSHIRE
6 · WARWICKSHIRE
7 · WORCESTERSHIRE
8 · MONMOUTHSHIRE
9 · OXFORDSHIRE
10 · BUCKINGHAMSHIRE
11 · HERTFORDSHIRE
12 · MIDDLESEX

Cartography by RICHARD EDES HARRISON and staff

A History of England
and the Empire-Commonwealth

A History of England

and the Empire-Commonwealth

Fourth Edition

WALTER PHELPS HALL

ROBERT GREENHALGH ALBION
HARVARD UNIVERSITY

JENNIE BARNES POPE

BLAISDELL PUBLISHING COMPANY

A Division of Ginn and Company

WALTHAM, MASSACHUSETTS · TORONTO · LONDON

Preface

"A clear and fresh interpretation of an old and honored theme is the aim of this book." That opening sentence of the original edition in 1937 has proved to be just as true in 1961 in a revision and reappraisal that has left scarcely a page untouched. This apparent anomaly results from the reinterpretations stemming from recent scholarship and from the almost incredible transitions of the mid-twentieth century. The most prominent of the new viewpoints concern the social and economic aspects of the later Middle Ages, the political evolution of the later eighteenth century, and the various stages of overseas expansion.

This fourth edition has been entirely revised, with much new writing, and extended to 1961 by Pope and Albion, with the exception of the new chapter on literature, which was originally written by Hall. In the first edition, ending with the abdication of Edward VIII, the sections on literature were written by Hall throughout and most of the constitutional, military, and naval aspects by Albion and Pope. The period from 1066 through the peace settlement of 1815 was the work of Albion and Pope. The non-institutional pre-Norman account and much of the part since 1815 was originally written by Hall, with extensive collaboration, particularly in foreign and colonial affairs, by Albion and Pope. In the second edition, Albion and Pope wrote the new section that carried the story to the surrender of Japan at Tokyo Bay in 1945. The third edition was the work of all three authors and continued the account to the coronation of Elizabeth II in 1953.

The authors express their gratitude to publishers of their former writings for permission to include, without quotation marks, occasional passages from those writings: Albion, *Forests and Sea Power,* Harvard University Press, 1926; *Introduction to Military History,* D. Appleton-Century Company, 1929; "The Communication Revolution," in *Transactions of the Newcomen Society of Great Britain,* 1933. Albion, in collaboration with Pope, *The Rise of New York Port,* Charles Scribner's Sons, 1939; *Seaports South of Sahara,* Appleton-Century-Crofts, Inc., 1959. Hall, *British Radicalism, 1791-1797,* Columbia Studies in History, Economics and Public Law, 1912; *Empire to Commonwealth,* Henry Holt and Company, 1928; "The Three Arnolds and Their Bible," in *Essays in Intellectual History,* Harper & Brothers, 1929; *Mr. Gladstone,*

W. W. Norton & Company, Inc., 1931; *World Wars and Revolutions,*
D. Appleton-Century Company, 1943; *Iron out of Calvary*, D. Appleton-Century Company, 1946. Hall and Beller (Eds.), *Historical Read-
ings in Nineteenth Century Thought,* D. Appleton-Century Company,
1928. Pope, *Early European History,* Oxford Book Company, 1936.
Albion and Pope, *Sea Lanes in Wartime,* W. W. Norton & Company,
Inc., 1942.

The authors wish to acknowledge their continued indebtedness to
many colleagues and other friends, too numerous to mention.

Contents

List of Maps

A History of England
and the Empire-Commonwealth

Chapter One

Celt, Roman, and Saxon

Off an open beach some few miles to the north of Dover lie Roman galleys. From them heavily armed soldiers jump into the shallow water. They fight with blue-eyed native Britons, whose eager leaders drive their lightweight chariots into the sea. The Romans reach land; the Britons disperse. The inevitable fortified camp is constructed; Caesar's first invasion of Britain begins.

Just why Julius Caesar made this attack in 55 B.C. is not known. It had been reported to him that certain rebellious Gauls had received aid from Britain, and this had to be stopped. It was also said that certain sundry articles of value which might be of use to him as the political leader of the Roman popular party were to be found across the Channel. Caesar had seen with his own eyes gold coins minted in Britain; and even if he found little gold, there were men and women to enslave. His own popularity at Rome had long been enhanced by a steady inflow of both gold and slaves. Perhaps thoughts like these came to the Roman general as he looked at the chalk cliffs of Albion.

Caesar intended to live off the country. His foraging parties, however, met with ill success, and storms wrecked many of his galleys. Taking a hostage or two, he withdrew to Gaul. The expedition was a failure, but it was not so announced at Rome. The following year Caesar came back with an army twice as large. Powerful British tribes were now his allies; maltreated, so they said, by other Britons, they thirsted for vengeance. On his second coming Caesar cut his way from the southeastern shore to the Thames and signally punished some tribesmen just across that river. The Britons decided to treat with their conqueror, who made peace on easy terms. Threatening revolts in Gaul demanded Caesar's presence, a sufficient number of Britons had been captured for the Roman slave market, and his base camp on the coast was too distant for continued campaigning. Upon promise of a yearly tribute to Rome, Caesar and all his troops departed.

The history of the British Isles as a matter of written record begins with the Roman invasion; but there is a history which makes its record elsewhere, which antedates all written symbols, which leaves its mark either upon the surface of the earth, architecturally, or else below the surface in caves, in the scattered weapons of the chase, in burial mounds, in the skeletal remains of what, once, were men. From the time when we have the first record of man's existence England seems to have shared in almost every one of the various stages of progress from the several stone ages into those of copper, bronze, and iron.

Apparently from earliest times wave upon wave of immigration had swept over Britain. It was an easy land to reach. At first, it would seem, men could walk dry-shod to England; even after the sea came through, forming the Straits of Dover, only twenty-one miles of water separated the island from the mainland. In later years, after England learned that her true defense lay in a guardian fleet, that narrow strip of Channel was to prove a bar to invaders and allow England to develop her own individual civilization unmolested. But in these earlier times the land lay invitingly open, with its coast line nearest Europe indented with harbors, with rivers leading into the interior, and with no part more than seventy miles from the sea. The rich lowlands of southern and eastern England were easily overrun time and again; but when the newcomers advanced toward the west and north, rugged highlands barred their way. Had nature set those inhospitable hills nearer the Channel shore, England would have been less open to invasion and her history might well have run a very different course.

The last of these early invaders were the so-called Celts, the first of five conquerors —Celt, Roman, Saxon, Dane, and Norman —about whom there is some written knowledge. Who the Celts were and what their origin was no one is sure. Julius Caesar referred to part of the barbarians to the north and west of Italy as those "who in their own language are called Celts, and in our language Gauls." The term "Celt," so far as English history is concerned, is more a matter of language and civilization than of race; for we do not know the extent to which the Celtic newcomers may simply have imposed their tongue and their customs upon the men whom they found already there. These Celts seem to have poured into the British Isles, perhaps in several floods. The language of the so-called Goidelic, or Gaelic, Celts, noticeable chiefly in Ireland, differed somewhat from that of the Cymric, or Brythonic, Celts. The latter possibly reached Britain about 500 B.C., near the time when the Greeks were repulsing the Persians at Marathon, and made the land theirs. They knew the use of iron, which the softer bronze of their predecessors could not withstand. The Belgae, apparently a branch of the Brythonic Celts and also closely allied to those Gauls whom Caesar conquered, seem in their turn to have taken the southeast corner of the island, including the valley of the Thames. The Celtic peoples of Britain all made the clan, a small family unit, the center of their organization.

By Caesar's coming these Britons, although less advanced culturally than those upon the Continent, had progressed a long way from the life of the yet more primitive peoples they had displaced. In the days long before, those earlier islanders, as far as we know, had not even dared occupy the lowlands, where wolves and other wild beasts prowled; instead they sought refuge on the uplands, the moors, the treeless places where one could see to fight by night. By Caesar's time, however, they had driven the beasts to cover and had learned to cultivate the soil. They were expert in working bronze, tin, and iron, and knew something of art also, decorating pottery with curved designs. When fighting, they wore metal helmets beautifully ornamented and inlaid, and those who lived in south Britain had a coinage modeled on that of Macedon in the fourth century before Christ. Nor was this strange, for the British Celts were after all probably the far-western wing of the Celtic family which stretched to the Danube.

In religion a priestly caste, the druids, about whom little has been ascertained, conducted sacrifices and interpreted omens. They were apparently leaders of public opinion and were singled out for punishment by the Romans for stimulating patriotic resistance rather than for their religion. They seemingly enjoyed many privileges; their persons were sacred, and the mistletoe, grown on the oak, was their emblem. They were the guardians of the law, setting penalties for its violation, determining inheritances, and assessing fines. On the island of Anglesey (Mona), off the northern coast of Wales, was their most sacred shrine. At Stonehenge and Avebury are mysterious structures apparently built before the Celtic invasions, but perhaps connected with druid worship. The hardened Romans reported the druid religious rites to be marked by practices which even to them seemed cruel. The druids, according to tradition, occasionally offered living sacrifices on their altars, incinerating victims in large wicker baskets to propitiate their gods.

Such was the island Caesar invaded, and his account of the people remains the chief source of our meager knowledge of them. After his withdrawal the Romans did not return in force for nearly a hundred years—a century which saw the birth of Christ and the Roman Empire at its peak. The friendly attitude of the Britons toward the economic penetration of their island by the Roman traders appears to have staved off trouble. Meanwhile the numerous tribes in Britain had combined into two or three so-called kingdoms, though the organization undoubtedly remained simply tribal. Not long before the renewed invasions by the Romans, the largest and most important of these was ruled by a friend of Rome, the Cymbeline of Shakespeare's play. He encouraged the Roman traders and so helped to prepare his people for Roman ways. Following Roman custom, he offered sacrifices at Rome itself and, if we may judge from the number of coins which bear the inscription "Cunobelinus Rex," grew wealthy.

Thus it was in the days of the eccentric Roman emperor Caligula, who countermanded orders for a new invasion of Britain before a boat took to the water, but decorated the troops as though they had won astonishing victories. The emperor Claudius had trouble with mutinous Gauls who had revolted at the instigation of the druids. Furthermore, Cymbeline in his old age had his power undermined by certain of his sons. These reasons were sufficient for Claudius to order his general Plautius to conquer the island in 43 A.D.

The Britons under Caractacus, a son of Cymbeline, resisted stoutly; but the Romans now knew the terrain and by superior strategy marched quickly through what is now Kent to advance past London to Colchester in Essex. Claudius came over in person for the last fight and returned to Rome after a week or two, the accredited victor, leaving Plautius in charge of a new Roman province. He campaigned for four years, carrying the Roman arms north to a line from the Mersey River to the Humber, and as far west as Wales and Cornwall. Caractacus, however, though driven out of England, stirred up the tribes in Wales in the west, while in the east, another tribe, the Iceni, alarmed at Roman threats to disarm them, revolted. Caractacus was captured and sent to Rome, where, if we may believe the Roman historian Tacitus, he made a successful plea for clemency at his public trial.

Still the Britons would not give over, and general after general was sent against them. Finally a determined Roman governor decided to break their morale by capturing Anglesey, the sacred center of druid mysteries. "Seek your auguries," he told his soldiers, "in the quivering intestines of the druid priests." Simultaneously with the slaughter of the druids came the revolt (A.D. 61) of Queen Boudicca (Boadicea), widow of the late king of the Iceni. She was publicly whipped, and her daughters were violated by Roman officials. Thereupon her tribesmen, in tremendous fury, massacred the inhabitants of Colchester, a center of the Roman occupation. Other disaffected Britons joined Boudicca, who found herself at the head of many thousand rebels. The

Roman "Newport Gate" at Lincoln (Lindum). Through it ran Ermine Street, joining another great road, Fosse Way, just outside.

most part military. Britain was an outlying province and made little impression on the Roman world. The Roman soldiers sent to guard Britain from the still wild tribes near-by stayed there long years, often permanently, according to the Roman custom, and married the native women. Soldiers were far from being the only Romans in Britain: officials, merchants, and scores of other civilians came for business and sometimes stayed. Rome wanted to make this northern province, like her others, pay its way as far as possible.

With their usual flexibility in utilizing native authority wherever feasible, the Romans won over tribal magnates to Roman ways, confident that the lesser Britons would follow their example. (The later British Empire would likewise utilize Indian rajahs and African paramount chiefs.) Out on the northern and western frontiers, to be sure, the army took full control, but in the south and east, the Romano-British notables enjoyed country villas and town houses.

Towns with forums, columns, baths, and other less desirable features of Roman life and extensive villas, with plumbing better than in many present-day English villages, have been revealed by excavation. Some of the towns, which probably numbered ten to fifteen (depending upon classification), were fairly sizable. London, from its setting where land and sea traffic could converge, was predestined to be a leading city, though it was overshadowed for a while by some administrative centers, such as Colchester. Commercially, it was pre-eminent from the start. Vessels could bring cargoes the forty-odd miles up the Thames from the sea to this site, where high banks made it easy to bridge the river so that roads could spread out in all directions.

Important archaeologically was the small town of Silchester, where excavation was fairly easy because no other town had been superimposed upon it. Laid out in checkerboard form, it had contained a forum; four

Roman troops, returning from Anglesey, crushed the revolt; Boudicca took her own life, and thereafter much of southern Britain lay quiescent under Rome.

The victorious Romans rested on their laurels until another restless tribe, to the northward, soon necessitated more campaigning. In A.D. 78, Agricola, a famous general, seems to have led his army in seven different campaigns far into Scotland, to have sent a fleet to circumnavigate Britain, and to have won the confidence of the Britons in the south of England. His conquests were not permanent; but his conciliatory statesmanship was effective, and in the southern part of the island, where Rome held sway, the Britons began to give up their own way of life for that of the Romans.

In the south, consequently, lay the civilization of Rome. Unfortunately, there are but few written records, and those for the

temples and a small Christian church; public baths; administrative buildings; many shops; some small houses; and a few large residences with painted wall plaster, mosaic floors, and numerous water pipes. Without its gates was an amphitheater.

Scattered throughout the countryside were the villas of the important native Britons and of Roman officials and many farmhouses of lesser folk. The lack of fortifications indicate a feeling of security in Romanized Britain, but the agricultural system remains so far a mystery. It is now known, however, that what were thought to have been Celtic villages, when first excavated, were instead single farmsteads, surrounded by flimsy outbuildings. The fragmentary traces suggest that many Britons were only slightly influenced by Roman ways.

Even more important, perhaps, to Britain than the Roman town was the construction, for purposes of defense, of substantial military highways. The most famous were the Fosse Way, from Exeter in the southwest to Lincoln in the northeast; Watling Street, from London to Chester; and Ermine Street, later the Great North Road, leading from London up past York to the northern frontier. Thanks to these splendid stone highways, communication was quicker and easier in Roman Britain than it was to be at any later period until the end of the eighteenth century. Although these roads degenerated into muddy lanes after Rome's withdrawal, they still helped to link the country together. A definite heritage from Roman Britain is the gauge of most railroads. Early wagons and coaches were built to fit into the ruts made by Roman wheels; and the first railway coaches had that same width.

In the continued fighting on the north and west frontiers, the legions stood constant guard. Their principal stations were at Chester and Caerleon on the borders of Wales and at York in the north. Raids and punitive expeditions were constant. In A.D.

120, the emperor Hadrian, growing weary of these fruitless forays, built a wall some seventy-two miles in length, from the Solway to the Tyne, to shut off trouble from the north. Originally of turf, the wall was supported by a large number of forts only a mile apart, connected with one another by blockhouses and military roads. A hundred years later it was rebuilt in stone thirty feet high and wide enough for three men to walk abreast from one tower to the next. "Manned by every breed and race in the Empire," the wall was guarded by most of the legionaries in Britain during the middle period of the Roman occupation. Behind the wall lay Roman settlements which developed, for the amusement of the garrison, "one roaring, rioting, cock-fighting, wolf-baiting, horse-racing town from Ituna on the west to Segedunum on the cold eastern beach." To the north of Hadrian's wall was no man's land. True, another shorter wall, still farther to the north, was built later, but was soon abandoned. Beyond Hadrian's wall, during most of the Roman occupation,

A surviving section of Hadrian's Wall, showing one of the larger forts and some "mile castles." Kipling described life there in "Puck of Pook's Hill."

there were only savages, called "Picts" by the Romans, who claimed their bodies were painted. Hadrian's wall was to stand firm for almost three centuries, even when Roman defense was crumbling in Asia and beyond the Danube. Britain was to be in serious danger from only one direction, the sea.

Around the year A.D. 300 Britain prospered under two strong emperors—Diocletian and then Constantine, who happened to be at York when he was proclaimed emperor. Even before Diocletian, however, Saxon pirates from what is now Germany had begun to raid the Channel coast—the vanguard of the eventual all-conquering Anglo-Saxon invaders. As a result, Britain was made into four subprovinces and the troops divided among three generals. One commanded the north and the wall; another, the reserves; and the third, the Count of the Saxon Shore, held the key position against piratical forays, as commander of the fleet and the eastern garrisons.

Not long after the death of Constantine the Roman Empire began to crumble as barbarians from the Germanic regions, pushed on by the Huns, fierce invaders from the east, hewed and hacked at the imperial frontiers. Some of the former defeated the imperial legions in the Balkans, A.D. 378, and actually invaded Italy itself. From the distant provinces legions were called home, including the Sixth (Victrix), which had been in Britain two hundred years; and one by one these outlying districts were abandoned to their own resources. The collapse of the Rhine barriers brought Germanic tribesmen deep into Gaul and almost severed the line of imperial communication.

With political paralysis at Rome the occupation of Britain was shattered by renewed invasions from the north, the west, and the sea. From the middle of the fourth century, the Picts and the Celtic Scots from northern Ireland made intermittent forays which steadily grew more intensive and alarming. They made such headway that before the fifth century opened the Romans had abandoned the wall and had twice to recommence the conquest of Britain north of London. More serious as an omen for the future, the Nordic pirates, barbarians of the same general stock as those who were harassing other imperial frontiers, were growing bolder in their frequent coastal raids. Roman commanders in Britain, intent on their own glory and the emperorship itself, added to the plight of the island. Two such officials, less than thirty years apart, setting out on vain quests for the imperial purple, took many legionaries to the Continent with them; and these troops never came back to Britain, where they were sorely needed to stem the invaders. In A.D. 410, three years after the second withdrawal, Rome itself was sacked by German barbarians, and with this Britain was no longer Roman. Scattered as the legion garrisons had become, it is doubtful that they all left at once; some perhaps never left. All that is known is that the glory of Rome had faded into darkness.

The Anglo-Saxon Invasions

During the next two hundred years, England became Engla-land. Following the trail of the earlier German pirates, fresh invaders—Jutes, Angles, and Saxons—overran the country in the middle of the fifth century and, unlike the Romans, stayed. These fair-haired Nordic newcomers hailed mainly from the Jutland peninsula of Denmark and from northern Germany. All three tribes were closely akin in everything that concerned religion, language, customs, and blood. While their differences blended quickly in England, they long remembered their German origin. All lived on the ocean almost as much as on the land at this early period, although before long they turned to a more settled agricultural life. Perhaps from the first only the more adventurous had spurned the prosaic raising of crops to become "the terror of all neighboring coasts, equally famed for merciless cruelty and destructiveness, sudden as lightning in attack and retreat, of an incredible greed for plunder, laughing and joyous in danger. They chose the tempest in which to sail, that they might find their enemies unprepared, and wherever the winds and waves drove them, there they ravaged."[1]

According to legend, in the year 449 their reputed leaders, Hengist and Horsa, invited in by the Britons to aid them against the Picts, soon turned on their hosts with fury. To quote from the history of the Venerable Bede, the leading authority, the newcomers "plundered all the neighboring cities and country, spread the conflagration from the eastern to the western sea. . . . the prelates and the people, without any respect of persons, were destroyed with fire and sword. . . ."

Roughly speaking, this new conquest continued for more than two centuries, while at the same time the Britons continued to be frequently hard pressed by the Picts and the Scots. The Saxon conquest was never carried on systematically. Wandering bands of "Anglo-Saxons" went up the English rivers in their lightdraft boats and crossed overland to sack and destroy such villas and towns as they happened upon. They were not city dwellers and also avoided settling along the Roman roads. They tore down the stone-constructed Roman villas and built new crude huts for themselves. The miserable Britons fled before them or hid themselves whenever opportunity offered, sometimes in the heating chambers underneath the hollow floors of Roman villas.

[1] S. A. Brooke, *English Literature from the Beginning to the Norman Conquest* (1907), p. 38. By permission of the Macmillan Company, Macmillan & Co., Ltd., of London, The Macmillan Company of Canada, Limited, publishers.

Ruins of Roman fortifications at Richborough (Rutupiae) for protection against Saxon raids. Just north of Dover, it was a key port, and headquarters of the "Count of the Saxon Shore."

From the little that has been learned of those two "lost centuries" between Roman and Saxon times, it would seem that the Saxon invaders had a fairly easy time in occupying the civilized southeast but encountered sturdy opposition as they pushed farther inland. At one time in the fifth or sixth century, under a mythical King Arthur, the Britons seem to have made a successful counterthrust, winning twelve battles; in the last one "960 men fell in one day at one onslaught by Arthur and no one felled them but Arthur alone." This account was probably written several hundred years later and the author may have invented the name of Arthur. The Arthurian legends have strongly appealed to the imagination of his fellow islanders, and have reappeared in literature down through the centuries.

For the most part the Roman-Celtic people apparently vanished, perhaps into the recesses of the Welsh hills or the tip of Cornwall, or into other remote corners, or even across the Channel. Some, who did not flee, lived on as slaves worth about eight oxen apiece. But the land of England was theirs no longer. Both Celtic and Roman influences were largely swept away by the heathen invaders, as far as the England of the Roman occupation was concerned. Yet throughout English history since that time the Celt has made himself felt, whereas Rome's legacies have been negligible. The four centuries of Roman occupation left little permanent impression on later England. On the other hand, in the "Celtic fringe" surrounding England, in Wales, in Ireland, in the Scottish Highlands, and to a lesser degree in Cornwall, have been preserved the language and many of the customs and characteristics of the Celts even into modern times. The organization of the clan, for instance, continued into the eighteenth century in the Scottish Highlands. Risky as it is to generalize, a strain of imagination and quick impulsiveness is found to this day among many of these Celtic people, making the Celt quite different from the average Englishman in both thought and action. Yet even the Englishman probably has in his veins some of the blood of the Celts and their predecessors; for in conquests such as this the victors often took the women, even though the men were driven off or slain.

For several centuries the Saxons dominated the island and in blood, in custom and in tongue left an indelible imprint on the history and the lives of English-speaking peoples to this day. Most of the population seems to have been displaced by the new Germanic groups. In their piecemeal and long-protracted invasions the Saxons sometimes retreated with their booty and sailed back to their homeland; sometimes they stayed and occupied the land. Then they would send eastward for their wives and children and the less restless of their number, who had stayed behind. Once settled in this new country, the Saxon, devoting himself to the soil rather than to the sea, was now the farmer above all else; but he continued to be a stalwart fighter.

At that same time other Germans were attacking other parts of the Empire. In the old Roman province of Gaul, for instance, these Germans (the Franks, who were to give their name to France) found the Gallo-Roman civilization more firmly rooted than the Romano-British. The result was that Frenchmen in subsequent centuries represented a more equal mingling of Celtic, Roman, and Teutonic strains than Englishmen, who were overwhelmingly Teutonic. The Goths and Lombards, who invaded Italy, likewise encountered a well-established civilization, which they absorbed rather than supplanted. So the story went: where the Germanic barbarians invaded definitely Romanized parts of the Empire, their imprint was less evident than in the remoter sections.

The Anglo-Saxons found it easy enough to kill Britons, but very difficult to deal with one another. They had no traditions of national unity, nor did they have a supreme leader. Kings there were in plenty, but not kingdoms in the modern sense. Many so-called kingdoms rose and fell during these dark ages. Only slowly and almost imperceptibly did seven take on sufficient form and substance to be recognized as such. Of this so-called Heptarchy there were Kent, in the extreme southeast, Sussex to the west of Kent, and Wessex still farther to the west; Essex and East Anglia were small kingdoms to the north and east of London, fronting on the North Sea; Mercia, a sizable central kingdom; and Northumbria, the largest of all, stretching from south of York to the north beyond Edinburgh (for Scotland, as a separate country, did not exist).

Before England could become a nation, these kingdoms somehow had to be united. Northumbria in the seventh century and Mercia in the eighth in turn managed to attain a sort of overlordship over the others;

but the forces of decentralization were too strong to be overcome until the rise of Wessex, in the ninth and tenth centuries. Civilization was at a low ebb. These warriors in the early days of the Saxon period had no cities, no commerce, and scarcely any communication with the outside world. Such literature as they possessed was in the form of unwritten songs, passed down from generation to generation; for they could neither read nor write. Furthermore, their religion, aside from a fine appreciation of courage and endurance, was devoid of ethical significance.

Yet by the commencement of the eleventh century there was to be an England, thanks to Christianity on the one hand and to the Danes on the other. Christianity was to bring England back into the circle of Western civilization, teach manners and morals to the wild tribesmen, make them think, no matter how crudely, about life's meaning. And to the gentler message of the Church there was to be added the menace of a Viking conquest, a fresh attack from overseas by men quite competent to hew and slay.

The Anglo-Saxons, when they came to England, had a religion of a sort, but not clearly defined. They believed in a group of gods presided over by Thor, the Thunderer, and by Woden, or Odin, God of Magic and Poetry, to whom most of the Anglo-Saxon kings traced their ancestry. The priests were apparently few, and not influential. In Northumbria, their social status seems to have been questionable. Their sole duty seems to have been confined to offering sacrifices, originally bloodthirsty in character but by the time of the first Christian missionaries limited apparently to animals. One virtue, valor, was emphasized. The Saxons did not fear anything, even their own gods, who were regarded more as boon companions in the hereafter than as supernatural life-directors. If one was fortunate enough to die fighting, one went to Valhalla, there to feast and to

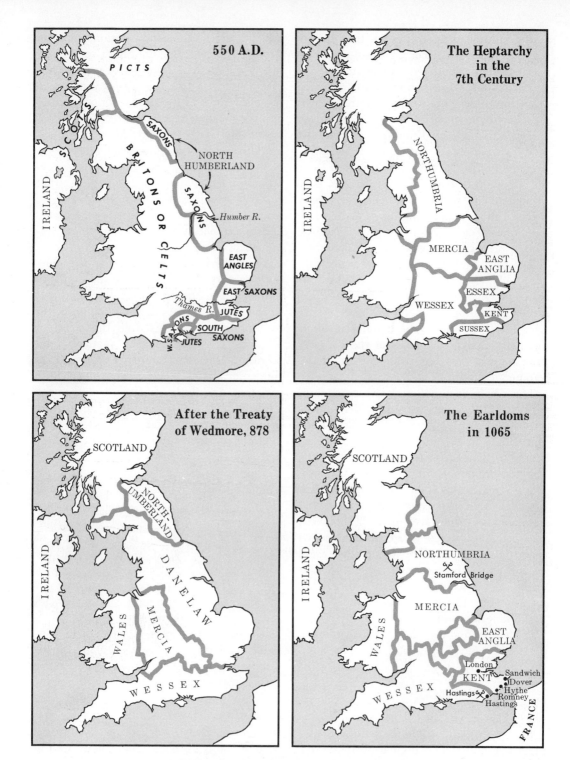

550 A.D.

PICTS

IRELAND

SCOTS

BRITONS OR CELTS

SAXONS

NORTH HUMBERLAND

SAXONS

Humber R.

EAST ANGLES

EAST SAXONS

Thames R. JUTES

W. SAXONS

SOUTH SAXONS

JUTES

The Heptarchy in the 7th Century

IRELAND

NORTHUMBRIA

MERCIA

EAST ANGLIA

WESSEX

ESSEX

KENT

SUSSEX

After the Treaty of Wedmore, 878

SCOTLAND

IRELAND

NORTH-UMBERLAND

DANELAW

WALES

MERCIA

WESSEX

The Earldoms in 1065

SCOTLAND

IRELAND

NORTHUMBRIA

Stamford Bridge

MERCIA

WALES

EAST ANGLIA

London

KENT

Sandwich

Dover

Hythe

Romney

Hastings

Hastings

WESSEX

FRANCE

ANGLO-SAXON ENGLAND

drink with the gods at a perpetual banquet. Occasionally the dead were cremated, together with their weapons and dogs. More frequently they were buried, the heroes having mounds or barrows raised over them. Superheroes became clothed with a kind of divinity; thus the distinction between God and man was made rather shadowy.

Scarcely a trace of any other formal religion has been found among the Saxons. The ideals of life which they cherished were of the simplest, if we may judge from their one great pre-Christian poem, Beowulf. The hero of this epic was a mighty fighter. Usually he and his comrades made the forest their home, but sometimes the "wavepath":

Who are ye of men, having arms in hand
Covering with your coat of mail, who, your
   keel a-foaming,
O'er the ocean street, thus have urged along,
Hither on the high-raised sea? Never saw I
   greater
Earl upon this earth than is one of you.
'Less his looks belie him, he is no home-stayer.
Glorious is his gear of war, aetheling his air.

Thus were Beowulf and his fighters greeted. Most certainly he was no home-stayer. He lay in wait for the monster, Grendel, who was wont to break the bones and drink the blood of sleeping men. "In the wan darkness, while the warriors slept, the shadow-stalker drew near from the Moorland; over the misty fells Grendel came ganging on; under the clouds he strode." Beowulf wrestled with him, tore off an arm. There followed then the encounter with Grendel's mother in a cave beneath the sea. Beowulf "saw hanging on the wall an old sword . . . and seizing the gold-charmed hilt, he smote at the sea-wolf's neck. The brand gripped in her throat, broke through the bone into the body." The hero rose through "the bloody sea," and his men acclaimed him. Finally Beowulf, grown old, and now king of his

people, came home to stay. A dragon, vomiting fire, terrorized the neighborhood. Beowulf found "his last foe and his death." His sword slipped, and the dragon got his claw on Beowulf until "the life bubbled forth in waves."[2]

The dying man cut the dragon in two with his ax and sang his death song—swearing no oaths which he did not keep, being true to kinsmen. Such a man personified the ideal of the Saxon before Christianity entered his life.

The Coming of Christianity

It happened in the late sixth century that Pope Gregory the Great was intensely interested in missionary activities among the pagan peoples. He knew of the Anglo-Saxons from observing blond youngsters from England in the Roman slave market. Also he was aware that the wife of the king of Kent was a Christian and that through her influence there might be an opportunity for an entering wedge in England. Therefore he selected Augustine, a monk, to head a mission thither in 597.

Waving banners and singing litanies, Augustine and forty followers landed in Kent, where the king received them courteously: "Because ye are come from afar into my kingdom, and, as I conceive, are desirous to impart to us those things which you believe to be true and most beneficial, we will not molest you, but give you favorable entertainment . . . nor do we forbid you by preaching to gain as many as you can to your religion." They converted the king and many of the people, to the Pope's delight. He made Augustine an archbishop and laid plans for further conversion of the English.

Although they met some setbacks both in Kent after the king's death and elsewhere, the missionaries were particularly successful in Northumbria, which was then at the

[2] S. A. Brooke, *English Literature from the Beginning to the Norman Conquest*, pp. 71, 73, 76-78.

height of its glory, stretching from Edinburgh on the north almost all the way to London on the south. Again the influence of a woman paved the way. Edwin, the king for whom Edinburgh is named, was married to a princess of Kent, and in her train was Paulinus, a Christian bishop who had been sent to further the work of Augustine. Paulinus plied the king hard, and the Pope wrote letters to Edwin and his wife, urging her active support. Edwin consented to a conference, just thirty years after Augustine had landed in Kent. It is memorable for a much-quoted speech by one of his chieftains: "The present life of Man, O King, seems to me, in comparison of that time which is unknown to us, like to the swift flight of a sparrow through the room wherein you sit at supper in winter . . . The sparrow . . . whilst he is within is safe from the wintry storm; but after a short space of fair weather, he immediately vanishes out of your sight, from one winter to another. So this life of Man appears for a short space, but of what went before, or what is to follow, we are utterly ignorant. If, therefore, this new doctrine contains something more certain, it seems justly to deserve to be followed." The people apparently took wholesale to the Christian assurances about the future life, destroying their idols. Paulinus traveled everywhere, baptizing thousands, and it was soon reported "there was then such perfect peace in Britain, wheresoever the dominion of King Edwin extended, that . . . a woman with her new-born babe might walk through the island, from sea to sea, without receiving any harm." The Pope made Paulinus an archbishop, so that there was now one at Canterbury and one in the north at York.

Doubtless all would have gone well for Christianity had it not been for Penda, king of Mercia, a most redoubtable heathen. He waged such successful war against Northumbria that Mercia replaced it as the leading kingdom around A.D. 650. Penda

did not persecute Christians, but he had contempt for them; and their church went under a partial eclipse. Paulinus, fleeing south, became a bishop in Kent.

Shortly thereafter the Church was to be revived from another quarter. Thanks to Constantine, the first Christian emperor, Christianity had first come to Britain long before Augustine, while the Roman legions were still there. His edicts in 311 and 313 had placed Christianity on an equal footing with other religions. British bishops were reported as attending church councils on the Continent as early as the fourth century. In fact, Christianity was indirectly one of Rome's few lasting legacies to Britain; but with the coming of the pagan Nordic invaders it disappeared from view. Some devout souls cherished the Christian belief in Wales, and from there it seems to have spread to Ireland, where, owing to the activity of Saint Patrick and Saint Bridget, it made rapid strides. Whence or when Patrick came to Ireland is uncertain, but it is clear that Ireland, culturally speaking, in the seventh century was one of the most advanced countries in Europe. Although Roman armies had never brought it within even the outer rim of Roman civilization, its monks now made it famous. Their enterprise was astonishing, their illuminated manuscripts artistic, and their scholarship excellent. "The literary output of the seventh century was small throughout western Europe, but there is enough to show that the Irish kept up the tradition of learning." The monks, indeed, were untiring. Within Ireland they built many monasteries which were educational as well as religious centers. Outside of Ireland—in England, in Scotland, in northern Germany, in France, in Switzerland, and even in Italy itself— their missionary enterprises were led by men of ability and wide culture.

Such a man was Columban. With his monks he went to Brittany, thence to Burgundy, to build a famous monastery in the Vosges Mountains; and afterward to build another, even more famous, in Italy. Such a one, also, was that other Irish monk, Columba. To make amends for the blood he shed in fighting in early manhood, he was exiled from Ireland by his fellow monks until he had won for God souls equal in number to those he had slain. Forthwith, at the age of forty-two, he sailed for the west coast of Scotland, made his headquarters on the island of Iona, and from thence spread Christianity in Britain. This sailor, soldier, poet, and first abbot of Iona lived austerely in a tiny hut within his monastery, with a stone for a pillow; but he also lived gently, ever compassionate for the poor and the distressed, whether man or beast. Hardly a day passed but pilgrims came to seek refuge on Iona; and Columba and his men went on repeated missionary tours by sea and land, winning converts everywhere.

As Northumbria relapsed into barbarism after the victories of Penda, it happened that a prince of Northumbria, Oswald, sought asylum in Iona. Victorious in war, he regained Northumbria, and, remembering the kindly monks, he asked them to send him a bishop. On the island of Lindisfarne this Irish bishop established his see, which was soon to become a center of learning second only to Iona. And from now on, in the words of a chronicler, many Irish "came daily into Britain, and with great devotion preached the word to those provinces over which King Oswald reigned . . . Churches were built in several places; the people joyfully flocked together to hear the word; money and lands were given of the king's bounty to build monasteries . . ."

Christianity forthwith began to sweep all before it. The much-feared Penda was slain in battle, and Mercia was converted. And as this occurred the Anglo-Saxon kingdoms of the south and east fell under the sway of the new religion. The question as to whether England would acknowledge one Catholic Church alone or have two hierarchies, the Roman and the Irish, called for immediate decision. The Celtic monks differed in discipline and in the date of Easter from the missionaries sent direct from Rome. Also, they shaved their hair from ear to ear instead of in a circle on top of the head. These differences were trivial, but the question involved far more than haircuts and Lenten fasting.

The issue was joined at the Synod of Whitby (664). Over it presided Oswy, king of Northumbria, who said "it behooved those who served only one God to observe the same rule of life . . ." In the long and closely argued debates the bishop for the Irish Church could only quote certain old traditions, but the spokesman for Rome had traveled widely and could affirm that in Italy, France, Greece, Africa, Asia, and Egypt the Roman date for Easter was the universal practice. He also could argue that Peter had been given the keys of heaven, and that the Pope, as Peter's successor, must be obeyed (the Petrine theory). Since the Irish bishop did not deny Peter's primacy, the king decided for Rome, saying, "lest when I come to the gates of the kingdom of heaven, there should be none to open them, he being my adversary who is known to possess the keys." The Celtic churchmen withdrew, discomfited, to Scotland.

Possibly the king had called the council simply owing to his annoyance at having court life disrupted because some began their Lenten fasting when the rest were completing it. But however trifling the reason, the results of Whitby were to have a far-reaching significance in English history. The decision in favor of Rome saved England from stagnant isolation by binding her more closely to the Continent, with all that it had to offer.

The Roman Church

A particular advantage was the introduction of a system far more clean-cut than anything the Anglo-Saxons themselves produced. The church throughout this period set the state a shining example of orderly

Anglo-Saxon farming, showing sowing and reaping, the basic seasonal activities of the bulk of England's population, changing little through the centuries.

organization. Under the guidance of the Popes, the Roman Church gave western Europe its only practical example of effective international organization during the Dark Ages. However divided into petty jurisdictions Europe might be politically, the Church gave uniformity, not only in belief and religious practices but also in administrative machinery. The Irish Church was purely monastic without the continuing everyday ministrations of a parish priest as such.

The far-reaching dominance of the Roman Church rested upon its tremendous role in the life of the medieval populace. Only through the Church was salvation possible. Life after death was emphasized in every way. The Church alone could open the gates of paradise to the true believer or, by closing them, could doom the recalcitrant to hell fire. Consequently the average man with faith in his church never

questioned any of its ideas or methods. In a particularly vital way the Church entered the life of every individual from birth to death through the sacraments—baptism, confirmation, marriage, Holy Eucharist, penance, ordination, and extreme unction. The infant was baptized shortly after birth; the youth, by confirmation, became an active communicant and thereafter regularly attended Mass, received Communion, and did penance after confession. When dying, the communicant received extreme unction. Nearly everyone came in contact with six sacraments, but marriage and ordination to the priesthood were normally contradictory, since churchmen were not allowed to wed. This deep connection between the Church and the daily life of the individual explains the effectiveness of the two church weapons for punishing violation of its commands: excommunication, which cut off an individual from the services of the Church, and the interdict, which prohibited most church services within an entire region.

The word "catholic" characterized the universal, or all-embracing, character of the Church throughout western Europe at this period. Everyone belonged to it, as time went on, as a matter of course, or else was branded as an outcast from society, a heretic. The Church stood as the one unified institution in Europe when the barbarian invasions had broken down almost everything else. The medieval people, with their heritage of the Roman Empire, longed for unity in their disrupted life and and found it only in the Church. They took comfort in the knowledge that at the same hour, in every Christian hamlet throughout western Europe, priests were chanting the same Latin service.

On the administrative side, western Christendom was neatly blocked off into definite units, each with its responsible head, subordinate to an immediate higher authority, from the Pope at the head, down through the hierarchy of archbishops and bishops, to the parish priests. There was discipline and control from top to bottom. The members of the religious orders—abbots, monks, and later the friars—were likewise under papal control. In addition, papal ambassadors, known as legates, often represented the Pope in the various countries. Eventually, at a time when the Anglo-Saxon period was drawing to a close, a group of prominent churchmen was organized into the "college of cardinals," to elect the Pope and to act as his advisory body. Occasionally councils, composed of the important churchmen of many regions, were called to discuss special church problems.

To what extent the bishop of Rome's ecclesiastical primacy over this vast network had been recognized in the beginning is not certain. A Roman Catholic might point out that it existed because Peter was the first bishop of Rome; a Protestant might argue that at first the bishop of Rome had

been no more important than other bishops. Because Rome, however, had long been the capital of the world, churchmen naturally turned there for guidance; and soon that bishop began to give unsolicited advice and even orders. Italy had already looked to him for leadership, since during the barbarian invasions he was often the strongest man there. Two exceptionally able Popes, Leo the Great (about 450) and Gregory the Great, added immensely to the dignity and prestige of the office. By the so-called **Petrine** theory, cited at Whitby, the Roman bishops claimed that they had succeeded to the power of Saint Peter and that because of this legacy their church had the purest doctrines.

At that time most of Europe was under the Roman Church except some parts of the still heathen north. The Balkan region, in the southeast, however, was to have its separate Christian Church, the Greek Catholic, or the Greek Orthodox, which was to be completely distinct from the Roman Church, centered at Constantinople, the capital of the still extant Eastern Roman, or Byzantine, Empire.

The vast area under the sway of Rome was divided into provinces, each controlled by an archbishop. The leading archbishop in each country was called the "primate" and was directly subordinate to the Pope. Each province was divided into dioceses. A bishop managed each diocese, throughout which he administered the sacraments of confirmation and ordination. In its turn the diocese was subdivided into parishes, one for each community, with several in the larger towns. The parish priest administered the sacraments of baptism, Mass, penance, marriage, and extreme unction, as well as attending to other duties among his parishioners. Archbishops, bishops, and priests were called *secular* clergy (from the Latin *saeculum*, "world"), because they came into direct contact with the outside world. Contrasted with them were the *regular* clergy,—the monks and nuns,—so called because they lived according to a "rule" (Latin, *regula*). The three branches of the regular clergy were the monastic orders and the later military and mendicant orders. The idea of the "rule" was introduced by Saint Benedict in the sixth century, when he set up his pioneer monastery at Monte Cassino, in Italy, in 529, thirty-odd years before Columba established the less formal Irish monasticism at Iona. The Benedictine Rule called for the triple vow of poverty, obedience, and chastity in a community life of service and prayer. Each of the scores of monasteries and nunneries, headed by its abbot or abbess, was pretty much a little world in itself, usually claiming independence of the authority of the bishop of the diocese and acknowledging only the superior authority of the Pope. In the tenth century the monks of Cluny, in France, sought more rigid control by establishing subordinate monasteries under their immediate supervision, not only in France but also in England and other lands.

Without the monks the Middle Ages would have been an even harsher period. Their service was fourfold: missionary, economic, social, and cultural. Not only were they frequently first in the work of conversion, but had it not been for their monastic outposts of Christianity in remote regions more than one converted land would quickly have returned to paganism. Their economic service lay in their demonstration of the dignity of labor by themselves working with their hands, particularly in agriculture, during the early days. Their interest in trade sometimes led to the rise of towns around the abbeys. In social service they cared for the sick, the aged, the poor, the friendless, and the orphaned. The monasteries were also shelters for the traveler. In those rough times, these communities were a refuge, especially for those who wanted to work and study, and to prepare for the future of their souls. Their cultural contribution lay in preserving and copying ancient manuscripts, when no one else cared

about them. Later, moreover, nearly all the schools, such as they were, were held in the monasteries.

England was given a more carefully defined place in this system five years after Whitby, when Theodore of Tarsus was sent to be head of the English Church. Born in Asia Minor and educated in Athens, he was a brilliant scholar and a thorough disciplinarian. Though nearly seventy, he spent twenty energetic years in establishing orderly church organization through England. He was Archbishop of Canterbury, and so the "primate," or head, of the English Church, although a junior archbishop was continued at York for the northern provinces. Theodore cut down unwieldy bishoprics. From this time priests ceased to be wandering missionaries and were given definite parishes to administer. Practically every township or group of hamlets was eventually set up as a parish with its own priest.

The Anglo-Saxons were generous in their support of the Church. As in other lands, everyone had to pay the tithe, theoretically a tenth of all he produced each year, for the support of the priest and higher churchmen. In addition, bishoprics and abbeys received rich grants of land from the kings. All this helped to submerge the freemen toward their new status of serfdom; that was the price of the spiritual and cultural leadership which Roman Christianity gave to England. The Church, moreover, was the better able to instill its example of organization into the State because, when the king looked about him for responsible, educated officials, churchmen were practically the only men who could meet those qualifications.

The introduction of Christianity proved of benefit to England in several ways: manners were softened and morals were improved; impetus and direction were given to scholarship and to the growth of English literature; and the unification of the English nation was aided enormously. Of the ideals of Christianity a famous English historian wrote: "From the cradle to the grave it forced on the Englishman a new law of conduct, new habits, new conceptions of life and society. It entered above all into that sphere within which the individual will of the freeman had been until now supreme, the sphere of the home; it curtailed his power over wife and child and slave; it forbade infanticide, the putting away of wives, or cruelty to the serf. . . . It met the feud face to face by denouncing revenge. It held up gluttony and drunkenness, the very essence of the old English 'Feast' as sins."[3]

During the century and a half after Whitby, Christianity likewise stimulated a literary movement, wherein a curious blending took place between pagan and Christian ideals. This may be seen in the poetry of Caedmon, Cynewulf, and others, who took their themes either from Holy Writ or from the early traditions of the Church. For all that, they remained men of the north, their imagery copied from that which was familiar to them, their inherited love of heroism and brave deeds making the familiar Bible stories appear in unusual perspective.

According to Bede, Caedmon, a humble monk, was the first poet to use Early English. He "was born a heathen and his work bridged the river between the pagan and the Christian poetry." Ascribed to him or to his school is a Saxon version of Genesis, in which Abraham is pictured as a great earl, leading his warriors against the men of Sodom, with "hard hand-play, crashing of weapons, storming of death-darts, tumult of battle. From out the sheaths men snatched their ring-decked, keen-edged swords." This does not seem altogether like the King James version.

Somewhat later came the poems of Cynewulf, a poet whose name remains shrouded in mystery. He may have lived around 800,

but that he wrote superbly there are none to question. In his poems was stressed the early Anglo-Saxon love of the sea. Thus in his *Elene,* when the mother of the emperor Constantine set forth to seek the Cross, we read: "Most speedily a band of earls began to hasten down into the deep water. Along the sea's margin stood harnessed ocean-steeds, fettered sea-stallions floating on the sound. Then was the lady's journey to be known, when she sought out the tossing floods with all her train." The gentler side of Jesus' life seems to have made but slight impression on these Saxon poets. "Jesus is the victory-child of God, his death a king's death." In *The Dream of the Rood* Cynewulf had the Cross speak thus: "The Hero, young—He was Almighty God—did off His raiment, steadfast, stout of heart, with valor in the sight of many men, He mounted up upon the lofty gallows, when He would fain redeem mankind."[4] Rome or no Rome, early Christianity in England, if we may judge from this poem, bore a peculiarly Teutonic impress.

Meanwhile, thanks to the new religion, schools of learning flourished throughout the country. At Canterbury, the mighty Archbishop Theodore was patron, and there Aldhelm, later abbot of Malmesbury and one of Europe's best scholars, studied Roman law, metrics, arithmetic, and astronomy. He was well acquainted with sacred as well as classical literature, as his letters and poems indicated.

Another center of learning was the monastery at Jarrow, on the Tyne, where for forty years labored the Venerable Bede, "the Father of English History." He wrote textbooks, theological expositions which were extraordinarily learned for his day, and showed a good knowledge of Greek. Above all, his *Ecclesiastical History of the English People* is our foremost, and frequently our only, source for nearly two

---

[3] J. R. Green, *The Conquest of England* (1883), p. 8.

[4] C. W. Kennedy, *The Cynewulf Poems* (1910), p. 307. By permission of E. P. Dutton & Co., Inc., George Routledge and Sons, Ltd., and the author.

The Ruthwell Cross, showing the Crucifixion story, is an example of Anglo-Saxon religious art.

of the age; a born teacher; pupil and master of York, which was then the greatest school in Europe." Truly the Anglo-Saxons had advanced far since Augustine's singing monks had landed in Kent.

Altogether Christianity as an institution began to pave the way for national unity. The clergy were a caste apart, and continuously became more and more influential. Not only did they know more than the rough Saxons, but they were armed with spiritual thunderbolts which men feared. The clergy threw their support to the establishment of law courts, partly to curb blood feuds and partly to protect the estates granted them.

Christianity brought also in its train knowledge of contracts, of written documents, and, above all, of the Latin alphabet. The crude symbols of the Saxons were of no use as far as written records were concerned, but once the alphabet became general it was possible to draw up written agreements. "A book ceased to be a tablet of beechwood and became a book of parchment." As soon as this took place, the clergy had a new weapon wherewith to coerce wild tribesmen into some semblance of social and political unity. Taxes and tithes made it possible to start schools, to build churches, to introduce art, architecture, literature, and leisure into England even though such expenditures often turned freemen into serfs.

Partly because of the pressure of the new religion, the number of independent kingdoms was gradually reduced from seven to three (Northumbria, Mercia, Wessex), and ultimately but one, England. Northumbria, originally so powerful, never regained its old political pre-eminence. Although strong culturally, politically it became weak, owing to a succession of feeble, inefficient, and short-lived kings.

The star of Mercia, meanwhile, rose in the eighth century, and so strong did this central kingdom become that it seemed for a time as though it might consolidate all

hundred years of English history. It contains suspiciously miraculous yarns, but none the less it is written in such pure and limpid Latin that even in translation it is a pleasure to read. The feature which makes his history really distinctive, however, is the spirit of research, which led him to track down the story of things as they really happened, either from documents or from the participants.

At the cathedral school at York, founded by the archbishop who had been a student of Bede, was one Alcuin, a teacher of grammar, arts, and science. So capable was he that even Charlemagne heard of him. This emperor (768-814) of the lands that composed much of western Europe decided to start a school of his own and placed Alcuin at its head. It was said that "in him were united all the qualifications which Charles desired. A man of Teutonic race, learned with a learning far above the level

England. Two kings of Mercia reigned for a period of nearly eighty years, an almost unparalleled record in those days of rapine and murder. The second, Offa, spreading the boundaries of Mercia in every direction, absorbed East Anglia, gained control of Kent, and built a great dike, or earthen rampart, for a distance of one hundred and thirty miles as a defense against the Welsh. His capital was at Lichfield, and, ambitious for ecclesiastical independence as well as for political power, Offa established there an archbishopric. By the Pope he was greeted as *Rex Anglorum;* and had his successors measured up to him in ability, Mercia might have absorbed the other English kingdoms.

This role, however, was left for Wessex, the smallest of the three kingdoms which survived as independent states at the opening of the ninth century. On ascending the throne, Egbert, its ruler (802-839), found himself surrounded on the north and east by Mercia and on the west by the Welsh. Striking first to the west he conquered West Wales (Cornwall). Then, taking advantage of revolts in Mercia, he swung to the north, defeated the Mercians, and was acknowledged as Bretwalda, or overlord, by all England south of the Humber. Next he turned farther north. The Northumbrians did not fight but "met him and offered him obedience and peace." The north Welsh, meanwhile, were "humbled," and Egbert could regard all England, temporarily at any rate, as under his direct or indirect control.

The supremacy of Wessex was to be a lasting one, owing to a new factor, the Danes. As a centralizing influence Christianity had proved powerful; but it alone might have been incapable of bringing together in one nation these unruly Anglo-Saxons had there not been the absolute necessity of unity if effective resistance was to be made to threatening new invasions.

Chapter Two

King Alfred, Danes, and Dooms

The comparative serenity of England was again roughly disturbed in 787, when, according to the Anglo-Saxon Chronicle, "first came three ships of Northmen out of Haeretheland [Denmark] and then the reeve [sheriff] rode out to the place and would have driven them to the king's town, because he knew not who they were: and they slew him. These were the first of the Danish men who sought the land of the English nation."

These Danes, Vikings, or Norsemen were of similar blood to the Saxons, but hailed from Scandinavian regions, farther to the north. They loved the sea, craved adventure, and had frequent famine in their cold homeland. These or other reasons led them far afield for pillage. They infinitely preferred piracy to peace; and their raids terrified the peoples of the coast communities throughout most of the ninth century and on into the eleventh.

If we may judge from name and deed, their ferocity was unbounded. Erik Blood-Ax, Harold Bluetooth, and Thorkill the Skull-Splitter were some of their names; and they were worthy of them. They made a business of war, and on select occasions worked themselves into frenzies of rage, howled like wild wolves, and gnashed their teeth on their iron swords. Not alone did the people of the British Isles have cause

to pray, "From the fury of the Northmen, O Lord deliver us." In all directions far and near where oars and wind might carry them they cruised and settled (see pages 35 ff.).

They were as expert in seamanship as in war, and they were skilled shipbuilders—almost of necessity. After plunder, commerce was their next thought; and both as pirates and traders, they had to have good craft. Some of their vessels, slender open boats with the lines of cup defenders, have been dug from the sand and mud in recent years. Generally such vessels had a mast and a square sail. A high prow and stern customarily tapered off into the form of a serpent or a dragon. On a platform at the stern stood the helmsman with a long steer board, whence the English word "starboard." Thwarts on either side of the ship provided for oarsmen. Without a deep keel, tacking was impossible in contrary winds; so oars were needed to supplement the sail. The Northmen were devoted to these ships, or "keels," calling them "Raven of the Wind," "Reindeer of the Breezes," and like titles of affection. In them they descended upon England, to drench that land in blood just at a time when Christianity was beginning to lessen strife.

These Danes, as the Vikings who descended on England were generally called,

At left: Remains of a Viking ship, preserved in museum at Oslo; at right, Northumbrian carving, around 700, showing warriors of the Beowulf period in chain mail.

at first merely pillaged, and, successful, they came again and again to strike at England, Scotland, and the east coast of Ireland. They apparently liked the land so much that they commenced to spend their winters there, and then to make permanent settlements. If we trust their sagas, intermediate between sober history and legend, they harassed England sorely. One of their earlier attacks, on Northumbria, was led by Ragnar Lodbrok, or "Hairy Breeks," who supposedly obtained his name by freezing hairy blankets to his trousers to protect his legs from the serpents which he drove out of his native Sweden. Ragnar, so it was told, led his men to Constantinople; to Dublin; up the Seine to Paris, which he sacked (845); to the bleak Orkney Islands, north of Britain; and eventually to Northumbria, whose king presumably thrust him into a den of snakes. As they slowly devoured him he sang of his past glories, each stanza beginning, "We hewed with our swords." And so until the end, when he sang: "I willingly depart! . . . The moments of my life are fled, but laughingly I die."

The sons of Ragnar, so the story goes, afterward returned and exacted memorable vengeance for their father's death. All northern England was overrun with Danes, who spread southward and infested the Wessex coast. Egbert spent the last years of his reign (see page 19) in stemming the tide. Driven back, the invaders would reappear from another direction. In 871, so it is said, they rowed up the Thames and attacked Wessex again. They were opposed by a new king, Egbert's grandson, who engaged in prayer as the Danes struck, but his younger brother, Alfred, led the Wessex fyrd (militia) to a signal victory, which, it has been said, saved Christianity in England. That same year, Alfred at twenty-two succeeded his brother as king.

Along with his military prowess, Alfred was inclined toward scholarly ways at a time when few other Saxon laymen could read or write. He had been unusually well educated, having traveled twice to Rome. For many years, he had no time for cultural pursuits as the omnipresent Danes won victory after victory. He had to flee to the wilder parts of his kingdom where he prepared for a new war. This was so successful that in the Peace of Wedmore (878) the Danes agreed to retire from Wessex and their king was baptized a Christian.

The treaty divided England between Dane and Saxon roughly along a line from near the mouth of the Thames to Liverpool. To the south and west lay Wessex ruled by Alfred, including London. The region to the north and east became known as the Danelaw (see map, page 10) with its Danes partly pagan but rapidly becoming Christianized.

The Danish conversion to Christianity was typical of the way the Viking invader usually adopted the customs of the lands he originally had plundered. But the Saxon was not much more civilized than the Dane at this time, and his background had been very similar, so that the Viking learned less in England than he did in regions with a more highly developed civilization than his own. Unlike the Saxon, the Dane did not lose his maritime interest when he turned to farming. As he settled down in the Danelaw brisk trading undoubtedly began to flourish on the coast there; for commercial enterprise was always the outlet for Viking energy when the first lust for plunder was surfeited.

The Peace of Wedmore did not end all troubles with the Danes, nor did it prevent the ravaging of the Channel coast from time to time by other Norsemen; but there appears to have been a respite until the last years of Alfred's life, when he again had to devote most of his time to war. It has been suggested that Alfred's military reforms (see page 24) and his fortification and permanent garrisoning of major towns, together with his building of a navy with which to fight the Danes before they might land, may have made it harder for the Danes to sweep all before them.

Alfred also sought to raise the general level of culture in England. The Danish wars had destroyed many, if not most, of the monasteries, the only centers of such meager culture as there was. Alfred, who wrote, "To give money to a school is to give to God," founded a school in which both English and Latin were taught, and like Charlemagne, he summoned many learned men to his court to help with it. The pupils, for the most part, were the sons of the nobility, who were compelled to attend. The king ordered that all well-born youths should be taught English, and that important Latin books should be translated for their benefit. Those boys who showed ability were to be trained in both English and Latin, particularly if they desired promotion in his service —a premium on knowledge such as no Saxon king before Alfred had ever thought to place.

The king meanwhile gave all his spare time to literary pursuits, particularly to the translation into English of certain standard Latin books. He first selected *Pastoral Care*, by Pope Gregory the Great, a book of instructions for priests, copies of which the king ordered sent to all bishops. "I remembered," he said in his preface, "how the law was first known in Hebrew, and when the Greeks had learned it how they translated the whole of it into their own language, and all other books besides. And again the Romans . . . and also other Christian people turned some parts of these books into their own tongue . . . we too should turn into the tongue which we all can understand certain books which are most necessary for all men to know."

Alfred may also have translated the Venerable Bede's *Ecclesiastical History* so that Englishmen could read it in their own language, but there is considerable doubt about this. Likewise uncertain is what he did in connection with the Anglo-Saxon Chronicle. Most important of a series of chronicles, which vary in value as source material with their authors' knowledge and discrimination, it was written in English instead of the usual Latin. Alfred stimulated the writing of it and apparently encouraged increasing the number of manuscript copies. Like most chronicles, it was originally simply a monastic table of important happenings made year by year; around this time, the scope of those entries began to widen gradually into more of a chronological history.

From the literary point of view, Alfred's best work was his translation of the *Consolation of Philosophy* by the Roman philosopher Boethius, who shows the influence of Christianity to such an extent that at times it is difficult to tell whether he was pagan or Christian. But Alfred changed the original, so that it became virtually a confession of his own faith. The following passages, for instance, are not in Boethius but are placed there by the royal translator: "He that will have eternal riches let him build the house of his mind on the foot-stone of lowliness, not on the highest hill where the raging winds of trouble blow or the rain of measureless anxiety." "A man will not be the better because he hath a well-born father, if he himself is naught." Thus wrote Alfred, who did his best to bring his crude and rough country within the circle of European civilization—such as there was of it in the ninth century.

This versatile king also stood far above his contemporaries in the practical administration of his government and in improving the condition of his subjects. His work was probably more a matter of restoring whatever had been weakened or destroyed in the recent invasions than of innovation. While the chronicles, dooms, charters, and wills give considerable information, it is impossible to disentangle Alfred's particular contributions, just as it would be extremely difficult to draw any sort of detailed and

The opening passages of the laws of Alfred, with manuscript picture of the King himself.

accurate picture of the institutional growth in any part of the six centuries between the arrival of the Anglo-Saxons in England and the coming of the Normans. Yet so far-reaching were the effects of the customs and institutions of this Anglo-Saxon period upon the later development of the country that certain significant features must be considered here, although description of the "systems" will be postponed until the coming of the more orderly-minded Normans, in 1066. Since social lines and governmental functions were seldom determined with precision and went through a process of constant evolution, it will be necessary to refer forward to the changes wrought by the Norman Conquest in order to appreciate the lasting effects of the earlier developments.

Whereas the Anglo-Saxons were formerly credited with most of the popular safeguards in law and government, together with the spirit which made England distinctive as a free country, more recent research indicates that some of the major developments came from other sources. Nevertheless, the Anglo-Saxon influence played a vital part, especially in the field of local government. Another difficulty in the way of a definite analysis of the social, economic, or political aspects of the period is the Anglo-Saxon avoidance of any preconceived, clean-cut systems of procedure. They have bequeathed to later generations of Englishmen this practice of "muddling through." They went ahead with their continual informal experimenting, apparently trusting that time and common sense would evolve methods which would work. That reluctance to conceive a rigid mold and then to jam everything into it crops up again and again in later English history.

The three principal occupations of the Middle Ages were fighting, praying, and farming. As time went on, the first two became highly paid specialties, supported by forced tribute from the masses who tilled the soil. The Church had since Whitby brought England into its system. In addition to the churchmen, there seem to have been four main classes in Anglo-Saxon society. The noble, or eorl; the ordinary freeman, or churl; and the slave, or thrall were important from the beginning. The fourth class, the partially free man, later called serf or villein, developed slowly at first, but finally increased so rapidly that it threatened to engulf most of the population. The earliest stages were more democratic than the later, because the ordinary freeman at first made up the bulk of the population, and there was not enough wealth to make inequality obvious.

Anglo-Saxon Society and Agriculture

The hereditary earls composed the Anglo-Saxon aristocracy at the outset; but gradually a more numerous lower nobility based at first on services rather than upon birth, developed in the thanes, or thegns.

They seem to have been an outgrowth of the German *comitatus,* or band of specialized fighting men, who had originally attached themselves to the king or to some powerful noble. The general "fyrd," or militia, was inadequate in many ways, so that regular fighting men with superior training and with better equipment, such as armor, were found among the thanes. They were rewarded for their military service not only by an honorable social status but later by grants of land also. Alfred's military reforms particularly concerned the thanes; he increased the number of those who were equipped to hurry on horseback to the scene of an attack by the fast-moving Danes. On the whole the thanes occupied a position similar to that of the knights of the feudal period and the country gentry of later centuries. At first the honor of thanehood was bestowed only for the particular service of an individual, but gradually it tended to become hereditary. Prosperous merchants trading in foreign parts were also granted the "thane right," as were those freemen who acquired five times the nomal amount of land. In the eyes of the law a thane counted, for certain purposes, as much as several ordinary freemen. By the end of the period the aristocracy consisted of three groups: the athelings, or princes of the royal family; the great earls, who dominated whole shires or groups of shires; and the far more numerous thanes.

The freeman was the substantial small farmer, who had his own land, who owed no forced agricultural service to a lord, and who was free to move about as he saw fit. All freemen were liable to military service in the general fyrd, or militia. Alfred appears to have reorganized this more efficiently by dividing the freemen so that, while some did the fighting, others might care for the crops, and still others garrison his newly fortified towns. This method prevented the former danger of being caught unprepared by a surprise attack of the enemy, perhaps when most of the fyrd would have to be at home reaping the harvest. Yet by Alfred's time the fyrd was probably not called out much because of its lack of armor and its primitive weapons, which made it vulnerable to the attack of the well-equipped Danes. The freeman is an elusive figure in English history. His was the most common status in the early days of the Anglo-Saxons, and the freeman was taken as the normal unit in the rudimentary politics and law. Gradually, however, he became the exception rather than the rule.

The growth of that large semifree class, which became the serfs of the Norman period (see page 48), came from several causes, some of which are obscure. The dread of the Danish invaders may have led some free communities or individual freemen to place themselves under the protection of a strong man who continued to exact services long after the danger had passed. The king and his advisers, too, might have transformed the old free communities into estates, which were granted as regular property to churchmen or nobles whom they wished to reward. The Anglo-Saxons had no single specific term for these men who sank below the rank of freemen. Many varying classifications and conditions later were to be blended into the fairly uniform status of the serf, "tied to the soil."

If serfdom was to mean a descent for the vast majority, it at least meant advancement for the lowest of the old English classes— the thralls, or slaves, who, not long after the close of the Anglo-Saxon period, gradually merged into the mass of serfs. A slave differed from a serf in that he could be sold as property and removed to other land. Some slaves were war captives, some owed their status to a legal penalty, and, in certain cases, parents even sold their own children into slavery. The port of Bristol is said to have carried on a thriving business in selling English slaves, both men and women, to Ireland.

At least nine out of ten of the people of these various social classes lived in agricultural villages, which were for centuries the commonest economic and social units in England. The usual village consisted of anywhere from a dozen to fifty thatched huts ranged along a narrow street and occupied by peasants, who derived their scanty living from work on the surrounding land. Generally these bleak, damp hovels were of the most primitive type, without windows or chimneys. Other buildings were the mill, the church, and the great house of the local lord or his representative, who dominated the village. Sometimes this residence was fortified so that all the village might take refuge there in time of danger.

The village lands consisted of the "arable," or plowed, fields for the raising of crops; the meadow for hay; the pasture for the grazing of horses, cattle, and sheep; and a woodland which provided acorns for the pigs, as well as firewood. In addition, small garden plots were attached to the various cottages, with a larger one for the great house. Often a stream ran through the lands, and sometimes there might be a fish pond. As in many other branches of medieval life, the individual was subordinated to the community. The pastures and wastes were "common" land, undivided among the separate peasants. Even in the arable land and the meadows the distribution of land and the agricultural practices were strongly influenced by this same communal relationship.

One of the most significant features of European history in the medieval and early modern period is the fact that, while most of the people spent their lives at farming, practically no changes in agricultural methods occurred between Roman days and the eighteenth century. The personal status of the agricultural population underwent certain slow changes, but the methods of raising crops went on in the same time-honored, inefficient manner from century to century. Meanwhile the small, active minority of the population not so engaged was making rapid advances in government, in-

Husbondrye

Plowing an open field strip, from the first published work on English agriculture, 1525.

fields in long, narrow strips of only a half acre or acre each. Nothing but little ridges of turf separated each strip from those on either side. A considerable part of the working day was thus wasted in trudging around among various isolated strips. The system doubtless arose from a desire to give each man a fair share of the best, the average, and the poorer soil of the community. Sometimes a redistribution of strips was made each year, and such a transfer of strips discouraged the peasant from improving his holdings. Actually each peasant simply had a fifteen-acre or thirty-acre share in the community arable land. Whether the open-field system came down from the Roman villas or originated in the Saxon free communities is strongly disputed. Whatever the source, this decidedly wasteful practice prevailed throughout much of England.

The "two-field" aspect of medieval agriculture further helps to explain the meager crops. Not until the eighteenth century was England to realize that turnips and other root crops could restore the nitrogen removed from the soil by the growth of grain; the best the early medieval farmers could do was to give the land a complete rest every other year. Consequently the peasant with thirty acres could use only fifteen in any given year. All the arable land was divided into two roughly equal fields, in each of which was half of each man's strips.

One of the few important changes in agricultural methods during the long centuries of conservatism was the gradual shift to a "three-field" system. Some farmers slowly realized how wasteful it was to leave half the land idle, and began to slide an extra crop into the fallow field. Eventually, with a partial knowledge of "rotating" crops, one-third of the land would be used for the basic wheat or rye and then the next year be sown with a different crop, usually barley or oats, so that it would lie fallow only the third year. But common action for this came very slowly, with some parts of

dustry, commerce, culture, and much else. Even if more effective agricultural methods had been devised, the communal situation hampered any deviation from custom. As a result the rural village remained on a subsistence basis, producing little if any more than was necessary for its own existence. Only when a considerable portion of the population had been lured away to towns and cities did agriculture finally undergo a revolution to increase its productivity. Two of the principal reasons for the inefficiency of medieval agriculture were the "open field" system of land distribution and cultivation, combined with the system of crude rotation of crops.

Under the "open field" system the average peasant held from fifteen to thirty acres of arable land. They were not, however, in a single, compact, fenced-off block where he could concentrate his energy. Instead, they were scattered widely through several open

England still clinging to the old "two-field" plan at the end of the Middle Ages.

The crude implements and field work were even more inefficient. Wooden plows, generally only tipped with iron, had to be drawn by eight undersized oxen and, as a peasant seldom owned more than two, it was necessary to co-operate for this work. Seed was wastefully scattered broadcast. Crops were harvested by back-breaking short sickles. The result of all this was that an acre yielded only eight or nine bushels of wheat, even in a good season, whereas modern agricultural methods produce several times as much. In bad years famine was likely to stalk through the land.

Yet the farmers raised enough at least to survive in a simple manner. From the wheat or rye they had their porridge and bread; from the barley came their principal beverage, beer. Their livestock could supplement this scanty diet with beef, mutton, or pork, usually salted for preservation, as well as with chicken, eggs, and milk. From the sheep, also, came wool, which could be spun and woven into crude cloth; from the cattle came leather for shoes and sometimes jackets.

Altogether, the village was a self-sufficing entity, producing almost everything necessary for its needs. In the early stages it had its own simple industrial specialists, such as a miller, a carpenter, and a smith. Its few outside demands seldom went beyond salt for preserving meat, iron for plows and tools, wax for church candles, and possibly silk, or other finer textiles than homespun, for the lord and his lady or the priest. Because of this self-sufficiency and because of the formidable obstacles to trade in the matter of robbery, tolls, and bad roads, there was almost no commerce or concentrated industry. Later the towns began to take over those functions, and the villages, specializing more than ever in agriculture, developed a sufficient surplus to exchange for the wares of the townsmen.

Anglo-Saxon Government

Englishmen have been particularly proud of their racial blend, government, and dominion on the seas and overseas, and their history emphasizes these in turn. At this point, when the mingling of Celtic, Roman, Saxon, Danish, and Norman influences is about to reach its climax, the historian picks up the thread of constitutional development, or the growth of English forms of government. That story keeps recurring down through the centuries until so good was the unique method of government worked out that many other nations have copied its essential features. The story of England's success on the seas still lay far in the future.

Compared with the specific, precise document which the American statesmen drew up in 1787 as a constitution, England's has always been vague and indefinite. That arises apparently from that Anglo-Saxon unwillingness to define and to confine precisely in words the exact status of their institutions. This has resulted in a desirable flexibility, in which governmental functions can mold themselves to changing circumstances without going through the rigid formality of amendments. The only attempt at a comprehensive written constitution lasted barely five years, and the three documents often piously regarded in recent centuries as the "bulwarks of English liberty" are mainly negative in character and deal with immediate and specific royal abuses. Even today the crown has tremendous theoretical power which has never been taken away by definite enactment; but the ruler and all Englishmen understand perfectly that the actual power has been whittled down by custom to almost nothing. The later sharp distinction between legislative, executive, and judicial functions did not exist in men's minds in those days. There was certain public business to be done, and the various individuals or bodies handled it as it came along, without speculating upon whether they were making laws, enforcing laws, or interpreting laws. If they occasionally used terms which now have a very definite meaning, such usage by no means implied that they gave them the present-day clear-cut significance.

The central government of the Anglo-Saxons was so ineffective that the Normans were to transform it almost completely. The local institutions, on the other hand, were permitted in many cases to continue without fundamental change, and consequently were to have permanent importance. The four main political units were, in order, the kingdom, the shire, the hundred, and the township, though the functions of that lowest unit remain obscure.

The prestige of the kingship, despite the inadequate machinery for central government, increased during the six centuries of the Anglo-Saxon period. At the outset every little tribe had had its own king, who had either held that office on the Continent or was a temporary war leader raised to permanent leadership. Whatever democratic control may have limited the kingship back in Germany and Denmark disappeared shortly after the arrival in England. After the kings of Wessex had gained leadership over all England, the royal influence grew considerably. The direct acquisition of crown lands from which the king derived a steady income, the influence of royal leadership against the Danes (particularly that of Alfred), and the support of the Church in matters of both theory and practice all probably contributed to this increased prestige. But the royal power fell far short of that which the first Norman king was to wield. England was still far from being a really united country, in spite of the nominal headship of the king. Remains of provincial independence lingered in the outlying regions, which remembered that they had been separate kingdoms, and which were controlled by powerful earls who enjoyed more real authority there than did the king. The services performed by the central government were not extensive or impressive. Local units administered most of the law and were charged with the triple duty (*trinoda necessitas*) of military service in the fyrd, the repair and guarding of fortified places, and the building and repair of bridges. Relatively little fell upon the king's central government except the conduct of foreign affairs and leadership in time of war, together with efforts to supervise the law and, in the case of the specific Danegeld later collected to buy off the Danes, to levy taxes (see page 33). A few "household" officials, such as the butler, chamberlain, marshal, and, later, the chancellor, assisted in administration.

Associated with the king in the central government was the body known as the witan or witenagemot. It was composed of the principal nobles and churchmen of the land, together with certain other prominent men whom the king saw fit to summon. It was not a representative body, for the members were invited because of their personal importance and not as representatives of particular regions. The witan advised the king on important matters of policy; served as a high court for certain serious cases, though not as a regular supreme court of appeal; and co-operated with the king in issuing statements of the law. Ordinarily it did not serve as a check upon the king's authority; for he summoned its members when he saw fit, presided over its meetings, and initiated the business. Under a minor or a weak king, however, this gathering of the "wise men" might take the authority into its own hands. When a king died, the witan elected his successor, normally a royal "atheling," or prince, provided he seemed adequate for the position. At times, however, it selected an outsider as king. The witan was significant, for the Great Council of the Normans and the subsequent House of Lords may be regarded as its direct descendants.

The most important subdivision of the kingdom, then and ever since, has been the shire, or county, as it came to be called after the Norman Conquest. Yorkshire, the largest, has an area greater than the state of Connecticut, but the rest are much smaller. Most of the forty shires had come into existence by the end of the Anglo-Saxon period. Some, like Kent and Sussex, represented former little kingdoms which had been absorbed; others, like Worcestershire and Leicestershire, bore the names of towns which were administrative centers around which they developed. The head man in the shire was the ealdorman, or earl, though that title did not have the same exact significance as "eorl" in the early Anglo-Saxon aristocracy. He was in charge of the military establishment of the shire, presided at its assembly when present, and received the "third penny" of fines levied in the shire court. At first the ealdorman was appointed by the king; but there was a tendency for the office to become hereditary, and hence more independent. Some time after Alfred's reign, moreover, certain earls extended their power over several shires until at one time there were only four earls. Next to the ealdorman came the sheriff, or shire reeve, whose office did not become hereditary and who served as a more direct representative of the king. The office grew out of the functions of the local reeves who collected rents from the crown lands. As time went on, particularly after the earls ceased to confine themselves to a single shire, the authority and duties of the sheriff increased. After the Conquest his influence was to be still further augmented, for he was the all-important link between the central and the local government. Those two officials, together with the bishop, presided at the meetings of the shire moot.

This shire moot, which met twice a year, was to prove one of the most significant Anglo-Saxon political institutions. It was primarily a court for cases which had not already been settled in the hundred moots; but in the undivided condition of public

business in that day it frequently handled other business of common interest as well. In theory all freemen of the shire were entitled to attend its sessions and participate in its judgments; in practice most of them were too busy to take the time, and attendance was probably confined chiefly to the thanes, together with representatives, perhaps, from the various subdivisions of the shire. Alfred is said to have been specially interested in the administration of justice and to have had both the shire and hundred courts meet more regularly.

Each shire was divided into several "hundreds," or "wapentakes," as they were called in the region of the Danelaw. The origin of these names is obscure. The hundred moot, which met usually every four weeks, served as a sort of police court and handled the bulk of the ordinary cases. It was more democratic in its actual make-up, having a larger proportion of ordinary freemen, who did not have to travel as far as they would in attending the shire moot.

These moots of shire and hundred embodied the principle of popular participation in government. That principle lasted on after the Norman period and helped to give the English people a practice in political affairs which was lacking in most regions on the Continent. Some have even seen in the shire moot the germs of the national Parliament which later arose.

The older histories told also of tun moots in the various townships, and those were regarded as direct ancestors of the New England town meetings which still exist. Men of the township may have gathered occasionally to settle questions of land distribution and other local matters, but there is little evidence of a regular moot which handled law cases, as did the assemblies of hundred and shire. Even if such may have existed, they were absorbed into the courts of the local nobility, which were even to encroach upon the hundred

Women engaged in carding, spinning, and weaving.

their emphasis to specific penalties or to the announcement of new offenses. Alfred was one of those kings who had comprehensive dooms drawn up and proclaimed. Much of the basic law was simply unwritten custom, preserved in the minds of the "wise men" of the community, so that any codification was decidedly useful. Criminal cases were the main business of the local courts, with the commonest crimes homicide, assault, and cattle-stealing. Consequently, criminal law loomed far more prominently than civil, which consists chiefly of private disputes over property. In the latter the royal dooms made one extremely rational provision: that all sales must be made publicly, in town or hundred, in the presence of at least two sworn witnesses who would be bound to testify to the transaction before a court. A third category of moot jurisdiction consisted of religious cases, tried in the presence of the bishop; but separate church courts were not set up in England until after the Norman Conquest.

In criminal law the striking feature of the early dooms was the principle of cash compensation for crime. The primitive Germans, with their strong ties of family, seem to have handled early criminal offenses by means of personal revenge and to have engaged in bloody feuds. It was a long step toward the preservation of the peace when the injured party or his kinsmen were persuaded to accept cash compensation instead of going out to exact a literal "eye for an eye and tooth for a tooth." As a result the early dooms give a regular list of prices for various forms of physical damage. Compensation for death was known as "wergild," or man money, and was paid to the kinsmen; the "bot" for injuries went to the victim himself; while an additional sum, known as the "wite," often had to be paid to the moot. The laws of Alfred, for instance, are delightfully specific in their details of the cost of bodily damage: "If a man strike off an-

courts. In some of the boroughs, or larger towns, the organization was more definite than in the rural townships, and some may have had regular hundred organization. Towns were the exception in that day, however, and — except for London — were often little more than overgrown villages.

Anglo-Saxon Law

Not until a full century after the Anglo-Saxon period did English law begin to take on familiar aspects, either in the nature of the law itself or in the methods by which it was administered. The justice dispensed in the shire and hundred moots was based on principles strange today and was arrived at by methods highly unscientific. From time to time the kings and their witans issued "dooms," or rude law codes, which throw considerable, but by no means complete, light on Anglo-Saxon legal principles; for these dooms devoted most of

other's nose, let him make bot with LX shillings. If a man strike out another's tooth in the front of his head, let him make bot for it with VIII shillings: if it be the canine tooth, let IV shillings be paid as bot. A man's grinder is worth XV shillings. If the shooting finger be struck off, the bot is XV shillings; for its nail it is IV shillings." There was a separate price for each toe, ranging from twenty shillings for the big toe to five for the little one. The scale did not stop with classifying injuries: there was a separate tariff of prices for each social class. It cost forty times as much to kill an ealdorman or bishop as a churl, and the price of king slaughter was prohibitive.

In two particular features the law differed from the present. The wergild, for homicide, was determined without regard to those considerations of motive which now result in varying penalties for first-degree and second-degree murder, manslaughter, and justifiable homicide. Then, too, the injured party himself had to hale the offender into court, to prosecute the case, and to collect the fine. That was frequently difficult, because the very fact of injury implied that the offender was the more aggressive of the two. Only toward the end of the period were certain particularly flagrant offenses regarded as crimes against society in general, to be punished by the king.

The court procedure in the shire and hundred moots seems strangely irrational today, but it is partially explained by the strong faith in oaths and miracles, and the smallness of the communities which enabled the assemblies to have a fairly good idea of the relative character of the contesting parties. On those two foundations, rather than on the weighing of evidence, justice rested. The case was opened before the assembly when the plaintiff, or injured party, swore his complaint under oath. Then the defendant, or accused, swore his denial. The work of the whole assembly consisted in determining which party

should proceed to prove his case and by what method. Ordinarily the proof was left to the defendant. If the crime was not too serious and if the defendant had some standing in the community, he was allowed to try to clear himself by compurgation, whereby a stipulated number of compurgators or oath helpers swore that they believed his denial was true. Simply what would be now called character witnesses, they did not attempt to introduce either an alibi for him or even any direct evidence bearing on the case. They were under oath, however, and penalties for false swearing, both immediate and in the next world, were serious enough to make a man think twice before committing perjury. Also, the fact that a man could find the necessary number of compurgators indicated that he had a fair standing in the community. If the offense was particularly grave, or if the accused was a stranger or lacking in friends, he was liable to be forced into the grim test of the ordeal, where pain and the probability of adverse judgment awaited him. This ordeal was a religious ceremony, based on the theory that if God considered the man innocent he would perform a miracle to rescue him from otherwise almost certain failure. Three favorite ordeals were by hot iron, hot water, and cold water. The royal doom laid down the procedure in full detail, including the religious ceremonies. In the case of the witnesses to the ordeal, for instance, it was decreed, "Let there go in an equal number of men of either side, and stand on both sides of the ordeal, along the church; and let these all be fasting, and abstinent from their wives on that night; and let the Mass priest sprinkle holy water over them all, and let each of them taste of the holy water, and give them all the book and the image of Christ's rood to kiss." In the first two ordeals the accused had to carry a piece of red-hot iron several paces or pluck a stone out of a kettle of boiling water. "If it be a single accusation, let the hand dive after the stone up to the wrist; and if it be three-fold, up to the elbow." Then the hand, inflamed from the iron or the hot water, was tightly bound up. If, on the third day, the skin was not infected, which would be considered a miracle, he was deemed innocent; otherwise he was guilty. The third ordeal consisted of lowering him, bound hand and foot, into cold water; if he floated, he was judged guilty, on the supposition that the water refused to receive anything evil. If the guilty man could not pay a fine or if the crime was too serious to be settled on a cash basis, there were penalties of death, mutilation, or outlawry; for the Anglo-Saxons had no jails for imprisonment.

Much of this development had come by Alfred's reign, but a few of the features took form only in the century and a half between his death (about 900) and the coming of the Normans. Among these later changes was, in particular, the extension of the Wessex kingship all over England by Alfred's son and grandson. Alfred's grandfather, Egbert, to be sure, had been acknowledged Bretwalda; but this was only a precarious overlordship, like that previously wielded by the kings of Northumbria and Mercia. Under a Bretwalda there were still separate kingdoms with their own kings; but in the tenth century the lesser kings had disappeared, their former subordinate kingdoms were administered by earls, and England had only one king, the ruler of Wessex. Unity was thus achieved with this increased prestige of the crown, although the machinery of actual government still left much to be desired. Because of this lack of the central government the unification of the kingship paradoxically led to a scattering of administrative functions among the local nobility. At this period it was ruled that "every man must have a lord" to answer for him before the law. Previously his kinsmen had had that responsibility; but England was outgrowing the family stage, yet had not attained the modern conception of the state's full responsibility for law and order.

Alfred's son, Edward the Elder, not only absorbed Danish Mercia, East Anglia, and Northumbria into Wessex but also won the partial, if not complete, submission of Scotland. According to the Anglo-Saxon Chronicle, "The King of Scotland with all his people chose him [Edward] as father and lord," a statement utilized long afterward by Norman kings of England as proof of their alleged suzerainty over Scotland. Athelstan, the grandson, went further. He consolidated his father's victories over Welsh, Danes, and Scots, and was definitely recognized king of all Britain. This reign—unless we include that of Edgar the Peaceful, concerning which the Anglo-Saxon Chronicle tells us practically nothing—marked the peak of the house of Wessex. A succession of weak kings, plots, and counterplots made, for the most part, a sorry tale of England's political history for the rest of the century.

One strong man, and one only, appeared on the horizon—Dunstan, abbot of Glastonbury, afterward Archbishop of Canterbury. Folklore in regard to Dunstan's miracles are many, but facts in regard to his career are few. He did much to reform English monasticism, purifying it on the model of the contemporary reform movements on the Continent (see page 16). He repaired many monasteries, brought a new influx of Irish monks to England, and wrote a good deal of ecclesiastical music. He was also something of a statesman and did all that he could to uphold the falling fortunes of the Wessex line. Upon the accession of Ethelred the Unready (978), however, he lost influence, and England was now harassed by fresh forays by the Danes. Their ninth-century raids had given them the Danelaw —half of England; these renewed attacks were to put the whole country under Danish rule.

Ethelred did not choose to fight these Danish pirates but bought them off by silver, a practice which led to his undoing. The tax levied for this purpose was called the Danegeld. Within a quarter century seven payments of this tribute had totaled more than seventy tons of silver from the thinly settled and impoverished land! Even this did not keep the Danes away; the more Danegeld they received the more frequently they came. In 994 a Danish leader, Sweyn Forkbeard, attacked London, spent the winter near Southampton, and returned to Denmark to fight successfully for that throne; but England was not rid of him for good.

Ethelred, whose "life was cruel in the beginning, wretched in the middle, and disgraceful in the end," now shifted from bribery to blood in his dealings with the Danes. In the year 1002, according to the Anglo-Saxon Chronicle, "the king ordered all the Danish men who were in England to be slain on St. Brice's Day." Since Danes and Saxons had intermarried for generations, the absurdity as well as the viciousness of this command was apparent. It is extremely doubtful, however, if any such wholesale massacre occurred, and perhaps certain Danes in Wessex, who were suspected of plotting against the king, were the only ones slain. The story that among those killed was a sister of Sweyn, beheaded by the special order of the English king, rests on doubtful foundation; at any rate, this time Sweyn, now king of Denmark, vowed vengeance upon the timorous "Unready." Such revenge must have looked easy to him if it is true that he received about this time a letter which read: "The land is a fair land and rich, but the king snores. Devoted to women and wine, he thinks of everything rather than war, and this makes him hateful to his subjects and ridiculous to foreigners. The generals are all jealous of one another; the country folk are weak, and fly from the field at the first crash of battle."

Sweyn Forkbeard landed in 1013 and within a year held all the north country.

London resisted for the time being, and Sweyn rushed past it to Bath, where the English thanes fell over one another in their anxiety to acknowledge his overlordship. Ethelred fled the country, seeking refuge with his wife's relatives in Normandy; and Sweyn presumably would have conquered all England had he not died, after a brief month as king of England.

The witan invited Ethelred back from exile; he returned, worthless as ever. For three years Saxon and Dane engaged in bitter strife for power, under the leadership of two able youths, each barely twenty. One was Edmund Ironside, upholding the cause of his father, Ethelred; the other was Sweyn Forkbeard's son, Canute, whom the witan had passed over in favor of Ethelred. With the death of Ethelred, in 1016, Ironside as king continued to fight valiantly against terrific odds. London alone stoutly resisted the Danish attacks. Treachery helped to end this fitful moment of Saxon resistance; and when Edmund died, after a heroic seven months' reign, Canute became king of all England, at twenty-two.

Danish Rule

This plundering young heathen, who had recently sent a group of hostages ashore with hands and noses lopped off, was quickly transformed by responsibility into a wise, efficient, Christian king—one of the best in English history. From slaughtering and looting the English, he devoted himself to governing them well—so well, in fact, that he soon became popular. Backward as Anglo-Saxon England might be, it was more advanced in many respects than Scandinavia. Coming from that adaptable Viking breed, which would take ideas and practices as readily as they would steal property, Canute respected English laws and customs, partly because they were better than those of his native land. Within a year he sent his army back to Denmark and made himself at home, proceeding to build churches on the sites of battlefields, and to

Left, Edward the Confessor and Harold; right, Harold's coronation, from the Bayeux Tapestry.

marry Emma of Normandy, Ethelred's widow. He played no favorites; he trusted the Anglo-Saxons and was trusted by them in turn. He published a law code which kept in the main to Alfred's. Anglo-Saxon prelates were retained in ecclesiastical positions. Aside from a small body of housecarls (personal retainers), he maintained no military display, and for twenty years he kept the peace, an unusual boon for war-trodden England. But of literary remains of Canute's reign almost nothing survives.

King of England, and soon afterward, at the death of an older brother, of Denmark as well, Canute aspired to further glory. He intrigued with the nobles of Norway and drew many of them away from their ruler. Commanding a great Anglo-Danish armada, he next attempted to conquer Norway. The king's dragon ship was said to have had sixty rowers, but despite his naval strength he was foiled by the skillful stratagem of the Swedes, allied to the Norwegians. In a second try Canute added Norway to his English and Danish thrones. Already before this time he had visited Scotland, where he is said to have received the submission of the king. For the time being, it seemed as though a great Scandinavian empire might arise, to be ruled from England.

This was not to be, in that time of difficult communication; but the maritime nature of Canute's dominions was to increase England's interest in her sphere of future

greatness, the sea. Canute's wide holdings gave increased opportunity for trade, so that London, which had relapsed from its activity of Roman days, received a powerful impetus toward its future career as a center of commerce.

Canute died in 1035, and his three sons inherited his three kingdoms, Denmark going to Hardecanute, Norway to Sweyn, and England to Harold Harefoot. Queen Emma was the mother of Hardecanute only, and she desired England for her son. In consequence, although the majority of the witan voted for Harold Harefoot, Wessex, where Emma's influence was strong, stood up for Hardecanute.

Neither of these two measured up to their father. Harold Harefoot proved to be an extraordinarily bloodthirsty tyrant, who died just as his brother, Hardecanute, prepared to contest the throne with him. This brother "devised no kingly deed during all his reign, and he caused the dead body of Harold to be taken up and shot into the marsh." He increased the Danegeld beyond reason, wrought frightful vengeance with his housecarls on those who refused to pay it, and, only two years a king, died apparently of strong drink. The English, now surfeited with Danes, had forgiven or forgotten the iniquities of Ethelred, and so they welcomed his son, Emma's child by her first marriage, to the English throne. Thus began the strange reign of Edward the Confessor (1042-1066).

Chapter Three · 1042-1087

The Coming of the Normans

Only twenty-four years after the Danish rule came to a close with the death of Canute's second son, England was to be conquered by another band of former Vikings, the Normans. While the Danes had contributed little that was new to Anglo-Saxon England, these Normans, although originally from the same northern regions, were to transform England radically as a result of their two centuries of sojourning in France.

In the beginning the only difference between a Dane of the Danelaw, a Norman of Normandy, a Varangian of Russia, and the other Vikings (or Northmen or Norsemen, as they were variously called) may have depended simply upon the direction from which the wind happened to be blowing upon the day when each group set sail from Scandinavia. A wind from the north or west may well have sent certain of these fierce and restless adventurers to raid the French or Russian coasts, while an easterly breeze may equally have settled the fate of shore communities in England or in Ireland, or even have tempted the earliest explorers past Iceland to Greenland and Vineland (America). The most important streams of these sea raiders headed down the North Sea toward the more settled parts of Europe, even past Gibraltar. Thus it happened that as Alfred strove with the Danes,

northern France was ravaged, even to the danger of Paris itself, by other Northmen. Both English and French saved themselves by buying off the invader with grants of territory. The French equivalent of the Danelaw was given in 911 to Rollo (Hrolf), the Norse leader. This, the duchy of Normandy, was a compact region, extending from the coast halfway up the Seine River toward Paris. Here lived the Normans who were to conquer England.

All the Vikings were quick to slough off their own crudeness and to adopt the civilization of those lands in which they settled as a conquering minority. Thus in France they became Roman Catholic in religion and genuinely French in language and in ways of living; in Russia, Greek Orthodox and Slavic; in England, Roman Catholic and Anglo-Saxon. The Northmen found more that was worth imitating in France than in England, where the Anglo-Saxons were not much more advanced than themselves. Normandy and the Danelaw soon had little in common except Viking ancestry; for France, even in the so-called Dark Ages after Charlemagne's reign, preserved at least a semblance of Latin culture, law, and unity, and was, moreover, working out that unique social system known as feudalism (see page 43).

William's Normans landing at Pevensey, showing typical ships; Bayeux Tapestry.

Owing to this contact and to their own energy the Normans became temporarily the most influential people in all Europe, dominating western and northern France and Sicily, as well as England. They were ahead of the rest of the world in their organizing ability, which they learned partly by observing and copying the workings of the Church. Their numbers were small; but, none the less, as noblemen, merchants, and fishermen they lorded it over the older peasant stock of Normandy, a Celtic, Roman, and Germanic mixture. Some were of the shrewd, hard-headed type which made excellent lawyers and administrators. More conspicuous were the restless, proud, and quarrelsome warriors who had been quick to adopt the latest military devices, and who stayed in the pink of condition as a result of constant warfare. While Anglo-Saxons and Danes still hewed at their foes on foot with battle-axes, the Normans were already using horses for their more important warriors, new weapons such as lances and crossbows, and, for defense, fortresses built on mounds. In spirit, ability, and equipment they were pre-eminent.

In 1035 the leadership of Normandy fell to one who was to rise from Duke William the Bastard to King William the Conqueror. His mother was not the duchess but a tanner's daughter whom Duke Robert (called the Devil by his foes and the Magnificent by his friends) had briefly loved. Duke Robert desired that, in default of a child born in wedlock, this illegitimate son should succeed him. Consequently, before embarking for a pilgrimage to the Holy Land from which he was never to return, he forced all his barons to swear allegiance to the boy. Thus William, eight years old, became duke of the most turbulent baronage in Europe, under the double handicap of being a minor and illegitimate.

Only a person of extraordinary force and ability could have conquered the difficulties which beset William almost from the cradle. "How to deal with men he learned, when to smite and when to spare," at a very early age. First, in his own duchy, the barons, especially in the west, rose to take instant advantage of a boy ruler, and his cousin, with a legitimate claim to the dukedom, sought to oust a tanner's grandson. William was fortunate in his guardians, and although only fourteen when they were murdered, he already knew how to fight. His liege lord, the king of France, assisted him at his decisive victory of Val-ès-Dunes over his barons. There William showed himself a justly severe but on the whole a merciful conqueror; for after the battle no blood was shed, and the punishments consisted merely of fines, the giving of hostages, and the surrender of castles. By nineteen he was the master of his own duchy, which flourished under his intelligent and forceful rule.

William next gave his attention to the neighboring counties and duchies—Anjou,

Maine, Brittany, and others. The jealous Count of Anjou persuaded the fickle king to turn against the young duke, whose authority he had just helped to establish, whereupon William, "the Iron-Cutter," proved himself not only a powerful warrior whose blows could cleave horse and man in two but also a skillful strategist. Despite revolts and invasions he kept his duchy intact, and so extended his power that he became foremost of all vassals in France, stronger even than the king. Flanders became his semi-ally by marriage, and without the friendship of that rich province on the Channel it is doubtful if he could have conquered England. The little county of Maine, to which he had some legal claim, became his by force. When the garrison of one town hung raw oxhides on the walls to taunt the tanner's grandson, he inflicted terrible punishment upon them all. And Brittany meanwhile was "reduced to submission by a single march."

The ability and aggressiveness of the duke as a soldier perhaps were natural inheritances from his pirate forebears, but his exceptional executive power and statesmanship resulted from his own genius. He righted wrongs no matter who the wrongdoer might be, and in consequence much else was easily forgiven him by his subjects, grateful in those unquiet times for law and order. William ever put himself on the right side of the law through craft and cunning, and some of his most oppressive acts were within the bounds of technical legality. Though short, fat, and bald-headed, William was powerfully built, with broad shoulders and long arms. Aroused, he had all the Northman's brutality but he usually kept his violent passion in check. His grim aspect and forbidding eye intimidated his court, and his life in some ways was solitary. His marriage to Matilda of Flanders, however, was said to have been a happy one; for, although not always faithful, he was devotedly attached to his wife. Even she, as legend has it, tasted his fierce tem-

per after scorning his first advances because of his birth. He rode headlong to her father's capital, found Matilda walking in the town with her maids, dragged her about by the hair, and then rode off—apparently this won her undying devotion. In his own way William promoted good men, valued education, protected the poor, patronized commerce, and altogether made Normandy into a compact, prosperous state. Because of his absolute authority he became the envy of all contemporary rulers. This was the man who now began to turn interested eyes across the Channel; and in view of his record it is surprising that even slothful England worried so little at his covetous glances and his friendship with her childless king.

But England, in these years between 1042 and 1066, was already experiencing a sort of preliminary Norman Conquest; for the throne was occupied by the much overrated Edward the Confessor. Had not Canute's younger sons been so notoriously worthless, the witan would probably have overlooked this colorless son of Ethelred the Unready and Emma of Normandy. Although he came from the old Wessex line in direct descent from Alfred, the Norman blood seemed to predominate in him. In education, in friends, and in interests he was thoroughly Norman. His mother had fled with him to her brother's court in Normandy when her husband, Ethelred, had proved himself so notoriously "unready" against the Danish menace. When she returned to England as Canute's bride, Edward remained behind with those monks who had taught him as a boy and who had ever remained his closest intimates. His personality received so deeply religious an impress that the Church became his main concern, and it later canonized him as Saint Edward, the Confessor.

Even in the disorganization and stagnation of these twilight years of Saxon England an energetic ruler might have built a firm government; but this petty-minded and charmless, albeit kindly, "French monk" was not the man to do it. In after years, when the yoke of Norman kings seemed oppressive, the English, as all people are apt to do, looked back with affection to the "laws of good King Edward"; yet, to quote one authority, "so far as we know he never made a law. Had he made laws, had he even made good use of those that were already made, there might have been no Norman Conquest." In that case, "Edward would never have gained his fictitious glories . . . as the last of the English kings of the English."

The Confessor's only policy—if even this could be dignified by such a name—was to introduce Norman ideas into England. Forced in middle age to rule across the Channel, he clung tenaciously to all things Norman, particularly in the Church. Among the many Norman prelates whom he placed in prominent benefices was Robert of Jumièges, who was Bishop of London and then Archbishop of Canterbury. So much did Edward rely upon him that it was rumored that if Jumièges "said a black crow was white, the king would rather trust to his mouth than to his own eyes." The Confessor also put the so-called Cinque Ports—Dover, Sandwich, Romney, Hythe, and Hastings—under Norman control. This was particularly galling for these proud seaports, which even then were important for their location on the southeastern coast, nearest the Continent. These ports, to which Rye and Winchelsea were later added, were to furnish most of the ships and men for the royal naval service until the end of the Middle Ages, and in return were to receive extensive privileges. Norman barons were also set to guard the important frontier districts known as marches; Norman wine merchants were given a wharf of their own at London; and Edward drew an ever-increasing number of Normans to the royal court.

This peaceful Norman penetration was to arouse the hostility of many Saxon English-men, including certain powerful nobles. They wanted to keep England for the English, without interference from either Dane or Norman; but they were too jealous of one another to act in unison. Foremost was Godwin, related by marriage to Canute, who had raised him from simple thane to Earl of Wessex. This vigorous and able Saxon, about whom unfortunately little is known, appears to have had much to do with Edward's elevation to the throne. Apparently hoping to become the power behind the throne, he found himself balked by too many Norman favorites. He succeeded, nevertheless, in marrying his daughter to the king, from whom he received so many favors that ultimately he and his sons through their many earldoms controlled most of England, except the north country, where the Saxon earls of Northumbria and Mercia were his only real rivals. Chief opponent of Norman influence in England was Earl Godwin.

In 1051 the ill-feeling between Saxon and Norman burst into flame, following hard upon an episode at Dover, where a party of Norman knights, returning from a visit with the king, were denied lodgings. A brawl followed; Normans were killed; and the king ordered Godwin to punish this insult to his guests. Godwin refused and civil war would have followed had he not fled with his sons. Within a year public opinion, inflamed by the rumor that Edward had made Duke William his heir, brought about their triumphant return. Although they sacked the Channel ports on their way home, southern England rose to join them with the cry "Live or die for Earl Godwin!" Terror-stricken Norman favorites fled as Godwin sailed up the Thames to dictate terms at London. For the remainder of the Confessor's reign Saxon interests, or at least those of the Godwin family, were uppermost in England. Robert of Jumièges was replaced as archbishop by a Saxon, Stigand.

In the year of his return Godwin died, and for a time his sons succeeded to most of his power. They were an interesting lot. One led his forces into Scotland to dethrone the king, Macbeth, immortalized by Shakespeare; another, the worthless Tostig, was exiled after kidnaping a nun and misruling his earldom, only to return in the year of the Conquest to distract the Saxon resistance; and finally there was Harold, the ablest of all, who succeeded his father as Earl of Wessex. These various earls paid little heed to royal authority, just as William, duke of Normandy, gave scant consideration to the wishes of the king of France.

With this submerging of Edward's Norman friends, the Norman Conquest would have probably dwindled to a mere gradual adoption of the more progressive ideas from across the Channel had Edward of England abided by the customary royal duty of providing an heir to his throne. Instead, on his wedding day he followed his marriage vows with an unusual oath, one of perpetual chastity. The monk who chronicled this performance praised Edward's pious act, but others in the realm felt that he was betraying his land by leaving it a prey to rival heirs and covetous Normandy. Primogeniture, to be sure, was not then as firmly established in the English royal line as it was later, and, of course, the real authority in deciding the succession was the witan's but, even so, it would seem that the monk in Edward had triumphed over the king.

Upon his death early in 1066 there were several claimants for the throne. He had named as his heir Harold, who was lucky enough to be at hand. The next of kin was Edgar the Atheling, of the old Wessex line, but he was a mere boy. Harold, the leading noble, traced his descent on his mother's side from Scandinavian kings; and he was at once duly named "King" by the witan. No voice appears to have been raised for the dispossessed Atheling; but a clamor arose elsewhere, particularly from Duke William of Normandy. Another possible claimant was Harold Hardrada of Norway, a de-

scendant of Canute. Some asserted that he was in the field only to support William, but whatever Hardrada's motives, his activities came at the most propitious moment for that duke. William himself declared that he was the rightful and legitimate king of England on several rather questionable grounds. Although illegitimate, he was related to the English royal family. He insisted that Edward had named him his heir. To be sure, it was not legally a gift in Edward's power, and a scantily attended witan had elected Harold; but William ignored that. In addition, Harold once had been shipwrecked on the French coast and, in the custom of those days, became with his ship, cargo, and crew legitimate prize of the shore community. William had taken advantage of this to force Harold to swear to help him gain the English throne; and Harold found to his cost that, unbeknown to himself, he had performed the oath over sacred relics, which made it a serious religious offense should he later break his word. In contrast to the modern view, the religious mind of the Middle Ages considered the exploiting of wrecked sailors a legitimate act, but falseness to an oath, given over relics, was one of the blackest sins, a fact of which William made good use.

Nevertheless, Harold, at the start, was able to outplay his rivals, since he was on the spot and had been lawfully elected and crowned. But his success was short-lived; he was faced with too many foes, and he had an apathetic England at his back. As the chronicler summed up his nine months' reign, "Little quiet did he enjoy the while he wielded the kingdom." The disunity of Anglo-Saxon England, which was to prove her undoing, helps to explain why more than a million Englishmen so readily submitted to a few thousand foreign adventurers. Harold could rely only on the earldoms in the south under his direct rule. The earls of Mercia and Northumbria were playing a waiting game, and his own brother Tostig was openly aiding Hardrada.

The Norman Invasion—1066

While Harold was anxiously patrolling the south coast in fear of the rumored arrival of William of Normandy, Hardrada and Tostig with a fleet of some three hundred vessels landed on the north coast and headed for York. Harold rushed north and offered his brother his old earldom of Northumbria back again, but Tostig asked what Hardrada was to get. "Seven feet of earth, perhaps more, seeing that he is a tall man," came the answer. There was to be no brotherly reconciliation. At Stamford Bridge, near York, Harold won a smashing victory; both Tostig and Hardrada were slain. The English had no time to celebrate. Three days after Stamford Bridge, William landed on the unguarded south coast at Pevensey.

The duke was making no haphazard foray upon the English shore. He had put his usual energy and thoroughness into preparations for what was to be one of the most successful military expeditions in history. To win European public opinion by propaganda, he sent Harold a message, reminding the latter of his oath, and promising both his daughter in marriage and control over a large part of England to Harold were he to support William's claims. The duke expected nothing from this, but it was a good thing to have on record. Whereas the active Norman diplomats were telling the story of the broken oath in many European courts and condemning Harold's "usurpation" of the crown, Harold himself was doing little to turn sympathy his way. The Pope, who was indignant at the irregular ousting of Archbishop Robert of Jumièges in favor of Godwin's Saxon candidate, Stigand, denounced Harold's broken oath and, probably forseeing that it might be as well to be on William's side anyway, gave him a banner and a blessing.

All this moral support bore practical results in stimulating the recruiting of adventurers from many lands. To the spiritual rewards of a "holy war" now were added promises of English estates, for William realized that an ordinary feudal levy for the forty days' service would be insufficient. Medieval statistics are notoriously inaccurate, but William's followers probably numbered around six thousand, many of whom were Frenchmen from regions other than Normandy. These men joined the duke in investing a considerable amount to secure the most up-to-date military equipment available and to provide provisions and boats. The conquest has been described not inaptly as "a joint-stock investment," and few investments have paid higher dividends. Prepared to set sail in mid-August, the expedition was delayed by contrary winds during the six weeks when Harold was carefully patrolling the south coast. Then the winds turned favorable just at the unluckiest moment for Harold, when the threat from Scandinavia was drawing him northward.

Upon news of William's landing, Harold hurried his exultant but weary army from Stamford Bridge back to London, two hundred miles, in five days! Meanwhile William acted upon the prime rule of strategy that the proper objective is not a geographical point, but the enemy's main army itself. He remained on the south coast, keeping open his line of retreat by sea and devastating the countryside to entice Harold into premature action. Harold, who up to now had acted with remarkable energy and intelligence, erred in hastening on through London without resting his men or waiting for reinforcements; but possibly apathetic and divided England might never have sent further troops to his assistance anyway.

Harold finally halted his foot-weary men to guard the London road on a steep hill, some eight miles inland from Hastings on the sea. Harold's men were brave, but they were placed under a desperate handicap, since their arms and tactics were hopelessly out of date. At Stamford Bridge they had just fought infantry of their own type, using

Normans charging the English lines at Hastings; Bayeux Tapestry.

similar weapons and tactics; at Hastings they were outclassed by the Normans, whose army was the best-equipped in Europe. As in many other ways, Saxon England had been stagnating in military science, while the Normans were using cavalry and archers to support the infantry. Harold had a powerful nucleus of real soldiers in his "housecarls," or regulars; but the bulk of the Saxon army was made up of thanes, and of the old regional fyrd, an ill-disciplined and ill-armed militia of farmers, in some cases equipped with nothing better than scythes or clubs.

At about nine, on the morning of October 14—so far as one can reconstruct the story of the battle—the Normans advanced to the attack, coming down their own hill, crossing a little valley, and struggling up the steep slope where Harold's army waited. First William used archers, but arrows made little impression against the line of Saxon shields. Next came the infantry, no more successful than the archers. Even the first crashing charge of cavalry recoiled, with men and horses gashed and split by the great battleaxes of the housecarls. It was then past noon, and a lesser general than William might have given up the attack, but his quick eye saw a way to penetrate the unbroken wall of shields. Part of the undisciplined fyrd had broken line to pursue the retreating left wing of William's cavalry. He thereupon launched a new cavalry attack, apparently with orders to feint

retreat. The fyrd fell into the trap, broke its line, and was cut to pieces or driven away. The stanch housecarls still stood firm around Harold and his banners of the Dragon and the Fighting Man. They repulsed charge after charge until William finally directed the archers to fire high in the air, so that a galling shower of arrows would fall into the inner ranks. Even at that the gallant band fought almost to the last man. At dusk Harold fell with an arrow through his eye, and a few survivors disappeared into the forest behind them. That night the sun set on the last of Anglo-Saxon England.

Once again William paused—this time, according to the chronicler, for "the nation to make known its submission," or, as it has more starkly been put, like a master waiting for a cowed dog to heel. The delay proved wise, for there was a general scramble to gain the Conqueror's favor, whereas a more rapid advance might have led the northern earls to unite against the small invading force. William moved cautiously against London as the Dover garrison surrendered; he ravaged Kent and Sussex, but spared Canterbury; next he turned westward, making a wide sweep about London to cut off its food supply from the interior. The witan meanwhile, in a panic, had elected the Atheling as king; but this stripling prince had the good sense to go to William and offer submission. Finally, since no help was forthcoming from the northern earls, of Northumbria and Mercia, London opened its gates to the Conqueror, and the witan elected William its third king that year. On Christmas Day, 1066, while Normans rioted with townspeople, he was crowned in Westminster Abbey.

Proclaiming himself the true king, who had ousted a usurper, he promised to introduce no foreign law, nor to make arbitrary confiscations except in the case of those who had actively opposed him. He began building the Tower, to keep London in submission, and he felt relatively secure when he saw that the earls in the north showed no stomach for fighting. In the spring he recrossed the Channel to attend to his duchy; for it must be remembered that he remained duke of Normandy and that for the next five centuries the kings of England were to own land in France.

No sooner had he left England than revolts broke out, continuing until 1072. The most serious of all came in the north. Danish fighters from the Continent came over to aid one of these uprisings in the old Danelaw. Exasperated at this reaction to his mild rule, William determined to teach the north country a lesson it would never forget. He and his barons laid waste the region so thoroughly that, as the old chronicler reported, "so great a famine arose that . . . they ate the flesh of human beings, horses, dogs, and cats . . . ; so severe was it that some sold themselves into perpetual slavery. . . . Nor was anyone left to bury the dead, for all were wiped out either by the sword or famine, or had departed from their homes on account of hunger. . . . broad wilderness existed for nine years. Between York and Durham nowhere was there an inhabited village." Thus at last did William pitilessly play the role of Conqueror. All England lay under the grip of the little group of Norman adventurers. Within a generation the great castle and cathedral of Durham arose as a sign of Norman domination of the north country. The native English chafed under the iron heels

of their local Norman masters, but no serious revolt was attempted again. The last stand, made by one Hereward the Wake in the swampy fens around Ely, near Cambridge, was finally subdued, and the sullen Saxons settled down under the new regime. William, during this period, had shown himself sparing of death sentences, though he had been callous in ordering the gouging out of eyes and cutting off of hands. His favorite and practical form of punishment was to confiscate rebel lands, wherewith to reward his followers.

This Norman conquest was not like the coming of the Anglo-Saxons six centuries earlier. The Anglo-Saxons had almost completely displaced the earlier inhabitants, whereas the Normans were never more than a ruling minority of a few thousand in a land of more than a million Anglo-Saxons, most of whom continued in the centuries-old routine of primitive agriculture. They had been cheered by William's coronation decree: "This I will and order that all shall have and hold the law of King Edward as to lands and all other things, with these additions which I have established for the good of the English people." This seemed to indicate little intention of making changes, and there were not many as far as new legislation was concerned. William made only three new laws, the most striking dealing with his reservations of vast forests for the royal hunt: "the rich complained and the poor murmured, but . . . they must will all that the king willed."

Although William had achieved a power "unprecedented among European kings," it seems likely that he wanted to make only such changes as were needed to reward his Norman followers and to ensure good government in the disorganized land. Instead of making far-reaching theoretical plans for reorganization, his practical mind apparently simply utilized such Norman precedents as seemed applicable as situations arose. His clever statesmanship avoided useless friction by permitting the

Durham, with its bishop's dual role, was "half church of God, half castle 'gainst the Scots." The castle was at the right of the Cathedral, shown here.

retention of pre-Conquest customs wherever they did not cross his purposes.

Nevertheless, there were many changes of fundamental importance in William's twenty-one-year reign. Most salient among the innovations were (1) the introduction of the political feudal system; (2) the tightening and centralizing of the royal power, though local government was left largely as it had been; (3) the Normanizing and improvement of the Church, which was more definitely separated from secular affairs; (4) the importation of a higher culture and a Latinized language which eventually merged with the Anglo-Saxon; and (5) the closer linking of England with the Continent. The coming of the Normans probably did not mean a great deal to the bulk of the population, the lower peasantry, who simply changed from one master to another, though frequently the new Norman barons were harsher than the old Saxon thanes.

The upper-class Anglo-Saxon leaders, the thanes and high churchmen, suffered most in the transition, for their lands and their power were William's rewards to his followers.

The Feudal System

The most revolutionary of all the Norman changes was the transplanting to England of that system of "land tenure based on military service" which had gradually grown up in Europe during the two centuries following the break-up of Charlemagne's empire—the so-called *feudal system*. Under it the ablest fighters received estates from the king and higher nobles in return for military service. In the chaotic days which followed the barbarian invasions in Europe, the rulers lacked money but had plenty of land. The only way for a noble to become wealthy and powerful was to secure a vast acreage; for, in the absence of modern industrial and financial capital, land was almost the only source of wealth. The feudal system was associated with, and is often confused with, its economic basis, the *manorial system,* which was the way these landowners managed their own estates. The feudal system was a political and military relationship between the king and the nobility or knights, while the manorial system was primarily an economic relationship between each man in the feudal system and the peasantry on his particular estates. The same men of the upper classes were thus involved in both systems: the noblemen received land from their king in return for military service and subdivided that land on the same terms among other nobles or knights, according to the feudal system. Every one of this fighting aristocracy from the king to the poorest knight was the "lord of the manor" on that part of his land which he kept for his own use and support, and as such had important functions in the manorial system in relation to his serfs. Some writers prefer to call these the political and the economic feudal systems. The latter was already partly developed in Anglo-Saxon England, but the political feudal system was almost a complete innovation. Before showing how it was introduced by William, we must describe its general organization. It is worth studying and remembering in detail; for even the national government was run on a feudal basis for several centuries, and one cannot, for instance, understand the terms of Magna Carta (1215) unless one is familiar with the workings of this political feudal system. The details of feudalism differed in various sections of Europe, but the Norman-French variety is what came to England.

Under the political feudal system all the land of a country belonged in theory to the ruler. He always retained a portion of it as a *demesne* (royal domain, or crown lands), to provide himself with his direct private revenue, while the remainder was divided among his more important followers for military reasons. These retainers, in turn, likewise kept a demesne for themselves, and, if their portion was large enough, parceled out the rest to retainers of their own. This process generally continued down through at least three or four stages, until the pieces of land became so small that they could serve only as a demesne without further subdivision. The land thus transferred was known as a *fief,* which in Latin is *feudum* (hence, "feudal" system). The donor of the fief was always the *lord,* and the recipient the *vassal;* but every man involved in this relationship belonged to the upper classes. A lord might be the vassal of someone else, and as the interchange of land for military purposes became more complicated a vassal might have several different lords. Those who held direct from the king were known as *tenants in chief.* The unit by which the size of the estates was measured was called the *knight's fee,* in return for which the holder furnished one man-at-arms, fully armed and mounted, usually for forty days each year. For example, a lord might grant to A certain holdings valued at thirty knight's fees. Out of these A might keep six as a demesne and grant land worth eight fees each to B, C, and D. B might keep two as a demesne and grant one each to E, F, G, H, I, and J. These last would receive so small a portion that the division could go no further. Although perhaps not originally intended to be inherited, the fiefs by custom soon passed from father to son.

When a vassal received a fief from his lord, he went through the dual ceremony of giving *homage* and swearing *fealty.* In homage the vassal knelt and placed his two hands between those of the lord and promised to be his "man" (Latin, *homo*), in more or less the following words: "I become your man, from this day forward, of life and limb and of earthly worship, and unto you shall be true and faithful and bear to you faith for the tenements that I hold of you." In the ceremony of fealty which followed, the vassal swore on the Bible to be faithful to his lord, with words such as these: "Hear this, my lord, that I shall be faithful and true unto you and faith to you shall bear for the lands that I hold of you, and that I shall lawfully do to you the customs and services which I ought to do, so help me God and his saints." There was a third oath which a vassal took to only *one* of his lords. Whereas a vassal, holding land from several different men, had to pledge homage and fealty to each of them, this oath, *allegiance,* a sort of superfealty, was a promise to support this one liege lord against all others should a dispute arise among his various lords.

The feudal system was really a contractual relationship, with mutual advantages for both lord and vassal. The lord, in addition to granting the fief, was supposed to protect his vassal's interests, while the vassal had several obligations — the so-called "incidents" which arose only at rare intervals — in addition to the primary and constant one of military service. There were the three feudal *aids,* which were cash payments due upon the knighting of the lord's eldest son, the marriage of the lord's eldest daughter for the first time, and for ransom in case the lord should be captured. *Relief* was a sort of inheritance tax due from an heir before he was allowed to take over his father's fief, and probably it was designed originally to make it clear that, while the custom of inheritance was observed, the land still fundamentally belonged to the lord. By *escheat* a fief was forfeited to the lord if the vassal died without heirs or was convicted of crime. Sometimes the lord, especially if he was the king, had the right of *premier seisin,* which allowed him to enter into possession of a fief, on a vassal's death, and take measures for the satisfaction of all claims against the estate before finally turning it over to the heirs. If the heir was a minor son under twenty-one or a daughter under fourteen,

The ceremony of a knight receiving his sword from the king; vignette from a thirteenth century manuscript preserved at Durham Cathedral Library.

the lord became the guardian; and his *wardship* might be very profitable, since he could keep the fief's revenue over and above the amount needed for the ward's support and education. In addition, the lord controlled the *marriage* of all female wards, and might betroth them to any suitor of equal social rank unless the ward was permitted to pay heavily to escape an unwelcome husband. Again, the vassal had to give his lord *hospitality,* should he travel in the vassal's fief; and, finally, he had to attend the lord's *court,* where he judged and was judged by his fellow vassals. Frequently the lord, particularly the king, abused these privileges, and the vassals brought pressure to have fairly fixed rates established, especially in the case of relief, wardship, marriage, and premier seisin. In fact, the system was far less legal than it appeared, and too often rested on force.

The military tenure, with its forty-day

knight service, was the customary feudal relation, but it was not universal. Some vassals received land on other terms. Most of the church lands were drawn into the system of knight service; but some religious institutions held land in *frankalmoign,* by which they were simply to pray for the souls of the lord's family. High and low officials of the court ordinarily received land in *grand* or *petty sergeanty,* in exchange for civil rather than military duties.

In England, William had a unique opportunity to wipe the slate clean and to modify Norman-French feudalism to his own liking. Not only had he and his followers known no other system, but land was all he possessed wherewith to reward those avaricious men, from whom he had to have the feudal return of military service to garrison the conquered country. He did not realize, however, the full value of what he was giving away so lavishly; considering what his vassals got and what they had to give in return, they were certainly overpaid. He claimed that the Conquest gave him title to the estates of all Anglo-Saxons. Some of the earls and thanes who had not opposed him received back part of their lands, at least temporarily; but those who were at Hastings and in the subsequent rebellions lost everything. Dividing most of this land among his followers on feudal terms, William obtained the service of some five thousand knights and men-at-arms.

William had been, and still continued to be, as bad a vassal to his liege lord, the king of France, as it was possible to imagine; but he had no intention of being so treated by any of his own vassals. English feudalism consequently became more centralized than the Continental variety. The royal power was strengthened, and much of the troublesome private warfare between nobles, which so distracted medieval Europe, was eliminated. The king broke up the old English earldoms, so that no subject in the future would be able to enjoy such power as Godwin had wielded

in Wessex. The piecemeal nature of the Conquest, starting in the south and only gradually extending to the north, accounted for the scattering of the holdings which each vassal received. Some historians think that this was a deliberate policy on William's part to prevent anyone from becoming too strong; but there is no proof that it was not a purely accidental occurrence: every time more land was confiscated, it was divided among the Normans. The chief distinction between English and Continental feudalism was that the lower vassals in England came gradually to owe their military service not to their immediate overlord but to the king himself. William, as duke of Normandy, held the allegiance of his vassals and led them "legally" against the French king; William as king of England saw to it that no vassal could do the same to him. He was said to have called his great landowners to Salisbury Plain in 1087 to swear "they would be faithful to him against all other men, even against their own lords." Many question, however, whether this ever occurred.

William did not put entire reliance on the Norman feudal army obtained by this distribution of fiefs. He used it to put down Saxon revolts; but he kept the old Saxon militia, or fyrd, as a check on the barons' power. Disappointed at his curtailment of the feudal individualism to which they had been accustomed on the Continent, the barons revolted in 1075. The king put down the rebellion with the help of the conquered English.

The Manorial System

The manorial system was the economic partner of feudalism. Land was the source of most wealth, because the manorial system was so arranged as to pay the bills of the king, lords, knights, and churchmen involved in the political feudal system. The land unit, the manor, was the whole or part of the private demesne which the vassal kept for his own use. An agricultural unit, with a village, fields, pastures, and woodland, it was in effect the Anglo-Saxon village under new management, still practically self-sufficient, since its inhabitants produced nearly everything they needed (see page 25). The Normans changed this village life very slightly as far as local customs were concerned, except that most of the inhabitants — including many former freemen, together with most of the remaining slaves—were crowded into the common status of serf or villein. Also, the manor, or village, became linked with the feudal system, since its new Norman masters were feudal lords and vassals; thus the distinction between the political feudal system and the economic manorial system must be kept clearly in mind to avoid confusion. The manorial relation, unlike the mutually advantageous political feudal relationship, was most unequal; for it gave almost everything to the lord and almost nothing to the peasant. In return for meager protection, which as times grew more settled was scarcely needed, the peasant was forced to toil all his life on the land for the benefit of the small group of feudal fighting aristocracy. As on the Continent, the English serf with his family was "tied to the soil," and his descendants inherited this bondage. He remained with the land when it changed owners, and could not be sold outside the manor. He was allowed the use of a small bit of land, to raise crops for his family, and he might keep livestock in the common pasture and cut a specified amount of firewood in the wood lot; but all this might be done only in the spare time left from his prime duty of working for the lord. With the extremely inefficient agricultural methods — in particular, the wasteful open-field system, with its scattered plots (see page 26)—the serf, even in years of good harvests, worked from dawn to sundown and was at best able to eke out only a wretched and meager existence for himself. His home was still the bare hut of the Saxon peasant, and in time of war

Two views, from an early manuscript, of the life of the aristocracy; above, the lord and lady dining at high table; below, hawking, then a most popular form of hunting.

he had to crowd into the manor house or castle for refuge. It is small wonder with so many chances for exploitation that landowning was such a source of wealth for the feudal aristocracy.

Fortunately, the Conqueror's Domesday Book, a kind of minute census compiled in 1086, enables us to reconstruct manorial conditions with much more accuracy than is possible for most other features of medieval government and society. William wanted to know whether he was getting all that he should in the way of revenue from the country; so his agents went out to every village to inquire the status of all the land and all the people, not only that year but also as they had been on the eve of the Conquest. No other such exhaustive census was made in all Europe for centuries, before or after. The name Domesday probably came from the "dooms" of Saxon law, though some related it to the day of judgment, or "doom," from which none could escape. As one chronicler wrote, "So narrowly did he cause the survey to be made that there was not one single hide nor rood of land, nor—it is shameful to tell, but he thought it no shame to do—was there ox, cow, or swine that was not set down in the writ."

The most startling revelation of the Domesday survey was that about 84 per cent of the rural population, or more than five men out of six, were rated as unfree serfs. Of the rest, 13 per cent were freemen or small landholders. The small remainder—barely one man in thirty—composed the feudal aristocracy of great vassals and lesser vassals who were fighting men and high church officials. From that small group came the lords of the manors, who lived at the expense of the serfs. Not included in the survey were some of the few townsmen and some of the lower clergy.

The principal source of revenue for the lord of the manor was the *manorial demesne.* Just as in the political feudal system, where the lord kept out certain demesne manors for himself, so, on the manor a generous share, often half, of the arable and meadow land was kept out when the rest was divided among the freemen and the serfs. Sometimes this was a separate tract, set off by itself; more often it consisted of a portion of the scattered strips in the open fields. Everything produced on that manorial demesne went to the lord, who managed it through his bailiff. Occasionally he might pay for a little of the work, but most of the cultivation came from the required labor of the serfs. The heaviest burden was *week work,* whereby the serf had to spend a certain number of days each week, usually three, working on the lord's land. In emergencies, such as threatening storms or harvest time, the serf must also do extra *boon work,* tending the lord's crop first, even though it might mean the ruin of his own crop and starvation for his family. In addi-

tion, the serf had to make still further payments from the produce of his remaining time, which was spent on the portion of land allowed him for his own crops. Extra gifts of chickens or eggs were often required on special occasions, such as Christmas or Easter. The serf, moreover, was mulcted by the manorial *monopolies:* he had to use the lord's mill, oven, bridges, and the like, and to pay a fee each time. When the serf died, his heir had to give the best ox or some other valuable gift as a *heriot,* corresponding to the "relief" in upper feudal circles.

Not only did the serf have to work and pay in these various specified ways, but he had no freedom of action. He and his family could not leave the manor for even a brief time without the lord's permission. That was seldom granted because, since the lord received more than half of the results of the serf's labor, he suffered a financial loss any time a serf was away. The serfs were not allowed to go away to fight. If a serf wanted to marry his daughter to someone on another manor or to send his son to school, he had to pay compensation for the services the lord would lose. A serf had no rights under the law or government outside the manor; for justice he was dependent upon the manor court, under the control of the lord's steward. A runaway serf — such escape was difficult — became automatically free if he reached a town and avoided capture for a year and a day.

Even among the serfs there were varying degrees. The ordinary "villein," the most numerous category, held fifteen to thirty acres and was better off than the "cottar," who had very little land and somewhat different duties. At the time of Domesday Book there were still some bondsmen, or landless laborers, a relic of the Saxon slaves, but they gradually merged with the mass of serfs.

The freemen, whom the Saxons had called churls (ceorls) and later centuries were to know as yeomen, stood midway between the feudal aristocracy and the serfs. They were not aristocrats, but they differed from the unfree serfs, not only in their landholding but even more conspicuously in their political, legal, and military status. The freemen held their land from the lord of the manor, but they generally gave him rent instead of servile labor. They might have three or four times as much land as the serf, and sometimes they hired laborers to assist them. They could move to another manor if they saw fit, and without the lord's permission could marry their daughters outside the manor or send their sons to study for the clergy. They could take part in the activity of the hundred and shire courts; later they could carry their grievances to the royal courts and serve as jurors, vote for members of Parliament, and sometimes even sit in the House of Commons. They were eligible and liable for military service in the fyrd. While the feudal aristocracy alone could afford the expensive cavalry equipment, the freemen formed a tough infantry. Three centuries later the longbows of those yeomen would vanquish whole French armies.

A typical manor was Crawley, five miles from the old Wessex capital at Winchester, one of the dozens of manors owned by its bishop. The financial accounts of the church have been preserved since Alfred's day. The village was "a short winding street of houses and outbuildings running up the hill from the pond to the church." Population remained fairly stationary down through the centuries—about fifty households, or some three hundred souls in all. At the time of the Domesday survey there were no freemen; only six of the heads of households were even ordinary villeins; twenty-five were cottars, and twenty were slaves. Before long, however, all were merged into the general status of serfs. Scarcely a quarter of the manor's thirty-six hundred acres were used for crops; the "home farm," or lord's manorial demesne, comprised about half of that arable land. The soil was chalky, and water was scarce, so that

sheep-raising was a particular source of profit. A century and a half after the Conquest each serf had an average of twenty-five sheep, two head of cattle, and ten swine, while half of them owned a horse apiece. In addition, the lord kept nearly two thousand sheep. The bishop's annual income from Crawley during the thirteenth century averaged about £75, ranging from £29 in the poorest year to £130 in the best. A serf, it would seem, was worth about thirty shillings a year to his master.

As to the machinery of government, the Normans introduced new features which were to be developed further by four great kings of the Middle Ages. The feudal system was the particular innovation of the Conqueror. Later, Henry I (1100-1135) built up a strong central government; Henry II (1154-1189) developed royal courts and the system of common law; and Edward I (1272-1307) further improved the laws and started Parliament on a regular basis.

The Conqueror quickly established definite authority over his new realm. Edward the Confessor and numerous other Saxon rulers had been kings in little more than name, for the real power was scattered among the earls (see page 28). After 1066 authority in England lay unquestionably wherever William happened to be. Orders given in his name were treated with respect, because men feared the penalty for disobedience. In his Great Council of nobles and prelates he preserved the functions of the Saxon witan (see page 56). Two of his particular devices for making his authority effective were the Domesday survey and the sheriff.

Into each county, or shire—except the border regions, with their special government—William sent a sheriff to administer government in his name. This official took his name from the old Saxon shire reeve, and some of his functions from the Norman vicomte; but he was, for a century at least, more powerful than any previous district officer. He was endowed with great authority in the administration of law, the collection of taxes, and the raising of armed forces. William thus broke the old local power of the earls, who became little more than figureheads in the shire administration. He preferred to rely upon these new men, who were dependent upon him for favor.

While the Conqueror was strengthening the central power, he left relatively untouched the old machinery of local government (see page 28). Most of the earldoms were broken up; but the Saxon courts of shire and hundred were allowed to continue, as far as the king was concerned. The country had become so thoroughly feudalized, however, that the manorial courts of the barons absorbed most of the local cases and frequently threatened the hundreds. The shire courts, bolstered by the royal authority of the sheriff, had vitality enough to resist most of this feudalizing influence (see page 29).

Church and State

The Conquest also brought new developments to England's century-old relations with the Church. The Conquest now made even closer those bonds established by the Council of Whitby in 664, with the all-inclusive international system of the Roman Church (see page 15). The somnolent Anglo-Saxon Church received valuable cultural and disciplinary stimulus from this contact, but at the same time the new relationship led to political friction.

The Roman Church, through the sorry centuries of the Dark Ages, had performed an invaluable service in giving Europe a powerful example of unity in a period of general chaos. In the absence of effective political government it had taken over many of the functions of a state, with its regular hierarchy of officials, its courts, its financial system, and its diplomatic corps. Now stronger rulers emerging in France and central Europe, as well as in England,

resented what they considered papal interference in their own secular functions. For more than two centuries Europe was to see a series of disputes, sometimes very violent, between Popes and kings. In England the three chief sources of this friction were the power to appoint bishops and abbots, the jurisdiction of courts, and taxation.

One of the strongest men in the whole history of the papacy held sway in Rome at this time. Even before he became Pope as Gregory VII in 1073, Hildebrand was for many years the real power in the Holy City. Educated in the strict monastery of Cluny, he had set out zealously to reform not only the monasteries but also the morals, learning, and general tone of the clergy. He was particularly vigorous in his attacks upon the appointment of prelates by political rulers (see page 59). Gregory, moreover, in his *Dictatus* proclaimed that the Pope was superior to any political ruler and that his word was law throughout Christendom.

This doctrine of universal power naturally ran counter to William's determination to be supreme authority in England. Both were strong and clever men. Gregory, involved in a long and bitter struggle with the Holy Roman Emperor over the appointment of prelates, did not relish a second major fight over this problem. William owed Gregory gratitude for his support of the Conquest. The result was a compromise. William kept the appointing power in his own hands; but he selected first-rate men to replace the Saxon prelates, who lost their bishoprics and abbeys one by one. He heartily co-operated with Gregory in his efforts to reform the tone of the clergy, but he flatly stated that no papal decree had validity in England without the king's consent. William removed the bishop from the shire court and established separate church courts for ecclesiastical matters. Within a century these courts would create friction between Church and State (see page 76).

In these church relations William had the

able co-operation of the noted Italian scholar Lanfranc, whom he made Archbishop of Canterbury in place of the Saxon, Stigand. Lanfranc had been prior of the Norman abbey of Bec, one of the leading intellectual centers of Christendom. Even before the Conquest he had become William's intimate and able adviser in intricate problems of State and Church. Never a "yes man," he once so strongly opposed the Duke that he was ordered into exile. A lame horse was the best that the monastery could afford for his departure. Overtaken by the angry William, who was impatient at his slowness, Lanfranc retorted, "Give me a better horse and I shall go quicker." This so amused William that the breach was healed. As Archbishop of Canterbury, Lanfranc worked hand in glove with his king and deserved much credit for the marked improvement in the quality of the Church in England. The bitter conflicts between English kings and Roman Popes still lay in the future.

A fourth result of the Conquest was a new language. The Normans came to England speaking their local variety of French, derived from their century and a half of contact with the Latinized civilization of France. For the next three centuries three different languages were heard in England. The churchmen, the scholars, and sometimes the lawyers used the international language, Latin. English remained the tongue of the bulk of the population; for we must remember that there were perhaps a million native English and only a few thousand Normans. The new Norman French was the polite tongue of the royal court and of the dominant feudal minority. Even today, the royal assent to a bill passed by Parliament is given in Norman French. By the middle of the fourteenth century the old English and the Norman French would be blended into a new common English language which could be understood both by the lord and by the peasant. English today shows traces of both with the simpler, more homely words from the Saxon heritage and the French or Latin influence found in the words for abstract ideas, the niceties and refinements of life, and in political, military, legal, religious, and artistic fields where the Norman aristocracy was active. As Scott pointed out in *Ivanhoe*, the words for the common domestic animals—cow, calf, sheep, and pig—are Germanic, whereas the meat from those same animals—beef, veal, mutton, and pork—are French. The English tended the animals; but the choice roasts found their way to the high table of the manor house.

The Normans also brought a Continental culture more advanced than that which they found in England. No particular literature of importance was produced in England in the early Norman period. French and Latin, rather than English, were generally used by such few writers as there were. The creative side of Norman culture was to find more prominent expression in the architecture of cathedrals and abbeys (see page 97). The Conquest itself left a unique artistic record in the so-called Bayeux Tapestry, woven possibly under the direction of William's queen and giving a graphic picture of the stirring events of 1066.

As a fifth and somewhat less definite consequence of the Conquest, the Normans linked England more closely to the Continent. For many years, barons and churchmen often held lands on both sides of the Channel, and there was constant passing and repassing between England and France. One result of this stimulus was the beginning of the rise of towns devoted to industry and commerce (see page 91). England was thus brought into contact with the main currents of the day and saved from the stagnant isolation which threatened Scandinavia.

The transition to Norman domination was probably not a happy one for most Anglo-Saxons. The earls, thanes, and prelates who were pushed out of their high positions to make room for Normans had particular cause for bitterness. So too did those formerly free peasants who were submerged in serfdom. For the bulk of the peasantry, it simply meant the changing of one set of masters for another. We cannot believe that all the Normans were as cruel as Abbot Thurstan, who had his archers shoot down the monks because they refused to sing the new Norman chants, or Robert of Bellême, the able but devilish Earl of Shrewsbury, who refused to ransom his prisoners because he preferred to torture them, and who, according to the chronicler, acting as godfather at the baptism of a vassal's infant, gouged out the baby's eyes because it cried while he held it in his arms (see page 61). Rough discipline was the price England had to pay for the new efficiency and for the benefits which were to become more obvious as centuries passed.

Altogether, the Norman Conquest did not have the thoroughgoing consequences of the coming of the Saxons, but it had more permanent influence on later England than had the invasions of the Celts, Romans, or Danes. The Saxon descendants were to form the bulk of England's future population, and their speech and customs were to have a lasting importance. The Normans were too few to replace the English, as the English had replaced the Celts; but the Conqueror and his followers had an impact out of all proportion to their numbers. They shook England out of her lethargy and bound that remote island more closely to the Continent; they introduced new elements of language and culture; and, above all, they provided such an efficient, centralized government, based on feudalism, that England's constitutional development may be traced in orderly fashion from 1066. And from that date the country contained the various major elements which were to make up its distinctive and highly satisfactory blend.

Chapter Four · 1087-1154

Centralization and Disruption

The Conqueror died in action. In the summer of 1087 he led from Normandy one of his perennial border raids into the lands of the French king, who had taunted him about his fatness. His horse stumbled in the street of a burning frontier town, and the high iron pommel of the saddle cut deep into its royal rider's stomach. Three weeks later William died at Rouen. His body, stripped by thieving servants while yet warm, was left lying around for days. Everyone had ridden off to protect his own interests in the emergency; there is good cause for alarm when a powerful dictator dies. For twenty-one years William's iron will had directed the Normanization of England. The turbulent baronage now saw a chance to strike for liberty, and chaos would have followed had not the Conqueror's deathbed wisdom robbed them of their opportunity and paved the way for nearly a half century more of powerful rule.

His last instructions had been that his second son hurry to England to be crowned by Lanfranc, while the eldest son, Robert, "Curthose," inherited simply Normandy. Even then the first-born customarily succeeded; but William knew his three sons, whom he had completely dominated, and realized his eldest was not the man to be king of England. Although Robert was brave and superficially chivalrous, he was also weak and futile. Because of this he twice missed a chance at the English throne; he even lost Normandy; and he died in imprisonment. Such a man was the natural choice of the self-seeking English barons. Henry, the third son, wily and somewhat of a scholar, received only a grant of money, but William is said to have made, along with the bequest, the cheering prophecy that some day he would win all his father's lands.

William II (1087-1100) was a good fighter and an unquestionably strong ruler, who brooked no interference with the law and kept the nobles in order. Little else that is good is known about him, but England at that moment needed his strength; without it, the work of the Conquest might have been undone. Evil in character and ugly in temper, he had, according to his kindest biographer, already sunk so low in vice at twenty-seven that there was no hope for betterment. It was also said of him that every morning he got up a worse man than he had lain down, and every evening he lay down a worse man than he had got up; the country folk fled to the woods at the approach of this vicious king and his boon companions. Yet the barons feared him, too. His extortions would seem to prove the charge that he wanted to be the heir of every landholder in England. His appearance was intimidating: very fat, with a constant sneering expression, a noticeable stammer, and such a beefy red face that it gave him the name "Rufus."

The barons lost no time in trying his mettle. They wanted Robert, with his inability to say No; and, since many of them held fiefs in both England and Normandy, they disliked two separate suzerains. They revolted under the Conqueror's half brother Odo, bishop of Bayeux and Earl of Kent, who had swung a lusty mace at Hastings— and only a mace, because a churchman was forbidden to shed blood. Rufus cannily appealed to the Saxon common people and, as the chronicle says, "set forth to them his need and prayed their help and promised them the best laws that ever were in this land and that he would forbid all unjust taxation and give them back their woods and hunting." Most barons seem to have joined the revolt; but most churchmen sided with the English townspeople and peasantry. The uprising failed; and so did a second one, seven years later.

Rufus's fine promises were not kept. They might have been had Lanfranc lived. Leaving the Canterbury See vacant for four years, that he might pocket its rich income, Rufus chose as his chief advisor his low-born, unscrupulous, and ingratiating boon companion, Ranulf Flambard, bishop of Durham. This Flambard, the "Fiery Torch," seems to have licked up everything. Justice in the courts depended upon the size of the pocketbook; agriculture was burdened by a species of general land tax; and bishoprics and abbacies were left vacant, as Lanfranc's had been, that the king might use their revenue.

Rufus, in a fit of remorse on his sickbed, finally appointed an Archbishop of Canterbury. For the second time an Italian abbot of Bec was chosen, the gentle, unworldly Anselm, sixty years old and perhaps the foremost scholar of his day. So loath was he to leave the contemplative life that he had to be dragged to the king's bedside. Once in office, however, Anselm defended his prerogatives with vigor. Lanfranc had been willing to regard the English Church as a branch of the Norman monarchy under the king, but Anselm considered it to be merely a part of the international religious system, under which his allegiance was due not to the king but to the Pope. Both to Rufus and to his brother Henry, Anselm proved a stumbling block whenever they tried to interfere with his strict version of the rights of the Church. He had a series of squabbles with Rufus and in 1097 went to Rome to lay his case before the Pope. He remained in Italy until after the death of Rufus, who had once more seized the rich Canterbury lands. The appointment of Anselm marked the beginning of the long-standing friction between Crown and Church in England—a friction which eventually led to a complete break from Rome.

England had almost no part in the tremendous wave of religious-military enthusiasm which sent thousands of Europeans to the Holy Land in the First Crusade in 1096; nevertheless Rufus profited from it (see page 81). It was primarily a French enterprise, and the French were so prominent in it that Europeans for centuries afterward were called "Franks" in the Near East. The many Normans, some from Sicily and some from Normandy itself, included the romantic, impractical Robert. He had already sold part of his duchy to his younger brother Henry, and had lost a part to Rufus. Now, in order to raise funds for the crusade, he pawned the remainder to Rufus, and finally returned penniless. Rufus and the Norman barons in England, however, remained at home, distrustful of one another and fearing what might happen during so long an absence.

Not content with securing control of Normandy from Robert, Rufus launched border raids against Wales and Scotland, and was on the point of seeking further

French lands when an arrow laid him low in 1100. He had been shot by one of his companions on a hunting party in the New Forest, perhaps accidentally.

Henry I

Although Robert's interests, like other Crusaders', were supposedly safeguarded this time and although he had long since received homage and fealty as Rufus's heir, Henry was at hand and that was what counted. Within two days, before most of England had heard of the king's death, the Conqueror's third son had rushed through his coronation and seized the royal treasury at Winchester. His swift actions left no chance to question his claim too closely.

The achievements of Henry I (1100-1135), one of England's best kings, were solid, like those of his grandson, Henry II, rather than of the spectacular sort which leaves a popular reputation. Clearheaded, self-controlled, prudent, and painstaking, he was at his best in all that concerned orderly, effective administration. Fattish, like most of his family, black-haired, and rather short, he was slow, obstinate, and parsimonious. His nickname, "Beauclerc," implies he could probably read and write more than most contemporary rulers. Some call his a naturally pleasant disposition, but others say that a man had cause to worry when Henry smiled at him. Now and then traces of the family cruelty might crop out: once he pushed a Norman rebel to his death from a high tower. A good general, but a better diplomat, he avoided fighting whenever possible. The machinery of government interested him more than anything else, and good work in the daily business of law or administration was a sure way to his favor. With all his more prosaic qualities, Henry continued the family tradition by ruling with such a strong hand that the chronicler could write, "He made peace for man and beast." He granted a few concessions at the outset, but never was he weak. The nation might groan under his heavy taxes and

Effigy in crusading chain mail of William Marshall, Earl of Pembroke and able regent of England after the death of King John.

savage penalties, but it knew that, unlike his brother Rufus, he usually played fair, and hailed him as the "Lion of Justice" predicted by the seer Merlin. The fact that an offender was a great baron did not save him from the same harsh treatment dealt out to lesser men.

The king, in some early conciliatory acts, aimed to please all kinds of people: the nobles by a Charter of Liberties and the arrest of the rapacious Flambard; the churchmen by recalling Anselm and filling vacant church offices promptly, instead of appropriating their revenue; and the old English populace by marrying Matilda (Edith), niece of the Saxon Atheling, the nearest blood kin of the Wessex line. The Norman nobles might sneer at her, but to the people this fulfilled the old prophecy that England's troubles would end when the green tree (Saxon line), cut from its root, should be rejoined and bring forth fruit. Since then, all occupants of the throne have had in their veins the blood of both Alfred and the Conqueror.

In the Charter of Liberties, Henry promised to abstain from the worst abuses of Rufus—the first legal limitation of the virtually absolute royal power established by the Conqueror. The gradual reduction of the king's authority, a process which lasted six centuries, has been the main thread of English constitutional history, which is just the reverse of French history, where the story centers around the gradual increase of royal control. Henry and his immediate successors frequently repeated similar promises, which formed the backbone of the terms which the barons forced upon Henry's great-grandson in the Magna Carta, a century later. The process was to go on, through the Petition of Right and the Bill of Rights, until eventually the king had become little more than a figurehead. Henry gave the promises voluntarily, and then did not keep them all; but they are worth remembering, because Englishmen came to look upon them as part of their rights and to feel that there were certain limits beyond which even the king might not go. Specifically, Henry agreed that the king should no longer profit by allowing high church offices to remain vacant; that abnormal exactions in relief and wardship should cease; and that various other sharp practices in connection with the feudal relationship should be modified. Actually, this Charter of Liberties was a strictly feudal document, aimed to secure the support of the powerful barons and churchmen because Henry's claim to the throne was rather shaky. To win more popular support as well, however, Henry urged these lords to treat their subordinates as he promised to treat them.

Central Government

The thirty-five years of Henry's reign left England with an efficient central government. It was not as today, however, concentrated in a capital city, with a palace or White House, halls of Parliament or Congress, and office buildings full of busy bureaucrats. Instead, a little group of men transacted business wherever they happened to be, as they traveled, often on horseback, around the king's lands in England and France. The Conqueror had gathered the central power into his own hands, but even he needed ministers to conduct his government efficiently. Henry's orderly mind gave definite administrative functions to the men who were closest to the king. In analyzing constitutional development it should be recalled once more that it is difficult, if not impossible, to state definitely when certain institutions first began or what their exact functions were.

There was no efficiency in that unwieldy body of "advisers" which the Anglo-Saxons had called the witan; which the Normans continued, somewhat feudalized, as the Great Council; and which still exists as the House of Lords. This was only an occasional assembling of the powerful nobles and churchmen to give the king advice, to assent to his decrees, and to choose his successor. Under a weak king, it might virtually carry on the government; but with men as strong as the first three Norman rulers it was scarcely more than a rubber stamp. One of the feudal duties was attendance at the lord's court; thus in order to keep an eye on his restless vassals, William I, as supreme lord, had summoned his tenants in chief to gather with him three times a year: at Easter in Winchester, the old Wessex capital; at Pentecost in Westminster, now part of London; and at Christmas in Gloucester, in the southwest. Such a body was too large and too temporary to be of service in managing affairs of state. After the barons and prelates rode home from these Great Council meetings, someone had to remain with the king to handle the multitude of details involved in governing a kingdom.

The answer to that problem was the

"Curia Regis," or King's Court. This name sometimes had been applied to the Great Council, but from now on it will be used to denote the "permanent standing committee" of the larger body. This smaller group, which took definite form during the reign, remained with the king after the others dispersed. Its functions made it the direct ancestor of three very important parts of the present government. As a little group of intimate advisers to the king the Curia Regis was the forerunner of the Privy Council and the present Cabinet. As a supreme court of justice it was the nucleus out of which grew the principal law courts. As the "Exchequer" it commenced a formal and regular financial administration which has continued under that name to the present.

With the formation of the Curia Regis came the introduction of three powerful officials as its leaders. The earlier kings, both in England and on the Continent, usually had delegated ministerial duties to "household officials," such as the butler, seneschal, constable, and marshal. Some of these officials continued as members of the Curia Regis; but they were overshadowed in administrative power by three new dignitaries.

Foremost was the justiciar, who was chief minister while the king was in the country, and who wielded full authority as viceroy or regent, when the king was elsewhere. The first justiciar, Roger, bishop of Salisbury, had attracted Henry's attention by the speed with which he could rattle through the Mass when the king was impatient to go hunting. He held this position through most of Henry's reign and into the next, and shares with the king credit for the efficient organization of the Curia Regis. For more than a century the justiciar was the most influential government official, but by 1300 the office had been abolished. Next to the justiciar in importance came the chancellor, keeper of the great seal and in charge of all secretarial work, such as the issuing of

The "Man of Law," typical of those who rode circuit with the itinerant justices, as pictured in one of the earliest editions of Chaucer's *Canterbury Tales.*

charters and the conducting of correspondence, both domestic and foreign. Chancellors there had been before, so far as the name went, but now the office became important. Before long the chancellor will be found presiding over a "Chancery Court," which developed a peculiar type of legal jurisdiction (see page 75). With the disappearance of the office of justiciar the chancellor became for several centuries the chief minister. Even today he holds a position of great dignity and presides over the House of Lords. The third of the new officers was the treasurer, whose functions and importance are obvious from the title. His duties today are performed by the Chancellor of the Exchequer.

These officials and some of the other members of the Curia Regis might meet one month as the "Exchequer," to handle financial matters, and the next as the supreme court of law. And in the meantime they might serve their third purpose of advising the king on matters of policy. Some of their subordinates might be specialists in financial matters, while others were particularly trained in law. The officials of the Curia Regis were largely recruited from the lesser barons or the clergy, among whom the shrewd, legalistic, hardheaded type of Norman was most likely to be found.

Royal Finances

As a financial body the Curia Regis derived special importance under Henry I. Its members were known as the "Exchequer" when they met to verify the revenue. The name came from the checkered cloth on the table upon which twice a year they received the payments from the sheriffs, collected from the income of royal estates, court fines, and other sources of revenue. Calculation of large numbers was a difficult process without arabic figures and a decimal system, both unknown to medieval England; so the checkered cloth served as an abacus. The lower Exchequer officials moved their chips or counters around the squares, verified the total, and cut notches on a stick which was then split in two, half being given to the sheriff as a receipt. The amounts were also recorded on long sheets of parchment, which were finally rolled up to be saved for future reference. The earliest of these so-called "pipe rolls" which is still preserved dates back to 1130. The Curia Regis, when it met for Exchequer purposes, verified these accounts of the sheriffs and settled disputed cases. This introduction of system into the royal accounting enabled the king to see to it that the sheriffs were collecting and turning in all that they should, and it also made it possible for him to ascertain at a glance the amount of most of his income. No other king in western Europe had anything comparable to this Exchequer.

That lone "pipe roll" of Henry I reveals the source of the ten tons of silver collected in 1130 as royal revenue. It accounts for some £25,000, and the few missing counties would bring the total to about £27,000. One tenth of this came from the Danegeld, which was the only equivalent of a regular modern tax, collected on a broad, uniform basis. The remainder came from the king's relation to the feudal and manorial systems as chief feudal lord of England, as though the nation were his private estate. In times of peace the king was expected to "live of his own" from the revenue of the demesne which he controlled directly and from the fiefs allotted to vassals. Under the heading "crown lands and rights" about £11,000 was collected from the demesne manors and towns. This amount could be depended upon regularly; for the sheriff had to turn in the same stipulated amount, or "farm," each year. If he collected somewhat in addition, that was his affair. The almost equal amount derived from the various payments in connection with fiefs was less dependable, since the lucrative dues from relief, escheat, wardship, and marriage were contingent upon variable circumstances. A year when barons and bishops enjoyed uniform good health thus meant a decline in the royal revenue. One of the heaviest individual contributors in 1130 was the widowed Countess of Chester, who paid a relief of £166 for the inheritance of her father's lands, and who also offered £333 that she might not be obliged to marry again within five years. A lesser vassal paid £6 13s. 6d. to be allowed to marry at will. Despite his promise in the Charter of Liberties, Henry collected, as a sort of wardship, £935 from the vacant bishopric of Durham.

The pipe roll reveals some less creditable sources of revenue. In addition to the usual court fines, Henry accepted bribes to influence court judgments. In a case where a Norman was being sued for a debt by three Jews, the king was offered £133 by the former and got £25 cash down from the latter; it was understood that the loser's bribe would be returned. The Jewish moneylenders, who began coming to England in the Conqueror's wake, and whose usurious interest rates sometimes reached 86 per cent a year, were called the "king's sponges" because they were tolerated by Henry at the price of frequent heavy fines on trivial pretexts. They had a monopoly of money-lending in the early Middle Ages because the Church forbade Christians to lend money at interest. The Jews of London, in the same year of this pipe roll, were, for instance, fined £2000 because a sick man was said to have died at the hands of a Jewish doctor. Gradually, regular taxes would replace these feudal and haphazard sources of royal revenue.

The pound sterling then had far more buying power than today, being literally a pound of silver, the twelve-ounce Troy pound. The only coin in regular circulation was the silver penny, about the size of a very thin dime or sixpence. One little penny could buy about four pounds of meat, or six pounds of wheat, or hire an ordinary foot soldier for a day. A farm laborer would work all day for twopence, and a fully armed knight's hire was only eightpence a day. A good penny would do all that; but there were too many bad pennies in circulation. Kings did not themselves begin officially to debase the currency until about 1350. In the time of Henry I, bad pennies were sometimes the work of the "moneyers," licensed by the king for a heavy fee to coin official money in some fifty different towns. They might debase the currency either by making the coins smaller or by putting in more copper alloy than the legal one-twelfth necessary for toughness. Then, too, the general public did their part by clipping a little silver from the edges of the pennies which passed through their hands or by actual counterfeiting. The situation became so bad, according to the chroniclers, that anyone going to market with a whole pound of pennies could find scarcely twelve acceptable to the merchants. News of this reached Henry in Normandy. Bad coins

meant a loss of revenue, so he had all the moneyers gathered at Winchester, where each had his right hand amputated in addition to other more serious mutilation. Thus Henry upheld the important principle of a sound currency.

In its legal capacity the Curia Regis of Henry I probably took the first steps toward many of the very important reforms under Henry II. The latter probably owed to his grandfather more than was formerly supposed, but the introduction of "itinerant justices" was the only certain contribution by the elder Henry (see page 68). When this Curia Regis accompanied the king on his travels, Henry from time to time sent justices out from that body into the counties to inspect the local administration. The justices thus acted a role similar to that of the "King's Eyes and Ears" of the old Persians or of the *missi dominici* of Charlemagne. Probably at first they went primarily on financial business; but, while they were attending the shire courts, they might at times have sat as justices in royal cases.

Investiture Contest

While perfecting the machinery of his own government, the king ran afoul of that still more extensive organization, the Church. Prospects for friendly co-operation between Church and State seemed good when Henry recalled Anselm and quickly filled a rich vacant bishopric. Anselm aided the king by approving the legality of his marriage, which had been threatened by the charge that Matilda was a nun. The queen insisted that she had been forced to wear the veil by her aunt, an abbess, as protection for a young girl in dangerous times, and Anselm agreed to sanctify the marriage.

But he was adamant on the investiture problem. Like taxation of church property and lay versus clerical courts, this was a chief bone of contention between the Popes and the medieval rulers. It centered around the question as to whether the Church or

Manuscript drawing of a bishop applying the tonsure, symbol of clerical status, which carried the advantage of "benefit of clergy."

bishop or abbot controlled more land, owed more military service, and enjoyed more income and influence than many a feudal lord. In royal eyes, the rich landholdings put the bishops and abbots in much the same category as earls and counts with both the powers and duties of feudal lords and vassals. Many of the highest officials of the Curia Regis were bishops, partly because churchmen alone had the requisite education and a rich bishopric was an easy way to pay a valuable man without expense to the royal treasury. Both points of view are understandable, and obviously they would clash with the churchmen's dual roles of spiritual duties and feudal obligations to their king.

The reform movement which had just swept through the Church under the influence of Pope Gregory VII (see page 50) placed particular stress upon these evils. Churchmen were strictly forbidden to receive the insignia of office from lay hands. The king, however, had a powerful trump. He need not hand over the church lands, upon which the income of a bishopric or abbey depended, unless the candidate was was a man of whom he approved and one who would give homage as the king's vassal, with all that it entailed. Anselm and Henry each sent missions to the Pope to present their points of view; and Anselm himself, with Henry's approval, once more took the road to Rome. "Know all men present," declared the king's advocate to the Pope on one occasion, "that not to save his kingdom will King Henry lose the investiture of the churches." "And before God," came the sharp reply, "not to save his head will Pope Paschal let him have them." Neither Henry nor Paschal, however, wanted a repetition of the scene twenty-odd years before at Canossa, where the investiture dispute kept the Holy Roman Emperor kneeling three days in the snow humbly awaiting Pope Gregory VII's forgiveness. No one except Anselm seems to have wished to carry the matter to a final de-

the ruler should appoint the prelates and "invest" them with the insignia of office. This selection of bishops and abbots was supposed to lie in the hands of the clergy of the diocese or the monks of the abbey, but ordinarily someone important behind the scenes, perhaps the Pope or ruler, dictated the choice. Thus, although the word "investiture" referred to the initiation *ceremony,* the real quarrel hinged about the *choice* of the prelates. Naturally, churchmen felt that it was wrong for a layman, often a wordly and ungodly one, to select a man for a spiritual position, and to go through with the traditional religious ceremony. The churchmen also considered it wrong that bishoprics and abbacies should be bestowed as political plums to party henchmen. At the same time, the Church had become so deeply enmeshed in the feudal system through gifts of extensive fiefs that a prominent

cision. Henry's hands were fully occupied with Robert's efforts to win the crown, and he did not want Anselm to seem a martyr in the public mind. He and Paschal exchanged conciliatory and sometimes contradictory messages, while the English bishops did their best to dodge the ticklish question.

Finally, in 1107, two years before Anselm's death, the opposing parties concluded the "Compromise of Bec." Its terms are not known, but it was apparently a royal victory. Henry relinquished the *ceremony* of investing with ring and crozier; but he kept the *right* to choose the prelate and to receive his homage as a feudal vassal. The Church retained little more than an empty ceremony, but it seems to have been satisfied with this token victory, or perhaps it decided that the strength of the English monarchy made it necessary to yield. A few years afterward the bitter German investiture struggle ended in a similar compromise. However another Church-Crown quarrel of longer duration gave indication of starting in this reign—one that involved the royal "squeezing" of money out of church property, usually through the fiction of demanding "free gifts." The third source of friction, the contest for court jurisdiction, lay a half century in the future, when another stubborn Archbishop of Canterbury carried things so far that he was murdered.

Along with constitutional changes and church disputes, there was plenty of fighting in England and Normandy. Henry had not been long on the throne when his brother Robert, having won renown as a Crusader, came home fully expecting to find the English throne awaiting him. He had not lost title to Normandy, which simply had been pawned as a private debt to Rufus. The English barons backed him because they wanted an easy-going king, and for once he had money in his pocket, thanks to the dowry of his new wife, daughter of the famous Norman crusader, Robert Guiscard. So, in 1101, Robert's chance for victory looked bright when he invaded England, but, so the story goes, his kindly chivalry kept him from seizing Winchester, with the royal treasure, because the queen was giving birth to a child there. As it was, Henry had the support of the Saxon English, and even of Anselm. A treaty was struck by which Robert gave up for the bait that was ever his undoing—ready money; he surrendered his heritage merely for the promise of an annual allowance, and recognition as heir presumptive. He kept Normandy for a few years more, until Henry got that away from him, too.

This affair made the barons disgruntled; for they had hoped to dislodge Henry. They persisted for a while in their sedition, under that thorn in the side of the king, the notoriously cruel Robert of Bellême, Earl of Shrewsbury. He finally was ruined, after a persistent struggle (see page 52), and with him ended the power of the great vassals. The barons thereafter were less powerful as individuals, and could be strong only when united. As the chronicler Orderic Vitalis summed it up, "And so, after Robert of Bellême's flight, the kingdom of Albion was quiet in peace, and King Henry reigned prosperously three and thirty years, during which no man in England dared to rebel or hold any castle against him."

Normandy, however, furnished sufficient rebellion and fighting to keep the reign from dullness. Robert's misrule, or rather lack of rule, had created anarchy there, indicating what would have probably happened had he become king of England. The barons with estates overseas urged Henry's intervention. So did the Church, which always suffered in such disorders, and which, despite the Anselm dispute, Henry desired to conciliate. His own lust for more lands doubtless influenced him, too.

To the popular mind, the English avenged their defeat at Hastings when Henry's expeditionary force to Normandy crushed his brother's Norman army at

Tinchebray, in 1106. Normandy thereby came under Henry's rule. Robert, captured in the fight, was thereafter kept a prisoner, despite the pleas of the Pope and others. Henry maintained that it was not imprisonment but simply a secluded life in utmost comfort. Others gave a different story.

Tinchebray, however, did not bring general peace. The Norman barons rallied around Robert's able son, William "Clito," who was also supported by the king of France and by the adjacent little county of Anjou. But by 1120 Henry had the Normandy situation well in hand, and also had re-established the old Norman claims of overlordship in Brittany and Maine. The Count of Anjou betrothed his eldest daughter to William, Henry's only son and heir.

Then as everything was going well for Henry, came a disaster after which he was said never to have smiled again. Prince William, returning to England with his bride, set sail with other young nobles on the "White Ship." So wild was the revelry that the bride was escorted by the king on another ship. With the crew evidently as drunk as the passengers, the "White Ship" struck a rock a short way from shore and sank with practically all aboard her.

The king's grief at the loss of his son was coupled with fears for the future of his dynasty. He would still have none of his obvious successor, William Clito. One of Henry's bastards, Robert of Gloucester, might have been his wisest choice; but in those days of church reform there was some prejudice against another illegitimate king. Henry, long since widowed, remarried, but had no son. In the meantime many intrigues were on foot, with the prospects of a disputed succession. The Count of Anjou gave his second daughter to William Clito, who had his usual bad luck, for the Pope annulled the marriage.

Matilda or Maud, Henry's daughter, was the next pawn in the king's efforts to secure the succession. She had been sent to Germany as the bride of the Holy Roman Emperor, Henry V, at the age of nine. Her husband had died shortly after the "White Ship" disaster; and the Germans, it is said, were even ready to bestow upon her the crown of the Holy Roman Empire. Reluctantly, at her father's behest, the empress returned to England where her father forced her to become the bride of Geoffrey, son of that same Count of Anjou. To the shy, proud Matilda of twenty-nine, who for twenty years had occupied the highest position possible for a woman in Christendom, this marriage to a rough, boisterous youth in his middle teens must have been both repulsive and humiliating. The English and the Norman barons too were displeased at this alliance with the despised, loud-mouthed Angevins. By the time Henry I died, six years later, this ill-mated union had produced the coveted grandson.

Stephen vs. Matilda

The death of Henry I, in 1135, ended a period of nearly seventy years during which the first three Norman kings had been strong enough to consolidate the effects of the Conquest and to establish a firm central government. The next nineteen years almost wrecked that system. During that anarchy, men appreciated that if Henry had made heavy exactions, he had given something of value in return. With his death, according to the Anglo-Saxon Chronicle, "there was tribulation soon in the land; for every man that could forthwith robbed another."

The dispute for his crown complicated matters. The barons had promised to accept Matilda as her father's successor, but being in France at the time, the emergency caught her unawares. Her delay was fatal to her interests, for in those days of slow communication it meant much to get news first. Her cousin, Stephen of Blois, who was near the Channel, dashed over to England and was immediately crowned. Technically, according to the principles of succession,

Walls of Pevensey Castle on the southeast "invasion coast" near Hastings. An outer, lighter Roman wall surrounds these powerful Plantagenet fortifications.

Matilda, as daughter of the Conqueror's son, had a stronger claim than Stephen, as son of the Conqueror's daughter, Adela, who had married the French count of Blois. But England had already seen the technical rights of the Conqueror's eldest son, Robert, set aside in favor of Rufus and then of Henry. Matilda's sex, her unpopular Angevin marriage, and her haughty personality all told against her succession. The barons transferred to Stephen their oaths, which were to prove once again short-lived and worthless. It is doubtful if either Matilda or Stephen was the sort that could have kept the turbulent baronage in hand, even if there had been no disputed succession. The next nineteen years were, strictly speaking, Stephen's reign; for although Matilda was crowned by the rival faction, he never abdicated.

Stephen was charming, generous, and chivalrous, but he lacked strength and good sense. England was soon to learn that "the country of an affable prince" was no man's land. "When the traitors perceived that he was a mild man, and soft, and good, and did no justice, then did they all wonder," states the Anglo-Saxon Chronicle. The English barons "were all forsworn and forfeited their troth, for every powerful man made his castles and held them against him." This illegal castle-building was a sure sign of royal weakness. The Conqueror had forbidden his vassals to build castles, except on the borders as defense against the Scots and Welsh. It was not hard to stop the building of castles; but once up, even the inflammable wooden structures on huge earthen mounds, which often passed for castles, ordinarily could withstand a siege from a feudal army which melted away after its forty days of military service. So many a petty baron built his unlicensed, or "adulterine," castle, where he could defy the royal forces and from which he and his henchmen could sally forth to harass the countryside with robbery and torture.

The whole period (1135-1154) was complicated by an intermittent and none too clearly defined civil war between Stephen and the adherents of Matilda. The barons kept constantly shifting from side to side, and one scarcely knew how they stood from day to day. There were fights, sieges, and executions all over the country for nineteen years, since even when the barons were not supporting Matilda they were at least defying the king. The fortunes of war kept shifting. The first major engagement came in 1138, when the Scots under their king, David, Matilda's great-uncle, invaded England. Stephen repulsed them in the so-called "Battle of the Standard," but let the fruits of victory slip through his fingers. The next year Matilda herself landed in England, and the west coast rose to her support. Stephen, in his chivalry, gave up a chance to capture her and was soon taken prisoner himself. Matilda was crowned, not as queen but only as "Lady of England." She quickly overplayed her hand. Even her bastard half brother, and chief supporter, Robert of Gloucester, remarked that "when the Empress was in such power so cruel and proud was she that men might suffer it not." She had to flee; Robert, captured and exchanged for Stephen, soon died, and her fortunes went from bad to worse. Trapped and almost starved in Oxford Castle, she made a spectacular and risky night escape through the snow and left England. Her husband was too busy conquering Normandy to help her in England. Stephen in the ascendancy could do little to check the anarchy.

The whole nineteen years of Stephen's reign were a period of rapine, pestilence, and general misery, with the possible exception of London and the southeastern part of England, where towns continued to develop. The peasant gave up tilling his field; the townsman fled from his home.

"Thou mightest go a whole day's journey," said one chronicle, "and not find a man sitting in a town nor an acre of land tilled."

Grim tales of these days have been preserved by the anonymous author of the *Acts of Stephen*. Geoffrey of Mandeville was a particular devil, who dominated the fen country around Cambridge and Ely. With his "formidable host of mercenary soldiers and freebooters" Geoffrey "devastated the whole country by fire and sword; driving off flocks and herds with insatiable cupidity, sparing neither age nor profession, and freely slaking his thirst for vengeance. The most exquisite cruelties he could invent were instantly executed on his enemies. Meanwhile "all the northern counties were subjected to the tyranny of the Earl of Chester, who subjected the king's barons in the neighborhood to his yoke, surprised their castles by clandestine assaults, and wasted their lands by hostile incursions; . . . John, also, that child of hell, and root of all evil, the lord of Marlborough Castle, was indefatigable in his efforts to create disturbance." Down in the southwest the men of Bristol, having plundered everything available in their own region, "quickly found their way into every part of England where they heard there were men of wealth and substance, and either violently laid hold on them, or got them into their power by fraud; then, bandaging their eyes and stopping their mouths, . . . they conducted their captives, thus blinded, into the middle of Bristol, and there, by starvation and torture, mulcted them of their property to the last farthing."

Yet this was a period of extraordinary expansion of monasteries and religious building, perhaps because, in such times, men were the more ready to withdraw from this world to contemplate the next. Especially significant was the coming to England of the Cistercian monks, with their practices and discipline so much stricter than those of the Benedictine monasteries, of which they were an offshoot. The order was founded by an Englishman, Stephen Harding, but its influence was spread by Saint Bernard of Clairvaux, leader of the Second Crusade. At this time also began the first teaching at the incipient university at Oxford. The monks began to go into trade more than ever, and the Cistercians were to make a particular success in raising and gathering wool. Altogether, the Church grew stronger; for, with the strong hand of royal power removed, the Pope interfered more, and this brought the English Church more directly under the guidance of Rome.

The years of trouble finally drew to an end. Matilda's son Henry had made one abortive attempt to challenge Stephen's rule at the age of sixteen. But three years later, in 1153, he returned to England and was so successful that he secured the compromise known as the Treaty of Wallingford. By this, Stephen was to continue to rule until his death, and then, since his own son was dead, Henry would be accepted as his heir. This long-delayed peace, with its provisions for the destruction of unlicensed castles and other lawless things, was scarcely needed. Stephen was to die within a year.

Henry II's accession gave England a new line of kings which was to rule until 1399. Sometimes this is called the Angevin line, because Henry was the son of the Count of Anjou; sometimes Plantagenet, because the counts of Anjou had the habit of wearing a sprig of the broom plant (*planta genesta*) as a distinctive sign. Nine generations of these counts, always a Fulk or a Geoffrey, had gradually extended the frontiers of tough little Anjou, lying astride the river Loire, until it had absorbed the rich county of Touraine. The Angevin family, scorned by the Normans as uncouth and provincial, but well known for its vigor and fiery temper, now stepped into power, in the person of its ablest and most energetic member, as probably the chief family of Europe.

Effigy of Eleanor of Aquitaine, heiress-wife of Henry II, in the Plantagenet burial vault at Fontrevault, next to that of her son Richard the Lion-Hearted.

Henry II

Henry II (1154-1189), by inheritance or by marriage, was direct ruler of more than a third of France as well as all of England (see map facing page 72). His title to Normandy, as to England, came through his mother, daughter of Henry I; but his father, Geoffrey of Anjou, had made it doubly sure by conquering Normandy himself. From him also came Anjou, including Touraine, and likewise the county of Maine, which lay as a buffer between Anjou and Normandy. Greater in area, if not in importance, than Henry's inherited French lands was the duchy of Aquitaine, which he secured for himself by marrying Eleanor, heiress of the tenth duke. Comprising most of southwest France, it included the three regions of Poitou, Guienne, and Gascony. Thirty to his nineteen years, the high-spirited Eleanor came to Henry with more lands than reputation; for she had just been divorced, not without good reason, by Louis VII of France. All these lands were under Henry's direct rule; he also had, like some of his predecessors, shadowy overlordship or suzerainty of the big, barren, Celtic duchy of Brittany, which jutted far out into the Atlantic. These holdings gave him more actual power in France than was enjoyed by the French king, whose authority was pretty well limited to the royal domain, about the size of Normandy, centering on the upper Seine, around Paris. The English king, of course, was vassal to the French king for his French lands; but this did not mean a great deal until the advent of the strong Philip Augustus, in the last years of Henry's reign. Englishmen take pleasure in the fact that English kings once ruled much of France: the French, however, can point out with equal truth that those kings were Frenchmen ruling England. Like some of his Norman predecessors, Henry proclaimed a hazy overlordship over Wales and Scotland, as over Brittany; and later he penetrated into Ireland.

A tremendous task faced the nineteen-year-old Henry in this huge "Angevin Empire." With his lands stretching from Scotland to the Pyrenees, he had the problems of reconciling different people and different ways of doing things; of long distances; jealous neighbors on all sides; a Church grown stronger with appeals to Rome during the unsettled years; an uncontrolled baronage, with its illegal castles; the bitter feelings always left by civil war; serious economic dislocation; and a total breakdown of his grandfather's administrative machinery, with consequent loss of all law and order.

"Affable, modest, and humble," was Henry, who spoke Latin as easily as French, and was said to understand many other languages as well. His energy and eagerness were so great that he nearly wore out his court with his dashing about from one place to another. He was so completely master of his own energy, it is said, that he never felt tired night or morning. Like other Angevins, he had a horrible temper which at times almost reached insane rage. He chose priests for their celerity in getting through Mass, and he had no use for anyone who could not keep up with his speed and versatility of accomplishment. So wide a range of territory did he control that his court was cosmopolitan in nature, with men from many places. Though the Exchequer sat almost continuously at Westminster, the real center of government was that little group of horsemen on the move. The itinerary of his movements fills one with amazement, considering the travel conditions in that day—London, Winchester, Gloucester, and York, and then Rouen in Normandy, Le Mans in Maine, Angers or Tours in Anjou, and Bordeaux in Aquitaine.

At a later time England's landholdings in France became a liability, because they distracted the attention, energy, and resources of England's rulers; but in Henry's day that was offset by the fact that wherever he went in his travels, he noticed what was being done and what needed to be done. He constantly transplanted ideas and methods of government from one region to another. All profited by the interchange, and England was left far richer by Henry's great innovations in the law, a valuable permanent contribution.

Common Law and Crusading

Although most school children have heard of Richard the Lion-Hearted and John, scarcely anyone who has not studied English history knows about their father, Henry II, "one of the conscious creators of England's greatness." Yet his effective system of uniform law, under royal control, was so well adapted to the peculiar English needs and tastes that its fundamental features today provide law for some three hundred million people, not only in England herself but also in many lands beyond the seas where Englishmen have gone to settle or to rule. These reforms, to be sure, may have arisen from a selfish desire to increase the royal power and revenue; but, whatever their original purpose, they helped to make life and property more secure throughout the kingdom, both then and later.

Henry found English justice in a jumbled condition, because of faulty organization and the anarchy under Stephen. Too many people were striving to administer too many kinds of law. The Conqueror and his sons had kept fairly well their promises to preserve "the laws of good King Edward"; but Saxon legal practices differed widely from region to region and, even at their best, left much to be desired. Already, Norman impatience with the unscientific and too often ineffectual Saxon efforts to achieve justice had brought about some changes, as we have seen, particularly in the foundations laid by Henry I. Unification is essential for an effective system of law, and herein lay the chief difficulty for the necessary expansion of the royal jurisdiction. Centralization could be achieved only at the expense of three other existing systems of courts—popular, baronial, and ecclesiastical—a difficult task, since barons and churchmen were trying to increase the scope of their own tribunals, realizing, like the king, that legal jurisdiction meant power. He who ran the court also pocketed the fees and fines.

Before the Conquest the old Saxon moots of the hundred and shire had conducted most of the legal business; but that was gradually being whittled away by the threefold attack of barons, Church, and king. The shire, or county, court remained as a very important unit in the English legal system, but the private baronial courts had absorbed many of the hundred courts, and there was danger they might seize even wider jurisdiction. Then, and for centuries afterward, many feudal lords on the Continent, unchecked by any effective royal power, dispensed "high, low, and middle justice," dealing out penalties all the way from death sentences to petty fines. Had Henry not overcome the anarchy of Stephen's reign, jurisdiction in England too might have been cut into small pieces.

The baronial courts represented an absence of system; the church courts, on the other hand, threatened to draw most of England's legal business into a uniform international system with its supreme judge at Rome. The Church had built up an elaborate court organization which had provided some kind of unity in the feudal anarchy of the Dark Ages. The Conqueror, in removing the bishop from the shire court, had led to the establishment of separate church tribunals. The Church's canon law, just before Henry's time, had been arranged by one Gratian into a comprehensive code which provided for a wide range of civil and criminal jurisdiction. The churchmen claimed the right to try all clerics for all offenses, and all cases as well in which sacraments or oaths were even remotely involved, such as marriage settlements, orphan guardianships, and wills. Their courts were popular, partly because they were well systematized, partly because the penalties set were frequently less harsh than those of royal courts.

Henry took the offensive against these three rival systems of the popular, baronial, and church courts. He drew legal business away from them partly by command and partly by offering a superior method for arriving at justice. Many of his most important reforms were incorporated in decrees which he announced to the assembled barons and prelates. The most far-reaching, the Assize of Clarendon (1166), outlined in twenty-two articles most of the basic features of his new legal system, providing for the relation of royal judges to the county courts and the use of the jury as part of the judicial system. This assize is not to be confused with the Constitutions of Clarendon, two years earlier, which dealt with church matters. Less important were Henry's three later decrees, the Inquest of

Sheriffs (1170), providing for a closer check-up of those powerful officials; the Assize of Northampton (1176), somewhat modifying the Assize of Clarendon; and the Assize of Woodstock (1184), harshly reaffirming the forest laws. Henry was much aided in establishing his legal system by two able justiciars, Richard de Lucy and, later, Ranulf Glanvill.

Itinerant Justices

A most essential feature of the new reforms was the linking of the royal justices with the old shire courts. Henry I occasionally had sent justices from the Curia Regis out into the counties on financial legal business. The Assize of Clarendon made this a regular practice. The shire, or county, court was to meet in its old form, at regular short intervals, for ordinary business (see page 59); but when the king's justices came around to hold their sessions, the king required a full attendance, including not only the barons and clergy of the county but also representatives of all the hundreds and lesser units. This preserved the old idea of the Saxon popular assembly, but linked it to the central government through the itinerant justices and the sheriff. It emphasized also the idea of representation; and when Parliament developed, it had a similar make-up, on a national basis, of barons, churchmen, and representatives of the lesser political units. Henry eventually divided the counties into seven circuits, with three itinerant justices, or "justices in eyre," for each; but the system was too ambitious for the time. Roads were wretched and travel was slow, so that some of the more remote counties often went for long intervals without official visitations. The main body of the Curia Regis, in the meantime, followed the king in his constant travels around the country. As some counties were neglected by the justices and as civil cases could be heard at first only before the Curia Regis, this became a costly nuisance. One man complained that he had trailed the court

The Court of King's Bench, early 15th century.

nor even primarily connected with law. The practice apparently was found among the Franks of Charlemagne's time, or even earlier, and was among the French customs which the Normans had adapted. Originally a special device for fact-finding, its name comes from the Latin for "oath," and the early jury seems to have been a group of men gathered by a royal official and sworn to give truthful information concerning facts probably more often financial than legal. This sworn inquest apparently was used by the Conqueror's agents in gathering facts for the Domesday Book. The original juryman, thus, was more a witness than a passive judge of right and wrong. Witnesses, as distinct from jurors, were not introduced into regular English law trials until nearly 1500. Any facts which they did not know already the early jurors were supposed to find out for themselves, outside of court, from general information or gossip presumably spread through any small community. The modern juror, on the other hand, is expected to base his decision only on what is presented in open court. He is supposed to come with a mind which is open, and which too often is blank. He may be excused or debarred if it is felt that he has too much previous knowledge about the merits of the case. It was the older type of witness-jury which the king applied to both criminal and civil justice.

By Henry's time criminal and civil law were setting out upon the separate paths which they have followed ever since. The layman is apt to associate judges and courts with the sentencing of criminals, but most lawyers are likely to think first of the fat fees in civil cases. A civil case is one in which an individual brings suit against another, usually over a question of property. The state, by furnishing a court, simply acts as umpire. In the Saxon period, criminal cases were usually treated on that same basis. If A cut off B's arm or occupied B's land, either action was regarded simply as an offense against an individual. It rested

from town to town and county to county for five years, and that, when he finally was awarded the disputed property, his profits had disappeared in expenses, lawyer's fees, and bribes. To remedy this, five of the justices remained sitting regularly at Westminster, where, not long after Henry's death, the Curia Regis split into three distinct courts: Common Pleas, for private civil cases; Exchequer, for governmental financial cases, largely concerning taxation; and King's Bench, chiefly for criminal cases.

Juries and Court Procedure

The jury, also a vital part of Henry's reforms, was the forerunner of the "grand" jury of the present day; the "petty," or trial, jury did not appear until the next century. It was formerly thought that the jury must have come from Anglo-Saxon origins, but later research indicates that origins were not Anglo-Saxon, nor popular,

upon B as plaintiff to bring A as defendant into court. If B won the decision, he was to collect and pocket the damages. In other words, crime was on a cash basis and seldom punished as an offense against the state (see page 30). Gradually, however, the idea developed that cutting off an arm was harmful not only to B but also to society as a whole. The state therefore accused A as a disturber of the peace. This prosecution of a crime by the state was accomplished by the enlargement of the scope of what was meant by violation of the "king's peace." This had always been an offense to be tried in the royal court. Originally applying merely to brawling in the actual presence of the king, it was then extended to the vicinity of the royal palace, and later to the king's highways. Finally all major crimes committed throughout the land were regarded as violations of the king's peace and came under royal jurisdiction. It was no longer necessary for B to bring the offender into court and conduct the case as a "common plea." It became a "plea of the Crown," when the state became plaintiff as well as umpire, and the case, as the lawyers would cite it, changed from "B v. A" to "Rex v. A." This extension of the king's peace, which had begun late in the Saxon period in connection with very serious crimes, appealed to Henry not only because it promoted peace and order but also because he was now the one to pocket the fine. The state's new relation to criminal cases is seen also in Henry's order that every county provide a jail; but an adequate police system, to make the relationship complete, had to wait for many centuries. Questions of property still remained "common pleas," with the individual as plaintiff and the state serving merely as umpire.

The jury's first function in the criminal field was to point out what cases should be tried before the king's justices as disturbances of the king's peace. The sheriff of each county was instructed by the Assize of Clarendon to assemble twelve good men from each hundred, together with four from each township, to report all crimes which, in their opinion, ought to be tried. It was felt that any serious crime or any suspicious person naturally would be known to such a group. Under the old system, where the burden of starting a criminal prosecution rested on the injured party, he might be bullied into silence by threats of revenge from the man who had injured him. It was expected that the new jury would be free from such intimidation. This early jury was the forerunner of the present grand jury, whose function is to present cases for trial. Its indictment did not necessarily imply that the defendant was guilty, but simply that the matter seemed worth looking into further. When the royal justices received the jury's "presentments," the question of guilt was at first determined either by the old Saxon water ordeal or by "wager of battle," the judicial duel introduced by the Normans. The ordeal, common at the start, was abolished by a church council in 1215. Wager of battle likewise soon fell into disuse, although the English neglected to abolish it officially until 1819, after an ingenious defendant had claimed his right to trial by that almost forgotten practice. Gradually most cases came to be settled by a second jury, the direct forerunner of our modern petty, or trial, jury. In cases of mild guilt the justices might settle the cases with fines which found their way into the royal treasury, but for more serious offenses the penalties were savage. In the first regular circuit of the itinerant judges in 1166, in the vicinity of London alone fourteen men were hanged and fourteen mutilated by the loss of hand or foot. Many criminals who escaped hanging were banished from the realm. The king confiscated the property not only of murderers but of the murdered as well, and heavy fines were imposed not only on actual offenders but even on counties and individuals if justice was not handled in exact accordance with the Assize of Clarendon.

Henry II assumed criminal jurisdiction by decree; but the plaintiffs in civil cases for the most part voluntarily shifted from the feudal or regular shire courts to the royal courts because the jury system offered a better chance to secure justice. There were plenty of civil cases in this reign, for much property had been seized by force during the anarchy under Stephen. The complications of feudal land tenure led to many delicate and intricate points of legal dispute. The old system decided these by wager of battle or a development of compurgation known as "wager of law." Even the devout began to question whether God settled fine points of land law through the relative merits of two husky professionals swinging pickaxes at each other, or through a system whereby, as an old Norman chief justice put it, "any dishonest man with six rascals to aid him could swear any honest man out of his goods." Possibly, with a weak case and a strong arm, one would prefer the wager of battle; but ordinarily it seemed far more sensible to leave the question to a dozen responsible individuals from the neighborhood, who presumably would have some factual knowledge of the case.

Henry put his new jury system at the disposal of private litigants and even decreed that certain types of civil cases must be settled through a jury and royal judge. The general use of the jury, however, was still treated as a royal privilege, and it was necessary to ask for specific permission to bring one's case before it. This was done by applying at the chancellor's office for a "writ," a written order directing the sheriff to assemble from a particular locality twelve good men to determine a specific kind of question. The case would be tried before the royal justices, who would render judgment after putting questions of specific fact to the jury. If this body seemed to bring in a false verdict, the verdict might be reviewed and the jurors, if guilty, fined. There was a particular specified writ for each of the principal types of cases which arose in civil law. The most celebrated of the early writs indicate the kind of questions to be settled. If the plaintiff complained that someone had seized land which he himself formerly had occupied, he asked for a writ of *novel disseisin*. If a stranger occupied property upon the death of the plaintiff's parent or close relative, the proper writ was *mort d'ancestor*, while the writ *utrum* was designated for questions of whether particular church lands were held by regular feudal tenure. There was also the *Grand Assize*, which drew into the royal courts cases concerning basic title to land, instead of simply the occupation of it. For a while the chancellor created new writs, defining new types of cases as occasion arose; but gradually the writs became rigidly limited to certain well-defined questions, and the chancellor began to settle in his own court and in another way special matters which did not fall into regular categories (see page 75).

The Common Law

Out of Henry's new legal system grew that distinctive English creation known as common law. The name implied that there was now a uniform law for all England in place of heterogeneous local customs. Other nations, with a law of a different type, have also secured legal uniformity, to be sure; but the distinctive feature of the English common law was the development of the so-called "case system." In disputed questions of law or court procedure the judge has been, from Henry's time, governed in his rulings by precedents established in previous cases. The justices of the royal courts drew up written reports of cases tried before them, pointing out their opinions on new features which arose in the trial, or instances where they saw fit to depart from earlier precedents. By the next century the more important of these reports were gathered into "Year Books," which enabled the justices to keep

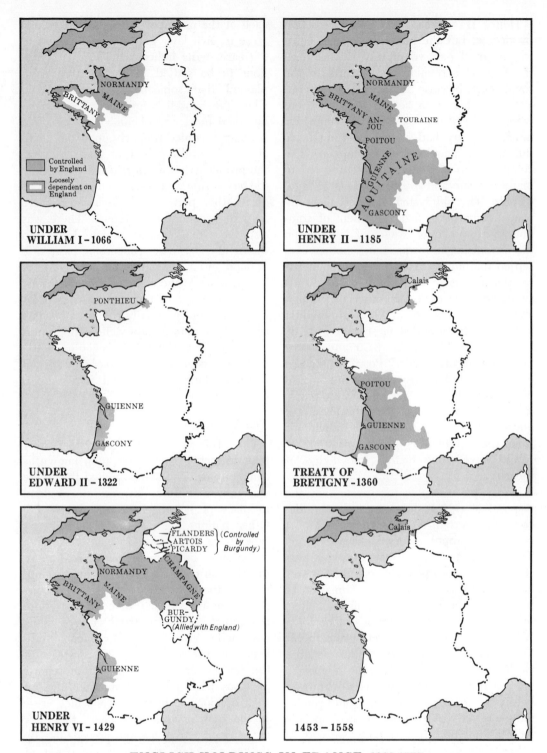

Controlled
by England

Loosely
dependent on
England

UNDER
WILLIAM I – 1066

NORMANDY
MAINE
BRITTANY

UNDER
HENRY II – 1185

NORMANDY
MAINE
BRITTANY AN-
JOU
POITOU
A Q U I T A I N E
GASCONY
TOURAINE

UNDER
EDWARD II – 1322

PONTHIEU
GUIENNE
GASCONY

TREATY OF
BRETIGNY – 1360

Calais
POITOU
GUIENNE
GASCONY

UNDER
HENRY VI – 1429

FLANDERS
ARTOIS
PICARDY
} (Controlled
by
Burgundy)
NORMANDY
MAINE
BRITTANY
CHAMPAGNE
BUR-
GUNDY
(Allied with England)
GUIENNE

1453 – 1558

Calais

ENGLISH HOLDINGS IN FRANCE, 1066-1558

up to date on the decisions of their colleagues. Justice B, for instance, finding an unusual feature in a case of *novel disseisin* in Devonshire, might follow the precedent established by Justice A in Yorkshire five years earlier, or, if his case seemed slightly different, might decide otherwise, whereupon his new decision would serve as a precedent for the rest of the justices. This practice has gone on continuously down through the centuries, making the common law a living organism which gradually can be adapted to changing conditions. From time to time the principles established in the courts might be crystallized into statutes (see page 103), while other statutes might become the subject for common-law interpretation. The citing of precedents has made it necessary for the modern English and American judge and lawyer to have access to hundreds of volumes of legal reports. It became increasingly difficult to run back through all the earlier reports for every case, so that digests summing up the principal cases under various headings began to appear. Some of these have been simply mechanical compilations; a few have had great influence in molding legal opinion and practice, such as those by Glanvill, the justiciar of Henry II; by Bracton, who by 1250 analyzed some five hundred decisions; by Coke (*c.* 1620); and by Blackstone (*c.* 1770). In addition to analyzing points of law, the English system also developed forms of court procedure still in use today. A unique feature of criminal practice in this respect is the right to jury trial, and the right of the accused to be faced in open court by his accusers. Finally, the development of the English system led to the theory that the law was supreme, and that even the king and his agents were not free to disregard it.

A well-trained legal profession was one explanation of the unity and permanence of the common law. Even in Henry's time, laymen were replacing churchmen on the bench, and lay lawyers soon began to accompany the justices on their circuits. Training for the common law in the later Middle Ages was to be had at Lincoln's Inn, Gray's Inn, and other "Inns of Court" in London. As in a law school at the present day, the students read law by day, and in the evenings, after dinner, held "moots," where they argued intricate hypothetical cases before older lawyers. Three languages usually were necessary to the lawyer's equipment: English for one's clients; Latin for the official records; and, above all, Norman French, which was used both in court and in the reports. Phrases like "oyer and terminer," as well as many commoner terms such as "plaintiff" and "defendant," still remain as relics of that tongue, which persisted in legal circles long after it was supplanted in common use by English. When the student had shown sufficient ability, he was "called to the bar" of his Inn and became a barrister who might plead in court. The more successful barristers were promoted to the grade of "serjeant," which became a prerequisite for appointment as a royal justice. The whole "bench and bar" of the common-law courts thus became a compact body, all trained in the same fundamentals from generation to generation.

Roman Law and Chancery

The common law was almost strangled at birth and again in infancy by the rival system of Roman law, which in modified form still prevails on most of the Continent. Legal reform was in the air in the twelfth century, in Italy as well as in England. Gratian organized the Church's canon law, based in part on Roman law, into an orderly system (see page 68); but the potent threat came from the slightly earlier work of Irnerius at Bologna. He rescued from virtual oblivion the *Corpus Juris Civilis*, the code of Roman laws, compiled at the order of the Byzantine emperor Justinian about A.D. 530. Thousands flocked to hear Irnerius expound it in the schools, which soon devel-

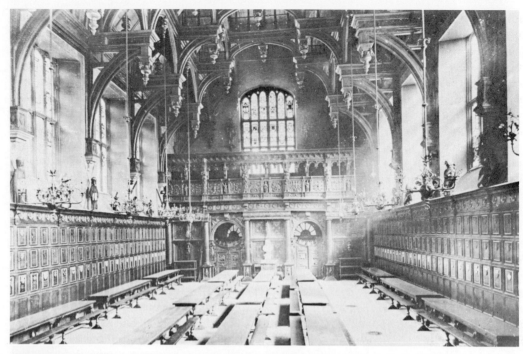

The great hall, with typical Tudor carved oak, of the Middle Temple, one of the four "Inns of Court," where lawyers were trained.

oped into the University of Bologna, and then scattered to teach it throughout Europe. One of these "civilians" had come to England in Stephen's reign. Henry II might easily have adopted it, admiring its systematic efficiency and its support of royal power. For a long time Roman law was a powerful threat to the common law; it was a "law of the books" rather than a "law of the courts." Its basis was usually a comprehensive code, like Justinian's, drawn up under the direction of a ruler and covering minutely and definitely the various phases of the law. Emphasizing abstract principles rather than practical experience, it was modified, not by actual case precedents, but by the philosophical opinions of scholars. It was better organized, more clean-cut, and simpler to administer than the English system; but it lacked the popular elements which Englishmen came to consider guarantees of personal security. The final de-

cisions were made, not by the help of a jury, but by judges who were active inquisitors, often hunting up evidence themselves. In place of the open English trial, where the accused must be faced by his accusers, trial under the Roman law was usually one in which the judges gathered evidence from the different parties separately. Finally, Roman law was often made the tool of an absolute ruler who could influence not only the original code but also the work of the judges. The common law has prevailed with notable exceptions, in much of the British Commonwealth, except Quebec and South Africa, and in the United States, except Louisiana.

The English legal system received the Roman law in what have been called occasional small doses, which acted as a tonic but were not strong enough to drug or to kill the distinctive English quality. Men like Bracton helped to systematize the common law and develop its fine points from Roman legal principles, but the influence of Roman law was most marked in the special courts which grew up outside the common-law courts of King's Bench, Common Pleas, and Exchequer. Its effects were noticeable in the Admiralty courts, which arose in the later Middle Ages for maritime questions; and it was closely related to the canon law which was used in the church courts, where matters of probate of wills and cases arising from marriage were tried for many centuries.

Foremost among these courts influenced by Roman law was Chancery, which would become around 1400 a regular court under the chancellor, who had long been exercising a special jurisdiction. This court dispensed "equity," a rather indefinite principle which was applied to situations where the strict letter of the common law could not or did not settle matters in a way which seemed fair. One use was to fill in gaps in the common law. The time came (1258) when the chancellor was restricted in his power to issue new common-law writs to meet new situations. As society became more complex such new situations were bound to arise. Chancery, unfettered by precedents, could advance to meet them more rapidly than Common Pleas. A plaintiff might be told that there was no writ to fit his case for trial in Common Pleas, but that he might get a "bill" which would bring the case directly before the chancellor or his subordinates in Chancery. There the trial, without jury, resembled Roman-law rather than common-law procedure. Chancery could be used also virtually to overrule a common-law decision which to the chancellor, as "keeper of the King's conscience," did not seem "equitable" because of the rigid stiffness of common-law procedure. As time went on, large numbers of cases, starting in Common Pleas, were later carried into Chancery, which would order the winner in the other court not to take advantage of his favorable decision.

This practice led to strong protests from the common-law justices and from litigants, but it was extremely profitable to the lawyers. Chancery also had special power through the "injunction." Whereas common-law courts could deal only with accomplished facts, Chancery, on threat of punishment for contempt of court, could "enjoin" an individual from committing an act. If someone, for instance, threatened to cut down a man's valuable shade trees, Common Pleas could do nothing but award damages after the trees were felled, whereas Chancery might prevent the cutting. This power has been used in recent times, particularly to limit the action of strikers. At first each case in Chancery was supposedly settled on its own merits, but gradually the court developed a body of procedure and precedents of its own. Chancery was influenced both by Roman and by canon law (the early chancellors being bishops or archbishops), and men preparing to practice before Chancery went more often to Oxford to study Roman and canon law than to the Inns of Court, which emphasized common law. Chancery at the outset was supposedly a short cut to justice; in later years the name became synonymous with tedious and costly delay, since cases sometimes dragged on for years or for generations.

This general survey of the English legal system has carried the development well beyond the time of Henry II, but one may easily appreciate the importance of his contributions. A century after his time Edward I crystallized some of the more important legal principles into statutes, and the common law appears later as something with which even the king was warned not to tamper.

Scutage

Henry's zeal for strong and efficient government also led to two innovations in military policy with a far-reaching influence upon England's social structure as well as upon her fighting efficiency. Both measures tended to curb that dangerous power of the barons and knights, richly endowed with lands in return for forty days of military service each year. Such a concentration of undisciplined fighting force was risky, as the reign of Stephen had shown; moreover, it was inefficient. The short-lived armies produced by the feudal system were inadequate for lengthy sieges and for service in France. Early in his reign Henry II extended the practice of *scutage,* or "shield money," with which Henry I had experimented. Instead of calling upon his vassals to furnish so many armed men for forty days, the king at times would demand a certain amount of money for each knight's fee. With that money he then hired mercenaries, either English or foreign, who could be held together long after the brief period of feudal service expired. This may be regarded as the first step in the transformation of the fighting baron into the peaceful country gentleman—a process which was to go on for several centuries. In the north and west, out toward the Scottish and Welsh borders, the fighting tradition continued for more than three centuries; but in the more settled parts of England the claws of the former fighters were clipped, their grim donjon fortresses were transformed into more comfortable country houses, and, still enjoying the rich profits from the manorial system, they gradually devoted themselves more and more to hunting, drinking, politics, local administration, and the supervision of their estates. Not until the sixteenth-century Tudor period, however, would the transformation be fairly complete.

Henry's other military innovation, the *Assize of Arms,* was a systematic extension of the old Saxon fyrd, or militia. Every freeman, even down to artisans in the towns and the meanest freeholders, was required to maintain certain military equipment and to be ready for the king's service in case of emergency. Henry was inclined to be auto-

cratic and absolute; but he maintained no standing army in England to enforce his will, and his despotism was sufficiently popular so that he dared to trust many men with weapons. By thus extending the number of potential soldiers Henry further weakened the former fighting monopoly of the feudal lords. Within two centuries the bold yeomanry would show their mettle on foreign fields and learn that they could hold their own with the proud knights on horseback.

Henry's military and legal reforms had much in common. In both he was trying to increase the royal power and make it more efficient. In both he played off the lesser freeman against the barons, whom he desired to curb. While the barons were losing their fighting monopoly they were also being deprived of jurisdiction; while the freemen were arming themselves at royal command they were also being given new importance as jurymen.

Church Courts and Becket

Henry's efforts toward making the royal courts paramount at the expense of the church and feudal courts naturally aroused opposition. In this dispute he met the most serious reverse of his career. This problem, like lay investiture and taxation, was a fruitful source of church-state quarrels in several countries. In England the conflict degenerated into a personal clash between Henry and his former faithful lieutenant, one Thomas Becket. Becket came from a prosperous family of the merchant class, but family reverses caused young Thomas to be placed at an early age in the household of an important archbishop. Here he learned all the ramifications of church business and rose quickly, becoming chancellor under Henry. Close friends, they worked together hand in glove, for Becket's businesslike methods were an asset to Henry's clever statesmanship. In foreign affairs and domestic, even where church privilege was involved, Becket acted as Henry's second self and ally. Perhaps because Pope Adrian IV (1154-1159), the former Nicholas Breakspear, was a native Englishman (the only such Pope in history), and perhaps because the prelates were Henry's own appointees, the king had peaceful relations with the church for a while. When the Archbishopric of Canterbury fell vacant, Henry wanted to see Becket in that coveted position. Nevertheless, a certain amount of irregularity was involved in Becket's appointment in 1162, as he was merely a Canterbury archdeacon and was rushed within twenty-four hours through all the other church ranks so that he might be invested archbishop.

To the stunned surprise of the king, Thomas came from the investiture a different man. As one chronicler expressed it, ". . . this change of habit was preliminary to a change of heart also; for he now renounced secular cares and attended only the spiritual concerns of the church and the gain of souls." The luxury-loving man of the world now went dirty and hungry, with a hair shirt next his skin. Henry was aghast, for he had envisioned in this appointment the link that would bring the Church closer to the throne. Instead, Thomas resigned the chancellorship and became as unreasonable a die-hard exponent of church privileges as Anselm at his worst.

The real trouble centered about the clashing jurisdiction of royal and ecclesiastical courts. The latter had asserted and had enjoyed complete jurisdiction over many sorts of cases, including the trial and punishment of "criminous clerks" (churchmen), whatever their offenses and their rank might be. This privilege of "benefit of clergy" was claimed not only by regular prelates, priests, and monks but also by many professional men, students, and others, some of whom had no stronger claim to church connection than their ability to patter off a few lines of Latin. Benefit of clergy was decidedly worth while, for the penal-

ties of the church courts were notoriously more lenient. A canon, for instance, had recently cleared himself of murdering a knight by a simple oath in the bishop's court. Henry, in 1164, attempted to bring the clergy under royal law with his Constitutions of Clarendon. According to this code, a "clerk" accused of a crime was first to be brought into a secular court to plead guilty or not guilty. He was still to be tried, as before, in the church court. If found guilty, he was to be unfrocked and turned over to the king's court, where he would receive the regular punishment for his crime. Becket's bitter stand against this meant that thousands were exempted from the liability to harsh punishment for the worst crimes. The logic of the royal stand that all Englishmen should be subject to the same law ran directly counter to the equally logical claim of the primate that the churchmen should be tried in church courts.

After a few months Becket left England; and so stubborn was he that even his own bishops were ready to compromise. Six years later Henry wanted to have his eldest son crowned king before his own death. The Archbishop of York performed the coronation ceremony. This infuriated Becket; but after a meeting with Henry in France, he came back and suspended or excommunicated the prelates assisting in the coronation. They hurried to Henry in Normandy. In one of his not-uncommon moments of sudden Angevin rage the king made a rash exclamation about this troublesome Thomas of whom no one would rid him. Four knights, taking this passionate outburst far too literally, hurried without the king's knowledge to Canterbury and burst into the cathedral. Then, and for long afterward, a church was usually respected as a safe sanctuary, even in the case of red-handed criminals; but on this occasion Canterbury itself was not safe for its own archbishop. The knights called for "the traitor, Thomas Becket"; he stepped down

The murder of Thomas Becket at Canterbury in 1170, taken from an almost contemporary drawing.

to meet them; bitter words were exchanged; and then they cut him down. One knight even drove his sword into the skull of the dying primate. The spot where he fell became England's most sacred shrine.

Like many people in a temper, Henry had not meant all he had said; but those rash words cost him a serious loss of prestige and a crushing defeat in the court dispute. The Canterbury murder scandalized and horrified public opinion everywhere. The immediate victory went to the dead archbishop. Henry went to Canterbury as the most groveling of penitents, and "barefoot and clad in woolen garments, walked the three miles . . . his tender feet being cut by the hard stones, a great quantity of blood flowed from them to the ground." "When he arrived at the tomb," continues the chronicler, "it was a holy thing to see the affliction which he suffered with sobs and tears, and the discipline to

which he submitted from the hands of the bishops and a great number of priests and monks." All of which may have been true, for Henry realized that the murder had seriously damaged his power. He had to withdraw some of the terms of the Constitutions of Clarendon, and, although "benefit of clergy" finally gave way before royal power, the "criminous clerks" continued to get off easily for many years. Henry's efforts, however, blocked the continual expansion of the church courts into new fields, together with the rest of the spreading power of the Church.

The murder of Becket coincided with the start of England's relations with Ireland, a sorry and tangled story that has run down through the centuries. In scarcely a year in all that time have relations been satisfactory to both English and Irish. Henry, not content with his immense Plantagenet empire, claimed, like some of his predecessors, overlordship of the Scots and Welsh; and his outstanding contact with the "Celtic fringe" was the start of the Irish problem, between 1169 and 1171.

Ireland had dropped out of English history after 664, when the Council of Whitby had decided in favor of the Roman Church instead of the more informal Christianity introduced by the Irish monks. It had continued in a primitive state of civilization, devoted chiefly to the tending or stealing of cattle, together with a little agriculture. The Vikings raided the island, but they were finally limited to Dublin and a few other towns on the east coast. There had been constant political turmoil, for the Celtic temperament was not as well adapted as the Saxon or the Norman to orderly government beyond the tribal stage. Sometimes seven kings ruled Ireland; sometimes there were more; occasionally a single ruler, like Brian Boru (1002-1014), might gain temporary ascendancy. But the chronicles of Irish history are little more than monotonous annals of feuds and sudden death.

Henry had toyed with the idea of conquering Ireland in the very first year of his reign, and supposedly had support from the English Pope, Adrian IV. The chief initiative came from a border baron, Richard de Clare, Earl of Pembroke, popularly known as "Strongbow," whose Norman-Welsh henchmen invaded Ireland in 1169. Strongbow himself soon followed, his knights in chain mail easily overcoming Irish resistance. Henry suddenly realized the dangerous possibility of an independent Norman state there and, doubtless anxious to distract public attention from the Becket murder, went over in 1171 and received the submission of a good part of the island. The Irish, with their traditions of tribal rule, probably did not realize the significance of the feudal homage which they gave to Strongbow and to Henry. The invading barons, however, took it at its face value and tried to rule accordingly. For the next three or four centuries Ireland fell into three zones, as far as English contact was concerned. The "Pale," extending some thirty miles around Dublin, had fairly effective rule along English lines. Far off in the west there was virtual independence. In between there was a very tangled situation, with the feudalized Norman-Welsh leaders and the old Irish paying only such respect to the king's representative at Dublin as they saw fit. Ireland seems to have had a remarkable capacity for absorbing its invaders. Before long the descendants of these barons—the Fitzgeralds, Lacys, Burkes (de Burgh), and the rest—became "more Irish than the Irish themselves." So it was with later waves of invaders—until the wholesale plantation of grim Presbyterians in Ulster about 1600, newcomers could be quickly absorbed.

Of Henry II it has been said that he could rule every house but his own. He and Eleanor had four sons, Henry and Geoffrey, dying before their father; Richard and John succeeding him in turn. The king seems to have been as much too soft in spoiling his sons as William I had been too harsh in repressing his. The ingratitude of the young Angevins was all the more marked because of their father's generosity during his lifetime. To honor them and to facilitate their inheritance, he had his eldest son, Henry, crowned king of England; Henry also received Normandy, Maine, and Anjou, while Richard was given Aquitaine, which he was to hold as a fief directly from the French king. Geoffrey, who had married the heiress of Brittany, received that duchy, which he was to hold as a fief from his elder brother Henry. John was nicknamed "Lackland" because he was too young to participate in the original distribution, but he later was granted the lordship of Ireland. Not one of the sons was content and they constantly intrigued against their father to make their nominal ownership actual. In this they were abetted by their mother, Eleanor, who was notoriously, and perhaps for good cause, hostile to Henry. The younger Henry, in league with the kings of France and Scotland and many barons, led a dangerous revolt in 1173; but the king finally crushed it.

Then came the treachery of Richard. In Philip Augustus (1180-1223), son of Eleanor's first husband by his third wife, France found a strong monarch. He utilized every chance to make the Plantagenet French lands his own, and Richard joined with him. The young prince shamefully humiliated his father in the ensuing conference, where all Richard's claims were perforce accepted. Sick at heart at this and at his favorite son John's involvement with Richard, Henry died in tragic bitterness in 1189.

Richard I and Crusading

The spectacular Richard, called Cœur de Lion, or Lion-Hearted, by his admirers, was anything but an asset to his kingdom. So little did it interest him that he was in England less than ten months of his ten-year reign (1189-1199), and his two brief visits were merely money-raising affairs. The rest

The capture of Richard the Lion-Hearted while returning overland in disguise from the Third Crusade. The English had to pay the Duke of Austria a huge sum for his ransom.

of the time he spent in quarreling with Philip over French lands, crusading in the Holy Land, or in captivity. Despite the intrigues of his brother John and others during his long absences, his father's work had been so thorough that, for once in medieval England, the government could be safely managed by ministers alone. Governmental details, left uncompleted at Henry's death, were, moreover, so well worked out under the highly capable Hubert Walter, eventually Archbishop of Canterbury and justiciar, that the reign even saw some constitutional advance.

Richard has come down in history and in legend as the embodiment of the romantic medieval knight. Endowed with a magnificent physique, this absentee king was brave, dashing, and at times chivalrous. He was a commander of considerable ability, but he was apt to spend his efforts along unpractical lines; and his subjects paid heavily in taxes for the reflected glory he brought them. Chivalrous he could be on occasion, ordering that the soldier who gave him his death wound be pardoned, but he also blinded fifteen of Philip's captured knights, leaving a sixteenth with one eye to lead the rest back to their king. Philip, "so that he might not appear inferior to Richard," sent back fifteen of the English king's knights completely blinded and led by a woman.

The motive force of Richard's existence was the crusading movement. The Crusades commenced after the Seljuk Turks, sweeping in from central Asia five years after Hastings, had routed an army of the Byzantine Empire and occupied most of Asia Minor and of the eastern-Mediterranean lands, including the Holy Land of Palestine. In 1095 the Byzantine emperor at Constantinople begged the Pope, Urban II, to come to his aid. Urban recognized this as an opportunity to enhance his own power by winning the Holy Land for western Christendom, and hoped at the same time to reunite under his leadership the Eastern (Greek Catholic) with the Western (Roman Catholic) Church. Fighting for the expansion of Christianity might turn the feudal nobility from their civil strife, which for some time the Church had been trying to curb in various ways, such as the "Peace of God," protecting noncombatants from warfare, and the later "Truce of God," forbidding fighting on weekends. The Turkish occupation, moreover, was potentially harmful to European pilgrims to the Holy Land, where formerly the Arabs had been more tolerant.

Passing on the emperor's appeal to the crowds at the church council summoned by him at Clermont, in France, the next year, Urban aroused an amazing response. To gain recruits for the proposed expedition, a "crusade," the Church promised volunteers forgiveness for their sins, protection for their forsaken families, and reduction of their debts. The emperor had hoped for some well-trained troops, not for the general exodus of western Christendom into his empire. The Pope too was surprised and disturbed when swarms took up the Cross and headed eastward to free Jerusalem from the infidels. People of all sorts flocked to the new adventure. Nobles were eager to gain fame, wealth, and, above all, new lands for themselves; merchants bethought themselves of trade; debtors sought freedom from creditors; criminals hoped to escape punishment; others saw in the Crusade a chance for travel or excitement; and, of course, to the truly devout the rescue of the Holy Sepulcher from infidel hands was a holy duty. Of such stuff were the Crusaders, who dashed eastward, occasionally in roughly organized bands, more frequently in armed expeditions led by knights and princes. Regarded in its broadest light, it was the positive expansion of western Christendom toward the East, under the inspiration of the Roman Catholic Church, the principal creative force of medieval Europe. The Crusades were thus one more act in the frequent resurgence of Europeans and Asiatics into each other's lands, which had been going on for over fifteen hundred years. They occurred midway between the deep inroads by the Moslem Arabs into Christian lands in the seventh and eighth centuries and the later conquest of the Byzantine Empire in the fifteenth century by the Moslem Turks, who thus established a long sway over the Christians of southeastern Europe.

In all, there were several Crusades in the next two centuries, and of these the Third (1189) most concerned England. The First Crusade occurred during the reign of Rufus, but few if any English barons participated (see page 54). It consisted of various parts, the first group composed of devout but poorly equipped pilgrims, led by Peter the Hermit and other religious enthusiasts, who went to what proved certain failure. The main expedition, in which Duke Robert took a minor part, wrested the Holy Land from the Saracens; and for themselves its lucky leaders gained states there which survived for some time. A second Crusade, called in 1147 by Saint Bernard, leader of the Cistercian reform movement, accomplished little.

Then, in 1187, a brilliant, spirited, and chivalrous leader, Saladin, who had arisen among the Moslems, recaptured Jerusalem, the center of the chief state of the Crusaders. All Christendom was aroused. Henry II himself took the cross—rather reluctantly —but rebellion interfered. His decision left one lasting trace in the "Saladin tithe." With the customary church tithe as a model, Henry levied a tax of 10 per cent on the personal property and income of all persons *not* going on the Crusade. This helped to pave the way toward regular taxation as distinct from the usual feudal sources of revenue.

The Third Crusade was particularly distinguished by the presence of four great leaders. On one side was Saladin, the outstanding commander of the Saracens; on the other were Richard of England and two of the most celebrated medieval monarchs: the aged, red-bearded Holy Roman emperor, Frederick Barbarossa, and that astute perennial enemy of the Angevins, Philip Augustus. The Christian triumvirate, each of whom was accustomed to the limelight, did not last. Barbarossa lost his life and most of his army during the difficult overland passage through Asia Minor. Richard, after scraping together all the money he could possibly lay his hands on, went by sea with Philip Augustus. Relations became strained when, at Cyprus, Richard married the beautiful Berengaria of Navarre, breaking his engagement to Philip's sister. With real skill Cœur de Lion captured the seaport of Acre, where he massacred nearly three thousand Saracens whose ransom was not forthcoming. Then Philip went home on a plea of ill-health, really in the hope of seizing some of Richard's French lands. From Acre, Richard

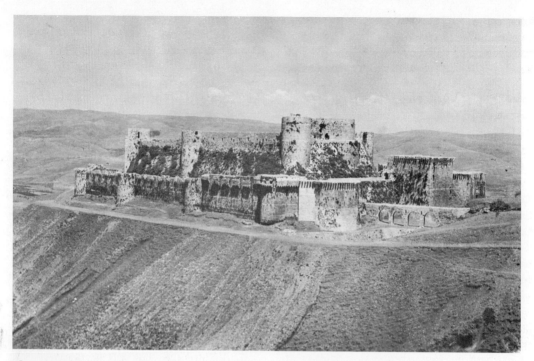

The powerful Krak des Chevaliers was built by the Crusaders in 1142 to protect their Kingdom of Jerusalem. It was finally captured in 1188 after a long siege.

made a grueling march down the coast and inland toward Jerusalem, while the wily Saladin constantly harassed his progress. News came of troubles at home, and Richard, within sight of the Holy City, reluctantly gave up the campaign. On his return he was shipwrecked in the Adriatic and tried to make his way overland through Austria in disguise. He was captured, dressed as a kitchen hand, in an inn near Vienna by followers of the Duke of Austria, who had several old grudges to settle, and imprisoned in a castle. There—as the story goes—he was finally found by his faithful minstrel, Blondel, who had sung all over Austria hunting for him. It cost England some £100,000, the equivalent of three or four years' normal revenue, to free the king; for ransom was one of the special feudal aids for which vassals were liable.

Of the other Crusades, the Fourth saw the sacking of Christian Constantinople by the Crusaders themselves; another Crusade was briefly successful under a reluctant Crusader, Barbarossa's grandson, the Holy Roman emperor Frederick II; while two others, under Saint Louis, grandson of Philip Augustus, were failures. The Holy Land remained under Moslem control until the British captured Jerusalem from the Turks during World War I.

Some historians assert that the change from medieval to modern Europe began with the Crusades; other claim much less for them. According to one authority (Munro), "Their real significance lay in the fact that they brought people of different nationalities together and caused an interchange of ideas and customs." The introduction of improved methods of fighting and of luxuries and comforts into western Europe and hence into England was definitely the result of this movement. Politically the kings gained power by taking over the estates of nobles who died on the Crusades, for some of the most turbulent and restless of the fighting barons left their bones in the Holy Land.

John, Philip Augustus, and Innocent III

Richard spent the last five years of his reign in France, engaged in constant squabbles with Philip Augustus and with his own French vassals. In a petty fight in Aquitaine in 1199, he was killed by a cross-bowman's arrow. As he had no son, the throne went to his younger brother, John. The rightful heir by primogeniture was the child Arthur, the son of Geoffrey, the deceased older brother, but he was another victim of the medieval preference for a grown man in a succession. Richard had designated John his heir, and in Normandy and England he was backed by such men as Hubert Walter, Archbishop of Canterbury; Geoffrey Fitz Peter, justiciar; and William Marshall, Earl of Pembroke; and by his mother, Queen Eleanor. Arthur had his supporters, too: his mother, Constance, through whom he had Brittany, while Anjou, Maine, and Touraine declared for him.

John was not long crowned when people realized that Henry II had had too many sons for England's good. John, generally called her worst king, had personal courage and high ability in political craft and in generalship. An excellent administrator, he failed because of his unnecessary cruelty, his indolence, his unwillingness to carry things through to conclusions, his utter faithlessness, and his lack of reliability. Some modern historians, however, point to the other side of his reputation. It was his bad luck to have as antagonists two of the strongest personalities of the Middle Ages, Philip Augustus of France and Pope Innocent III. Baronial hostility to him and his loss of Normandy naturally prejudiced the writers of the period against him. Yet like his father he kept close watch on the Exchequer officials and interested himself in the royal courts. That personal influence doubtless accelerated the expansion of royal justice; in his constant journeying about the land, he often sat as a judge. Nonetheless, other historians are inclined to find John a difficult subject for much white-washing. His was the darker side of the Plantagenet character in which the fiery Angevin temper and arbitrary will were not balanced by the wisdom, seriousness of purpose, and sustained activity of his father. Energy he had when he surmounted seemingly hopeless situations; but those moments were swamped in his self-indulgence or counterbalanced by deeds of wanton brutality. Sooner or later he alienated nearly everyone with whom he had any dealings, through greed, heartlessness, or complete disloyalty.

Three major conflicts dominated the reign and by their consequences made it a significant period. The climax came, first, with Philip Augustus over the Plantagenet empire; secondly, with Pope Innocent III over investiture; and, lastly, with the English barons, who forced the granting of Magna Carta.

To further his purpose of bringing more of France under his direct control, Philip Augustus played John and Arthur against each other in a long series of petty campaigns in which the mothers, Eleanor and Constance, did their part. The eighty-year-old Eleanor energetically arranged a marriage between her granddaughter, Blanche of Castille, and Philip's son. This brought about a temporary truce in which Philip threw over Arthur's claims in return for the "relief" to be paid by John for Richard's French fiefs, together with some minor cession of territory.

John's own action, as always, quickly canceled this temporary success. He had just secured the annulment of his marriage to the childless heiress of Gloucester; and while awaiting the return of envoys who were seeking the sister of the Portuguese king for his second bride, he suddenly fell in love with a twelve-year-old beauty, Isabel of Angoulême, already betrothed to one of John's own vassals in Aquitane. But not even the seriousness of a medieval betrothal daunted John, and he married the girl. That gave the ever-watchful Philip his chance. As John's suzerain, he summoned him to his court to explain this insult to a vassal's honor. John refused to comply because, though he might technically be Philip's vassal for the French lands, he was as king of England equal in rank to Philip. The latter thereupon returned to Arthur all the disputed French fiefs except Normandy, which he wanted for himself. John, during one of his bursts of energy, rescued his mother, who was being besieged by Arthur's forces, and captured his young nephew. That was the last that is known of Arthur. Contemporary rumor held John responsible, either directly or indirectly for the boy's death; it was never denied by John or by anyone close to him. These ugly rumors caused Philip to redouble his efforts against John, who did not produce Arthur when so ordered by his suzerain.

By the end of 1204, most of John's vassals and strongholds were lost to Philip. Even the strongest castle in western Europe and the key to Normandy itself, the Chateau Gaillard (Saucy Castle), Richard's proud monument, fell to the French with scarcely a struggle. It is said that John did not bother to carry out his excellent plans for its defense. In five years, he lost all the Plantagenet empire north of the river Loire —Normandy, Maine, Anjou, and even part of Poitou, in Aquitaine. They passed forever out of English history, except for a brief interlude in the Hundred Years' War. The only overseas heritage left was part of Aquitaine. By this careless throwing away of Plantagenet lands, John unwittingly did England an excellent turn. She came to realize that territory on the Continent was a serious liability, causing more trouble than it was worth. After 1204, moreover, the "half-and-half barons," who owned estates in northern France as well as in England, had to choose between France and England. This led to a baronage more exclusively concerned with England and her affairs.

The Plantagenet crown was shortly to become more tarnished in the lengthy duel between John and Innocent III over the vacant see of Canterbury. No ruler was the match for that invincible Pope, who compelled even the strong-willed Philip Augustus to take back the Danish bride whom he had rudely repudiated on the morning after their wedding. It had long been customary for the monks of Canterbury to choose the archbishop; but here, as elsewhere, the choice ordinarily was dictated by someone higher up, usually the king. This time some of the younger monks stole a march on the king by secretly selecting one of their number to succeed Hubert Walter, and in short order had the new archbishop duly started on his way to Rome for Innocent's approval. John, enraged at hearing this, insisted upon the election of the bishop of Norwich. Upon arriving at Rome, neither was approved by Innocent, who put forward his own candidate, Stephen Langton, for election. Thus everyone concerned violated the correct procedure: the monks by their secrecy, John by his insistence on his personal candidate, and Innocent by his suggestion of the third candidate. But it may be said in justification of Innocent that Langton was an excellent choice. Born an Englishman, he had won a great reputation at the University of Paris and had risen to be a cardinal.

In the duel between John and Innocent each had powerful weapons. John took the first step, either expelling the Canterbury monks or at least causing them to rush fearfully into exile. Taking over the rich Canterbury lands, he threatened reprisals against all the English clergy should Innocent continue his insistence upon Langton. Innocent, not one to be defied, placed an interdict upon all England. In its strictest interpretation, it would have cut the people off from all public church services and most of the sacraments. In this devout age, when most of the people had been brought up to believe that very careful participation in all church rites was essential to their future salvation, an interdict might cause them to rise against their ruler, lest they risk eternal damnation. As a matter of fact, certain sacraments, including baptism, confirmation, penance, and marriage, were continued under restrictions, while Christmas, Easter, and some other church festivals were exempted from the general prohibition. The feature of the interdict which bore most heavily upon the people was the necessity of burying their dead, without services, in unhallowed ground. John, in retaliation seized the lands of most of the bishops and also of the lesser clergy, to whom he left only a bare allowance for a very little food each day. He is said even to have ordered clemency for a highwayman who had murdered a priest because he had slain the "king's enemy." After two years of this, plus fruitless negotiations, Innocent launched his second weapon, excommunication, against John himself. This cut off any given individual from contact with the church, and he was supposed to be shunned by all members of society, high and low. John took steps to prevent such ostracism by instilling fear of cruel reprisals.

Outside England, John's position seems to have suffered little from this double indignity of interdict and excommunication; for there were three other excommunicated princes at the time, among whom was the Holy Roman Emperor. Within England itself there was no immediate outburst. The people, as a whole, were accustomed to resent papal interference, and the confiscation of clerical property momentarily lightened the demand for scutage and other feudal dues. The power of John's effective mercenary troops probably had much to do with England's outward calm. Before long, however, the country was seething under

his reign of terror. The chroniclers were discreetly silent about this period; but as one of them put it, "No one durst speak." One unfortunate archdeacon was so ill-advised as to wonder, aloud, whether he ought to stay in the service of an excommunicated king. With an appallingly heavy weight of lead on his head, he was incarcerated in a cell, too small for either sitting or standing, until he starved to death. John also demanded as hostages the children or other dear ones of any noble family whom he suspected of disloyalty. The wife of de Braose, a prominent suspect baron credited with knowing the fate of Arthur of Brittany, refused to trust her son as a hostage to "Arthur's murderer." John thereupon imprisoned her with her son in Windsor Castle, with only raw bacon and some uncooked oats for food, until they died. By such methods the king stifled open criticism —for a time.

The despotic power which had been built up and ably used by Henry II was now in the hands of a "disliked and despised man." Arrogant foreigners were installed as sheriffs and overstepped the usual bounds of authority. Increased forest exactions and new illegal tolls made the reign burdensome even to the poorest and least likely objects for royal extortion, like the Bristol Jew whose teeth were knocked out one by one each day until on the eighth he promised to pay what the king demanded. The pipe rolls indicate exaggeration by the chroniclers here, but there is no doubt of John's frequent and generally illegal demands of money. He went too far in all things; and, as whispered tales passed from mouth to mouth, arousing widespread bitterness, gradually resistance took form.

Warnings of a conspiracy reached John in 1212 on the western border, where he had summoned the feudal levies for an invasion of now hostile Wales. The situation seemed so threatening that he sent home the feudal forces, whose loyalty was in question; but not before he publicly executed twenty-eight boy hostages from prominent Welsh families. John next cleverly tried to win the common people with promises of relaxation of the forest laws, lessening of illegal tolls, and royal commissions to hear complaints; but those fair words could not offset the cumulative effect of his cruelty. The articulate opposition came particularly from the barons, who had suffered both in purse and in honor; for it was reported that no woman, no matter how nobly born or well married, was safe from John's desire.

In the meantime Innocent, simply to scare John into submission, suggested to Philip Augustus that he seize John's throne for himself. Philip, however, took Innocent's idea seriously and joyfully made ready for the conquest of England. John, knowing his baronage was an uncertain quantity, neatly slid out of the dilemma by accepting Innocent's demands in 1213. Considering John's long defiance, these were comparatively moderate: acceptance of Langton, recall of exiled ecclesiastics, compensation for the losses of the clergy, and John's co-operation in a future Crusade.

John went even further: he gave England itself to the Pope, and then received it back as a fief, with promises of annual tribute. Humiliating as this sounds, and though later Popes tried occasionally to capitalize the matter financially, the act was of slight importance and meant little beyond a small matter of loss of dignity. Other princes of the time had done likewise. On the other hand, it proved an ace of trumps for John, who had the gleeful satisfaction of seeing the disgruntled Philip forbidden by Innocent to invade a papal fief!

Chapter Six · 1214-1297

Barons and Parliament

Except for the wild years of Stephen's reign, the restless and powerful barons had been kept well under control by a series of iron-handed monarchs for a century and a half after the Conquest. Then, in the last years of John's reign, they commenced a series of more orderly efforts to secure a share in the government, and several times during the next century they would adopt further measures to curb the formerly absolute royal power. Not one of the purely baronial movements secured lasting results, but they helped to pave the way for the successful rise of Parliament, where barons and commoners together finally gained a major share of the power once monopolized by the king.

Although John was now the Pope's vassal with England a papal fief, Stephen Langton, the new Archbishop of Canterbury, was, from the moment he landed in England, the guiding spirit of the baronial movement to check royal despotism. On at least one occasion he even read the Charter of Liberties of Henry I to an assemblage of barons, and advocated its use to curb John's arbitrary actions (see page 56). The king, however, was apparently blind to this new danger. Relieved of the threat of French invasion, he decided to take the offensive himself and to regain his lost provinces in

France. The failure of this further attempt at reconquest overseas, with the resulting additional loss of royal prestige, was the last straw to the baronial impatience with misrule.

John, as usual when he put his mind to it, was an excellent strategist. He had planned to catch Philip Augustus between two fires. John himself would strike from Aquitaine, while Holy Roman Emperor Otto, his sister's son, together with several lesser princes in English pay, would attack Philip Augustus from the north and east. The scheme was delayed by the refusal of many English barons to serve overseas, but John finally took over a force composed chiefly of expensive mercenaries. His own campaign failed, and the whole scheme came to grief in the Flanders marshes in July, 1214, when Philip Augustus routed Otto and his allies at Bouvines. That battle greatly increased the French king's popularity; it cost the German emperor his throne; and it meant serious trouble for John.

In England, signs of discontent had been multiplying since the refusal of some of the barons to accompany John or to pay the scutage which he had levied at a heavier rate than ever before. For perhaps the first time since the Conquest the majority of

One of the original copies of the Magna Carta showing the beginning articles.

Englishmen sided with the barons against the king. All classes had felt the burdens of John's rule, and not only had his military exploits been more expensive than Richard's, but he had given England no glory in return for her money. Starting north to punish the recalcitrant barons, John was dissuaded by Langton, by now the unquestioned leader in the widespread demand for immediate reform. John, who by the close of 1214 was feeling the loss of prestige at Bouvines, tried unsuccessfully to win over the churchmen and the Londoners with special concessions; but the barons grew constantly more restless. By Easter week in 1215 they gathered in force and a month later occupied London. There was some desultory campaigning, but John soon realized that the odds were too heavy to contest.

Magna Carta

On June 12, 1215, one of the most dramatic moments of English history occurred at Runnymede, a meadow on the Thames. The king had ridden over the short distance from Windsor Castle to meet the large force of the barons and their followers who had come up the river the twenty miles from the capital. Langton, more than anyone else, gave form and direction to the events which followed. The barons brought with them a series of demands, and to this provisional document John set his seal. By the end of the week, after long discussions of details, the two sides had agreed to the sixty-three points of the famous Magna Carta, or Great Charter.

This celebrated document, which has been variously called a treaty, a statute, and a declaration of right, was drafted in the conventional legal form of a charter or contract such as was used in granting a fief. The modern reader is struck by several strange features. Unlike the American Declaration of Independence of 1776 and the French Declaration of the Rights of Man of 1789, it did not indulge in political philosophy or in sweeping generalizations about the freedom of the people. Its sixty-three articles, clauses, or "chapters" dealt with immediate, specific problems. They were arranged in a rather haphazard manner, covering a wide range of subjects. The most numerous items centered around questions of feudal dues, law courts, and administrative abuses. One needs to be familiar with technical feudal relations to appreciate those articles designed to keep the king within reasonable bounds in the matter of reliefs, wardships, aids, scutage, and similar points where he had abused his relations with his vassals. The legal articles show that, on the whole, the barons appreciated the value of the new court system established by Henry II, even though it cut into their own jurisdiction. Only in major cases of land title did they object strongly to the new writs. They felt that a royal court should be established permanently in one place for the convenience of litigants; they stipulated that penalties should be reasonable; and they hinted at John's abuse of the legal system in the celebrated fortieth clause, "To no one will we sell, to no one will we refuse or delay, right or justice." The specific attempts to check administrative abuses imply further shortcomings of John. He was to appoint as officials "only such as know the law of the realm and mean to observe it well" (article 45); the sheriffs, who had become very powerful as royal agents, were to be curbed (article 24); committees were to investigate abuses of the forest system (article 48); and royal officials were to be checked in the "purveyance," or commandeering, of property and labor (articles 28, 30, 31). Certain clauses, dealing, for instance, with weights and measures (article 35), fish weirs (article 33), and bridge-building (article 23), seem strangely out of place in company with the weightier ones. Finally, near the end, several clauses refer to the immediate, temporary situation. John was to return all hostages (articles 49, 56-59); discharge certain unpopular officials and all his mercenaries (articles 50, 51); restore illegal fines and seizures (articles 52, 53, 55); and grant a general pardon (article 62). Langton and the barons, knowing the man with whom they dealt, were giving John no excuse to say that he did not know exactly what they meant.

Scholars have not yet ended their discussion of the exact nature of Magna Carta. One has called it a guarantee of liberty "to every being who breathes English air"; others, probably more accurately, belittle it as a selfish feudal document. The barons, interested in safeguarding their own interests, naturally emphasized the clauses on feudal dues. A few items, however, clearly extend the privileges of Magna Carta to other classes, in just recognition of the widespread support which the barons had received. All the advantages which the barons gained from the king were definitely extended to their own vassals (article 60). The freedom of the Church was recognized (articles 1, 63), while the men of London and the other towns were promised "all their liberties and free customs" (article 13). In the first clause "all the underwritten liberties" were promised "to all freemen of our kingdom" forever, but this excluded the mass of unfree villeins, or serfs—roughly four men out of five. The only reference to them in the Charter was the provision that a serf might not be deprived of his growing crops or his plow as legal punishment; he was not to be rendered unable to perform his full services to the lord of the manor.

Two famous articles of Magna Carta were later interpreted as implying far more than presumably was intended. The twelfth stipulated that, with certain reasonable exceptions, "no scutage nor aid shall be levied in our kingdom, unless by the common consent of our kingdom." This was later stretched to imply the principle of "no taxation without representation" and was considered "the germ of Parliament." The "common consent," as spoken of in the Charter, however, was simply that of the leading barons and prelates, who actually represented no one but themselves, while the scutage and aids were feudal dues rather than taxes. The thirty-ninth article stated that no freeman should be arrested or otherwise molested "unless by the lawful judgment of his peers" and "by the law of the land." Although later generations expanded this into a guarantee of jury trial for everyone, it seems to have been originally a reactionary feudal protest against the royal courts. The barons wished to free themselves from trial by juries and royal judges, whom they did not regard as "peers" or social equals.

The real significance of Magna Carta is not to be found in its detailed provisions. They were conservative on the whole, designed to preserve conditions already time-honored, and many of them soon became obsolete. Its lasting influence lay rather in its general implications. Later generations of Englishmen were to remember particularly that John had given his assent to two principles upon which English constitutional development was based: that certain laws and customs were of greater authority than the king himself, and that, if the king did not observe these laws, the people reserved the right to force him to do so. Regarded in that general light, Magna Carta quite rightly ranks among the most important documents of history.

Magna Carta had a checkered career in later English history. Although its immediate effect was slight, subsequent medieval kings reissued or confirmed it in modified form about forty times (see pages 100, 108). Then it apparently dropped from sight under the popular Tudor absolutism (1485-1603). Shakespeare's play about King John, written about 1595, did not mention it. Some thirty years later, the Parliamentary party used Magna Carta as a weapon against the Stuart kings and read into it some exaggerations. Since then, it has been regarded as one of the fundamental bulwarks of English liberty, with countless orators calling upon it to strengthen arguments of every sort. England, of course, has no written constitution of the type drawn up in the United States in 1787, but a famous English statesman once declared that Magna Carta, the Petition of Right (1628), and the Bill of Rights (1689) form "the Bible of the English Constitution."

Three months after Runnymede the Charter was less effective than it was to be six centuries later. To enforce the terms, the barons had thought of no better device than a committee of twenty-five who could authorize civil war if the king failed to keep his word. Whether the blame lay with John or with some of the more hotheaded barons, civil war soon broke out. Innocent III absolved John from obedience to the terms of Magna Carta, but Langton still strove to maintain the Runnymede settlement. During that last year of his life John waged an energetic, ruthless, and fairly successful war against the barons. They finally called for help from Philip Augustus, who dispatched a considerable force under his son, later Louis VIII. The invaders occupied London and part of southeastern England while John conducted a campaign all the way from the Welsh border to the eastern counties. While carelessly taking a short cut across an arm of the sea without due regard to the tide, John lost all his baggage and treasure and part of his men in the quicksands. Furious and disheartened, he recklessly overindulged in peaches and new cider, a meal which spared England a long civil war.

John's death left his nine-year-old son to reign for fifty-six years (1216-1272) as Henry III. For once, the accession of a child to the throne was accepted enthusiastically by the barons, who preferred even John's son and a child to a Frenchman. With the French holding most of the south and east, Henry had to be crowned in the west of England. He was lucky in his regent, the ninety-year-old but still able William Marshall. Within a year, the energetic English defeated the French on land and also won a signal victory at sea, which has sometimes been termed the beginning of English naval history. Hubert de Burgh, the doughty commander at Dover, appreciated the maxim that the best way to handle invaders was to "drown them in the sea before they ever could set foot on the land." A storm had scattered the defense squadron long enough to let Prince Louis land with part of his French forces, but de Burgh was able to beat off Louis's reinforcements. The French, in consequence, soon abandoned the invasion. The regency, at Marshall's death within three years, was carried on by de Burgh and three powerful churchmen until Henry at twenty began to rule in his own name.

He was to reign through more than half of the thirteenth century; for his first forty years, England's political history was relatively uneventful, but it was an era of social change and intellectual awakening. The "Dark Age" was beginning to lighten about the time of the Conquest. The twelfth and thirteenth centuries were thus really forerunners of what is called the Renaissance—with their new interest in the world beyond one's own manor, the growth of towns with their guilds and active artisans, the renewed vigor of the Church through the mendicant orders, the rise of new universities, the building of cathedrals, and all the thriving, busy life of the later medieval period.

The Rise of the Towns

Especially significant were the towns with their growing trade and industry. During the Dark Age town life had pretty much disappeared. The manor had been able to supply most of its own simple needs. Some of the manorial workers had taken time off from their farming to spin and weave wool for their clothing, to tan leather, to make shoes, and to do the necessary tinkering and the like. In the late tenth century, for the first time since Roman days, town life began to flourish on the Continent, especially in Flanders, the Rhine Valley, and northern Italy, the only locality where it had been holding its own. The towns began to specialize in the making and exchanging of wares. The manors limited themselves, on the whole, to the raising of crops. The surplus food was brought to town to exchange for cloth, shoes, hardware, saddlery, and other articles produced by people who devoted themselves to particular crafts. Most of this industry was still on a local scale, but articles from distant regions began more and more to circulate in trade by way of the towns. This new activity in manufacture and exchange produced a surplus of wealth by which the more successful townsmen became prosperous. They developed into a new middle class; some of them came perhaps from the lower knights, but many of them

Calais around 1390; barely 20 miles from Dover, it was in English hands from 1347 to 1558. It was the chief, and sometimes only, staple town for wool exports to the Continent.

were recruited from escaped serfs, who became free if they could remain in a town for a year and a day.

Considering her remote, northern position, England had had a fair share of Roman towns, as names like Chester, Worcester, and Gloucester indicate by their derivation from the Roman *castra*, or "camps." At the time of the Conquest, the hundred so-called towns also included Saxon and Danish communities which had grown up around fortified places or abbeys with names often ending in "ton," "by," or "ham." Most of these were simply overgrown villages; few had developed industry and trade which made the later towns distinctive.

The Conquest gave English towns a temporary setback; for many were burned, and others were partly torn down to make room for castles. The Norman, however, gave more than he took, in this as in most ways.

Law and order meant that traders could move about in greater security. The coming of the Jews, the easier contacts with Normandy and Aquitaine, and the Crusades all shared in stimulating trade and industry with the demand for new articles. By 1300 the hundred English towns had grown to two hundred, and nearly every one had gained in activity, wealth, and importance.

London, with forty thousand inhabitants, less than half as many as Paris, was then and for centuries afterward, the only community of any size in England. The average town had probably about five thousand. The townsmen devoted most of their time to handicrafts or trade. The first stage was apprenticeship. A boy was bound for seven years, more or less, to a master who taught him his trade and fed and clothed him; in return the apprentice worked without pay. Then he became a journeyman, working for the master for wages. If successful, he might become a master himself, with a shop of his own, working alongside his apprentices and journeymen, and selling the goods which he had helped to make. In the master was thus combined both capital and labor, industry and trade.

In England, as on the Continent, the townsmen organized themselves into guilds, which secured official charters. Some of these might be simply social, but the two most important types were the merchant guild and the craft guild. The former, which developed first, was a sort of local chamber of commerce, composed of the leading masters in the various crafts. Its chief function was to protect the interests of its members, giving the townsmen a monopoly of the business at the expense of outsiders. The merchant guilds also acted together in securing special privileges for the town, and often virtually took over the town government. The craft guild was more like a modern labor union, except that it was composed of all men concerned, both employers and employees—masters, journeymen, and apprentices. Each craft, such

as the carpenters, masons, weavers, tanners, shoemakers, goldsmiths, coppersmiths, and blacksmiths, would have its own guild in each town, including all local workers. Each guild had regulations designed to ensure the size and quality of the products. Gradually the craft guilds became so rigid in excluding newcomers that the system broke down. In their day, however, the merchant guilds did real service in securing special privileges for the towns, while the craft guilds maintained a high quality of workmanship.

For the exchanging of local goods each town usually held a market at least once a week. The countrymen would bring in their produce and would purchase what they needed from the masters' shops. For the more elaborate articles coming from a distance there would be fairs, held once or twice a year at certain places. Most celebrated was the Stourbridge Fair near Cambridge, which attracted traders from many lands.

At the outset the political status of the towns was quite indefinite. Some were in little better condition than villages of manorial serfs and were dominated by officials of the king or by some noble or churchman. Gradually, however, the townsmen bargained—usually in the beginning with the king—for special privileges which gave them much greater freedom. There were various things which they desired: the right to pay a lump sum to the king instead of various petty tolls and rents; exemption from tolls throughout the king's lands; the right to a town court, instead of the regular hundred or shire court, for everything outside royal court jurisdiction; the right to elect local officials in place of having a royal official; and, finally, the right to a merchant guild. The borough, if it paid enough, would secure a charter granting one or more of these rights. London had all of them from a charter given in the reign of Henry I and confirmed in Magna Carta; it could deal directly with the king like a powerful vassal. Towns had better luck in securing charters from the king than from barons or churchmen. Borough charters were granted in large numbers by Hubert Walter, the justiciar, to raise money for Richard's costly ventures, and John followed this example in his zeal for more money.

In the towns carnivals, pageants, and religious plays were common, as well as brawls and riots. Large sums were spent on the beautification of the churches as well as in alms to the poor. All in all, the towns gave England, as they did the Continent, the busy, creative work of the artisan which did so much to make the Middle Ages memorable. Today, their picturesque remains give an idea not only of crowded quarters and unsanitary conditions, but of the charm of crooked streets, overhanging houses, busy market places, profusely decorated guildhalls, and imposing churches. The towns, moreover, with their newly acquired wealth, would be given their share in the national government during the reigns of Henry III and his son.

Monks and Friars

The thirteenth century saw the Church at the height of its power, for Innocent III had built it solidly from within while enhancing its external political prestige. The papal hold on England was particularly strong under Henry III. Where previous kings had resisted church encroachments, Henry was thoroughly subservient to the Pope, who took full financial advantage of this fact. In return England profited greatly in education, architecture, and other fields where church influence was paramount. To the approximately five hundred monasteries in England by 1200, one hundred and fifty-seven new ones were added during this reign. In the seven centuries since Saint Benedict, however, the monastic system had lost much of its early vigorous simplicity. The early monasteries had served as frontier outposts in carrying Christianity to the barbarians and had fulfilled many valuable social and cultural functions (see page 16). The intellectual, the peaceful, and the weak, as well as the pious, had found valuable refuge in them. The very piety of the monks, however, led to their decline. In England, as on the Continent, dying reprobates were prone to leave much of their wealth to monasteries in order to help win forgiveness for their sins. The monks no longer had to work in the fields, for as the owners of manors they had serfs. Therefore many Benedictine monks, well provided for in this world's goods, tended to become lazy and sometimes degenerate. Foremost among the reform movements started in European monasteries was that at Cluny in the middle of the tenth century, and the one at Clairvaux in the twelfth (see page 50, 64). The latter establishment was the home of the extremely strict Cistercian order, many of whose members came to England during the reign of Stephen. But prospective donors, feeling that the prayers of the stricter monks might be more effective, left their lands to them, so that they too were tempted to become soft, lax and worldly. The Cistercians, the least corruptible of the orders, set an extraordinarily able example in estate management and effectively developed sheep-raising for the wool trade.

Although few monastic establishments came into being in England after the thirteenth century, an energetic new type of "regular" clergy appeared (see page 16). Unlike the monks, who spent their lives shut up in a community, the so-called mendicant or begging orders, or friars, went out among the people, to share in their poverty and distress, to set an example of Christian living, and to teach pure doctrine. Part of Innocent III's work was his sanctioning of Franciscan and Dominican friars. He recognized the need for reform in the wealth and worldliness of many of the upper clergy and the lazy ignorance of many of the lower. He finally sanctioned the proposals of Saint Francis, who had been a rich, pleasure-loving youth in the Italian town of Assisi before he determined to try to reproduce the simple life and the helpful services of Christ. A few years later the Pope gave his approval also to the Dominicans, named after their founder, the Spanish scholar Saint Dominic. Alike in being wandering mendicants, the two orders differed in their aims and activities. The Franciscan "Gray Friars" (later robed in brown) were like social workers in their close contact with the people and in their efforts to supplement the work of negligent parish priests. The more intellectual Dominicans, the "preaching friars," with their white gowns and black hoods, devoted themselves to combating heresy, especially in southern France. These Dominican "Black Friars" never attained the popularity of the Franciscans; for they became the chief agents of the hated Inquisition, and men punned on their name to dub them "the Hounds of God."

In England, where the Dominicans arrived in 1220 and the Franciscans four years later, there was little heresy to combat, and even little feeling against the papacy until Henry III's actions finally aroused it. Yet as the last of the foreign influences to reach England directly, the work of the friars reached wide proportions. The Franciscans, the "jolly friars," in particular made a tremendous impression upon the lives of the poor. They brought tales of the outside world to isolated places. They preached and administered the sacraments in simple language and made themselves always readily accessible to the downtrodden and forlorn. In the towns they were a godsend to the crowded people, especially in the healing of the sick. Unlike the monks, with their isolated communal life and landed wealth, they did not pose as examples to the people but went into their hovels to aid them personally. At this time both orders sided with the people against the king when political troubles arose; but by the time of the religious reformer, Wycliffe, a century later, they were no longer popular.

Oxford and Cambridge

The two mendicant orders were also intimately associated with the early history of the two great English universities. The rise of Oxford and Cambridge was part of the general appearance of higher education throughout Europe. Schools, which had largely disappeared during the barbarian invasions, had been somewhat in evidence at the time of Charlemagne and Alfred, but were chiefly used for training the local priesthood. Not until the eleventh or twelfth century did real universities start. They were composed virtually entirely of men and brains, and lacked almost completely campuses, as well as libraries and other buildings. A medieval university at the beginning was simply an informal group of students, who gathered around some teacher with a reputation as a lecturer. Most of the student body might migrate en masse to some other center at any time, and occasionally it did so. The universities were under the protection of the Church, and the teachers at first were clerics. Even modern students enjoy a certain amount of "benefit of clergy" in disciplinary matters when a dean assumes police-court functions. Some early universities were guilds of students, as at Bologna (noted for its law), where the students managed everything and paid the teachers. Others were guilds of teachers, as at Paris (noted for its theology), which served as a model for the English universities. The students, whose ages ranged from the teens to middle age, normally listened to lectures and took notes, for books were too scarce and too expensive. Degrees at first were simply licenses to teach. A full-fledged university, or *studium generale,* had four faculties: theology, civil or canon law, medicine, and the lesser faculty of arts. The term "philosophy" then, and for centuries later, included much that is called science today, and was strongly influenced by the work of Aristotle.

Various legends of the early founding of Oxford and Cambridge have grown out of the rival claims of the two places for priority. Oxford seems to have been the center of some scholarly activity about 1170, when the quarrel between Henry II and Becket led many English students to leave the University of Paris and to settle there on the Thames. Cambridge seems to have received its first big impetus in the thirteenth century when a sanguinary town-and-gown riot at Oxford caused large numbers to migrate to the sister institution in the eastern fen country. In 1248 Henry III gave Oxford a charter which afforded the students more privileges than the townsmen and gave the university chancellor legal jurisdiction in addition to that of the mayor. The college system within the universities developed because of inadequate living conditions. Three of Oxford's colleges, University, Balliol, and Merton, came into being late in the reign of Henry III. Many of the students came from the lower middle class and went into the Church, which offered the most promising path to advancement.

Among the thinkers of Henry's long reign was Robert Grosseteste, a pioneer in England's literary and scientific development. From a humble Suffolk home, he studied law, medicine, and natural science at Oxford, where he became chancellor. He was the first rector of the school established there by the Franciscans in 1224, and he built up such a reputation that he has been called the foremost mathematician and physicist of his age. He finally became Bishop of Lincoln, and we shall hear more of him as a bold, outspoken opponent of the designs of Pope and king to subordinate the English clergy. He was the close friend and patron of another graduate of Oxford. This was the Franciscan friar Roger Bacon, who went from Oxford to Paris and who gained such a high reputation as a scientist that

Except for its graceful 14th-century spire, Salisbury Cathedral was built from 1220 to 1266.

he was suspected of black arts. Twice he was forbidden by the church authorities to spread his radical views and once was even imprisoned, but a more liberal Pope personally asked him to write his celebrated *Opus Majus* about 1267. Like Francis Bacon later, Roger was distinctive as a pioneer in the study of scientific method. He found out a good deal by actual experimentation in regard to chemistry—or alchemy, as it was called then—which included the science of weights and the listing of "metals, gems, stones, colors, salts, oils, bitumen, etc." The study of optics also fascinated Bacon, and he became familiar with the use of the convex lens, "both for the magnification of objects [the simple microscope] and as a burning glass." He apparently knew something about gunpowder, and a great deal about geography. Other Englishmen, chiefly Franciscan and Dominican friars, shared these speculations with Bacon, but none of them were revolutionary in their ideas when it came to philosophy and theology.

Literature

Outside the work of such scholars, little literature of lasting consequence appeared in England during the three "almost dumb" centuries following the Conquest. Such writing as there was consisted chiefly of chronicles and romances. The Anglo-Saxon Chronicle dwindled away to a disgruntled finish, in very bad English, within a century after Hastings, but various monks, writing almost always in Latin, took up history. The chronicler generally went back to Creation for a running start and boldly adapted previous works until he came down to his own time. William of Malmesbury, who wrote in the reign of Henry I, has been called the first real English historian since Bede. By the reign of Henry III a remarkable center of chronicling was the abbey of St. Albans, on the Great North Road, where the monks, in entertaining travelers, made the most of their opportunity to find out what was going on. Its leaders were Roger of Wendover, whose *Flowers of History* carries the story to 1236, and Matthew Paris, who continued it to 1259.

The literature of the period reflected the new chivalry (from the French word for horseman or knight) which was rapidly becoming the code of the aristocratic military class. Its precepts and practices were drilled into the young men first as pages, then as squires, and finally as knights. An early and very masculine form of chivalry in vogue at the time of the Conquest, with loyalty and valor its ideals, found favorite expression in the *Song of Roland,* which was sung at Hastings and makes only one casual reference to a woman. By the thirteenth century a strong feminine influence was pervading chivalric thought and deeds. The softening effect may have come partly from the Church, which, in an endeavor to modify the harsh brutality of war, pro-

claimed the Peace of God, enjoining fighters to spare women and other noncombatants. But far more potent was the pagan influence of the gay regions of southern France. Both Eleanor of Aquitaine and Henry III's wife came from there, and their presence at the English court undoubtedly attracted French minstrels (troubadours, jongleurs, and the like), who were specialists in the new doctrines of romance. Love was uppermost in the new chivalry: every knight must be in "spiritual vassalage" to some fair lady; every lady must have a cavalier lover. One's own husband or wife had little to do with the system. Chivalry led knights to joust for the favor of proud ladies and to seek opportunities to rescue damsels in distress. The songs of chivalry created a world of unreality. The former rough fighting men took on more polished manners under the influence of "courtesy." In the main, the ladies were of their own aristocratic class; chivalry did not extend to townsmen or villeins. The new feminine influence even extended to ecclesiastical fields; for churches were now being dedicated to "Our Lady," in the hope that the Virgin Mary would intercede against harsh divine justice at the Judgment Day.

That new atmosphere of chivalry was particularly receptive to the legends of the mythical King Arthur (see page 8), about whom an amazing collection of tales began to flourish in this period. Arthur figured prominently not only in the very readable but thoroughly unreliable collection of Celtic legends written in Latin, in the name and form of history, by Geoffrey of Monmouth, a Welsh bishop, but also in a long poem, *Brut,* written about 1200 by one Layamon, a parish priest of the west country and based on the old legend that the Britons were descended from one Brutus of Troy, a descendant of Aeneas. These tales, together with romances and stories of various sorts, transmitted by minstrels from one land to another, found eager listeners in thirteenth-century England.

Besides the chronicles and the tales of chivalry, dealing in Latin or French with the affairs of the upper classes, a few scattered fragments of verse in Middle English indicate a love of nature on the part of the middle or lower ranks of society. Perhaps the earliest example of English lyric verse is the "Cuckoo Song" (about 1240), which has three verses, beginning "Summer is icumen in. . . ." By the time of Chaucer, a century and a half later, the different languages and the different interests were merging to form a real English literature.

Architecture

The artistic and creative element in medieval England found its chief outlet in magnificent cathedrals and other church buildings. The architects so combined technical skill with their art that their creations still last to inspire a more worldly age. Styles in church architecture gradually changed with the centuries, but the building usually took the form of a cross, the top of which was represented by the choir or the apse, which contained the altar and generally pointed toward the east. The two transepts, at right angles, formed the crossbar, while the lengthy nave, stretching westward, was the main portion. Frequently two towers flanked the western entrance; sometimes a great central tower rose at the junction of nave and transepts.

The earlier churches, until late in the reign of Henry II, were of the type known as Romanesque, modeled originally upon the old Roman basilica or law court. This type had round arches, massive pillars, thick walls, and small windows. The Anglo-Saxons had built many churches in what is generally called the crudest type of Romanesque in Europe. The Norman bishops and abbots replaced every Saxon cathedral and large church building with a new structure in sturdy Norman Romanesque. Only in the smaller parishes were the Saxon churches spared. The noblest survival of

Norman building energy is found in the yellow-stone cathedral, with its adjacent castle, on the river bank at Durham, "half house of God, half castle 'gainst the Scot," as befitted the dual role of the earl-bishop, guardian of the northern border.

A more graceful type of architecture, known as Gothic, began to appear in northern France about 1150. It was characterized by pointed instead of round arches and by a great increase of window space at the expense of the hitherto massive walls. The most exquisite expression of this new architecture was reached in such French cathedrals as Amiens, Reims, and Chartres; but the influence quickly spread to England, which developed a distinctive Gothic of her own, rather more dignified and restrained than the exuberant French. Gothic passed through three stages in England: the Early English type, with its lancet windows, from about 1180 to 1280; the more elaborate Decorated Gothic, with broader windows, from about 1280 to 1380; and finally, from about 1380 to 1530, the Perpendicular, with flatter-pointed arches and the familiar square towers.

The pointed arches of the Gothic style reached England late in the reign of Henry II. Canterbury Cathedral was partly destroyed by fire just after Becket's murder, and one William of Sens was brought over from France to direct the rebuilding. After he fell from a scaffold, William the Englishman carried on the work, which was the first important example of Early English Gothic. The beautiful cathedral at Lincoln began to take form in Richard's reign, and by the time of Henry III the graceful new style was well established. That long reign was a very active period of building new churches and abbeys, as well as rebuilding the simpler Norman ones. Stonemasons were not the only artisans needed for this work. The enlarged windows were resplendent with colored glass; paintings and mosaics in brilliant hues filled the interiors; and sculptured figures were set in niches

Canterbury Cathedral dates principally from around 1180, but there was earlier and later construction. At right, 13th-century stone masons and carpenters.

both inside and out. This artistic development was quite to the king's taste. He undertook at his own expense the rebuilding, in Early English Gothic, of England's most famous church, Westminster Abbey, originally built by the Confessor. Salisbury Cathedral, regarded as one of the most beautiful, came into being between 1220 and 1266. Such rapidity was unique, for most of the cathedrals were not products of any one reign or even any one century. Bishops were constantly being tempted to pull down a transept, nave, or choir and to rebuild in the latest style; and if the body of the church was satisfactory, they could at least add new towers. The "minster," or cathedral, at York, built over the foundations of a seventh-century Saxon church, underwent at least one major operation in rebuilding or addition every fifty years between 1070 and 1472.

Architectural activity, of course, was not

limited to churches. During most of the Anglo-Saxon period there was nothing worthy of the name of castle. The characteristic early Norman castle was a wooden tower on an artificial mound of earth, probably surrounded by a ditch and a wooden stockade. The Conqueror built the Tower of London and two other castles of stone, but not until about the time of Henry III did one find the gaunt, square, stone "keep" rising straight from the ground to a considerable height, with walls sometimes as thick as fifteen feet. The Crusaders brought new ideas in castle-building back from the East. The keep was surrounded by outer walls which gave much more protected space and served as first lines of defense. Towers arose at intervals along the walls, and curved lines replaced straight ones, to eliminate "dead space" where the arrows of the defenders could not reach. This new castle architecture reached a climax in

Cœur de Lion's Château Gaillard in Normandy and led to several powerful frontier castles in England. The manor houses of barons and knights were at first built with defense strongly in mind, and toward the Scottish border they long retained a resemblance to the castle keep. In the quieter portions of England more comfortable structures, utilizing wood and plaster, gradually replaced the earlier fortress-home. The main feature of all manor houses was the great hall, the center of social activity, used as a dining-room, and often, except for the master's family, as a sleeping-room. At their best the medieval homes of even the proudest barons lacked most of the modern comforts. They were too often smoky and drafty, privacy was lacking, and sanitary arrangements were primitive. A country house underwent even more constant and radical transformations through the centuries than did a cathedral, so that pure medieval examples are very rare today. The poor lived in mean, thatch-roofed hovels or in the crowded, overhanging houses of the towns.

Henry III and Outside Influences

Henry III resembled in his piety, his inept weakness, and his un-English sentiments, the flabby Edward the Confessor. He was physically brave, extremely devout, devoted to his beautiful, clever wife, and a cultivated liberal patron of art as well as religion. On the other hand, he was recklessly extravagant with his subjects' money, and was often ready to sacrifice English interests to Popes or to Frenchmen. He was ungrateful to deserving supporters, his "heart of wax" being easily moved by the flattery of intriguing adventurers. He had that combination of obstinacy and indecisiveness which leads to irritability when crossed. Like his father, he was false, shifty, and undependable. Lacking both vision and executive ability, he was nothing of a statesman. Dante, the Italian poet, consigned him to the purgatory of children and simpletons.

His reign very quickly resolved itself into a bitter contest between the English and non-English interests. The latter were represented by four separate waves of foreigners who came over to enjoy high influence and fat offices. During most of the earlier part of the reign these outsiders were in the ascendancy. Prominent after William Marshall's death was Peter des Roches, an unscrupulous adventurer from Poitou, a part of Aquitaine, to whom John had given a rich bishopric. He brought the first wave of alien parasites; a nephew enjoyed an income as sheriff in sixteen shires and then became treasurer. Next came more Frenchmen, in the train of Henry's charming bride, daughter of the Count of Provence. Her four uncles all found remunerative posts, one as Archbishop of Canterbury, and so did many of her other poor relations. Henry's four half brothers comprised the third lot. His mother, widowed young, had married her original betrothed, from whom John had taken her. Henry's spoils system provided well for their children.

The fourth swarm of invaders came from Rome to make the most of John's grant of England as a papal fief. The papacy was ready to "milk dry" any land where the ruler did not object. Early in the reign two papal legates took part in governing the country. Heavy financial demands upon the English Church were made, and paid, even up to a fifth of its income. Then the Pope began to fill English church offices with foreigners, chiefly Italians. By the "provisor" system he claimed the right to "provide," or promise to appoint, a man to a church position as soon as it should become vacant. One Pope even demanded that three hundred English positions be reserved for members of Roman families. Many of these alien appointees never bothered to visit England, but drew a goodly income while allowing the actual work to be done by underpaid deputies.

Under these foreign influences, the king

was drawn into a foolish, costly, and impractical foreign policy. The papacy persuaded him to chase an alluring but futile will-o'-the-wisp in placing his son Edmund on the throne of the Two Sicilies (Naples and Sicily), a matter in which England had no possible interest. The English treasury therefore paid heavily for the empty and short-lived honor. Henry's brother, Richard of Cornwall, received an equally hollow title with his election as successor to the Holy Roman Emperor. In the meantime the French were closing in on Aquitaine. For a while Henry lost it almost completely. With difficulty and at great expense he finally recovered a part, hereafter known usually as Guienne.

During all this time the "England for the English" party fought the foreign influences with varying success. The first strong champion was Hubert de Burgh, victor of the sea fight off Dover and one of the first little group which governed England for the boy king. For eight years, as justiciar, he stoutly contested Peter des Roches's power, but was finally dismissed in shameful disgrace. The son of William Marshall led a revolt which was crushed. The Poitevins were finally ejected, only to be replaced shortly by the new queen's relatives. Three times Henry was forced to reissue Magna Carta, for he was ever ready to evade the most solemn oaths. Bishop Grosseteste of Lincoln (see page 95), the leader of some prelates who stood out against the alliance of Pope and king, believed in the normal authority of papacy, but felt that it could command obedience only when its orders were in keeping with the teachings of Christ and his apostles. While rigidly reforming morals and discipline in his own diocese, he fought successfully against the Pope's exorbitant financial demands. Grosseteste pointed out that the foreign churchmen, appointed under the "provisor" system, were annually carrying out of the country an amount at least equal to the regular revenue of the king; and he flatly refused to find a place

in his diocese for a nephew of the Pontiff. Rome started to punish him, but hesitated because of his influence, scholarly renown, and popularity. Meanwhile, the king's foreign ventures were increasing in cost and bringing nothing in return. By 1254 his debts equalled several years of normal income.

All this finally resulted in several efforts to set up machinery for the limitation of the royal power and led to the beginnings of Parliament on a broad national basis. There was constant constitutional experimenting from the middle of the thirteenth to the end of the fourteenth century. Chance events, determined by the outcome of a battle or of the political exigencies of the moment, have taken on unusual significance in later days because they marked the obscure beginnings of Parliament, which became the most successful constitutional body in all history.

Baronial Unrest and Montfort's Parliament

The storm first broke early in 1258. Henry summoned to London what was already being called a "parliament," though it still consisted of only the officials, nobles, and churchmen of the old Great Council. "Parliament," which comes from the French for "talk" or "discuss," has been defined as "any meeting of the King's Council that has been solemnly summoned for general business"; and for a half century more there was little uniformity in the elements of its membership. A chronicler dubbed this the "Mad Parliament," a fitting name if one uses "mad" in the sense of "angry." Henry needed more money than usual and proposed an extraordinary levy. The clergy discreetly withdrew, but the barons defied the king. When, after adjournment, Parliament met again at Oxford that summer, the barons came fully armed. They forced upon Henry the "Provisions of Oxford," which transferred the royal powers to a number of baronial groups. Business was to be conducted in the name of the king through a council named by one baronial committee and constantly checked by another. Several reforms, particularly the expulsion of the foreign favorites, were contemplated. This has been called the high-water mark of the baronial efforts to rule, but it did not last three years. The barons, though united in opposition to the king, were torn by selfish dissensions when they came to administer the royal power themselves. The Pope annulled the Provisions. The king and barons laid their claims before the French king, Louis IX (Saint Louis), for arbitration, and he also decided in favor of Henry in the so-called "Mise of Amiens" early in 1264.

That led at once to civil war and brought to the foreground a remarkable baron, Simon de Montfort. Strange to say, this new leader of the "England for the English" party was a native Frenchman who had once been one of the most unpopular of the foreign favorites. His father, of the same name, had with cruel thoroughness harried the heretics of southern France for Innocent III. The younger Simon had come to England to secure the lands and high position which went with his title of Earl of Leicester, inherited through his mother. He married the sister of Henry III and served as governor of Aquitaine. Eventually the two brothers-in-law fell out. Simon was harsh, domineering, and impetuous, but he threw his heart, his energy, his common sense, and his real military ability into the fight for political reform. There was some brisk campaigning around the southeast coast, and finally the rival armies met in May, 1264, at Lewes. Prince Edward, the future Edward I, drove deep into Montfort's center with a sweeping cavalry charge, but Montfort overcame the rest of the royalists, and took many prisoners, including the king himself. That battle made Montfort master of England for fifteen months.

This brief period is memorable because, for the first time, representatives of the towns were summoned to sit in Parliament. On at least one occasion, in 1254, each shire had been directed to send to a parliament a number of knights. Montfort added the final element of the present-day Parliamentary membership when he called for two representatives from each of certain cities and boroughs. It is highly improbable that Simon had any democratic motives for this action, but he did not want to neglect any possible element of strength. Montfort's Parliament was a partisan one, drawn from his own supporters. For this reason, and also because it was not summoned by the king, it did not establish a precedent for future Parliaments. Nevertheless, Montfort's example had much to do with the summoning of a similar "model" Parliament by Edward I thirty years later. Beyond setting that all-important example, Montfort accomplished little that was constructive during his brief period of power.

The royal forces quickly counterattacked with success. Having escaped from confinement, Prince Edward, with a greatly superior force, trapped Simon at Evesham, in a bend of the river Avon toward the Welsh border in August, 1265. The one-sided fight was quickly over, and Montfort's body was hacked to pieces. To the people he became a martyr.

As in the case of Magna Carta, the ultimate influence of the baronial opposition was greater than its immediate result. Neither the people nor the crown forgot that kings had been forcibly called to account for their misrule. The wiser monarchs profited by the lesson. Some of the more foolish suffered deposition and even death because they failed to take into account the teachings of Runnymede, Oxford, and Lewes. The barons had shown themselves unable to set up a satisfactory government of their own. They were torn by too many selfish motives, and their rule did not rest upon a sufficiently broad basis. They had served, however, as indispensable shock troops in the struggle for English liberty; for at that time they were the ones best equipped to offer successful resistance to absolutism.

Fortunately for England, before Henry died, within seven years, the control of royal policy had passed to the able grasp of his son, named for Edward the Confessor. Montfort's work did not die with him, for Edward was sufficiently intelligent and magnanimous to profit by his rival's example. Some of the best features of the baronial reforms were incorporated into law two years after Simon's death, and Edward showed an open mind in his continued experimenting with the idea of representative government.

England's four strongest medieval kings each left a lasting contribution to the nation's constitutional development. The Conqueror brought over the political feudal system; Henry I built up a centralized administration; Henry II organized the legal system; and Edward I (1272-1307) contributed further legal reforms and added much to the development of Parliament.

Edward I (numbering started with the Conquest) was the first king since the Conquest to be regarded as primarily English; his predecessors had been essentially French. Six feet three in height, with a magnificent physique and a strong, attractive personality, "Longshanks" was every inch a king. Always clear-headed, he drove his tremendous energy along lines best calculated to bring results and overcame those traces of the Angevin impulsiveness which had marred some earlier Plantagenet careers. An enthusiastic sportsman and a first-rate fighting man, he was also a statesman, with a realization of the needs of the present and future. Like his father, he led a spotless private life; he was religious, but without subservience to Rome. He believed strongly in royal power and would never yield until compelled. The tradition of baronial resistance had been built up in the two preceding reigns, however, and Ed-

ward had to give in occasionally. Had such a man followed directly upon Henry II, royal absolutism might well have become firmly entrenched.

Edward was absent on the futile last major Crusade when the news of his father's death reached him. Everything was so quiet in England that he spent two years in a leisurely return, stopping to do homage for his fiefs in France, where the king received him with noticeable coolness. For the first twenty years of his reign he was remarkably successful. Wales was conquered, and he made reforms of lasting value in law and government. Then foreign complications arose on every side, and the barons grew restless. "Longshanks" suffered several setbacks, but he left Parliament as a lasting heritage of the utmost importance.

Edward I's Statutes

Edward has been called the "English Justinian" for his legal reforms. He was scarcely back in England before he began to make effective use of a very important new device, the statute. This was a kind of legislation issued by the government and intended to be permanent, which had received the assent of both the king and of what was soon to become Parliament. For temporary and minor matters the king and his small council might often issue ordinances, but for matters of fundamental importance it became customary after Edward's time to secure the assent of Parliament to a legislative act. Edward's six great statutes, from "Westminster the First" in 1275 to "Westminster the Third" in 1290, may not all have received the concurrence of the shire knights and the burgesses in that experimental period, but they have come down through the centuries with all the authority of full-fledged acts of Parliament. Only a few in the reign of Henry III antedate them in the long record of "statutes of the realm." Statutes became the law of the land, overriding all previous customs, decrees, or decisions which might conflict with them. The legislation of Edward I, which covered a wide range of matters, was of lasting importance in improving the legal, administrative, and financial work of the government.

Henry II had set up the machinery of royal courts which had led to the development of the common law. Edward perfected that machinery, but his more important contributions consisted in defining by statute certain major features of the law itself. In the century since Henry II gave them their start, the royal justices had by their decisions been molding the law and even making new law. The statutes took precedence over this judge-made law. To a certain extent Edward's legislation was a codification of the law as it had thus developed, but in some cases he introduced new features which were an advance upon the existing law. The royal courts, often to their displeasure, had to recognize the superior authority of these statutes. Edward did his work so thoroughly that, in the words of Maitland, a leading student of English law, "For ages after Edward's time, king and Parliament left private law and civil procedure, criminal law and criminal procedure, pretty much to themselves."

His legislation left its most permanent traces in the field of land law. His statutes De Donis and Quia Emptores, known, like papal bulls, by their opening words, dominated the conditions of landholding in England for centuries. They reflected the decline of the old political feudal relationship, already weakened by the introduction of scutage a century earlier. The vassal's duties of fealty, homage, military service, court attendance, and the like were being discarded as the fighting men became country gentlemen, and the economic, landholding side of feudalism alone remained important. The relationship of "lord and vassal" was shifting to that of "landlord and tenant." The king and chief barons, as the principal landlords, were interested in retaining all they could of the feudal features which were still profitable—the relief, wardship, and escheat which might come at the death of the vassal-tenant. The new legislation, therefore, was aimed against any transfer of property which would diminish those profits. The statute De Donis established the practice of entail. Land would be granted to a tenant and to the "heirs of his body." Such land could not be disposed of as the tenant or the succession of eldest sons saw fit; they had only a life use of it; and if the line of direct heirs ran out, the land reverted by escheat to the lord. This tended until fairly recent times to keep family estates intact and to concentrate the ownership of land in the hands of a relatively small group. The statute Quia Emptores was directed against the former practice of subinfeudation by which a vassal could grant part of his land to a subvassal who would owe to him the profitable relief, escheat, or wardship. Such a subvassal now became the direct vassal or tenant of the granter's overlord. This eventually increased the number of tenants who held directly from the king.

Edward also aimed the Statute of Mortmain (1279) against transfers of property to the Church without his consent. The "dead hand" of the Church never relinquished any property which it once received; and as the Church was a perpetual organization, which never died, the overlord lost all hope of future reliefs, wardships, or escheats. The judges and lawyers of the royal courts, who were never enthusiastic about these statutes anyway, quickly developed legal fictions whereby entails could be broken and the Church could receive the benefits of new grants.

In perfecting the legal and administrative machinery established by Henry II, Edward ordered the barons to show by what authority (Quo warranto) they were still exercising jurisdiction in their courts. This roused strong opposition, for few could show charters, and one stoutly stated that his sword was his authority. Edward did not press the matter too far, but his action led to the gradual decline of baronial jurisdiction except for villeins' cases in the manor courts. Chancery, as a regular court, had not yet come into being, but the separate existence of the courts of King's Bench, Common Pleas, and Exchequer was recognized. These had all sprung from that small body of officials known as the Curia Regis or King's Council, which grew up under Henry I (see pages 56 ff.). This council still retained an important place in giving advice to the king and in settling important or tangled questions which did not fall into the regular business of the law courts or government departments. A new administrative branch known as the "wardrobe" was growing more influential. More directly under the king's eye than the Exchequer or the chancellor's office, it took on an increasing amount of financial and other governmental business. A well-trained corps of civil servants was growing up to handle these various branches of official activity.

By military reform, another feature of Edward's legislation, he systematized and improved upon the Assize of Arms by which Henry II, a century before, had laid the broad foundations of a national militia (see page 76). As in the earlier legislation, Edward stipulated that the lesser freemen maintain the modest equipment for infantry service, while all men with an annual income of at least £20 from land were required to accept knighthood, which involved the more costly paraphernalia of the cavalry.

Finally, innovations in the national finances were instituted because the cost of government was steadily increasing while the king's normal income remained fairly stationary. Henry II had managed with an annual average revenue estimated at £25,000. Under John this rose to £40,000. The average for the long reign of Edward I was £67,000, and in three different years it exceeded £100,000. With Edward III (1327-1377) the average was to rise to about £140,000. The earlier kings had been able to meet most of their expenses from their relation to the manorial and feudal systems. They received roughly £10,000 from the manors and towns of their royal demesne, and about an equal amount from feudal incidents such as reliefs, wardships, escheats, and vacant bishoprics, together with court fees and fines (see page 67). They might at times increase the amount by levying an arbitrary "tallage," or tax, upon the towns or a scutage upon the vassals, but the "hereditary revenues" of the crown remained fairly constant at about £20,000. To meet the steady increase in their expenses, the balance had to be found elsewhere.

The year 1275 is a landmark in the history of English revenue, because customs duties then appeared on a permanent, recognized basis. Edward was granted, as a part of his regular revenue, specified export duties on wool and leather. This was welcome, as the burden fell principally upon foreigners. By the end of the reign, the king was receiving as much from the customs as from the hereditary revenues, and before long two or three times as much. Import duties of two shillings on each tun, or cask, of foreign wine, and a penny on each pound's worth of merchandise, were also imposed. Hence these duties came to be known as "tunnage and poundage." Royal efforts to stimulate foreign commerce soon followed (see page 163).

The king meanwhile cut off one old source of royal revenue in 1290, when he banished all Jews from England. The earlier kings had allowed them to make fortunes at lending money and then had fleeced them regularly (see page 58). Edward's edict, which met with popular approval, kept the Jews banished until about 1650. Their place as moneylenders was taken by Italian bankers, chiefly from Florence (see page 131).

The combination of hereditary revenues and customs duties was generally enough for normal times of peace; but such occasions were scarce under Edward I, with his costly campaigning in Wales, Scotland, and France. The government finances were still regarded as the king's personal affair, and the people felt that he should "live of his own" from those two regular sources. If he needed more in an emergency, he was no longer to get it by levying arbitrary tallages and scutages but by means of a special direct tax on movables, with the consent of the taxpayers. The chief precedent for such a direct tax lay not so much in the Danegeld as in the Saladin Tithe which Henry II had levied in 1188 upon all who were not going on the Crusade. They were to pay one tenth of the value of their movable goods, which meant generally the surplus produce of a manor or the townsman's stock of wares. This Saladin Tithe opened royal eyes to a rich source of income, and the tax on movables became the basis for later subsidies. There were a few of these under John and Henry III, but the practice became prominent under Edward I, who was granted nine subsidies totaling more than £450,000. Each of the three main taxpaying groups—feudal landowners, churchmen, and townsmen (the villeins were not involved directly)—determined the rate at which it would pay. The normal grant by the laymen was "a tenth and fifteenth," that is, a levy of 10 per cent on the townsmen and of nearly 7 per cent on the landowners. The normal yield of such a grant was about £40,000. The clergy voted a separate "free gift," sometimes a tenth, sometimes a fifteenth. This voting of money became highly important, not only as a financial measure but also as the main cause of the growth of Parliament (see page 100).

The Model Parliament, 1295

During a period of constant experimenting, between 1250 and 1400, England's national assembly was developing from a Great Council, limited to great barons and churchmen, into a Parliament, where those

A London river scene around 1480, showing shipping, the Tower of London and its Traitors' Gate, and, in the background, London Bridge.

"Lords Spiritual and Temporal" shared power with a new House of Commons, representing the middle classes of town and country. The first half of the period saw the "commons" gradually admitted to the assembly; the second half saw them organize and gain in influence. The year 1295 is commonly taken as the standard date for the beginning of Parliament. In that year Edward I summoned the so-called "Model Parliament" which contained commons as well as lords. To legal-minded Englishmen, Montfort's Parliament of 1265 was not a valid body, because it had not been summoned by the king. There is a danger, of course, of attributing too much to the Model Parliament; for though it has been called "more thoroughly representative than any England had yet seen," it by no means had all the functions and features of the modern Parliament, which is clearly divided into a House of Lords and a House

A representation of the Model Parliament in 1295, showing Edward I, flanked by Alexander of Scotland, Llewellyn of Wales and the archbishops, with lords, and others, in foreground.

of Commons, and which devotes its energy principally to the making of new laws. One of the reasons why Parliament ultimately became so highly successful is that, instead of suddenly being organized in a definite form, it "just grew." Because of constant adjustments and compromises, it became particularly well adapted to the needs of the nation.

The most influential members of the Model Parliament were naturally the barons, bishops, and abbots, who had been summoned for centuries to consult with the king and to give assent to his proposed measures. The witan of Anglo-Saxon times had been such a body, and so, too, was its feudalized successor, the Great Council of the Norman kings (see pages 28, 49). In the Norman theory these men were the king's chief vassals, whose feudal duties included attendance at their lord's court. This group ultimately developed into the House of Lords, whose members still receive individual summons, not as representatives of any region or group but because of their rank.

The novelty in the Parliament of 1295, as well as in that of 1265, lay in the development of representation. The writs summoning the Model Parliament contained the phrase, which probably did not mean anything definite to the men of those days, "What concerns all should be approved by all" ("all," of course, excluded four men out of five as unfree villeins). In small communities it has often been possible for every free man to have a direct voice in the local government. The Greek city-state and the later New England town meeting provide examples of such direct government. It was obviously out of the question, however, to gather all the free men of a whole nation into one place for deliberation. The thirteenth century offered a solution by having the various scattered districts and communities select representatives, empowered to speak and act for them in the central assembly. Some claim that Parliamentary representation was simply an extension of the practice of the shire courts, where each hundred, town, and village was instructed to send representatives to sit with the nobility, gentry, and clergy of the county. Others see a closer precedent in the national gathering of the Dominican friars, to which each local group sent its representatives. Whatever the inspiration may have been, the effect of representation has been all-important in the government of England and of many other lands.

The representatives of the "commons" fell into two categories which have remained distinct for centuries—the county members and the borough members. Each of the forty counties, or shires, was directed to send two "knights," while one hundred and fourteen chartered cities, or boroughs, each sent two "burgesses," in addition to London's representatives. Normally only about eighty boroughs sent members during the Middle Ages.

The knights of the shire were more important than the townsmen, not only on account of their social position but also because they represented larger political units. Knights had been summoned to Parliament at least as early as 1254, eleven years before Montfort sent invitations to the townsmen. The knights represented the lower grades of the landholding feudal class. In theory they were fighting men, but actually they were leaving fighting more and more to the professionals and were settling down into peaceful country gentry, or "squires." Such men, belonging to the feudal aristocracy, might have been expected to have more in common with the great barons than with the upstart townsmen. Over on the Continent, men of similar position were rated as part of the nobility, a distinct caste whose "blood" separated them from the commoners by a wide gulf. England never developed such sharp barriers of caste, and one of the sources of her strength was the middle position occupied by this substantial group.

The inclusion of the borough members, a practice which had been employed on more than one occasion during the thirty years since Montfort's Parliament, was a recognition of the rapidly increasing importance of the towns. The townsmen were a comparatively new element in medieval society (see page 91). Their making and selling of goods, while not yet considered fully respectable, was generally recognized as profitable. The more prosperous townsmen could often lay their hands on more ready cash than could the proud barons. The townsmen, however, for a long time did not consider Parliamentary representation a privilege or an honor. To them it was generally a burdensome duty, much as jury service is still regarded. The borough had to pay its representatives for expenses while they were on Parliamentary duty, and at least one borough sought and gained permission to be exempted from the burden of representation. The townsmen probably realized that when their members reached Parliament they would be silenced by a general inferiority complex in the presence of the great men of the land and would probably simply be bullied or cajoled into agreeing to further taxes.

The nobles, the bishops, and the commoners from county and borough still continue as members of Parliament, but the representatives of the lower clergy in the "model" body of 1295 withdrew from later sessions. The Church preferred to vote its money to the king through its own body, known as Convocation. The bishops, because of their positions as extensive landholders, continued to sit in Parliament as well as in Convocation, and so did the important abbots until the monasteries were abolished around 1540; but the lower clergy before long sat in Convocation only.

While the members from shire and borough in theory represented the whole country, the huge body of villeins and other lesser workers had no say whatever in the choice of members. Not until the latter part of the nineteenth century was voting for members of Parliament placed on a uniform, democratic basis.

The next problem was the organization of the members after they assembled. The Estates-General, summoned as a French national assembly seven years after the Model Parliament, remained clearly divided into three separate estates: the clergy, the nobles, and the "third estate," principally townsmen. The result was that the third estate, overshadowed by the two privileged orders, had no effective voice in the government. The Model Parliament probably divided in a similar manner, as each estate voted its own rate of taxation; but before long the English followed a different course from that of the French. The clergy's withdrawal had left the landowners and the townsmen. Far-reaching effects came then from the "knights of the shire," the equivalent of the lower French nobles, joining with the townsmen. Had they joined the great barons instead, the borough representatives alone might have sunk from view, as they did in France. The knights, however, seem to have felt that they could get along better with the townsmen than with the lords. Their decision was a gradual one, and it was almost half a century before one finds a distinct House of Commons, representing both county and town. The union of the knights with the burgesses gave the Commons a broad enough basis and a substantial enough membership to hold its own against the House of Lords. Around 1600 the Commons were to overshadow the Lords and by 1700 were more important than the king as well.

That "model" gathering in 1295 foreshadowed the basis of Parliament's membership; the "Confirmation of the Charters," two years later, pointed the way by which Parliament was to rise to power. Edward was in immediate need of large amounts for campaigns against both France and Scotland (see page 115). He had managed to antagonize all three of the classes which mattered: the barons were muttering at overseas orders and forest laws; the churchmen were ordered by the Pope not to submit to taxation; and the merchants were exasperated at the king's high-handed seizure of all the wool they were exporting. The result was that Edward, already over in Flanders to start his fighting, reluctantly agreed to the so-called "Confirmation of the Charters," in which he repeated the terms of Magna Carta and other royal concessions and also made an agreement that the crown would abstain from further "maletotes," or irregular exactions (such as the seizure of the wool), "without the common consent of the realm." The significance of this lay in the fact that it gave, by implication, the power of the purse to the new Parliament of Lords and Commons.

By the end of the thirteenth century, therefore, the foundations of Parliamentary development had been laid, both in personnel and in financial control. Parliament's organization, functions, and power were still vague and indefinite; but throughout the fourteenth century it gradually took form, acquired influence, and built up sufficient prestige to become an integral part of the English government.

Beyond the Borders

Edward I won three popular titles: "Long-shanks" for his height, "the English Justin-ian" for his constitutional reforms, and "the Hammer of the Scots" for his aggressive northern policy. Also like the Roman em-peror Justinian, he expanded his territory. French strength made unlikely the recovery of the Plantagenet lands in France, lost through John's carelessness, but conditions in the distant reaches of the British Isles opened the way for Edward's intervention.

Had it not been for the inaccessible, rough, and mountainous country of western and northern Britain, each of England's in-vaders might well have overrun the entire island and absorbed the Celtic strain cen-turies before. Those remote wildernesses likewise blocked national unity for the island. In Wales and also in Scotland still lived the primitive Celts, with their dis-tinctive language, habits of living, and crude tribal or clan organization.

In Wales they lived in flimsy huts of boughs as they followed their flocks and herds from valley to mountainside with the seasons. The old racial stock had escaped contact with the Saxons of England; but certain adventurous Norman lords, encour-aged by their king, carved out estates for themselves, in Wales. As a whole, they made their way up the river valleys of southern Wales; but, even in the lowlands, forest and marsh were barriers against their progress. These "marcher lords"—so called because, in feudal parlance, remote, dan-gerous border fiefs were generally known as "marches"—built themselves castles and remained in power until the sixteenth cen-tury when this part of Wales was brought under close royal control. Though their in-dependence and their private armies were sometimes troublesome to the crown, they were tremendously useful buffers between southwestern England and wild Welsh raiders.

Most of the expansion of these marcher lords occurred between the reigns of Wil-liam I and Edward I. Part of the inhabi-tants of a region generally fled, at the ap-proach of the barons, to higher places where they might keep their old ways un-molested; but others stayed to live around the new castle under the lord's control. Time, however, was on the invaders' side, with their constant reserves of people and supplies. The marcher lords introduced agriculture, permanent dwellings, and some trade to their communities. The people came to represent a mixture of Norman, Saxon, and Welsh blood. For all this, peace did not come with the marcher lords. Even the Welsh of their communities clung to their own language (which even today can produce the word "Llanfairpwllgwyngy-llgogerychwyrndrobwllllantisiliogogogoch") and to other distinctive features, such as special music, sung in parts and rarely in unison. They were inclined to help their brethren in the remote hills in frequent raids upon the marcher lordships. "In the hills, tribe fought against tribe, and in the valleys, baron fought baron, while every baronial valley was at war with its tribal hills."[1]

Such were the conditions on the eve of Edward's Welsh conquest, with South Wales, to this extent, in the hands of Norman marcher lords, but with North Wales utterly primitive. From time to time before this, English kings—Rufus, for instance, and Henry I—had on occasion sent help to the Norman lords in their struggles with the Welsh. During the disorder under Stephen the Welsh regained some territory, and Henry II accepted homage from some of the native Welsh chieftains. It was in his day that the marcher lords from Wales, under Strongbow, undertook the initial conquest of Ireland (see page 78). Independent Wales reached its peak during the long reign (1194-1240) of Llewellyn, "the Great," a prince of North Wales who came close to uniting the whole wild western peninsula under his rule. Patronizing the bards liberally, he aroused Welsh patriotism through a revival of poetry and of pride in tradition. He meddled steadily in the turbulent politics of England, siding sometimes with king and sometimes with baronial factions, while the borders suffered from a constant series of raids and reprisals. He married an illegitimate daughter of John, but later broke with him on the eve of Magna Carta (see page 86).

The grandson of Llewellyn the Great, Llewellyn "ap Griffith," the last native prince of Wales, likewise fished in the troubled waters of English politics. He sided with Simon de Montfort, whose

[1] G. M. Trevelyan, *History of England* (1926), p. 208. By permission of Longmans, Green & Co.

daughter he later married; but in 1267 the aging Henry III made a generous peace with him. In exchange for rendering homage to the English king, the last Llewellyn was to receive homage from virtually all Wales, even from most of the marcher lords. This success apparently turned his head. Whatever his motives, he rashly refused to render homage to young Edward I or to attend his coronation, stopped paying the indemnity he had promised, and kept on ravaging the borderlands. Thus Edward had ample provocation and legal feudal sanction for his attack on Wales in 1277. Before coming to the throne he had been on the western border as Earl of Chester and knew the situation well. While Llewellyn was ignoring his threats, Edward was being told by his Italian bankers that an export duty on wool would give him the money needed for a campaign (see page 104).

The Conquest of Wales

The expeditions of Edward into Wales were the usual story of such fighting by trained troops against primitive ones. In his well-planned invasion, he had a broad road torn through the forest to avoid ambushes, and he sent his supplies by sea, in ships of the Cinque Ports, to simplify his line of communications. Llewellyn's men retired to their mountain stronghold on the slopes of Snowdon; Edward's capture of the granary of Wales, the island of Anglesey, threatened them with starvation. By the terms of his submission, Llewellyn's holdings were whittled down to a small region around Snowdon; and he was required to render homage and to agree that at his death the title of prince would revert to the English crown.

Celtic impatience hastened the complete conquest of Wales, restive under the rough methods by which Edward's officials tried to introduce English law. Llewellyn's brother, David, who had sided with Edward in the first war, suddenly captured in

Harlech, one of the four strong castles built by Edward I to keep North Wales in order. The Welsh song, "March of the Men of Harlech," is said to date from the Wars of the Roses, when Harlech was the last Lancastrian stronghold.

1282 the castle of the English justiciar of North Wales, who was badly wounded and kidnapped. Edward invaded Wales more ruthlessly than before. Llewellyn unwisely sallied from his inaccessible stronghold and was killed in a skirmish. David was captured and hanged, drawn, and quartered. Thereupon, the defeated country was at Edward's disposal.

He strengthened his hold by building powerful modern castles with series of outer walls, practically impregnable to the crude siege machinery of the day. At one of these, Carnarvon, his son, later Edward II, was to be born. According to doubtful legend, Edward introduced the newborn baby to the Welsh as the prince he had promised them, who would be a native of Wales and could speak no English. The eldest sons of England's rulers have since borne the title "Prince of Wales."

In 1284, by the Statute of Rhuddlan—sometimes simply called the Statute of Wales—Wales was definitely declared to be under the English crown and was divided into shires. English courts and law were established. A merchant class was encouraged to build up towns and trade, as well as to furnish a prosperous group of taxpayers to help with revenue problems. The towns became English, but the old Celtic speech and habits lingered on in the wilder regions.

Although the settlement at Rhuddlan ended Welsh independence, the final complete union with England did not come for two and a half centuries. The marcher earls were left relatively undisturbed in their old powers, and their feudal fights, combined with the tribal troubles in the hills, made Wales a land of chronic disorder, pillage, and sudden death. Around 1400, Owen Glendower, a Welsh gentleman of magnetic personality and dauntless courage, aroused the spirit of nationalism in a brief spectacular and successful attempt to recreate Llewellyn's united Wales. But, although he took advantage of England's difficulties in the old Welsh way by allying himself with the rebellious vassals of Henry IV, it was all to no avail (see page 141). Eventually Welsh turbulence was controlled by Henry VIII, who decided to show the lawless land what government really meant. Some well-timed executions, combined with an act of Parliament, did the work. The Act of Union (see page 188) in 1536, a forerunner of similar acts for Scotland in 1707 and for Ireland in 1801, swept away the marcher lordships and other special Welsh features. Wales was incorporated definitely into the English government, with twelve regular shires and twenty-four representatives in Parliament.

Edward I and Scotland

In summarizing England's relations with the "Celtic fringe," it might be said that Wales was completely conquered; Ireland, partly conquered; and Scotland, never conquered. It is hardly accurate, however, to class Scotland, which was next to receive Edward's attention, as a Celtic nation. In blood and background, to be sure, insofar as any definite statement can be made about the Celts, the majority of Scots belonged to that race (see page 8). But the Scottish government and dominant society took their form, speech, and spirit not from the examples of Ireland and Wales, with their loose tribal organizations, but from Saxon and Norman England. A relatively small part of Scotland, the southeast, was eventually to give tone to the whole land. This had early been overrun by Anglo-Saxons, and with the Conquest, more of them left England for these Lowlands (see page 9). After them came various Norman barons, who established a regular feudal system. The Scottish kings looked to England not only for wives but also for forms of government. Three in particular—Malcolm, a contemporary of the Con-

queror; David, who ruled in the time of Stephen; and William the Lion, his successor—borrowed freely from the south, copying English shires, boroughs, and laws. They endowed churches on the English model while their barons were building castles of the English type. From that wealthy and dominant southeast corner, moreover, spread a modified English speech throughout the Lowlands. In the northern half of the kingdom, beyond the "Highland line," primitive Celtic tribal customs continued to hold full sway until after the final revolt of 1745; but the Scotland with which Edward and his successors had to deal was a feudal kingdom, built on English lines and able to present a fairly united front.

In 1290, the high point of Edward's reign, there seemed to be every chance of his achieving mastery of Scotland by the easy means of a marriage contract. Scotland's king, falling over the edge of a cliff on horseback one dark night, had left as heir only a three-year-old granddaughter, the child of his deceased daughter and the king of Norway. Scotland ran the risk of absorption by Norway or England. Edward, after lengthy negotiation with the Scots and the king of Norway, achieved the engagement of the infant queen to his son, the slightly younger Prince of Wales, in 1290. Edward, by treaties, promised that, in the event of this dual rule of Scotland and England, Scottish laws and customs would be respected. Unfortunately, this peaceful union was not realized, for the "Maid of Norway" died on the rough wintry voyage from her father's country. A divided nation and a disputed succession were her troublesome legacy. Of some thirteen claimants for her crown, the choice narrowed down to John Balliol, grandson of William the Lion's eldest niece, and Robert Bruce, son of her next younger sister.

Edward saw a way to capitalize on this situation. Before the Conquest there appeared to have been some acknowledgement by Scottish rulers of subservience to the English crown (see page 32), and at times, thereafter, homage had been demanded. Except in the case of Henry II, who had received homage for all Scotland, this probably was simply for certain fiefs held across the border in England, just as the English kings did homage for their French lands. Nevertheless, Edward now declared that, as overlord of Scotland, he would take over the government until the rightful king was selected. The Scottish barons, on the brink of civil war, were in no position to resist this ultimatum, but this foreign highhandedness was deeply resented among the people. Balliol and Bruce both hastened to gain Edward's favor by taking the oath of homage to him. Edward referred the claims to a commission chosen by himself and the two rivals; Balliol was eventually announced as king. This choice, based on primogeniture, apparently satisfied the majority of Scots; and had Edward kept his hands off, England might have long retained this nominal suzerainty with little outspoken objection from the Scots.

But Edward treated Scotland as if it were merely his feudal fief, with Balliol his vassal. In particular, he insisted that appeals could be made from the Scottish courts to his jurisdiction. Begun during the interregnum, this unpopular practice was deeply resented by the Scots. Balliol found himself treated as a subordinate in other matters, as when Edward demanded that Scotland furnish troops for English wars. At last, in 1295, goaded by the popular temper and by his barons this weak-willed king made an alliance with France. He followed this with a raid across the border, refused Edward's summons to explain these actions, and thus renounced homage.

Edward now acted quickly and openly as the conqueror of Scotland. The border town of Berwick was captured, and then, in the battle of Dunbar, the Scots were so overwhelmingly defeated that most of their leaders gave themselves up. Edinburgh next surrendered, and so did Balliol—both his crown and himself. Edward took over the government, and appointed English officials to rule in his absence. In five months of 1296 Scotland had been completely vanquished—for the time being.

Trouble with France and the Papacy

Balliol's alliance with France was the beginning of nearly three centuries of close Scottish-French friendship and alliance, a combination that was often to trouble their frequent mutual enemy, England. Philip IV, "the Fair" (1285-1314), was one of the strongest kings of medieval France. Like Philip II, "Augustus," who took over so much of the Plantagenet empire (see page 84), his determined eye was upon the fief of Aquitaine, still in English hands. Philip, firmly building up his royal power in France on the sure basis of ample royal revenues, took the same attitude toward his vassal Edward as that king had with Balliol; but Edward balked at stricter overlordship in Aquitaine. The seagoing French subjects of the two monarchs, Philip's Normans and Edward's Gascons from Aquitaine, had been fighting each other for some time, and Philip summoned his vassal Edward to answer for the Gascon depredations. Upon Edward's ignoring the order, Philip declared Aquitaine forfeit to himself. Edward's answer to this was to construct an anti-French alliance and to declare war in 1294. Philip's alliance with Scotland, however, gave England more immediate concern at home, and not until Balliol's collapse, in 1296, was Edward free to turn to the French troubles again.

By that time Edward, like John, was pitted not only against a strong French king but also against a powerful Pope. The newly elected Boniface VIII (1294-1303) began at once to resist the efforts of both Edward and Philip to make their clergy help pay the costs of war. This was not Edward's first trouble with the Church. Opposed earlier by Archbishop Peckham, he

SCOTLAND

0   50   100
-Scale of Miles

ORKNEY ISLANDS

Pentland Firth

The Minch

North Sea

HEBRIDES

Inverness ● ●Culloden 1746
Loch Ness
R. Spey
R. Dee
●Aberdeen

Sea of the Hebrides

✕Glencoe 1692

R. Tay
HIGHLAND LINE
●Scone ●Dundee
●Perth

L. Lomond
Stirling ✕1297
Bannock-burn ✕ 1314
Edinburgh
Dunbar ✕ 1650

Falkirk ✕1298, 1746
Pinkie 1745
Preston-pans 1745
Halidon Hill 1333
Glasgow ●
R. Clyde
R. Tweed
Flodden Field 1513

Solway Moss 1542 ✕

IRELAND

ENGLAND

Irish Sea

had silenced that prelate effectively in 1279 by the Statute of Mortmain, which limited the transfer of property to the Church (see page 103). In 1294 Edward demanded a heavy income tax from the clergy, who had no leader, since the Canterbury see was vacant after Peckham's death. Philip was making similar demands. In 1296 Boniface issued a bull, *Clericis Laicos,* which forbade any lay authority to demand money from the clergy without special permission from Rome. Philip replied with a decree forbidding all precious metals to leave the country, thus shutting off the Pope from any revenue from the French clergy. Edward took up the fight with his new Archbishop of Canterbury, Winchelsea, who flatly refused to make any church grant to the king. Thereupon Edward declared the clergy outlaws, beyond the protection of the laws, and seized the archbishop's lands so that he had to live on charity. Both sides finally compromised. Boniface, in a later bull, permitted the clergy to use their consciences in the matter, and the king was able to secure "free gifts" which were often not as voluntary as the name implied.

In the meantime many of Edward's barons had been resenting the steady increase of royal power. Some of them openly defied him when he gathered them at Salisbury to discuss the French campaign. The marshal of England refused to go to Gascony, claiming that his office entitled him to accompany the king to Flanders. "By God, sir earl, thou shalt either go or hang," cried Edward. "By the same oath, sir king, I will neither go nor hang." The merchants were in a similar mood, for Edward had seized all their wool at the ports. Archbishop Winchelsea fused the combined discontent of clergy, barons, and merchants into a common resistance to Edward's desperate efforts to raise money and troops for his French wars and the revived trouble in Scotland. At Ghent, Edward reluctantly agreed, late in 1297, to the "Confirmation of the Charters" (see page 108). The chronic baronial opposition, coupled with the financial demands of foreign wars, thus pushed further along England's remarkable constitutional development.

Pope Boniface was soon removed from his powerful position by Philip. Though forced to compromise on financial matters, Boniface in 1302 made an extreme claim of papal power in the bull *Unam Sanctam*, declaring that all were heretics who denied the supremacy of the papacy in temporal matters. The war of words was ended by force. An adviser of Philip led a troop of Frenchmen into Italy, where they handled the aged Pope so roughly that he soon died. Shortly thereafter the papacy came

for nearly seventy years (1309-1377) under direct French influence. During that so-called "Babylonian Captivity" the Popes were Frenchmen living at Avignon, surrounded by French lands and under French influence.

Edward and Philip never came to a conclusive show of strength in their war begun in 1294. Both were busy with their respective quarrels with the papacy, and both found themselves defeated by nearer and weaker neighbors, Edward in Scotland and Philip by the burghers of Flanders. They finally patched up a peace of sorts, with Aquitaine restored to Edward. Had these energetic rulers, with their strong governments, been free to fight each other unhampered, the Hundred Years' War between England and France would probably have been under way forty years earlier. As it was, the way was paved for it.

Scottish Rising under Wallace

In Scotland, there suddenly arose a guerrilla leader from the class of lairds or lesser gentry. Tall, strong, and magnetic, William Wallace quickly stirred his fellow Scots to an intense pitch of democratic nationalism, virtually unheard-of in feudal times, except perhaps among the Swiss mountaineers. Feudal lords, as the English crown had learned in Normandy and Aquitaine, tended to be either internationally-minded or class-minded or both, and often put special interests before national ones. So it was with the Scots; some nobles looked down on Wallace as an upstart commoner; others, with holdings on both sides of the border, were as apt to be for as against Edward. Those aroused to hot anti-English patriotism were mostly lairds and the more solid peasantry. They developed a fighting formation to repel the armored man on horseback: infantry pikemen would form a solid line of bristling spears, against which the advancing cavalry was likely to be impaled.

In 1297, just a year afterwards, Edward's conquest of Scotland was undone in the spectacular defeat of English forces by Wallace at Stirling Bridge at the gateway of the Highlands; his Scots made belts from the tanned skin of an unpopular official slain there. Hurrying back from France, Edward himself with a formidable force and a new infantry device ended Wallace's ascendancy at Falkirk. Again the hedgehog lines of pikemen stopped the English horsemen in their tracks, but the arrows from Edward's longbow archers cut wide gaps in the pikemen. With the next cavalry charge, the surviving Scots fled in wild disorder. This use of the longbow, learned from the Welsh, would later have equally devastating effect upon the French. For six years, Edward made piecemeal gains in Scotland and held them with scattered castle garrisons. Then, as he was about to transplant English forms of government as in Wales, the spirit of Scottish nationalism flared anew under Robert Bruce, grandson of the original claimant to the throne in 1290. Wallace just before that had been tried for treason at London, and hanged, disemboweled, and quartered. The gory remains were sent to four northern towns, and his head was stuck up on London Bridge. Escaping death at Falkirk, he had been betrayed into English hands in 1305. His fame was to inspire his countrymen, as Bruce carried on his work to a more successful conclusion. The latter's temper flung him into sudden prominence, when he stabbed a rival Balliol claimant for the throne before a church altar in 1306. His followers completed the murder; and the clever Bruce realized that his only chance now lay with those opposing Edward, although his record showed much past pro-English dealing. Outlawed, he fled into hiding but not before hastening to have himself crowned at Scone, the ancient seat of Scottish kings. The Scots, finding themselves with a new leader and one whose family position and royal blood gave him a wider basis for support than Wallace, broke out in sporadic revolts. So ill that he

had to travel by litter, Edward started north in 1307, only to die before reaching the border.

Edward II and Bannockburn

One of England's ablest kings, he left much unfinished work, an empty treasury, restless barons, various scattered enterprises —and a most incapable heir. Edward II (1307-1327) had his father's good looks and tall athlete's body; in all else, Edward of Carnarvon, first English Prince of Wales, was an almost pitiful contrast. At times, he whipped his flaccid will to spurts of energy, but he was incurably lazy and incompetent. Primarily the playboy and sportsman, he nevertheless slid away from any risk of personal danger. He was clever with his hands but did not bother his brain with anything serious. His companions were the frivolous, the dissipated, or the lower-born, perhaps because of the scorn of his father's friends. He seemed intent on opposing much that his father had done and all whom he had liked. Only in his marriage, apparently, was he to keep his father's plans; but the twelve-year-old Isabella, daughter of Philip IV of France, just half his age, was to be the instrument of his undoing. Although faithless and unscrupulous, she would have made the better ruler. The marriage incidentally was to give England a claim to the French throne.

The Scottish policy of the first Edward may have been a mistake, but the weak apathy of his son prevented any chance of its success. The campaign to vanquish Bruce frittered away to nothing under the son's careless and lukewarm attitude. Not even Longshanks's legendary last command that his bones, boiled clean of flesh, should accompany the troops into Scotland, could furnish a talisman for victory. Young Edward quickly found an excuse for returning home.

Bruce, thus left pretty much unmolested for some six years, built himself up from a hunted man with a mixed following to leader of most Scottish factions. He raided the border almost with impunity, and one by one Edinburgh and other strongholds fell to him. When he besieged Stirling, almost the last castle in English hands, Edward and his disaffected barons were stirred into a brief co-operation against the common peril of the Bruce. This belated activity in 1314 led to one of the most crushing English defeats. At the Bannockburn, a stream just outside Stirling, the English outnumbered the Scots three to one, but, badly directed, became jammed together in a bog. The archers could not discharge their arrows; the reserves could not get into action; and when, finally, some Scotch camp followers feigned a flank attack, the English fled in panic.

Bannockburn won Scotland her freedom for three centuries. An independent and troublesome neighbor, she was often allied with France. Time and again, Scottish raiders, carrying only a little oatmeal for their meager rations, swept over the English border to plunder and ravish; time and again English armies struck back. The English had the geographical advantage, being within easy reach of Edinburgh and the most prosperous part of Scotland, while the Scots invaded only the barren and sparsely settled northern counties. But the Scots were still a free nation when their own Stuart king, James VI, inherited the throne of England in 1603; they remained a separate kingdom even after that for a century and, still independent, joined England voluntarily in 1707 to form the kingdom of Great Britain (see pages 221, 286).

Baronial Unrest

At home Edward II was not wholly to blame for the baronial unrest. In fact, it has been said that his father's legacy to him had been not only heavy debts but "policies which could neither be abandoned nor continued with safety." After a strong king like him and with memories still green of the halcyon days under weak Henry III, the baronage were set for trouble. It is significant that Parliament and the machinery of government continued to function throughout the disorders not only of this reign but of the whole disturbed period of the fourteenth century and the first half of the fifteenth century. Actually Parliament was strengthened, since both king and barons called upon it from time to time to support their respective positions, and thus the commons were brought into their councils. Under a continuous series of strong rulers, an absolute royal autocracy, like the French, would probably have resulted. This would have killed, in their feeble youth, the seeds of middle-class supremacy and democracy that were to make England's government distinctive. In fact, she probably "needed her weak kings to keep her growth well-rounded and to give her special constitutional institutions a chance to develop."

Edward opened the way for his baronial difficulties by putting in place of his father's experienced ministers the very men whom his father had disliked. Chief of the favorites to anger the barons by their presumptuous usurpation of the king's functions were Piers Gaveston, exiled by Edward I to get him away from his son, and the two Hugh Despensers. Instantly recalled, the exuberant Gaveston from Gascony insisted that all matters for the King must be cleared through him. Almost immediately, baronial enmity returned him to exile, softened by Edward with the governorship of Ireland. Again recalled and again exiled, he returned once more in 1312 at Edward's urging, only to be seized by his enemies and beheaded. After this the Despensers, the son and the grandson of a former justiciar, so grossly mismanaged the government for their own ends that they pushed their king yet faster toward disaster.

In the meantime, in 1310, only three years after his accession, the government was taken out of Edward's hands by the barons, as in 1258 it had been taken out of

Henry III's. They put twenty-one so-called "Lords Ordainers" in charge, most of whom were lay barons, with a few ecclesiastical leaders such as the returned exile, former Archbishop Winchelsea. They issued, the next year, the "Ordinances of London," which were much like the "Provisions of Oxford," but, by ignoring the new Commons, were not in line with the constitutional progress of the country. These ordinances provided for the punishment of favorites and forbade any appointment of officials or any declaration of war by the king without the Ordainers' consent. The Ordainers, however, who owed their existence to Edward's personal unpopularity, were to prove only a temporary constitutional innovation. Their main attack was upon the management of the royal household, a heterogeneous mixture of official and semiofficial functionaries, whereby Edward was able to find plenty of loopholes to get his way by varying the functions of the various departments.

The King's Household

This interference with the king's household was to lead the way to important developments in methods of administration. In theory, at least, the government was regarded as the king's household, and for years certain titles, such as "Steward," "Chamberlain," and "Marshal," had carried with them certain governmental functions. Naturally the men who handled the every-day running of the details of government, together with the collecting and disbursing of money, were in a position of influence, whatever their titles might be. Gradually some of the offices, starting with royal domestic duties, turned into regular public administrative posts. The chancellor, for instance, developed a legal court of equity and was the keeper of the great seal which was attached to official business. The Exchequer was taking over much of the financial business (see page 57). In keeping with the household idea, much was trans-

acted by the "chamber" under the chamberlain. The men who held these offices were conspicuously in the public eye, and their actions, naturally, were closely watched. The result was that this reign saw the marked acceleration of a movement, already begun several reigns before, to start new administrative offices which would not be so much in evidence and which would be more closely under royal control. Thus the "wardrobe," originally simply the little room outside the royal chamber, took over many governmental functions, including war finance, and its keeper began to use a little seal in place of the chancellor's great seal. The barons, attacking the royal administration, in 1312 set up a separate keeper of the Privy Seal. That too became a public and powerful office, so that before long a "secret seal," or signet, was devised for business which the king or his advisers did not want to submit to the chancellor or Privy Seal. Eventually this keeper of the secret seal also became one of the most important administrative officials. There was no orderly defining of what particular sort of business belonged to each office. With this purposely left vague, and with each office carrying with it plenty of potential power, Edward II and other kings could simply "dig underneath" if one part of the royal household were attacked, and could accomplish the same ends through another. A fairly permanent corps of trained under-officials eventually came into existence, so that even when baronial squabblings led to new men in the high offices, the routine business of government continued to function smoothly. It was from such irregular and indefinite beginnings that most of the chief administrative departments of modern government have come.

The barons, with their Lords Ordainers, managed no better than Edward's favorites, partly because their leaders (such as the king's cousin Thomas, Earl of Lancaster) were just as self-seeking and no more able. The country was in evil plight, with high taxes, unsuppressed fighting among the baronage, Scottish raiding in the north, and generally poor government. Finally Edward's anger, which had boiled helplessly at Gaveston's execution, pushed him into action in 1322, after the Despensers had been exiled and his queen had been insulted, while traveling, by the refusal of hospitality at the castle of Leeds. With a spurt of energy worthy of his father, Edward defeated the baronial party in battle. Lancaster was executed, many others were exiled, and the Ordinances were revoked, as Edward turned to Parliament and the Commons for co-operation.

Quickly Edward relapsed into his old indolence, the Despensers returned, and once more the king's incapacity alienated everyone. Meantime, Queen Isabella had been sent to negotiate with her brother, the king of France, about Aquitaine. In France, she fell in with the disaffected baronial exiles and made herself so notorious as the mistress of one Roger Mortimer that her brother, the king, asked her to leave. Edward had been writing her for months to come home; consequently she now started, but brought the exiles with her for an invasion of England. Stopping in the Netherlands, she betrothed her son, the future Edward III, to a local count's daughter, whose dowry provided money for more troops.

Landing in England with this escort, Isabella carried all before her. With scarcely a friend left, Edward wandered a frantic, hunted man, until captured. Parliament, called in, enthusiastically declared for Edward's twelve-year-old son and forced his own resignation. He stepped aside in 1327; but the implacable Isabella, not forgetting the early humiliations of her marriage, had him imprisoned. But she still was not content; and when Edward was living on after months of abuse, murder, thinly veiled from public knowledge, occurred one night in Berkeley Castle. No regency was welcome in the Middle Ages, but this one might have been among the worst, as the queen and Mortimer spent most of the kingdom's revenues upon themselves. But in three years, Edward III (1327-1377), at fifteen years, suddenly seized Mortimer for execution and sent his mother to a distant castle.

Edward III and Friction with France

This spectacular monarch wore the crown for fifty years, but the most important developments of that significant half century of transition were not his work. He had no interest in finance or administration. Like Richard the Lion-Hearted and Henry V, he was the sort of king who lives on in storybooks; but constitutional changes came about only as by-products of his flashy war policy, and he concerned himself little with the welfare of his subjects. Handsome, charming, chivalrous, generous, albeit vain, tricky, and immoral, he reveled in the pomp and glamor of the dying days of feudalism and was in close accord with baronial ideas. Dragging England, without adequate reason, into a century of struggle with France, he himself participated in some of the amazing but sterile victories. He was a first-rate tactician on the battlefield, but a blundering strategist who had no clear conception of where he was going or why.

Edward first turned his martial instincts against the Scots, who were in turmoil with increased French intrigues, border raiding, and the Bruce dead. Edward whipped them at Halidon Hill, near the border, and helped establish on the throne another pro-English Balliol, John's incapable son. Bruce's son, however, soon returned from his French refuge to gain the throne.

Edward was already otherwise engaged with the French, with whom there were now immediate causes for friction, along with the heritage of hostility. First there were the perennial bickerings over Aquitaine, the last of the Plantagenet empire still held by England's rulers as vassals of the French crown. The French monarchy, increasingly powerful, was inevitably encroaching upon those remaining English holdings, while the English kings, also growing stronger, were more reluctant to perform even ceremonial homage. The constant friction between Edward I and Philip IV (see page 115), which had never disappeared, was to help drag the two nations toward a long, exhausting conflict.

French designs on Flanders, one of the richest parts of Europe and vitally linked with England's economic life, were another important consideration. Flanders lay in the southern section of the so-called "Low Countries," in what was to become Belgium and the northeastern corner of France. This region was destined to cause national rivalries and to suffer repeated invasions (see page 278). The lack of definite natural boundaries in its flat country-side to link it clearly with France or Germany was recognized nearly five centuries earlier, when at Charlemagne's death, his empire was divided in three parts: France, Germany, and a long middle strip between them, running from the North Sea to Italy and including the "Low Countries." Yet, located at the crossroads of Europe's main trade routes, this was one of the most prosperous regions in all Europe, with its business particularly flourishing in the fourteenth century. Bruges, and later Antwerp, became the chief centers for the exchanges of wares from north, south, east, and west. They not only reaped their percentages on the goods passing through their hands, but with neighboring cities greatly increased the value of some wares by means of manufacture. Flanders was the chief consumer of raw wool, England's chief export.

Edward III's concern over Flanders was intensified because its ruler was a pro-French count. Then, its merchants and artisans, dreading French aggression, and the consequent interruption of the English trade, set up in his place a commoner of Ghent, Jacob van Artevelde, who naturally looked to England for support.

The rough mariners of the Channel were a further source of Anglo-French complications. With the expansion of commerce and shipping, their rivalry stopped at nothing. Every clumsy merchantman went heavily armed, not only for defense but also for offense. The border line between peaceful merchantman, warship, and pirate was a hazy one. Even the seaports were not immune from raids.

Finally, to crystallize all these latent sources of friction and to protract the war long after all excuse for it had ceased, came the English claim to the French crown. Philip the Fair's three sons, each reigning briefly in turn, died without heirs. Their sister Isabella, the mother of Edward III, and a cousin, the son of Philip the Fair's brother, were the next of kin. As in England in the case of Matilda and Stephen, the question of the succession lay between a female claim in the senior line and a male claim in the junior line. The French obviously did not want a foreign king, but by strict primogeniture Edward's was the better claim. To prevent this, the French courts, stretching an old rule of the Salian Franks, a tribe in northern France nearly a thousand years before, declared that a woman might not inherit a throne herself nor might her son obtain it through her claim. Thus did Philip the Fair's nephew become king by "Salic Law," which neither side would have held sacred under other circumstances. Before long, however, Edward assumed the title of "King of France," and during most of the next four centuries it was used solemnly and officially by English monarchs.

Underneath all these specific causes lay England's aggressive mood. Although considerably smaller than France in area and population, she was probably the most compact and effective state in the Europe of that day. Henry II and Edward I had built up strong machinery of centralized government, so that royal power could make itself felt throughout the counties in matters of taxation, justice, and military organization. In sharp contrast stood the loose feudal structure of France, where power and jurisdiction were still largely in the hands of the feudal nobility. And so, with a king who wanted glory, merchants who wanted secure commerce, and soldiers who wanted plunder, England was ready to utilize genealogy for an attack on her bulky, but disorganized, traditional rival.

The Longbow and Free Companies

For fighting purposes England's social system gave her an advantage over France at this time. The French still relied upon feudal armies of the type which had flourished for centuries—the horses, armor, and lances of the proud, undisciplined nobility, with their stipulated military service. Between those nobility and other ranks there was a wide, impassable gulf. In England the classes shaded off from top to bottom with less clear divisions. England too had her proud barons and her knights, but she had, besides, her less military land-holders, the future country gentlemen, and also—very important for the work at hand—the free small farmers, or yeomen. Sturdy, self-reliant, and tough, they were to stiffen the English armies with a rank and file of a quality unequaled in most lands on the Continent. In addition, by the military legislation of Henry II and Edward, the equipment and organization of all these classes had been stipulated and standardized (see pages 76, 104).

England was in a position to take full advantage of a profound revolution in military methods. For nearly a thousand years, since the decay of the Roman legion, the aristocrat on horseback with his expensive equipment had held full sway on the battlefield. Now, infantry was about to establish lasting superiority over cavalry. In Switzerland rugged mountaineers with long pikes were learning to check their feudal oppressors, while in England the longbow was forging to the fore. This longbow, the cross-

Sir Robert Knollys with the mercenaries of his private "great company," who were some of the most persistent plunderers of France in the first part of the Hundred Years' War.

bow's rival, was of the primitive standard bow design, made of yew wood, about five feet high, and shot arrows a yard long. Every village green had its archery practice, and by 1300 the sturdy yeomen were achieving remarkable speed and accuracy with this new weapon. The longbow in skillful hands could be deadly at two hundred yards and could send off approximately six aimed shots a minute, which could penetrate a horseman's armor. Edward I had learned its use from the Welsh and had employed it effectively against the Scots at Falkirk in 1298 (see page 116); but it became generally known—more suddenly than most new weapons—through its deadly work against French horsemen in the early battles of the Hundred Years' War. A third arm of military service, artillery, just coming into being, was still too crude to do much more than scare horses on the battlefield; before long its siege guns would fur-

Crécy, 1346, showing longbows in foreground.

turned to the professionals of the free companies. During the next three centuries the average free companies in Europe might be composed of men of a dozen different lands; those in English pay were largely Englishmen. All free companies fought for anyone, as long as their pay came regularly. During intervals of peace, and consequent unemployment, they would live off the country, and any luckless peasant at their approach knew that neither he himself, his crops, his home, nor his womenfolk were safe. Such bands, both English and French, were to ravage the French countryside year after year.

That war, by no means a century of continual heavy fighting, fell into two very similar periods. Each began with an English invasion of France, resulting in one or more crushing English victories, followed by a burst of French patriotism which ousted the invaders. The famous battles—Crécy (1346), Poitiers (1356), and Agincourt (1415)—all went to the English, but the final success was French.

Edward started the war with a fruitless invasion of France in 1339. In the following year he was present at the naval victory off Sluis, really an infantry fight at sea. A fleet of English merchantmen destroyed the French sea forces so that the English were able to cross the Channel and bother the French whenever the spirit moved, a role which England was to enjoy for centuries thereafter. Her south coast might be occasionally raided, but she escaped the sort of serious invasions that she was busily inflicting upon France.

Crécy and Poitiers

The battle of Crécy in 1346 was the most celebrated victory yet won by English arms, and their longbow made it also a dramatic turning point in general military history. Edward, invading France with some twenty thousand men, led them in a blundering, aimless fashion up the Seine on a ravaging expedition almost to the gates of Paris. The

ther weaken the feudal lord by destroying his castle.

Yet another military innovation, particularly stimulated by this progress of infantry, was the professional, or mercenary, soldier. Two centuries earlier, when scutage began to appear, Henry II had appreciated the advantage of hiring the fighters who would stay under arms for more than the conventional feudal forty days (see page 75). The system became general during the Hundred Years' War. Contractors—or, as the Italians called them, *condottieri*—would promise to furnish a ruler so many fighters for a certain price. These men were not necessarily of the same nationality. The contractor would then sign up the necessary number of "free companies," or units which were ready to sell their services for ready money. The first armies sent to France during this war were general levies based on the military legislation of Edward I; then, England

Sluis in 1340 was the first major English sea fight and the first major encounter of the Hundred Years' War; like most naval actions before 1588, it was, as the picture indicates, essentially an infantry fight at close quarters.

French king, in pursuit, nearly caught him in a strategical trap between the Somme and the sea. Then Edward demonstrated that battle tactics were his forte, though he was outnumbered three or four to one. At Crécy, he secured a strong defensive position on a crest, with his flanks well protected. He bade his proud horsemen dismount in order that they might give a solid defense to the archers with their longbows. Thus armed and lined up, the English awaited the French attack. As at Hastings and at Waterloo, they were standing firm on the defensive against the cavalry attacks of the French. At Hastings the Normans had the advantage of up-to-date methods; at Crécy the French were handicapped by clinging to the traditional disorganized charge of feudal cavalry. It was late afternoon when the French approached the English position; good sense called for a halt to rest their tired army, but the impatient horsemen would not wait. Rushing headlong, they rode down their own Genoese crossbowmen and in one impulsive mass hurled themselves on the English position. Then the longbow twanged. The English archers, wrote Froissart, the chronicler, "shot their arrows with such force and quickness that it seemed as if it snowed." The French armor was no protection to the riders, while the horses, maddened by pain, charged back into the oncoming mass of French men-at-arms. A few Frenchmen pushed through to the English line, but there the dismounted Englishmen, fighting side by side—king, lord, and commoner—pushed them back. So they fought until dusk, when the French retired, leaving many thousands, including "the flower of French chivalry," dead upon the field. Twice more in this war this great victory was to be repeated.

Edward's initial good fortune continued.

Two months later an invading army of Scots was routed by the home forces at Neville's Cross, and in 1347, after a long siege, Edward captured the important port of Calais. Just twenty-odd miles from Dover, it was the nearest port to England; and for two centuries, even after all else in France was lost, it was to remain in English hands as a trading post and a jumping-off place for expeditions into France.

Ten years after Crécy, England won another striking victory at Poitiers under Edward's eldest son, the "Black Prince." That much overrated paragon of chivalry led a raiding force from the south of France, with the French king in pursuit with an army ten times as large. Once more French strategy was better; the English were cut off from retreat to the sea. But once more their battle tactics triumphed. In a powerful defensive position, protected by hedge and ditch, the greatly outnumbered archers and dismounted men-at-arms cut the French army to pieces and captured the king. In 1360, the Treaty of Bretigny gave Edward complete sovereignty over all Aquitaine, as well as Calais and certain adjacent territory. France had to pay a crushing indemnity for the release of the king, whom many of his subjects considered not worth ransoming. Edward, in turn, agreed to drop his claims to the French throne.

The war, however, was soon resumed, and dragged on its desultory course for many years. There were minor battles and constant, cruel ravaging of the French countryside by the English free companies. Finally disgrace and misery aroused a successful patriotic resistance in France. The Black Prince found his match in a tough, able Breton, Bertrand du Guesclin. For a while, the fighting was shifted to Spain where the French and English supported the rival contenders for the throne of Castile.

The romantic spirit of the time has come down to us in Jean Froissart's thrilling chronicle of many deeds of valor. The acts and words of kings, earls, knights, and even squires are given at great length. To Froissart they alone counted—not the stout yeomanry, whose arrows won Crécy, nor the French peasantry, who went through hell for generations as a result of the war. Froissart is partly responsible for the inflated reputation of the Black Prince. He shows how the prince's chivalry led him to sacrifice even military advantage. To prove that England did not fear the military prowess of the captive Du Guesclin, the prince released him for a heavy ransom—thereupon, Du Guesclin quickly cleared France of the English invaders. Like Richard the Lion-Hearted's, the chivalry of the Black Prince and his fellows was reserved for the well-born; toward the common people, they showed a callous cruelty. Upon hearing of the death of Sir John Chandos, his friend and right-hand man, he assuaged his grief by storming Limoges and having two thousand men, women, and children put to the sword without mercy. There was no Froissart to write the grim story of such forgotten men and women, who suffered murder, pillage, and torture. Even at home the free companies took what they wanted. One expedition, waiting at Southampton two weeks for the arrival of transports to carry them to France, were billeted in a nunnery. There they had their will of all the inmates and carried off a few of the nuns with them when they sailed. The pious chronicler of this cruel episode relates that God finally looked out for "his lambs"; for a storm arose, and, even though the superstitious soldiers threw the nuns overboard, the whole expedition was wrecked.

Even for those who escaped physical violence, the war meant crushing taxes. The desperate French peasantry rose in a brief but savage revolt just after Poitiers; the English peasants twenty-odd years later staged a more orderly but nevertheless dangerous rebellion against their terrific taxation (see page 129). In the earlier stages of

A contemporary representation of the wholesale burial of the dead during the Black Death.

the war the English people had not murmured so loudly, for they were receiving the glorious news of Crécy or Poitiers in return for their money; but as the struggle dragged on, its futility became more apparent. By 1377, when Edward died, the French military revival had been so successful that only the ports of Calais, Bordeaux, and Bayonne remained to England. The war was to lapse for more than thirty years before a second active and successful invasion ushered in its second stage.

Yet England had achieved something intangible. The French wars, on top of the Scottish troubles, had brought forth a national spirit which for the first time broke down provincial bounds. Men began to think of themselves as Englishmen and grew proud of their country. The prowess of English arms at Crécy and Poitiers inspired a healthy respect on the Continent. Indirectly, too, the war influenced the political development of the nation: the yeomen, with a longbow in every home,

were able to look the barons more squarely in the face, and Parliament was increasing its powers because of the king's constant need for money. At the same time, less spectacular but more fundamental forces—social, economic, cultural, and religious—were also at work and by the end of the century were becoming noticeable (see page 130 ff.).

The Black Death

When Edward crossed the Channel for the Crécy campaign, in 1346, he left about four million subjects in England. Three years later scarcely two and a half million remained; the Black Death had done for the rest. This terrible epidemic, a sort of bubonic plague, which had somehow slipped in from Asia, swept over France and some other European countries also. It started on the southwest coast of England in 1348 and from there quickly spread. The unsanitary conditions in which men lived—with sewage dumped in the streets, no adequate water supply, and almost no bathing —made the people of the Middle Ages vulnerable to disease at all times and defenseless in epidemics. "People perfectly well on one day were found dead on the next," wrote one chronicler. "A few noblemen died . . . but innumerable common people and a multitude of monks and other clerks known to God alone passed away." "After the pestilence," wrote another chronicler, "many buildings both great and small in all cities, towns, and boroughs fell into ruins for want of inhabitants, and in the same way many villages and hamlets were depopulated, and there were no houses left in them, all who had lived therein being dead . . . the sheep and cattle strayed in all directions without herdsmen, and all things were left with none to care for them." In some regions, at least, the ravages of the Black Death were by no means that serious; but probably three Englishmen out of eight perished. Although the war continued without interruption, such a tremendous dislocation naturally caused great social and economic readjustment. For the next half century England was to wrestle with the problem of a "dearth of servants." Parliamentary attempts to preserve the old economic relationship were futile, even in Edward's time (see page 128).

Last Years of Edward III

Edward III lived too long for the good of his reputation. His last three years were a sad anticlimax. His grip loosened on the reins of government, for his mind and morale were weakened by a senile infatuation for one Alice Perrers. So secure was her hold on the doting old king that she would enter the law courts to bully the judges, and the Pope himself wrote to enlist her cooperation. She even abandoned her royal lover as he lay dying, after stripping the rings from his fingers.

Only one person was more powerful in these last days of Edward—his fourth son, John of Gaunt, duke of Lancaster since his marriage to the rich Lancastrian heiress. Most of the contemporary accounts pay more tribute to his cleverness than to his character. With all the cunning and methods of a modern political boss, he made himself the strongest man in England. Surrounded by a few confederates of his own sort, he built up a political machine for power and plunder. His older brother, the Black Prince, lay dying, disgusted by this state of affairs.

The situation produced political factions which were to torment England for a century, with rivalry based on lust for power rather than on principles. At the moment all the better elements joined in opposition to John of Gaunt and his clique. The so-called "Good Parliament" of 1376 went so far as to strike at the evil influences, attempting, in the first use of the new weapon of impeachment, to remove John of Gaunt's henchmen from power and to separate Alice Perrers from the king. That last stroke however, went too far for Edward's aquiescence, and he nullified most of Parliament's well-designed legislation.

Edward went to the grave in 1377, a year after the disheartened Black Prince, who missed the crown by that narrow margin. The succession went to the prince's eleven-year-old son, the second Richard (1377-1399), whom some had feared might die as had young Arthur who had stood in John's way to the throne. It was a sorry heritage. For a while, at least, the royal power would be exercised by some of the grasping group of nobles. At home there were bitter quarrels over religion, and the disgruntled peasantry were about to break forth in revolt. Abroad the invincible reputation of English arms was becoming dimmed by defeat after defeat, and the vast holdings won in the Peace of Bretigny had been whittled away to almost nothing. On the seas Frenchmen harried English shipping and were bold enough to raid the south coast. The future looked black, and was to prove so.

Turbulence and Ferment

The later Middle Ages in England have long been looked upon as a dreary and unproductive interlude between the high achievements of Edward I and the later glamor of the Tudors. A strain of melancholy and disillusionment in some writings and the tales of fruitless baronial fighting gave that impression—and other usual historical source material was meager. Later research, however, is steadily mining out from long neglected or newly unearthed sources a new conception of those years. There is a growing realization that the period from about 1350 to 1485 saw an unusually thoroughgoing transition in various phases of economic life, with consequent social changes which shook the security of part of the population, while opening up new opportunities for the rest. Those years witnessed also a serious questioning of, and growing hostility to, the authority of the Pope, the clergy, and some church doctrines; the emergence of a literature in the new English tongue; and the increasing influence of Parliament, especially the House of Commons.

The shadow of impending strife among the descendants of Edward III did not prevent the peaceful acceptance of his grandson, Richard II, son of the Black Prince, as king in 1377. That grown men of the caliber of his uncles were passed over for a child of eleven, popular though the boy's father was, shows the growth of the principle of primogeniture. The regency for Richard's minority included his mother but none of his uncles, not even John of Gaunt, the most prominent man in the kingdom in the later days of his father's reign.

Brooding discontent among many kinds of people characterized the early reign of this boy king. Economically and socially England had been unable to adjust herself to the tremendous dislocation of labor caused by the Black Death some thirty years earlier. Even before that, there had been signs of modifications of manorial restrictions, together with some rise in prices. The plague hastened matters, and so did the Peasants' Revolt of 1381. Although they have often both been credited with causing the end of serfdom, they were actually only part of several forces at work in that direction during the century. The pattern was rather confused; developments varied from decade to decade, from county to county, and even from manor to adjacent manor. But one thing was clear: eventually the manorial setup in England broke loose from the rigid post-Conquest mold (see page 46). The old inefficient methods of raising crops underwent little change; the difference came in the relationship of the men involved in the process. In the course of the changes, many of the rich became less rich, while many of the poor became prosperous.

The changes centered not upon the serfs' own strips of land, where they raised their slim subsistence crops, but upon the lord's demesne, where they had been required to work for three days or so each week without recompense, in addition to their other manorial burdens. Those demesne products, often sold by the lord for cash, were what made the manorial system profitable to him and explained why the serfs had been "tied to the soil." Early in the fourteenth century, however, a prolonged "agricultural depression" severely cut down such income. Some landlords tried to offset this by demanding more free work than ever from their serfs. Some began to "commute" the duties for cash, and then hire day laborers. Still others, no longer trying to operate the demesne, rented it for a fixed price, usually to prosperous peasants. Such lords lost interest in the personal bondage of their serfs, now that "week work" and "boon work" were no longer demanded. Those trends were already underway before the Black Death made labor so scarce. So many serfs or villeins died that crops lay ungathered and fully a third of the arable land was left totally uncultivated. The remaining workers, realizing the situation, demanded and in many cases received modifications of the old manorial terms. Many serfs, however, fled from their manors; some made for the towns, while others wandered about, seeking the highest wages they could find from the hard-pressed landlords. In the towns the free laborers, whose ranks were being rapidly swelled by these runaway arrivals from the country, were even more aware of the changing circumstances of their employment. The lower groups were becoming so crowded that the opportunities of rising to be a master workman were greatly reduced.

Parliament vainly tried to legislate against this tide of increased workers' independence. Barely had the Black Death receded when the Statute of Laborers was passed (1351). This was an effort to maintain the scale of wages and of prices as they had been on the eve of the plague. On pain of imprisonment, no one might give up his job in order to get higher wages, and all unemployed of both sexes under sixty years of age must take any job offered at the old rate of wages. No able-bodied beggar might longer be given alms. Anyone, moreover, who paid wages above the old level was liable to a heavy fine, which would go to the informer. Also, commodity prices were to be kept down where they had been before the pestilence. Shortly afterward laborers were further forbidden to leave their own communities in search for better jobs. Like many subsequent attempts, this effort to offset economic changes through legislation failed. Stronger than this Parliamentary law was the economic law of supply and demand, which was to make competition, not regulation, the decisive factor in wages and prices. Consequently, in spite of wholesale arrests and fines, wages and prices continued to go higher, in defiance of the Statute of Laborers.

In the course of the next century, serfdom gradually diminished as a result of these varied causes. There was no act of Parliament freeing the serfs, and there were still a few unfree villeins well into the sixteenth century. Large numbers of more fortunate peasants, on the other hand, had taken advantage of the opportunity to rent demesne land or otherwise advance into yeoman status. At the same time, many of the nobility and landed gentry were feeling the pinch of reduced income from their manors just when the manner of living and styles in dress were becoming more expensive. This led to the intrusion of businessmen, lawyers, and other outsiders into the ranks of the country gentry. This process would continue for centuries, partly as a matter of "status seeking." Such newcomers usually had the necessary capital for their new way of life, particularly for the conversion of estates from the now unprofitable raising of crops to that of sheep, which called for far fewer laborers. Sheep raising would lead by the late 1400's to "enclosures" of common lands, which would uproot many peasants (see page 168). It was said of the new businessman type of landlord that he inclined to be more grasping and less considerate of his peasants than the old gentry had been.

But in the fourteenth century those early manifestations of independence on the part of the hitherto humble led to much bitterness. Naturally the landowning aristocracy were shocked at this upheaval in their manorial life, while the rich townsmen were equally incensed at the new attitude of their employees. The poorer classes were losing much of their old deference for their betters, as indicated in the resentful rhyme

> When Adam delved and Eve span,
> Who was then the gentleman?

The poor distrusted the dubious role which John of Gaunt was suspected of playing. Furthermore, the renewal of the French war had gone badly, with French raids on the southern coast, much expense, and no compensating victories. The landowners and merchants in Parliament, feeling that their share of the tax load was too heavy with the usual land taxes and custom duties, levied a poll tax to spread the tax burden. This called for one shilling from every man and woman in England over fifteen years of age, except beggars. Such direct taxation was bound to be unpopular, because it was obvious to the person taxed and, being uniform, naturally bore heavily on the poor. A storm of protest broke out. At first the tax was shamelessly evaded. When collectors were sent out to investigate the delinquents, rioting began.

At once (June, 1381) the Peasants' Revolt, often called Wat Tyler's Rebellion, was in full swing. Although concentrated into this one month, it was a grave menace. At the

The death of Wat Tyler; at right is young king who then boldly dispersed the rebels.

same time, it was far more restrained than the terrible rising, after Poitiers, of the French peasantry, with its savage atrocities and reprisals. The English revolt centered in the two eastern counties below London, on the Thames. In Essex it began with the mobbing of the Chief Justice; in Kent a leader was found in one Wat Tyler, who was said to have killed a tax-collector for insulting his young daughter. A "Mad Priest," John Ball, fired the revolutionary spirit with democratic harangues. Manor rolls, with their lists of old peasant obligations, were destroyed, particularly on church estates. The men of both counties marched on London, where it was feared the discontented artisans might join them. The gates were flung open, and the rebels sent a list of their grievances to Richard, who had taken refuge in the Tower.

The young king, only fifteen, showed his mettle in personally calming down the aroused peasants. Bravely keeping his head, he came to confer with them and agreed to their demands, including the abolition of serfdom and other vexatious manorial services. Many rebels, well pleased by this lenient royal attitude, set out for their homes. Others remained in London for a night of rioting, during which the Archbishop-Chancellor and the Lord Treasurer, who to the public mind were most responsible for the hated poll tax, were murdered. Lawyers, clergy, and officials were special targets for the mob's wrath. Again the following day the king rode out from the Tower. Wat Tyler, flushed with success, was insolent and threatening; the Lord Mayor struck him down, and one of the king's squires killed him. Before the seething mass of peasants could draw their bows on the king's small retinue, the fearless Richard boldly cantered toward them, shouting that he would now be their leader. Won by his courage and by his kindness in granting pardons to all, the remaining rebels dispersed, well satisfied. For all this apparent success, the Peasants' Revolt nevertheless failed. The king's ready promises, many of which had not been within his power, remained mere words; Parliament answered the revolt by a re-enactment of the Statute of Laborers; and a number of reprisals were inflicted locally upon the peasants.

Wool and Woolen Cloth

One reason for that conversion from crops to sheepruns was the sweeping change that was taking place, at that same time, in English commerce and industry. In the century following 1350, England moved away from its passive economy and began to acquire rich extra profits by offering woolen cloth to the world instead of exporting raw wool. Around 1300 England was exporting some 35,000 bales of wool; by 1450, these had dropped to 8,000. But in the meantime, her exports of woolen cloth had risen from 4,700 pieces in 1354 to 38,000 in 1461 and would be 102,000 in the

Dyeing cloth, 1482; much English woolen cloth was dyed in Flanders.

1530's. By then, much of that would be carried in England's rapidly growing merchant marine (see pages 162 ff.), which had been very small in 1350.

It is hard to realize that the same England which in later days so aggressively pushed her own manufactures in her own ships into ports all over the world had in the earlier Middle Ages passively left most of the profits available from such activity to foreigners. A passive region, such as she was then, only produces raw materials. An active one engages in commerce and industry, buying such raw materials, converting them by manufacture into finished products, selling them again, and also bringing outside products which the passive region may want in exchange. Raw wool around 1300 accounted for some 93 per cent of England's exports; the chancellor today sits on the "woolsack" in presiding over the House of Lords, as symbolic of that early economic foundation. But such sacks of raw wool were worth only about half the value of that same wool after it had been manufactured into cloth and sold to outside regions. The major profits went not to the English woolgrowers but to the foreigners who carried away the wool, spun and wove it into cloth, and sold it again as a finished product.

Three groups of foreigners were particularly active in English trade during that passive period. In many cases, they operated in England even, not only establishing themselves at London or other seaports, but going into the inland counties to sell their imports or to pick up wool.

Most intimately involved in this down through the years were the Flemings of Flanders (see page 120), who consumed more English wool than any other region. Insisting upon it as the best available, they made much of the finest cloth in Europe at Bruges, Ypres, and Ghent. Bruges was, moreover, an entrepôt—a place where various commodities from every direction are brought together and exchanged. It was the busiest in northern Europe until supplanted late in the fifteenth century by Antwerp in nearby Brabant. Though the Flemings were not active in shipping, their merchants long made themselves at home in England.

The cities of northern Italy, particularly Venice and Florence, were also extremely influential in England's commercial relations. They not only gathered most of the trade of the Mediterranean into their own hands but also established relations with eastern Asia for spices, silks, and other exotic products. These they aggressively peddled throughout the rest of Europe. At least once a year Venice sent northward a trading fleet, the "Flanders galleys," part of the ships going to Flanders and the rest to England. This Italian trade built up a surplus of capital; and Florence became Europe's leading financial center, some of its great banking houses becoming involved in English royal loans. It was also the only city to rival Bruges, Ypres, and Ghent in the making of fine cloth, and it, too, insisted upon English wool.

A third body active in English trade was the Hanseatic League, or Hanse, a union of Hamburg, Bremen, Lubeck, Danzig, and other cities of the Baltic and inland Germany. Allied so effectively that they could bargain for privileges in outside regions, they offered wax, timber, furs, and other northern products and brought back outside wares in exchange. Their vessels, moreover, conducted an active carrying trade for passive nations which lacked adequate merchant marines of their own. The "Hansards" were not concerned with England's raw wool, but would later become a major market for her woolen cloth. They had commercial outposts at Novgorod in Russia, Bergen in Norway, Bruges, and London, where their "Steelyard" enjoyed amazing special privileges on better terms than English merchants themselves enjoyed. They were to retain those even after they crowded the English merchants out of Danzig, Bergen, and most other northern ports.

A fourth commercial area was in a somewhat different status. From Bordeaux and neighboring ports in Gascony came England's heaviest import, great quantities of wine. A part of Aquitaine, this region was, of course, long under the English crown. For a while, the Gascon merchants operated in England, but this was the first of the big trades where English shipping eventually secured the lion's share.

English merchants, who had been handling barely a third of the raw wool exports, gradually secured most of them around 1350, and more important, woolen cloth began to be made in England for export. A succession of official measures were formerly considered to have been an indication of far-seeing wisdom in steering England toward a more positive economic role. Now, they appear to have been the incidental result of efforts to finance the Hundred Years War. Edward I, when the wool trade was developing into England's first "big business," had realized that export duties on wool could become a major part of the national income; that it was in the government's interest to stimulate the trade; and that he could borrow money in exchange for trade concessions, particularly to the Italians who replaced the Jews as moneylenders (see page 104).

Efforts to pay for the costly campaigning in France were to lead to more extreme moves along those lines. Edward III turned to the Italian bankers for heavier loans than ever. When he repudiated those debts, he contributed to the failure of two large Florentine banking houses. He next obtained big loans from small groups of the wealthiest Englishmen, using a monopoly of wool exports as bait. By 1350, these men were bankrupt, while in the meantime Parliament was reflecting the anger of the wool-raisers, for the monopolists were paying them less for their wool. Four years later, Parliament agreed to give the king a substantial regular "subsidy," which was based on an increase of the wool export duties to 33 per cent or more. It also agreed to a monopoly on a wider basis, in the hands of the 300 to 400 members of the Merchants of the Staple, the semi-official pioneer of England's trading companies. To exercise full control, the exports had to pass through one or more "staple" towns; very shortly, Calais became the sole staple town. This Stapler arrangement did not include the Italian trade, but it did crowd the Flemings out of the wool export business.

By that time, the English output of woolen cloth was getting under way. The cloth industry, formerly in the hands of the town gilds, spread out into the country where labor was cheaper and far more plentiful. The Flemish weavers, brought over at the king's invitation to instruct the English, may have contributed something to this, but the major stimulus is now recognized as having come from English initiative in technique and organization.

The earlier cloth industry, centered in Norwich and other towns of eastern England, had been cramped by the inelastic practices of the craft gilds. Useful as they had been in earlier times (see page 92), they now operated under unrealistic price regulations that disregarded the law of supply and demand; and their membership was restricted lest there be too many workers to share the business. They were thus not in a position to expand production for foreign markets.

One cause of the shift to the country was the introduction of water power for "fulling" the woven cloth to clean it and shrink it. Formerly this process had been a matter of stamping with bare feet, but now water power came into general use—four centuries before it was applied to spinning and weaving. Thus the industry tended to spread to the westward where streams were more plentiful.

More credit for the new development, however, belongs to an anonymous class of "cloth merchants," "merchant clothiers," or to use the economists' phrase, "entrepreneurs." They were working out the so-called "domestic" or "putting-out" system which would dominate English textile production until almost 1800. "Already by Chaucer's day, the rural cloth industry was being organized by the capitalist clothier, who bought the wool and distributed it for carding and spinning to country cottages. . . . He collected the spun wool, and took it to the weavers, thence to the shearers, the fullers, the dyers—from craftsman to craftsman until the finished cloth was ready for him to carry on his pack horses to market."[1]

Such a system was capable of indefinite expansion. It involved a separation of functions, because the entrepreneur, who

[1] A. R. Myers, *England in the Late Middle Ages* (Pelican History of England, Penguin Books Inc., 1956), p. 56.

owned the goods, furnished the capital, and found the market, was a separate person from the master workman, who, under the old guild system, had combined in his person both capital and labor, industry and commerce. No longer was it necessary to gather all the workers under one roof. There was no question of an exclusive guild which would arbitrarily limit the number of workers. Those workers, moreover, had considerable economic freedom: they could work long or short hours as they saw fit, being masters of their own time. They could shift from one employer to another at will. Besides, they were not always dependent upon industry alone, for they could generally till little gardens, do extra work at harvest time, and perhaps keep a cow, sheep, or geese for food. The new system had the great advantage of elasticity, not only in meeting the seasonal export demands on time, but in increasing output as overseas markets continued to grow.

The broadcloths quickly overtook the raw wool exports with their handicap of heavy duties. Only three per cent was levied on the cloth, an important difference for the foreign buyer. The Flemish and Italian cloth-making gradually declined as the English output boomed.

This shift from wool to cloth tremendously widened England's foreign markets, for it could be sold anywhere, whereas the wool demand was limited to the few cloth-making cities. The aggressive quest for new outlets would do much to stimulate England's maritime growth. Around 1400, Englishmen were selling the cloth in Iceland, Norway, Prussia, Spain, Portugal, and many other places. The term "merchant adventurers" was sometimes applied to almost everyone who ventured beyond the seas, except the Staplers, but it became particularly associated with the powerful London company which eventually shipped much of the cloth to Antwerp, to be sold at its fairs for distribution throughout Europe. By mid-fifteenth century, the Hanseatic League was crowding the Englishmen out of Danzig, Bergen, and other northern ports, but was itself selling English cloth in large quantities. Around 1480, for intance, the exports of cloth averaged £134,000 a year, of which the Merchant Adventurers handled £75,000, the Hanse £28,600, and the other aliens, chiefly Italians, £29,900. The exports of raw wool came to £68,000, with the Staplers monopolizing everything except the £10,000 of the Italians. The raw wool paid export duties of £26,000, or 38 per cent, whereas the cloth paid only £4,500, or three per cent. By that time, Edward IV was giving strong royal support to commerce, and before long Henry VII would be giving still more. As part of this trade expansion, England's merchant marine was growing (see pages 162 ff.). Altogether England has come far toward an active economic role.

Religious Discontent

Discontent with the Church, especially among the rebellious poorer classes, was steadily increasing among the English during the last quarter of the fourteenth century. Since the Conquest there had been a tendency to resent papal interference in English affairs. For the nearly seventy years (1309-1377) that the Popes were Frenchmen, living at Avignon under the domination of the king of France (see page 115), they were naturally unpopular in England, which was at war with France. This led to two important antipapal acts of Parliament under Edward III. The Act of Provisors, in 1351, was directed against the filling of church offices in England by foreign nominees of the Pope (see page 99). The Act of Praemunire, two years later, penalized certain efforts to appeal to the Pope from the decision of an English royal court. In 1366 Parliament refused to continue the payment badly in arrears of the annual tribute promised by John when he made England a papal fief. Although the so-called "Babylonian Captivity" ended in 1377, when a new Pope decided to return to Rome, some of the cardinals preferred to keep the papal center at Avignon. As a result, in the so-called "Great Schism," from 1378 to 1417, there were two rival popes. The nations of Europe lined up behind either the pope at Rome or the pope at Avignon, with England naturally supporting the one at Rome. Unity, one of the great sources of papal power, was thereby badly weakened.

While thus distrusting many actions of the papacy, many Englishmen were also becoming at this time antagonistic to their own clergy, with their vast lands and increasing wealth. Economic discontent and religious dissatisfaction, indeed, were closely interwoven, and both are evident in the teachings and influence of England's great contemporary religious leader, John Wycliffe.

In the year following the Peasants' Revolt the authorities at Oxford were disciplined for permitting the followers of John Wycliffe to preach within university walls. Officially, Wycliffe was at this time only the humble rector of an insignificant parish in northern England. Yet his voice, slashing at fundamental doctrines of the Catholic Church, of which he was and remained a priest, and urging incessantly the need of a religious revival based directly on the Bible, is the clearest which comes down to us from these troubled times.

Wycliffe, a forceful writer in the vernacular as well as Latin, became the foremost critic of those ecclesiastical and economic relationships which tied England to the papacy. He advocated the disendowment of the Church, poverty as a way of life, and a ban on the export of precious metals to Rome. He is said to have given credence to the proverb passed around the papal court at Avignon that "the English are good asses, for they carry well all the loads laid upon them." An enemy of ecclesiastical luxury wherever found, he attacked the sloth and ease in the monasteries; also he felt the perpetual monastic vows were unrighteous. Futhermore, he was almost, if not quite, a heretic. He did not deny the miracle of the Mass but had queer ideas about it. Not only did he openly defy papal authority in his own country, but he refused to obey an order summoning him to Rome. Meanwhile he was perfectly safe, for he was protected by that able, unscrupulous politician John of Gaunt, who apparently used Wycliffe's brain and pen for purposes of consolidating his own power. Thus throughout his long life he was unmolested, but after his death his bones were dug up and burned by order of the Pope.

Wycliffe translated the Bible for the first time into English, and he organized and inspired a religious revival, which unfortunately came to grief as a result of the Peasants' Revolt. The supreme test of authority, according to him, lay not in the Church but in the Bible, "a charter written by God," "the marrow of all laws." Futhermore, according to him, the New Testament was the common possession of all; therein the simplest and rudest of men might find all that was necessary to salvation and it ought to be available to all. To carry out his idea, he and his friends translated into English the entire Vulgate (the Latin Bible of an early Church Father). The influence of this was limited, however, for in those days before the printing press it was expensive to copy even brief portions by hand.

Wycliffe also was the founder of an order of "poor priests" who went forth to convert and to civilize England, "clad in russet robes of undressed wool reaching to their feet, without sandals, purse or script, a long staff in their hand, dependent for food and shelter on the good will of their neighbors, their only possession a few pages of Wyclif's Bible."[2] Known as Lollards, a word of obscure origin meaning either

[2] H. B. Workman, *John Wyclif* (1926), Vol. II, p. 203. By permission of the Clarendon Press.

singers or lazy folks, they resembled the Franciscan friars in their early and more kindly days. Over the Lollards, however, there was neither bishop nor Pope. They lacked any kind of official authorization except that of Wycliffe, a village rector who, learned though he might be, had opposed the wishes of the Pope's representative in England.

Then, as this form of unconventional, simple, evangelical preaching spread through England, came the Peasants' Revolt. John Ball, the priest-agitator, was said to have confessed that he drew his inspiration from Wycliffe, but just how much connection there was between Lollardry and the revolt is not certain. Wycliffe personally, it may well be assumed, was not involved; for he was a quiet and secluded scholar most of his life. He did not denounce the peasants but spoke sympathetically of their cause; nor did he withdraw the Lollards from their work among the poor but urged them on to fresh activity. In the *Short Rule of Life,* written on the eve of the revolt, not only did he advise the peasants "to live in meekness and truly and wilfully to do their labour," but he also urged that lords "govern well their tenants, and maintain them in right and reason, and be merciful to them in their rent, and suffer not their officers to do them wrong or extortions."

Whether or not the Lollards were in any way responsible for the revolt, it gave the Church an excellent opportunity to suppress heresy. The Archbishop of Canterbury, by accusing the "poor priests" of stirring up the people, succeeded in practically ending this potentially dangerous movement. From England, it is true, it secretly spread to Bohemia, where the writings of Wycliffe made a profound impression on John Huss. Luther (see page 179) took Huss's doctrines and, with certain modifications, made them his own. In his country, however, the following of Wycliffe, whether he was a heretic or a prophet of the Protestantism that was to come a century and a half later, grew less and less until it practically ceased to be.

Middle English Literature

Like other fourteenth-century writers, Wycliffe had written his more popular works in what is known as Middle English, a half-way house between the Old English of the Anglo-Saxon period, which is unintelligible to the average man today, and Early Modern English of the late fifteenth and the sixteenth century, which is understandable to all. In the neighborhood of 1350, "John Cornwal, a maystere of gramere," is said to have "chaunged the lore (teaching) in gramere scole and construction of Freynsch into Englysch," and shortly afterward the law courts also adopted the new English vernacular for pleadings. Poets did likewise; and the changes taking place in the English language and in the undercurrents molding English life in the fourteenth century are to be found in the poetry of William Langland and of Geoffrey Chaucer.

The poem, *Piers Plowman,* was the work of Langland, of whom little is known except that he apparently "yearned up out of the farmyard mire to the cloister and the school." Medieval in form, written as a series of allegories, its spirit is modern, revealing the author's interest in the actual life of the world—courts of law, mendicant friars, disease and pestilence, and improvident marriages. There is throughout real sympathy for the harsh and cruel life of the poor. Langland must have been a vigorous fellow; for he seems to have antedated Thomas Carlyle and the gospel of work by five centuries.

> In dykinge or delvynge, or travailing
>   in prayers—
> Contemplatyf lyf or actyf lyf—
>   Crist wolde men wroughte.

Geoffrey Chaucer (c. 1340-1400), a most prolific and entertaining poet, was a wine

Chaucer, drawn at Thomas Occleve's request, with woodcuts of the knight, wife of Bath, and friar from early edition of his *Canterbury Tales*.

merchant's son upon whom fortune shone. His wife was the sister-in-law of John of Gaunt, and he himself, after long experience in the diplomatic service, became, in succession, Comptroller of the Customs and Clerk of the King's Work, a post with varied duties ranging from the custodianship of the king's palaces to the repair of bridges across the Thames and the construction of wooden stands for knightly tournaments.

Both from the standpoint of historical significance as well as of literary technique Chaucer ranks among the greatest English poets. In his *Canterbury Tales,* his major work, may be found reflected the life of fourteenth-century England, at once curiously medieval and at the same time prophetic of change. A number of pilgrims, on their way to Canterbury, whiled away the time by telling one another stories; and these, loosely connected with sundry oc-

currences at the tavern or on horseback on the way to Canterbury, comprise the poem. The company was very mixed; in it were a knight, a miller, a man of law, a pardoner, a shipman, a prioress, a middle-class widow from Bath, and several others. Each spun a yarn. The knight's tale was of old-fashioned chivalry; the miller's tale was indecent, and Chaucer apologized for telling it; and the man of law told a most pathetic little story. The Wife of Bath, who had rejoiced in five husbands—"Three of hem were gode and two were badde"—discoursed on marriage, attacking with vigor the medieval glorification of celibacy. One of the best of these stories was told by the Nun's Priest, who under the guise of animal dialogue makes sport of human foibles.

The *Canterbury Tales* give a kaleidoscopic picture of life as it actually was in fourteenth-century England. Religious dissatisfaction was everywhere; but although fun was poked at relics, there was as yet no indication of any religious upheaval. New social classes were beginning to press forward, and people like the Wife of Bath represented a sturdy, independence-loving middle class. Faith in the accepted order was waning, but not very sharply. Strong traces of other-worldliness—that major characteristic of the Middle Ages—appeared in Wycliffe, Langland, and to some extent in Chaucer. All three had a new slant on life, a fresh interest in everyday affairs; and in Chaucer this new leaven was predominant.

Dissatisfaction with Richard II

While Wycliffe and Chaucer were writing, English politics were by no means dull. Several violent episodes in Richard's reign led eventually to his deposition. Courageous and clear-headed as he showed himself at the momentary crisis of the Peasants' Revolt, he was to prove too self-willed and impetuous for a successful king. His mother, who had been a restraining influence, died when he was eighteen, and the control of the government fell into the hands of five courtiers, particularly Michael de la Pole, earl of Suffolk, and Robert de Vere, earl of Oxford. The power of such a group naturally aroused resentment and jealousy; and an opposition party made headway under Thomas of Gloucester, who, like the rest of the king's uncles and their equally ambitious sons, was still excluded from all share in the government. The ensuing struggle for control came to actual fighting more than once. It was the forerunner of similar conflicts which distracted England through most of the coming century, when Edward III's descendants were to continue this selfish scramble for the spoils of power, using high-sounding patriotic aims as the pretext for fighting.

Gloucester and his confederates came to be known as the Lords Appellant because they "appealed," or accused of treason, first Suffolk and then the rest of Richard's courtier group before Parliament. In 1388, after a victory over the royal forces, five Lords Appellant, headed by Gloucester, took over the government. This, like the Provisions of Oxford of 1258 and the Lords Ordainers of 1311, proved to be one more short-lived baronial effort to master England. After a year of this rule, no better nor worse than before, Richard suddenly announced that, being now of age, he would take the reins into his own hands. He did so without bloodshed; and there followed eight good years of what may be termed constitutional government, for Richard ruled well and in harmony with Parliament. He even retained some of the Lords Appellant in his council.

Livery and Maintenance

During this period Parliament endeavored to curb a serious evil, revealed in the recent turbulence, by an act against "livery and maintenance." This was part of a widespread pattern of "bastard feudalism," in which many great lords had retainers by the hundreds or even thousands, held in line by pay instead of by the land tenure and lord-vassal relationship of normal feudalism. Most numerous among these retainers were the fighting men, recipients of "livery and maintenance" from the lord, who thus had a regular little standing army of his own, which wore his livery with his particular device, or coat of arms, and which was supported in his pay or protected in case of trouble. The English armies in the Hundred Years' War consisted of many such groups, for whose services the lord was compensated from the royal treasury. In between campaigns, they did little beside "brawl and bully," sometimes fighting the forces of a rival lord, more often terrorizing the countryside. Not only fighting men were included in a lord's sphere of influence in this newer feudal setup, but also lesser gentry, yeomen, lawyers and other professional men, and many others in the counties. This was of mutual advantage; the lord's jealously guarded prestige rested in part on the number of his retainers, and these other folk found that advancement of interest, and even basic safety, depended upon having a powerful patron.

That effort of Parliament to break up this setup under Richard did not succeed. In defiance of the weak royal authority, great lords, supported by their retainers and tenants, had taken matters into their own hands. Men were ambushed by large armed bands and slain on the highway for incurring the enmity of some local potentate. Disputed lands were seized by force from weak claimants. The personal and family correspondence of the Pastons, a substantial middle-class family of Norfolk, tells how three different noblemen, with large bands of retainers, captured three different Paston manors; in one case, the sheriff informed Paston that the offending lord was too powerful to be defied. The justices of the King's Bench and Common Pleas still rode their circuits, but no longer rendered effective justice. Even when armed bands did not terrorize the assizes, these royal judges themselves were openly partisan and not above the suspicion of bribery. And one such, a justice of Common Pleas, laid an ambush, with five hundred men, for a peer; when called to account, he claimed not to know that he had broken the law. Besides overawing judges and juries in the shires, the power of the lords extended far up into the central government, sitting as they did in the House of Lords and sometimes in the Council as well. With the threat of their private armies, some were able to force the election of their henchmen to Commons. Altogether, the continued existence of such bands of armed ruffians increased the factious and disturbing rule of the nobility for a full hundred years more.

After 1397 Richard's good government suddenly changed into absolutism. This trend toward tyranny has been attributed to that frequent source of discord, Parliamentary criticism of court extravagance. Whatever the cause—whether this thwarting of his imperious will or the loss of his first wife, Anne of Bohemia, to whom he was deeply attached—Richard showed himself a despot who brooked no curb, even that of English law. He drove the Lords Appellant into exile or to execution; he intimidated Parliament with four thousand archers, so that it meekly yielded to his wishes. His forced loans and other arbitrary acts were deeply irritating; but he overstepped himself early in 1399 when, without excuse or provocation, he seized the vast lands of his uncle, John of Gaunt, who had just died. Since this was an attack on private property, which upper-class Englishmen have defended for centuries, it caused particular resentment.

John of Gaunt's son, Henry of Lancaster, returned with a small band from abroad to take over his father's confiscated estates. He was an experienced soldier, who had campaigned from the Baltic to Jerusalem, but this time he did not have to fight. Men flocked to the standard of this unjustly despoiled scion of the royal line. Richard was stormbound in Ireland, where he had gone because of his deputy's murder. Henry discovered that not merely the family lands but the throne itself was his for the taking. Probably reminded of the fate of Edward II, Richard abdicated, and Parliament at once announced his deposition.

The Lancastrians and Parliamentary Growth

This quick revolution, which made Henry IV king (1399-1413), is taken as the end of the straight Plantagenet line and the beginning of the Lancastrian. Richard had no children, but the next of kin was not this cousin Henry IV, the son of Edward III's fourth son. Another cousin, the eight-year-old Edmund Mortimer, Earl of March, as the grandson of Edward III's third son, had a better technical claim. The name of Lancaster came from the family of Henry's mother; and his father, John of Gaunt, had been created Duke of Lancaster after the marriage. Henry IV; his son, Henry V; and his insane grandson, Henry VI, belonged to this line.

The deposition of the last direct Plantagenet was constitutionally far more significant than that of Edward II. In the earlier instance the natural heir apparent became king, while this time Parliament changed the succession by skipping over Edmund Mortimer to select Henry of Lancaster. The events of 1399, moreover, did away with the royal absolutism which was threatening to undo the century of Parliamentary development. The year 1399 may consequently be considered a peak in the growth of Parliament. The most significant of these steps were concentrated in the fourteenth and the seventeenth century. This transferring of the crown to the Lancastrian line was the climax of the earlier century of development, just as another threatened despotism in 1688 again resulted in Parliament's changing the succession and securing what was to prove a permanent supremacy in England.

The Hundred Years' War helps to account for this rapid rise of Parliament. The fighting in France meant the constant need for money in large amounts. Increasingly the king was unable to "live of his own," particularly in wartime. No previous king had been forced to ask for such frequent and heavy grants of money as Edward III. To him, moreover, the war was so important that he was ready to make concessions of all sorts to obtain these funds. Probably neither Edward nor his Lords or Commons realized the full future significance of thus yielding to Parliamentary wishes; for henceforth Parliament began to make a regular practice of capitalizing the financial needs of the crown. It learned that here was a way to get whatever it wanted from the king. To the money grants, consequently, were added all sorts of Parliamentary petitions to the king for reforms. The two being thus coupled, the king had to assent to the petitions when he approved the grants of

revenue to himself. Parliament also began to appoint committees to check up the collection and expenditure of the funds. These practices became more and more fixed as the century wore on.

The House of Commons was the chief agent in thus coercing the king through his financial needs. It was about 1340, the year of the opening naval battle of Sluis, that the House of Commons as such began to meet as a separate body. The lower clergy had withdrawn to their own Convocation and were no longer part of Parliament. The knights of the shire had taken the all-important step of aligning themselves definitely with the burgesses rather than with the lords, thus greatly strengthening the influence of the Commons. From this time the Commons began to come into their own as the distinctive feature of the two-bodied Parliament, the Lords having long before met as the Great Council. Steadily the House of Commons was to grow to a position of power which far outshadowed the prestige of the House of Lords, with its purely hereditary membership.

While achieving this control of finances by the close of the fourteenth century, Parliament was also endeavoring to secure a similar dominance over legislation. The king, to be sure, had to agree to petitions for reforms in order to get his money grants; but before these reforms were enrolled as statutes, he or his ministers could alter or suppress them. He might also, through his council and independently of Parliament, make ordinances as distinct from statutes (see page 102). It came to be understood that royal ordinances were temporary measures, while Parliamentary statutes were relatively permanent. The Statute of Laborers, for instance, was an emergency ordinance, issued by king and council in 1349, before it became a regular Parliamentary statute two years later. Gradually Parliament began to submit regular bills to the king, in place of its original petitions. As the system finally evolved, a bill went through three stages before it became a statute, or act of law. It would originate in either the House of Lords or the House of Commons, then be passed by the other House, and after receiving also the royal assent become law. Of course, the other House might kill a bill or the king might veto it by withholding his assent. In either case the bill was finished for that session of Parliament. Ordinances, however, continued to be used for special purposes and in modern times exist as Orders in Council.

In connection with financial grants and lawmaking, Parliament sought also, at times, to direct the policy of the government. It might accomplish this by refusing grants; but it began a more direct and effective method in the "Good Parliament" of 1376, when apparently it first used the weapon of impeachment. Preserving the old idea that the House of Lords, as the successor of the former Great Council, was the highest court in the land, the House of Commons acted as a sort of grand jury in presenting offending ministers to the Upper House for trial for high offenses, particularly treason. Parliament thus kept the view that the king himself could do no wrong, and so avoided open rebellion; but at the same time it evolved the idea that it was an offense to give the king bad advice or even to obey bad orders given by him. The fact that this weapon of impeachment of ministers hung over them often affected the policies of both king and ministers. The net result of the century's development was that by its close Parliament had complete control over finances, a fair hold over legislation, but less direct influence upon policies.

The next sixty years under the three Lancastrian Henries have been termed a period of premature constitutional government, for they acted hand in glove with Parliament. The fourth Henry owed his title to it; the fifth needed money for French wars; and Henry VI was an infant when his reign

began, and insane at its close. No major constitutional changes occurred, but certain details of procedure were rounded out. Among them were efforts to secure freedom of speech in Parliament (Richard II, for instance, had secured a death sentence against a member who criticized his extravagance, although the sentence was not carried into effect); freedom of members from arrest on civil charges while Parliament was in session or even while they were en route between it and their homes; the principle that revenue bills must originate only in the lower house (a practice continued today in national and state governments in the United States); and, finally, a certain control by Parliament itself over the election of members. In 1430 Parliament ruled that knights of the shire were to be elected by all freeholders possessing land worth an annual income of forty shillings. This provision, lasting four centuries, gave considerable importance to the yeomanry, or the lesser freeholders of moderate means; but it kept the great bulk of tenant peasants and agricultural laborers from voting. The borough, or town, on the other hand, chose its members of Parliament on any basis it saw fit, and retained that method until 1832 (see pages 404 ff.).

From 1460 to 1603, under the Yorkist and Tudor kings, Parliament did not expand its powers (see page 148). The traditions built up, however, during the earlier period of growth were strong enough to keep alive at least the forms of Parliament, so that in the seventeenth century it was able to forge ahead.

Henry IV, whose crown had come so easily, was to find it another matter to keep it. He had average ability and ample energy (until it was sapped by chronic illness and worry over holding the throne); but revolts and border wars filled the first two thirds of his reign, preventing much constructive work. Parliament continued co-operating with the king, even going so far at first as to nominate the members of his council. The chief piece of legislation, the statute of *De Heretico Comburendo,* authorized the burning of Lollards or any other heretics (1401); and the first martyr was hurried to the stake just as the law was being enacted.

Once, however, the direct royal line had been broken, there were many candidates for the throne of England, and before Henry had been king a year the revolts began. After the first of these uprisings Richard II, who had been retained in imprisonment, was murdered.

The elimination of Richard did not lessen the revolts. The most serious menace came from Wales. There Owen Glendower, a Welsh gentleman of magnetic personality and dauntless courage, had aroused the spirit of Welsh nationalism to a last fitful flame. For several years he made Wales a virtually independent principality, as the great Llewelyn had done in the thirteenth century (see page 110). Following the old Welsh policy of taking advantage of English political troubles, he allied himself not only with the Scots and the French but also with rebellious English vassals.

The situation became grave for Henry in 1403, when the Percys, one of the great families of the north, made an alliance with Glendower. Their head, the Earl of Northumberland and his son "Harry Hotspur," had helped put Henry on the throne and had kept the Scots beaten back; but they were alienated by what they felt was insufficient gratitude to them and by his attitude toward the family of the rival Yorkist claimant for the throne, the Earl of March, a relative of Hotspur's wife (see page 138). By a mere matter of minutes the royal army under Henry's young son caught the Percys unexpectedly at Shrewsbury and routed them before they could reach Wales to join Glendower. Their kinsman, the Archbishop of York, had already been captured and beheaded. Not long after this the Scottish threat collapsed when the heir to Scotland, on his way to France, was taken by the English and brought to Henry's court as a hostage. France, which had been decidedly hostile since the death of Richard, who was related to her king, went so far as to dispatch a small expedition to Wales; but the Hundred Years' War was not renewed in force, for France was having internal disputes of her own.

In 1408, the royal forces finally closed in on Northumberland, who was killed. The rebellious elements were well in hand; but Henry's remaining five years found him ill and harassed by the ambitions of his restless son, Shakespeare's wild "Prince Hal," who eagerly succeeded as Henry V (1413-1422). He was the ablest of the Lancastrians, but all his energies were bent on the barren quest of military glory.

Revival of The Hundred Years' War

In 1415, without provocation, he commenced the second active phase of the Hundred Years' War. Since the death of the Black Prince the war had been spasmodic, with minor raids on both sides. Henry's revival of the fighting arose from his own youthful zest for military glory and from the disrupted condition of France. A born soldier, an excellent organizer and disciplinarian as well as fighter, at seventeen he had commanded the royal troops at Shrewsbury. In France the strong king Charles V (1364-1380) had been followed by an insane son, Charles VI (1380-1422), whose alternating spells of lucidity and madness seriously weakened the monarchy. As a result, for nearly thirty years France was disrupted by the rivalry of two younger branches of the royal house—a situation similar to that which was to distract England in the latter half of the century. At the head of one faction, the king's able uncle, the Duke of Burgundy, held not only the section of that name in the east but also Flanders and other rich lands in the north. The other leader was the king's attractive younger brother, the Duke of Orleans, with extensive but scattered lands.

Attack on fortified French town, showing siege gun, crossbows and longbows.

The quarrel of the original rivals was kept up by their sons, Frenchmen taking sides with the red scarf of Burgundy or the white scarf of Orleans. This naturally prevented a united front when Henry V rejected all French efforts at conciliation in his energetic reopening of the war.

Henry captured the port of Harfleur, at the mouth of the Seine, the first town taken by the English with artillery. Then, with about a third of his force, he decided to strike north to Calais. His strategy and battle tactics were similar to those at Crécy (see page 122). A French army at least five times as strong blocked his way and met him at Agincourt, midway between Crécy and Calais. The French crowded their great army into too small a space and so lost their numerical advantage. The English archers let fly their deadly arrows, and then with axes rushed the enemy lines to kill or capture thousands of Frenchmen

too heavily armored to run. Fearing a counterattack, Henry ordered the slaughter of these thousands of prisoners; but this brutality was unnecessary, for the remaining French fled. Many of the French dead were, as at Crécy, noblemen. The English losses of all ranks were only a few hundred at most. Agincourt was to be the last great English military victory on the Continent for three centuries.

For another fourteen years the war continued to favor the English. In 1417, again invading, they overran Normandy and starved Rouen, the Conqueror's old capitol, into surrender. Normandy, which had been French since John lost it in 1204, was to remain in English hands for thirty-odd years. French hope for unity was destroyed in 1419 with the murder of the Duke of Burgundy by the pro-Orleanist heir to the throne (or by his men). The resulting alliance of the Burgundians with the English invaders lasted sixteen years. The English successes were sealed in the Treaty of Troyes in 1420. By this Henry was recognized as the next king of France upon Charles VI's death and was to marry the latter's daughter at once. In the meantime, as regent of France, Henry was to control Normandy and other lands formerly held by England. While undertaking a third invasion two years later to consolidate those gains, Henry died at thirty-five from the effects of exposure at a siege.

Perhaps he was fortunate to die while he was the most influential prince in Christendom, and he did not see that the price of his glory was, like Edward III's, "immediate misery for France and eventual confusion for England." His success had aroused national pride at home and made a profound impression abroad; also his part in ending the Great Schism had enhanced his prestige. But most of his achievement was of a transient military nature, to be completely lost within forty years and to prove the undoing of his Lancastrian house.

The English crown went to an eight-months-old baby, who with the death of his grandfather, Charles VI, three months later, was also proclaimed king of France, in accordance with the terms of Troyes. Thus began the troubled thirty-nine-year reign of Henry VI, who was to be cursed by the inheritance of insanity from his French grandfather. Others constantly overshadowed him, from his valiant, strong-minded wife to the regents who ruled during his long minority and after the onslaught of his disease. Even in the decade between these two periods he did little actual ruling, for his gentle, retiring, and unsuspecting nature made him a helpless pawn. The founding of the famous boys' school at Eton and of King's College at Cambridge University was evidence of his keen interest in education and letters.

The regency for an infant led, as usual, to keen rivalry among several grown men of the royal line. Of Henry V's two surviving brothers, the elder, John, Duke of Bedford, a man of first-rate ability, was made regent in France, and Humphrey, Duke of Gloucester, popular but harebrained, was put in nominal charge at home. Also there was Bishop, later Cardinal, Beaufort, whose good sense and excellent grasp of foreign affairs had had much to do with Henry's successful part in ending the Great Schism. Beaufort was one of four illegitimate children of John of Gaunt, who had eventually married their mother, Catherine Swynford; and the following year Parliament had legitimatized these children. The importance of the so-called Beaufort branch of the royal line was to increase, for from it would come the powerful Tudor dynasty.

During the next seven years, the English gave every appearance of being triumphant conquerors, while the apathetic French, appalled at the terrific devastation of their land, seemed to lose hope. Actually the English situation was steadily worsening; and Parliament grew ever more reluctant to pay the increasing costs. The occupation, instead of being a source of profit, was a constant drain because of the ravaged state of the conquered territory. Despite Bedford's capable leadership, moreover, the new campaigning fell far short of the earlier English successes.

Then to the French from an unforeseen and unusual source there came such mysterious aid that the tide of war was turned dramatically in their favor. This turning point came in 1429 at Orleans, key to the few remaining unconquered regions and besieged by the English. Suddenly a young French peasant girl, Jeanne d'Arc (Joan of Arc) appeared at the court of the timid, vacillating Dauphin, who had been disinherited by the Treaty of Troyes. She told impassionedly a strange story of mystic voices in her native woods of Domremy, bidding her free France from the invaders. Incredulous at first, the Dauphin was finally persuaded to let her join the army for the

Joan of Arc, drawn by a scribe in the original records of her trial in Rouen. This is the only sketch made during her lifetime.

rescue of Orleans. She insisted that she could drive out the "goddams," as the English were called, no matter how numerous they might be. Clad in white armor on a white charger, she so inspired the defenders that Orleans was miraculously saved from almost certain doom.

Next this dauntless girl achieved the coronation of the Dauphin, at Reims, as King Charles VII, a step he had not dared risk himself. Joan then seems to have felt that her Heaven-sent mission was over and begged that she be allowed to go home; but, unluckily for her, Charles wanted to keep her inspirational presence with his troops. She was soon captured by the Burgundians, and they sold her to their English allies. Ungratefully, Charles did not lift a finger to save her when she was charged with bewitching the English troops so that they could not fight. She was brought to trial by the church authorities at Rouen and

then burned at the stake. Some English soldiers, so it is said, were to murmur, as she bravely died, "We have burned a saint"; and five centuries later she was made a saint by the Church which had condemned her.

Joan's work lived after her in the new national enthusiasm among the French. The English steadily lost ground. Gloucester and later Bedford antagonized the Duke of Burgundy by their marriages, which brought into their hands lands which he had coveted. By 1435, consequently, the Burgundians broke their English alliance to join forces with Charles VII, who, at last aroused, was showing himself to be an excellent leader. In that same year Bedford died and was succeeded by a less competent leader. At home Gloucester wanted to push the war, but Beaufort worked for peace. Finally, in 1444, England agreed to abandon everything but Normandy and part of Aquitaine. Henry VI's marriage was arranged with the niece of the French king, fourteen-year-old Margaret of Anjou, "passionate, spirited, and indomitable."

Two years later the English foolishly broke this favorable truce. In the meantime the French had organized a very efficient army, especially strong in the new artillery. By 1450 Normandy was lost for good. The following year England's possessions in Aquitaine crumbled away. In 1453 England sent a last expedition in a vain attempt to recover the lost ground, but it was cut to pieces by the French artillery in what proved the final battle of the war. Bordeaux, which England had held ever since Eleanor had brought it as a dowry three centuries earlier, reverted to France. The Hundred Years' War was over. Of all England's vast holdings in France there now remained only the port of Calais. That same year, 1453, six weeks before that last battle, the Eastern Roman, or Byzantine, Empire had come to an end when Turkish invaders from the east captured its capital, Constantinople.

Despite the spectacular English victories at Crécy, Poitiers, and Agincourt, France had finally won the Hundred Years' War. Nevertheless, this loss was to prove a blessing in disguise for England. In earlier years the relation with Normandy and Aquitaine had been an asset because of the cultural contacts which they afforded, but in later years the French lands had become more of a liability. The loss of these possessions freed England from entanglement in many of the petty continental squabbles into which she had been drawn hitherto. England learned so well this lesson of the futility of Continental conquests that she rarely sought again Continental territory as spoils of victory. Centuries later, 1689-1815, England and France were to contend in another "Hundred Years' War," but that time England sought colonies overseas. Her victories in the second contest led to permanent acquisitions which became valuable parts of the British Empire. Canada and India were to prove more useful than Normandy and Aquitaine. One lasting advantage, aside from this lesson to avoid Continental conquests, did England gain from the first Hundred Years' War—the rise of Parliament's power occasioned by the king's need of money for military purposes.

The English of that day, however, did not see these benefits of defeat. When, along with the bad news from France, law and order was going from bad to worse after a century with "livery and maintenance" still unchecked, they turned savagely against the Lancastrian government. Henry's marriage had been unpopular from the first because it had entailed the loss of land in France instead of the usual gains of territory through a dowry. Besides, Margaret, an exceedingly able person, never accepted the self-effacing role expected of a king's consort. Her strong will and violent prejudices were frequently to carry her into rash and overly arbitrary acts. Through her influence, William de la Pole, of the same family as Richard II's favorite, and like him, eventually Duke of Suffolk, supplanted Gloucester and Beaufort as leading minister in 1445. Two years later Gloucester was charged with treason in Parliament and almost at once was found dead, presumably murdered, in his bed. With Cardinal Beaufort's death soon after, Suffolk was left supreme and alone in power, but was to find himself blamed for all the disasters in France and the troubled conditions at home.

In 1450 Suffolk, the focal point of criticism, was threatened with charges of treason, and for his own safety was sent into exile by the king. On his way to France he was seized from the ship and murdered. His followers, however, retained control at court for a few months until, when news of the loss of Normandy reached England, the men of Kent and adjacent regions marched on London under Jack Cade, an Irish adventurer and some substantial gentlemen and yeomen. Their demands were for a more efficient government. In London the mob of followers ran riot, alienating the townspeople, and Cade was among those killed. Although practically nothing immediate was gained, the demonstration nevertheless had some effect. The power wielded by Suffolk passed to another friend of the royal couple, the Duke of Somerset, a Beaufort, who had conducted the recent French campaign badly, and was not the man whom the discontented elements wanted in charge of the government.

Yorkists versus Lancastrians

Their hopes pointed to Richard, Duke of York, who stood next in line to the throne, and whose hereditary claims to it were equal if not superior to those of Henry VI. These rival claims of the Lancastrians and the Yorkists to the throne went back to various sons of Edward III. The line of the eldest son, the Black Prince, had ended with the death of his son, Richard II; the second son of Edward III had died young, without heirs; but the next three sons—

Lionel, Duke of Clarence; John of Gaunt, Duke of Lancaster; and Edmund, Duke of York—each had descendants. Ordinarily, by strict primogeniture, which was becoming the rule of the English crown, the children of an older son would have priority over those of a younger one; but in 1399, it will be recalled, Parliament had passed over a boy of the Clarence line to put on the throne of John of Gaunt's son, Henry IV, the first of the three Lancastrian Henries. Now, a half century later, in the able Richard of York the malcontents had a candidate for the throne with an exceedingly strong claim because of his descent from Edward III through both father and mother. Whereas the Lancastrian line came only from the fourth son of Edward III, this Yorkist was descended through his mother, the great-granddaughter of Lionel of Clarence, from that third son of Edward III, as well as through his father from the fifth son, Edmund of York. Genealogy would not have figured so prominently had it not been for the strength of the Yorkist Richard in contrast to the weakness of the Lancastrian Henry VI. With a good record as a soldier in France, Richard was also free from all blame in the crisis of affairs, since he had been in Ireland, sent there by the king, undoubtedly to get such a popular figure out of the limelight. The influence of Cade's Rebellion, in which Richard's share is disputed, brought Richard back from Ireland; and from that time events moved rapidly to open hostility between him and the Lancastrians.

As events in France approached their humiliating end in 1453, two developments suddenly complicated matters. In August, Henry showed the first traces of his French grandfather's mental disease; in October came the birth of a son, which automatically excluded Richard of York from the probable succession. With Henry incapacitated, York was placed in charge of the government by the House of Lords; and he ruled well, but this improved government did not last. An unfortunate element in Henry's illness was its periodic character, and within eighteen months he had recovered. Queen Margaret, who had always resented York's popularity, then showed an unwise tendency to push her advantage too far. This characteristic was often to bring to nothing her deeply loyal and dauntless efforts in her husband's behalf. Through her vindictiveness at this time, not only was Somerset returned to his old power, but York and his friends were completely excluded from the government. The royal attitude forced York to take to arms, to save himself and his followers further vengeance, and civil war was thus precipitated.

Barely was the Hundred Years' War over, therefore, when the rival interests of Lancaster and York were involved in the intermittent thirty-year struggle known as the Wars of the Roses because the white rose was the symbol of York and the red rose, at least in retrospect, was the badge of Lancaster. With no particular principles or theories of government involved, the Wars were simply a conflict for purely personal ends between rival royal lines, each backed by groups of strong noblemen. The nobility, with their private armed forces, held by "livery and maintenance," were fairly evenly divided between Lancaster and York, and frequently shifted sides as their own interests of the moment seemed to indicate.

Foremost of this group of nobles and typical of their strength was Richard Neville, Earl of Warwick and nephew of Richard of York. The Neville family had practiced successfully the policy of obtaining land by marrying heiresses. Warwick is said to have held some hundred and fifty manors, in many parts of England but chiefly in the north country. He owned more lands than any subject had ever previously held; his income was even greater than the king's; and as a result many thousands wore his private badge of "the Bear and Ragged Staff." With this private army and these vast resources he

THE WARS OF
THE ROSES

North
Sea

TOWTON •York
1461

Ravenspur

WAKEFIELD
1460

Irish Sea

Trent R.

W A L E S

BOSWORTH
1485

MORTIMERS CROSS
1461

NORTHAMPTON
1460

Ouse R.

TEWKESBURY
1471

Severn R.

ST. ALBANS
1455, 1461

Milford
Haven

BARNET
1471

Thames R.
London

Dover

Calais

English Channel

0   50   100
Scale of Miles

was able to play the role of "Kingmaker" in the Wars of the Roses. First he put a Yorkist king on the throne in place of a Lancastrian; and then he lost his life in trying to pull him off again.

These were brutal wars. Many of the soldiers employed by the lords were foreign mercenaries, and the queen showed no hesitation in importing such men for the main part of her army. The mercenaries brought with them many savage practices developed in the Continental wars. In the actual fighting, both sides being armed with the longbow, neither had any particular advantage. For the bloody work at close range both used the "bill," a broad knife on

the end of a staff. In most of the battles the heaviest casualties were suffered by the armored noblemen and mounted knights; for the footmen of the defeated army generally escaped slaughter by running away. Each side was inclined to follow victory with the execution of prominent prisoners —London Bridge was decorated with the severed heads of Lancastrian and Yorkist leaders in turn.

Throughout the long struggle the bulk of the people were indifferent to its course. Not a single town was sufficiently interested in either side to withstand a siege, but instead opened its gates to whatever force came along, as the easiest way. On the whole, the towns and the more advanced southern counties tended to favor the Yorkist cause, particularly after the plundering excesses of the queen's troops. Of course, London was the chief prize; whoever held it had control of the government. Consequently a number of the most important battles were fought in the vicinity of the metropolis.

The mixture of melodrama, intrigue, genealogy, and homicide which went to make up the Wars of the Roses is not worth following in detail here. The major fighting fell into four distinct parts: the opening battle of St. Albans, in 1455; the nine months in 1460-1461 which placed the Yorkists on the throne; the brief Lancastrian restoration in 1470-1471; and the final battle of Bosworth Field, which brought the Yorkist rule to an end in 1485.

In 1455 the actual fighting began with a Yorkist victory in the old abbey town of St. Albans, thirty miles from London. Somerset was killed. Shortly afterward, York took over again the role of Protector when the king fell ill. Before long, however, with his recovery, Margaret—now the undisputed leader of the Lancastrian cause—regained control. Fighting began again in 1459, and after two small battles the leading Yorkists—notably Richard of York, his son Edward, and Warwick—had to flee into exile.

They returned in the summer of 1460, to start nine of the most violent months of the wars. At Northampton, Warwick won a victory, took Henry VI prisoner, and gained control of the government. Richard of York claimed the crown for himself, citing his double descent from Edward III; but Parliament refused to dethrone Henry. It did, however, designate Richard as the king's heir instead of recognizing Henry's son. Two months later Richard was killed in a Lancastrian victory, and his head, derisively decorated with a paper crown, was displayed at York. Margaret, relentlessly bitter at the disinheriting of her son, then

led a plundering army of northerners toward London and, in a second battle at St. Albans, rescued the king. Then the queen for once missed her opportunity. With the capital close at hand, the Lancastrians and their king might have returned to power. Instead, the queen's army retreated up the Great North Road, ravaging all the way.

Thereupon Warwick seized the first of the chances which gave him his title of "Kingmaker." Summoning York's nineteen-year-old son from the Welsh border, where he had just won a victory, Warwick had him crowned by a very irregular assembly at London as Edward IV in 1461. His throne was not secure, however, as long as the Red Rose had a powerful army in the field. The southerners, enraged at the damage inflicted by the Lancastrian army, joined Edward's army in large numbers. Shortly, the two armies met at Towton, near York, in what has been called the bloodiest battle on English soil. After seven savage hours in a blinding snowstorm the Lancastrians lay dead in thousands upon the field. Henry, Margaret, and their young son fled for safety to a precarious exile in Scotland. Towton placed the Yorkist line firmly upon the throne, and Parliament confirmed to the son the title it had refused to give his father the year before.

After sixty-two years under the three Lancastrian Henrys, England was to have twenty-four years under three Yorkist kings before the White Rose, in turn, gave way to the great century of the Tudors, 1485-1603. Most of the Yorkist period was filled by the reign of this Edward IV (1461-1483); for his young son, Edward V, was king (in name) for only a few months, and his brother, Richard III, ruled only two years.

Edward IV was to give England a more efficient rule than the Lancastrians had, at the expense of Parliamentary co-operation. Parliament's last show of independence was its refusal of the crown to Richard of York in 1460. The next year it entered a century and a half of relative obscurity. Edward, like his Tudor successors, showed the effects of the new, crafty, calculating methods of statecraft which Europe was beginning to learn from Renaissance Italy (see page 175). By clever financial management and by avoiding costly foreign wars both Edward and the Tudors freed themselves from such constant dependence upon Parliamentary grants as the Hundred Years' War had entailed. Realizing that England would forgive much to a king who would help to restore law, order, and prosperity, they enjoyed much of the power of autocratic rule; but they were wise enough not to boast of it as Richard II had done. Edward, again like the Tudors, knew the art of cultivating popularity among the people in general and among the commercial classes in particular. He realized, too, that occasional high-handed acts against proud nobles would be condoned as long as the people were not constantly nagged with petty vexations. Edward, however, did not attain the Tudor success, partly because too many of the disruptive feudal elements still remained uncrushed in the England of his time, and partly because he did not work hard enough at the job of being king.

A tall and handsome man with a winning personality, Edward was indolent and inordinately fond of a good time. He had real ability as a soldier, and his keen intelligence might have made him equally successful in other fields had he bothered to apply it. Upon his coronation he threw himself into a constant round of pleasure-hunting, dancing, eating, love affairs. Among his many mistresses were the wives of various London citizens; yet by no group was he better liked than by the Londoners, with whom he freely mixed and whom he frequently could flatter into making generous loans. Edward's spasmodic bursts of energy quickly gave way to longer spells of laziness, and he would never push himself to spend the necessary long hours on administrative detail.

The "Kingmaker" was before long to regret his choice. Warwick wanted an alliance with France, which was making a remarkably thorough recovery, and Edward, appearing to agree, allowed Warwick to negotiate for his marriage to a sister of the French queen. But Edward was already secretly married to the widow of a Lancastrian knight, originally Elizabeth Woodville. He had indulged in that rare luxury for royalty, a love match. Politically it was unwise; not only Warwick, but many other Yorkist supporters were incensed at the honors and riches heaped upon the queen and her numerous upstart relatives. Warwick held his peace for five years more, working for a French alliance, but Edward instead allied himself with the rash Duke of Burgundy, the rebellious vassal and archenemy of the crafty French king, Louis XI.

Warwick, his patience at an end, revolted against his king. After a ten-year lull the Wars of the Roses broke out anew. Warwick and Queen Margaret, who after long wanderings had taken refuge at the French court, staged an invasion which drove Edward temporarily into exile. Henry VI, who had been a prisoner in the Tower and whose mind was sadly deranged, was after a decade now replaced upon the throne by the "Kingmaker." His restoration lasted only six months.

In 1471 Edward IV returned from overseas, quickly gathered an army, and won a crushing victory over the Lancastrians at Barnet, near London. Warwick was killed. A few weeks later the Yorkists also routed the queen's army at Tewkesbury, in the west. Margaret was captured and her son, the Lancastrian heir, was killed. Before the month was out, Henry VI had died in the Tower, presumably murdered. The direct Lancastrian line was thus wiped out, and until the death of Edward IV, twelve years later, his Yorkist rule remained scarcely challenged. The Wars of the Roses were over except for the final critical fighting which was to end the Yorkist line in 1485.

The latter half of Edward IV's reign was relatively uneventful—a welcome relief for harried England. In 1475, in alliance still with the Duke of Burgundy, Edward invaded France; but Louis XI bought him off for some £15,000 cash and payments of £10,000 a year for life. Edward was not the only English king who was to receive gold instead of glory at the expense of France (see pages 168, 265).

Otherwise, the restoration of order went on without outside distractions. Edward now increasingly neglected his duties for gay times with one Jane Shore and other favorites; but he found so many sources of revenue that he did not have to call upon Parliament for a penny during the last eight years of his reign. With his handsome allowance from France; fines from lawbreakers, who were finding royal justice once more active; the confiscation of the rich estates of Warwick and others; and profits from trading on his own account with his own merchant ships, he was able to balance his budget and even build up a surplus. On the occasions when he needed more ready money, he resorted to "benevolences" or loans rather than apply to Parliament. The only time he called Parliament was to pass a death sentence upon his troublesome and treacherous brother the Duke of Clarence, who was quarreling with a third brother, Richard, Duke of Gloucester, and who was too ambitious for Edward's peace of mind. Clarence, it is said, had a unique execution, being drowned in a butt of his favorite wine.

Suddenly, in 1483, Edward died, worn out at forty by overindulgence. His death led to two grim years which spelled the doom of the Yorkist party. Little Edward V, his twelve-year-old son, had the shortest and probably the saddest reign in English history, from the spring until summer only.

The obvious candidates for the regency were Edward V's unpopular mother, Elizabeth Woodville, and his uncle, Richard of Gloucester. The latter, short and thin, with a sad, suspicious face, had a hitherto good record both as soldier and as administrator. Lust for power, however, was suddenly to give him a place among England's few royal villains. In this moment of his young nephew's succession Richard acted with promptness, energy, and complete lack of scruple. He won over some of the Council by bribes and executed or imprisoned the others. Declared regent by this method, he secured the custody of Edward by force. Accusing the queen of witchcraft, he announced that her children were illegitimate because her marriage had been irregular. With Edward V thus made ineligible for the crown, Gloucester overawed Parliament with armed forces and had himself declared king as Richard III. All this he accomplished before his brother Edward IV had been three months in the grave.

Had Richard stopped even there, he might have achieved a successful reign; but what happened next shocked the whole nation, even in that callous age which had witnessed so much cruelty. The child, Edward V, had been sent to the Tower, where his younger brother was soon confined with him. These boys disappeared from their cell. Richard, so rumor whispered, had had them smothered to death by pillows while they slept. Neither the boys' death nor Richard's guilt was certain at the time; but two centuries later some workmen repairing a staircase in the Tower found the bones of two youths. In 1933 a coroner's inquest exhumed the bones and laid the blame upon Richard III, exonerating the next king, Henry VII, whom some had suspected of the crime. Some, however, continued to disagree with that verdict; the death of the princes would still seem to be among the unsolved mysteries.

That same autumn (1483) the Wars of the Roses entered their final stage when rebellion broke out in the west against Richard III. The rebels planned to place upon the throne a young Lancastrian, Henry Tudor, Earl of Richmond, the future Henry VII.

Richard III

His Tudor grandfather was a Welsh gentleman who had married the young French widow of Henry V; through his other grandfather, a Beaufort, son of John of Gaunt, he inherited an indirect Lancastrian title to the throne. It was proposed to marry him to Elizabeth, the eldest daughter of Edward IV, and thus unite the rival claims of Lancaster and York. Since the last Lancastrian disaster at Tewkesbury, Henry had been in refuge in Brittany. Richard crushed this revolt even before young Tudor had joined the rebels. Two years were to pass before Henry's second and successful try for the crown.

In the meantime affairs went badly for Richard and gave him little opportunity to show his apparent ability. Rumors of a French invasion led to costly preparations and forced loans. Richard's unpopularity increased, while death carried off his wife and only son. Rumors about the princes in the Tower dogged his efforts at good government and rendered them worthless. Instead, repression became the order of the day as the reappearance of Henry Tudor grew imminent; a man was even executed for posting an insulting doggerel couplet about Richard in St. Paul's Cathedral.

In the summer of 1485, Henry Tudor sailed from France with a small force of mercenaries, furnished him by the French queen, and landed on the west coast, flying the banners of both Wales and England. He was joined first by Welshmen and then, as he advanced eastward, by malcontent Englishmen. Richard hurried to meet him with a force twice as large, but reluctant and untrustworthy in spirit. On Bosworth Field, almost in the center of England, the armies met. As battles went, in the Wars of the Roses, it was not a large encounter, but in significant results it outranked all the rest. Richard's half-hearted army broke and ran; but he laid about him bravely with cries of "Treason! Treason!" until the enemy blows brought death. The Wars of the Roses were over; so too, one might say, was medieval England.

Modern Portents

According to legend, the battered English crown was picked up at Bosworth Field and placed upon the head of Henry VII. This accession of the first Tudor was long taken as the traditional date, 1485, for the end of medieval and the beginning of modern England. Yet most of the changes took place so gradually, and from region to region so unevenly, that not only did the men of the time fail to visualize their significance but even today, with the perspective of many centuries, it is difficult to say with any certainty just where medieval history ends and modern history begins.

The present-day historian rejects the positiveness of the earlier textbook writers who printed in large type the dates 476, when the Roman Empire "fell" in the West, and 1453, when Constantinople fell in the East, implying that the light of civilization was suddenly turned off at the earlier date and suddenly turned on again at the latter, leaving the intervening thousand years as stagnant "time out." There have been recent tendencies to push the end of the Middle Ages either farther back or farther ahead. The beginnings of the revival of learning, once the traditional dividing line, have been found to be rooted farther and farther back toward the Dark Ages, with references even to "the twelfth-century Renaissance." Some would end the Middle

Ages proper at some such early date as 1270, the last Crusade. Others insist that the full transition to modern times did not take place until the late eighteenth century. Up to then, the latter point out, agriculture remained the chief occupation, and the manorial system for the most part continued, so that everyday life for the bulk of the people was still closer to that of medieval than of present times.

As a whole, however, the latter part of the fifteenth century is generally accepted as the period of transition, and a variety of dates explain why. The one-time popular date of 1453 not only marked the end of the Hundred Years' War but, more important, the Turkish capture of Constantinople, which put an end to the Eastern Roman Empire and was credited unduly with stimulating the revival of learning and the age of exploration. Another favorite, 1492, witnessed not only the discovery of America by Columbus but also the fall of the last Moorish stronghold in Spain and the death of Lorenzo de' Medici, the famous patron of art in Italy. Besides England's particular date, 1485, Spain has 1479, the accession of its joint rulers, Ferdinand and Isabella, who united the nation; and France, 1483, the death of Louis XI, called her last medieval and first modern king.

Gradually, the medieval state of affairs

was giving way to new conditions. First, a new interest in learning, long chiefly a monopoly of the clergy, was developing. Secondly, Europe was ceasing to be contained within itself. Voyages of discovery began to spread European peoples and influences overseas, until this so-called expansion of Europe brought most of the world for a while under the control of Europeans or of their overseas descendants. With the new discoveries, business increased, banking developed, and trade routes changed from a Mediterranean to an Atlantic center, which made the location of England far more important. Thirdly, the whole general nature of the governments of western Europe was undergoing a transformation. The loose feudal kingdoms, with nobles powerful and kings often weak, were developing into national states, and with this went the growth of autocratic royal power. Finally, never recovering the prestige lost through the "Babylonian Captivity" and the Great Schism, and weakened by the new spirit of questioning, the Roman Catholic, or universal, Church, the main unifying institution of medieval Europe, was about to be broken into many parts by the Reformation, or Protestant Revolt. Each of these changes came sooner or later to England, sometimes in a modified form because of the peculiar circumstances of her separate island position. Sometimes England was ahead of Europe, sometimes she was slower to take the new ways to herself.

The word "Renaissance" has a broad and spacious meaning to the modern scholar. An older generation thought of it as rather specifically a rebirth of interest in classical scholarship and Greco-Roman civilization which, widening into a fresh, invigorating interest in affairs of this world rather than the next, led men to cast aside the supposedly confining shackles of medieval thought, to create new cultural patterns, to paint new and glorious pictures, to build new and magnificent palaces. More re-cently, the Renaissance has come to be taken as comprising the sum total of those changes which culminated in the fifteenth century and made their influence felt in western Europe in literature, philosophy, art, government, geography, and economics.

One aspect of the Renaissance, the Revival of Learning, or renewed interest in Greek and Latin literature, first appeared in Italy. Men known as Humanists became absorbed in the study of the classics, began to ferret out from monastic libraries forgotten Latin writings, began to edit and to make numerous copies of old Latin books, and to popularize classical ideas. Enthusiasm spread to the Greek language, the study of which had become practically extinct throughout western Europe. Classical libraries were made; Italian families, such as the celebrated Medici of Florence, becoming wealthy through trade and commerce, acted as patrons; and one of the Popes, Nicholas V, placed himself at the head of the Humanistic movement.

Love of classical literature led to new interest in sculpture, painting, and architecture. One phase of this new spirit was the so-called "many-sided man," with interests and ability in several such lines of activity. Pagan as well as Christian subjects began to be chosen by artists, who now enjoyed painting Venus as well as the Madonna. Pagan myths in addition to Biblical subjects served as themes for the imagination of sculptors. The merchant princes of Italy gave a new stimulus to architecture by ordering the construction not of new churches to the greater glory of God but of handsome palaces to their own glory.

There had been traces of the new learning in Chaucer's day; for the model of the *Canterbury Tales* had been Boccaccio's *Decameron,* and Chaucer himself had spent much time in Italy. Humphrey, duke of Gloucester, had also aided the introduction of Humanistic learning (see page 143). As a man and as a prince, he was contemptible; but he loved classical lore, and his library, the best in England, included Livy, Pliny, Cicero, Ovid, and a number of Greek authors in Latin translations. A patron of Oxford, he presented that university with nearly three hundred volumes, a very valuable gift indeed in those days before printing. No wonder the university said that he "was to Oxford what Caesar had been to Rome, what Hector had been to Troy."

The New Learning in England

The revival of learning came late to England, for the anarchy of the Wars of the Roses slowed down all cultural advance. The printing press, for instance, was invented about 1450, but not until 1477 was one set up in England. The honor of printing the first English book belongs to William Caxton, a London merchant. In 1464 while in Bruges to negotiate a commercial treaty with the Duke of Burgundy, he became interested in the new art of printing, retired from politics, and printed no less than ninety-six different books in ten years, mostly tales of chivalry translated from the French into English. Caxton's press, however, was a commercial venture, and England had to wait for quieter times and greater prosperity before scholarship, as such, could receive much attention, either from printers or from anyone else.

A major difference between the revival of learning in Italy, in the fourteenth and fifteenth centuries, and that which occurred north of the Alps, particularly in England, from about 1485 to 1525, may be found in the quasi-religious quality which was manifest almost from the beginning in England. In Italy, in contrast, the movement was not directly concerned with religion, except perhaps in a negative sense. A number of the Popes, patrons of the new learning, became less religious in both word and deed as they came in contact with it; but in Germany and England its effect, for some generations at least, seems to have been in the opposite direction. The study

of the classics, particularly Greek, tended in northern Europe to make men more concerned about religion, as may be seen in the careers and the writings of Colet, Erasmus, and More.

John Colet, a wealthy young Englishman, son of a Lord Mayor of London, and a graduate of Oxford, profoundly versed in the classics, spent considerable time in Italy with the foremost Humanists. Returning to Oxford to lecture, he astonished everyone by his simple analysis of Saint Paul's Epistle to the Romans. To him "the epistles of Saint Paul were not a string of riddles but the real letters of a real man, and he wanted to get at what that man meant."

The freedom, frankness, and passionate earnestness with which Colet spoke at Oxford attracted wide attention, and soon after the turn of the century he became Dean of St. Paul's Cathedral in London, where he preached to huge congregations. Like Wycliffe, he thundered at the corruption of the clergy, and with astonishing boldness he denounced a war upon which Henry VIII's heart was set. Despite his riches Colet lived modestly, giving away large sums to charity. He founded St. Paul's School, in which both Greek and Latin were to be taught; for it he wrote a celebrated grammar, and to it he left all his wealth.

Among his warm personal friends was Erasmus, most celebrated of all northern Renaissance scholars. Erasmus, an international Humanist, born at Rotterdam, the illegitimate son of a priest, lived successively in France, England, Italy, and Switzerland. Of these four countries he praised England the most, and England, in turn, adopted him as a son. A young English nobleman, meeting him in Paris, introduced him to England, to Oxford, to the English Humanists, and even to the young boy soon to be Henry VIII. Colet urged Erasmus to stay permanently, but he was restless and longed for Italy. Twice again he returned, the second time to remain for five years, during which he was appointed professor of divinity at Cambridge; was given a comfortable church living; and for the first time in his life had no real financial troubles.

These posts were sinecures, amounting in effect to an English subsidy, and Erasmus so considered them. Spending no time on his parish, Erasmus translated the New Testament and the writings of an early Church Father, Saint Jerome. The former task was one of his most important contributions to scholarship. Just as the Church disapproved of Wycliffe's translation of the old Vulgate from Latin into English (see pages 134ff.), so, for a somewhat different reason, it did not encourage this translation from the original Greek into Latin. Defective as the standardized Vulgate might be, the Church felt that a new translation might imply a challenge to accepted authority. The severely orthodox "felt, and quite truly, that any jarring of the foundations might bring the whole structure of ceremonies and usages in which they were thriving about their ears."

Erasmus, on the whole a conservative, advocated reform but not revolt. The temper of his mind, which reflected that of Renaissance England, may best be demonstrated by his description of a pilgrimage to the shrine of Saint Thomas Becket: "they expose to be kissed the shoe of Saint Thomas, which is, perchance, the shoe of some harlequin; and in any case what could be more foolish than to worship the shoe of a man! . . . When the shrine was opened, the abbot and the rest fell on their knees in worship. . . . All this seemed to John Colet, who was with me, an unworthy display; I thought it was a thing we must put up with until an opportunity should come to reform it without disturbance."

A friend of Colet and Erasmus was Sir Thomas More, one of the choicest spirits of the Renaissance. A son of a judge of the King's Bench, he was brought up as a page in the household of the Archbishop of Canterbury. At Oxford he so distinguished

"Plan of Utopia" from 1518 edition.

himself that his father, alarmed at his son's literary and religious inclinations, hastily withdrew him. More then studied law; but he never ceased to be interested in the revival of learning. He lectured at an early age on Saint Augustine, and wrote in both Latin and Greek on social and religious topics. When scarcely more than a boy, he opposed the wishes of Henry VII in Parliament, for which act his father was sent temporarily to the Tower. As a young man he won a celebrated lawsuit for the Pope against the crown, thereby attracting the attention of Henry VIII, who, charmed by More's learning and personality, visited him and his family frequently, and became such a nuisance that More had to feign stupidity to rid himself of his royal visitor. Henry, however, knighted More, sent him on a diplomatic mission, and finally insisted that he become Chancellor of England, which proved a fatal post (see pages 179, 183).

Best known of his writings is *Utopia,* which has perhaps converted more Englishmen to socialistic ideas than the later writings of Karl Marx. *Utopia* purports to be a conversation between More and a learned and much-traveled seaman, who compares England with the mythical kingdom of Utopia, much to the disadvantage of the former. He is amazed at the cruelty of the laws in England and suggests that if, instead of hanging men for thievery, the authorities found work for them, such severe punishment would not be necessary. He finds too many men who "not only live in idleness themselves, but also carry about with them at their tails a great flock or train of idle and loitering servingmen, which never learned any craft whereby to get their livings." He attacks the enclosure movement, seeing that on the farms sheep have taken the place of men (see page 168). "They consume, destroy, and devour whole fields, houses, cities." In *Utopia* everyone lived a simple life, following his own craft. A six-hour day sufficed; for all worked and lived without ostentation, sharing their goods in common. They found their major delight in good health, in good conversation, and in reading aloud from Greek writings. Wars were avoided; "for with bodily strength (say they) bears, lions, wolves, boars, dogs, and other wild beasts do fight." In religion, the Utopians were extraordinarily tolerant. Some worshiped the moon, others the sun, while the more enlightened worshiped an unknown power, "everlasting, incomprehensible." They took rather kindly to the idea of Christianity, but when one of their number was baptized and then reproached his fellows for their wickedness, they banished him "as a seditious person and as a raiser up of dissensions among the people." "Idleness they utterly forsake. . . . For whatsoever unpleasant, hard and vile work is anywhere, from the which labour, loathesomeness and desperation doth freight other, all that they take upon themselves willingly and gladly."

This most unusual book was widely popular in Europe. Originally written in Latin, it was translated into French, Italian, and German, and published in four Continental cities before being translated into English. That the writer could remain a Catholic in good standing and afterward become canonized, as a saint, perhaps may be partially explained by the fact that the Catholic Church always has distinguished between the four cardinal virtues, wisdom, fortitude, temperance, and justice, and the three theological ones, faith, hope, and charity. Paganism at its best had been characterized by the former, and *Utopia* was founded on them. More was, in a way, writing a satire on the so-called Christian society of his own day, implying that it fell far short of even the cardinal virtues of his own Church. Not only was there no attack on Catholic dogma but there was emphasis on Catholic practice, and, in a sense, *Utopia,* if it pointed forward to socialism, pointed also backward to earlier and more simple Christian ideals. Its critical tone made it a Renaissance book; yet it was also a Catholic one, since it denied the worth of individualism, greatly stressed by the Renaissance. Furthermore, the author remained assiduous in the exercise of his Catholic faith, not merely externally by attending Mass, but privately by wearing a hair shirt next his skin. In More, indeed, the medieval and the modern were strangely blended.

Beginnings of Overseas Expansion

The revival of learning was but one aspect of the Renaissance. Of equal and perhaps more importance, from the standpoint of English history, were the geographical discoveries. They, as well as the study of the Greek New Testament, were influential in bringing about a revaluation of social ideals. If the Renaissance led to renewed curiosity and interest in man, it did likewise in regard to the world.

The world map was suddenly unrolled before the eyes of an amazed Europe dur-

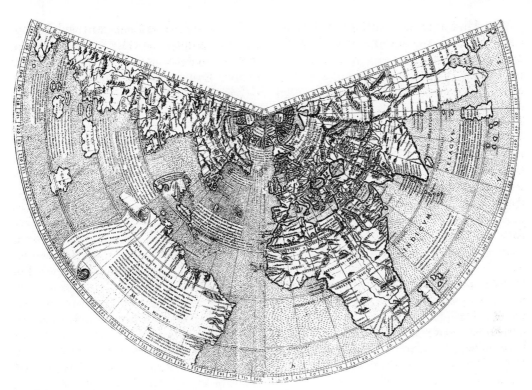

World map, drawn in 1508 by Ruysch, showing newly discovered areas in the Americas.

ing the last years of the fifteenth century. In 1485 Europe knew almost nothing of the other continents, except where Asia and Africa touched the Mediterranean. A solid belt of hostile Moslems prevented penetration in that direction. Part of the African coast had been explored. Marco Polo, an Italian, had written of his travels to the Far East. The Americas were unknown, for Viking voyaging centuries before had been forgotten. Fifteen years later, by 1500, Europeans had sailed around Africa and had established direct relations with India. They had discovered and explored the Americas, north and south. Portugal and Spain were laying the foundations of overseas empire. Once started, the movement was to continue until Europeans or their descendants controlled nearly the entire globe.

England played a minor part in that sudden unrolling of the map, but the story of what the other nations accomplished in exploration is essential here because of its tremendous bearing on later England. The shift of European maritime activity from the Mediterranean to the Atlantic changed her relative geographical importance. Hitherto remote on the outer edge of the European world, now she was to lie directly across the important new lines of sea communications to the new lands. England waited until others had experimented before entering wholeheartedly into the race for maritime and colonial power; but, once she started, she proved more successful than any of her rivals until eventually she controlled a full quarter of the earth's surface and a quarter of the earth's population. Just as the mingling of the races was the significant key to the early chapters of English history, and constitutional development made distinctive the middle portion, so maritime and colonial activity has been

England's particularly noteworthy achievement in the modern period.

Few episodes in history have been more fascinating and more far-reaching in their consequences than this expansion. Its high points may be compressed into five short periods of significant changes. The original explorations centered around 1500, when Portugal and Spain opened the new sea routes and commenced their empires. Exactly a century later three new rivals— England, Holland, and France—entered the colonial race. Holland took Portugal's best colonies, but was soon left behind. In 1689 England commenced the duel for empire which was to give her most of France's choicest possessions. The two decades before 1900 saw the feverish spread of a new imperialism into Africa and Asia. Finally, from 1947 onward, most of those same regions began to break loose from colonialism.

Spices stimulated the remarkable crop of early discoveries. Dreams of gold and glory or the spirit of crusading may have played their part, but the great captains sailed primarily to secure cargoes of the pepper, ginger, cinnamon, and nutmegs which grew on rich islands just southeast of Asia. Europe needed those spices in the days before refrigeration to make meat palatable. For centuries the spices had come to Europe by indirect routes. Arab traders had carried them to India and thence, part way by water and the rest of the way by caravan, to the eastern Mediterranean ports. There the Venetians and Genoese had secured the supply and had distributed it throughout Europe, amassing in the process the riches which helped to endow the glories of the Italian Renaissance. After 1400 the spread of Turkish power threatened to close the old caravan routes. The actual fall of Constantinople in 1453 has been overrated in this connection. More important, Europe was growing tired of paying the high prices of the Italians. A direct sea route to the source of the spices would reduce the cost

of transportation and cut out the profits of various middlemen. The opening of the new sea routes was to short-circuit the old, indirect Eastern trade and leave Venice and Genoa at one side. Yet the names of Columbus, Vespucius, the Cabots, and others show that some of the most prominent explorers who thus contributed to the decay of Italian trade were themselves Italians sailing under the flags of various Western nations.

It may seem strange that the two out-of-the-way nations, Portugal and Spain, took the lead in overseas enterprise. They were just emerging as compact states after seven centuries of intermittent fighting with the Moslem Moors who had occupied their peninsula and who had developed a high degree of civilization there. Little Portugal, remote in the west, was the first to drive out the Moors; following suit came the smaller Christian states of northern Spain, and finally a united Spain ejected the last of them. The restless energy hitherto spent in fighting infidels at home needed a new outlet. These states bordered on the Atlantic, and there lay their future.

If any one man started Europe's overseas expansion, it was Prince Henry "the Navigator," a younger son of the Portuguese king and his English queen. In the very year 1415, when one grandson of John of Gaunt was winning at Agincourt, this other grandson was laying the foundations for more lasting achievement. The seagoing English like to think that his maritime initiative came through his English mother. Prince Henry conceived the idea of sending ships around Africa to India. This would mean a further triumph of Christendom over Islam, and would add to the glory of Portugal. It would satisfy geographical curiosity as well; and, above all, it might prove extremely profitable by bringing spices direct by sea, thus eliminating the expensive freight and the middlemen's profits of the old indirect routes of the Italians. Retiring in 1415 to a bleak cape,

Henry devoted the rest of his life to the promotion of exploration, gathering the best available maps, shipbuilders, and mariners. Fortunately, he had ample resources; for exploration then, like space flights today, needed financial backing. Henry himself never "navigated," but for almost half a century he sent captain after captain down the west coast of Africa to find a way around to India.

It was slow work. The superstitious sailors believed the tales of boiling seas and terrific monsters. The actual terrors were bad enough. The invention of the mariner's compass, followed by that of the astrolabe, an ancestor of the sextant, for determining latitude by "shooting the sun," made it no longer necessary to hug the shore; but the clumsy, top-heavy ships were no larger than modern tugs. One captain declared that the sailors continually had the pumps in their hands and the Virgin Mary on their lips. It was a triumph for exploration when one of Henry's captains finally rounded a cape on the Moroccan coast. Thereafter things went a little faster. Gold and slaves were brought home, and merchants sent out expeditions in hope of profit. But Henry, wanting more than that, kept urging his captains to make new records. They had nearly reached the equator at his death in 1460.

His work bore rich fruit in the last years of the century. Early in 1488 Bartolomeu Dias worked around the stormy tip of Africa and found himself sailing up the eastern coast. That was only the means toward an end, for the Portuguese were interested in Africa only as the obstacle in their path eastward. For nearly four centuries Europe was to neglect Africa save for the slave trade. But now the way was clear for India, so that the king called that southern cape "Good Hope." Ten years later Vasco da Gama, continuing this route, at last arrived at the center of the spice trade in India. He loaded a heavy cargo of spices in spite of bitter opposition from the Arab merchants, who saw their long-standing trade threatened. Da Gama's leaking squadron, absent two years, finally limped back to Portugal. The cargo yielded a sixtyfold profit. Europe was relieved of dependence on the Arabs, caravans, and Italians. Portugal was on the threshold of a brief but brilliant imperial career.

Midway between the voyages of Dias and Da Gama, Christopher Columbus, apparently a Genoese, had made the most important of all explorations. The Portuguese had simply been paid agents, following out the plans laid down by Henry the Navigator. The world might be flat as far as they were concerned. Columbus was one of the minority in Europe who believed that it was round. He was a spice-hunter like the others, but he proposed to get his spices by sailing westward into the Atlantic. He tried persistently to "sell" his idea to someone who would give him the necessary financial backing. The Portuguese, intent upon the African route, rebuffed him. But Queen Isabella of Spain enabled him to equip three vessels by advancing the equivalent of five thousand dollars. From the financial standpoint that was to prove the most successful investment in history.

On October 12, 1492, ten weeks out from Spain, Columbus sighted one of the Bahama Islands. America was discovered—by accident. Columbus thought that it was Japan, with the Spice Islands of the Indies not far off. The names "Indians" and "West Indies" have come from his error. Spain went wild with joy, and laughed at the Portuguese who had been working nearly eighty years without results. The latter could only point out that Columbus had brought back no spices. The rest of his story is an anticlimax. He made three more voyages to the Caribbean, but he lacked the force and tact for successful administration of the new lands he had discovered. Even in the naming of the new continents he lost out to a second-rate explorer

Americus Vespucius, who had a better flair for publicity. The first voyage of Columbus, however, was probably the most significant in the whole history of exploration.

Two weeks before Da Gama started from Lisbon on his momentous voyage in 1497, the English flag had been planted on the shores of the New World. The initiative in this English exploration came from an Italian, known as Giovanni Caboto back in Genoa and Venice, but called John Cabot by Englishmen. He found financial backing from the merchants in the seaport of Bristol, who were interested in the Atlantic route because of the port's frequent fishing voyages to Iceland. Sales of English woolens in the Baltic, moreover, had given them surplus money to invest in new adventures. Henry VII gave Cabot and his sons "full and free authority, leave and power, upon their proper costs and charges, to seeke out, discover and finde whatsoever isles, countries, regions or provinces of the heathen and infidels, which before this time have been unknown to all Christians." Cabot sailed from Bristol with eighteen men in the little *Matthew*. Details of his voyages depend largely upon the account written many years later by his son Sebastian, who seems to have been somewhat of a liar. It appears likely that late in June, 1497, Cabot landed on the tip of Cape Breton Island and also sighted the larger island still known as Newfoundland. At any rate, he was back in England that summer a popular hero. "Vast honor is paid him," wrote a Venetian from London, "and he dresses in silk; and the English run after him like mad people." The king promised generous support for another expedition the next year "and has also given him money wherewith to amuse himself till then." The privy-purse accounts of the tight-fisted first Tudor contain the item "To hym that found the New Isle, £10." Henry also granted him a pension of £20 a year, which John seems to have lived only two years to enjoy. In 1498 he and Sebastian made a second voyage, apparently discovering Labrador and penetrating into artic regions, probably the pioneers in that long and dangerous quest for a "northwest passage" around the top of America to the Indies. Sebastian himself found a more liberal paymaster in the king of Spain, for whom he helped to open up the Rio de la Plata near the present city of Buenos Aires, in South America. Long afterward he returned to England, and as late as 1551 was promoting explorations of a "northeast passage" around the top of Europe. Bristol profited from its initiative and investments; for after the American colonies developed, it secured much of their trade and was for many years the second largest city in England.

In spite of this early start, England quickly dropped out of the expansion race for the time being. The Tudors were too busy with their Continental foreign policy, and the lands which the Cabots discovered were cold and barren, yielding neither spices nor precious metals. Yet those Cabot voyages revealed to England something that in the long run was to bring her more wealth than Portugal's pepper trade or Spain's silver mines. In the fogs off the Newfoundland coast lie the shallow Grand Banks, so teeming with cod that they are the best fishing grounds in the world. The Cabots, so Sebastian said, caught them simply by lowering buckets over the side. At any rate, Portuguese and Frenchmen, as well as Englishmen, almost immediately swarmed to the new fishing grounds and, in spite of cold, danger, and hard labor, made huge catches of cod, salted and dried them on the barren shores of Newfoundland, and returned with wealth wrested from the sea. When England a century later began to plant colonies in North America, she could claim the rights of discovery because of the Cabot voyages.

The third great voyage ranking with those of Columbus and Da Gama, was the circumnavigation of the earth by one of

Magellan's ships between 1519 and 1522. Balboa, a Spaniard, had crossed the Isthmus of Panama in 1513, and was the first European to see the Pacific Ocean. Six years later Spain sent a Portuguese mariner, Ferdinand Magellan, to find out what lay beyond the American continent. He discovered the strait which bears his name, and then pushed across the Pacific. Magellan himself was killed in the Philippines, but one of his ships continued through the East Indies and around the Cape of Good Hope, the first to sail around the world. By that time Europe had unrolled the map enough to realize the extent of the outside world, although there were still plenty of dark corners for men to explore.

Colonization followed close upon discovery. The nations which had backed the explorers proceeded to establish overseas empires, taking political and commercial control over the new lands which had been claimed in their names. As soon as Columbus returned in 1493, the Pope, as the highest international authority, divided all the lands beyond the seas between Spain and Portugal. As things worked out, with slight stretchings of this papal "line of demarcation," the Americas—except for the Portuguese Brazil—were Spain's and the East—except for the Spanish Philippines—was Portugal's. This decree theoretically excluded England from a share in overseas territory, but Henry VII disregarded it in authorizing Cabot's voyage, thereby alarming the Spanish envoy at the English court. Within forty more years England was to cast off papal authority, not only in geography but in religion as well. After that the papal decree was to last only as long as the guns of the Portuguese carracks and the Spanish galleons could uphold it.

From that day to this, European expansion in the tropics and in temperate regions has followed separate courses. The climate and products of the former led to colonies of exploitation, where an ever shifting handful of Europeans dominated vast numbers of natives. The temperate regions made possible colonies of settlement (see page 229). To these, European populations migrated to make permanent homes overseas. Men brought their families to the latter type of colonies, but almost never to the former. Some colonies, like part of Spanish America, represented a mixture of the two types.

Spain's vast empire included most of Central and South America and even extended into the southern part of the present United States. Ruthless, daring *conquistadores,* with their little bands, overcame the frightened natives, who had never before seen horses or guns. Rich silver and gold mines gave special importance to Mexico and to Peru, where the high-handed work of Cortes in 1519 and Pizarro in 1532 overthrew the semicivilized states of the Aztec and Inca Indians. The natives died like flies in the unaccustomed forced toil of mining, until a humane official introduced African Negroes in order to save the remaining Indians for Christianity. Spaniards came over by the thousands. Some, in the more temperate regions, managed to preserve a pure European strain down through the generations. But the majority had no scruples about promiscuous interbreeding, which led to a mixture of white, Indian, and Negro blood.

Government and trade were rigidly regulated in the sole interest of the mother country. Powerful viceroys at Lima and at Mexico City passed on to the local governors orders from the king and the Council of the Indies at home. Trade was limited to annual fleets of galleons. A few companies secured control of commerce, to the exclusion of all foreigners and even of Spanish free traders. Silver and gold poured into Spain, the king receiving his royal fifth. This helped to make Spain the leading power of Europe in the sixteenth century; but it led to an abnormal jump in prices, and it made the Spaniards scornful of humdrum industry.

Portugal, in the meantime, was building up a somewhat different sort of empire in the East. It was out of the question to dominate those lands of ancient culture and well-developed civilizations as completely as Spain was dominating America. The Portuguese empire therefore became a series of armed trading posts, with little political authority over the interior. The center was Goa, in western India. Under the stimulus of Alfonso Albuquerque, Portugal's power soon spread all along the coasts of India, into the Spice Islands, where the cinnamon and pepper grew, and even to China, where she gained a permanent foothold, in addition to stations along the African coast. Those thousands of miles of her scattered coastal claims were held together only by sea power and a few garrisons.

The Portuguese people did not settle in India to any extent, for they were not numerous enough. A steady succession of officials spent three-year terms amassing as much money as they could. With them went a swarm of ne'er-do-wells who could live in a style far beyond anything possible at home. Very few Portuguese women migrated to India, so that a race of half-breeds was inevitable. Saint Francis Xavier and other churchmen tried to spread Christianity, but the natives were more impressed by the cruel arrogance of the average Portuguese. Trade, as in the case of Spain, was confined to the annual fleets which carried the spices to Lisbon. The king conducted the entire business as his private monopoly, but dishonest officials pocketed more than half the profits.

Those beginnings overseas were an important part of what has been called the "Commercial Revolution." During the transition from medieval to modern times European economic life underwent several significant changes. Business outgrew its old local character. England and the other monarchies organized commerce on a national basis, with the government regulat-

ing and encouraging it. This led to the decline of those old cities unrelated to strong states, especially Venice and the other Italian cities as well as the Hanseatic towns of the north. To provide the sinews of war in that day of mercenary soldiers, a well-filled treasury was considered essential. And the more prosperous the population the more it could pay in taxes and customs duties. In alliance with the businessmen, the new monarchs utilized the national resources of legislation, diplomacy, and even war to improve business conditions and to acquire colonies. Out of this grew the so-called "mercantile system," which reached its prime in the later seventeenth century (see page 226).

The English kings, having achieved a fairly centralized government ahead of their Continental rivals, had for a considerable time been using the machinery of government to stimulate business on a national basis (see pages 130 ff.). Now England was trying also to secure the additional profits which come from freight charges paid for carrying exports and imports. The English merchant marine was small, and even when Englishmen traded abroad they frequently had to hire foreign vessels. In 1381, early in the reign of Richard II, Parliament had passed a "navigation act" forbidding exports except in English ships. This was premature for there were not enough such ships to handle the trade, and the law could not be rigidly enforced. Its renewal under the first Tudor was also not carried out to the letter; but it was the forerunner of the celebrated Navigation Acts of 1651 and 1660, which finally did much to build up England's maritime supremacy (see pages 247, 263). From the fourteenth century also came efforts to establish England's "sovereignty of the seas," partly so as to reduce piracy and to extend the king's peace to adjacent waters. This led to the practice of forcing foreign vessels in those waters to dip their flags to the English as a symbol of this authority.

The hectic years of the middle fifteenth century saw little advance in this economic legislation. Gradually the English extended their commerce, however, with Bristol becoming rich in selling woolen cloth to Baltic ports. Edward IV did something to stimulate trade, although he extended still further the privileges of the Hanse in return for loans. The first Tudor adopted a positive policy of expanding England's influence on the seas. Besides having encouraged Cabot in his voyages of discovery, he began to develop a regular royal navy, in place of the haphazard gathering of armed merchantmen from the Cinque Ports and elsewhere in wartime. He likewise showed himself a modern king by his persistent use of legislation and diplomacy to increase England's commerce. A treaty with the king of Denmark promoted trade with Scandinavia and Iceland at the expense of the Hanse. There were treaties with some of the Hanse towns themselves, but more often there were reprisals and discriminatory duties. Efforts were made to break the Venetian commercial hold by dealing with rival Italian cities. A treaty with Flanders, known as the " Great Intercourse," removed many of the artificial barriers of trade with that region, which was still a valuable market. Within a hundred years the Flemish, the Venetians, and the Hanseatic League would pass from their old leadership of European commerce, as those city units were overshadowed by the new national economic systems. Altogether, two centuries of national endeavor had transformed England's economic role and had pointed the way for her to develop into "a nation of shopkeepers," "the workshop of the world," and "mistress of the seas."

The new era saw England, as well as the rest of Europe, coming more and more to a cash basis. In the earlier Middle Ages the relationship between lord and vassal and lord and serf had been based on personal service; now payments were made instead. The influx of precious metals vastly increased the amount of available money. Finance was becoming more important as a separate sphere of economic activity. The earlier functions of the Jews and Lombards were expanding until moneylenders developed on such a scale that they could sometimes determine whether or not a monarch might fight. Antwerp, with its flourishing commerce and its stock exchange, was the important financial center of the sixteenth century, to be followed by Amsterdam and then by London. The Italians had developed drafts and other forms of commercial paper which made it possible to conduct distant transactions without the actual constant transfer of bullion. Previously, borrowed money had not been generally used for productive purposes; men now realized that a judicious use of capital and credit could lead to the production of new wealth. England, however, lagged behind Italy, Germany, and the Low Countries in the development of banking.

Centralized Royal Governments

A third great change was the growth of national states with strong, centralized monarchical governments. In the Middle Ages, with its feudal organizations, wherein the great holdings of the barons sometimes rivaled the royal domain, men were apt to think of themselves primarily not as Englishmen or Frenchmen but as men of Kent or Cornwall, of Brittany or Anjou. In England this decentralization was not as marked as on the Continent; for William the Conqueror, Henry II, Edward I, and others had set the example of strong central government. The troubled times of the fifteenth century, however, had almost thrown England back into the old feudal disorder.

Gradually, various forces had worked to exalt the monarchs at the expense of the nobles. Many of the feudal lords perished in the Crusades, in the Hundred Years' War, and in such local fighting as the Wars of the Roses. Not only were those troublesome individuals removed but their estates often went to swell the royal domain. The protracted fighting of the Hundred Years' War served, too, to increase the feeling of national patriotism. The victories of Crécy and Poitiers had given Englishmen a national pride; Joan of Arc had done much to produce the same result in France. The long centuries of fighting the Moors had engendered a similar national feeling in Portugal and in the Christian kingdoms of northern Spain. The substitution of professional armies of mercenaries for the inadequate feudal levies had also been accelerated by these long struggles. Thus the original basis of the feudal system, land tenure in return for military service, gradually disappeared. The remaining lords, however, although they had lost the original justification for their generous holdings, clung to their privileges for centuries until, in some cases, they were dispossessed by revolution. Only an ample royal treasury could afford these new armies of mercenaries, so that one more bulwark was built about the growing royal power. Just as the rise of infantry was diminishing the value of the man on horseback, so the use of gunpowder further weakened the position of the fuedal lords; for the new cannon of the royal siege trains could batter down their hitherto almost impregnable castles. As the nobles declined in power the kings found good allies in the men of the rising middle class, who were excellent potential taxpayers and who favored strong government because it was good for business. With the tendency toward increased royal absolutism, national assemblies such as the French Estates-General gradually lost their power; even the English Parliament was to lose its influence temporarily. Administration, military control, justice, and finance passed from feudal into royal hands.

In the late fifteenth century two large European states—France and Spain—and one small one—Portugal—were also reaching this status of strong centralized monarchies. The French king Louis XI (1461-1483) had utilized the feeling of nationalism aroused by Joan of Arc and the close of the Hundred Years' War to enhance his power. Using craft and cunning against his barons, he further extended the royal domain so that before his death Brittany, the last of the semi-independent provinces, was brought under the control of the crown. Spain, the leading nation of Europe during the coming century, was united by the marriage of the rulers of her two energetic northern Christian kingdoms, Ferdinand of Aragon and Isabella of Castile, who soon completed the centuries-old fight against the Moors by capturing their last stronghold in 1492. The Holy Roman Empire, on the other hand, the loose government of the German and Austrian lands, was too decentralized to become a real national state until the nineteenth century; but the emperors, generally chosen from the Hapsburg family, enjoyed a powerful position in Austria and their other hereditary lands which they had been building up by marrying heiresses. By 1500 one of these marriages was to join these extensive holdings to the strongly centralized Spanish monarchy by the accession of Charles V (see page 176). Likewise Italy was made up of small states and was not united until the nineteenth century. The old Eastern, or Byzantine, Empire was experiencing autocracy from her new Turkish masters, but included too many diverse peoples for nationalism. Russia was just beginning to free herself from centuries of rule by the Tatars in China. The Scandinavian countries were developing into two monarchies: Sweden and Denmark (including Norway). Poland, long a powerful state, was following meanwhile a trend quite different from that of the west by disintegrating under an excess of feudalism.

Tudor Beginnings

In England, the nationalistic spirit had developed during the long war with France, while the Wars of the Roses had eliminated many feudal lords. The country, weary of the pointless civil war, craved peace and order, and by this time was ready to forgo some of its liberty to that end. A strong king was needed to accomplish this, and England found him in Henry VII. Although only twenty-eight at the time of his accession, he was old beyond his years, hardened by exile, intrigue, and disappointed hopes. Lean, sharp-featured, hardheaded, Henry had neither the presence nor the personality that makes for popularity; but England did not ask for a popular or romantic king in that hour of disordered confusion.

At this distance the steps by which Henry VII built up the new royal power may be traced; but it must be remembered that to the men of his day he was for a while simply another temporarily successful dynastic rival who had gained the throne by one battle and might lose it by another. Fifteenth-century England had seen so many rapid rises and falls that it was some time before the Tudor line was accepted as a fixture. In many respects the role of Henry VII resembled that of Henry II. Both found England in feudal turmoil; both quickly restored law and order and then proceeded to make lasting contributions to the development of their country. Both have been overshadowed in popular reputation by their sons, whose spectacular achievements were made possible only by the substantial but less showy achievements of the fathers. Like Henry VII, too, in shrewdness, unromantic realism, and strength, were his Continental contemporaries who also were laying the foundations for the glory of later generations—the kings of France and Spain and, to a lesser degree, the Holy Roman Emperor. So far as policy was concerned, the rule of the Yorkist Edward IV had much in common with that of the Tudors; but England was not quite ready for it then, and Edward IV too often sacrificed business to pleasure (see page 149).

Henry lost no time in establishing his

Henry VII, in 1505, by an unknown Flemish artist.

position. Six weeks after Bosworth Field, writs were sent out for a new Parliament. It took time, in those days of wretched roads, for the writs to reach the borders of Scotland and Wales and for lords and commons slowly to assemble, but in two months more the first Tudor Parliament met at Westminster. The Tudors were to keep Parliament in the passive role into which it had fallen under the Yorkists. They respected the old forms, but, for a whole century to come, Parliament's role consisted chiefly in acquiescence to royal wishes. The Council, a small group of officials and nobles with important executive and advisory functions, tended to overshadow Parliament in influence throughout the Tudor period. Henry's first Parliament complacently gave him his royal title without saying much about the embarrassing point of hereditary right to the throne. The votes of Lords and Commons simply ratified the verdict of battle, and the *de facto* king became king *de jure*.

Not content with Parliamentary sanction alone, Henry strengthened his position by marriage. Just as Henry I had married into the Saxon line to widen the hereditary background of the royal house, so Henry VII, representative of the Red Rose, married a representative of the White Rose, Elizabeth of York, daughter of Edward IV, to whom he had been earlier betrothed. The birth of a son (Arthur) in whose veins flowed the blood of York as well as of Lancaster served to bring the rival factions closer together, although the reconciliation was not complete.

The three main problems facing Henry were the suppression of the nobles, the filling of the treasury, and the improvement of foreign relations. Sterile as they had been on the whole, the Wars of the Roses had accomplished something by killing or driving into exile many of the turbulent lords. When Henry's first Parliament met, there were only eighteen lay nobles in the House of Lords, whereas there were thirty spiritual peers. Some of these surviving nobles, however, were strong enough to give trouble, for the legislation of a century earlier had been ineffective in suppressing the evils of "livery and maintenance" (see page 137). To break up the private armies of the nobles, Henry set up a special tribunal, composed of the Council together with the two Chief Justices, and authorized to handle cases without any hampering common-law precedents. The most arrogant noble could not browbeat such a court; and it brought to heel one stubborn offender after another. This Court of Star Chamber (so called from the room where it generally met) was the first of several special Tudor tribunals created to meet particular emergencies. Although the later abuse of their special powers led to the abolition of those courts, they were very effective in the immediate situations for which they were designed. Peace gradually settled upon the counties. Members of the old nobility who escaped with a simple clipping of their wings were lucky, for many were heavily fined and some were executed. Few members of the English peerage can trace their titles farther back than 1485; for the House of Lords was gradually filled with "new men," lesser landholders and the middle-class men of business, whose interests coincided more closely with those of the king.

Henry found the royal coffers bare when he came to the throne; when he died, twenty-four years later, they were so full that their contents were estimated at £1,-300,000 to £1,800,000, "the richest treasury in Christendom." It was a strange phenomenon to find a king who could not only balance his budget but also salt away a considerable surplus nearly every year, yet with a minimum of Parliamentary grants. He did not want to antagonize the middle class, whose support he desired, by asking too much from the House of Commons, where that group was strongly represented. Only five times in his whole reign did he request the Lords and Commons for money —only twice in his last eighteen years. He managed to do this by rigid economy, which at times degenerated into stinginess; by his regular income from crown lands and customs duties; by the acquisition of escheated lands of dead men; and by irregular high-pressure methods of extortion, which represent the seamy side of the picture. The crown lands now yielded about £100,000 a year. The customs duties, which Parliament granted him for life, were worth about £30,000 a year at the beginning; but Henry so encouraged commerce that the figure had risen to some £40,000 by the end of the reign. The extortions caused bitter complaints. The name of his bishop-chancellor appeared in a tax-collecting device called "Morton's fork," by which, in the words of Francis Bacon, "the sparing were to be pressed for money because they saved, the lavish because they spent." The brunt of the odium fell upon Henry's two overzealous and unscrupulous lawyers, Sir Richard Empson and Edmund Dudley, who continually dragged out the most flimsy pretexts to fine and confiscate in the king's interest. One of the first popular acts of Henry's son was to execute this hated pair; but without their work the treasury would certainly not have been so full.

Henry constantly had to keep his eyes beyond the borders. The time would come when he would play high politics with France and Spain; but first he had to watch the dangerous pro-Yorkist hostility closer at hand in Scotland and Ireland, as well as in Flanders, where the dowager duchess of Burgundy, Margaret, sister of Edward IV, was an implacable enemy.

These three immediate foes struck at him by launching two Yorkist pretenders. The first, posing as Edward's nephew, who was Henry's prisoner in the Tower, appeared in 1487 in the person of one Lambert Simnel, simple son of an Oxford tradesman. Coached by a priest, he received an enthusiastic reception and coronation in disaffected Ireland, and then crossed to England, backed by a force of German mercenaries sent by the duchess Margaret. Henry crushed the invaders in a single battle and sent Simnel to work in the royal kitchens. Five years later, with the murder of Edward's sons in the Tower still a debated question, a more persistent and dangerous pretender, Perkin Warbeck, made a natural appeal to the popular mind posing as the younger prince. With strong Continental backing, he intrigued for five years. Three attacks in his name were blocked; and general disaffection caused a mob of Cornish miners to march on London. Henry's spies, however, kept close track of the intrigues; and by 1497 Warbeck submitted to the king, who had him executed two years later.

In connection with Scotland and Ireland, Henry took steps which foreshadowed England's later relations with those British neighbors. The Warbeck affair had led to

Scottish invasions. Henry tried to relieve this menace by arranging in 1502 a marriage between his elder daughter Margaret and James IV, king of Scotland. Some of his advisers warned him that it might lead to the absorption of England in Scotland; but Henry, citing the case of Normandy, pointed out that "the greater would draw the less." So it resulted; for that marriage brought the great-grandson of James and Margaret southward as England's first Stuart king just a hundred and one years later.

Ireland, on the other hand, was reminded more strongly than ever that she was a dependency of England. Relations had been irregular for many years, and Yorkist Ireland supported both pretenders. Henry sent over a capable soldier, Sir Edward Poynings, who was unsuccessful in subduing the wild outlying provinces, but who managed to get some important legislation through the Irish parliament in the "Pale." These "Poynings's Laws" of 1494, later heartily damned by the Irish, made their parliament definitely subordinate to the English crown and to the English Parliament. It could meet only when the crown agreed, and take up only such legislation as the crown approved; whereas all English Parliamentary laws were valid in Ireland, even if counter to Irish acts.

In foreign affairs Henry dabbled steadily in international diplomacy of the trickiest sort. He held his own fairly well against astute rivals, although many of his wily schemes came to nothing. In 1489, desiring the prestige of a first-class alliance, he joined with the crafty Ferdinand of Spain, who wanted English help in acquiring some French territory in the Pyrenees. This was sealed by the betrothal of two infants, Henry's first-born Arthur, and Catherine of Aragon, daughter of Ferdinand and Isabella—a match, like the Scottish, destined to have important consequences. Henry successfully bargained for a heavy dowry.

Only once did matters lead to declared

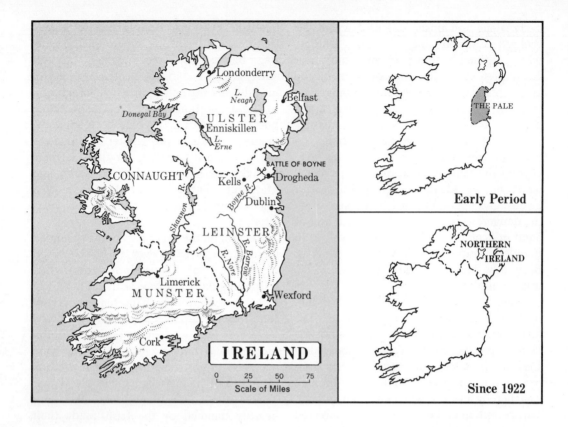

Londonderry
L. Neagh
Belfast
Donegal Bay
ULSTER
Enniskillen
L. Erne
BATTLE OF BOYNE
CONNAUGHT
Kells
Drogheda
Shannon R.
Boyne R.
Dublin
LEINSTER
R. Nore
R. Barrow
Limerick
MUNSTER
Wexford
Cork

IRELAND

0   25   50   75
Scale of Miles

THE PALE

Early Period

NORTHERN IRELAND

Since 1922

war, and then it was a war of a mercenary, unromantic type that would have made Richard Cœur de Lion and the Black Prince turn in their graves. The campaign of 1492 was glorified blackmail. Henry secured a very generous war grant from Parliament, and then, in the very week when Columbus reached America, crossed to France with a large force. He laid siege to Boulogne, not particularly wanting it but aware that France was so busy in preparing to invade Italy that she would not want to be bothered with an English war. To Henry's gratification and his army's disgust, he was bought off before any serious bloodshed occurred, as Edward IV had been twelve years before (see page 150).

Economic and Social Changes

Whereas the changes of overseas expansion, the new learning, and the strong national monarchies affected other European nations as well as England, two economic innovations, the "enclosure movement" and the "domestic system," were quite distinctively English and also influenced the life of many Englishmen (see page 132).

Like much else in England's early economic life, both were closely connected with wool. The increasing demand for it, both for domestic manufacture and for export, had given great impetus to the enclosure movement, which was to produce grave consequences throughout the Tudor period. Under the old manorial system, which had continued with the simple substitution of cash payments in place of forced service, a considerable part of the manor land was used in common (see page 46). This unchanging system of agriculture was so inefficient and wasteful that it produced little more than subsistence for the workers. Shrewd landowners, observing the riches which had come to the Cistercian monks through their raising of sheep and selling of wool, realized how much more productive the common lands on their estates could be. The word "enclosure" came from the practice of fencing off the former common lands and thus excluding the peasants from their share in the meadows, woods, and even much of the cultivated land. They might be left with small plots for their own cultivation, but no longer could their livestock run at large. A manor which might have had fifty peasants tilling the soil under the old system would need only three or four shepherds to tend the sheep on those same acres; yet the wool from those sheep would be worth much more than the former meager products of the soil.

There had been some enclosures in England as early as the thirteenth century, but with the Tudor period the process became very general. Sheep raising was particularly adapted to the barren north country, but the practice spread over much of the nation. By 1600 about half the manors of England, it was estimated, had experienced in some degree enclosing for sheep raising. It is easy to understand why the landlords desired enclosures, and it was the landowners who sat in Parliament and dominated local government. But the new process meant a tremendous dislocation of the former agricultural workers, who were rudely displaced with nowhere to go. For a whole century the roads were filled with "lusty beggars" and wandering rogues, while the weaker unemployed, left in the villages, had scant means of holding body and soul together. Two centuries later England was to have another epidemic of enclosures—that time for more efficient raising of crops (see pages 332 ff.).

These economic developments were partly responsible for certain shifts in the importance and well-being of the various social classes in Tudor England. In the main, the "new men" of the middle groups profited at the expense of the peasantry and nobles. The squires, or country gentry, rose in prosperity and power; so too, to a lesser degree, did the "middle class" proper, the businessmen of the towns, engaged in trade or industry. Henry VII was deliberately interested in beating down the power of the great nobles, and, at the same time, did little to prevent the exploitation of the peasantry.

While typical members of these various social groups may easily be identified, class lines were not drawn as rigidly in England as they were in France or most other parts of the Continent. In the Middle Ages both England and France had had their fighting feudal aristocracy, their suppressed serfs, and their small group of middle-class townsmen. In France those sharp distinctions still continued; a man was a nobleman or he was not, and a vast gulf in prestige, privilege, and mode of life existed between social classes. The unprivileged paid most of the taxes and did all the work, but were not allowed to participate to any extent in the government. In England, there was, to be sure, a difference between "gentle" and "simple" folk; but the social frontiers were hazier, blending all the way from dukes down to farm laborers, and also were easier to cross. England was consequently more of a unit and was better able to escape the terrible revolt against the privileged noble caste which was later to tear France apart.

The difference between the English and French social systems was particularly noticeable and significant in the case of the lower and most numerous ranks of the landed aristocracy. On both sides of the Channel they enjoyed the leisure and social position that came from the family possession of land. In France this lower aristocracy all held titles of nobility and as such formed a distinct caste. In England titles were of less consequence. Many of the lesser peers differed little from the squires, or gentlemen, whose acres might be just as extensive. A small group of important Englishmen held the titles of duke, marquess, earl, viscount, or baron, which entitled them to membership in the House of Lords. They alone, strictly speaking, comprised the English nobility, or peerage. The king might create as many new peers as he saw fit; but the power was used sparingly, and the House of Lords never exceeded a few hundred in size. Another influence which kept the peerage small was the fact that the English title descended only to the eldest son—"the first of the litter," as a later statesman sneered at the House of Lords. Edward I, as we have seen, had helped to crystallize this practice of primogeniture and entail, whereby the family lands as well as the title went intact to the eldest son. The younger sons were commoners, with no automatic social rank or privilege beyond what they might achieve for themselves, and were free to carry their heritage of class into many diverse fields. It was through them in particular that the English social system came to possess more flexible features than the Continental. In France, and elsewhere on the Continent, every son of a nobleman was a nobleman also, rigidly limited by caste in the occupations which he might select. The class thus increased in geometric ratio, until in Poland, as an extreme case, it was estimated that there was a nobleman for every four acres of land.

The bulk of the landed aristocracy in England were known simply as "gentlemen" or "squires." A few might enjoy knighthood and prefix "Sir" to their names; the majority at the most might use "Esquire" or "Gent." after their names. The term "gentleman," however, was used in a more restricted sense in those days, generally implying a good family and a fair amount of property, together with the possession of a family coat of arms and the theoretical right to challenge even an earl to a duel.

With the curbing of the Nevilles, the Percys, and the other proud and tempestuous feudal lords, the gentry came into their own in the Tudor period and remained the dominant element in English political as well as social life until the nineteenth century. Their rise, to be sure, had extended over several centuries (see pages 24, 169). They were counterparts of the Saxon thanes and Norman men at arms who had received land in return for military service. Although that original reason for their landholding had begun to disappear with the introduction of scutage in the twelfth century, they still retained the power and profit which went with lordship of the manor. The Black Death had accelerated the substitution of cash for service in the manorial relationship. The abolition of the monasteries under Henry VIII, moreover, was to give many townsmen, previously engaged in trade or industry, an opportunity to improve their social position by acquiring landed estates.

These landholders formed a leisure class, for their rents gave them an income without exertion on their part. Most of them were content with life on their estates, but some joined the lively, ambitious group at court. This was a period of elaborate and costly dress. As the century progressed, broad neck ruffs, together with tights for the men, made costumes even more extreme. More than one good grove of oaks was slashed down so that the owner and his wife might cut a proper figure at court. Such outlay might, however, prove a good investment, and Englishmen then as now were good gamblers. The Tudor monarchs favored "new men"; and the experience of the Seymour and Cecil families is an indication of how high country squires might rise if they made the most of their opportunities in the royal presence. Many a family fortune of later days was based upon the cleverness and presence of mind of some ancestor who had used his head at court in Tudor times.

The true habitat of the squire, however, was not the glittering society of London, Windsor, or Hampton Court. The typical country gentleman spent most of his days on his estate, in close contact with his

Typical Tudor country house: Charlcotte Hall, the home of Sir Hampton Lucy, in Shakespeare's Stratford-on-Avon.

tenants and retainers and with a social circle generally limited to the other "county families." Some squires might take an active interest in the raising of crops on the demesne land with hired laborers; many, however, found it simpler to lease the demesne to tenant farmers. A considerable part of the squire's ample leisure was spent in chasing the deer, the hare, or, later, the fox with horse and dogs, or birds with trained hawks.

The country houses took on a new charm in the Tudor period. The stately "great hall" of the older manor houses gave way to more comfortable and livable quarters in which elaborate staircases and rich oak paneling were prominent features. Glass windows began to come into common use. These Tudor countryseats, often long and rambling, with broad chimneys, were sometimes built of stone or were half-timbered with oak and plaster; but most common

was warm, red brick. Altogether they were a happy adaptation of the Renaissance to the spirit of the English squirearchy.

These same hard-hunting, hard-drinking squires controlled England's local government in the rural districts until late in the nineteenth century. In the earlier Middle Ages, we remember, they had enjoyed some local power through their manorial courts; but the kings had relied primarily upon the sheriffs as their direct representatives in running the shires (see page 49). As time went on, however, those functions passed more and more into the hands of the gentry, who exercised them not as feudal individuals but as unpaid justices of the peace, definitely commissioned by the central government and theoretically subject to the king and his Council. While major legal cases were usually held for the periodic assizes, at which the itinerant royal judges presided, the ordinary run of court work was in the hands of these squire-justices. Such a justice could settle minor cases alone, without a jury, and could bind offenders over for regular court trial, administering bail if he saw fit. For cases too grave for such summary jurisdiction but not weighty enough for the King's Bench assizes, there were the county "quarter sessions" four times a year, presided over by two or more of the justices of the peace. In addition to their legal work, the justices of the peace had supervision of the collection of taxes and served as officers of the militia. In fact, they were the agents for carrying out locally nearly everything, affecting the immediate community, enacted by Parliament or decreed by the central government. They had been entrusted with the administration of the old Statute of Laborers and would be given extensive further duties in carrying out the social and economic legislation of the later Tudor period. This service was rendered without pay, but sense of duty or love of influence provided an adequate supply of such "J. P's." The work gave the country gentlemen prestige and valuable experience. A trained bureaucracy of royal officials of the French type would doubtless have been more efficient; but England in that case might not have had its unique record of thwarting an absolute monarchy at such an early period.

The Tudor tendency toward autocracy prevailed only because it rested upon the approval of the majority of these country gentlemen who administered local government. The crown possessed no standing army or other adequate force under its own control, and its decrees could never have been enforced unless these amateur administrators out in the counties had seen fit to do so. Their political role was not limited to the sphere of local government. They were gradually taking over the House of Commons and formed a majority of the Privy Council, all-important in Tudor administration (see page 195).

The preparation for this life of the country gentleman involved more education in Tudor times than it had in previous centuries. An increasing number attended Oxford and Cambridge, and there were protests that the young aristocrats were crowding out the sons of the poor who had formerly sought a university training as preparation for the Church. Many others, too, attended the Inns of Court in preparation for their work as justices of the peace. With some, foreign travel also was a part of the preparation, and already many were taking what would later be called the "Grand Tour," bringing back from France or Italy new ideas of the Renaissance. With the system of primogeniture, only the eldest son, as we have seen, looked forward to inheriting the estates, with the comfortable life of a peer or a squire; and his younger brothers, because of this unique feature of the English social system, had to shift for themselves. The favorite fields for younger sons in later days were army, navy, and Church; but in Tudor times the armed forces rested on too uncertain a basis to give career opportunities. London offered openings to engage in law or business, which were taboo for the aristocracy on the Continent. This did much to break down the class lines between the gentry and the middle class and between manor and town. Just as the squire might have sons in business and law, so many a prosperous townsman of humbler birth was able to purchase an estate and become a squire himself. An heiress, moreover, whose fortune came from woolens or the Levant trade was no mean match for a young squire.

While the gentry were rising to their position of importance in Tudor times, that same middle class was also steadily improving its position. The "domestic system" of cloth manufacture made possible the accumulation of capital far beyond the normal wealth of a master craftsman of the Middle Ages, while England's constantly expanding foreign commerce led to fortunes in London, Bristol, and other ports.

The ambitious middle-class youth had before him several marked examples of such success: "Jack of Newbury," who was said to have employed a thousand workers in the woolen industry; William Canynge of Bristol, with his scores of ships and hundreds of sailors, extending English commerce into new fields; and, more important in legend than in fact, Dick Whittington, Lord Mayor of London. There had been, to be sure, a Richard Whittington who became a wealthy merchant and Lord Mayor of the City; but he was the son of a prosperous squire rather than the legendary poor orphan whose sole capital was his cat. Nevertheless, the active middle class, interested keenly in making money, were steadily to gain in prosperity and prestige until finally they challenged the squires for control of England in the early nineteenth century.

The last years of Henry's reign were somewhat of an anticlimax. Some attribute this to the death of his wife in 1503. At any rate, most of Henry's constructive work was accomplished before that time, and most of the meaner and more sordid phases of his reign fall within the later years. He made a fool of himself in his fruitless quest for a second wife, even going so far as to talk of marrying his widowed Spanish daughter-in-law; for Arthur had died a few months after that marriage in 1501, and Henry wanted to be sure that the dowry remained in England. But, at the worst, Henry was only somewhat ridiculous and somewhat more grasping than before; if England did not continue to go ahead as she had done in his earlier years, at least she did not slip back. The kingdom which he left to his son Henry in 1509 was an immeasurably stronger, happier, and more prosperous country than it had been when he took it over on the day of Bosworth.

What was true of this first Tudor's reign was to be re-enacted in later Tudor reigns, so that it is no exaggeration to call the battle of Bosworth Field a turning point in English history ranking close behind the dates of 1066 and 1688. The three great Tudors—Henry VII, his son Henry VIII (1509-1547), and Elizabeth I (1558-1603), his most successful grandchild and England's greatest queen—managed to combine force with a remarkable tact in understanding and handling people. They gave the English an almost absolute rule and made them like it. Their word was virtually law, but only because they had sense enough to know what England needed and wanted. Their absolutism was always disguised by respect for traditional forms; for they preserved Parliament, though they were generally able to obtain the votes they needed from it. Their ability stands out all the more clearly when one contrasts it with the stubborn blundering of the Stuart kings who were to follow them. It is much to the glory of the Tudor family that the first one, on coming to the throne in 1485, found the country disrupted by feudal anarchy, the treasury empty, trade disorganized, and foreign prestige at low ebb, but that when the fifth and last Tudor died, in 1603, England had a stable, powerful government, order and prosperity at home, and deep respect abroad, and was experiencing the greatest period of her history.

Chapter Ten · 1509-1558

Tudor Politics and Religion

The cold, calculating Henry VII had never been able to arouse spontaneous enthusiasm, but the reverse was true of his eighteen-year-old son, Henry VIII. The political security, foreign prestige, and financial surplus laboriously built up by the first Tudor, however, made possible a spectacular reign for the second. "Nature could not have done more for him," wrote the Venetian ambassador. "He is much handsomer than any other sovereign in Christendom. . . ." Young Henry could wear out eight or ten horses in jousting and the hunt; he was an enthusiast at tennis. His zest for heavy feasting had not yet begun to ruin his figure. He was a good musician, could speak four languages, and was so able and so enthusiastic a scholar that he roused high hopes among the intellectuals. His charm of manner and personal magnetism won loyal support from all sides. England in 1509 did not foresee the later Henry, grown fat and coarse, with an inflexible will which could smash the papal hold on England, and a violent temper which made it equally perilous to serve him as a minister or as a wife. In the meantime the nation cheered the news that one of the young king's first acts was to execute his father's lawyer-ministers, Empson and Dudley, whose legal extortions had helped to amass the royal

treasure which Henry was to spend with a lavish hand.

For the time being, the king left most of the details of government in the capable hands of the ministers inherited from his father. Occasionally he spoke with force and authority, but most of his time was spent in sport and revelry. The internal affairs of the kingdom were running smoothly, so that the main interest in the first part of Henry's reign centered in foreign relations.

Italy was in the foreground as the "battleground of Europe." Ever since a French invasion in 1494 had shown how easily it might be conquered, there had been a scramble for possession or control of the peninsula. Its wealth from trade made it a tempting prize; its many political divisions laid it open to plunder. As an Austrian minister sneeringly remarked three centuries later, Italy was simply a "geographical expression." Foremost among its numerous states was the rich, strategically located region around Milan, in the north. The maritime republic of Venice also owned enough north-Italian land to excite envy. The Pope, as ruler of a strip running diagonally across central Italy, often seemed more interested in local politics than in religion. Then, too, there was the larger, but poorer, state including Naples, southern Italy, and Sicily, and known as the Kingdom of Naples or the Two Sicilies. It was a glorious but hectic period in Italian history. In the very years when Raphael, Michelangelo, and Leonardo da Vinci were producing immortal masterpieces of art and when Machiavelli was embodying the realistic principles of Renaissance statecraft in his *Prince,* the mercenaries of France and Spain were struggling to bring as much of Italy as possible under foreign domination.

England had no positive interest in securing Italian territory for herself. France and Spain, however, each hoped that an English attack might distract the other from her Italian designs, or that England, with her well-filled treasury, might at least assume the role of "paymaster of the allies," which was to become a familiar British function in the future. In this game young Henry was pitted at first against three crafty men with whom his father had matched wits: Ferdinand (Isabella had died), who still ruled Aragon and controlled Spain; Maximilian, the Hapsburg Holy Roman Emperor; and Louis XII of France. This veteran trio expected to take advantage of the impetuous inexperience of England's new king.

Henry's first foreign venture confirmed their hopes. He still clung to his father's Spanish alliance, which had been cemented by his own marriage to his brother's widow, Catherine, daughter of Ferdinand and Isabella. Ferdinand in 1512 induced Henry to send an expedition to the Bay of Biscay in the hope of regaining some of the lost lands of Guienne. There was mutiny on the expedition; it accomplished nothing; and Henry realized that his foxy old father-in-law had used him for a cat's-paw.

The next year, however, Henry in person crossed the Channel, besieged and captured two towns, and won an encounter at Guinegate, called "the Battle of the Spurs" because of the speed with which the French knights fled from the field. Three weeks later, against the Scots, England won an

Henry VIII, in 1540, one of the many English portraits by Hans Holbein.

even more decisive victory. Following tradition, the Scots had headed for England as soon as the English sailed for France. They came down the east coast, crossed the Tweed, allowed themselves to be maneuvered out of a strong position, and were crushed on Flodden Field, a battle in which they lost their king and the flower of their nobility. That summer's fighting of 1513 restored England's international prestige. A peace was arranged with France, which included the marriage of Henry's lively eighteen-year-old sister Mary to Louis XII, who died within three months.

Francis I, Charles V, and Wolsey

Ferdinand and Maximilian followed Louis to the grave by 1519, to be succeeded by two men who were even younger than Henry and whose names were to be intimately associated with his for some thirty years. In 1515 the French crown passed to

Francis I, who ruled until his death in 1547, two months after Henry. Francis, like Henry, was an enthusiastic sportsman and athlete, loved pageantry and dancing, prided himself upon his physical prowess, and was, besides, a liberal patron of the Renaissance arts. He was brave in battle, a place where Henry, for all the vaunted Tudor courage, never appeared personally. Vacillating and irresolute, he was much influenced by women, of whom there were, in his debauched career, a larger number than in that of the much-married English king.

Marriages and deaths put in the hands of Charles V a combination of lands greater in extent than those of his contemporaries, Henry and Francis, combined. His vast heritage was the culmination of the marriage policy of the House of Hapsburg, whose diplomats were always on the lookout for eligible heiresses. A single marriage might determine the political destiny of a region for centuries, and it was by a constant succession of those marriages that the Hapsburg family built up its extensive but unnatural empire. One great-grandfather of Charles was the Duke of Burgundy, Charles the Bold, whose death in battle left his lands to a daughter Mary. Hapsburg diplomacy secured her as a bride for Maximilian, in spite of her previous engagement to the French heir. For the son of Maximilian and Mary the Hapsburg diplomats found an even richer wife in Joanna, elder daughter of Ferdinand and Isabella and sister of Henry's wife, Catherine of Aragon. With the hand of Joanna, known as the Insane, went the rule of Spain and her possessions. Charles therefore had an extensive inheritance from each of his four grandparents. From Mary came the Netherlands and the county of Burgundy; from Maximilian, Austria and the other hereditary Danubian lands of the Hapsburgs; from Ferdinand, Aragon and parts of Italy; and from Isabella, the rest of Spain, as well as the new colonies in America, with their

many silver mines. The Hapsburg tradition, too, made Charles the logical candidate to succeed Maximilian as Holy Roman Emperor. His election to that position gave him nominal control of Germany, in addition.

Unlike his exuberant contemporaries, Francis and Henry, Charles was cold, reserved, levelheaded, conservative. Even in times of peace, to administer so many countries, held together only by a personal tie and each with its peculiar form of government, involved complex responsibilities. But other problems made peace difficult. It happened that the Ottoman Empire had reached its greatest power and extent in the same years as the Hapsburg empire. Under its ruler Suleiman the Magnificent, Janizaries came surging up the Danube valley to the very gates of Vienna, as his corsairs raided and kidnaped along the Mediterranean shores of Charles's domains. Then, again, Charles had to deal with the first outburst of Protestantism in the Reformation, and the Protestants of northern Germany were for years a thorn in his side. Finally, he was drawn into chronic conflict with Francis. The dominions of Charles almost completely surrounded France. Wherever a Frenchman looked outside his country, he saw either Hapsburg territory or the sea. French foreign policy for nearly two centuries consisted in efforts to break that "Hapsburg ring." Francis tried often and in vain. Each side in that conflict sought allies. Suleiman was a natural ally of France. The German Protestants might also be counted upon normally to oppose Charles. The doubtful element was England.

Just before Francis and Charles came upon the scene, Henry found a remarkable minister who was to guide his relations with these rival monarchs. Thomas Wolsey, son of middle-class parents and a graduate of Oxford, had attracted royal attention by unusual speed in traveling to the Continent and back on a diplomatic mission, and he

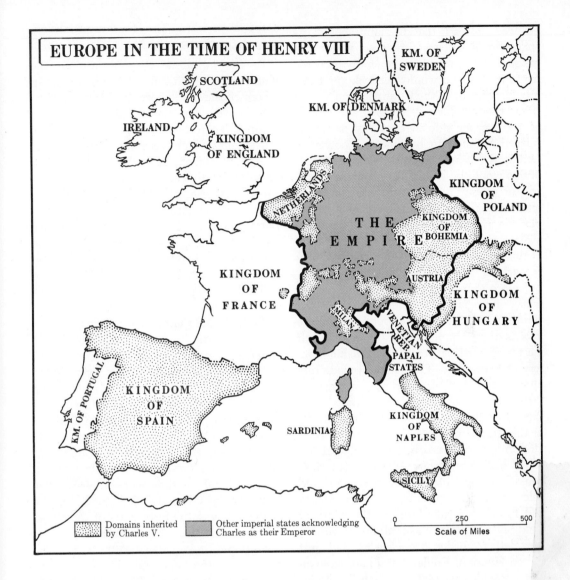

EUROPE IN THE TIME OF HENRY VIII

KM. OF SWEDEN

SCOTLAND

KM. OF DENMARK

IRELAND

KINGDOM OF ENGLAND

NETHERLANDS

KINGDOM OF POLAND

THE EMPIRE

KINGDOM OF BOHEMIA

AUSTRIA

KINGDOM OF FRANCE

KINGDOM OF HUNGARY

MILAN

VENETIAN REP.

PAPAL STATES

KM. OF PORTUGAL

KINGDOM OF SPAIN

SARDINIA

KINGDOM OF NAPLES

SICILY

Domains inherited by Charles V.

Other imperial states acknowledging Charles as their Emperor

0   250   500
Scale of Miles

lost no opportunity to demonstrate his usefulness around the court. His organizing and negotiating ability had much to do with the military and diplomatic success against France in 1513 and 1514. From that time on, his rise was meteoric. In addition to receiving several rich bishoprics, he became in short order Archbishop of York, cardinal, and papal legate, and he hoped to become Pope. He was also made chancellor, and in that capacity he gathered most of the threads of administration and justice into his own hands. Impressive in

appearance, effective in negotiations, and tireless in industry, Wolsey for fifteen years virtually governed England. The "proudest prelate England has ever seen" enjoyed a magnificent income and lived in almost regal splendor. He referred to "ego et rex meus"; but there were times when even Wolsey had to adjust his policy to the imperious Henry.

Wolsey's special forte was diplomacy. He realized the futility of trying to seize actual Continental territory, as had been attempted in the Hundred Years' War. He believed, instead, that England should exercise the balance of power—a policy she has since followed pretty generally. According to it, England would not seek any territory for herself on the Continent but would throw the influence of her men and money on the weaker side in case any nation or ruler threatened to become too powerful. Ordinarily, it was hoped, the mere threat of this would be enough to maintain peace, and so Wolsey hoped to uphold England's international importance by means of diplomacy rather than war.

Strange to say, Wolsey's own application of this was not a success. He tried to play the arbiter between Charles and Francis, but more than once he backed the wrong horse. Francis no sooner came to the throne, in 1515, than he slipped around the guards of an Alpine pass and made himself master of northern Italy by a crushing victory at Marignano. This triumph made him appear stronger than Charles, who began to take over his various thrones immediately thereafter. By 1520 Wolsey was intervening in the grand manner. The nobles of England and France nearly bankrupted themselves and "wore their estates upon their backs," because of the extreme pomp and splendor of the meeting between Henry and Francis on the "Field of the Cloth of Gold" near Calais. Negotiations, nevertheless, led to little; for Charles had just visited Henry in England and had made an alliance which was effective when Charles and Francis began their first war the next year. England intervened on the side of Charles and sent a rather ineffectual army to invade France. Wolsey's error was evident in 1525, when Charles overwhelmed the French at Pavia, in Italy, and even captured Francis himself. English aid had helped to make Charles master of Europe, quite contrary to the principle of the balance of power. Even the two million crowns received as indemnity from France did not offset the disadvantage of having helped to put Charles securely in the saddle.

The Protestant Revolt

In the meantime, Europe was in the midst of the so-called Reformation, in which considerable portions of western Europe broke away from the Roman Catholic Church. There had been rumblings of this movement, which many scholars call the Protestant Revolt, as early as the twelfth and thirteenth centuries, owing to widespread criticism of certain church abuses, such as simony, broken monastic vows, marriage of the clergy, the general ignorance and laxity among the lower clergy, and the wealth and corruption of the higher clergy. Heretical agitation, notably the Waldensian and Albigensian, had been evidence of this dissatisfaction. Pope Innocent III, about 1200, had made numerous reforms, including the authorization of the mendicant friars (see page 93), and these are said to have helped to postpone the crisis some three centuries. The prestige of the papacy had been badly impaired by its removal to Avignon, under the French influence; and the English in particular resented this bringing of the head of the universal Church under the apparent control of the king with whom they were at war. That "Babylonian Captivity" led to a further serious blow in the forty years of the Great Schism, when the existence of two or three rival popes shook men's faith in the supremacy of the Pope and his direct spiritual descent from Saint Peter. The Renaissance too did its part in weakening papal prestige, so contrary was the spirit of that movement to the old ideas of faith and submission to the authority of church teachings. The rediscovered pagan classics were full of joy in life and love of beauty—for the most part earthly life and physical beauty, and for that very reason somewhat alien to traditional Christianity and unlike the medieval subordination of the individual and emphasis on the other world.

Even yet, strong, pious Popes might have saved the Church from dismemberment. Instead, the healing of the schism was followed by a series of worldly Popes. Alexander VI, a cruel and debauched Spaniard with a criminal character and a notorious son, Caesar Borgia, represented the papacy at its very lowest; Julius II devoted his energy to playing the role of a petty Italian prince; and finally there was Leo X, one of the Florentine Medicis, whose absorption in Renaissance art rather than in spiritual affairs was to bring the issues of dissension to a head in the Reformation in the early sixteenth century.

The expensiveness of Leo's plans for the beautification of Rome, especially for the rebuilding of the church of St. Peter, made essential a drastic increase in papal revenues. For this, Leo turned largely to the old device of the indulgence. A truly penitent sinner might by an indulgence, procured ordinarily by the payment of a sum of money to the Church, reduce the future punishment in purgatory for a sin. One might also purchase an indulgence for a deceased relative or friend. This did not mean that a cash gift to the Church alone won forgiveness for sins; for an indulgence was supposed to be operative only in the case of those already truly penitent. Nevertheless, it was the energetic, careless, and "high-pressure" selling of indulgences in Germany and elsewhere that was the center of the storm.

The sale of indulgences, however, was but one of the sparks that set off the Reformation; for the decline of papal prestige had made more outspoken and dangerous the criticisms which had been muttered for centuries. Of these new critics perhaps the most famous and influential was Erasmus, of whom we have heard as the inspiration of the English Humanists, those Oxford reformers, Grocyn, Linacre, Colet, More, and others (see pages 154 ff.). Like most Humanists, Erasmus conceived of a renaissance of Christianity. No one was more scathing in satirizing clerical abuses than was he in his *Praise of Folly;* but he wanted

merely to reform from within and sadly rued the impetus he had unintentionally given to the Protestant Revolt.

Of quite another sort was the German monk Martin Luther, who, because of his unusual and brilliant explanation of Biblical beliefs, was the most popular lecturer at the University of Wittenberg. Luther, after wrestling with personal worry about his own soul's future, stressed the old conclusion that, to win God's forgiveness for sins, men should be justified before God by inner faith—the so-called "justification by faith"—rather than by "good works" and outward acts. He wanted to bring back simple, primitive Christianity where (from the Protestant point of view) man was his own priest and where the clergy were simply guides pointing out the way to God. He had his own interpretation of other features, such as the Mass, confession, saints' relics, and the marriage of the clergy.

In 1517, when the sale of indulgences was at its scandalous peak, Luther nailed to the local university church door at Wittenberg his famous "ninety-five theses." These were merely subjects, posted like any modern university notice, which he intended to discuss; but the list was such a suggestive one, containing the question of indulgences and justification, as well as other of his unconventional ideas, that his hammer blows sounded the break-up of the centuries-old Catholic unity. Within a few months not only Germany, which was seething with all sorts of discontent—economic, social, and political—but most of western Europe as well had heard of his theses, which had been translated from Latin into the vernaculars. The sale of indulgences fell off alarmingly. Before long, Luther allowed himself to be argued into decidedly heretical statements. At the same time, he won important German princes to his side by urging them to reform the church within their own borders—in their eyes a God-given chance for more wealth and power in the heterogeneous Empire.

The Pope excommunicated the recalcitrant monk, but Luther boldly burned the papal bull. The Church, having thus fired its strongest weapon in vain, appealed to the emperor. Young Charles V summoned Luther before an imperial diet, a sort of parliament, at Worms in 1521, where the ban of the Empire was placed upon him, rendering him an outlaw whom anyone might kill. Luther, however, was spirited away by a powerful noble, in whose castle he remained hidden until the tumult quieted. But he had started far more than he was to approve. All the discontented classes of Germany, from the knights down to the peasants, found this the signal for revolt. They rose in Luther's name, though political and economic considerations were also important causes.

Another priest, Zwingli of Zurich, was inflaming the people of Switzerland in much the same way and for many of the same reasons as Luther. He was, however, more radical in some of his religious ideas and more politically minded. For a time South Germany as well as half of Switzerland seemed to look to him for spiritual leadership, but he was killed in one of the first battles between Protestants and Catholics. Most of his followers either turned toward Luther or toward the Frenchman John Calvin, the third great Reformation pioneer.

Forced to leave France, Calvin made his home in Geneva, a free city and a willing convert to his teachings; it to all practical purposes came under his control. It speedily became the center of a peculiarly virile and effective form of Protestantism, which spread rapidly northward even into Scotland. Calvin's teachings were formulated in his *Institutes of Christianity*, published in 1536. In them he stressed above all else the sovereignty of God, who from the beginning had a "definite, individual, and unchanging purpose" for every person. According to this doctrine of predestination, man cannot change his own future,

because it is predetermined by God's will. Calvin, a stern man, emphasized duty, obligations, responsibility, hard work, and discipline rather than forgiveness and gentleness, laying especial stress upon the Old Testament. From Geneva he issued affirmations and denunciations as though he were a species of Protestant pope.

All northwestern Europe was thus aroused by the middle of the sixteenth century. The Protestant Revolt took a somewhat different form in nearly every country, but region after region was lost to the papacy. Northern and central Germany accepted Lutheranism and later developed some Calvinism. The three Scandinavian kingdoms also went over to Luther. Calvin's ideas spread to France, Holland, and, through the stern John Knox, to Scotland, while in England his influence came to permeate Puritanism. Even Bohemia and Poland became Protestant for a while.

Ample evidence indicated that the English people were as ready for change as those on the Continent. There was, for instance, the lasting influence of Wycliffe's example. The new learning had broadened the people's vision. Colet and other Humanists had talked freely of reforming church abuses. Furthermore, the Englishman of Henry's day could look back upon four centuries of royal opposition to the Pope. The quarrels which had started with Anselm and Becket had continued into the thirteenth century with King John. The reign of Edward I saw the Statute of Mortmain limiting church landholding; that of Edward III saw two more hostile statutes, Provisors, to check the foreign church appointees, and Praemunire, to check appeals to Rome. The Church, however, had found means to avoid some of these laws, and in the early sixteenth century the Pope still enjoyed power and profit from his relationship to England. Every newly appointed bishop and abbot had to pay "annates," or "first fruits," the first year's income of his benefice, into the papal treasury; while the "Peter's pence," an annual contribution of one penny, supposedly voluntary, for every hearth in England, also went to Rome. In spite of the Statute of Praemunire, marriage annulments and other dispensations from the canon law were still obtained from the papal see. The church lands continued to grow, for the kings granted frequent exceptions to the Statute of Mortmain. The Church in England was decidedly wealthy with its annual income estimated at £320,000 a year, considerably more than the royal treasury normally received. Of that amount about £100,000 was monastic income. There was a growing feeling that many of the clergy did not do enough in return for their special privileges (see pages 133 ff.).

The scene was thus set for change, even if there had been no Henry VIII and no royal marriage problem. The king, with his usual Tudor political sagacity, utilized all these aspects of discontent by making Parliament his instrument in the whole personal matter of the dissolution of his marriage when the Pope refused his assent, and this tended to give a more national aspect to the English Reformation. The importance of Parliament, for once during this Yorkist-Tudor period of neglect, was increased when Henry thus made it his ally, instead of depending solely upon consultation with a church gathering presumably subservient to Rome.

On the other hand, it must be remembered that at first the question was not fundamentally one of belief, and interpretation of the Bible, as on the Continent, but was, rather, the question of the supremacy of the Pope over England. In fact, Henry was so incensed by Luther's ideas that he himself wrote a pamphlet defending the seven sacraments against such an attack; and so grateful was the Pope for this royal literary outburst that he bestowed on Henry the title of "Defender of the Faith." Not only did Henry keep this high-sounding title but even to this day the Prot-estant ruler of Protestant England retains it. Henry was thus apparently a Catholic in most of his beliefs to his deathbed, in spite of his bitter antipapal fight. The result was that in England the Reformation took an extraordinarily middle-of-the-road course, with but brief excursions into either camp.

Henry VIII's Marriage Problem

By 1527, if not a few years earlier, Henry had become seriously obsessed with the necessity of putting aside his wife, Catherine of Aragon, the younger daughter of Ferdinand and Isabella of Spain. During the last years of Henry VII's reign, Catherine had come to England as the bride of his older son, who soon died. Thereupon, a second marriage was arranged for her with her brother-in-law, the future Henry VIII (some five years her junior), in order to keep her rich dowry. A deceased brother's widow, however, was within the prohibited degrees of marriage, so that a special dispensation had been obtained from the Pope to permit the new wedding on the ground that Catherine was said to have been a wife in name only to her sickly young bridegroom of a few months. Catherine bore to Henry several children in rapid succession, but only a daughter, Mary, survived infancy.

Now, after eighteen years of marriage, Henry began to profess horror because he was living in sin with his widowed sister-in-law. Although the desire to marry her maid in waiting, the black-eyed, vivacious Anne Boleyn, was to hurry Henry's determination, his worry over the lack of a male heir was noticed long before Anne came upon the scene. Heretofore England's one experience with a reigning queen, it must be remembered, had been with the unfortunate Matilda and anarchy. Had not Henry desired so desperately a legitimate son, he would perhaps not have bothered to lead Anne to the altar any more than he had his other mistresses.

Although usually referred to as the "divorce" problem, it was technically something different; divorce was prohibited by the Church, which claimed sole jurisdiction in all legal matters connected with marriage and other sacraments; consequently it was unheard-of in pre-Reformation Europe. Marriage, as one of the seven sacraments, was considered indissoluble except by the hand of God in death. To be sure, annulment of marriage was not uncommon if the Church was shown that some serious impediment, such as too close kinship of the couple or the forcing of one of them, had prevented the marriage in question from being a true sacrament. Henry wanted an annulment on the ground that since the queen was his brother's widow, they were within the Church's prohibited degrees of kinship. Under ordinary circumstances it would have been granted speedily and easily to one in his regal position, with the need of an heir so obvious. In Henry's case, however, there was a snag that made annulment virtually impossible. Impediment to the marriage there had seemed to be, but it had been declared nonexistent by the Church in a special dispensation *before* the wedding! Before the present Pope, Clement VII, might annul the marriage, he would first have to show that the earlier papal dispensation, based on affidavits that Catherine had been a wife in name only, was an error. That seemed out of the question. The Church had permitted the marriage with Henry only because all concerned were certain that Catherine was making her first real marriage. Her appearance at this second wedding in virgin white, with her hair hanging down her back, had impressed this vividly upon the public mind. Catherine was the aunt of Charles V, who not only controlled Italy, after an especially savage sack of Rome in 1527, but also even held the Pope as prisoner for a while; and Charles would scarcely countenance the proposed humiliation of his mother's sister. Also, many knew of Henry's

past liaison, with Anne Boleyn's older sister; that placed Anne within the prohibited kinship degrees. It was obvious that Pope Clement VII was in a tight place when Wolsey began the negotiations to free Henry from his marriage.

Wolsey made a strenuous effort to help Henry; but he was in a difficult personal position, since he had his eye on the papal succession. Failure met him on all sides, partly from the oversubtle efforts at compromise to avoid prejudicing his own papal chances; partly from Henry's own premature plans, about which he kept Wolsey in the dark; and partly because of that serious difficulty of the previous dispensation. Henry was ready to accept any expedient, even bigamy or the entrance of Catherine and himself into holy orders, with, of course, the assurance of his own later absolution from his vows in order to wed again.

Catherine soon got wind of the "divorce plans" and made a dignified protest, backed by the whole force of Hapsburg power. Wolsey, in the meantime, continued his efforts, despite his aversion to the Boleyn marriage; but the Pope procrastinated in the evident hope that time might solve the dilemma. Finally Cardinal Campeggio was sent from Rome to England to act as a legate in conjunction with Wolsey on the question of the validity of Catherine's first marriage. The Pope gave Campeggio a so-called decretal bull, with orders not to let out of his hands. In the form which Wolsey had asked, this bull would have made the decision final, with no possibility of Catherine's appeal to Rome. But its final form did not make this clear, and Catherine did appeal. The Pope then revoked the whole Campeggio-Wolsey mission and summoned the case to Rome in 1529. This spelled doom for Wolsey. Campeggio's baggage was searched at Dover in vain for the decretal bull which in English hands might have saved the day. Wolsey was arrested, charged with violating the Statute of Praemunire because he was a legate, a position which he had held at Henry's own special request for fifteen years! The marriage impasse was not the only cause of his fall; Henry had grown impatient with him and wanted to take over more of the ruling. Wolsey resigned most of his offices and, with much of his wealth confiscated, was allowed to retire in order to take up his neglected duties as Archbishop of York. Anne's influence was growing, and she hated Wolsey. Late in 1530, at the instigation of enemies who feared that his popularity in the north might return him to favor, Wolsey was arrested, this time for high treason. Ill and in bitter disgrace, he died en route to London, thereby probably cheating the block.

Serving as Henry's ministers was a thankless and risky task. Two of them were beheaded within the next ten years. First was Wolsey's immediate successor, Sir Thomas More, the gentle, high-minded author of *Utopia* (see page 155). The other of sterner, coarser fiber was Thomas Cromwell, who had attracted attention by his skillful and loyal work in managing Wolsey's business affairs. More died because he was too good a Catholic; Cromwell, because he picked out too unattractive a royal bride.

The Break with Rome

Upon the advice of Thomas Cranmer, who was soon to become very helpful as Archbishop of Canterbury, Henry next asked numerous universities in Europe for their opinions upon the merits of the "divorce" matter. The replies were not conclusive. Then, in 1530, he bullied the English clergy into submission. As they met in the Convocations of Canterbury and of York, Henry informed them that they, like Wolsey, were guilty of violation of Praemunire, and would be relieved only upon payment of £100,000. Coupled with this, they had to recognize Henry, in this "Submission of the Clergy," as the supreme head

of the Church in England. The combined demand was a bitter pill, but they chose the safer and more practical course in following their king rather than remaining loyal to the Pope. This stand was to prove decidedly to their advantage in changing the anticlerical tone of public opinion. They accepted the king as supreme head, however, only with the evasive clause "as far as the laws of Christ allow."

Not depending upon the churchmen alone, Henry turned to Parliament to use it as his ally in attaining his religious objectives. Late in 1529, just a month after Wolsey's fall, one of the most prolific Parliaments in English history began seven years of sessions that were to be memorable for the legislation which definitely severed the Church of England from Rome. In fact, it was ready to give the king practically everything he asked, except money.

Parliament's first step, in 1532, was to decree that the annates, or first fruits, were thereafter to be paid to the crown instead of to the Pope. The papal confirmation of bishops was also ended. At these affronts to the Pope, More resigned the chancellorship, his first step toward execution.

By the next year, Anne had given in to Henry's advances, after cleverly holding out for the title of Queen for nearly five years, and it became doubly necessary to speed the "divorce." Henry found a complaisant Archbishop of Canterbury in the scholarly Thomas Cranmer, who in March, 1533, gave Henry, through an English church court, the long-desired "divorce" from Catherine. At the same time, Parliament passed an act forbidding appeals to Rome, in even stronger terms than the old Act of Praemunire, so that the action of Cranmer's court was final. It was none too soon. Henry now married Anne publicly (he had supposedly married her privately about the beginning of the year); but the people were not pleased, and not a cheer enlivened Anne's rather dreary coronation procession.

In September, she gave birth, not to the hoped-for son, but to the king's second daughter, the future Queen Elizabeth I.

Thus Henry, with Parliament passing antipapal laws and the primate of England supporting his ideas, obtained a new queen and defied the Pope. In 1534 Parliament passed the Act of Supremacy, the climax in the breaking of papal power in England. It established the Church of England or Anglican Church, which is directly related to the Protestant Episcopal Church in the United States. The king, not the Pope, was its head. It was a national church, with all foreign control and interference at an end, and an "established" church, because of its official connection with the government. To be sure, the Pope excommunicated Henry and declared his English "divorce" null and void, but most of England regarded this as an idle gesture. In its own words, the act made the king and his successors "Protector and Supreme Head on earth of the Church and Clergy of England," as wrested from the Convocations four years earlier. Every Englishman was required to take the Oath of Supremacy, recognizing the new substitution of king for Pope. Failure to do so was high treason. In an Act of Succession, Parliament also recognized the legality of the "divorce" and secured the crown to Elizabeth or any other children of Anne at the expense of Catherine's daughter, Mary, who was declared illegitimate. The definition of treason was widely extended, largely to enforce the new legislation and to prevent public criticism.

Various executions followed refusal to take the Oath of Supremacy, including More's. He had hoped to avoid trouble by withdrawing from the world, after resigning the chancellorship; but others did not hold their tongues. A monk preaching before Henry told him that if he continued on his wicked course "dogs would lick his blood"; a nun was so rash as to prophesy the king's imminent death. As a result of such remarks, four monks, one of them the head of the Carthusian order in England, were hanged, cut down alive, and disemboweled, and their heads were stuck up over London Bridge. The king feared that others might copy the defiance of More and Bishop Fisher of Rochester, who had been lodged in the Tower together. Both were tried for high treason and beheaded. More, a clever lawyer, used as his defense that no one could prove that he had ever uttered a word against the "divorce." "For this my silence neither your law, nor any law in the world, is able justly and rightly to punish me." At the scaffold, his last words were: "I die the King's good servant, but God's first."

Changes were now introduced in the church services, such as the use of English instead of Latin in the Lord's Prayer and elsewhere. An English translation of the Bible, probably by one Coverdale, a friend of the Tyndale whose earlier translation in 1526 had been suppressed as heretical, also was adopted. The canon law was overhauled and its study discouraged, which incidentally increased the importance of the lay courts. Relics and images were destroyed, and the old miracle-working shrines, expecially that of Thomas Becket at Canterbury, were discredited. In dogma, however, the changes were very slight, for Henry was not interested in becoming a Protestant. Two years after the Act of Supremacy the Ten Articles declared the Bible and the creeds to be the sole authority in matters of faith, but this was merely a clerical pronouncement and lacked royal authorization. By 1539 Henry would clamp down on the reformers with the Six Articles, which definitely dragged dogma back into old forms.

Thomas Cromwell, the king's next chief minister, was not made chancellor, but was given a new title, "Vicar-General of the Church," which gave him power to handle the business end of the new religious situation. As clever a statesman of the Machiavellian school as any king might desire,

Ruins of a suppressed monastery: the abbey of Whitby in Yorkshire, site of the synod that decided in 664 for Rome, and home of the poet Caedmon.

Cromwell saw further financial possibilities in the break with Rome. Already the royal treasury had been enriched by the diversion of annates, Peter's pence, and other former payments to the Pope. Cromwell proposed nothing less than the abolition of the monasteries, which owned about one-sixth of all the land, and the transfer of their wealth to the rapidly emptying royal treasury.

Abolition of the Monasteries

Undoubtedly there was some serious corruption among the seven hundred monasteries and nunneries. Wolsey had pointed the way by taking the money of certain monasteries to establish a college. In the new spirit of the times the virtual monastic monopoly of education was giving way to educational institutions with relatively little emphasis on church connections. The impulse which had led men into the mon-

astic life centuries before had lessened; fewer men were willing to isolate themselves. Since Henry III few new monasteries had been established. The old ones still continued, well endowed by rich gifts of land through the centuries; but monks and nuns no longer commanded quite the old general respect. The main question was whether the monasteries were still held in high enough esteem to prevent Cromwell's plan.

He ran into no serious opposition when he presented the matter to Parliament. It was ready to sanction the dissolution of the monasteries, in addition to the breach with Rome, because the more money the king could get from the Church the less he would need from Parliament. It consequently authorized a commission to investigate the general condition of the monasteries. Cromwell sent out commissioners who doubtless were told what kind of reports were expected. It is uncertain how far their findings corresponded to the facts. Their questions fell under three main heads: the wealth of the establishment, its superstitious practices, and its immorality. Numerous institutions, even under the circumstances, were reported as satisfactory in the last two respects, but from many came tales of miraculous shirts, girdles, or bones of saints which could cure headaches or relieve the pains of a childbirth, while there were a surprising number of pieces of the True Cross. The reports told of monks who made merry with married and single women and of nuns who had become unwed mothers. The reports undoubtedly blackened and exaggerated conditions, but they produced the desired Parliamentary acts. In 1536 Parliament decreed the end of some 376 lesser monasteries and nunneries which had an annual income of less than £200 each.

Southern and eastern England accepted the abolition quietly, but the conservative Catholic north rose in arms. Cromwell, who was to be called "malleus monachorum," the "Hammer of the Monks," had identified himself conspicuously with the reformers, and this, added to his low social origin, annoyed many people. The northern monasteries, moreover, were noted for their works of charity among people already aroused by the enclosure movement. The revolt started in Lincolnshire, and in Yorkshire it received the name of "the Pilgrimage of Grace." By clever negotiations the first revolt was easily suppressed, but it soon broke out again. This time, the leaders were executed, but Henry was fairly lenient with their common followers. This revolt led to the establishment of another special Tudor tribunal, which had unusual powers outside the regular courts and laws. This Council of the North, composed of powerful officials, sat at York and, like the Court of the Star Chamber of Henry VII, was given full authority to handle emergencies.

So far as stopping the suppression of the monasteries was concerned, the rising failed. The larger monasteries were dissolved by 1539. A few voluntarily closed their doors, foreseeing their inevitable end; the rest were abolished by royal coercion. By 1540 not a monastic establishment was left in England. Their annual income of some £100,000 was a temporary boon to the royal treasury. The actual financial gain to the government, however, was slight; for about two thirds of the lands went by sale to Henry's friends and favorites at bargain prices, and these lands continued as large or medium-sized estates. Many family fortunes date from the sale of monastic lands. Numerous prosperous townsmen took advantage of the opportunity to rise in the social scale by becoming landholders. Among them were the ancestors of George Washington, who spent town-earned money to purchase the manor of Sulgrave, formerly a priory. The poor, moreover, suffered from the change; for the new landlords were generally harder masters than the monks and were more inclined to dispossess tenants in order to enclose the land for sheep raising. The poor also felt the loss of the social services of the monasteries which had served as hospitals and centers of charity (see pages 15 ff.). It was soon necessary for inns to be introduced, to take the place of the former monastic hospitality. With the abbots removed from membership, the former clerical majority in the House of Lords gave way to a lay majority which clearly outnumbered the bishops (see page 196).

In 1539, the year the remaining monasteries were abolished, Parliament passed the Six Articles. These were intended to pacify both those who wanted still more church reform and those who wanted to retain as much as possible of the old faith. Cromwell sided with Archbishop Cranmer and Bishop Latimer in the wish to push reform further, but Henry was reluctant. This so-called "Whip with the Six Strings" was a victory for those of Henry's persuasion (ap-

Catherine of Aragon

Anne Boleyn

Jane Seymour

Anne of Cleves

Catherine Howard

Catherine Parr

parently the majority of Englishmen); for in many ways the articles reaffirmed the faith, yet emphasized the break with Rome. Unlike the unofficial Ten Articles, they were legally passed by Parliament. They decreed that (1) transubstantiation was a fact; (2) confessions and (3) private Masses were essential; but (4) Communion in both kinds was not; (5) priests must not marry; and (6) vows of chastity must be kept. The penalty for failure to concur was death for the first article and severe punishment for the others. Thus did England separate from the papacy but not essentially from the old faith.

Henry, in the meantime, was again looking for a new wife. Anne Boleyn, after dashing his hopes for a son, was sent to the block in 1536, charged, as an unfaithful wife, with treason to her husband, the king. Directly after her execution Henry married her maid of honor, Jane Seymour,

who died the following year at the birth of the future Edward VI. To cement the Protestant German alliance and to fill the vacant place in the royal bed, Cromwell suggested another Anne, the Protestant sister of the German duke of Cleves. Over-persuaded by Cromwell and by an unduly flattering portrait by Holbein, Henry completed negotiations to marry her, but suddenly the Protestant alliance no longer seemed essential in the constantly shifting diplomatic scene, and on top of this came the arrival of the unattractive bride. The marriage was carried through by the reluctant Henry, who openly expressed his opinion of the "Flanders mare." Within eight months this diplomatic error, added to his doctrinal defeat in the Six Articles, sent Cromwell to the block, and Anne, complaisant in the arrangements made for her, retired from court, divorced. Henry's fifth wife, gay young Catherine Howard, was soon executed, like her kinswoman Anne Boleyn, charged with traitorous adultery, while her successor, Catherine Parr, a charming widow, outlived him. Thus of Henry's wives the two foreign princesses were divorced, and of the four English girls, two went to the block.

Henry trusted no more in ministers but, fat, coarse, diseased, and dangerous, headed a government more absolute than ever. Parliament had given up some of its own authority by permitting the king to make valid laws simply by proclamation, and it had dangerously extended the scope of treason. It was unsafe to murmur even mild discontent against a ruler who did not hesitate to behead.

Foreign wars, which had been set aside during the years of religious activity, broke out again in 1542. Charles and Francis had been drawn together temporarily by the threat of an English alliance with the German Protestants; but with the repudiation of Anne of Cleves they were free to resume their fighting. There was friction between France and England because Francis was behind in his payments promised in past treaties. The immediate trouble came with Scotland, the perennial French ally. Henry had recently completed the absorption of Wales into the English system of government (see page 112). England had hoped for a peaceful control over Scotland, but that was blocked by the dominant Cardinal Beaton, who hated both England and Protestantism. A series of border raids by both sides led to a decisive but quite bloodless English victory over the Scots at Solway Moss. The news of that reverse killed the Scottish king, James V, son of Henry's sister Margaret. The Scottish throne was left to his week-old daughter, the famous "Mary Queen of Scots." Two years later an English force, attacking from the sea and burning Edinburgh, antagonized Scotland further. In the meantime Henry had allied himself with Charles and had invaded France. The Channel port of Boulogne was captured, but little else was accomplished. Charles made a separate peace, and the French actually sent a fleet to invade England. The French made a temporary landing on the Isle of Wight, but Henry had created a fairly effective navy and had strung a series of forts along the south coast. The French abandoned the attempt, and peace came in 1546. The fighting had given Henry a little temporary glory at a crushing expense to the treasury; but, like Wolsey's earlier meddling in Continental affairs, it was a sterile conflict, without benefit to England.

However much this second Tudor may have degenerated in his later years, he had given England a great reign. His wars and pageantry left no permanent results on the map, but they at least stimulated national pride and for a while raised England in the eyes of Europe. His religious changes, however trivial their causes and however selfish their motives, had permanent and important consequences. Henry may have played the arbitrary despot at times, but it is doubtful whether Parliament and the people would have followed him as they did through such momentous decisions had not the nation as a whole been in general sympathy with what he wanted.

At his death, January 28, 1547, England was to pass through the short and sorry reigns of Edward VI (1547-1553), son of Jane Seymour, and of Mary I (1553-1558), daughter of Catherine of Aragon, before reaching the long and glorious rule of his third child, Elizabeth I (1558-1603), Anne Boleyn's daughter. The religious question, initiated by Henry, was to make very stormy the reign of Edward, under whom England went over to extreme Protestantism, and that of Mary, who dragged it back to Catholicism, before Elizabeth quieted the turmoil with a clever compromise. The Tudor line ended with her, possibly because of Henry's venereal disease. Edward and Elizabeth never married, and Mary, fortunately for England, was disappointed in her efforts to continue the Tudor line with a child of her husband, the Catholic Spaniard, Philip.

Edward VI and Protestantism

As Edward VI was only nine years old and was to die at not quite sixteen, his reign was dominated by others. Many were the men ready to enter that risky scramble for influence during the king's minority. A clever stroke might bring lands, wealth, even the control of England; a single misplay might mean the block. In this period the three outstanding families were the Howards, the Seymours, and the Dudleys. In the course of twelve years two Howards, two Seymours, and two Dudleys were beheaded, including a Seymour and a Dudley who for a short time had each been virtual ruler of England. The habit of referring to a man by his title is confusing, for family relationship is hard to trace through a maze of titles. The conservative and generally Catholic Howards, the oldest and proudest, were almost the only family of pre-Tudor nobility to retain both life and power. Cropping up throughout the Tudor period, generally in high place at court and in command on land or sea, all the way from Flodden Field to the Armada, they furnished Henry VIII with the two wives whom he beheaded. Their bid for supreme power just before Henry's death led Surrey to the block and almost caught his father, Norfolk, too. Compared with the Howards, the Seymours were upstarts. They had been simple country gentry; but after their Jane became queen and gave Henry a son, they rose rapidly to wealth, influence, and high command. Edward Seymour, Earl of Hertford, better known as Duke of Somerset, was the most powerful noble in England at Henry's death; his brother, the admiral, married Henry's widow. Of the three generations of clever, rascally Dudleys, the founder of the house was Edmund, the extortionate tax-gatherer of the first Tudor. Henry VIII executed him, but much of the money he had gathered stayed in the family and contributed to the rise of his son John, successively Viscount Lisle, Earl of Warwick, and Duke of Northumberland. John's son Robert, later Earl of Leicester, was prominent at Elizabeth's court (see page 199).

Henry VIII had intended that a council, composed of men of varying views, should conduct the government during Edward's minority; but Somerset (Seymour-Hertford), the young king's uncle, quickly assumed the title of Lord Protector. He was ousted late in 1549 by Northumberland (Dudley-Warwick), who continued in control until Edward's death. Alike in their ambitions for power, the two men were radically different in their methods; Somerset, a champion of the oppressed classes, meant well, but was ineffectual. Northumberland, one of the most desperate political gamblers in English history, was a clever, scheming, hypocritical opportunist. Their problems were for the most part inherited from Henry's reign.

Their foreign policies were failures. At Henry's death, negotiations were on foot to unite England and Scotland by the marriage of Edward VI to the little Scottish queen, Mary, granddaughter of Henry's older sister. In order to hasten the betrothal, Somerset invaded Scotland. In the battle of Pinkie he killed some ten thousand Scots and then devastated the region near Edinburgh. Naturally he failed to win the bride for Edward. Instead she was sent to France, where she was soon betrothed to the Dauphin and some years later became queen. In the meantime France renewed war against England and succeeded in recovering Boulogne.

Although Henry VIII had inherited from his father an amazingly well-filled treasury, he left an empty one to his son, for the wars of his last years had not only exhausted the church spoils but run the country heavily into debt. Regular taxes could not meet the expenses; Somerset and Northumberland therefore carried to extremes the inflation of the currency started by Henry. They debased the currency to the lowest level in English history, ordering the mints to turn out shillings which were only one-quarter silver and three-quarters alloy. The great influx from the Spanish mines of Mexico and Peru was already beginning to lower the value of silver radically by increasing its supply, even without this deliberate inflation. Prices jumped, and there was widespread distress.

Altogether, times were bad, and the rich seemed to be growing richer and the poor poorer. The dissolution of the monasteries had resulted in a wholesale change of property titles and conditions. By carrying out a late order by Henry for the abolition of various other religious and semireligious endowments, the religious functions of the guilds were ended, and much of their property was seized. Craft guilds proper still continued, sleepily inactive. The "chantries," endowments for perpetual saying of prayers for the dead, were suppressed, on the plea that they increased superstition. The chantry priests, along with praying for the dead on special requests, frequently maintained schools in connection with their establishments, and only a few were transformed into "King Edward grammar schools." The guilds, moreover, had been exceedingly useful to the poor through their charities, which were now cut off; for the wealth thus confiscated went the way of the monastic riches—chiefly into the pockets of courtiers. The enclosure movement still continued to oust many peasants. Somerset tried to legislate in the interest of the poor; but he antagonized the upper and middle classes and only aroused false hopes in those he sought to help. Northumberland crushed serious uprisings in various parts of England with the help of foreign mercenaries. Then he was able to get rid of Somerset, who, having already sent his own brother to the block, followed him to it.

The most significant feature in the reign of Edward VI was the religious drift toward extreme Protestantism. Somerset began this moderately; but under Northumberland it was pushed much farther. Strange to say, the man who left the strongest lasting influence upon England out of all that period of active, positive men was the timid, vacillating, compromising Cranmer. From the time he became Archbishop of Canterbury and immediately gave Henry his "divorce," his political record was weak and shifting; but his rich and mellow scholarship, with his remarkable command of language, enabled him to produce an enduring monument in the Book of Common Prayer (1549). Its beautiful phrases still live, with few changes, in the Anglican ritual. Cranmer retained a good deal of the old Catholic prayer book, yet introduced some noticeable breaks with the past, particularly the use of English instead of Latin. The new Protestant ideas found in his writings were vigorously reinforced by the able and forceful sermons of Hugh Latimer, who courageously denounced the personal profits which politicians were making from church spoils. In 1549 Parliament passed a mild Act of Uniformity, which stipulated that the new prayer book was to go into use throughout England on a particular Sunday. Somerset's aversion to persecution was also shown in the repeal of the "Whip with Six Strings" and the legitimizing of clerical marriage (see page 187). This toleration was perhaps premature; for, on that first Sunday, thousands rose in protest in the west, and a few elsewhere, demanding the return of the Six Articles and the former service book. The radical Protestants, on the other hand, whitewashed many church frescoes, smashed irreplaceable stained-glass windows, and destroyed beautiful statuary in their desire for Protestant simplicity. All in all, the writings of Cranmer and the sermons of Latimer helped to swing England from the Catholic beliefs and practices which Henry had retained, and planted the ideas of the Reformation so strongly that in the next reign hundreds were ready to die for them.

Under Northumberland the trend toward extreme Protestantism increased markedly, in spite of the hopes that his rise to power had given the Catholics who had supported him against Somerset. Englishmen and foreigners, steeped in the doctrines of Luther, Zwingli, and Calvin, swarmed over from the Continent. These "Hot Gospelers" wanted to push England much farther away from Rome than Cranmer's compromise had carried it. The Reformation in England reached its extreme point in 1553, when the principles of belief were embodied in "Forty-two Articles," following close upon a revision of the Book of Common Prayer, still ornamented by Cranmer's beautiful prose. Both these measures showed the marked influence of Zwingli and even of Calvin. The revised prayer book did not mention the word "Mass," and the elaborate vestments of the clergy were forbidden. Neither of the prayer books was sanctioned by the body of the clergy, but both had the potent backing of Parliament. Had Edward lived, precocious mentally and strongly Protestant as he was, he might have taken as strong and unpopular a stand for the new Protestant teachings as his sister Mary was soon to take for the old faith.

The Forty-two Articles, however, were the last legislation signed by the dying Edward. The young king trusted Northumberland, but the people saw that the duke "rang as false on the counter as one of the bad coins issued by his government."[1] Consequently his attempt in 1553 to change the succession was foredoomed. Henry VIII had provided that if Edward should die without heir, the throne should go to Mary, the Catholic daughter of Catherine of Aragon. Northumberland, knowing what his own end would be if that happened, produced a rival for the crown in Lady Jane

[1] G. M. Trevelyan, *History of England* (1926), p. 317. By permission of Longmans, Green & Co.

Grey, a sixteen-year-old girl remarkably well educated and admirable in every way. If one excepted Elizabeth, because of the questionable legitimacy of her birth in the midst of her father's "divorce" difficulties, Lady Jane was the next Protestant in line for the throne, since she was the granddaughter of Henry's younger sister Mary, who, after her three months as queen of France, had married an English courtier. Northumberland arranged Lady Jane's marriage with his own son, and persuaded Edward, who was fond of her, to name her possible male heir as successor to the throne in order to avoid a change in religion. Northumberland then altered the will to make Jane queen in her own name, and at Edward's death had her so proclaimed.

Englishmen, however, rallied to Henry's daughter; for they saw in the little-known Lady Jane only Northumberland's daughter-in-law. Not yet had the issue between Catholicism and Protestantism reached the point of bitterness where England would let it count in choosing a sovereign. Mary, in the meantime, ignoring Northumberland's summons to the court—and probably to her death—was quickly crowned by her supporters. All England hailed Mary, while poor Lady Jane Grey, the "nine-day queen," was imprisoned in the Tower with her young husband. Northumberland tried to save his head, cheered for Mary, and turned Catholic, but he did not escape the ax.

Mary Tudor and Catholicism

The spontaneous enthusiasm for England's first reigning queen since the Matilda fiasco did not last long. Unfortunately for herself and for England, Mary, "the most honest" of the Tudors, was a fanatic in religion. The humiliation of her mother and herself during the "divorce" days, was enough to leave a lasting mark on any girl; and to one of Mary's narrow nature the psychological damage was incalculable. Forced, moreover, by her father to deny her faith, she was apparently always seeking to expiate that act. At first she seemed kind and rather tolerant, but secret opposition and open rebellion soon started her upon that road of persecution which was to give her the epithet of "Bloody Mary." If the people had distrusted Northumberland, they soon came to hate far more this somber woman of thirty-seven. The five years of Mary were to give the English a long-enduring hatred for Catholicism, and for Mary, her Spanish husband, and her wholesale persecutions. This reaction, from the same people who shortly before had cheered Henry even in his tyrannical last years and were soon to love Elizabeth, whatever she did, may perhaps best be explained by Mary's ignorance of popular opinion, a fault not characteristic of the other Tudors.

Mary's flouting of the people's wishes began with her betrothal to the bigoted and ardently Catholic son of Charles V. It was natural that Mary, after her difficult young years in England, should have turned with homesick eyes toward her mother's Catholic Spain for a husband; but a long-faced Spanish husband accentuated the criticism of Mary's own unpopular Spanish characteristics. Unluckily, the Queen fell in love with the coldly disdainful Philip, who was to ignore and to humiliate her. He wanted England; the unattractive queen was merely a necessary evil in the bargain. Charles V was soon to abdicate his various thrones and to divide his too burdensome heritage. His brother was to receive the German Hapsburg lands and the imperial title; his son was to become Philip II of Spain, and to inherit along with it the Netherlands, parts of Italy, and the rich Spanish colonies beyond the seas. If a son were to be born of this marriage, England feared that, like the Netherlands, she might perhaps become a hereditary dependency of Spain, to be added to those many other regions drawn into the Hapsburg net by royal marriages. Exhortations that Mary either remain single or marry an Englishman fell on deaf ears. In vain the popular temper showed itself with boys in the London streets pelting the imperial negotiators with snowballs.

Early in 1554 the news of the impending marriage, combined with the threatened restoration of Catholicism in full force, led to a dangerous revolt, Wyatt's Rebellion. Various notables of the Northumberland party plotted to put Mary's Protestant sister, Elizabeth, on the throne and to marry her to an Englishman. The revolt in the Midlands failed, but the men of Kent, under Sir Thomas Wyatt, followed much the same course that the rebels from that same county had taken in 1381 under Wat Tyler and in 1450 under Jack Cade. They marched on London, and with a little more boldness might have carried the day. Mary, endowed with the usual Tudor bravery, met the situation with the same coolness that Richard II had shown. She promised that she would not marry without the consent of Parliament, and the Londoners barred the way to Wyatt's men. Numerous executions followed, including that of Lady Jane Grey, whom Mary might have spared had she not been a focus for plots potentially too dangerous. Even the canny Princess Elizabeth, with her perennially deaf ear to plots and her professed loyalty to Mary, lay in the Tower in the shadow of the block. Parliament, with the usual compliance of such Tudor bodies, finally approved the marriage terms, which, thanks to the efforts of the patriots in the Council, were very favorable to England, imposing careful safeguards against any exercise of royal power on Philip's part. The combination of Philip and Mary was not a legally joint rule like that of William III and his wife (see page 274).

Had Mary made a moderate return to the faith of her forebears, England undoubtedly would have acquiesced. Moderation, however, was not in her nature, and those who would not return to the Roman fold were to be burned as heretics. When

Mary felt that she was serving God, no one could swerve her from her purpose. Three hundred men and women died in agony in the fires of Smithfield and elsewhere—an unusual number of executions even for callous Tudor England. A compliant Parliament sanctioned the repeal of all antipapal statutes since the beginning of Henry's "divorce" problem, and the revival of the old heresy laws. It would vote to meet new royal ideas in reconciliation with Rome and in dogma, but not to restore the seized monastic lands, in which some members were personally interested. No great spiritual revival accompanied the return to Catholicism. The Venetian ambassador remarked that "with the exception of a few pious Catholics, none of whom are under thirty-five years of age, all the rest make this show of recantation yet do not effectively resume the Catholic faith." Even three quarters of the parish clergy and a few bishops made the change. Lip service was enough to save life and property, and most Englishmen were ready to take that easy way. Some, however, would not. The victims of the Smithfield fires were mostly of humble origin, but attention centered upon three prelates who had been most active in pushing England toward Protestantism. Cranmer, in fear of the flames, at first recanted his Protestantism; but finally he announced his real faith and boldly thrust into the flames the hand that signed the recantation. Latimer and Bishop Ridley of Rochester were burned together at Oxford. "Be of good comfort, Master Ridley, and play the man," said Latimer; "we shall this day light such a candle by God's grace in England as, I trust, shall never be put out." He was right. These executions helped to bring about a tremendous reaction against Catholicism that lasted for centuries. John Foxe's *Book of Martyrs*, written with minute detail and a bitter anti-Catholic bias, kept alive the memories of the fires of Smithfield. Mary's open subservience to Spain and the Pope,

moreover, injected a patriotic element into the anti-Catholic movement. Even a century and a half later England took a stupid German for king simply because he was a Protestant.

Mary's foreign policy brought her into difficulties too. Partnership between Philip and Mary meant that Spain could use English resources without giving England any compensating privileges. The royal marriage did not enable the queen's subjects to enter the king's rich closely guarded colonial empire in America. That led, in Mary's reign, to the effort to reach the East by way of a northeast passage around the top of Europe, free from Spanish influence. Two captains, Willoughby and Chancellor, undertook the difficult voyage around the North Cape. The former was wrecked and lost; the latter reached the White Sea and opened trade with the semibarbarous Russian state of Muscovy through Archangel. With this attitude of "What's yours is mine and what's mine is mine, too," Philip persuaded Mary to drag England into a war against France, using English men and English money for purely Spanish purposes. A French general boasted that he could capture Calais in seven days; and he did, to a day, in the first week of 1558. That loss ended the five centuries of English ownership of land in France. Since the end of the Hundred Years' War, Calais had been the sole holding, and it was considered a useful commercial outpost, as well as a landing place for expeditions against France. Its loss proved no fundamental detriment to England; but it was a severe humiliation, and Mary declared that at her death the word "Calais" would be found graven on her heart.

Before the year was out she died, and London that night was merry with bonfires and cheering. Not the least cause of joy was that now with Philip II out of the picture, England had escaped from becoming enmeshed in the Spanish—Hapsburg coils.

The Glorious Age

Bitter resentment toward Mary made England skeptical about a second Tudor queen. The country could not foresee that Mary's sister, made of different stuff, was about to lead it into the most glorious period of all English history, a half century charged with dramatic action, high achievement, and keen zest for living. Inheriting "the shakiest throne in Europe," Elizabeth gave the nation forty-five years of internal prosperity, high international prestige, and splendid achievement, both on the seas and overseas. Another queen regnant, three centuries later, was to have a reign almost as great; but Victoria scarcely deserved the fame given to the imperious virgin daughter of Henry VIII and Anne Boleyn, for the accomplishments of Elizabethan England were in no small measure attributable to her own sagacity, tact, and inspiration.

Elizabeth at twenty-five when she came to the precarious throne radiated that "personal magnetism that Henry VIII had never lost." "Her appearance . . . was still very young and fragile," with a skin "of a glowing paleness" and smooth red-blond hair. Her hands were unusually beautiful. That magic of hers "was admitted even by those who distrusted and disliked her."[1]

[1] Elizabeth Jenkins, *Elizabeth the Great*, pp. 36, 62. © 1958 by Elizabeth Jenkins. By permission of Coward-McCann, Inc., and Victor Gollancz, Ltd.

An excellent Renaissance scholar, she was at home in French, Italian, and Latin; quick in repartee and brazen in deception, she could more than hold her own in matching wits with the most brilliant; ever the realist, with a clear sense of practical values, her shrewd mind proved a dependable brake upon her strong-willed, impulsive nature. Her hectic girlhood, when she had been the natural object of plots, was a hard school. Thanks to her own native wit and to a caution beyond her years, she had survived those perilous days which once had brought her close to the block. Stripped of illusions and cynical to boot, she had gained the knack of analyzing men and motives. With her father's ability to handle people, she knew how to say the right thing at the right moment. She could rebuff a minister, a suitor, or a Parliament more gracefully than many could grant a favor. She enhanced the power of the crown by colorful pageantry, not only in her gay and glittering court, but by showing herself frequently to the cheering Londoners and by making numerous "progresses" out into the counties. Despite this smiling, cheerful surface, there was iron in this "spirited and haughty" woman with her "genius for authority, who thoroughly enjoyed the exercise of power." Before she had been on the throne many months, England knew that this was a queen who could and would rule as well as reign.

The success of her reign depended to no small degree on her choice of capable ministers, whom she supported loyally. Almost none of importance came from among the playboys of her court. She might flirt with them, but only rarely entrusted them with serious business. Her ministers were members of the Privy Council, a group of a dozen or so "experienced, devoted, and grossly overworked" public servants, who really ran the government for her. Other rulers had had some such group; some highly efficient, like Henry I's Curia Regis, while others, staffed with prominent nobles, were far less so (see pages 57, 143). The system was particularly effective under the Tudors and responsible for much of their success. Selected largely from middle-class "new men," many of them served in the "great offices," such as secretary, treasurer, chancellor, and admiral. Collectively, they handled a tremendous variety of business, ranging from foreign policy to minor local details; they also divided into advisory committees for particular subjects. Their proclamations had the force of law, a power that Parliament would challenge in the next century. Much like the later cabinet they differed mainly in being responsible only to the Crown, rather than to Parliament, and in there being no specific "prime minister" (see pages 293 ff.).

Two members of Elizabeth's Privy Council towered above the rest. For forty years, her chief adviser was William Cecil, later Lord Burghley. Although never assuming the pompous magnificence of a Wolsey, Cecil, a great Parliamentarian, was one of the most capable and useful ministers in all English history. He came from the middle class, like most Tudor ministers; was educated at Cambridge; served as secretary to Somerset and to Northumberland; and managed to keep alive under Mary. Shrewd, practical, and tireless, cool and cautious, he saw eye to eye with

A "progress" of Elizabeth, attended by courtiers, with the younger Cecil in foreground.

Elizabeth on the role of the Reformation in England's future and on the "ruinous waste of war." And "in their life's business, the art of government, they recognized no distinction between work and pleasure." "To wait and see how things fell out, how others would commit themselves, and then to intervene at the last possible moment, was her method all her life." Her habit of taking "the credit to herself" when a policy succeeded but when "she had endorsed a failure or what threatened failure," to blame others sometimes goaded Cecil to complain.[2] Younger and somewhat more impulsive than Cecil was Francis Walsingham, who first served as ambassador to France. He organized an extremely efficient secret service, all important with the constant plots and tangled negotiations of those days.

[2] *Ibid.*, pp. 63, 80, 147.

Though Parliament exercised little real power under the Tudors, both houses underwent structural changes. Henry VIII's first Parliament contained two archbishops, nineteen bishops, and twenty-eight abbots to only twenty-nine lay peers. With the dissolution of the monasteries and removal of the abbots, the number of prelates dropped, while with new lay peers being created their number rose to eighty-two (see page 186). Although the House of Lords was to be more and more overshadowed by the Commons, the individual peers were increasingly able to influence the choice of borough members in the Commons. Originally required to elect bona-fide residents of the borough, the townsmen were now giving their votes more to non-resident country gentry—a class which had served from the beginning as shire or county members (see page 106). To the squires, these seats began to look increasingly desirable, whereas the townsmen were often relieved at not having the burden of supporting one of their number at Westminister, since no pay was attached to such service. The voters, being a very small group, tended to be easily influenced or bribed.

Problems of the gravest sort faced Elizabeth and Cecil in the last days of 1558. Edward and Mary had left their sister a sorry heritage. Feeling ran high and bitter. Finances were in a weak state, with a debased currency, dislocated trade, a heavy national debt, and poor governmental credit. In foreign affairs it was necessary to liquidate the unfortunate French war into which Philip had dragged England. Thus divided, England would be fortunate to escape absorption by Spain or France. To make matters worse, Elizabeth's own title to the throne was none too secure. She had been declared illegitimate by Parliament, and she had in Mary Queen of Scots an influential rival with a good Tudor claim to the crown.

Nevertheless, before she had been on the throne two years, Elizabeth and her ministers had brought about a remarkable recovery in finance, religion, and foreign affairs. Strict economy quickly restored the shattered national finances. Elizabeth in her first six months spent only 40 per cent of what Mary had spent in her last half year. The debased currency was called in, and sound money was issued. Sir Thomas Gresham, who founded the Royal Exchange and whose name is associated with the economic law that "bad money drives out good," was able to pay off the heavy loans incurred by Mary and to report by 1560 that England enjoyed better credit than any other nation in Europe. Elizabeth throughout her reign fully appreciated the advantages of a balanced budget, and her efforts in that direction brought her, like her grandfather, under charges of stinginess.

The "Elizabethan Compromise"

Elizabeth also realized that were she to follow either the Protestant extremes of Edward VI or the Catholic extremes of Mary, turmoil and disunity would continue. Her compromise was clever if not noble. She herself probably had no strong religious convictions. She was bound closely, however, to the antipapal side, since the intimation of her coming birth had hastened the "divorce" of Catherine and Henry, thereby accelerating the breach with Rome. Elizabeth herself could not, had she so wished, have been Roman Catholic *and* queen, since in the eyes of Rome she was illegitimate.

The "Elizabethan compromise" was designed to include as many Englishmen, Protestant and Catholic, as possible. The first Parliament of the reign passed most of the legislation essential for this, and a later Parliament ratified the beliefs of the Anglican Church in the Thirty-nine Articles, a modification of Cranmer's Forty-two. In addition, a Parliamentary Act of Uniformity required all Englishmen to conform to the Church of England. The Court of High Commission, a special Tudor tribunal, like the Court of Star Chamber and the Council of the North, was established to handle cases arising under this act. At first, however, the recusants, those who refused to conform, were let off rather easily. Not until after 1569, when the Catholics had become very active with plots and rebellion, was the act enforced at all harshly.

In general, independent of Roman control, as it was, the Church of England was regarded as Protestant, especially in the doctrinal belief embodied in the Thirty-nine Articles, although it still kept some Catholic aspects, such as the rubric (the directions for public worship placed in italics in the prayer book). This contradiction was illogical, but English institutions both then and now have never been noted for logic. What Elizabeth and the English people wanted was a comprehensive church which would include as great a variety of Christians as possible. Uncompromising Catholics were dissatisfied, for the Church denied both transubstantiation and the authority of the Pope; the more extreme Protestants also were displeased; and both these minority groups remained outside the Church. The new arrangement, however, was flexible enough to include both the High Church element, which approached Catholic practices in elaborate ritual, and the opposite group of many Protestants who wished to "purify" the Church still further from Romish influence, particularly in regard to vestments and ritual. These "Puritans" comprised the Low Church group in the Elizabethan establishment; and, like the Catholics and extreme Protestants, they were later to cause trouble. For the time being, however, the majority of Englishmen had had quite enough of church broils and were content with the easygoing compromise.

The Church of England was more than a matter of dogma and ritual. As an "established" church, it was also a part of the government; its bishops were appointed and its policies were determined by the political authorities. Elizabeth herself, to spare the feelings of moderate Catholics, substituted, in her titles, the expression "and so forth" where her father and brother had used "Supreme Head of the Church"; but she kept the full authority. It was, for example, even decreed that Wednesday, in addition to Friday, should be meatless, in order to encourage the fisheries.

The Church of England lacked the vital force that goes with more positive settlements. Religious fervor was seldom one of its features, and its services often lapsed into perfunctory formalism. At that price Elizabeth spared England the terrible excesses which were marking religious disputes in many other lands during her day. She had, moreover, a united England at her back when she faced Catholic France and Spain.

Precarious Neutrality

Elizabeth's foreign problems were not settled so quickly and easily. They required the closest attention and cleverest handling. It is no small tribute to her and to Cecil that they gave England a quarter century of nominal peace, the longest such period since Henry III. Peace meant economy in national finances and a breathing spell in which the nation could build up commercial prosperity. Many forces, however, threatened to draw England into open conflict.

European political and diplomatic relations were seriously complicated by the movement which Protestants call the Counter Reformation and Catholics, the Catholic Reformation. Rome did not accept without a struggle the terrific dismemberment it had sustained during the first half of the century (see pages 178 ff.). It sought, partly by cleaning house and partly by intrigue and force, to recover as many as possible of the lands which had turned, or were threatening to turn, to Protestantism. The Church had called a council in 1545 in the Alpine city of Trent to consider reforms. The Protestants were invited in the hope that they would return to the fold, but they held aloof. For almost twenty years the Council of Trent held its intermittent sessions, doing much to purify the Church of past abuses. It reaffirmed the Catholic belief in the seven sacraments, in papal supremacy, and in other orthodox doctrines. The Counter Reformation found invaluable agents in the new Society of Jesus, an order resembling friars, and founded by a former Spanish army officer, Ignatius Loyola. These Jesuits received a remarkably thorough training, submitted to an extremely rigid discipline, and often showed fearless devotion in the face of death. They did great work as educators and missionaries and were very energetic in their political activity, which Protestant England came to regard with grave suspicion.

The Counter Reformation ensured to the Roman fold Poland, Bohemia, the southern Netherlands (now Belgium), south-central Germany, and most of France. It was the signal for a century of bitter religious wars, which broke out about the time Elizabeth came to the throne. In the name of religion, men indulged in some of the dirtiest fighting Europe has ever seen west of the Balkans. Religion, to be sure, was often only a pretext for political or economic disputes, which might be carried out the more ruthlessly in that name. France and Spain, the two most powerful countries in Europe, might use religion as a cloak for their designs upon English independence; but they, like Scotland, both had their own religious civil wars between the Catholics and the Calvinists. In France, dominated by Catherine de' Medici through her three weak sons as successive kings, troubles with the Calvinist Huguenots distracted the nation from 1562 to 1594 in a long and bewildering series of civil conflicts in which both Catholic and Huguenot partisans were guilty of excessive brutality. The bloody climax came on Saint Bartholomew's Eve, 1572, on the occasion of the wedding of the king's sister and the Protestant Henry of Navarre, when the Catholics massacred between ten thousand and thirty thousand Huguenots. When this Huguenot leader finally came to the throne as Henry IV, the first Bourbon king, he turned Catholic to win the support of Paris; but at the same time he granted toleration to the Huguenots in the famous Edict of Nantes. Philip II of Spain, archchampion of the Counter Reformation, used energetic and cruel means in a vain effort to stamp out Protestantism in the Netherlands. In 1567 a "Council of Blood" under his viceroy there found victims by the hundreds; yet his powerful regiments of Spanish infantry, the best troops in Europe, could not crush the revolt, which continued under William the Silent, prince of Orange. The southern Netherlands (now Belgium) remained Spanish and Catholic; but the northern provinces, commonly called Holland, eventually won their freedom in an "eighty years' war" with Spain, fought vigorously on land and sea. By the close of Elizabeth's reign the Dutch were virtually free and about to enter upon a period of commercial prosperity. Scotland, converted thoroughly to Calvinism by John Knox, rebelled against her Catholic regent. During all this period the papacy itself interfered frequently in international and internal affairs.

Faced with this situation, Elizabeth and her ministers followed a course which was bewildering in the details of its tactics but was quite consistent in its general strategy. They kept the country out of open war until it should be strong enough to fight successfully. They accomplished this by means of frequent double-dealing, quick changes of face, downright lying, and occasional abandonment of allies. Walsingham and the more enthusiastic advisers urged a more heroic championship of Protestantism. Elizabeth and Cecil, however, after one unfortunate venture in France, were too calculating to be drawn into such activity. They were ready to sneak money and even men to aid the Huguenots, the Dutch, and the Scottish Presbyterians; but Elizabeth did not want openly to encourage rebellion against a lawful monarch. She herself, with the questionable legitimacy of her birth, was too vulnerable. The other countries were employing similar, but less successful, methods to bring about a revolt of the English Catholics. Elizabeth also condoned the raids of her seamen on the Spanish Main—a further example of how far a nation could go without actually declaring open war. Elizabethan England was full of men who were ready to fight papists or to chase galleons, with the clear understanding that if they should fail, Elizabeth and Cecil would disavow their acts to protesting ambassadors. Thus it was that England was steered in a safe but tortuous course, guided by general considerations of balance of power.

An unmarried Elizabeth was a very valuable diplomatic asset in these efforts to prevent war. The possibility of sharing the English throne kept more than one foreign prince in line. During her first two years as queen Elizabeth had fifteen proposals, coming from eight different countries. Philip II tried to continue the advantages he had enjoyed as the husband of Mary. An Austrian archduke, a very persistent Danish prince, and later even Ivan the Terrible, Czar of Russia, were among her suitors. To hold France in line, Elizabeth dallied with two brothers of Charles IX in turn; her flirtation with the younger one, a rather stupid young man with a huge nose, lasted until she was nearly fifty. Some Englishmen too aspired to the honor. Perhaps, as rumor says, the only man Elizabeth ever cared for was Robert Dudley, whom she later made Earl of Leicester. His father, Northumberland, and his grandfather, the tax-collector, had both been beheaded; but that did not injure his career. When his neglected young wife, Amy Robsart, was found dead of a broken neck, England buzzed with gossip that Lord Robert was clearing his way to the throne. Although a crop of scandals attached themselves to the queen's reputation, modern research has indicated that Virginia was not misnamed. Parliament, fearing the dangers of a disputed succession if Elizabeth should die unwed, kept urging her to marry, but she persistently procrastinated. England, she said, was her husband.

Mary Stuart and Scotland

Elizabeth's name is always associated with that of her younger and more attractive cousin and rival for the throne, Mary Stuart. "Queen of Scots" in her own name since babyhood, temporarily queen consort of France, and, as great-granddaughter of Henry VII, enjoying a title to the English throne almost as good as Elizabeth's, Mary was in a powerful position. Tall, with an exquisite pale skin and beautiful dark-brown eyes and hair, Mary had a feminine charm so irresistible that she is ranked as one of the most fascinating women of history. Passion and impulse, however, led her to throw away her many advantages and to be at times incredibly foolish. Her English cousin sacrificed the woman to the queen; Mary sacrificed the queen to the woman every time. So it was that eventually Mary lost her life at Elizabeth's order.

Scottish affairs loomed large at the outset of Elizabeth's reign. French influence was strong at Edinburgh; for Mary's French mother, of the strongly Catholic Guise family, was the regent. Mary herself, at sixteen, had just married the heir to the French throne, whose brief reign as Francis II was about to begin. England feared a French invasion through Scotland, her "postern gate." It was, however, a restless, poverty-stricken, and far from united land (see pages 286, 307), with religion contributing to the unrest. The Calvinism brought over by the stern John Knox appealed strongly to a large proportion of the Lowland Scots, and they were up in arms against the French-Catholic regent. Elizabeth gave active aid, by land and sea, to the rebels. By 1560 Cecil secured a favorable treaty at Edinburgh, which virtually eliminated the French influence.

A year later Mary, a widow of eighteen, accustomed to French gaiety, returned to her chill somber northern homeland. She was not content to be simply queen of that barren realm, and she was to spend her remaining years in intrigue for a more impressive title. She was soon in conflict with sober John Knox, who disapproved of everything about her. In 1565 Mary married her cousin, Henry Stuart, Lord Darnley, a Protestant, who like herself was descended from Henry VII. A weak and drunken debauchee, he soon aroused Mary's contempt.

The three years following were filled with melodrama in which Mary's folly sealed her fate. She was soon paying too much attention to her Italian secretary, David Rizzio. In March, 1566, Darnley and others broke into Mary's sitting-room and murdered Rizzio before her eyes. Three months later Mary had a son, the future James VI of Scotland and James I of England. In February, 1567, Darnley, who was convalescing from an illness at a little house just outside Edinburgh, was visited by Mary. That night the house was blown up, and his strangled body was found outside. Letters, possibly forged, later found in a silver jewel casket, seriously incriminated Mary. Scotland was, on the whole, glad to be rid of Darnley, but it was shocked three months later when Mary married the Earl of Bothwell, a "glorified border ruffian" supposedly involved in Darnley's murder. Some contended Bothwell used force, but Mary had shown him previous favor. At once the nobles revolted,

defeated the queen's supporters, and ten weeks after her third marriage, forced her to abdicate in favor of the infant James. Mary was imprisoned, made a dramatic escape in 1568, was again defeated, and fled to England, where she threw herself on the mercy of Elizabeth.

Elizabeth and her ministers did not know how to dispose of the Scottish queen. They might have sent her back to Scotland, but they distrusted her word and feared further troubles north of the border. They could foresee that kept in England, on the other hand, she would become the center of Catholic plots, domestic and foreign, to win England, by means of her coronation as its queen, back to Rome. This latter risk, however, seemed the lesser of the two evils, and so Mary began her nineteen years of mild imprisonment in England.

Her presence was partly responsible in 1569, the year after she arrived, for the one serious threat of rebellion in Elizabeth's reign. This was partly a political intrigue by various nobles, under the Duke of Norfolk, to oust Cecil and partly a Catholic revolt in the north, which, still remaining feudal and conservative, disapproved of the rapid changes going on in southern and eastern England. Led by some northern nobles, hundreds of sincere peasants, wearing the red cross of crusaders, took up what crude arms they could find, occupied Durham, and held Catholic services at a discarded altar in the cathedral. Elizabeth's government acted with speed and vigor. Before the rebels could free her, Mary was whisked away to a safer place of confinement, and loyal forces, although outnumbered, dispersed the rebels. Norfolk went home sick and was arrested. Elizabeth's reign had not witnessed a single execution for religious or political purposes—a remarkable contrast to the previous Tudor reigns—until the aftermath of this revolt spoiled this record.

A year later the Pope issued a bill excommunicating Elizabeth, calling her a usurper, and releasing her subjects from obedience. In 1571, also, Walsingham discovered a fantastic plot, formed by one Ridolfi, an Italian banker, to put Mary Stuart on the throne with the help of foreign force. Norfolk, the ranking peer and last remaining duke in England, was seriously implicated in this plot also, and paid for it with his head, thus putting the Howard family ahead of the Dudleys in the matter of executions. Mary was to remain in confinement, at one country estate or another, for seventeen years more, until she became the center of a new crop of plots so serious that her death was deemed necessary.

In foreign relations England was shifting from Spain to France. The French were no longer an active menace in Scotland, while Philip II was assuming more and more the role of political champion of the Counter Reformation. Part of his war against Protestantism consisted of support of Mary Stuart for the English throne. England, therefore, began to give secret aid to the Dutch rebelling against him, opening for a while her ports to the "Sea Beggars" who were making serious depredations upon Spanish shipping.

The Sea Dogs

One reason which led to strained relations between England and Spain lay three thousand miles away. Spain had followed up the discoveries of Columbus with conquests which gave her most of the southern part of North America, Central America, and most of South America (see pages 159-161). Spain's chief interest in those American possessions lay in the silver mines of Mexico and Peru, which annually provided the equivalent of millions of dollars. Commerce with those regions was rigidly regulated. Each year a great fleet set out from Spain, the cargo vessels being conveyed by warships. On reaching the West Indies, it generally split, one part sailing to Veracruz, where the Mexican silver was brought

down from the interior, the rest of the ships heading for the Isthmus of Panama, for the Peruvian silver, which was brought by ship up the Pacific coast and carried across the Isthmus by mule trains. Then the two divisions would rejoin at Havana in Cuba for the return to Spain. The "royal fifth" of the American silver went into the national treasury. Spain neglected the normal economic demands of her colonists, who wanted slaves and other commodities which the mother country failed to provide in adequate quantity. At the same time Spain kept her colonial empire a rigid commercial monopoly and forbade the colonists to trade with any other nation.

This situation strongly appealed to England. Early in Elizabeth's reign we find the beginning of persistent Anglo-Saxon efforts to get a share of those riches, which Spain tried to monopolize. The English sought to supply articles to that large but neglected market, and eventually also to plunder the plate fleets, and the cities of the Spanish Main, where the treasure was collected.

Much of the glamour of Elizabeth's reign comes from the adventures of her most colorful subjects, the "sea dogs." These tough mariners, most of whom came from Devon and operated from Plymouth, on the southwest coast, spent part of their energy in exploring arctic wastes and in trying to plant new colonies, but a great deal more in their daring adventures in breaking Spain's monopoly on the seas and in the lands beyond the seas. Until that was accomplished, England could not expand into the maritime and colonial field where she was eventually to be the most successful nation. Even after Philip II's marriage to Mary, Spain would permit no peaceful infringement of her colonial monopoly.

Force, then, was England's only pathway to colonial fortune. The sea dogs were eager to apply that force against the galleons, seaports, and treasure trains of His Catholic Majesty. The drawback, as the cautious Cecil kept emphasizing, was that inroads on the Spanish colonies might well lead to war with the strongest power in Europe. The legal status of the sea dogs, moreover, was anomalous; a monarch could not properly commission them to prey on neutral shipping in peacetime. They were technically pirates, but with royal connivance. Elizabeth, more ready to take a chance, secretly invested in their commercial ventures, lent them warships of the royal navy, and took her very generous share of their profits. At the same time, she tried to preserve the appearance of peace, by profusely apologizing to the Spanish envoys for the actions of her unruly subjects. For a whole quarter of a century, those "pious pirates" harried the Spanish Main before they finally goaded Spain into war on England, which was by then in a position to smash Spanish sea power.

The pioneer of the group, John Hawkins, later Sir John, the son of a prominent Plymouth merchant and shipowner, conceived the idea of selling African negroes as slaves to the Spanish colonists, in spite of the fact that the colonists were forbidden to deal with foreigners. In 1562, he picked up a cargo of Negroes on the Guinea coast and successfully peddled it along the Spanish Main. Two years later he set out with a more ambitious expedition for which the queen lent a worn-out warship. In view of the Spanish regulations and warnings by Elizabeth and Cecil not to provoke Spain too outrageously, he had to resort to subterfuges. He would put into a colonial port ostensibly in desperate need of water or supplies or refitting. If he could not bribe the authorities, he would fire his guns or land men so that the local officials could report that they had been trading under compulsion. The colonists themselves were delighted to have a chance to buy the slaves. Hawkins's second voyage netted a profit of 60 per cent. His third voyage, in 1567-1568, however, came to grief. All along the coast of Spanish America he found that the authorities had strict orders to have nothing to do with him. Finally he put in at Veracruz, in Mexico, to refit. While he was there a powerful Spanish fleet arrived to convoy the treasure ships. In a desperate, one-sided fight, only two of the English vessels escaped. Many of Hawkins's men were imprisoned, and some were burned as heretics. The more fortunate settled down in Mexico with native wives.

Hawkins was soon overshadowed in reputation by his stocky, brown-bearded, daredevil young cousin Francis Drake, later Sir Francis. Drake had taken part in that disastrous third voyage and had escaped from Veracruz. More impetuous than Hawkins, he did not bother with pretenses of "legal" trading but went out boldly for loot. Autocratic, violent in temper, and with an insatiable thirst for glory, Drake had a resolute will and a breezy, magnetic personal charm. Before he was thirty, he was a terror to Spain and an idol to England. He sailed from Plymouth in 1572 on a voyage of reckless adventure with two little vessels and a youthful crew of seventy-three. On the Isthmus of Panama, where the treasures of Peru were brought overland, he ambushed a rich treasure train, leaving fifteen tons of silver behind because the other loot was more valuable.

Then Drake conceived an even bolder design. He realized that the Spanish Main was by this time well on guard; but the Spaniards on the Pacific probably were taking no such precautions with their ships bringing Peruvian silver to Panama. Elizabeth made a secret investment in his risky project, warning him to keep his plan from Cecil. Late in 1577 Drake led one of the most famous expeditions in English history out of Plymouth harbor. Following Magellan's course, he led his little squadron through the tortuous and treacherous Strait of Magellan, only to run into a terrific gale on the Pacific side. One vessel was lost, another put back to England, and Drake kept on alone in the *Golden Hind.* Catching the Spaniards completely off guard, he raided up the coast, overhauled an unsuspecting treasure ship, and had her cargo of precious metals transferred to the *Golden Hind* till she could hold no more. Now came the question of getting home. Drake knew full well that the Spaniards would be waiting for him at the Strait of Magellan; so he pushed on up the coast into the fogs of Vancouver, hoping to find a passage back to the Atlantic. Failing in that, he dropped back to San Francisco Bay and took possession in the name of Elizabeth, and named it New Albion. Then he set out westward across the Pacific. Once more Drake picked up the course of Magellan's voyage sixty years earlier, and came back around the Cape of Good Hope. Finally, after an absence of nearly three years, the *Golden Hind* rode into Plymouth harbor, the first English ship to circumnavigate the earth. Whole wagon loads of treasure were carried to London; the queen made a personal profit of some £163,000, which was about 40 per cent of the total booty. The other investors made nearly a fiftyfold gain on their shares. The Spanish ambassador protested as usual, but Elizabeth herself knighted Drake on the deck of the *Golden Hind.*

Having tasted so freely of Spanish treasure, the English returned again and again to the Spanish Main; but no subsequent raid yielded either the romance or the profit of Drake's great voyage. Meanwhile another sea dog, Martin Frobisher, tried to find a northwest passage around America, as an English short cut to the East. North of Labrador he discovered the bay which bears his name. John Davis also left his name on the Arctic map.

In 1585 English seagoing activity took a more constructive form when Sir Walter Raleigh attempted to plant a colony in Virginia. Raleigh was too versatile and too elegant to be classed simply as a sea dog. He represented, in extreme form, the Eliza-

bethan expression of the many-sided man of the Renaissance who, finding any single field too narrow for his ambitious ability, made a considerable mark in several fields. Raleigh was at times explorer, naval officer, and promoter of colonization; but he was also courtier, soldier, poet, historian, economist, and businessman. Like Hawkins and Drake, he was a product of Devonshire, the son of a prominent landholder. He left Oxford to fight in the French religious wars, lived in London for a while as one of the gayest of young bloods, and went to Ireland as an officer in the army sent against the rebels. Several cruel acts marred his record there before he was sent back to court with dispatches. That event marked the beginning of his rapid rise. Adept at intrigue, he made a habit of criticizing his superiors to their superiors and rose rapidly. He soon won the favor of the queen, who from time to time presented him with lucrative monopolies, and sufficient estates in England and Ireland to make him the most extensive landholder in the country. Historians question the familiar story of the cloak and puddle, but it was perhaps typical of the tactics by which he became the chief favorite of Elizabeth in the period between Leicester and Essex. Few men were more thoroughly hated; he was considered an insolent upstart, untrustworthy and unscrupulous. Elizabeth characteristically never entrusted him with any really serious business of state, although she made him captain of her guard and piled riches upon him, until he married without her knowledge or permission.

He deserves much credit for his stimulus to colonization. The transplanting of Englishmen into overseas regions was to become a distinctive feature of the country's greatness, and, while the first permanent settlement was not founded until four years after Elizabeth's death, Raleigh was pointing the way by 1585. Several expeditions were sent to the deserted region, north of

Landing in 1585 of short-lived Roanoke colony near Hatteras, carried home next year by Drake; drawn by John White who headed 1587 "Lost Colony" there.

Spanish Florida, which he is supposed to have christened Virginia in honor of the queen. Those first settlers, however, were disappointed in their search for gold and silver. One group, on little Roanoke Island, disappeared completely, and other colonists were brought back in a starving condition. Raleigh, meanwhile, was credited with having introduced tobacco and the potato to Europe.

The domestic situation had quieted down after the rebellion of 1569 and the Ridolfi plot two years later. By 1580, however, new Catholic agents were arriving in England. These Jesuits, after receiving training in seminaries on the Continent, returned to engage in the risky attempt to restore England to Rome (see pages 197 ff.). Manor houses, especially in the north country, had secret "priest holes" for these devoted men, who not only held surreptitious Mass for those who remained Catho-

lic, but soon became engaged in plots to assassinate Elizabeth and to bring back Catholicism with foreign aid. In 1586 the most serious conspiracy, the Babington plot, aimed to kill Elizabeth and her ministers at court and to rush Mary Stuart to the throne. Philip II sent money, but Walsingham's spies were in the innermost councils of the conspirators. The Scottish queen, still a prisoner after all these years, was the center of the plotting. Elizabeth's ministers persuaded her that the security of England demanded the death of Mary. Elizabeth hesitated and finally tried to throw the responsibility on others, but the unfortunate Queen of Scots was beheaded at Fotheringay Castle on a February morning in 1587.

That execution accomplished what Drake's raids had failed to do. Philip and the other Catholics had kept hoping that Mary might yet be queen of England. Now, motivated by both religious and by national interests, Philip began to gather warships for an expedition to crush the obstinate heritics, to make England Catholic, and, incidentally, to put a stop to the humiliating raids of the sea dogs. The latter, however, acted upon the principle that "the best defense is the offensive." Drake swept down on Cádiz and destroyed some of the fleet which Philip was assembling; then cruising off St. Vincent, he inflicted further damage by intercepting vital supplies. This "singeing of the King of Spain's beard" postponed the final showdown until the following year.

Hawkins, after the Veracruz disaster, had undertaken a more prosaic but very important task ashore as principal administrative officer of the royal navy. Henry VIII had given the navy a good start, but Hawkins found and fought conservatism and corruption. By the development of a new type of warship, he probably did more than anyone else to defeat the Spaniards. Their clumsy galleons with very high forecastles and poops were designed for the old style of fighting—laying alongside the enemy for an infantry battle at sea—and Spain had the best infantry in Europe. The new vessel, with which the sea dogs were experimenting, had its forecastle and poop sharply cut down and its lines enabled it to be navigated with more speed and efficiency. Above all, it made close-range boarding action obsolete, for it was equipped with plenty of guns that could outrange and pound the enemy from a distance without his being able to come to grips. The royal navy itself was still small; but in those days the line between warship and private ship not being sharply drawn, it was reinforced with the ships of many sea dogs and other mariners.

The Spanish Armada

By 1588 Philip had repaired the damage of Drake's Cádiz raid and had concentrated most of Spanish sea power in an "Armada" of some one hundred and thirty vessels and thirty thousand men for the conquest of England. Only eight thousand of his men were sailors; most of the rest were infantry, who were to prove useless against the English long-range tactics. Spain's best admiral, a veteran of fifty years at sea, died just as the preparations were approaching completion. Philip chose as his successor the Duke of Medina Sidonia, whose chief asset was his high social rank, which was then considered essential to control highborn captains. The duke tried to dodge the responsibility: "I know by experience of the little I have been at sea that I am always seasick and always catch cold. Since I have had no experience either of the sea, or of war, I cannot feel that I ought to command so important an enterprise." Philip remained stubborn; so the "Golden Duke" took command of the expedition which helped to end Spanish greatness.

For command of her fleet, Elizabeth also picked a titled name, Lord Howard of Effingham, a Protestant member of the otherwise Catholic Howard family. A fairly able naval officer, he deferred in his decisions to the foremost seaman of England, Sir Francis Drake, his vice-admiral. Hawkins was rear admiral, and other sea dogs were also prominent. Drake once more wanted to raid the Spanish ports before the Armada set sail, but the queen's hesitation prevented him. Late in July the Armada appeared off the southwest coast, driven by a wind which held the English bottled up in Plymouth. By desperate work they towed their warships out into open water, and then, in a running fight all along the south coast, the Spanish "floating barracks" got a taste of the English tactics. The lighter, faster English ships, about two hundred in number, hammered the Spanish craft, which could not reply effectively. Spanish strategy was hampered by the Armada's orders to head for the Netherlands to convoy the Spanish army of its governor, the Duke of Parma, to England.

The Spanish Armada off Start Point in Devon, pursued by the more maneuverable English fleet, July 22, 1588; from engraving based on contemporary tapestry.

That was an impossible task: the Low Country's ports were too shallow for the big Armada ships to come close, and had Parma's troop barges attempted to go out unprotected, they would have been snapped up by Dutch warships off the coast. This had been pointed out to Philip, but he ordered the Armada to sail regardless. Medina Sidonia, harried by the English who had the wind at their backs, was pursued across the Channel to Calais. To dislodge him, the English let blazing fire ships loose in that port, whereupon the terrified Spaniards cut their moorings and straggled out into the gale. The whole Armada was nearly driven ashore on the Flemish sandbanks. The English followed, pounding them mercilessly as long as their powder lasted; the winds, then, completed England's task. The crippled Spaniards rounded the north end of Scotland, leaving wrecks wherever they were swept. Several

of their ships went ashore on the Irish coast, where the crews were massacred. Medina Sidonia finally struggled back to Spain with only a fraction of his original proud force; even on those ships, men continued to die by the hundreds of scurvy and typhus. "The Armada had been sent, too weak and too scantily supplied, on an impossible mission. . . . There is a tendency of late to speak more kindly of Medina Sidonia, to recognize his courage and his administrative ability, but no one has yet said he could not have done better. It is at least arguable, however, that no one could."[3] For a full century, Spain had been the first country of Europe; those terrible days of gunnery and gales off the British coasts began her decline.

Until Elizabeth's death, the sea dogs were to continue their tormenting of Spain,

[3] Garrett Mattingly, *The Armada* (Houghton Mifflin Company, 1959), pp. 270, 275.

both at home and on the Spanish Main. Cádiz itself was once more raided under Raleigh, while Drake and Hawkins both died in the Caribbean in 1595 on an unsuccessful expedition. In the most famous post-Armada encounter, an English fleet was sent to the Azores, in 1591, to intercept the treasure convoy from America. The Spaniards forewarned, fell upon them with a greatly superior force. To cover the escape of the other English vessels, Sir Richard Grenville, who at the last minute had replaced his cousin Raleigh in the little *Revenge,* stood off fifteen Spanish warships, all larger than his own, from midafternoon to dawn. With her masts gone and her decks slippery with blood, she was battered into a hopeless wreck. Grenville then got a taste of Spanish close-range tactics, in a long grim cutlass fight, in which the Spaniards lost heavily. At last, with hope long since past, Grenville wanted to blow up his ship, but his subordinates persuaded him to surrender. Gravely wounded, he was taken to the Spanish flagship and treated with all courtesy; but, after crushing wineglasses and swallowing the fragments, he died before reaching port. The *Revenge,* too, the only English warship captured by Spain in the whole period, sank before reaching port.

The breaking of Spanish sea power immediately opened distant regions to England, Holland, and France, both in the East and in America. Philip II's seizure of the Portuguese throne in 1580 gave Spain a brief monopoly of European contact with the other continents (see page 161). Once her control of the seas had been broken, she had only strength enough to preserve the colonies which she had already established in America, from Florida southward, fairly intact for more than two centuries longer; and her silver fleets from America continued to come regularly until 1804. She could not defend nor could she keep others out of the Portuguese possessions, centering in the Spice Islands and the coast of India, as well as in the American region north of Florida that she neglected because it was "too much like Spain."

The influence of the Armada's defeat is shown by the rush of England, Holland, and France into these two regions. By 1596, English and Dutch squadrons were seeking out the weak points of the rotting Portuguese empire in the East. On December 31, 1600, Elizabeth chartered the English East India Company; two years later the Dutch East India Company came into being. In 1605, the French settled Port Royal in Acadia (Nova Scotia) and in 1608, Quebec. In 1607 the English made their first permanent American settlement at Jamestown. In 1609 Henry Hudson, sailing for the Dutch, explored the river which bears his name and which shortly became the scene of a Dutch settlement.

Troubles in Ireland

A more sordid undertone ran throughout Elizabeth's reign in the bloody chapter written into the sorry story of Anglo-Irish relations (see page 167). Henry VIII tried to placate the turbulent tribal chieftains by honorary English titles, and tried to hold them in line by a series of able deputies. English authority, however, meant little beyond the "Pale," which was still limited to about twenty miles around Dublin. The religious reforms were extended to Ireland under Henry VIII and Edward VI; but they were not taken seriously outside the Pale, and the principal effect was felt in the abolition of the monasteries, the only centers of learning and culture in the land. Ireland was to maintain a costly and unattended Anglican Established Church until 1869; but the English religious policy might have caused no particular trouble if the Jesuits had not stirred up religious feeling to embitter the already existing political and racial hatreds. Ireland became one of the most devoted Catholic regions in the world. And, in those days of Elizabeth, with Catholicism went Spanish influence.

It became a byword that "England's necessity is Ireland's opportunity"; so Philip II, hoping to open a side door by which to attack England, joined with the Jesuits in arousing the natives of the "other island."

There were three very serious Irish revolts during Elizabeth's reign, one in the early years, another in the middle, and the third ending only a year before her death. The principal centers of the revolts were Ulster, the seat of the O'Neills in the north, and Munster, the stronghold of the Desmonds in the south. English influence was fairly strong in the eastern province of Leinster, while the western province, Connaught, was too remote for serious trouble. The story of those revolts is a monotonous record of treachery and atrocities. Just as before and since that time, England did not use sufficient force to subdue Ireland as thoroughly as she had Wales; and half measures were enough to antagonize and to embitter but not to crush. Englishmen, who were horrified by Spanish cruelty to Dutchmen and Indians, murdered men, women, and children in cold blood, or so devastated the land that thousands ate weeds or grass until they died of starvation. "The eagles flew to the Spanish Main," it was said, "while the vultures descended on Ireland"; some sea dogs hunted the "wild Irish" between voyages. The Irish, on their part, would generally begin a revolt by a surprise massacre of every "Saxon" in the region. This Irish fighting cost the English treasury nearly fifteen times as much as the repulse of the Armada.

The third Irish revolt was marked by the dramatic fall of Elizabeth's third favorite, Leicester's stepson, the Earl of Essex. Young, handsome, and chivalrous, he was a fool in matters of discretion and judgment. The honors and privileges which the queen heaped upon him went to his head. This spoiled darling of the court, a magnet for all the exuberantly adventurous young bloods of England, led them in several ventures on land and sea, only one of which was successful. Elizabeth departed from her usual rule when she entrusted him with the chief command in Ireland in 1599. He abused his power and neglected his duty. When finally called to account, he conspired with the rebel leader whom he had failed to defeat. Returning to England, he continued his plots to seize the throne by force, and was executed for treason in 1601. The Irish command, in the meantime, had gone to Lord Mountjoy, a real soldier, who broke the revolt and gave to Elizabeth, in her last year, a control over Ireland which no previous English monarch had enjoyed (see page 231).

The next reign was to catch the full force of the Parliamentary protests which began to appear during Elizabeth's last years. The defeat of the Armada brought an increased feeling of security and strong national enthusiasm, but it also produced a new feeling in Parliament. For a century that body had acquiesced in Tudor tactics which sometimes had tended strongly toward absolutism. As long as England was threatened by foreign foes, religious discord, or fears of a disputed succession, Parliament was ready to waive a certain amount of freedom in the interests of security. Now, however, everything seemed secure. The first session of Parliament after the Armada was ready for more fighting, but grumbled even at the moderate cost of that tremendous victory. Its grant was given reluctantly and was collected very slowly. In later sessions Parliament attacked certain royal prerogatives, particularly the granting of monopolies to favorites. Yet, out of respect and gratitude to the old queen, Parliament saved its real attacks for her successor.

Twice during the reign, however, Parliament tackled social and economic reforms which were to remain at least nominally in effect for more than two centuries. As in the previous Tudor reigns, the lower classes were in a bad way, although it was a period of prosperity and pleasanter living for those of higher estate. Now that a man's home did not have to be built like a castle for protection, the nobility and gentry, in many instances enriched from earlier monastic loot, were building comfortable, rambling homes, with broad chimneys and mullioned windows. The long nominal peace also swelled the profits of merchants and tradesmen. On the other hand, there were the tens of thousands, uprooted and unemployed, and whole villages emptied because of the enclosures for sheep grazing (see page 169). Partly to remedy this, Parliament passed in 1563 the Statute of Apprentices (or Statute of Artificers), which placed upon a national basis the regulation of industry and labor, formerly handled locally. Requiring many to remain engaged in agriculture, it tried to check the march from country to town. The act stipulated that everyone must have an occupation, but only those who had served an apprenticeship of at least seven years could participate in town industries; and admission to apprenticeship in some fields required a specified family income. Each year the local justices of the peace were to determine the proper wages for the various industries. Long before the act was formally repealed in 1814 it was widely felt to have cramped economic development. Even under Elizabeth, Parliament was unable to legislate everyone into a job; multitudes of "valiant and lusty beggars" were elements of disorder during a considerable part of the century, while the "lame, ympotente, olde, blynde, . . . poore and not able to worke" had been in misery, particularly after the dissolution of the monasteries. The early 1590's saw grave famine and distress, and Parliament in 1597 and again in 1601 tried, with as little success as Somerset (see page 190), to strike at the enclosure movement itself. In its "Poor Laws" it at least did something to alleviate the consequences of enclosure by making the parish the responsible unit for its own poor and by trying to end the wandering and begging. Savage penalties were aimed at the able-bodied vagrant who was to be either banished or "stripped naked from the middle upwards and shall be openly whipped until his or her body be bloodye." More constructive was the companion act to improve the "miserable estate of the godly and honest sort of the poor subjects of this Realm." Each parish appointed four overseers of the poor, who, with the church wardens, had the power of compulsory taxation for poor relief. The money thus raised was to be devoted to binding out poor children as apprentices, buying raw materials to give work for the unemployed, and building workhouses for the very poor. This act was the basis of subsequent poor relief in England, where it was to remain in force, virtually unchanged, for two centuries; and its system of decentralized, local responsibility also spread to America.

Shakespeare

William Shakespeare was the most famous of all the Elizabethans; yet surprisingly little is known about his life. He was born in 1564 at Stratford-on-Avon, of old yeoman stock, his father a man of some local importance, his mother a peg or two higher in the social scale. Apparently he attended the local "grammar school," and as a young man led a rather reckless life at Stratford. In London he rose slowly from obscurity to a reasonable degree of contemporary fame as poet and playwright, and made sufficient money by 1600 to buy a handsome property in his native town, where he died in 1616.

Like many men of letters, Shakespeare reflects his own environment. He held "the mirror up to nature"; but it was an Elizabethan glass which reflected the interests and the enthusiasms of his own generation. In him is found a man of the late Renaissance, interested in music, in rural games and pastimes, a sportsman, a man of the world, absorbed in the human drama, fond

Portrait of Shakespeare, engraved by Droeshout, on the first folio of his works, 1623.

of society, of adventure, and of all that was new and amazing in the astonishingly fresh and springlike Elizabethan day.

The stage of the theater of that day was simply a raised platform with no scenery, open to the sky, and with performances given only in daylight. Close and somewhat below the stage was the pit with the cheapest admission. Around the stage and the pit were roofed balconies, and here gathered the élite. On one side of the stage a flimsy hollow structure could be used as a cave, a grave, a balcony, battlements, or even as a bed for Desdemona. Feminine parts were always played by boys. Here was the rough setting for Shakespeare's glorious portrayal of humanity.

The most striking way in which Shakespeare reflected Elizabethan England was in the men and women he created. Whatever else may be said of those magnificent free lances, they are most distinctly non-

medieval. Whether or not Shakespeare was himself a religious man has been hotly disputed. As Hazlitt writes, "he was in one sense the least moral of all writers; . . . his talent consisted in sympathy with human nature in all its shapes, degrees, depressions and elevations." He was not interested in narrow codes of morality as such, but his adherence to the basic Christian ethic shines through in his plays.

Both he and the creatures of his imagination cleave fast to their individualism with extraordinary tenacity. To a considerable degree this was a characteristic of his time. The old standards had faded into dust; the new standards were not yet established. The Renaissance had proved a disruptive force, and the Reformation was as yet too recent to have established its mastery. England, from the point of view of intellectual and psychological freedom, was perhaps freer than ever before in her history. To some degree this may account for the superb vitality and striking individualism of Shakespeare's men and women.

Noticeable in Shakespeare is his warm patriotic fervor for the house of Tudor and the England which he loved. It is significant that in one of his early historical plays, *Richard III*, the ultimate victory of the Tudors in the Wars of the Roses is celebrated. As for England, he speaks of this "scept'red isle" as "This blessed spot, this earth, this realm, this England." In *King John*, he declares that she "never did nor never shall, lie at the proud foot of a conqueror."

Like most Elizabethans, Shakespeare was fond of the countryside and sport. He knew his little rivers that "make sweet music with th' enameled stones." Flowers delighted him—"Where honeysuckle ripened by the sun"—and he was also familiar with the chase and falconry. "Poor dappled fools" he calls the deer in the Forest of Arden; and again: "Sweep on, you fat and greasy citizens!" as the herd dashes by the injured buck.

Common folk were seldom introduced into his plays, and when they were it was as a foil or background. His crowds and mobs either were ludicrous or else, as in *Julius Caesar*, they smelled vilely. Clownish characters were now and then described, but his art, his admiration, and his love were reserved for those of higher degree in the essentially aristocratic society of his day.

Even without Shakespeare, this would have been a period noted for its literary output. Among his fellow playwrights, Christopher Marlowe, from whom he appears to have borrowed much, was outstanding. In poetry, Edmund Spenser is called one of England's greatest poets, especially for his *Faerie Queen;* and Francis Bacon, scientist and philosopher extraordinary (see pages 219 ff.), may be considered Shakespeare's peer for his prose.

But none of these men could justly contest Shakespeare's place as the representative Elizabethan man of letters. Far more,

he belongs to the ages. Perhaps the finest tribute ever paid him came from a modern Oxford scholar: "He too learned that in the duel with Fate man is not the hunter, but the game, and that a losing match nobly played is his only possible victory."

He was to write his major tragedies after Elizabeth's death. By then most of the great Elizabethans of the original group associated with her were dead: Drake, Hawkins, and Frobisher, as well as Burghley, who had guided the ship of state so shrewdly for forty years. Active, imperious, and tactful to the end, Elizabeth remained mistress of England until death took her, at seventy, on a March morning in 1603 at Richmond. Considering with what she started and what she accomplished, her forty-five years on the throne well deserve the title of "the Golden Age," just as does she herself, that new designation, Elizabeth the Great, coming into use in the mid-twentieth century.

Chapter Twelve · 1603-1629

Commons and Colonies

On a Saturday evening late in March, 1603, a young English courtier galloped into the courtyard of Holyrood Palace at Edinburgh. By wearing out successive relays of horses in dashing up the Great North Road at the rate of one hundred and sixty miles a day he had established a speed record between the English and Scottish capitals. There was reason for haste. Elizabeth had died on Thursday, and James VI of Scotland was awaiting with quite improper impatience the news that he had become James I of England (1603-1625). Thirty hours later, official messengers of the Council, sent by Cecil's son, confirmed the tidings that the English crown was transferred from the House of Tudor to that of Stuart. England and Scotland were at last joined under a single crown.

At the end of the Elizabethan Era, England was to find herself involved in a century of civil difficulties and overseas expansion which were eventually to set her far in advance of her neighbors. The long-drawn-out conflict between Parliament and the four Stuart kings, based on money and religious difficulties, was to transform England into the first modern constitutional monarchy, with the House of Commons, not the king, the real ruler. The disturbances brought about by this Parliamentary conflict were to give impetus to the plant-

ing on the Atlantic coast of North America of some of the sturdiest colonies any nation has ever owned. Ever since the Norman Conquest, England had been drawn into Continental problems and had developed, despite her insular peculiarities, on the same general pattern as the rest of western Europe. Now she was to turn in the opposite direction. In a period which has been called "the Age of Absolutism" in Continental history, a time when royal autocracy was reaching its height in the chief European countries, the English Parliament was to force the crown to submit to its domination.

Immersed as she was in her particular home problems, England showed less interest than usual in foreign affairs. France easily forged ahead to front rank on the Continent. The Holy Roman Empire was nearly wrecked by the prolonged devastation of its politico-religious conflict, the Thirty Years' War (1618-1648). Holland and Sweden rose to temporary prominence out of all proportion to their natural capacities. Spain continued to decline from the proud position she had enjoyed before the Armada. France, however, swept along unhindered in her "glorious age," until England, having put her house in order, turned her attention to checking French power.

A nightmare had been haunting England

for many years—who would follow Elizabeth? She objected to any talk about it and consistently refused to name a successor, until on her death bed, she is said to have mentioned Mary Stuart's son, James VI of Scotland. According to Henry VIII's last Act of Succession, Edward Seymour, Lord Beauchamp, the descendant of Henry's younger sister, Mary, the grandmother of Lady Jane Grey, was favored over the descendants of Henry's older sister Margaret, who had married the king of Scotland in 1503, an exact century before Elizabeth's death. In this latter line, which Henry had probably set aside because it was Scottish, were the thirty-seven-year-old James, king since babyhood, when his mother abdicated the throne, and the unfortunate Arabella Stuart, who, like Darnley, was descended from Margaret's second marriage. When the crucial moment came, however, King James succeeded Elizabeth without disturbance, as he and most others had anticipated. Robert Cecil, the son of Lord Burghley (who had established Elizabeth upon the throne), proceeded to do a similar service for James.

James I

To follow Elizabeth was enough to tax the ability of the cleverest and most magnetic person; but in place of such there came to England a singularly unattractive, pudgy, and pedantic Scot. That this uncouth James, with his driveling mouth and overlarge tongue, should have been the true son of the fascinating Mary Stuart and the handsome Lord Darnley seems almost incredible. James was stupid in everyday matters and in many affairs of state, but was interested in learning. In some ways, such as his desire for peace, his views were ahead of his time; but he was on the whole merely an uninteresting encyclopedia of facts and theories, with an overweening confidence in his own infallibility. Despite his books and writings, and occasional displays of wit, the king seemed incapable of sensible action. Through tactlessness and petty insistence on details he alienated that public opinion which the able Tudors had known how to cajole. On his triumphal ride into his new realm, he showed quickly his utter inability to comprehend English justice when, in a self-righteous display of swift retribution for evildoing, he ordered the immediate hanging, without trial, of a pickpocket caught red-handed. He not only always tended to do the right thing at the wrong time, but also too often displayed cowardice and timidity. A contemporary French minister called him the "wisest fool in Christendom."

Handicapped as he was by background and character for English leadership, James faced, in a country apparently tranquil and well disposed, a very difficult situation. Ever since the Armada's defeat, a new feeling of security and self-confidence was producing a quiet but increasing hostility to strong royal power, which was beginning to seem irksome and unnecessary. The Tudor family had brought law and order to an England torn by civil strife, and its virtual despotism had seemed a safeguard against civil bloodshed and foreign invasion. The people, however, had forgotten the trying years of chaos; the Scots were now harmless and the Spaniards no longer terrifying, while the exactions of royal control became constantly more wearisome. Respect and loyalty for Elizabeth had kept most of this discontent beneath the surface until now.

To make matters worse, both James and his son Charles talked too much about their rights. One of James's strongest beliefs was in the "divine right of kings." God, according to that theory, had placed the monarch on the throne, to rule as his viceroy; and anyone who disobeyed or crossed the king's slightest wish was thus deliberately acting against God himself. This theory was held generally by royalty in that period and was, on the whole, accepted placidly by their subjects. The Tudors had acted upon it, but they had not brought the matter up for discussion. They had received due respect without demanding it. They had been despotic enough; but the two Henrys and Elizabeth were statesmen of note, while outside circumstances had helped to explain the shortcomings under Edward and Mary. The former trio did as they pleased, while keeping the surface tranquil by not unnecessarily irritating the country. They had understood the English mind, and consequently the people had reacted to any tune they chose to play. At the same time, they had respected Parliament as a body with a definite and not unimportant place in the state. James, on the other hand, ignored Parliament's powers and privileges, as his family had long treated its Scottish counterpart; and he alienated one group after another by his didactic manner and bullheaded stubbornness about the slightest detail. By overstressing their rights the Stuarts were to cause more trouble for England in this century; but they perhaps saved her from the bloodier revolutions which the Continent later experienced by pushing her, ahead of the times, toward her peculiar seventeenth-century experimentation with limited monarchy.

As James came to the throne, a slight flurry of plots arose, but they did not reach a serious stage, for Englishmen as a whole were deeply relieved that the dreaded day of Elizabeth's death had come and gone so quietly. A so-called "Main Plot" was hatched by Raleigh and some others, to get rid of the younger Cecil because he wanted to end the Spanish war, and the plans even extended to placing Arabella Stuart upon the throne. Closely following upon this came the "By-Plot" of certain Roman Catholics to seize James and thus get rid of Elizabethan laws against their religion. The net results were a few beheadings and the twelve-year imprisonment of the versatile and illustrious Raleigh. The Catholics, further disappointed at not receiving the favors they had expected from the son of Catholic Mary Stuart, went further. In 1605 a group planned to blow up not only the king but also both houses of Parliament. A gentleman from Warwickshire was leader of the plot; but when one of the conspirators gave away a clue, it was one Guy Fawkes, a former soldier, who was found with the kegs of powder under the House of Lords. His name has been attached to the "Gunpowder Plot," and November fifth has since been celebrated as a holiday, "Guy Fawkes Day." The penal code was stiffened against Catholics, now more in disfavor than ever.

The Puritan element, strong in the House of Commons, expected as much from a king from Calvinistic Scotland as had the Catholics from the son of Mary Stuart. The Elizabethan compromise had been a master stroke because of the number of people it satisfied; but the extreme Protestants and the inflexible Catholics remained outside. Throughout Elizabeth's reign they had remained quiet, though since the Armada they had grumbled more and more audibly. Both groups hoped for recognition from James, and both were to be disappointed.

The nickname "Puritan" had been applied by an archbishop in Elizabeth's reign rather indiscriminately to those left-wing Protestants within the Church of England who demanded simpler church rites and a more Calvinistic theology. The early Puritans grew steadily more radical, became known as "forward" or "advanced" Puritans, regarded bishops with dislike, and, as a whole, generally favored a Presbyterian form of church government. Some of them became "Separatists," desiring to break with the Church of England. Of the latter a few, called Brownists, set up independent meetings of their own and adopted a Congregationalist form of government, which made the individual congregation an independent unit and even did without the presbyteries. (The presbytery familiar in Presbyterian Scotland was a body composed of both clergy and laymen, governing a certain number of congregations—the Calvinist substitute for the bishop and his diocese.) The Elizabethan Act of Uniformity had kept these extremists either quiet or in hiding. Upon James's accession they proceeded immediately to present the monarch with the "Millenary Petition," named for its supposed signatures of one thousand clergymen, but actually signed by only eight hundred.

The petition was mild enough, but trouble came from it. The king invited the signers to a conference in 1604 in Hampton Court. There was mention of the word "presbytery" which enraged James. Shouting "no bishop, no king," he threatened to harry out of the land all who did not conform to the Established Church. No good came of the conference except the King James version of the Holy Scriptures, which for more than three hundred years was the standard translation of the Bible into the English language. It was, incidentally, the one achievement to result from James's learned interests. From now on, the Puritans, in many instances wealthy and influential, were to be counted as foes of the king.

The Puritans and Parliament

James never mastered the significance of the position of Parliament in England. The Scottish Parliament was simply a "court of record," and he failed thoroughly to appreciate the prestige which the English body had accumulated in its three centuries. Two months after rebuffing the Puritans at Hampton Court, he again came face to face with Puritans in large numbers when he met his first House of Commons. That first session of 1604 heard the opening guns of the eighty-four-year fight between the Stuart kings and their Parliaments—a stubborn fight, with varying fortunes, until in 1688, with victorious Parliament in full control, the grandson of James had to flee the country.

Underlying all the particular disputes which marked that long contest was the question of sovereignty. The unwritten English constitution was characteristically hazy as to whether the last word lay with king or Parliament. Both the undefined "prerogatives" of the king and the "rights and liberties" of Parliament might be stretched by the interested side, as, for the first time, the rival forces met openly on the issue. In earlier periods there had not been any well-established ascendancy of Parliament over king or of king over Parliament. A satisfactory compromise, dividing sovereignty bewteen the two, was apparently inconsistent with efficient government. With each side vigorously seeking supreme power, it was to take Parliament nearly the whole seventeenth century to secure victory.

Before resorting to sword and musket in the 1640's, the rivals turned to history for their weapons. Parliamentary lawyers and royal officials searched musty records to find precedents which could be stretched or twisted to give an aspect of legality to their claims. This search for precedents was natural in a nation accustomed to the procedure of the common law. Parliament, on the whole, had to hunt farther back in history than did the royalists. Magna Carta, not even mentioned by Shakespeare in *King John,* was dragged from oblivion and set up as a precedent for Parliamentary claims. The Commons could draw heavily upon the experiences of the fourteenth century and the Lancastrian period of the fifteenth, when Parliamentary influence was strong (see page 139). The century and a half of Yorkist and Tudor rule, however, had added little to the increase of Parliamentary power; in fact, Parliament had been fortunate to survive those absolutist tendencies. It had at least been preserved as a matter of form, and at the same time, under the Tudors, had evolved highly effective methods of procedure, such as the committee system. Moreover, the crown had had to take the potential opposition of Parliament into account; but, for the most part, Parliament had been quite complaisant in agreeing with the will of the monarch.

In Parliament's earlier periods of importance the House of Lords had tended to overshadow the Commons. From 1604 onward, however, the story of Parliament is largely that of the burgesses and knights of the shire rather than of the Lords Spiritual and Temporal. The Upper House had changed in complexion during the Tudor period. The first Parliament of Henry VII had contained two archbishops, nineteen bishops, twenty-eight abbots, and only twenty-nine lay peers. The dissolution of the monasteries, by removing the abbots, gave the Lords Temporal a majority (see page 170). The first Stuart Parliament had eighty-two lay peers and twenty-six bishops. This Upper House was to play only a minor role in the ensuing struggle. The House of Commons had nearly five hundred members, of whom about four hundred represented boroughs. The bulk of its membership, however, was composed of country gentry; for it was no longer the custom to require a member of Parliament to reside in the constituency which he represented, and, while the boroughs occasionally sent up some of their own merchants or town officials, they were more apt to choose a substantial squire. Another group, however, influential out of all proportion to its numbers, was the lawyers, whose training and technique were all-important for leadership in the work at hand.

Theoretically, the House of Commons perhaps represented all Englishmen and Welshmen, but in practice the franchise was in the hands of a relatively small part of the population. Such public opinion as there was, however lacking in uniformity or logic the basis of franchise may have been, filled the Stuart Lower House with a majority of strong, sober men of Puritan persuasion, most of whom had little to gain personally. Unlike many of their successors in the next century, they did not seek seats in order to enrich themselves or their relatives and friends at the public expense. It was a strong indication of the politico-religious temper of the Puritan element that that sturdy group, which might have remained comfortably at home, was ready to incur the inconveniences, and even the threat to its liberty and property, which accompanied membership in Parliament.

In 1604 no definitely established rules existed about the particular rights and immunities of members of Parliament nor the frequency of Parliamentary elections and sessions. During the century Parliament would put these matters on a definite basis. In the matter of personal liberties there were questions of freedom of speech in Parliament, freedom from arrest for members, and the right of Parliament to determine the qualification of its members in cases of disputed elections. The frequency of elections and sessions, depended entirely upon the king. He called Parliament only when circumstances forced him. When he had what he wanted, or encountered too stubborn opposition, he might either prorogue that same Parliament for a later session or he might dissolve it completely so that a new House of Commons would have to be elected. Of James's four separate Parliaments, only the last escaped being dissolved.

Linked closely to the Parliamentary situation were the courts of law. The three common-law courts—King's Bench, chiefly for criminal cases; Common Pleas, for private civil suits; and Exchequer, for government financial cases—were all operated upon the basis of precedents which had accumulated since their origin in the Plantagenet period (see page 69). The Court of Chancery, dispensing equity under the chancellor, was more directly under royal control, while the king had even more influence in the special "prerogative" courts, such as Star Chamber and High Commission, which had been established by the Tudors with extensive powers unfettered by common-law procedure. The common-law courts were regarded as bulwarks of English liberty, and their judges were supposed to be impartial umpires in cases where the interests of king and subjects might conflict. That role was weakened by the power of the king to dismiss judges at will. The common law found a doughty champion in Sir Edward Coke, Chief Justice of Common Pleas and later of King's Bench. A thoroughly disagreeable person in public and private life, Coke was, nevertheless, remarkably well grounded in the origins of the common law, his one love in life; and he proved a tough fighter in its defense. His chief contention was that the law was superior to the king, whereas James aimed to make the judges agents of royal policy—"lions under the throne," as Francis Bacon, then his attorney general, expressed it.

The King's Finances

The principal key to Parliament's rise to power lay in the king's need for money. Inflated prices seriously affect governments as well as individuals dependent on fixed incomes; and the influx of Spanish-American silver had increased many items of governmental expenditure while the traditional sources of royal revenue, from the crown lands and the like, remained stationary. Only the customs duties kept pace with the rising costs because the volume of English commerce increased. Elizabeth had felt the effects of those rising costs, but her rigid economy had kept her budgets well balanced. She had carried England through a highly successful reign, including very grave foreign complications, with an annual income which rarely exceeded, and frequently fell well below, £400,000. By her economy she had avoided serious dependence upon Parliament, although she left her successor saddled with a considerable debt. James, however, in spite of occasional instances of thrift, generally threw Elizabethan parsimony to the winds. Anomalous as it may sound for a Scot, he spent like a drunken sailor. In the years of waiting in his barren, impoverished kingdom, he had looked forward eagerly to the day when he should have plenty of money. The wealth of England had aroused Scotland's envy just as the wealth of Spain had incited England's envy. James was not long on the throne before the regular expenditures jumped to £600,000 a year, even with peace, while income lagged about £150,000 in the red. A court which was faster and coarser, but less clever, than Elizabeth's helped to account for this unbalanced budget. There were three ways to deal with the constantly mounting debt. One was economy, which James generally failed to practice; the second was dependence upon the hostile Puritans in the Commons; and the third was the collecting of money by novel methods beyond Parliament's control, a practice which Stuart Parliaments would stubbornly resist.

The first clash in the struggle between Crown and Parliament arose over which was to decide the qualification of members of the Commons in disputed elections. The king had directed that such cases should be referred to the Court of Chancery, but the Commons won the right to settle them themselves. Rival views of the status of the Commons were exchanged. The king told the Commons that they "derived all matters of privilege from him and by his grant." They replied that their "privileges and liberties are of right and due inheritance no less than our very lands and goods," and that "they cannot be withheld from us, denied, or impaired, but with apparent wrong to the whole state of the realm."

A cargo of currants from the eastern Mediterranean was the innocent cause of the next encounter. James tried to increase his revenue without Parliament's consent by boosting the customs duties. Like his predecessors, James had recieved at the beginning of his reign a life grant of "tunnage and poundage," or customs duties, at the regular specified rates. In 1606 he "imposed" an additional duty on currants. John Bate, a merchant in trade with Turkey, carried the case to the Exchequer Court. The judges went out of their way to give James a favorable decision, citing Tudor precedents to demonstrate that the king had full powers in matters of regulation of trade. Thereupon James had a new "Book of Rates" drawn up, increasing the duties on all kinds of imports. The House of Commons, aroused to the danger of this flank attack upon its control of the purse, passed a bill against impositions; but it was killed by the Lords, and James continued to collect his increased duties throughout the reign.

James was also trying to do without Parliament in the making of laws. Henry VIII had been empowered to issue, through his Council, proclamations which had the force of law. Such proclamations, like the earlier ordinances (see page 102), could be—as they still are—a useful and necessary device to meet temporary emergencies, especially at times when Parliament was not in session. If carried to extremes, however, these royal proclamations might supplant Parliamentary statutes as the law of the land. James showed a tendency in that direction, particularly in defining new offenses which were to be tried in the "prerogative" courts of High Commission or Star Chamber. The House of Commons and the common-law courts joined forces against this practice which threatened to injure them both. Coke and three eminent colleagues, when summoned before the Council, boldly stated that the king had no right to create any new offenses by proclamation, and declared that the king had no prerogative but what the law of the land allowed him. This alliance between the Commons and the judges helped to check the threatening practice for some time.

James's first Parliament had thus come into conflict with him on several points during its five sessions between 1604 and 1611. The second Parliament, called in 1614, was dissolved after two stormy months of deadlock. It declared that the king had no right to impose taxes without Parliamentary consent, and it refused to give the king a money grant before discussing its grievances. James consequently dissolved it and sent four members of the Commons to the Tower.

There was no meeting of Parliament now for seven years, nearly a third of the reign. James began in earnest to scrape together money from every possible source in order to keep the government running without Parliament. "Benevolences," or supposedly voluntary contributions, and forced loans were exacted from prosperous individuals, who had little hope of ever seeing their money again. One man, who used strong language of protest in declining to contribute, was sent to the Tower. Altogether, less than £43,000 was raised in three years by this method. Old debts and fines were collected with relentless vigor. Titles were shamelessly put up for sale. One might become a peer, with a seat in the House of Lords, for £10,000, and a new title of hereditary knighthood, baronet, was invented and put on sale at £1000.

In 1616, the year of Shakespeare's death, James struck a powerful blow at the independence of the common-law courts by removing Chief Justice Coke. With Parliament in abeyance, these courts alone were in a position to offer official resistance to the royal policy, by means of decisions which might arise in various sorts of cases. Coke twice strongly resisted the efforts of the king to interfere in trials while these were in progress. After his dismissal, he was to continue his opposition to James from the floor of the Commons. As long as the judges held precarious office, dependent upon royal pleasure rather than upon good behavior, the common-law courts lost their independence. Other chief justices were removed during the Stuart period; but the common-law courts were not perverted as much as they might have been, because the crown preferred to divert cases to Star Chamber and other prerogative courts which were unhampered by past precedents.

If the king could get rid of a chief justice, Parliament could strike back by removing his chancellor. The Parliament of 1621, which James was forced to summon because of the foreign situation, assembled in a friendly mood, but friction quickly developed. Parliament, thereupon, dragged out the weapon of impeachment, which had not been used since Henry VI's reign (see page 140). This was less cruel than the favorite Tudor weapon, the bill of attainder, whereby Parliament might vote a

The versatile Sir Francis Bacon, in his robes as Lord Chancellor.

man to death without regular trial; in impeachment, a verdict of guilty simply involved dismissal. The first impeachment victims were two courtiers, charged with abusing their grants of monopolies (see page 208); such grants would be declared illegal by the next Parliament.

The Commons then impeached no less a man than Francis Bacon, not only chancellor but also scientist, philosopher, essayist, lawyer—and by all odds, the greatest English intellect of the day. He had been attorney general before the chancellorship, and had just been created a peer. He exercised a wide influence through his writings —his Essays, the Advancement of Learning, and particularly the Novum Organum. Like the medieval friar, Roger Bacon (see page 95), he was a pioneer in the field of scientific methods of research. Later generations have hailed his arguments for the inductive method, based on observation;

but his *Novum Organum* was over the heads of most Englishmen, including the learned James, who said that it resembled the peace of God, which "passeth all understanding." All the Commons saw in Bacon, however, was the royal henchman, guilty of the not uncommon practice of receiving bribes, while in office. In his defense, he admitted accepting presents, but claimed they had not affected his judgment; the Lords, however, fined him heavily (though later remitting the fine) and barred him from all office holding. Three years later, the Lord Treasurer was likewise impeached.

This Parliament of 1621 also ventured into the sphere of foreign affairs, where the precedents for interference were less certain. Not only did it give the king less than ten per cent of the money grants he had requested, because of the complicated situation with Spain and Germany, but it advised him against a Catholic Spanish marriage for his son. Elizabeth, when repeated Parliaments had tried to give her similar advice, had rejected it, but had cleverly smoothed the ruffled feelings of the Houses. James, instead, bluntly told the Commons not to meddle in the mysteries of state, whereof they were ignorant. Parliamentary control over foreign relations has always been a ticklish matter; for any government is loath to reveal, for public discussion, the progress of delicate negotiations. The squires, to be sure, were quite unversed in the "deep matters of state"; but they answered the king in an outspoken "protestation," reaffirming their privileges and liberties as hereditary rights, and declaring that "the arduous and urgent affairs concerning the king, state and defense of the realm, and of the Church of England . . . are proper subjects and matter of counsel and debate in Parliament." James soon sent for the journals of the Commons and, in the presence of his Council, with his own hands tore out the page with that offensive protestation. As in 1614,

several members of the Commons were sent to the Tower, and Parliament was soon dissolved.

The fourth Parliament, in 1624, more harmonious, approved of the foreign policy of the moment and gave James a much larger percentage of the funds he requested. It also passed the sole piece of constructive legislation of James's four Parliaments—their importance had lain rather in their defining points of resistance to the royal claims of divine absolutism. This act was against the practice of granting monopolies, which had caused dissatisfaction since the later days of Elizabeth. It was one thing to grant an inventor a monopoly of the sale of his invention for a period of years, but when courtiers received monopolies of the sale of common commodities, such as soap, glass, or coal, in which they did little if anything to stimulate trade, the practice resulted in an unjustifiable tax on the consumer.

The first Stuarts were unfortunately dependent upon favorite courtiers, and unlike Elizabeth, their choice was generally bad. Any good-looking young man, preferably with a Scottish burr, so it was said, would go far with James, so surprisingly lavish for a Scot with gifts for his favorites as well as titles and high posts. Lord Salisbury, the younger Cecil, acted as a check upon James until he died in 1612, when a young Scot, Robert Carr, the future Earl of Somerset, was raised to highest favor for his handsome face, it would seem, since certainly he had no other qualifications. Scandal and worse soon followed. He fell in love with the Countess of Essex, whom he married after her divorce, granted unfairly on James's orders. Then, the two were tried for the murder of a man who had threatened blackmail in connection with the divorce proceedings. All that James did for his favorites was spare them the death penalty. Their much-publicized trial advertised, and perhaps exaggerated, the scandals of the court.

The young and good-looking George Villiers, eventually Duke of Buckingham, was more able than Somerset and exceedingly charming, but failed to leaven his ambitious ideas with common sense. Rising with extraordinary rapidity under the favor of James, he was the dominant figure in English policy, both foreign and domestic, until his murder early in the next reign. James took his advice, when the great Francis Bacon was just as available; but Bacon was not the type to have influence with this king.

Strange Foreign Policy

In foreign affairs James was essentially a pacifist. He gave England peace throughout his entire twenty-two-year reign except for the first year (until the war inherited from Elizabeth could be stopped) and the last, when Buckingham led the country into a series of mad adventures. James's foreign policy had some strange and unpopular features; but his pacifism, a unique phenomenon, brought the country a more genuine peace than the quarter century of quasi-war under Elizabeth and the elder Cecil.

As far as Scotland was concerned, James brought up the matter of union with England as soon as he came to the throne; but Parliament, perhaps fearing that the wealth of the southern kingdom might be used to relieve the poverty of Scotland, was not even interested in naturalizing Scots as English subjects. A court later ruled that Scots born after 1603—the *postnati*—might enjoy English status; but, except for that, James found that he could not go beyond the present loose personal union. This at least made England more secure by removing the danger of border raids and the perennial alliances between France and Scotland. Not for another century would England and Scotland be actually united with a common Parliament.

England continued to be engaged in the Spanish war, which had opened in the 1580's, but the leaders at court were divided on its continuation. Raleigh and other surviving Elizabethan adventurers were determined to humiliate Spain still further, but Salisbury (Cecil) and others favored peace. After Raleigh's arrest following the "Main Plot," Cecil, with the king's support, ended the war.

Not particularly acceptable to Parliament, this Spanish peace was even more unpalatable to the seafaring elements. James utterly neglected the navy, and the seaports smoldered with hostility for years. England no longer insisted that its flag be saluted in home waters, while pirates from the Barbary coast of northern Africa raided ships and towns with impunity. James's naval neglect proved costly to the nation's international prestige and nullified most of his diplomatic gestures. This policy of James, moreover, ran counter to the wishes not only of his people but also of Parliament, and his playing the diplomat, with his penchant for Spanish, or at any rate, Catholic alliances, made England a joke on the Continent for some time to come.

The twenty-year peace brought one strange result. Count Gondomar, a very brilliant grandee, Spanish ambassador to England, became one of the most influential men at court. He intrigued James by the tantalizing suggestion of a Spanish infanta for a daughter-in-law, while Gondomar himself kept his keen eye upon the prospect of a re-Catholicized England. As a result of his partisanship, life was made easier for the English Catholics, who had suffered severely from the penal code since the Gunpowder Plot. This would have galled the Protestant Englishmen anyway; but Gondomar's presence at court was emphasized by the spectacle of a hundred priests released from prison to escort him on a trip to Spain. The hostile populace retaliated by several angry anti-Catholic demonstrations. The French embassy, hitherto always favored over the Spanish, was no more pleased than were most Englishmen by this haughty grandee strutting about the English court as though he were chief minister.

The most shocking display of his power was yet to come—the execution of Raleigh. With the fall of Somerset, who had been completely the tool of Gondomar, James was persuaded to release Raleigh for an expedition to seek gold in Guiana. Sent out with strict orders not to fight the Spaniards in that Spanish-infested quarter of the world, and with thoroughly inadequate equipment, Raleigh was to return a beaten man, with no gold. Unavoidably, it would appear, he had attacked a Spanish settlement. The old Elizabethan hero, the hard hater of Spain, was sent to the block by James on an old and ridiculous charge of treasonable relations with that country; and this at the insistence of Gondomar, who was threatening war. Such was the fate of one who had outlived his glorious generation.

In that year, 1618, the beginning of a long war in Germany further complicated James's already confused foreign policy. Trouble had been brewing in the Germanies since the Protestant Revolt. By a compromise in 1555, permission had been granted the rulers of the various states within the Holy Roman Empire to choose between Lutheranism and Catholicism, but no recognition had been given to Calvinism. Fermenting during the years of the Counter Reformation and the religious wars elsewhere, the bitterness caused by this broke out in 1618 in the Thirty Years' War, a bloody and devastating conflict which has been called the last of the religious and the first of the political wars. It began when James's son-in-law, a Calvinist prince of the Rhineland, Elector of the Palatinate, accepted the crown of Bohemia in defiance of the traditional rights of the Catholic Holy Roman Emperor. This "Winter King" was quickly deposed; and by 1629, four years after James's death, the Catholic imperialists were fully victorious,

despite the intervention of Denmark and England. Then Protestant Sweden quickly and permanently turned the tide under her famous king, the "Father of Modern Warfare," Gustavus Adolphus. Politics now definitely overshadowed religion as a war motive; for France, under her two great Catholic cardinal-ministers, Richelieu and Mazarin, entered the war on the Protestant side because of French hostility to the Hapsburgs and helped to consolidate Protestant victories and to smash the surrounding ring of Catholic Hapsburg territory. The Spanish Hapsburgs naturally sided with the German Hapsburgs. The war was to end in 1648 with (among other results) France powerful and Holland free, while most of the Germanies were so devastated that it took them a full century to recover.

The marriage in 1613 of James's daughter Elizabeth to Frederick of the Palatinate was to be of subsequent importance, for thereby George I inherited the throne a century later; for the time being, it tended to draw England into the war. The nation, being Protestant, was interested anyway, and James, despite his pacifism, had too much family interest to stand aloof. The situation became very complicated when a Spanish invasion threatened to cost Frederick his own territory, the Palatinate. In 1621 it looked as though king and Parliament for once had something upon which they could agree—saving the Palatinate from Spain. Gondomar was in a difficult position; but he met it ably, offsetting the threat of war by continued prospects of a Spanish marriage for Prince Charles.

The threatened war against Spain evaporated; but the Spanish marriage remained to plague England. Prince Charles was far more attractive than his father, but fully as unreliable and lacking in good sense. His deceased elder brother had rejected such a marriage, as he did not want "two religions in one bed"; but Charles was attracted by Spanish glamour. The thoughtless, impulsive young prince and the Duke of Buck-

Frederick V, elector of the Palatinate and "Winter King" of Bohemia, and his wife Elizabeth, daughter of James I. Their grandson, elector of Hanover, came to the British throne in 1714 as George I, starting the Hanoverian line.

ingham now decided with James's private approval that it would be a clever stroke, as well as good fun, to dash off to Spain incognito, woo the Infanta, and bring her back a bride. England was thoroughly discredited by the antics of the irresponsible pair, Spanish decorum was profoundly shocked, and, despite the extravagant concessions of Charles in the matter of Catholicism, it soon became obvious that the marriage idea was simply bait to keep James in line. The two young men returned to find themselves popular heroes, so glad was England that her prince was "still a live man, a Protestant, and a bachelor!"

Buckingham was so entranced with his own popularity that he turned against Spain, begged for war, and obviously fancied himself the Protestant champion of Europe. The breach with Spain was now an accomplished fact. James, unable to stand out against Charles, Buckingham, and the strong popular sentiment, seemed to lose all interest in his country and to let Buckingham manage everything. The king's death in 1625 and the accession of the prince, as Charles I, made scarcely a ripple.

Between 1624 and 1628 Buckingham was in full control, and he dragged England into a mad orgy of war. Though England was in no condition to handle even a single foe, expeditions were dispatched to Spain, to France, and to Germany—six expeditions in four years, and every one a miserable failure! It always has taken England a considerable time to recover from the military stagnation of a long peace; for the Englishman engaged in civilian pursuits is quite unwarlike. There was no rush to arms; press gangs had to recruit by forced draft. Few communities allowed their better men to be rushed to what, in a time of unpreparedness, meant probable death by starvation or disease, if not on the battlefield. The army was composed of riffraff; the navy had been allowed to decay. England was small, in comparison with France, Spain, and the Hapsburg empire, and so were her forces. Under such circumstances Buckingham's schemes, badly conceived and muddled as they were, were foredoomed.

The first of those ventures, the most shameful failure in English military history, was England's sole effort at armed intervention in the Thirty Years' War. Early in 1625, two months before James's death, Count Mansfield, a swashbuckling German freebooter, was sent to free the Palatinate from Spanish control with twelve thousand English troops — untrained, undisciplined, ill-clothed, ill-fed, and mutinous. France denied them permission to cross her territory, and the poor wretches were unwelcome guests in Holland, where they had landed. By the time James died, three quarters of them were dead of disease, exposure, and starvation; the remainder melted away without reaching the Palatinate or striking an honest blow. The navy did no better with an expedition against the Spanish port of Cádiz that same year. It had twice been successfully raided by the Elizabethan sea dogs under Drake and Raleigh, but this was a hopeless attempt for the ill-planned, unequipped, untrained force that set sail in rotten ships.

In the meantime relations with France were complicated. Charles I had been on the throne barely ten weeks when Buckingham brought over Henrietta Maria, the fifteen-year-old sister of Louis XIII of France. The duke knew that a French Catholic queen would be almost as distasteful as a Spanish one, so the marriage was rushed through before Parliament met. Such deliberate defiance deepened the disgust at Buckingham's "statecraft." The marriage became a devoted one. Charles, like Louis XVI of France and Nicholas II of Russia, who were likewise executed by revolutionary subjects, was a good family man, but weak and of mediocre ability. All three

might have been able to hold their thrones under normal conditions, but when crises arose, their foreign wives, with stronger characters, urged them into extreme stands, so that they often turned stubborn on the worst possible occasions.

The friendship with France was short-lived. Buckingham was no match for the astute and masterful Cardinal Richelieu, the real power under Louis XIII. During the marriage negotiations Buckingham had not only committed indiscretions with the queen of France but also made sweeping promises about improving the condition of the English Catholics. But Charles, declaring the agreement only a formality, dismissed his bride's French Catholic attendants. Further trouble came when eight English vessels, lent to France for an expedition to Italy, were ordered against the seaport of La Rochelle, the chief stronghold of the French Huguenots, which Richelieu was trying to capture. The English crews mutinied rather than fight against Protestants.

Three English expeditions were sent to La Rochelle to relieve the Huguenots from the besieging French royal forces. The troubles with France might have been ironed out; but Buckingham and Charles recklessly added Richelieu to the list of their enemies, as though complications with Spain and the Palatinate were not sufficient. In 1627 Buckingham led an expedition, ill-founded as usual, to the Isle of Ré, just off beleaguered La Rochelle. While awaiting naval reinforcements which never came, his men were attacked by the French and most of them were slaughtered. Early in 1628, a naval expedition to La Rochelle returned in disgrace; Richelieu had had the approaches barred by strong breakwaters. Later that year a third Buckingham fleet was about to sail when the duke was murdered by a disgruntled naval officer at Portsmouth. The nation broke into wild rejoicing, as Charles mourned his best friend. The Huguenots were finally starved into surrender, while the English fleet vainly demonstrated outside the Rochelle breakwater.

Parliament was linked with these foreign fiascos. Approving efforts on behalf of Protestantism abroad, it had been fairly generous with money grants in 1624, the only relatively harmonious session under the first two Stuarts. But the three Parliaments crowded into the first four years of Charles's reign displayed a different temper. They starved Buckingham's expeditions, distrustful of him after his trickery over the French marriage, and then used his failures to refuse further funds. "Our honor is ruined," they said, "our ships are sunk, our men perished, not by the enemy, not by chance, but by those we trust." The very cost of these expeditions threw the king into dependence upon Parliamentary grants. The House of Commons, realizing its strategic position, went much farther than it had in the preliminary sparring under James. Foremost among the able Puritan squires was Sir John Eliot, a prosperous Cornishman, who was to guide them through their stormy sessions, and consequently, die in prison. Important also was Sir Thomas Wentworth (later Lord Strafford), a supporter of royal authority and no Puritan, but strongly opposed to Buckingham; subsequently a royal minister, he was to die by the vote of the House of Commons he was now guiding. Three of the other country squires were John Hampden, John Pym, and Oliver Cromwell.

Charles angrily and quickly dissolved the first two of these Parliaments. They were determined to take up grievances before granting the money he needed. The first gave him tunnage and poundage for one year, instead of life, as was customary; the second impeached Buckingham.

Finding that he could not get money from Parliament without accepting humiliating terms, Charles tried to collect it as though it had been voted. "Forced loans," equivalent to the amount of a normal grant,

were demanded from the nation. The more prosperous who refused to pay were imprisoned; the poorer were drafted for the army. The general indignation was increased at the plight of these soldiers and of the unlucky civilians in whose homes they had to be billeted since the king was too short of funds to build barracks. From many quarters came stories of looting, rape, and other violence. Martial law was ordered, which gave officers in courts-martial power to deal out immediate punishment, even to civilians involved in cases with soldiers.

The Petition of Right

Under such conditions, the elections for the third Parliament in 1628 brought to Westminster a House of Commons unusually high in quality and particularly bitter against Buckingham. The Commons took immediate advantage of the fact that because foreign complications made a money grant necessary, they could force the king to admit the illegality of his acts. They drew up the Petition of Right, which like its precedent, Magna Carta, was limited chiefly to stated grievances—arbitrary taxation, arbitrary imprisonment, billeting, and martial law; neither document dealt in generalities. Passed by Commons and Lords, it received specific, formal royal assent on June 7, 1628. It thus became virtually, if not technically, a regular statute, a valid part of the law of the land. Neither this nor Magna Carta prevented the king from continuing his abuses, but he could no longer claim a legal right to do so. Charles was rewarded for his assent with five subsidies, equivalent to about £350,000.

Parliament's second session, early in 1629, brought further friction as the king still continued to collect tunnage and poundage without a grant. He had even seized the goods of a member of the House of Commons, a merchant who refused to pay the duties. The Court of Star Chamber had ordered a man's ears to be cut off. Archbishop Laud then tried to introduce High Church features into the Church of England, the beginning of an activity which thoroughly aroused the Puritans. By March 2 the temper of Parliament was such that Charles commanded the Speaker to leave his chair if anyone attempted to speak. Determined to register a protest before adjournment was thus forced upon it, the House had the doors locked to prevent anyone from leaving and to keep out the royal official who was pounding for admission. While several members forcibly held the Speaker in his chair, the Commons passed by acclaim three measures drawn up by John Eliot, condemning the new "Papist innovations" in religion and the illegal customs impositions with anyone declared a traitor who paid them. Then the Commons voted their own adjournment while the royal serjeant still thundered at the door. That was the last sitting of Parliament for eleven years. Nine members were arrested; Eliot died in the Tower in 1632, and two others were still there when the next Parliament met in 1640.

Overseas Expansion

Just two days after that last stormy meeting, Charles granted a charter to "the Governor and Company of Massachusetts Bay in New England" to establish a new Puritan colony in America. England was about to enter upon a remarkable period of colonial expansion; for during the eleven-year "long vacation" of Parliament the number of Englishmen overseas jumped from some nine thousand to more than sixty-five thousand.

England's empire was already well under way before it received this stimulus. Elizabethan propagandists had argued the value of colonies and had made initial experiments; Elizabethan sea dogs had cleared the way for expansion by crippling Spanish sea power. Under James the actual permanent foundations had been laid, both for colonies of exploitation in the East and for colonies of settlement in North America and the West Indies (see page 161). Spain, Portugal, France, and Holland, as well as England, established successful colonies of exploitation, where a handful of Europeans went out to dominate a huge native population of yellows, browns, or blacks, while parts of Spanish America were a combination of exploitation and settlement. England, on the other hand, was unique in attaining success with regular colonies of settlement, where family groups left home permanently to set up a fairly normal European society in some region of temperate climate beyond the seas.

Colonial expansion was stimulated by the doctrines of "mercantilism," which were influential among the European maritime nations from the sixteenth century through the eighteenth. According to mercantilism, a nation should sell more than it bought in dealing with other nations to secure a "favorable balance of trade." At first, stress was laid upon the "bullionist" theory that an excess of exports would pile up silver and gold in a nation. Climatic conditions prevented the European nations from meeting all their economic needs with home products. Colonies, consequently, were considered desirable in order to produce under one's own flag what otherwise would have to be purchased from foreigners. Colonies of exploitation in tropical regions could provide for exotic needs; colonies of settlement in more temperate zones could not only supply further desirable products but also could buy the surplus manufactures of the mother country.

Three particular types of desirable colonial products were stressed by the early English writers. First, there were silver and gold, such as Spain was receiving in tempting quantities from Mexico and Peru. Secondly, spices—pepper, clove, cinnamon, and nutmeg—which had served as the original impetus for the great explorations a century earlier and had brought Portugal prosperity through her monopoly of the spice-growing islands in the Far East. Thirdly, tar, hemp, and other naval materials, for which England was dependent upon Sweden, Russia, and other lands of northern Europe, were essential to a nation's shipping. The English colonies met with no particular success with any of those, although sugar, tobacco, indigo, tea, and similar materials eventually did much to round out a self-sufficient empire. The Elizabethans had also pointed out that colonies might serve as a dumping ground for what they considered the surplus population of England. The "sturdy beggars" who had prowled around the land through the whole Tudor period gave the impression that there were too many Englishmen, whereas the population was actually dislocated by enclosures and other economic changes. The wise legislation of Elizabeth's last years had remedied that trouble, as the slow emigration during James's reign clearly demonstrated. When Englishmen finally began to swarm overseas under Charles, it was not because there were too many at home but because they were too discontented there.

The pioneer colonial empires of Spain and Portugal had been direct royal ventures in which the crown provided the initiative, capital, and control. Elizabeth and the Stuarts were not disposed to take such full responsibility, and the cost and risks were too great for successful individual initiative, so most of the early English colonization was carried on by private corporations, known as joint-stock companies. A group of individuals would subscribe to shares in a venture, to provide the necessary capital, and would then divide the profits, if any. A half century before successful English colonization got under way, the joint-stock company had been introduced for trading purposes. In 1553 the Muscovy Company was organized for trade with Russia, with a capital of £6000, divided into shares of £25 each. Its success caused others to follow in its wake. In 1581

Elizabeth contributed £42,000 from her share of Drake's plunder as half the capital of the Levant Company, formed for trade with Turkey and the East. Even the voyages of Drake and Hawkins had been temporary ventures of this type, with various individuals contributing shares of capital and receiving dividends from the profits, which were generally bigger than those of most of the later colonizing companies.

The East India Company

The most successful and long-lived was the East India Company, or, more fully, "the Governor and Company of the Merchants of London Trading into the East Indies," chartered by Elizabeth on December 31, 1600. The charter gave the company a monopoly of trade in the entire East between the Cape of Good Hope and the Strait of Magellan, with full political and military power in such posts as it might establish. It was formed to exploit the rich but rotten colonial empire which Portugal had built up in India and the East Indies. Portugal was temporarily under the Spanish crown at the time, but after the Armada defeat Spain could do no more than protect her own established colonies in America. England had shown a keen curiosity in the East even before the sea lanes were opened. Anthony Jenkinson, traveling for the Muscovy Company, had explored some of the trade routes of central Asia in the 1560's, while Ralph Fitch, at the time of the Armada, was making an overland trip even deeper into the rich eastern region. Shortly afterward an English sea captain was prowling about the Indian Ocean and exploring the Spice Islands.

The chief problem of the East India Company was not so much the ousting of the Portuguese as the rivalry of the Dutch East India Company, formed in 1602. Holland, entering upon her half century of remarkable maritime success, had rushed into the Eastern trade even more vigorously than England. With her ships heavily out-

Capture of huge, richly-laden Portuguese carrack in the Straits of Malacca in 1602 by early East Indiaman under Lancaster, aided by the Dutch.

numbering the English in the East, she finally secured control over the Spice Islands, the richest part of the Portuguese empire. The English tried to share this, but in 1623 the Dutch tortured to death the ten Englishmen on the clove island of Amboina and after that had the spice monopoly pretty much to themselves.

The English had to content themselves with the mainland of India. European contact with India then and for a century more was restricted to a few small coastal trading posts, called "factories." About the time that Elizabeth became queen, a powerful Moslem invader gained control over most of the peninsula. He and his five successors, the "Mogul" emperors, ruling the land from Delhi, were so strong that the European posts were maintained only by their sufferance. Not until after the sixth "Great Mogul" died in 1707 could European influence penetrate into the interior.

By 1613, after a successful fight with the Portuguese, the English East India Company set up a "factory" at Surat, on the northwest coast, and before long a ship or two returned each year to England with cargo worth about £50,000. Finding few spices, the English imported some saltpeter, an essential ingredient of gunpowder, and indigo for dyeing, but concentrated on the cheap cotton cloth (whence the terms calico, madras, gauze, and seersucker), which was a welcome substitute for expensive linen and silks. With India desiring few English goods in return, most of the payment was in silver. The profits of the East India Company showed a marked jump in the latter half of the century, when annual dividends sometimes reached 20 and even 50 per cent, though the English company could not match the dividend record of its Dutch rival, which averaged 18 per cent for two centuries. By 1700,

Surat was overshadowed by the "big three" of British India: Bombay, on the western coast; Madras, on the Coromandel Coast (southeast); and Calcutta, in Bengal (northeast).

Settlements in America

While England was beginning her colonies of exploitation in India, she was making a more distinctive experiment with colonies of settlement in North America and the West Indies (see map, page 302). The defeat of the Armada had thrown open not only the Portuguese East but also the temperate seaboard north of Florida.

The efforts to colonize Virginia, begun by Raleigh in 1585 (see page 203), were crowned with success in 1607 with the founding of Jamestown, England's first permanent colony. It was a rather sorry beginning. The hundred and five adventurers who were deposited on that malarial peninsula included no women, and the majority were rated as "gentlemen" who hoped for easy wealth without hard work. Within four months half were dead, and supplies were nearly gone. Instead of planting crops, they exhausted their strength in factional fights and futile searching for gold. In constant peril from famine, fever, and Indians, iron discipline on the part of a few strong leaders alone saved Jamestown. Even at that, in 1610, the discouraged colonists, reduced to a handful by a terrible winter of starvation, had started down the river for home, only to meet a fleet with reinforcements from England. Before long the colony found its economic salvation in tobacco. King James had written a "Counter-Blaste" against smoking; but that did not prevent its popularity, and the ten tons of tobacco shipped to England in 1617 were the beginning of a lucrative business which gave Virginia a definite niche in the self-sufficient empire. In 1619, a Dutch ship landed "twenty Negars." The gradual introduction of Negro slavery, together with the labor of indentured servants who had to work for several years to pay for their passage, eventually enabled the Virginia planters to lead a comfortable existence with a minimum of physical exertion.

That same year saw the first step toward colonial self-government, a continuing distinctive feature of English colonization. Virginia, which by that time had several thousand colonists, opened a legislature composed of representatives from its dozen scattered communities. The following year came another experiment in self-government in Massachusetts. The English colonies of settlement were thus permitted to manage a considerable portion of their own internal affairs. Except to a limited extent in the Dutch settlements in America, such self-government scarcely appears in the colonial history of the other European nations. It was the natural consequence of the Englishman's willingness to migrate, coupled with his traditional insistence upon his political rights.

Other colonies sprang up quickly. Part of a squadron headed for Jamestown in 1609 had been wrecked at Bermuda, which became the second permanent English settlement. In 1608 the French established Quebec as the center of their American colonization, which not only included the St. Lawrence valley but spread down the coast to Maine, where it ran into conflict with some abortive English colonial attempts. After Hudson, an Englishman in Dutch pay, explored in 1609 the river which bears his name, the Dutch soon founded fur-trading posts on the sites of New York City and Albany. Between those French and Dutch spheres of activity, the next English efforts were centered in present New England.

In 1620 an English colony of settlement quite different from Jamestown was planted on the sandy shores of southeastern Massachusetts. Its leaders were extreme Protestant nonconformists, or "Separatists," from eastern England. They had slipped away to Holland in order to worship more freely,

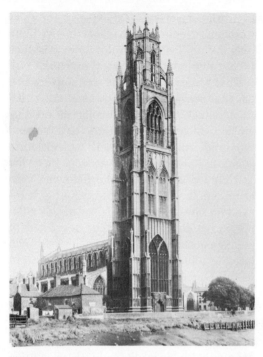

"Boston Stump," church tower at old East Coast port for which Massachusetts port was named.

Cape Cod Bay, as at Jamestown, almost half the group died during the first few months, but the survivors were of tougher fiber than the Virginians. They resisted starvation and were soon on a self-supporting basis.

The charter granted by Charles to the Massachusetts Bay Company in 1629 bore quick results. The leaders of the venture were more prosperous than those at Plymouth, and their followers were much more numerous. By the summer of 1630 nearly a thousand settlers had been landed in and about Boston, some thirty-five miles north of Plymouth. A second thousand joined them within a year. By 1640, when Virginia had some eight thousand colonists, Massachusetts Bay alone had about fourteen thousand, while offshoots in Rhode Island and Connecticut, the "old colony" at Plymouth, and scattered settlements up the coast in New Hampshire and Maine brought the New England total to about eighteen thousand.

Massachusetts and Virginia became the outstanding examples of two radically different types of society, which finally came into violent conflict more than two centuries later. This was partly attributable to the types of settlers. The New Englanders were much more homogeneous than the Virginians, who represented the social extremes, with a few aristocrats and a large number of indentured servants too poor to pay in advance for their passage. The Massachusetts settlers, chiefly from eastern England, the stronghold of Puritanism, were mostly of the middle classes, either townsmen or small landholders. The harsh deputy governor of Virginia complained in 1611 that his colonists were "so profane, so riotous, and so full of mutiny that not many are Christians but in name." The first governor of Massachusetts Bay wrote proudly that "God sifted a whole nation that he might send the choicest grain into the wilderness." The New Englanders claimed then, and long afterward, that they had

but after a dozen years at Leiden some of them determined to migrate to America. They secured financial backing from some London merchants who saw possible profits from furs and fish. In September, 1620, 102 "Pilgrims" sailed from Plymouth in the *Mayflower* with only a third from Leiden and the rest gathered from London. The Jamestown pioneers had included only men, and cargoes of girls were sent over for wives, but nearly half the *Mayflower's* passengers were women and children. Late in November they reached the tip of Cape Cod, farther north than they intended. Before anyone went ashore, every man signed the Mayflower Compact, an instrument of colonial self-government which all agreed to obey. The dominant Leiden group had drawn this up to keep the restless Londoners in hand, and the colony was spared the factional fights which distracted Jamestown. At Plymouth, on the west shore of

come to America in order to worship as they pleased, but it seems likely that free land provided another incentive. The combination of religious, political, and economic conditions in early Stuart England seemed so intolerable that it dislodged many who might otherwise never have been willing to take such a chance.

The members of the Massachusetts Bay Company, instead of remaining in England, came to America and brought their charter with them, so that they secured even more complete self-government than Virginia or Plymouth. The Puritan church members, though a minority, dominated the colony and its numerous towns. Showing a harsh intolerance toward all who differed in religion, the Puritans severely regulated not only the beliefs and worship but also the morals of the community. The combination of Calvinistic influence, long, rigorous winters, and energetic efforts to wrest a living from the forests, the sea, or rugged farms developed a stern toughness of character, together with shrewdness, clear thinking, and tireless energy. Each new town quickly built not only a meeting-house but also a schoolhouse; for every child was to be well grounded in the three R's. Such emphasis was placed on education that Harvard College was founded as early as 1636, more than a half century before Virginia's William and Mary.

From the economic standpoint England regarded New England as the "most prejudicial" of her overseas settlements; for it refused to fit into the scheme of a self-sufficient empire. It might have produced useful naval materials, but it co-operated only to the extent of sending masts. Barely able to sustain themselves with agriculture, the New Englanders devoted their attention to lumbering, fishing, and shipbuilding, and then actively peddled their products wherever they could find markets. Instead of rounding out the needs of England, they were competing with her.

The "great emigration" during those eleven years when England was without Parliament was by no means limited to Virginia and to New England. Some fifteen hundred colonists went to Maryland, established in 1634 under tolerant Catholic auspices, with a feudal form of government under its "proprietor," Lord Baltimore. The West Indian Islands attracted even more settlers than all the mainland colonies together—the little island of Barbados, only twenty-one miles long and less than fifteen miles wide, having more settlers than all New England. At first these islands raised tobacco; but the Dutch finally demonstrated the advantages of sugar cane, from which sugar, rum, and molasses could be derived. Negro slaves were introduced, and for a long time these few little dots on the map were worth more to England than either the mainland colonies or India.

Along with overseas settlements a colonizing venture was being carried out nearer at hand. After the crushing of the Irish rebellion in the last years of Elizabeth's reign, it was decided to hold Ireland in hand by transplanting thither Englishmen and Scots. Six of the nine counties in Ulster, the northern province, were given over to settlers from Britain. Some of these were English, but a considerable number were Scottish Presbyterians. Hitherto the Celtic Irish had absorbed the Danes, Normans, and Englishmen who had gone among them, but these dour Scotch-Irish of Londonderry, Belfast, and other parts of Ulster have remained sharply distinct and hostile. A century later large numbers of the Scotch-Irish were to go to America, bringing Presbyterianism with them to the middle colonies and out to the frontier.

Those critical years of the first two Stuarts not only saw England approaching a crisis in its constitutional development but also saw English history spreading out from the little island kingdom into distant regions which must thereafter be taken constantly into account in any history of the English people.

The Puritan Revolt

The contest between king and Parliament reached its height in the middle of the seventeenth century. For eleven years Charles governed England without summoning Parliament. Once it assembled, antagonism was so sharp that both sides soon resorted to arms—king against Parliament, Cavalier against Puritan. Charles lost his head, and Oliver Cromwell, Parliament's general, in more ways than one kept his. The monarchy of England was submerged beneath the flood; and Cromwell, a species of saint to many, a most decided devil to others, became dictator of an English republic. At his death, chaos almost reigned until Charles's son returned in full glory as King Charles II.

By means of various pretexts, Charles I managed between 1629 and 1640 to scrape together sufficient money without Parliamentary aid. He could collect enough to govern the country on a peace basis, but war was a luxury he could not afford. By 1630, peace treaties had ended English meddling in France, Spain, and Germany. It has been remarked that "James made many mistakes, but at least he had a European policy; Charles had no European policy at all." The Thirty Years' War continued its intricate and devastating course; but, much as Charles wanted to help his sister's cause, England was forced to remain aloof. Sweden rose to a brief greatness; Richelieu intervened to smash Hapsburg power; Holland slowly fought her way to complete freedom. But in all that, England stayed at one side, sullenly fermenting with domestic dissensions.

The royal officials left no stone unturned to bring money into the treasury without resorting to Parliamentary grants. No possible source of income was overlooked: even the stumps of oaks in the royal forest were sold. The customs duties were still collected in spite of the recent protests of the Commons and the temporary resistance of the merchants. Courtiers formed companies to secure the obnoxious patents which had been denied to individuals, except inventors, by Parliament in 1624. The ancient limits of the royal forests were retraced, and many who had lived for years within the forgotten boundaries were heavily fined under the rigorous forest laws. Fines had to be paid in London before new buildings might be constructed, and in the country before old ones might be demolished. According to an unrepealed statute of Edward I, all landholders with a stipulated income (originally £20, later £40) were required to become knights (see page 104); this had been designed to provide a properly equipped force of armed horsemen. Now, when £40 incomes had become far more common, this "distraint of knighthood" was revived to mulct a very large group. Men had to pay a heavy fee if they became knights, and they were fined if they refused.

The most celebrated of these financial attempts was the collection of "ship money." It was an ancient custom that in time of war, when the rest of England was called upon for military service, the seaports of the south coast were to furnish ships for fighting purposes. Now, although the country was at peace, not only were these seaports asked for money in place of ships, but so were the inland counties as well.

The navy, to be sure, was impoverished. James had allowed it to decay, and its low efficiency had been glaringly evident in the ill-starred ventures of Buckingham. Not only was the royal navy ineffective as a weapon of offense; it was unable even to protect the coasts of England. Barbary pirates from Algiers were raiding with impunity the shores of the British Isles. In 1635 they descended one night upon the seacoast town of Baltimore in Ireland and carried away some two hundred of the inhabitants, who were sold in the slave markets at Algiers—the women for the harems, the men for toil in galleys or stone quarries. Ten years later England sent commissioners to Algiers to redeem hundreds of English, Scottish, and Irish men and women at the prices they had fetched in the slave sales.

The needs of the navy were one thing, and the ship money, that went into the celebrated *Sovereign of the Seas*, Phineas Pett's masterpiece, at least was well spent. But the methods of collecting ship money were another. The former Puritan members of the House of Commons stiffly resisted this flank attack upon Parliament's power of the purse. John Hampden, one of the foremost Puritan leaders, and one of the wealthiest men in England, refused to pay

Charles I, 1631

the twenty shillings levied upon one of his estates. In his trial, he vigorously combated the crown. In spite of the past removal of obstinate judges, the king won his decision in 1638 by only a vote of seven to five. But the wide-spread publicity gave Hampden a moral victory.

Archbishop Laud

By that time another source of irritation, becoming daily more exasperating, was Charles's new chief adviser, William Laud, a scholarly little churchman with "prim mouth and sharp, restless eyes." One-time Oxford don, through Charles's favor he had won not only the chancellorship of Oxford but also successive promotion through three bishoprics until, in 1633, he became Archbishop of Canterbury. By nature a disciplinarian, he expected royal authority to back up church discipline, and, in turn, he argued strongly for royal prerogative and sat high in royal courts and councils. He was able, pious, honest, conscientious, and courageous; but his ideas ran counter to those of most Englishmen. He tried to order men rather than to persuade them. By his stubborn persistence in pursuing his unpopular aims he probably did more than any other to bring on the Civil War, which ruined the king whom he so sincerely and energetically tried to serve.

Laud had forced the Oxford students into caps and gowns; now he tried to force England into similar external uniformity in worship. As far as doctrinal beliefs were concerned, Laud was possibly more broadminded than the Calvinistic Puritans whom he hated. He wanted to link the Church of England with the traditions of the past and to base it upon more than the simple Puritan interpretation of the Scriptures. To Laud it was a matter of utmost importance that the Communion table should be placed in the east end of every church and that all should bow when the name of Jesus was mentioned. His vicar-general made tireless visitations to enforce such ceremonial regulations, distasteful to the majority of the clergy and to a greater proportion of laymen whose interest lay rather in what their preachers had to say. The poet Milton objected to the emphasis on "palls and mitres, gold and gewgaws"; Cromwell condemned such "poisonous Papist ceremonies." Laud took vigorous measures to suppress the Puritan preachers, marking for promotion only the minority who agreed with his High Church views. Laud, with his passion for authority, did not stop there. During his rule the church courts meddled with the morals and daily life of the people. Laud himself, sitting on the courts of Star Chamber and High Commission, took a vigorous part in several savage sentences upon men accused of libel for criticizing the government and the religious innovations. A preacher was fined £10,000, sentenced to long imprisonment, flogged, and placed in the pillory, where his ears were lopped off, his nose slit, and his cheeks branded "S.S." ("sower of sedition"). Such practices help to explain the extensive Puritan migration across the Atlantic during those years.

Scottish Reactions

The archbishop's innovations caused irritation enough in England; the results were more immediately violent in Scotland, with its warlike feudal nobility and its lowlanders saturated with Presbyterianism. When Laud held the work of John Knox "not a reformation but a defamation," trouble started. When a new prayer book, incorporating Laud's ideas, was forced upon Scotland, everyone blamed the "pope of Canterbury," and it was read in few places. The attempt of the Bishop of Edinburgh to use the new service in the great church of St. Giles in June 1637 was met with a stool hurled at his head by an angry woman. With the mob outside shattering the church windows, he rode home amid a shower of stones. From that violent outburst may be traced a regular and rapid series of events leading to the Civil War.

Seven months later Scotland produced her famous document, the National Covenant. In this the Scots declared their loyalty to the king, but bound themselves to reject all religious innovations which had not first been approved in free assemblies of the Scottish Church (Kirk). After the clergy, nobility, and gentry had signed it, the Covenant was spread on a tombstone in the churchyard of Greyfriars' Church in Edinburgh, where thousands of common folk, raised to a high pitch of emotion, added their signatures. Circulated around the country, it was subscribed to by most of the people. A general assembly of the Kirk at Glasgow definitely repudiated bishops and all innovations in religion.

Charles determined to punish his stubborn Scottish subjects, but he had neither men nor money enough for a successful campaign. Nevertheless, in the spring of

Scottish Presbyterians signing the National Covenant in 1638 in Greyfriars church-yard; Edinburgh Castle in the background.

1639 he summoned the nobles and the militia of the northern counties and headed for Scotland with an ill-led, ill-trained, reluctant army. At the Tweed, which separates the two kingdoms, he came face to face with a Scottish force better prepared than his own and strengthened by veteran Scots from the Thirty Years' War. There was no fighting, and this "First Bishops' War" soon ended with a truce. A year later the Scots were to force Charles to end his long rule without Parliament.

That autumn the king took a new chief adviser, Sir Thomas Wentworth, better known to history by his new title (1640) of Earl of Strafford. Scion of prominent Yorkshire gentry, Wentworth had gone to Cambridge, had studied law, and had become an experienced parliamentarian. Although he was always loyal to the king he disapproved his arbitrary acts and wanted him to take Parliament into ac-

count as the earlier Tudors had done. In the stormy session of 1628 he tried his best to work out a compromise between Commons and king, but Charles would not agree. Thereupon the leadership in the Commons passed to Eliot, who pushed through the Petition of Right. Wentworth would not stomach Parliamentary supremacy and was thenceforth one of the stanchest supporters of royal power. In a few months, he was sent to York as head of the Council of the North. In 1633, he went as deputy to Ireland, where during the next six years he did what he could for the Irish: restoring order, remodelling the army, reforming the corrupt civil service, stimulating education, and doubling the volume of trade by encouraging the linen industry. An efficient executive, and an impatient one, he secured his ends by high-handed methods which he himself described as "thorough." He carried those same principles into his brief but all-powerful period as chief minister of Charles, to whom he offered much of his private fortune and his efficient Irish regiments.

With Charles still bent upon punishing Scotland, Wentworth, now Strafford, advocated the calling of Parliament in 1640 as the only means to secure adequate funds. He seemed not to realize that a Parliament could not be manipulated as easily in England as in Ireland. When the Commons assembled, pent-up grievances of eleven years found voice. They would not grant the king a shilling until he listened to them. He had no intention of doing this, and dissolved this "Short Parliament" in three weeks.

Strafford gave England a final brief taste of royal absolutism. There were riots, but the ringleaders were executed. Several members of Parliament were imprisoned. Press gangs rounded up crowds of riff-raff for a new army to invade Scotland. But, in the "Second Bishops' War," the Scots took the initiative and invaded England. It was a sort of friendly invasion; for they knew that the mass of Englishmen would welcome the forcing of the king's hand. Before Strafford could get his reluctant conscripts to the border, the Scots had advanced as far as Durham. They might have continued on to London; instead they adopted a clever course which must have warmed the heart of every Scot. They simply remained about Durham, running up bills of £850 a day and announcing that they would not leave until Charles paid those bills.

The Long Parliament

Thus, for the second time in 1640, the king had to call Parliament. The presence of the Scots kept the king from another quick dismissal of its members. Some of them were still sitting in 1653—hence the name, "Long Parliament." Even in 1660 those who still survived were called together once more for a final settlement of the twenty intervening years.

The Long Parliament had able guidance in John Pym, "burly and shaggy and vigilant as a watchdog." A Puritan who "thought it part of a man's religion to see that his country be well governed," he combined breadth of vision, keen ability in political tactics, and the will to transform Parliament from a protesting into a dominating body. Next to him ranked John Hampden, of ship-money fame, with "long, thoughtful face, thin lips, and bright, melancholy eyes," high-minded, clear-headed, and keen-witted. They, with a few other prominent Puritans, had kept in close contact during the eleven-year recess, and they remained together for constant counsel and action in the crisis which approached. Missing from the Commons were its two leaders of eleven years before: Eliot had died while imprisoned by the king, and Wentworth as his right-hand man was now its archenemy.

Eight days after the Long Parliament assembled, the Commons impeached Strafford and then Laud. It was a case of "my head or thy head"—if the Commons had not impeached Strafford when they did, he was ready to have Pym and his associates condemned for treasonable relations with the Scots. Parliament substituted for impeachment a speedier and more certain action, namely, an act of attainder, whereby the accused could be voted to death without the formalities of a trial. This had been used against Thomas Cromwell a century before. Strafford had given himself up with the solemn promise of protection from Charles; but howling mobs scared the king into signing the act, which two days later sent his faithful, if over-zealous, adviser to the block. With the words, "Put not thy trust in princes," Strafford met his end with dignity. The little archbishop was not executed for four years.

As in the French Revolution, a century and a half later, most of the permanent,

constructive work of the English revolution was accomplished in the early months before conditions grew violent. The Long Parliament did away with Star Chamber, High Commission, and other royal-prerogative courts, which had served useful purposes when created by the Tudors, but which had been perverted by the Stuarts into instruments of oppression and ran counter to the ideas of the Puritan gentry. Ship money, distraint of knighthood, and penalties for forest encroachments were permanen   also
passed ce
prevent th

In cons
absolutisr
much as
business
army it k
The Cor
from the
"root an
altogethe
a consic
had vot
purely

The
news fr
As so
Irish re
savage
ford's i
Catholi
the Pro
that no
tury.
thing l
and v
open;
and m
in the
der u
Proba
origin
later. The wild rumors which horrified England, however, magnified those figures manifold; the widespread contempt for the

"wild Irish" turned into bitter hatred. Everyone wanted to punish them, but they were to wait eight years for that vengeance; neither the king nor Parliament would trust the other with the command of an army for fear of its use in England.

The new Royalist party in Parliament began to stand out by itself. The closeness of the division was evident in the last days of 1641; the Puritans introduced the "Grand Remonstrance," a lengthy appeal to the people, reviewing previous evils of the reign and suggesting further reforms. er long and stormy debates, it was lly passed by the narrow margin of ven votes. That night Oliver Cromwell uoted as saying that if the measure had led he would have left England forever, bably for New England.

Then Charles blundered. In the first ek of 1642 he attempted, illegally, to peach Pym, Hampden, and three other ders of the Commons for high treason. e Lords refused to act. The next day harles himself, at the head of several ndred swaggering, armed "gentlemen," vaded the House of Commons to arrest e five members. Forewarned, they had caped down the Thames by boat. The ng, muttering that the birds had flown, tired with much loss of dignity and restige. The City of London, aroused, took arliament under its protection to save it rom the king's bullies. Hundreds rode in rom the adjacent counties to assist in the lefense. The king's high-handed action ave Parliament a powerful ally; for London, in addition to its numbers and its wealth, possessed the only adequate armed force in the country in its "trained bands."

A few days later Charles rode north from his capital, which he was not to see again until he returned a prisoner. The Long Parliament suffered the first of the great cuts that were to slash its membership, for many of both houses went northward to join the king. About thirty of the one hundred and fifty Lords and three

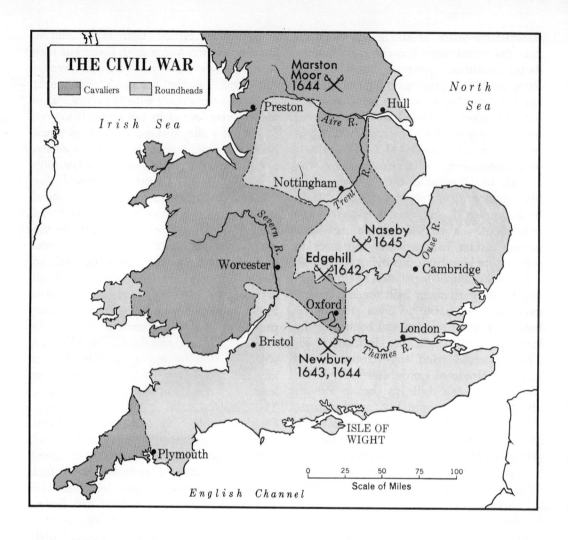

THE CIVIL WAR

Cavaliers   Roundheads

North Sea

Irish Sea

Marston Moor 1644 ✕

• Preston   • Hull

Aire R.

Nottingham •

Trent R.

Severn R.

Naseby 1645 ✕

Ouse R.

Worcester •   Edgehill 1642 ✕   • Cambridge

Oxford •

London •

• Bristol   ✕   *Thames R.*

Newbury 1643, 1644

ISLE OF WIGHT

• Plymouth

0   25   50   75   100

Scale of Miles

English Channel

hundred of the five hundred members of the Commons remained behind to conduct, in the name of Parliament, the government of England.

For eight months both sides prepared for the approaching war between the Royalist "Cavaliers" and the Parliamentarian "Roundheads." Parliament fortified several seacoast towns, took over the command of the militia, and in July organized a force of twenty-four thousand men under the Earl of Essex, the son of Elizabeth's onetime favorite. That same month the navy declared for Parliament, remembering its grievances over Stuart neglect. A considerable number of men rallied around the king, but they lacked discipline and equipment.

Gradually England took sides. For some men, loyalty to king or to Puritanism made the decision easy; many more took their stand reluctantly and with heavy hearts. The Civil War was not primarily a war of section against section nor of class against class. It was more a war of one set of ideas against another. Unlike the French Revolution, no one class stood as a whole for either king or Parliament. There was, however, a tendency for the great nobles and their retainers to side with the king, and for the moderate squires, the sturdy yeomen, and the townsmen to incline toward the Parliamentary cause, though no clean-cut line separated the classes in the struggle. Actually, two minority parties from the upper and middle classes fought the war; the bulk of the peasantry was barely affected. Geographically the division was almost as vague, although a line drawn from Hull to Portsmouth divided roughly and not too accurately the territory of the two sides. The conservative, fairly feudal, sparsely populated north and west of England thus generally supported the king, while Parliament was strongest in the more advanced south and east, which, in addition to agriculture, included most of the nation's commercial and industrial activity. The large counties of Yorkshire and Lancashire, however, were divided. Isolated in the Royalist southwest, Plymouth, the home port of the Elizabethan sea dogs, and the port of Bristol, the second largest city in England, stood for Parliament.

Outbreak of the Civil War

On August 22, 1642, Charles formally began the war by raising the royal standard at Nottingham in the presence of a rather slender crowd who cheered in the rain. Essex neglected his chance to fall upon the poorly equipped and smaller royal forces, which slipped off to the west, where the king developed a cavalry force under his dashing young nephew, Prince Rupert, third son of the late Elector of the Palatinate. Essex, in pursuit, missed him, and both armies raced for London. At Edgehill, hard by Stratford-on-Avon, they met in an indecisive encounter, for neither army was adequately trained. Charles advanced to the university town of Oxford, sixty miles above London, and made it his gay headquarters during most of the war.

For at least a year after Edgehill the tide of war favored the king. Much of the fighting was on a small scale; although some 140,000 men were under arms, it was unusual for a single force of 15,000 to engage in battle. There were many attacks on towns and on garrisoned country houses; and the larger forces marched and countermarched in surprising ignorance of the enemy's whereabouts. The Royalists evolved a scheme of grand strategy: three separate armies, from the north, the west, and the southwest, were to push aside the Parliamentary forces and to converge below London, thus cutting off the capital from the sea. The battle of Newbury, in which the stubborn London apprentices acquitted themselves well, blocked the most threatening Royalist approach to the city. Bristol and other Parliamentary towns fell to the king's men, and nearly two thirds of England was in his hands; but the three armies did not converge as planned.

Parliament, seeing that the fighting was going against it, sought outside aid. In the summer of 1643 it made a "Solemn League and Covenant" with the Scots, who gave military aid without which Parliament might never have been victorious. The Scots, however, demanded their price, not only in cash but in religion, and Parliament agreed that England was to become Presbyterian. The latter was a very heavy price, and was the germ of much serious trouble later. A body of divines, known as the Westminster Assembly, began its thousand wordy sessions, which by 1648 produced a Presbyterian code still important in Scotland and America.

By the end of 1643, Pym and Hampden had both died, the latter in battle. For the time being, no man of equal caliber arose to fill their places; the eventual leader, who would overshadow them, was busily drilling cavalry. Oliver Cromwell, distantly related to the famous minister of Henry VIII, had grown up in the swampy fen region around Cambridge, and for a year, in which his chief interest seems to have been athletic, he attended the university. Then he settled down as a prosperous landowner. He became strongly Puritan but with independent views opposed both to the Anglican and to the Presbyterian

Cromwell, 1653

cavalry was made up of men representing many independent shades of Puritan belief; but along with their prayer meetings, they underwent tireless drill and iron discipline. His "Ironsides" had thus become a force able not only to deliver a crushing charge like Rupert's, but to remain under control to complete the work in other parts of the battlefield.

They showed their worth on a long July evening in 1644 at Marston Moor, seven miles west of York. It was the largest gathering of troops of the war: 18,000 Royalists faced 27,000 Roundheads and Scots. Both armies were drawn up in the conventional battle order of the day. Cromwell, again with Scottish assistance, carried the day by keeping his Ironsides in hand and by using them to crush the stubborn infantry regiments of the king. That battle lost northern England to the king, and it made Cromwell.

Marston Moor revealed that the other Parliamentary commanders and troops did not measure up to the high efficiency of Cromwell and his Ironsides. Cromwell himself grew increasingly impatient with Lord Manchester, the supine Parliamentary commander in chief. In that autumn of 1644 Manchester's inactivity allowed the outnumbered royal forces to escape disaster in the second battle of Newbury. A month later, in Parliament, Cromwell launched an open attack upon his inefficient chief, with two results. First was the "Self-Denying Ordinance," whereby all members of Parliament in military service were to resign their commissions within forty days; thus the dead wood at the top was removed. The command was reorganized, with Fairfax at the head and Cromwell second in command, with particular charge of the cavalry. Second, early in 1645, came the creation of a "New Model Army," based on the efficient discipline of Cromwell's Ironsides. This, incidentally, was the first army to adopt the famous red coat as the regular English uniform.

forms of church government and worship. By 1628 he was in the House of Commons, and he sat again in the Long Parliament, where Hampden and more than twenty other members were relatives of his. He spoke only occasionally, with more force than grace. A cavalry captain at the battle of Edgehill, he realized that the Parliamentary forces needed strong cavalry more than anything else. As he told his cousin, Hampden, their troops were mostly "old decayed serving men and tapsters," who lacked the spirit of Prince Rupert's "gentlemen of resolution." The effectiveness of the heavy cavalry charge particularly impressed Cromwell from studying the innovations of the great Swedish king, Gustavus Adolphus, whose military genius had done much to turn the Thirty Years' War into a Protestant victory. Within six months after Edgehill, Cromwell had trained for his command eleven hundred troopers. His

The new Model Army in June, 1645, blundered into the royal army at Naseby for the decisive battle of the war. As at Marston Moor, Cromwell's charge carried away the opposing cavalry wing; then he turned his disciplined horsemen upon the stubborn Royalist infantry. A thousand Royalists fell; four thousand were captured, and so were the king's private letters. These contained such damaging proof of intrigue that their publication did irreparable harm to Charles. Naseby, to all intents, ended the Civil War. Quickly the remaining royal army was crushed, and one by one the king's isolated strongholds were seized. Charles, reduced almost to the status of a wandering refugee, fled to the Scottish troops. By the spring of 1646 the Roundheads had unquestionably triumphed.

The Four Factions

The victorious Parliamentary side was now faced with the problem of reconstruction. The bitterness that was to characterize later Cavalier defeats was scarcely aroused at this time. Religious toleration as a general basis of settlement, with restraint on the part of the victors in making the vanquished pay for the war, might have healed more wounds than anything else and have brought earlier tranquillity to the divided land; but such toleration, unfortunately, for the time being proved impossible, since there were four factions, each determined on its own stubborn way in bigoted fashion: Parliament, the Parliamentary army, the king, and the more or less interested Scots.

The war was won in the name of Parliament; but what did Parliament represent? Never fairly representative of all England, it did not now stand even for dissenting England. At this time it was largely Presbyterian in sentiment, in a country where Anglicans, Independents, and others were very numerous. Yet even the common desire with the Scots to impose the National Covenant on England did not bring these two of the diverse elements into common action, perhaps because of the Scots' lesser interest in the military and political situation and their greater readiness to give Charles what he wished. The army, on the other hand, the winner of the Parliamentary victories, was composed largely of various other sects, some of them extreme in their fanaticism, but chiefly Independents, who wanted self-governing groups to worship freely without outside control and who were almost as ill-disposed to presbyters as to bishops. Since the army had given Parliament its power, it was not to be ignored or snubbed with impunity. These divergent elements on the winning side led Charles, not unnaturally but most unwisely, to try to play off Parliament, army, and Scots one against the other. A dangerous game for the cleverest, this juggling of such inflammable political material; and when the player was a prisoner, and not trusted by any group because of his notorious inability to keep any promise, failure was inevitable. Yet the king, in the minds of many, was still the symbol of law and government. His personal disaster made military dictatorship practically inevitable.

Between the various factions stood Oliver Cromwell, the focal point of the whole tangled situation. When Charles, on that wintry January morning, had invaded the House of Commons with his soldiers, Cromwell already was forty-three years old and by no means recognized as a leader of men. Yet within four years he forged to the front as a famous soldier, and within four more was to become dictator of his country. Circumstance and not desire made him such; of this we can be reasonably certain. Very little else may be affirmed of him without qualification. He was a Puritan of the Puritans, devoutly religious; but at the same time he kept a relatively clear head in matters of faith. Although far from radical in his political ideas, he did not hesitate, roughly and illegally, to execute his king. He believed with all his heart in constitutional methods; but he threw three Parliaments out of Westminster by the scruff of the neck because of their ineptitude. None could deny that he was an opportunist who moved this way and that among the stubborn, set ideas of Parliament, king, Scots, and army until the decision was in his hands. Nevertheless, when he decided upon action he was always confident that the Almighty had made the decision. Tragically enough, Cromwell's way ended for the time being the very constitutional ideas of government for which he had fought. The force of circumstances, combined with his own personal idiosyncrasies, fashioned out of this conscientious opponent of tyranny one of the most absolute rulers England has ever endured.

Before Cromwell found himself master of England, the first step in the series of futile moves was the presentation by Parliament, with the consent of the Scots, of certain peace terms to Charles at Newcastle, in the summer of 1646. Charles played for time, hoping to widen the breach between the Presbyterians and Independents. Although in the power of the Scots, he remained constant in his hatred of Presbyterianism. He was apparently ready, among other things, to compromise on the Covenant for three years, pending a religious settlement under the joint auspices of certain Presbyterian clergy and others to be appointed by himself. The Scots, disgusted at this stand, permitted Parliament to take him into custody upon payment of certain sums due them for their aid in the war, and withdrew homeward.

Parliament, with Charles as prisoner and with the Scots for the moment out of the picture, embarked upon an arbitrary course of religious persecution and wanton taxation of all and sundry. Not content with driving the Anglican clergy from their parishes and forbidding the prayer book,

it began deliberately to persecute the Independents and to treat other sects harshly. Lasting resentment was aroused among the Royalists over the confiscatory fines charged against them as "rebels," which in numerous cases forced the sale of their family estates. But Parliament in this was only following the easiest way of making the losers pay the bills. Its more conspicuous folly came in its treatment of the army purely as paid employees. Composed, as it was, of many different sects, the army had long been annoyed at Presbyterian dominance, and now was infuriated by religious persecution. When Parliament directed that most of it be disbanded without pay and ordered most of the rest to Ireland, its patience broke.

Acutely aware that it had put into power the very Parliament that was treating it in such a manner, the army now took the lead in negotiations with Charles, a task made easy by kidnaping His Majesty's person in the summer of 1647. Although Parliament itself had seemed sterile in original ideas for governing the country, political theories were rife in the army. The present day may laugh at the "Fifth-Monarchy Men," who hoped to see the prophecy of Daniel fulfilled by the rule of Christ and the saints as successors to the Assyrian, Persian, Macedonian, and Roman empires; but it can appreciate the "Levelers" and others who clamored for democracy this early. "The poorest he that is in England hath a life to live as much as the greatest he, and a man is not bound to a government that he has not had a voice to put himself under," declared one of their spokesmen. Although very advanced for the time, their suggestions of universal suffrage and government actually in the hands of the people found ready listeners among the unpaid and religiously dissatisfied soldiery. The radicals began to show, by open personal criticism, an increasing distrust that was to be the ruin of Charles. Nevertheless, Cromwell held the radical elements so well in check that the actual terms sent to Charles, the so-called "Heads of the Proposals," were moderate, tolerant, and less discriminatory against Royalists than any others in those unquiet years.

But the king's oversanguine character and impulsive unsteadiness now pushed matters rapidly to the end of the monarchy and his own life, whereas his acceptance of these terms would probably have extended both. Not only did Charles foolishly refuse them, perhaps from loyalty to many of his followers who would receive no amnesty, but, late in 1647, he fled to the Isle of Wight. There, however, he was soon to find himself in custody again. The soldiers, under the Levelers' influence, now wholly disgusted at this evidence of the king's instability, could no longer be controlled by Cromwell. They demanded that the whole settlement be referred to the people in a then unheard-of popular referendum, with the proposal that the monarchy be at once abolished and that one house of Parliament, with no Lords admitted, be substituted for the two houses. While Cromwell was successfully keeping these extreme doctrines from being put into effect, the king again thought that he could get the situation into his own hands by playing the various factions one against another. He even called in the Scots. This last piece of stupidity convinced England of Charles's utter duplicity and untrustworthiness.

This Scottish invasion in 1648 opened the Second Civil War, a short affair. A Welsh royalist uprising was put down, as well as others in Kent and Sussex; and the attempt of some warships, turned pro-Stuart, to block the Thames came to nothing. The invading Scots and their Royalist allies were cut in two by Cromwell at Preston, in the west—the only major encounter, and a fatal one for the Royalist cause.

The army was now finally and definitely in control. An attempt by Parliament to come to terms with Charles a month later only precipitated Oliver's dictatorship. When the Independents got wind of the pro-Presbyterian, monarchical tone of those negotiations, the army took the king into closer custody. On the morning of December 6, 1648, one Colonel Pride, on Cromwell's order, stationed armed men at the door of the House of Commons as it was about to meet, and excluded those who were in favor of Presbyterianism or the king. This "Pride's Purge" delivered Parliament into the hands of the army and Cromwell. Of the five hundred members of the Commons who had gathered in 1640, barely a hundred remained. Some humorist dubbed these the "Rump" (the part which was sitting), and that name has ever since been attached to this small but powerful remnant of the Long Parliament.

The army was in possession of the king's person, and gave orders to the Rump. Politically the army was divided into two wings. One, the left, was composed of radicals and Levelers and was bitterly hostile to the monarchy. The right wing, including most of the officers, was conservative in tone, willing to negotiate further with the king. Ever since 1646, there had been conflict, open or concealed, between these two wings.

Cromwell's position was somewhat enigmatic. He knew that his was the more influential voice, yet Fairfax was his commander in chief. He was divided between his own conservative instincts and his deep loyalty to his soldiers. Furthermore, Charles's perpetual evasions had aroused his anger. So, as was his wont, he looked to Heaven for a sign. He would give Charles another chance and let God decide. An envoy was sent to the king, with another offer from the army, but His Majesty refused it. God had spoken, as Cromwell informed the Commons: "If any man whatsoever hath carried out the design of deposing the king, and disinheriting his posterity, or if any man hath yet such a de-

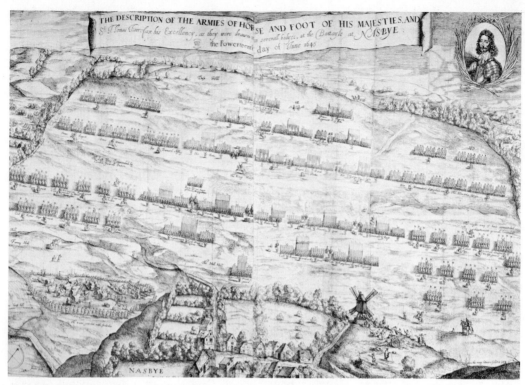

THE DESCRIPTION OF THE ARMIES OF HORSE AND FOOT OF HIS MAJESTIES, AND
S.r Thomas Fairfax his Excellency, as they were drawn in severall bodies, at the Battaile at NASBYE
the Fowerte-nt day of June 1645

NASBYE

Naseby, June 14, 1645, with Parliamentary forces in foreground, royalists in rear.

sign, he should be the greatest traitor and rebel in the world; but since the Providence of God hath cast this upon us, I cannot but submit to Providence . . ."

The Rump, with the approval of Cromwell and his friends, now brought the king to trial as a traitor to his country. Treason had hitherto been an offense against the king, but Charles Stuart as an individual was now charged with acting against the safety of England. The handful of Lords objected in vain, for the residual Commons insisted that all power was vested in them. A week's trial before an illegally constituted court of commissioners, including Cromwell, made a farce of justice; the king was not even heard on his own behalf. He was charged with intrigues with the Scots against Parliament, with Parliament against the army, with the army against both Scots and Parliament, and with foreign sympa-

thizers against all three. Nevertheless, the reasons for his death were entirely political, for he had committed no crime recognized by English law. In January, 1649, he went to the block on a balcony at Whitehall. In his last hours he showed himself a man of kingly stature, brave, calm, dignified. No cheers, it is said, greeted this execution— only deep, pitying sighs. The unfair trial and the execution at its close did much to turn England back toward the Stuarts even at this time, and more surely during the next kingless eleven years. "Not to royalists only, but to all who had a care for the human decencies, it seemed that a cruel wrong had been done and that innocence had been outraged. . . . It is clear, from contemporary letters and parish records and the diaries of obscure folk, that there fell on the land the horror of a great sacrilege. . . . That January day in Whitehall did not wash the balm from kingship, but gave it a new anointing."[1]

The army under Cromwell had had its way; but it was to find that it was not the way of the nation. Many of the Anglicans, Catholics, and even Presbyterians went so far as to wish for a king again. Among the few who liked the new order was the still unpaid army, which wanted a more radical democracy than the Rump was ready to grant. Dangers threatened on all sides: the Irish, the Scots, and some of the colonies were openly in revolt in the name of the second Charles, for whom there was a growing sentiment in England. Foreign powers, deeply disturbed at the execution of a brother monarch in that heyday of royal absolutism were so openly hostile that English trade, sea power, and colonial possessions seemed threatened.

Cromwell and the Commonwealth

The result was the Commonwealth, an experiment in republican government. Cromwell, as always during the coming years, held the reins in his own hands, though for a while his authority was disguised. The radical republic advocated by the Levelers, as well as too much Parliamentary power, considering the personnel of the Rump, were to his mind undesirable. Yet the latter's immediate dissolution might bring dangerous disorder, with the probability of the control being seized by either conservative Royalists or Levelers. To ensure order Cromwell for the time being supported the Rump and approved the formation of an executive Council of State, whose members were to be appointed annually by Parliament. The office of king was formally abolished; so also was the House of Lords. For nearly five years the Council of State was the nominal authority in meeting the various crises; but actually the successful restora-

tion of order throughout the British Isles and of British prestige on the sea and abroad was the work of Cromwell, ably assisted by the great admiral Blake and by John Milton.

John Milton (1608-1674), one of England's greatest poets, had hitherto stayed out of the main vortex of politics. Now he was appointed to the "secretaryship of Foreign Tongues," for which a scholar was necessary since much of the diplomatic correspondence was in Latin. His sympathies lay with the Puritans, but his life had been dedicated to literature. His more famous minor poems, *Il Penseroso, L'Allegro,* and *Comus,* had already been written, and he longed for peace and quiet to complete a long epic poem or a tragedy. His siding with the Presbyterians against the king had led to his wife's returning to her Royalist parents, a fact which caused Milton to advocate divorce. The Presbyterians therefore had attacked Milton, and he had deserted them for the Independents, coming to the conclusion that "New Presbyter is but Old Priest, writ large." Early in the Civil War, Milton had written, "Give me the liberty to know, to utter, and to argue freely according to conscience above all other liberties." This was the theme of the *Areopagitica,* his important plea for freedom of the press and not displeasing to Cromwell, who also disliked the Presbyterians. Therefore came Milton's appointment, which he was to regard as that of a pamphleteer at large for Cromwell's administration. A flood of pamphlets followed until the writer became blind. Possibly, owing to this latter circumstance, he was permitted to live quietly in England after the return of Charles II. During that time he wrote *Paradise Lost,* in which are to be found the best qualities of Puritanism: constant courage, if not mercy; quiet confidence, if not humor; unshaken will, even if gloomy; and a spiritual exaltation, mysterious, overwhelming, which sometimes approaches the sublime.

[1] J. Buchan, *Oliver Cromwell* (1934), p. 256. By permission of Houghton Mifflin Company, Hodder & Stoughton, Ltd., and the author.

Ireland and Scotland

The attention of the Commonwealth was next turned to Ireland and Scotland, both of which seemed dangerous as bases for a Royalist reaction. In two years and two weeks (August, 1649, to September, 1651) Cromwell overcame the two regions by force. For the first time all the British Isles were united under a single powerful authority.

Ireland presented a menacing Royalist front under the Duke of Ormond, the Lord Lieutenant, who had united both Catholic and Protestant Ireland in opposition to Parliament. His formidable forces, strengthened by some English Royalists, threatened to gain complete control of the island. In August, 1649, Cromwell went over with fifteen thousand men, and in ten months had Ireland at his feet and a serious blot on his reputation. He had gone in the vengeful spirit of an Old Testament leader, mindful of the massacres of 1641, which to him called loudly for reprisals upon a despised people (see page 237). Quickly after landing, striking at the seaport of Drogheda, he ordered the massacre of the garrison. The Royalist commander, who had fought in England all the way from Edgehill to the last little battle of the war, had his skull smashed with his own wooden leg; hundreds perished by cold steel in the streets; and when seventy took refuge in a church steeple, it was set afire. Similar treatment was dealt out to the garrison at Wexford. There were many scattered operations against an elusive enemy, and Ireland was well humbled by the time Oliver returned for his Scottish work.

The name of Cromwell, however, has been particularly hated in Ireland for his land settlement, under which Ireland was to suffer for two centuries and a half. It was a different sort of settlement from that of the "plantation of Ulster," where both landowners and peasantry had been moved out of a considerable portion of the northern province to make room for Scottish and English colonists forty years before. Now, from two thirds to three quarters of the rest of the land in Ireland passed to Protestant English landlords. The great majority of the peasants were left in southern Ireland, still predominantly Celtic and Catholic, but many were transported overseas, particularly to the West Indies. The new landowners were in part adventurers, who had helped to finance the invasion, and in part officers and soldiers of Cromwell's army. Many of the latter sold their shares to wealthier men, who built up extensive estates. Some of the lesser English landowners ultimately mingled with the native Catholic Irish; but the Protestant aristocrats tended to remain aloof from their oppressed tenantry. Often absentee landlords, they rarely visited the estates in which their only interest lay in the money which their stewards could squeeze from the tenants. The twentieth century was to come before England finally took effective measures to undo the unfortunate effects of this Cromwellian settlement.

Oliver did not remain behind to parcel out the land, but left that to his sons-in-law and then his son. Late in June, 1650, three weeks after he returned from Ireland, a ship arrived in Scotland bearing a cynical, charming young rake whom the Scots had already hailed as Charles II of Scotland and England. The dour Presbyterians had persuaded Charles to accept their distasteful Covenant as the price of their support in recovering the Stuart thrones. Scotland was preparing to invade England to restore the monarchy. Consequently Parliament decided to strike first, and Cromwell took sixteen thousand men up the Great North Road to Edinburgh. He approached the Scots in a mood quite different from his bitter contempt for the Irish. The army of the Scots was twice the size of his, and he knew from Marston Moor that they were good soldiers. He tried to appeal to the clergy of the Kirk, who controlled the situation; "I beseech you, in the bowels of Christ," he wrote, "think it possible you may be mistaken." But the enemy remained stubborn, and the Scots nearly trapped Cromwell at Dunbar, with his back to the sea. A counterattack, however, in the September dawn brought victory to the Roundheads. Ten thousand Scots were prisoners and three thousand dead, while barely twenty Englishmen had died.

Dunbar broke the ascendancy of the Kirk. Cromwell took Edinburgh and overran the Lowlands; but the Scots rallied a new army on a broader national basis than Calvinism. They held an impregnable position at the gateway to the Highlands, and Cromwell could not dislodge them. Then in the next summer, 1651, he resorted to daring strategy, luring them out by leaving the road to England open. A force of Scots and Royalists started down the west coast under their new king and pushed on far past Preston, where Cromwell had beaten them three years before. He raced down to head them off, and met them, a year to a day after Dunbar, by the old cathedral city of Worcester, far down on the Welsh border. Among the few who escaped was young Charles Stuart. Disguised as a servant, he was spirited from house to house by loyal Royalists. He had many narrow escapes, at one time hiding for hours in an oak while the Roundheads searched the woods. Taking ship, he left for nine more years of exile on the Continent. A Cromwellian army of occupation brought relative peace to the unruly Highlands. "The very ruined nation," as Cromwell called it, was not happy under its red-coated masters, but it gave England no further serious trouble for many years.

The First Dutch War

There was trouble enough elsewhere. Five weeks after Worcester, Parliament passed an act which quickly led to foreign war. Under Elizabeth, England and Holland had often worked together in opposition to Spain. The decay of Spanish sea power, however, turned the former allies into rivals. They had raced for the spoils of the Portuguese Indies, and the Dutch had secured the lion's share (see page 227). All sea routes, moreover, led to Amsterdam, which became the leading seaport and financial center of Europe. It was a case of "he that hath, to him shall be given"; for Amsterdam, with all its wealth, could finance maritime ventures at a low rate of interest, and each venture led to more wealth. The trade of the Baltic, the Mediterranean, and many of the byways of commerce came under Dutch control; and, as one of their lesser ventures, the Dutch had established New Netherland in America for the fur trade.

The Dutch practice which caused deepest resentment in England concerned the carrying trade. Holland not only bought and sold in large quantities but also provided ships for the merchants of other nations who wanted to sell their own goods or to buy. If a London merchant wanted to bring wine from Bordeaux or masts from Danzig, he was likely to use Dutch ships, because of lower freight rates. Holland was now at the height of her power; for her complete independence from Spain had finally been recognized in 1648, after an eighty-year struggle, and she had built up a strong navy. Nevertheless, Parliament struck against this Dutch carrying trade in 1651 with the first Navigation Act, which provided that European goods must be imported into England only in English vessels, with crews at least half English, or in vessels of the producing nation. Wine, for instance, might be brought from Bordeaux in English or French vessels, but no longer in the Dutch ships which had been generally employed. In trade with Asia, Africa, and America, however, only English ships could be used.

England now had a navy with which to support this provocative legislation. In 1648

Parliament's control of the seas had been threatened when eleven warships, more than a quarter of the navy, declared for the king in the Second Civil War. Prince Rupert, the erstwhile cavalryman, took them on a far-flung piratical raid. The Commonwealth sent a soldier to sea to catch him — short, stout Colonel Robert Blake, hero of two sieges in the west country. Fifty years old when he first took command of a warship, Blake in the remaining eight years of his life won a naval reputation which places him with Drake and Nelson among England's greatest seamen. He chased Rupert to Ireland, to Portugal, to Spain, and around into the Mediterranean, demonstrating to England the strategic importance of that sea. Rupert swept over to the colonies, and Barbados and Virginia became temporarily Royalist; but he was pursued, and his squadron dispersed. By 1651 Parliament was powerful on the seas and had re-established its firm hold on the colonies. The fleet was doubled in size. With its eighty warships and its energetic seagoing military commanders, it was ready to challenge the Dutch.

There was no surprise when the Navigation Act led, in 1652, to a two-year naval struggle with Holland. It was closely contested, with the honors fairly even in the various stubborn combats, waged in and around the Channel. Van Tromp and De Ruyter could hold their own with the doughty Blake. But while the Dutch shared the fighting honors, they were so thoroughly dependent upon sea-borne commerce that its interruption hurt them far more than the English. The harbor of Amsterdam became a forest of masts of idle ships; financial ruin was imminent. Peace was made in 1654, and the Navigation Act remained in force. Two more Dutch wars (1665-1667, 1672-1674) were to be necessary, however, before Holland was eliminated as an active competitor on the high seas.

The recurrent crises in the British Isles, together with the bold foreign policy, necessitated heavy taxation, considerable censorship, and other rather harsh measures which began to produce a reaction against the Rump and its executive body, the Council of State. In addition, "blue laws," upholding the extreme ascetic Puritan ideals of conduct and morals by repressive restrictions, were a constant, everyday source of irritation. At the same time the army, not even yet paid its arrears, was restive. Cromwell, apparently well aware of the dissatisfaction with the Rump, waited until that body took the unwise step of preparing to fill vacant seats by nomination instead of by election. On April 20, 1653, his impatience produced one of the most dramatic scenes in English history. He rose from his seat and roundly denounced the Rump for its injustice and inefficiency. "I will put an end to your prating," he shouted; "you are no Parliament." He called thirty musketeers into the chamber. Turning to the mace, the symbol of the Commons' authority, he cried: "What are we to do with this bauble? Take it away." As the members crowded out, Cromwell flung individual invectives at them. Then, in characteristic Cromwellian fashion, he called to them, "It's you that have forced me to this, for I have sought the Lord night and day that he would rather slay me than put me upon the doing of this work." So ended in violence the thirteen years of stress in which at least a portion of the Long Parliament had been sitting regularly.

At last the power of the army was no longer cloaked. A provisional council, composed largely of army officers with Cromwell at its head, replaced the former Council of State. Cromwell still felt that a Parliament was necessary, but one that must be kept under control. Consequently he and the Council selected the members from lists of "suitable" men compiled by the Independent preachers of the country. This new "Nominated Parliament" — or "Barebones Parliament," as it is sometimes known, because one of its members rejoiced in the name Praise-God Barebones—naturally was composed of the more extreme religious fanatics. All sorts of measures—some too extreme for the times, like the abolition of tithes—soon alienated every faction in some way or another. The Barebones Parliament lasted from July to December, 1653; then Cromwell again used soldiers to expel such members of this overactive body as did not join in a self-denying motion to dissolve.

The Protectorate and Army Control

This second violent ending of a Parliament led to the Protectorate in place of the Commonwealth (although some use the latter term to include the whole interregnum between the reigns of Charles I and Charles II). The army officers offered England her first and only written constitution, the "Instrument of Government." By this Cromwell was to be Lord Protector for life. A Parliament, to be elected by a fairly generous franchise, omitting Catholics and those who had borne arms against Parliament, was to meet for at least five months every three years. The Protector's power and that of Parliament were both to be limited, one by the other.

The first Protectorate Parliament, in 1654, determined to reduce the army and whittle away the Protector's power, at once debated the Instrument of Government. After five months, this Parliament also was ended; Cromwell, his patience exhausted, told it: "Instead of mercy and truth being brought together, weeds and nettles, briars and thorns have thrived under your shadow."

A second Protectorate Parliament asked Cromwell to take the crown. The Protector hesitated long before refusing, but he could not bring himself thus to affront his old comrades in arms. The office of Lord Protector, however, he was willing to accept. A new Parliament was elected, and a second House—not called the House of Lords but simply "the other House"—he filled by appointment.

Meanwhile Cromwell's foreign policy continued vigorous and aggressive, although in some ways unusual, since, toward the end of his rule, he ignored the balance of power by his co-operation with France, the strongest nation in Europe. At first it even looked as though he might become head of a great league of Protestant nations against the Catholic powers. He did succeed in extending England's prestige among European nations to a point which it had never before attained. His hand fell heavily upon the Spanish empire. Late in 1654 Admiral Penn, father of the founder of Pennsylvania, took a fleet to the West Indies, and a year later captured Jamaica, soon to become England's richest colony. Admiral Blake made the Mediterranean all but a British lake. His dying act was the annihilation of a Spanish treasure fleet from America. Cromwell made an alliance with Mazarin, France's second great statesman-cardinal; and three thousand redcoats helped to win the battle of the Dunes over the Spaniards, as a result of which the port of Dunkirk fell to England as a prize.

In domestic affairs the Protector was not so fortunate. As a temporary solution, to offset the all-prevailing internal disorders, he parceled England out into wide districts, over each of which he placed a major general with full administrative jurisdiction. A peaceful, conforming England was obtained by their harsh rule, but underneath surged a bitter weariness and an increasing desire for a Stuart restoration. The Stuarts at their worst had done nothing as generally unpopular as the enforcement of the blue laws by redcoats. Theaters, cockfighting, church festivals, and other forms of merriment dear to the hearts of the people were prohibited. England was forced to endure the negations of the harsh, gloomy Puritan Sabbaths, when walking was deemed an unholy pleasure and one could travel only with formal permission. Severe morality was enforced; swearing was forbidden, let alone flirting. But the atmosphere of Massachusetts Bay rested poorly upon England; and Cromwell, who was fond of music, horses, and all field sports, doubtless would have put a stop to this extravagant righteousness had not his own end been near.

He died in September, 1658. With his strong hand removed, England passed through a troubled year and a half under the threat of a new civil war. During half this period Cromwell's elder son Richard held nominal authority as Lord Protector; but "Tumbledown Dick," lacking force and ability, soon dropped from view, while the Rump was recalled and threw its influence behind the civilian discontent as army commanders maneuvered for power. At last, in the first week of 1660, General Monk, who had commanded the army of occupation in Scotland, led his redcoats through the border town of Coldstream (from which the first regiment of the reg-ular army was to take its name) and marched southward to back the civilians in their demand for a free Parliament. All the surviving members of the Long Parliament were called back to join the Rump; the Long Parliament issued a summons for a new election; and the resultant "Convention" Parliament recalled Charles II from his long exile. The turbulence of the interregnum at last gave way to the less heroic gaiety of the Restoration, and the Puritan revolt was at an end.

Its failure for many a long day was to cast a shadow upon Puritanism in general and upon Cromwell in particular. The former, at its worst, had been a nightmare; but at its best it had sought to raise to high and worthy levels the entire life of the English people. As for Cromwell, he remains something of an enigma. Like Caesar, like Napoleon, he bent a nation to his will. Unlike them, he was a man most humble of mind, baffled by problems beyond his powers to solve.

Restoration England

In May, 1660, a dark, slender Stuart celebrated his thirtieth birthday by returning to London as King Charles II. He rode into the capital "with twenty thousand horse and foot, brandishing their swords and shouting with inexpressible joy; the ways strewed with flowers, the bells ringing, the streets hung with tapestry, fountains running with wine." London was madly exuberant. The grim repression of the reign of the saints was over; so, too, was the dread uncertainty which had followed the death of Cromwell. There was gratitude to General Monk, who had made the decision to bring the monarchy back; to the rather irregular Parliament which had extended the invitation; and to Admiral Montague, who had brought the new king over from Holland in a flagship with the name *Royal Charles* hastily painted over *Naseby*.

The social system of this England, to which this Stuart son returned, differed in many ways from that of France, where he had spent many of his impoverished years of exile (see pages 169 ff.). At the close of the Restoration period a writer made some estimates which indicate the numbers in the various English social classes and occupations. His guesses were "generally accepted at the time as reasonable," with the following number of heads of families in each group: 160 temporal lords, 26 spiritual lords (archbishops and bishops); 800 baronets; 600 knights; 3000 esquires; 12,000 gentlemen; 5000 persons in greater offices and places; 5000 persons in lesser offices and places; 10,000 merchants and traders by sea; 10,000 in law; 10,000 clergymen; 160,000 freeholders (yeomen); 150,000 (tenant) farmers; 15,000 persons in liberal arts and sciences; 50,000 shopkeepers and tradesmen; 60,000 artisans and handicraftsmen; 5000 naval officers; 4000 military officers; 50,000 common seamen; 35,000 common soldiers; 364,000 laboring people and outservants; 400,000 cottars and paupers; and an indeterminate number of "vagrants, as gipsies, thieves, beggars, &c." The blanket phrase "gentry" would include the 16,400 baronets, knights, esquires, and gentlemen, while the phrase "middle class" would probably include the group ten times that size, engaged in public office, the professions, commerce, trade, and industry, and as naval and military officers. The yeomen and tenant farmers, some 310,000, formed a sort of agricultural middle class; the remainder, more than half the population, made up the lower classes.

England still had an essentially agricultural economy, with most of her wealth coming from the ownership of land and the vast majority of workers tilling the soil. The land, not yet disfigured by industrial development, was about half under cultivation, the rest being pasture, woodland, moor, or fen. The once vast oak forests were being devoured as charcoal for the iron furnaces; and the navy was beginning to worry about timber wherewith to build its ships. But much that was still wild and primitive remained, especially in the barren northern and southwestern counties. London was long since, of course, a metropolis, and there were some towns of medium size.

Of all the social classes, the most conspicuous but the least characteristically English was that surrounding Charles at his Whitehall palace. That little group, probably the wealthiest in the land, included many of the highest titles in the peerage—not a few newly created from among the king's boon companions. Aping the new French society at Versailles and led by a monarch who was a fitting master of revels, the Restoration court lived in a constant round of showy and licentious gaiety. Men with clever, cynical wit and boldness of action strove for the bounties which were lavishly granted by a king too poor to pay his sailors or repair his ships; while maids of honor, whose actions belied their titles, shamelessly sought to make the most of their opportunities, to the scandal of a land just emerging from Puritan repression. Not the least shocking to the nation was the prominence of the royal mistresses. Some of these had no small influence on the course of events: Barbara Villiers, who became Countess of Castlemaine and eventually Duchess of Cleveland; the French Louise de Querouaille, who was made Duchess of Portsmouth; and "pretty, witty" Nell Gwynne, a vivacious redheaded actress who held first place in the king's affections during the later years of the reign.

But this gay group at Whitehall was not typical, even of upper-class England. Many of the peers and most of the gentry, the true landed aristocracy, seldom visited the capital unless attending Parliament. The country squires (see page 170) still held their dominant position in local and national government, though many of them spent a considerable part of their days in hunting the fox, and their nights in emptying the bottle. Harsh game laws, passed by a Parliament of landowners and enforced locally by the justices of the same class, barred lesser folk from hunting. Worcester, Leicester, Gloucester, and similar shire towns were to the county families what Whitehall was to the great lords and courtiers; and the quarter sessions of the shire courts were apt to be accompanied by a local social season. This localism helped to produce a stubborn and sometimes ignorant prejudice. "Toward London and Londoners" according to Lord Macaulay, the squire "felt an aversion which more than once produced important political effects." Calling him an uncouth, crude boor, with little education, Macaulay yet admitted that he was "essentially a patrician, and had in large measure both the virtues and vices which flourish among men set from birth in high place, and accustomed to authority, to observance and to self-respect." Macaulay's estimates have of late years been discounted as Whig prejudice toward the generally Tory squires and clergy. It must be remembered that Hampden, Eliot, and Pym were among those from this same class of gentry, which had no small part in the Puritan opposition to the first two Stuart kings and now gave loyal support to the third.

In the rural classes lower than the gentry were the vast majority of Englishmen, making what living they could from the soil. Most prominent were the yeomen, who owned their land as freeholders, and a like number of tenant farmers, who rented land to cultivate. Economically similar, both groups actually worked the land themselves, often with a farmhand or two. In some respects, the yeomen, belonging to that sturdy minority which had maintained independence since Saxon days and had furnished the victorious archers of Crécy and Poitiers (see pages 48, 121), could hold their heads higher. As freeholders with land yielding at least forty shillings a year, they could vote for county members of Parliament—and had no landlord to coerce their choice.

Then came the great mass of peasantry proper. Of these, the cottars lived in the little cottages of the rural villages, tilling a small strip or plot, of ground, for which they generally paid rent, keeping a few geese or animals on the common land, and sometimes acting as spinners and weavers for the "clothiers" in the domestic system of industry (see page 132). Still lower in the scale were farm hands, the agricultural laborers who worked for wages for some lord, gentleman, yeoman, or tenant farmer. It was estimated just after the Restoration that about one third of the whole population, chiefly the cottars, made barely enough for subsistence, while another third was unable to live without poor relief. Some of these poor lived in London slums, but most of them were rural.

Yet, with all that, the land probably came nearer to being a "merry England" than it was to be for succeeding generations after the Agricultural and Industrial Revolutions had made the nation more efficient at the expense of individual well-being. The peasants, to be sure, toiled hard and lived on the edge of poverty; and not for two centuries more would they have a voice in the government. The month-after-month, year-after-year routine of planting, cultivating, and reaping was broken by frequent holidays and festivals in which they could make merry in keeping alive the old customs. All England went into the woods before dawn on May Day; Christmas, Michaelmas, St. Valentine's Day, and many another occasion had its observances for the peasant as well as his betters.

London

The remaining fifth of England's population were to be found in London and the towns. This "middle class" was engaged in commerce and industry, which were to become more and more distinctive of modern England. It was estimated that more than one tenth of England's five million inhabitants lived in London, perhaps the largest city of its day. In that vast settlement on the Thames, forty miles from the sea, there were then, as now, the "City" proper, the business heart of the nation, and a mile or so farther up the river, connected with the City by the Strand and Fleet Street, Westminster and Whitehall, its political center. Slums stretched to the eastward of the City, where the shipping, a regular forest of masts, lay below London Bridge. Other parts of the north bank, and to a lesser extent the south bank, already were growing with the steady increase in London's citizens.

The City within the lines of the Roman walls had once been practically all there was to London. It enjoyed special privileges, some of them dating back to Henry I. The king, for instance, might not enter the City without permission; and it had a special municipal organization, with a Lord Mayor and other colorful functionaries. Within its walls merchants, men of influence in national affairs, negotiated for the purchase or sale of goods from all parts of the world, and there most of the major financial transactions were conducted. The port of London was constantly increasing its activity and by 1730 would catch up with Amsterdam. Many merchants had their homes within the City; and many lesser buildings, chiefly of timber and plaster, were crowded within it, their gables almost touching over the narrow, winding streets, until the Great Fire of 1666 wiped out a large number of them.

The Westminster district had long been the center of England's government. Within

View of London in 1616, just half a century before the Great Fire which changed the appearance of the City, from the south bank of the Thames.

a stone's throw of Westminster Abbey, the national shrine, lay Westminster Hall and St. Stephen's. The highest courts of law had sat for centuries in Westminster Hall. St. Stephen's was the meeting place of Parliament until fire destroyed it in 1834, and the new Parliament buildings rose on the site. In Restoration times the real center of interest and activity was in the royal palace of Whitehall, close at hand. A conglomerate assemblage of buildings of varying sizes and shapes, it stretched along the Thames for almost half a mile. It housed not only the king himself but also the chief ministers of state and the great array of servants of every kind—a small edition of the glittering court which Charles's cousin Louis XIV was building for the French at Versailles. In and around that mass of buildings, pageantry, play, intrigue, and serious business went on steadily. Anyone might come to see the king praying in his chapel or dining

in his stately banqueting hall; anyone might walk in the long stone gallery, where men of all kinds, with errands and schemes of as many sorts, met, chatted, and exchanged rumors. There were more exclusive places to which the king might withdraw: to the anteroom, where he met the foreign ministers; to the great bedchamber overlooking the Thames, where the real business of state was transacted; to the council room; and finally, for much-needed solitude, to the "king's closet," where he kept his prized clocks, watches, maps, ship models, and "old masters." Beyond Whitehall stretched St. James's Park, where he sauntered with his spaniels or took his exercise at tennis or "pall mall." The color, glamour, and excitement of Restoration Whitehall have disappeared, save perhaps for the daily guard mount of the Horse Guards or the royal spectacle at the opening of Parliament. Yet in Downing Street, in the Parliament build-

The medieval St. Paul's Cathedral with its square tower dominated the skyline; the Globe Theater, associated with Shakespeare, is just below it in Southwark.

ings, at the Admiralty, and in other near-by buildings the principal governmental business of the nation and the empire is still transacted.

Shortly after Charles came to the throne, London was struck by two calamities in rapid succession. The Plague in 1665 was the last violent outbreak of the same scourge which had cropped out from time to time since the Black Death three centuries earlier. This time its effects were limited pretty much to London, where at least seventy thousand are estimated to have died in a few months, when there was, as Pepys wrote, "little noise heard night or day but the tolling of bells."

The following year (1666) the Great Fire raged five days. In the City proper it destroyed some thirteen thousand homes and eighty-nine churches, including the old Gothic cathedral of St. Paul's. It spared the slums to the eastward and did not extend far toward Westminster. Fortunately, one of England's greatest architects, Sir Christopher Wren, was at hand to design a more beautiful and sanitary London on the ruins.

London's half million inhabitants followed a mode of life quite different from that of the rural manor or cottage. London may best be seen through the eyes of Samuel Pepys, who left behind a remarkable diary. The middle-class son of a London tailor from Cromwell's fen country, and a Cambridge graduate, his start toward success came at the Restoration when his cousin, Admiral Montague, secured him a post on the Navy Board, from which he rose to become the secretary of the Admiralty. In his official capacity Pepys has been described as one of the most valuable public servants England ever had; for he managed well a chronically bankrupt navy and prospered in the process.

During the first nine years of the Restoration he confided daily in shorthand to his diary an uncensored and lively account of what he saw, what he did, and what he thought and felt. Between the "up betimes" and the "so to bed" each day he crowded more varied activity than a fox-hunting, hard-drinking squire would encounter in months. He shows the domestic life of a successful middle-class man of the city, and of his pretty but rather simple wife, "poor wretch," who must have found him trying, for he wrote of his "tousling of wenches" and his more serious amours with a candor which few others would trust to paper. Outside, in the capital, his insatiable curiosity left little undescribed. He hobnobbed with peers and high officials; carried drunken admirals home at night; relished the latest gossip about the royal mistresses and others of the glittering court; engaged in learned discussions on science, politics, and economics; hunting out hangings and cockfights; and, altogether, missed little of the gay and complex life of the capital. The unwashed denizens of the slums to the eastward seldom appear in his diary; to him they merely gave London its importance in quantity.

Some new features came into London life with the Restoration. In addition to the usual wine and beer, tea and coffee made their appearance. The coffeehouse became a daily rendezvous for the Londoner and served as a clearinghouse for rumors and theories of every sort. The theater, too, took on a gayer tone with women now in the place of boys for feminine roles. Night after night, Pepys went to the plays, going cautiously about the unpoliced streets, which were dangerous after dark and dirty at all times. With no theater-going during the Puritan interregnum, Londoners were making up for lost time.

Restoration Literature and Science

Plays were, in fact, the most distinctive feature of Restoration literature. Most characteristic of the period were the comedies of manners, often witty and generally notorious for licentious dialogue. The 1670's produced a luxuriant crop, written to suit the tastes of the courtiers and men-about-town.

The outstanding literary figure of the period was the versatile and prolific John Dryden, England's first poet lauriate, dramatist, and writer of excellent prose. Milton, to be sure, was writing *Paradise Lost*, but was keeping well out of the public eye (see page 245). In his early days Dryden was among the playwrights turning out those popular comedies, but unlike some of them, he also wrote tragedies. As a poet, he still wins high praise, especially for his *Absalom and Achitophel*, in which he satirized the Whig leaders, and *The Hind and the Panther*, in which he defended the Catholic Church, which he joined to please James II. He also dealt with various timely subjects, from the Dutch wars to the Great Fire.

There was, however, outside the capital, a writer of different mold, named John Bunyan. A private in the army of Parliament, an itinerant preacher, a mystic, a fanatic, and a Dissenter of Dissenters, Bunyan had little to recommend him to the Restoration wits. There have been many other allegories, but none with quite the vividness and stark simplicity of *Pilgrim's Progress*. "Images came crowding on his mind faster than he could put them into words, quagmires and pits, steep hills, dark and gloomy glens, soft vales, sunny pastures, a gloomy castle of which the courtyard was strewn with skulls and bones of murdered prisoners, a town, all bustle and splendour, like London on Lord Mayor's Day, and the narrow path." Released from prison by the king's pardon, Bunyan became a kind of informal wandering bishop to the lowly. *Pilgrim's Progress*, printed on the roughest of paper and circulating only among the poorer folk, lived on to become a celebrated English classic.

Science as well as literature now flourished. In the days of Cromwell learned men, interested in "Physick, Anatomy, Geometry, Astronomy, Navigation, Staticks, Magneticks, Chymicles, Mechanicks, and Natural Experiments," had met informally at Oxford. They apparently became the nucleus of the Royal Society, to which Charles II granted a charter in 1662. The Royal Society investigated "soils and clays for making better bricks"; took note of "all physical receipts and secretes, instrumentes, tools, engines"; and fostered new methods "of brewing ale and beer, manuring with lime, devising a new cider press, and a lamp for hatching eggs." A wide correspondence was begun with foreign scientists; and when Leeuwenhoek, in Holland, invented the microscope, the society sent two of its members there to investigate. The transactions of the society became internationally famous. A museum and a library were opened. The society grew steadily in influence and authority and remains a most respected organization.

The Cities, the Church, and the Armed Forces

After London, Bristol, the busy seaport on the southwest coast (see page 160), and Norwich, the center of the East Anglican woolen industry, were next in size. Each had not quite thirty thousand inhabitants. Below them the population dropped off again sharply to the ten thousand of York, "capital of the north," and to that of Exeter, "capital of the west." The other county towns, centers of the business and social life of the shires were even smaller. Many of them continued the old forms of the guild organization, although industry had spread out into the country under the domestic system. The future big centers of the Industrial Revolution—Manchester, Leeds, Birmingham, and Sheffield—still had only a few thousand inhabitants.

Agriculture and industry still continued in much the same old medieval ways, though changes lay just around the corner.

So too with communication; for there was no novelty in the wretched roads, which only grew worse each spring with their deep ruts and holes.

The Church of England was settling down into relative apathy after the tense excitement of the earlier part of the century —an apathy which was to become more marked in the next century. It was opposed to Catholics and Dissenters, but at this time it had little beyond empty formalism to offer. It was "established" as a virtual branch of the government, and its support was compulsory through the collection of tithes. Macaulay's view of the clergy, like his opinion of the squires, has also been found to be extremely biased by recent writers. Yet the country parson had influence in the community second only to the squire, and was to be ranked among the strong elements of Toryism which grew up, late in the Restoration period, in support of royal power. With all its lack of vital force, the Church of England received the loyalty of a large proportion of the people.

Connected with the Church were the two universities, Oxford and Cambridge, which had, together, about four thousand students. Neither was then a center of vital intellectual activity. Like the Church, they were slipping toward their eighteenth century apathy. Cambridge was generally a little more active and a little less fashionable. The students as a whole fell into two groups—sons of the nobility and gentry who often went simply for the college life, and a numerous class of "sizars," or self-help students, generally training for the ministry, who either received scholarships or did menial jobs for support. The rules against Dissenters robbed the universities of a supply of excellent potential material.

The standing army was still in its infancy. The English had long had a prejudice against a regular royal force, and the experience of the Cromwellian period had deepened this aversion. The beginning of

The Battle of Solebay in the Third Dutch War on May 28, 1672, a hard-fought but indecisive encounter between the fleets of the Duke of York and De Ruyter.

the regular army dates from 1661, when one of Monk's regiments became the Coldstream Guards (see page 250). Several other regiments were gradually formed, but were not popular with Englishmen. Several regiments of Englishmen were in military service in the pay of Holland or other foreign powers, so that a force of trained men might be called upon in an emergency; but domestic military service was not in high repute.

The more popular royal navy maintained a regular force of fighting ships, no longer depending, as in Tudor times, on using converted merchantmen in an emergency. After the period of neglect under the early Stuarts it had risen to high efficiency under Cromwell, and was kept in fighting trim through the three Dutch wars, in spite of constant financial starvation which it required all the ingenuity of Pepys to offset. Even at that, rotten ships and ill-fed, un-

paid crews too often hampered naval operations. The later remarkable breed of professional naval officers had not yet developed. Some were courtier captains, who could barely keep their feet planted on deck in a moderate sea; others were crude, unlettered, but effective "tarpaulins," who had risen from the forecastle. According to Macaulay "there were gentlemen and there were seamen in the navy of Charles the Second. But the seamen were not gentlemen; and the gentlemen were not seamen."

The Return of Charles II

Charles, who had borne his long exile and hardships with good humor, was one of the most astute of all the English kings. Excessive laziness and cynical indifference masked this latent cleverness well. Only in mental acuteness did Charles have anything in common with Cromwell. But whereas Cromwell was essentially an Englishman born and bred, Charles was foreign in heritage, upbringing, and attitude. Even his grandparents had little English blood, being Scottish, Danish, Spanish, and French. His mother's French strain, accentuated by his formative years of exile spent principally in France, predominated in Charles. He knew how to capitalize his infectious smile and ready wit to win men to his cause. An assiduous pursuer of pleasure and possessor of a bevy of fascinating mistresses, the "Merry Monarch" was a fit leader for the quarter century of boisterous license into which England lapsed after her overdose of Puritan grimness. His open scandals shocked the more sedate elements in England, who were even more disturbed by his careless neglect of royal duties. A thorough cynic, he took few things seriously and held still fewer sacred. Yet Charles's keen mind kept him from playing the fool to any dangerous degree; and whenever matters grew threatening, his ability saved him from his father's fate on the block or his brother's exile. Lacking their determined stubbornness, in emergencies Charles would gracefully modify his policy as seemed expedient in the face of opposition. More than once his clever manipulation of hostile situations must have aroused the admiration of his harshest critics. Steady, plodding, everyday attention to his duties was not for him; but brilliant, masterly statecraft he could show on those rare occasions when he bothered to make the effort. Through all the tortuous shiftings of his policy ran one firm intention—to live and die in his own England. Though his insidious schemings were traitorous and though his selfish personal desires threatened England with the two things the people hated most—French domination and Catholicism—he still held their affections on his deathbed. With his remarkable facility for dealing with individuals and with situations, one can only wonder what a less lazy, less selfish, or less cynical Charles might have done for England.

Charles II

Yet, for all the wild acclaim of 1660, Charles was not restored to all his father's prerogatives—a lesson his stubborn younger brother, James II, never learned. It was a restoration of Parliament as well as of king, after a period of dictatorship. All the lawmaking of the turbulent years since 1642, because it had not gone through all the normal three stages of Commons, Lords, and king, became null and void, except a few laws which were re-enacted through the regular channels. This interesting evidence of the English legal spirit is shown graphically in the collection of Parliamentary acts known as the Statutes at Large. At the top of one page is the last act to which Charles I had given his formal assent; following it, without the skipping of even a line, is the first act to which his son gave royal assent in 1660. While, in the eyes of the law, the whole intervening period was "time out," the lesson of those unsettled years tempered the course of Restoration politics. Therein are to be found all the incipient stages of the modern Parliamentary system, including even the first political parties. Although Charles knew that he was inheriting most of the theoretical powers enjoyed by his father, except those few prerogatives, like the Star Chamber, abolished by the Long Parliament (see page 237), he admitted the increasing authority of Parliament. At Breda, in Holland, where he accepted the recall to the throne, he promised to let Parliament decide the religious settlement, provided no law-abiding sects were persecuted; to pardon all rebels, except those whom Parliament should designate; to leave to Parliament the question of restoring Royalist lands; and to pay the wages of the army, which was about to be disbanded. Also, sensing that part of his father's troubles had come from a tendency to act as his own ministry, Charles avoided many pitfalls by delegating much of his governmental business. This worked out admirably for him: he had more leisure, and the ministers were blamed when matters went badly.

First among his ministers was Sir Edward Hyde, his father's faithful friend and Charles's chief adviser throughout the years of exile. Hyde did much to bring about Charles's return, whereupon he was made Earl of Clarendon, Lord Chancellor, and head of the Privy Council. After seven years of power he ended his days in exile, bearing the brunt of popular disfavor. The next six years saw the five ministers of the so-called "Cabal," followed by the Earl of Danby. Charles dropped these helpers by the road whenever it seemed expedient. Thereafter he was pretty much his own chief minister, profiting by the theory that "the King can do no wrong."

The so-called "Convention Parliament," which had called Charles to the throne, realized that revenge was profitless. For the most part, the Roundheads, with two grim exceptions, escaped the reprisals which too often accompany restorations. The bodies of Cromwell and of two of his lieutenants were dug up, dragged to Tyburn, where common criminals were executed, publicly hanged until sundown, and then buried at the foot of the gallows. A dozen or so of the "regicides" who had been active in the death sentence of Charles I were carried living to the gallows and there cut to pieces before the crowd, while others fled to precarious exile on the Continent or in America. But for the rest, an "Act of Indemnity and Oblivion" in 1660 was designed to heal the nation's wounds. England was ready to forget those intervening years as a bad dream.

The discontented loyalists, however, dubbed this an act of "Indemnity for the king's enemies and Oblivion for his friends." No attempt was made to restore all the lost Cavalier estates. The general restoration applied to those lands directly confiscated by the revolutionary governments from the crown, the Church, or private owners. Many of the Independents, who had invested in such property, were ruined. But most of those more numerous estates which had not been actually confiscated but which the Royalists had had to sell in order to meet the crushing taxes or fines imposed by their enemies remained in the hands of their new owners. Many of those were Presbyterians, a group well represented in the Convention Parliament, who thus established themselves in the gentry, occupying the places of the disgruntled Cavaliers who had had to part with their cherished ancestral acres.

From this time on, one may more properly refer to land*owners* instead of simply land*holders*. At the time of the Conquest, William I, acting upon the principle that all the land was his, had granted most of it to "tenants in chief," or principal vassals, who owed him in return not only military service but also the various feudal incidents, such as relief, escheat, wardship, and similar payments. Under the Conqueror's son nearly half the royal revenue came from that source. Even after the average tenant in chief had abandoned military activity and was paying scutage instead of his forty-day service, Edward I had managed to preserve many of the old incidents (see page 103). So matters had persisted throughout the intervening centuries. The squire, to all intents and purposes, owned his land; but the survival of the payments of feudal incidents kept alive the theory that the land really belonged to the king. This ended when the Convention Parliament abolished all the old feudal dues. The squire might still have to pay as much to the government, but his ownership of the land was now more definite.

The abolition of the feudal dues was part of the well-meaning but clumsy attempt to place the national finances upon a more stable basis. There were still heavy debts from the interregnum; the army, in particular, had to be paid. Parliament, urged by Charles to make a satisfactory financial arrangement, substituted a direct tax for the old feudal dues. This land tax fell most heavily upon the landed aristocracy, while the men of business escaped. Charles still had his hereditary revenue from the crown lands, the equivalent of the old demesne of the feudal system (see page 44), and Parliament granted him for life certain items from taxation, estimated to give him a regular annual income of about £1,200,000 for the running of the government. That, however, was not enough even for normal peace-time expenditure; and the national finances quickly fell into heavy arrears, which became worse during the remaining Dutch wars. Lacking an adequate coordination between receipts and expenditures, England had to wait some thirty years longer for a more satisfactory financial system (see page 280).

This Convention Parliament had not been a strictly legal body, because it had not been summoned by the king. In 1661 regular elections were held. A final rising of those military extremists, the Fifth-Monarchy Men, had just been suppressed, and England, in a burst of loyal enthusiasm, returned hundreds of Royalist squires to the House of Commons. The resultant "Cavalier Parliament" was so favorable to Charles that he knew he could never again secure its equal. Consequently, in contrast to the previous short-lived Stuart Parliaments, this one was kept by Charles for eighteen years, long after it had ceased to represent the temper of the nation.

If the Convention Parliament restored the monarchy, the Cavalier Parliament restored the Church of England. It was to prove hostile both to the Dissenters, who represented the interregnum harshness, and to the Catholics, who seemed to many to represent the sinister influence of France. Severe restrictions, which in some cases lasted nearly two centuries, were placed upon both these minorities which failed to come within the broad compromise of the Elizabethan settlement.

The religious legislation was aimed at all non-Anglicans; but the first crop of laws bore particularly upon the Dissenters. This was a blanket term often used to include Independents, Presbyterians, and numerous other sects (although occasionally they were termed "Nonconformists," a milder expression which later supplanted "Dissenter" in referring to Protestants outside the Church of England). Between 1661 and 1665 Parliament passed the "Clarendon Code," four acts to curb the power of the Presbyterians and others outside the Church of England. The Corporation Act excluded all but Anglicans from the corporations which governed the towns, thereby affecting the election of borough members of Parliament. The Act of Uniformity required that the clergy agree to everything in the prayer book; two thousand Dissenting ministers were expelled for refusing to do this. The Conventicle Act imposed savage penalties for attendance at meetings, or "conventicles" where any but Anglican services were used. The Five-Mile Act forbade any nonconformist minister to teach school or to come within five miles of any organized town unless he promised that he would not "endeavor any alteration in Church or State." Since most of the Dissenters were in the towns, this deprived them at once of their religious worship and their education. In Scotland there was a tumult at similar laws against the "Kirk."

Although Clarendon's name was popularly attached to these acts, modern research indicates that his judgment was against such extreme measures; he was more a political opportunist than an ardent Anglican. Charles suggested the exemption of the Presbyterians from the "Clarendon Code." His pro-Catholic leanings led him toward toleration, for he foresaw that this wave of persecution would turn next against the "papists." The real responsibility for the harshness seems to rest with the great majority of the squires and churchmen in Parliament. They pushed through the program which drove the moderate Dissenters into at least lip service to the Church of England, while many of the others found arrest, hiding, or exile their fate. John Bunyan wrote his famous *Pilgrim's Progress* while imprisoned for violation of the code.

Clarendon, hard-working, morally severe old Stuart friend, paid heavily for this Anglican victory. He further alienated Charles by his constant criticism of the court life, the royal mistresses, and the royal neglect of state matters. In addition, the Cavaliers had long been angry because he had not arranged the return of all their lost estates. Parliament resented his rather high-handed demands for money, while the Dissenters hated him for the code. His daughter's marriage to Charles's younger brother, James, Duke of York, which made him father-in-law to the heir to the throne, was called presumptuous by the court. He did not belong to this young Restoration generation, and the times had outlived his belief in

royal power and the insignificance of the Commons.

Popular suspicion also laid at his door Charles's unpopular marriage to the Portuguese princess Catherine of Braganza, who surrounded by her nuns, was rather lost and pathetic in the gay court. Clarendon was suspected of having chosen a princess who he knew was unlikely to have children, in order to ensure the throne to his own grandchildren, James's daughters, the future queens Mary and Anne. Catherine's dowry brought to England the port of Tangier, in Morocco, just across from Gibraltar, which was retained for twenty years; and, more important, Bombay. These distant acquisitions did not offset, to the Englishman of the day, the sale to hated France, in 1662, of the near-by Dunkirk, won by Cromwell's redcoats a few years before. Probably unjustly, Clarendon was blamed for this and for filling his own pockets in the process. His sumptuous new London house was jeered at as "Dunkirk House," while a scurrilous rhyme referred to

> Three things to be seen—
> Dunkirk, Tangier and a barren Queene.

When, on top of all these undercurrents, three major disasters of plague in 1665, fire in 1666, and a victorious Dutch fleet in the Thames in 1667 (see pages 255, 263) descended upon England, Clarendon was the obvious scapegoat. Two months after a mob had howled around his new house in rage at the naval disgrace, he was dismissed, and then impeached by Parliament. He fled once again to the Continent. That exile left English history richer for the magnificent prose of his autobiography and history of the Civil War.

The next step in ministries, after Clarendon's fall, was the Cabal. Although not the first group of ministers to be called a cabal, this time, by strange coincidence, the initials of the new set of Charles's advisers spelled the word, and since then "Cabal" has generally meant these five particular men. Of them Clifford and Arlington were Roman Catholics; Buckingham was the son of the earlier Stuart favorite; Lauderdale, a Scottish peer and strong Anglican, was Charles's deputy in Scotland; and Ashley-Cooper, later Earl of Shaftesbury, the most important of the five, was a frequent turncoat during the Stuart period, a clever rascal whose ideas happened to be along the line of England's future development. Theoretically the Cabal was simply a committee of the Privy Council on foreign affairs, and that foreign sphere remained its main interest as well as the chief issue during its period of power.

In the meantime, Charles and Parliament saw even less eye to eye in foreign affairs than in religion. He was pursuing a tortuous course between his own friendly inclinations toward Catholic France and the general English hostility toward her as a traditional enemy; the activities of Holland were a further complication. The latter was still in the heyday of her maritime greatness despite Cromwell's naval war and the territorial cupidity of the French king. Parliament, for its part, had kept its fingers in foreign policies from the beginning.

Parliament in 1660 had renewed and amplified as a regular statute the Navigation Act of 1651 and further extended it in 1663. This not only reaffirmed the principle of "English ships with English crews," which had led to the First Dutch War in 1652, but extended the principle more rigidly to the colonies. The mercantile system (see page 226) was at its height, and its principle of "Sell more than you buy in foreign trade" was embodied in the new legislation. The ideal function of a colony was to furnish the mother country with materials which could not be produced at home, and in return to purchase its outside necessities from the mother country. The new Act consequently "enumerated" certain articles which must be sent only to England. On this list, as it gradually expanded, were sugar from the West Indies, rice and indigo from the

Carolinas, tobacco from Virginia and Maryland, and masts from New England. The colonies might send their flour, fish, and lumber wherever they pleased, but they could send the enumerated articles only to Bristol, London, or to some other English port, whence the surplus would be sold to the Continent, the extra profits going to English merchants. The colonists, moreover, had to buy virtually all their imports from England. This code was not altogether a hardship to the colonies: their shipping enjoyed all the privileges of "English ships with English crews," and the Northern colonies were to profit richly thereby. It was, however, a further blow to the Dutch, who had been energetically supplying the English colonies with various necessities and luxuries from abroad and, in turn, disposing of their colonial produce.

This renewed legislation helped to bring on the Second Dutch War (1665-1667). A year before war was officially declared, an English squadron swooped down upon a Dutch post on the African coast and then upon New Amsterdam. As a result, New Netherland became the English colonies of New York, New Jersey, and, later, Delaware, thus rounding out the English control of the Atlantic seaboard between the French holdings in the north and the Spanish in the south. For a while the captured region was under the direct proprietorship of the Duke of York, hence the name "New York." The war itself was pretty much a repetition of the previous one, with stubborn, hard-fought battles in the North Sea. The English won the first big battle; the second lasted four days and was a sanguinary draw; and then, by 1667, the navy became bankrupt, in spite of all that Pepys could do, and some of the big ships were laid up inactive at Chatham, near the mouth of the Thames. There the Dutch made a raid, caught the English unprepared, burned five men-of-war, and sailed away with the greatest ship of the royal navy—that very *Royal Charles* which had brought the king home from Holland. At the peace treaty, however, which quickly followed, England kept her American seizures, although many Englishmen would have preferred the little East Indian spice island of Puleroon to all New York.

Relations with Louis XIV

To Charles, France had been a haven, his mother's country, where his preferred religion was established, and where his beloved young sister "Minette" was the wife of the Duke of Orléans, younger brother of the French king. To England, almost since the days of the Conquest, France was the enemy to watch and to mistrust.

In the seventeenth century she was the most powerful nation in Europe, just as Spain had been in the sixteenth. France had been raised to this pre-eminence largely by the work of two able cardinal-ministers: Richelieu, who held the power during most of the reign of Louis XIII, and Mazarin, the subtle Italian who ruled in the long minority of Louis XIV. Richelieu's wish to extend France to her "natural boundaries" of the Rhine, the Alps, and the Pyrenees involved the smashing of the "Hapsburg ring," which had surrounded France since Charles V had come into his tremendous inheritance (see page 176). As we have seen, Richelieu, cardinal though he was, attacked the Austrian Hapsburgs in the Thirty Years' War, by bringing France in on the Protestant side, and also fought the Spanish Hapsburgs. Mazarin reaped where Richelieu had sown by taking full advantage of the defeated Austrian Hapsburgs at the Peace of Westphalia, in 1648, and then, aided by Cromwell's army, humbling the Spanish Hapsburgs at the Peace of the Pyrenees in 1659 (see page 249). At the same time the two cardinals had built up royal authority in France. Richelieu crushed the nobles, dismantling their fortified castles, and executing some of the most exalted for treason. The Huguenots too received drastic treatment in losing their fortified towns. In inter-

nal affairs Mazarin, despite several factious uprisings, continued Richelieu's policy, so that the young Louis found himself inheriting a kingdom that realized Richelieu's ambition of "the king first in France and France first in Europe."

This ambitious young ruler had his own way in Europe during the first part of his long reign, because no other country was in condition to stop him. The Austrians were busy defending themselves from the last outburst of Turkish energy in the Danube valley; most of the German states were still prostrate from the Thirty Years' War; Spain was a beaten nation; and Prussia was barely beginning to rise as a nation. Unhindered, Louis was free to expand France in the Rhine region and the Spanish Netherlands (present-day Belgium), and even to threaten Holland's independence. His victorious progress was remarkably well served by exceptional generals and first-rate ministers. Above all, the versatile Colbert was almost a whole cabinet in himself. An ardent exponent of mercantilism, he tried to co-ordinate his various departments of finance, industry, commerce, colonies, and navy into a general scheme which, if followed, might have given France an empire as great as that which England later won. Louis, however, preferred banging away at the Low Countries and the Rhine for more territory in Europe.

At home France was enjoying a Golden Age such as England had had under Elizabeth. At Versailles, with its magnificent new palace, Louis completed Richelieu's subjection of the nobility by making it clear that those who expected governmental favors must be in constant attendance on the king's person. Consequently the nobles thronged to Versailles instead of plotting revolts on their distant estates. Ultimately this glittering court was to hasten the revolution which convulsed all France in 1789, because it widened the breach between the parasitic nobility and their peasant tenants, who had to pay for the gaiety of their absent masters. For the time being, however, the scintillating life of Versailles became the envy of all Europe. France was recognized as the arbiter in matters of letters, art, and society; French became the language of diplomacy and the polite world.

In 1668 the three Protestant maritime nations, England, Holland, and Sweden, joined forces to check the formidable power of France. Within two years, however, Louis had broken up this Triple Alliance by buying off the kings of England and Sweden.

In the case of Charles this was accomplished by the Treaty of Dover, negotiated in 1670 through his sister "Minette." One of the most audacious and dishonorable in the nation's diplomatic history, this treaty was bound to be unpopular with most Englishmen. It contained two parts, one more secret than the other. Charles showed to all the Cabal his agreement to help Louis in attacking Holland, in return for cash; he kept the other outrageous arrangement from all but the two Catholic ministers. In return for more cash, and troops if necessary, Charles agreed to turn Catholic himself and convert England into a Catholic absolutism. The French sent over charming Louise de Querouaille to hold the susceptible monarch in line.

That agreement to help France attack Holland ran counter to two cardinal principles of English foreign policy: the balance of power, and the protection of the Low Countries from falling under the control of a strong nation which could threaten England's insular security. Nevertheless, in the spring of 1672 Charles dragged England into the unpopular Third Dutch War (1672-1674). For the third time in twenty years the rival fleets exchanged broadsides, and the valiant Dutch held their own fairly well against the combined navies of England and France. But Holland had more than navies to worry her in her vulnerable land frontier over which the most powerful army in Europe was advancing. In the

grave crisis of invasion a slender, taciturn young man of twenty-two, the third William of Orange, was brought to the head of the government. Sixteen years later he was also to be the third William to rule England. By 1673 Parliament refused further funds for the Dutch war, and a year later Charles had to make peace. Although Holland fought the French four years more, she emerged without loss of territory.

The strain, however, of the constant fighting on land and sea dragged Holland down from the proud position which she had held in all things maritime during the earlier part of the century. She still kept her rich spice islands in the East, together with some other colonies; Amsterdam remained for some time to come, until overtaken by London around 1730, the commercial and financial center of Europe. But the exhaustion of war removed Holland as an active contender for the highest honors on the seas and overseas. She joined Portugal and Spain as unsuccessful rivals of England's expansion. The turn of France would come next.

Two days before the Third Dutch War started, in 1672, Charles took his first step toward the other half of the Dover bargain. He tried to lessen the penal restrictions on English Catholics by issuing a "Declaration of Indulgence for Tender Consciences." In this declaration, he was exercising the "dispensing power" by which the king claimed the right to set aside the operation of certain laws. Along with the Catholics, Dissenters were included in the act of grace, in order to make toleration seem a general principle. The Dissenters, however, suspected this, and hesitated to take advantage of the favor.

The Cavalier Parliament, with its Anglican squires, struck back at the king and the Catholics with its Test Act in 1673. This excluded from all civil or military office under the crown anyone who refused to take the Sacrament according to the Church of England. Although leveled at the Catholics, just as the Clarendon Code had been aimed at the Dissenters, the latter were included in its terms, but were gradually relieved. The immediate effect was to remove many high officials; in particular, Charles's brother, the Duke of York, who had turned Catholic, lost his command of the navy. Some of these disabilities lasted until 1828.

Thus, within two years of the Treaty of Dover, Parliament had stopped both the Dutch War and the Catholic project. Charles's point of view was somewhat comprehensible; he was perpetually short of money, between his own extravagance and a niggardly Parliament, but he was too wise to resort to his father's illegal money-raising. He had, however, badly misjudged the temper of his people, and, though he quickly learned his lesson, his reign had come to a turning point. He was about to enter a period of serious dissension with Parliament, lasting until 1681, while hysterical fear of Catholic and French intrigue swept all classes in England in a reign of terror.

The Cabal had broken up when one of the Catholic members was forced from office by the Test Act. At about the same time, Charles dismissed Ashley-Cooper, recently promoted to be Earl of Shaftesbury, who soon began to build up a powerful opposition to the king. Charles's chief minister for the rest of the troubled seventies was Thomas Osborne, who held successively six different titles from baronet to duke, but is best known as the Earl of Danby. Strongly Anglican and anti-French, he was a shrewd and not particularly honest politician, who saw to it that, whatever his private inclinations, he pleased his sovereign. Adept at modern party-machine tactics, he got his way in Parliament by buying votes with such a lavish hand that the Cavalier Parliament won the additional nickname of "Pensioned Parliament." Danby's appointment was another milestone toward England's constitutional development, for he was the first chief minister to be appointed

because he was the leader of a faction in Parliament. Consequently, he was the real founder of the Tory, or pro-king, party, just as Shaftesbury became the founder of the Whig, or anti-king, party.

The widespread popular resentment against everything Catholic and French burst into flame in 1678 with the false testimony of a perjured informer, Titus Oates, who revealed what he claimed was a Popish Plot to murder the king, burn London, seize England with French and Irish troops, and massacre all Protestants who refused to turn Catholic. In the panicky temper of the time, men did not question Oate's reliability, and he became a popular hero with opposition helping to fan the flames of anti-Catholic hatred. Many Catholics, most of them innocent, were hunted down and dragged into the courts, where several were condemned to death until Lord Chief Justice Scroggs had the courage to defy the popular clamor by questioning the flimsy evidence.

The Popish Plot gave stimulus to Shaftesbury and his opposition, soon to be known as Whigs. They brought up the question of the succession. Charles remarked that he had no fear that anyone would depose him in favor of his Catholic brother James whose secretary had just been executed for treasonable correspondence with France. The succession apparently would go to James's Protestant daughters, Mary and Anne, the former married to the Protestant Prince of Orange, her cousin. Yet many favored having Charles divorce his present wife and marry again, or else divert the succession to one of his illegitimate sons, most of whom were dukes. Of these, the rather attractive Duke of Monmouth, born while Charles was in exile, was the favorite of the Protestant opposition in Parliament, which was doing its unsuccessful best to pass an Exclusion Bill to keep Catholic James from the throne.

The year following the Popish Plot saw an end of Danby's ministry and the eighteen-year-old Cavalier Parliament. Its members were no longer the enthusiastic loyalists they had been in 1661; a steadily increasing number were following Shaftesbury into opposition. Charles had been playing fast and loose with Louis as well as with Parliament, taking what money he could from each and then doing as he pleased. The new Dutch marriage of James's daughter had annoyed Louis, so he revealed a damning letter from Danby requesting more French funds. That Danby had reluctantly written it at the king's order was carefully concealed. Parliament, already at fever heat over the Popish Plot, cried for impeachment. To save Danby and to avoid incriminating himself, Charles for the first time dissolved Parliament.

The Beginning of Political Parties

In the midst of these disputes there came into being the party system, an all-important device which was to influence strongly the future political life of England, the United States, and many other nations. A political party has been defined as "an organized group of the electorate who attempt to control the action of the government through the election of its candidates to office." The closest approach to a political party in England's previous history had been the organized Puritan opposition in the early days of the Long Parliament, under the skillful leadership of Pym.

There were bound to be differences of opinion among the five hundred men who composed the House of Commons, as well as among the hundred-odd peers, at any time, but the events of seventeenth-century England seemed to drive them toward more sharply opposing points of view. They tended to fall into four different general attitudes toward political policy; reactionary, conservative, liberal, and radical — terms that are often misapplied. In their earlier connotation, and perhaps to oversimplify, the reactionary was one who wished to go back to former conditions; the conservative

was psychologically or economically opposed to any considerable change; the liberal was ready to preserve what seemed good in the old but was equally ready to make changes; and the radical, as the Latin derivation indicates, wanted to get at the roots and start anew. These viewpoints came to be designated by the position in which the various groups arranged themselves in the parliaments which eventually developed on the Continent: reactionaries, extreme right; conservatives, right or right center; liberals, left or left center; radicals, extreme left. At this time of the birth of political parties, the extreme reactionaries and radicals were less important than the two great groups, conservatives and liberals, who gave England a normal basis for her two-party system. Such divergent points of view had been reflected in previous Parliamentary debates and actions, of course; but effective results were not to be expected as long as individual members of Parliament acted without any common organization or plan of action. The function of the political party was to provide that necessary cohesion and strategy.

If any one year can be taken as the definite beginning of England's regular party system, it would probably be 1675, when, under the guidance of Shaftesbury, a number of prominent members of both houses formed the Green Ribbon Club, with headquarters at a London tavern, to co-ordinate the liberal "country," or Whig group in opposition to the conservative Royalist-Anglican "court," or Tory element headed by Danby. Numerically this "country" opposition was strong, as the Test Act had shown; but until it built up a machine, it could scarcely hope to compete successfully with the king and Danby who had all the resources of government for bribery and patronage. Shaftesbury and his colleagues quickly created such a machine and soon developed the party devices familiar in later politics. For their appeal to the electorate, the Whigs had a slogan, "No Popery!"

They had also a platform: Protestantism, toleration, liberty of the subject, commercial advantages, and Parliamentary supremacy. Their particular source of potential strength lay in the alliance of a few great peers with the men of London and the towns, where dissent was strongest. Some squires also might adhere to this view, though squires and clergy on the whole were inclined to favor the conservative side. The Whig platform, then, was one which would appeal particularly to the middle-class Dissenters. Every election was carefully managed, candidates were selected and supported, and well-timed propaganda was prepared both for the electorate and for the members of Parliament. The new party was even able to call out a London mob to howl for effect at the proper moment. The election of a majority did not end Whig activity; they proceeded to see that their members voted effectively. In its sessions, the Green Ribbon Club carefully discussed the next day's course of action, and lest there be any slip-up, often decided just who should propose a measure and who should second it. The Tories were not as well organized. With the executive power in the hands of Charles and Danby, they had less need to be, but they made ample use of a practice which like the Whig tricks was to become a feature of party rivalry. This was patronage, or the bestowal of the favors of government—such as offices, pensions, and even bribes—upon those who voted right, a practice which the Whigs would develop even further when their turn came in the next century (see page 298). The Tories, too, had a platform stressing their support of the Church of England, with opposition to toleration of any other faith, together with a preference to let the crown, rather than Parliament, have the last word. Danby was the Tories' first leader; but when the Whig opposition drove him to the Tower for five years, he was succeeded by others of the king's more conservative advisers, and finally by Charles himself.

The names of the two parties were bestowed by their rivals as insulting epithets. "England owes her greatest party names to Titus Oates. He used to croak 'Tory' at any man who dared to question the plot, and his admirers took up the word. And as soon as one side thus called its opponents after the Catholic bandits who waylaid the Saxon settlers among the Irish bogs, it was an obvious retort to hurl back the name of the Covenanted 'Whigs' who murdered bishops on the Scottish moors."[1] For a century and a half the Whigs and Tories were to dispute elections and to sit on opposite sides in Parliament; the names then changed to "Liberal" and "Conservative" but the rivalry went on.

Capitalizing the anti-Catholic feeling during the frenzy of terror, the Whigs now dominated Parliamentary elections. Charles, after keeping one Parliament for eighteen years, dissolved three within the next two years, because of their Whig majorities. The Tories had not contested the elections vigorously; for, while they were normally ready to support the king, they too feared Catholic domination.

In the first of these short Whig Parliaments, elected in 1679, Shaftesbury once more pressed for an Exclusion Bill to substitute Monmouth for James in succession to the throne. Charles dissolved this Parliament quickly, but not before it had passed a celebrated act which became a permanent safeguard of liberties throughout the English-speaking world. This Habeas Corpus Act definitely established the old practice that anyone arrested had the right to be shown by what authority and for what reason he was being detained.

Late that summer, elections were held, but for more than a year Charles refused to assemble Parliament, relying upon the freshness of the memory of civil war in the minds of most Englishmen to avert a seri-

[1] G. M. Trevelyan, *England under the Stuarts* (1926), p. 411. By permission of G. P. Putnam's Sons and Methuen & Co., Ltd.

ous crisis. When, after strong Whig petitions, that third Parliament finally met in the autumn of 1680, Shaftesbury once more pressed for exclusion, and Charles dissolved Parliament before it had granted him any money. Once again in 1681, the country returned a Whig majority. Charles summoned this Parliament to Royalist Oxford, where it would not have the support of a London mob. At Oxford and along the roads to it, he assembled considerable military strength. Within a week Charles appeared without warning in the college hall where Parliament was meeting and suddenly dissolved it.

In the remaining four years of his reign Charles was virtually absolute, ruling by himself without Parliament or even an outstanding minister. His bold coup, which put an end to the brief Whig ascendancy, had taken Shaftesbury and his followers completely by surprise.

Mystified at the source of the king's independence of Parliament, they fled in terror from Oxford. The explanation was that by strictly secret negotiations, oral this time, Charles had arranged to receive a new and larger allowance from Louis of France. He consequently no longer needed Parliament. His action in taking matters into his own hands met the hearty approval of the Tory clergy and squires, who had feared that the Whigs were pushing the country toward civil strife. Now that the king had apparently dropped Catholicism, they were ready to support him in everything else, even the threat of absolutism. The doctrine of nonresistance spread among them: one Tory went so far as to state that a lawful ruler, even if he were a Nero, should be obeyed in everything. These Tories, it must be remembered, had most of the local government in the shires in their hands; and while the Tory clergy preached nonresistance, the Tory justices of the peace harried the Dissenters with renewed vigor. The Whigs, as Charles had foreseen, overplayed their hand. Shut out from legitimate

Parliamentary opposition for the next seven years, some of them plotted to assassinate Charles and James and to start an insurrection. Public opinion was alienated; Shaftesbury fled to the Continent; and several other prominent Whigs were executed with scant show of justice. Charles then struck at the towns, strongholds of Whiggery and Dissent. For centuries no king had challenged their medieval charters; now Charles called them in on flimsy pretexts, and issued new ones which placed the power in the hands of his Tories. Tory town governments would now send safe borough members to Parliament, and Tory sheriffs would select jurors who would be harsh to Dissenters.

For all that, Charles's last years saw general prosperity; the French subsidy lightened the tax burden; and some of the enthusiasm of the early Restoration once more centered about the king. He had safely ridden out several threatening storms and had not "gone on his travels again." He had remained the Anglican king his people required, but as he lay dying in 1685 he is said to have received the sacraments of the Catholic faith.

James II

That absolutism of Charles's last years might have become permanently fastened upon England had not his successor been a devoted Catholic. Despite the past Whig efforts at exclusion, the Duke of York came to the throne as James II. Probably his age, already fifty-three, and the fact that his Protestant daughters were his only heirs, helped to counteract his hated religion and his unpleasant personality. Had he learned the significant lessons from his family's experience, he would have kept his throne more than three years. He inherited much that was favorable: a small standing army, and subjects who were tired of the disturbing results of opposition. Unfortunately for himself, this second James was as tactless as the first, without the latter's erudition; as stubborn as his father, with none of his more attractive qualities; and in politics he was a fool as compared with his older brother. James had a fixity of purpose in his support of Catholicism, but most Englishmen violently disagreed with this aim. About the only thing he ever did well was his excellent management of the navy, before the Test Act forced his resignation.

Five months after James came to the throne, Charles's bastard son, the Duke of Monmouth, plunged into a revolt which was hopeless from its inception. Despite his facile charm, the weak and sometimes vicious Monmouth was doomed to be someone's gullible tool. The Whig exiles on the Continent easily persuaded him that he had but "to show his handsome face among the shouting crowds" and the English crown was his. With only a handful of followers, he landed on the southwest coast, where four or five thousand men, chiefly devoted peasants, flocked to his standard. Most of England held aloof, however, from this ill-equipped and ill-disciplined force. The royal regiments of regulars easily closed in, crushing his bravely fighting followers at the battle of Sedgemoor. Hopeless and ill-advised as was this "last popular uprising in the old England," too drastic vengeance fell upon all participants. Monmouth was executed after an extremely bungling job by the headsman. More than a thousand others, even persons only remotely involved, were either hanged or sentenced to virtual slavery in Barbados. Lord Chief Justice Jeffreys, later rewarded with the Lord Chancellorship, presided at the trials, the "Bloody Assizes." He was charged with extreme brutality. One Alice Lisle, for instance, a lady of good family, who unwittingly had harbored two starving refugees, was beheaded as a merciful alternative to his original sentence of burning at the stake.

James was determined to make England Catholic, not seeing that his religion, even if still kept as a private affair, caused general irritation and uneasiness. No sooner was he on the throne than he began to attend Mass publicly. He expected co-operation from the Anglican High Church clergy because they shared his hostility to Dissenters. It had been one thing for Charles II to persecute the Dissenters, a minority; one of the most stupid of James's many blunders was to antagonize the powerful Anglican Tories by his efforts in behalf of the Catholics. Nine months after this accession, Englishmen were given a vivid illustration of Catholic political domination when Louis XIV revoked the Edict of Nantes, which Henry IV had granted to protect the Huguenots, and began a brutal persecution of those Protestants.

The religious question cost James an excellent chance for Parliamentary co-operation. The charters had recently been taken away from London and many other municipalities; the new ones were designed to curb or eliminate the power of the Whig Dissenters in voting for members of the Commons. Consequently, James's first Parliament was strongly Tory and so loyal that it was ready to vote him a generous financial grant if he would only relieve its religious fears. Instead, James insisted that he had the right to appoint Catholics to any position, Test Act or no Test Act. Since Parliament would do nothing under those conditions, he suddenly dismissed it; a second Parliament never met.

Since Parliament would do nothing for him, James proceeded to appoint Catholics to high places, using the so-called "dispensing power" by which he claimed the right to set aside the operation of the laws in the cases of certain individuals (see page 265). A Catholic was placed at the head of the Irish government and another in command of the fleet. Many were made justices of the peace or mayors; others were promoted to the House of Lords; and some were even admitted to the Privy Council, including a Jesuit, Father Petre, who enjoyed considerable influence with the king. There was particular concern when James began to replace Protestant army officers with Catholics, for there were sixteen thousand regulars encamped on Hounslow Heath, just outside London, where they could easily overawe the capital. When Hales, a Catholic, was appointed governor of Dover, the port closest to France, the matter was carried to the courts; but the judges, as in earlier Stuart days, held office at the royal pleasure and gave James a favorable decision. Emboldened by such success, James moved against the Church of England, proposing a religious court similar in nature to the old Court of High Commission, which had been abolished by the Long Parliament. In spite of the violent protest of the fellows, he also placed a Catholic at the head of Magdalen College at Oxford, a particular stronghold of the Anglicans.

Along with this James tried toleration. In 1687 he issued a Declaration of Indulgence to Dissenters as well as Catholics, similar to that of his brother fifteen years earlier. William Penn, the Quaker founder of Pennsylvania and sometimes called the one good man among James's advisers, urged this. The Dissenters, released from their prison cells by the hundreds and free once more to worship in their own way, might have forgiven the recent persecutions had not James issued a second Declaration of Indulgence the next spring (1688), designed to legalize his granting of important civil and military posts to Catholics. Seven bishops were bold enough to protest, and James, by ordering them tried for seditious libel, further infuriated the Anglican Tories. London cheered loudly in the last days of June when the jury acquitted them.

James was no more intelligent in his foreign policy, steering an indecisive course when his interests called for a close alignment with France. He got all the odium of an alliance with Louis XIV, yet received none of the advantages. He early asked Louis for money, but promised nothing in return. James might have strengthened his position by taking advice from Louis with his similar religious policy, but fortunately for English constitutional development he did not.

The second Declaration of Indulgence was the first of the events that were to make 1688 one of the most significant dates in English history as the year of the "Bloodless," or "Glorious," Revolution. With James's daughter Mary as his heir, a safe Protestant succession had seemed guaranteed. But after fifteen childless years of his second marriage, a son was born to his second wife, Mary of Modena, an Italian Catholic. England now seemed likely to have a succession of Catholic rulers far into the future, for this son would of course inherit before his half sisters. His birth was consequently the spark that ignited the smoldering resentment against the rapid accumulation of grievances. The more moderate, who had been inclined to wait out the reign, were now almost as ready as the discontented Whigs for immediate change.

Thus were hastened the negotiations to bring William of Orange from Holland to secure the succession for his wife, Mary. Her claim as the daughter of James II and Anne Hyde far outweighed the fact that William himself was also a grandchild of Charles I, as the son of his daughter. William was the obvious champion for the enemies of James. For sixteen years, ever since he had cut the dikes to save Amsterdam from the invading Frenchmen, he alone had stood up against the tremendous power of Louis XIV. The great end to which he devoted his career was freedom for Europe—freedom from the danger of French domination. His vision took in something more than Holland alone or England alone, something more than Protestantism alone. He, more than anyone else, deserves the credit for the final realization of that aim.

And now this cold, cautious man was

being urged to enter upon a desperate gamble. William had no particular interest in the English crown for its own sake. It appealed to him because it would bind firmly one powerful ally in the league which he was forming against France. He had no intention of following Monmouth to the block; it was not enough to tell him that he had but to land on England's shores and an enthusiastic nation would rally to his standard. He insisted upon a formal written invitation from some of the leading men of the nation, so that their fates would be bound up with his. Such a risky but essential document was signed by seven prominent Whigs and Tories on the June day when the seven bishops were acquitted.

Fate or fortune carried William successfully through several narrow escapes during the next few months. If any one of a number of things had gone wrong, England would have missed a "bloodless" revolution. In the first place, had Louis XIV, about to set out upon another war of conquest, headed for the Low Countries again, William would have had to stay at home to defend his own land. Instead, however, Louis struck at the middle Rhine region, which suffered terrific devastation. Then William had to secure the consent of the Dutch, with their complex and cumbersome system requiring the approval of the various jealous provinces and cities; with the French menace temporarily removed, they finally agreed. Unlike Monmouth, William went well protected by Dutch warships and regiments. But that too involved risk: if he had to fight the English navy or army, his position, even if he were victorious, would have been that of a foreign conqueror. Fortunately, the command, as well as the rank and file, of both navy

and army were not averse to the change of rulers. Even the wind blew in William's favor. The English naval commander saved his face by anchoring his fleet where it was held immobile by wind and tide while William's ships sailed past; then he pursued them at a safe distance. William landed at Torbay, not far from Monmouth's landing place. The remaining hazard of the English army, some thirty thousand strong vanished with the defection of the commanders, headed by John Churchill, the future Duke of Marlborough. Though he owed his whole advancement to James, Churchill wrote the king that under the circumstances he would not oppose the advance of William (see pages 282 ff.). If James had used his Irish troops, all England would have been exasperated into open revolt.

James, virtually at the mercy of the Dutch invader, might still have saved his throne had he been willing to summon a new Parliament and descend to the role of a limited constitutional monarch. This he would not do. Dropping the Great Seal in the Thames to stay the legality of official action, he hurried to the coast to escape to France. Some zealous fishermen apprehended him and turned him over to the authorities. It was best to have him out of the way—to say that he had abdicated, instead of having the necessity of deposing him. Consequently, after some fruitless efforts on James's part to negotiate for terms, he was permitted to slip quietly out of the country. Soon the last Stuart king took refuge at the court of his cousin Louis XIV, for the remainder of his life. The way was clear for the "Revolution Settlement," which permanently ended real royal power in England.

Limiting the Monarchy

The year 1688 stands as one of the most significant turning points in all English history marking as it does the final triumph of Parliament in the century-old struggle to limit the royal power. From that time on, the idea of divine right was dead, for it was definitely understood that the sovereign owed his title to Parliament. Within thirty-five years Parliament was to work out a method for exercising its new power. The resultant system of a limited monarchy with responsible government was England's unique contribution to the field of constitutional development. Other nations by the dozen were to imitate the forms which England gradually achieved. The English are proud of their "Glorious" and "Bloodless" Revolution of 1688 not only for those constitutional results but also because it was carried out without the savage and lurid episodes often accompanying political change in other lands. This was all the more remarkable since the central actor was the ruler of a foreign nation, which only fourteen years before had been at war with England. Yet William of Orange came, not as William the Conqueror after a bloody victory over Englishmen, but as the invited guest of some of the most important men of the nation.

By only a narrow margin did the revolution prove bloodless. The departure of James had left England without a lawful government, and anarchy threatened. As soon as the news of the royal flight leaked out, London mobs worked off their anti-Catholic belligerence by two nights of violent rioting. Even the embassies of certain Catholic countries were not spared, while Judge Jeffreys of the "Bloody Assizes," although disguised as a laborer, barely escaped being torn to pieces. All over England anxious men patrolled roads and town walls, for rumor told of marauding bands of armed Catholics. To make matters worse, one of James's last acts was to disband the standing army, and fear of these rough soldiers added to popular terror.

Such disorder frightened the responsible elements, Tory as well as Whig, into a common readiness to support that earlier invitation given William and to accept amicably the summoning of a foreign ruler. A hasty gathering of peers and former members of the Commons, together with some London magistrates, now asked William to take over the administration temporarily. In his name invitations were sent out for the election of a Commons in the usual way. This resulted in another irregular "Convention Parliament," similar to that which had called home Charles II; neither was summoned in a legal manner because no king had signed the writs of summons. This met early in 1689 to discuss what should be done with the vacant throne. The precedent of 1399, when Richard II had been deposed in favor of one not in the direct line, was freely discussed as was the fact that at "Bloody Mary's" death, her husband, Philip II of Spain, to England's good fortune, had lost all authority in her affairs (see pages 138, 192). Some wanted to make William regent for his absent father-in-law. Others favored making Mary queen, with William merely administrator of the government during her lifetime. William would have none of either proposal. He would be king himself for life or return at once to his own land. Never would he tolerate the subordinate position of being tied to his wife's apron strings, as Parliament proposed. Consequently, the Convention Parliament declared the throne vacant because James, "having endeavored to subvert the constitution of the kingdom by breaking the original contract between king and people," had "abdicated the government"; and it agreed that William and Mary should be joint sovereigns, with the chief administration in the husband's hands.

Thus did this tight-lipped, cold little Dutchman, who made up in character what he lacked in charm, become the third William to occupy the English throne, in addition to remaining the third William of Orange to govern Holland. From the critical moment of his initiation into power in 1672, with French troops overrunning Holland, this great-grandson both of William the Silent and of James I had shown an indomitable courage, a dogged determination, and a native shrewdness which were to stand him in good stead in his new land. As a soldier he lacked the smashing ability of Cromwell, but he was clever at keeping diverse allies in line. All in all, he was one of the strongest English kings in modern times. Mary was of slight consequence as Queen. She was to die after five years, but William would continue to rule some seven years longer.

The Revolution Settlement

Before bestowing the crown upon the new king and queen Parliament ensured its dominant position by the so-called Declaration of Rights. A deathblow to the idea of the "divine right of kings" in England, it made it obvious that only Parliamentary decree had given the crown to William and Mary. Like the two earlier safeguards of English liberty, Magna Carta and the Petition of Right, this did not deal with broad generalities of political theory but was specific and largely negative in character. The misdeeds of James II were recounted in detail and their illegality cited. The declaration pronounced illegal, without the consent of Parliament, the making or suspending of laws; the royal exercise of the dispensing power; the levying of taxes, forced loans, or other money payments; and the maintenance of a standing army. The definite rights of subjects were stipulated in regard to petitioning the sovereign, keeping arms, reasonable bail in case of arrest, and several other matters. For Parliament itself there were to be frequent sessions, free election of members, and freedom of debate. Some months later, after the Convention Parliament had been regularized, this Declaration of Rights, with the added specific provision that the crown of England might never be worn by one of the Roman Catholic faith, was embodied in the Bill of Rights, a regular statute, by which name it is more generally known.

This was further strengthened by several subsequent acts which, together with it, made up the so-called "Revolution Settlement." The compression of so much reform into a brief period of time was to be typical of much of the course of future English development. In the legislation following 1688 the liberties of the subject were still further guarded in the Treasons Act (1696), which protected the accused in treason trials from arbitrary condemnation, and also in that part of the Act of Settlement (1701) which secured the independence of the bench by basing the tenure of judges on their good behavior, as decided by Parliament, instead of on the royal pleasure. Parliament ensured regular meetings for itself by the Mutiny Act (1689), which authorized, for a limited period only, the trial of soldiers by court-martial, previously forbidden in the Petition of Right. This act, renewed at least annually ever since, gave Parliament more control of the army. Without such yearly renewal the crown would have no legal way of keeping the armed forces under discipline. Together with the granting of appropriations for one year only, the Mutiny Act prevented the king from ruling long years without calling Parliament, as Charles I had done. The Triennial Act (1694) prevented the king from keeping the same Parliament in office year after year without new elections, as Charles II had done for eighteen years with his Cavalier Parliament. As its name indicates, it stipulated that a new Parliament be elected every three years; but before long this was extended to seven years and much later reduced to five.

Finally, in the Act of Settlement (1701), Parliament showed the strength of its new authority by deciding for the future which royal line should be given the succession. It had already indicated that it controlled the choice of the ruler, both in its offer of the throne to William and Mary and in the provision of the Bill of Rights that at their death the crown should pass successively to the children of Mary, to her sister Anne and her children; and, in default of such heirs, to the children of William by a second wife. Before William died, however, it was obvious that Anne would have no surviving children, and William did not remarry. Consequently, the throne might go to Anne's half brother James, the "Old Pretender," and his children, who were by strict primogeniture the direct line. Such a possibility being anathema to most of England, with the current hysteria over popish plots and papists, Parliament decided to make the provisions yet more specific. In the Act of Settlement it designated as Anne's successor her next *Protestant* kin, her second cousin Sophia, granddaughter of James I, and wife of the Elector of Hanover. England is still ruled under this act; for Sophia's son was to come to England as the first king of the Hanoverian line.

The Revolution Settlement helped to smooth over religious dissension by the Toleration Act (1689), which granted freedom of worship to most Dissenters. Technically the act was more limited in scope than it actually proved in practice. It required that dissenting clergymen accept most of the Thirty-nine Articles, and all political disabilities remained in force. Neither the Clarendon Code, nor the Test Act, nor the earlier acts of the Tudor period were repealed. Catholics and those Dissenters who did not believe in the Trinity were specifically excluded. Nevertheless, most Dissenters were fairly well satisfied, and most Englishmen thereafter were permitted to worship as they pleased. William and the Whigs had been ready for equal political rights regardless of religious belief; but the Tories prevented the extension of toleration as far as that for a long time to come. Dissenters of all sorts, as well as Roman Catholics, were still excluded from the higher offices of the state, the army, the navy, and the universities. The Dissenters, however, were permitted to hold some positions, particularly in local government, on the condition that they practice "occasional conformity," which merely entailed taking the Anglican Sacrament once a year. Many were willing to make this gesture of conformity.

Scotland and Ireland

William was not accepted in this easy fashion in the other parts of the British Isles. The Lowland Scots recognized this break in the Stuart line with equanimity; for not only did they retain their laws, but their Parliament, during the confusion of 1688-1689, had been able to make Presbyterianism the Established Church of Scotland, which the land of John Knox had long desired. Beyond the Highland Line, however, Viscount Dundee, who, like some of the other Scottish nobles, hated this supremacy of the Presbyterian clergy and the House of Orange, "drew his sword for King James." Certain of the wild clans gathered about him and swept down to crush the regular troops at Killiecrankie (1689). Dundee fell at the moment of victory, and the leaderless Highlanders scattered to carry their booty back into the hills. Recognizing their extreme poverty, William hit on the scheme of buying the support of the chieftains; all but one clan, the Macdonalds of Glencoe, took the oath of allegiance to the king as specified. They delayed their submission until the last day, and by the time they had trudged through many miles of snow to find the proper official, the legal time limit had expired. The leading royal official seized this opportunity to display the strong arm of government to the Highlanders, and, with the consent of William, who did not know the full circumstances of the delay, proceeded to exterminate the clan. A force of regular soldiers, deliberately selected from among the bitterly hostile Campbells, visited the clan in its wild glen, and after accepting two weeks of cordial hospitality, slaughtered everyone in the night. This "Massacre of Glencoe" was not complete, because some of the clansmen escaped into the woods; but it left the blackest stain on William's name.

In Ireland the opposition was far more menacing under the leadership of James's Lord Lieutenant, the Earl of Tyrconnel. The Catholics, bitter at the Cromwellian settlement which had established Protestant landlords over them (see page 246), rose everywhere. James II, supported with

funds and with men by Louis XIV, arrived in Ireland early in 1689 to use Ireland as a back door to regain the English crown. He called an Irish parliament in which the Catholic element predominated. It passed laws giving the land back to the Catholics. In the meantime the Scottish Presbyterians of Ulster were at once besieged. The river port of Londonderry put up a valiant fight against starvation, and was saved when the relief ships from William finally broke the boom stretched across the river by the Catholic besiegers. On the same day Enniskillen drove off the army at its gates.

William, aware that any war on the Continent against his enemy Louis XIV would be folly with this danger in his rear, sent over an army to clear up the situation. This expedition, poorly equipped and ill-managed, as was usual in English military efforts after an interval of peace, fared badly in the face of adverse weather and disease. William went over himself; and in July, 1690, met James at the River Boyne. Fording the stream in the face of enemy fire, he routed his father-in-law's army. James threw away his cause in Ireland by fleeing to the Continent after this one defeat.

His garrison of Limerick held out until generous terms were granted. Irish Catholics were to retain all the religious privileges given them under Charles II, and their estates were not to be sequestered. This Treaty of Limerick (1691), however, would become a source of intense bitterness, for William, listening to the Protestant clamor for revenge, quickly repudiated it. England now subjected the Catholic Irish to new and even harsher laws, which, among other things, prevented Roman Catholics from teaching in schools and from serving on juries or as constables or in the Irish parliament or in the military or naval forces, forbade their voting, subjected them to a fine if they refused to work on Catholic holy days, and even made it illegal for a Catholic in Ireland to own a horse above the value of £5. The hatred engendered in those years lives on, and there are still free-for-all fights when the Orangemen celebrate the anniversary of the Boyne on July twelfth, Northern Ireland's counterpart to Saint Patrick's Day on March seventeenth. Many Catholic Irishmen enlisted in the French army, where they could fight England and be paid for it. Even the Ulster Protestants soon found ground for complaint, for selfish trade laws excluded their linen and other products which might have brought them prosperity. Consequently many of them, after 1700, found their way to the American colonies, where they formed the tough, stern "Scotch-Irish" Presbyterian element of the frontier.

"The Second Hundred Years' War"

William was now ready for the work which had drawn him to accept the English throne—war against Louis XIV, who for nearly thirty years had worked his will on most of his weaker neighbors. England's king had been in his pay, Austria had had her hands full with Turkish invaders, Spain was too weak to interfere effectively, most of Germany still lay exhausted from the Thirty Years' War; and, finally, the best generals and the ablest ministers of the day were French (see page 264). Only little Holland had stood up to that menace, and William, who had had to flood his land by cutting the dikes to stop the French, had bided his time for revenge. Since about 1682 the picture had been changing. Colbert and the leading French generals were dead; the Turks had been driven from the gates of Vienna; much of Europe had been aroused by Louis's persecution of the Huguenots; and, to cap it all, Louis's bitterest enemy was now no longer merely stadholder of Holland but king of England as well. Undeterred, Louis had already set out for new conquests. Luckily for William's purpose, he headed first for the central Rhine valley instead of for the

Low Countries; otherwise, William would not have been free to try for the throne of England.

The ensuing war was to be the first of six major encounters between England and France in the next century and a quarter. For more than half those years the two nations were to be actually engaged in warfare. The series has been called, with some justification, the "Second Hundred Years' War." In the first Hundred Years' War, England had tried to seize and to dominate territory in France herself and had even sought the French crown, only to realize the futility of so doing. This second series developed into a duel for empire, with sea power, commerce, and colonies as prizes. Each of these six wars involved fighting beyond the seas, but in the first two wars the colonial aspects were simply side shows. England, throughout the long series, generally paid allies to keep the French busy on the Continent so that she could more readily concentrate her own energies in the maritime and colonial field. The conflict ended with the choicest of France's overseas possessions in English hands (see Chapter 16).

The War of the League of Augsburg

In the first war, known variously as the War of the League of Augsburg or the Palatinate War (1689-1697), William was the organizer and mainspring of a widespread anti-French alliance in which England, Holland, and Austria were the chief members, with Spain, Sweden, and others less active. Interest centered in the Spanish Netherlands (Belgium) and in the rivalry of the navies.

This was not the first nor was it to be the last time that English participation in a general European war centered in the region in and around the Spanish Netherlands. Here, in the most familiar foreign soil in England's military history, lies the dust of Englishmen who have fallen in battle all the way from Bouvines, in John's

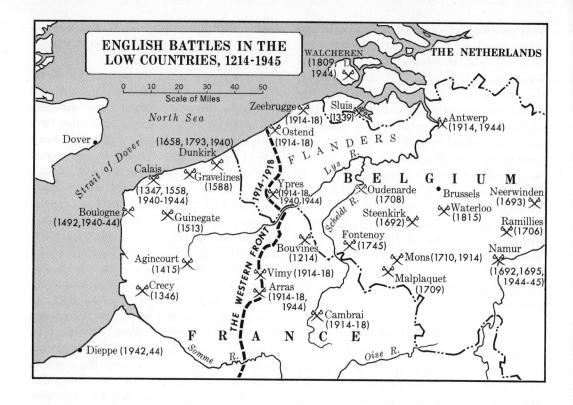

ENGLISH BATTLES IN THE
LOW COUNTRIES, 1214-1945

0   10   20   30   40   50
Scale of Miles

North Sea

THE NETHERLANDS

WALCHEREN
(1809; I.
1944)

Dover

Strait of Dover

(1658, 1793, 1940)
Dunkirk

Zeebrugge
(1914-18)
Ostend
(1914-18)

Sluis
(1339)

FLANDERS

Antwerp
(1914, 1944)

Calais
(1347, 1558,
1940-1944)

Gravelines
(1588)

Lys R.

Ypres
(1914-18,
1940,1944)

Scheldt R.

BELGIUM

Oudenarde
(1708)

Brussels Neerwinden
(1693)
Waterloo
(1815)

Steenkirk
(1692)

Boulogne
(1492,1940-44)

Guinegate
(1513)

Ramillies
(1706)

Fontenoy
(1745)

Agincourt
(1415)

Bouvines
(1214)

Mons (1710, 1914)

Namur
(1692,1695,
1944-45)

Crecy
(1346)

Vimy (1914-18)

Arras
(1914-18,
1944)

Malplaquet
(1709)

THE WESTERN FRONT

Cambrai
(1914-18)

FRANCE

Dieppe (1942,44)

Somme R.

Oise R.

reign, to the western front in the World Wars. This region has been a "cockpit of Europe" for centuries, lying, as it does, exposed to France and Germany, and belonging clearly to neither by geography or population. To England the possession of Belgium by a strong power has been a major menace because of the narrowness of the dividing sea; and since the days of the French threats to the Flemish wool trade in the fourteenth century (see page 120) England has more often than not entered a Continental war when Belgium was involved. This critical little region had come into the possession of Spain from the dukes of Burgundy, through the marriages which led to the empire of Charles V. In the days of Philip II Spanish occupation of Belgium disturbed England because of Spain's strength (see pages 176, 198). Now, however, France was the threat, and Spain lacked the strength either to keep out the French invaders or to prevent Louis XIV's

permanent absorption of some of the border towns. Holland's interests at this time ran parallel to England's, for the Dutch wanted Belgium to remain a buffer state between them and France.

The Low Countries, moreover, had the ideal terrain for military operations. It was a flat country with many navigable rivers (particularly the Meuse and Scheldt), connected by canals. In those days of bad roads such waterways were invaluable for moving artillery, munitions, and bulky supplies.

In his fighting against the armies of Louis XIV in this region William pursued much the same course as George Washington, who, like him, was a good but not a brilliant general. William lost the two major battles of the war, Steenkirk and Neerwinden (or Landen). Fighting in Belgium in this and some other wars has been less a matter of pitched battles than of slow siege operations against the fortresses guarding every strategic point. In this siege warfare, the French had their Marshal Vauban, the great military engineer who was bringing the art of fortification and siegecraft to its peak of perfection. Unlike the medieval castles, with their high walls vulnerable to artillery fire, the new "star-shaped" forts were "sunk in the ground" and only a series of grassy earthworks met the eye. A whole city would be surrounded by such defenses, designed in intricate geometric patterns. To capture such places, Vauban developed an attack by "parallels," whereby the besiegers built a successive series of earthworks around the fort, advancing from one to the next as their artillery silenced the guns of the defenders. Siegecraft became a systematic game with fortresses classed by the number of days they could normally hold out.

The allies, after a serious initial defeat, were more successful at sea. Colbert had built up a powerful French navy which in 1690 roundly whipped a somewhat weaker force of English and Dutch off Beachy Head on England's south coast on the very day before William's victory on the Boyne. This was one of the very few occasions in the whole Second Hundred Years' War when the French were to enjoy even temporary command of the sea; but they wasted the opportunity. They might have cut off William's army in Ireland and have invaded defenseless England; all they did was burn one small coast town and capture some merchantmen. Two years later James was waiting with a strong force of French regulars and Irish troops at La Hogue to cross to England as soon as command of the Channel was secured. This time the tables were turned: in a five-day running encounter, a superior force of English and Dutch drove the French back. Many of their finest ships were run into port, where the English followed in small boats and burned them. That was the end of Colbert's magnificent navy. For years thereafter, the allies were able to move pretty much as

they pleased at sea, while the French simply resorted to bold privateering against English and Dutch commerce.

In the meantime on a much smaller scale, the English and French colonists in North America were fighting their King William's War. Count Frontenac, greatest of the governors of New France, not only saved Quebec from an attack by New Englanders but also devised an effective and devilish scheme of counterattack. Bands of Indians led by French officers were sent on surprise raids upon the isolated English frontier settlements. Traveling on snowshoes, these stealthy invaders would swoop down at midnight. Then followed war whoops, burning homes, the massacre of some colonists with the tomahawk, and for the rest —men, women, and children—the long, cold route back to Canada, dragged along as captives. Schenectady in New York, Deerfield in Massachusetts, and Fort Loyal (Portland) in Maine were among the victims. English settlers disappeared from Maine for a quarter century. Not until the French were finally dislodged from Canada could the pioneers on the outskirts of the English colonies breathe freely.

The Peace of Ryswick, in 1697—only a four-year truce — restored matters very much to the *status quo ante bellum* (the situation before fighting began). While William's victory was not striking, Louis's triumphant spread of French power had been unquestionably checked. William obtained his recognition by Louis as the rightful king of England instead of James II.

The National Debt

This war cost England even more than previous ones, for in addition to her own heavy military and naval costs, she was starting her familiar role as "paymaster of the allies." The Revolution Settlement survived because it developed a new method of meeting these heavy expenses in 1693 through the establishment of a permanent national debt, whereby part of the heavy extra war costs were charged to the future. Earlier English kings had tried to pay for their wars while these were in progress or soon afterward, partly through extra taxation and partly through short-term loans. Parliament now met about two thirds of this war's costs by taxation, but balked at the heavy taxes which would have been necessary for a completely "pay as you go" policy. As a result the remaining third of the costs was left to future generations by "funding" the debt. In other words, the government borrowed money wherewith to meet its expenses and agreed to pay interest at a specified rate. The nation was like an individual with a fairly fixed income who suddenly incurs heavy extra debts in an emergency. He might keep this a "floating debt" until he could pay the bills bit by bit out of his income; but such a practice works an injustice to his impatient creditors, while his own credit suffers. Consequently he funds his debt by borrowing from the bank, settling his bills at once, and paying interest to the bank for the use of the money. The bank, to ensure repayment, often takes a mortgage on his house or demands some other safeguard or "collateral" of value. The collateral for the national debt was the general credit of the government. Nothing was said about paying back the principal of these loans, and the national debt tended to become permanent. When William came to the throne, England had a floating debt of about £1,000,000 in unpaid bills, but with the funding of the debt she owed more than £18,000,000 at his death; and this national debt had risen to some £850,000,000 by the end of the Second Hundred Years' War, in 1815. Some later finance ministers, to be sure, experimented with "sinking funds," whereby money was to be set aside each year for paying off the principal; but these efforts to reduce the debt were generally failures, and England kept on paying interest on money borrowed for wars long past, until interest charges alone came to more than the total annual cost of government in William's time. In view of all that England gained by her ultimate victory over France, that heavy borrowing was a profitable step; but a national debt presented a constant temptation to wage war more frequently and more extravagantly perhaps, since it gave an opportunity to shift a portion of the burden to the shoulders of future generations.

The creation of the national debt led directly to the founding of the Bank of England in 1694. England had lagged behind Italy, Germany, and Holland in the matter of organized banking (see page 163). Jews and Lombards had performed such services in earlier centuries; later the goldsmith, with whom men deposited their money, carried on banking functions of sorts. Banks could serve two useful purposes: individuals with surplus money might deposit it where it would not only be fairly safe but also pay interest. The bank could pay interest because, on the basis of these deposits, it was able to lend money or discount notes and thus to promote business activity. Underlying the whole financial system was the principle of credit, from the Latin word for "believe"—in this connection, belief that the money could be repaid. When the government was seeking loans for the national debt, it not only tried to attract the general public with various schemes of annuities and lotteries but also to get certain companies to take over portions of the debt in place of their capital stock, in return for special privileges. It therefore welcomed the proposals of one William Patterson to organize a Bank of England, which would lend the government £1,200,000 and use the national credit as its capital for doing a general private banking business of deposits, loans, and discounts. The Bank, established in London in 1694, has since been a bulwark of the English financial system. The Bank of England was later given full management of the national debt and the exclusive right to issue bank notes which might pass as currency. In spite of this close relation to the nation's finances, it remained a private institution until 1946. Other banks were authorized later, but none had the privileged position of the "Old Lady of Threadneedle Street."

Political Parties and the War

Financial considerations strongly affected the attitude of the two political parties toward the war. When the government determined to pay two thirds of the costs as it went along, its chief device for raising the extra funds was a land tax on the rental income of landowners. Nominally four shillings in the pound, or 20 per cent, it was actually nearer 10 per cent. It fell with particular force upon the Tory squires, who complained that the Whig monied interests not only escaped such taxation but also profited during the war from interest on government loans, war contracts, and the extension of world markets. An income tax was proposed, to make the business and professional men pay their share, but the Treasury was unable to work out an adequate system of collection. The Tories disapproved likewise of the concentration of power in the Bank of England. Besides war costs, another reason for the sharp, bitter dissension was the vital interest Whigs had in preserving the Revolution Settlement, in which much of their money was invested. During this reign and the next, it was nip and tuck between them; the absence of a few Whigs or Tories from the Commons for a cock fight or a party might be enough to change a vote.

Triumphant in its Revolution Settlement, the Commons had yet to work out an orderly way of exercising its new supremacy. Ultimately this was to be achieved by linking the ministers of the cabinet with the party which controlled a majority in the Commons, and there were already gropings in that direction. William was suspicious, and with cause, of his ministers, as well as of his generals and admirals, more than one being in secret correspondence with the exiled James in France, with a view to a possible restoration. Although the king began by choosing ministers from both parties in order to win as broad a support as possible for his government, he soon saw that the Whigs were more inclined to see eye to eye with him on the matter of the French war. By 1694 he had an incipient party cabinet composed entirely of Whigs, hoping that they would assure more unity of action with the majority in the Commons. This group was known as the Whig "Junto," implying, like "Cabal," a conspiracy of a suspicious nature.

With the close of the war, William's crabbed temper grew worse, and his favoritism toward foreigners in English offices alienated many men. The Tories, winning a majority in the House of Commons, directly flouted him by cutting the army to only seven thousand, despite his request for a much larger force and also by taking away estates which he had granted to some of his Dutch friends. Meanwhile, however, affairs on the Continent grew so threatening to England's security that by 1701 even the Tories were ready for another war against Louis XIV. William lived long enough to organize one more big alliance against Louis.

Queen Anne and the Marlboroughs

His wife's sister Anne (1702-1714) peaceably succeeded him on the throne. Not a murmur was raised against the accession of this younger daughter of James II and Anne Hyde, whatever may have been the private thoughts of those who did not like the Revolution Settlement. Anne's father had died just before William, and the Loyalists transferred their allegiance to her half-brother, another James, whose birth had precipitated his father's overthrow in 1688. These Jacobites (so-called from Jacobus, the Latin for "James") now performed certain ceremonies at their secret meetings, such as squeezing an orange and holding their glasses over bowls of water in drinking to "the king over the water"; they even toasted the "little gentleman in black velvet" (the mole over whose hole William's horse had stumbled, causing his death). But this animosity to the Revolution Settlement seldom came into public evidence.

The new reign, like those of two other queens regnant, was to witness much national glory and high literary achievement. To be sure, only part of the credit for this success may be attributed to the dowdy invalid queen, worn out at thirty-six by the births and deaths of "at least fifteen babies," only one of whom survived infancy. Anne's mind has been called "slow as a lowland river"; yet she had more than the usual Stuart share of common sense, and she slaved conscientiously at the details of government in spite of almost steady illness and acute pain. Her stolid husband, Prince George of Denmark, a heavy drinker but withal kindly and devoted to her, was either "too stupid or too shrewd"[1] to interfere.

During the first two thirds of the reign three very able persons joined with Anne in governing England: Sarah Churchill, later Duchess of Marlborough, in the queen's chamber; her husband in the field; and Sidney, Lord Godolphin, as chief minister. Sarah, girlhood friend and inseparable companion of Her Majesty until seven years before the queen's death, was as brilliant as Anne was slow. Less clever than the Marlboroughs, but steady, methodical, and thoroughgoing, was Godolphin, whose family wealth had come from Cornish tin mines. Off duty, he enjoyed gambling and horseracing; his Arabian stallion was one of the three ancestors of most of England's later famous race horses. His son married the Marlboroughs' daughter, and, as Lord

Treasurer, Godolphin was to give Marlborough efficient co-operation from home for his military campaigns. As Charles II had once said of him, "Little Sidney Godolphin is never in the way and never out of the way."

The outstanding member of the trio, John Churchill, Duke of Marlborough, was perhaps the greatest military genius who ever fought for England. He was also fully the equal of William III in keeping together ill-assorted and jealous allies. In a day of generally static methods of warfare, with siegecraft predominating, Marlborough injected a boldness and originality into strategy, and on the battlefield his keen mind and quick eye seemed always to pick out the best tactical movements. It was not only as a strategist and battle tactician that he excelled. No small part of his success came from his meticulous foresight for every detail: his soldiers always had food, clothing, shelter, and pay, and came to the battlefield in the pink of condition. Whereas there is general agreement about the military ability of the handsome and remarkably gracious Marlborough, such unanimity does not exist about his character. Avarice and disloyalty repeatedly rear their heads. Yet more friendly critics than his contemporary Swift or the later Macaulay have laid his avarice to his indigent youth, when he had to live on an ensign's meager pay at Charles II's extravagant court, and his apparent disloyalty at times to forethought for England's ultimate advantage rather than for his own. Presumably untrue were many of the charges against him, such as that of sending his officers into dangerous positions in battle so that he might resell their commissions. Nevertheless, all in all, the charges against him seem to total a sorry indictment. John received his first commission in the Guards when his sister, Arabella, became the mistress of James II, then Duke of York. The favor of James, coupled with his own ability, quickly raised him to a responsible

<hr>

[1] G. M. Trevelyan, *England under Queen Anne*, Vol. I, pp. 167, 168. By permission of Longmans, Green & Co.

position. He smashed the Monmouth rebellion, and in 1688 his last minute shift of allegiance from James to William probably did more than anything else to make it a "Bloodless" Revolution. Created Earl of Marlborough by William, but jealous of the king's favor to foreigners, he has been accused of betraying to France a projected naval attack on Brest. He was forced to leave England. Incidentally, the French seem to have already received that information, possibly from Godolphin. In his last year, William, faced with a new war, recalled Marlborough. Some of his intrigues with the enemy during Queen Anne's reign have a somewhat suspicious look, but his loyalty to her was not questioned. His military genius rose pre-eminent to win for England some of her greatest victories in the War of the Spanish Succession (1701-1713), which soon ended the short-lived Peace of Ryswick.

War of the Spanish Succession

The new conflict arose from the lack of a direct heir to the Spanish king, Charles II, who died childless late in 1700. The marriage of his aunts and sisters into the French Bourbon and Austrian Hapsburg families had made sons of those lines his next of kin. Other nations were only too ready to intervene in this rich and rotten kingdom. William was particularly determined to prevent the union of Spain with France, which would close a considerable part of Europe and the New World to English and Dutch trade. Besides, French control of the Spanish Netherlands would threaten the security of both Holland and England. At an international conference, Louis seemed ready to co-operate with William. The French had a somewhat better case than the Austrians, because the Spanish mother and wife of Louis were both older than their respective sisters, who were married to Hapsburgs in Vienna. The elder Spanish infantas, to be sure, had officially given up their claims to the Spanish

throne, whereas their younger sisters had not. Such genealogical details may seem trivial, but they were to lead Europe into a dozen years of war. Both Louis and the emperor claimed the Spanish throne in the names of their second grandson and second son, respectively, because neither were their own direct heirs. A compromise on Charles II's own choice for his heir of the Bavarian elector's young son, another grandson of the Austrian Hapsburgs, came to naught with his early death. Afterwards, the Spanish grandees, who wanted to keep Spain's holdings intact, apparently persuaded Charles, just before he died, to will his entire lands to the second grandson of Louis XIV. Such temptation was too much for Louis; he accepted that bequest for his grandson, who was crowned Philip V of Spain. Although as a younger grandson, he was not in direct line for the French throne, England felt that the balance of power was gravely menaced by this double kingship of the Bourbons. Louis at once threw French troops into the Spanish Netherlands in his grandson's name, and going back on his Ryswick agreement, told the dying James II that he would support his son "James III" for the English throne. Thereupon, in September, 1701, William organized the Grand Alliance, which included the three chief allies of the preceding war, England, Holland, and Austria, against the Franco-Spanish combination.

The war was fought on several fronts. England and Holland were primarily interested in the fighting in the Low Countries. Austria centered her efforts in Italy, where she hoped to recover lands from the Spanish. The defense of the Rhine region was left to those German states which were wheedled onto the side of the allies, Brandenburg-Prussia being bribed by the promotion of her ruler from elector to king, while Hanover came in because of the elector's interest in the English throne (see page 275). As a side show, England and

Holland, with Portugal, unwisely tried to put the Austrian claimant on the throne of Spain by a campaign there. Except for the Mediterranean, little happened on the sea. The only major naval battle was a draw; but the English and Dutch helped to bring victory by keeping the sea lanes barred to French and Spanish shipping, while they themselves moved troops and cargoes freely. As in the other contests of the Second Hundred Years' War, the War of the Spanish Succession spread to America, where it was known as Queen Anne's War. Except for his brilliant campaign in 1704, Marlborough concentrated his efforts in the Low Countries, where he pushed back the French at the outset of the fighting in 1702 and opened important lines of communication. In 1704 Austria was almost forced out of the war when Vienna itself was threatened by a joint French and Bavarian army. Disguising his intentions from the allies (for he well knew that they would never allow him to leave the Low Countries undefended), Marlborough rushed by secret rapid marches the several hundred miles to the Danube. En route he joined forces with Prince Eugene of Savoy, the very able Austrian commander, who alone knew of the plans. With some fifty thousand men, they met an equal number of French and Bavarians at the hamlet of Blenheim on the Danube. With half the enemy killed, wounded, or prisoners and the rest in disorganized flight, Marlborough won his most spectacular victory. Europe was amazed, for French regiments had been invincible for half a century.

Back in the Low Countries, Marlborough cleared the French out of the entire Spanish Netherlands after another smashing victory at Ramillies in 1706. At the same time Prince Eugene drove them from Italy. In 1708, after the French had recovered part of Belgium, Marlborough inflicted a third decisive defeat upon them at Oudenarde and captured Vauban's masterpiece, the fortress at Lille, in France itself.

The following year at Malplaquet he won again, though he lost three men to the French two. After that his part was less noticeable. He had a reputation as the first soldier of Europe; Parliament had voted a huge sum to build him a palace; and even two centuries later men still sang, on the Continent, "Malbrouck s'en va t'en guerre" (to the tune "We won't go home till morning").

Already by the time of Ramillies the Grand Alliance had achieved its two chief objectives, the expulsion of the French from the Netherlands and from Italy. Despite increasing failures, the Spanish campaign of the English and Dutch, with Portuguese support, to oust the Bourbon Philip V in favor of the Austrian claimant, still dragged on. Although the campaign was a costly blunder, two important byproducts came of it. The treaty with Portugal provided for the exchange of English woolens for Portuguese port and Madeira wine. This tended to replace the use of light French wines in England. More essential, a week before Blenheim an English fleet captured the weakly defended Rock of Gibraltar, the key to the Mediterranean; four years later Minorca, in the Balearic Islands, also fell to the English, who made it a permanent winter naval base inside the Mediterranean. Thus England, which had first seen the value of the Mediterranean in Cromwell's time, and which had come to realize the need of a naval protection there after her rich "Smyrna convoy" had been captured in 1693, now took her place as a power there.

By 1709 France, bled white, was ready for peace. On top of defeats and an empty treasury from such prolonged warfare, she was faced with famine after a bitter winter, the "Great Frost," which froze crops in the ground and peasants in their huts. Louis, ready to concede almost anything, agreed to all but one of forty allied demands—that French armies must join in driving his own grandson from his Spanish throne. There-

The taking of Gibraltar, 1704, by an Anglo-Dutch fleet under Sir George Rooke.

upon, with cruel stupidity, the blame for which must fall mostly on England, which rallied to the cry of "No peace without Spain!" the war was continued, with the French putting up a stubborn fight.

Union with Scotland

In the meantime, at home, England and Scotland were uniting to form the kingdom of Great Britain, with a single Parliament, an event which proved of lasting advantage to both countries. James I had tried to achieve this when the two kingdoms had been brought under the same crown in 1603, but England at that time would have none of it. The experiment of one king and two separate Parliaments had not been a very happy one. The rulers were inclined to govern Scotland from London, and the Scots felt, with some justice, that their interests were being sacrificed. Cromwell had joined the two nations by force, but

the regime of Monk's redcoats had not endeared the English to the Scots.

On the eve of the union, English writers were calling the Scots "bloody, barbarous, inhuman butchers" and were turning up their noses at their "nastiness and ill manners," while Scots referred to England as "insolent and proud like hell." Englishmen disliked the bulk of the Scots as Presbyterians or Jacobites, while Scotland still remembered Flodden and Glencoe. Nevertheless, underneath the surface, each nation had a respect for the other, which unfortunately did not characterize Anglo-Irish relations. Not friendship, then, but a shrewd realization of the mutual advantages of union brought the two together.

Poverty, more than anything else, drove the Scots to give up the independence they had made secure at Bannockburn (see page 117). Their thrift, which hundreds of jokes have emphasized, was forced upon them by the niggardliness of nature in their bleak country. Their harsh, dour characteristics had been nourished on a monotonous diet of oatmeal, whisky, and Calvinism. The per-capita wealth of Scotland was reckoned at less than one sixth of that south of the border. Some lairds struggled to keep up appearances on half as much as thousands of English yeomen made. Between poor soil and crude methods, the peasantry could do little more than exist on their meager crops. There were few towns of account outside Edinburgh, the capital, where a considerable population was crowded into a small space, living in gaunt, gray, stone buildings, seven or eight stories high. Industry and trade were in a feeble state, and the foreign commerce of Leith and Glasgow was negligible.

Beyond the Highland line was another Scotland, wilder, less civilized, and even poorer. The clansmen of the Highlands cared little for the authority of Kirk or king; to them the paternalistic chief was everything. Their Celtic inheritance was also preserved in their speech, in their belief in the supernatural, and in many other ways. In religion many were still Roman Catholic. No Sir Walter Scott had yet appeared to give to Lowlanders and Englishmen a glamorous picture of this Highland life; to the outsiders the kilted clansmen in their plaids were dangerous relics of an older and lower civilization. But the Act of Union was primarily a Lowland matter; the Highlanders would be heard from later —in 1715 and again in 1745.

The bait which lured Scotland into the union was the commercial and colonial system established by the Navigation Acts, with their exclusive emphasis on English ships and English sailors. England was obviously growing rich: the profits from her commerce were estimated at £2,000,000 a year in 1700, and the contrast was all the sharper because Scotland was staggering from two recent economic blows. A succession of bad crops in William's time had brought famine and widespread death from starvation. To make matters worse, every Scot who could scrape together a few pounds had invested them in the "Company for Trading with Africa and the Indies," which had sent a few ships toward India and had planted a colony at Darien, on the Isthmus of Panama in 1698. This colony, planted in the heart of the monopolistic empire, died a quick and miserable death from Spaniards, fever, and dissension, while England did not lift a finger to save it. In addition, the Scots had been kept out of India by the monopoly of the English East India Company. Thus running afoul of two rigid overseas monopolies, the Scots could appreciate the advantages of being on the inside rather than the outside of such systems. The loss to the investors would have been serious even in England; to the Scots it was a tragedy. England helped to pave the way for the Act of Union by reimbursing the investors, with interest thrown in for good measure.

The price which Scotland paid for commercial rights was the loss of her separate parliament. But that body was even less representative than England's Parliament. The deeper loyalty of the Lowland Scots was to the Kirk, the highly organized Presbyterian system established by John Knox. In its various bodies, from the parish "session" through the presbytery and synod to the annual national General Assembly at Edinburgh, the layman took part as well as the preacher. Scots of all degrees had far more opportunity for actual participation in the Kirk than in the regular political organization. This was a valuable democratic influence. Their rising in 1638 was not because of political reasons but because Laud was tampering with their Kirk (see page 234). As long as the union left that undisturbed, the Scots would more easily forego their parliament.

After several years of negotiations, during which there was the constant possibility that on Anne's death the Scots might set up an independent kingdom under the Pretender, as "James VIII," thirty-odd commissioners from each kingdom met at Whitehall in the spring of 1706. As a result of sharp bargaining, they arrived at the essential terms of the Act of Union. Scotland was not only to retain her own Kirk, which has ever since remained separate from the Church of England, but also to preserve Scotland's particular legal system, based on elements of feudal and Roman law, quite different from the English common law. Scottish ships with Scottish crews would thereafter enjoy the same trading privileges as ships from London and Bristol or colonial Boston and New York. With the abolition of her own parliament, Scotland was to send forty-five members to the House of Commons at Westminster, while the Scottish peers were to select sixteen from their number to sit in the House of Lords. In each case this was less than one tenth of the number from England and Wales.

In spite of protests and riots in various parts of Scotland, the Scottish parliament signed its own death warrant. On May 1, 1707, the Kingdom of Great Britain came into being. England celebrated that May Day in gay fashion; but in Scotland, it is said, some of the bells played "Why should I be sad on my wedding day?"

The act paved the way for relative prosperity in Scotland. Commerce began to flourish at Glasgow, Leith, and other ports. The canny shrewdness of the Scot contributed much to the success of the kingdom and the empire. By the end of the century, too, the names of Adam Smith, Robert Burns, and James Watt indicate Scotland's accomplishments in thought, literature, and invention. Only from 1707 on may one properly refer to the "British" government, "British" army, and so on. Within forty years the British army in particular was to become more effective with regiments of those wilder Scots of the Highlands, who in 1707 had been untamed troublemakers.

Whig and Tory Rivalry

Soon afterwards, the refusal to make peace "without Spain" gave weary Europe four years more of fruitless war. This was largely the result of the party situation in England. The balance between the parties was as close as it had been in William's reign, and feeling ran higher. Anne, moreover, was not the person to keep such a contentious rivalry in hand; for, although she always conscientiously presided at her cabinet meetings, she was not able to control them as William had done. Consequently, Godolphin for some eight years was virtually a prime minister. Anne wanted a general equable mixture of parties represented in the government. "All I desire is my liberty in encouraging and employing all those that concur faithfully in my service, whether they are called Whigs or Tories, not to be tied to one nor the other." But instead, she found the parties to be "such bugbears that I dare not venture to write my mind freely of either of them without a cypher for fear of any accident. I pray God keep me out of the hands of both of them."[2] To add to the confusion, the Tories were now split into a High Church group—extreme Anglicans and some of Jacobite persuasion—determined upon harsh punishment of Nonconformists and the ending of the practice of "occasional conformity," and into a Moderate group, desiring a middle course. Combined, the Tories would have outnumbered the Whigs; but they did not stay together. The control of Parliament, therefore, gradually changed from united Tories, at the beginning of the reign, to a combination of Moderate Tories and Whigs, and then to Whigs alone, who favored vigorous prosecution of the war. In the election of 1705 large numbers of Whigs came into the Commons, but Anne's attitude kept

[2] G. M. Trevelyan, *England under Queen Anne* (1932), Vol. II, pp. 170, 385. By permission of Longmans, Green & Co.

many Tory ministers in office until about 1708, when the Whigs obtained complete domination. Marlborough found it expedient to change from Tory to Whig. Between 1708 and 1710, however, as the war dragged on, Whig popularity began to wane in the country at large.

With that came the eclipse of the trio who had been so closely associated with Anne. Sarah had already lost the queen's friendship in 1707; Godolphin was dismissed in favor of a Tory in 1710; and the duke fell from power a year later. They had brought England victories abroad and the union with Scotland at home, but they were replaced by three less worthy individuals who were to bring about peace but fall out over the succession. Sarah was ousted from favor by the amiable and ingratiating Mrs. Abigail Masham, a poor relation of hers, whom she had introduced into the queen's household. The steady, dependable Godolphin was to give way to Robert Harley, whom some called a slippery backstairs politician. He was a Moderate Tory in policy, careless in administration, and remarkably well informed through his efficient secret service—Mrs. Masham was his tool more than once. His ally and later archenemy, the High Tory, Henry St. John, later Viscount Bolingbroke, was one of England's most brilliant statesmen, a master of oratory and diplomatic negotiation. Yet he was a profligate debauchee, not to be trusted in matters of finance or loyalty. His desperate gamble in Anne's last hours was to ruin his own future permanently and his party's for half a century.

The overthrow of the unpopular Whigs was hastened by the excessively High Tory sermon of one Dr. Sacheverell in November, 1709. In scathing denunciation he virulently attacked Godolphin and the whole Revolution Settlement. Since the Church was established, the government took action. Sacheverell was impeached by the House of Commons and tried by the Lords, who found him guilty by a small majority. His sermon, however, had been in tune with the popular feeling of the moment. The Lords gave him the lightest sentence in their power, and Sacheverell, a popular hero, took triumphal possession of a new and lucrative living. The fickle London mob, which had attacked Catholic chapels in 1688, now turned upon those of the Dissenters.

Then the changes came thick and fast. During the next six months Anne quietly dismissed her ministers one by one, sending even the faithful Godolphin merely a curt note to break his staff of office, without a word of gratitude for his many services. A general election in this same year, 1710, gave the Tories a powerful majority, with the Moderate and High factions temporarily united. Harley became chief minister. The more rabid St. John, also coming into office, immediately began to stir up a group of wild young bloods, in the October Club, who were talking of the return of the Pretender.

Plotting permanent confusion to all Whigs, the Tories now turned to literary talent to spread their propaganda. Pamphleteering swept the country in 1710 and 1711; rarely have such able writers been marshaled to use their pens for political purposes—the violently High Tory Swift, the more moderate Addison and Steele, and Defoe, who had been Harley's ear to the ground and now took money from both sides. The Tories pushed through legislation designed to keep everyone except squires from the House of Commons, to prevent Nonconformists from qualifying for official positions by "occasional conformity" (see page 275), and to close all Dissenting schools. None of these laws, however, was to have permanent effect.

Even before the end of the Godolphin regime there had been secret negotiations for peace with France behind the backs of England's allies. Now St. John rapidly and shamelessly carried these forward to achieve at once the Tory aim of peace "without Spain." In the summer of 1711, by a clever move in which he did not lose a man, Marlborough pierced the French lines and had almost a clear road to Paris; but in that very month St. John had completed preliminary peace terms in which England received a great deal at the particular expense of Holland. Marlborough, whose popularity had withstood the party changes, stood in the way. To break his influence, efforts were made to discredit him by charges of bribery and of keeping for himself part of the money granted for the hiring of mercenaries, though that was the usual way generals acquired secret service funds. Without investigating, Anne dismissed him. Unfortunately his hands were not as clean as they might have been yet these charges were much exaggerated, if not untrue. To avoid prosecution, he went abroad for the rest of the queen's life. He received high rewards from four English monarchs, and to Anne alone was he relatively loyal (see page 292).

The House of Lords was another obstacle to peace. To ensure a majority to support the Commons' desire for immediate peace, Anne, at a single stroke on New Year's Day of 1712, created twelve new peers, including St. John and Mr. Masham. This was an important constitutional development; for it showed a way to override opposition in the Lords. The sovereign, of course, was entitled to create as many new peers as he or she saw fit. After this precedent the mere threat of its repetition was to be sufficient to overcome resistance in the Lords (see pages 405, 499).

That same month the peace conference assembled in the quiet Dutch city of Utrecht, but the fighting continued without an armistice. Prince Eugene and the other allied commanders were planning a further invasion of France; but Bolingbroke, to use St. John's new title, sent secret orders to Marlborough's successor to avoid fighting for the present, stating that a copy of the letter was being dispatched to the French court. By the summer of 1712, to the disgust and dismay of the deserted allies, the British troops were hurried back from the front, with the soldiers, so it was said, in tears from shame and from losing the anticipated booty.

Peace of Utrecht

By the spring of 1713 the various treaties which bear the name of Utrecht were signed. They reflect shrewd work by Bolingbroke, but England's desertion of her allies won for her the epithet of "Perfidious Albion," which was to be repeated half a century later. Several royal deaths affected the settlement. The Austrian Hapsburg claimant to the Spanish throne had become Emperor Charles VI, and the Spaniards retained as their king the Bourbon Philip V for whom they had been fighting. Both the son and the grandson of Louis XIV, however, had just died, leaving only a great-grandson, the sickly infant who would soon be Louis XV, between Philip V and the French throne. Thus there were now Bourbons on both sides of the Pyrenees, and France need fear no longer the "Hapsburg ring." The agreements stipulated that the same men should never occupy both the French and the Spanish thrones; but during the coming century there were to be frequent renewals of a Bourbon "family compact," which forced England to keep her navy as large as the combined French and Spanish fleets.

Both France and Spain, however, paid heavily for this dynastic concession. The Peace of Utrecht marked England's first successful looting of the French colonial empire. While Marlborough had been keeping the French busy on land, English admirals had gained ascendancy on the sea, and the colonies had sustained "Queen Anne's War." England received from France a clear title to the disputed regions of Hudson Bay and Newfoundland as well as part of Acadia (Nova Scotia). Louis once again officially recognized the Protestant succession in England at the expense of the direct Stuart line. In the Mediterranean, England kept the island of Minorca and, more important, the key position at Gibraltar, the huge rock fortress which she had also taken from Spain and successfully defended against all the Franco-Spanish attempts to recover it. She also received valuable trading concessions in the hitherto closed preserves of Spanish America, where, in the "Asiento," Spain gave England a thirty-year monopoly of her colonial slave trade and permission to trade with one ship a year (see page 201). England did not share these maritime concessions, obtained in the preliminary secret negotiations, with her ally Holland, who, exhausted by the long wars and thus abandoned by her ally, dropped from her brief moment in the ranks of the first-class powers to a comfortable berth among the lesser nations. For added security against France, Holland was given authority to occupy a string of barrier forts in the Belgium region, though these were far from being the complete safeguards she desired. Belgium, previously the Spanish Netherlands, became the Austrian Netherlands, being shifted to the other branch of the Hapsburg house because Austria was too remote to be a menace to either Holland or England. Among other advantages, Austria gained considerable territory in Italy. That did not particularly concern England, whose interest in Continental territory, aside from the security of the Low Countries and the acquisition of Gibraltar, remained a negative one. The quarter century of conflict had removed the French menace and saved the balance of power.

Tory Scheming

With the Spanish succession out of the way, the question of the English succession loomed larger. It lay between Anne's Protestant cousin of the Hanoverian line, stipulated by the Act of Settlement in 1701, and her Catholic younger half brother, the Jacobite Pretender, whose birth had precipitated the Revolution of 1688. And on this issue, Tories were to split. Bolingbroke, steadily building up a High Tory faction, was apparently turning more and more toward the Pretender. An urgent crisis seemed imminent at Christmas of 1713, when Anne fell dangerously ill. Oxford (Harley), with his moderate policies, stood in the way of Bolingbroke's plans, which began to materialize feverishly as Anne grew worse. Working in conjunction with the faithless Abigail, who had shifted from Sarah to Oxford and who now intrigued to oust Oxford, Bolingbroke found himself balked; for Oxford clung on, despite increased carelessness and sullen inactivity, in his high post of Lord Treasurer. Bolingbroke pushed through Parliament in June the Schism Act, which closed all Dissenting schools "down to the meanest" (see page 288), hoping to embarrass Oxford and provoke the Nonconformists to revolt. In that case Louis XIV had promised to send over the Pretender with French troops.

Anne, disgusted with Oxford's strange apathy and neglect, and by now too weak to resist the steady pressure of Bolingbroke and Abigail, dismissed Oxford. No one but the dying queen was now Bolingbroke's immediate superior. Whether he was actually plotting a Jacobite restoration, as many of his acts seemed to indicate, or whether he was merely trying to get the power into his own hands, to be in a strong position for the Hanoverian succession is not clear. But, that he himself intended to be the center of whatever stage he was setting is obvious: and with the situation temporarily in his hands, he had to work fast. But he did not realize just how short the time was to be; less than three days did the Lord-Treasurership lie vacant and Anne did not trust Bolingbroke enough to give him this key position. Oxford had been dismissed late on Tuesday; on Friday the Privy Council hastily met on learning that the queen was sinking fast. The Jacobites and Bolingbroke apparently were caught unawares. The Whigs and Moderate Tories were ready with a nominee for Lord Treasurer, a trusted Moderate Tory peer; and Anne acquiesced. Until midnight this group, whose authority was greater than that of the cabinet alone, worked feverishly, sending orders throughout the land to make ready for the peaceful succession of the Hanoverian heir. Bolingbroke, with his hopes of power dashed to earth, meekly signed the papers with the others. Sunday morning Anne was dead, and with the proclamation at St. James's Palace of the Hanoverian elector as King George I (1714-1727) cheers went up all over London. That night the city blazed with bonfires before the homes of the prominent peers, even that of Bolingbroke.

The Accession of the Hanoverians

Had Anne died a few months earlier, she would have been succeeded by another queen, a lively, clever old lady in her eighties, Sophia, the dowager electress of Hanover. Sophia's mother had been the daughter of James I, her father that "Winter King" of Bohemia whose aspirations had started the Thirty Years' War, and her brother Prince Rupert of Civil War fame (see pages 222 ff., 239, 248). Just as the marriage of a Tudor princess to a Scottish king had brought a Stuart to the English throne a century later, so now the marriage of that first Stuart's daughter to a German duke was to bring in the Hanoverian line a hundred years later. Sophia had married a rather insignificant German noble, of a branch of the House of Brunswick. In 1692, as the price of his military support, the Hapsburg Holy Roman Emperor had made him Elector of Brunswick-Lüneburg, usually called Hanover after its principal city. Hanover was one of the lesser German states, touching the North Sea near Hamburg and Bremen. Sophia is said to have intrigued for years to become Queen of

England and then missed it by four months. Instead, the throne went to her son, who regarded it as something of a nuisance. When the news of Anne's death reached Hanover late in the night, the British minister, it is said, awakened the elector and saluted him as King of Great Britain; but unlike James of Scotland who waited restlessly for Elizabeth's death, George merely grunted and went back to sleep. Nevertheless, the British throne was too important to refuse, and before seven weeks had elapsed a reluctant, homesick, and somewhat bewildered George arrived in England, accompanied by two elderly and grasping mistresses, whom the disrespectful dubbed the "Maypole" and the "Elephant." These German countesses became English duchesses, but George's own wife never saw England; she had been divorced and even for a while imprisoned for a youthful indiscretion for which her alleged lover had been murdered.

The first two Georges were stolid, stodgy, and colorless Germans; the third alienated many and then went insane; the fourth George was probably the coarsest of English monarchs; and his brother, the fourth William, was stupid and uninteresting. England became attached to the Hanoverians not from affection, admiration, or respect but because, except for George III, they interfered little with the running of the government and, by occupying the throne, they kept out a rival line which might have threatened Protestantism and the control of Parliament.

England's foreign policy between 1714 and 1837 was often complicated by her kings being also electors of Hanover; their solicitude for that state affected the insular independence of England's policy. The first two Georges in particular took Hanover very seriously into account in their foreign policy. The royal navy could prevent an invasion of England, but it could not defend the frontiers of Hanover from French or Prussian aggression. England was to breathe a sigh of relief when, at Victoria's accession, the tie was broken by German custom, which barred a woman from ruling Hanover.

The Whig regime coming into power with George I, who owed them his throne, lasted until George II's death in 1760. So badly discredited was the Tory party by Bolingbroke's fiasco and other events that it ceased to exist as an effective opposition. A few diehards were returned to Parliament, but the moderates turned Whig. Much of this Whig power lay in the hands of some seventy great landed families. Under such leadership, which was inclined to raise as few disputed points as possible, England enjoyed a period of sleepy prosperity.

Before settling into that somnolence, however, England was stirred in the year after George's accession by a Jacobite uprising remembered as the "Fifteen." The Jacobites, caught unprepared by Anne's death, were now all ready to fight—the exiles in France, including Bolingbroke; the malcontents in England; and some Scottish chiefs. With better plans and more solidarity among themselves, the Jacobites might well have shaken George's throne. Not only was there woeful bungling, but many, still undecided as to whether they wanted to bring "James III" home, were determined to keep in the good graces of both sides until they could see how events were shaping themselves. Marlborough, back home from exile and the nominal head of George's army, was sending money to the Pretender. One Scottish peer betrayed the Jacobite plans to the government, but kept his son in the Pretender's army. The standard was raised prematurely in the Highlands; the government knew the plans through the double-dealers almost as soon as they were formulated. A small band of Highland clansmen was joined by a few Catholics from northern England. Had there been time to rouse the Lowlands, the revolt might have had a different ending; for

there were only about eight thousand soldiers stationed in the British Isles. Yet even before the Pretender landed, the Jacobites had been twice defeated. Louis XIV had died on the eve of the Pretender's departure, and the regent for the infant Louis XV made no move to aid James, who fled back to France, where he lived out his life in exile. The rebels were treated with a leniency which later events indicated was perhaps mistaken.

The only other serious threat to the new regime came from the wild financial frenzy of the "South Sea Bubble" in 1720. The South Sea Company was a joint-stock organization formed by Harley in 1711 to handle the trade with Spanish America to be opened by the "Asiento," which he was even then negotiating. In 1720 the company become involved in government high finance. To fund the large floating debt, the government naturally turned to the great companies with concentrated wealth at their disposal. The Bank of England and the East India Company had already taken over portions of the national debt in this manner, substituting government securities for their regular capital (see page 280). Now it was the turn of the South Sea Company, which, by an act of Parliament, received monopoly privileges and other advantages in exchange for taking over £30,000,000 of the debt. But, whereas the other two organizations had remained on a conservative basis, the stock of the South Sea Company was manipulated into an abnormal boom, all the more easily because, ever since Elizabethan days, Spanish America and its silver mines had suggested fabulous wealth. Within three months after the act was passed, speculation had driven £100 South Sea shares to a peak of £1060. Taking advantage of this bull market, unscrupulous promoters gathered capital for various wildcat schemes; a thousand gullible fools even subscribed to "a company for carrying on an undertaking, but nobody to know what it is." As is usual, the bubble suddenly burst; millions in paper profits were wiped out overnight; sound companies were dragged down with shaky ones; and thousands were ruined. The public suspected graft in high places and clamored for victims. The Chancellor of the Exchequer, who had made some £800,000 by his illegal manipulation, was expelled by the House of Commons; another high official committed suicide; the royal mistresses were involved. Altogether, it was a sorry scandal.

As a result, Sir Robert Walpole was advanced toward a position of prominence, from a junior capacity in the ministry. This shrewd, if not brilliant, Norfolk squire, with his marked financial ability, had advised against the South Sea act; his hands had remained clean while his colleagues' were besmirched; and he did an able job of straightening out the tangle afterward. Even Lord Stanhope, the captor of Minorca, the dominant man in George's first ministry, who had handled foreign affairs with remarkable ability, was acquitted in the Commons by only three votes, though his part in the "Bubble" was apparently innocent. Lord Townshend, nominally the senior member of the cabinet, continued in office; but he had been overshadowed by Stanhope, and now was to be overshadowed by his brother-in-law, Sir Robert Walpole, until eventually, in annoyance, he retired to his estate for his pioneer achievements in agriculture (see page 331).

Walpole and Responsible Government

Walpole was to be hailed in later years as England's first prime minister. This in effect he was from 1721 to 1742, although he never had the title and always denied that he was any such thing, for the phrase had in those days an unpleasant significance, suggesting a royal favorite. An odd circumstance, arising from the refusal of the German king to learn English, gave Walpole the opportunity to usher in a

Walpole (left) talking with Speaker Onslow in the House of Commons, by William Hogarth.

most important constitutional development. George, with his heart in Hanover, where his word was law, did not bother to attend cabinet meetings—the first monarch to neglect this duty. William had dominated his cabinet, and Anne had at least gone to the meetings. George refused to sit through long conferences of which he could understand nothing. This left the power and the responsibilities in the hands of ministers, though not concentrated at first in those of a single minister. Walpole had the ability and personality to assume the dual role of control over the cabinet and leadership of the majority in the House of Commons. He thus combined the role of a party leader with that of chief agent for the king, with whom he could communicate in bad Latin. As this worked out, the cabinet ministers, who carried on the government in the king's name, remained in power only as long as they could command support in the House of Commons. This brought about a combination of the executive and legislative; for the executive power came to be directly dependent upon the elected legislature, which, in theory at least, represented the will of the people. Thus arose "responsible government," by which Parliament finally gained the machinery for exercising the control it had won in 1688.

Shortly after this time, a French political philosopher, Montesquieu, ascribed the secret of the success of the English government to its distinct separation of the executive power as represented by the king and the legislative as represented by Parliament. The United States adopted this in her Constitution in 1787 with a sharp separation of function between President and Congress, to which the colonists were accustomed in the disputes between governors and assemblies. But the English government, far from separating those powers, was uniting them more and more in the person of the prime minister through this system of responsible government.

In 1707 England had passed another constitutional landmark, practically unnoticed at the time, but important in retrospect. It will be recalled that before it could become an act, a bill which had passed Commons and Lords must receive the royal assent, as given in the words "Le roy (la reine) le veult." It was within the power of the ruler to withhold assent, with the words "Le roy s'avisera" (The king will consider the matter). That was equivalent to a veto. William III had withheld his assent from four bills, and the last instance of a "royal veto" occurred when Anne refused assent to a Scottish militia bill. Thereafter, every bill which has passed the two houses of Parliament has received the royal assent as a matter of course, though the form of making an act the express will of the ruler is still preserved. It might be still possible for the crown to exercise the veto power, but the fact that it fell into abeyance gave added importance

to the legislative branch of the government in its extension of power into the executive field.

Gradually, during the eighteenth century, Parliament continued to work out the system of making the cabinet responsible to the majority in the Commons. As it finally developed, there were three courses which a cabinet might take in case of an adverse vote there. It might resign at once, whereupon the king would ask the opposition leader to form a new cabinet. It might call for an "appeal to the country," that is, a general election for an entire new House of Commons. Finally, it might disregard a few adverse votes in hope of recovering its majority; but if the Commons voted a "lack of confidence" in the ministers, resignation was necessary. The possibility of an "appeal to the country" at any time theoretically gave the electorate a strong influence on the affairs of government; but that was used sparingly, and the average term of a cabinet during the first two centuries of responsible government was almost identical with the arbitrary four-year term of an administration in the United States. From the period of George I the king tended to become more and more a figurehead, exercising a varying degree of *influence* but little real *power*. Practically the only direct political function left to the crown was the choice of which leader of the opposition to call in as prime minister when a cabinet fell; theoretically, it might be said, of course, that extensive powers and prerogatives still remained to it.

It is characteristically English that this cabinet, which for two centuries has been the mainspring of the government, does not exist in the eyes of the law. The legal authority of its members rests partly on their particular official positions and partly on the fact that they all belong to the Privy Council and can transact business in its name. The Privy Council had been important for centuries, particularly under the Tudors. It had become too large and unwieldy for effective work by the time of William III, who gathered about him some of its most influential members as a Cabinet Council, so called because it met in his cabinet. As a body the members discussed general matters of policy; as individuals most of them were administrative heads of particular departments, transacting business in the king's name. During most of the eighteenth century the cabinet usually consisted of eleven members. The prime minister was never officially known as such, but usually held the office of First Lord of the Treasury. The others were generally the Lord Chancellor, Lord Privy Seal, Lord President of the Council, two secretaries of state with general administrative authority (particularly in foreign affairs), Chancellor of the Exchequer (for finance), First Lord of the Admiralty, Paymaster-General of the Forces, Lord Lieutenant of Ireland, and Secretary for Scotland. Later there were special secretaries for "home affairs," colonies, war, and India. Other officers were added from time to time, until the cabinet grew so large that in a crisis a small inner group assumed special authority. The meetings of the cabinet have long been held at No. 10 Downing Street, the prime minister's residence, close to Whitehall.

There was nothing unique about the cabinet simply as a group of ministers. Every ruler, even the most absolute, had to have certain men upon whom he could depend for the running of the various branches of the government. The Curia Regis of Henry I had been such a group, and the Cabal of Charles II was a more recent example. Several distinctive features, however, gradually developed after Walpole's leadership of the cabinet began in 1721. First, there was the authority of the prime minister, ordinarily the definite leader of the cabinet. He selected the members, and the administration was known by his name. At times, however, he might be merely a figurehead, overshadowed by abler colleagues. Secondly, the cabinet was a

unit: its members assumed collective responsibility for each others' actions, and resigned in a body in case of defeat, instead of being nibbled away one by one like Godolphin's cabinet. Thirdly, from this it followed that the members of the cabinet generally all belong to the same party; the experiments of William and Anne with mixed cabinets had not been successful. During the long period of Whig domination, from 1714 to 1760, rivalry among different groups in the Whig party overshadowed opposition from the Tories. Fourthly, unlike the practice in the United States, the cabinet members all belonged to Parliament and sat in either Lords or Commons. A practice grew up by which each of the various departments was represented in each house; if the cabinet minister was a peer, his undersecretary would serve as departmental spokesman in the Commons, and vice versa. The ministers occupied the "Treasury bench," where they sat facing the "Opposition bench."

Since the term of the cabinet rested on the majority in the House of Commons, the prime minister and his colleagues had the problem of keeping the majority in line. Walpole demonstrated to his successors the methods that would maintain such a mastery of the House of Commons. That was a far simpler matter in his time than it is today, when Commons depends upon the approval of a democratic electorate numbering millions of men and women. In that period the electoral system was so arranged that scarcely one man in ten of legal age, so it has been estimated, could take part in choosing members of Parliament; and only in a few unusually democratic constituences were the members really chosen by popular election. A handful of peers, usually from among those seventy-odd dominant Whig families of landowners, were very often able to control this majority in the House of Commons. The head of the family in such cases often sat in the House of Lords, providing seats in the Commons for

"The Cockpit," one of Hogarth's satirical pictures of English society.

his sons and for friends who were fairly sure to vote as he wished. This situation naturally simplified the control of Parliament. Walpole had only to placate a sufficient number of those who controlled the seats, and he was then free to do as he pleased. He is credited with the cynical remark, as he once looked over the Commons, "All these have their price." Anything but an idealist or a reformer, he knew how to secure their election and their votes. An analysis of the "unreformed Parliament" as it existed between the Restoration and the Reform Act of 1832 (see page 405) shows how such a small group of landowners could control the government. The House of Commons, so imposing in its entirety, loses some of its dignity when the methods by which it could be elected and managed come to light.

The size of the Commons remained stationary at 560 members from the Scottish union in 1707 until 1801, when 100 Irish members were added. Of that total, 45 were from Scotland, 24 from Wales, and the remaining 491 from England proper. The heavy English representation consisted of 82 from the counties and 409 from the boroughs, including the two universities. Normally each county and borough sent two members.

The chief fault in the system lay in the representation of a large number of "rotten" boroughs, containing few inhabitants or, in one case, none at all. The fact that a Plantagenet, Lancastrian, Yorkist, or Tudor had once given them the right to representation continued them in that right even though they slumbered, almost deserted, in memories of a more important past. Most common in this class were the decayed seaports along the southern coast. Remote Cornwall, a stronghold of royal influence jutting into the western sea, was most notoriously over-represented with 44 members in Commons, only one less than all Scotland. One small Cornish district only twenty-eight miles long and twelve wide, with some 350 voters among its 15,000 inhabitants, returned 18 men to Parliament—more than Middlesex, Westminster, Southwark, and the other populous constituencies which made up London!

Even in these boroughs the franchise was restricted in strange and devious ways, unlike the counties, where every "forty-shilling freeholder" was entitled to a vote. The 203 English boroughs fell into four general groups, about equally numerous: scot and lot, burgage, corporation, and freeman. The scot and lot, or "pot-walloper," franchise was the nearest approach to a uniform, democratic system; for every householder who had resided in the borough for six months and was not a pauper was generally entitled to a vote. In the burgage boroughs the vote went to the owners of the houses, or sites of houses, of original voting householders. The franchise in the corporation boroughs was limited to the members of the municipal government. In the final category it was restricted to a special group known as "freemen," often members of the trade guilds.

The vote in many of these boroughs could easily be manipulated in return for cash or other valuable considerations. It was no longer the practice in England that the member must be a resident of the constituency which he represented, as is the custom in the United States; consequently anyone with sufficient money or family connection might acquire a seat in the Lower House. Some came so completely under the control of an individual that they were known as "pocket" or "nomination" boroughs. The "scot and lot" boroughs, with their wide franchise, were the most difficult to manipulate, though in little ones a majority of the votes might be purchased at relatively small expense. In those days before secret voting, the candidate who paid for votes at least knew he was getting his money's worth. In the burgage boroughs it was comparatively simple to buy up the real estate which carried the right to vote. Out of the hundred burgages in one borough, a certain peer owned ninety-nine, including one which was deep under water. Ramshackle sheds and pigsties might carry the right to vote if they stood on the proper site. Perhaps the most notorious of the rotten boroughs was Old Sarum, the "hole in the wall," on the site of the original city of Salisbury. Every one of its inhabitants had moved away, and there was not a single permanent building on the forty acres of plowed land. Yet those acres continued to be represented in Parliament, the owner sending whomsoever he pleased and erecting a tent on the ground for the "election" formalities. The small number of voters made corporation boroughs easy to manage. Some of the more honest corporations contented themselves with extorting from the candidates promises of presents to the town, such as a hall, bridges, or the deepening of a river or harbor. The corporation system was sometimes perverted by the intrusion of outsiders; thus the corporation often became simply a machine for choosing members of Parliament, to the complete neglect of the municipal government. In some of the "freeman" boroughs there were too many freemen and in others not enough. Some boroughs created a swarm of "honorary freemen," solely for election purposes. Dunwich, which was being eaten away by the North Sea, supplemented its forty-five regular freemen with five hundred outsiders. Some boroughs granted the vote to anyone who had ever been a freeman there, though he might have been absent for years. Candidates would sometimes canvass the London alehouses to gather ex-freemen from the borough in question and transport them back to vote. On the other hand, some boroughs went to the opposite extreme, and their freemen were an extremely exclusive group. In the little decayed port

"The Poll," one of Hogarth's pictures of 18th-century election methods.

of Rye the election to the House of Commons was at one time in the hands of six men! With the right to vote in such places often handed down to the eldest son or son-in-law, a freeman's only daughter needed no other dowry; her husband might be paid enough in one election to support him until the next.

This system produced an influential group, known as borough patrons and boroughmongers. By making judicious expenditures, they could become reasonably sure of controlling the vote. The Duke of Newcastle was one of the most powerful. Another, Sir James Lowther, for instance, generally had a well-disciplined squad of eight or nine nominees in the Commons, all of whom were supposed to vote as he dictated or else resign.

Patronage was what made boroughmongering profitable and linked it up with the question of the control of Parliament. The control of appointments to government position, formerly—and still nominally—a function of the crown, passed to the prime minister. His most effective means to keep his majority secure was the bestowing of the best offices upon those who controlled the votes. A regular spoils system resulted in which everyone from earls, admirals, and archbishops down to the meanest subordinates in the customs, excise, and dockyard services received appointments in return for in expectation of political support.

The Commons might also be manipulated through the House of Lords. The surest way to a peerage was to control votes in the House of Commons. Admirals and generals might occasionally find their way into the House of Lords, but at least two thirds of the peerages were granted to borough patrons like Lowther, who became Lord Lonsdale in return for the votes of his squad. Even when such a man reached the peerage, he might still have dangled before him the prospect of promotion from baron to viscount or from viscount to earl.

The borough patron not only could gratify his social ambitions with a peerage but could also make financial profit out of boroughmongering. He might secure fat army or navy contracts, or he might gain the privilege of lending the government money at a high rate of interest. Best of all were the official appointments, where drawing a salary was frequently the only work involved. Some, like the post of Master of the King's Buckhounds, involved absolutely no work. More frequent was the practice of accepting a post and then appointing a deputy to do all the work for a small fraction of the salary. One George Selwyn, who controlled two or three votes in the Commons, was "at one and the same time, Surveyor-General of Crown Lands, which he never surveyed; Registrar of Chancery at Barbados, which he never visited; and Surveyor of Meltings and Clerk of the Irons at the Mint, where he showed himself once a week, in order to eat a dinner which he ordered but for which the nation paid." Such appointments were sought not only for oneself but also for sons and relatives and for the families of those whose votes were necessary in the boroughs. If a son was unable to earn a normal living, or if poor relatives clamored for aid, they might be supported at the expense of the government. Members of Parliament spent much of their time bullying or begging for such positions, so that a "patronage secretary" was created to save the time of the department heads. The qualifications of the candidates for office mattered little; newly appointed clerks and copyists sometimes had to be granted leave of absence so that they might learn to write. Outworn offices, no longer necessary, were perpetuated simply to provide more posts.

Walpole's ministry of twenty-one years reflected his motto "Let sleeping dogs lie." Unlike the Tories at the end of Anne's reign, the Whigs left undisturbed the Anglican churchmen, Tory and reactionary though most of them were, while the squires, also with Tory traditions, were allowed to manage the local government as justices of the peace without interference. Because of this tolerance toward potentially dissatisfied elements, and because of shrewd methods in bribery and corruption, the Whigs, really only a minority, went their way virtually unchallenged. Walpole encountered only three serious crises: in 1727 the accession of a new and already hostile king, in 1733 the rejection of his own unpopular excise bill, and in 1739 the declaration, against his will, of war on Spain.

Already a man in his thirties when his father became king, the second George (1727-1760) was another dull monarch whose mind seemed incapable of rising above petty details. He lacked either the intelligence or the ambition to play any more active a role than his father. There was danger, however, that his accession might be the end of Walpole, simply because he had been the minister of the first George, with whom the second had quarreled most of his life. Luckily the high character and intelligence of the latter's German wife, Caroline, commanded her husband's respect if not his fidelity. Her appreciation of Walpole's ability kept him in office.

Walpole, termed "the first great commercial minister since the days of Thomas Cromwell," was chiefly interested in economic matters. He had sought, with only partial success, to lower the interest rate which the government was paying on the national debt, and to use the money thus saved to reduce the principal of the debt itself. He had also done much to straighten out the financial confusion after the South Sea Bubble. In commercial policy his views were advanced; some of his liberal measures were along the same lines which England was to follow a century later. He announced that his policy was "to make the exportation of our own manufactures and the importation of the commodities used in the manufacturing of them as practicable and as easy as may be." Accordingly, he proposed the removal of export duties on more than a hundred articles of British manufacture and on nearly forty raw materials. Some colonial restrictions were specifically relaxed, and in other matters he winked at colonial violations of the existing regulations (see page 320). He made a substantial cut in the rate of the land tax, which fell most heavily upon the country gentry and nobility.

Another major item of governmental income, customs duties, was collected not only upon all articles imported for consumption in Great Britain but also upon the large quantities which were re-exported to foreign nations. In the latter case the government gave a drawback, or refund, of the duties paid. In this cumbersome refunding Walpole's logical mind saw wasted effort and money and an additional opportunity for graft. He proposed to have duties collected only on goods which were to remain for internal consumption. This would greatly facilitate the re-export trade and incidentally reduce the alarming prevalence of smuggling. Such a step, he said, would "make London a free port and by consequence the market of the world." As a start, he proposed in 1733 to apply it to tobacco and wine. Unfortunately, he called the measure an "excise" bill, which to the popular mind had an ugly sound, suggesting new internal taxes. Walpole's enemies implied that excise officers would soon be snooping into homes and that bread and other necessities of life might be taxed. The popular clamor was so great that Walpole, rather than face an adverse vote in Parliament, withdrew the bill, which might have been passed by any other name.

This was one rare instance in eighteenth-century England when public opinion affected governmental action. Another occurred six years later, in 1739, when Wal-

pole's era of peace came to an end, much against his will. The years since Utrecht had not seen England engaged in a major war. France, too, wanted peace, so the two traditional rivals for a while had worked together to keep Europe quiet. It was a busy era, however, for the diplomats, who created a constant succession of leagues and alliances; and even the royal navy saw some service. Year after year a fleet sailed into the Baltic, where Sweden and Russia were fighting, partly to ensure the safety of England's supply of masts and naval stores. In the Mediterranean Spanish ambitions actually led to a desultory war during which the British destroyed a Spanish fleet. Later, however, when many of the Continental powers engaged in a "War of the Polish Succession," Walpole kept aloof and could proudly say to Queen Caroline, "Madam, there are fifty thousand men slain this year in Europe and not one Englishman." But England, bored with smug prosperity, was spoiling for a fight. The apparently decadent Spanish colonial empire looked like easy loot, and war was started on a very flimsy pretext (see page 306). Walpole worked hard for peace, but his hands were forced by the war party.

The declaration of war was a bitter pill for him. Today a prime minister in such a situation would at once go out of office with his cabinet. There were no precedents at that time for such circumstances. Walpole did twice offer his resignation, but George refused. So for another three years Walpole remained until, conducting a war of which he heartily disapproved, his control of the House of Commons gradually melted away. Finally, two days after receiving a peerage, he retired from office with his cabinet and took his seat in the House of Lords as Earl of Orford.

His great ministry of twenty-one years, however, had laid secure foundations for the new system of responsible government, which enabled Parliament to utilize the supremacy it had achieved in 1688.

The Duel for Empire

A restless England ended Walpole's long peace in 1739, and until 1815 would be engaged in war two-thirds of the time, with France the principal enemy. The Second Hundred Years' War (see page 277), revived in full force, became essentially a "duel for empire." England had taken her first colonial loot at Utrecht in 1713; exactly fifty years later the French were to be stripped of most of their choicest overseas possessions. Largely responsible for this was 1759, the *annus mirabilis*—the wonderful year that simply "rained victories," with the brilliant seizure of Quebec, with successes in India, and with two French fleets crushed by the royal navy. British world power had come far since England under William III had first challenged the might of Louis XIV. But even that was not to end the rivalry.

At the outset of the Second Hundred Years' War in 1689, France had an overseas empire which looked very impressive on the surface. It occupied more space on the map than the British.

In North America the territory claimed by France almost completely hemmed in the English colonies in their narrow strip between the mountains and the sea. The center of New France was the St. Lawrence valley, with the capital at Quebec and Montreal an important post farther up the river. French power was also well entrenched in Acadia, the present Nova Scotia. The explorations of various intrepid Frenchmen had given France title to the region of the Great Lakes and to the valley of the Mississippi and its tributaries. New Orleans, to be established in 1718, would command the outlet to that vast interior region. The ownership of Newfoundland, close to the valuable fishing banks, and the Hudson Bay region, with its fur trade, was disputed between the English and the French.

In the West Indies, France held a string of sugar islands of which the richest was Haiti. Except for Guadeloupe and Martinique, they were to drop off, bead by bead, under British attacks.

Out in the East, France had arrived much later than her rival; but after Colbert revived the French East India Company in 1664, it made aggressive advances. The principal seat of French power was Pondicherry, some seventy miles down the coast from Madras, the chief English post. Chandernagor was established in the northeast, as a counterweight to the English station at Calcutta near by. The French also had a slave-trading post on the Guinea coast of Africa.

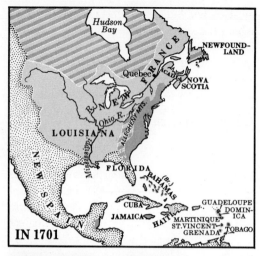

THE STRUGGLE FOR NORTH AMERICA, 1701-1783

British holdings and claims   French holdings and claims   Spanish holdings and claims   Bands indicate conflicting claims

But, despite its impressive extent, there were grave elements of weakness in the French colonial empire. In North America the long record of English colonies failed to produce such a galaxy of spectacular men as those French explorers whose names still live: Champlain with a lake, Cadillac with an automobile, Père Marquette with a railroad, and Joliet with a prison. Nor did any English governor attain the stature of Count Frontenac, whom Louis XIV had

sent to America to get him away from the ladies at Versailles. Nevertheless, while the English colonies were rapidly being filled with thousands of substantial middle-class settlers who multiplied so rapidly that their numbers doubled every twenty years, few Frenchmen were willing to migrate to an overseas colony of settlement. France had established Quebec a year after the English founded Jamestown. Although several times larger, France, unlike England, had to make continual official efforts to attract or force settlers to America. Regiments of regulars were disbanded in New France, and land was given to officers and men; cargoes of prostitutes and kidnaped peasants were shipped to the St. Lawrence; bounties were offered for babies. Yet the population remained small, with only about fifteen thousand in Canada in 1689, and even after almost a century and a half of effort, only some fifty-four thousand by 1750. At both those periods there were some twenty English settlers in America for every Frenchman. Even peasants who came over were reluctant to settle down as underdogs in the transplanted manorial system, and sometimes ran off into the woods, where they often married Indian wives and became *coureurs de bois,* or forest rangers, trapping for furs and forming an unstable element in the population. No small part of England's colonial population came from her religious malcontents; but France, to keep her colonies safely Roman Catholic, finally forbade her Protestant Huguenots to migrate to them. Consequently that substantial, hard-working commercial class, which might have built up solid colonial prosperity, found its way to the English colonies instead, settling in such places as New Rochelle, near New York.

Another source of French weakness was that despite Colbert's grand visions of coordinating industry, commerce, navy and colonies into a profitable unity (see page 264), most French colonial ventures did not pay. France formed commercial companies, like the English and the Dutch, but whereas Dutch East India stock yielded average dividends of 18 per cent, and English East India stock half that amount, French colonial stock paid no dividends. Since none would invest unless coerced, the government finally had to take over the ventures.

Some fundamental strategic considerations in the home countries also help to show the causes of French colonial weakness. Whereas England could concentrate most of her military spending upon a navy which not only would serve as an adequate defense at home but also would be useful as an instrument of aggression on the seas and overseas, the Continental nations had land frontiers to defend. Even Holland, primarily interested in maritime activity, was exhausted by trying to stem French aggression on land (see page 264). Despite Colbert's pleadings, Louis XIV much preferred to spend his energy banging away at the frontiers, and, throughout the Second Hundred Years' War, Frenchmen, if they could be lured into a land fight, tended to neglect naval and colonial warfare. England, by means of generous grants of gold, "hired" Austrians, Prussians, and whoever else would take the money, to keep the French busy on land. Then the royal navy would scour the seas, pick off neglected French colonies, and, without suffering many serious casualties, make more than enough from increased commerce to offset the grants to the allies who suffered the heavy battles losses. This system caused the Anglo-French duel for colonial empire to become entangled with the Austro-Prussian duel for control of European territory.

Static Fighting Methods

In these days of constant innovation in instruments and methods of warfare, it is hard to realize the unchanging conditions of eighteenth-century fighting. A description of the British ships, regiments, and tactics of 1740 serves almost as well for sixty years later. A warship eighty years old, used in 1782, was little different from the newer ships, and Marlborough's soldiers would have found few changes a century later. War was a well-regulated game in which everyone knew the common rules until Napoleon on land and Nelson at sea by their originality won surprising victories at the end of the century. But they used the same old instruments of war.

England's chief pride and interest, the royal navy, probably enjoyed a longer record of power and success than any other fighting organization in history except the Roman army. It then consisted of three or four hundred vessels, about a hundred of which were ships-of-the-line. Counterparts of later battleships, they were used in squadrons or fleets to fight the major battles. Of these, most common was the "seventy-four," so called from the number of her guns. A few larger three-decked ships of the line served as flagships, but the two-decked seventy-four was the largest that would sail well and fight well under most conditions. Her hull ranged some two hundred feet from the figurehead under the great bowsprit to the stern. Broad in proportion to her length, her beams measured more than fifty feet between the bulging sides. This breadth robbed her of the speed of the little frigates, but it gave her strength to withstand terrific buffeting in battle. Much was crowded between the decks of that stout hull. The fighting decks were flanked with long rows of muzzle-loading guns on wooden trucks. In those cramped quarters some six hundred men lived at sea for months and sometimes years.

Throughout this period the heads of the royal navy worried about its supply of wood for building such ships. The "seventy-four" required for the hull some two thousand oak trees, averaging a hundred years old, and England was cutting down her oaks much faster than she was replacing them. England had to send to the Baltic for the planking of the bulging yellow sides. From there also came the masts of middling size —in all Britain there were no trees suitable for masts. The little spars had generally grown on some Norwegian mountainside; but for the great lower masts, anywhere from two feet to forty inches in diameter, the royal navy depended upon the colonial pines in New Hampshire and Maine. More than once the navy was to be handicapped when its supply of masts or oak was curtailed.

Next in importance came the frigates, corresponding to cruisers. Lighter and faster than the heavy ships of the line, they had one fighting deck with some twenty-eight to thirty-eight guns. They served as the "eyes of the fleet" in major operations, and were used also for patrolling; for the protection, regulation, or destroying of commerce; and for the bearing of dispatches. Various minor types of warships ranged from sloops and gun brigs down to fire ships.

The royal navy generally had excellent officers. A naval commission was one of the most attractive goals for younger sons of good family. Becoming midshipmen at twelve or thirteen, their promotion was fairly rapid at the start, and one was frequently a frigate captain in the twenties; but then there was a long wait before seniority might bring an admiral's flag. Those naval officers were inclined to be arrogant, but they usually had ability as well. In those days of slow communication, the commander in distant waters often had to act on his own judgment in weighty matters, serving as diplomat as well as admiral.

There was a vast gulf between quarter-deck and forecastle. The crew were cramped in stuffy quarters, engaged in laborious and dangerous duties for little pay, and were too often at the mercy of a martinet who could have them lashed for minor infractions of discipline. It is small wonder that the navy did not attract volunteers. To man the fleets, Parliament time and again authorized impressment, which was virtual kidnaping. Sailors in the merchant marine, returning from a long voyage, would often find themselves taken off for naval service before they reached land. The men of the coast towns were always on guard against press gangs which made sailors, willy-nilly, out of anyone upon whom they could lay their hands. Once caught in this way, the poor devils often had to remain in naval service until death or disability released them. Yet mutinies were scarce, and these reluctant conscripts generally made excellent seamen.

The naval tactics of the period were rigidly standardized. The opposing squadrons or fleets, ranging ordinarily from eight to thirty ships of the line, fell in behind one another in a long line of battle and lay alongside the enemy line, each ship picking out a single adversary. Then they would blast away at close range until something gave way. So conventional was the plan of battle that in one encounter, where the British outnumbered the foe, the extra ships lay at a distance for want of anything better to do. The frigates frequently engaged in single combat, in which the principal trick was to get the "weather gauge," where one could maneuver with the wind at one's back.

While the British navy was the best in the world, the same cannot be said for the British army at this time. The redcoats were brave, but the French generally outclassed them in the size of their military establishment and in their natural genius for leadership. England was inclined to neglect the army, partly from the widespread opposition to a standing army, partly from the feeling that its naval defense was adequate (see page 257). While the French army was usually kept at one hundred thousand men at least, the English sometimes dropped as low as fifteen thousand, and had to be expanded with more speed than efficiency in time of war.

As in the navy, the gap was wide between officers and men. All army commissions up to colonelcies had to be purchased, and this operated as a social restriction. The life of the army officer in time of peace was less exacting than in the navy. The enlisted men, often from the dregs of society, were generally lured into service by recruiting officers who slipped the "king's shilling" into the hand of the prospect while he was too drunk to realize its significance. On occasion, vagabonds were drafted, and more than once the jails were emptied to swell the ranks. The tactics of the day called for "well-drilled marionettes," and it took about two years of hard discipline to whip a recruit into shape. Man for man, the redcoats were as good as any soldiers in Europe, but too often they were "lions led by asses"; for in battles like Bunker Hill the men executed, with utmost bravery, stupid orders which should never have been given.

The nature of the battle tactics made well-disciplined troops an absolute necessity for effective work. The infantry customarily advanced in two long, thin lines, in parade-ground formation, without firing a shot until within fifty or a hundred yards of the enemy. Then the lines would halt, deliver a series of crushing volleys, and finally, if the enemy still stood fast, charge with the bayonet. Against cavalry charges the infantry formed a square so that there would be no flanks to turn. Such formations, suicidal later, were thoroughly effective in the era of the "Brown Bess" musket. It was smooth-bored, loaded at the muzzle, and discharged by a "flintlock" outside the gun. It had to be reloaded after each shot and could not be fired more than three or four times a minute. It was likely to misfire, especially in the rain, and was not effective anyway at more than a hundred yards. To save ammunition soldiers were ordered not to fire "until you see the whites of their eyes." The artillery or cannon were of the same crude, smooth-bore, muzzle-loading type. The gunners simply aimed in a general direction and trusted to luck. Cavalry, much less important than infantry, was used for scouting and to give a heavy shock in battle at the critical moment.

Warfare in this century probably disturbed the general population less than at other times. The severely disciplined troops did not terrorize the non-combatants as in earlier wars. They were skilled professionals, usually lacking in religious or nationalistic zeal. The idea of universal military service did not gain headway until the French

Revolution. The wars, moreover, were generally of a limited nature, designed to gain some special border or colonial objective rather than to crush the enemy completely.

War of Jenkins's Ear

England used a very trivial excuse for ending this quarter century of peace. At Utrecht in 1713, she had at last made a real breach in the rigidly guarded trade of Spain's vast American colonial empire, upon which she had been casting greedy eyes since Elizabethan days (see pages 201, 249). By the "Asiento," England was given the monopoly of supplying slaves to Spanish America and was also permitted to send one ship a year to trade at Porto Bello, on the Isthmus of Panama. Keeping within the letter of the law, the English had anchored a ship off that port and had replenished her apparently inexhaustible hold from the cargoes of other ships, thus maintaining almost continuous trade. Some Englishmen took further advantage of the situation for illegal trade and naturally ran afoul of the Spanish coast guards. Finally one Captain Jenkins began to tell a wild tale in the taverns of England. He exhibited a withered ear, which be asserted had been cut off by the Spanish coast guards. Summoned before Parliament, he was asked what he had then done. He replied, "I commended my soul to God and my cause to my country."

In spite of Walpole, that withered ear and popular restlessness led to a declaration of war against Spain in 1739 (see page 300). London celebrated with wild enthusiasm. "They now ring the bells," remarked Walpole; "they will soon wring their hands." The navy performed better than the long-disused army. Admiral Vernon immediately seized Porto Bello. Admiral Anson followed Drake's track to the west coast of South America, picked off the Philippine galleon, and circumnavigated the world. In a joint naval and military attack on Cartagena, the key port of the Spanish Main, the bewildered general, taunted by the contemptuous admiral, missed his chance to rush the city. The yellow fever was more deadly than the Spaniards. For weeks the sharks in Cartagena Bay feasted on the corpses of redcoats thrown by thousands from the pestilence-ridden transports. The armament was then turned against Cuba, but felt too weak even to attack. Barely a tenth of the men who had set out to conquer the Spanish Main returned home. By 1742 the "War of Jenkins's Ear" had died of inertia, becoming involved in a more general European conflict.

War of the Austrian Succession

In the meantime, two German rulers, approaching death, were full of apprehension about what might happen under their heirs. The Hapsburg emperor, Charles VI, having no son, knew there was no possibility of his daughter, Maria Theresa, succeeding to the shadowy title of "Holy Roman Emperor." His worry was that in view of the old German prejudice, she might as a woman be kept from inheriting the family holdings in Austria, Bohemia, and elsewhere. Hoping to forestall their partition among greedy neighbors, he secured by persuasion and concessions the agreement of the other European states to a "Pragmatic Sanction," recognizing her as his rightful heir. Frederick William I of Prussia was otherwise troubled. A thoroughgoing militarist, he had devoted his life to building up a powerful army, gathering tall soldiers from wherever he could and drilling them into a perfect machine. It was irony that his reign began in 1713, when one major war ended, and closed in 1740, when another started. His son Frederick had literary inclinations and loved to play the flute. Little did old Frederick William realize that such a son would become one of the foremost soldiers of history.

The deaths of these two rulers in 1740 was the signal for a struggle between

Hapsburg and Hohenzollern for first place in Germany, a rivalry which was not finally settled until 1866. Young Frederick II (later called "the Great"), disregarding the Pragmatic Sanction, threw his father's excellent army into the rich Hapsburg province of Silesia. This private German quarrel spread into the war of the Austrian Succession and was quickly linked up with the Anglo-French colonial rivalry. France, true to her old anti-Hapsburg policy, allied herself with Prussia, Bavaria, and Saxony, hoping to cut Germany into several weak states which would come under French influence. England, with Hanover and Holland, backed Austria, taking full credit for supporting the sanctity of the Pragmatic Sanction.

The hostilities lasted from 1740 to 1748. England and France at once sent armies to support their respective allies and were actually battling each other long before their formal declaration of war in 1744. The English campaigns on the Continent were not decisive. In 1743, George II was in command, the last time an English king led an army into battle. He campaigned aimlessly until the French caught his starving army in a trap at Dettingen, near Frankfurt. His horse, startled by the musketry, bolted far to the rear with the mortified king, who returned and finished the fight on foot. He won an undeserved victory, for the French plans went awry. The command soon went to his young brother, the Duke of Cumberland, who was outclassed by the able French commander Marshal Saxe, one of the reputed three hundred children of Augustus the Strong, ruler of Saxony and Poland. For five years the two armies fought in the familiar Low Countries. The high point came in 1745 at Fontenoy, on the Scheldt. Cumberland attacked a position strongly fortified by Saxe, a classic example of the formal tactics of the era. The British infantry made one of the most remarkable attacks in its history. Forming under heavy artillery fire, the thin red British line advanced slowly in perfect order for a half mile, constantly closing up the gaps torn in the ranks and not firing a shot until within fifty yards of the enemy. A French commander, according to legend, stepped out in front of his line, bowed low, and requested the English gentlemen to fire first; an English officer responded by proposing a toast to the gallant foe. Then the British fired, and several crack regiments of the French army simply melted away under their crushing volleys. But the attack was in vain and the British had to retire, for their allies had not cleared away their sections of the enemy. It was one of the bloodiest battles of the century, the British losing nearly six thousand of their fifteen thousand infantry in killed and wounded, while the French lost even more. Thereafter, Saxe generally had the upper hand and gradually gained control of the Austrian Netherlands (Belgium). At least, the French were being kept busy at home.

In the summer of 1745 England was suddenly faced with a serious domestic menace. Less than three months after Fontenoy, the "Young Pretender," grandson of James II and son of the "Old Pretender," who had invaded England in 1715, landed in Scotland with only seven companions. The Highlands rose to support him as they had his father, thirty years before. Edinburgh was occupied, the redcoats in Scotland were roundly whipped, and a small, motley Jacobite army invaded England. The people were apathetic, and the Pretender's forces penetrated as far as Derby, less than eighty miles from London, which was in panic. A hurried concentration of the scattered troops in England, however, caused the Scottish invaders to retire to their own land. The Duke of Cumberland and some of his regiments, recalled from the Continent, pursued the Scots and finally crushed them the following spring at Culloden in the Highlands. Cumberland won the name of "Butcher" from the ruthless punishment of the vanquished. The popular "Bonnie

The attack on Louisburg in 1745 by the New England troops under Pepperell, shown landing in fishing boats under the protection of British warships.

Prince Charlie" was spirited out of the country and off for France by loyal Highlanders. After that venture he led an aimless, drunken life in Europe for more than forty years. The death of his younger brother, the "Cardinal York," in 1807 ended the direct Stuart line.

After the "Forty-five" the Highlands were definitely opened to civilization. England wisely capitalized on the martial ardor of the clansmen by enlisting them in her service. Highland regiments were formed in the British army—the "Black Watch" and many others. Still wearing their distinctive kilts and tartans, they did remarkable work in America, in India, and wherever else the empire called them to service.

As for the War of the Austrian Succession, as soon as England and France went formally to war in 1744, it spread far afield. The linking of the Austro-Prussian and the Anglo-French rivalries was summed up in

an epigram: "Because a monarch robbed a neighbor he had promised to defend, red men scalped each other by the Great Lakes of America, while black men fought on the coast of Coromandel."

In America, the rivals had already clashed in "King William's War" and "Queen Anne's War," as the Americans called the contests with Louis XIV. The terror spread by Frontenac's policy (see page 279) of French and Indian raids along the northern English frontiers of settlement continued as long as France held Canada. The New England colonists had unsuccessfully attempted to take Quebec, the capital of New France in 1690, and twenty years later a British expedition there was wrecked. The British did capture Acadia, which as "Nova Scotia" was ceded to them at Utrecht. On their adjacent Cape Breton Island, the French erected at great cost a powerful fortress at Louisburg, where they threatened the cod fisheries, vital to New England's economic existence. In 1745, a force of New Englanders under Sir William Pepperell aided by a naval squadron captured it after a short siege. This colonial victory, at a time when the regulars were meeting defeat in France and Scotland, was very impressive. The Yankees then urged the conquest of Canada, but England had other uses for her ships and soldiers.

In India, until this time European contact had been limited chiefly to a few trading posts along the coast (see page 227). Shortly after the Portuguese arrived, most of India had come under the sway of Muslim invaders, who ruled the land from Delhi. For six generations these Mogul emperors remained strong, and the Europeans stayed only at their sufferance.

The charter of the East India Company had granted political and military powers, but these had been restricted to the immediate settlements at Madras, Bombay, and Calcutta, with a few lesser posts. The Company was still essentially a trading corporation, sending to England the cotton cloth of India, together with tea, silks, and other wares brought over from China. There was only a handful of Englishmen in those posts. Mortality was heavy in that climate. But many of these who survived returned to England where they were known as wealthy "nabobs." Two governors of Madras about 1700 left a lasting influence from their wealth. Elihu Yale contributed part of his gains for the first building for a little New England institution founded "to educate ministers in our own way"; and Thomas Pitt, on an annual salary of £500, managed to buy for £20,000 a famous diamond. Later its sale for several times that amount firmly established his family, which was to give England two of her foremost statesmen. The French posts at Pondicherry, Chandernagor, and elsewhere were also primarily devoted to trade, though their business was only a fraction of that done by the English company.

Then began a fundamental change in the relationship of the Europeans to India. Aurangzeb, the last of the strong Mogul emperors, died in 1707, and, with the control from Delhi relaxed, the various lesser potentates of India engaged in a scramble for power. Freebooting bands plundered far and wide, and India was faced with anarchy. With rival claimants for many of the thrones, intrigue was the order of the day. François Dupleix, the French governor of Pondicherry, saw an opportunity to increase French influence in India by mixing into this maze of intrigue. He developed the practice of supporting one of the pretenders to a disputed throne, in return for special commercial privileges to the French. The few European troops were vastly superior to the huge ordinary armies of the Indian states; so, too, were the "sepoys," Indian troops led by white officers and trained in European methods. It was with such troops that Dupleix planned to set a candidate on a native throne and to keep him there.

Barely had his new scheme begun to take form when the War of the Austrian Succession spread to India in 1744. For a while the French enjoyed naval superiority in those waters under an energetic admiral who, with Dupleix, managed to capture Madras. Some of the English escaped to a smaller post down the coast.

Colonial Conflict Between the Wars

The War of the Austrian Succession ended in 1748, with the Treaty of Aix-la-Chapelle. Except for Frederick the Great's retention of Silesia, there was a general return to the *status quo ante*. To the disgust of the New England colonists, Louisburg was returned to the French; to Dupleix's disgust, Madras went back to the English. Aix-la-Chapelle was simply a breathing spell between two Anglo-French wars. During the next eight years of nominal peace, the French and English kept on fighting in America and in India. By then the colonial aspects of the struggle were definitely overshadowing the Continental.

In India, the English resumed their trading, but Dupleix began more actively than ever to build up his connections with native rulers. The ruler of the Deccan, which covered a considerable part of southern India, died in 1748, and Dupleix supported one pretender while the English supported another. The French candidate won the throne, and another protégé of Dupleix received the subordinate post of nawab of the Carnatic, which included the Coromandel coast, where Pondicherry and Madras were located. By 1751 the situation at Madras was grave. The English native pretender was closely besieged by the pro-French nawab, with vastly superior forces. The officials at Madras were in despair when a young man of twenty-five, destined to be one of the foremost builders of the British Empire, turned the tables. Robert Clive, a clerk for the East India Company, had become thoroughly bored keeping ledgers, and had managed to secure a commission as captain in the Company's forces. To relieve the pressure of the siege, he hit upon the daring scheme of capturing Arcot, capital of the pro-French nawab. With only a handful of redcoats and sepoys, he took Arcot, and then sustained a long, desperate defense against the nawab's numerous forces, who relaxed their Madras siege to save Arcot. Clive's little garrison was nearly starved. When help came from a powerful native chieftain who was impressed by their courage, Arcot was saved, and also Madras. Clive won further victories, and when he returned to England, in 1753, he left English influence uppermost in southeastern India. Dupleix was recalled in disgrace a year later. After a temporary lull, Clive and the English soon reappeared in the northeast, around Calcutta.

The French, during this interval between the wars, were taking the initiative in America. La Salle's discovery of the Mississippi had given them a claim to the valley of that river and its tributaries, which they now proceeded to fortify. Fort Duquesne was erected where two rivers join to form the Ohio, the site of the present Pittsburgh. Some English colonies also claimed this region by virtue of their original charters, which had given them title from sea to sea. In 1753 the governor of Virginia dispatched young George Washington with a letter to the commander of Fort Duquesne warning him that he was trespassing on English territory. Washington was received courteously after his long and perilous trip through the wilderness, but the French laughed at the English pretensions. The next year Washington was sent back with a force of colonial militia and was defeated at Fort Necessity by the forces from Duquesne. Then, although the two countries were nominally at peace, England sent over two regular regiments under General Edward Braddock to support her title to the Ohio valley. Braddock marched on Duquesne, but was caught unawares by the French and Indians. Accustomed to the formal fighting of Flanders, he kept his soldiers lined up in close formation to be shot down by foes they could not see. He was killed and Washington helped lead back the shattered remnants.

During this interval the British took two steps to protect Nova Scotia and offset the restoration of Louisburg to the French. In 1749, several thousand ex-soldiers and their families were settled in the vicinity of an excellent harbor, which as Halifax became an important naval base. This was the only community in America founded by direct action of the British government. Secondly, British settlers were being threatened not only by French and Indian raids but also by religious propaganda among the French inhabitants of Nova Scotia. With war imminent in 1755, the British deported most of these Acadians by sea to various colonies to the southward, a tragic uprooting which is deplored in Longfellow's poem *Evangeline.* Many found their way to French Louisiana, where their descendants are called "Cajuns."

The Seven Years' War

This peace-time fighting in India and America led France and England into open conflict again in the Seven Years' War, 1756-1763. Once more the Anglo-French rivalry was tied up with the Hapsburg-Hohenzollern fight in Germany. Englishmen continued to fight Frenchmen, and Prussians to fight Austrians, as in the previous war; but this time they changed partners. There was a "diplomatic revolution" in which France and Austria became allies, whereupon England made an alliance with Frederick the Great, paying him generously for keeping the French occupied in Europe. This time the best navy (England's) and the best army (Prussia's) were on the same side; consequently the results were far more decisive than in the previous war, where they had been opposed.

At the outset, however, the war went badly for England. The French captured Hanover, and, in the Mediterranean, Minorca. The British admiral whose lack of energy lost the latter was condemned by a court-martial and shot on his quarterdeck. In America the British tried but failed to take Louisburg, while the frontier was once more aflame with French and Indian raids. There was even a fear that the French would invade England.

Then William Pitt came into power and within three years demolished the French colonial empire. To appreciate the situation, it is necessary to explore briefly some of the sordid records of political intrigue. The Whigs remained in undisputed power, but there were various factions within the party. Walpole had finally ended his long ministry in 1742 and for a year was succeeded as prime minister by the colorless Earl of Wilmington, who was overshadowed by Lord Carteret (later Lord Granville) in charge of foreign affairs. Then control passed to the Pelhams—Henry and his older brother, the Duke of Newcastle. Henry, a man of moderate ability and considerable tact and common sense, was prime minister from 1743 to 1754, when he was succeeded by his brother, who had been a secretary of state for thirty years. Newcastle was one of the wealthiest landowners in England, and perhaps the most proficient boroughmonger and Parliamentary manipulator the nation has ever seen. One weakness of responsible government was that high cabinet positions, requiring statesmanship, depended on a majority in the House of Commons, which could be built up by the arts of the politician. Newcastle was a master politician, but a ridiculous statesman. A fussy little man, who enjoyed power for its own sake, he bustled around with an air of great importance. According to one wit he always "lost half an hour in the morning and spent the rest of the day in running after it." He could marshal a sizable block of members in the Commons, and through his hands passed the appointments of bishops, judges, admirals, and the many lesser spoils of patronage (see page 298). When after his fall from power, he was snubbed at a court levee, he looked at the formerly obsequious bishops, murmuring, "Even the fathers in God forget their maker."

A group of the younger Whigs had commenced an attack on the corrupt methods of governing back in Walpole's time. Foremost among them was William Pitt, a grandson of "Diamond" Pitt, the governor of Madras, who had purchased Old Sarum, the rottenest of the rotten boroughs (see page 296), through which William entered the Commons fresh from Oxford. With his commanding presence, flashing eye, and impassioned though somewhat flowery oratory, he was also a master of invective, and soon antagonized the king by attacking Hanover's influence in British foreign policy. He had a burning patriotism, with a desire to make England foremost among the powers, and he was unique in that day in his refusal to join in plundering the public funds. Such a man was disturbing to the somnolent atmosphere of mid-Georgian politics, but he was too insistent to be ignored. The Pelham brothers had had to resign in order to force the reluctant king to accept him in their ministry. As they were indispensable, the king accepted Pitt as paymaster of the forces. There was a chance for tremendous profit by gathering interest on huge sums before they were paid, but Pitt did not take a penny beyond his salary. Chafing at Newcastle's bungling mismanagement as a war minister, he broke with the incompetent arch-politician, despite the former Pelham support. "I am confident," declared Pitt, "that I can save the country and that no one else can." In the autumn of 1756 Newcastle was ousted, and the Duke of Devonshire became prime minister, with Pitt as the guiding genius. He began to inject new life into the prosecution of the war, but without Newcastle's well-organized voting power in the Commons the ministry could not make headway. Early in 1757 Pitt was dismissed from office. Immediately a storm of protest arose in loyal support of the "Great Commoner." Before the year was out, a compromise was made. Pitt, the statesman, joined forces with Newcastle, the politician, who, as prime minister, was allowed to keep control of the patronage and maintain a majority in Commons. Pitt, as secretary of state, had full control of running the war. Under that arrangement, which lasted four years, the Old Empire was brought to its peak.

Pitt clearly perceived the value of keeping France occupied on the Continent while England gathered in her overseas possessions. He generously financed Frederick the Great, remarking later that he had "won Canada in Germany." Vigorous young men who had demonstrated their ability were given responsible command, in the place of the gouty generals and admirals who had let matters drift. The whole nation, moreover, was roused to a high pitch of national and imperial enthusiasm.

The situation in America reflected the change. In 1758, Louisburg was recaptured and Fort Duquesne was at last taken (see page 310). The next year three armies approached from three directions to capture Quebec. In over-all command was Sir Jeffrey (later Lord) Amherst celebrated in the song of the college named for him. He was to come from the south by way of Lake Champlain. A second force from the west was to capture Fort Niagara. A third force, commanded by young James Wolfe, was to attack from the east, going up the St. Lawrence with naval support. The British troops were reinforced by large colonial forces, while Frederick the Great was doing his part in the conquest of Canada by keeping the French so occupied that they did not adequately support the Marquis de Montcalm, their American commander. The southern and western expeditions captured their initial objectives; but the long distances in the wilderness delayed their push through to Quebec, where the brunt of the attack there fell upon Wolfe and his supporting admiral.

Quebec, situated on a high bluff rising sharply from the river, was a difficult position to attack. One British effort after another failed. Summer passed into autumn, when the river would soon freeze, thus necessitating a British withdrawal. Wolfe was both capable and lucky. The French had nearly twenty miles of land above the city exposed to attack. Day after day, boats full of redcoats drifted up the river with the tide and then dropped back again, while the weary French trudged along the shore to prevent a landing. Wolfe eventually spied a narrow path leading up the cliffs to the "Plains of Abraham" above. Complete surprise was essential; if the French had warning, they could defend it easily. One night Wolfe attacked and found the path lightly guarded. By day-

A compressed view of the British attack on Quebec, 1759, showing the landing from warships, ascent of the heights, and battle on the Plains of Abraham.

light the French, to their dismay, found several British regiments lined up on the Plains of Abraham. In the sharp battle, Wolfe and Montcalm both fell mortally wounded. After a century and a half, the French fleur-de-lis was hauled down from the citadel of Quebec. Montreal and the remaining startegic points soon fell, and within a year New France was in British hands.

Nearer home, during that "glorious year" of 1759, the French had gathered flatboats at Havre to convey the troops for an invasion of England. Three British fleets went out to block them. One destroyed the flatboats; another caught the French Mediterranean fleet as it was coming round to join in the attack; while the third, under Admiral Hawke, encountered the main Atlantic fleet at Quiberon Bay, pursued it relentlessly through dangerous rocky channels in a storm, and smashed it thoroughly.

Once more England was clearly mistress of the seas. On land a combined force of British and Hanoverians defeated the French at Minden.

In the meantime England was laying the foundations of her great empire in India. Whereas the earlier rivalry had been centered in southeastern India, in 1756 the principal seat of action was suddenly transferred to Bengal, in the northeast. Its native ruler, Surajah Dowlah, resented the presence of the British at Calcutta far more than he did the French up the river at Chandernagor, who were to play only a subordinate role. The Bengal prince was annoyed at the defenses which the British began to make at Calcutta with the outbreak of the Seven Years' War. He swooped down on the city, captured it, and herded one hundred and forty-five Englishmen and the half-caste wife of one of them into a little room, the "Black Hole," barely

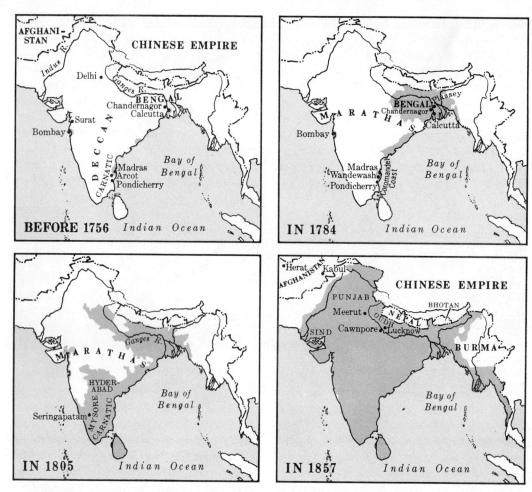

DEVELOPMENT OF BRITISH POWER IN INDIA, 1756-1857

Boundary shows extent of British India in 1900

eighteen feet long and fourteen feet wide. All day and all night the suffocating group called vainly for air and water. In the morning only twenty-three remained alive; among these was the woman, who was taken to Surajah Dowlah's harem. Clive, sent up hurriedly from the south, recaptured Calcutta early in 1757; he then moved against Surajah Dowlah, who had fifty thousand native troops. Clive had less than a thousand white troops and about two thousand sepoys, but intrigue helped to compensate for this disparity. Mir Jafar,

Surajah's second in command, agreed to betray his master. In perilous dependence on this treacherous Oriental, Clive boldly attacked the Bengali army at Plassey; Mir Jafar kept his troops at one side until he saw how the battle was going, before coming to Clive's assistance. That battle initiated the spread of British power into the interior of India. For a while the British exerted their influence through Mir Jafar, set up as a puppet nawab in Bengal, but Bengal was virtually theirs. Later Clive and Hastings adapted the East India Company into a ruling force for the millions of inhabitants of Bengal.

Back on the Coromandel Coast around Madras, the British came to final direct grips with the French during the Seven Years' War. Count Lally, sent out to capture Madras, tried to do so; but early in 1759, a British squadron saved the besieged town. The English then wrested from French control the strip of seacoast stretching northward toward Bengal. In 1760 Sir Eyre Coote definitely broke French control in India by defeating Lally at Wandewash, and a year later Pondicherry fell.

Pitt won the war; but he was not in at the finish. For political reasons his power was undermined (see page 317). He learned in 1761 that France and Spain had secretly renewed their Bourbon "family compact" and that Spain would probably declare war on England as soon as her annual plate fleet from America should arrive (see page 161). Pitt urged immediate British declaration of war against Spain in time to capture the silver; but his new colleagues disagreed, and he resigned. Spain duly entered the war, and England promptly punished her. British squadrons captured Havana and Manila and also snapped up several French islands in the West Indies. Pitt had supported Frederick the Great, but that financial and military backing was now withdrawn. The Prussian king continued to battle against heavy odds and managed to retain Silesia, but once more a Continental ally had occasion to complain of the practices of "perfidious Albion."

The Seven Years' War ended with the Treaty of Paris, early in 1763. France withdrew completely from the mainland of North America. England received all of Canada, Cape Breton Island, and the rest of Nova Scotia, together with the region between the Alleghenies and the Mississippi. All that remained to France in the north were two barren little islands, Saint Pierre and Miquelon, off Newfoundland, suitable only for drying fish. In the West Indies, France ceded to England four islands (Grenada, Saint Vincent, Dominica, and Tobago), but kept her more important sugar colonies of Guadeloupe, Martinique, and Haiti. In Africa, England took the slaving post at Senegal, but let France keep Gorée at Cape Verde. In India the changes were not reflected on the map; for France was permitted to retain Pondicherry and her other trading posts, but the French renounced all political ambitions in connection with the native rulers. Minorca, captured in 1756, was restored to England. Spain ceded Florida to England, and in compensation received from France New Orleans and that portion of "Louisiana" west of the Mississippi.

Altogether, this meant a tremendous extension of overseas power for England and marked the height of the Old Empire. The old French colonial empire had virtually disappeared, and France, moreover, had received a severe setback as a commercial and maritime power. Yet the peace terms were unpopular in England. It was pointed out that Pitt could have won as much in 1761, and there was nothing to show for the additional British successes of the following year. The peace was already signed before the news of the capture of Manila reached Europe. The mercantilist conception of colonial values was reflected in the argument of many that it would be better to take the sugar island of Guadeloupe instead of Canada. While the latter would "color the map red," its scanty trade in beaver skins would not offset the burden of defense and administration, whereas a sugar island would mean immediate profits, even though only a dot on the map. The final decision in favor of Canada is said to have been influenced not only by the desire to remove the French menace to the thirteen colonies but also by a lobby of the powerful British planters of Jamaica, who did not want another sugar colony enjoying imperial privileges.

George III and the Whigs

Britain had now entered upon a decade of political changes which upset the comfortable and secure domination enjoyed by the Whigs since the accession of the Hanoverian line. The twenty-two-year-old grandson of George II began his sixty-year reign in 1760 as George III, his father having died nine years before. That first decade has been subjected in recent years to a thoroughgoing reappraisal, particularly a revaluation of the young king and an analysis of party structure and politics. As a result, on the two hundredth anniversary of his accession, the new views ran as follows: "Historians now recognize that George III was a much maligned man, both in his own day and in the writings of history. It so happened that his opponents, the Whigs, had all the best writers; they had not only most of the men of genius but the future with them, and they fixed the legend of George as a corrupt tyrant, acting unconstitutionally, engaged in a conspiracy against English liberties. None of this is true."[1]

That old Whig legend, eagerly amplified in America, has long prevailed. According to this legend, George, influenced by the Tory Bolingbroke's idea of a "Patriot King," who would restore the former powers of the crown, had set up a tyrannous rule in place of the authority of Parliament, so carefully developed since 1688. He had, it was believed, deliberately driven wedges between the Whig factions, playing off one group against the other until he had time to build up a Tory party of his own. His principal weapon had been patronage, such as Newcastle had used to keep control of Commons. But as later research has emphasized, the two-party responsible government of 1760 was by no means what developed later, nor was the House of Commons, with its strange election methods, responsive to

public opinion (see pages 296, 399). While George did a good many stubborn and stupid things, his methods were not "illegal," for the crown was still supposed to be responsible for the executive side of the government. He was trying to achieve effective government by Parliamentary methods.

As for George personally, he has been found to have been "a clear psychotic case . . . lethargic and rather stupid; he had been brought up piously by his mother . . . in great innocence of the world."[2] He leaned almost pathetically upon the opinion of his confidential adviser, the Earl of Bute, a smooth and well-connected Scot, "with a cultivated mind and well-turned leg," whom the gossips called his mother's close friend. George fell madly in love with the charming fifteen-year-old daughter of a peer; but told firmly by Bute that he could not marry an English girl, he turned resignedly to a list of eligible German princesses. He was one of the few English kings to be a faithful husband. It was his misfortune that he came to the throne just in time to encounter the powerful impact of three Revolutions—the American, Industrial, and French. George with his stubborn obstinacy could not adjust to those stresses; and ultimately he went insane.

George's accession coincided with the break-up of the old Whig control. From 1760 to 1770 there were seven different prime ministers, and a resultant lack of controlled and consistent policy at a critical period when the colonial situation in America required intelligent handling. This situation was a far cry from later clear-cut practices when a whole cabinet would be replaced by another whole one. For some years the Whigs had been gradually disintegrating into a number of cliques, with some sufficiently close-knit to be called parties themselves. Individuals shifted from one combination to another, occasionally for reasons of principle or policy, but more often for plunder or personal grudges. Outstanding among

[1] A. L. Rowse, "New and Kind Light on George III," *New York Times Magazine*, October 23, 1960. By permission.

[2] *Ibid.*

the leaders who found such difficulty in co-operating was Pitt. He still appealed strongly to the popular imagination but behaved like an egoistic prima donna, turning down one cabinet suggestion after another rather than accept anyone else as leader or even equal. The better of the two major "party" groups, the "Old Whigs" under the Marquess of Rockingham, came largely from long standing Whig families, and were harder working and less corrupt than the "Bloomsbury gang" under the arrogant Duke of Bedford. George III definitely disliked most of the Whig leaders, particularly Pitt's brother-in-law, George Grenville, the only one he actually dismissed. He realized, however, that he had to devise some sort of combination among them to keep the government going.

Shortly after George came to the throne, Pitt resigned his cabinet post in 1761 and the prime minister, Newcastle, did so the next year after disputes with their colleagues. Newcastle dropped from prominence fairly quickly, but not too gracefully, for others were now distributing the patronage he had so long bestowed. George made his friend Bute prime minister; he was generally unpopular and resigned shortly in 1763, sensitive over criticism of his handling of the peace terms. Unable to find anyone else who really satisfied him and could manage Parliament, George reluctantly turned to Grenville, though he said, "I would rather have the devil in my closet." Grenville was stubborn, narrow-minded, and a "bullying prig," who did much to antagonize the American colonies; yet he was a fairly able administrator, particularly in finance. He received support from the "Bedford gang," who had no set principles, but who kept together for bargaining purposes. In 1765 Grenville omitted the king's mother from a proposed regency bill; so George dismissed his ministry and turned to the "Old Whigs" and the Marquess of Rockingham. Pitt could not be persuaded to join their ministry, which was strained by

American problems and gave way in 1766. Thereupon Pitt became prime minister with a very ill-assorted cabinet. The "Great Commoner" lost a great deal of popularity by accepting a peerage as Earl of Chatham, the name by which he is often called to avoid confusion with his prominent son, the younger William Pitt. His oratory, an important asset in the House of Commons, had far less effect in the Lords. He was a complete failure as prime minister; his gout crippled him, and his mind seems to have become affected. His colleagues consequently did pretty much as they pleased, particularly the erratic Chancellor of the Exchequer, Charles Townshend. The next year Chatham virtually retired from public life, and the nominal headship of this "mutinous crew" went to the Duke of Grafton, a descendant of Charles II and Lady Castlemaine.

In 1770, after a decade which had seen Newcastle, Bute, Grenville, Rockingham, Pitt, and Grafton as prime ministers in rapid succession, that cabinet instability gave way to Lord North's twelve-year Tory ministry. Some new light on those "King's Friends" makes them less sinister than they had been in the Whig-American interpretation. As early as 1766, a large number of independent members of Commons, as well as King George, had been annoyed and frustrated by the selfish bickerings of the Whig chieftains. With personal feelings becoming increasingly more bitter, while the American situation was calling for firmness and stability, a good many of these, "losing their normal antagonistic attitude" to the crown, became "anxious to serve any cabinet which knew its mind and was certain of its future. These were the 'King's Friends' . . . They were not in fact a group organized even as that century knew organization."[3] They found a leader in Lord North, amiable son

[3] J. S. Watson, *The Reign of George III, 1760-1815* (Oxford History of England, XII, 1960), pp. 146-147. By permission of Oxford University Press (Clarendon Press).

A distorted caricature of Lord North, prime minister during the American Revolution.

ministerial policy, a rare occurrence with the almost complete absence of popular suffrage; but Grenville allowed such an opportunity to arise. In 1762 John Wilkes, a clever courageous rascal and a reprobate member of Parliament, started a review, the *North Briton,* for the express purpose of attacking the royal policy. In issue No. 45 there were some particularly scathing remarks about a speech by the king. George instructed the ministry to issue a general warrant for the arrest of the authors, printers, and publishers for libel. Wilkes was apprehended and sent to the Tower; but a justice of Common Pleas soon freed him on the ground of his privilege as a member of Parliament and further declared illegal such general warrants, which did not specify by name the individual to be arrested. Thereupon the House of Commons expelled Wilkes as a member, and he was attacked in the Lords for an indecent, but unpublished, "Essay on Woman." Early in 1764, after an adverse judgment in the court of King's Bench, he fled to France and was declared an outlaw.

He returned in 1768, just on the eve of a seven-year general election for Parliament. The county of Middlesex, which included a considerable part of London, was one of the few places in England with a really democratic franchise. It elected Wilkes, popular for his defiance of the king, as one of its representatives, but the Commons expelled him. Three times Middlesex elected him, and the third time, in spite of bitter protests both within and without Parliament, the Commons voted that his opponent, who had received only a few votes, ought to be seated. An anonymous author bitterly attacked the king and his ministers in the *Letters of Junius,* while the London mob howled for "Wilkes and liberty." Wilkes was sentenced on the old libel charge, and the mob tried to rescue him from prison; he was even elected an alderman while in confinement. The colonists in Pennsylvania named a town

of an earl and cultivated Oxford graduate, whose principal political asset was his easygoing approach to problems as they came along. Not associated closely with any of the rival groups and, like Walpole, ready to let sleeping dogs lie, he was altogether a welcome relief to the king, to whom he was thoroughly loyal. He successfully retained adequate Parliamentary support with the help of the patronage he now commanded. The Whig factions went into disgruntled opposition. North's first four years, during which he achieved some successful results in India and elsewhere, were in contrast to the critical American situation from 1774 onward, when two faulty decisions helped to precipitate matters. After that, despite repeated efforts to resign, he stayed and shared some of the opprobrium brought on by the king's stubbornness.

Long before North came into power, London rigorously voiced its disapproval of

(Wilkes-Barre) for him and for Colonel Barré, another opponent of the royal policy. From this outburst of popular indignation may be dated the commencement of a radical demand for Parliamentary reform which was to culminate in 1832. Even Pitt, who had formerly denounced Wilkes as "the blasphemer of his God and the libeller of his king," began to realize that an organic change was necessary in the British electoral system. For the time being, however, England was not yet a democracy, no matter how the mobs might howl or Middlesex might vote.

Colonial Friction

While the Whig party was disintegrating, there were serious rumblings heard in the American colonies. They were warnings of the approaching conflict that would disrupt the Old Empire, which reached its climax at the Peace of Paris in 1763. In fact, the outcome of the Seven Years' War was linked closely with the causes of the American Revolution. In at least three ways the Americans were affected. Ever since Count Frontenac had started the policy of French and Indian raids, the English frontier colonists had lived in terror of the French menace to the north and were comforted by the fact that British regulars could help them in an emergency. Now that menace was removed. Experiences such as Braddock's defeat, moreover, had shown the colonial troops that in some types of fighting they were better men than the haughty regulars. Finally, and more immediately, the cost of the Seven Years' War led England to think of measures whereby the colonists might share part of the cost of empire.

In addition to Canada and Nova Scotia, the "continental" colonies had become thirteen in number with the founding of Georgia in 1733. The combination of a high colonial birth rate and constant immigration led to a doubling of the population about every twenty years, until they were almost one third as populous as the mother country herself. They were, moreover, well trained in self-government. Every colony had its assembly, with members elected by popular vote, which raised taxes for local purposes and legislated for the needs of the community. Any acts of the colonial legislature might be overridden by the governor, appointed from England, or his council, which he nominated, and were subject to review by the Privy Council in England. Nevertheless, the governors used their veto power sparingly, because the assemblies could withhold their salaries. The Board of Trade and Plantations, to be sure, was apt to check up on violations of the Navigation Acts and other trade laws, but during the easygoing period of Walpole and Newcastle the colonists had violated even these with impunity. They had been enjoying a greater degree of latitude than England originally intended.

When Grenville looked over imperial finances in 1764, he decided that the colonists should bear a share of the cost. The Seven Years' War had increased the national debt by some £130,000,000, part of it incurred in defending the American colonists. England did not expect them to pay for that, and had even reimbursed the colonies for their military expenses during the war. At its close, however, a serious Indian threat in the West made it seem desirable to keep a considerable force of regulars in America. At least the colonists might pay for their own protection in times of peace. Without a central colonial government with which to deal, the simplest way seemed to be a stamp tax, whereby all legal documents and similar papers must bear a revenue stamp of specified value. In 1765 Parliament accordingly passed the Stamp Act, which was expected to raise some £100,000 a year. Benjamin Franklin, in England as a colonial agent, saw no objection to the scheme. To the general surprise of the English, however, the cry of "No taxation without representation" resounded through the thirteen colonies, and in several places the stamps were destroyed. Representatives from the seaports gathered in a "Stamp Act Congress" and agreed solemnly to import nothing further from England until the obnoxious act was repealed.

That was an argument which touched deeply the London merchants. England's trade with the thirteen colonies amounted to more than one-eighth of her total overseas commerce, not including Ireland. Increasing at a faster rate than any other region, America's average annual total of exports and imports rose from £500,000 to £2,800,000 between the years 1700-1710 and 1760-1770, just ahead of the India-China increase from £500,000 to £2,500,-000. The West Indian sugar islands, with an area less than Connecticut's, remained in first place, at £900,000 to £3,400,000, though the rate of increase was slower. Altogether, the empire was becoming more and more profitable. In 1700-1710 the British trade with Europe, at £7,600,000, had been more than four times as heavy as the colonial. By 1760-1770, the empire total had more than trebled, to £9,800,000, almost catching up with the £11,700,000 European total.

While Grenville's mind was on America, he also tightened up the colonial customs service and ordered a rigid observance of long-neglected regulations. The colonists called this an infringement of their rights. In fact, it has been said that the Revolution started when he began to read the colonial dispatches. Since England had little use for their lumber, fish, and flour, the northern and middle colonists had exchanged them at Jamaica, Barbados, and other West Indian islands for sugar, rum, and molasses. By this triangular trading, the Yankees were able to pay for the British manufactures they needed.

England did not object as long as the Yankee trade was with British islands, but its extension to Guadeloupe, Martinique, and other foreign sugar islands was different. Parliament in 1733 had passed a Molasses Act, which levied an almost prohibitive duty on products of the foreign islands; but in the period of Whig neglect smuggling and violations, with official connivance, became common and contributed much to the building of colonial fortunes. Some of the governors protested, but to little avail. The Molasses Act was now revised as the Sugar Act (1764), with lower duties, designed to reduce smuggling and to produce revenue rather than to prohibit such trade.

The pressure from the British merchants was effective, and in 1766 the Stamp Act was repealed by the Rockingham administration. But Parliament as a face-saving measure declared that it had a right to tax the colonies—a theory much argued ever since. As the colonists objected to the stamps as internal taxation, England next tried external taxation. In 1767 Charles Townshend pushed through an act imposing duties on glass, paint, paper, and tea imported into the colonies. The new income would be devoted to the salaries of colonial governors and judges, thus rendering them independent of the colonial assemblies. Once more the colonies angrily protested. Pitt, whose attitude toward the colonies was favorable, was too ill or too neglectful to prevent this further source of irritation. In 1770 North had the duties removed on everything but tea; the tax was maintained on that, he said, simply to show England's right to tax the colonies.

While England and America were slowly drifting toward war the government had another imperial problem in India. Since Clive had placed his puppet on the throne of Bengal, the East India Company had to assume a new function. Hitherto primarily a trading concern, operating through a few posts of limited area, it became more and more directly the sovereign power in Bengal, a region several times the size of England, with a population of some thirty millions. In 1760 Clive returned to England at the age of thirty-five with a huge fortune and became Lord Clive.

In his absence, the Company's officials shamelessly plundered the natives and built up fortunes for themselves. Clive, sent back in 1765 to clear up the situation, put affairs on an honest basis, and secured from the Mogul emperor the Company's right to the financial administration of Bengal and two adjacent states. After two years, he went home, where an attempt was made to impeach him for a forged treaty and illicit gains. Clive remarked that when he thought of what he might have taken, he marveled at his moderation. Only partially cleared of the charges against him, he died in 1774, apparently a suicide. By making a scapegoat of Clive, and later of Hastings, England perhaps salved her conscience about the seizure of Bengal; but no one proposed to give it back to the natives. Some four million pounds sterling had reached England as a result of the battle of Plassey, including Clive's half million; and more would come later.

The East India Company, as a trading organization with a royal charter, was not under Parliamentary control, but in view of its new political functions it seemed proper that the government should have more authority. Lord North's India Regulating Act of 1773 combined the three separate presidencies of Bombay, Madras, and Calcutta under the authority of a governor-general who would have his seat at Calcutta. It gave him a council of four men and ruled that all decisions should be made by the majority. The first governor-general appointed under this act was Warren Hastings, already governor at Calcutta. Hastings planned carefully the administration of Bengal and wisely laid the foundations of the remarkable system whereby the British long ruled India (see page 448). He also had to fight certain native chiefs who were threatening British power. His solid constructive work in Bengal ranks him with

Clive as one of the two principal founders of British India.

The East India Company indirectly caused further complications in America. Since the Company's finances were in bad condition, and it had a large quantity of unsold tea on its hands, Lord North had permitted it to sell the tea directly to the colonists without paying duties. Tea was already a sore point with the Americans: they had protested when Townshend taxed it; now they were angered at its cheapness, for the regular merchants could not compete with the Company's special price. At Boston a group disguised as Indians rowed out to the tea ships and dumped their cargoes into the bay. From that time on, things moved fast toward revolution. Tea had been spilled or sent back at other ports, but Boston from the outset had been the principal source of trouble. In 1774, the same year which saw the generally wise and liberal Quebec Act for the new province of Canada (see page 324), North had Parliament punish the Bostonians, in spite of pleadings for conciliation from Edmund Burke. The Boston Port Act closed that port to all shipping, while companion acts put the Massachusetts government under royal control and prohibited public meetings. A soldier, General Gage, was sent to govern Massachusetts, supported by a strong force.

That stirred the people into united action. Delegates from most of the colonies met at Philadelphia in the autumn of 1774 in the First Continental Congress. It was agreed to suspend all trade with England until more satisfactory treatment could be secured. There was no intention of war or independence. Each side seemed to be waiting for the other to back down; each remained stubborn; and the drift toward war continued, with no one in apparent control of the situation. Massachusetts organized part of its militia as "minutemen," who would be ready to seize arms at a moment's notice.

The American peace commissioners in 1783—Jay, Adams, Franklin, Laurens, and Franklin's grandson, by Benjamin West, who was unable to finish the painting.

The American Revolution

On April 19, 1775, Gage sent eight hundred men to destroy some military stores gathered by the colonists at Concord, about twenty miles from Boston. The colonists were warned, and when the British reached Lexington they found a force of minutemen drawn up on the common. The first shots of the war were fired, eight minutemen fell, and the redcoats went on to Concord. There they were stopped by a larger group of "embattled farmers" and had to retire. The British were shot at from behind trees and stone walls; by the time they reached Boston again, they had lost more than a third of their men.

The older American schoolbook accounts of the Revolution pictured it as a struggle in which every American was a "patriot," engaged for eight years of hardship in heroic efforts to eject the British, who were tyrants to a man. The older British ac-counts, so far as they gave more than passing mention to the war, often spoke of the Americans with extreme contempt. Today the majority of American and British historians agree that instead of being primarily a war between America and England, it was more properly a civil war within the British Empire. Loyalties were divided on both sides of the Atlantic. It has been estimated that among the American colonists about 20 per cent were active "patriots"; 15 per cent were "Loyalists," or "Tories," who positively favored the king; and the remaining two thirds were relatively indifferent. In England the king and the ministry supported the war; but the Whigs opposed it on the ground that if George III stamped out American liberties, he would next proceed against the liberties of Englishmen. Such division explains the anomalous facts that New York raised some fifteen thousand Loyalist troops, while in

England prominent members of Parliament cheered American victories. Some of the outstanding generals and admirals had Whig loyalties and either declined to fight or, like the Howe brothers, fought half-heartedly.

The American fighting, which began in 1775 at Lexington, continued for six years, until the fall of Yorktown in 1781. But England had far more on her hands than the rebellious colonists alone. France, Spain, and Holland were also finally ranged against her, and most of the rest of Europe was hostile. The navy was engaged not only on the American coast but also in home waters, in the West Indies, in the Mediterranean, and even on the coasts of India. During this contest it was to receive its most serious setbacks.

In America, each side had certain marked advantages and disadvantages. The British had organization, wealth, and authority on their side. Their experienced troops were well trained, and usually well equipped and well fed. These were assisted by thousands of professional "Hessians," hired from German princes at so much a head. The British navy could move troops rapidly from one part of the coast to another, leaving the Americans guessing where they would strike next. The Americans, on the other hand, lacked money and supplies for even the small regular army which they managed to hold together. They could count on the militia to turn out when their immediate region was in danger; but these untrained men were not dependable in battle, nor were they interested particularly unless near their own homes. There was no adequate central political authority to co-ordinate American activity. Yet all these British advantages were offset by certain other factors. The British had to wage war three thousand miles from home, a fact which entailed problems of supply and control; and they had to subdue a vast region before the rebellion could be crushed. The Americans simply had to make the British so weary of the war that they would let the colonies have their own way. When the Americans retired inland, the British would follow and immediately find themselves in trouble. Distances were great, communications were bad, and there was constant danger of being cut off by a rising of local militia. Altogether it developed into an endurance contest, but at times it looked as though the Americans would not hold together long enough to wear out the British.

A few personalities must also be taken into account. Shortly after Lexington, the Continental Congress wisely put the military command in the hands of George Washington, a Virginia planter, one of the wealthiest men in the country (see page 310). A competent, but not a great, general, he lost many of his battles, but maintained American resistance against the disheartening odds of intrigues, apathy, short-term enlistments, local jealousies, and few trained men. In England the most significant figures were not of the military but two cabinet ministers responsible for the direction of the war, Lord Sandwich, in charge of the navy, and Lord George Germain, in charge of military affairs. Sandwich, a cynical debauchee, won immortality of a sort by inventing the sandwich so that he could lunch without leaving the gambling table. By neglecting the material condition of the ships and by alienating the Whig admirals, Sandwich probably did more damage to the navy entrusted to his care than any hostile French admiral had ever done. Germain was a fitting colleague. At the battle of Minden in the Seven Years' War, the British cavalry failed to complete the victory when ordered to do so. Germain, the responsible officer, had been court-martialed and forbidden ever again to serve in a military capacity. Yet, because of the king's friendship, here he was in full control of operations! With more adequate leadership, the British might have crushed Washington's main army, an operation easily possible on several occasions, or they might have made it a purely naval war, with a rigid blockade to cut off the Americans from all outside communications and trade. Instead they engaged in blundering land campaigns combined with naval support.

The main fighting began around Boston and worked south to New York and Philadelphia during the first three years of the war; then it moved to Georgia and worked up through the Carolinas to Virginia during the next three. There were several varied operations farther west.

The news of Lexington and Concord brought some sixteen thousand colonists to the vicinity of Boston to form an army. Gage missed his chance to nip the revolt in the bud. In June the British lost more than a thousand men in winning the battle of Bunker Hill, across Boston Harbor, where they made a brave but stupid frontal attack on entrenched colonials. That winter an American force, which had made a remarkable march through the wilderness, was defeated in an effort to take Canada. England's wisdom in giving the French Canadians their old religion and law by the Quebec Act, the year before, was now demonstrated; the Canadian settlers disappointed the Americans by their lack of interest. In March, 1776, the Americans seized the hills around Boston, and the British evacuated the city by sea. That summer, while the Continental Congress was signing the Declaration of Independence at Philadelphia on July 4, the British were beginning to concentrate against New York, which they captured after defeating Washington on Long Island. New York remained in British hands throughout the rest of the war. Washington's dwindling army was pursued across New Jersey into Pennsylvania; but on Christmas night he crossed the ice-choked Delaware and captured the garrison of Hessian mercenaries at Trenton by surprise. Ten days later, when the British were concentrating on him there, he slipped away from certain defeat by superior forces,

and routed the British rear guard at Princeton, thus recovering most of New Jersey and reviving American morale.

Later in 1777 General John Burgoyne, an able playwright who had opened the impeachment attack on Clive, brought an army down from Canada through Lake Champlain to the upper Hudson. There he was surrounded by a swarm of Americans and in the autumn surrendered his army at Saratoga. General Sir William Howe, instead of going up the Hudson from New York, captured and occupied Philadelphia. In the spring of 1778 Sir Henry Clinton, his successor, started across New Jersey for New York. Washington fell upon him at Monmouth; but a jealous subordinate threw away the battle, and Clinton reached New York, where he remained for the rest of the war, with Washington watching him nearby for three years.

Meanwhile the news of Saratoga brought France into the war as an ally of the Americans in 1778. The French had built up a first-rate navy, which, for once, was to enjoy superiority over the British navy, weakened by Sandwich's misrule. One after another the best British admirals declined to serve and took their places on the Whig opposition benches in Parliament. Things grew so bad that it was necessary to put an eighty-year-old veteran in command of the Channel fleet. On the American coast, in the West Indies, in India, and even in the Channel, France enjoyed naval superiority. In 1779 France determined to invade England; troops were ready; and a combined fleet of French and Spaniards, who had also come into the war, swept down on the south coast. Allied seasickness and lack of co-operation saved England; her outnumbered naval "first line of defense" had fled for safety.

After the war certain Englishmen asserted that America owed her independence to the winds. Time and again throughout the war came the tale of squadrons scattered and ships rendered useless, while worn-out masts split open and tumbled into the sea. Ever since Cromwell's time the navy had depended on New Hampshire and Maine for its great masts; but the colonists had cut off the supply at the opening of the war; and Sandwich neglected to seek substitutes elsewhere. When France entered the war, she dispatched a fleet to America. Admiral Byron, the poet's grandfather, was sent with thirteen ships to head them off. A mild gale struck his squadron in mid-Atlantic, the rotten masts broke, the ships limped away in every direction, and only one reached New York ahead of the French. So it went throughout the war.

England had tried to impose a similar shortage of naval materials upon France by intercepting neutral cargoes from the Baltic. Many of these were being carried in Dutch ships, until England forced Holland into the war in order to capture those ships more easily. Under the leadership of Catherine II, empress of Russia, the Baltic nations joined in an armed neutrality to protect their neutral shipping against British attack. It was England against the world: America, France, Spain, and Holland in open war against her, while most of the rest of Europe viewed her with undisguised hostility. For once she had no continental ally to keep France busy in Europe.

In America active operations had moved to the south. The British took Savannah, Georgia, in 1779; then they captured Charleston, in South Carolina. From that base Lord Cornwallis campaigned with varying success through the Carolinas. Then he headed for Virginia and established himself at Yorktown, on a broad river near Chesapeake Bay, while the French and Americans closed in on him. But British generals always felt that, as long as they could remain near the sea, the royal navy would rescue them if they got into trouble. This time the royal navy failed Cornwallis. A French fleet guarded the entrance to Chesapeake Bay and beat off the English fleet. For once in history, England was to

feel to her cost the influence of sea power. The French and American siege lines closed in on Cornwallis who surrendered his army on October 19, 1781. The redcoats marched out with their bands playing "The World Turned Upside Down." That surrender virtually ended the American fighting and established the independence of the thirteen colonies.

But England in 1782 was able elsewhere to offset some of her earlier misfortunes in the war. In the West Indies, Admiral Rodney, redeemed from the creditors who had been hounding him, tried a new tactical maneuver of cutting through the enemy line instead of lying alongside it. It worked to perfection in the "Battle of the Saints," near Dominica; he crushed the very fleet which had secured the Yorktown victory. Meanwhile France and Spain had been besieging Gibraltar for three years. A final desperate attempt to capture it with powerful floating batteries was beaten off by tough old Sir Gilbert Elliot, with red-hot shot, and England kept Gibraltar.

Though the final peace treaties did not come until 1783, negotiations were opened in the fall of 1782. The Americans, French, and Spaniards had agreed not to engage in separate negotiations; but when the Americans learned that the French and Spaniards were working behind their backs to limit American acquisitions, they began their own dealings with the British. Lord North's ministry had fallen after Yorktown (see page 362), and Benjamin Franklin, in charge of the American negotiations, was a friend of the new British prime minister, Lord Shelburne, who was generous in his dealings. In September, 1782, England recognized the independence of her former thirteen colonies as a new republic, the United States of America. The Americans managed to secure the region between the Alleghenies and the Mississippi up to the Great Lakes, a concession which had not originally been expected, and were granted fishing rights off Newfoundland and in the Gulf of St.

Lawrence, as well as free navigation of the Mississippi. The restitution of confiscated estates of Loyalists was to be recommended to the states by Congress, but when the states disregarded that, England herself gave the Loyalists compensation elsewhere (see page 459). The final definitive Treaty of Paris was signed on September 3, 1783, the same day England signed the Treaty of Versailles with France and Spain. Minorca, England's naval base in the Mediterranean for three quarters of a century, returned to Spain, as did Florida after twenty years in English hands. France gained little from her costly participation beyond the satisfaction of humbling England. It has been estimated that it cost England some £110,000,000 to lose the American colonies; France spent £55,000,000 to help the Americans gain their independence; and the Americans, who gained most, paid only £20,000,000. That recognition of independence, with the loss of the most populous of the colonies of settlement, marked the end of the Old Empire, which had reached such a proud height just twenty years before.

Chapter Seventeen

The New Wealth

The eighteenth has been called the most comfortable century in English history, because, after the alarm over the Jacobites at the beginning, the country dozed complacently through the long middle years until the specter of the Jacobins arose to cloud the end. On the surface this was true, for certain segments of the population, for others it was most decidedly uncomfortable. Economic readjustments, both in industry and in agriculture, were bringing fortunes to many, but the status of far more was sharply deteriorating. The word "revolution," ordinarily associated with sudden changes in a country's government, such as in America in 1776, in France in 1789, and in Russia in 1917, is also used in an economic sense, in which it refers to the changes in the way many of the people at a certain time and place make their living. Three different but interlocking revolutions were taking place in the world of economics: one in agriculture, a second in industry, and a third in communications. The England which finally emerged from the revolutionary impacts was a more complex nation on the threshold of modern capitalism. Democracy, nationalism, factories, labor problems, and long trousers all marked the passing of the good old days.

The agricultural upheaval came first. In 1750 barely a quarter of the population lived in towns and cities. The village was still the center of English life. The rental of acres, rather than the earnings of factories, ships, or banks, was still the usual and the most respectable source of wealth. The cultivation of those same acres remained the most common form of labor. It was estimated in 1770 that the national income from agriculture was £66,000,000; from industry, £27,000,000; from commerce, £10,000,000; from interest on capital and from the professions or governmental services, about £5,000,000 each. More than half of England's wealth, according to these figures, came from the soil.

The land had been owned for centuries by a surprisingly small part of the population. The vast bulk of Englishmen have been, and still are, tenants paying rent to some landlord. No reliable statistics for the ownership in the mid-eighteenth century of England's thirty-six million acres are available; but in 1688 there were about 175,000 landowners in a population of some 5,000,-000 (see page 251), and in 1874 about 1,000,000 landowners in a population of some 23,000,000. Even these figures do not fully indicate the remarkable concentration

Huntsmen and hounds, engaged in the favorite outdoor sport of the aristocracy.

of landowning in the hands of a favored few. In 1874, 250,000 persons owned nine tenths of the land, while 4200 owned half of it.

Theoretically this land originally had all belonged to the king. William the Conqueror, it will be recalled, had divided England among his followers, receiving military service and feudal dues in return. Gradually, this was coverted to a non-military cash basis. The agricultural labor of the manorial system likewise shifted to a cash relationship (see pages 43 ff., 103, and 128 ff.). The landlords still continued to derive plenty of gain from those below them. Their principal income, from renting out their holdings, amounted annually to about ten shillings an acre in the middle of the eighteenth century.

These great landowners of the eighteenth century generally owed their prosperity to their families' past perspicacity or good luck in marrying well or in being on the right spot in a troubled time of wholesale changes in land ownership. Few great houses had such an ancient record as the Percys, owners of half of Northumberland and much else, who traced back some title deeds to the Conqueror's liberality. The

dukes of Bedford received their vast acres from their Russell ancestor who was high in royal favor when Henry VIII was handing out lands confiscated from the abbeys and nobles. Besides at least a hundred thousand acres in various parts of England, they collected, and still collect, very profitable rent from a large portion of central London. The Cavendish dukes of Devonshire had equal cause to be thankful for the dissolution of the monasteries. The earls of Grosvenor, later dukes of Westminster, owned another large section of London, because a Restoration ancestor had married an eleven-year-old heiress. The dukes of Grafton and Richmond, on the other hand, owed their start to royal love affairs of Charles II.

Those English aristocrats and gentry of the eighteenth century were born into very pleasant surroundings. Upstarts from the middle class had enjoyed power under the Tudors and to a less extent under the Stuarts, but the landowners reached their zenith under the Georges. No longer subject to the will of a monarch from above, they were not yet at the mercy of a democratic multitude from below. Theirs was a compact and homogeneous society with a common background, education, and mode

The "hunt" is pictured in full pursuit of the fox, the huntsmen in "pink" coats.

of living (see pages 170, 252). They led, on the whole, a less artificial life than the more polished French nobility, and they had by this period far more education and cultural interests than the Prussian. Hard drinkers, frequently immoral, sometimes callous and grasping in their treatment of the lower classes, these peers and country squires nevertheless, as a group, utilized their leisure well and demonstrated a strong sense of duty, particularly as justices of the peace (see page 172). The calm, strong, handsome faces which look down from the paintings of Gainsborough, Reynolds, and Romney reveal their self-satisfaction and contentment with life in general. It is small wonder that their century of domination witnessed only one decade of reform. It naturally seemed folly to tamper with what to them was the best of all possible worlds.

Their closely knit social system is partly explained by their early training. Their sons were usually sent to Eton, Harrow, Winchester, or one of the other great "public" schools, whence they often proceeded to Oxford or to Cambridge. The universities were at much lower ebb in this century than in the seventeenth, Oxford being described as "steeped in port and prejudice," and Cambridge called not much better. Most young aristocrats did little more than grace the university with their presence, receiving a "pass" degree without examination. When Charles James Fox, who developed a real passion for learning, left Oxford to travel abroad for a few months, his class in mathematics was suspended until his return, since the others were not interested. Yet even some idlers apparently acquired a taste for the classics as reflected in their libraries and some of their later Parliamentary speeches.

The "grand tour" generally finished the young man's education. Armed with letters of introduction and of credit, and often accompanied by a tutor, he spent several months or even a couple of years on the Continent. The memoirs of the day reveal these young English "milords" at nearly every social gathering, "losing their hearts in one palace and their money in another." Lord Chesterfield's letters to his son show that the aim was to evolve the grand gentleman, with "that engaging address, those pleasing manners, those little attentions, that air, and those graces which all conspire to make that first advantageous impression upon people's minds. . . ." The grand tour did much to give "this most necessary varnish" to Georgian society.

After this there was a parting of the ways, for only the eldest sons could look forward to inheriting their fathers' acres. Frequently these found their way into the House of Commons. If they belonged to the inner circle, they were before long "sailing on a sea of claret from one comfortable official haven to another," passing through the undersecretaryships and sinecures to cabinet positions, often with no further recommendation than their family connections. It was a fast society which spent much of its time gambling at the clubs—the Whigs at Brooks's and the Tories at White's. Stakes were heavy, one young nobleman losing £11,000 at a sitting and winning it back on a single hand. Wit was a premium—the gossipy letters of Horace Walpole, Sir Robert's son, stand in the front rank of the clever literary products of this group. At Bath, the fashionable watering place, Beau Nash dictated manners and fashions, as did Beau Brummel later in London.

For younger sons the army, the navy, and the Church offered the principal openings, though many went into government civil service, law, or, occasionally, business. Although embryo naval officers often became midshipmen at twelve, the purchase of commissions was the custom in the army. In the Church, political influence increasingly dictated the filling of lucrative positions. The "two-bottle parson," a gentleman by birth, was often better known for hunting prowess than for spiritual zeal; yet with the proper backing, he might still become a bishop. In those three fields, in the family of Lord Cornwallis, not only did he himself hold very high military command and become governor-general of India and viceroy of Ireland, but there was also another general, a ranking admiral, a bishop, and even an Archbishop of Canterbury. In business, the English younger son had an advantage over his French counterpart, automatically barred from such an occupation as degrading.

The country house still remained the true habitat of the English aristocracy. The squires were on their estates most of the time. Even the fashionable London group, with their town houses, were accustomed to spend much time on their country estates. Under the influence of the grand tour, the rambling, gabled features of Tudor and Jacobean days gave way in the Georgian country house to simple, dignified rectangular lines, often accentuated by classic pillars. Many older mansions and college buildings in the United States show the effects of this architecture. The chaste white interiors, and the furniture designed for them by Chippendale, Heppelwhite, and Adam, were in keeping with the stately Georgian simplicity. The paintings on the walls often included old masters as well as old ancestors. Some of the landed aristocracy, like the dukes of Bedford, took an active interest in the supervision and improvement of agriculture; but the majority were to be found more often following the hounds. The stables were an important part of every estate, and the running of the first Derby in 1780 probably aroused much keener interest than the contemporary maneuvers of Cornwallis in the Carolinas.

Along with an assured income without much risk or effort land-owning carried with it a social and political prestige that money obtained from trade did not. George III would raise no man to the peerage unless he owned land; and a long-standing rule, not strictly enforced, forbade anyone to sit in the Commons unless he had an estate worth at least £300. It is not difficult, therefore, to understand Parliament's vital interest in law, order, and sanctity of property, especially large landed property. London merchants and bankers, East India "nabobs," and West India planters purchased estates if they expected to count for anything in society and politics.

Except for those most severely depopulated by the Tudor enclosures, the eighteenth century village, still a string of thatched cottages along a single street, differed little from its ancestor, the manor (see pages 25 ff., 46 ff.). At least half of them operated their acres more or less on the old communal basis, by which no peasant had a permanent interest in any particular portion of the waste, meadow, or tilled land. In more than a thousand years English agriculture had seen few important improvements in the time-honored methods, wasteful and inefficient though they were. A farmer of Alfred's day would probably have noticed little that was unusual either in the practices of Queen Anne's time or in those of ancient Rome. The farmer still spent a good bit of his working day in moving himself and his crude tools from one scattered strip to another of the six acres he tilled of the three open fields, one still lying fallow annually. Reaping about ten times as much as he sowed, he had a net gain of some 300 bushels of grain, half wheat and half rye or barley. He had also milk, wool, eggs, and occasionally meat from his livestock. Besides his rent, he had to pay every tenth sheaf of grain to the Church's tithe proctor. The larger tenant farmers usually hired cottagers to work in their fields. Agriculture, being largely seasonal, cottagers and farmers alike had another important source of income in spinning and weaving in the "domestic system" (see pages 168 ff.).

The Agricultural Revolution

By the middle of the century England was beginning to feel the first effects of the "Agricultural Revolution," closely related to and closely followed by the still more sweeping changes of the "Industrial Revolution." These two movements were in a way complementary; both secured efficiency and increased production at the expense of the workers. The surplus tillers of the soil, uprooted by the Agricultural Revolution, found their way into the new factories of the Industrial Revolution. And, since the factory workers could not themselves produce bread and beef, the agricultural communities underwent still further changes to meet the new demand.

In these movements, as in many others, various obscure pioneers paved the way. The first prominent name in agriculture was that of Jethro Tull, an Oxford graduate who had made a close study of European agricultural practices on his grand tour, and who then had settled down to experiment. In 1733 in his *Horse-Hoeing Husbandry*, he argued that the soil could be made much more productive by breaking it up into small particles by means of double plowing at the start, followed, even after the grain began to grow, with frequent hoeing by a horse-drawn cultivator. This made it necessary to plant seed in rows, instead of the customary broadcasting. To the amazement of rural England, Tull showed that a reduced amount of seed would produce more grain to the acre than ever before.

Lord Townshend, Walpole's brother-in-law, won the nickname of "Turnip Townshend" by experimenting upon his estate (see page 293). He showed that a usable root crop, like turnips, would restore the fertility of the third field by replacing the missing nitrogen and would obviate the necessity of leaving it fallow. The turnips could then be fed to the livestock, which had hitherto often gone hungry in the winter months for want of fodder. Townshend urged that barnyard dung be spread on the fields instead of being left piled in unhealthful heaps, and advocated lime and marl to give increased fertility for longer periods.

The possibility of thus providing winter fodder turned attention to breeding. The pioneer in this was Robert Bakewell whose findings transformed English sheep and cattle. His object was an increased supply of meat, whereas farmers had formerly thought primarily of wool from sheep, milk from cows, and hauling from oxen. By constantly inbreeding, he achieved chunky, compact, and larger animals to supplant the rangy, long-shanked ones. Sheep and cattle were now much larger in size and fatter. "Symmetry well rounded" was his watchword; visitors came from the Continent to see his famous ram Twopounder, whose descendants by the hundreds of thousands were to provide mutton for Englishmen. The records of Smithfield Market at London show that between 1710 and 1795, when Bakewell died at seventy, the average weight of sheep rose from 28 to 80 pounds, while cattle jumped from 370 to 800 pounds.

When the landlords heard that hitherto barren wastes were producing rich crops with heavy increases in rental value, they wanted to introduce the new methods, but were balked by the old communal system of village agriculture. The small farmer lacked the capital to buy the apparatus required for Tull's "horse hoeing" and to pay for the expensive fertilizing. He could not experiment with rotation of crops by himself; for the village as a whole decided each year what everyone should plant in the two active fields. He could not hope for success in improving the breed of sheep or cattle, since his beasts would have to roam "unchaperoned" among their lanky neighbors on the waste. For success, a farmer would have to shut off his own particular plot of land instead of continuing the old open-field system. Such considerations led to the wholesale agricultural enclosures of the Georgian period. These must not be confused with the Tudor enclosures, usually intended for sheep-grazing (see page 169).

A village tragedy was enacted on two thousand occasions in the last forty years of the century. The church door one Sunday morning would bear a notice that Parliament was about to be petitioned for an enclosure of the common lands. The lesser villagers might protest or even riot; but with Squire himself or his friends in Parliament, and with that body composed, anyway, largely of landlords, the bill would ordinarily pass. Soon commissioners would

appear to put an end to the immemorial communal life of the village. The common waste land would disappear, and probably the meadow and tilled land also. Each individual who shared in the old common tillage—and this did not include the cottagers—would be allotted a particular piece of land which he was to fence in, or "enclose," for his own use. The squire and the larger freeholders or tenants would receive enough to make their cultivation more profitable under the new methods; but the lesser tenants, who were losing their free fuel and the pasturage for their livestock, could seldom afford the compulsory cost of enclosing their little allotments and would have to sell out their rights for a song. For them three courses were open. They might emigrate to America, or become factory hands in the new factories, or stay in the village as laborers. The cottagers, receiving no land of their own and losing their old common privileges, went the same way. The landlord might argue that "God did not create the earth to be waste for feeding a few geese, but to be cultivated by man." The answer came back, "Parliament may be tender of property; all I know is that I had a cow and an Act of Parliament has taken it from me."

The former happy, inefficient population of the villages dwindled away to a fraction of the old number; yet that small remainder, following the new methods of Tull, Townshend, and Bakewell, made the village acres far more productive than they had ever been before. Bread and beef were thus supplied for a while to meet the demands of the rapidly increasing industrial population. Between 1761 and 1801 there were exactly two thousand enclosure acts, affecting nearly a tenth of the total area of England; and the following forty years saw nearly as many more.

Without the enclosures England could scarcely have made good use of the new agricultural discoveries, have fed a larger population, or even have defeated Napo-

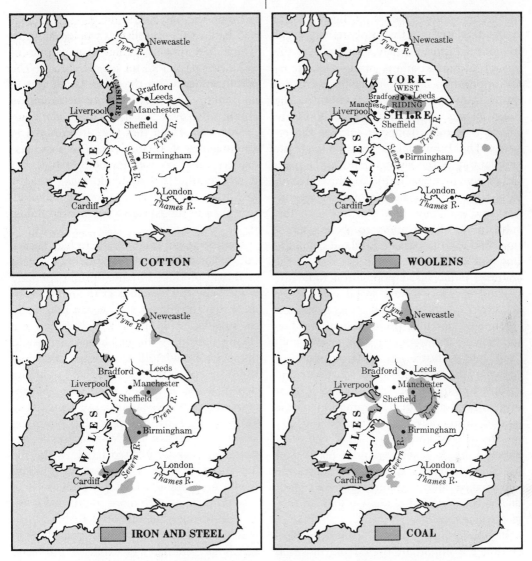

INDUSTRIAL ENGLAND IN THE 19TH CENTURY

leon. To some extent, therefore, most Englishmen benefited, but mainly the landlords, who, being rich, became richer still. Some of the new wealth percolated down, naturally, to the intelligent farmer, a term always used in England to denote a person who rents a farm and who tills it in person, an agricultural laborer working for wages never being called a farmer. But the lesser folk at the bottom paid the penalty for the advance of science. As the contemporary poet Goldsmith has it in his *Deserted Village,*

Ill fares the land, to hastening ills a prey,
Where wealth accumulates, and men decay:
. . . a bold peasantry, their country's pride,
When once destroy'd, can never be supplied.

The Industrial Revolution

A considerable portion of that bold peasantry was "decaying" in the factories and slums of Manchester, Leeds, and other mushroom centers created by the Industrial Revolution, perhaps the most striking event in modern history. Briefly stated, it was the change in human affairs brought about by the application of power machinery to industrial processes. "Manufactured" (the Latin *manus* and *facio*) originally meant "made by hand." Today it implies the reverse. The Industrial Revolution was the supplanting of the human hand in the making of commodities by the machine. It was to change the very nature of society, politics, and economic life. Starting with this substitution of machinery for handwork, it uprooted a large part of England's population and set it down in another part of the country; it increased population radically; it emphasized two new social classes, the wealthy capitalistic, middle-class bourgeoisie and the landless proletariat of the factory towns; it introduced women and children into industry on a large scale; it brought about a new and hitherto undreamed-of discipline in industrial life; it overthrew the political domination of the landed aristocracy; it substituted the city for the village as the important center of national life; it gave England a position of increased importance in world commerce and finance; and it gave the working class, during the period of change, a half century of extreme misery.

Beginning just before the American Revolution the important period of transition lasted about sixty years. It represented the fourth main stage in the development of English industry. In the early Middle Ages such industry as there was, centered in the self-sufficient manor. Then, about 1100, came the towns with guilds and workshops. By 1400 they were being supplanted by the "domestic," or "putting out," system (see pages 25, 46, 91 ff., 172 ff.). England's rapidly expanding foreign commerce stimulated the demand for manufactures, and the introduction of machinery and factories was the answer. Textiles and iron were the special fields of the new activity.

From the later Middle Ages, England had had a well-established woolen industry which had quickly achieved a surplus of cloth (see page 130) for export abroad. The cotton industry, on the other hand, was in its infancy. The English were becoming so enthusiastic over the new cotton cloth imported from India that they determined to manufacture it themselves. The new machinery could be used for both textiles, but it was natural that it should make quicker headway in the newer cotton manufacture than in the conservative woolen industry.

Under the old methods there had been a fair balance between the amount of yarn or thread produced by the upright spinning wheels and the demands of the hand looms on which the thread was woven into cloth. As early as 1733 John Kay invented the "flying shuttle," with which one man could operate a broadcloth loom where two had been necessary before. The hand spinning wheels could not keep pace with this increased speed of weaving until James Hargreaves, in 1764, invented his "spinning jenny," the first of the four big textile inventions popularly associated with the beginning of the Industrial Revolution. Really a spinning wheel lying on its side, it could turn eight or more spindles at once, instead of only one. In 1769 Richard Arkwright patented a new spinning machine in which a number of rollers produced tougher threads than those from the jenny. This was called a "water frame," since it could be operated by water power. Samuel Crompton in 1779 combined the principles of the jenny and the water frame in his "mule," which could spin a thread both fine and tough. By this time the old situation was reversed, and the looms could not keep up with the greatly increased supply of thread until, in 1785, the Reverend Edmund Cartwright invented the power loom. This came into general use more slowly than the spinning machinery; but by 1833 there were 85,000 power looms in England,

and the original balance between spinning and weaving was restored. The final need was for an adequate supply of raw cotton, which was to come from the United States, where Eli Whitney about 1793 invented the cotton gin, which separated the fiber from the seeds. This gave to the southern part of the United States its principal source of wealth.

The flying shuttle and the spinning jenny could be used at home under the "domestic system"; but the new looms were too large, and they also required water power. This led to the gathering of workers into factories near swift streams, which could turn the wheels. Many were located in lonely valleys in the northwest, especially in Lancashire, with its little streams flowing from the hills. Not until the advent of the steam engine was it possible to concentrate these factories in cities.

Hand in hand with the textiles went developments in iron. Iron deposits existed in many parts of England, and for centuries there had been a fairly active iron industry in the southern counties, where the large groves of oaks provided the charcoal necessary for smelting. By the middle of the eighteenth century, however, the oaks were disappearing so fast that the government was seriously concerned over the future supply of naval timber. But in the Midlands and in the north were large coal deposits, with plenty of iron close at hand. "Sea coals" had long been carried from Newcastle to London for fuel, but only gradually the idea developed of using coal instead of oak charcoal for smelting.

Between 1708 and 1754 the Abraham Darbys, father and son, made a series of successful experiments in smelting with coke made from coal. This led to a shift of the iron industry to the coal regions. It was difficult to get the fire hot enough to melt the ore thoroughly, however, until an engineer invented a blowing engine for the coke blast furnaces at the Carron works in Scotland. The blast furnace turned out pig or cast iron containing from 2 to 5 per cent carbon, which made it too brittle for many purposes. Then, to produce malleable wrought iron by removing this carbon, a "reverberatory furnace" was invented; but real success came in 1784, when Henry Cort perfected the process of "puddling," which made possible the efficient conversion of pig into wrought iron on a large scale. Cort, working with one Purnell, also developed the rolling mill, which turned the wrought iron into sheets and other forms needed in industry and engineering. Sheet iron was useful for boilers, tanks, and later for shipbuilding; while bar and other structural iron was used in bridges and canals, and later for rails. The immediate demand for iron led to a wholesale opening of foundries and mines in the "Black Country" of the Midlands and the north.

There still remained the need of producing steel on a large scale. Steel is tougher than cast iron and more easy to work into shape than wrought iron, and because of its strength it is more valuable than iron for many purposes. It must have just the proper proportion of carbon—less than cast iron and more than wrought iron. It was produced in excellent quality but small quantity by the cutlery works of Sheffield and elsewhere, but large scale production had to wait until the inventions of Bessemer and others in the middle of the nineteenth century. Steel thereupon replaced iron in many of its former uses.

Particularly important was the development of the steam engine during the mid-eighteenth century. As early as 1705 Thomas Newcomen invented one which was used to pump water out of mine pits and to work the blowing engines for blast furnaces. It was inefficient because energy was wasted in heating and cooling the cylinder for every stroke. James Watt, a young Scot, mathematical instrument-maker at the University of Glasgow, observed this drawback when he was called upon to repair a Newcomen engine. Developing a separate condenser, he made the first practical steam engine. By closing both ends of the cylinder, he introduced the steam into it by alternate jets. He also added the flywheel, thus making rotary motion possible, an indispensable improvement if the engine was to be of general utility; and later he invented the governor, or speed-regulator. In 1769, Watt took out his first patent; and shortly afterward he and Matthew Boulton, a Birmingham manufacturer of note, formed a partnership to manufacture the "Boulton and Watt" engine, particularly for the iron and coal industries. In 1785 one of these engines was first used in a cotton mill; then it gradually replaced water power and made possible the concentration of factories in large cities. The steamboat and the locomotive were other results of Watt's invention (see pages 346, 401). Until partially replaced by electricity, steam was the principal source of power for industry and transportation. This invention naturally increased the demand for coal; and hundreds of new mines were opened, in addition to those connected with iron-smelting.

The new inventions tremendously increased production. In 1764, the year of the spinning jenny, England imported 1500 tons of raw cotton; in 1833, she imported 150,000 tons! The increase in the production of iron was almost as great. In 1740, 59 furnaces produced 17,350 tons. Just a century later, 378 furnaces were producing 1,348,000 tons.

Growth of Population

Population as well as production was profoundly affected by the Industrial Revolution. As long as most Englishmen were engaged in subsistence agriculture, with its old inefficient methods, population grew very slowly. In nearly seven centuries, between the Domesday survey and 1750, it rose from about 1,500,000 to only about 6,500,000. Then it began to grow by leaps

and bounds as industry became increasingly more important: 8,890,000 when the first regular census was taken, in 1801; 13,800,000 in 1831; 17,900,000 in 1851; 22,700,000 in 1871; and 32,500,000 in 1901. After that, the rate of increase slowed with only 42,600,000 in 1951. Those figures are for England and Wales alone. Scotland and Ireland, which remained more distinctly agricultural, grew more gradually, with some 7,000,000 inhabitants in 1801 and only 8,500,000 in 1901, a figure which remained practically stationary for forty subsequent years, the moderate gains in Scotland having been offset by heavy losses in Ireland. The increase in population was caused in part by medical discoveries and by improvement in hygiene, which cut down infant mortality.

A second effect on population was its shift northward and westward from the southern and eastern counties. The heaviest exodus was from the region most severely affected by the Georgian agricultural enclosures, a strip running from near the Isle of Wight northeastward toward Norfolk. The cotton industry became located in Lancashire, in the west, just above Wales, partly because its moist, even climate prevented the threads from breaking as they would in drier air. The center of the woolen industry moved from Norfolk to the West Riding of Yorkshire. The iron industry converted into a "Black Country" parts of the Midlands and of the north, where coal was plentiful.

The third effect was that the typical English worker became a city dweller instead of a countryman. In 1750 about three quarters of England's population was rural; in 1851 the rural and urban populations were almost exactly equal; and in 1901 more than three quarters of the population was urban. The four most important cities built up by the Industrial Revolution—Manchester and Leeds in the textile industry and Birmingham and Sheffield in iron—grew at least tenfold in the century following 1760. Towns of about 5000 inhabitants in 1685, they had about 30,000 in 1760 and 300,000 in 1860. Manchester jumped from 17,000 in 1757 to 142,000 in 1833 and continued rapidly toward the half-million mark. Birmingham rose steadily until it was second only to London in size, displacing Bristol, now completely overshadowed by the rival port of Liverpool, the outlet for Lancashire. Newcastle-on-Tyne, over on the east coast, waxed great with coal and shipbuilding, while Bradford flourished with the woolen industry. And many another small town grew rapidly into a populous and grimy city.

Social Effects

The social results of the Industrial Revolution were many and profound. In the days before power machinery, class lines between employers and employees were few. That gulf had existed between noble and commoner, landowner and peasant; but under ordinary circumstances an industrious apprentice, who saved his money, had in the early days every expectation of rising in the ranks, often becoming a master. The simple, inexpensive, and portable tools were at first the personal property of those who used them. True, under the domestic system a class of middlemen arose between producer and purchaser; but class lines still remained vague. The steam engine ended all this. The expensive and bulky new machines could not easily be moved. Instead of being the worker's personal property, they came under the head "capital goods." Capital has been defined as wealth which is used to produce more wealth; the new machines and the factories which housed them were thus capital. There had been no such thing as capitalism, in the sense that the tools of production belonged to men who did not operate them, until the domestic system, and then the amount involved was very slight as compared with this new concentration of capital. The old social unities began to disappear. Now the

capitalist or employer did not live with his men. He "hired and fired" his "hands." At first, in the smaller factories, he frequently continued to know each individually; but as they grew larger and larger personal relationships disappeared. Occasionally a factory hand might rise to the status of employer; but this became the exception rather than the rule. The employers, who owned the tools, became a class apart. Without land, without property, without guarantee of employment, the working class, the so-called "proletariat," sank in the social scale.

The enterprising and often self-made group who created, owned, and operated the factories, foundries, and mines profited greatly by the Industrial Revolution. Almost overnight some of them built up fortunes rivaling those of the landed aristocracy. This "middle class," the so-called "bourgeoisie," was not new in England (see page 172), but never before had it been so prominent. It grew steadily more powerful during the nineteenth century, acquiring political power along with wealth. The Reform Act of 1832 and the repeal of the Corn Laws signalized the victory of these capitalists over the landowners, who had monopolized the government for so long. Under the influence of their new wealth, the government adopted a *laissez-faire*, or "hands-off," attitude toward business, with the result that for many years little was done to improve the lot of the factory workers (see page 391).

Along with this hardening of class lines came an enormous increase in the employment of women and children in industry. The new machinery, particularly in the manufacture of textiles, now put a premium on quickness and agility rather than on strength. Not only did a child occupy less space on a crowded factory floor than an adult, but little fingers were more flexible in tying broken threads, and above all else child labor was very cheap. The results were unfortunate. Women, drawn from their homes, competed with men in the labor market, thus depressing the wage scale; and children placed in factories were subjected to harsh and inhuman treatment.

In early factories in the remote regions, the children were generally orphans or paupers, leased out in batches as apprentices by the guardians of the poor. They were herded in barracks and forced to work from twelve to fourteen hours a day. On Sundays they had to clean the machines and go to church. If they went to school once a week (on Sunday), that was considered sufficient. By an act of 1747 "an apprentice could appeal to a magistrate against his master's ill-treatment, and if the case was proved, could obtain his or her discharge."[1] But just how a ten-year-old or twelve-year-old child was to avail himself of this protection was not stated.

As steam succeeded water power the number of child laborers increased. With the congestion of factories in the new industrial towns, it was no longer necessary to hire pauper children, for children of the local working class were available. The conditions remained much the same. From the age of eight and sometimes younger, children in most mills worked from six in the morning until seven at night with an hour off at noon. Not until 1802 was any act passed by Parliament specifically for their protection. Other acts, increasingly protective, followed in 1819 and 1833 (see pages 408 ff.). In the meantime, the children continued to work, doing their bit to defeat Napoleon by adding to England's wealth. An unfounded tradition has accredited William Pitt, the great war prime minister, with advising the mill owners, discouraged and disgruntled because of high taxes, to recompense themselves with child labor. Such advice was already being followed. More than one generation of children grew up without

education, and with such strenuous labor they were worn out physically far too young, even when they did not lose their jobs, as they became adults, to younger competitors.

The effect on home life of this work by women and children was not the least of its evils. Long factory hours left women neither time nor strength to clean dark and cheerless rooms of what were anyway crowded, unsanitary tenements. With no time for cooking, the family meals became largely a matter of baker's bread. The children were dirty, undernourished, and often half sick. Bad enough as these conditions were for the strong and well, they were the more deplorable for the sick and the aged, for whom there was neither money enough nor room. The too frequent presence of the unemployed husband and father, spending his days idly in the nearest "pub" or in half-hearted attempts to improve the housekeeping did not help.

Before the coming of power machinery the hours of work had been as long, sometimes longer; but the worker generally chose those hours as he saw fit. To work thus with machines was impossible. Instead of the worker's finding satisfaction in making a complete article, he was more and more limited to guiding a machine monotonously through some separate part of the process, because this new "division of labor" was more efficient. Machines, moreover, were never tired; therefore those who tended them were subjected to a necessary but irksome discipline. "The workman was summoned by the factory bell; his daily life was arranged by factory hours; he worked under an overseer imposing a method and precision for which the overseer had in turn to answer to some higher authority; if he broke one of the long series of minute regulations he was fined."[2] A spinner was fined a good part of his meager day's pay, if he was found with his windows open, dirty at work, washing himself,

[1] J. L. Hammond and B. Hammond, *The Town Labourer* (1917), p. 149. By permission of Longmans, Green & Co.

[2] *Ibid.*, p. 19.

Industrial landscape in Yorkshire, 1814, with child workers in foreground.

whistling, or five minutes late, to mention only a few offenses.

The Industrial Revolution brought about the urbanization of life—new cities grew with astonishing rapidity and without direction. Speculative building went on apace, "jerry-built" houses being the rule rather than the exception. Rents had to be low and the collection of them was not always easy or regular. Many little houses in which the industrial proletariat swarmed were built back to back, with no windows in the rear, to economize space and brick. In other cases, a number of closely packed houses would front on a tiny court, into which garbage and sometimes sewage were dumped. Frequently both methods of construction were followed at the same time, and the result from a sanitary point of view was alarming.

The slums of Glasgow in 1839, with between fifteen thousand and thirty thousand inhabitants, were described by a royal commissioner, as consisting of "narrow alleys and square courts, in the middle of every one of which there lies a dung heap. . . . In some of the sleeping places . . . we found a complete layer of human beings stretched upon the floor, often fifteen to twenty, some clad, others naked, men and women indiscriminately."

In Manchester, a prominent contemporary economist, wrote thus: "In one place we found a whole street following the course of a ditch, because in this way deeper cellars could be secured without the cost of digging—cellars not for storing wares or rubbish, but for dwellings for human beings. *Not one house of this street escaped the cholera.* In general the streets of these suburbs are unpaved, with a dung heap or ditch in the middle; the houses are built back to back, without ventilation or drainage, and the families are limited to a corner of a cellar or garret." According to a doctor who wrote in 1837, out of 6951 houses 6565 needed whitewashing within, 1435 were damp, and 2221 were without even privies.

It is small wonder that men did not flock willingly to the factory towns and wanted nothing more than to continue the old life undisturbed. That was out of the question, for the "domestic" workers, already deprived of their cows and their fuel by the enclosure movement at just this period, could not compete with the new machinery. One man, or even one child, operating a factory machine produced more than several men using the old methods. Textile prices were so reduced by the new large-scale production that the handworkers had their choice—unless they preferred to sink to the level of farm laborers or migrate overseas—of becoming factory hands or else of slowly starving to death upon the reduced income from their spinning and weaving. Exile from familiar surroundings was hard enough; but besides that, as part of the landless proletariat, they were completely at the mercy of the fluctuations in the demand for labor, with no garden plot, cow, or geese to serve as reserves in times of depression. The medieval serf was pitied because he was tied to the land; the factory worker was to be pitied because he had no land at all. No longer master of his time, he was subject, with his wife and children, to appallingly long hours under severe discipline; and, when his work was done, the filthy slums in which he lived were in sad contrast to the former village. From robust, generally contented, though often slow-witted beings, many English workers were transformed into sickly, stunted, and disgruntled members of society, potentially dangerous because they had a grievance.

Such was the growth of industrial England. Hard enough as such life was when there was work to do, it became desperate when mills shut down in periods of depression, as happened with a certain degree of regularity in the fluctuations of modern world business. Whatever the causes, and they are many and complex, the effect upon the worker and his family was tragic, for all sense of security was gone. Yet too dark a picture must not be painted. Not all the new houses were jerry-built slum tenements; and a good many people became far more prosperous than they had ever been.

The Workers' Reaction

How did Englishmen react toward these astonishing changes in their economic life—this physical dislocation of huge numbers of men from southern and eastern England to the north and west; this change from countryside to city, from plow to loom; new wealth for some, new poverty for others? The poorer folk, the depressed classes, who stayed in the country appeared more resigned to their fate than their brothers who migrated to the cities. The old economic order had changed in the village; but this did not mean that the old moral order had disappeared. The squire was still the squire, a justice of the peace. The church was still the church; and where, as occasionally happened, the villagers flocked to the ministrations of some itinerant Methodist preacher, they still listened to sermons which stressed obedience to the powers that be. Proposals made in Parliament for a minimum wage never had a chance of enactment, but the Poor Law (see page 209) did intervene to some extent to prevent actual death from starvation. With this the dwindling minority on the farms had to be content. They were even barred by an old law of Charles II from shooting game unless they were freeholders or large leaseholders. A great number risked poaching, however, despite severe penalties if caught, and death-dealing traps set for them in the woods by gamekeepers. During the reign of George III poaching increased rapidly.

Aside, however, from poaching and occasional rick and barn burning, there was general submission by the rural poor. A

View of cotton factory on Union Street, Manchester, in 1835.

feeble rebellion flared up in 1830 as the result of improved threshing machines; but it was quickly suppressed, and the agitators were sent to the penal colonies in Australia. The atmosphere of the village was not conducive to revolt.

Not so the atmosphere of the town. Here the living symbols of traditional authority were lacking—the squire, the clergyman, perhaps the old grandfather in the chimney corner. In place of them, it is true, were superintendents, overseers, factory owners; but these men carried no traditional, inherited authority. Usually risen from the ranks, they inspired no awe in those beneath them. With workers from all over Britain and Ireland thrown together pell-mell, there was a chance for the agitator to make himself heard. Some of these workers could read, and the pamphlets of Thomas Paine and other radicals were in circulation.

The cotton workers, for instance, were hostile to Richard Arkwright, inventor of the water frame. They attacked his first mills in Lancashire at the time of the American Revolution, destroyed most of the machinery, and burned the buildings. The mills, nevertheless, increased in number. In 1789, the year of the French Revolution, the first Watt steam engine was started in Manchester. For several decades in that bleak northern city, there followed dull misery, bitter hate, and numerous strikes. The government in alarm introduced soldiers and spoke of French influence. The weavers and spinners alike knew little of France and cared less. They were hungry, ill-fed, ill-clad, and ill-housed, and wanted higher wages. When they were not striking, or breaking up machinery, they were either drawing up petitions to Parliament for a minimum wage or else attempting to organize themselves into unions, an action then forbidden.

In Yorkshire, to which the woolen and worsted workers migrated, there was never quite so decided a concentration either of population or of capital as in the upstart cotton industry, but the woolen workers had centuries of tradition behind them. Their principal animosity was directed against the "gig mill," which raised the nap in cloth far faster than by hand work. Some employers did not use the new machine, so violent was the feeling; and its introduction was gradual. As late as 1836 there were still some 14,000 worsted weavers at Bradford competing against the steam engine.

The same general features characterized the efforts of the Spitalfields silk weavers, workers in the lace trade, and the "stockingers"—namely, strikes, lockouts, arson, troops. In the midst of the Napoleonic Wars riots started in the stocking trade, where unemployment, combined with the high cost of living, led to the destruction of the "frames," as the machinery was called. Since they were widely scattered in small houses, it was difficult to prevent their wreckage. So great was local sympathy that the government at times sent soldiers to guard the courthouses where the rioters were tried. The movement spread to other industries. The "Luddites," as these bolder workers were called, were suppressed in the Midland counties, but shortly appeared in Lancashire, burning mills and smashing machinery. The government was quick to act: there were eight death sentences, and Lancashire became quiet. Then, the frenzy broke forth in Yorkshire. Again it was stamped out thoroughly, with some hanged, and others transported. Little more was heard of the Luddites. Though using spies, the authorities seem to have acted with decent, albeit harsh, respect for legal rights. But England at this time, it must be remembered, was at war with Napoleon, and if many were convicted, many more were acquitted.

More intelligent than breaking machines were the workers' efforts to unite in unions to force higher wages and better working conditions. Joining together gave them more equal conditions for bargaining with employers; otherwise the cards were stacked against them. While the discharge of one employee who tried to get more pay or shorter hours for himself would count for nothing in the running of a factory, the strike, or refusal to work, of all the workers, for the purpose of enforcing their demands, would temporarily disorganize business. From 1799 to 1824, labor was prevented from using this device of collective bargaining by the Combination Acts. These stated explicitly that any workmen who combined "to get an increase in wages or a decrease in hours" were liable if convicted to "be sent forthwith to jail for three months." Even to attend a meeting for such a purpose, or to urge others to attend, or to help to collect money for holding such a meeting was held a criminal act. Rigidly enforced during the Napoleonic Wars, they remained the chief weapon against the workers until repealed in 1824.

Thereafter, the trade union was to become a powerful factor in England. By "trade union" is meant the combination of the workers in a trade; this was the usual workers' unit in the English movement. Its most common weapon was the strike, or the cessation of workers from their jobs in order to gain some end. The more radical "general strike," designed to stop all industry by all unions striking at one time, was later used. Partly because of the unions, the proletariat was to secure more political power in a few generations than the scattered agricultural peasants had gained in centuries. By 1867 a large proportion of the factory workers would secure the vote. By the end of the century there would gradually develop a Labor party, which after World War I would be more than once the largest party in the House of Commons.

One may wonder how the intelligent and educated men who governed England in the early decades of the Industrial Revolution, were so blind to the plight of the workers, to child labor, and to other factory abuses. One explanation is that they, like everybody else, confused by the sudden impact and onrush of the Industrial Revolution, could not see clearly what was taking place. There were no historic precedents to guide men's actions in regard to the new wealth. The energetic, hard-working businessman, who was rising fast in the economic scale, had little time to reflect on the social significance of what he was doing and was apt to adopt the prevalent view that the employer was beneficial to the community, "whatever the wages he paid or the conditions he imposed . . . the employer had only to say that all the profits of his industry depended on his last half hour, and the kindest people saw that it was cruel to give the workmen a little leisure at the risk of their livelihood."[3] The leading economic thinkers, such as Adam Smith and Malthus (see pages 357, 413), were in general agreement with such a point of view. For the most part, however, few bothered to ponder over economic theories. Another explanation was the panic created by the French Revolution and heightened by Napoleonic victories on the Continent (see page 367). A third might possibly be sheer selfishness, rationalized into devotion to law and order. For a fourth it is necessary to have in mind the evangelical religious revival of the times (see page 354). Strange as it may seem, if one trusts to evidence drawn from the writings of that ever-popular writer Hannah More and from the speeches of William Wilberforce, an influential member of the House of Commons, poverty was generally considered to be good for the soul. Workingmen were expected to remain patient under affliction and to look forward for better days to heaven alone. At the same time, private benevolence was considered

[3] J. L. Hammond and B. Hammond, *op. cit.*, p. 209.

a duty of the well-to-do, and many of them spent time and money in humanitarian work. But even these failed to see any connection between religion or justice and the necessity for dragging a whole social class out of the gutter.

The Communication Revolution

Simultaneously with the Industrial Revolution came the beginning of a "Communication Revolution." Unlike the contemporary transformation of agriculture and industry, its benefits were not secured at the expense of the workers. Developments in transportation and communication have linked the world closer together, have broken down the old provincialism, have facilitated the exchange of commodities and ideas, and have added much to the possible pleasure of life, while they have created still further new wealth. They have helped men to explore and settle the wilderness, and to centralize business and government both at home and overseas. This "revolution," which began in the England of George III with canals and turnpikes, later developed the steamboat, railway, telegraph, cable, telephone, automobile, and airplane, and still continues with radio, television, and space exploration.

The changes were certainly revolutionary. Goods, men, and messages did not move as fast in 1760 as they had done in Roman times. Every decade since 1760 has seen a greater development in communication than took place in the whole fifteen hundred years before that date. The normal rate of travel on the main roads was about forty miles a day, while freight moved at about half that speed. In France, where a start had already been made in improving roads, the rate was somewhat faster, while in America it was slower. The narrow, deeply rutted, and muddy English roads were responsible for these relatively slow rates. Travelers of the eighteenth century have left most uncomplimentary accounts of them, even on the main lines of

The Birmingham Tally-Ho! Coaches passing the Crown at Holloway, 1823, showing the conditions of fashionable travel in the pre-railway era.

communication, where they often followed the track of the splendid Roman highways (see page 5). In 1760 the stagecoach, springless and uncomfortable, had been in use for about a century, and it took two weeks to travel the four hundred miles between the English and Scottish capitals. Except on the main roads, it was often necessary to go by horseback. For freight, four-wheeled wagons, carrying a ton or two, were in use on the main highways; they took three weeks between London and Edinburgh. Over the poorer roads or paths the pack horse was the common means of transportation, and it took seven of these to carry a ton of coal.

Freight was transported by water whenever this was possible, although freshets, droughts, and mud banks made river traffic unreliable, while coastal voyages were often protracted to unreasonable lengths by the contrary winds. Six weeks was good

time for a transatlantic voyage, but head winds might extend this to ten weeks or more. In 1759 it took thirty-three days for London to hear of Wolfe's victory at Quebec, the nearest American port to England. The East Indiamen required about six months for the voyage to or from Calcutta, while the expedition which first settled Australia was eight months on the way.

Even the maximum speeds attained under such general conditions were not impressive. Ordinarily the best records were made by couriers riding night and day with frequent changes of horses. The young courtier who had carried from London to Edinburgh the news of Elizabeth's death had averaged only one hundred and sixty miles a day. When the first shots of the American Revolution were fired at Lexington, near Boston, in 1775, a messenger, dispatched immediately to carry the news southward over the main post roads, with

The pioneer canal designed by George Brindley for the Duke of Bridgewater, opened in 1761, is shown crossing the River Irwell by a high aqueduct.

all possible speed, reached New York in four days. A fuller account, sent over the same route two days later, was carried through New Jersey at a maximum speed of 100 miles a day, but this slackened in the Southern colonies with their still poorer roads, cut by broad inlets of the sea. Altogether, it took three weeks from Boston to South Carolina. This may be taken fairly to represent colonial land communication at its fastest, an average of about 55 miles a day. Had the winds been favorable all the way, the message would have gone quicker by water.

Now, as a result of the developments in communication, messages are sent almost instantaneously around the world, and that distance is being traveled in fewer and fewer days. The progress may be summarized by recalling a dozen dates when new developments reached a fairly practicable stage. In 1761 the first bargeload of coal was shipped over Brindley's Bridgewater Canal. In 1803 Thomas Telford inaugurated scientific road construction on a large scale in Scotland. In 1807 Robert Fulton's *Clermont* steamed up the Hudson from New York to Albany. In 1825 George Stephenson's locomotive opened the Stockton and Darlington Railway in England. In 1844 Samuel F. B. Morse sent from Washington to Baltimore the first long-distance telegraph message. In 1866 transatlantic cable service was permanently established, after an abortive attempt eight years earlier. In 1876 Alexander Graham Bell sent to his assistant the first telephone message. In 1879 a little electric train at the Berlin Exposition foreshadowed electric power on railways and local lines (see page 401 for railway beginnings). In 1887 Gottlieb Daimler operated the first gasoline-propelled automobile. In 1901 Count Marconi, in Newfoundland, heard the three dots of the Morse code S sent across the Atlantic from his wireless station in Cornwall. In 1903 Wilbur and Orville Wright made the first successful airplane flight at Kitty Hawk, on the Carolina coast. In 1915 the human voice was transmitted from Washington to Hawaii by wireless, paving the way for the rapid development of radio and television—to say nothing of later fantastic developments in outer space.

The coming of the Industrial Revolution, and particularly the necessity of moving iron and coal, called for improved methods of transportation. Canals, the first answer, had been used on the Continent, but in England the earliest was a short one designed in 1761 by James Brindley for the Duke of Bridgewater to connect his coal mine with Manchester ten miles away. Freight costs were radically reduced, and soon all the important industrial parts of England were linked with a network of canals.

Then came the building of turnpikes. The word "macadamize" has given lasting recognition to the success of Thomas Telford and John McAdam, about 1800, in giving the roads a hard surface of crushed rock. The principal reason for the poor roads of the earlier period was the old duty of each community to maintain the roads which passed through it; now turnpike companies were formed to undertake the costly new construction and were permitted to charge tolls to reimburse themselves. Stagecoaches could now travel twelve miles an hour, and freight could be moved much more easily than had been possible under previous conditions.

The steamboat's chief value lay in relieving shipping from dependence upon the whims of the winds. The effects of this new regularity and dependability were most noticeable in short coastal voyages and in the harbor functions of tugs and ferries, while steamboats could also be used to ascend rivers with swift currents. Steam was not so essential upon the high seas,

and not until 1838 did steamships begin to take the place of the swift sailing packets on the transatlantic shuttle. The old sailing square-riggers clung even longer to ordinary ocean freight-carrying, and not until the last quarter of the nineteenth century was the tramp steamer quite generally supplanting them (see pages 401 ff. for railways).

The new developments were to have a particular effect on freight, most noticeable in the bulky commodities, such as coal, and the perishable ones, such as food. In the eighteenth century transportation was so slow that herrings began to smell before they had been carried many miles inland. Now, with the further application of refrigeration to modern carriers, the "roast beef of old England" comes fresh from the Argentine or the plains of the United States, while mutton comes from "down under" in Australia and New Zealand. No longer does a community have to depend upon the seasonal supply of fruit and green vegetables from local gardens, and even milk, which spoils quickly, may be brought from long distances.

Business too has felt the effect of improved communications. The term "venture" was aptly applied to the sending forth of a shipment, as it was not known whether it would reach an empty or a glutted market. Advance information of important matters, even a few hours before the information became public, might mean a fortune. Financial giants like the Rothschilds maintained an elaborate service of correspondents and couriers; but even they lacked the full and fresh business information that is to be found in any metropolitan daily today. World prices, too, have tended to become equalized. The buyer now can ascertain quickly the current prices of a desired commodity, even in different continents. After taking freight and other charges into account, he will normally buy in the cheapest market, thus bringing into close competition commercial centers thousands of miles apart. The financial world also became involved in the various agencies of communication. The coming of the railway meant heavy depreciation of canal and turnpike securities, and for nearly a century the locomotive held full sway on land, moving nearly everything and everybody that had to travel more than a few miles. Profits were good, and transport was an absolute necessity; consequently railroad securities became favorites with conservative as well as speculative investors. Of late years, the railways have been fighting against the fast increasing inroads in their former passenger and freight monopoly by the private automobile, the bus, the truck, and the plane.

Rapid communication has also made possible the concentration of political authority and responsibility, especially in colonial and foreign affairs. When an interchange of messages with the home government involved weeks and even months, governors, admirals, generals, and diplomats had to be endowed with wide powers to meet emergencies. The ministers at home frequently had no control in important crises. The new methods of communication transformed those in authority on distant stations from plenipotentiaries into "nothing but damned errand boys at the end of a wire." London is in far closer communication today with the farthest capitals of the Commonwealth than it was with Oxford or Portsmouth in 1760. British rule might well have not spread in India had there been a cable connection in the formative period. Even in Britain itself, it formerly took weeks to send out writs for a new election to Parliament and to assemble the members from the distant shires; now a new Parliament can gather at West-

minster within a week of a general election. Downing Street keeps its finger at all times upon the course of events all over the world. Warfare likewise has been affected by the possibility of concentrating armies rapidly in large numbers, of relieving threatened positions quickly, of improving the situation of the wounded, and of extending the campaigning distance from the base of supplies. At sea as well as on land, tremendous changes have been wrought in strategy and tactics.

By no means the least important influence of the revolution in communications has been the broadening of the horizon of the individual. The average village was practically cut off from the outside world, and news of great events trickled in slowly. Most people never in their lives traveled more than fifty miles from their birthplace. The railway did much to increase travel; but cars, always available at one's convenience, and jet planes, enabling one to lunch in England and dine the same day in America, have done infinitely more in giving individuals a new control over their movements. Cheap and rapid postal service, together with the telephone, have helped to increase outside contacts. Provincialism has been still further broken down by the instruments of mass communication—the newspaper, the moving picture, the radio, and television; important events, occurring anywhere in the world, can be reported to millions within the hour. And that has been accomplished without those grim accompaniments—the grinding discipline, the dreary factory towns, the labor problems, and the squalid slums—which marked the companion movement, the Industrial Revolution.

Chapter Eighteen

Thought and Letters from Newton to Burke

Eighteenth-century Englishmen excelled in war, in economics, in thought, and in letters. By land and by sea British arms were victorious. Soldiers and sailors, merchants, colonial administrators, and, more especially, colonial mothers formed and fashioned a fine empire—only to lose the choicest part of it. A host of miners tapped the coal and iron mines of England. The steam engine began its miraculous career. Textile mills appeared in many places in the north. Bristol continued to thrive on the West Indian trade. London was rapidly moving toward world primacy in commerce and finance.

Almost simultaneously with the economic revolutions of the century there was taking place what has been called "a revolution in men's minds." The printing press, the book store, and the laboratory, as well as the countinghouse and the royal navy, were high in popular esteem. Philosopher and scientist, poet, pamphleteer, and historian were all participating in this intellectual revolution. It seeped in slowly, with just sufficient changes here and there to make it possible to subdivide the story into three parts, associated with Alexander Pope, Dr. Samuel Johnson, and Edmund Burke.

To men of letters and to the social philosopher the eighteenth century will ever remain one of the choicest in English history. It was an era spacious, rational, and tolerant in spirit; interested in things of the mind, but not forgetful of the body; sufficiently static, socially, to permit cultural standards to form; sufficiently dynamic, intellectually, to keep them alive. The century had a fair heritage in the Revolution of 1688. The Stuart exit meant more than the death of the divine right of kings: it signified at once the end of Restoration immorality and of Puritanical bigotry. Although weary of dissipated Royalists, England did not yearn for the return of the "saints." Instead good-natured compromise was sought. Its idealized expression may be found in the music of Handel and in the English words written in 1740 as a libretto for his *Il Moderato*.

> Kindly teach, how blest are they
> Who nature's equal rule obey;
> Who safely steer two rocks between,
> And prudent keep the golden mean.

The era of the coffeehouse and the tavern was at hand. Prosperous London drew like a magnet the English world of fashion, of wealth, and of culture. Dandies flocked hence to dazzle society and themselves by the gaiety of their waistcoats and the expensiveness of their wigs; and to dine and to gamble at White's or, later, at Brooks's. Solid merchants met to exchange gossip and to hear the latest maritime news at Lloyd's. Literary folk gathered at Will's to listen to the serious-minded Addison or to laugh with "Dick" Steele.

The Augustan Age

In its opening decades the century was far from introspective. Men did not wear their hearts upon their sleeves nor did they worry much about their souls. Literature was "urban and urbane," conversational in tone, devoted primarily to one theme, man —his foibles, prejudices, and behavior. *The Spectator,* with its "Sir Roger de Coverley Papers" and famous essays, was a successful as well as an original venture in periodical literature, selling occasionally as many as ten thousand copies of a single issue. Swift, Addison, Steele, Defoe, and Pope were in their glory. England was a cheerful place for the "Queen Anne wits." It was difficult, then as now, to make a living by the pen, but politics helped. Whig and Tory bigwigs freely bestowed sinecures of one kind or another in return for service rendered and pamphlets written. The Drury Lane Theater helped to fill the bottomless pockets of Mr. Richard Steele. There was the Church of England and its sister, the Church of Ireland, with a deanship for Jonathan Swift. The writers of the "Augustan Age," as the first three or four decades of the century are aptly called, did not complain of an unappreciative world.

Literary men in general turned to the classics, because Greco-Roman civilization had been stable and not given to emotional vagaries. Style and diction then had been formalized. The eighteenth-century man liked this; for it was quiet, peaceful, and, above all, reasonable. He was, on the whole more Roman than Greek, preferring the more permanent and substantial model offered by the Augustan Age of Rome.

If the Revolution Settlement had laid stress on classical values merely as the result of sheer exhaustion, the new age might have been purely imitative. But the early eighteenth century imitated only the form, not the substance, of classicism. Its foundations were laid in certain new ideas, the key to which may be found in the mathematics of Sir Isaac Newton and in the philosophy of John Locke. Although their main work came in the late seventeenth century, their influence upon the thought of the entire eighteenth century is difficult to exaggerate.

Sir Isaac Newton (1642-1727) was a modest man of science, content to ponder twenty-one years over his discoveries before publishing them. A professor at Cambridge at twenty-seven, he became indignant at the efforts of James II to interfere with the universities, and he entered Parliament to fight on their behalf, thereafter remaining more or less in political life. In 1687 his major work, *Principia,* almost instantly made him famous at home and abroad.

The *Principia* explained the Newtonian law of gravitation—"the forces which keep the planets in their orbits must be reciprocally as the squares of their distance from the centers upon which they revolve." From this mathematical formula it followed that the sun, moon, stars, earth, planets, and comets—indeed, the universe itself—are controlled, directed, and kept in place by a universal law of gravitation. The implications of this new theory went far beyond the realms of astronomy. The Newtonian laws made it possible to estimate the size of the celestial bodies, but they also led man to revolutionize his social and religious ideas. The law of gravitation did not abolish God, but it made him decidedly less personal, a kind of glorified watchmaker who wound up the universe and then retired to the background. It led also to a firm and implicit belief in natural law, applicable to the birds of the air, the beasts of the field, and even man. A scientific sanction was thus given to the compromises of Greco-Roman civilization.

Complementing the work of Newton on the political side was that of John Locke (1632-1704), from whom English and American statesmen drew heavily for political and constitutional arguments. Of Puritan ancestry, he was a student at Oxford during the Commonwealth; but he became so disgusted over the theological wranglings of Presbyterians and Independents that he became an Anglican. Even in that, however, he was an extreme latitudinarian, much more interested in chemistry and in meteorology than in dogma. He practiced medicine for a while, but showed so much interest in politics that he found it expedient during Charles II's reign to live in France. He returned to Oxford, incurred the displeasure of James II, went into exile in Holland, and came back with William and Mary. His famous essays on *Toleration,* on *Human Understanding,* and on *Government* did not appear until the final decade of the seventeenth century.

Key words to an understanding of Locke are "probability," "reasonable," "compromise." And a key sentence in his *Civil Government* runs thus: "Man . . . hath by nature a power to preserve his property— that is his life, liberty and estate—against the injuries and attempts of other men." In other words, there must be government; but it must not be confiscatory, tyrannical, or illiberal. Such a government may best be secured by a system of checks and balances, with the power of both king and legislature limited. Kings, lords, and commons, and likewise a judicial system calling for independent judges and for juries, should balance each other in a way reminiscent of Newtonian natural law. If a balance were found between governmental functions, a reasonable civic society would flourish; otherwise revolution might also

occur. "Whenever law ends," he wrote, "tyranny begins, if the law be transgressed, to another's harm; and whosoever in authority exceeds the power given him by the law, . . . ceases in that to be a magistrate, and acting without authority may be opposed . . ." Here surely was a justification of revolutions in general. But as a good Whig, he was more intent upon justifying the Revolution Settlement of 1688 than in proposing new ones. As time passed, however, Tories also accepted his main conclusions.

The major currents of early-eighteenth-century thought flow from these scientific and philosophic ideas and find their best reflection in the works of Alexander Pope and of Joseph Addison. The premier poet of the period was "Mr. Pope of Twickenham" (1688-1744), a writer vastly popular in his own day, much derided in the nineteenth century, and now returning once more to his own.

Pope, a Roman Catholic, without political privilege, a malformed cripple unduly sensitive to ridicule, was so brilliant that he was virtually subsidized as a young man to translate Homer. By this he made £8000, a fabulous achievement in those days of pirated copyrights. Augmented by an inheritance from his father by no means inconsiderable, it made him financially independent. His country place at Twickenham on the Thames, near London, was for years the Mecca of the learned. Here in his famous grotto he entertained the élite, gossiped freely and sometimes venomously, and polished and repolished his poems in his own inimitable manner. Although an authority on the technique of poetry and poetical forms, he is renowned as a historic figure mainly because his writings sum up an epoch.

One of the clearest landmarks in the intellectual history of Britain is the year 1733-1734, the date of the publication of Pope's *Essay on Man,* a long poem written in the form of the heroic couplet and divided logically into four epistles, each dealing with certain philosophic questions which long have perplexed humanity. The first epistle treats of man's relation to the universe and implies that it is foolish to fuss too much about trying to discover God's purposes. Every animal is provided for by Providence: strength is given to bulls, fur to bears, mind to man. The next epistle takes up man's knowledge of himself:

> Know then thyself, presume not
> God to scan;
> The proper study of mankind is man.

That study should be undertaken with due respect for Newtonian principles of balance weight and counterweight, attraction and counterattraction. Ease and toil, humility and pride, avarice and prudence, sloth and philosophy—all are in evidence. But this is not contradictory to beneficent natural law. It is desirable that the hero should have pride, that the merchant should toil; so does Nature provide by a kind of law of social gravitation. The two remaining epistles deal with man's relation to society and happiness. Pope, like most eighteenth-century men, is very much concerned about happiness. "WHATEVER IS, IS RIGHT" he puts in large type. If you would be happy, do not question but accept. Rich and poor alike all have an equal right to happiness, and may obtain it only by a recognition of the fact that

> Reason's whole pleasure,
> all the joys of sense,
> Lie in three words, health, peace,
> and competence.

Now health, peace, and competence, to say nothing of reason, had but remote resemblance to the three virtues of Christianity: faith, hope, and charity. Furthermore, an abstract first cause, called by courtesy "God," who never interfered with the cold, passionless laws of Nature, did not resemble to any striking degree the God of historic Christianity. Thus there were some who intimated that the morality taught in this poem was dubious and that the author did not believe in God. Whereupon, to answer this charge, Pope wrote a hymn, reaffirming the existence of God, as a kind of impersonal deity.

In this "civilized and sophisticated society," where reason reigned, the prose was characterized by wit, kindliness, taste, and judgment rather than by warmth and enthusiasm; comedy was preferred to tragedy, laughter to seriousness, and smiles to laughter. Two of its best-known representatives, Joseph Addison (1672-1719) and Richard Steele (1672-1729), collaborated closely in bringing out first *The Tatler* and then *The Spectator,* the simple and unpretentious forerunners of the modern magazine. Addison was the more serious of the two, with a somewhat more polished style; Steele was the more lovable, the more irresponsible, with a lighter style. Both were, however, fundamentally alike in determining like Pope to make the best of what was, content with their lot and with the world.

Together they invented a group of imaginary characters headed by the squire Sir Roger de Coverley, and first one and then the other of the two authors discoursed upon their fictitious heroes. Sir Roger, according to Steele, was in "his fifty-sixth year, cheerful, gay and hearty, keeping a good house both in town and country." One of his friends is "gallant Will Honeycomb," upon whom "time had made but little impression, either by wrinkles on his forehead or traces in his brain." Steele finally leads Sir Roger into paths which seem not altogether respectable to the more prudish Addison, and the latter ends the life of his hero lest he die with blemished character. *The Spectator* was compounded of such trivial sketches, interspersed with essays on taste, on the theater, on poetry, on the passing show, now serious, now tragi-comic, but never boisterous, extreme, passionate, or partisan. Politics were excluded, and in place of controversy there was kindly comment and subdued humor.

Different in approach was Jonathan Swift (1667-1745), whose writings reflect his tragic life. To Thackeray, Swift was a species of ogre; but to later critics "his misanthropy is a kind of perverted philanthropy." Swift was an ambitious man of talent, a Tory pamphleteer whose career was checked by a long period of Whig ascendancy, whose love was thwarted by adverse circumstances, and whose health grew steadily worse. He did have a sinecure deanship in the Church of Ireland, but to him Dublin was virtual exile.

Gulliver's Travels, his best-known book, is the most celebrated satire in the English language. It is not characteristic of its age, in its savage invective and in its belittlement of man, "the most pernicious race of little odious vermin that nature ever suffered to crawl upon this earth." On the other hand, Gulliver has distinctively eighteenth-century earmarks. It is in no way sentimental, and is so realistic as to describe imaginary minutiae with the utmost plausibility. It is also a distinctly non-theological, impersonal work of art, wherein life is faced as it is.

The Reaction Toward Sentiment

By the fourth decade of the century philosophers and thinkers began to question the pleasant, easygoing compromise by which Pope and his friends had simply accepted the universe without thinking very much about it. Literary men began to feel the need of more emotional warmth. The Augustan Age had specialized, perhaps overspecialized, in wit; and to appreciate wit one must be highly cultured. The rapidly rising middle class, which the new wealth was bringing to the fore, was not; but many members of it had intellectual interests and were not content with simply making money. They too, as well as the aristocracy, wanted to read books and to talk about them. They were at one and the same time interested in the why and wherefore of life and in reading which would not unduly tax their intellectual capacity.

In consequence the intellectual and literary history of the century may be considered as entering a second stage. The distinctive ideals of the first stage were now challenged both by the advocates of the cult of sensibility, who were the forerunners of English romanticism, and by the Methodists and evangelical leaders in the Church of England, who advocated a more emotional type of religion. In this new stage, approximately from 1740 to 1789, Augustan ideals were largely on the defensive but were defended well and stanchly by Dr. Samuel Johnson, who held the fortress of the accepted order, although breaches were made in the ramparts.

The first major challenge to the Augustan conception of life came from the sentimentalist writer with his cult of sensibility, exemplified by the Reverend Laurence Sterne (1713-1768). He was born in Ireland, the son of a poor army officer who had influential relations. Owing to their help and to his natural wit, Sterne was graduated at Cambridge, took holy orders, and received a living near York. He was an unusual clergyman, even for the easygoing Church of England. Much of his early manhood was spent at "Crazy Castle," where a club, the "Demoniacs," held sway.

In 1759 his *Tristram Shandy* greatly scandalized York and soon made Sterne famous in London, France, and Italy. His *Sentimental Journey* was even more widely read. Sterne was a man of the world, but in a way different from the "Queen Anne wits," who believed in quiet self-restraint. There was nothing controlled about the emotions of Sterne: the heart was what mattered, not the head. Sterne reveled in both tears and laughter. His humorous stories in the *Sentimental Journey* and *The Life and Opinions of Tristram Shandy, Gent.* were noted for their whimsicalities, or "shandyisms," as they came to be called.

Tristram Shandy, although seemingly without plan or plot, did have a purpose: to reveal character by dialogue, and incidentally to poke fun at all prigs. Mr. and Mrs. Shandy, Uncle Toby, Corporal Trim, and Dr. Slop converse wittily on all kinds of topics from noses and baptismal names to varieties of cursing.

Part of the cult of sensibility was the cult of the natural man. Writers in the mid-eighteenth century fancifully idealized the residents of the South Sea Islands, of Lapland, and even of Chile as noble savages. They knew nothing of those distant regions, but in their imagination they peopled them with excellent creatures, bold, simple, free. The descendants of the natural man were found also in Wales and the Scottish Highlands, living simple and virtuous lives, and delighting in bards rather than in neo-classic poets, and in gloomy shades and wild, desolate forests. This idealization of simplicity came nearer home in the humble crofter and the village laborer.

These notions, stressed by the forerunners of the Romantic school of English writers (see pages 400 ff.), found their reflection in Gray's "Elegy Written in a Country Church Yard," which intimates democratically that there may lie, unknown to fame, "mute inglorious Miltons."

This double cult of sensibility and of the natural man was easier to describe than to explain. It was not satisfactory to say that the English derived these ideas from the contemporary French philosopher Rousseau, for they blossomed forth in English literature before Rousseau wrote. Perhaps the best explanation is that Newtonian philosophy led to the exaltation of reason, and it is difficult for man to live by reason alone. Furthermore, reason led to further reasoning, particularly concerning God. "Is he willing to prevent evil but not able? Then he is impotent. Is he able, but not willing? Then he is malevolent. Is he both able and willing? Whence then is evil?" These questions were asked by David Hume, contemporary philosopher and historian in the *Dialogues;* and such thoughts were widely current and headed straight toward skepticism. The eighteenth century, not wishing to follow reason to that logical end, invented something new to stifle lurking doubts: the reason of the heart, delight in emotional reaction. Presumably these sentimental emotions in their purest form would be felt by simple people. Hence the return to nature. If we add to this argument the pleasure which humanity feels in contemplating what is contrary to its everyday experience, the cult of nature is explained further. Eighteenth-century England, relatively speaking, was a wealthy, civilized society, and thus liked its opposite.

Another reaction to Newtonian philosophy was Methodism. To many there seemed to be only two alternatives, the skepticism of Hume and a return to historic Christianity. A large number chose the old trail rather than the new. This helps explain the Methodist revival and the contemporary evangelical movement within the Church of England, which stressed personal salvation. The Church of England in the middle of the century had become, more or less, an intellectual backwater, losing steadily in influence and power. Its clergy, affected by the contemporary deism (belief in an inactive and remote deity), did not pay much attention to their duties. Enthusiasm was frowned upon, and there was little inner zeal. This was the situation until the arrival of John Wesley (1703-1791), the founder of English Methodism.

He and his brother Charles, while at Oxford, sought to re-establish the simplicity of life and the spiritual fervor of the Christian Church in its first century. They organized a little group of about twenty-five, called Methodists by undergraduates in derision because of their unusual devotion to religious exercises. For some time their activity was confined to members of the Church of England, in which both brothers became ordained clergymen.

In 1738, on a May evening "about a quarter before nine," John Wesley wrote, "I felt my heart strongly warmed. I felt I did trust in Christ and Christ alone for salvation." This experience was the real commencement of Methodism. He began to preach with such warmth and abandon that his own church would have none of him. He then went forth like an apostle all over England and many times to Ireland, traveling five thousand miles a year and preaching fifteen sermons weekly. As his followers grew in number he assumed one function of a bishop in appointing ministers in his own right. The younger brother, Charles, far less celebrated as an evangelical preacher, wrote innumerable hymns, many of them among the more famous in the English language.

Wesley did not preach without violent opposition. His life was threatened again and again. Frequently he was charged with making a disturbance; but inasmuch as the latter consisted simply in getting people to rise in the early morning, to sing hymns, and to convert others, the magistrates were forced to release him. Wesley thrived on excitement. Some cried, " 'No, no, knock his brains out; down with him, kill him at once.' Others said, 'Nay, but we will hear him first.' "

Thus Methodism originated, and the author of it continued in the active service of his new church until his eighty-eighth year. His followers, for the most part, were of lowly rank; but the movement was instantly felt in the Church of England, where, in the middle of the century, evangelicalism, or emotional conversion, became strong. It included within its ranks such literary celebrities as William Cowper and Hannah More.

Samuel Johnson

As literary England turned first toward one of these paths and then toward another —toward sentimentalism, toward the nature cult, toward religion, and occasionally toward agnosticism (refusal to affirm or deny the existence of God)—one man of letters, Samuel Johnson (1709-1784) never veered an inch from the old loyalties. The son of a provincial bookseller, he was used to poverty from youth. His rise to fame was slow but steady; and after his dictionary was completed, in 1755, he became the foremost star in the English literary firmament. He was very much of a fixed star, a sturdy fighter for the old cause of common sense, neoclassical literary standards, a Christianity not too fervent, not too cold, suspicious of all "isms" and all cults, devoted to old England as it had been.

The famous Doctor scarcely can be considered an original thinker or a first-class writer. His novel, *Rasselas,* was better philosophy than fiction; his articles in *The Rambler* and *The Idler* do not match the better essays of Addison and Swift; his life of the poet Savage is a good biography but of a second-rate poet. As a dictionary-maker Johnson was an eminent figure, but he is remembered for his conversations, as recorded by his faithful friend and devotee James Boswell, the "perfect biographer." In Boswell's *Life of Johnson* the character of this great man stands out in clear and complete relief. As his well-known letter on patrons to Lord Chesterfield bears witness, Johnson is no toady; on the other hand, he is not a rebel, for he gratefully accepted a pension from King George III. He is a sincere, gruff defender of the old order and of the old ways of thinking. Dr. Johnson had no use for those who spoke in sentimental vein of distant lands. He hated America and Americans, and he disliked Scotland almost as heartily. "Let me tell you," he says to Boswell, "the noblest prospect which a Scotchman ever sees is the high road that leads him to England." Johnson also treated with disdain the idea that crude living in the wilds made for happiness. Abhorring sentimental talk, he was known for his own kind heart, but always went out of his way to conceal its existence.

On matters of religion and politics the opinions of Dr. Johnson were equally frank. He was a stanch upholder of the Church of England and genuinely devout, as a number of his written prayers amply attest. He disliked Voltaire, the cynical and bitingly sarcastic contemporary French philosopher, and his fellow agnostics; he disliked even more Rousseau, with his ideas of a "social contract" between the ruler and the "sovereign people," and the other sentimentalists. Quakers and women preachers annoyed the Doctor greatly. "Sir," he observed, "a woman preaching is like a dog walking on his hinder legs. It is not done well; but you are surprised to find it done at all." The Methodists also annoyed him with their belief in the inward light, "a principle utterly incompatible with social or civil security." Incited by Boswell, Oliver Goldsmith, and other friends, Dr. Johnson continued to lay down the law in this fashion. He knew very little about economics, politics, or government, but he spoke as freely on such topics as he did on literature.

He was an ardent Tory and abominated Whigs. "Sir," he declared, "I perceive you are a vile Whig." The Whigs, in reality, were aristocratic enough; but from Johnson's point of view they were jealous of the power of the crown and on that account to be condemned. This did not mean that he advocated an absolute king. On the contrary, all that he had in mind was a perfect balance of power, that liberty might be guaranteed. He was not much of a politician, and he never sat in Parliament. What he loathed was anything in the way of a leveling principle. Society should be divided into social classes. He wanted for himself both superiors and subordinates, and fixed, invariable rules for the distinction of rank.

Among those who gathered in friendly intercourse with the mighty Doctor at the Turk's Head Tavern were Reynolds, the portrait painter; Sheridan, the playwright; Burke, the rising young politician; Garrick,

the actor; and Goldsmith, the novelist. The last mentioned was especially protected by the favor of Johnson and was made the special butt of Boswell and of others who showed little appreciation for the unfortunate Irishman.

Oliver Goldsmith (1728-1774), author of "The Vicar of Wakefield" and "The Deserted Village," occupies a place in English literature intermediate between the sturdy Johnson and the sentimentalists. He is like the former in his approbation of wealth and civilization; he resembles the latter in his tender-heartedness and simplicity. Many of the ideas found in the satiric writings of Voltaire appear faintly in what he wrote— the attack upon pompous authority, the absurdity of certain customs, the unfair treatment meted out to the poor. But in Goldsmith, the sentimentalist, the sting is missing from the satire.

There were many other notable writers in the middle years of the eighteenth century, among them Fielding, the author of *Tom Jones*, said to be the most perfect novel in the English language, and Richardson, who described at interminable length in *Pamela* the adventures of a poor servant girl in defense of her chastity.

Historians, Economists, and Scientists

History was extraordinarily popular with the average reader; and many thousands of pounds were paid in royalties to the three important historians of the period: Hume, Robertson, and Gibbon. History, as popularly conceived, was a branch of literature, not a science. It portrayed the past on a broad canvas, with a big brush. Rarely did the eighteenth-century historian attempt details. Even had he chosen to do so, he would have failed; for collected material in the way of sources was lacking. On the other hand, he devoted more attention to form and style, and in consequence was more readable.

David Hume (1711-1776) and William Robertson (1721-1793) were Scotland's chief eighteenth-century historians. Both were of rather humble parentage, both attended Edinburgh University, both were read widely and so made much money.

By a strange irony of fate, Hume won more contemporary renown as historian than as philosopher, although his early ambitions lay all the other way. Educated for the law, he secluded himself for years in France to write philosophy, and sought in his *Treatise of Human Nature* "to produce almost the total alteration of philosophy." He failed to win a philosophy professorship at Edinburgh because of accusations of skepticism; and so he became a historian.

The history of England was his field: his first two volumes dealt with Stuart England; the second two with the Tudors, and the last two with early England. Imbued with the eighteenth-century belief in natural laws, his psychology was at fault; and his analysis of historical characters, like Luther and Joan of Arc, was based on the assumption that their reactions were the same as his own. On the other hand, Hume's style was easy and flowing, and his scholarship was much better in the periods nearer to his own day. For the first time the English people found in his history a clear and readable account of their own past from its early origins.

Robertson, a Presbyterian clergyman, was an even more distinguished historian. He rose to fame early by writing a history of Scotland which won the warmest praise from distinguished men of letters, although it was a trifle ponderous. Robertson next wrote a massive biography of Emperor Charles V, for which he was paid £4500. The book was hailed with enthusiasm and so also was his *History of America*, which had to do mainly with the voyages of discovery and the Spanish conquests.

Finally there was Edward Gibbon (1737-1794), ablest of all English historians. Gibbon was the grandson of a wealthy army contractor and therefore, fortunately enough, excused from the necessity of earning a living. He was educated largely at home, owing to his poor health. He went to Oxford, but learned nothing much there except to become a Roman Catholic. His horrified father dispatched him forthwith to Switzerland, to study other doctrines. The young Gibbon spent five years there, reading omnivorously. He became a Protestant again, but a lukewarm one, his studies tending rather toward agnosticism than toward a rejuvenated faith. He returned to England, took some insignificant part in public affairs, and became a member of Johnson's club. According to Boswell, he was "an ugly, disgusting fellow." The worthy Boswell doubtless was jealous. With the exception of Dr. Johnson, Gibbon towered high above his contemporaries.

For a long time Gibbon hesitated in regard to a subject for his projected lifework. His final choice was *The Decline and Fall of the Roman Empire*. To prepare himself for this task, he traveled extensively in Italy and read every scrap of the original Greek and Latin that he could find. He finished his first volume in 1776, the year of American independence, and his last in 1787, two years before the French Revolution. His greatness lay in his mastery of form. Every event and every actor in this majestic enterprise falls into its proper place. Since his day *The Decline and Fall* has been assailed because of the unreliability of many of the authorities upon which he depended and the unfairness of his treatment of the early history of the Christian Church. Despite such blemishes no one can cavil at the completed work, with its dignified and comprehensive style and its sustained eloquence and power.

Economic thought in the eighteenth century was both stimulated and transformed by the new wealth. The prevailing economic doctrines at the beginning of that era were those of the mercantilist school, which upheld the omnipotence of the state and the subordination of the individual to it (see pages 162, 226). The first attack on mercantilism developed in France in this century. The so-called physiocrats began to argue that governments would do well to leave business alone. Deducing their ideas from the Newtonian faith in natural law, they believed that there were natural laws in economics, which were as immutable as the natural laws of astronomy. Laissez faire (let things alone)—let nature run its course—and all will be well, these men proclaimed. Living in an agricultural country, they considered agriculture to be the principal source of all wealth. In Scotland a more practical man, Adam Smith, gave expression to their ideas in somewhat different form in 1776 in his *Wealth of Nations*. This book was a landmark in economic thought (see page 414).

Experimental science had a wide vogue in the eighteenth century. Amateur laboratory experiments were common; and the "enlightened" man of the day was intensely interested in the new discoveries, particularly those relating to physics and chemistry. The major scientific discoveries of the century were made by German, French, and English scientists with some collaboration from other countries. In England, besides the great Newton, there was Edward Jenner (1749-1823), doctor and naturalist, who had charge of the zoological specimens brought back by Captain Cook from the South Seas (see page 443). As early as 1775 Jenner had begun his investigation which set the world free from smallpox. Before long he was able to prepare from a sick cow a serum which, injected into the human blood, made man immune to smallpox. By the end of the century his discovery was accepted everywhere by intelligent doctors, and a grateful government twice honored him with large grants of money.

Then there was Henry Cavendish (1731-1810), a wealthy nobleman and a recluse, who dabbled in all sorts of scientific experiments. "He was the first who, by purely inductive experiments, converted oxygen and hydrogen into water, and who taught that water consisted of these gases." Even better known for chemistry experiments was Joseph Priestley (1733-1804), a famous Unitarian clergyman and political radical (see page 360). Priestley specialized in gases, which he studied carefully in English breweries and elsewhere. He proved that the theory that "combustible bodies are composed in part of an invisible and highly combustible substance" was impossible. He must be credited also with the discovery of oxygen, while he and Cavendish between them made possible the later work of the Frenchman Lavoisier, the founder of quantitative chemistry. Later in life Priestley, because of his radical political ideas, was to flee from England to spend his last years in Pennsylvania.

Burke and the French Revolution

A third chapter in the intellectual history of the century began almost simultaneously with the French Revolution of 1789. The fall of the Bastille in Paris made an astonishing impression on English minds. English writers as well as English statesmen began to take sides both for and against the new ideas so boldly proclaimed across the Channel (see page 367). The England of Newton, Locke, and Alexander Pope had withstood with some degree of success the attack made upon it by the cult of sensibility, by the nature-worshipers, by the Methodists, and by the rather mild agnosticism of men like Hume. Now that same old England faced a fresh assault, more vigorous and more threatening. In the England of 1770 one might favor the democratic doctrines of Rousseau or the skepticism of Voltaire without appearing to threaten British institutions; to do so in 1790 was a somewhat different matter. The old order was dashing to destruction in France, and many suspected that the wild storm might spread to England. Some Englishmen hoped that it would. The "new wealth" had created new areas of social and economic friction and had accentuated many old ones. Compromises that seemed reasonable in 1700 wore the appearance of illogical, if not tyrannical, maladjustments by 1790. "Liberty, equality, and fraternity" was a French slogan; but it was heard also in London, even within the halls of Parliament.

The spread of the new French ideas was checked in England by a number of factors, predominant among which was the long war against France. This conflict, however, was not waged entirely by ships and men. It was a literary and an intellectual war as well, in which England had a redoubtable champion, Edmund Burke. His role in English letters at the end of the century, in certain respects, was like that of Dr. Johnson in the middle decades, namely, to inspire his countrymen with a love of English ways and to defend the established institutions of his country against revolutionary criticism.

Burke (1729-1797) was Dublin-born and, like Swift and Goldsmith, a graduate of Dublin's famous Trinity College. The years of his early manhood were spent in comparative obscurity in London, where he supported himself, after a fashion, as a hack writer. Slowly he emerged as a literary free lance, became private secretary to a peer, and then entered Parliament, in the Whig interest, from a rotten borough. Within little more than a decade he was one of the foremost statesmen of England—an astonishing fact when we remember that he inherited neither a great name nor a fortune, that he was an Irishman, that his wife was a Roman Catholic, and that his relatives were not to the aristocratic manner born. On the other hand, he knew how to charm his friends. Even Dr. Johnson, who despised all Whigs, said of him, "I love his knowledge, his genius, his diffusion and affluence of conversation." And as Burke talked, so he wrote, with a wealth of imagery and sustained enthusiasm.

He never rose to high rank as a practical statesman, nor did he ever enter a British cabinet; but his pen and his voice were the most influential in Britain as the century closed. He took a leading part in three great controversies: in the American Revolution, in the investigation of alleged scandals connected with British rule in India, and in Britain's relations to the French Revolution (see pages 321, 448, 366). His name has become traditional as the distinguished foe of the French Revolution.

Within two years, 1774 and 1775, Burke wrote one letter and composed and delivered two speeches which laid the foundations for his fame as a leading exponent of conservative British political philosophy. In the letter written to the electors of Bristol, which he then represented in Parliament, he made clear that he was not elected merely to act as their delegate. "Your representative owes you," he said, "not his industry alone, but his judgment; and he betrays it, instead of serving you, if he sacrifices it to your opinion."

The two speeches, on taxation and on American reconciliation, dealt with the approaching revolution overseas, and are packed with phrases which came later to be recognized in England as the quintessence of good statesmanship. Burke refused to discuss theoretical rights. "What is the use of discussing a man's abstract right to food or medicine? The question is, What is the method of procuring and administering them." The author was for taking a practical yet at the same time a long view of the American controversy. "The question with me is not whether you have a right to render people miserable; but whether it is not your interest to make them happy. It is not what a lawyer tells me I may do, but what humanity, reason, and justice tell me I ought to do." Throughout, Burke was determined to ignore complicated legalities. He insisted that the fact that the Americans were sensitive, that their inheritance was nonconformist, and that their religion was "the dissidence of dissent and the Protestantism of the Protestant religion" must be remembered. "An Englishman," said Burke, "is the unfittest person on earth to argue another Englishman into slavery." Then, too, there was the empire to consider. "Magnanimity in politics is not seldom the truest wisdom; and a great empire and little minds go ill together." Contemporary England recognized to some extent the validity of these views, even if official England was so foolish as not to act in accordance with them.

Not, however, until 1790, when he publicly broke his friendship with Fox, the Whig champion (see page 366), and when he published his *Reflections on the French Revolution,* did he win recognition as the chief literary and philosophic representative of old England. As a contribution to the history of the French Revolution his book was well-nigh worthless. What raised it to high place in English letters was that it incarnated the political and social traditions of his own countrymen. "People will not look forward to posterity," says Burke, "who never looked backward to their ancestors." The present should be blended with the past, and the future blended with the present; for it is unwise to hew and to hack at the roots of any society. Among the British roots which Burke cherished were private property, the Established Church, the law of entail (see page 103), and the aristocratic tradition. He had no more confidence in democracy than in absolute monarchy. "Of this I am certain, that in a democracy the majority of the citizens is capable of exercising the most cruel oppression on the minority." Equality of rank was absurd to his mind, because certain occupations are honorable while others are not. Liberty, may best be secured by relying on checks and balances. "Property," he affirmed, "is sluggish, inert, and timid, and it never can be safe from the invasions of ability unless it be out of all proportions predominant in the representation." Therefore he thought that the House of Commons in large measure should represent property, with kings and Church, Lords, and Commons balancing one another. What held his respect was a society which is cautious in regard to change.

Now Burke, thus far, had followed mainly in the paths indicated by Locke and Newton. It is true that he stood for traditions; but he was also sensitive to his own day, and in that he differed from Locke and Newton. The Romantic movement in literature (see page 400) was in bud; and Burke, as a part of this movement, emphasized the validity of the nonrational and mystical, and held to a type of religious experience different from that which characterized the age of Pope. At the commencement of the century, Locke had based his philosophy on individualism and on natural rights. Burke, toward the close of the century, based his philosophy on a "religion which so much hates oppression that when the God whom we adore appeared in human form he did not appear in the form of greatness and majesty but in sympathy with the lowest of the people, and thereby made it a firm and ruling principle that their welfare was the object of all government." That these sentiments were expressed by a man who believed in the perpetuation of social classes, ranks, and grades was paradoxical; but it must be remembered that Burke's philosophy was, in a sense, a throwback to earlier centuries, when the natural man was considered evil rather than good and when it was held necessary for strong and powerful forces to save him from the follies inherent in his weakness.

Burke's *Reflections* raised the conservative standard, and to it flocked the gentlemen of England. It helped to bring about the deadening Tory reaction to all liberal trends (see page 366). On the other hand, it met with a bitter, uncompromising, and by no means negligible radical attack, which likewise was to be interwoven with the history of English thought and letters.

Prominent among the many opponents to

the *Reflections* were Priestley, the scientist; Holcroft, the dramatist; and Thelwall, a popular lecturer and pamphleteer. Possibly the most representative were Mary Wollstonecraft (1759-1797), schoolmistress and later mother-in-law of Percy Bysshe Shelley; Thomas Paine (1737-1809), former excise collector, and pamphleteer extraordinary on two continents; and William Godwin (1756-1836), ex-clergyman, and subsequently the second husband of Mary Wollstonecraft.

First in the field in reply to Burke was Mary Wollstonecraft's *Vindication of the Rights of Man.* "I perceive," she wrote to Burke, "that you have a mortal antipathy to reason, but if there is anything like argument or first principles in your wild declamation, behold the result—that we are to reverence the rust of antiquity, and those unnatural customs which ignorance and self-interest have consolidated into the sage fruit of experience." The schoolmistress had no respect for the British constitution. It guaranteed property, no doubt, but at the same time "the liberty of an honest mechanic is often sacrificed to secure the property of the rich." "Why cannot large estates be divided into small farms? Why does the brown waste meet the traveller's view when men want work?" As for the much-praised House of Commons, its members were in her opinion but puppets. "After the effervescence of spirit raised by the opposition and all the little tyrannical acts of canvassing are over—quiet souls!—they only intend to march rank and file, and to say yes or no."

Mary Wollstonecraft was well-nigh forgotten amid the bleatings of timidity, exclamations of hatred, and shouts of approval that greeted the writings of Thomas Paine. He embodied the spirit of radicalism as Burke did that of conservatism. This was recognized by everyone of the period, as the discussion of Paine in the contemporary literature and the numerous replies called forth by his pamphlets demonstrate. It was

further indicated by the venomous hatred of Paine in certain circles. We are told that it was fashionable to wear Tom Paine shoe nails, that he might be trampled underfoot. The burning of Paine in effigy was a common sight, while, on the other hand, celebrations were held to do him honor.

It is rather difficult nowadays to account for the horror with which Paine's *Rights of Man* was received. It is true, his language in defense of France was violent; but his proposals for the reform of England were not particularly immoderate. His principal ideas were to make the government more democratic, to abolish entail, to create peasant proprietorship, to lessen expenditure on the court, the army, and the navy, to finance the country by an income tax, to pay old-age pensions, to give bonuses for births and marriages, and to spend a good deal for education. Very likely if he had not included royalty in his diatribes, always calling the king "Mr. Guelph," he would not have been hounded out of England.

Finally there was Godwin, a most unassuming little person who wrote the most radical book of the decade, more radical than most contemporary French theory. *Political Justice*, published in 1793, was an attack on private property, the greatest evil of the day in the author's opinion, since it was responsible for the lack of an independent spirit. The glorification of property Godwin considered much more detrimental than the swollen pension roll of the government, because "hereditary wealth" with "a premium paid to idleness." He held that private property retarded not only the development of genius but the growth of intelligence as well; for property either surfeited those who held it or, by its unequal distribution, compelled others to spend their days in sordid cares.

Had it not been for protracted war with France, it is probable that these radical writers would have made more of a dent in English public opinion than they did. There was much which needed reforming: corrupt politics, outrageous penal laws, grave economic injustice brought about by the Industrial Revolution, and still much deep-rooted religious and social bigotry. Furthermore, as we shall see, the younger Pitt was a genuine reformer; and England, after the loss of the American colonies, was in a mood to clean house. The war with France, however, hushed, for the time being, the radical note in England. The country gentry tightened their grip on their country. To be a radical was to be a French sympathizer and therefore unpatriotic. Not until some time after Waterloo was there a change. When the eighteenth century had dawned, England had been relatively weak in comparison with France under Louis XIV; when it closed, she was mistress of the ocean and the leading commercial power of the world.

But the comfortable mood of the century was changing, and the old shibboleths of placid worldliness and contentment seemed no longer valid. The cult of sensibility in literature was deepened and broadening into romanticism. In Burke the new Romantic movement showed its conservative side, but with others it took a different form. Robert Burns, for instance, struck a democratic note and insisted on the value of all human life, even that of the humblest crofter. And William Blake, artist, engraver, poet, and religious mystic, expressed a hope for days to come:

> I will not cease from mental fight,
> Nor shall my sword sleep in my hand,
> Till we have built Jerusalem
> In England's green and pleasant land.

Needless to say, the Jerusalem of Blake's dream has not yet appeared; but there were more Englishmen eager for its coming in 1804, when this poem was published, than there had been a hundred years earlier, when one did not worry about "Jerusalems" but sought instead the measured comfort of the London coffeehouse.

Reaction and Napoleon

Two decades of war with France and the postponement of her own reform movement were the immediate effects of the French Revolution upon Britain, but its results went deeper than that. Like the rest of Europe she was never to be the same after the passionate outburst of the revolutionaries; for democracy and nationalism had seriously affected the secure existence of the privileged classes of the old regime.

But for that revolution, England would have been ready for extensive reforms after the loss of the thirteen colonies. The news of Yorktown in 1781 had caused the Whigs, who had opposed the king and his Tory ministers throughout the war, even occasionally cheering for the Americans, to attack the luckless ministry with renewed energy. Not only was Germain, whose blundering was in no small measure responsible for the failure, thrown overboard, but Whig efforts did not slacken until the powerful majority which North had built up by bribery and corruption had melted away. Five months after Yorktown the "King's Friends" were out of office with the resignation of North himself, "the genial old man who for twelve years had done the king's dirty work."

After twenty lean years the Whigs now had their chance; but this time, they were to be out within two years because of internal dissension. Divided more by personalities than by principles, the party split into two strong and jealous groups. One leader, the Earl of Shelburne, later Marquess of Lansdowne, a man of high ability, knowledge, and industry, the intimate friend of Adam Smith, Benjamin Franklin, and other intellectuals, had made exhaustive studies of the existing political and economic ills. But an impression of secretiveness made men distrust the "Jesuit of Berkeley Square." His rival, the lovable, unselfish, impulsive Charles James Fox, seldom went to bed before sunrise and squandered a fortune on cards, women, and horses. Admired by later generations for his fight for liberal reforms, after most others had turned reactionary, he had only himself to blame for being left the solitary champion of forlorn hopes. Shelburne, a follower of Chatham, was content to give the king a reasonable share in the government. Fox, hating George as much as George hated him, wanted thoroughgoing parliamentary supremacy. The two Whigs agreed on most essential points of policy, including the reforms for which their party had long clamored.

Yet because of Fox's jealousy and dislike of Shelburne, the victorious Whigs remained united barely a hundred days. Lord

Rockingham, a high-minded and liberal old Whig aristocrat, who had also been prime minister earlier when the Stamp Act was repealed, persuaded both of them to join his ministry. They quarreled violently over the American peace negotiations. Rockingham died, and the king asked Shelburne to form a new ministry. To the general surprise and disgust of the nation, Fox, refusing to serve under Shelburne, allied himself with North, whom less than a year before he had been threatening with impeachment. The ratio of power in the Commons was roughly as follows: Shelburne, 7; North, 6; Fox, 5. Hence no one of the three could command a majority by himself. Unable to stand alone against this unnatural alliance, Shelburne resigned in less than nine months when Fox and North carried a vote of disapproval of the peace negotiations as finally completed by Shelburne. Fox and North were finally called in by the king under the nominal leadership of the Duke of Portland. Their ministry lasted a few days less than Shelburne's, being ended by a high-handed royal maneuver. When the Commons passed Fox's bill for a reorganization of the government of India, the king sent word to the Lords that he would regard as a personal enemy anyone who voted for it! It was defeated by thirteen votes. Then, in spite of the majority in the Commons, George defied the principle of responsible government by dismissing Portland and asking the twenty-four year old Tory, William Pitt, to be prime minister.

England's first reaction to the change was mild amusement at "A nation trusted to a school-boy's care." The "school-boy," however, quickly won "one of the most desperate battles in English Parliamentary history." A ministry normally resigns when it meets defeat in the Commons; but Pitt, backed by the king, continued after a dozen defeats. Taking consistent advantage of Fox's blunders, he wore down the hostile majority to one vote! Then he asked for a general election. The voters, still angered at the Fox-North combination, returned a substantial Tory majority; 160 of Fox's "martyrs" lost their seats. With the backing of the king, the Lords, the Commons, and the people, Pitt was in a more powerful position than any prime minister had yet enjoyed. This marked the end of the Whigs' power for almost fifty years.

William Pitt the Younger had inherited his father's brains, his self-assurance, and—for a while at least—his popularity; to his older brother had gone the title of Chatham. At Cambridge he studied classics and mathematics and at twenty-one entered Parliament. After his maiden speech a wit remarked, "It's not a chip from the old block; it's the old block itself!" At twenty-three, as Chancellor of the Exchequer under Shelburne, he was vigorously attacking the Fox-North alliance. From twenty-four until his death at forty-six, except for a brief voluntary retirement, he was prime minister, holding that office years longer than anyone else except Walpole. His speeches lacked his father's fiery vehemence; but he was never at a loss for the right word and was a master of sarcasm. Though far less able than his father as a war minister, he was a genius at finance. Also he quickly showed he was more adept at Parliamentary tactics and knew just how to keep the essential Commons majority in line. Many of his constructive proposals were not his own, for he was always ready to use good ideas whatever their source. He always held himself under rigid control; his very youth may have caused him to assume a solemn and haughty austerity, an icy barrier only the chosen few ever penetrated. He was distinguished for the purity of his private life; his nearest approach to a bad habit was his lifelong zeal for port, which had been prescribed for him as a sickly boy. He never married, partly because he felt he could not afford it. His private income was only £300 a year; but, although he ran deeply into debt, he followed his father's example in refusing to take a relatively respectable official sinecure worth £3000 a year. In finance, millions passed through his hands; yet his absolute integrity was never questioned. He created peerages by the score, nearly doubling the House of Lords, but did not take one himself. His thirst was for power, and few men have had a better chance, outside a despotism, to gratify such an ambition.

With him a new Tory party came into being. It was Tory insofar as it supported the king and was aided by the country squires, but it differed from the Jacobite Toryism of Bolingbroke or the sordid submission of the "King's Friends" under North. Those Tories had put the royal power first; Pitt's Tories saved the crown from complete nullification at the hands of the Whigs, yet they were the first positively to establish the prime minister as the most powerful individual in the kingdom (see page 293). Pitt's was a Toryism of the future rather than of the past, and it began with such high promise of liberalism that during his first ten years Pitt has often been claimed by the Whigs. In the four Tory decades, the party increased, absorbing ex-Whigs until that party diminished to a mere "rump." In reaction to the French Revolution, the Tories became more and more conservative.

Only once after 1784 was Pitt seriously threatened by a Whig return. In 1788, when George III showed the first touch of an intermittent type of insanity, the Whigs proclaimed that by right the Prince of Wales should immediately become regent, with full royal powers. Pitt realized that Fox would be called into office if his friend, that coarse and jovial prince, the future George IV, were made regent. The Tories consequently upheld the claims of the Commons and the ministry against such a regency. The king returned suddenly to apparent sanity before any steps were taken.

The Post-Yorktown Reforms

During these years since Yorktown, the movement for reform was making headway. That humiliating defeat had created a determination to overhaul the rotten system which had helped to cause so much trouble. In fact, even before the peace, England had begun to put her house in order, and she continued to do it under the leadership of Shelburne, Fox, Pitt, and others.

Parliamentary corruption had existed as far back as Walpole's day, but that Whig corruption had not lost a war. After North's resignation the first step was the disfranchisement of the government revenue officers, who comprised about one sixth of the total national electorate, and had found it expedient to vote as the Treasury had dictated, to swell the ministerial majority. Next, contractors for the army and navy were forbidden to sit in Parliament. Burke's Economy Act of 1782 made drastic reductions in lucrative sinecures (government positions involving little or no work); in the number of pensions; and in the amount of the secret-service funds sometimes used for actual cash bribery of foreign officials. Here the Parliamentary reforms stopped until the Reform Bill of 1832 (see page 405), although Pitt tried three times to eliminate the rotten boroughs, only to meet defeat (once by only twenty votes).

Adam Smith, in his *Wealth of Nations* (see page 357), denouncing the arbitrary barriers imposed by the mercantile system, had urged a general adoption of international free trade, with each region producing the things for which it was best adapted. Pitt proceeded to put the economist's theories into practice. But the mercantile interests in Parliament killed his proposal for free trade between Great Britain and Ireland. He was more successful in his short-lived reciprocity treaty with France in 1786, which opened rich new markets for English manufactures in France until war intervened.

In finance, his achievements resembled those of Alexander Hamilton, the American, shortly afterward. The American Revolution had nearly doubled the national debt, increasing it from £126,000,000 to £240,000,000. Besides the funded debt (see page 279), there was a considerable floating debt, with many salaries and bills for supplies, unpaid for several years. Credit was so low that governmental securities sold for only about 57, little more than half their nominal value. Pitt soon raised them to 96 by funding the floating debt and selling the equivalent of present-day "bonds" in open sale to the highest bidders, instead of allotting them at special rates to political supporters, as North had done. Arrangements were next made to pay back the principal on the national debt, which had tended to become permanent, with consequent heavy annual interest charges. Pitt hoped to wipe it out by a sinking fund, for which a certain amount was to be set aside each year, to accumulate at compound interest until it would automatically pay off the debt. The plan broke down when the government borrowed money at 5 per cent to gather interest at 3 per cent in the sinking fund!

Pitt was also determined that Britain should pay as she went, instead of charging so much to the future. He tried to balance the budget by increasing the government's income and reducing its expenditures. The widespread smuggling which was conducted shamelessly all along the coast, especially in tea, silk, tobacco, and wine caused a tremendous loss in customs duties. To make it less worth while, he had the duty on tea drastically reduced and took action to authorize the seizure of any vessels "hovering" suspiciously off the coast. To offset a probable loss in tea duties, he laid excise, or internal, taxes on a queer assortment of articles, chiefly luxuries, including ribbons, race horses, ale licenses, windows, and servants. Also he combined the bewildering array of special accounts for items of income and expense into one general Consolidated Fund into which everything was paid and from which everything was drawn. Since the "bonds" were secured against this fund, they were popularly known as "consols." Pitt achieved a surplus of income over expense during the years of peace. These financial reforms were perhaps his most valuable work, and (combined with the economic strength and prosperity born of the Industrial Revolution) they enabled Britain to act as "paymaster of the Allies" during the long struggle just ahead. When war costs once more began to mount, he introduced an income tax, so that business and professional men would pay their share of the burden (see page 281).

Among various other reforms suggested, was the removal of the disabilities against Dissenters and Catholics, but this came to nothing for another fifty years. The society organized by Pitt's evangelical friend William Wilberforce for the abolition of the slave trade, however, would win its fight in 1807 through the work of Fox. As a result of this decade, then, Britain had a purer, if still unrepresentative, Parliament; a new and more liberal attitude toward the regulation of commerce; an improved financial system; and a public awakened to the need of further reform. Overseas, relations with India and Canada improved, while beginnings were made in the settlement of Australia. This reform movement, which began so auspiciously, might have continued to gain momentum had not events across the Channel suddenly hardened Britain's heart against reform for at least thirty years.

The French Revolution

In France, with her absolute monarchy and her parasitic nobility, revolution reared its head in 1789. Beginning as a liberal movement, which copied some English constitutional features, it grew into a radical upheaval with many lurid episodes and involved Europe in more than twenty years of war. Its legacy of nationalism and democracy continued to ferment during the next century and altered many aspects of government and society in the world at large. England, flattered at first by the attempted imitation, finally reacted in alarm and became the most persistent enemy of revolutionary France.

The French Revolution was essentially an effort of the intelligent middle class, such as doctors, lawyers, and merchants, to secure equality of opportunity with the nobility, who—unlike the English aristocracy—did practically nothing to justify the extensive and exclusive privileges of special rights before the law and virtual exemption from taxation. It was not primarily a revolt of the peasants, who were better off than most peasantry outside of England. The Estates-General, the counterpart of the English Parliament—with its groupings of first estate, or clergy; second estate, or nobles; and third estate, comprising the other 97 per cent—had not met for 175 years. Middle-class royal officials appointed by the king fulfilled the duties of the aristocratic English justices of the peace. Whereas in Britain the aristocracy had power rather than privilege, in France they had privilege rather than power. The well-meaning but incapable Louis XVI (1774-1793), and Marie Antoinette, his spirited Austrian queen, were totally unfitted to deal with the crisis.

During the eighteenth century the ignored middle class was growing increasingly resentful. The contemporary French philosophers gave them ample ammunition to bolster their personal grudge: Montesquieu, with his guarded attack on absolute monarchy (see page 294); Voltaire, with his merciless, logical sarcasm directed against all things traditional, from monarchy to Church; Diderot, with his provocative definitions of established institutions in his *Encyclopedia;* and, above all, Rousseau, with the new idea that the people were the

sovereign power and could set up a new government if the king failed to keep his "social contract" with them. The times were ripe for the Revolution. England set an example by her long record of constitutional development, and so, too, did the American Revolution, aided and abetted as it was by French money and forces. Consequently the bankruptcy of the government, caused in part by the American Revolution, which had been a luxury France could ill afford on top of all her other wars, gave the middle class their chance. When, as a last resort, Louis XVI called the Estates-General in 1789, the third estate, with its largely middle-class membership, finding that the privileged nobles and clergy would be enabled to override it with a two-to-one vote on every measure, set itself up as a distinct body and refused to disband until it had given France a constitution.

For a year or so the French Revolution continued to be comparatively respectable, constructive, and "English." France became a limited monarchy; the special feudal privileges of the nobles were renounced; and "liberty, equality, and fraternity" were proclaimed. With its high principles and lack of bloodshed, it looked like an imitation of the "Glorious Revolution" of 1688 to the English, who felt flattered. Correspondence societies sprang up for the exchange of liberal ideas. Then an increasing number of French noblemen began slipping quietly over to England. The story went round that this revolution was not as roseate as it had appeared. It seemed that groups of radicals were getting control of the government, that peasants were sacking the châteaux of the nobles, and that many of the nobility were fleeing across the Rhine or the Channel. English aristocrats thought of the possibility that their own half-starving peasantry might burn looms and tear down enclosures. Long before the real Terror began in France, they were using their imaginations with unpleasant results.

THE *Contrast*

1793

ENGLISH Liberty

French Liberty

Religion   Morality
Loyalty Obedience to the Laws
Independance Personal Security
Justice Inheritance Protection
Property Industry National Prosperity
        HAPPINESS

Atheism   Perjury
Rebellion Treason Anarchy Murder
Equality Madness Cruelty Injustice
Treachery Ingratitude Idleness
Famine National & Private Ruin
        MISERY

Which is BEST

Cartoon contrasting the nature of liberty in England and revolutionary France.

Burke and Reaction

Then England turned reactionary. Edmund Burke, one of her foremost liberals, threw his eloquent influence on the conservative side. In November, 1790, appeared Burke's *Reflections on the French Revolution* (see page 358). Not an aristocrat himself, Burke felt that Britain's security was bound up in the interests of her dominant landed aristocracy. He predicted that unless the French Revolution were checked, its pernicious ideas would permeate all Europe and that law, order, religion, and society would disappear in democratic anarchy. The mass of the wavering English landowners became firmly convinced that the revolutionary ideas meant their destruction. This view was soon strengthened by Tom Paine's radical *Rights of Man*, which argued that England needed a really representative republican government, with the abolition of the hereditary power of king and Lords. The establishment of the French republic, the execution of the king and queen and of thousands of others on the guillotine, and the excesses of the extreme radicals simply confirmed the idea that Burke was right.

In Parliament, the Whigs split, the majority following Burke over to the Tory camp, and backing the harsh reaction that set in. It was the turning point in the career of Pitt, hitherto a liberal. His government was turned into an instrument of oppression, crushing liberals as well as radicals. By the spring of 1792 a proclamation was issued against "seditious" writings, first of the harsh measures which silenced many and punished ruthlessly those who would not keep silent. There followed an Aliens Act, a Seditious Meetings Act, a Treasonable Practices Act, and the Combination Acts, which made trade unions illegal (see page 342). Suspension of habeas corpus, much of the time until 1801, made possible imprisonment without trial. Government spies sneaked into every sort of gathering, and some excellent men whose views were only a little more liberal than Pitt's had been earlier were transported to Australia for their "treason." Lord Erskine's eloquence successfully persuaded a jury to acquit Horne Tooke and others on trial for high treason for having advocated "representative government, the direct opposite of the government which is established here"; but that was an exception.

Fox, almost alone, kept liberal ideas alive in Parliament during the black reaction of the nineties. A few Whigs remained with Fox, registering persistent but ineffectual protests against the muzzling of the nation. Gradually most of them slipped away in disgust to their estates, and Fox, with a few of his "young men," was left to carry on. He expressed views which would have led to instant arrest from a less prominent person. He was able at least to register vehement disapproval of the panicky reaction and his "young men" would successfully revive the dormant liberalism after 1815.

In the meantime war descended on most of Europe. Revolutionary France wanted to convert the world. The course of events there was arousing the absolutist states, particularly Austria, Russia, Prussia, and Spain, more than it had Britain. In 1791 a joint declaration by Austria and Prussia expressed the hope that the European rulers would act together to restore Louis XVI to his full powers. By 1792 a French republic had been proclaimed, the moderate revolutionaries were out of the picture, and soon a radical "Convention," with its executive Committee of Public Safety under Robespierre, was entering upon a mad career. In the hectic rivalry the question of war or peace became too often a political football. Relations with Vienna grew constantly more strained, and on April 20, 1792, France declared war on Austria. This automatically brought in Austria's ally, Prussia.

In France, the government and finances were shaky. Mutinies were widespread in the old standing army; the new raw volunteers left much to be desired; and most titled officers had left or been ejected. Rochambeau and Lafayette, who had been at Yorktown eleven years before, led two armies. At the first sight of the foe, the French ran. This left the offensive to the allies. Had their well-trained forces marched at once against Paris they could probably have ended the Revolution then and there, but various complications held them back. The French call for volunteers brought them swarming by the thousands, singing the new Marseillaise. At Valmy, in September 1792, the French artillery fire caused the invading Prussians to withdraw. One of the "decisive battles of the world," it saved the Revolution; and the next day France was declared a republic. Encouraged, the French soon overran the Austrian Netherlands (Belgium), which had been in revolt. The French Convention proclaimed that the river Scheldt, which, with its port of Antwerp, had been closed to navigation by international agreement ever since 1648, was once more open to shipping.

That news shortly brought Britain into the war through her perennial dread of a strong power in the Low Countries (see page 278). Pitt called Belgium the "chain which unites England to the Continent" and declared that any powerful nation controlling the Scheldt "holds a pistol pointed at the heart of England." Hitherto he had favored peace with France. The British reaction was by no means unanimous. At Sheffield workers celebrated the French success by barbecuing an ox and parading ten thousand strong with the revolutionary tricolor. In the Commons, Fox made a strong pro-French speech which at least kept fifty members from voting unanimous support of Pitt's stand.

Both nations, however, pushed steadily

toward war, neither being in the mood to give way. The four principal men involved were under thirty-four. The French foreign minister and the ambassador at London were inexperienced and enthusiastic; Pitt and Grenville, his foreign minister, were so cold and so haughty that they often verged on insolence. Pitt immediately called out part of the militia and put the navy in a state of readiness. In reckless self-confidence, the French Convention had voted to "grant fraternity and assistance to all people who wish to recover their liberty," and later to "revolutionize all countries where its armies are or shall come." In the meantime it annexed Savoy. Britain offered to leave the French Revolution alone if it would confine itself to France. The French announced their determination to secure their "natural frontiers"—the Alps, the Pyrenees, the Rhine, and the ocean. This, of course, involved Belgium and a part of Holland. Then came, on January 21, 1793, the beheading of Louis XVI. Apparently forgetting the fate of Charles I, England denounced this as "the most odious and atrocious crime in history." Having now a high moral purpose, as well as her more practical reasons of state, Britain was ready for war. The French ambassador was given a week to get out of London. The actual declaration of war came from France on February 1.

Within a few weeks the French also declared war on Spain and Holland. Prussia, Austria, and Sardinia were already at war with them, and the other German states of the "Empire," together with several small nations, joined the contest by the end of March. France, in a reckless mood, had taken on all comers and was ringed around with enemies who were known as the "First Coalition," a phrase which implies a more effective alliance than this was. All the allies gave lip service to the "cause of kings" and to the fight against nationalism and democracy, but most of them had their own special reasons which outweighed the common cause. Austria and Prussia hoped to seize some French frontier territory and were busy with other diplomatic juggling. George III and Burke sincerely wanted to crush the revolutionary ideas, but Pitt's prime interest was the security of the Low Countries. Practically the only strong bond in the whole coalition was the hope of securing gifts or loans from the British treasury, which Pitt had filled so successfully. Looking at the situation through the eyes of the financier, he underestimated the fighting power of France, with her exhausted treasury and demoralized administration. He put too much faith in the power of gold, overlooking the importance of the will to win. He took over his father's policy of "hiring" Continental countries to fight the French; but the recipients were so involved in their own particular intrigues that Britain did not always get full value for the millions which she poured into their coffers. She was to remain the "paymaster of the allies" throughout the long struggle and to take the initiative in building up a succession of coalitions which the French proceeded to destroy. It was not until 1813 that Austria, Prussia, and Russia, all three at the same time, would join in alliance with England and finally beat the French.

The intrigues and individual problems of Britain's allies seriously hindered united action. Austria, who, next to Britain, was France's most persistent enemy, bore the brunt of the attacks. Behind the pomp at Vienna and the imposing armies of whitecoats was not a nation but the shadowy Holy Roman Empire and a heterogeneous conglomeration of regions and races—German, Magyar, Slav, Italian, Belgian—accumulated by Hapsburg marriages and conquests. After an overdose of royal reform under two "benevolent despots," Maria Theresa and her son Joseph II of Austria had lapsed into stiff-necked conservatism. Francis II, narrow-minded, pedantic, and shy, met all problems by "Let us sleep upon it," so irresponsible court adventurers controlled affairs. As for Prussia, Frederick the Great would have turned in his tomb could he have seen how she had slumped in the twenty years since his death. Frederick William III was weak, and his predecessor had neglected the army and had bankrupted the state. Prussia's role in the coming struggle was marked by apathy and sordid haggling. She was to stay at peace with France from 1795 until 1806, when a crushing defeat shocked her into a thoroughgoing national revival. Russia's Catherine II, on the other hand, established as high a record for ability as for immorality. Whereas Peter the Great was said to have made Russia a European power, Catherine made her a great one. The backward condition of Russia offset her size; but the reason she did not do more in the French situation was that Catherine's prime interest was in Russia's own expansion against Turkey in the south, Sweden in the north, and especially Poland in the west. Spain, only a shadow of her former greatness, with probably the most worthless of all the contemporary crowned heads for king in Charles IV, used her mediocre forces first on one side, then on the other. Of the lesser states there were Holland, with civil war recently within her borders; Piedmont, or Sardinia, Italy's chief independent nation, to be the nucleus of a united Italian kingdom; Sweden, whose role was unimportant; Denmark and Portugal, about which none of the allies bothered much; and the three hundred and sixty-odd virtually independent units in Germany, loosely held together in the Holy Roman Empire, but acting separately as each selfish interest dictated. As for Poland, where the turbulent rule of the nobility gave her neighbors, Russia, Prussia, and Austria, a chance to intervene, she had disappeared with three partitions by 1795.

This was the heyday of the old secret diplomacy, with double-dealing the rule; and more than one foreign minister would draw up a treaty of alliance with one nation when the ink was barely dry on a similar one with its rivals. The general system, as later, was that if one or two powers showed designs on new territory, the others would bluff them out of it by a show of force, share in the spoils themselves, or demand "compensation" elsewhere. Pitt and his foreign minister, Grenville, had made their own alliances and three times prepared the royal navy for action as a threat. Twice that was sufficient: in 1786 to keep the Dutch ruler on his throne; and four years later to stop a Spanish attempt to bar fur-hunting English ships from Nootka Sound on Vancouver Island, on the Pacific coast of North America. But in 1791, Pitt's objection to Russia's expansion on the Black Sea coast against Turkey—a grave threat in English eyes to the safety of her possessions in India—came to nothing, partly because of the lack of Parliamentary support. Britain also balked the Austrian plot to exchange Bavaria for Belgium for fear of Belgium's falling into French hands.

Now, with the long war once under way, England's constant building up and paying of alliances was to be a very important factor in the ultimate French defeat; but her function as a belligerent did not end there. The army and navy were quickly drawn into action in many places—altogether too many—with disheartening reverses at first. Pitt showed poor judgment in selecting his war ministers. His own elder brother, the second Earl of Chatham, was worthless as First Lord of the Admiralty. Pitt's close friend Henry Dundas, the political boss of Scotland to whom he entrusted the general supervision of the fighting, already had his hands full with the control of Indian and home affairs. In ignorant optimism, Dundas frittered away its strength in giving the army far more tasks than it could adequately perform.

The navy was in fair condition, thanks to the preparations in the Dutch, Spanish, and

Russian crises. As soon as the press gangs had kidnaped enough crews, the ships of the line were sent off to the usual stations in the Mediterranean, the West Indies, and so on. The Channel fleet did not clap down a proper blockade and several French squadrons slipped out to cause unnecessary alarm and damage. The demoralization of the French fleets, which had been so effective in the last war, aided the British. As in the army, with the titled officers leaving or being ejected by mutineers, lieutenants or merchant marine officers were raised to high command and discipline disintegrated. Britain cut off the supplies of masts and other naval stores needed to put the ships in condition.

The British army was in bad shape with widespread abuses unchecked. Too many officers were interested in the bottle, to the complete neglect of tactics and strategy. The old rank and file were good, but all too few. There was little inducement to volunteer in a service which offered inadequate food and clothing, flogging for drunkenness and, besides the usual perils of bullets and bayonets, the likelihood of freezing to death in the Low Countries or of perishing of yellow fever in the Caribbean. Consequently large numbers were dragged into service by methods almost as crude as the kidnaping by the navy. As usual, England supplemented her forces by hiring large numbers of Hessians and Hanoverians.

Although at the outset, Britain had fewer than twenty thousand men available, Dundas undertook tasks requiring five times that number. The most obvious was the Belgian front where the French were starting a dash for Holland. There were opportunities also to assist rebellions in various parts of France, and the temptation to seize the French West Indian islands. Dundas tried them all and failed in each.

There was no time to lose in the Low Countries. For the moment the British and Austrian troops saved Holland, cleared Belgium, and even had a clear road to Paris. Again, a determined advance might have ended the French Revolution; but the allies wrangled over their prospective spoils and neglected to beat the French first. They wasted most of 1793 in trying to capture cities for themselves; Britain wanted Dunkirk.

Lazare Carnot, "Organizer of Victory," was meanwhile transforming the French army from a disorganized rabble into a formidable fighting force. He was undeterred by an empty treasury and worthless paper money—insuperable handicaps in Pitt's eyes. Carnot appealed to the spirit, as Pitt had not, and so marshaled all the resources of the people—women, older men, children even, as well as fighting men. Shirts and shoes were requistioned by the tens of thousands, and every eighth pig gave up its life to feed the army. With the waning of initial volunteering, conscription was instituted. Rigid discipline stamped out mutinies. New tactics were developed for the partly trained new troops. Great massed columns of infantry were to crush through the thin lines of the enemy. For high command there was a career open to talent; sergeants and privates, Jews and foreigners, might become marshals. The guillotine awaited the commander who failed to crush the enemy. The general who drove the British from Dunkirk was beheaded for not having whipped them more decisively. These French armies, even with conscription, fought with a fervor quite lacking among their professional opponents, where commissions depended on social rank and men were units hired at so much a head.

The reorganized French forces began to win victories in every direction. Belgium was recovered; and by 1795 they had Holland as well. Hundreds of British soldiers there, neglected by Dundas, actually froze to death. Rebellious royalists within France fared no better. Late in 1793 the British Mediterranean fleet, at their invitation, occupied the great naval base at Toulon; but the allies did not send troops enough to hold the hills commanding the harbor. The French rushed the hills; and a young artillery lieutenant, named Bonaparte, helped to drive out the British ships, which left in too much of a hurry to carry off or destroy half the French navy lying there at their mercy. Nearer home in answer to appeals to co-operate with strong royalist uprisings near the French coast, Dundas "sent a boy to do a man's work." One inadequate expedition after another failed after raising false hopes and exposing the royalists to additional vengeance. But, even worse, in the West Indies, superior British sea power failed to take an easy prey, the rich French sugar islands. Delays, blunders, and injudicious intervention in Haiti, where the Negroes had risen against the French planters, resulted in lost opportunities and terrific losses from yellow fever.

Aside from the Toulon affair, the principal naval action of the early war was only technically a British victory. In the spring of 1794 France, on the verge of starvation, was dependent upon American grain. A flotilla of 120 merchantmen loaded with essential supplies sailed from Chesapeake Bay, protected by only a small convoy of warships. The British might have captured the whole expedition as it left American shores or blockaded the French ports to prevent its arrival. As it was, the French fleet put out from Brest to make a sacrifice play, by engaging the British Channel fleet while the grain ships slipped safely into port. The French lost more than a quarter of their ships of the line in that "glorious first of June," as it was called by the British.

By the summer of 1795 the First Coalition had nearly fallen to pieces. Only Austria and little Sardinia remained British allies. Holland, overrun by the French, had to join them. Spain made peace with France and soon appeared on her side. Prussia, more interested in the third parti-

tion of Poland and quite bankrupt, agreed to withdraw, provided France would not disturb northern Germany. So, too, did several of the smaller German states.

That year was a quiet one. The British army had withdrawn from the Continent, contenting itself with a single raid on the French coast. The rival navy forces in the Mediterranean engaged in ineffective encounters. Redcoats continued to die like flies in the West Indies, where Negro rebellions complicated the situation. The British captured the Dutch colonies, including the Cape of Good Hope and Ceylon, holding them "in trust" for the regular pro-British Dutch ruler.

The situation then grew worse. France undertook a triple campaign to put Austria and Sardinia out of the fight. Two of her most experienced generals attacked Austria from the Rhine and the Danube, but were stopped. A third force struck at Italy—a sideshow which revealed the military genius of a young man of twenty-seven, who was to occupy the center of the stage for nearly twenty years. Napoleon Bonaparte's family was of the lesser aristocracy but very poor. An artillery officer, he had first distinguished himself with his batteries in helping to eject the British from Toulon. Intense, quiet, and studious, he almost at once revealed the qualities which were to give him a place among the greatest soldiers of history. A master of strategy and tactics, he could also inspire his men. He knew all the conventional rules practiced by his rivals and was capable of constant originality in developing new movements to surprise them.

It was a grave day for England when this short, dark, and, at that time, slender soldier was given the opportunity to show his ability. Approaching by the Riviera, between the Alps and the sea, he rapidly put Sardinia out of the fight and deftly parried the attacks of one Austrian general after another. Northern Italy quickly came under his control, new republics on the

French model were set up, and the loot from Italian cities helped to replenish the empty French treasury. By the spring of 1797 he had his sixth Austrian opponent on the run, only sixty miles from Vienna, when Austria made peace. Napoleon deliberately gave Austria lenient terms so that France might concentrate her energies against Britain, now without allies.

But those twenty-one miles of Channel put Britain in an entirely different category from the Continental nations which the invincible French armies had overrun and would continue to overrun for years to come. Infantry, cavalry, and artillery could not bring Britain to terms as long as her royal navy held the sea. Yet, while she remained unconquered, her diplomacy and gold would continue to bring together alliances to fight France. In the course of ten years France was to try four different ways of putting her out of the fight; by armed threats at Ireland, at India, and at England herself, and finally by economic pressure.

The royal navy blocked all those attempts; yet that same navy was seething with mutiny in 1797. Many sailors were there against their will; their pay, disgracefully low, was badly in arrears; the iron discipline sometimes degenerated into tyranny. Trouble started at Spithead, off Portsmouth, when as the Channel fleet was ordered to sea, the crews refused to sail until their pay was raised. Parliament, recognizing the justice of their claims, tardily redressed some grievances. That leniency led to a less justifiable and more violent mutiny in the North Sea squadron. This time the government hanged eighteen ringleaders. Order was restored in home waters; but mutiny spread to the squadron off Spain, to the West Indies, and to the Cape of Good Hope.

In spite of the mutinies, some of these very ships won two decisive victories that same year. The French navy had pretty much gone to pieces, but they hoped to make use of the two ready-made navies of Spain and Holland. Spain had become an ally, while Holland, already overrun, had part of her icebound navy captured by French cavalry. By the autumn of 1797, however, Britain had shattered the Spaniards off Cape St. Vincent, near Gibraltar, and the Dutch at Camperdown, in the North Sea. France was thrown back on her own depleted naval resources. Part of her vessels were used for fruitless expeditions to discontented Ireland (see page 375), but a more dramatic role was selected for the Mediterranean fleet.

Bonaparte returned from his Italian triumphs a hero. He was urged to overthrow the corrupt government, but felt that "the pear was not yet ripe." Desiring to be out of the way, meanwhile, he struck at Egypt, an attempt which might be a threat to British power in India. In 1798 he sailed from Toulon with fifteen ships (all that France could scrape together), narrowly missed the British Mediterranean fleet, and landed in Egypt, which was nominally subject to Turkey but actually governed by the Mamelukes, professional soldiers, whom Bonaparte defeated in the shadow of the pyramids.

Then his plans were wrecked by Horatio Nelson, the greatest of Britain's sea heroes. Son of a clergyman, he had gone to sea at twelve as a midshipman, and had run up through the grades with extraordinary rapidity—captain at twenty, rear admiral at thirty-nine. He had dash, daring, and magnetism, and was highly unconventional in everything from dress to morals. He had burst into fame the previous year in the battle of Cape St. Vincent, where his bold boarding action forced the surrender of two of the Spanish ships. He was an exceedingly vain little man, but his officers and men swore by him, and in battle he had that same brilliant advantage over conventional rivals that Bonaparte enjoyed on land. He had already lost an eye and an arm in battle.

Admiral Horatio Nelson in 1797, just after he lost an arm at Teneriffe.

At Abukir Bay, at one mouth of the Nile, the French were first to experience the "Nelson touch." Their fleet anchored in a single line fairly close to shore, expected the attack in the regulation single line, with the ships pairing off one by one for duels. But Nelson, seeing that with careful steering his ships could get between the French and the shore, attacked in two lines, one outside the French, the other inside. Each French ship was thus caught between two fires, and one after another succumbed as Nelson rolled up their line. The great French flagship blew up; most of the rest were captured; and Bonaparte's army was marooned on the wrong side of the Mediterranean. Then Nelson, forgetful of his wife in England, fell under the spell of Lady Hamilton, the beautiful wife of the British minister at Naples, and for two years this infatuation kept him in that vicinity. In this most bizarre episode of an unconventional career, he even used the fleet to meddle in Neapolitan affairs.

Bonaparte, meanwhile, had started up the Mediterranean coast toward Turkey, but was checked at Acre, where a British squadron aided the Turks. Abandoning his army, which was later conquered by British redcoats, he slipped off to France in 1799 and by a bold stroke overthrew the corrupt Directory, then in control. He was to be master of France, for five years as First Consul and for ten more as Emperor. While he was busy in Egypt, England had built up a Second Coalition, with Austria, Russia, and Turkey. They had recovered Italy and had undone all his work there; but he crossed the Alps, got between them and their base, and in a crushing victory at Marengo broke up the Coalition in 1800.

Then Bonaparte, newly allied with Russia, planned to join the northern European nations to close the Baltic to Britain. Denmark controlled the entrance. Without a declaration of war, a British fleet was sent in 1801 against Copenhagen, with Nelson only second in command, because of the scandal. He had a bold plan to attack the Danish fortifications through a shallow channel risky for great ships. His superior reluctantly agreed, but when he saw the situation becoming serious, he hoisted the recall signal, generously giving Nelson, with the advance force, a chance to retire. Nelson, however, with his telescope to his blind eye, declared he could see no such signal. He thoroughly smashed the Danes; the pro-French Czar of Russia was assassinated as the result of a domestic plot; and the Baltic remained open.

In 1802 France and England signed the Peace of Amiens, in which most captured places were restored. During this two-year breathing spell, Bonaparte accomplished much of lasting value for France in legal, educational, and religious reforms. At the same time he made active preparations for renewed conflict. But England let the navy lapse to a peace basis to save money.

Irish Revolt and United Kingdom

During those last years of fighting the ever-smoldering Irish problem had flared up violently, as it so often did in English emergencies, since only at such times could the Irish hope to gain anything. During the American Revolution, they had demanded free trade and a free parliament. The leadership was Protestant, with the moral support of the Catholics; for the easygoing atmosphere of the century had quieted religious animosities. With 100,000 Irish Protestants under arms, and only 5000 redcoats to check them, Parliament in 1782 gave Ireland the most satisfactory government she had had in centuries. Many trading restrictions were lifted, and Poynings's Laws (see page 167) were repealed. Ireland was given her own parliament at Dublin, commonly known as "Grattan's Parliament" because Henry Grattan (a Protestant, like many of Ireland's national leaders then and later) was largely responsible for it. This arrangement, to be sure, left much to be desired. The Irish boroughs were even more "rotten" than the English. Only Protestants might sit in parliament and, at first, only they might vote for its members. The executive power was still in the hands of English appointees at Dublin Castle, who opposed any reform of Ireland's main grievances—the exclusion of the Catholics from its government; the rent to the English landlords, imposed by Cromwell; and the payment of tithes by Catholics to an established Protestant Church which they did not attend.

Nevertheless, with relative prosperity for a time and the population almost doubling in eighteen years, Protestants and Catholics worked together to gain whatever they could for their unhappy island. The penal code was modified, and Catholics were given the vote, but not membership in the Dublin parliament. Then came the French Revolution, and the Irish radicals sought French help. A revolutionary society was organized by one Wolfe Tone. By 1797, Dublin Castle unearthed the revolutionary plots, and decided to stamp them out by force, but unfortunately chose as its agents the unruly Protestant militia who used the opportunity to settle old scores. Men and women were stripped on the streets and punished if they were wearing as much as a ribbon of the revolutionary green; some were flogged, hanged, or shot down in cold blood. These methods prevented rebellion in the north; but in the south it flared out in 1798, and the rebels were equally ruthless. Militia companies were massacred in their barracks, and a barn containing nearly two hundred men, women, and children was burned to the ground. A powerful French fleet nearly made a landing, but was dispersed by gales; a smaller French force got ashore, but finally had to surrender. The main body of the rebels was defeated at Vinegar Hill, and vengeance was once more visited upon them. These events gave rise to the famous Irish song with the refrain "They're hanging men and women for the wearin' of the green."

Having crushed the revolt, Pitt decided that something must be done to remedy the conditions which provoked it. An independent Irish legislature seemed dangerous, so he decided to draw Ireland more closely to the British government by having Irish representation in the British Parliament instead. Scotland in 1707 had received trade advantages in exchange for her loss of legislative independence. Ireland's compensation, Pitt agreed, was that full political rights should be given to the Catholics and that they should no longer have to pay for a church they did not want. By means of heavy bribes in peerages and gold, Grattan's Parliament was persuaded to terminate its existence and to agree to a legislative union with England.

On the first day of the nineteenth century, January 1, 1801, the Kingdom of Great Britain, which had been formed in 1707 by the inclusion of Scotland, was expanded into the United Kingdom of Great Britain and Ireland, which lasted until 1922. The Irish were to have 32 members in the House of Lords and 100 in the Commons, as compared with 16 in the Lords and 45 in the Commons for Scotland. The union did not please the Irish, for they did not receive the compensations they had been led to expect. This was primarily the fault of George III, who opposed granting new Catholic rights, calling it a violation of his coronation oath. While the last royal veto had occurred in 1707, this stubborn stand of the intermittently insane monarch amounted to virtually the same thing, and long embittered Anglo-Irish relations.

In the face of this royal opposition Pitt resigned, and was succeeded (1801) by Henry Addington (later Lord Sidmouth). A dull, well-meaning man, his weak ministry came at the time of the one breathing spell in the French wars. Soon after the contest was resumed, popular demand brought Pitt back in 1804.

Renewal of War and Threat of Invasion

The technical excuse for the resumption of hostilities in 1803 was England's failure to restore Malta as agreed at Amiens. That little island, strategically situated where it could dominate the narrow passage between the eastern and the western Mediterranean, had long belonged to the military crusading order of the Knights of Saint John. Bonaparte, on his way to Egypt in 1798, had seized it; but the French had treated the inhabitants so wantonly that they welcomed the British, who soon occupied it. They now clung to it as an excellent site for a naval base, all the more necessary because Minorca had been lost in 1783.

With the resumption of hostilities England was faced with as grave a menace of invasion as in 1588, but once again the royal navy rose to the occasion. Bonaparte's Grand Army was encamped at Boulogne, where artisans were hard at work making flatboats in which to transport it across the Channel. It remained only for the French navy, strengthened by many new ships, to hold off the British warships long enough to get the troops across those twenty-odd miles of water. Once they were across, England would have no forces capable of effective resistance. In naval strategy, however, France had always been under a heavy handicap. The Spanish peninsula lay between her Atlantic coast with its base at Brest near the Channel and her Mediterranean coast with its Toulon base. Bonaparte planned to have the Toulon and Brest fleets join to gain temporary control of the Channel.

Britain clapped down a close and continuous blockade on the enemy ports and, despite terrific difficulties, maintained it for twenty grueling months. While the French veterans were practicing getting into flatboats, and panicky land-defense measures were being taken in England, the British warships kept their stations. Admiral Cornwallis, whose brother had lost Yorktown, kept guard off Brest while Nelson watched the Toulon fleet. Lesser squadrons cruised before lesser ports, including those of Spain, again a French ally. England's numerical superiority of 55 ships of the line to the enemy's 42 was necessary from the nature of the work. The enemy had their ships based together for use at any moment, whereas the forces outside were liable to be scattered by storms or diminished by the need to refit. The blockaders had a negative mission, requiring constant vigilance, and they had to be strong enough to drive the enemy back into port. The constant service on blockade kept the crews well trained, while the enemy lay inactive; but it was a severe test for unsound ships. And there were plenty of unsound British ships, for there was no timber for repairs. English oaks were constantly growing scarcer, and even the available supply was in the hands of a powerful monopoly which refused to give any to the navy unless its old graft were restored. Consequently complaints came in from the various stations of British squadrons, which were weakened by wear and tear while the enemy grew stronger in port. "My crazy fleet are getting in a very indifferent state," wrote Nelson off Toulon, "and others will soon follow. The finest ships in the service will be destroyed. I know that if I was to go to Malta, I should save the ships during this bad season; but if I am to watch the French, I must be at sea, and if at sea must have bad weather; and if the ships are not fit to stand bad weather, they are useless." "However," he wrote in closing, "you may rely that all which can be done by ships and men shall be done." They made good that promise. So did the forces on the other stations, from one of which an admiral wrote, "We have been sailing for months with only a copper sheet between us and eternity." By 1805 the Admiralty had yielded to the monopolists and had hastily patched up some of the decrepit ships—none too soon. The enemy now outnumbered the British blockaders by fifteen ships; but still the blockade held fast. "The world has never seen a more impressive demonstration of the influence of sea power upon its history," wrote Mahan in his study of sea power. "Those far-distant, storm-beaten ships, upon which the Grand Army never looked, stood between it and the dominion of the world."[1]

Trafalgar and Continental System

Then, in the summer of 1805, while Nelson's forces were temporarily scattered by a storm, the Toulon fleet slipped out of port and headed for the West Indies, to draw the British away from their sentry duty. Nelson, after a hurried search of the Mediterranean, followed them to the Caribbean and back. The Toulon fleet put into Cádiz, joining forces with the Spaniards. Bona-

[1] A. T. Mahan, *Influence of Sea Power upon the French Revolution and Empire* (1898), Vol. II, p. 118. By permission of Little, Brown & Company and Sampson Low, Marston & Co., Ltd.

parte, now Emperor Napoleon, put a more energetic admiral in command; but before he could reach Cádiz, the combined French and Spanish fleet, in a gesture of despair, sailed out to challenge the British. The result was a decisive battle off Cape Trafalgar, just outside Gibraltar, on October 21, 1805.

The enemy had thirty-three ships of the line to Nelson's twenty-seven, but he inspired a high morale and kept his men in fighting trim. The enemy straggled out in the single conventional line. Nelson headed for its center with his ships in two parallel columns. Signal flags were run up from his flagship, the *Victory*, with a characteristic Nelson touch, "England expects every man to do his duty." The lazy breeze brought the fleets together at barely a mile an hour; but at last they joined in a melee. A marine from an enemy seventy-four's fighting top fired at Nelson. He fell, and was carried below to the dark cockpit among the other wounded, where he died after learning that the enemy fleet was routed. Not until 1916 was Britain's main fleet again to engage in battle with an enemy of fairly equal strength.

Nelson died thinking that he had saved England from the Grand Army at Boulogne, for word had not reached the fleet that it was now on the Danube. Pitt had persuaded Austria and Russia to join England in a Third Coalition, with her, as usual, paying a generous share of the bills. Napoleon, determining to break up the alliance before it could get under way, secretly withdrew the Grand Army from Boulogne and hurried it eastward across Europe by forced marches, much as Marlborough had done in the Blenheim campaign. Four days before Trafalgar, he caught one whole Austrian army by surprise. Then he entered Vienna and in December crushed an allied Austrian and Russian army at Austerlitz.

When Pitt saw his Third Coalition crumble away before Napoleon's onslaught, he said, "Roll up the map of Europe; it will

Trafalgar, 1805, with British ships of the line smashing the enemy fleet.

not be needed these ten years." Early in 1806 he was dead. There followed a succession of mediocre prime ministers, each of whom was overshadowed by at least one member of his cabinet. Lord Grenville, whose father had pushed through the Stamp Act in 1765, headed a "Ministry of All the Talents" including several Whigs, particularly Fox, who, with only a few months left to live, crowned his career with the abolition of the slave trade. In 1807 the innocuous Duke of Portland (see page 363) again became titular head of a cabinet which included the sharp-tongued George Canning, later famous as a liberal Tory, and Lord Castlereagh (eventually Lord Londonderry), handsome, cold, and competent, who guided England's military policy and foreign relations during most of the ensuing years of war and of peace negotiations and won a name for being a worse reactionary than he really was. By 1809, after these two men

had fought a duel and Portland had died, came Spencer Perceval, a clever Parliamentary tactician and a good hater of the French. His assassination in 1812 came just too late to avert war with the United States (see page 381). He was followed by the fifteen-year ministry of the "arch mediocrity" Lord Liverpool, who was obscured by Castlereagh and other able subordinates. These men, stubborn, dogged, and level-headed, deserve credit for Napoleon's final downfall, but the distant gunfire from the Continent deafened them to the smashing of looms by the distressed handworkers and the complaints of the starving rural workers at home. George III went permanently insane in 1811, and until his death in 1820, his eldest son, the future George IV, served as Prince Regent.

Austerlitz had put Austria out of the fight for the third time, and the Russians withdrew; but Prussia, who had kept out of the fray for eleven years, suddenly took up arms. Had she done so a year earlier, when Pitt was desperately urging such a course, the Third Coalition might have been another story. As it was, Napoleon routed her rusty army at Jena, in 1806, and showed his contempt by imposing humiliating terms. Russia still remained; but after two desperate and bloody battles, Napoleon and Czar Alexander met amicably at Tilsit, in 1807, to "divide the world between them." Until 1812 Napoleon's power was at its height. Most of the Continent was to be either under his control or at least in alliance. There was a lull in the major campaigning, and Europe listened to his commands.

Napoleon and Britain were continually engaged, however, in economic warfare on a grand scale. Napoleon was determined upon a final effort to bring her to her knees. His thrusts at Ireland and at India through Egypt had failed; Trafalgar had shown that direct invasion was out of the question. But as long as Britain remained untamed, her gold and diplomacy would go on building up coalitions to challenge his power. To dry up the source of much of that gold, Napoleon issued in 1806 his Berlin Decree which closed the ports of his empire and dependencies to all ships from Great Britain; made British goods liable to seizure; and declared the British Isles in a state of blockade. At Tilsit he had secured the adherence of Russia and Prussia to these terms, and Denmark also joined. Later in 1807, his Milan Decree declared all neutral ships liable to seizure if suspected of trade with the British. Britain had countered with Orders in Council (similar to the old ordinances and proclamations); the severest of these, issued in 1807, declared Napoleon's coasts in a state of blockade and practically required all neutrals to trade through British ports. Neither side had ships enough for a literal blockade on such a wide scale; their announcements on "paper" that a port was blockaded made all shipping trading there liable to capture. Despite all efforts to keep the Tilsit terms secret, even to staging the conference on a raft in the river, England learned of them quickly. Within two months a British fleet repeated Nelson's work of six years before by smashing the Danes at Copenhagen without a declaration of war, and carrying their navy back to England. Albeit illegal, this prompt action kept the Baltic open.

Either Napoleon's "Continental System" or Britain's "Continental Blockade" could have practically ended European commerce if the original edicts had been enforced at their face value. But, as each side wished to maintain its own trade while crippling the enemy, there arose a license system of "trading by exception" through maritime indulgences. Both sides adopted this maritime hypocrisy which sometimes went to ridiculous lengths. When Napoleon was preparing to invade Russia, he bought vast quantities of overcoats in England; and his old mother put the money he gave her into English consols, to ensure herself an income whether he won or lost. England, while fighting in Spain, paid the armies by means of drafts which passed through the bankers of Paris.

After Trafalgar, the royal navy's ships of the line had little fighting to do, and smaller craft took up the navy's burden of enforcing the Continental Blockade. Britain gave a remarkable demonstration of "the noiseless, steady, exhausting pressure with which sea power acts, cutting off the resources of the enemy while maintaining its own, supporting war in scenes where it does not appear itself or appears only in the background, and striking open blows only at rare intervals."[2] Frigates and sloops by the hundred were necessary for this; even the ten guns of little gun brigs were enough to make a merchantman heave to and prove

[2] A. T. Mahan, *Influence of Sea Power upon History, 1660-1783* (1890), p. 209. By permission of Little, Brown & Company, and Sampson Low, Marston & Co., Ltd.

that its papers and cargo satisfied Britain's commercial regulations.

For their own trade, the British constantly sought loopholes in the Continental System. There was a certain amount of leakage, even where it was enforced most rigidly. British secret-service agents kept the government informed of the situation in the various ports, particularly where the officials were negligent or corruptible. Scores of merchantmen, under naval convoy up to the last minute, would descend on ports reported "safe" with Britain's commercial offerings. Europe craved some products which England alone could bring from her empire, such as coffee, tea, chocolate, and tobacco, but for the West Indian sugar, scientists had just found an adequate substitute from beets. Textiles and hardware from Britain herself were in high demand, too. Also, the landowners of northern Europe wanted an outlet for exporting their grain and timber which lay rotting at the ports. Even if officials were occasionally changed, and some zealous newcomer seized ships and publicly burned cargoes of English woolens in the square, the profits on successful cargoes were enough to offset such losses. Although the quantity of Britain's exports decreased, that very scarcity enhanced their price, so the trade expanded in value. From some £50,000,000 in 1805, exports rose in 1809 to £66,000,000 —higher than ever before. "Because they were better at the price," Britain did not have to force her wares on unwilling foreigners. Her sea power enabled her to set her goods ashore, where they were taken by "the willing hands of the people whom Napoleon claimed to be rescuing from her commercial tyranny."

Neutral Trade and the War of 1812

Each side had to use neutral flags if their commerce were to survive the edicts of 1806 and 1807. The British flag was as vulnerable in a Continental port as the French flag at sea. Each side had to use neutrals,

but each distrusted them. England had a long record of opposing the sanctity of neutrality. If the doctrine of "free ships, free goods" were allowed, she would lose the whole advantage which command of the seas gave her in cutting off enemy trade. For centuries, suspected merchantmen had been brought to by a shot across the bow from a British warship; whereupon the "right of search" would be exercised with cold insolence, and would frequently end with a prize crew's taking the vessel to England for trial in an Admiralty court. There were neutrals and neutrals. Some were legitimate, exporting their own products in their own ships or carrying the wares of others. There was also a farcical prostitution of neutrality: the tiny merchant marines of free German cities, which had their own flags, were sometimes expanded a hundredfold overnight in time of war by wholesale registration of belligerent ships. A French or British brig might secure shelter behind the sacred protection of neutrality by a mere scratch of the pen and a liberal use of money. Suspicious boarding officers might have the stern of the vessel scraped to see what name and hailing port had been originally painted underneath. Pitt voiced the British point of view when he asked in Commons "whether we are to suffer neutral nations, by hoisting a flag upon a sloop or a fishing boat, to convey the treasures of South America or the naval stores of the Baltic to Brest or Toulon." But Britain herself had to use neutral "flags of convenience" when she approached the ports of Napoleon's domains. Her attitude toward neutral shipping, like that of most nations, depended wholly upon whether she was a neutral who wanted to trade (see page 423) or a blockading belligerent.

The outbreak of the Anglo-French war in 1793 had been a boon to the United States, most conspicuous of the legitimate neutrals. Her old colonial commerce had been knocked askew by the Revolution, but building new ships by the score, she now did a lively business carrying wares for both England and France. From the start, many of her ships ran afoul of the regulations of one belligerent or the other; but that carrying trade laid the foundations of many a Yankee fortune. When the Napoleonic decrees and the Orders in Council increased the chances of seizure, the owners and the mariners still wanted to take the risk, but President Jefferson pushed through Congress in 1807 an Embargo Act. This forbade all foreign commerce in American vessels, but was soon modified into "nonintercourse," and Britain and France were told that the Americans would trade with the one which repealed her decrees. Napoleon made a gesture of doing so. Prime Minister Perceval refused to relax the Orders in Council. There was a bitter feeling against England's exercise of the right of search, together with the impressing of seamen from American ships on the charge that they were British deserters. That, combined with irritation over the British relations with the Indians in the Northwest, and a hope that Canada could be easily captured, led the United States to declare war on Britain in 1812. That very week, following Perceval's assassination, the new ministry revoked the Orders in Council, but it was too late!

The so-called "War of 1812" is a radically different story as told in American, Canadian, or English accounts. The Americans dwell upon the naval exploits. They had devised frigates strong enough to whip most of the British frigates and fast enough to run away from anything stronger, so that the *Constitution* crushed the *Guerrière* and *Java*, and the *United States*, the *Macedonian*. But despite this blow to British pride, the royal navy soon blockaded most of the American ports, swept American merchantmen off the seas, and even captured two of the frigates. The Americans also emphasize the triumphs of their improvised flotillas on the lakes, and of the smashing defeat of veteran redcoats by backwoods riflemen at New Orleans (a battle fought after the peace had been signed). The Canadian versions are likely to dwell upon the repeated and unsuccessful efforts of large but unprepared American armies to conquer Canada. The British barely mention the indecisive war, treating it as a subordinate "sideshow" to more weighty events on the Continent.

Wellington and the Peninsular War

To them, the War of 1812 was completely overshadowed by the contemporary "Peninsular War." Those six years in Spain and Portugal, where the army fully offset its long lack of accomplishment, loom particularly large in British annals. This war had its origin in the Continental System. Napoleon had assumed a crushing burden when, in order to cut off British trade, he undertook to keep all the nations of the Continent from trading with Britain. He could not afford even a single breach in the wall. England's old ally Portugal in 1807 was still outside his sphere of influence. He persuaded the weak Spanish Bourbon government to allow him to send troops through Spain to bring Portugal to terms. He did so; and the British escorted the Portuguese government safely to Brazil. Spain's turn was next. Using the Portuguese expedition as an excuse, Napoleon filled the strategic spots in Spain with French troops. Then, bullying the weak king and also his worthless son into abdication, he persuaded a packed council to accept his brother as king. Holland and Westphalia, in Germany, had each accepted a Bonaparte brother as king; and a stepson had become ruler of Italy. But with Spain it was different. The Spaniards, loyal to their legitimate ruler, worthless though he was, at once revolted.

Thus Napoleon tasted the first violent reaction of that same fierce national spirit which had enabled France to conquer her neighbors but now was to roll back upon the French and to wreck their super-state. This Spanish war was of a sort which

The Duke of Wellington, c. 1827

munications. He later made the unpleasant but apt comparison of the Spanish war to an ulcer which drained away the strength of his empire. French reverses came quickly. One general with eighteen thousand men was trapped by the Spaniards and forced to surrender.

What the Spanish "nation in arms," with its fierce and irregular guerilla methods, needed was a small, well-disciplined body of troops to serve as a nucleus for its resistance. That was what England sent in the summer of 1808 and kept there until it had driven the French out. The slender, austere general of thirty-nine in command was one of Britain's foremost soldiers. Clearheaded, shrewd, and painstaking, Sir Arthur Wellesley, who would be Lord Wellington next year, and later Duke, came from a family of Anglo-Irish aristocrats of that governing caste for which Ireland blames Cromwell. He had served skillfully in India, where his older brother was viceroy. He never won the affection of his officers and men, as Marlborough or Nelson had done; but he commanded their entire confidence. Napoleon's men affectionately called him the "Little Corporal"; the coldly self-controlled Wellington was to be known as the "Iron Duke."

A month after that French general surrendered his army in Spain, Wellesley landed at Lisbon, which Britain was always glad to use as a convenient jumping-off place. British generals always felt more secure with their backs to the sea; and seldom did the royal navy let them down as it had Cornwallis at Yorktown. Before long Wellesley ran the French out of Portugal, but in Spain the French had ten men to his one. Consequently he adopted a "hit and run" policy. He found that he could disconcert the enemy by darting at their lines of communications and then hurrying back to his powerful triple series of field fortifications around Lisbon. Here, he stripped the countryside of anything the French could eat, and so rested secure after his hide-and-

puzzled and annoyed Napoleon. It was not like fighting the Austrians or Prussians, who came out on the battlefield according to the regular rules and could be put out of the fight in a battle or two. A treaty would be signed, a little more land annexed, and that would end the episode. But in the sort of war the Spaniards waged—*guerrilla*, they called it, or "little war"—everyone might fight, even priests and women. An army would vanish from sight, and there was no telling where the scattered detachments might turn up next. A whole brigade of cavalry had sometimes to accompany the courier if a message were to have a reasonable chance of getting through the Pyrenean passes to France. There was no glory in winning such a war, and there was a very good chance of losing, as Napoleon was to find out. He had to keep some 300,-000 troops in the Peninsula, but many of them were simply guarding vulnerable com-

seek. Unlike the generals of the other nations that fought Napoleon, Wellington retained the effective old "thin-line" tactics (see page 305), which enabled every soldier to use his musket against an attacking force. This, combined with his remarkably efficient supply system, gave him a decided advantage over the French, who clung to the vulnerable mass formations devised for green troops early in the Revolution, and who tried "living off the country," a difficult feat in sun-parched Spain and Portugal. So it went until 1812, when Napoleon began to withdraw troops for his Russian campaign. Wellington grew bolder: he forced, at terrific cost in men, the fortresses guarding the two mountain gateways from Portugal into Spain; and then "beat forty thousand men in forty minutes" at Salamanca. After one more winter at Lisbon, Wellington in 1813 took the offensive, and after a month's rapid campaigning smashed the French at Vitoria and drove the Bonaparte government out of Spain. It was still hit and run; but now Wellington was doing all the hitting and the enemy all the running. By autumn he was crossing into France.

Napoleon's Downfall

The effort to maintain the Continental System had helped to ruin the Corsican genius. Europe had grown more and more restless under its restrictions. When Alexander of Russia decided to withdraw from the system, Napoleon invaded Russia in 1812 with 600,000 men, drawn from his many subject regions. Russian armies were often inefficient outside their own borders, but on the defensive they had both the tremendous distances and the terrible weather on their side. Napoleon found Moscow burning, so had to start back; winter caught him; and only a pitiful remnant of the Grand Army ever returned. Meanwhile Castlereagh was carrying on Pitt's old work as a coalition-builder. This time almost all joined in the killing—Austria, Russia, Prussia, and many lesser powers. Prussia after a remarkable national revival now had an effective army, thanks to an ingenious system of universal military training. In the fall of 1813, while Wellington was crossing the Pyrenees and an American commodore on Lake Erie was writing, "We have met the enemy and they are ours," these various allied foes whipped Napoleon in the three-day "Battle of the Nations" at Leipzig. Deftly parrying the blows from several different armies, he fought a series of brilliant rearguard actions as he retired toward Paris, ever hoping that his luck would change. It did not; and in April, 1814, he abdicated his power, to become "emperor" of the little Mediterranean island of Elba, off the coast of Italy.

Europe breathed more freely; the quarter century of French threats seemed over. The stodgy Bourbon brother of the late Louis XVI was placed on the French throne. A grateful nation made Wellington a duke, and he took his place with Castlereagh as Britain's spokesman at Vienna, where the potentates of Europe gathered to redraw the map which had been so strangely altered since 1792.

But the fighting was not over. Napoleon escaped from Elba in March, 1815, and landed in France, where many of his old soldiers gathered around him. He went back to the throne as emperor, and in the following "Hundred Days" Europe wondered with dread what he might do. But, whichever way he turned, allied armies blocked the roads. Britain, as usual, was most interested in the Low Countries; so Wellington waited across the road to Brussels with a mixed force of British, Dutch, Hanoverian, and other troops. Near by was rough old Marshal Blücher, with his Prussians. Napoleon turned toward Brussels; and so to Wellington fell the brunt of the defense.

The final battle was fought at Waterloo, near Brussels, in June, 1815. The "thin red line of heroes" beat off the massed columns

Waterloo, 1815, with Scottish Highlanders beating off French cuirassiers.

of infantry which Napoleon hurled against them; when the cavalry charged, the British "formed square" and drove them back, too. Thus it went until, late in the day, a large body of troops was seen marching from the east. It might be the Prussians under Blücher; it might be a French corps; anyway these fresh forces would probably turn the tide. They wore the Prussian blue, and the day was saved. After vainly shattering the "Old Guard," the choicest of his crack regiments, against the stubborn wall, Napoleon got into his coach and drove furiously for the coast. Blücher was after him, swearing to hang him if he caught him. Finding that he could not escape to America as he had planned, he went aboard H. M. S. *Bellerophon* and threw himself on the mercy of the British. This time no chances were taken: England carried him to exile on her bleak and lonely island of St. Helena, far down in the South Atlantic, where he died six years later. The diplomats, the captains, and the kings went back to finish up the peace settlement which he had so rudely disturbed.

Chapter Twenty · 1815-1832

The Approach to Reform

In 1815 Britain had won her heart's desire, peace with victory. She was mistress of the seven seas; Napoleon was a captive in her hands; and Castlereagh, her chief representative at Vienna, was obtaining here and there throughout the world a few strategic places which would prove useful in the future of her empire.

She was on the threshold of a transitional period of seventeen years during which she was gradually to readjust her attitude in foreign and domestic affairs. Her close cooperation with the Continental powers, which had contributed much to the downfall of Napoleon, was gradually to give way to a policy of "splendid isolation," coupled with support of various nationalistic aspirations for independence. At home she was still more slowly to free herself from the deadening Tory repression.

The peace negotiations at Vienna, begun in 1814, after Napoleon's first abdication continued despite the Hundred Days. The representatives of the powers were laboring to establish a lasting peace and, at the same time, to get for their respective countries as much as possible. This Congress was carried on amid constant social revelry which nearly bankrupted the Austrian government. Some important decisions were made during dinners, balls, or hunts, and

formal sessions were rare. With the map of Europe being redrawn, bullying and bargaining went on feverishly before frontiers became fixed. Hundreds of delegates, from every European country save Turkey, were present; but the power to make the real decisions rested with a few men.

The dominating figure of the congress was Count Metternich, chancellor of Austria, who had probably taken the heaviest punishment, having five times challenged France to fight. Naturally, her persistent opposition gave Metternich a commanding position. Calculating, cynical, and conceited, a thorough realist and reactionary, he had spent years as a diplomat at various European capitals fighting the ideas of the French Revolution, and with characteristic self-glorification, he took the credit for Napoleon's downfall. His aim was to restore Europe as far as possible to its condition before the French Revolution. In particular, he was determined to have Germany and Italy so reorganized that Austrian influence would be increased and the French doctrines of democracy and nationalism stifled.

British interests were in the capable hands of Lord Castlereagh, the most influential man in English politics during the ten years preceding his death in 1822. His

The Congress of Vienna, 1814-1815, showing Metternich standing at left; Castlereagh seated, behind chair; and Talleyrand seated at table, extreme right.

reputation is beginning to emerge from the bitter opprobrium many heaped upon him (see page 392). Yet there seems to be no question about the penetrating and straightforward quality of his intellect, or that his diplomatic success owed much to his charm, graciousness, and persuasiveness in intimate company, although he was cold in public and a poor speaker. He steered his way with force and adroitness through the maze of intrigues at Vienna, whither he had even brought his own maidservants to prevent spies from serving in his household. England had been even more persistently than Austria the foe of France, and her prestige was further enhanced by Wellington's recent victories. With England's having no designs on Continental territory, Castlereagh could act in a more disinterested fashion on his declared policy "to bring back the world to peaceful habits." Although he disapproved of some of Met-

ternich's views, he was inclined to side with Austria against the disturbing ambitions of Russia and Prussia.

The same Czar Alexander who, at Tilsit, had suddenly changed from stubborn battling to enthusiastic co-operation with Napoleon played something of a dual role. On the one hand, as an idealist he injected an atmosphere of religious mysticism into his proposals for a "holy" basis for future peace. Yet his ministers were engaged in the most successful land-grabbing at the congress.

Talleyrand, though spokesman for defeated France, overshadowed the representatives of Prussia, the fourth victorious great power. Subtle, dishonest, disloyal, unscrupulous, albeit charming, Talleyrand, always the opportunist, had served France and himself since 1789 by always moving ahead to whatever side was coming into power. A noble and a bishop in pre-Revolutionary France, a moderate during the early Revolution, foreign minister under both the Directory and Napoleon, sponsor of the restoration, he now utilized the disagreements among the victors by siding with Metternich and Castlereagh against Russia and Prussia. Though his influence has perhaps been overrated, he helped to popularize the view that Napoleon, not France, was the defeated enemy and that the keynote of the congress should be "legitimacy."

This "legitimacy" meant the restoration of the legitimate prewar monarchs to their thrones. The powers adhered to this policy, however, only in those cases where it suited their interests. Bourbons were restored to three former thrones—a dull king in France, a worse one in Spain, and the worst of all in Naples. More than three hundred "legitimate" political units in Germany, however, were compressed into thirty-nine. The former independent states of Venice and Poland were not revived. In general practice the great powers took what they wanted, and the medium nations were compensated at the expense of the small ones. Russia received Finland and a generous share of territory formerly Polish; Prussia's gains were chiefly in Germany; while Austria became paramount in Italy and head of the new loose German Confederation, which arose in place of the defunct Holy Roman Empire. Belgium (the former Austrian Netherlands) was joined to Holland under the Dutch king, to form a buffer state on the northern frontier of France. For a like reason the ancient republic of Genoa was granted to the House of Savoy, in order that its kingdom of Sardinia (or Piedmont), the future nucleus of a united Italy, might better guard the French southeastern frontier.

The treatment accorded France was remarkably lenient. Castlereagh and Metternich had been willing to work with Talleyrand to prevent the aggrandizement of Russia and Prussia and to whittle down the demands made for the punishment of France. The French lost only a few valleys on the frontier. An indemnity, imposed as punishment for the Hundred Days, was light, and when it came to paying, the British made borrowing easy; in the interim, allied troops were to occupy French territory.

As for England, the rival French, Dutch, and Spanish fleets had virtually disappeared, and the royal navy ruled supreme on the seas. In the matter of overseas territory Castlereagh might have taken almost anything England desired, but instead he restored many former enemy colonies. Principally for strategic bases, he kept Malta to replace Minorca; Heligoland in the North Sea; the Cape of Good Hope; Ceylon and Mauritius in the Indian Ocean; Trinidad; and part of Guiana. He also obtained the assent of the powers to the abolition of the slave trade (see page 365). Freedom of the seas and neutral rights, however, were not discussed.

Before adjourning, the powers arranged to continue their co-operative action for twenty years. England, Austria, Prussia, and Russia late in 1815 signed at Paris a treaty forming the Quadruple Alliance "for the safety of their governments and for the general peace of Europe," and, in view of the fact that "revolutionary principles might again convulse France and endanger the peace of other countries," they guaranteed the territorial and dynastic settlements which they had made. France joined in 1818, making it a Quintuple Alliance. It was arranged to hold occasional congresses to discuss policies. Metternich set considerable store by this, and Castlereagh thought that it was more desirable than the secret methods of individual diplomatic intrigue. This alliance is often confused with the so-called Holy Alliance, a pet idea advocated by Czar Alexander for permanent international peace. He wanted all the monarchs of Europe to join in a Christian union of peace, love, and charity, and most of them humored him in the matter. To Castlereagh

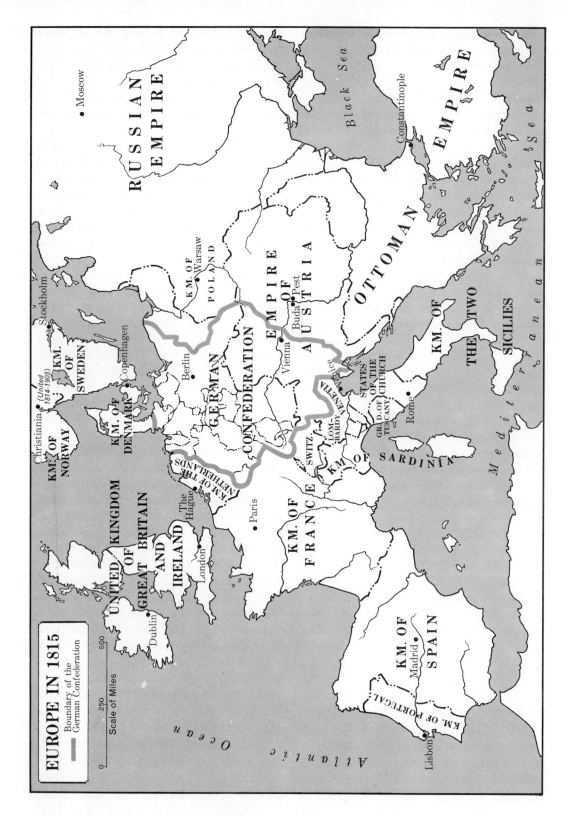

EUROPE IN 1815

Boundary of the
German Confederation

Scale of Miles

0   250   500

RUSSIAN EMPIRE

• Moscow

Black Sea

OTTOMAN EMPIRE

Constantinople •

KM. OF Warsaw POLAND

EMPIRE OF AUSTRIA

Vienna •
Buda • Pest

Stockholm •

KM. OF SWEDEN

Christiania • (United 1814–1905)

Copenhagen •

KM. OF NORWAY

KM. OF DENMARK

Berlin •

GERMAN CONFEDERATION

Venice

VENETIA

STATES OF THE CHURCH

LOM-
BARDY

SWITZ.

Rome •

KM. OF SARDINIA

KM. OF THE TWO SICILIES

Mediterranean Sea

UNITED KINGDOM OF GREAT BRITAIN AND IRELAND

The Hague •

KM. OF THE NETHERLANDS

Paris •

KM. OF FRANCE

London •

KM. OF SARDINIA

GR. D. OF TUSCANY

Dublin •

Atlantic Ocean

KM. OF SPAIN

Madrid •

KM. OF PORTUGAL

Lisbon •

it was a "piece of sublime mysticism and nonsense"; and England did not join this Holy Alliance.

The Metternich System

The machinery thus set up, as well as the way in which it was used, was so much the work of Metternich that the next thirty-odd years are known by his name. There were no wars between the great powers for nearly forty years, but constant political unrest seethed among the liberal elements on the Continent. Metternich led the anti-revolutionary, repressive movement which characterized the period until the upheaval of 1848. He repressed liberalism in the Austrian, German, and Italian regions under his control, and he sought to use the Quintuple Alliance as his tool for intervening in revolutions outside that zone. The years 1820-1821, 1830, and 1848 saw the main revolts against this "Metternich System," which survived the first two epidemics of revolution.

Castlereagh, in supporting the Quintuple Alliance, had interpreted it as simply guaranteeing the new territorial boundaries and preventing a return of Napoleon or his family. Metternich considered it an alliance to suppress liberal and revolutionary movements within states. When a liberal revolt broke out in Spain early in 1820, Metternich and Alexander were determined to crush it. Castlereagh, in a powerful state paper, made it clear that England would not participate in such interference in the domestic affairs of another nation. The Alliance, he wrote, was not "intended as an union for the government of the world, or for the superintendence of the internal affairs of other states." England, to be sure, had joined in the precautions against revolutionary France; but that was on account of her military menace, and not directed "against the democratic principles. . . . Our position, our institutions, the habits of thinking, and the prejudice of our people, render us essentially different." England, he declared, would act if actual danger menaced the territorial system of Europe; but not "upon abstract and speculative principles of precaution."

Austria, Russia, and Prussia decided to go ahead, without England; and at the Congress of Troppau, later in 1820, authorized the Austrian troops to suppress the revolts which had broken out in Naples and Piedmont. Simply an interested observer at Troppau, Castlereagh refused to participate in the policy of intervention; but took care not to break openly with his old allies. Intervention in Spain remained unsettled (see page 393).

Castlereagh also improved relations between England and the new United States. The Treaty of Ghent, concluded during the last days of 1814, simply ended the indecisive War of 1812, and did not even mention the questions of neutral rights and impressment of seamen which had caused the Americans to fight. By the Rush-Bagot agreement, in 1817, each nation agreed to maintain not more than one warship on the Great Lakes, where an expensive naval rivalry was continuing after the war. This has been called one of the most successful disarmament agreements in history. The long frontier between the United States and Canada was retraced. Each side continued to fortify strategic points along this border for a half century; but they were never put to the test, despite serious mutterings of war in the forties over the Maine-New Brunswick boundary in the East and the Oregon territory in the West. Each country was the other's best customer, and had the common heritage of Anglo-Saxon backgrounds.

Altogether, Britain's external position seemed enviable. She had fought the good fight with gold, with redcoats, and particularly with ships of the line. She was undisputed mistress of the seas, and her early start with the Industrial Revolution gave her pretty much a monopoly of the world market for manufactures. The new wealth was breeding capital, too; and London, rather than Amsterdam, now became the foremost financial center to which borrowers turned.

Domestic Difficulties

Yet almost instantly the fruits of victory tasted sour. The stress and strain of protracted war had taken a heavy toll from Englishmen. With their trade in confusion, their treasury empty, their taxes high, and their national debt colossal, peace found their morale shattered. The government, which had been spending millions of pounds a year in providing for its own fighting men and in subsidizing Continental allies, now bought but little, and impoverished Europe proved an equally poor customer. England was consequently overstocked with goods, which, thrown upon the market, drove prices down so rapidly that many firms failed. The resulting widespread unemployment of miner, artisan, and agricultural laborer was made worse by the competition of some 300,000 disbanded veterans for the fewer jobs. Furthermore, over field and factory and countinghouse hung the shadow of the national debt, by that time some £850,000,000.

Those economic aspects were serious enough, but in addition a new spiritual uneasiness was abroad in the land. The grit and courage which had buoyed up the people in the face of many a Napoleonic triumph seemed exhausted. The panic aroused by the French Revolution paralyzed those more generous impulses toward social and political reform which had made the late eighteenth century bright with hope (see page 367). England in 1815 was more "Old England" than she had been just before the French Revolution. Patriotic emotion sanctified old laws, old customs, the old Church, and particularly the old constitution. The suggestion that anything might be unjust or irrational in the established order angered and at the same time frightened the country gentlemen, whose

rule had brought the country through more than twenty years of desperate crises. The postwar period was full of confusion, with the extremists overshadowing the moderates. As a result, the more moderate Whigs were out of the picture. Lord Liverpool's Tory ministry was still enjoying an overwhelming majority in the Commons, while repression obsessed the Tory mind (see page 392). The Tory Parliament did not hesitate to repeal the Habeas Corpus Act, to bring suit for criminal libel against pamphleteers, to place a heavy stamp tax on newspapers, and to suppress public meetings.

Of the radicals, some blamed the new machinery for putting men out of work and, here and there, urged its destruction (see page 341). Others considered that the true remedy lay in national instead of private ownership of land. Francis Place, London tailor, busied himself with the organization of trade unions, and quietly but effectively proved himself a good political manipulator. "Orator" Hunt preached everywhere that hope for England lay in universal suffrage and in annual Parliaments. The best-known of these radicals were Robert Owen, wealthy cotton manufacturer, who urged the protection of factory workers by law, and William Cobbett, the caustic editor of a popular political weekly, who advocated the repudiation of the national debt and the devaluation of the currency.

Owen combined shrewd business ability with unselfish idealism. Born of poor Welsh parents, he made a fortune in the early days of the Industrial Revolution; but he became so shocked by the appalling conditions of the factory system that he later impoverished himself in trying to remedy them. Through his marriage he became a large shareholder and, later, manager of the New Lanark Mills in Scotland. There some five hundred children, largely five- and six-year-old "poor house" children, worked from six in the morning to seven at

The model industrial community at New Lanark, near Glasgow, developed by Robert Owen between 1800 and 1828 as an experiment in "Utopian" socialism.

night; while among the fifteen hundred adult employees conditions were also bad. Attempting much in advance of his time, Owen made this into the first "model" factory. He established the first schools for factory children in Britain, shortened the hours, raised wages, improved housing, started a co-operative store. He was also an advocate of the inadequate First Factory Act, of 1802 (see page 408), and a pioneer in the trade-union movement (see page 397), presiding at the first congress. He also tried to reform the whole basis of society itself. Probably it was in connection with his theories that the term "socialism" was first used; but his was not the later socialism, which was opposed to the private ownership and operation of industries. Known as a Utopian socialist, after the book *Utopia*, by Sir Thomas More (see pages 155 ff.) he believed that individuals acting upon their own initiative, could create model co-operative enterprises. Like the other highly idealistic Utopians, of whom there were many in France, he hoped to achieve such an ideal community that the rest of the world would copy it, and competition would give place to co-operation. His most ambitious attempt, which was in the United States, was a dismal failure and so, too, were his schemes in England.

More influential among his contemporaries was Cobbett, a former plowboy and ex-sergeant-major in the army, who began his public career as a violent Tory pamphleteer. The government subsidized him for his writings, until he began to attack it. Sentenced to prison, and his papers confiscated, Cobbett sought refuge in the United States. Returning to England, he revived his weekly *Register*, which with its cheap price and clear, incisive style soon had a tremendous circulation. He plunged into the limelight as "an all-round reformer," the vigor of his words frequently making him appear more radical than he was. Interested primarily in the welfare of the peasantry, he rode back and forth through rural England making incendiary attacks on the wealthy; by his speeches and his paper he caused less intelligent men to take the law into their own hands.

All the radicals, even Place and Cobbett, were agreed on the need for Parliamentary reform as a first step. The old Parliamentary reform movement which was sponsored by Pitt before the French Revolution had never died (see page 364). Taking on new vigor with the return of peace, what originally had been a cautious move to readjust inequalities in elections grew rapidly into a demand for universal suffrage and annual elections for Parliament.

In the midst of this agitation the Tories themselves offered reforms, of a kind. The duty on imported grain (Corn Laws) (see page 396) was raised to prohibitive heights, to ensure landlords against heavy loss in farm rentals during the depression. The income tax was repealed, to please the well-to-do middle class. The sum of £1,000,000 was voted for the erection of new buildings for the Church of England in the industrial north, where the towns had outgrown the rural parishes.

Altogether, these panaceas aided the Tories little. Although they still controlled the government, they were faced with numerous riots. In 1816 a huge meeting at Spa Fields, on the outskirts of London, was dispersed by force, but not until it had passed a resolution that there were "four million of people on the point of starvation, four million with a bare subsistence, four million in straitened circumstances, and a half million in dazzling luxury." From the north in the following year came the march of the "blanketeers," unemployed workmen tramping to London; and in 1819 a strike of cotton-spinners at Manchester made fertile soil for radical propaganda. A large

demonstration for universal suffrage was held there in St. Peter's Fields. The local magistrates lost their heads. An attempt to arrest the ubiquitous "Orator" Hunt resulted in the so-called "Peterloo Massacre." Cavalry were launched into the milling throng, with the result that eleven persons were killed and several hundred wounded. This "military victory" was dubbed "Peterloo," in derisive comparison with Waterloo.

It resulted in the famous "Six Acts," by which the Tory government effectively if temporarily gagged adverse public agitation. These acts speeded the trial of offenders, prohibited military drilling without authorization, empowered justices of the peace to search dwellings, authorized the seizure of printed libels, banned public meetings, and subjected all political publications to a stamp tax.

Meanwhile the pathetic figure of George III, aged, blind, and insane, wandered aimlessly through the corridors of Windsor, until his death in 1820. His eldest son, "a debauchee, a gambler, a disobedient son, and a cruel, treacherous friend," had already as Prince Regent forfeited the nation's respect. His accession as George IV (1820-1830) changed neither his character nor his behavior. He brought divorce proceedings against Queen Caroline, only to make her a heroine with the masses. She was not above suspicion, but the public rightly sensed that she was more sinned against than sinning. Popular discontent took the form of insults to the sovereign. Castlereagh, overworked by his combined burden of managing Parliament and foreign affairs, cut his throat with a penknife in 1822—and crowds cheered the news (see page 385). His excellent record in diplomacy counted for little in the popular mind, which blamed him for the domestic depression.

Affairs began to take a turn for the better. A reorganization of the cabinet, still Liverpool's, brought forward more liberal and enlightened Tory leaders, particularly

George Canning, William Huskisson, and Sir Robert Peel. The government took on a new lease of life, blazing a new trail in foreign policy and inaugurating measure after measure of reform.

Canning and Nationalism

At the Foreign Office, Canning, during the remaining five years of his life, won a secure place among England's foremost statesmen. Throughout a tortuous career of nearly thirty years, he had never been a regular party man, but everyone recognized the political ability and brilliance of this self-made man. Unlike Castlereagh, he was a magnetic orator and won widespread popular support for his foreign policy. These two had once fought a duel, but Canning continued many of his predecessor's policies and pushed them even further along a distinctively British course. His particular achievements were a complete separation from the Metternich system and the support of nationalistic efforts for independence.

He was barely in office when he struck a telling blow at the congress system. The Italian revolts of 1820 had already been stamped out by Austria, but the liberal Spanish government, set up by revolt in the same year, was still in operation, and the powers were assembling at Verona to discuss its suppression. Canning had no sympathy with the "European police system" which Austria, Russia, and Prussia were trying to enforce. On his instructions, Wellington announced that England would not take part in measures against Spain, and then left the congress. The congress system never recovered from this abrupt withdrawal. Two further attempts to summon congresses failed, largely because Britain flatly refused to participate. France alone intervened in 1823 to crush the Spanish revolutionary government.

Britain had good reason to be keenly interested in the revolts in Spanish America, also. Ever since the days of the Sea Dogs she had sought an entrance into that jealously guarded preserve where the Spaniards, intent on silver and gold, were allowing rich normal commercial opportunities to go to waste. The Asiento at Utrecht had been an entering wedge into this valuable market, and the "War of Jenkins's Ear" had been an effort to drive it farther (see pages 290, 306). By 1812, during Spain's internal troubles with Napoleon, revolts began to break out in her American colonies; during the next dozen years, these spread successfully except in Cuba and Puerto Rico. England had aided and abetted these uprisings: "patriot" expeditions had been openly fitted out in British ports, with British ships, soldiers, and seamen all aiding the revolutionary movement. "We are fighting the battles of British commerce," wrote one South American merchant, and cargoes of Lancashire cottons and Birmingham hardware found their way into ports newly opened by the revolutionaries. The revolt of 1820 at home further weakened Spain's hold on her colonies; the rebel armies made rapid headway, and republics were set up all the way from Mexico southward.

Canning had a difficult problem there to protect the new trade. He had to keep France and the other European powers from restoring Spanish rule, while at the same time he had to prevent the United States from stealing all the credit for supporting the new republics. As a republic, she was more free than Britain to extend diplomatic recognition, but Britain alone had a navy strong enough to keep the European powers from restoring Spanish rule by force.

Canning played his cards well and accomplished both ends. In 1823 he proposed to the United States minister that their two nations make a joint declaration opposing European intervention; but an agreement upon terms could not be reached. Thereupon, John Quincy Adams, the American Secretary of State, drew up a powerful single-handed declaration which was included in President Monroe's annual message to Congress late that year. This "Monroe Doctrine" stated that "the American continents, by the free and independent condition which they have assumed and maintain, are henceforth not to be considered as future subjects for colonization by any European powers" and that any European effort to interfere with the new republics would be regarded as "the manifestation of an unfriendly disposition towards the United States." This was more than Canning had wanted, and caused him to fear the formation of an American league of republics. He quickly stole much of the Yankee thunder by telling the world that he already had sent an ultimatum to France, which had overrun Spain, that Britain would fight any attempt of France to recover Spain's colonies. The Spanish-Americans were given to understand that they owed their liberty more to this threat, backed as it was by the royal navy, than to the bold words from Washington. When the Spanish king asked for a congress to discuss the recovery of the colonies, Canning flatly refused to participate. In 1824, while the revolutionists were crushing Spain's last army in America, Britain at last accorded full diplomatic recognition to several of the new states. This showed how far Canning had cut loose from England's former allies. He told the House of Commons, "I called the New World into existence to redress the balance of the Old." Brazil broke away from Portugal at this time, under the son of the Portuguese king, and Canning soon gave recognition. He became a hero to the Latin Americans, and Britain received the lion's share of their trade.

The revolt of the Greeks finally drew Canning into active participation in the Near East, which was to loom large in British foreign policy for a full half century. Between about 1250 and 1550 a succession of powerful Turkish Sultans had spread their conquests along the eastern and southern shores of the Mediterranean and up into the Danube valley. The Eastern Question resulted from the gradual decay of this huge Ottoman Empire, which fell into four main parts. Only Asia Minor, where the Ottoman dominion began, had a considerable Turkish population. To the south and east lay a vast area peopled largely by Arabs—like the Turks, Moslems, but differing in race and background. Egypt and the piratical Barbary States of North Africa had a mongrel population under loose, nominal control. Most important in the eyes of nineteenth-century Europe, were the predominantly Slavic Balkan Christians—the semi-independent Rumanians, the Greeks, the Serbs and Montenegrins, and the Bulgarians, closest to Constantinople. In the course of the century these various peoples were to break loose from their Turkish masters.

This Balkan nationalism in the disintegrating Ottoman Empire became closely entangled with European ambitions, causing the peninsula to be known as the "tinderbox" of Europe. Russia, whose eyes had long been on Constantinople, with its strategic position on the Straits at the entrance to the Black Sea, abetting these revolts, claimed to be the natural protector of the Balkan Christians, most of whom, like her own people, were Slavic in race and Greek Orthodox in religion. She thus hoped to push Turkey out of Europe. Austria, likewise with Balkan ambitions, opposed the revolts, which if successful might cause her own subject Slavic peoples to rebel. France, too, and Germany, after her unification in 1871, mixed in Balkan affairs; but their interests were less obvious than Britain's. Her policy was a purely negative one. She wanted no Turkish territory; but she was vitally concerned with preventing Russia from getting too close to Constantinople, because that might menace British trade in the eastern Mediterranean and especially communications with India. Instead of the powerful Russia, which she was to fear throughout the century, Britain consequently preferred a weak Turkey, the "Sick Man of Europe," at the Straits, even one cruel to her subject Christians. Already for more than a century, Russian armies in war after war had been encroaching on Turkish territory around the Black Sea. In 1791 the younger Pitt had wanted to interfere, but Parliament would not empower him to do so. As the Turks grew weaker, their rule became more brutal, and corrupt. Russian agents were constantly attempting to stir up revolts.

Europe was too busy with Napoleon to bother with the first, the Serbian uprising; but in the Greek revolt in 1821, the powers, hoping to prevent international complications, sought to localize the conflict. Meanwhile Greeks and Turks slaughtered one another with the atrocious savagery of most Balkan wars. Then, in 1825, the Sultan called in the efficient army of Egypt, which threatened to exterminate the Greeks. The powers no longer remained indifferent. Russia seemed ready to intervene on behalf of the Greeks, however opposed Czar Alexander might be to revolutions elsewhere. That would bring Russian power unpleasantly close to the Mediterranean—the last thing Canning wanted. At the same time, he wanted particularly to help the Greeks. If Russia wanted to intervene, therefore, England would too. Numerous Englishmen who admired ancient Greece went out to fight for the freedom of the modern Greeks. Byron died at Missolonghi, and Admiral Cochrane, with his Chilean job finished, went over to command the Greek navy. British bankers made heavy loans to the Greeks, charging stiffly for their services. But Canning realized that still more was necessary to prevent the Russians from acting alone. England, Russia, and France agreed at London in the summer of 1827 just before his death to impose an armistice upon the Turks and Greeks, by peaceful means if possible. A combined fleet of the three, under a British admiral, blockaded the Egyptian navy. That fall there was an "accidental" encounter in Navarino Bay; when the smoke cleared away, the Sultan's ships were no longer afloat. That virtually ensured Greek independence. After protracted delays, during which Russia fought Turkey alone after all, Greece was declared independent. A German prince was selected as her king, and a British frigate bore him to his new realm.

Huskisson and Free Trade

In co-operation with the Board of Trade and the Exchequer, Canning also used diplomacy to push Britain toward free trade. William Huskisson, president of the Board of Trade, was keen in his grasp of economic principles, broad and far-seeing in his vision, and tireless in pushing his new ideas in the face of business skepticism. The French wars had interrupted this movement initiated by Adam Smith's theories and first put into practice by the younger Pitt (see page 364). Huskisson, with the co-operation of Robinson, Chancellor of the Exchequer, had to begin anew. The principal reforms were modification of the Navigation Acts, readjustment of colonial regulations, abolition or reduction of tariff duties, and diplomatic pressure through reciprocity or reprisals.

Conditions had undergone great changes since the Navigation Acts and old tariff codes had been enacted. Holland was no longer a rival to be feared; the United States, on the other hand, now outside the colonial system, threatened lively maritime competition. Latin America was being opened to British commerce. Britain had made such strides with the Industrial Revolution that, except perhaps in grain, she needed little tariff protection against outsiders, while reduced tariffs would mean a cheaper supply of raw materials. Financially, London was fast becoming the money market of the world. The Rothschilds, Barings, and other great banking houses lent some £100,000,000 overseas during the first quarter of the century. The interest rates were high, but the risks were considerable —fully a quarter of that vast amount was defaulted. Since Britain was the creditor country, the tariff walls needed to be low enough to admit wares from the debtor foreign nations, as these borrowers would naturally find difficulty, except through building up a surplus by selling goods to England, in paying back interest and capital. Except for the landowners, who wanted protection for their grain, Britain was ready to apply Adam Smith's theories.

The old Navigation Acts had required that all goods from America, Africa, and Asia be brought in British bottoms. England still tried to keep those profitable "long hauls" for her own shipping, but had to adjust conditions to the new American republics. The harsh limitations on imports from Holland also were relaxed. Adjustments were made in the old prohibition against foreigners trading with British colonies; for the British West Indies had suffered from the restriction of their supply of food and lumber from the United States. Many of the former stipulations about "English ships with English crews," however, were to remain on the statute books until the final abolition of the Navigation Acts in 1849.

In liberalizing the colonial restrictions, Huskisson threw open colonial ports to foreign trade, though keeping in Britain's hands the shipping with her own colonies. He also introduced a system of "colonial preference" whereby British goods would enter colonial ports at a somewhat lower duty than foreign goods, while, conversely, colonial goods would enjoy a tariff preference in British markets. That principle was not continued by his successors, although strong efforts were made to revive it later in the century.

In the overhauling of the customs regulations, the Chancellor of the Exchequer had to be brought in; for customs duties formed no small part of the national revenue. More than a thousand acts were scrapped and the whole scale of duties compressed into a compact system. Export duties were completely eliminated, while many import duties were abolished and others reduced. To render less profitable the work of the smugglers of Romney Marsh, the duties on articles of large value in small bulk, wine, brandy, and silks, were reduced with the hope that greater quantities of such goods would enter legally through the customs. Finally, the resources of Canning's diplomacy were used to secure advantages from other countries in the matter of tariffs, port duties, and the like, with reciprocity for the nations which would co-operate and reprisals for those which would not.

In one field, however, rigid protection stood firmly entrenched. Industry and commerce, because of their superior advantages, could well afford to take chances in the removal of restrictions. Agriculture, however, was exposed to the competition of cheap grain and flour from the Baltic and America. The landowners, still dominating Parliament, were protected by the Corn Laws. These 1815 laws had flatly forbidden the importation of foreign "corn" (which included wheat) until prices in England should have reached a certain fairly high price. Gradually they were made less rigid, and a sliding scale of duties was introduced; but the principle and practice remained until the middle of the century. Huskisson was killed by a locomotive at the opening of the Liverpool and Manchester Railway; but the drive for free trade continued until, by 1860, only twenty-six tariff duties out of more than twelve hundred remained (see pages 418 ff.). This had been the beginning of Britain's conversion from "a country of high protection and fierce economic nationalism into one that was free from all commercial regulations and believed in open competition for traders of all nations."[1]

[1] A. P. Newton. *A Hundred Years of the British Empire* (1940), p. 141.

A further step toward the abolition of old restrictions was the repeal of the harsh Combination Acts (see page 342) which had been passed during the reaction against the French Revolution. In theory they had been directed against combinations of employers as well as of employees. In practice, however, they bore heavily on the working class alone, making it "illegal for any body of workmen to meet, even peacefully, for the purpose of discussing wages." These laws had proved unenforceable as well as unjust. Their repeal in 1824 came through the skillful manipulation of Francis Place, who secured a favorable member of Commons to call for a committee and act as its chairman, and then quietly brought before it witnesses to give overwhelming evidence against the laws. Immediately many violent strikes broke out. Consequently within a year a new law was passed to clip the wings of the trade unions, now springing up everywhere. Not for several decades were they to obtain full legal recognition, but their rapid progress during the century was to make them a power in the nation.

Huskisson also brought about the repeal of another often violated statute, which prohibited the emigration of artisans. British mechanics had been enticed to Prussia, and others had slipped away to aid in the beginning of the cotton industry in the United States. Since it was impossible to prevent such men from carrying the plans of the new machinery in their heads, it ultimately became expedient to repeal another statute against the exportation of machinery.

One cannot tell to what extent the economic advance during the next few years was occasioned by this reform movement or by a change in the economic cycle. Doubtless trade would have improved even without new laws. From both North and South America, as well as from the Continent, came an increased demand for British goods and British capital. Prices began to rise; new mines were opened; new factories were established; and those who held office received the credit.

Another liberal Tory, Sir Robert Peel, the son of the wealthy calico manufacturer of the same name (see page 408), was a paragon of virtue and ability. His ambitious father had sent him to Harrow and to Oxford, where he had done well in his studies. Thereupon, a seat was purchased for him in the House of Commons, where he won fame in debate and also the friendship of the younger Pitt. Before Waterloo he served as Chief Secretary for Ireland, and in 1822 he became Home Secretary in Liverpool's cabinet. Peel, by antecedents and by nature, was first of all a man of business and loved order and efficiency, as well as power and prestige. His rise from the middle class possibly accounts for his being somewhat aloof and self-conscious.

Within certain limits a reformer, he improved the prison system, the method of deporting prisoners, and the way in which judges were paid. He also ended the practice of employing spies among workingmen; stopped the persecution of radical newspapers; and in London established the first civilian force of trained police, known as "Peelers" or "Bobbies." Above all, he gave the criminal code a long-needed overhauling. In the early nineteenth century the punishment was death for over two hundred offenses, including picking a pocket, stealing a fish or five shillings from a shop, robbing a rabbit warren, or cutting down a tree. This state of affairs tended in some cases to cause oversevere punishment, and in others to discourage juries from bringing in a verdict of guilty. For a decade before Peel became Home Secretary, law reformers tried time after time to revise this barbaric code. Sir Samuel Romilly devoted his life to the cause with small success; and although his successor in this work, Sir James Mackintosh, secured a great deal of publicity, not much was done. Building upon the labor of these early reformers,

Peel succeeded in having the death penalty removed from a hundred offenses.

Catholic Emancipation

The Tories approached religious reform in gingerly fashion. The Toleration Act of 1689 had permitted most nonconforming Protestants to worship as they pleased; but the political disabilities of the Test and Corporation Acts still remained, along with certain restrictive laws particularly directed against the Catholics (see page 276). By the strict letter of the law both Nonconformists and Catholics were thus debarred from all civil and military positions under the crown, from municipal corporations, and from the universities.

Opposition to the relaxation of these laws on behalf of the Nonconformists was not particularly strong, as they had tended to lapse in practice, but to some, it went against the grain for Nonconformists let alone Catholics to be on a basis of equality with members of the Church of England. "Occasional conformity" (see page 275) had been permitted during most of the intervening years, and it was customary to pass an annual bill of indemnity pardoning them for holding office illegally. Many people feared, however, that an official lowering of the bars in favor of the Nonconformists would encourage agitation for the repeal of further restrictions which applied to Catholics alone. Consequently, the repeal of the Test and Corporation Acts was delayed until 1828. Then, as many had dreaded, emancipation for Catholics followed during the next year.

The Elizabethan legislation and the penal code against the Catholics in both England and Ireland still made it illegal to hear Mass, to make Catholic converts, to conduct Catholic schools, or to engage Catholic tutors. The worst of these legal discriminations had been removed; and most of the others had long been a dead letter in England. Only recently, Catholics had won the right to vote—but only for Protestant candidates. Nevertheless, certain grave restrictions remained. In particular, they could not be elected to the House of Commons; they could not serve upon grand juries, in whose hands lay much of the local government of Ireland; and if peers, they could not take their seats in the House of Lords.

Vigorous protests against this state of affairs came not only from Ireland but from Great Britain, where there were not more than a hundred thousand Catholics. These were mainly well-to-do, and with the death, in 1807, of the last male heir of the direct Stuart line the last political reason had disappeared for depriving them of civil rights. Most Irish Catholics, on the other hand, were poor peasants. During the French Revolution and Napoleonic days many had taken up arms against the king (see page 375). Although the younger Pitt had resigned when George III refused to allow the Irish Catholics a share in the government in 1801, at the time of the Act of Union, most Englishmen continued to feel that it was better to play safe and to watch all Catholics. Some years later Catholics were almost given the right to hold office; the measure was defeated over a minor matter.

Thereupon appeared a new leader, Daniel O'Connell, a Dublin barrister, who disliked England and all things English, and had been connected with revolutionary Irish societies. He firmly believed that Ireland should be independent, or, at least, self-governing. Realizing that it would be impossible at this time to secure repeal of Pitt's Act of Union, he felt that Catholic emancipation might be a step in that direction. Furthermore, O'Connell, politically ambitious and a magnetic speaker, was determined to gain admission to the Commons, law or no law. He organized in Ireland the Catholic Association and drew into its membership huge numbers of his countrymen. Parish priests joined, and preached its cause before the altar. Its members marched and countermarched throughout Ireland, contested Parliamentary elections, and elected O'Connell despite the law which would prevent him from taking his seat.

The English authorities, fearful of civil war, did not dare to advocate openly a change in the law, since George IV threatened to veto any such measure. On the other hand, to exclude O'Connell, duly elected by his constituents, was dangerous. Ireland seethed with economic discontent and was fully capable of starting serious trouble for the landlords.

Canning had been favorably inclined toward emancipation, but by 1828 he was dead. Lord Liverpool, after fifteen years as prime minister, had retired in the spring of 1827, and Canning, succeeding him, had died four months later. Then followed Lord Goderich (Robinson), who had recently served well as Chancellor of the Exchequer, but who as prime minister proved an ineffectual figurehead and lasted only five months. Early in 1828 the Duke of Wellington next agreed to head the government. Thus there were four prime ministers, all Tories, within ten months! Although Wellington had been very vehement in opposition to emancipation, he now decided upon a strategic retreat. His ministry was already seriously weakened by the withdrawal of Canning's friends, who resented his sharp military manner. He realized, too, that the landlord class would not stomach rick-burning and cattle-maiming. Consequently Wellington approached George IV. The king, fortified by much brandy, invoked the memory of his sainted father and dismissed his ministers. He soon changed his mind, however; for he preferred Wellington and Peel to Whigs and radicals, even at the price of surrender. Consequently, by 1829 the Catholics became eligible for most offices under the crown, with a very few exceptions such as the Lord Chancellorship.

Emancipation, however, had a joker within it. As Catholics won the right to elect men of their own religion to Parliament, many of them lost the right to vote at all. The forty-shilling freeholders—small landholders, of whom there were some 190,000—were disenfranchised in Ireland. Wellington had insisted on this minimum safeguard. This was the last reform of the liberal Tories, who now, for the most part, were to line up with the rest of their party in opposition to constitutional reform, which almost immediately was to become the principal question of the hour.

The Unreformed Parliament

The British constitution was extraordinarily complex and intricate in regard to Parliamentary government. The political center of gravity rested in the House of Commons, as a result of the constitutional struggles of the seventeenth and eighteenth centuries (see pages 215, 294). The Industrial Revolution, with the rapid growth of new towns had intensified the inequalities in borough representation, which had been flagrant enough in the time of Walpole (see page 296). Only two new boroughs had been created since 1625, when great industrial centers like Leeds, Birmingham, and Manchester were only tiny hamlets. In 1830 these great new cities had no representation in Parliament except through the two members elected by the shire, or county, as a whole. On the other hand, many small towns which had decayed, or actually disappeared, were still represented in the Commons by two members each. Because of the ease with which the votes of "pocket" and "rotten" boroughs, with their bewildering lack of franchise uniformity, could be manipulated, the control of the House of Commons remained in the hands of a few. It has been estimated that an actual majority in the Commons could be elected by fewer than fifteen hundred votes. This system had drawn the fire of reformers in the late eighteenth century and even more after Waterloo. It was not completely undemocratic; for some "pot-walloper" boroughs allowed every householder who was not a pauper to vote. But it was archaic and illogical, as well as grossly unfair to the progressive industrial areas of the Midlands and the north.

For the first five years after Waterloo no single question was discussed more vigorously in Britain. Then, curiously enough, nearly ten years elapsed before public opinion again actively concerned itself with Parliamentary reform. Between 1820 and 1830 one particularly notorious "rotten" borough, Grampound, was disfranchised; but Lord John Russell, second son of the Duke of Bedford, tried in vain to increase the membership of the House of Commons by one hundred members, giving sixty to the counties and forty to the unrepresented cities. But until 1830, Parliament gave little heed, and the public apparently lost interest in Parliamentary reform.

Among the contributing factors in this was the noticeable increase of interest in religion, both within the Church of England and outside. This surging tide of pious sentiment was to emphasize otherworldliness, saintly living, and patient endurance. But democracy did not concern its many representatives in Parliament, many of whom were wealthy, particularly the Quakers. The "Saints" were reformers of a kind, with slavery their particular bête noire. They also urged educational and prison reform. Thus most of the Nonconformists resembled the Church of England evangelicals in taking little if any interest in politics.

Meanwhile the country gentry were wellnigh unanimous in fighting against Parliamentary reform; and they knew how to fight for the power which they had wielded for centuries. Unlike the French nobility, they were the mainstay of English society as the backbone of the House of Commons, and as the administrators of the law in their local communities (see page 169). Furthermore, their ranks were not shut against the more wealthy of the middle class. Many a poor boy, having made a fortune in India,

in industry or in commerce, bought landed property, intermarried with some socially eligible family, and in his own person or in that of his descendants became one of the favored few. The elasticity of the British aristocracy enabled it to survive: it bent, but it did not break. It had, however, no intention of bending unless self-preservation so dictated.

Although there was a two-party system in the House of Commons, both parties drew their strength from the same aristocratic class. The Greys, Russells, and Hollands, famous Whig families and wealthy landowners, were as closely identified with the aristocratic tradition as the Tory families. In fact, party lines between 1820 and 1830 almost melted away, and between the more liberal of the Whigs and the liberal Tories (often called Canningites) there was little to distinguish. The Whigs, although willing to criticize the laws sponsored by the Tories, were not yet willing to adopt Parliamentary reform.

Writings of the Romantic School

More significant than the evangelical movement or the party seesaws was the reaction of the public mind to the long struggle with Napoleon. This is indicated in English letters of the time which were conservative in trend and dominated by the brilliant and versatile Romantic school. After twenty years of warfare, discouraged humanity sought relief in books which appealed to the imagination rather than to the critical faculties.

Sir Walter Scott, Britain's leading literary figure, afforded such relief. His novels deal with Britain's past—with old ways, old customs, old virtues. "They set forth a Tory view of life, not a Tory program. . . . Whether the scene be laid in the court of Prince Charlie, or in the England of Richard Coeur de Lion, or in the struggles of the Crusaders, . . . the same attempt is made to show man at his best when most conforming to the usages and institutions of society.[2] Scott, with his glowing imagination and warm heart, was in no wise a dispassionate critic of the contemporary scene; he was a country gentleman, happy in his environment, believing with all his heart in a society of fixed classes.

Also characteristic of the Romantic school was the love of nature. No man personified this more completely than the poet laureate William Wordsworth. Cities to him were obnoxious, and virtue dwelt in the untrodden ways of the countryside, the abode of beauty, truth, and wisdom. Man, according to him, should seek his place in the universe by mystic communion with Nature. He had little confidence in man's capacity to raise himself by his own efforts. In consequence Wordsworth, although a radical in his youth, grew conservative with the years. Liberty, Equality, and Fraternity were to him false gods, partly because they were French gods, for his patriotic reaction against Napoleon had been severe.

Coleridge and Southey, England's two other "Lake poets" (a term applied to poets who lived in the Lake country of northwestern England), were as disillusioned with revolutionary France as was Wordsworth. Coleridge became more and more a mystic, preoccupied with religion and the glorification of the national Church. Southey was radical in economic ideas and conservative in political theory. Political democracy was anathema to him and as a contributor to the *Quarterly Review* he fought all proposals for Parliamentary reform.

The influence of these four more than offset that of the more rebellious Lord Byron and Percy Bysshe Shelley. In many ways Byron was not a radical; he was not, for instance, particularly interested in democracy. He exalted liberty, but it was of freedom in the national sense that he sang —the freedom of Greece or of Italy from alien tyrannies. He attacked the morals, do-

mesticities, and kings of Georgian England; but he was not the sort to lead a mob, nor did he offer any constructive theories for a new society. Byron's influence was more Continental than British. His fellow countrymen read his poems; but they disapproved of the author, and were in no way inclined to accept him as a radical prophet.

Shelley, however, was a true revolutionary, imbued with a flaming idealism which only an untimely death could quench. There is a revolutionary bite and tang to all his political poetry. But for Shelley, his day was not yet. The weather vane of British literature during the first third of the century continued to point rather steadily in the conservative direction. Religion, politics, literature—all three buttressed the old order.

Despite these retarding elements there was at work one unceasing influence which made change inevitable: the economic revolutions in industry and communication. Sooner or later the constant demands of the middle class—industrial entrepreneurs, bankers, manufacturers, merchants, who were growing wealthier and more numerous—for a redistribution of Parliamentary seats must be answered.

The Coming of the Railway

The Communication Revolution was now entering on a new stage. No matter how good the turnpikes, or efficient the canals, the full force of the new power machinery could not be realized until some cheaper method of transportation was available. George Stephenson and his locomotive made a national market possible, and ensured the ultimate rise of the middle class.

The railway came in dramatic fashion. The novelty lay not in the use of rails but in the new motive power. For some time rails had been used to reduce the friction of wheels in hauling coal, but the power had been provided by horses and mules. Occasionally gravity was used, and some-

[2] Crane Brinton, *Political Ideas of English Romanticists* (1926), p. 109. By permission of the Clarendon Press.

times empty coal wagons were hauled up steep grades by means of inclined planes. That locomotives could haul long trains for any considerable distance was, before 1825, purely a matter of speculation. A Cornishman, Trevithick, to be sure, had invented what to all practical purposes was a steam automobile, but his engine had little power and could haul nothing. He also invented a locomotive which performed useful service in the coal districts, pulling coal wagons upon rails. But all these inventions had but slight practical value.

George Stephenson, son of a poverty-stricken miner, began earning his own living at the age of eight and taught himself to read when he was eighteen. By occupation he was a plugman, watching the old-fashioned pumping engine at work in order to plug the suction holes in its pipes when the pit was drained. Adept at repairing stationary engines, he studied Trevithick's invention and discovered that flanges on the wheels of both cars and engine would do away with the clumsy cogwheel method. Then came the Stockton and Darlington railway, begun by enterprising Quakers to carry coal over the forty miles from the mines at Stockton to the sea at Darlington, near Newcastle. The question of motive power was left undecided between horse-cars, stationary engines drawing cars by cables, or a "traveling engine." Stephenson was invited to make the latter, and the history of the locomotive dates from its first successful run in 1825. It was a crude affair, but it worked. "A man on horseback rode in front of the train to drive off cows and careless farmers. . . . At times the horseman had to break into a gallop so swift was the speed of the train." The traveling engine hauled passengers as well as freight, and it halved the price of coal at Darlington.

Four years later an improved Stephenson locomotive demonstrated more fully to the public the possibilities of the modern railway. The cotton manufacturers of Man-chester and the cotton importers of Liverpool saw that a railway for the thirty miles between their two cities would relieve the congestion on the canal which joined them, and would break the monopoly of the canal owners. Opposition to this was loud and powerful. The canal companies feared the loss of their generous dividends, and there was an immense amount of capital invested in stage lines, in turnpike companies, in taverns. Engineers testified in Parliament that the cars would fly off the tracks upon rounding curves. It was stated that "cows would not graze nor hens lay if locomotives were to roar past; . . . that farm houses near the line would be burned up . . . ; and that boilers would burst and blow passengers to atoms." But for Huskisson's influence and the expenditure of many thousands of pounds, permission for any sort of railway would have been refused. The railway was completed before the directors decided its motive power. Various proposals were made: that the cars might be propelled by hoisting sails or by the use of bottled gas or by stationary engines and cables. Finally, the directors of the railway advertised a prize of £500 for the best locomotive. Stephenson had done the preliminary work of building the line, bridging the swamps, and digging the tunnels. The battle of the engines in 1829 was a sporting event witnessed by thousands. Among the competitors was John Ericsson, a Swedish engineer, later the inventor of the screw propellor and of the Civil War's ironclad warship *Monitor*. Of the four entries, all broke down except Stephenson's *Rocket*. Crude as it was, it more clearly resembled a modern locomotive than did the other entries.

For a time the railway—or railroad, as it is more generally called in the United States—made slow progress. The first really long one, the London and Birmingham, was not authorized until 1833. Then the pace quickened; by 1840 Britain had no less than 1331 miles of railway and by 1860

The Parkside station on the pioneer Liverpool & Manchester Railway, where William Huskisson was killed when he stepped in front of Stephenson's "Rocket."

the "railway mania" had run the total up to 10,410 miles. In the United States, with its longer distances, the railway mileage was about double that of the English at those dates.

The railway did not directly precipitate Parliamentary reform. Nevertheless, the forces which brought about reform were in the last analysis the same as those which brought the railway into existence—surplus capital seeking investment, and surplus capital in the hands of an unrepresented but proud and self-conscious class of capable men who were knocking insistently at the gates of political privilege. To be sure, the radical agitators wanted votes for everyone; but the money and the organization for their agitation came from the new middle class, which by the Reform Bill of 1832 was to win a measure of political power commensurate with its economic importance.

The Parliamentary Reform Agitation

Two years before that a tidal wave of revolution more widespread than the previous one, of 1820, swept over a large part of Europe and partially disrupted the settlement of 1815. In France the rule of the feudal nobility was abruptly terminated with the overthrow of the king and elevation to the throne of Louis Philippe, who belonged to another branch of the royal family. With the new king the French middle class rose to power, a fact of which the English middle class, already clamoring for political privilege, speedily took note. Wellington had proved a thoroughly unpopular prime minister. He was disliked by many Whigs, who had been willing to cooperate with Canning; by his own die-hard Tories, who felt he had given way unnecessarily in the matter of Catholic emancipation; and by other Tories because he ordered them around, instead of treating them with the finesse due their rank and importance. Here, then, was an opportunity for the Whig opposition to reopen the old question of Parliamentary reform, to take advantage of the ever-increasing pressure of the middle class and to overturn Wellington.

The Duke, less adroit than usual, took the offensive upon opening Parliament in 1830 and praised the present system to the skies. It answered, he said, "all the good of purposes of legislation, and this to a greater degree than any legislature had ever answered, in any country whatever." This speech angered the Commons, and his majority melted away. Defeated on a minor issue, he resigned, and Lord Grey came into office.

Apparently the Whig cabinet's idea was to keep the old system with some minor changes, but it contained radicals as well as conservatives. Grey's son-in-law, Lord Durham, who was later to recommend responsible government in the colonies (see page 461), did not belie his name of "Radical Jack." Also Henry Brougham, a celebrated radical and law-reformer, was an advocate of Parliamentary reform. With such members, the cabinet under the pressure of popular opinion turned toward the left.

"Orator" Hunt emerged from obscurity and was elected to Parliament. Cobbett took up his pen again with unsurpassed bitterness. O'Connell started an antirent campaign in Ireland. At London and at Birmingham huge crowds angrily protested. It was evident that no halfway measure would do. Consequently, early in 1831, Lord John Russell introduced a more far-reaching bill than had been originally intended.

It proposed to redistribute the seats in the Commons and to extend the franchise. The first it would accomplish by taking away representation from boroughs with a population under 2000, and cutting down the representation from two members to one for those with a population of from 2000 to 4000, thus eliminating most of the rotten boroughs. In their place it was proposed to create new seats for some of the industrial cities and for several counties which had grown rapidly. Secondly, a uniform borough franchise was provided in place of the bewildering and entirely irrational old system. As finally modified, the franchise in the boroughs was to be given to all men who owned or rented a house of the annual rental of £10 over and above all taxes. While this extended the franchise to many, it disfranchised some voters. In the counties the franchise was retained by the forty-shilling freeholders who actually resided on their freehold. It was extended to men with certain long-term tenures worth £10 a year, and to still others with more precarious tenures at £50 a year, thus enfranchising well-to-do farmers who leased but did not own land.

Opposition to the measure was vehement during sixteen months of violent agitation. It did not provide for annual or even triennial elections of Parliament; and the ballot, or secret voting, was rejected. Reverence for the old system was strong, and in its favor three main arguments were advanced. First, under the old constitution England had become the foremost country in the world. Secondly, the rotten boroughs, through the nomination of a patron, had introduced into Parliament young men of great promise in their early twenties, such as Burke, Pitt, and Peel. The rotten boroughs also provided a safe refuge for elder statesmen of worth and value who were unwilling to go through the hurly-burly of contesting elections. Finally, it was argued that the Commons should represent interests rather than numbers. The English constitution, as it had evolved throughout the centuries, provided for this. The very poor were represented in those "pot-walloper" boroughs where almost everyone could vote, and the agricultural interests by the counties. The mercantile and manufacturing interests were represented indirectly, since any man willing to spend sufficient money could buy a borough. These arguments could not prevail in the face of the actual facts. The evidence of Parliamentary corruption was overwhelming, the unfairness of the failure to recognize that the population of England had shifted was too patent, and the pressure of the inadequately represented middle class was too powerful. The bill passed its second reading, but by a majority of only one.

Then it was defeated, to all intents and purposes, by a successful motion that the representation in the Commons be not reduced; and in April, 1831, Grey, persuading the king to dissolve Parliament, appealed to the country. "The bill, the whole bill, and nothing but the bill" became the slogan of Whigs and radicals alike. The combined pressure of the middle class and the workingmen, together with the potent influence of government patronage, was irresistible. The Tory strength in the counties was almost wiped out, and in the boroughs, greatly reduced. In the autumn of 1831, it passed the Commons by a sizable majority, but not the Lords. Wellington, deciding to dig himself in, advised the Lords to reject the bill, and they did so.

All England rang with revolt at the presumption of the peers. The castle of the Duke of Nottingham, a well-known boroughmonger, was destroyed. The jails were opened at Derby and the inmates freed. A mob fired the town hall at Bristol and burned the bishop's palace. The Birmingham Political Union, with its affiliated branches, staged huge demonstrations, and a national union of workingmen was organized to attain universal suffrage. At Oxford young Mr. Gladstone, feeling that the British constitution was in danger, warned other undergraduates against the bill. On the other hand, John Stuart Mill, equally young, wrote "if the ministers flinch or if the peers remain obstinate, I am firmly convinced that within six months a National Convention chosen by universal suffrage will be sitting in London."

Passage of the 1832 Reform Bill

In 1832 the bill was introduced for the third time. To conciliate the Tories a few slight changes were made, the most important being that wealth as well as population should be given weight in determining the boroughs to be disfranchised. This time the Commons accepted the bill by a two-to-one vote, but the Lords tried to kill it by amending it. Thereupon Grey sought authority from the new king, William IV (1830-1837), to follow the precedent of 1712 by creating a sufficient number of new peers to pass his bill unamended through the Upper House. Failing to obtain this, the prime minister resigned.

Once more Wellington became prime minister; but as he did so the church bells began ringing throughout England, and workmen threw down their tools. The king was hooted in his coach, and a run was started on the Bank of England. "To stop the Duke, go for gold," was the brilliant idea of Francis Place. It was effective. The Iron Duke promptly withdrew, and the king sent once again for Grey.

William IV, the "Sailor King," was not brilliant, but in character he was an improvement upon his elder brother, the late George IV. This time Grey was able to persuade him to create the necessary number of peers, and, fortified by the king's written promise to that effect, Grey accepted office. Wellington saw the fight was lost. Rather than have the House of Lords swamped by a host of new peers he and a hundred of his Tory followers absented themselves from Parliament and the bill, passed by a rump of the Lords, became law at last on July 7, 1832. Even after its final passage, it was popularly called the Reform "Bill" because of the prominence it had gained before it had become an act.

Thus did the British people accomplish a kind of revolution. It did not dethrone a dynasty; but it did destroy what amounted to a semi-feudal monopoly of the government in the hands of the landed aristocracy. The contemporary revolution in France provided one vote for every two hundred citizens; in Britain the bill gave the vote to one in every thirty, almost doubling the voters in the counties. The revolution, if it may be called such, was characteristically British. It changed old methods and practices somewhat roughly, but it did not end them altogether. The political power of the landlord class was reduced, but the middle class was not put in the saddle. The upper middle class, however, became elevated to approximate equality with the country gentry. As for the working classes; laborers were too poor to occupy £10 houses. In cities such as Leeds they live in houses with rents from £5 to £8, and only about 10 per cent of the artisan class received votes. What the bill gave with one hand it took away with the other: the "pot-wallopers" and the "scot and lot" men lost the franchise, and so, in certain boroughs fewer voted after 1832 than before. Furthermore, the extension of the franchise in the counties added in a curious way to the political influence of the wealthy landlords. Before 1832, when only landowners could vote in the counties, the yeomen, or lesser landowners, held the balance of power in a number of constituencies. Now they were heavily outnumbered by the voting tenants who stood in fear of losing their leases if they voted against their landlords; for all voting had to be done in the open.

The great Reform Bill of 1832, in short, was a compromise. It set a precedent and was an important landmark in the advance toward democracy: it was to be followed by four similar acts (1867, 1884, 1918, 1928) which finally gave Britain universal suffrage. Another precedent was strengthened. Although the House of Lords had surrendered none of its power in theory, nevertheless the fact remained that when faced with the repetition of Queen Anne's mass creation of new peers it had yielded against its will to the popular demand as expressed in a parliamentary election. The strategic retreat of Wellington in 1832 was not forgotten in later days (see page 499).

Chapter Twenty-one · 1832-1865

The Victorian Compromise

For more than thirty years after the Reform Bill of 1832 Britain enjoyed one of her most prosperous and fruitful periods. The era is intimately associated with the name of Queen Victoria, constituting as it did nearly half of her long reign, which commenced in 1837. Britain was enjoying the fruits of the Industrial Revolution at their richest; for material growth continued, and outside competition was as yet negligible. Abroad her prestige was high, backed by the royal navy; in no uncertain tones, she exerted her influence not only in guarding her own interests but also on behalf of those struggling for the English type of liberty. Under that placid façade, however, there was slowly stirring ferment of social unrest, for it lay upon a foundation of widespread human wretchedness. And upper-class England, warding off democracy for the time being, was making only a moderate effort to adjust the nation to the new conditions.

Moderate men controlled Parliament. The fears of the Duke of Wellington lest the gentlemen of England should no longer serve their country in the House of Commons were groundless. Most of those elected were still gentlemen in the narrow sense that they did not have to earn their own living. The electorate evidently preferred to remain loyal to the old tradition.

Party rivalry was in a transitional state. Before 1830 there had been almost a half century of Tory domination, preceded by a similar period of Whig supremacy. After 1860 came relatively compact and disciplined Liberal and Conservative parties. In the interim Parliament was divided into several groups, no one of which could command a majority by itself. There were the aristocratic old Whigs, fairly conservative by nature; conservative Liberals and liberal Conservatives; die-hard Tory squires, who regretted the changes already made; the radicals, as they chose to call themselves, clamoring for universal suffrage and the secret ballot; liberal reformers; and usually some independents, whose views and support were at times problematical. Consequently as in later Continental parliaments, a ministry often consisted of a very unnatural alliance of several such groups. Each would seek places in the cabinet; each would seek support for certain policies; and some, at least, would not hesitate to shift to the other side upon due provocation. On the whole, the Whig-Liberal combinations had the upper hand, since they were in office three quarters of the time between 1830 and 1867, and for two more years had a share in a coalition ministry.

After pushing through the Reform Bill,

the Whigs, first under Grey and then under Melbourne, were to remain in power for nine more years, save for the five-month ministry of Sir Robert Peel. The Tories, under the latter, proved a chastened group. Many of the die-hards had either retired from politics or been rejected at the polls. Peel was determined "to look forward to the future." The Tories apparently would not be a brake on progress that kept within reasonable limits. Grey, in the meantime, presided over a motley group ranging from old Whigs to radicals and including a number of reformers.

The Crop of Whig Reforms

The Whigs put reform after reform through Parliament. By 1835, scarcely knowing themselves, they had abolished slavery, enacted factory legislation, revolutionized the Poor Law, and reformed the British municipalities. Then, curiously enough, their zeal was to abate; and they relapsed into comparative inactivity.

Ever since Waterloo there had been a cry for the emancipation of the slaves, of whom there were some 750,000 in the British colonies. Wilberforce, who had led the successful campaign against the slave trade in 1807, now spearheaded the fight against slavery itself, which others carried through to victory in 1833 (see page 365).

In 1833, also, was passed the first effective law for the protection of children in British factories. For some strange reason the evangelical reformers, who had worked hard for the welfare of the Negroes, remained indifferent to that of the child laborers. From the early factories in the late eighteenth century the labor employed had been chiefly children; and the conditions generally shocking (see page 338). The first remedial legislation in 1802, achieved partly through the efforts of Robert Owen and Sir Robert Peel, the Elder, forbade employment of children for more than twelve hours, exclusive of mealtime, and in certain cases night work;

and ordered the factories whitewashed for sanitary reasons. It was of slight benefit, being limited to those employing apprentices, and it lacked proper enforcement. Again in 1819, Peel was instrumental in securing an act forbidding employment under nine years of age and limiting actual work of those between nine and sixteen to twelve hours, but it applied only to cotton mills and again was without machinery for enforcement, essential in factory legislation. By then the steam engine had made it no longer necessary to locate near water power, so the large cities were becoming industrial centers; but the employment of children under harsh conditions continued, except that now they were usually the children of the laborers themselves (see page 338).

Three Tories deserve the credit for the next factory reform. Michael Sadler in the Commons, by his fiery denunciations of what went on with children behind factory walls, brought about the appointment in 1831 of a royal commission. Operatives and medical men testified freely of children of eight and even younger at work twelve hours, of stunted bodies and consumptive lungs, of bad ventilation and brutal overseers. Their tale of iniquity was long and grim. The necessary pressure behind Sadler's efforts came from mass meetings, at which Richard Oastler fearlessly and loudly cursed conditions as he had seen them in factory towns of Yorkshire, where he was steward of the estate of a wealthy squire. He had first been interested in the abolition of slavery, until taunted by friends with indifference to what was taking place nearby. It was his custom to watch parents carrying their sleeping children to work before daylight; to get evidence as to the use of the whip, of food covered with dust and lint, of arches and insteps broken, of legs supported by iron braces. The conscience of England was now touched, and the prospect of a ten-hour working day for boys and girls under eighteen seemed bright; then, in the scramble for the vote in 1832 Sadler was defeated, and the manufacturers held the whip hand in Parliament. Asserting that the royal commission had been ill-advised, they counseled futher delay, and the work of years seemed lost.

The third advocate for factory regulation appeared in the Commons. Lord Ashley, who, like his ancestor the founder of the Whig Party, later became Earl of Shaftesbury, was an aristocrat to his finger tips, and a convinced opponent of democracy; but he took over Sadler's work on the understanding that it had nothing to do with trade unions. In 1833 he sponsored a bill forbidding the employment of all children under nine, and providing that no person under eighteen was to work more than ten hours a day (eight on Saturday). But even these mild terms were too drastic for the average M.P. of that time. The opposition, sparring for time, secured the appointment of another royal commission. Although this commission was unable to refute the evidence of Sadler's commission, it denounced the agitation for a ten-hour day and produced medical evidence (of a kind) indicating that children over thirteen needed no special care, since "at that age, the period of childhood properly so-called ceases." Supported by this, the House approved by a large majority thirteen years as the top age limit for the ten-hour day. The law as finally enacted forbade employment under nine except in silk mills, limited labor between the ages of nine and thirteen to nine hours a day, or a total of forty-eight hours a week, and permitted a twelve-hour day for workers from thirteen to eighteen. For adults there was no time limit, because it was felt that one would interfere with the sacred right of free contract. As one and a half hours were to be allowed for meals, the regular factory day for those over the age of twelve was fixed at thirteen and a half hours; and these hours were to be be-tween 5:30 a.m. and 8:30 p.m. This law applied to most textile mills, and inspectors were to be sent out from London to enforce it.

Ashley had won a real victory; although his original bill had been trimmed, the provision for inspectors gave teeth to the law. It was passed by Parliament as a nonpartisan measure, but the Tories deserved the greater measure of praise. Their economic interests being primarily agricultural, they had welcomed this opportunity to criticize the manufacturing and commercial classes, and as Tories they were less indoctrinated with the laissez-faire principles of Adam Smith than the Whigs. Nevertheless, since the latter had a huge majority over Tories and radicals combined, the bill would never have become law without Whig support.

Factory legislation, begun in earnest in 1833, was to continue at intervals throughout the century, with Ashley for many years its principal champion. In 1842 he was a leader in efforts to improve conditions in the mining industry, which were reputed to be worse than in the mills. To cite extreme instances, according to the report of a royal commission, children of six and seven years were employed as trappers, staying underground twelve hours a day to open and shut doors which provided for the ventilation of the mines. They were also used to haul coal wagons through passages too small for adults, and sometimes "were harnessed like dogs in a go-cart." Women and girls were employed underground with the men, frequently working half naked, with their skin hardened by toil. A thirty-eight-year-old coal-putter testified that carrying coal caused her "to miscarry five times from the strains, and was gai ill after each. Putting is no so oppressive; . . . I have wrought below now thirty years and so has the guidman; he is getting touches in the breath now. None of the children read, . . . when I go below lassie ten years of age keeps house and makes the broth or stirabout." These were probably extreme cases and not general.

Ashley proposed a bill barring boys under thirteen and women of any age from mine work. To secure the approval of the House and more particularly to meet the opposition in the Lords, where the mining interests were strongly entrenched, the minimum age of boys was cut to ten in the Mines Act which became law in 1842. Ashley, now Earl of Shaftesbury, continued his fight for the ten-hour day for younger workers between thirteen and eighteen in the factories. For years that "Ten-Hours Bill" hung fire, finally to become law in 1847. Altogether, as a result of this legislation no child under nine was permitted to work in mines or in most textile factories; no woman or girl might work underground in the mines; in the factories children under eighteen might not work more than ten hours a day. But there was still no limit on the hours for boys or men in the mines, nor for men or women in the factories.

Women at work in a cotton factory, c. 1835.

The third great reform tackled by Parliament was that of poor relief, which had grown constantly more perplexing since Tudor days. The basic Elizabethan legislation had been little changed, except for the system which was originated by the justices of the peace at Speenhamland in 1795 when the wartime cost of bread was aggravating the sufferings of the poor. It guaranteed agricultural workers a certain minimum income by supplementing wages out of taxes. Consequently, whether the cost of bread went up or down, a family would get the designated minimum amount. This principle, that all poor persons were entitled to doles, entirely on the basis of need, resulted in an incredible increase in the number of paupers. Farmers reduced wages, knowing that the laborers could obtain sufficient relief from the poor rates to keep body and soul together, and many manufacturers did likewise. Lower wages forced independent workingmen into the ranks of pauperdom. The greater the number of paupers the higher became the taxes and the more wages fell. With many taking advantage of this to avoid work, poor rates became an intolerable burden.

Parliament's answer was hard and cruel; poverty was to be treated as a crime and made so unbearable that the individual would put forth every effort to avoid public support. Deciding to make every individual fend for himself, Parliament decreed, in the Poor Law of 1834, that poor relief should be centralized at London under three commissioners, who were to curtail drastically all outdoor relief or assistance to the poor in their own homes. Instead, with sexes segregated, they were to be herded into large workhouses, where they were purposely to be subjected to a lower standard of living than the lowest-paid independent workingmen. After entering a "bastille," a man could no longer live with his wife;

for that might make him contented. Food and heat were to be kept at a minimum. Paupers—and this age classed all the poor as such—were not to be buried in parish churchyards.

The same group of philanthropic Tories who labored so unceasingly for the factory acts violently opposed this "indoor relief." Christianity taught the reverse of the projected law, and that was enough for them. The aged Cobbett denounced it as "the poor man's robbery bill," and even the *Times* attacked it. But public opinion was determined to force national economy as well as prevent graft. Consequently this act, hated by the poor of England for many decades—judging from Dickens's *Oliver Twist* and Arnold Bennett's *Clayhanger*—was added to the accomplishments of the new Parliament.

The Municipal Corporations Act of 1835, completing this major legislative program, did for the cities what the Reform Bill did, more or less, for the nation. It straightened out a tangled mess of local customs and gave to all cities (except London, which already enjoyed a considerable degree of self-government) a common form of local government. It wiped out the system by which municipal control had rested in a small self-perpetuating body, the corporation, often corrupt and generally negligent, which let out to private companies or left to separate authorities the monopolies of water supply, lighting, and sewerage. Now municipal councilors were to be elected for three years by all ratepayers (taxpayers), who included practically anyone who occupied a house. These councilors then elected part of their number as aldermen, to serve six years. Councilors and aldermen comprised the city council, which chose a mayor to serve one year, and also had power to regulate all public utilities. Thus, in a way, the Municipal Corporations Act was a more thoroughgoing reform than the Reform Bill.

Parliament then rested on its laurels for the next thirty years except for further factory legislation and the repeal of the Corn Laws. This did not mean the cessation of political life—far from it. Ministries rose and fell. Cabals and party alignments formed and re-formed; one foreign war and several frontier wars were fought. This long period was one of excellent administration that led to adjustments here and there in the British political system. Nevertheless, the fact remains that those who ruled Britain, the landed aristocracy and the middle class in joint harness, were well content with their work. Convinced that on the whole this was the best of all possible worlds, they were unwilling to embark on futher untried paths.

Queen Victoria

Five years after the Reform Bill a slender, attractive girl of eighteen, niece of George IV and of William IV, came to the throne as Queen Victoria (1837-1901). Her reign, the longest in English history, ranks with that of Elizabeth I as one of the most successful in all fields of activity. Perhaps her most distinctive contribution was the restoration of the crown to a position of respect which it had lost under the Georges. She was the personification of respectability, and the term "mid-Victorian" still connotes the ultrapropriety of "middle-class morality" in that period when legs were "limbs" and many other things were unmentionable. Later generations might laugh at such extremes, but this was a decided improvement over the coarseness of George IV. An incidental result of Victoria's accession was the end of England's connection with Hanover, which had been joined to the British crown since 1714 (see page 291). Since a woman might not rule there, her uncle became king of Hanover, and Britain was rid of that vulnerable point in her foreign relations.

Victoria herself selected her cousin, the conscientious and somewhat stiff Prince Albert of Saxe-Coburg-Gotha for her hus-

Promoted by Prince Albert, the "Crystal Palace" in Hyde Park housed the "Great Exhibition" of 1851. Six million visitors saw its 13,000 exhibits from all countries, and were amazed at the percentage of goods made in Britain.

band and Prince Consort. Through his family connections and through the marriage of some of their nine children, Victoria became closely related to many of the other rulers of Europe. Theirs was an unusually devoted marriage; his death twenty-one years later left her inconsolable.

Although on the whole she accepted the role of constitutional monarch, the young queen was determined that the crown should have much more than decorative importance. At times this seemed almost to threaten the normal workings of responsible government, particularly as her husband; her uncle, king of Belgium; and her confidential adviser, Baron Stockmar, were all Germans, brought up on political theories far different from those of English limited monarchy. In 1839, her stubbornness kept the Tories from office. Sir Robert Peel refused to form a ministry unless she would replace the Whig ladies

of the bedchamber with Tories. Victoria would not, and the Whigs stayed in office, though it was later agreed that "the ladies should retire with the ministers." Her chief interference was in foreign affairs, where her prejudices were conservative and strongly pro-German. In 1850, when Victoria was shocked by the way in which Lord Palmerston was conducting foreign affairs (see page 420), Stockmar drew up a constitutional memorandum with Albert's approval. This stated that the monarch should be the permanent prime minister, ranking "above the temporary head of the cabinet" and exercising "supreme authority." The detachment of the crown from politics was called a dangerous "constitutional fiction." Palmerston was presented with a demand that the queen see important dispatches before they were sent, and that they should not be changed after her approval. When, after agreeing to this,

Palmerston went his old way, she was instrumental in bringing about his dismissal. More than once she tried to keep him from returning to the cabinet, but popular pressure was too strong. In the army too, where her cousin became commander in chief, she tended to stress royal against Parliamentary control. It has been said that "Victoria's widowhood saved the British constitution."

The "Victorian Compromise"

Despite those theories and practices involving the relation of the crown to Parliamentary government, she was in accord with the general sentiment of the time in accepting the organization of society as she found it—an organization firmly based on what has been called the "Victorian Compromise." Its tacit terms were that the aristocracy and the middle class divided political power between them to the exclusion of the working class. The two dominant classes were willing to compromise on voting privileges, provided that these did not go beyond the act of 1832. They did not deny that it might be improved, but it was held final in placing the control of Britain in the hands of trustees, capable, tried, trustworthy representatives of the aristocracy and of the middle class.

As a corollary of the Victorian Compromise, workingmen were not to be ignored by the government, for in a Christian country it would be unseemly to let the poor starve. A moderate amount of protection for the "down-and-out," the inefficient, the pauper, the depressed classes should be given (witness the Factory Acts and the Poor Law); but laziness must not be encouraged. Deep in the psychology of the middle class was the conviction of a link between poverty and wickedness. The successful Victorian businessmen had worked hard; and in frugality, hard work, and temperance lay the salvation of the lower classes, so they thought. These virtues must not be weakened by a paternalistic society that looked out for the less able.

The loosely drawn alliance between the aristocracy and the middle class, which controlled the government in mid-century, conformed to a rather definite extent to the political and economic ideas of three earlier writers. Tories, Whigs, and particularly radicals, were influenced in varying degree by Jeremy Bentham (1748-1832), a rich recluse rarely seen by the public. Benthamism or utilitarianism did not sweep over England without stirring strong countercurrents; but consciously or not, it set the direction of government policies and reform —legal, social, economic, and political—for most of the century.

Bentham's concepts were tangible, covering a vast range of human interests. His fame dated from his frontal attack on Blackstone (see page 73), the foremost legal authority of that period. From this was to emerge eventually a drastic simplification and codification of English jurisprudence. After the French Revolution Bentham interested himself in a number of varied reforms and became a recognized authority on constitutions.

Benthamism was based primarily on two concepts, utility and happiness. They were correlated, the value of every human institution or custom depending exclusively on whether or not it furthered human happiness. "Good" and "happiness" according to Bentham were well-nigh interchangeable terms. Since everyone was best fitted to know what was most conducive to his own happiness, any interference with an individual retarded his advance, and so lessened his opportunity for personal happiness. Since the welfare of any society was determined by adding up the happiness of its various individuals, the goal of government should be to secure the "greatest happiness of the greatest number." From a laissez-faire beginning, Bentham's followers developed a doctrine of social reform.

The second intellectual pillar of the Victorian Compromise, Thomas Malthus (1766-1834), was an English clergyman, who occupied the first professorial chair in political economy in Great Britain. His fame rests on his *Essay on Population* (1798), in which he had held that under normal conditions population increased faster than food. This meant inevitable human suffering because an unchecked population would in time outrun the food supply, if not held back by war and disease or by humanity voluntarily refraining from reproduction. Victorians tended to concur in his theory as they saw their population increasing by leaps and bounds along with poverty and hunger in the towns. The Malthusian argument, after years of oblivion, was to come to the fore again in the mid-twentieth century when overpopulation became an acute world problem.

Adam Smith (1723-1790), a Scot who had studied at Glasgow and Oxford before becoming a professor of logic, was the third member of the middle-class trinity of social philosophers. His *Wealth of Nations*, long accepted as a chief authority on economics, had been published back in 1776 (see pages 357, 364). Its main doctrine was *laissez faire*, that is, the absence of most restrictions on trade and industry, in contrast to the narrow economic regulations of the earlier period. Monopolies, the regulation of labor, the fixing of wages, trade unions which limit apprenticeship, tariffs, every kind of restraint on trade, Smith called injurious. Government, in his opinion, should not interfere with business and should keep taxes at a minimum. A keen individualist like Bentham, he felt that man "by pursuing his own interests frequently promotes that of society more effectually than when he really intends to promote it."

The ideas of Bentham, Malthus, and Smith indicate pretty much what the middle class believed in such as the right of free contract; free trade; the necessity for peace; reform in certain outdated institutions, like the game laws; the sanctity of private property; imprudence, including having too many children, as the cause of poverty; individualism as the right social philosophy. In other words, taxation should be low, extravagance should be checked, and governments should confine themselves principally to enforcing contracts and to preserving the peace. A few of the more radical of the middle class-aristocracy alliance went so far as to advocate universal suffrage, as a logical deduction from Bentham's teachings. Some of the more conservative had their doubts about individualism and harked back to earlier, semifeudal ideas which held the ruling class responsible for the welfare of society.

Meanwhile the Commons were ready to enact into law various reforms in harmony with the spirit of the age. Jews were permitted to enter Parliament. The Anglican religious establishment, both in England and in Ireland, was improved by curbing certain weaknesses. A "Truck Act" was passed making it illegal to pay wages simply in credit at company stores. Cheap postage was introduced. The formation of savings banks was encouraged. Assent to the thirty-nine articles of the Church of England was to be no longer required of students for matriculation at Oxford and Cambridge Universities.

The Oxford Movement

That the Victorian Compromise proved so acceptable to English public opinion was largely because of the indirect influence of the Oxford Movement, fear of the Chartists, the success of the anti-Corn agitation, the popularity and influence of Lord Palmerston, and economic prosperity. The Oxford Movement was a religious revival which began in 1833 as a protest on the part of certain talented Anglican churchmen who were disturbed at the prevailing ignorance of the principles upon which the Church of England was founded; at the passage of certain laws by Parliament (such as the repeal of the Test and Corporation Acts, and Catholic emancipation) which undermined the exclusively Anglican character of the government; at what they called "Erastianism," which exalted the State over both Bible and Church; and at a growing demand that the Church do something for the money paid it. The last manifested itself in a successful attack on the Irish Church and an unsuccessful one on the English Church.

The leaders, prominent Anglican clergymen like John Henry Newman and Edward Bouverie Pusey, were passionately devoted to the Church as an institution, and as scholars of Oxford they looked to the past of the Church to find inspiration for her future. They tended to stress more and more the idea of Apostolic succession and of one Holy Catholic Church. Their message, which made an eloquent appeal to reason as well as to emotion, was extraordinarily successful at first. In vain did Dr. Arnold of Rugby, England's famous schoolmaster and Low Church champion, contend against it. The movement grew rapidly at the expense of both Low Church and Broad Church because of its color, its fervor, its more brilliant preachers, its profound scholarship, and its greater contrast to the lay progressivism of the period, which exalted the steam engine, commercial prosperity, and the accumulation of wealth while manifesting distrust of ancient ways and modes of thought. The movement reached a climax in 1845 with Newman's conversion to Catholicism. This religious revival, the parent of the later High Church movement, though not directly concerned with the Victorian Compromise, negatively abetted its acceptance by proclaiming religion as something apart from economic and political life. The drift of High Church sentiment in after decades was to reaffirm various aspects of the social gospel of the primitive and medieval Church; but this Oxford group, intent on trying to prove that the Church of England was not Protestant but truly Catholic, just about let the battle go by default in matters that were merely of lay concern to them.

The Chartists

The Chartist movement crystallized rapidly in the late thirties, came to a head in 1839-1840, continued with various ups and downs, as a serious threat to the Victorian Compromise as late as 1848, and virtually disappeared ten years later. Its members, largely radical agitators of varied hue, were drawn from artisans of the lower middle class and from workingmen. Some were motivated by disillusionment over the compromises of the Reform Bill, and others over the failure of Owen's abortive experiment with a trade union, but the majority probably came in because of the continuing industrial distress and exploitation, especially in the north (see page 341). These elements combined to bring about "one of the most dynamic movements of working class agitation so far known in England."[1]

William Lovett, a cabinet maker concerned with education of the depressed classes and founder of the London Workingmen's Association, and Francis Place (see pages 392, 397) drew up as the program for that group of artisans, a "People's Charter." Its six points embodied the aims of what became known as Chartism: universal (male) suffrage, the ballot (or secret voting), equal electoral districts, no property qualification for members of Parliament, payment of members, and annual elections. The movement turned much farther to the left with its organization on a national scale. This resulted largely from the revival of the Birmingham Political Union by a Birmingham banker, Attwood, who had made it effective in 1832. His purpose was inflation of the currency; but to win over the workingmen he subordinated this to a demand for universal suffrage. After missionaries of the Union had met with great success in Scottish cities, Attwood proposed a National Convention of

[1] David Thomson, *England in the Nineteenth Century* (1815-1914) (The Pelican History of England, Penguin Books Ltd., 1950), p. 83.

Workingmen in London. Meanwhile, the Chartists enlisted their largest membership among the workers of the industrial north, now further distressed by the new Poor Law. Foremost among the northerners was Feargus O'Connor, Irish landowner, editor of a widely circulated radical Leeds newspaper, and son of a United Irishman (see page 375). A born demagogue, large in stature and bold of speech, he was prodigiously active in denouncing the "big-bellied, little-brained, numskull aristocracy." His activities and the idea of the forthcoming "convention" caused serious but, as it happened, unnecessary concern.

At this convention in 1839, the Chartists frittered away weeks in argument, while awaiting the gathering of what they claimed were a million signatures on their first petition for their charter. It was received courteously by the House of Commons, but rejected almost six to one. Thereupon the convention ordered a general strike, which was cancelled before it was due. No money was available, the trade unions held aloof, and fierce quarrels broke out in the ranks. Many were alarmed at the wild talk of insurrection emanating from certain of their comrades, and all of them were impressed by the army's preparations to nip civil war in the bud. Some were arrested for incendiary speeches; and more were sick of the whole affair. Disheartened, the convention agreed to disband.

But Chartism was not to die easily, despite the continuing disagreements on common tactics. The so-called "physical-force" Chartists started an abortive revolt among the Welsh miners, which was easily put down. The ringleaders, tried for treason, were condemned to die, but instead were transported. Although O'Connor had conveniently absented himself in Ireland during this affair, after Place's resignation, nevertheless, he gradually assumed undisputed leadership.

In 1842 a second petition, supposed to have over three million signatures, was car-

ried on poles to Parliament, where it had to be broken into segments to get it through the doors. Macaulay, who was among its attackers, declared that "universal suffrage would be fatal to all purposes for which government exists. . . . I conceive that civilization rests upon the security of property." Russell held that "even to discuss such demands would bring into question the ancient and venerable institutions of the country." The House rejected the petition 289 to 49. Chartism now entered a new phase, in which O'Connor tried experiments in land settlement, with his Cooperative Land Company, a forerunner of the movement that was to dot England with cooperative stores.

In 1848, an epidemic of revolutions broke out on the Continent. Many German, French, and Italian revolutionaries came to London. With a successful revolution (followed by a Second Republic) in France, with a national parliament assembling in Germany, with Italy up in arms against Austria, and with the Austrian Empire aflame with revolt at home, the old Metternich system of reaction and oppression dominant since 1815 was rapidly breaking up. The Chartists took advantage of the general confusion to circulate a third petition and call another convention. A spectacle again was staged in the streets of London, with O'Connor, now a member of Parliament, presiding over it.

The government took no chances in that year of revolutions. Troops were located in strategic places by the aged Wellington. A quarter of a million special constables were sworn in, among them Louis Napoleon Bonaparte, soon to be president of the new French Republic and then, like his uncle, emperor of France. There was, however, no disturbance. O'Connor, in a speech to his followers, urged them to put their faith in the 6,000,000 signatures on their third petition; and the crowd dispersed quietly. When the suspicious government counted the names thereon, it found only 2,000,000 including Victoria, Duke of Wellington, Pug-nose, and No Cheese. Soon after this fiasco, the movement faded into oblivion. O'Connor died insane.

Yet, this "first widespread and sustained effort of working-class selfhelp" was not the failure it seemed. From it came some of the impetus that led to the later Parliamentary reforms and to trade union development. As for its six political demands, all except the annual election of Parliament were enacted by 1918. At the time, however, the growing prosperity and an increasing awareness of social ills, soon replaced Chartism in the public's mind.

The Anti-Corn-Law League

The strength of the Victorian Compromise also lay in the success of the Anti-Corn-Law League, a well-officered, well-financed association which outbid the Chartists for the support of the working-men and helped to push Britain still further toward free trade. The Corn Laws in 1840 differed little from those of 1815 (see pages 392, 396). They had been the target of desultory attack for many years, but the landed interests, both Whig and Tory, championed them.

Two textile manufacturers, Richard Cobden and John Bright, made it otherwise. Cobden, moderately wealthy, was, in every sense of the word, a self-made man. Protracted travel in both the United States and Europe and the constant study of economic institutions as living realities had convinced him that Britain ought to buy in the cheapest and sell in the dearest market. He looked forward with misgiving to the increase in her population and to her economic competitors' growing strength. Cheap bread he believed essential to the country's welfare; for it would give the working classes more money with which to buy British manufactured goods. At the same time the repeal of the Corn Law would, in his opinion, stimulate agriculture in the United States and thus give the Americans more money with

which to buy from British firms. Only the landlords had received the advantages of protection, and they had not passed these down to the laborer or to the farmer but had kept rents high.

Cobden believed in following Adam Smith to his logical conclusion by allowing the natural laws which supposedly governed economics to operate unhindered. Poverty, he believed, was caused primarily by interference with these laws. These ideas were not new; but the energy, skill, and moral fervor of Cobden and Bright gave them an unwonted vitality and freshness. As leaders of the so-called "Manchester school," their views were particularly acceptable to the cotton manufacturers, who realized that cheaper bread would make it possible to pay a lower minimum wage to their workers. The development of the Anti-Corn-Law League was Cobden's great achievement. His "fresh and sanguine temper" made the whole enterprise throb with energy. He mapped out his campaigns in minute detail, pressing forward on half a dozen fronts. None excelled him when it came to raising money, writing pamphlets, and directing missionaries. He enlisted not only the middle class but some workingmen and even a few aristocrats.

The League carried on a war on both the Chartist and the conservative fronts. It was necessary to convince the working class that the ballot, the vote, and the other four points of the charter were not as important —at least at the moment—as cheap bread; and, above all, to persuade them that the League, financed by the manufacturers, was not their natural enemy. At the same time the squires had to be made to feel that their continued monopoly of agriculture was uneconomic, unjust, and wrong.

It was fortunate for the League that it had money. In 1843 alone its financial status was so satisfactory that it had sufficient funds to publish nine million tracts and to send out eight hundred persons on missionary tours. The following year £100,000 was added to its treasury. In 1845-1846, as the climax approached, no less than £525,000 poured into its coffers.

It was fortunate also in possessing an extraordinarily good orator in John Bright, of Quaker descent and industrial background. Not many Englishmen have surpassed his spoken word for simplicity and directness of diction, pugnacity, and moral fervor. After Cobden spoke, Bright modestly remarked, "I used to get up and do a little prize fighting." Cobden gave facts, ferreted out conditions, exposed fallacies, laid foundations; Bright stirred the conscience and steeled the will. The League could depend on Bright to convince the popular mind that the poor paid and the rich reaped the profits. With his scathing indictments of the callous rich, he drew workingmen from the Chartist camp. Some have charged the League with hypocrisy, for Bright and others of his persuasion had a blind spot to certain aspects of social reform, but most of them apparently were sincerely convinced that free trade would be good for the whole country as well as for Manchester. Nevertheless, most manufacturers probably considered their contributions to the League a good investment.

The landed aristocracy, meanwhile, did its best to frighten the missionaries of the League away from the countryside. Even convinced free traders in the Commons, like Macaulay, refused to appear on League platforms. The *Times* spoke of Cobden, Bright, and their allies as "capering mercenaries who go frisking about the country." As for the Chartist opposition, it was hopelessly outclassed by the League.

Time and tide worked in the League's favor. When the long Whig ascendancy ended in 1841, the Tories, now beginning to be called Conservatives, returned to power, only to face the "hungry forties." Unemployment was rife, the price of bread high. The economic depression arose from causes larger than the Corn Laws, but politically they provided a scapegoat. Peel,

now prime minister, was pledged to maintain them; but he was a businessman, who recognized facts when he saw them, and weather became all at once a decidedly potent one, influencing history to an exceptional degree.

Potato Famine and Corn Law Repeal

Rains fell incessantly on the British Isles throughout the summer of 1845. England's wheat crop failed, but infinitely more serious was the situation in Ireland, with its undue dependence on potatoes. They rotted in the ground and actual famine stalked the land. As the sober British census later described it: "Agriculture was neglected and land in many places remained untilled. Thousands were supported from day to day upon the bounty of outdoor relief. . . . The disorganization of society became marked and memorable by the exodus of over one million of people, who deserted their homes and hearths to seek shelter in foreign lands, of whom thousands perished of pestilence and hardships endured on shipboard. . . . Generally speaking, the actually starving people lived upon the carcasses of diseased cattle, upon dogs and dead horses, but principally upon the herbs of the field, nettle tops, wild mustard and water cresses, and even in some places dead bodies were found with grasses in their mouths."

In the face of this crisis, Peel, convinced by Cobden that Corn Law repeal was inevitable, resigned. Russell and his Whigs had their golden chance, but did not take it. The overwhelmingly Tory House of Lords would throw out any Whig repeal bill. The Whigs, with no stomach for a struggle with the Lords, pretended that they could not form a new ministry, and "passed back the poisoned chalice" to Sir Robert.

There followed the "great betrayal." Peel had become a free trader. He felt that the constant talk of rich versus poor was not a good thing for the possessing classes, and that the sooner the League accomplished its purpose, the sooner it would disband. He realized that the Tory party might be temporarily broken up, but he looked beyond the political exigencies of the moment to the nation's future needs. Furthermore, he was sure that the Tory Lords would do the bidding of Tory leadership in the Commons.

Peel's motion passed the Commons with the assistance of the timid Whigs; and it passed the Lords because Wellington said that it must. "Rotten potatoes have done it," he said; "they put Peel in his damned fright." The Duke, old and deaf, did not care about the Corn Laws; but he did know that the government had to be carried on. Thus the Corn Laws were repealed in 1846.

This repeal meant the rise of Benjamin Disraeli. This curious interloper in that first club of Europe, the House of Commons, determined to make himself Tory leader (see pages 465 ff.). He drove the rapier of his vitriolic scorn into Peel with unerring skill and drew the support of the country squires, who knew a leader when they saw one. Disraeli seemed never to think the issue one of economics or even a question which concerned all Britain. Instead all he seemed to see was the betrayal of the country gentlemen, who had made the nation great in the past. He gave them his loyal and romantic devotion, and at the same time found his way into high office.

Again, the repeal marked a serious schism in the Tory party. The majority followed Disraeli; the "Peelites," as they were nicknamed—few in number but brilliant in intellect, among whom stood Gladstone—remained true to the fallen leader. With really two Tory parties instead of one, came a long period of Whig-Liberal rule.

The repeal was also a signal victory for laissez faire over the protective tariff, although customs duties survived on commodities other than grain. Nevertheless, free contract, free sale, free trade, were henceforth to be the rule rather than the exception for the rest of the century. In this con-

PAPA COBDEN TAKING MASTER ROBERT A FREE TRADE WALK.

Peel, dragged toward free trade by Cobden, complains "That's all very well, but you know I cannot go as fast as you do."

nection the repeal registered the finality of the last shift from an agricultural to an industrial economy; from now on, Britain was to become more and more an industrial country.

Palmerston and Foreign Policy

Lord Palmerston, another bulwark of the Victorian Compromise, was for thirty years the guiding spirit in British foreign relations, even as prime minister and home secretary. Others might command greater respect, but not one could arouse the widespread affection which Englishmen felt for "Pam." A "statesman-aristocrat of sporting proclivities," this bluff peer had all the background of family, wealth, and education which Britain still looked for in her leaders; a gay bachelor until well past fifty, he had, too, wit, joviality, undisciplined exuberance, and a frequent rough arrogance which won the multitude; yet he was a tireless and painstaking worker, a remarkable master of details, who did not shrink from the drudgery of administrative routine. With reports pouring into the Foreign Office at the rate of a hundred a day, he boasted that he read them all, "down to the least important letter of the lowest vice-consul." Blessed as he was with unusual vitality, the cares of office left him at seventy-five still "springy and elastic" and looking "as if he did not care one straw for any man or thing on earth."

That last quality, perhaps, was what endeared him most to his countrymen and made him politically indispensable. Britain was not in a modest mood and rejoiced at his arrogant tone used all too freely even toward the great powers of Europe. The people were pleased when he declared that British subjects everywhere should have the same claim to protection which ancient Rome had given her citizens. They cheered even when the claims to British protection were as diluted as those of the Portuguese Jew born at Gibraltar, for whom a fleet was sent to Greece to collect questionable claims, or of the Chinese vessel which helped to bring on a war because of an insult to her British flag which she no longer had the right to fly. It was a risky sort of belligerent patriotism which kept the army and navy in a nervous state of constant expectancy; but the public enjoyed the prestige.

His public career reflected the political shifts of more than half a century. Entering public life fresh from Cambridge in 1807, Palmerston was a Tory until after Canning's death. Briefly a junior Lord of the Admiralty, he was then Secretary for War, until, with other Canningites, he "mutinied" against Wellington in 1828. Never essentially a party man, he joined forces with Grey's Whigs, and might thereafter be called a conservative Liberal. Under Grey in 1830, Palmerston assumed charge of foreign relations, which henceforth were to be his absorbing specialty. Except for the five

months of Peel's first Conservative ministry (1834-1835), he remained steadily in office in the Liberal ministries of Grey (1830-1834) and Melbourne (1834-1841). After his "longest vacation" from office, during the second Peel ministry (1841-1846), he returned to the Foreign Office in the Liberal ministry of Lord John Russell (1846-1852). Dismissed for a glaring indiscretion, he was out of office during Lord Derby's ten-month Conservative ministry when Disraeli at the Exchequer was the real leader (February-December, 1852). This "stop-gap government without a majority and without a policy" quickly gave way to a Conservative-Liberal coalition under Lord Aberdeen (1852-1855), in which Palmerston, considered too dangerous at the Foreign Office, was Home Secretary. The need for more aggressive leadership in the Crimean War brought in Palmerston in 1855 as Liberal prime minister. He held that office, interrupted only by a brief second Derby-Disraeli ministry (1858-1859), until his death ten years later.

His international problems ranged from the pine forests of Maine to the hongs of Canton; but his attention was centered particularly upon the Continent, where numerous delicate situations arose from the various crops of revolutions, the breakup of the Metternich system, and the perennial crises in the Eastern Question. It was fitting that, as Canning's avowed disciple, he assisted at the births of the new kingdoms of Belgium and Italy and encouraged elsewhere those who sought new constitutions, modeled, of course, upon England's.

Palmerston had a strenuous initiation in his first application of this principle in 1830. The Belgians, united with the Dutch at Vienna in order to provide a strong buffer state against France, had just revolted and sought independence. Britain had repeatedly fought to keep France out of these former Burgundian provinces, which since the Middle Ages had belonged in turn to Spain, Austria, France, and Holland (see pages 278, 368). Now again, France had designs upon Belgium. On the other hand, if the antirevolutionary powers—Austria, Prussia, and Russia—supported the Dutch king in recovering her, France might fight and thus plunge Europe into a general war. Palmerston steered such a clever and careful course that the powers at London in 1831 agreed that Belgium be independent, with her neutrality perpetually guaranteed by the five great powers. That was intended as a safeguard against absorption by France. Leopold of Saxe-Coburg-Gotha, uncle of the future Queen Victoria, had declined the Greek crown, but accepted the Belgian, as a limited monarch on the English pattern. It took eight years of persuasion and armed pressure from England and France to bring both the Belgians and the Dutch to terms. In 1839 the representatives of the five great powers gathered again at London to sign a final treaty guaranteeing Belgium neutrality (see page 565).

Palmerston also supported the unification of Italy, a "geographical expression," as Metternich described it. Austria's influence was strong among its varied states, and she had crushed the revolts of 1820, 1830, and 1848. By that time Piedmont (Sardinia), which led the opposition to Austria, realized that a free and united Italy could be achieved only with outside aid, and the only two possible allies were Britain and France. Piedmont allied herself with them in their Crimean War against Russia, so as to have the Italian situation brought up at the peace conference. Both nations were impressed: England gave assurances of moral support, and in 1859, during a war between Piedmont and Austria, France invaded Italy and inflicted two bloody defeats upon the Austrians. Although the French emperor, Napoleon III, suddenly stopped, with the Austrian defeat only half completed, Piedmont annexed Lombardy by the peace treaty. Next, at the suggestion of Palmerston and Russell, then foreign minister, the small states of central Italy were permitted to vote upon their political status; and they heavily favored union with Piedmont. The dramatic raid of an Italian patriot, Garibaldi, and his "Red Shirts" upon Sicily and Naples (the Kingdom of the Two Sicilies) brought the southern part into the newly forming kingdom of Italy, a limited monarchy on the English model, under the ruler of Piedmont. He expressed unbounded gratitude to England, which had not spent a shilling or lost a man in Italy's cause, while the French outpouring of blood and treasure was offset by the fact that French troops still guarded Papal Rome, Italy's natural capital. Fully united with the inclusion of Venetia and Rome by 1870, Italy became the sixth great power, albeit rather a marginal one.

For a considerable time, Palmerston had his hands full with the Eastern Question, (see page 394), for the Ottoman Empire continued to disintegrate under constant pressure from outside, with England continually trying to check that process. It was pointed out at the time that it is extremely difficult to maintain the status quo in a decomposing carcass. Canning's imperious cousin, several times ambassador at Constantinople, did what he could to resist Russian encroachments. One of Palmerston's diplomatic masterpieces came in 1840 when the ambitious ruler of Egypt, backed by France, marched northward in a successful attack upon his Turkish overlord. Palmerston and the British fleet intervened, and Turkey was saved.

The Crimean War

"Pam's" popularity rose to its greatest heights during the stupid and useless Crimean War (1854-1856), when England and France supported Turkey in fighting Russia. The fact that British ministries were short-lived, with five different foreign secretaries in fifteen months, probably encouraged the Czar to proceed against Turkey. When he told the British ambassador that Europe had a very sick man on his hands and that

A very early military photograph, taken in 1855, showing the harbor at Bala-clava in the Crimea, with tents and huts of British troops in foreground.

it would be well to consider the disposal of his estate, Britain was put on guard. She joined in nearly a dozen ineffectual efforts for peace, while Russian troops occupied Rumania, and Russia demanded of Turkey full control over the Balkan Christians. Confident of British support, Turkey refused and went to war with Russia. After a Turkish squadron had been annihilated, Britain early in 1854 entered the war, accompanied by France, which had a rather trivial grievance against Russia.

The allies, having blundered into the war, continued to blunder through it. They concentrated their military and naval efforts upon the strong Russian naval base at Sebastopol, on the Crimean peninsula, which juts into the Black Sea. The scene of action was far distant, and their army poorly led, poorly organized, and insufficiently supplied with food and clothes. There were several bloody battles; but the Russians, snugly en-sconced, had for a long time little difficulty in driving off the French and British attacks, and the allies lost heavily in men and morale. Then winter set in, with bitter cold and heavy storms. The commissariat having broken down, there was no hay for the horses, no medicine for the sick, no overcoats for the men. At home the ill-assorted coalition ministry under Aberdeen, who did not approve of the war anyway, made little headway.

In the face of "party anarchy," England clamored for "Pam's" aggressive leadership. He was over seventy, but still a fighter and the public fed upon his noisy patriotism. So he became prime minister and sent recruits, supplies, and munitions to the Black Sea. Finally Sebastopol fell, after allied efforts in which the French outshone the British. The principal tangible results from Britain's only major conflict between Waterloo and the Boer War arose from her own shortcomings. Tennyson's poem "The Charge of the Light Brigade" commemorated one more instance of British valor in a suicidal military blunder; Florence Nightingale's work on behalf of the sick and wounded, in the face of glaring military neglect, was a step toward the founding of the Red Cross; and an eventual thorough overhauling of the nation's military administration obviated some of its gravest defects. The Treaty of Paris, which ended the war in 1856, among other terms, neutralized the Black Sea, from which Russian and Turkish warships were to be barred; but it did not push Russia back from the Balkans and the route to India as decisively as Britain had anticipated (see page 474).

The American Civil War

Except for sixteen months of Conservative government, Palmerston remained prime minister for the rest of his life, with "Little John" Russell as his foreign minister. In 1861, a four-year civil war broke out in the United States between the populous industrial and commercial North and the slave-holding, cotton-growing South. Britain was bound to be concerned in such a conflict. The factories of Lancashire depended on Southern cotton, just as Flanders had once depended on English wool. The South was eager for British recognition of its Confederacy as an independent state, and hoped that the royal navy might break the Northern blockade, slowly strangling Southern economic life. But the North was England's best foreign customer, and Northern grain was beginning to feed Englishmen, though the aggressive Yankees of the North had been giving Britain a close run in the early fifties with a merchant marine almost equal to the British in size and decidedly superior in quality. Britain's upper classes saw in the Southern planters the closest American approach to the English landed aristocracy; her commercial classes saw a chance to weaken a lively business rival. On the other hand, the radicals Cobden and Bright, together with the factory workers of Lancashire, saw in the North the champion of the same democratic principles for which they were contending in England. Palmerston and Russell steered a fairly correct and neutral course, alert for trouble but hoping for peace, though their actions frequently seemed pro-Southern in the eyes of the United States minister at London.

Matters came to a crisis late in 1861, when a Northern cruiser stopped the British mail steamer *Trent* on the high seas and removed two Southern diplomatic agents en route to England. This breach of international law sent British troops rushing to Canada. Palmerston and his colleagues drafted a strong note which might have meant war; but Victoria's dying husband toned it down. The North, losing battles at that stage, could not risk British intervention and disavowed the *Trent* affair. In this whole blockade matter, the Napoleonic situation was reversed (see page 380). Each side could throw back the other's old arguments, but both realized that their roles of blockader and protesting neutral might be reversed again. Britain did aid the South in the matter of the Confederate raiders, particularly the *Alabama,* which was built near Liverpool and allowed to slip away to sea despite protests from the Northern minister. Dread of the raiders sent up insurance rates on Northern shipping; as a result, scores of United States vessels were transferred to British registry, accelerating the decline of the American merchant marine. That fear sent the rates much higher than the actual damage warranted; for such destruction as there was, Britain later paid substantial damages (see page 471). When President Lincoln proclaimed the freedom of the slaves, the English attitude toward the conflict began to change. The tide of war turned in the summer of 1863, and the North emerged victorious in 1865.

In the meantime there were cabinet difficulties. The Liberal party had become a

"BEGGAR MY NEIGHBOUR."

Punch cartoon of 1861 showing Palmerston topping Napoleon III's ironclad warship *Gloire* with the *Warrior* and asking, "Is not Your Majesty tired of this foolish game?"

more compact unit in 1859 with the final adherence of the former liberal Conservative followers of Peel. Its three leaders each came from a different direction: Palmerston was a former Canningite Tory; Russell, an old Whig; and Gladstone, the Chancellor of the Exchequer and future leader of the party, a Peelite. As long as Palmerston lived, there were enough conservative elements in the party to prevent any radical extension of the franchise beyond the 1832 basis. He and Gladstone, however, did lock horns on the rival issues of free trade and military preparedness. In 1860, through the negotiations of Cobden, a free-trade treaty was arranged with France. Gladstone wanted to go farther and repeal the duties on paper, arguing that this constituted a tax on knowledge. Palmerston opposed that additional loss of revenue at the very time when Britain needed to spend heavily for defense to protect herself against what he considered

the dangerous ambition of the French Emperor Napoleon III. The House of Lords, fearful of higher income taxes, retained the paper duties. Gladstone was furious, but his day would come. A new election in 1865 entrenched "Pam," now eighty-one, still further in power; but before the year was out he was dead.

Industry and Exports

A final aspect of the Victorian Compromise was the growing prosperity which characterized the mid century. Thanks to her long head start in the Industrial Revolution, the "workshop of the world" was turning out enough manufactures not only for her own growing needs but most of those of other nations as well. British ships were gaining added profits by distributing these wares, and the surplus capital was being lent abroad to bring back still further riches in the form of interest. In deliberately devoting herself to industry, England, in the repeal of the Corn Laws, had shown a readiness to sacrifice agriculture, but for the time being did not have to pay the price.

The most striking feature of Victorian commerce was that cotton goods formed the most valuable single article of export, while raw cotton led the imports until finally overtaken by foodstuffs. The chancellor might well have changed his woolsack for a bolt of calico to symbolize the new mainstay of British prosperity. The huge hoop skirts and multiple petticoats of the middle decades had something to do with the nearly three billion yards of cotton cloth exported a year. That naturally meant lively business for the plantations of Georgia and Alabama, for the factories of Lancashire, and for the busy seaports of Liverpool, New York, and New Orleans. In 1860, out of £35,000,000 worth of raw cotton, England exported £52,000,000 worth of cotton cloth, yarn, and thread in addition to meeting the heavy domestic demands. By the 1880's, rival factories in Germany, the United States, and elsewhere would be

FOREIGN TRADE OF THE UNITED KINGDOM, 1820-1910
(Showing Principal Articles of Export and Import in Millions of Pounds Sterling)

EXPORTS

	Total	Cotton Goods	Other Textiles	Iron, Steel, etc.	Coal	Re-exports
1820	48	16	6			10
1850	197	28	18	9	1	21
1880	286	75	38	40	8	63
1910	534	105	52	85	37	103

IMPORTS

	Total	Cotton	Wool, Silk, Flax, etc.	Grain and Flour	Meat	Dairy Products	Sugar	Tea
1820	32	2		1			5	2
1850	100	21	9	12	1	1	10	5
1880	411	42	40	66	26	19	22	11
1910	678	71	46	77	48	41	25	11

competitors. Woolen cloth lagged far behind its rival with exports at £16,000,000, less than a third in value. Linen, chiefly from Ireland, followed at £6,600,000, while silk and finished apparel were each £2,400,000.

The sudden boom in iron and steel exports, noticeable in 1860, arose from the invention by Henry Bessemer, four years before, which produced steel cheaply in large quantities (see page 335). For a while, this gave Britain a lead in steel manufacture, with orders pouring in from all directions, particularly for railroad material. Closely associated with iron and steel was the making of machinery, for which the foreign demand was also heavy. Earlier its export had been forbidden to keep its mysteries secret; Huskisson had removed the restrictions (see page 397). Britain now took her profits while she could, even though the products of the exported machines might later compete with her own. Unlike cotton, the raw materials for her iron and steel industry did not have to be imported.

Coal, too, came from England's own "Black Country"; and she gradually increased its export to nations like Italy, with little or no coal of their own. Coal exports were more important than their value indicated; for they gave British shipping a useful outward cargo. Germany and the United States would gradually enter into keen competition in this also.

Among the imports, sugar and tea, two good old "colonial wares," remained fairly steady throughout the century. Far more significant were the import figures for the grain and flour, meat and dairy products formerly produced by Britain herself. In 1830, with agriculture well protected by the Corn Laws, these amounted to only £3,500,000. By 1850 they had risen four fold. British agriculture remained in fairly good condition until the late seventies, when bad crops at home coincided with good crops in the United States, and the invention of the refrigerator ship flooded the market with American beef and Australian mutton. By 1880 food imports had risen to £111,000,000. The landlords at last were feeling the effects of industry's political victory, and Britain was lapsing into that state of dependence upon foreign food which was to render her dangerously vulnerable to blockade. But for the time being, agriculture still had little ground for complaint.

Additional profits in foreign commerce came from Britain's "entrepôt" trade in re-exports. Tea from China, would be brought to London and reshipped to Spain; wine from Spain would be carried by way of England to Brazil or New Zealand; and in such instances England would be the richer from commissions, insurance, freight, and the like.

Geographically the distribution of British foreign trade in 1860 had changed (see page 320). The United States stood first both in imports and in exports; and the well-beaten ocean trail between New York and Liverpool became the most important of sea routes, while both those ports steadily crept up on London, the busiest seaport of the world. Thanks to cotton, imports from the United States amounted to more than the total for the whole British Empire. Out of the total exports of British products (not including re-exports) of 136 (in millions of pounds sterling), the United States bought 21.6 with India next at 16.9, while Australia, Canada, and South Africa combined were only 14.4. The British West Indies, once the pride of the empire, had dwindled to 2.4. Of the European customers, Germany was an easy first at 13.3, while the Latin American total of 10.8 showed the value of Canning's diplomacy.

By 1860, although imports were running ahead of exports, certain "invisible" items indicated that the balance was not "unfavorable," as the old mercantilists would term it. An extremely rich foreign source of British wealth was the interest on capital lent abroad, mainly by the great private banking houses at London (see page 395),

on ventures such as a railroad, a revolution, or a government bond issue in outlying regions. By 1825 British foreign loans have been estimated at about £100,000,000, and by 1885 at more than £1,000,000,000. Railroads were particularly favored; it was said that in 1857 England had invested £80,-000,000 in United States railroads alone, about a quarter of the amount invested in British railways. In such a case the profits of the loan were not limited solely to the interest, for much of the money would probably be spent in Britain for iron, steel, and machinery.

Shipping: Shift to Steam and Iron

Marine freight earnings also constituted another important "invisible" source of wealth from foreign trade, for about three fifths to two thirds of Britain's foreign commerce was carried in her own ships, even after the repeal of the Navigation Acts in 1849. With some bulky commodities like coal and timber, the freight often amounted to more than the original value of the article.

In 1860, Britain had 25,000 sailing vessels totaling 4,000,000 tons, and 2000 steamers totaling 400,000 tons. By 1883, steam tonnage had caught up with sail. By 1900 sailing vessels, both merchantmen and warships, had been crowded out of all important business by steel and steam. After the success of Fulton's *Clermont* in 1807 (see page 345), steamboats had been rapidly adopted for river and harbor work and for other short runs where relief from dependence on the winds was vital. By 1820 they were linking England with Ireland and France. On the high seas, however, regular transatlantic steam navigation only dates from 1838, when, within a few hours of each other, the *Sirius* and *Great Western* arrived at New York from British ports. The following year Parliament granted to a Nova Scotian, Samuel Cunard, a generous annual subsidy to carry the mails from Liverpool to Halifax and Boston, later to

New York. About that same time, another famous British steamship line, the Peninsular and Oriental, cut the time of communication with the East, carrying mails through the Mediterranean to Alexandria, and then by land to Suez, on the Red Sea, whence other steamships continued the trip to India and China. Next came the screw propeller, safer and more powerful than the early paddle wheels, and the iron hull, which relieved shipping of the limitations imposed by the size of timbers, and allowed more cargo space because the sides did not have to be so thick. The introduction of iron, of which she had plenty, in her ships gave Britain a great shipbuilding advantage over the United States, which had hitherto built ships much more cheaply because of her great forests. For long after that, sailing vessels continued to carry the bulk of the ordinary freight, but gradually they were supplanted by steel "tramps." The steamship could make more runs in a year, with greater regularity; and that off-set the fact that coal cost money, while wind was free.

Steam and iron came even more slowly to naval warfare. The Admiralty was conservative, and, since Britain's navy was larger than any other, she was not eager to introduce changes which would render it obsolete. The paddle wheel was too vulnerable for warships, and interfered with the broadside batteries; but the screw propeller, meeting those objections, was introduced into the wooden ships of the line. In the meantime a former Napoleonic colonel was responsible for explosive shells instead of solid shot in naval guns. From the navies the cry went up, "For God's sake, keep out the shells!"; and various nations began to experiment with armor plate. In 1859 the French launched the *Gloire*, the first regular armor-plated warship, and began a big force of such ships. The British for once were worried about their naval supremacy, and despite sceptics in high naval circles, Britain soon had her iron *Warrior* as an answer to the *Gloire*.

Britain was moving slowly in more ways than one toward a vastly different way of thinking and living. Even within two years of Palmerston's death, the landed aristocracy and the middle class themselves opened the doors to political control on a broad democratic basis, although the full impact of this would not make itself felt until the next century. In the meantime, the middle class reaped the major profit from British prosperity; yet the condition of the poor did improve as real wages (the amount of goods which money wages would buy) increased and unemployment decreased. Goods and commodities beyond the reach of the workingman in 1830 were familiar to him thirty years later.

Chapter Twenty-two

Victorian Thought

Victorian thought was nourished and grew to maturity in a bourgeois world where the tempo and quality of cultural achievement depended on the approval of middle-class Englishmen. It was formed in the hurly-burly which marked the onward sweep of the Industrial Revolution, and was profoundly affected by the development of the natural sciences. An intellectual revolution was born as the Industrial Revolution reached a climax. Together the perfected steam engine and the theory of evolution changed profoundly the currents of life and thought.

Science, in the broadest meaning of that word, is the main key to Victorian thought. Applied science—namely, the invention of engines and power machinery—increased the prestige and power of the middle class; pure science—specifically, the conclusions of geologists and biologists as to man's origin—changed the Victorian conception of the universe. Together they, directly or indirectly, colored Victorian literature, religion, art, and philosophy.

Science in industry, in manufacturing, in transportation, and in shipping made the Industrial Revolution the most obvious and the most universal material factor in the life of Victorian England. The attitude of thoughtful men toward these changes is indicated in certain influential writers: John Stuart Mill, the foremost English economist of the nineteenth century; Thomas Carlyle, spokesman for eternal truths; John Ruskin, art critic; Charles Kingsley, blunt yet sentimental Anglican clergyman; Cardinal Manning, of the Roman Catholic Church; and William Morris, the English socialist.

John Stuart Mill

John Stuart Mill (1806-1873) was brought up in extraordinary fashion by his father, James Mill, a fanatical disciple of Bentham (see page 413). From the age of three the lad was drilled on lists of Greek words. His education continued to consist in "storing the mind" with Latin, logic, economics, and history. Novels, music, and physical games were under the ban. The boy's exercise was to walk with his father, who utilized these occasions to discuss with his son his outside reading. Happily the young Mill tore himself loose from this discipline, learned to read poetry and to enjoy it, and fell in love. He became an editor, wrote books, and entered Parliament. A comfortable income from the old East India Company, which he served for more than thirty years, kept him from financial worries.

Mill was, for his time, perhaps the foremost apologist and defender of the middle class, and of the Industrial Revolution which filled its pockets. He did not, however, unreservedly uphold the contemporary economic structure of society; in certain respects he was an advanced thinker and a radical. He approved of trade unions for purposes of collective bargaining. "In that contest of endurance between buyer and seller [of labor]," he wrote, "nothing but a close combination among the employed can give them even a chance of successfully competing against the employers." He even had a kind word to say for the communists of the Continent, afterward called the Marxian Socialists (see page 433), who advocated in one form or another the transfer of the ownership of capital from the few members of the bourgeoisie, or middle class, to the many members of the proletariat, or propertyless class. He went so far as to state, in his *Principles of Political Economy:* ". . . if the institution of private property necessarily carried with it as a consequence, that the produce of labour should be apportioned as we now see it, almost in an inverse ratio to the labour—the largest portions to those who have never worked at all, the next largest to those whose work is almost nominal, and so in a descending scale, the remuneration dwindling as the work grows harder and more disagreeable, until the most fatiguing and exhausting bodily labour cannot count with certainty on being able to earn even the necessaries of life; if this or Communism were the alternative, all the difficulties, great or small, of Communism would be but as dust in the balance."

Mill believed in private property, but looked forward to having it diffused among many more people without a change in the ownership of the fundamental basis of wealth. A better distribution of economic goods was his remedy to be accomplished by peasant proprietorship, heavy taxes on land, and inheritance levies. "It is only in the backward countries of the world," he wrote, "that increased production is still an important object; in those most advanced what is needed is better distribution." Production of wealth, he thought, was determined by natural law, and to production he devoted the first section of his *Principles.* Like his contemporaries he was under the spell cast by Malthus (see page 413) and believed in the ever-present latent danger of a race between population and production. The poor should limit their numbers; would do so of their own accord, he was sure, once they were better educated.

Consequently, to Mill laissez faire in business was a good principle, if not carried too far. He clung fast to self-interest as the dynamo of human activity. If every man were allowed to follow his own interests unhindered, society as a whole would be benefited. "All tendencies on the part of the public authorities to stretch their interference . . . should be regarded with unremitting jealousy." Believing individual liberty was the wellspring of progress, he feared that governmental encroachment on individual lives would make society static. Mill believed in a circle that should be generously defined and sacredly guaranteed "around every individual being which no government, be it that of one, of a few, or of the many, ought to be permitted to overstep." There had never been "more necessity for surrounding individual independence of thought, speech, and conduct with the most powerful defenses, in order to maintain that originality of mind and individuality of character which are the only source of real progress, and of most of the qualities which make the human race much superior to any herd of animals." In other words, governments could and should intervene in the distribution of economic goods, but not in their production, for that would bring inevitable disaster. Mill was in accord with the democratic, liberal reaction to the Industrial Revolution, that private property was one great foundation of personal rights, and laissez faire, within reason, was another.

Thomas Carlyle

Thomas Carlyle (1795-1881) was a Tory, a democrat, and a religious revivalist, all in one. He hated the Industrial Revolution and he fought Benthamism, laissez faire, and individualism tooth and nail. His Toryism was not conservatism, as popularly understood, but rather a vital faith in certain truths, absolute and eternal, which to him must be remembered if England were to live. He was democratic, but at the same time he hated Chartists and scoffed at universal suffrage. Like his fellow Scot, Robert Burns, who wrote, "A man's a man, for a' that," neither rank, nor wealth, nor brains, nor blood, but inherent character determined manhood to his mind. He was also a revivalist; but he did not go to church, nor did he hold with creeds. Yet few in Britain had greater faith in God than did this vitriolic and impassioned writer.

The son of a stonemason, destined for the Kirk, he went to Edinburgh University, taught school and disliked it, found himself unable to stomach any of the numerous brands of Presbyterian theology, and so became a free-lance writer. He was past forty before the world of letters noticed this fiery, independent, and hard-working Scot. Meanwhile he lived a life of bitter poverty, shared by a talented wife; wrote voluminously and well for reviews and periodicals, as chance offered; and on a rough and lonely farm at Craigenputtock compiled *Sartor Resartus* (first published in a periodical, 1833-1834), which attracted little attention at the time. In 1837 his *French Revolution* established his reputation, and was followed by *Past and Present,* a clear criticism of Victorian England, *Oliver Cromwell,* and eventually *Frederick the Great.* *Sartor Resartus* and *Past and Present* are interpretive of the Industrial Revolution in its broadest sense. The former is the more philosophic. It purports to be an explanation of the writings of a Professor Teufelsdröckh of Weissnichtwo, who elaborates a philosophy of clothes. The style is boisterous and gusty, and the meaning obscure, but it had a message for an England confused and baffled by the Industrial Revolution.

"Two men I honour," wrote Carlyle in *Sartor,* "and no third. First, the toilworn Craftsman that with earth-made Implement laboriously conquers the Earth and makes her man's. . . . A second man I honour and still more highly: Him who is seen toiling for the spiritually indispensable; not daily bread, but the bread of Life. . . . These two, in all their degrees, I honour: all else is chaff and dust, which let the wind blow whither it listeth." Carlyle, at once democratic and aristocratic, honored the honest worker, but thought he in turn should seek leadership outside of himself and exalt, honor, and obey the leader.

Although not well received in Britain, *Sartor* was popular in the United States, owing to the influence of Ralph Waldo Emerson. Carlyle felt encouraged; and he and his wife moved to London, there to depend entirely on the slender reed of literature. When the tide turned in his favor, he gave his attention to Cromwell, but he was diverted by contemporary conditions on the eve of the Corn Law repeal (see page 418). Carlyle found himself pulled first to the right in his sympathy with some Tories and then to the left toward certain Radicals. Putting *Cromwell* aside, he wrote *Past and Present* quickly, at white heat, but as the fruit of long thought and passionate feeling. To him there were two Englands: not, as in Disraeli's *Sybil,* an upper England of the possessing classes and a lower of the disinherited, but an England past and present. England past had been crude beyond belief; but at least there had been Englishmen who had ruled, in honor bound to help and to protect those under them. England present was given over to Midas worship. Between man and man there was only payment, either cash or credit. The indolent aristocracy refused to accept the responsibility of "noblesse oblige." The "millocracy," the manufacturers, worked hard, but for themselves only, and they also refused to accept such responsibility. Carlyle told the landed aristocracy, ". . . you did *not* make the Land of England; and by the possession of it, you *are* bound furnish guidance and governance to England!" And again: "My lords and gentlemen —why, it was *you* that were appointed, by the fact and by the theory of your position on the Earth, to 'make and administer laws' . . . you were appointed to preside over the Distribution and Apportionment of the Wages of Work done; and to see well that there went no labourer without his hire . . ."

Past and Present made few specific proposals for bettering society. Carlyle refused to write on the unrepealed Corn Laws, which he considered too absurd to survive much longer. He favored more stringent factory acts, high standards of living, the encouragement of emigration, and large sums for education. All these remedies he hinted at, but left practical details to others because his heart was absorbed in his one great theory of life: that some were born to rule, others to obey, and that great men of heroic mold must arise, seize power, and prove worthy of it. This idea is discussed in his *Heroes and Hero Worship.*

John Ruskin

John Ruskin (1819-1900) represents the reaction of the artist to the Industrial Revolution. Ruskin was a childlike, petted, talented, and lovable person, the only son of a frugal wine merchant who left him his large fortune. After Oxford, the young Ruskin traveled extensively and expensively, particularly in Italy, and wrote voluminous essays on painting, sculpture, and architecture. He came to know almost everyone who was worth knowing in contemporary England, and was extraordinarily popular as the prophet of new principles of beauty and aesthetics. He objected to the Indus-

trial Revolution because it was physically ugly and carried with it false spiritual values. In his criticism of the new industrial age and in his aesthetic approach, he was a forerunner of and an influence upon the Age of Decadence of the 1890's (see pages 503 ff.). He was not only a critic of artists but told businessmen how to run their affairs, professors what to teach, writers how to write, architects how to build houses, economists the why and the wherefore of their science, workmen how to use their spare time, women how to conduct themselves, and clergymen how to interpret the will of God.

In 1869, appointed to the Slade Professorship of Art at Oxford, he quickly became its most popular lecturer. Crowds came to hear him interpret the painters of the Renaissance; but whether he lectured on Botticelli, Alpine flowers, or religion, his appeal to youth was magnetic and diversified. Young Arnold Toynbee drew from him the inspiration to establish university settlements; and young Cecil Rhodes was inspired to paint the map of South Africa red (see page 529).

Charles Kingsley

Charles Kingsley (1819-1875) is the best known clerical writer on the subject of the Industrial Revolution, and his economic ideas typify those held by the Broad Church group in the Church of England. In character he was a true John Bull, hale and hearty, pugnacious, and honest. Kingsley began his career in a poor agricultural parish, where he became angry at the way in which agricultural laborers were treated. Excited by the Chartist agitation, he joined with a number of the younger clergy in a "Proclamation to the Workmen of England," counseling against violence, but friendly and full of sympathy. Kingsley wrote many tracts and novels, such as *Yeast, Alton Locke, Westward Ho! Hereward the Wake,* and other contemporary best sellers, and was appointed professor of history at Cambridge and canon of Westminster.

No one was left in doubt as to his views. "I assert," he said, "that the business for which God sends a Christian priest into a Christian nation is to preach and practice liberty, equality and brotherhood, in the fullest, deepest, widest, simplest meaning of those great words . . . All systems of society which favor the accumulation of capital in a few hands, which oust the masses from the soil which their forefathers possessed of old, which reduce them to the level of serfs and day-laborers . . . or deny them a permanent stake in the Commonwealth, are contrary to the kingdom of God which Jesus proclaimed." Here was the essence of the Christian Socialism in which he believed. The bishops of the Church of England, for the most part, did not like this preaching, but they were powerless to stop it. By speech and by pen Kingsley drove his message home. In *Cheap Clothes and Nasty*, he paid his respects to sweatshop methods in the tailoring trade: "The charming Miss C—is swept off by typhus or scarlatina, and her parents talk about 'God's heavy judgment and visitation.' Had they tracked the girl's new riding habit back to the stifling undrained hovel where it served as a blanket to the fever-stricken slopworker, they would have seen *why* God had visited them." In *Yeast*, he portrayed the degradation of English village life. In *Alton Locke*, he attacked conditions in a factory town.

All this created a sensation at the time. The Christian Socialists were of some prominence, and were regarded with more approval than dismay by the ruling classes, probably because they were harmless. Their remedy for England's troubles lay in co-operative shops, manufacturing enterprises in which workmen supplied the capital or had it given to them by charitable men of wealth, and in substituting the blessed word "association" for the evil term "competition." They did some good by calling attention to the leaky roofs of thatched cottages and by pointing out that sewage was something which concerned society; but they did not succeed, as Kingsley had hoped, in convincing many people that Christianity and Socialism should be married. The Church of England was on the defensive at this time against the tendency of German scholarship to weaken belief the authority of the Scriptures. Kingsley and his allies were identified with the new advanced criticism; and partly on that account they were regarded with suspicion by those who held to the old theology, no matter how they might regard the new economics.

Cardinal Manning

Cardinal Manning (1808-1892) ranks with Kingsley as a clerical foe of the Industrial Revolution. Manning did not write much; but since he came to head the Catholic Church in England, his voice, to many, was more authoritative than that of an Anglican priest. As an Anglican clergyman, Manning had written bitterly of Newman's desertion of the Church of England and he had seen eye to eye on ecclesiastical matters with his friend Gladstone (see pages 414 ff.). Then Manning became an ardent Roman Catholic and an enemy of religious liberalism and of all English Catholics tinctured with it. Newman, whom he had attacked as a renegade Anglican, he now scorned for maintaining independent views as a Catholic. With the majority of English Catholics the new convert was unpopular; but the Pope, Pius IX, nevertheless appointed him a cardinal, believing that English Catholics needed discipline. The new cardinal drew tight the ecclesiastical reins, and stifled practically all discussion in Catholic circles.

But in all that had to do with economics Manning was radical. Now that he was head of the Roman Church in England he found that the great majority of his flock consisted of Irish immigrants, the poorest of the poor, ignored by the trade unions, and without guidance or hope. He delivered a celebrated lecture on the Rights and Dignities of Labor, which echoed the Marxian socialistic theory that all wealth comes from labor, that all men were entitled to work, and that society must provide it for them. "There is the absolute necessity of raising up and easing the labor of men in such a way that their lives may be human lives. . . . Long hours render . . . domestic life impossible." Manning's influence was impaired partly by his autocratic temper, his stern belief in discipline and authority, and his dislike and distrust of trade unions, but he took a prominent part in housing and educational reform, and at the time of the great strike of London dockers (see page 486) his was the most influential voice in favor of those downtrodden men.

William Morris

William Morris (1834-1896), the best-known English socialist of the late Victorian period, apparently never went to church, and there is no indication that he was influenced by the Christian example. Yet few men have ever loved their fellows more than this great, red-bearded man, born a gentleman yet by choice a craftsman. Morris was poet, novelist, painter, designer, architect, furniture-maker, and socialist. He was well-to-do, went to Oxford, became a friend of Burne-Jones and Rossetti, the "Pre-Raphaelite" painters, wrote easy-flowing poetry, and decided that the Industrial Revolution had made England ugly. He founded a firm to make beautiful things, such as murals, stained glass, metalwork, and furniture; he wanted to substitute simplicity and honesty for ostentation, and to seek after the beautiful in all things.

Literature supplanted furniture as his ruling passion. He wrote long poems on early medieval and Icelandic themes, and became interested in old manuscripts and in all that had to do with books, the art of printing, and the designing of new fonts of type. Rough, hearty, full-blooded, warmhearted, his interests eventually included a solicitude for the way in which the contemporary English lived and lured him into politics, first as a Liberal, then as a Socialist.

Not a "Utopian" like Robert Owen (see page 391), he followed rather hazily the new socialism of the German economist Karl Marx, which had just begun tardily to make its influence felt in England. Unlike the "Utopian" socialism, which aimed to establish a new organization of society, with more equitable opportunities for all, through the example of ideal communities, this was called scientific, because Marx stressed an "economic interpretation" of history which emphasized the influence of economic factors upon historical events. According to Marx, the age-old struggle between different social classes was at last converging into a two-sided conflict between the bourgeoisie, who owned capital, and the proletariat, who owned nothing but their own labor. With the growth of industry since the Industrial Revolution, Marx declared, capital was becoming concentrated in fewer and fewer hands, while at the same time the proletariat was steadily increasing in numbers. Marx did not want to end the private ownership of personal things, but attacked the private ownership of capital, or the wealth—such as land, mines, and factories—that is used to produce more wealth. Believing in an inevitable class struggle, he called on the workers to unite under an international revolutionary organization for the purpose of overthrowing the capitalistic organization of society. The *Communist Manifesto*, which he wrote in collaboration with another German economist, Engels, in 1848, but which stirred little comment in that year of revolutions, concludes with this ringing call: "The proletarians have nothing to lose but their chains. They have a world to win. Working men of all countries, unite!"

Morris considered himself a revolutionary socialist; but what he really wanted was to make the life of the poor clean, sweet, and beautiful. He hated railway trains, steamships, and the Industrial Revolution, commerce, ledgers, and the stock exchange, and he worshiped old England, old inns, old songs, and the old leisure. Lacking a wide knowledge of economics, he wanted to end a social system in which the people who did the most work had the hardest lot and to create a society characterized by honest craftsmanship and simple living. This he would achieve not by dividing the wealth but by ending surplus production and the fierce competition to create new markets, often for absurd, ostentatious, and useless goods. He at first joined the Democratic Federation (later the Social Democratic Federation), the English organization of Marxian socialists, but soon quarreled with its founder and Britain's foremost Marxian, Henry M. Hyndman (see page 487). Hyndman wanted to build up a political party, but Morris wanted revolution to attain the ends of socialism. Even today Morris would be classified as a left-wing socialist, using "left" to mean radical in contrast to "right," or conservative. He had scant patience with the idealistic Fabian Society of socialists, with its noted membership, which wanted to introduce social changes piece by piece through gradual legislation. As he wrote, "no program is worthy the acceptance of the working classes that stops short of the abolition of private property in the means of production. Any other program is misleading and dishonest." Seceding from the Social Democratic Federation, Morris founded the Socialist League. This in turn fell a prey to dissensions, and Morris quit it to found the Hammersmith Socialist Society; at its meetings, fiery young Bernard Shaw disputed with the now elderly Morris. He kept on addressing street meetings, waving red flags, publishing militant poems, subsidizing socialist magazines, and spreading propaganda until his death.

There were few authors and thinkers of any degree of eminence who did not regard the social results of the Industrial Revolution as highly unfortunate. Macaulay, the historian, refers only here and there in his book reviews to the new golden age, which he was inclined to regard as a marvelous era. To thoughtful and cultured Victorians the steam engine was seemingly a tribulation as well as a blessing, and the changes which followed in its wake perplexed and troubled them.

Darwin, Huxley, and Evolution

The theory of evolution filled the imagination and perturbed the thought of the Victorians almost as much as did the Industrial Revolution. This period was one of scientific activity, with many eminent names such as Faraday and Lister; but it was the theory of evolution that changed a static Newtonian world into a world of continuous change and development. Evolution was primarily associated with the life and work of Charles Darwin (1809-1882). After his day, man's belief in fixed, scientific laws, such as the law of gravitation, was broadened by a belief in evolution, modification, and adaptation to environment.

More then twenty years before Darwin published his famous *Origin of Species*, Sir Charles Lyell inferentially had hinted at evolution in his geology, and for years Darwin had been studying, in minute detail, fossils, barnacles, coral reefs, and pigeons. Slowly scientists had laid the foundations for the Darwinian theory; but of this the lay world knew nothing, and it awoke with a start when it read Darwin, who revolutionized man's entire conception of the universe. Galileo's telescope had done something of this sort when it demonstrated that the sun, not the earth, was the center of all things. Then came Darwin; and if what he taught was true, the Biblical account of creation was a myth. If life had developed slowly and gradually into a myriad of species out of earlier and simpler forms, it was dubious whether a Divine Creator had made every species of living thing and, separately and above all, man.

Darwin did not prove, in the sense that two and two make four, that the different species of animal life developed out of earlier forms. He did, however, amass a great deal of evidence to show the probability of such a thesis; and when the biologists applied it to man and drew attention to the similarities between man and the other mammals, the profound implication of this hypothesis had tremendous repercussions in both literary and religious circles. This new idea seemed to destroy hope for survival after death and to make it rather difficult to designate the particular stage in evolution when the soul was acquired. Victorian England was interested in evolution and its implications, and many nonfiction writers sooner or later had something to say on the subject. This is true of Huxley the biologist, Spencer the philosopher, Matthew Arnold the poet and critic, and Tennyson the poet laureate.

Thomas Henry Huxley (1825-1895) was the foremost exponent. "Darwin's bulldog," to use Huxley's description of himself, acted as the interpreter of the gentle biologist to a hostile and skeptical world. The layman reading Darwin's *Origin of Species* is soon bewildered by technicalities and scientific terms, but in Huxley's prose Darwin's conclusions are set forth simply and clearly.

Entering the royal navy as a surgeon at twenty-one, Huxley was assigned to a ship outward bound to make surveys in Australian waters. The youthful doctor's study of tropical marine life won his election to the Royal Society. Resigning from the navy, he accepted a chair at the London School of Mines. His rise in the world of science was rapid; a devoted worker and the author of a steady stream of scientific articles, he was one of three whom Darwin consulted about the publication of *The Origin of Species*. "If I can convince Huxley," said Darwin, "I shall be content."

Huxley thus became Darwin's popularizer and defender before the British public. At an Oxford meeting of British scientists in 1860, Bishop Wilberforce, suave, authoritative, and powerful, attempted to drown Darwin's theory in a flood of sarcasm. "And now," said the bishop in triumphant conclusion, "do you trace your monkey ancestry on your father's side or on your mother's?" "I would rather," replied Huxley, "be descended from the humble ape than to trace my ancestry to one who used his ability and position to discredit and to crush those who sought after truth."

Huxley called himself an agnostic, that is, one who refuses to affirm or deny the existence of God. Devoted to the discovery of truth, he thought of science as the only key to a better world. He felt that once science was given its proper place in the schools of England, civilization would become vitalized. In his inimitable lecture on *Evolution and Ethics* one sentence sums up his whole philosophy of life: "Let us understand, once for all, that the ethical progress of society depends not on imitating the cosmic process, still less in running away from it, but in combating it." In other words, man's first duty is to fight nature, and to do this he has one weapon—science.

Herbert Spencer (1820-1903) was the philosophic interpreter of biological evolution. In his *Synthetic Philosophy* he applied Darwinian theories to social institutions in order to explain their development. As a boy Spencer was stubborn and refractory, and made slight use of such meager educational advantages as his lower-middle-class environment offered. He disliked the classics and refused to study them. He served as a civil engineer on a railway-construction project. Abandoning this work for journalism, he wrote many articles for the reviews, and in 1850 published his first book, *Social Statics*. Within ten years his reputation had secured him several thousand dollars raised in the United States as advance payment for the great philosophy, not yet written. The ultimate publication of his *Synthetic Philosophy* was hailed as an important occasion, but the glory was short, and it is now all but forgotten.

Spencer believed it was possible to study humanity in the same way that Darwin studied pigeons, if only one were sufficiently rigid in excluding personalities, and were at the same time sufficiently exact in weighing verifiable fact. He never avoided facts; indeed he employed others to seek out and to classify more facts, with which his books are stored. The philosopher demonstrated to his own satisfaction that there was such a thing as a social science, embracing all human relationships. Social science took the biological principle of adaptation to environment and boldly applied it both to prehistory and to recorded history.

Spencer widened the application of laissez faire from economics to almost every form of human activity, believing that any interference with the individual was spoon-feeding the multitude and that "a creature not energetic enough to maintain itself must die." So widespread was his influence that Justice Holmes, of the United States Supreme Court, considered that the ideas of Spencer's *Social Statics* had become embedded in the decisions of that body. The majority of those educated in his day were thoroughly imbued with his sturdy individualism. He renewed for many faith in the potentialities of individual freedom, and also a hope that history offered possibilities for discovering laws governing conduct. For science was then making glorious strides, and to Spencer's contemporaries it held the promise of a new Jerusalem here on earth.

Matthew Arnold (1822-1888) was probably the most celebrated of the many in Britain who wished to apply evolutionary principles to religion. Just as the study of primitive forms of life by Darwin and Huxley led to biological evolution, and speculation concerning primitive social and political ideas made many believe with Spencer in social and political evolution, so did the detailed analysis of the Bible, and of the literary materials used in its composition, lead to an evolutionary interpretation of religion. It was Arnold's brilliant role to popularize this scholarship.

Arnold was the son of a famous headmaster of Rugby, a clergyman who held that some parts of the Bible were not inspired. The boy, going beyond his father in this direction, became the center of religious controversy. An essayist and poet, he was professor of poetry at Oxford; and later became an authority on secondary education. Throughout his life he was fascinated by the Bible, and his *Literature and Dogma* has become a landmark in its interpretation.

Arnold believed that people had been taught to accept the Bible too literally; they should instead "perceive that it is literature; and that its words are used, like the words of common life, of poetry and eloquence, approximately, and not like the terms of science, adequately." "What is called theology," he said, "is in fact an immense misunderstanding of the Bible, due to the junction of a talent for abstract reasoning combined with much literary experience." Arnold wished to cast aside the vast theoretical superstructure of religion and return to the original wellspring of inspiration: Jesus. He believed in neither prophecy nor miracles. In his opinion, miracles were comparatively insignificant in estimating the worth of Christ's message, and Christianity probably would have been better off without the rumor of their occurrence. "To profit fully by the New Testament the first thing to be done is to make it perfectly clear to oneself that its reporters could and did err. . . . To know accurately the history of our documents is impossible, and even if it were possible we should yet not know accurately what Jesus said or did." Arnold's ideas started a fight which still continues, especially in the various Protestant churches.

Alfred, Lord Tennyson

Finally, there was Alfred, Lord Tennyson (1809-1892), whose poetry, more than that of Rossetti, Arnold, or even Robert Browning, reflected the quintessence of Victorian ideals. Tennyson, poet laureate by royal patent, has borne the brunt of the anti-Victorian attack. Assaults have been made upon his old-maidishness. Objections have been raised to the long theological discussion in *In Memoriam,* and the *Idylls of the King* have been criticized as merely a romantic escape from the drab environment of industrialism. To all this there is some truth: Victorians, perplexed by their environment, sought another world in Tennyson's poetry. *In Memoriam,* written to commemorate Tennyson's friend, Arthur Henry Hallam, is inordinately long; but the Victorians did not mind, for to doubt the immortality of the soul on biological grounds was something new in Victorian England.

Tennyson's first poems were published in 1827, but he was not made poet laureate until 1850. Then, seeking privacy, he went to live on the Isle of Wight, where his home promptly became a Mecca for all English-speaking people. After twenty-two years here, he sought refuge in rural Sussex, to be rid of the crowds. For two more decades poems poured forth from his new retreat, while his fame increased.

His contemporary popularity is not to be accounted for purely on poetic grounds. His name overshadowed that of his contemporaries (with the exception of Browning) primarily because what he wrote coincided nicely with what middle-class Englishmen chose to believe and feel. They always had stressed the family as an institution. Both the children of the aristocracy, largely educated away from home, and the children of the working class were thrown on their own resources too early, and did not usually worship the family in the same intimate way as the middle-class family, which stayed at home. The middle class thoroughly believed in the Victorian compromise, and so did Tennyson. Freedom, precedent, and settled ways of government expressed his ideas and those of his readers. Both were bewildered by biology and demanded a message which would soothe their religious doubts. Tennyson wished to reconcile religion with evolution: "God must exist, because the human heart felt an instinctive need for his existence. The soul must be immortal, because any other solution was unthinkable."

The foregoing eleven writers offer a fair résumé of Victorian thought. The vogue of the novel was at its height in Victorian times, but novels were read for pleasure rather than for enlightenment. The middle class grew indignant with Dickens over the treatment of Oliver Twist, shed tears of laughter over Pickwick, and tears of sorrow over Little Nell. It enjoyed Thackeray, especially appreciating the cleverness of Becky Sharp in *Vanity Fair;* but all this did not involve thinking about what was right and just in the world, let alone speculating on the eternities.

Later writers, inoculated with Marxian doctrines, have not regarded the Victorians highly. Since capitalism in all the vigor of its early manhood characterized the Victorian day, that in itself is a signal for many to flay the bourgeoisie. One may point to the jerry-built slums of Glasgow, Birmingham, and Manchester, to the ostentatious furniture, to the somewhat crude and literal paintings of Watt (who covered canvas by the square yard), in order to justify an indictment of Victorian England. "I found myself," wrote Edward Carpenter, the poet, "in the middle of that strange period of human evolution, the Victorian age, which in some respects, one now thinks, marked the lowest ebb of modern civilized society: a period in which not only commercialism in public life, but cant in religion, pure materialism in science, futility in social convention, the worship of stocks and shares, the starving of the human heart, the denial of the human body and its needs, the huddling concealment of the body in clothes, the 'impure hush' on matters of sex, class-division, contempt of manual labor, and the cruel barring of women from every natural and useful expression of their lives, were carried to an extremity of folly difficult for us now to realize."[1]

Even Carlyle could find no harsher words than these to fling at his fellow Victorians. Yet, during Victoria's long reign, a little island set the pace for all mankind in industry, in law, in elevating the character and the dignity of the poor, in the advance of science, in spreading the Christian religion and Parliamentary institutions in all parts of the earth. Distant lands were peopled with Anglo-Saxons, and the dread of war grew less. In view of such accomplishments more and more appreciation is being given to the Victorians.

[1] Edward Carpenter, *My Days and Dreams* (1918), p. 320. By permission of George Allen & Unwin, Ltd.

The Changing Empire

In 1783, with the loss of the thirteen colonies, the British government also lost for a while some of its enthusiasm for empire. Britain had no desire to spend another £110,000,000 in a vain effort to hold unwilling members within the imperial family. The colonies were under a cloud; they were likened to fruit which dropped off when it became ripe, or to ungrateful children who ran away from home as soon as they were big enough. Why, then, men asked, should further British blood and treasure be wasted in gaining and defending overseas lands? At the outbreak of the American Revolution, the "Old Empire" had been at its height; by the mid-1870's, Britain, like several other powers, would be on the threshold of the imperialistic scramble in Africa and Asia. The intervening years saw the transitional "Second British Empire."

England still had a respectable overseas empire left in 1783. Jamaica, Barbados, and more than a dozen lesser islands in the West Indies, scarcely started on their long decline from sugar prosperity, were far more profitable than the other remaining American holdings of Canada, Newfoundland, Hudson Bay, the Maritime Provinces, Bermuda, and the Bahamas. There was Gibraltar, still guarding the Mediterranean; a few pestilential holdings in West Africa;

lonely St. Helena, far down in the South Atlantic; and India, with Bengal representing the first step inland. By 1815, England also had her spoils from the Napoleonic Wars, taken mainly for strategic purposes, ranging from Malta to the Caribbean, from Good Hope to Ceylon (see page 387). Compared with the remains of the other colonial empires, these were impressive. By that time, Spain's vast holdings in America were beginning to break loose in revolution; Portugal's Brazil would soon be free, leaving her only some shadowy remnants in Africa and Asia; Holland still had the rich spice islands, but little else; and France's empire had dwindled to not much more than some sugar islands and other scattered posts (see page 315).

The Second British Empire

The Second British Empire, differing in several respects from the Old Empire, presents a strange anomaly for nearly a century after the peace treaty of 1783. In contrast to the aggressive zeal of the elder Pitt and the later nineteenth century imperialists, there was far less official initiative in extending colonies; yet large new areas of the world map became colored in British red. A major readjustment involved the overhauling of the rigid mercantilistic commercial regulations; this eventually led to the opening of colonial ports to foreign trade and the abolition of the East India Company's long commercial monopoly (see page 454). Wholesale migrations, particularly to Canada and Australia, led among other things to increasing self-government for the colonies of settlement. The new humanitarian attitude brought activity in behalf of subject colonial peoples. Out of these varying features developed two opposing viewpoints. Some eager "colonial reformers" achieved new policies in colonizing and in colonial government, but a larger group of influential free trade supporters became "Little Englanders" who felt that the colonies of settlement no longer justified their expensive administration and defense.

Changes in Commercial Policy

The close of the American Revolution necessitated the first commercial changes. As foreigners now, the former American colonists could no longer send their vessels in the old triangular trade with Jamaica and the other sugar islands, which suffered keenly from the loss of that cheap supply of flour and fish (see page 320). The notorious "mutiny on the Bounty" in 1789 occurred during a British effort to secure a substitute food supply in the newly discovered breadfruit from Tahiti. The United States, no longer a colony forced to buy all her imports from Britain or to send thither all her tobacco and other enumerated articles, quickly developed direct trade with the Baltic, the Mediterranean, and other parts of the world. Her trade with India and China was particularly galling to most Britons, who were barred from those ports by the East India Company's commercial monopoly. Their vehement protests led to the ending of that monopoly in 1813 with India and 1833 with China. Also until the final repeal in 1849 of the Navigation Acts, which had called for British-built ships only for British registry. British shipowners

could no longer buy cheap wooden ships from American yards as in pre-Revolutionary days. Shipyards in Canada and the Maritime provinces were to help fill that gap, however, in time.

Far more sweeping were the colonial economic changes of 1825 as part of Huskisson's important steps toward free trade (see page 395). The rigid old mercantilistic regulations, aimed at a self-sufficient empire, had forced the colonies to buy everything they needed from England and to send many of their special products there (see page 263). Now the colonies were permitted to trade freely with foreign countries. For a while, certain colonial products, such as West Indian sugar and Canadian lumber and grain, were admitted to England at preferential duties lower than from foreign countries, but eventually those also went. Likewise, with that final repeal of the Navigation Acts in 1849, foreign vessels were even admitted to the trade between the colonies and Britain herself. The fact that the mother country no longer enjoyed the old monopolistic privileges in colonial trade was one of the arguments against keeping the colonies.

Emigration

In the wave of migration between 1815 and 1870, more than seven million people left the British Isles to settle beyond the seas. Although some two-thirds of these went to the United States, more than a million settled in Canada and a similar number in Australia and New Zealand, with smaller numbers in South Africa and elsewhere. Not since early Stuart days had there been such an impressive emigration. Even before the "hungry forties," economic distress and fast-increasing population were leading large numbers to try their fortunes in distant temperate regions where land was plentiful. The government looked favorably upon the movement, and local authorities often found it preferable to pay the fares to Quebec or Sydney rather than build more poorhouses. Eventually, the colonial reformers would devise systems whereby the proceeds of land sales could be used to bring out the "right sort" of settlers, particularly to Australia and New Zealand. By mid-century Britain was granting a degree of self-government, far beyond anything in the Old Empire, to these rapidly growing colonies of settlement (see pages 447, 458).

Humanitarianism and Slavery

At the end of the eighteenth century, as byproducts of the new evangelical movement (see page 354) came various humanitarian efforts, particularly to abolish slavery and to save the souls of the heathen. This so-called humanitarianism aimed at achieving a more humane relationship with the black, brown, and yellow peoples with whom the expanding empire might come in contact, and was akin to the reform movement at home in behalf of the underprivileged. Its leaders, sometimes dubbed the "Saints," were substantial and politically influential, often able to secure potent support from colonial secretaries and others in authority. In addition to the abolition of the slave trade and slavery, and missionary activities, much good resulted from the Parliamentary committee on the aborigines' problems in South Africa and New Zealand, sponsored by Thomas Buxton in 1835 (see pages 457, 447).

Although Britain herself had long been involved with both the slave trade and colonial Negro slavery, British humanitarianism was nowhere more strikingly evident than in its attack on those twin problems. Down through the eighteenth century, most of the colonial powers had maintained African slaving posts to supply their Caribbean and mainland American plantations; but it was Britain's trading posts on the Guinea Coast, her swarms of Liverpool and Bristol slave ships, and her rich sugar colonies that had been most successful in this lucrative exploitation of the unfortunate

blacks. Then suddenly, in 1807, Parliament, with William Wilberforce primarily responsible, abolished the slave trade, one of the final achievements of the Whig liberal Charles James Fox (see page 387). Not only had Britain decided to forego those high profits—slavery's turn would come next—but also to influence other nations to do likewise. The United States formally abolished the trade the following year; and at the Congress of Vienna, Britain received the agreement of the other nations, but it was half-hearted at best.

Down through the next half century British cruisers attempted to stamp out slaving in the West Africa-America sphere, despite the ravages of the pestilential climate and technical difficulties over the right of search. Britain even annexed Lagos, eventually the capital of Nigeria, to check the traffic. The Portuguese, with constant slave demands in Brazil, were the worst offenders; the Spaniards also, wanting slaves for Cuba and Puerto Rico, failed to cooperate. The United States was finally persuaded to give naval assistance in checking the trade, but with her strong Southern political influence, this was not too effective, and some Americans engaged in slave running, too. Long after this area ceased to be a problem, the trade continued in the East Africa-Arabia region despite constant efforts by British naval forces to curtail this also.

On the other hand, British colonial slavery was abolished at one stroke in 1833, effective in 1834. This was a further step in which Britain took self-denying action. Except for some Hottentots and other Negroes enslaved by the Boers in South Africa, the bulk of the 750,000 slaves were owned in Jamaica, Barbados, Antigua, and the other sugar colonies, where the loss of that slave labor would hurt the economy badly. Wilberforce was in the forefront of this effort also. The politically powerful West India planters delayed the legislation by their tenacious resistance to losing their valuable human property. Wilberforce, worn out by the struggle, was succeeded by Buxton, who first moved to free the Negroes in 1822. He collected an extraordinary mass of information to prove that in some cases at least Negroes were brutally treated on British plantations. He related that an expectant Negro mother had been punished for a trivial offense by 170 lashes; that other Negro women had been branded on their breasts. In 1815 a young slave who ran away to his mother "was hanged for endeavoring to rob his owner; his mother was imprisoned for life for receiving stolen goods." All Buxton asked was that Negroes born after a certain date be declared free. Canning approved this, but did not care to antagonize the planters. In consequence only a few reforms materialized in the crown colonies which did not have strong colonial legislatures like Jamaica. After the passage of the Reform Bill, however, antislavery agitation began again. As slaves were property, it was considered unfair to the owners to emancipate them at one stroke. Parliament, having rejected Buxton's scheme, proposed another, which in modified form became the emancipation law. It provided an apprenticeship stage of seven years, during which three quarters of the Negroes' time was to be at the service of the owners, who were to receive in addition £20,000,000. Despite gloomy prophecies, there was no accompanying bloodshed, but freeing the slaves was to accelerate the decline of the Caribbean sugar colonies from their former high prosperity and to lead the South African Boers to move inland (see pages 458, 457).

The Missionaries

Most continuous and widespread of the humanitarian efforts in the empire came from Britain's sudden entry into the mission field. In British colonization, commerce had always far outranked the other usual motives of conquest and conversion. The last had been more conspicuously lacking in the Old Empire than in the early colonizing activities of the Catholic powers with their Jesuits and other orders. Wholesale conversions had been conducted by Saint Francis Xavier in the Portuguese East; by Spanish missionaries in America, where the Jesuits in Paraguay and the Franciscans in California set up states with conversion as the primary motive; and by the French Jesuits in New France, where some of them suffered martyrdom at the hands of the Iroquois. Religion, to be sure, had considerable to do with the founding of New England; but the Puritans, except for a few missionaries like Eliot, gave scant thought for the souls of the Indians. British missionary activity is generally considered to have begun in 1792 when William Carey, cobbler, Baptist preacher, naturalist, and linguist, published his *Enquiry into the Obligations of Christians to use Means for the Conversion of the Heathens.* Within a few years, with the formation of missionary societies by various sects, the movement had grown so rapidly that missionaries were numbered by the thousands. Carey himself went out to India for forty years of remarkable work, although the East India Company had refused him passage on any of its ships because it did not want "any interference with the religion of the natives." While the saving of souls was their prime motive, missionaries were often teachers and doctors also. They also tried to stamp out barbarous customs. In India they helped to end both "suttee," whereby widows, either voluntarily or under the pressure of custom, were burned alive on their husband's funeral pyres, and also the sacrifice of infants. In the Fiji Islands they tried to bring humane ideas to the old chief who had set up 852 headstones, each for a human being he had eaten; and they interfered to prevent the strangling of another chief's principal wives when he died. In New Zealand too, they fought against cannibalism. Constant tribulations and setbacks were their lot, but every now and then came the triumphant report, "The natives are fully clothed and in their right minds." Some Lancashire manufacturers are said to have contributed liberally to the missionary societies because this pious concealing of nakedness meant a tremendous new market for English textiles. The Colonial Office might favor the missionaries at times, but the officials and settlers out in the colonies frequently found their activity an embarrassment.

The Colonial Reformers

Meanwhile, concerned about colonial settlement and administration, various reformers, such as Lord Durham of Canadian fame and the ubiquitous Edward Gibbon Wakefield, were making fresh approaches to those problems. Overseas possessions, except for India with its own form of control, were directed from what came to be called the Colonial Office, which differed little from the machinery of the Old Empire. At first a sort of administrative stepchild, the rather neglected part-time job of a lesser cabinet member, it was later to have a full time cabinet member as Colonial Secretary. The actual management of most of the details had been in the hands of a few officials, who followed the routine with little imagination. It was these men, checking up on colonial legislation, reading petitions, and handing out lucrative sinecures, who managed the far-flung organization of empire. Parliament, which had been paying scant attention, was now to be harassed by the criticisms of individual colonial reformers, who often held differing views. As one of these wrote: "Parliament exercises in fact hardly the slightest control over the administration of the laws for the colonies. In nine cases out of ten, it merely registers the edicts of the Colonial Office. . . . In some back room . . . you will find all the mother country which really exercises supremacy and really maintains connexion with the vast and widely scattered colonies of Britain. We know not the name or func-tions of the individual into the narrow limits of whose person we find the mother country shrunk." But when the establishment of the new post of permanent under-secretary in 1837, which was a step toward the desired closer control, ended this anonymity to a degree, then the reformers turned on its first incumbent as a fresh target for criticism. This was James Stephen, who had a long record of participation in the humanitarian group, especially for the end of slavery. According to a later verdict, he was an efficient administrator, whose impact "on colonial policy and administration during those formative years can hardly be overestimated." But some of the reformers, impatient at his rigidity, dubbed him "Mr. Over Secretary" and "Mr. Mother Country." Also exerting pressure on Parliament, but from a negative angle, was the larger group of "Little Englanders." To them, now that Britain had given up her special advantages in colonial trade, the colonies of settlement cost too much in administration and defense to keep. No matter how much the apathetic colonial administration or this group might say, "Go Slow," hardy settlers kept pushing across the plains of Canada, out toward the blue mountains in Australia, and in Africa inland from the Cape, while traders and missionaries clamored for the protection of the flag as they moved ever farther afield.

Cook's Voyages and Australia

Almost simultaneously with the loss of the American colonies a new part of the world was opened to British expansion in the South Seas, as the southern Pacific is called. Those waters and islands, discovered long before, had seemed to offer scant prospects of commercial profit. Widespread interest in them dates from the three naval voyages of Captain James Cook, between 1768 and 1779. He was originally sent out in the little *Endeavour* on a scientific mission, taking naturalists along to study the flora and fauna of the region.

First European contact with South Sea glamor: Captain Samuel Wallis of H.M.S. *Dolphin* greeted by Queen Purea of Tahiti in 1767, two years before Cook's visit.

After a successful astronomical observation at his primary objective, Tahiti, and the discovery of the idyllic charm of its native existence, Cook pushed westward to New Zealand, and then continued to the eastern coast of Australia. In 1772, going out on a second voyage, he spent three years crossing and recrossing the South Pacific to disprove the theory of a great southern continent. On his third voyage he discovered the Hawaiian Islands and fur trade possibilities of the American Northwest Coast. After passing through Bering Strait he returned to the Hawaiian Islands, where he was killed in a minor scuffle with the natives. His journals, when published, quickened popular interest in the South Seas.

Within ten years, his explorations bore fruit in the first colonization of Australia. This smallest of the continents, or largest of the islands, almost equal in size to the continental United States without Alaska,

had been visited several times previously, particularly by the Dutchman Tasman in 1642; but Holland had seen no possibility of profit in a colony there. A considerable part of Australia was desert, its northern tip reaching nearly to the equator, and the natives were perhaps the most backward on the face of the earth. The southeastern corner was a promising, temperate region, suitable as a "white man's country." Sir Joseph Banks, who had accompanied Cook on his first voyage, was particularly impressed with the possibilities of what he named Botany Bay, in the district which Cook, because of superficial resemblances, called New South Wales.

In 1787 the British government took one of its few positive steps toward extending colonization in this period by establishing a penal colony there. For more than a century it had been customary to commute death sentences to transportation to the colonies. The southern American colonies had received a large number of criminals, but now that outlet was shut off. The prisons became congested, and even the overflow prisons in old ships moored in the Thames were crowded. News reached England that France was preparing to send an expedition to the South Seas, possibly with colonization in mind. Botany Bay seemed to offer a chance to kill two birds with one stone: prison congestion would be relieved, and England might secure a strategic foothold in the new region of interest. Accordingly, a naval captain in the spring of 1787 headed for Botany Bay with an expedition which included about 750 convicts and some marine guards. They arrived early in 1788, but quickly moved to a better bay nearby, where the settlement named for Lord Sydney, the minister in charge of colonial affairs, came into being. Six days later the French expedition appeared on the scene. Whatever its intentions may have been, it departed after an exchange of greetings and was never heard from again.

The convicts were of all sorts: desperate criminals, men and women convicted of minor delinquencies, and not a few innocent persons who had been convicted wrongfully. It was customary, after the transported men had finished serving their term as prisoners, to assign them as laborers to the free settlers, who followed later. While still on parole, they were called "ticket-of-leave men;" once fully free, they became "emancipists."

The difficulties inherent in such a system were obvious. Many prisoners escaping to the wilds became bushrangers, and lawlessness was prevalent. "In 1833, when the population was about 60,000, there were sixty-nine death sentences."

Only gradually did New South Wales shake off its status as a penal colony. Australians might jokingly say, "We left our country for our country's good"; but they were eager to demonstrate that original convict stock died out and that most old families of Australia were descended from the honest sheep-raisers who followed them. A captain of the guards in early convict days noticed that the land seemed suitable for sheep-raising, and sent back for some merino sheep, whose wool commanded a high price because of its fineness. The woolsack became as symbolic of the basis of prosperity in modern Australia as it had been in medieval England. A free population, composed partly of soldiers of the guard whose enlistments had expired and partly of direct free immigrants from Britain, gradually overshadowed the convicts. During the early years of New South Wales the colonial governor was a naval or army officer with almost dictatorial power. One of these, the same Captain William Bligh, whose crew on the *Bounty* had set him adrift in those same seas, again provoked mutiny and was deposed by the colonists. Gradually the government became that of a regular crown colony.

From the first settlement, Sydney, soon the capital of New South Wales, explorers went forth in every direction, paving the way for what would become five more colonies, besides the original New South Wales. At the southeast corner developed the small but populous Victoria, with its capital at Melbourne. Beyond along the south coast came South Australia, with Adelaide. Out on the distant west coast, the British raised their flag just in time to forestall the French, and slowly built up Western Australia, with Perth as its capital. Northward, up the east coast toward the hot tropics was Queensland, with Brisbane. The sixth was the island colony of Van Diemen's Land (Tasmania), with Hobart.

The transportation of convicts to New South Wales ceased in 1840, and when the government tried to revive it nine years later, the aroused populace would not let them land. When Van Diemen's Land finally got rid of them in 1853, it changed its name to Tasmania in honor of its Dutch

Sydney, New South Wales, in 1802, from the west side of the "Cove."

discoverer. The government then considered South Africa as a dumping ground; Cape Town's grateful residents named their main street for the colonial reformer in Parliament who blocked this. While Australian settlers as a whole resented convict competition, the big landowners welcomed the cheapness of convict labor; and for that reason Western Australia continued to receive them until 1868.

Everywhere near the coast the land seemed fertile, so that the prospects were bright that Australia might provide for Britain's surplus people. That at once raised the question of how best to attract them. In Western Australia, on the Swan River, the mistake was made of granting huge tracts of land to private interests, who made some general promises about bringing out settlers. The project was poorly planned and the colony got off to a very slow start.

To South Australia came Wakefield, the most influential of the colonial refomers. A one-time young man of fashion, he had been sent to prison for abducting a sixteen-year-old heiress from her school and marrying her. While in prison in 1829, he turned his mind to the linking of colonial land sales with the attracting of proper settlers. He sought to apply his theory of colonization, popular at the time: land should be sold by the crown at a fairly high price and should never be given away, and the proceeds should be applied to a colonization fund to pay the traveling expenses of future immigrants. If the land were held at a fairly high figure, it was argued, the laborers would save money to buy land of their own. An orderly and conservative society, capable of self-government, would result, and an immigration fund, steadily augmenting, would bring in a constant flow of new settlers. The Colonial Office approved such a settlement in the colony of South Australia, with its capital at Adelaide, named for the queen of William IV, but it was not a success. Suspecting that among the promoters there were radicals and republicans, the Colonial Office gave only the granting of land titles to the company's commissioners, and kept control of the government, which led to friction between commissioners and the governor. Too many settlers dashed to Adelaide before farms could be surveyed. Badly managed, the colony was rescued from insolvency only by the able administration of Sir George Grey, who on several occasions saved other colonies in distress.

In 1851 boom days suddenly came to Australia. Just as the keen eye of an army captain had laid one foundation of Australian prosperity by deciding that the land looked good for sheep-raising, so now a prospector, fresh from the mad gold rush in California, decided that there might be gold in the hills of New South Wales. He was right: gold was found not only at Bathurst but also in various other parts of Australia. All normal work stopped. Sheep-raisers, storekeepers, clerks, and laborers all dashed to the gold fields to try for sudden riches. The clipper ships, built for the California gold rush, now brought new hordes of adventurers to Australia, and for a while there was difficulty in absorbing the wild swarm of riotous newcomers. But, as in the case of California, prosperity and increased population resulted. There were barely a quarter million colonists in Australia at the beginning of 1851; within a decade an additional half million had joined them. So much did the wealth, the importance, and the population of the six separate colonies increase, that within ten years all but Western Australia were granted self-government on the Canadian model (see page 461). Western Australia was kept in leading strings until 1890, since her scanty and scattered population did not seem to warrant such a degree of freedom. The original use of a secret ballot by voters occurred in 1856, first in Victoria, then in South Australia; New South Wales adopted it within two years. This Australian ballot became the usual voting method in democratic nations (see page 470).

New Zealand

By the time of the Australian gold rush, British colonization was making rapid progress on the large, beautiful twin islands, twelve hundred miles to the southeast, named by Tasman for the Dutch province of Zealand. Cook had visited them in 1769 and had noted the fertility of the valleys among the mountains. With their temperate and healthful climate, they were ideally suited for what they eventually became, the most characteristically British of all the overseas colonies of settlement. But New Zealand was far from that in the first quarter of the nineteenth century. Several thousand lawless whites had drifted to the islands—whalers, traders, escaped convicts, and other unregulated and irregular elements—held down by no law or authority and engaged in high-handed transactions with the native Maoris. Whereas the Australian natives represented the lowest form of development, the Maoris, like the American Indians, were among the strongest and most self-reliant of the races encountered by European civilization, and were tough fighters. A third group in those early days were the missionaries, who were trying to save the natives from the white man's rapacity for land and who were also working to curb the Maori taste for human flesh. The home government long resisted efforts to bring New Zealand under the British flag, and it went its lawless way until the actual planting of regular English settlers necessitated more definite control.

The colonization of New Zealand was carried out by middle-class British citizens under the spell of Wakefield's teachings. Displeased with his experience in South Australia, he had withdrawn from that enterprise and started another company, to colonize New Zealand. Because of the influence of the missionaries who considered that white colonization there would seriously hamper their labors, the Colonial Office refused to sanction the enterprise. The New Zealand Company, however, began to do business without a charter, dispatching a ship to New Zealand to make treaties with native chiefs for the purchase of land. French activity in the area then brought action; the government sent an officer who, early in 1840, hoisted the British flag and signed a treaty with the natives whereby the sovereignty of New Zealand passed to the crown, in return for which Her Majesty guaranteed the Maoris full ownership of their land unless they chose to sell it. On the south island, he was only a week ahead of the French. The company meanwhile had become popular in England with influential persons like Lord Durham, the colonial reformer, who became interested in its success, and in 1841 it received a charter.

The occupation of New Zealand went on apace during the next ten years. Wakefield secured the support of the religious groups by suggesting that they buy land from his company to establish semireligious settlements. A number of Scottish Presbyterians founded Dunedin, later famous as the point of departure for South Polar expeditions, while Anglicans named their settlement Canterbury. Nelson and Wellington were founded, directly under the company's auspices. Wakefield and his associates had made New Zealand; but the company was not to last a decade. It had trouble with the civil authorities; with its own settlers; and with the native chiefs, who found that the land which they had sold for a song was resold at a much higher rate.

Again it was Sir George Grey who put this colony also on a firm foundation (see page 447). His unfailing tact and firmness stood New Zealand in good stead during its formative years. It was given a generous measure of self-government in 1853. Shortly after came two wars with the Maoris, who were stalwart fighters and did not propose to see their tribal lands occupied by the whites, even if papers were signed to this effect. Their resistance was finally broken in 1864, and the rebellious chiefs were fined heavily. Since that time most of the Maoris have stayed on their reservations and have even slightly increased in number. Some, on the other hand, have been successful in business and professions, one becoming deputy premier.

This deliberately planned and regulated but unofficial colonization produced excellent results. The growth was steady, but not abnormal as it had been in Australia. In 1841, the year after New Zealand was taken officially into the empire, there were 6000 settlers; three years later, 15,000; and by 1865, 172,000. Of all the dominions since the loss of the thirteen colonies, New Zealand had the most purely homogeneous British stock. Partly for that reason and partly because of its isolation, it was to become one of the most loyal of all the overseas lands.

Expansion in India

In India, the most important of the colonies of exploitation, Warren Hastings, after organizing the government of Bengal on a stable basis under grave handicaps (see page 321), returned to England in 1785. Like Clive, he was faced by a bitter attack in Parliament for alleged unethical and highhanded acts, particularly in extorting large sums from natives by force. Burke led the Commons in a demand for impeachment, and another brilliant Irish orator, Sheridan, joined in heaping moral invectives upon Hastings; he was impeached on twenty-two counts in 1788. The trial before the House of Lords dragged on for years but he was eventually acquitted on all counts. Unlike Clive, he bore the sustained attack resolutely, thoroughly convinced of his own rectitude. The trial, however, left him financially impoverished, and he retired to the country, cheated of the peerage and other honors which his work in Bengal had certainly merited.

Pitt pushed through Parliament an India Act in 1784 much more thoroughgoing than North's Regulating Act of 1773 which had asserted Parliament's authority over the East India Company, without devising adequate machinery for exercising that control. With politics continuing to encroach upon trade in India, it seemed increasingly unwise for a trading organization to have command of a situation involving foreign complications and other considerations of national importance. Pitt's act of 1784 preserved the nominal authority of the East India Company while giving actual control of policy to the cabinet. The Court of Directors of the Company still kept up the appearances of rule, retaining in their hands the extensive patronage and management of the commercial affairs; but in all other matters the important decisions were to be made by a political Board of Control, dominated by its president, who was to be a member of the cabinet. That office went to Pitt's friend Dundas, the political boss of Scotland (see page 370). To all intents and purposes, he was the Board of Control. The governor-general at Calcutta, with authority over Bombay and Madras, was given increased authority. This act remained the basis of British rule until the end of the East India Company in 1858. By that time most of the Company's original justification for existence had gone; for in 1813 it lost its commercial monopoly, except the China trade, and that also was taken away in 1833.

The first governor-general sent out under the new act was Lord Cornwallis. Georgian England sometimes showed a strange sense of reward and punishment. Clive and Hastings, who laid the foundations of British power in India, came back to face humiliating attacks. Cornwallis, who had lost the American colonies by allowing himself to be trapped at Yorktown, was sent to Cal-

cutta to succeed Hastings. At any rate, Cornwallis did a much better job at Calcutta than he had done at Yorktown. He rounded out the work which Hastings had commenced in the administration of Bengal, in particular, placing on a permanent basis the land revenue, the chief form of taxation. The new regulation relieved the natives of the capricious rapacity of the native tax-collectors, whose rates had often fluctuated violently from year to year. With rates on a permanent basis, the Company could count upon some £2,750,000 a year from Bengal.

Cornwallis also retrieved part of the military reputation he had lost in Virginia. One of the hostile native threats to England's foothold in India was the state of Mysore, in the southwest. It had been seized by a Moslem adventurer who had fought Hastings and whose son Tippoo, now challenged Cornwallis. Moving against Mysore, Cornwallis was so successful in the field that Tippoo gave half his territory to the British to save his capital from being stormed. Cornwallis had no trouble with the other hostile element, the powerful Hindu confederacy of Maratha chieftains, whose various allied states formed a broad band across central India and which menaced Bombay in Hastings' time. He had sent Bengal troops to the rescue, and for twenty years thereafter the Marathas were relatively quiet. England had further trouble ahead, however, both with Mysore and the Marathas. Cornwallis returned home in 1793 and shortly became Lord Lieutenant of Ireland. For five years little happened in India.

In 1798, the future Marquess Wellesley arrived in Calcutta with a deliberately aggressive policy which aimed at nothing short of making British power paramount in the Indian peninsula. French intrigue was once more active at Mysore and among the Marathas, as it had been in Hastings's time. French officers were training their native troops, while Napoleon's Egyptian campaign was a distant threat against

British rule in India. Wellesley magnified the dignity of his office, engaging in constant pageantry to impress the natives; but India was impressed even more deeply by the spectacular success of British arms. Armies closed in on Mysore from two directions in 1799; Seringapatam was captured, and Tippoo died fighting valiantly to stem the final rush. Then Wellesley's younger brother, a colonel later the Duke of Wellington, inflicted some smashing defeats on the Marathas. They were brought partly under British influence, but would require further beatings. Wellesley also put pressure on several native rulers to place their states under British protection. Before his recall in 1805, because the Company considered his policy too costly and aggressive, British rule or influence had extended over more than a third of India, including not only Bengal and certain lands stretching westward up the Ganges, but also all the eastern coast and all the southern part of the peninsula. Whatever the authorities at home might desire, Wellesley had committed England to his policy of dominating all India. The huge central block of Maratha territory still remained relatively independent; but a third Maratha war, waged under another governor-general, finally brought that too under England's influence (see map, page 314).

As established at that time the British *raj*, or rule, in India long consisted partly of direct rule over certain territory and partly of indirect control over numerous native states. Bengal was the original example of the direct rule. Eventually "British India," including about sixty per cent of the territory and eighty per cent of the population of all India, came under this direct rule. First the officials of the East India Company, and later those of the crown, administered the region under direct rule, collecting taxes, dispensing justice, maintaining army and police, and performing the other necessary functions of government. The land tax was the principal financial support

of this entire region. It might amount to a quarter of the peasant's annual income, but it was no heavier than under native rule; and the British gave far more in return.

Native princes continued to maintain all the outward pomp and circumstance of rule in the protected states under indirect control until after India became independent in 1947. Altogether, there were seven hundred of these, of which the largest was Hyderabad. A British political "resident" remained in constant attendance as an adviser and as a check upon their actions. Their armies were under British supervision, sometimes officered by Englishmen. They were forbidden to make outside alliances or to employ foreign officers or advisers without British consent. In case of misbehavior or misrule such rulers were subject to deposition, and Britain later removed several, including two of the most powerful. Within these limitations native rulers were free to tax and to judge their subjects as they pleased. Because of their fabulous store of wealth in its most concrete form—gold, silver, and rare jewels—several Indian princes were reckoned among the world's wealthiest men. The system of indirect control was of mutual advantage: the British suzerainty guaranteed a prince against the old violence of intrigue and revolution, and Britain was relieved of the direct burden of administration. The native princes' subjects, however, had fewer of the civilizing benefits of the West than those in British India.

The close of the third Maratha war, in 1818, brought a temporary lull in fighting, and for a while attention was concentrated upon improving the condition of the Indian people, principally within the region of direct control. Most of the population was desperately poor; even under the best circumstances they were only able to scratch a bare subsistence from the soil. And when the annual rains failed in the interior, famines took a terrible toll. The British helped to relieve, if not to eliminate this threat, by digging canals to improve irrigation and railways to carry grain from the more fortunate regions. The latter meant a greatly increased market for Britain's rails, bridges, and rolling stock, thus enhancing India's economic desirability. Lord William Bentinck, governor-general from 1828 to 1835, made particular progress. The old Hindu practice of suttee or widow-burning (see page 442) had been attacked by the missionaries for some time and was finally prohibited by decree in 1829. Bentinck also stamped out the evil practices of the Thugs, assassins who engaged in wholesale killings as part of the worship of Kali, a goddess of death and destruction. During his beneficent administration Thomas Babington Macaulay, later famous historian, poet, and essayist, came out to Calcutta as adviser. Knowing nothing of Oriental tongues and despising them, he recommended that English be used in Indian education. Its adoption introduced the future leaders of India to English history and literature, thus giving the Indians a common tongue as well as nursing them in the traditions of English liberty, a lesson which they were to apply later to their own land, to the annoyance of their teachers.

Those Indian students might become the future leaders of India, but the immediate masters were the young Britons of the Indian civil service. Few governmental bodies in history have maintained a higher quality of personnel. Ignorant and lazy appointees might be sent by the Colonial Office to fill Caribbean sinecures; but even Dundas, that past master of patronage, in distributing Indian jobs among his deserving Scots picked first-rate material. The responsibilities were tremendous. Many officials were needed to administer regions under British direct control; others served as residents at the courts of native princes. Force, tact, and character were necessary in either case. Frequently a youth in his twenties might be the only white man within a radius of fifty miles or more, and the success of British rule in that

A magistrate of the Indian Civil Service holding court in Oudh in 1853, just four years before the Sepoy Mutiny.

region might depend upon his quick thinking or force of personality in an emergency. The Indians, with their ancient culture, were keen to sense a man's true character, and no small part of Britain's success in India depended upon the intrinsic worth of her responsible representatives there. She could not rule by force, having less than a hundred thousand white troops and a few thousand civil officials to maintain ascendancy over a vast region which even then was approaching a population of three hundred million. There were about a quarter of a million sepoy troops, to be sure; but they, in turn, depended upon the leadership of their few white officers. Consequently the quality of the Indian civil service was of the utmost importance.

Time and again during the second quarter of the nineteenth century the governors-general extended the Indian frontiers. In 1824 Lord Amherst, nephew of Lord Jeffrey, sent forces to conquer part of the old Indo-Chinese kingdom of Burma, across the Bay of Bengal from Calcutta; and later expeditions extended British authority in that region. But to the northwest of India the Afghans were tougher fighters than the Burmese. The Himalayas, the loftiest mountains in the world, gave India magnificent natural protection all across the northern frontier, but there were several narrow passes in the northwest through which Alexander the Great, the Moguls, and other invaders had come in the past, and beyond those passes lay Afghanistan. Now the specter of Russian invasion arose before the British officials at London and Calcutta. During the Napoleonic period, after absorbing the province of Georgia, south of the Black Sea, Russia had carried her expansion to the southeast to occupy the oases in the desert north of Aghanistan. Now a mixed force of Russians and Persians was attacking Herat, in western Afghanistan. To Britain this seemed to threaten a continued advance to the Himalayan passes and the valley of the Indus beyond. Against Russia's huge armies up there in the hills the royal navy, the chief defensive force, would be of no avail. Kabul, the Afghan capital, became a center of intrigue. The new ruler, or *amir,* who had vast troubles with his unruly tribesmen was also quarreling, among others, with the Sikhs, the puritanical and warlike Hindus in the Punjab, a part of northwest India not yet under British control. The British governor-general considered it more desirable to remain friendly to the Sikhs than to assist the distant amir, so the latter suddenly turned from Britain to Russia. His intrigues led to the first Afghan war (1838-1842) and to the occupation of Kabul by Anglo-Indian troops. The British found it easy to occupy Afghanistan, but unpleasant to stay there. The Afghans were ill-disposed to them and to their old ruler, whom British arms had restored. The British marked time while a nasty revolt threatened their army outside

Kabul. Trusting to the guarantees of the rebels, they finally retreated. Some 4500 fighting men and 12,000 camp followers were caught in the narrow defiles of the Afghan mountains. Only one man survived to tell the tale; the rest were victims either of the snow or of Afghan knives and bullets. To rescue the garrisons still there the British sent a punitive expedition to Kabul and burned the bazaars; then they returned to India. Afghanistan remained a buffer state between British and Russian expansionist ambitions; and forty years later, a second Afghan war repeated the story of murder and punitive expedition.

In the late eighteen-forties, two wars fought with the fierce bearded Sikhs, the best fighting men in India, brought the Punjab and Kashmir in the northwest corner under British rule. The large protected state of Oudh, on the upper Ganges, was absorbed into British India in 1856 according to a policy adopted by the British toward the protected native princes. This resembled the old feudal escheat, whereby a vassal's fief was taken over by the suzerain if he died without heirs or if he seriously misbehaved. Oudh had been badly misgoverned, and had no regular heir. Its annexation aroused widespread grumbling among the Indians. That same year the son of George Canning, about to sail for India to take up his duties as governor-general, made a prophetic remark at a farewell banquet of the Company directors: "I cannot forget that in the sky of India, serene as it is, a small cloud may arise, no larger than a man's hand, but which, growing larger and larger, may at last threaten to burst and overwhelm us with ruin."

The Sepoy Mutiny

The next year the British *raj* was shaken to its foundations. The repeated annexations of territory were not the only causes of native unrest. Macaulay's system of English education contributed something to the ferment. The Hindus, with a religion centuries older than Christianity, resented 'the energetic labors of the missionaries. A conservative country, skeptical of innovations, was mystified and worried by surveys for irrigation to improve the water supply, while the belching locomotives of India's first railway, built in 1854, heightened the apprehension. There was, moreover, a legend that British rule would only last a century, and it was exactly a hundred years since Clive had seized Bengal in 1757.

The immediate source of trouble lay among the sepoys, that quarter of a million of native troops trained in European methods and commanded by British officers. The proportion of sepoys to white troops in India had been increasing until it had become nearly six to one. The Crimean War had brought with it rumors of British decline. The Afghan war had wounded the religious susceptibilities of many sepoys. Now orders came that the sepoys to re-enlist must agree to serve across the salt water, which the Hindus believed would cause them to lose caste. The spark which set off the explosion seemed extremely trifling to European minds. The British army was replacing the inefficient old smoothbore "Brown Bess" muskets (see page 305) with the more accurate Enfield rifles, which were still muzzleloaders. The rifle cartridge, consisting of a paper pouch and containing the powder charge, was fastened to the bullet, greased to slip into the narrow bore. In order to load, the soldier held the bullet in his teeth, tore off the paper, poured in the powder, and then rammed in the bullet. Word spread among the sepoys that the grease on the bullets was beef or pork fat. That aroused both the Hindus, to whom the cow was sacred, and the Moslems, to whom the pig was unclean. They scented a plot to discredit them with their own religions and then make Christians of them.

Part of a cavalry regiment at Meerut, near the old Mogul capital at Delhi, refused to accept the cartridges in April, 1857. Thereupon they were arrested and sentenced to ten years' imprisonment. The other sepoys at the station rose in revolt, freed the prisoners, and shot most of the officers. The commanders of the white troops there lost a chance to nip the Sepoy Mutiny in the bud, and the whole valley of the upper Ganges was quickly aflame. At Delhi the sepoys and the mob killed most of the English, and a revival of the Mogul Empire was proclaimed. The British, taken unawares, were temporarily paralyzed, shut up in their cantonments. The most horrible atrocities occurred at Cawnpore, a border post of Oudh on the Ganges, where some four hundred English and eighty loyal natives, protected merely by a rough embankment, held out for three weeks in June against thousands of sepoys led by the Nana Sahib, the "archvillain of the Mutiny." Finally they surrendered, upon Nana's promise of safe conduct; but just as they were getting into their boats the entire garrison was massacred. Some two hundred women and children were spared for the moment; but later, as relief was approaching, they too were hacked to pieces and thrown down a well. The white garrison at Lucknow, the capital of Oudh, was more fortunate. Caught unprepared, the force of less than a thousand redcoats, assisted by loyal sepoys and civilians, fought for two whole months behind a rambling line of defenses. "Do not negotiate, but rather perish by the sword" was the word sent them; and they had nearly reached the end of their resistance when the distant sound of Highland bagpipes told them of Sir Henry Havelock's timely arrival with reinforcements.

The mutiny collapsed as rapidly as it began. Had all India, or even all the sepoys, joined the revolt, British dominion might have disappeared overnight. But most of the native princes remained loyal; and the Sikhs, those stout soldiers of the Punjab who had been conquered only twelve years before, showed their appreciation of kind British treatment and joined in the suppres-

Until 1947, the British flag flew over the Lucknow residency, battered in the Mutiny siege.

sion of the insurrection. British vengeance rested heavily on the mutineers. Thousands were hanged, and many were blown to bits from the mouths of cannon—a particularly terrible punishment, as the Hindus believed that the bodies could never be reassembled for the future life.

One particular victim of the Mutiny was the East India Company. Its prerogatives had been gradually shorn from it at various times since the days of North and Pitt. Now, in 1858, the "Honourable John Company," chartered by Queen Elizabeth, ended its existence. The British government took over responsibility for India in the name of the crown. The president of the Board of Control became the Secretary of State for India, and the governor-general was hereafter known as viceroy. The essential features of the system of rule, however, continued much as before, and Indian history was uneventful for some time to come.

The commercial interests in England welcomed the news that expansionist wars would cease in India with the British raj extended over the whole peninsula. In that period of skepticism about the economic value of most of the other overseas possessions, there was little question about the importance of India in British trade. India's earlier role of furnishing England with finished cotton goods (see page 228) was now completely reversed, with about one tenth of England's total exports going to India, which consumed, in particular, roughly one third of the Lancashire cotton cloth. Indian railroads, too, used British iron; altogether, India was becoming a market essential to Britain's whole economic system.

The Opening of China

The East India Company had long linked India with China, where it had had a monopoly of the British trade. From the early seventeenth century the English had tried to obtain a share in the lucrative China trade. Eventually the Company's "country" ships began to carry tea, silks, and "china" ware from Canton to India, whence they were sent to England. China, however, remained indifferent and almost hostile to this outside intercourse, except for a brief interlude about 1685. The foreigners found all Chinese ports closed except Canton, where they were forced to deal through the medium of specified Chinese "hong" merchants and were hindered by numerous other restrictions. China regarded herself as the "Middle Kingdom," or center of the universe, to which the outside "barbarians" brought tribute. Unimpressed by the achievements of the Western nations, they showed no interest in British diplomatic efforts to open more ports to commerce. In 1792 Lord Macartney, on such a diplomatic mission, was carried up the river on a craft with the inscription "tribute-bearer to the Emperor." He had to follow the emperor into the interior; and even when he found him, he was refused an audience unless he would perform the humble bowing gesture of kowtow. That was a bitter pill for a proud British peer; but he finally compromised on bending his knee. Even that brought no trade concessions; and Lord Amherst, a few years later, was not even permitted an audience.

The East India Company, however, continued to do a thriving business through Canton. Instead of having to bring silver or furs to exchange for tea, as the Americans usually did, it sent Indian opium, although from 1800 opium importation was forbidden by the Chinese government. The Company's monopoly of this opium trade ended in 1833, when other British merchants, and Americans as well, were permitted by England to carry Indian opium to China. Gathered at Canton, these unruly newcomers grew restive under the old, strict regulations that had been accepted by the servants of the East India Company. The Chinese announced that the newly arriving merchants must select a "head man" to do their negotiating with Chinese merchants. England, although fully aware what the Chinese meant, tried to use this situation to open direct diplomatic relations with the government; but in vain. Meanwhile opium was coming into China in increasing quantities; and the Chinese, disturbed at the consequent debauching of the people, without warning ordered their officials at Canton to confiscate all the drug they could find. Chests of British opium, grown in India, to the value of several millions were destroyed. In addition, the mandarin at Canton, infuriated by the inability or unwillingness of an English captain to turn over to Chinese justice one of his crew, launched a fireship against the British fleet. The reprisal came swiftly. Canton was bombarded; several Chinese forts were captured; and the Chinese, awakened at last to the effectiveness of Western methods, were compelled to yield. In the Treaty of Nanking, which ended this "Opium War" in 1842, Britain kept the island of Hong Kong, already occupied, which has remained a British colony. Shanghai and some other "treaty ports" were opened to trade with consular representation. At these ports extraterritoriality, by which foreigners were to be under the jurisdiction of their own laws and courts, was established because of the strange methods of Chinese justice, a privilege soon extended to the Americans and other foreigners. The Chinese naturally resented this concession, which Europeans had long enjoyed in Turkey. A supplementary treaty contained the "most favored nation" clause, by which China promised England a share in any privileges granted to other foreign nations. As this clause was also incorporated by France, the United States, and other powers in their later treaties, it did much to facilitate future foreign-trade expansion in China.

There was less justification for Britain's action in the second war (1858-1860). As a result of continuous piracy on the Chinese coast, bad blood between the Chinese and British continued. It reached the boiling point when the *Arrow*, manned by Chinese and flying the British flag as a result of former British registry, was seized by Chinese officials. A sharp British ultimatum, only partly met, brought on a new war. The French, enraged at the murder of a missionary, cooperated as allies of the British. The war dragged on until French and British soldiers finally marched on Peking and sacked the Imperial Palace in retaliation for the firing on a flag of truce by the Chinese and their brutal kidnaping and torturing of French and British negotiators. The treaty gave England and other nations a further entering wedge in Chinese trade.

It happened that anarchy was brewing in China at the time of that second British war. Known as the Taiping Rebellion, this disturbance centered in the valley of the Yangtze and threatened the lives and property of foreigners living in Shanghai, the treaty port. The European and American inhabitants there, in co-operation with Chinese officials, organized a miscellaneous force for defense, at first commanded by an American and then by Major Charles George Gordon, one of England's most popular military heroes (see page 527). His ancestors had fought for Prince Charlie in the "Forty-five" and for King George before Quebec. He himself had been in the Crimean War and now was to win the name of "Chinese Gordon" for the triumph of this "Ever-Victorious Army," composed mainly of Chinese that crushed the Taipings within a few years. The end of the rebellion saw the British, as well as other foreigners, firmly entrenched in Shanghai. Side by side with the old Chinese town of that name there now grew up rapidly a modern European and American city. Although built originally on swampy ground leased to the foreigners at a nominal rent, it soon outdistanced the old Chinese city. The new Shanghai became autonomous in all municipal matters, with separate courts, police force, and taxation. Before the end of the century it began to vie with Hong Kong as the center of British commerce in the Far East.

Between those two Chinese wars an American naval squadron had made two visits to Japan and had persuaded her to end her hermit isolation; and, just as the United States shared in the advantages England had won in China, so England shared in the American concessions gained in Japan. Thus were laid the foundations of the Far Eastern problem, which was to become the center of imperial attention at the end of the century.

Raffles and Singapore

Shortly after 1815 Britain had taken steps to safeguard the route between India and China. After her seizure during the Napoleonic Wars of the Dutch spice islands, in the East Indies, a very able colonial administrator, Sir Stamford Raffles, governed Java in masterly fashion. The islands were restored to Holland after the peace, but Raffles felt that England should keep a foothold in that region. Castlereagh and the East India Company did not favor his projects, but certain British commercial interests supported them. He cruised along the Malay coast, looking for a proper site, and finally hit upon the island of Singapore, at the tip of the Malay Peninsula. It was ceded in 1819 by a native sultan; and the surrounding "Straits Settlements" soon became a British colony, subordinate at first to the East India Company. Raffles had chosen the site of Singapore wisely; for, commanding the passage from the China Sea into the Indian Ocean, it became the foremost trading center of that part of the East and a naval base of high importance for a long time (see page 639).

South Africa

Though the British restored the spice islands to Holland in 1814, they retained for strategic reasons two other Dutch possessions which they had occupied. Ceylon, the big island off the southern tip of India, would present few problems, but the Cape Colony in South Africa would give continuing trouble arising from the interrelationships of Britons, Boers, and African natives.

The opening of the Suez Canal robbed the Cape Colony, at the southern tip of Africa, of most of the strategic value for which England had taken it from Holland during the Napoleonic Wars. As long as shipping had had to make its way around Africa, Cape Town was naturally a point of importance for the refitting of Indiamen and for naval control on the important sea route. Discovered by Dias in 1488, the Cape had been shunned as a land post by the Portuguese; but in 1652 the Dutch had taken possession of it and established Cape Town. The climate was favorable to a "white man's country," and gradually a colony of settlement developed at the Cape. Dutchmen as well as French Huguenots, who gradually adopted Dutch speech and ways, came out in considerable numbers. Many became farmers, or *boers*, and slaugh-

Typical wagon in which the Boers moved inland in the Great Trek, c. 1836.

tered or enslaved the native Hottentots. These Boers or Afrikaners remained the most numerous European element there. There were about 25,000 of them when England took over the Cape in 1795. It was restored by the Peace of Amiens, but was seized again in 1806, British title being confirmed in 1814 (see page 387). At that time the future of the colony did not seem bright. The Boers were disgruntled, and there was frequent fighting with the native Kaffirs. Britain soon made one of her few official efforts to send out free colonists. To strengthen the British element and to offset the Boers, some four thousand well-selected settlers, including many artisans, were taken to the Cape at government expense and planted to the northeast of Cape Town at Port Elizabeth. Like the later Durban in Natal, this settlement had a lasting influence in giving a distinctive British tone to that particular region in spite of the general Boer preponderance in South Africa.

Many of the Boers soon withdrew to the interior. They had resented outside control even in the days of the Dutch East India Company's rule. They were already ill-disposed toward their new British overlords when, in 1833, Parliament freed all the slaves in the British colonies (see page 441). This action infuriated the Boers, since payment granted them in compensation for their slaves could be collected only in London, and since they felt, furthermore, that it was wholly inadequate. Selling their land

for what it would bring on the spot, a large number of them with their belongings in oxcarts "trekked" away from the British. The exodus was not a mass movement; some went to the north beyond the Orange River and farther northward beyond the Vaal River. Some headed eastward to the region on the Indian Ocean called Natal by Vasco da Gama, but there they had been forestalled by the British. There was sharp fighting, and the Boers moved inland.

The British government was in a quandary. Since the Boers were technically British subjects, it was Britain's duty to defend all these scattered white men from the warlike natives. It was also her duty to defend the natives from the highhanded Boers, and back in England, the humanitarian "Saints" were taking an interest in these "aborigines." The expense of doing this, however, would be great; and since the Boers cared nothing for the British connection, Britain consequently proclaimed the independence of the South African Republic (the Transvaal), a vast region beyond the Vaal River in 1852. Two years later the Boers remaining in the region between the Orange and the Vaal River were likewise given independence as the Orange Free State. The political setup of South Africa was at last definitely outlined: two British colonies (the Cape and Natal) occupying the coast line and two Boer republics in the interior, the latter surrounded by a ring of native African tribesmen.

The two British colonies made headway slowly. Sir George Grey, of Australian and New Zealand fame, making his rounds as a governor throughout the British world, helped somewhat in settling troubles with the native chieftains. Representative institutions were established at the Cape in 1854; and responsible government came there in 1872, rather against the wishes of the inhabitants, who did not like the withdrawal of imperial troops which it implied.

British contacts with tropical Africa were still scattered and informal. Much of the "Dark Continent" was unexplored until after mid-century and even along the coast there were only occasional trading posts and missions. On the Guinea Coast in West Africa the humanitarian pressure led Britain to a complete reversal of her traditional role in the slave trade, in which Liverpool had been very active. With the trade's abolition in 1807, the royal navy was given the long, arduous, and often frustrating task of trying to suppress further slaving by other nations. Britain had a few scattered holdings such as Gambia, Sierra Leone, stations on the Gold Coast, and finally Lagos in what would be Nigeria. Over in East Africa, she developed important commercial contacts with the Arab sultan of Zanzibar.

Decline of the West Indian Sugar Islands

Across the Atlantic, during this middle period, the West Indian sugar islands, the brightest colonial jewels of the crown in the Old Empire, were actually falling backward. Those few dots on the map which had enjoyed a heavier trade with England than the whole thirteen colonies or the ports of the East India Company sustained a series of shocks beginning in 1783 which ruined their old prosperity. United States independence had knocked askew the old triangular trade which had been of mutual value to the mainland and island colonies. Rival sources of cane sugar developed in Spanish Cuba and in the United States,

while European scientists, during the days of the Continental System when "colonial wares" were cut off, had learned to make sugar from beets. Also the British trend toward free trade robbed the British sugar islands of their old preferential position. Perhaps the heaviest blow of all was the abolition of slavery in 1833. No longer could Negroes be forced to work. In the smaller colonies the Negroes had no alternative but to continue to work on the planters' land. In Jamaica, where there was much free land, "they deserted the estates and lived in their own villages, supporting themselves by primitive subsistence agriculture." To offset this labor shortage the planters imported large numbers of natives from India. In 1865 a Negro revolt in Jamaica alarmed both planters and Parliament. Up to this time Jamaica and the other islands had enjoyed representative government, with elected assemblies such as the thirteen colonies had had before the Revolution (see page 319). The following year, at a time when many other colonies in the British Empire had just advanced to a still further stage of self-government, Jamaica lost even that. The elected assembly was abolished, and the island was ruled by a governor and council. The same thing happened in most of the other British West Indian islands; little Barbados, however, like Bermuda and the Bahamas (just outside the Caribbean), still maintained its elective assembly.

Constitutional Pioneering in Canada

The American Revolution had taught Britain a lesson she did not forget in governing her remaining colonies of settlement. From 1774 to 1867, with Canada her experimental laboratory, she made a series of constitutional innovations there that demonstrated the adaptability and flexibility of her colonial system.

The term "Canada" until 1867 referred only to the present provinces of Quebec and Ontario. The rest of British North America now included in the Dominion of

Canada was under separate governments. There were in the east the Maritime Provinces of Nova Scotia, New Brunswick, and Prince Edward Island, and on the Pacific British Columbia (which came into being in 1858 after a gold rush). The vast region lying between those eastern and far-western possessions was loosely held by the Hudson's Bay Company. Newfoundland, which included part of Labrador, then played a lone role.

On the eve of the American Revolution, Britain had shown such good sense in handling Canada with its predominant French Catholics that the people generally remained loyal to England throughout the Revolution. The same Parliament that in 1774 goaded New England into revolt passed the Quebec Act that same year, which allowed the colonists to keep their Catholic religion and their old French civil law.

Within ten years, however, large numbers of "United Empire Loyalists," those "Tories" from the thirteen colonies who chose to stay under the old flag, had migrated northward. England generously demonstrated that loyalty was appreciated; for lands were granted to them, and they were compensated for at least part of the losses which they had suffered during the Revolution. Perhaps 35,000 of them went to Nova Scotia, where the part adjacent to Maine, set up as the separate colony of New Brunswick, became their special haven. Perhaps six thousand more trekked overland across New York to lay the foundations of what is now Ontario. A third group, numbering about a thousand, made their homes along the St. Lawrence in the present province of Quebec.

Pitt sponsored the Canada Act of 1791, to settle the problems rising from this migration. Two colonies were created, Upper and Lower Canada, the former to include the English-speaking settlers in the new region to the west of the rapids of the St. Lawrence beyond Montreal, the latter those of French blood in the lower valley of the St. Lawrence, from Montreal and Quebec to the sea. Pitt's idea had been to separate as much as possible the English-speaking people in Upper Canada from the French-speaking settlers farther down the river. Each colony was organized along the line of the original thirteen American colonies, with a governor appointed by the crown, and a legislature with two chambers, an appointed council and a representative elected assembly (see page 319). In Upper Canada provision was made "for the support and maintenance of a Protestant clergy" by setting aside for that purpose large areas of land (the clergy reserves). In Lower Canada the Roman Catholic Church retained its privileged position.

This splitting of Canada relieved an awkward situation, but it still left causes for friction. As before 1776, it was not always easy for an assembly elected by the people to agree with a governor appointed from England. The English minority in Lower Canada, moreover, felt itself at the mercy of the French Canadians, and the English majority in Upper Canada was displeased that a colony dominated by Frenchmen controlled its only outlet to the sea. The War of 1812 against the invaders from the United States temporarily lessened this friction (see page 381); but with its conclusion trouble broke out again.

Nor was it simply a question of colony against colony or colony against mother country. Upper Canada was affected more than any other region by the boom in migration from the British Isles after 1815. With only 10,000 inhabitants in 1784 and 94,000 in 1814, its population jumped to around 150,000 by 1825 and 400,000 by 1838. There were Englishmen, Irishmen, and Americans among the newcomers, but the Scots became most influential. The United Empire Loyalists and other early settlers in Upper Canada were none too friendly toward these newcomers, and they formed the so-called "Family Compact," to

Royal troops attacking the insurgents at St. Charles, Lower Canada, November 25, 1837, one of the few "shooting" encounters of the Canadian Rebellion.

try to keep the government in their own hands. They were willing to divide the church lands between the Presbyterians and the Church of England; but the numerous Methodists, left out in the cold, were resentful. William Lyon Mackenzie, the leader of the malcontents, hinted in his newspaper at the possibility of secession from the empire, and irate supporters of the "Family Compact" sacked the office where it was published. Mackenzie, however, got himself elected mayor of Toronto, after being five times elected to the legislature, and five times expelled by the "Compact" party.

In Lower Canada a feud arose between the legislative assembly, controlled by the French, and the upper house, the legislative council, nominated by the governor. It began over the payment of judges' salaries, but widened in many directions. Louis Papineau, Speaker of the Assembly, sponsored

a large number of resolutions granting to that body many rights not recognized by Pitt's Act, such as an elected legislative council, and elected representatives on the governor's executive council. When the government would not yield, Papineau and his party finally came to open rebellion. This rebellion of 1837 was a trifling affair from a military point of view: the adherents of Papineau were quickly put to rout with slight loss of life, and in the upper province an attack by Mackenzie on Toronto proved a fiasco. Nevertheless, the fact that there was fighting at all seemed ominous to English statesmen, who were determined to avert another American Revolution. In the following year Lord Durham, an advanced Whig called "Radical Jack," who had been active in drawing up the Reform Bill of 1832, was sent to Canada to diagnose its ills.

Under his vague commission, he was to

be "Governor-in-Chief of all the British North American Provinces except Newfoundland, and High Commissioner for special purposes in Upper and Lower Canada." He was accompanied by Wakefield and other colonial reformers. He was in North America for only five months, and he suffered from ill-health so that he accomplished but a small part of what he attempted. He also got into grave difficulties with the Colonial Office for illegally exiling participants in the rebellion to Bermuda. Nevertheless, his official report on the affairs of British North America, made to Parliament in 1839, is a monumental landmark in British constitutional history. Within a year it was reported to have "gone the rounds from Canada through the West Indies and South Africa to the Australias, and has everywhere been received with acclamations." Throughout the colonies of settlement it suggested and advocated the principles upon which dominion development was to rest.

Lord Durham and Colonial Responsible Government

Its importance lay in its recommendation of *responsible government*. There had been "self-government" or "representative government" in the British Empire ever since a legislature was established in Virginia in 1619, but the actions of the colonial assemblies were limited by the executive power of the governor and by the authorities in England (see page 319). Responsible government meant the dependence of the executive on an elected legislature, as in England (see page 294). Durham recommended that colonial governors should be instructed to select their ministers from those men who could command a majority in the lower and popular branch of the legislature. The governors, he argued, should be told that they should not look to London for advice or assistance on any domestic questions but were to act in the self-governing colonies as the crown acted in Britain,

holding themselves above the political battle. Authority, under this scheme, would lie with the popularly elected colonial assemblies. The only powers to be reserved for the imperial Parliament were over foreign relations, trade between the colonies and Great Britain, intercolonial trade, and the public lands.

Eventually the imperial government conceded to the colonies an even wider freedom than Durham had suggested. It took nearly a decade, however, and the endeavors of a group of eminent British-American statesmen to convince the government of the soundness of Durham's plan. In Canada the fight for responsible government was carried on by Robert Baldwin, a man much more moderate but no less determined than the fiery Mackenzie, now a fugitive in the United States. He was aided by Louis Lafontaine, a French-Canadian of similar views. In Nova Scotia the hero of the battle was Joseph Howe, who as leader of the democratic group in that assembly worked long and hard to compel the governor to select his advisers from men who were supported by a majority in it. He harassed governor after governor, and in a famous series of open letters to the Colonial Secretary put forward with complete courtesy yet unanswerable logic the case for responsible government. At last, after the Whigs had come into power in England in 1846, the new Colonial Secretary, Earl Grey, instructed the governors to rule through the medium of ministries commanding the confidence of the assemblies, "since it cannot be too distinctly acknowledged that it is neither possible nor desirable to carry on the government of any of the British provinces of North America in opposition to the opinion of the inhabitants."

In Canada responsible government was inaugurated during the governorship of Lord Elgin (1847-1854). The two Canadas had again been united in 1840. Durham, who desired to ensure an English majority in the legislature had recommended this, but the Act of Union allotted equal representation to the two provinces. As Upper Canada soon had more people than Lower, yet only the same number of members, the old jealousies revived; and ultimately a complete deadlock ensued. In the meantime, however, Elgin, a man of great intelligence and attractive personality, winning the confidence of the Canadians, accustomed them to the workings of responsible government and, by his frank acceptance of the principle that real power must rest with ministers backed by a majority in the Canadian parliament, cemented the connection with the mother country. At the same time he aided the economic life by negotiating a Reciprocity Treaty with the United States, and thus introducing a period (1854-1866) of relatively free trade across the border.

Responsible government was extended in the mid-1850s to Newfoundland; to the four Australian colonies of New South Wales, Victoria, South Australia, and Tasmania; and to New Zealand. Queensland was to have it from its beginning, as a separate colony in 1859. Cape Colony did not accept it until 1872. In each of these colonies the executive power lay, as in England, in the hands of a premier and cabinet responsible to the popularly elected legislature. Self-government was almost complete. The colonies could regulate their own trade, even to the point of erecting tariffs against the mother country, which Canada did very early. The only important reservation was the natural and necessary one that the control of foreign affairs should still lie with the imperial government. The governor became more and more a mere representative of the dignity of the crown, playing little part in the real business of ruling.

Britain was perhaps not entirely unselfish in granting such generous extensions of self-government to her colonies. During the middle of the nineteenth century in the British Parliament the many prominent "Little Englanders" looked forward to the day when the colonies of settlement might withdraw from the empire. Far from deploring this, they were anxious to make the separation as peaceful as possible. Self-government, in their opinion, would help to prepare the colonies for independence.

The reasons for such an attitude were largely economic, rising in part from Huskisson's ending of the mercantilist monopoly of the old colonial system (see pages 263, 396). Since his modifications of the Navigation Acts in 1825, the colonies were no longer forced to purchase for their outside needs from the mother country. The Manchester school (see page 417), looking at the colonies from the economic standpoint, considered them liabilities rather than assets. Their meager trade, it seemed, did not offset the heavy cost of defending and administering them. India, which was absorbing fully a tenth of British exports, was a different matter; but in Canada, Australia, New Zealand, and South Africa, the imperial game did not seem worth the candle in the eyes of the "Little Englanders." They could point to the former thirteen colonies as a demonstration that the actual bond of empire was not necessary for profitable trade. As politicians pointed out: "In 1844 we exported to the United States produce and manufactures to the value of £8,000,000, an amount equal to the whole of our real export trade to all our colonial dominions, which we govern at a cost of £4,000,000 a year; while the United States costs us for consular and diplomatic services not more than £15,000 a year, and not one ship of war is required to protect our trade with the United States."

Their most definite grievance against the colonies was that they would not pay for their own protection. Britain was ready to provide naval defense, but felt that they might at least pay for the redcoats maintained within their borders. Her efforts in 1764 to make the thirteen colonies pay for similar protection by regular troops had been the first step toward the American Revolution (see page 319). It was estimated in 1847 that about one third of her military costs went for these colonial garrisons, and that of every seventeen shillings which the British taxpayer spent in taxes one shilling went to keep redcoats in the colonies. The Indian forces were paid out of Indian revenue, but the troops in Canada, Australia, New Zealand, and South Africa were a direct burden on the mother country. Those garrisons gave the "Little Englanders" a talking point against the whole colonial relationship. According to one British peer: "One by one, the last rags of the commercial system have been torn away. We receive no tribute; we expect no commercial advantage in the ports of our colonies that we do not hold by merit and not by favor; yet we undertake the burden of defending them against attack. It is on this ground that certain politicians exclaim against colonies; that they denounce them as useless expense and would do away with them altogether." In 1869 the Colonial Secretary in the Liberal cabinet remarked regarding relations with North America that "the best solution of them would prob-ably be that in the course of time and in the most friendly spirit the Dominion should find itself strong enough to proclaim its independence." This view was far from universal, even among the Liberals. Lord John Russell, definitely not a "Little Englander," sarcastically declared: "When I was young it was thought the mark of a wise statesman that he had turned a small kingdom into a great empire. In my old age it appears to be thought the object of a statesman to turn a great empire into a small kingdom." After a quarter century of anti-imperial agitation the colonial garrisons were finally removed. Quebec had had a garrison of soldiers ever since Wolfe had taken the city; but on a November day in 1871 the last regiment marched down from the citadel with the band playing "Auld Lang Syne," boarded the troopship, and dropped down the river. Halifax, like the Cape of Good Hope, was so important as an imperial naval base that a detachment of redcoats was left there for defense; but Newfoundland, New Zealand, and Australia, with heavy hearts, saw their garrisons withdrawn, and in general the self-governing colonies were left to shift for themselves.

Gladstone and Disraeli

For fifteen years, after Palmerston's death in 1865, Gladstone and Disraeli dominated the public arena. Political labels had a meaning once more; the Victorian Compromise was speedily undermined; and men grew angry and heated over issues made all the more vivid by these two personalities, both forceful, determined, and powerful, but in no other respect alike. Almost immediately under their leadership, the aristocracy-middle class alliance relinquished their monopoly of power and made Britain a political democracy.

Only intermittently before 1866 had these two men crossed swords, but from then on, the duel was bitter and continuous. Disraeli first drew blood: within one year he defeated the Liberals and within another he climbed to the premiership—"the top of the greasy pole" (1868). Nine months later he was displaced by Gladstone's first ministry in 1868. Then, Disraeli returned in 1874. In their last encounter (1880) Gladstone won, and the battle doubtless would have lasted longer had Disraeli not died the next year. This long-contested fight meant more to England than a clash of personalities; it showed the shifting fortunes of the Liberal and Conservative parties.

William Ewart Gladstone, nearly fifty years in the House, was before the public eye somewhat earlier and a good deal later than Disraeli. He is said to have wanted to go into the church, but his father, a Liverpool shipping merchant, insisted on politics. Wealth, influential position, impressive appearance, superb health—all were Gladstone's. After Bright, he was probably the finest orator of his day. He was a loyal though not a slavish follower of Peel from 1832 until that statesman's death. Both sons of capable business men, they won highest honors at Oxford and entered the House as infant prodigies. Unlike Peel, whose seat was bought, Gladstone was the nominee of the Duke of Newcastle, a patron who handed out seats, not a boroughmonger. Gladstone was methodical, honorable, just, a hard worker, and conspicuously a success in matters of finance; but his mind worked slowly. He was also a man of violent passions, largely swayed by his feelings. Despite the brilliant promise of his youth, it was to take him more than thirty years to find himself.

In general, his tremendous admiration for Sir Robert had kept him within the Tory party until the breakup of 1846 (see page 418). Only by slow stages did the great English Liberal of the nineteenth century gradually separate himself from his former political allies. The slant of his mind was always toward the middle course. He preferred, other things being equal, to be a liberal Tory rather than a conservative Liberal. But the leadership of the Liberal party was much easier for him to attain than that of the Conservative; for after the repeal of the Corn Laws the county squires would not willingly follow a Peelite. Meanwhile the Liberals beckoned to him. Although hitherto opposed to political reform, he was genuinely liberal at heart in all that had to do with civil and religious liberty. He had defended Roman Catholic and Jew with warmth and been a stanch upholder of "peace, retrenchment, and reform." Although he had opposed Palmerston's Chinese policy, he was at one with him in regard to Italian unification (see pages 455, 421). Perhaps, for that reason, he served in Palmerston's cabinet in 1859.

The passing of time divorced Gladstone still further from the Conservatives. A masterful man, he took umbrage at what he considered the insolence of the House of Lords in rejecting his paper-tax repeal bill (see page 424). He loved Oxford, which he represented in Parliament, but could not stomach the petty Anglicanism of many of his university constituents. Furthermore, he was not immune to flattery. John Bright and other left-wing Liberals had picked him out as their man, and had assured him that he had it within his power to rise high in the Liberal party. After Oxford rejected him as her candidate in 1865, and South Lancashire, a manufacturing constituency, returned him to the Commons, he was henceforth to lead the Liberal forces.

Benjamin Disraeli was evidently not another darling of the gods—at least, not of English gods. A Jew (D'Israeli was the family name), he did not attend either public school or university. His family, to be sure, turned Anglican when he was thirteen, and he did study law at Lincoln's Inn. A failure in business, his first try for the Commons was rebuffed by the electorate.

EXTRAORDINARY MILDNESS OF THE POLITICAL SEASON

Punch cartoon of Gladstone and Disraeli, 1869, smiling, but ready to attack each other.

When he eventually won a seat, Whigs and Tories alike laughed at his first remarks. That this man, so flamboyant, so un-English in clothes, in manner, in speech, and a novelist to boot could rise to the command of the aristocratic Conservatives seems almost to defy explanation. Nevertheless Disraeli had the definite conviction that the British aristocracy must and could weld all classes in the country into one national body under its control and leadership. The poor, the weak, the lowly, yearned for this leadership and were entitled to it. Also, the aristocracy instinctively recognized that they could depend upon his loyalty. To him the English country gentlemen were identical with England; with them lay his heart. He could laugh and jest at all other things, and appear cynical, unscrupulous, and a charlatan to many who never fathomed the man. Profoundly ambitious, highly imaginative, conscious of his own ability in debate

GLADSTONE AND DISRAELI 465

and of the inability of his aristocratic followers to speak for themselves, he was willing to lead them to victory.

These two men, originally both Tories, took different sides in the Corn Law fight. Disraeli attacked Peel, believing it both undesirable and dangerous to permit the agricultural classes to decay. Disraeli, gradually settled in the saddle as Conservative leader, disliked Gladstone, whom he thought pompous, a trifle dull, and something of a prude. Gladstone naturally disliking a traitor to the great Peel considered Disraeli flippant and somewhat unprincipled.

Composition of the Rival Parties

The Liberal party of these years was composed of two main wings. Numerically the smaller, but rich and socially prominent, were the Whig landlords whose presence in the party was largely a matter of tradition, since in interests and prejudice they were much like Tory landlords. They were liberal in matters of trade, commerce, and civil rights, but were not enthusiastic about democracy and were largely content with the Victorian Compromise. The more aggressive, stronger wing of the party was dominated by the manufacturing and commercial interests, who were advocates of laissez faire and willing to extend the suffrage to the more intelligent workingmen. Some, like Bright, even believed that every man should vote as a matter of natural right. Regarding party rivalry as a contest not of rich versus poor but of landlord versus manufacturer, they felt that increasing the urban vote would strengthen them. The party also included those Nonconformists who wished to break the hold of the Church of England upon education (see page 469) and some scattered radicals, too few to form a party of their own.

The overwhelming majority in the more homogeneous Conservative party came from the landed gentry and those of the middle class socially and economically dependent on it, such as small-town merchants, butchers, grocers, and innkeepers. From the middle class, too, it attracted men of wealth and position in the business world who looked forward to buying estates and becoming country gentlemen. Also included, as far as cheering went (for they had no vote before 1867), were a few workingmen who were Conservative more because they disliked the middle-class Liberals, with whom they came in intimate business contact, than because of any special love of the gentry. The majority of the House of Lords, the officers of the army and navy, and Society, spelled with a capital "S," were all overwhelmingly Conservative.

Extension of the Franchise

In 1866 the opening gun of the new party war was fired for the Liberals by Gladstone, who proposed lower requirements for Parliamentary voting. His bill was moderate, giving the vote to the more skilled workingmen, which would raise the theoretical political power of labor in the boroughs from about one fourth of the votes to about two fifths if voting eligibility were based as he proposed on a lowered standard rental. He planned another bill for a more equitable distribution of Parliamentary seats, further reducing the number of unimportant or semi-rotten boroughs while creating new seats for cities which had increased rapidly in population during the preceding thirty years. Ever since the Reform Bill of 1832 there had been gestures in this direction by Disraeli and Lord John Russell, among others; but it had never been pressed to a vote.

Under Russell, who succeeded Palmerston as prime minister, the Liberal party now came out officially in its favor. The redistribution in 1832 had been inadequate even then. The success of the North in the American Civil War seemed to many to justify democracy. The British working classes had shown a decided advance in literacy. They had savings banks, and their trade unions were under conservative leaders. Chartism was no longer feared; but trade unions were here and there demanding an extension of the suffrage. Gladstone and the Liberals considered it better to give in to their demands before they became too articulate.

The wily Disraeli, meanwhile, awaited events. He knew that the Palmerstonian Liberals, for the most part the old Whig element, would be apt to balk at this. If the Liberals quarreled among themselves, Her Majesty's opposition, of which he was the shining light, might sail back into power. This was what occurred. The devoted followers of "Whiggery" revolted against Gladstone, holding down his majority to five votes. Finally, the Conservatives defeated the bill on an amendment and Russell resigned. Therefore, in June, 1866, they trooped triumphantly into office with Lord Derby, their nominal head, as prime minister, and Disraeli as leader in the Commons.

The next year, 1867, saw strange sights, both within and without Parliament. The people, hitherto indifferent to these Parliamentary skirmishes, suddenly became vociferous in their demand for Parliamentary reform. Huge mass meetings throughout northern England reflected in no uncertain way the nation's will; a mob even pulled down the fence around Hyde Park in London.

Disraeli decided that the Conservatives should adopt reform as their child and undermine Gladstone's popularity with the working classes by stealing his thunder. They would lower the franchise requirements of their own accord, in order to retain office. With unerring skill and patience Disraeli, having persuaded the Conservative party to adopt this idea, introduced a reform bill of his own. It went much farther in a way than Gladstone's, since it discarded property rights and income alto-

A LEAP IN THE DARK.

"Leap in the Dark" cartoon, based on Lord Derby's comment on the Second Reform bill of 1867, showing Britannia dashing into reform while others hold back.

gether as a yardstick and proposed to give the franchise to every male householder in the British boroughs who paid poor rates. To counter this radical step toward universal suffrage, however, Disraeli proposed so called "fancy franchises" which gave two votes to clergymen, university graduates, owners of government securities, and those who paid direct taxes of more than twenty shillings a year.

Gladstone, enraged, felt that he had been tricked by an unscrupulous politician. Falling upon Disraeli's bill with fury, he proposed amendment after amendment and attacked the "fancy franchises." In every instance Disraeli yielded gracefully; for to him the important concern was that every taxpayer should vote. Gladstone failed to block the bill, except for the deletion of the "fancy franchises," which Disraeli gracefully accepted. Not only did the bill become law, but its author, upon Lord

Derby's resignation early in 1868, became prime minister.

This Second Reform Bill, as passed in August 1867, was not only more revolutionary than that of 1832, but in its final form went further than any of the original proposals. It extended the franchise in the boroughs to all householders paying the poor rates and all lodgers of one year's residence, paying an annual rent of £10. In the counties, owners of land yielding £5 annually and occupying tenants paying £12 annually were enfranchised. Four of the large industrial centers received a third member in Commons, and other adjustments were made. Altogether, the electorate was increased from about one to two million voters. To all practical purposes, this meant that Britain was now a political democracy, with close to universal manhood suffrage in the populous centers.

Whereas in 1832 the balance of political control was shifted toward the middle, now it was pushed much farther to the left, toward the working class. The former's upper stratum was so interlinked with the aristocracy as to continue England's aristocratic tradition, modified but unrevolutionized. Now only after some decades would the full effects and the finality of their voluntary relinquishment of power in 1867 be brought home to the upper classes. At the time, Disraeli was confident that the working man would prefer Conservatives to Liberals; Gladstone was as confident of the reverse. The country as a whole approved, but even some Conservatives definitely did not, and Thomas Carlyle's pamphlet, *Shooting Niagara,* bewailed this grant of the vote to ignorant and unthinking men. Lord Derby, himself, though allowing that it had "dished the Whigs," called it "a leap in the dark."

Disraeli was not long to enjoy his triumph. His redoubtable enemy almost immediately launched a successful attack on him from a new angle, Ireland, and defeated him on a measure to "disestablish" the Irish Church.

Disraeli appealed to the country, confident that the workingmen to whom he had given the vote only the year before would stand by him. Their answer was, No! Once more, in December, 1868, the Liberals came back into power, with a majority of one hundred.

Gladstone's Great Ministry: Ireland

Gladstone, now for the first time prime minister, began his great ministry (1868-1874). First on its program was the pacification of Ireland. In the two decades since the Potato Famine its woes had continued to be many and vexatious. The Irish, apart from Ulster, were sullen, poverty-stricken, and ill-disposed toward England. Since an abortive revolt in 1848, Europe's year of revolutions, staged by Young Ireland, which had taken over from the more moderate O'Connell, the initiative had passed overseas. Irishmen, who had migrated, particularly in New York, established in 1858 the Fenian Brotherhood to collect funds to overthrow the British domination of Ireland. In 1865 two of its leaders, attempting to smuggle arms to another abortive uprising in Ireland, were arrested. Then came Fenian threats against Canada from the many seasoned Irish soldiers in the disbanding Northern army at the close of the Civil War. They crossed from Buffalo and briefly held a fort in Ontario, which gave Canadians one more argument for federation (see page 537). Two years later, the Fenians attempted a general uprising in Ireland, which failed. Then, a bomb explosion in England at a Manchester prison, designed to release two Irishmen, killed or injured 132 persons.

These events naturally had brought to the fore Ireland's troubles for which Gladstone proposed three remedies: the political and financial status of the Church of Ireland, reform of the land law, and reorganization of education. First, he resumed his attack on the established church, owner of some £16,000,000 whose services were not attended by most of the Irish, who crowded into their little Roman Catholic chapels, leaving its stately edifices almost exclusively to the landlords. Although he was a devout Anglican, it seemed to him wrong that an Anglican body should be a state organization in that Roman Catholic island. He proposed to take half of the assets of the Irish Church for charity and education, leaving the other half to a reorganized Church, divorced altogether from the government. The bill to this effect was pushed through the House of Commons without any determined opposition from Disraeli, who realized that some time must elapse before Gladstone's popularity would wane. The House of Lords, however, showed fight, and the queen and the bishops were incensed. Gladstone, willing to make financial concessions for the sake of peace, allowed the Church to retain a larger share of its own endowment. The Lords grumbled loudly, but feared to challenge Gladstone's large majority in Commons. Thus, the Church of Ireland was disestablished.

Irish Land Problems

Next came the more difficult question of the Irish land, most of which was owned by absentee landlords charging exorbitant rentals. "Rack-renting," as this abuse was called, was made easier by the absence of industries in which the peasants might have found alternate employment. The landlords, having the whip hand, took advantage of this by leasing land only from year to year. Since the peasants were generally in arrears, eviction for nonpayment of rent was frequent. The land was divided and subdivided into tiny strips until profitable cultivation became almost impossible, making Ireland more vulnerable to famine. Furthermore, outside of Ulster the land was rented unimproved, without dwelling houses, barns, stables, pigpens, or even drainage. The peasants realized the futility of trying to better their material condition when any such indication of improvement would mean a rise in rent.

Among various remedies proposed, John Stuart Mill, the economist, advocated for the landlord's protection a fixed rent, to be set, guaranteed, and collected by the government. To the peasant he would ensure fixity of tenure, as a guarantee against eviction. John Bright urged peasant proprietorship, by which the government would buy out the landlords and then let the peasants gradually pay the government for their individual bits of land. Both were too radical for Gladstone, who favored "Ulster custom." In Ulster, which alone of the provinces had escaped economic blight, there prevailed a custom more binding than many laws. If a landlord refused to renew a lease or insisted upon eviction, he must pay for improvements, and also further damages for disturbing the tenant. This was the nucleus of Gladstone's land law of 1870 for all Ireland. That he succeeded in winning the approval of Parliament for such a measure was little short of miraculous, with both houses composed largely of landowners. Only the gravity of the Irish economic crisis, the prestige of the recent Liberal victory, and Gladstone's indomitable will made Parliament accept a law that declared that the Irish peasants had certain legal rights to the soil simply because they tilled it. The outcome was disappointing. The landlords soon found a loophole: there was nothing in the law to prevent their raising rents. Nevertheless, the law set a valuable precedent, for from now on, it would be easier to modify property rights.

Other Gladstone Reforms

Gladstone, postponing the question of Irish education, turned his hand to English reforms. In higher education, he broke the monopoly of the Church of England, which closed fellowships and professorships in the universities to all but Anglicans. Henceforth such religious tests were barred. In elementary education Parliamentary appropriations for schooling had hitherto been very meager, partly because of the excellence of a few privately endowed schools, partly because of the prevalent theory of laissez faire, and partly because of religious strife. The people refused to divorce religion from education; yet they could not agree as to the kind of religious instruction. Gladstone's ministry proposed giving subsidies to the existing voluntary schools and setting up new national "board" schools in which there should be instruction in the Bible but no other religious teaching. This was the basis of the Education Act of 1870, for which W. E. Forster, of Gladstone's cabinet, was largely responsible. The Conservatives were amenable since most voluntary schools were controlled by the Church of England. But Gladstone's Nonconformist following objected to church schools' receiving tax funds and looked askance at "Bible teaching," which might include Anglican doctrines.

Gladstone, however, was too good a businessman to build new schools all over England when existing voluntary schools might suffice. Therefore the only compromise was an amendment to his bill which excluded "every Catechism and formulary distinctive of denominational creed." "We must educate our masters" was the cry after the general enfranchisement of 1867, and Gladstone began that process three years later. During the next twenty-one years elementary education was made compulsory and then free. In the short space of ten years the average school attendance jumped from about 1,100,000 to 4,000,000.

Other reforms followed. The civil service had been the happy hunting-ground of the sons of influential men, many of whom were not qualified to occupy the posts which wealth and family position secured for them (see page 298). Except for the Foreign Office, the civil service was now placed on a competitive basis, with examinations for government positions.

In due course came the army's reforms as proposed by Edward Cardwell, Secretary of War. These cut down its strength by twenty thousand men, withdrew garrisons from some overseas posts, changed long-term enlistments to short ones, organized a proper reserve, and abolished the purchase of commissions. "Purchase," an old British custom dating back to Stuart days, had not worked too badly in practice, for it was necessary first to be recommended as worthy of promotion. The system, of course, discriminated against officers who were poor. But it made for rapid promotion, as the common practice of retiring as captains or majors left vacancies by which distinguished officers might rise to high rank without having to wait for dead men's shoes (see page 304). Gladstone's resolve to end "Purchase" stirred up no small storm among the upper classes. The Lords determined to kill the bill, but they were completely foiled when Gladstone had it abolished by royal warrant. The royal warrant belonged to the same general type of non-Parliamentary legislation as the earlier ordinances, proclamations, and Orders in Council, and purchase had been started by this method. Disraeli had been firm for "Purchase," but the controversy seemed to him foolish; for even without "Purchase" the upper classes would control the army as long as an officer's pay barely sufficed for the upkeep of a polo pony.

A final important reform, the secret ballot for open voting in Parliamentary elections, had often been proposed by radicals. It had already been adopted in Australia and New Zealand (see page 447). British opinion, however, had felt that there seemed something almost un-English about the secret ballot, which might imply that a man was ashamed of how he voted. Gladstone himself had opposed this before 1867, arguing that voting was a public trust, and those who had the franchise should not hide their votes. Before 1867, with the franchise limited pretty much to those who had money, there was little danger of intimidation. Once let the poor vote, and the secret ballot was needed to protect them. An open vote against the candidate of an employer might mean a job lost. In this Gladstone ran counter once more to the House of Lords which, in 1871, threw out the ballot bill because it was "dangerous," "incoherent," and "contradictory." The following year, he promised if the Lords rejected it to dissolve Parliament and to hold an election on the issue. Consequently the ballot was at last adopted. His ministry also began in 1873 an overhauling of the judicial system that was to be continued over forty years (see page 500).

Gladstone's Foreign Policy

In 1873 the popularity of the prime minister was obviously waning, partly because of his very conciliatory foreign policy. He did not wave the Union Jack as Palmerston had done. He had protested Russia's violation of the Treaty of Paris (1856) in reinstating her warships on the Black Sea during the Franco-Prussian War of 1870-1871; but he had done so quietly, and Russia had ignored his protest (see pages 550 ff.). At that same time without blare of trumpets, he preserved strict neutrality while ensuring the neutrality of Belgium.

Nevertheless, many felt that he was too pacifistic in all these matters; and when his submission of the *Alabama* claims of the United States government to arbitration resulted adversely for Britain, angry patriots stormed him. In these claims the United States insisted that Britain had been negligent in enforcing international law in regard to the Confederate raiders built in Britain (see page 423), arguing that Britain might have stopped such action if it had earnestly desired to do so. An international court, consisting of an Italian, a Swiss, a Brazilian, an Englishman, and an American, met at Geneva in 1871. The United States tried to claim indirect damages, such as added insurance issued on cargoes, etc.; but the British refused to consider that. The court decided in favor of the United States in respect to those losses occasioned by the ac-

The heavy American "indirect claims" in the Alabama negotiations were satirized in 1872.

tual depredations of the rebel cruisers, *Alabama* and *Florida,* and to some extent in respect to those caused by the *Shenandoah.* Britain was directed by the court to pay $15,500,000 in gold, which she promptly did. Even at that Britain greatly profited by the crippling of American maritime competition. This case was important both because it preserved Anglo-American friendship and because it set a precedent for international arbitration. Many Britons, however, were much humiliated by the decision, British jurists were displeased with it, and Gladstone's enemies made much of it.

Meanwhile, in addition, each reform measure had antagonized some special interest. The Nonconformists were up in arms over the Education Act. The Irish Land Act had alienated many of Gladstone's old Whig adherents. The man in the street was somewhat disconcerted by the multiplicity of reform bills. A slip here and a slip there —a foolish tax on matches, ill-advised and premature temperance legislation—all combined to lessen Gladstone's grip on the electorate. In 1874 came defeat on a third Irish bill, which would have set up a university in Dublin, neither Catholic nor Protestant but broadly national. When Gladstone agreed to a proviso forbidding lectures in philosophy and modern history, the bill was doomed; and so was his ministry. Proportional representation, woman's suffrage, further extension of household suffrage to the counties, salaries for members of Parliament, the disestablishment of the Church of Wales—all these had been proposed during his premiership, and he had supported none. He did not approve of paying legislators. In his opinion the government was strong and fine because people of wealth and leisure gave their time freely without thought of pecuniary reward. The Great Ministry as the active agent of the middle class left its permanent mark on British history and freed the government from much which hampered an efficient and intelligent democracy.

Disraeli and State Intervention

The Parliamentary election of 1874, which brought Disraeli back for the second time as prime minister, led to an active intervention of the state on behalf of the poor, something new in nineteenth-century England, and also to a more aggressive colonial and foreign policy. Except for the ballot and Gladstone's education bill, practically nothing had been done during the long Liberal reign to brighten the lot of those who had to toil with their hands for a living. The Liberals had a most positive belief in self-help, rugged individualism, and laissez faire. If a workman did not rise from the ranks, it was assumed to be his own fault. All that the state should do, according to their laissez-faire viewpoint, was to remove restrictions which impeded individual initiative. Some of those who feared

the effects of "government meddling" went so far as to form a "Liberty and Property Defense League."

Disraeli, on the other hand, was the first of a trio of non-socialists, including Joseph Chamberlain and Lord Randolph Churchill (see page 488), who favored active government intervention. Although all individualists, they did not believe self-help was the invariable answer. Disraeli thought it possible to accomplish what Macaulay had said was impossible: to raise the level of a whole class by enacting laws. He was clever enough to realize the political advantages in thus improving the condition of the working class by positive legislation. What the working class asked for, in his opinion, was "better, healthier, more humanizing conditions in their own daily life. They wanted sanitary and commodious homes; they wanted regulations of their occupations so as to minimize risk to life and health; and to prevent excessive toil for their women and children; they wanted freedom of contract and equality before the law with their employers; they wanted encouragement and security for their savings; they wanted easy access to light and air and all the beneficent influences of nature."[1] By a long series of laws enacted over a period of years Disraeli did much to secure these wants.

Among the more important statutes enacted by the Conservatives were an "Artisans' Dwellings Act," a "Consolidating Factory Act," a "Rivers Pollution Act," and a number of laws regulating trade-union activities, the treatment of merchant seamen, and the enclosure of public lands. The Conservatives broke with the middle-class doctrine of laissez faire that the ramshackle tenements, the foul courts, the back-to-back houses, and other warrens in which the very poor lived were private property and

[1] W. F. Monypenny and G. E. Buckle, *Life of Benjamin Disraeli* (6 vols.; 1910-1920), Vol. V, p. 363. By permission of The Macmillan Company and John Murray.

therefore sacred. Instead they gave permission to municipalities to destroy unsanitary houses and to erect suitable ones. They also extended and consolidated in 1878 the various factory acts hitherto passed. They were likewise responsible for making the rivers cleaner by a law declaring manufacturers responsible for the condition of waters flowing from their establishments and by regulating sewage conditions. Gladstone had sided more with employers than with employees on the question of union labor, but the Conservatives did the opposite. By two bills they reversed the historic Liberal interpretation of "breach of contract," hitherto regarded as a breach of the criminal law when perpetrated by a union, and likewise the orthodox Liberal interpretation of "conspiracy" as applied to strikes. Employers and employees were now put on a basis of legal equality in these two respects, whereas hitherto the law had always favored the former. Furthermore, the conservatives supported a private bill introduced by Samuel Plimsoll, obliging all merchant vessels flying the British flag to treat seamen decently in regard to food, quarters, and safety. Finally, the government reversed the historic development known as the enclosure of public lands and commons. They not only forbade future enclosures but took steps to redeem public lands for public use by taking over Epping Forest and making it a public park. Grass, light, air, playgrounds for all—these were matters of real importance in Disraeli's shrewd and beneficial program.

The old-line Liberals, displeased with these measures, dubbed them "Disraeli's sewage policy." Government, according to their way of thinking, should concern itself with politics, with constitutions, with affairs of state. Disraeli went on his way undisturbed, developing what afterward became known as "Tory democracy." This meant the protection of the physical as well as the spiritual welfare of the many through intervention on their behalf of a wide-awake and alert aristocracy devoted to the interests of all classes—not selfishly intent on the interests of one.

Meanwhile Disraeli changed British policy in a different direction—toward more interest in the British Empire and toward a more spirited foreign policy. His imagination had long been fired by the East, and he felt that such a new outside interest would help to take Britain's mind from her threatening economic ills in the world depression of the middle seventies. Whatever the cause of the depression, its effect had been heightened by the industrial and agricultural expansion of the United States since the Civil War. England's agriculture after 1879 was never again to be as prosperous, and her manufacturers now saw Germany rising as a possible competitor. The Continent, as well as the United States, was moving toward higher protective tariffs. Cobden's old dream of world peace through free trade seemed far distant, and a reaction was setting in against the ideas of the Manchester school. Disraeli, although no economist, felt the breath of the impending changes, and, always the opportunist, knew how to turn them to account. In the field of empire he took the two dramatic steps of buying control of the new Suez Canal and having Victoria declared Empress of India (see pages 524, 533).

Disraeli and the Balkan Crisis

In Europe, the pot of Balkan politics was seething. Quickly recovering her Balkan ambitions after her Crimean defeat, Russia continued to stir up unrest and was ready to act whenever revolts occurred. Already she had helped Rumania gain her virtual independence, and when Europe was distracted by the Franco-Prussian War of 1870, she had successfully defied Britain in repudiating the 1856 treaty (see page 423).

When the next revolt came in 1875 in the northern provinces adjacent to Austria, she sought to bring pressure upon the Turks to reform and behave by concerted international action. Disraeli was, however, pro-Turk and anti-Russian, primarily because he was ever watchful lest Russia gain a Mediterranean outlet, that might threaten the route to India. Consequently he prevented measures against Turkey, even concentrating a fleet in her waters as a token of support.

Thus encouraged, the Turks kept on with their Balkan misrule; and the next year came their massacre of Bulgarians. Their revolt, the last of the subject nationalities to rise against their Turkish masters, was met by the slaughter of men, women, and children by the thousands by irregular troops, instigated by the Sultan. When rumors reached Britain of these terrific mass killings, Disraeli called them "coffeehouse babble," unwilling to have his confidence in the Turks destroyed, but when they proved true, it became more difficult for him to remain pro-Turk, though his bitter anti-Russian attitude did not waver. Gladstone, thoroughly aroused, wrote, "Let the Turks now carry away their abuses in the only possible manner, namely, by carrying off themselves . . . one and all, bag and baggage, shall, I hope, clear out from this province they have desolated and profaned." A considerable part of the nation agreed with him.

That same summer Serbia and Montenegro, autonomous, though not independent of Turkey, declared war on her. A conference of the powers, including Britain, assembled at Constantinople to bring pressure for reform upon the new Sultan, Abdul Hamid II, later to be known as "Abdul the Damned" and the "Sultan Assassin." When the indignant representatives opened their session, however, the wily Sultan announced that the previous day, Turkey had already become reformed, with a liberal constitution. There remained nothing for the exasperated conference to do, though, as many foresaw, the new constitution was not to remain in force a year. Turkey still felt secure in her English support.

In 1877 Russia declared war on Turkey and invaded the Balkans. Despite stubborn defense, the Russian army was at the gates of Constantinople early in 1878. Lord Beaconsfield, to use Disraeli's new title, took instant and militant steps. The British fleet was ordered to advance on Constantinople, while Parliament voted a heavy war grant. As a popular war song expressed the nation's attitude: "We don't want to fight, but by jingo if we do, we've got the men, we've got the ships, we've got the money, too." For a few days, things were tense. But Russia, in no condition to take on Britain too, suspended hostilities and in a few weeks made peace with Turkey at San Stephano, just outside Constantinople. Britain was particularly concerned because this called for a satellite "Big Bulgaria" with indirect Russian control over most of the southern Balkans, which could give Russia naval bases in the Aegean, as well as bring her dangerously near Constantinople.

The Congress of Berlin

Beaconsfield dramatically ordered a large force of Indian troops to Malta, and then demanded a thorough reconsideration of the whole Near Eastern and Balkan questions at an international conference. Otto Von Bismarck, "Iron Chancellor" of the newly united German Empire (see pages 550 ff.), declaring that he was acting as an "honest broker," seeking nothing for Germany, invited the congress to meet at Berlin and presided at its meetings there in mid-1878. Beaconsfield was a striking figure at this most important congress since Vienna. Even Bismarck admitted the influence and success of "the old Jew," whose preliminary bargaining bore fruit in the resultant Treaty of Berlin. Bulgaria, partly free from Turkish rule, emerged cut to a third of the size determined at San Stefano, thus keeping Russia away from Constantinople. Britain, moreover, secured the use of the island of Cyprus for a naval base in the eastern Mediterranean. Serbia, Rumania,

The Congress of Berlin in 1878, showing Disraeli in left center and Bismarck in right center, each talking with a Russian delegate.

and Montenegro were recognized as completely independent of Turkey, and Austria was granted the military occupation of two adjacent provinces; while Russia had nothing to show for her expenditure of blood and treasure except some minor gains in Europe and the region east of the Black Sea.

At the time seemingly it was a victory for Britain. Years later Lord Salisbury, Beaconsfield's lieutenant at Berlin, who succeeded him as head of the Conservatives, admitted that in backing Turkey "we put our money on the wrong horse." By that time Turkey had become still more disreputable in the eyes of western Europe through her wholesale massacres of Armenians; the new Balkan nations had enjoyed a vigorous growth; and British statesmen were less concerned about Russia in the Near East than in the Middle East and the Far East. The close relationship between England

and Turkey quickly dissolved, in fact, after Berlin; and Germany soon stepped into the vacant place as supporter of the Turks.

Few realized those implications in 1878 when Beaconsfield, returning to London, said proudly, "I bring peace with honor," and received the adulation of the people and thanks of the Queen-Empress. Without war England had greatly heightened her prestige. Yet two years later Beaconsfield was repudiated by the British electorate, Gladstone coming out of semi-retirement to defeat him at the polls. Now suddenly this man, who cared little about foreign affairs, returned to power on the heels of Beaconsfield's brilliant diplomatic victory!

The economic situation and the character of Gladstone largely account for this. During most of Disraeli's second premiership, British commerce, industry, and agriculture were in the doldrums following a lively boom which had reached its peak in

1872, immediately after the Franco-Prussian War. In that year the exports of British products (not including re-exports) reached a total of £256,000,000, the highest up to that time. They had fallen to £192,000,000 by 1878, the year of Beaconsfield's triumph at Berlin, and were slightly lower in 1879, the black year in which English agriculture, in hopeless competition with American grain, sustained a blow from which it never recovered. The world by that time was so closely knit together economically that trouble in one country tended to drag down others as well. The United States, Britain's best single customer, had undergone a severe financial crisis in 1873, and her purchases of British goods dropped from £40,000,000 in 1872 to £14,000,000 in 1878, accounting for nearly half of Britain's slump. Those were dark days for shipowners, manufacturers, landlords, and all those whom they employed. As British trade fell off, the era of budget surpluses did likewise. It had been easy enough for Gladstone to balance the budget in prosperous years. Now times were hard, and governmental expenses, instead of decreasing, were mounting. Therefore it was not difficult to persuade the unthinking that Beaconsfield was responsible for deficits and financial gloom. As for Gladstone himself, he was too imperious and too masterful to stay quiet for long. Furthermore, he was stung to the quick by the Bulgarian massacres. Religious people in general were indignant that Britain might justly be blamed for these. Gladstone made many believe that if Britain had not supported the infidel, he would not have slaughtered Bulgarians. Although Gladstone was no longer the official head of the Liberals, his personality turned the tide against the Conservatives. He was past seventy in 1880; but the British traditionally admire activity on the part of their elder statesmen. He spoke as he had never spoken before, sweeping through northern England and Scotland like a prophet of Israel. He addressed meetings from railway carriages, thus greatly shocking Queen Victoria. He made the British ashamed of their lust for military glory. He belittled the acquisition of Cyprus, as an island which Britain did not need or want. He blamed Beaconsfield for the loss of British lives on the fringes of empire, and accused him of marring the proud record of Canning, supporter of the oppressed. Intermittently he spoke of how well off he and the Liberal party had left the British treasury, and of how empty it had now become through neglect and extravagance.

So ran the campaign, with Beaconsfield taking little part in it. Hitherto it had not been customary for leading statesmen to make appeals to wide audiences outside their own constituencies. Five years older, tired, too, and never having cared for public meetings, Disraeli let the others talk. The people, he was sure, would vote for him again; he had done much for them.

Gladstone's Return

Gladstone triumphed in the election; but Victoria did not wish to send for him. She complained that he always talked to her as though she were a public meeting, whereas Disraeli, she had found, was flattering and charming. Lord Hartington, the titular head of the party, however, could not form a cabinet which did not include Gladstone, and the latter would not serve under Hartington—so Gladstone became prime minister for the second time. The long duel between the rivals was now about to close. The fierce encounters across the table in the House of Commons between the fiery, imperious Scot and the cynical, debonair Jew had already ended with the latter's withdrawal to the Lords. Never robust and already in failing health, he lived only a year and a half in semi-retirement. But despite that defeat at the end, he helped to initiate trends that would affect Britain's course for years to come.

The Rise of Irish Nationalism

In Ireland, England had her thorniest problem and met with her greatest failure. The royal standard might fly over Dublin Castle, the sons of Erin might enlist in British regiments and be elected to the English Parliament, and the king's writ might run from Cork to Derry; but this did not make a United Kingdom while in village church, in hut and cabin, in Dublin tenement, and in desolate Donegal there were hostile hands and hostile hearts. Economic distress and awakened nationalism were the interlocking causes of this hatred. Times were very bad in nineteenth-century Ireland, and nationalism was nowhere more rampant or more bitter (see pages 468 ff.). Of the three chief Irish problems, that of disestablishment of the church had been solved quickly (see page 469), and the land problem, though Gladstone's efforts had so far not brought satisfaction, was soon to be on the way to eventual settlement. But the third, home rule, was about to stir up the most bitter trouble of all, that would torment Ireland and worry England for many years to come.

The Irish peasant lived so close to starvation that any abnormality of weather brought acute misery. Overpopulation, too exclusive reliance on the potato, and land-lordism all shared the blame. Ireland's more than 8,000,000 inhabitants of 1841 had shrunk to only about 6,500,000 by 1851. About 250,000 had died of starvation; the rest had emigrated, chiefly to the United States. With this emigration continuing, Ireland had less than 4,500,000 people by the century's end.

Since his first land act had not alleviated the situation, Gladstone tried again during his second ministry (1880-1885). This bill involved "three F's": fair rent, fixed tenure, free sale. Rents were to be fixed by judicial bodies for periods of fifteen years each; peasants were guaranteed against eviction, except in certain circumstances, such as failure to pay rent; and if they chose to leave their holdings, they had the right to sell to the newcomer such permanent improvements as they had made. In such "dual ownership," the legal owner could no longer do what he wished with his own property, and the man who rented it obtained new legal rights by the mere act of occupancy. This semisocialistic bill of 1881 passed the Commons only after considerable difficulty, and the Lords after more. It might not have passed at all if Ireland had not been more disorderly than she had been in years (see page 404). Bad crops resulted in some thou-

An eviction in County Galway.

sand evictions in the first six months of 1880. The law was expensive and difficult to enforce. Also declining land values of the time tended to drop below the price fixed by the courts, so that those who had contracted to pay a given rent for fifteen years were soon in an impossible situation.

This legislation had, moreover, come too late. The Irish were already in the grip of a nationalistic fever, not to be allayed by such economic medicine. Their relations with England had changed sharply for the worse since Gladstone's first ministry. In 1874 a cultivated Irish gentleman, Isaac Butt, had organized a new political party pledged to obtain a separate legislature for Ireland. Promptly it had won more than fifty seats at the first Parliamentary election, vastly encouraging all who sought self-government. Given a fair hearing, Butt's followers discoursed eloquently on Ireland's wrongs.

Parnell's Parliamentary Policy

They did this annually, and apparently were content to do nothing more until there arrived in their midst Charles Stewart Parnell, a Protestant landlord. "The Uncrowned King" was of different fiber. A man of intense passion and icy manner, he had inherited his mother's hatred for England. Determined to make trouble, Parnell took advantage of the weight of Ireland's votes at a time when the parties were fairly even in strength. He advised the Irish members to object to everything, make speeches, amendments, more speeches, more amendments. "Refuse all invitations, don't try to make yourself popular, make yourself disliked, have no truck with the enemy, make him want to get rid of you, and above all else make it impossible for the Commons to transact business." Thus, he hoped to achieve a separate parliament in Dublin.

Butt tried to discipline his unruly colleagues; but one by one they were won over to Parnell's tactics. Succeeding Butt as their leader, he began to stage the famous "Irish nights" in Commons, in which the Irish Nationalists refused to obey the speaker and continued with their orations until removed by the sergeant-at-arms. And since they had to be removed one by one, and then repeated the performances when permitted to return, endless time was wasted, and British nerves began to fray. Yet the English did not want to adopt closure (arbitrary closing of debate). But to carry on Her Majesty's business something had to be done with these truculent fellows who thought nothing of talking all night and the next day as well about the petty activities of some unknown magistrate in County Galway.

Meanwhile there was Michael Davitt, peasant-born, embittered, and prematurely aged by eight years in a British prison. Sojourning in America, he had seen much of the Fenians (see page 468), the "physical force" Irish, but he preached a different

Parnell being ejected from the House of Commons in 1881.

doctrine—"the land for the people." Returning to Ireland, he started a Land League, to compel the landlords to sell and the government to buy. Arguing that the peasants had already paid in exorbitant rent more than the value of the land, he urged them to wrest it from the landlords. The league grew fast, and although Parnell despised Davitt's social ideas, the two were soon allied.

The combination became powerful; for the agrarian program was thus identified with the political. Parnell made the peasants conscious that they were Irishmen, with an economic as well as a political grievance. He kept reiterating that they must show the landlords that they intended to hang on to their homesteads and not again be dispossessed.

Parnell also sought aid from the Irish in the United States, where in a triumphant tour in 1879-1880, he raised large sums of money. The British government set a spy upon his tracks; but he was too clever to be caught in treason. He did not advocate actual violence, for he knew that the Irish could not successfully fight the British with bayonets.

Parnell also began to practice, through Davitt's Land League, another method. He himself kept cleverly within the law, but he and Davitt between them seem mainly responsible for the Irish reaction to the British defense of property rights. Following the League's advice, the peasants made life hot for the landlords by refusing to pay the rent demanded, by caring for the evicted, by maiming cattle, by burning barns, and by shunning "as if he were a leper" anyone who dared take the farms of the dispossessed. From this last process, used repeatedly against landlord as well as peasant, comes the word "boycott," the name of one of the first victims, a landlord's agent.

The more the British resorted to coercion in these disorders, the more violence there was. Furthermore, Parnell worked against the "three F's" of Gladstone's second land act, as its success might injure his case for nationalism.

Gladstone, very much perplexed, alternated force with milder policies. Now he had Parnell clapped into jail, the league suspended, coercion bills passed, and Ireland ruled by a kind of martial law. He appealed to the Pope and to the Irish people—all to little avail.

Gladstone then tried placating Parnell, who was released, and in return agreed to curb the rural agitation. The coercion acts were repealed. Lord Frederick Cavendish was sent over as chief secretary. Promptly he and the under-secretary were stabbed to death in a public park. Although Parnell and his leading henchmen denounced these Phoenix Park murders, the British resumed coercion. Trial by jury was suspended for three years, and the police were given greater freedom of search and arrest. Agrarian disorders, though not ending, decreased noticeably, however.

Land Purchase Loans

Parnell, discovering that nothing else was to be gained through Gladstone, began to dicker with the Conservative party. By swinging his votes in their favor on a non-party issue, he helped them oust Gladstone's second ministry in June 1885. The general election could not be held before December, because of the time required to put the recent redistribution of parliamentary seats into effect. Consequently, the Conservatives formed a temporary "caretaker" ministry under Salisbury.

Parnell got his reward that August when Salisbury pushed through the Ashbourne Act, which provided a fund of £5,000,000 for loans whereby the Irish peasants could buy their lands by installment payments, spread over forty-nine years, at low interest. Gladstone's 1881 Land Act had been a moderate step in that direction, but this was the important landmark as it gave the movement the needed strong impetus and was to be followed by several other Conservative acts by 1903. At the eve of World War I, nearly seven million acres had been bought by tenants from their landlords through such government loans, totalling some £75,000,000.

Making and Unmaking Ministries

The December 1885 election came out exactly as Parnell had hoped, with the Liberals having a plurality over the Conservatives, but not a majority without the Irish votes. The latter were now increased to eighty-six, reflecting the effects of the secret ballot act of 1872, which gave tenants more freedom to vote as they pleased, and the 1884 Reform Act, which trebled the number of Irish voters. Parnell thus had the balance of power he knew so well how to use; and he threw those votes in favor of Gladstone, who at seventy-six now entered his third ministry.

This lasted only from February to July, 1886, because of his efforts to settle the Irish problem once and for all with home rule. He had been moving in that direction for a long time, but that was known only to a few intimates until recently, when his son had indiscreetly let the news leak out.

The mere announcement of the main outlines of the first home rule bill created a whirlwind of opposition from all sides, not only from the Conservatives, but from many of Gladstone's own Liberals under Joseph Chamberlain, the chief heir to his party leadership. An Irish parliament was proposed of one house, but of two orders, one representing population and the other property. Normally, they would meet and vote together. Either one meeting separately could exercise a veto which would suspend a bill until a new election was held. The Dublin parliament was to control the Irish executive, thus introducing responsible government, and it was to have full powers except on such matters as were reserved for the crown. Among the latter were foreign affairs, the army, the navy, customs and excise duties, and, for the time being, the constabulary. Ireland was to contribute one fifteenth of the total expenses incurred by the British Parliament for imperial purposes. The Irish members were to be withdrawn from the Westminster Parliament, and an Established Church in Ireland was to be forbidden.

Gladstone's First Home Rule Bill

One objection, stressed by many of the insurgent Liberals, was that the Irish would be taxed without representation, because they would have no members at Westminster, and such a situation had proved fatal in the American colonies. Chamberlain spoke in favor of home rule all around, in the sense of imperial federation throughout the empire, but he opposed this bill, which called for separate parliaments with divided authority. Others insisted that the electorate had not realized it was voting for home rule in returning the Liberals, and that on such a momentous matter as breaking up the United Kingdom (see page 375) the people should make the decision. There were serious military and naval strategic considerations, too, with Ireland lying athwart Britain's main line of sea communications and near enough to serve as a back door for England's enemies again as it had before, even so recently as the French Revolutionary Wars (see pages 208, 276, 375). Some wondered why Gladstone was coupling this bill with a new land bill, which proposed to buy out all Ireland's landlords by using the credit of the British treasury; and they wondered, too, where he expected to find security for repayment. So argued Gladstone's opponents, and not the least vociferous was the Protestant majority in Ulster, which threatened revolt at the possibility of being under the control of a Catholic parliament in Dublin.

As the debate wore on, it became evident that the Liberal party would break in two over the bill. The enemies of home rule, fearing that the enormous prestige of Gladstone, assisted by Parnell's votes, might be enough to carry the bill through the Commons, left no stone unturned to defeat it. Particularly, they capitalized upon the religious antipathies of the loyal British citizens of Protestant Ulster. "Ulster will fight, and Ulster will be right," cried the inflammatory Lord Randolph Churchill, descendant of the famous Duke of Marlborough and father of the later statesman Winston Churchill. Ulster, meanwhile, made ready to fight, and many of Gladstone's Nonconformist adherents prepared to desert him in order to support it.

As a result of this widespread agitation the bill was lost, ninety-three Liberals voting against it. Gladstone appealed to the country. Thereupon the Liberal opponents of home rule hastily organized a party of their own, the Liberal Unionist, under Chamberlain, and entered the electoral battle in combination with the Conservatives. This coalition won a handsome victory, with a safe majority over both Gladstonians and Parnellites. Lord Salisbury returned, this time for six years (see page 489).

The chief reason for the defeat of home rule at this time lay in the inheritance of fear, hatred, and contempt which blinded men's eyes and steeled their hearts, destroying faith and confidence. Many of the objections might well have been solved in course of time by patient compromise and good-will. Nationality and religion summarize the failure. The midnight murders, the boycottings, the maiming of cattle, and the intimidations which had characterized the social disorder in Ireland naturally bulked large in the minds of Englishmen. With their own ordered lives reflecting the queen's peace, they did not know the extremity of misery, desperation, and squalor that lay behind such ruthlessness. Salisbury, comparing the Irish to Hottentots, expressed what thousands felt in England. In the matter of Catholicism, the Spanish Armada, Tudor glories, and Stuart treacheries might belong to history, but that did not prevent their influencing votes in 1886. Many in Britain, especially among the Nonconformists, felt profound suspicion of Catholics, while the Irish Protestants had been "top dog" too long to relinquish their ascendancy and feared home rule would bring both schools and taxes under Catholic control.

The victorious Conservatives, assisted by their allies, the Liberal Unionists, turned to two seemingly contradictory methods: economic reform, to "kill home rule with kindness," on the one hand, and the suppression of disorder on the other. The first involved further extension of the land purchase policy (see page 480). Evictions were made more difficult, and rentals, it was agreed, were to be revised every three years. Arthur Balfour, chief secretary for Ireland, in 1887 worked hard to redeem the congested districts in the west. He introduced light railways, built docks and bridges, gave away seed potatoes, and tried to revive the fishing industry. Despite that, he was called "Bloody Balfour" as this policy was supplemented by unadulterated coercion. The Crimes Act (a name used also for some of the earlier coercion acts) gave magistrates and police extensive powers; stipulated that certain criminal cases be tried in London; and authorized the chief secretary at Dublin Castle to suspend all constitutional guarantees whenever he considered it desirable. As a result Balfour proscribed the National League and put several Irish members of Parliament in prison.

Meanwhile the Irish Nationalists organized without Parnell a campaign whereby the peasants were to decide for themselves what rent they could pay and, if the landlords would not accept the proffered payment, were then to continue their old terrorist methods. In spite of Balfour's efforts, the economic situation remained bad. Cheap food from overseas spoiled the Irish market

in Great Britain, and the synthetic manufacture of fertilizers in Germany ruined the Irish exportation of kelp. Opportunity for Irish labor to work in British fields diminished as British farmers began to use new agricultural machinery. These facts added grist to Parnell's mill. But, above all, the appeal to Irish patriotism was kept alive and warm through the Irish Nationalist party, a perfect political machine, responsive to Parnell's will.

Something now happened which aroused deep sympathy for the Irish leader in the land he hated. The London *Times,* using letters which turned out to be forgeries, accused him of having approved the Phoenix Park murders in Dublin. He refused to trust himself to an English jury in a libel suit. A Parliamentary Commission investigated and found him guiltless, and for a time a remorseful British public made a hero of him.

All the good-will that Parnell had won in England soon faded, however, when one Captain O'Shea brought suit for divorce, naming Parnell as correspondent. The suit was undefended; for Parnell had long lived with Mrs. O'Shea and had a child by her. Gladstone's mail-bags were now full of letters denouncing Parnell, particularly from Nonconformists, whose preachers thundered their anathemas in the name of the Lord. Gladstone then privately sought Parnell's resignation from the Commons and, when he refused, told the Irish Nationalists that nothing could be done for them as long as they kept Parnell as leader. The effect upon the Irish M. P.'s was electric. They tore at one another's throats, the majority denouncing Parnell. Gone now was the united block of Irish Nationalist votes. The Irish could not agree; and the English, fearing them less, scorned them the more.

The Second Home Rule Bill

Nevertheless, in 1892 Gladstone by a narrow majority was returned to power for his fourth ministry, and the next year at the age of eighty-four, he introduced his second home rule bill. It bore a marked resemblance to that of 1886, but provided that Ireland could be represented at Westminster as well as in Dublin. It was a lost battle from the beginning. Even counting the Irish votes, Gladstone's majority was only forty. The Liberals, moreover, were not enthusiastic about Ireland's cause, and most of them supported it only as a compliment to Gladstone. The crux of the matter lay in the Irish contention that they were a nation, which neither Liberals nor Conservatives were willing to admit. Probably no compromise could have saved home rule at this time. The men who had opposed it in 1886 on the specific ground that Irish members were to be withdrawn from the British Parliament now fought it because the Irish were to remain there, and these same men would probably have opposed a separate parliament for Ireland under any circumstances. It apparently made no difference in the result whether or not Ulster was excluded from the bill. After many bitter scenes the bill passed the Commons by a close vote but met defeat in the House of Lords; in rejecting it the Lords performed a popular act. The schism in the ranks of the Irish Nationalists made it impossible for them to obstruct Parliament seriously any longer. It was apparent that there had been no real change of heart in England, and home rule seemed dead.

The Nationalist cause looked desperate in 1893, with disunion in their ranks and discouragement in Ireland. Long after Parnell's death his followers continued to quarrel over him. In England the political situation brought fresh disaster to Nationalist hopes. Gladstone had resigned in 1894, and the general election of 1895 brought in Salisbury for the third time (1895-1902). In addition, the Unionists (the new name adopted by the Conservative-Liberal-Unionist alliance) had a tremendous majority. The foes of home rule had triumphed with this victory at the polls, and, what was worse, its former friends among the Liberals had grown lukewarm.

John Redmond, who had been in Parliament since 1881, now came slowly to the fore as Nationalist leader there. Staunch follower of Parnell in defeat or victory, but not in method, he spoke seriously and persistently for a free Ireland within a free commonwealth.

Twentieth-Century Improvements

As the twentieth century opened, some Irishmen wanted their land to resurrect her native culture, and become self-reliant by looking to her own strength. One way attempted was to revive the old Gaelic (Celtic) language and use it in everyday activities. Another way was for Irishmen to reorganize their own economic life without British assistance. Owing largely to Sir Horace Plunkett, the Irish began co-operative buying, co-operative dairying and butter-selling, and even co-operative banking on the minute scale successfully put into operation by co-operative peasant banks in Germany.

The Conservatives, in power at the turn of the century under Salisbury, and then under his nephew, Balfour, resumed the latter's policy of trying to "kill home rule with kindness." The Irish County Council Act of 1898 revolutionized local government, previously controlled by the landed gentry, by placing it under local elected county councils. Still more important, the policy of lending the peasants money to buy their land, gaining momentum since 1886 (see page 480), reached a climax in 1903 with an act which eventually made some £100,000,000 available for the purpose. This land law, coupled with Plunkett's reforms and the general rise in the price of agricultural products, worked wonders. Emigration declined, and altogether Ireland enjoyed real prosperity.

Politically, the Irish situation remained unchanged. Prosperity or no prosperity, the demands of the Nationalists at Westminster were in no way abated. The renaissance of the British Liberal party in 1905-1906 (see page 491) made no difference, for the twentieth-century Liberals were wary of the Irish question after their party's two defeats on home rule. Also, their victory was so astonishingly complete that they did not need the Irish votes. Nevertheless, Redmond consistently supported them, aware that the real lion in the path was the House of Lords; he surmised that the Liberals would come into conflict with the Lords on some other question and that then would come Ireland's chance.

So it proved. The Lloyd George budget (see page 498) was thrown out by the Lords, and the Liberals, appealing to the country, secured, if one counted the Irish Nationalist votes on their side, a majority for the budget and for the Parliament Act. With the Irish holding the balance of power, the Liberal party once more embraced their cause, whether by a formal bargain as the Conservatives hinted or not.

The Third Home Rule Bill

In 1912 Asquith (prime minister, 1908-1916) introduced the third home rule bill. This created a parliament in Ireland and granted autonomy to a limited extent but did not give Ireland dominion status. To the British government were reserved certain functions, not only the army, navy, and foreign affairs, but also the control of the Royal Irish Constabulary, land settlement, old-age pensions, the National Insurance Act, the collection and, to some extent, the levying of taxes. The parliament established was to have a Senate nominated in the first instance by the government, and a House of Commons elected by popular vote. A ministry, exclusively Irish, was to be dependent on the new parliament. In the British Parliament there were to be forty-two Irish members instead of the current hundred-odd.

The two-year fight over this bill was extraordinarily complicated. In addition to the old difficulties of 1886 and 1893, there were new ones, mainly financial. The British had sunk a lot of money in Ireland in the twentieth century, particularly for the land settlement, and the old-age pension law (see page 493). The bill proposed the collection of Irish taxes by British officials, the deduction of what was due Britain, and the turning back of what was left to the Dublin parliament. As one Tory opponent put it, "the British go to the Irish taxpayer in the sole capacity of tax-collector, and the Irish government is the fairy godmother distributing gifts which have been collected by the British ogre."

Ulster Opposition

The main issue was Ulster, which as in 1886 threatened to fight any attempt to separate it from Britain. Although some two-thirds of Irish Protestants were in Ulster, it was by now Protestant by only a narrow margin, with the majority in the northeastern counties, the nucleus of the bitterest opposition. With most of the factories there, it was more prosperous than the rest of Ireland, and feared heavier taxes and crippled industries from a parliament at Dublin. It was alarmed lest the Roman Catholic south, with its numerical majority, attempt reprisals for the long years of Protestant oppression. "You may call it what you like," to quote one of their M. P.'s: "we in the north of Ireland believe that a Parliament in Dublin would be dominated by the Roman Catholic Church." The Ulstermen, moreover, were proud of their British citizenship. The Conservative leaders, recognizing this determination to remain British, promised them that they should neither be left in the lurch nor forced out of their country. Other possibilities were discussed, but the Unionists made it clear that they would agree to nothing except the complete defeat of the bill. A covenant, signed publicly in 1912 by thousands of Protestant Ulstermen, read, "We stand by one another in defending for ourselves and our children our cherished position of equal citizenship in the United Kingdom and in using all means that may be found necessary to defeat the present conspiracy to set up a Home Rule plan in Ireland." The open Bible, the Union Jack, and this Ulster covenant became the symbols of Ulster's resistance.

In January, 1913, the House of Commons passed the Government of Ireland bill, and the Lords promptly rejected it. Some months later it met the same fate. But the Lords' veto power had been clipped by the recent Parliament Act (see page 499), and if the Commons passed the bill once more it would become law.

Meanwhile, the Ulster Protestants, arming and drilling in preparation for fighting home rule to the death, soon had an army of considerable size. This hypothetical rebellion of Ulster obsessed men's minds, although there had been no overt act. The appeal of the Ulstermen was at once subtle and direct: they wanted nothing, they asked for nothing, except to remain the loyal British citizens they had been for centuries; and British public opinion tended to favor them.

When the bill came up for the third time early in 1914, Asquith, realizing how slender his majority was, except for the Irish votes, proposed that every separate county in Ulster should determine by plebiscite whether or not it chose to enter the new Ireland. If it voted for exclusion, for six years it was to remain a part of Great Britain; after that period, unless the British Parliament intervened, it would be included in Ireland. Redmond, as the Irish Nationalist leader, reluctantly agreed; but Ulster's spokesman, Sir Edward Carson, a south-of-Ireland barrister, remained adamant. Nevertheless, in May, 1914, the bill passed the Commons, and received the royal assent in September.

During the spring and summer, however, much else happened. At rumors that military force might be used to bring Ulster to terms, various army officers resigned to avoid such duty. The Ulster volunteers cut telegraph wires, and brought ashore and distributed ammunition. In southern Ireland, Sir Roger Casement, a Protestant, and other eager advocates of home rule organized national volunteers and sought to arm them. Redmond was reluctantly forced to recognize the necessity for this. Enlistments in the south grew rapidly, and by summer the national volunteers outnumbered those of Ulster. Because of the tense situation George V in July called a conference of political leaders in Buckingham Palace, but his efforts were futile. The day after, a parade of armed Ulster volunteers marched through Belfast, with no one interfering. The next day troops fired on National volunteers engaged in gun-running near Dublin.

Civil war seemed about to begin, but a blacker cloud than Ulster was close at hand —World War I. And so Redmond rose in the Commons to pledge Ireland's help in fighting Germany. The operation of the new act was suspended during the war. Catholic Ireland, it appeared, would fight for Britain and trust to the future. Yet before the war was half over, Dublin was to be in revolt.

The Broadening Base of Government

In 1886 a mob, led by men with red flags, broke the windows of the Carlton Club, looted shops in Piccadilly, turned respectable people out of their broughams in Hyde Park, and terrorized the fashionable West End of London.

One year later came "Bloody Sunday," a rough-and-tumble contest in Trafalgar Square between unemployed workingmen and the police. Law and order triumphed, but at the price of calling out the military. "No one who saw it," wrote a contemporary, "will ever forget the strange and indeed terrible sight of that grey winter day, the vast sombre-coloured crowd, the brief but fierce struggle at the corner of the Strand, and the river of steel and scarlet that moved slowly through the dusty swaying masses when two squadrons of the Life Guards were summoned up from Whitehall."[1]

Two years afterward the strike of the London dockers, fifty thousand unskilled longshoremen led by John Burns, a self-educated Scottish engineer, tied up all shipping. Destitute and ignorant though they were, these men had the courage, the per-

tinacity, and the discipline to win their strike. The extra penny an hour became theirs, and Britain realized as she never had done before, the pitiful way of life of her lower classes.

Although the great depression had been going on for a dozen years, these demonstrations heralded something new. Within thirty years democratic Britain was to appreciate that changed conditions were supplanting the Victorian compromise made by the middle class and aristocracy. The result would be the demise of laissez faire and the birth of the Labor party.

In the years of Gladstone's second ministry (1880-1885), just before these outbursts, the nation was very slowly emerging from the worst of the severe slump (see page 475), although agriculture was not recovering at all. Under the strain of the long depression, factories had closed their doors, farmers could not pay their rents, and agricultural laborers flocked to the cities to swell the ranks of the unemployed. To be sure, factory hours were shorter than in the earlier part of the century because of the factory legislation, and the workingman could buy more goods with his money because of the decline in prices. But all this was of no use to the penniless unemployed.

[1] J. W. Mackail, *Life of William Morris* (1899), Vol. II, p. 191. By permission of Longmans, Green & Co.

Police and rioters in Trafalgar Square, in the heart of London, during the serious disturbances of "Bloody Sunday," November 13, 1887.

Britain was the richest country in the world, but thousands of homeless, hungry men were tramping the streets of her cities.

Gladstone said that the bad times were only temporary and that the government could do nothing. Soon, however, he set up a royal commission which was to propose two highly conservative remedies: cheaper manufacturing costs and new markets. Apparently the alliance between the middle class and the aristocracy, firm in its belief in laissez faire, could think of nothing better and had faith in Macaulay's idea: "Our rulers will best promote the improvement of the nation by strictly confining themselves to their own legitimate duties. . . ."

British Socialism

But the doctrine of laissez faire toward social problems was under increasing attack. The 1867 Reform Bill had given the workingmen the power with the vote, al-

though the middle class and aristocracy had not yet had that brought home to them. The Marxian socialists in various countries were calling for benefits to mitigate the insecure lot of the workers. From Germany now came the example of a governmental program of "state Socialism" for insurance against sickness, accident, and old age. At home, Hyndman, the leading socialist, insisted that workingmen must strive for political power and for the abolishment of private productive property. Telegraphic and postal service, gas, and water were already state or municipal monopolies, and he wanted the government to continue nationalization upon a large scale. To persuade the conservative trade unions to his way of thinking, he started the Social Democratic Federation, hoping to build up an effective political party, but he accomplished relatively little. Added to his voice was that of Henry George, an American,

George Bernard Shaw, brilliant, colorful playwright and Fabian socialist.

vention, like Disraeli, whose chief successor as a "Tory Democrat" was Churchill (see pages 472, 481). Chamberlain was rising rapidly in popular favor. Gladstone had been compelled, for expediency's sake, to include him in his second ministry, although he disliked him as a pushing Birmingham manufacturer of screws, as well as for some of his unorthodox ideas. Chamberlain called on the upper classes to "stop talking so much about their rights and start to recognize their obligations and responsibilities." He had published what he called an "unauthorized program," which was anathema to old-time radicals like Bright, let alone Gladstone, who did not want the Liberals to become a labor party. It incorporated many socialistic schemes such as heavy graduated taxes on the income of the wealthy, municipal public works, and free educational facilities of the poor. It called for the purchase, by condemnation if necessary, of agricultural land, and its resale in small allotments. "Three acres and a cow" was to be the new slogan.

who advocated a single tax only, and that on land.

There was also the typically British Fabian Society, organized in 1883 to educate the public about socialism. It sought to introduce this gradually by legislation and without class war. Its membership, never large, included such brilliant young writers as Sidney and Beatrice Webb, H. G. Wells, and George Bernard Shaw (see pages 512 ff.). The pamphlet literature poured forth was vigorous, provocative, and in many instances the result of careful research. It probably helped to make socialism respectable in England, but its influence appears to have been much overrated.

This socialistic attack on the old order and on the gods of laissez faire was echoed in Parliament among the Liberals by Joseph Chamberlain and among the Conservatives by the less radical Lord Randolph Churchill. Both believed in governmental inter-

Third Reform Bill

Gladstone turned to some less controversial political reform to heal this split in his own party of the old Whig element and the old radicals on the one hand, and the adherents of Chamberlain and the new radicals on the other. In 1884, he pushed through Parliament the third Reform Bill, which gave virtual household suffrage to the agricultural laborers in the counties as the second Reform Bill in 1867 had done for the industrial workers in the towns. In 1832, the franchise included about one adult male in thirty; in 1867, more than half of them; and now in 1884, four out of five. Those males still excluded were mainly young men living in their father's home, servants, and others without separate households. In 1885, a redistribution of seats ended the remaining rotten boroughs and increased the House of Commons to 670 members, with 465 from England, 103 from Ireland, 72 from Scotland, and 30 from Wales.

The English party system seems to function best with two rival parties of about equal strength. There were long periods, however, when one party enjoyed predominance, such as the Whigs from 1714 to 1760 and the Tories from 1770 to 1830, while between the first and second reform bills the Whig-Liberals were in power about three quarters of the time. Never were the rivals so closely balanced in power as in the half century between Gladstone's first appearance as prime minister, in 1868, and the fusing of the parties into a coalition during World War I, in 1916. Each enjoyed twenty-four years of power. The Liberals were in the saddle during the four ministries of Gladstone (1868-1874, 1880-1885, February—July, 1886, 1892-1894), that of his successor Rosebery (1894-1895), and then, after a long Conservative interlude, those of Campbell-Bannerman (1905-1908) and Asquith (1908-1916). The Conservatives began with Disraeli (1874-1880), and then came the three ministries of Salisbury (1885-1886, 1886-1892, 1895-1902), followed immediately by that of his nephew, Balfour (1902-1905). This close balance explains the marginal importance of a group like Chamberlain's Unionists or Parnell's Irish Nationalists, whose members could swing the majority from one party to the other.

Party overturns came in unusually rapid succession in 1885 and 1886, while business was undergoing another sharp decline. Within a period of fifteen months each party fell twice from office. After Gladstone's second ministry ended in June, 1885, the Tory Lord Salisbury formed his first ministry, which was overthrown early in 1886 as the result of a general election (see page 480). Gladstone was back in power for the third time, but only for six months. Then another general election broke the Liberal party in two, Chamberlain and the anti-home-rule Liberals joining forces with the Conservatives (see page 481). This sec-

ond time Salisbury's ministry, thus reinforced, was to last six years.

The Irish home rule bill of 1886, for the time being, continued to distract the attention of the public from the main economic issue of the abandonment of England's old policy of hands off trade, commerce, and industry. The bill disastrously weakened the cause of the reformers by drawing their leader, Chamberlain, over toward the Conservative camp. He hated Irish Nationalists more than he did English landlords; and since he had to co-operate with the latter in order to defeat the former, his zeal for social reform lessened. He and his fellow rebels from the Liberal ranks organized their own party, the Liberal Unionists, who detested home rule but had scant enthusiasm for reform. Brilliant, eccentric Lord Randolph Churchill tried hard to commit the Conservatives to a strong labor program. But being in poor health, he resigned from the cabinet and died shortly afterward. There was no one to take his place. Salisbury, though at heart no reactionary was primarily interested in foreign affairs.

In the rival Liberal camp the supporters of social reform likewise were without a natural leader; for most of them had followed Gladstone on the Irish question, and his heart was set on one thing only—home rule for Ireland. He did not like the new ideas anyway; in benighted Ireland he was reluctantly prepared to sacrifice property rights, but not in progressive England.

The tide against laissez faire, however, had set in, and made it expedient for both parties to bid for the votes of the workingmen, who were more and more influenced by socialistic ideas. Chamberlain, in allying himself with the Conservatives, had not forgotten all his old enthusiasms. He did secure a part of his "unauthorized program" in an act facilitating the purchase of small holdings, and in another doing away with all school fees for the children of the poor. In 1888 the creation of County Councils removed most of the burdens of the local rural administration from the justices of the peace to popularly elected bodies. The "J.P.'s," who had virtually controlled English local government from Tudor times, only retained their functions as magistrates (see page 171). Chamberlain in the next election campaign even advocated old-age pensions; he did so, however, as an individual, for no important party in the nineteenth century would commit itself to such wild heresy.

Gladstone's Fourth Ministry

The Liberals, however, stole his thunder. Their social-reform group was strong enough to commit the party to their "Newcastle Programme." This was a curious mixture, ranging from home rule and a leash for the House of Lords, to local liquor option and parish councils. "It is an absurd programme, an impractical programme, a dishonest programme," thundered Chamberlain. Nevertheless, in the general election, that brought Gladstone into office for his fourth and last ministry (1892-1894); the Liberal candidates who stuck closest to it made the best showing.

This fourth ministry did scarcely anything for social reform. Once Gladstone's second home-rule bill was defeated by the Lords in 1893 (see page 483), it was evident to all that he was too old, too deaf, and too blind to carry on much longer. The following year at eighty-five, the Grand Old Man resigned and died within four years. His successor, the Earl of Rosebery, essentially a Whig aristocrat who owed his promotion to good manners, family position, and the Queen's favor, had three ambitions in life: to become prime minister, to win the Derby, and to marry an heiress—all of which he realized. His fifteen and a half months in office (1894-1895) were sterile of achievement.

The Cecil Decade

In 1895 the Unionists (a term now applied to Conservatives and their Liberal-Unionist allies) returned for ten years (1895-1905) with a thumping majority over both Liberals and Irish Nationalists combined. This decade has sometimes been referred to as that of the Cecil dynasty, owing to the influence of the two Cecil descendants— Salisbury and his nephew and successor as prime minister, Arthur Balfour, later Earl Balfour. No. 10 Downing Street was even jokingly called the "Hotel Cecil." It was a period of changes in British foreign policy, of vital importance in the empire, and of economic reforms in Ireland (see Chapters 29, 28, 25); but as far as social reform in England was concerned it was comparatively barren.

Victoria died early in 1901, surviving by only three weeks the nineteenth century, with which her sixty-four-year reign is so intimately associated. She had won the enthusiasm of her subjects once more in her later years, and the whole empire had joined in lavish tribute to her in her fiftieth and sixtieth anniversary jubilees. She was succeeded by her eldest son as Edward VII (1901-1910). Already nearly sixty and a grandfather, this thorough-going man of the world and sportsman was dignified, robust, kindly, and tactful. Throughout his long wait as Prince of Wales his mother had limited his role to the purely ceremonial appearances which she herself neglected during most of her widowhood. Edward had managed to enjoy life in unofficial ways, and many of the gayer places in France knew him well. He and his charming Danish wife were very much liked. In fact, he was not only an able king, but the most popular since Charles II.

The Attack on Free Trade

Next in influence to the two Cecils in the Conservative or Unionist party was Joseph Chamberlain, now colonial secretary, a post that appealed to him because it gave him a way to social betterment through trade expansion, imperialism, and colonial federation, rather than through direct governmental intervention in the affairs of the poor.

Four generations of royalty, 1894: Victoria and future Edward VII, George V, and Edward VIII.

To him, prosperity was the nation's prime need; to obtain it, he would abandon free trade, set up preferential duties on colonial products, and knit closer the economic ties of empire. Britain no longer enjoyed the long lead in industrial development which had made free trade safe in the middle of the nineteenth century. Behind high tariff walls the United States, Germany, and other nations were building up their own industries so successfully that they not only were becoming less dependent upon British textiles, metals, and coal but were actually invading free-trade England with their own products (see pages 425, 555). A protective tariff, Chamberlain felt, could pay for old-age pensions and the relief of the distressed classes.

His campaign against free trade was initiated directly after the Boer War. Balfour, having succeeded his uncle as prime minister in 1902, had slight interest in economic questions, and, in view of divergent views in the party, dodged the issue. Chamberlain thereupon resigned in 1903, to press his campaign for protective tariffs with greater vigor. Almost immediately that question divided the party into three factions. Some, the "wholehoggers," warmly supported Chamberlain's protectionist ideas. At the opposite extreme, the "free-fooders" were flatly opposed to any tax on bread. Between them, the "little piggers" approved with qualifications Balfour's scheme for food duties as part of a plan of imperial federation.

These dissensions caused joy among the Liberals, who rallied to the defense of free trade and the cheap loaf. The temporary economic boom made protectionist warnings less significant. British exports were increasing—£349,000,000 in 1902, £371,000,000 in 1904, and £460,000,000 in 1906; while unemployment was on the decline. The Liberals, also, had other strings to their bow: the unsatisfactory conduct of the Boer War and the financial scandals connected with it, Balfour's ultra-Anglican and unpopular Education Act, and the importation of Indian coolies into South Africa. But none of these rivaled in tactical importance the new heresies of Chamberlain. He was the bête noire of the Liberal party, which he had ruined in 1886 by "betraying" Gladstone; now, it was feared, he would "betray" the memory of Cobden and Bright!

The Liberal Decade

Balfour, with his majority in the Commons dwindling away, at the end of 1905, resigned and so paved the way for a decade of Liberal control. The new prime minister, Sir Henry Campbell-Bannerman, a Scot nearly seventy years old, had in his cabinet three men destined to achieve prominence in the next ten years: Herbert Henry Asquith, David Lloyd George, and Sir Edward Grey.

Early in 1906, a general election established the Liberals more firmly in power, with 380 seats of their own and, as potential allies, about 50 Laborites (including 29 of the new Labor party), and 80 Irish Nationalists. This left only about 130 Conservatives and 25 Liberal-Unionists in the opposition (the figures vary slightly in different sources). In securing the support of the Laborites and Irish, the Liberals assumed the obligation of promoting legislation desired by those two groups; and under their leadership legislation of great social and political significance was achieved.

The Laborites and Taff Vale

An immediate result was the arrival at Westminster of the Laborites. They invaded the staid precincts of the House of Commons wearing cloth caps instead of silk "toppers"—an ominous portent to the fast-dying Victorians, accustomed to considering government as the private preserve of the wellborn and the well-to-do. A conference in 1900 of representatives of the trade unions, the Fabian Society, Hyndman's Social Democratic Federation, and the Independent Labor party—the rival Marxian group—set up the Labor Representation Committee, which was to become in 1906 the Labor party. This conference had been planned at the Trade Union Congress the preceding year, "to devise means of increasing the number of Labor members" in Parliament. The socialistic organizations supplied the intellectual material, and the trade unions most of the membership. There were some twelve hundred and fifty trade unions, with a total membership of about two million. The trade unions, which had been legalized in 1871 and in 1876 (see page 472), had not been actively engaged in politics before the "Taff Vale decision" in 1901.

This Taff Vale case has become, in retrospect, a landmark of tremendous importance. It brought the trade unions toward the support of the Labor Representation Committee, and thus pushed to more rapid completion the new party's organization. In Taff Vale, an isolated valley in Wales,

the strikers on a short railway line carrying coal for the navy were sued for picketing. This practice of union patrolling, in an effort to prevent the hiring of substitute workers, was apt to involve intimidation. The case had been carried to the House of Lords, which, when acting as the court of highest appeal, consisted of the Chancellor and the few law lords. Their decision made trade unions financially liable for offenses committed by their agents in such disputes. Employers might now sue trade unions as legally responsible bodies if any damage were done. The Taff Vale decision eventually cost the Amalgamated Society of Railway Servants, which had no direct responsibility for this local strike, extremely heavy damages and costs. Consequently, to secure a reversal of this decision by Parliamentary act, the trade unions made common cause with the two socialistic groups on the Labor Representation Committee, but the latter lost much of their importance because the trade unions had long tended to vote with the Liberals and would scarcely support socialism. The Fabians, expecting the party to fail, continued to work through the old parties, while the Social Democratic Federation soon turned against the Committee. Although not overlooked by other parties, to whom the workingman's vote was of real concern, this development gave little indication at the time of its ultimate victories.

Social Legislation Program

Campbell Bannerman announced to Parliament that underlying every proposal of his government would be a policy of social reconstruction. Asquith, as Chancellor of the Exchequer, hinted strongly at radical measures. "Property must be associated in the minds of the people with the ideas of reason and justice." Spurred on by the Laborites, the Liberals would enact a whole series of laws which, from the standpoint of nineteenth-century liberalism, were socialistic in character and revolutionary.

One of the first, the "Workmen's Compensation Act" of 1906, increased the scope and made more stringent the provisions of two earlier acts (1880 and 1897) that had already established the principle of employers' liability for compensation to injured workmen. Before these acts a workman injured at work could gain compensation only by suing his employer, an expensive and lengthy process; but the principle of employers' liability made the employer legally responsible for such injuries to his workers unless the latter might be proved to have been willfully careless. The new statute of 1906 extended this principle to most workers who received less than £250 a year, not only in industrial accidents but also in many occupational diseases. Under this law a worker received about half his usual wages for the duration of his injuries or illness, while in case of death his dependents received a sum equal to three years' pay. Nearly six million workers were protected under this act.

The Trades Disputes Act, passed the same day, reversed the Taff Vale decision; for it granted unions the right "peaceably to persuade," or the right to picket, and also the right to boycott as long as these activities did not involve violence. The funds of unions, moreover, were safeguarded against such suits as the Taff Vale.

In 1908 a hot contest preceded the passage of the old-age pension bill, which provided, with certain stipulations as to minimum residence and income, a pension, on a sliding scale, of between one and five shillings a week at the age of seventy for every person of good character, who was not criminal, insane, or receiving poor relief at the time. Asquith, in his budget speech the year before, while carefully explaining that he was not a socialist, said that if the state intervened at the beginning of life's journey in matters of education, it was only logical that it should do so when an individual "spent out with a life of unrequited labour finds himself confronted in old age, without

fault or demerit of his own, with the prospect of physical want and the sacrifice of self-respect." This was completely at odds with the nineteenth-century idea that the individual, if compelled, could and would provide for his own old age. Balfour objected because of the difficulty involved in proving birth dates, to say nothing of character; and wanted to know where the government would find the money. But such arguments had scant effect; the majority in the Commons seemed to see little difference between a major general's pension and a laborer's. In reference to the character requirement, the Laborite Will Crooks retorted that an old man could not do much "on five shillings a week, whether his character is good or bad. . . . I said before, and I repeat it, if a man is foolish enough to get old, and if he has not been artful enough to get rich, you have no right to punish him for it. . . . It is sufficient for you to know that he has grown old." The bill became law, and by 1912 nearly a million aged people were receiving pensions at a cost of about £12,000,000, about half of the cost that year for naval construction and repairs. Later the amount of pension was doubled and the eligibility extended.

A Parliamentary committee in 1909 issued in forty volumes a report of three years' study of poor relief. Its wealth of statistical material revealed that one eighth of the population enjoyed nearly half the wealth. About one third of the employed adult workmen earned less than twenty-five shillings a week, while barely a quarter of them received more than thirty-five shillings. Such wages were barely enough for existence, even when they came in regularly, while there was no chance to set up a reserve to tide the worker through emergency periods of illness or unemployment. At a cost of about £15,000,000 a year the public was supporting some 600,000 fairly permanent paupers, in addition to many others who needed poor relief for shorter periods. The committee's recommendations to Parliament were divided into a majority and a minority report. The former was mild in its advocacy of changes, but the latter contained what at the time seemed very radical suggestions for social security. The Poor Law of 1834, which had supplanted the Elizabethan legislation, had dealt with poverty as an accomplished fact and with the best method of treating those who were already poor (see page 410). The minority report boldly advocated methods for alleviating some of its chief causes, such as sickness and unemployment. It consequently became a program for further important progress in social legislation.

The Labor Exchanges Act in 1909 embodied the moderate attack on unemployment which was advocated in the majority report. The more technical manufacturing became, the more difficult it was to obtain work for older and unskilled men. Following the German example, the government established several hundred public labor exchanges, which would serve as clearing-houses for job information, and so tend to decrease the wandering of the unemployed here and there in search of work. The project was successful to a moderate degree. By 1912 the labor exchanges filled roughly one third of the applications for employment.

Sweated labor also engaged the attention of Parliament in 1909, resulting in the passage of the Trade Boards Act. "Sweated" was an adjective applied to the unskilled labor conditions characterized by very low wages, excessive hours, and those bad unsanitary working conditions about which Charles Kingsley had written (see page 431). To lessen these evils, trade, or minimum-wage, boards, with a membership consisting of representatives of employers, workers, and government, were established to fix a minimum rate of wages. Only certain trades were covered, especially the manufacture of ready-made clothing, where women in particular, lacking unions to protect them, were often working very long hours for very meager pay. Inspectors were

to enforce the decisions of the local boards. The bill, as the government's spokesman asserted, was "the first occasion, certainly in modern Parliamentary times, in which any government has proposed machinery, first for deciding and secondly for enforcing a legal rate of wages." In older Parliamentary times, the Statute of Laborers and the Elizabethan Statute of Apprentices (see pages 128, 209) had set up machinery for deciding and enforcing a legal rate of wages; but those earlier acts were designed to keep wages down by establishing a maximum, and the machinery for enforcement had consisted of justices of the peace from the employer class, without the representation of the workers. The bill aroused much opposition. The tariff reformers declared that without a protective tariff, it would simply drive business out of England. Germany had introduced reforms of this sort, but she had high tariffs. The majority in the Commons was ready, however, to take the chance without protection. In 1912, after a serious coal strike, this principle was extended to the miners as well, even though they had their strong unions to protect them.

A third important piece of social legislation was the Housing and Town Planning Act of 1909. According to the census of 1901, millions were living in crowded tenements of only one or two rooms, not infrequently in cellars or basements. The industrial towns had grown in mushroom fashion with dingy houses, back-to-back, devoid of ventilation, and with almost no open spaces for back yards, let alone parks. In such towns the average "age of death of the gentry and professional classes was 44; of the tradesmen, 27; and among the laborers, only 19." The Liberal Government decided that the strong arm of the state was needed to help remedy this situation. As John Burns, the labor leader now in the ministry, declared, England was not that destitute of land. This act forbade the construction of back-to-back houses; gave medical officers increased powers; and made landlords at all times legally responsible for the condition of their houses. The demolition of certain dwellings was made mandatory, and opportunity to build better ones with state aid was assured. Municipalities were authorized to condemn certain areas and to create open spaces in accordance with such aesthetic and sanitary programs as they should see fit to adopt. Parliament also passed several lesser acts for the promotion of health and child welfare.

Finally, to crown the whole program of social legislation, there was the more radical and potentially more costly National Insurance Act, providing insurance against sickness and unemployment. Though proposed in 1909, it had to pass several hurdles before becoming law late in 1911. Sickness, it was pointed out, probably accounted for about 30 per cent of pauperism; sick workers lacked funds for doctors' bills and hospital charges, to say nothing of supporting their families during the period of enforced idleness. There was already a certain amount of private insurance against illness through mutual "friendly societies" and trade unions; but a large part of the workers who most needed insurance were unprotected. The act made sickness insurance compulsory for most workers (nearly fifteen million) receiving less than £160 a year. In this, the worker and his employer shared with the government in contributing a few pence each week toward the cost. In the event of illness the worker received not only doctor's services and hospital care but also for the support of himself and his family a specified sum each week. With wage-earners to be docked of their pay without their consent and doctors virtually dragooned into serving on boards, a storm of objections rose from all sides.

The government proceeded more slowly with the unemployment portion of the bill. It likewise called for contributions by worker, employer, and government, and provided, after one week of unemployment, for small weekly payments for a specified period, except for unemployment arising from the workers' own misconduct or from strikes, lockouts, or similar labor disturbances. Also, at sixty, if seldom unemployed, one might recover his own contributions to the fund, with the small accumulated interest. Whereas sickness insurance was extended to all trades, unemployment insurance had a modest start with about two and a half million workers in the engineering and building trades, where the seasonal nature of the work increased the risk of unemployment. Under such auspices began the great experiment which became the blessing or the curse of contemporary Britain—the "dole," as it came to be called in popular parlance—under which the postwar government would later support, with little or no contribution on their part, millions of unemployed in continual idleness (see page 595).

Thus, in the six years since they came into power, the Liberals had carried through an economic program breath-taking in its nature, which was entirely contrary to laissez-faire liberalism. Workmen's compensation, old-age pensions, and national insurance had helped to dispel somewhat the major worries which had continually hung over those with no economic margin of safety. Measures for housing, health, and child welfare had been passed to improve living conditions. The Trades Disputes Act had strengthened the trade unions, and the labor exchanges had to a minor degree relieved unemployment. This program, clearly following the German example, was the new Liberal answer to the economic ills of modern industrial society.

The rich had to bear most of the added financial burden, and the House of Lords, in trying to defend the interests of the upper classes, was shorn of most of its power. Now, after forty years, the upper classes were beginning to feel the effects of their abdication of traditional political control to the workers in the 1867 Reform Bill. Since command of the government depended upon a majority of the popular vote and since there were infinitely more poor men, the result was sooner or later inevitable, once labor appreciated its potential power. At any rate, ballots were less deadly than bullets, and Britain was so far spared the more violent forms of class struggle.

The Lloyd George Budget

Matters came to a head in 1909 with the "Lloyd George Budget." When Asquith replaced the dying Campbell-Bannerman as prime minister in 1908, his office as Chancellor of the Exchequer was filled by Lloyd George, the most prominent Welshman since Henry Tudor. Asquith, Grey, and others of the Cabinet were statesmen of the old school; but Lloyd George, short, dynamic, wiry, quick-witted, and persuasive, had the power of appealing to the masses, a useful quality in a democratic government. Almost at once, in preparing the government's annual budget for 1909, he was faced with the problem of finding about £14,000,000 additional revenue for old-age pensions, labor exchanges, and the projected national insurance, as well as for the construction of new warships in the costly naval race with Germany (see page 560).

He embodied three principles in his proposals. First, the burden of taxation should fall on all classes; higher import or excise duties on tobacco and liquor would do this. Second, the wealthy should pay more than they had in the past. To achieve this he would increase the income-tax rate, distinguishing between "earned" and "unearned" income; levy an additional supertax on incomes of over £5000; increase the "death duties," or inheritance taxes; and tax automobiles and gasoline. Finally, to bring in greater future revenues, he would clap a tax of 20 per cent on the increase of urban land values, along with a tax on unimproved agricultural land.

A chorus of protests broke forth against the budget, which many called a step toward socialism. These came chiefly from the rich, upon whom the heaviest burden would fall. It was argued that it would discourage private enterprise, leading to lower wages and increased unemployment; that capital would flee the country. Some said it would be impossible to distinguish between earned and unearned income. Less fundamental were the complaints that playgrounds would disappear and that it would discriminate against the workingman by increasing the price of whiskey but not champagne.

The major attack was against the land taxes, because Lloyd George proposed to take one fifth of the so-called "unearned increment." By this was meant the economic rent or the increase of value that came to the owner of land through circumstances other than his own efforts. This proposition was in some ways similar to Henry George's proposal for a "single tax" (see page 487) on the whole unearned increment to pay all governmental costs. It seemed unfair to both these men that a landowner in London, for example, should have his property soar in value through the years solely because thousands of new people happened to choose that locality to live and work. Without his doing a day's work in his life, the labor of other people increased his income. This unearned wealth of his, according to Lloyd George, was to be distinguished from that of a businessman who created his wealth as the result of initiative, risks, and hard work. In many cities large areas owned by a few proprietors, such as the Dukes of Bedford and Westminster in London (see page 328), were leased on long terms during which the owners did little to improve their value. A lease was seldom renewed except at a large increase in annual rent; and new houses were erected upon the land at the expense of the lessee, who, in addition, frequently had to pay an extra amount for the option of renewing his lease. Lloyd George felt it only right and proper that the owner of the

BRITISH REVENUE AND EXPENDITURES, 1908 AND 1912 (In Million Pounds)		
Revenue		
	1908	1912
Total	151	188
Customs	29	33
Excise	33	38
Income tax, etc.	33	44
Death duties, etc.	18	25
Stamp tax (documents)	7	10
Land-value duties		.4
Expenditure		
	1908	1912
Total	152	188
Navy	32	44
Army	26	28
Debt service	28	24
Education	17	18
Law and justice	4	4
Public works	3	3
Old-age pensions		12
Health insurance		2
Unemployment and labor exchanges	.1	.8

ground should make a special contribution to the state.

In the cities were many who virtually escaped taxation by leaving their land undeveloped, while throughout the country private parks, since they were unproductive, escaped taxation. The new budget put a small tax upon the value of undeveloped land unless it was useless for agricultural purposes or unless it was a park to which the public had access. Lloyd George's motives have been called social rather than financial, for they yielded only about the equivalent of the expenses of the royal family. He was interested in breaking up the abnormal concentration of land in a very few hands.

Attacks on the House of Lords

The budget passed the Commons with a safe majority. The House of Lords, however, was another matter. The Conservative peers, who comprised over four fifths of the House of Lords, had the power to throw the budget out if they dared, but it was contrary to custom to refuse assent to a money bill. The Lords had already defeated several Liberal measures, particularly those dealing with the liquor trade and with education, and had only grudgingly accepted the Liberal social-reform legislation. The time now seemed ripe to them for a rally in defense of the old order. They were especially angry at Lloyd George, the Welsh lawyer and pro-Boer agitator, whom they considered nothing but an inflammatory demogogue. They felt that a speech of his at Limehouse, in the slum section of London, exceeded the bounds of propriety when he had given instances and named names. He declared that it was not business but blackmail when the Duke of Northumberland, following a customary procedure of London ground landowners in renewing a lease, forced his tenant to submit to an annual increase of £4000, and in addition pay £50,000 and promise to put up certain costly buildings according to specifications supplied by the duke's architects.

Liberal feeling against the Upper House had been growing steadily more bitter since the later days of Gladstone. Whereas the House of Commons had adjusted itself to the democratic consequences of the Parliamentary reforms acts, the House of Lords had not. In the eighteenth century there had been little friction between the two houses (see page 298), since both were largely composed of landed aristocrats. Some peers also, through their control of boroughs, could dictate to their henchmen in the Lower House, who on the whole were fairly insensitive to the views of the particular constituencies which had elected them. Now changes had come with the rotten boroughs fast being eliminated, the electorate greatly expanded, party organization strengthened, and popular newspapers keeping the public in close touch with the political situation. The cabinet seemed to be growing more dependent upon the votes of the public than upon the votes of the Commons, whose individual members were thereby becoming less important. "What is outside Parliament seems to be fast mounting, nay to have already mounted, to an importance much exceeding what is inside," wrote Gladstone in 1880. The cabinet, supported by the electorate, seemed no longer the servant but the master of the Commons, with government policy therefore more sensitive to popular control. Consequently, when Lords and Commons disagreed, it was not an even contest between the free opinion of two groups, for the House of Commons was directly sensitive to the views of an electorate of several millions, while the Lords were responsible to no one. Most of them owed their seats to the accident of birth, and the ability which had won peerages for their ancestors was by no means always passed on to the later generations. As far back as 1885 there had been talk of "mending or ending" the House of Lords, and more recently the Liberals had passed a resolution through the Commons to the effect that "in order to give effect to the will of the people . . . the power of the other House to alter or reject bills passed by this House should be restricted."

Now the time had come for a final reckoning. The fact that it was a budget at issue seriously complicated matters. Even in the later Middle Ages, "money bills," or financial measures, always originated in the Lower House. It had become a well-established custom that the Lords might not alter a money bill, and their theoretical right to throw one out altogether had not been exercised for years. The Lords felt that it had been sharp practice for Lloyd

George to include his revolutionary and "socialistic" principles in a bill which traditionally enjoyed special privileges.

During the debates in the autumn of 1909 Lord Rosebery, the former Liberal prime minister, pointed out the danger in interfering in a financial measure. "My Lords, I think that you are risking, in your opposition to what I agree with you in thinking is an iniquitous and dangerous measure, the very existence of a second chamber. . . . The House of Lords has lived on menaces ever since I can recollect, and yet it seems to be in a tolerably thriving condition still. . . . The menaces addressed to you now come from a wholly different school of opinion, who wish for a single chamber and who set no value on the controlling and revising forces of a double chamber." Not surprisingly the Lords acted otherwise. This budget struck at landholding, with which their body had been identified since the days of the witan and the Great Council. It struck also at wealth, and their ranks included many of the men who would be liable for the heaviest income taxes and death duties in the whole kingdom. They were, moreover, Conservatives by a great majority. In November, 1909, they rejected the budget, over three fourths of them voting against it, and Asquith promptly asked King Edward to dissolve Parliament.

The general election early in 1910 weakened the Liberals' hold on the House of Commons. They returned with only a few more seats than the Conservatives, having lost many independent voters by their radical trend. This left them dependent upon the Laborite and Irish Nationalist votes, which they would receive only if they sponsored the measures desired by those two minorities.

The new House promptly passed the budget again, and this time the Lords did so as well, sensing the rising demand for a limitation of their powers. But they were too late, for the Commons were already discussing a "Parliament Bill" which would make it impossible for the Lords to delay for more than one month any bill certified by the Speaker of the Commons as a finance measure. It would also place upon the statute books any other sort of bill passed by the House of Commons three times within two years with or without the approval of the Lords. Thus, the legislative power of the House of Lords would be whittled down to a "suspensive veto" on nonfinancial measures.

In the ensuing violent disputes the Conservatives pointed out that this meant, in the last analysis, single-chamber rather than the old bicameral government. They considered the Lords as the defenders of British democracy, performing the valuable function of saying to the Commons, "Stop! Look! Listen!" and thus serving as a check upon precipitate action. The Liberals, with their Irish and Laborite allies, replied that the bill provided a quite sufficient check, since the two-year delay should be long enough for public opinion to manifest itself upon one side or another. The Liberals also pointed to the way in which the party situation was perverted by the constant heavy Conservative majority in the Lords: Conservative measures from the Lower House were passed almost automatically, whereas Liberal bills were rejected, modified, or twisted out of shape.

There was also the fundamental question of the composition of the membership of the Lords. Many objected to the pressure "to revise at ten days' notice the constitution of eight hundred years," but the pleas of the Lords that they were taken unawares and lacked sufficient time to reorganize were laughed out of court. They had, as a matter of fact, dallied with the idea of reforming themselves for several decades, but without indicating any serious intentions in that direction. Asquith, in reference to this current activity of theirs, quoted Dr. Johnson that "nothing concentrates a man's mind so much as the knowledge that he is going to be hanged." Now under fire, they had to defend their House as it was, "One-sided, hereditary, unpurged, unpresentative, irresponsible, absentee . . . with all its anomalies, all its absurdities, and all its personal bias." All through the late summer and the autumn a committee of four members from each party tried in vain to iron out the differences. The Lords would not pass the Parliament Bill, nor would the Commons accept their substitute measures.

Meanwhile Edward VII had suddenly died in the spring, after a reign of only nine years, and his conscientious, level-headed, and serious son had ascended the throne as George V. Asquith now secured from the new king an agreement to dissolve Parliament. In the second general election of that year, the principal issue was the Parliament Bill, as the Lloyd George budget had been in the first. The results were almost identical: Liberals and Conservatives were practically tied, the balance of power again resting with the Irish and Labor members. And the Irish wanted to break the Lord's vote because it would clear the way for home rule.

Once more, early in 1911, the Commons passed the Parliament Bill, and the diehards in the Lords determined to defeat it. The new king, however, followed the precedent of 1832 and agreed to create as many new peers as should prove necessary to pass the bill in the Upper House. This forced the issue; and in early August, with many members abstaining from voting, the Lords reluctantly passed the measure by 131 to 114 votes. Originally a bill might be defeated in any one of its three stages: during its passage by the Commons, during its passage by the Lords, or by royal veto. There had been no royal veto since 1707, so that now, with the curtailment of the power of the Lords, legislative power lay directly in the hands of the Commons. The Parliament Act also changed the maximum duration of a single Parliament. In 1694 the Triennial Act had set it as three years; in 1716 it had been extended to seven, and now it was reduced to five. Nothing definite was done concerning the membership of the House of Lords. The abolition of the absolute veto of the Lords opened the way for Irish home rule and the disestablishment of the Welsh Church. The latter's disestablishment, like Irish home rule (see pages 484 ff.), finally became law in 1914, after being three times passed by the Commons and three times rejected by the Lords. Both were then suspended during the war.

The House of Lords still maintained the highest position in the English judicial system, though its legislative functions were radically curtailed in 1911. For centuries England had left almost untouched the legal machinery established during the Middle Ages (see pages 68, 102). By a series of Judicature Acts between 1873 and 1910, this had all been co-ordinated into an orderly system. The three old common-law courts of King's Bench, Common Pleas, and Exchequer were merged into the King's Bench division of the High Court of Justice; the second division of the High Court was Chancery; the third division comprised the Probate Court and Divorce Court (subjects once handled by the Church) and the High Court of Admiralty. As in medieval times, the justices of these courts not only sat in London but also went on circuit to preside at assizes, as had the itinerant justices of Henry II. Cases might be carried from these divisions of the High Court of Justice to the Court of Appeals and from there, as a last resort, to the House of Lords. In its capacity as a supreme court, the Lords did not depend upon the decisions of the regular hereditary peers, unless they were judges or ex-judges; the legal business was handled by the Chancellor and a few "law barons" who were nonhereditary peers, fairly close counterparts of the justices of the United States Supreme Court.

In 1911 the House of Commons also voted salaries of £400 a year for its own members. This arose from a dispute with the Lords, acting in their judicial-appeal capacity. Their "Osborne Judgment" in 1909, like their earlier Taff Vale decision, was a blow at trade unions; for it made it illegal to assess union members with a "political levy" for the salary of Labor M. P.'s and forbade unions to engage in politics at all. If they paid their members, it was contended, they might control their votes, and the independence of the Commons would be threatened. As a matter of fact, the Labor members were required to take a pledge to vote as the party directed. It was also argued that the measure might cause men to enter Parliament to make money rather than to serve the state. Many Laborites, of course, lacked independent means. With close party balance the Liberals needed the Labor votes; consequently the salary measure was passed despite vigorous opposition. Thus one more of the old Chartist demands was realized. It was recognized that such a law tended to alter the character of the House, and succeeding decades were to witness surprising changes from the days when only gentlemen of independent means were members.

The Suffragettes

Meanwhile, England was confronted with the question of woman suffrage. Since the Industrial Revolution new conditions made it necessary for women to be more independent economically, as the average family could no longer support or find room in the home for dependent aunts, cousins, and sisters. The number of women in industry had been steadily increasing. In education they were admitted to the University of London in the late sixties, not long after that at Cambridge, and finally at Oxford, where eventually separate colleges were established for them. Agitation for enfranchisement had been proceeding quietly ever since the middle of the century, but without gaining many converts, John Stuart Mill being the only man of importance to advocate it. In 1903, however, under the leadership of Mrs. Emmeline Pankhurst and her daughters, Sylvia and Christabel, the Women's Social and Political Union determined to wake up England. Its members, not content with signing and circulating petitions, began to interrupt public meetings and to heckle politicians and statesmen in order to draw attention to their cause. Such conduct in England, on the part of women, was unheard-of, and the suffragettes, as they were called, were derided and denounced, but that only stiffened their determination. Year by year they took bolder steps. They padlocked themselves to the grillwork of the visitors' gallery in the Commons and shouted "Votes for Women!"; laid siege to Parliament Square; put chemicals in mail boxes; broke the windows of Bond Street stores; smashed porcelains in the British Museum; and slashed a Venus at the National Gallery. Rather than pay fines, they went to prison, where they endured much unflinchingly.

The cabinet, divided on the question, sparred for time, pleading that its social legislation must come first. Fearing a woman suffrage bill would alienate many of its supporters, it suggested a bill to overhaul the election laws. Should this be amended to give women the vote, it would not be the ministry's fault. The suffragettes accused the government of trickery and doubled the number of outrages, burning railway stations and cutting telephone and telegraph wires. Now they went on hunger strikes as soon as arrested. The authorities did not dare let them starve, and therefore they poured milk down rubber tubes through the women's noses. The public resented this brutal treatment and the suffragettes bravely persisted. Finally Parliament hastily passed the "Cat and Mouse" Act, by which the hunger strikers were released when dangerously exhausted on "license," but were returned to prison upon resuming their activities. They abandoned their agitation when war came in 1914.

Far from being content with the social

Arrest of suffragettes during their attack on Buckingham Palace, May 21, 1914.

measures in their behalf, the workers continued to clamor for more, both inside Parliament and outside. Though business was brisk, wages had not kept pace with the increased cost of living. The workers now turned to the unions for aid. Within ten years the total union membership had jumped from two to four million, while the process of consolidation and amalgamation had resulted in fewer and more powerful unions, better prepared than ever for concerted action. Other nations, as well as Britain, were experiencing labor disturbances in these same years. The Laborites did not consider the payment of members an adequate reply to the Osborne Judgment. In the Trade Union Act of 1913 they succeeded in having the scope of the term "trade union" extended and the right of the unions to use their funds for political purposes legalized, with the proviso that any member might refuse to pay.

The public was aroused by the tremendous epidemic of strikes in 1911 and 1912. Many of these were no longer local affairs. Through the new solidarity of the unions, it was possible to call a strike of all the workers in a particular activity, and even to secure sympathetic strikes of the workers in other fields. Three great labor groups were in a particularly advantageous position through their capacity to tie up the nation's business: the railway men, the dock workers, and the coal miners—and all three went on strikes during these troubled years. The railway men struck for the principle of the "closed shop," in which no one was to be employed unless he had a union card. For two days all transport was paralyzed. The railway unions merely obtained the right to elect their representatives on conciliation boards which were to decide disputes between employers and employees. The dock laborers and others in the Transport Workers' Federation also gained little in their strike. More was achieved by a million coal miners in the greatest strike which England had yet seen. They secured from Parliament inclusion in the minimum-wage provisions of the Trade Boards Act (see page 494). In 1914 these three unions formed a "triple alliance" for common action whenever they should agree. This was paving the way for labor's strongest weapon, the general strike. Some trade unionists, feeling that Parliamentary socialistic legislation was too slow a method, listened to the new doctrine of syndicalism, as taught in France, with its advocacy of violence as the best weapon. Even during the dark days of both World Wars labor would not hesitate to strike.

All things considered, Britain on the eve of the world conflict, was in a singularly nervous state. The government's home-rule policy (see page 485) had produced a serious danger of civil war in Ulster; growing bolder, the trade unions were staging more extensive strikes; and conservative folk of both political parties were much alarmed over conditions. No wonder the German observers thought the chances were good that Britain would stay out of a Continental war.

Chapter Twenty-seven · 1890-1916

Literary Crosscurrents

As the nineteenth century and Queen Victoria entered their last decade, a waning enthusiasm for many of the causes and achievements of the mid-Victorian years and an underlying apprehension for the future seem to have been largely responsible for the crosscurrents in English letters. These would continue into the early years of the new century under Victoria's amiable son—a period upon which the next generation, embroiled in war and chaos, would look back with envy as the "Edwardian Indian summer." But even in those years, the British actually had much to disturb them (see Chapters 25, 26, 29). Already in the making, and discernible in many directions, were the revolutionary forces of the twentieth century that would leave scarcely a sphere of life unchanged anywhere in the world. In particular, to the British upper and middle classes was finally coming a realization of the possible social consequences of their abdication of political power to the masses back in 1867 (see page 468). And abroad, imperial crises and the fast growing threat from Germany foreshadowed to some the approaching demise of the old, comfortable Pax Britannica.

It was, consequently, not surprising that this was a confused period in literature, with varying trends. Except for the early poetry, there did not seem to be much of a common denominator. A rather general disintegration was taking place in the former relative unity of ideas of the earlier Victorian period. The intellectual furor, for example, over Darwin's evolutionary theories was pretty well over. Social unrest, having become somewhat less noticeable, apparently did not present as much of a challenge to the creative writers. The socially minded among them were inclined to attack broader problems of society, rather than conditions affecting primarily the lot of the poor. Those who still concentrated on bettering the latter were apt to be motivated by the hope that this might be a way to improve the intelligence level of the newly enfranchised voters. All in all this period of mediocre poetry and great novels defied classification. The early poets turned to decadence and fantasy; the late ones were quite different; and the writers of fiction throughout the period pretty much followed several paths. Few of the novelists reacted to a common pattern: some turned to romantic adventure and others to current issues; some were buoyant in that day of imperial greatness, and others pessimistically anticipated the futilities and frustrations of the post-1914 world. And, as another gloomy portent of the future, science fiction for the young, even in the nineties, was bringing out the possible horrors of warfare in an age of advancing technology.

Aestheticism

The early poets—none of whom came anywhere near the stature of Britain's great poets—had much in common with one another. Their traits were drawn more from across the Channel in France than from the traditions of English letters. This influence was so dominant that some literary critics refer to this movement of the nineties by the French term, *fin de siècle*. More commonly, it has been called Aestheticism or more derogatively, decadence. This group lacked not only the technical skill but also the zeal of the French Symbolists with their protest against the scientific spirit, as well as the belief of the Realists and Naturalists that truth lay in the physical world. Even their understanding of Symbolism, to which they owed so much, was imperfect; only Arthur Symons, who wrote *The Symbolist Movement in Literature* and whose French translations influenced William Butler Yeats, (1865-1939) had any real knowledge of French literature. The Aesthetes might have given new life to their secondhand ideas, had they, like the Symbolists, made innovations in style. Their work seemed to justify the charge that they were superficial, for it never seemed to come to grips with any artistic creed. Perhaps its most marked characteristic was its concentration on the sensual. The Symbolists had used the techniques of the American Edgar Allen Poe in their efforts to reassert the mystery of life by obliterating barriers between the real and the dream world. Also like them, the decadents were poseurs in artistic selfconsciousness, cultivating the conception of ideal beauty, vagueness of expression, a languor of rhythm, and a liberal use of symbols or images. Both tended to dwell on sexual love and to go out of their way to

shock their readers. The artist was glorified as a being apart from the practical world and free from any responsibilities except to himself as he worshipped at the shrine of art.

In the beginning, the movement was strongly influenced by the "Pre-Raphaelite" poet and painter, Dante Gabriel Rossetti (see page 433) and by Walter Pater, the Oxford essayist, who was friendly with the "Pre-Raphaelites" though not of them. James McNeil Whistler was another artist who had some effect on the decadents. They copied the emphasis on beauty and the luxuriant imagery of Rossetti's poems but Pater's prose made a deeper impression. They followed their interpretation of his ideas in their actual living as well as in their literary practices. He stated in his *Renaissance:* "To burn always with this hard gem-like flame, to maintain this ecstasy is success in life." He meant a life devoted to "art and song," not, as the decadents thought, one of "high passions" and moral irresponsibility; he has thus been unfairly blamed for many of the excesses of his imitators. He anticipated much of twentieth century criticism in stressing that style and content were inseparable.

Yeats alone of the Aesthetes has been called of major significance; and he was with them only briefly in his youth or he might have shared their obscurity. The most flamboyant of them, Oscar Wilde (1854-1900), wrote with no apparent conviction in Aestheticism, but he played the role of its concept of an artist in society by wearing soft shirts, rolling collars, velvet coats, knee breeches, and oversized boutonnieres of a sunflower or lily. His ostensible explanation for this was to attract attention to the doctrine of beauty as its own justification. To little-known Ernest Dowson with his short lyrics has gone the credit for the best poetry of the group; but that is faint praise. Some cohesion was given to the Aesthetes when Yeats, Wilde, Dowson, and Symons, among others, founded the

Rhymers' Club, which included not only poets but artists, critics, and others interested in the movement. Members of the club published in two journals, the *Yellow Book* and the *Savoy;* but it was said of these journals that they contributed to the literary world only "a faint and unanalysable flavour."

Wilde's poetry would never have brought him literary fame; that came from his plays, called the wittiest comedies since the eighteenth century. The best known of these were *Lady Windemere's Fan, The Importance of Being Earnest,* and *An Ideal Husband,* which continued to be produced generations after his death. Their skillful plots and dialogue jested at Victorian sobrieties in the common mood of the "Naughty Nineties." It was a severe loss to the theater when this flow of comedies ceased after his notorious trial in 1895, with its sentence on a morals charge of two years in prison at hard labor.

Although in his young years, Yeats followed the Aesthetic pattern, in writing of the disparity between the real world and an ideal one, his ideal one, inhabited by the artist in solitude, was a delightful place peopled by Irish elves and fairies. He was, moreover, always aware that longing for the world of the imagination made one discontented with one's real surroundings. This tension between love of the ideal and the need to face the actual was what gave strength and meaning to much of his work. The symbols that he used in trying to capture the spiritual had a firm base in the lives and emotions of the people. Though he did not scruple to rewrite Celtic legends, his retention of traditional motifs gave his work a continuity lacking in other poetry of the nineties.

As the Aesthetic movement was dying out, Yeats and Lady Gregory in 1901 founded the Abbey Theatre in Dublin. At this time Yeats was already abandoning much of his cloudy romantic language and using more precise images. This theater proved detrimental to the spirit of Aestheticism as its aim as a national theater was to revive poetic drama and revitalize the stage by a new literary style. As for Yeats, his genius was a lyric rather than a narrative or dramatic one and his best works still lay ahead. To him belonged the credit of encouraging John Millington Synge (1871-1909), who was never a decadent, to leave Paris and come to Ireland, where he was to create a literary style based on the dialect of the Aran Islands. In *Riders to the Sea* and *The Playboy of the Western World,* Synge's dramatic imagination transformed the simple, dreary lives of those close to the soil and the sea.

An Era of Novelists

But the poetry shrinks into insignificance beside the novels and drama of those years at the turn of the century. Not only did novels dominate the literary scene, but they were part of a revolution in popular reading. The change in the reading public became discernible, along with different values in the fiction produced, even before the eighties. The Education Act of 1870 (see page 470) had much to do with this as it inevitably resulted in a tremendous increase in the number who could read and did, undistracted by radio or television. The tastes of this new army of readers were varied, and no one writer could hope to appeal to more than a segment of them. One particular result was that the old three-volume novel was doomed. The necessity to crowd the material into one volume forced a more tightly knit and more concise organization and treatment. Also, the novel began to divide into different types: thus there emerged not only the old "straight" novel, but the adventure novel, the mystery or detective story, the psychological novel, and so on. Along with the new short novel, the short story was found to have popular appeal, as Edgar Allen Poe's already had in the United States. The publishers as a whole only slowly awoke to this new situation. The big sale of Stevenson's *Treasure Island* (see page 507) in its one-volume form, after it had not gone particularly well in a boys' magazine, has been called one of the earliest factors in drawing publishers' attention to the way the wind was blowing. Easy reading, for which the desire had long existed, now had infinitely more voices raised in its favor. The novelists who met these popular requirements sold well; others could not or would not conform. Some of the latter, who were most acclaimed by discriminating critics for their style and creative part in the evolution of the novel, have been little read. Yet the fact remains that although only a few works of even the "great" writers deserved that adjective, an unusual amount of this vast bulk of fiction have been enjoyed even by a much later public.

Gissing, Moore, Butler

One group of these far from homogeneous novelists followed the tradition of the French Naturalists, the successors, in the second half of the nineteenth century, of Maupassant, Flaubert, and Zola. The spirit of the novels of George Gissing (1857-1903), George Moore (1852-1933), and Samuel Butler (1835-1902) was a far cry from that of the decadents' poetry. Their work demonstrated the changing form coming to the Victorian novel. Theoretically, in Naturalism, an almost photographic accumulation of facts was emphasized; after thus recording the details, a writer supposedly stood aside and let his characters work out their lives, like an elaborate chemical process, according to their heredity and environment. The English group, however, were rarely objective and on the whole were completely committed to things of this world. Gissing, who knew extreme poverty all his life, made all his heroes out of sympathy with their environment. They were men of the working class, who had educated themselves beyond it, yet, even when occasionally successful, were not wholly accepted into the aristocracy of birth. Like this title of his, they were *The Unclassed.* Such realism was not popular, though Gissing wrote well.

Moore, born in Ireland and educated as an artist in Paris, was inclined to be a poseur, but he had an admiring following. His most famous novel, *Esther Waters,* dealt with the uneventful life of a servant girl, starkly told. Her acceptance of her lot as a good one throughout her life, beginning with her seduction, revealed the nobility within her as she devotedly served her illegitimate child, her mistress, and her eventual husband. These writers did not blame the person involved when evil occurred, but rather the forces, mainly social, that they felt controlled man's destiny.

Butler's ideas, radical for his day, had considerable influence on Moore, Wells, Shaw, and Lytton Strachey (see page 513), as some recent literary criticism has shown. He was a satirist, somewhat like Swift, and aimed his bitter attack at the hidebound Victorian conventions and much else. He expected the machine eventually to ruin civilization. Darwin's theories interested him and led him to write some articles about them. He was also an artist whose paintings were exhibited at the Royal Academy. The grandson of a bishop, he told in his autobiographical novel, *The Way of all Flesh,* of a young man's revolt against his clerical home and family. Such rebellion against authority, whether of parents, church, or state, was a common subject at the time, but his vitriolic satire pretty well demolished some of the pious and hypocritical values of the Victorian compromise. Although the narrative, in the first person, was from the godfather's viewpoint, it was Butler himself piling vindictive evidence against his own family. Masterly though his satire of the parental portrait was, it has been criticized as too often merely spiteful and as clumsy compared to the more sophisticated methods of the American, Henry James.

Henley, Stevenson, Kipling

Another contemporaneous group—vigorous, affirmative, and lusty in spirit—further challenged the art for art's sake school. They strove, not unsuccessfully, to revive in British hearts Elizabethan joy in sheer living. On the whole, they were not popular in intellectual circles; they appealed rather to the average person who liked color and excitement in his reading rather than somber speculation and sober realism. They provided a strong counter current to the overniceness of those devoted to the exquisite phrase. Among those well in the forefront of the attack were William Ernest Henley (1849-1903), Robert Louis Stevenson (1850-1904), and Rudyard Kipling (1865-1936). A common thread united these three; its strength was indicated in one of Henley's poems:

> For still the Lord is Lord of might;
> In deeds, in deeds, he takes delight; . . .

Henley and Stevenson were at one time intimate friends—later, Henley was to resent what he felt was his friend's "unworthy popularity." Henley was largely responsible for popularizing Kipling, when the latter was a newcomer from India.

The versatile Henley was a poet, a dramatist, a literary critic, and editor of the *Scots Observer* of Edinburgh, which became the London *National Observer*. The son of a poor bookseller, he had tuberculosis of the bone from the age of twelve, but nothing seemed to crush the spirit of the author of *Invictus*, who lay month after month in a hospital, playing martial airs on a penny whistle. Like Pope, that other celebrated cripple of English letters, Henley was a harsh and waspish critic. At heart, however, he was warm and friendly, vying with Dr. Johnson as the hero of a dining club—dubbed the Henley Regatta. This included such well-known literary figures as Sir Gilbert Parker, Yeats, and young Kipling. The conservative *National Observer*

was an anti-Gladstone worshipper at the Disraeli shrine; but policy contradictions and clashes were usual with its strenuous editor. Though a Tory of Tories, he encouraged young writers—Hardy, Wells, Yeats, Shaw—though differing in political persuasion from himself.

The glory of England and death—his two main subjects—were in a sense both the result of his illness. His war against the body was a losing one; the battle for his country's supremacy had a firmer foundation and more lasting significance. Stevenson was in many ways similarly motivated; as he wrote to his friend, the novelist George Meredith in 1893, "I was made for a contest, and the powers have so willed that my battlefield should be this dingy, inglorious one of the bed and the physics bottle." Henley, who had loved violent exercise, was confined to the indoor life of the editor's chair; while Stevenson, likewise tubercular, had to live out of doors. They had much else in common; both wrote poetry and prose praising the active and sometimes violent life. They co-operated in writing plays; their correspondence with one another was voluminous. To Henley, Stevenson dedicated his *Virginibus Puerisque;* his courageous and masterful hero of *Treasure Island* flung his crutches over the stockade and defied the mutineers, very much as Henley was to throw his own crutches down the stairs after a departing Oscar Wilde.

Stevenson was to seek health in many lands—from Swiss sanatoria to California, to southern England, to Lake Saranac in the Adirondacks, and finally to Samoa in the South Seas, where he died. In his last six years, he lived like a Scottish laird in his home there. The Samoans called him Tusitala and turned to him for advice, especially in their dealing with the consuls of Britain and Germany who controlled the islands.

Despite his ever-recurrent hemorrhages, he was a prolific writer of poetry, short stories, essays, and letters as well as novels. He perfectly met the demands of the new reading public with his stress on romance and adventure, and with his finished style that has been called better than his context. He dreamt of being "the leader of irregular cavalry . . . at a hard gallop up the road out of a burning valley in the moonlight." Four novels showed how this came to pass in his imagination: *Treasure Island, Kidnapped, David Balfour,* and *The Master of Ballantrae.* Literary critics have sometimes scoffed at the first of these in particular as just another romantic tale for boys. But *Treasure Island* had more to it than that; there was the will to endure while life lasted, the concern with the psychology of character, and, as in most of Stevenson, skill in presentation.

Kipling's fame rested primarily on his portrayal in both verse and prose of the spirit of Britain's late Victorian empire, in general, and of her *raj* in India in particular. He wrote, too, of varied events elsewhere—all the way from Burma, East of Suez, where "the dawn comes up like thunder out of China 'cross the Bay"; on to South Africa where the prospector plunges into the wilderness lest "his neighbor's smoke shall vex his eyes"; and to the "Captains Courageous" on the foggy Grand Banks of the North Atlantic. But it was India with which his millions of readers associated his name.

He came naturally by that, for his father was in a cultural branch of the Indian civil service. Like most children of those Anglo-Indians, he and his sister were sent to England for their education for several homesick years. The later ones he spent in a school that prepared for Indian service, the setting for his unusual and popular story of three boys, *Stalky & Co.* At seventeen, he was back in India, where he soon found his stride as a young journalist. He was shortly to reveal to western eyes in direct and pungent verse and short story the manifold aspects of Indian life, fascinating, perilous,

and cruel. Though he has been charged with the naive belief that Victorian stabilities and imperial glories would last forever, his writings showed his awareness that life and government in India, three decades after the bloody Sepoy Mutiny, were poised on a precipice (see page 452). His characters were shown in a situation as it was and with its effect upon them; he did not go into deeper analyses. Almost every phase of government and society in India was reflected in his stories of the pukka sahibs of the civil service and the Army and their womenfolk. He pictured that hotbed of scandal, the cool hill town of Simla where officialdom sought relief from the unbearable heat of Calcutta, Lahore, and the other capitals; the devotion to duty of many of those officials burdened with never-ending tasks, in a pitiless climate even harder on their wives than on themselves; and those many others who succumbed to "What's the use?" and played around Simla or went home to a less exacting life. Now and then, as in his later short novel *Kim,* he wrote of the Indians themselves and his interest extended admiringly to the enlisted ranks of the "thin red line of heroes" as in his *Barrack-Room Ballads* of "Tommy Atkins" and "Danny Dever."

Sometimes, he voiced the spirit of the empire as a whole. Many Britons were grateful to have the verses of his "White Man's Burden" attribute unselfish motives to the often thankless tasks of empire (see page 548) at a time when doubts were creeping in. Yet he was not blind to future imperial implications. When Indian rajahs, African chiefs, and warships by the score were parading Britain's might at Victoria's Diamond Jubilee of 1897, his poem "Recessional" came like a dash of cold water with its warning "Lo, all thy pomp of yesterday, is one with Nineveh and Tyre" and its sombre refrain "Lord God of hosts, be with us yet, lest we forget."

At twenty-three Kipling had several volumes of stories published, of which *Plain*

Tales from the Hills was to be the best known; his first book had been verse. When he returned to England around this time, he went the long route by the Pacific, crossing China and the United States. In the latter he found no interested publisher; in fact, Harper informed him they dealt in literature; but in Britain his writings had already made him known. His themes— Anglo-Indian life, a dislike of democracy, a love for authority—all recommended him to the audience who had never ventured far from its insular armchair. His mastery of the new popular medium of the short story and the short novel, his easily-memorized verse, his command of rich and colorful language, and his concise journalistic techniques all insured that his name would soon become a household word. His growing reputation was further enhanced by Henley's publication of his poems, later collected as *Barrack-Room Ballads,* in his *National Observer.* One of these, "Mandalay," was perhaps the most popular of all he wrote; it was set to music, just as part of his "Gentleman Rankers" became embodied in Yale's famous Whiffenpoof song. After Kipling married an American, they lived for a while in Vermont, where some of his best work was done, including the immortal *Jungle Books,* that became familiar to children throughout the English-speaking world.

For a good many years, he was the object of scorn among most literary critics, but by 1960, the indications were increasing that the tide in his favor was well on the turn. During World War II, a famous English critic initiated a reappraisal, which brought a vehement rebuttal on both sides of the Atlantic. Kipling was castigated as a "sadist . . . morally insensitive and aesthetically disgusting," and condemned for "dedicating his talents to the praise of the practical man." One reason for the earlier chorus of disapproval, around 1900, was that he was outspoken in his opposition to the "precious poets" of the Aesthetic school; and they reciprocated. Oscar Wilde said of *Plain Tales*

from the Hills that it made the reader feel as if he "were seated under a palm-tree reading life by superb flashes of vulgarity," while Kipling made clear his dislike for those "long-haired things in velvet collars rolled" and the way they "moo and coo with womenfolk about their blessed souls." Kipling's glorification of force, his "flag-waving," his arch-conservatism (he has been quoted as feeling that even Stanley Baldwin, his cousin, was socialistic underneath), his didactic tendencies, all added fuel to the censure. Much of it would seem to have persisted because "the man and his works symbolize a part of British political and social history about which his countrymen have an uneasy conscience." That "the critics have underestimated and misunderstood the nature of Kipling's work"[1] would seem to be the status twenty-five years after his death.

Conrad

Joseph Conrad (1857-1924), one of the most original novelists of this varied period, has been generally called one of the greatest writers on the sea. Although he wrote in a language that he did not begin to learn until he was twenty-three, he achieved extraordinary color and rhythm in his prose; and under the name of Conrad, a shortened version of his own, his place in English letters was to become a unique and secure one.

Born a Pole, he became a British subject. He came of a family of landholders, who had long been active Polish patriots. His father, a poet and translator, was deported with his wife and family to northern Russia for his revolutionary leadership in the early sixties. His son, leaving home for good at seventeen, spent a few years in the French merchant marine. From the age of twenty-one, he was in the British merchant marine, rising from third mate to master, until his later thirties, when impaired health forced

[1] Noel Annan, "Kipling's Place in the History of Ideas," *Victorian Studies,* June 1960, pp. 323, 348.

him to leave the sea. He married an Englishwoman, and settled down in England, long his adopted country. His years at sea were often as exciting as his fiction, of which they were made a part. His various adventures were apt to find him on the side of his conservative and anti-imperialistic convictions. For example, when he was involved in gun smuggling on a French vessel in Spain, he was on the side of the royalist insurrectionists.

Like his voyages far and wide over the world, the settings of his novels were either at sea or in distant lands. He did not begin to write until toward the end of his sea career. His first book, which had Borneo as its locale, did not come out until 1895; its poor sale dismayed him, though it was praised as a "portent of something new" by H. G. Wells and others. *Nostromo,* sometimes called his best novel, was laid in an imaginary Latin American state, and *Lord Jim,* another of his more important works, in the Eastern seas. *The Nigger of the 'Narcissus,'* the story by which he felt he would "stand or fall" as a creative writer, took place entirely at sea.

His works were all adventure tales, but they were not on the order of Stevenson's, for Conrad's stories were dominated by his psychological analyses of his characters' inner conflicts. This unusual pattern brought him also somewhat into the category of his other contemporaries, who wrote of the problems of individuals and society. Not that his books showed "deliberate ethical purpose" or interest in society's welfare, but they had much to say of "tests of moral solicitude and estrangement, secret guilt, fear, and courage" in his searchings into his characters' souls and consciences. Frequently, he dramatized the man who in an irrational moment betrayed his fellows and then spent the rest of his life in trying to make up for that betrayal; Conrad emphasized that no one was without such a "plague spot." This happened with "Lord Jim," a mate on an old tramp ship crossing the Indian Ocean with hundreds of Moslem pilgrims en route to Mecca; she hit a derelict and Jim forgot his post and jumped for a lifeboat. He thus missed his chance to show the courage of which he had habitually daydreamed. This lapse kept him recurrently jobless until he met a romantically-minded trader who sent him to an island in the East Indies, urging that he "follow his dream" of heroic action instead of just brooding. Jim took over the rule of the island. Then, seeing his own image— had he not had this second chance—in a captured pirate, he freed him. When treachery and disaster followed, Jim took the blame and was killed. Conrad left open the question of whether Jim did this in religious atonement or simply in satisfaction of his own exalted ego.

Heart of Darkness, one of his shorter works, revealed similar concern. Although placed far from the sea in the "heart of Africa," it was a setting he knew well from a horror-filled trip of his own up the Congo which had left him too ill to continue at sea. His impressionistic picture of the creeping jungle, its primitive peoples, and the deterioration into savagery of the white men of the ivory stations provided an atmosphere of brooding evil for his probings into the potentialities of the "dark hearts" of his characters. Marlow, a seaman hired by an ivory company—his brutal predecessor had been killed by natives—pushed far up the Congo to rescue an agent, Kurtz, reputedly a genius, who had turned despot and gone viciously native. Throughout, Conrad stressed Marlow's identification with Kurtz's demoralization: "It is strange how I accepted this unforeseen partnership, this choice of nightmares forced upon me in the tenebrous land invaded by these mean and greedy phantoms."

Meredith

George Meredith (1826-1909) though better known for his novels, first wrote poetry and continued to do so at intervals. His earlier poems were in a simple lyrical mood; his later ones, like his novels, were dominated by his philosophical analyses of the human spirit and its struggles to rise above the brutalities of its original nature. But during the first half of the twentieth century, he failed to retain his earlier reputation in either sphere. For one thing, many of the problems of which he had written had lost their urgency. The pessimistic implications of Darwin's evolutionary theories no longer needed optimistic interpretations, nor did the growing freedom of women still require a champion against society's condemnation. But mainly Meredith's epigrams, his dazzling episodes of social smartness, and above all his verbose and tiresome style went out of fashion. His writing was not limited to novels and poems. Educated in Germany and intended for the law, he became a free-lance journalist, was briefly a war correspondent in the sixties, and then edited a review as well as being literary adviser to a publishing house.

Meredith has often been compared with the American novelist Henry James, who preferred England and the Continent to the crudeness he found in the United States. He settled in England in his early thirties but became her subject only in the last year of his life during World War I. As one of the most eminent writers of the day, he has sometimes been claimed by English literary circles also. He was a brilliant critic, whose analysis of novel techniques strongly influenced other writers. He was an extremely meticulous literary artist, sometimes so precise in his quest for the perfect word that his writings lost something in vigor. One of his favorite themes dealt with the American abroad, who might be subtly corrupted by the older civilizations of Europe. Meredith and James were similiar in their dramatization of the upper classes and of a traditional, highly developed society; and both portrayed people in their social interaction with one another.

Meredith's ideal character in both his fiction and his poetry possessed a fine balance of "blood, brain, and spirit." He felt that man, being a creature of the earth, must not attempt to make his will supreme against that of nature. His novel, *The Ordeal of Richard Feverel*, first placed him among the leading writers of the time, though not a popular success as *Diana of the Crossways* was to be some twenty-five years later. Richard Feverel's father believed that he could avoid or control his son's destiny by an ideal system of education. But Richard, by falling in love contrary to schedule, ultimately destroyed that illusion. By putting this love story in an idyllic natural setting, Meredith emphasized that the role of nature could not be ignored. In his long sonnet sequence, *Modern Love*, the tragic lovers destroyed themselves because their wit and brain made it impossible for them to communicate with one another. *The Egoist*, sometimes called his outstanding novel, was the story of a pretentious man, with overpowering self-regard, who thought of himself as a grand gentleman and benevolent person. He could only love where he could completely possess. When his fiancée fell in love with another man, he had to salvage his ego by making the world believe that he had rejected her. Meredith used what he called the comic spirit, "thoughtful laughter," to expose the self-deception, the pretense, and the inhumanity of characters like the "egoist" and Richard Feverel's father. Since, to him, their egoism and vanity came from their loss of a sense of proportion, the comic spirit by using irony could point that out and so restore them to a more sensible attitude, that did not defy nature.

Hardy

Thomas Hardy (1840-1928), like Meredith, wrote poetry as well as novels. Although the latter brought him fame and a modest subsistence, his "true genius," according to later critics, was the more "securely represented" in his poetry. Taken together, his prose and poetry showed the "continuity" between the two centuries that his life bridged. His novels belonged wholly to the Victorian era—the famous group centered in southwestern England appearing between 1874, when the popular success of *Far From The Madding Throng* enabled him to marry, and 1895, when *Jude The Obscure* met with a particular blast from his hostile critics for his "barnyard morality" and "blasphemy." Hardy himself indicated that he felt his novels were the means to permit him to devote himself to his true vocation, poetry. Most of this appeared in the twentieth century, although some of it had been written before his novels. On the whole, critics have been unanimous in their high praise of his many short lyrics, but their reaction to his long epic on the Napoleonic Wars, *The Dynasts,* has been mixed.

Hardy was born in Dorset, a part of King Alfred's long extinct "Wessex," where his forbears on both sides had been rooted. Living in that region most of his life, he knew and loved it well. An architectural apprentice in his youth, his work on the restoration of old churches and his own wide reading on the subject made him an expert on early English ecclesiastical architecture. In fact, he was undecided between that profession and writing. The publisher who rejected his first novel had done so on the advice of Meredith, who asked, however, to meet its author. It was to be Meredith who persuaded Hardy to choose writing as his career.

His novels bore a strange likeness to the Greek tragedies; in *Tess of the D'Urbervilles*, Aeschylus of Greece appeared almost to have been born again in "Wessex." Hardy believed in predestination as firmly as the bleakest covenanter in Scotland. In telling of what he saw without hope, yet without fear, he seemed to sense the end of an era he disliked and the advent of one for which he had no enthusiasm. Although his characters have been called stereotyped and his plots without depth, his vivid descriptions of the English countryside, his quaint humor, and his "gift of anecdote" made him a colorful storyteller. His intense love of nature in all its phases resulted in his becoming an expert on birds, flowers, and trees. "Fair prospects," he wrote "wed happily with fair times; but what if times be not fair?" They did not seem fair to him; and he brooded much. Yet interfused in the gathering gloom was his humor and his overflowing appreciation for all the manifestations of nature and for simple folk subject to her vagaries. His characters, largely peasants, artisans, and yeomen, lived usually in his own region, as did Arnold Bennett's (see page 513). Some, like *The Return of the Native*, however, were placed in a setting of a rougher land of scattered farms and villages. His detailed accounts of cider making, thatching, dairying, and other rural pursuits indicated his own thorough familiarity with country living. One sees the little carts and wagons, slowly winding around hill and dale, rambling across moorland and heath, as slowly the peasants whom he knew so well pondered their problems, made love, withstood the buffets of an unfeeling universe, or yielded to them.

Wells

H. G. Wells (1856-1946) was a versatile writer who did not limit himself to fiction. It has been said of him and of Shaw, the dramatist, that the often-used term "end of century" should never be applied to these two; they were "turn of the century," looking as they did to the future and its betterment. They were radical reformers, belonging to the Fabian Society (see page 488). Along with Bennett, the novelist, they were of the middle class, but far lower down the social ladder from him, Wells's family barely clinging to its lowest rung. His fight against extreme poverty was, moreover, to be made particularly hard by his bad health. He loved to read and read everything scientific that he could find. A drapery clerk, he was twice discharged; once in error for a theft and next for fighting. Eventually winning a scholarship, he went to the Royal College of Science, where Huxley was lecturing (see page 435). Then he obtained a post in a second-rate school, only to fall ill. In bed for months, he experimented with writing, mainly science fiction. His fascinating stories about invaders from Mars, a machine which took its operator backward and forward in time, and other yarns sold well.

By 1900, he was turning to more serious fiction. He was a fast writer, with at times more of the techniques of a propagandist than an artist. He himself said he was primarily a journalist and that his ideas were the first consideration; but his humor was of the type of Dickens and greatly enriched some of his earlier books. As time went by, he wrote prolifically, not only fiction, but essays and even a history of the world. He felt that future security required an overall government for the world. Even his fiction at this time seemed to be primarily intended as propaganda.

Previously, his novels had been widely read; they had good plots, humor, and sometimes the quality of the romantic adventures of his early science fiction. But their unique value came from the way they gave a better understanding of British life just before and during World War I than probably any other account. In *Tono Bungay*, Wells moved his hero from one environment to another until several levels of English society were described: the stately way of life on a great estate before taxes became astronomical and servants virtually disappeared; the extreme evangelical atmosphere in a country baker's home; and the household of an apothecary, in transition to extreme wealth due to his patent medicine, mostly water, Tono Bungay, an early success of commercial advertising. Another novel in this group, *The New Machiavelli*, based on an analogy with

the *Prince*, by the sixteenth-century writer, Machiavelli, gave an excellent analysis of the political trends leading up to the 1909 Lloyd George budget. The plot concerned a young Cambridge graduate, bent on a Parliamentary career, and his baffled efforts to decide his party preference. Socialistic in his thinking, like Wells, he entered the Commons as a Liberal, only to turn Tory in voting against that budget.

One of the first novels of World War I, and Wells's outstanding contribution in his portrayals of British life and thinking was *Mr. Britling Sees It Through*. In this, Wells kept alive an unforgettable picture of the British relaxed in their security after a century without a major war when the unbelieveable befell them in 1914. The humor and pertinacity that was to symbolize British endurance in the great wars ahead and the strong undercurrent of what came to be called old-fashioned patriotism, as depicted in Wells' easy, fluid style, have given this book historical importance in understanding the early twentieth century.

Bennett

Arnold Bennett (1867-1931) was born in Staffordshire, the pottery region of the industrial midlands. His lawyer father pushed the family from the ranks of the low middle class to a higher level; it has been said that whereas Wells's family were of the servant class, Bennett's was to become among the employers of servants. Bennett went into his father's law office as an unpaid clerk, but winning a prize for a short story turned him to a literary career. He first wrote beauty hints and advice to the lovelorn in a fashionable weekly magazine, of which he rose to the editorship. In his early thirties after his first novel appeared, he went to France to write, later marrying a French actress. But despite the fact that he turned out a large quantity of writing, he was over forty when *The Old Wives Tale* established him as one of the foremost novelists and itself among the best novels of the century.

Bennett, like that other sojourner in France, George Moore, approached the novel from the Naturalist viewpoint, but in Bennett's case, there was much more warmth and comedy, and less objectivity. His "whimsical, impudent, and realistic" imagination made ordinary happenings seem extraordinary. This was especially true of his group of novels, considered his best, that centered like *The Old Wives Tale* in the pottery towns of his native region—the early *Anna of Five Towns* and his trilogy, *Clayhanger, Hilda Lessways,* and *These Twain.* Though both he and Hardy concentrated on specific regions, their attitude toward them was miles apart. Hardy loved his "Wessex" all his life; to him it was the place of all others to return. That was the basis of his stories. But Bennett had left the "five towns" as young as he could and never went back for more than a few days. To him, they were provincial and so he wrote of them, although he was as steeped in their atmosphere and traditions as Hardy was in those of his countryside. In these regional novels, generally considered his outstanding achievement, he unrolled "the panorama of life" with the "tiny, detailed incidents of its thousand acts." Beyond that careful picture, he did not analyse problems or characters.

During their lifetimes, Bennett like Wells achieved amazing public prominence. This came not so much from their novels as such but because they played the role of journalists in being ready to serve as oracles on any subject under the sun. In the drama, George Bernard Shaw's popular reputation had a similar basis; and the three became the most highly paid writers of the English-speaking world.

Galsworthy

John Galsworthy (1867-1935) has been bracketed with his contemporaries, Wells and Bennett, in the top rank of the novelists of the first half of the century. Unlike them, he was also a popular playwright and, as he came from an aristocratic family of means, his writing never had to be his livelihood. He went to a prominent school, Harrow, where he was a good athlete as well as student, and to Oxford, where jurisprudence was his major interest. He continued with the law at Lincoln's Inn, marine law being always his speciality. He spent much time traveling about the world on freighters to familiarize himself with the legal problems of ships and seamen. On one such voyage, he came in contact with Conrad, then a mate; a lifelong friendship resulted despite their different backgrounds and outlook.

His best-known work was the popular *Forsyte Saga,* a compilation of five previous novels dealing with a family of his own class, whom he made live for his readers. The first of these, and generally considered the most interesting, *The Man of Property,* referred to Soames Forsyte, who viewed his unhappy wife—helplessly tied by the current divorce laws—as his private property, in exactly the same category as his paintings and his land. His life story ran through the whole *Saga;* in some parts he was the key character, less often he was in the background. But he was overshadowed by his family, even down to cousins and in-laws. Its many members, all sharply portrayed by Galsworthy's keen analysis, were tied together by love of possessions. *To Let,* the last of these novels, climaxed the tragedy that had been brewing from the first; Soames found that neither he nor all he possessed could help the one person he had ever loved, his daughter. In characteristic irony, Galsworthy called the family "half England, and the better half, too, the safe half, the three per cent half, the half that counts. It is their wealth and security that makes everything else possible; makes your art possible, makes literature, science, even religion possible."

Although he had had no experience in writing for the stage, his plays from the first were effective and, like Shaw's, were generally popular productions. In his plays, his interest in ethical and social problems was more evident than in his novels. His treatment of opposing points of view in his characters showed his scrupulously judicial effort to be fair. Three noteworthy dramas of those produced before World War I were *The Silver Box, The Eldest Son,* and *Justice.* The last, perhaps the most famous, was a scorching indictment of the English divorce laws at the time, and of English penology.

After his death, Galsworthy's work was considerably disparaged by some critics. His weakness, it was pointed out, was his tendency to take sides and, unlike Bennett, his failure to conceal his own feelings about his characters. In the case of Soames Forsyte, for instance, Galsworthy's sympathy obviously increased until at the end he seemed to be identifying Soames with himself. Furthermore, in contrast to Bennett, Galsworthy tried to analyze and assess a situation or problem, a characteristic which could lead to partisanship. Yet to other critics, Galsworthy was "a subtler artist and more penetrating critic of life" than Bennett. He continued to be praised for his "strong sense of character" as well as for the undisputed value of the broad picture he drew of British upper-class society. He was charged generally with being unable to "escape from his own class" and thus with lacking feeling for the poor; yet his writings, particularly his plays, showed him to be always on the side of the underdog.

Dramatist: Shaw

George Bernard Shaw (1856-1950), the dramatist, unlike some of the novelists, increased in stature over the years; he would seem to have achieved a high place in the whole long history of the English theater. He possessed an extraordinary combination of talents—clear insight into the root of social problems, the gift of comedy, exceptionable originality, and above all, a brilliant mind. In addition, he was a hard

worker, meticulous in the form of his writing and equally so in the details of play production. During his long career, however, the attention of the general public was perhaps focused less on his genius than on his startling pronouncements on all sorts of things and his flamboyant appearance. His flaming red beard, bristling eyebrows, and ever-ready repartee often drew crowds on London streets in his younger days.

He was born in Dublin; his middle-class parents were definitely on the down-grade, his father being a drunkard and his mother, seemingly indifferent to her son, eking out the family living by music lessons. After a meager education and an early job as an office clerk, Shaw at twenty went to London to write novels. As no one would accept his novels, he went to work for a telephone company, and then turned to earning a few pounds as a music critic. He was soon welcomed with open arms to the Fabian Society (see pages 434, 488) for which he wrote many tracts. It had been the intellectual aspects of Fabianism that had drawn him, but his ardent espousal of Marxism in speech and writing went far beyond the moderate Fabian approach and his own convictions. Only once, in fact, did he march in a parade of workingmen demanding revolution, and then he admitted his presence was incongruous.

During the last five years before the turn of the century, his fame as a playwright was already beginning to mount. He found ideals and realities sadly commingled in a mixed-up world. Always delighting in controversy, he fostered it by turning everything possible upside down in his plays. His ridicule left little untouched; the army, the church, landlordism, marriage, the medical profession, contemporary sex mores, as well as much else were all his targets. Most of his plays were entertaining, thanks to his wit, and a few, such as *Candide, The Devil's Disciple,* and the much later *Caesar and Cleopatra,* were relatively free from his usual propaganda. He was a reformer who believed that nothing should be hidden that concerned the welfare of society, and he began to write in an era that believed that social ills were better left unmentioned. Consequently he seemed wicked and immoral in many conventional eyes. Furious controversy was aroused by one of his earlier plays, *Mrs. Warren's Profession,* which brought prostitution—a subject particularly taboo in polite society—into the open. Although Shaw's portrayal of vice made it anything but attractive, the play was barred from the stage in England and elsewhere for many years.

Among his later plays which preached a moral was *Androcles and the Lion,* a frontal attack on Christianity. The introduction—always an important part of Shaw's works and in this case longer than the play itself—provided in essence an essay on Christ's religious ideas. According to Shaw, Saint Paul had twisted the original intent of Christ's teachings into what came to be known as salvationist Christianity, making slaves of its adherents and blocking all hope of social progress.

In *Man and Superman,* perhaps the closest Shaw came to declaring his own philosophy, the chief character did not want to be tied down by marriage and a family. Yet the so-called life force, the primitive urge to have children, was to push him into marrying an unscrupulous woman. Shaw would not accept a personal God, but here he indicated his belief in an interrelation between man and nature in a curious blend of mind and instinct. To him, all that was best in the artistic and the active world was created by men of genius "selected by nature to carry on the work of building up an intellectual consciousness of her own instinctive purpose." He did not mean the single superman of German philosophy, but the selective breeding of many supermen, who would be capable of governing or recognizing the capacity for government and benevolence in others.

Georgian Poets

As George V succeeded his father, Edward VII, four years before World War I, new poets, protesting rather vaguely against their Aesthetic predecessors, were to be called Georgian. Their lyric poems, although dissimilar, generally followed a somewhat sentimental and pastoral pattern, with their form simple and their subjects quite unsophisticated. Included among them were Walter de la Mare, Rupert Brooke, Harold Munro, and John Drinkwater. They were to be strongly criticized for their lack of depth and avoidance of harsh reality. Particularly annoying to later generations were the idealistic and at the time extremely popular war poems of Brooke, who had been killed in 1915 before modern warfare had approached its crescendo of horrors. Another movement during the later war years was short-lived Imagism. Although in point of time technically "Georgian" poets, the Imagists were very different; they opposed vagueness by trying to render the image in their verse in clear, concise terms, free from all traditional poetic forms. Its chief, most successful sponsors were Americans—the young Ezra Pound, Amy Lowell, and Hilda Doolittle (writing as "H.D."). Their work overshadowed that of the main English Imagist, Richard Aldington, who married "H.D."

Although these less noteworthy poets, as well as some of this indeterminate period's outstanding prose writers, would continue to produce for many more years, younger writers were soon to be seeking actively for new techniques in their efforts to combat the frustrations and futilities of a drastically changed Britain.

Dominion Over Palm and Pine

A striking change in the attitude of the average Briton toward his empire came during the last three decades of the nineteenth century. It was heralded by the delivery of Sir John Seeley's lectures on the expansion of England, which gave the impression that Englishmen were uniquely, if not divinely, appointed to rule over Negroes in Africa and brown men in India. Indifference and apathy gave way to enthusiastic zeal two or three decades later when Rudyard Kipling was pouring forth poem after poem praising the pluck and daring of Britons overseas, and emphasizing their "dominion over palm and pine." In Africa, in Asia, in Canada, and in Australia, to say nothing of old England, there came a rebirth of imperial feeling, in respect both to the self-governing colonies of European stock and to those of exploitation; and this was soon translated into action by an enlarged empire acreage and a new empire unity.

Britain was not alone in this new "imperialism" or "colonialism," as it came to be called by the colored races. She was more or less pushed into it by the aggressive expansion of France and other continental powers. During the next quarter century, they would extend European influence over much of Africa and many other parts of the world. For decades Britain might have taken almost anything she wanted around the world in the way of colonies and protectorates all the way from the Guinea Coast out to the Fiji Islands, but the "Little Englander" spirit had opposed that, along with its negative attitude toward the colonies of settlement. As late as 1865, a Parliamentary committee had resolved that "all further extension of territory or assumption of government, or new treaty offering any protection to native tribes, would be inexpedient." It was only when other nations threatened to stake off claims that might bar Britain's traders from former markets that in self-protection she joined in the scramble, first in Africa and then in China.

"Map Coloring" and "Financial Imperialism"

This new imperialism shared certain features with the old colonial system. Overseas possessions were still expected to be markets for the expanding industry of the mother country, and to furnish exotic products to round out her national economy (see page 226). Now appeared two new features. One was "map coloring" where imperial authority "showed but did not pay" in contrast to the old colonizing which

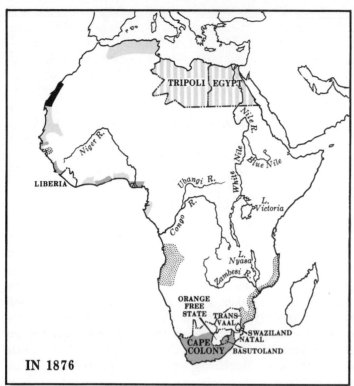

EUROPEAN
HOLDINGS
IN
AFRICA

1876 and 1914

Boundaries used are
those of 1914

IN 1876

MAP KEY

British holdings

French holdings

Portuguese holdings

Spanish holdings

Turkish holdings

Belgian holdings

German holdings

Italian holdings

Independent or
unorganized

IN 1914

was expected to be profitable. Secondly, "financial imperialism" "paid but did not show," whereas in the old colonies the mother country's flag, armed forces, and officials made her authority obvious to all. With plenty of the world map already colored in British red, Britain did not go in for that gratification of national vanity as did France with her annexation of the Sahara Desert and Italy with her acquisition of various other sandy wastes that, before the days of oil, no one else wanted. The financial imperialism developed from lending money at high rates of interest to backward regions, which were allowed to go through the forms of self-government even though the real authority was exercised from London, Paris, New York, or elsewhere. Egypt and China would be prime examples of this process. Though the new overseas acquisitions were advertised as possible outlets for surplus population, the "colony of settlement" aspect was not prominent in the new imperialism, which, because temperate regions were already preempted, centered in tropical areas and not in good white man's country. Germans or Italians who wanted to migrate were far more apt to head for the United States, Brazil, or the Argentine rather than Kamerun or Eritrea. So far as Britain was concerned, Canada, Australia, New Zealand, and the other self-governing areas were not part of imperialism proper, and it was only gradually that interest in them gained momentum.

The Scramble for Tropical Africa

The opening of tropical Africa by renewing European interest in the Dark Continent probably did more than anything else to usher in this new era of imperialism. Back in the later fifteenth century, it had attracted attention when the Portuguese were seeking a way to India; but thereafter, it had figured mainly in popular imagination as the place where Negro slaves had been obtained. There had been some ex-

perimentation with colonies of settlement at the southern tip (see page 456) and in Algeria, where French enterprise had begun to be active in the middle of the nineteenth century. Africa as a whole, however, until the sixties and the seventies, had been largely a land apart, vast, unknown, completely mysterious.

During these two decades came the more important explorers, a few of them French or German, but the majority British. To David Livingstone, Scottish missionary, and to Henry Morton Stanley, Welsh-born American journalist, belongs the chief credit for making the world "Africa-conscious" by revealing the hitherto unknown geography of its tropical interior. Livingstone traced the whole course of the Zambesi, discovering Victoria Falls, while after his death, Stanley was to do likewise for the mighty Congo. Both did much to show the pattern of the great lakes in eastern Africa. Stanley, star reporter of the *New York Herald*, had fought on both sides in the Civil War before he first went to Africa, sent by his paper in search of Livingstone, who had disappeared in the jungles of East Africa. Stanley located the elderly, ill Scot on the shore of Lake Tanganyika, where he greeted him with his famous "Dr. Livingstone, I presume." Livingstone continued his work in East Africa, where he died before long. His funeral in Westminster Abbey took place just two months after Disraeli succeeded Gladstone in 1874. Five other Britons explored the lakes of East Africa—Speke, Grant, Burton, and the Bakers, husband and wife, who between them demonstrated that the White Nile had its source in the great Lake Victoria.

The first enthusiastic convert to African possibilities was Leopold II, the Belgian king who summoned an international conference in 1876 at Brussels; this led to the "International Association for the Exploration and Civilization of Africa" with committees in the various countries. The particularly active Belgian committee later

Henry M. Stanley's greeting: "Dr. Livingstone, I presume," when he located the missing missionary at Ujiji on Lake Tanganyika, November 10, 1871.

employed Stanley, who by 1884 had mapped out for it in the heart of Africa some 900,-000 square miles, shortly to be recognized as the Congo Free State. This quasi-international state, under the control of the Belgian king, started the major rush of the European powers for African loot.

There they directly annexed territory for their empires without the polite disguises of spheres of interest, concessions, or leases often employed by them elsewhere. The French, already in North Africa, secured the north side of the Congo basin and also extended their control over other parts of West Africa. This spread of French influence alarmed the British and German merchants who had long been trading in that pestilential region. At their simple little "factories" or trading posts they had swapped various European manufactures for African commodities, particularly palm oil, an important ingredient of soap. Some

of them had established steamship services to link up their scattered posts. Their governments, however, were not yet interested in starting or increasing their political controls in the region. Fearing they might now be shut out of the areas where they had been trading freely, the British and the Germans began to form colonial trading associations.

Then almost overnight, Germany blossomed forth with a sizeable colonial empire, with Bismarck's reversal of his former negative attitude toward imperialism, and the great scramble was on. In 1884, Britain suddenly awoke to what was happening when Gustav Nachtigal went down the west coast in a gunboat hoisting the German flag in what became the little colony of Togoland and the much larger one of Kamerun (Cameroons). In the latter, the British lost out by a week—their consul was rushed down to take it over only to find the Germans already there. He did, however, quickly have the British flag hoisted over what would become part of the great colony of Nigeria just to the northward. Down in the vast barren region in southwestern Africa, the British took one port, Walvis Bay, but despite urgings from the Cape, refused to proceed further. But that same year, 1884, the Germans took over the rest as their colony of Southwest Africa.

Nigeria and Gold Coast

On the low, swampy, malarial west coast Nigeria, which was then, next to India, the largest dependency directly subject to the crown, dated back to 1879 and the formation of the United African Company, a successful business enterprise which exploited the lower Niger valley. Reorganized twice, this corporation, later the Royal Niger Company, received a charter in 1886; and to its charge was delivered the British protectorate proclaimed the preceding year over the Niger delta and a considerable distance up that river. For fourteen years the company continued its role as political overlord and extended its sway far into the interior, at one time claiming no less than half a million square miles. By the end of the century it could boast that it had an army of its own, commanded by a modern conquistador, Colonel Lugard, already celebrated for his exploits as an empire-tracker in East Africa (see page 522). As a result, it had rid the country of slave raids and had kept trade and communication open all the way from the ocean to Sokoto. Having done this, it sold all its war material and administrative buildings to Britain and retired from the political field.

The Colonial Office now created two large divisions, Southern Nigeria and Northern Nigeria. The first, including the old British colony of Lagos, was already pacified. The second, two thirds of the whole, was a much wilder region, where the company had clung closely to the rivers, and

had warily stood aloof from the fierce Moslem tribes of the interior. The Hausas, pure Negroes, had been driven headlong before these tribes, with a resulting reign of terror. Lugard, now Sir Frederick, was sent to end it. Speedily three chieftains submitted to his rule, and shortly afterward a fourth, an old slaver who had boasted that he would die with a slave in his mouth, like a cat with a mouse. In 1903, Lugard subdued the last remaining tribe, the Fulani, who, entrenched in their walled town, had forced all Northern Nigeria to pay tribute. New friendly emirs were installed, and wandering tribes of robbers were brought to heel.

An indirect government was set up with rule through native chiefs. All non-official Europeans, such as missionaries and traders, were refused admittance to the region. British residents were placed over the various provinces, some the size of England or Scotland, into which the land was divided, but were not to interfere with the barbaric customs beyond forbidding poison for suspected criminals, throwing of people to crocodiles, or forcing of twin babies, believed to be fathered by the devil, into gourds. In contrast to the system in British East Africa, the land was left in tribal holdings. In 1914 all Nigeria was united under the governorship of Lugard, recalled from Hong Kong for this post, but the indirect rule was retained in the northern part.

Smaller than Nigeria but relatively more prosperous was Gold Coast to the westward. It had slipped into the empire much more gradually, for the Royal African Company had had posts there back in the days of the slave trade, and by 1871 the British had bought out the former Danish and Dutch interests. Time and again all through the century Britain sent punitive expeditions against the fierce Ashantis in the interior; least successful was the first when the governor was killed and, as a tribute to his bravery, the Ashanti king ate his heart and used his skull as a drinking cup. Aside from the gold which gave the region its name, and the usual palm oil, Gold Coast eventually grew rich from cocoa. A native in 1879 returned from contract labor at an island in the Gulf of Guinea with some cocoa plants; by the turn of the century natives were growing them all over the colony assisted by government agricultural stations. Eventually Gold Coast, later Ghana, would become the world's leading producer.

Unlike East Africa with its temperate regions, there were only a handful of Europeans in West Africa. This was partly because of its wretched climate; also Europeans were forbidden to acquire land. In Nigeria in 1911, for instance, there were only about 1000 whites in a population of some 17,000,000. That was one reason why eventually the British could give up Nigeria and Gold Coast without the stresses caused by the well entrenched white settlers in Kenya or French Algeria (see pages 705 ff.).

East Africa

On the eastern coast, out of the rivalry of the British and the Germans, were to arise German East Africa (Tanganyika) and British East Africa (Kenya), as well as two other British possessions, Uganda and Zanzibar. Until that time the entire region from Portuguese East Africa (Mozambique) to the Gulf of Aden supposedly belonged to the sultan of Zanzibar, who had tried to lease all his land to a British merchant at Zanzibar in 1877, but England would have none of it. Thereupon Dr. Karl Peters, a very energetic German promoter of imperial expansion, intrigued at Zanzibar with native chieftains and signed innumerable treaties; and almost before the British realized it, the German East African Company was born, claiming some sixty thousand square miles, lawfully acquired. While all this was going on, the Portuguese revived their old, but badly neglected title to huge tracts— Angola, bordering on the Atlantic in West Africa, and Mozambique on the Indian Ocean in East Africa. At the end of 1884, Bismarck assembled an international conference at Berlin to ratify all these sudden sizeable acquisitions, which had brought much of the Dark Continent under European control.

In East Africa, Sir William Mackinnon, head of the big British India steamship line, challenged Peters's ambitious claims. The Foreign Office then entered the picture; and a bargain was struck with the Germans, whereby they were to keep to the south in the present Tanganyika and the British to the north in the present Kenya and Uganda.

The Imperial British East African Company was formed to exploit the land reserved for British enterprise. As a business concern it was not successful; for though it had some 170,000 square miles at its disposal, they were difficult of access, and capital was limited. But as a political agent for the extension of the empire the company proved invaluable.

Particularly important was its activity in Uganda, lying roughly between Lakes Victoria and Albert, the Congo and the Nile. The Germans made bold efforts to obtain it. Reaching Uganda, Peters found disorder, with French, German, English, and Moslem missionaries contesting for the souls of the black men and with the sons of the late king at each other's throats. He secured a general treaty of friendship for Germany with various native chiefs, and then hurried back to report his progress. Meanwhile Captain Lugard, in command of the troops of the British East African Company, also penetrated Uganda with some fifty Sudanese soldiers and likewise obtained a treaty, which placed the country under company's protection (see page 521). Then he too left Uganda, disappearing into the bush on a hunting trip. The company offered to retain control if the government would finance a railway from the coast; but Lord Salisbury, prime minister at the time, would advance only a meager amount to survey the route. Eventually the British won out in this region, however, for in 1890 the Germans acquiesced in their control of Uganda and the present Kenya and in a British protectorate over Zanzibar, obtaining in return for the latter the island of Heligoland, in the North Sea, which they were to make into a superbly fortified naval base.

In 1895 the British government bought out the Imperial British East African Company; Mackinnon and his associates lost heavily by the ungenerous terms, though they had done their part in extending the empire.

Next came the building of a railway from the port of Mombasa on the malarial coast; it rose rapidly to a splendid plateau several thousand feet high, where altitude offset latitude to make good white man's country. Through those "white highlands" of Kenya, the line went to Lake Victoria and on to Uganda. Some of the Indian coolies brought over to build it were chewed up by the lions of the region. Though scarcely a hundred miles south of the equator, Nairobi, the sophisticated city which quickly developed, was so cool at night that wood fires were to become quite usual. Joseph Chamberlain offered a generous tract of these Kenya highlands to the Jews as a national home, but they insisted on Palestine instead. Subsequently, thousands of these fertile acres were granted on easy terms to British settlers who came to farm. In this lay the germs of much future trouble, for the natives resented being dispossessed by these intruders.

Almost every European country of major importance participated in the new imperialistic enterprises. Russia pushed forward toward the borders of Afghanistan and toward the Pacific. France absorbed a large part of northwest Africa. Germany, a new contender in the colonial field, commenced in the eighteen eighties to earmark colonies, where opportunity offered, in Africa, China, and the South Seas. Belgium found herself the inheritor of the Congo basin, mainly as the result of King Leopold's misconduct, that monarch having been ap-

pointed a kind of international trustee for civilization over the Congo. Italy, also entering the competition late, ran into a hornet's nest in Ethiopia (Abyssinia), and was forced for the time to be content with Eritrea, on the inhospitable coast of the Red Sea, and part of Somaliland. Finally, Britain, in addition to entrenching herself firmly on her Indian frontiers, now aimed at ultimate control from "Cape to Cairo" and carved out a great and largely new African empire.

Disraeli and Empire

Disraeli was long credited with being the prophet, if not the founder, of the new empire, whereas Gladstone was known as its opponent. It is true that the initial wave of popular enthusiasm came during Disraeli's second ministry. That wave receded, for the time being, with Gladstone's victory in 1880, which might be regarded as the last successful protest of the ideas of the Manchester school against the incoming tide of economic and national imperialism. But that conclusion regarding their roles had "slight justification. Neither appreciated the meaning of the two new phenomena: the rise of nationality in the dominions, and the conquest of the tropics by capitalist industry. . . . Though Disraeli yearned to hold the gorgeous East in fee, and acquired control of the Suez Canal in order to attain that end, his imperial policy largely consisted of grandiose gestures in the realm of foreign policies."[1] Ever sensitive to the way the wind was blowing, he had taken advantage of the awakening British interest in imperial expansion, evidenced by the creation of the Royal Colonial Institute in 1868, by Sir Charles Dilke's *Greater Britain* in 1869, and by John Ruskin's injection into a lecture on art at Oxford the idea that Britain should "found colonies as fast and as far as she is able, formed of her most energetic and

[1] C. E. Carrington, *The British Overseas* (1950), p. 667. By permission of Cambridge University Press.

worthiest men; seizing every piece of fruitful waste ground she can set her foot on." These words would be translated into action by one of his undergraduate listeners, young Cecil Rhodes (see page 431). Consequently, only a few years after Disraeli had declared that the colonies were "a damned millstone around our neck," and that England should "give up the settlements on the West Coast of Africa," he declared in 1872 that "the Empire shall not be destroyed;" and imperialism was one of the things that helped to bring him to power in 1874. But beyond two spectacular moves he did relatively little constructive work. That would have to await the advent of Joseph Chamberlain as Colonial Secretary, who would do much with the dominions as well as the new regions of exploitation. The real political high priest of imperialism, however, was a Frenchman, Jules Ferry, who gave great impetus to the movement during the eighteen eighties, creating situations which would lead Britain and Germany into defensive activity.

The Suez Canal and Egypt

For many years, the British had been interested in developing speedier contact with India and the East than the long sea route around Africa. By the 1840's, they had opened an "overland route" whereby mails and passengers after coming through the Mediterranean to Alexandria by steamship proceeded by way of Cairo across sandy wastes to Suez at the head of the Red Sea whence another steamship sailed for Bombay. Heavy cargo, however, still had to go around the Cape of Good Hope. In the mid eighteen fifties Ferdinand de Lesseps, a French diplomat, made a significant arrangement with his friend Said, the new viceroy or "Khedive" of Egypt, an autonomous province of Turkey. He proposed to dig a 100-mile canal through the sandy isthmus from the Mediterranean to Suez. This would obviously be a short-cut to the East; the voyage from London to Bombay

would be reduced from 11,220 to 6332 miles. DeLesseps formed a private corporation and allotted a large block of the stock to the Khedive in return for forced peasant labor and 99-year use of the route. Palmerston was furious, regarding it as a French threat to British interests in the East, but was unable to stop it. The Suez Canal was formally opened late in 1869; a procession of steamships traversed the whole route from Port Said, named for the Khedive, to the Red Sea at Suez.

British shipping was quick to take advantage of the new route, which left Cape Town neglected. In 1875, Disraeli made one of his most dramatic strokes. Under Said's extravagant successor, Ismail, Egypt was becoming badly enmeshed in financial imperialism, borrowing at excessive rates far more than she could pay back (see page 519). The French bankers were not eager to advance more money to the spendthrift monarch. Disraeli saw his chance: without consulting Parliament he asked the great Jewish banking house of Rothschild for nearly £4,000,000 with which to purchase Ismail's canal shares. When questioned as to the security, he replied, "The British Government." Disraeli received the money, bought the shares, informed the queen that they belonged to the British crown, and then sought Parliamentary sanction for what he had done. It was an audacious act, but Parliament approved. The shares were to prove immensely profitable, although they did not give Britain actual control of the canal company. The purchase was to lead to the British occupation of the Nile valley.

The acquisition of the Suez Canal had given Britain, to all practical purposes, a half partnership in the development of Egyptian resources. The inevitable followed quickly. The ambitious and extravagant Khedive Ismail borrowed too much money in Europe, mainly from French and English bankers, who floated Egyptian bonds for him; and soon he was unable to pay the exorbitant rates of interest on the bonds,

Disraeli and the Sphinx—celebrating his coup in buying control of Suez, the "Key to India."

ranging from 12 to 15 per cent. His debt rose in twelve years from £3,000,000 to £91,000,000. The situation was impossible, and Egypt was bankrupt. The international bankers then brought pressure on their governments, to good effect. It was suggested to Ismail that the financial control of his country be assumed by the two powers in question (the "dual control"), an Englishman to collect the revenues, a Frenchman to disburse them. In 1877 this division of financial authority was arranged, with the Khedive's agreement. Europe approved, especially Germany, where Bismarck was always glad to distract France's attention from Alsace-Lorraine, annexed in 1871 at the close of the Franco-Prussian War.

All seemed propitious for this international experiment in the liquidation of a bankrupt country, but just as Beaconsfield died, the seed which he had planted in Egypt was to bear astonishing fruit. Glad-stone, pacifistic if not a pacifist, was left to deal with it.

There was a military revolt, brought about by favoritism shown in the Egyptian army to Turks and Circassians. As it spread it changed from an anti-Turkish protest to an antiforeign uprising. The new Khedive (Ismail had been deposed earlier), was weak in character and in brains, and appealed to the dual control for assistance. Not receiving it, he yielded to the rebel ringleader, Arabi Bey, appointed him minister of war, and summoned a council of notables. The latter interfered with the dual control, with the cry of "Egypt for the Egyptians!"; and matters went from bad to worse. The Khedive and Arabi intrigued against each other; some fifty Europeans were killed in riots in Alexandria; and the warships of France and England converged on that port. At the last minute, a ministerial crisis at Paris caused the French, to their lasting regret, to withdraw. So the British acted alone. Their warships bombarded and destroyed Arabi's batteries. Fiercer antiforeign riots followed, more Europeans lost their lives, and Arabi threatened to blow up or to block the Suez Canal. The British reply to that was instant. General Wolseley beat Arabi's forces at Tel-El-Kebir, seized the canal, marched on Cairo, exiled Arabi, and mastered the country.

It proved easier to enter than to leave Egypt. The Egyptian government had long been paralyzed. Foreign bondholders had to be considered, European residents had to be protected, a nasty outbreak of the plague had to be fought, and the Sudan was to be an immediately urgent probelm (see page 527). If Turkey, whose Sultan was the hereditary overlord of Egypt, had been able or willing to assume responsibility for it, the British would probably have left the country altogether. The Turks, however, taking French advice, refused to give any guarantees. Europe shrugged its shoulders. The international financial obligations of the Egyptian government were now over

£100,000,000; and the drop in cotton prices, coincident with the recovery of the Southern states after the American Civil War, seemed to preclude the economic recovery of Egypt.

Britain was to get out of these troubles under the clever management of a member of her great banking family, Sir Evelyn Baring, afterward Earl of Cromer, who was consul general at Cairo from 1883 to 1907.

A strange multiple system of controls resulted. While still legally part of the Turkish Empire, Egypt was to all intents and purposes a part of the British Empire. As head of the western Moslems, Turkey's Sultan was always an important factor in Egypt, and in addition received a yearly tribute as overlord. The Khedive appointed and dismissed all officials, supposedly formulated policies, and signed and enforced decrees. The Caisse de la Dette, an international commission representing European bondholders, still retained control of certain taxes and from the receipts subtracted interest charges. In addition, by the "capitulations," or customary privileges granted foreigners, consular courts and mixed tribunals had jurisdiction over criminal cases in which Europeans or Americans were involved; and, more serious yet, the capitulations forbade the levying of any direct tax on foreigners. Finally there was the British consul general; all he did was to *advise* the Khedive. But British troops paced the streets of Cairo, and that was sufficient reason for the new Khedive to accept Cromer's suggestions.

The choice of an Egyptian prime minister, the appointment of the Egyptian cabinet, the desirability of new legislation, the wisdom of selecting various Englishmen as advisers to the heads of the financial, judicial, and educational departments, the nomination also of an Englishman as sirdar of the Egyptian army—upon matters such as these the Khedive consulted with the consul general. To a resourceful mind such as Cromer's, this gave an opportunity to embark on an extensive program. The rehabilitation of Egypt on the material side went on rapidly under his direction. His first definite accomplishment was to redeem Egypt from bankruptcy, by adding to the Egyptian debt and by spending the money on irrigation. The magnificent but half-completed dam on the lower Nile, the work of French engineers, was finished, and at the First Cataract, at Aswan, a second great dam was constructed which made possible, through the new irrigation, two crops a year in place of one. The "Three C's"—courbash, corvée, corruption—now drew his attention. The courbash, or whip of rhinoceros hide, which was freely used on native workers, was banished. The corvée, compulsory and unpaid labor on the canals, was done away with. Political corruption, for which Egypt was notorious, almost disappeared. The consul general kept an eagle eye upon his civil service. Carefully recruited at home, where Cromer was said to have accepted men only from Oxford, Cambridge, or Trinity College, Dublin, it was well paid and highly honored.

In the interim Egypt began slowly and painfully to reconstruct her cowed and beaten army. Without pay, officers, or discipline, it had only feebly resisted the occupation. When Colonel Herbert Horatio Kitchener became sirdar, or commander in chief of the Anglo-Egyptian forces, in 1892, things began to hum. No married officer might hope to serve under Kitchener. The army was Kitchener's life; it must be that of his subordinates also. To every native Egyptian battalion he assigned three Britons, two to serve as majors, one as a noncommissioned drill sergeant.

With the twentieth century the growth of Egyptian nationalism brought discontent. This movement, partly religious, partly political, was directed toward the expulsion of foreigners and toward Egyptian independence. The British gave in to it in part by recalling Cromer, who although just, had been unbending in his relations with the

Egyptians. His successor was less autocratic, but Egypt became more restless. There were two reform factions; the new consul general advised the Khedive to appoint the leader of one to head the government. The appointee was promptly murdered; and ex-President Theodore Roosevelt of the United States, emerging at this time from hunting big game, proclaimed in a public speech in Cairo that the British should either withdraw or else rule Egypt with a firm hand. The nomination of Kitchener as consul general indicated that they chose the latter course. Tackling his new work with speed and dispatch, he came to the rescue of the poorer peasantry by a law which made it impossible for usurers to seize their land. He also increased the number of elected members in the Egyptian legislative council and gave slightly increased powers to that assembly. Whether Kitchener would have succeeded is problematical, for World War I intervened.

Statue of General "Chinese" Gordon at Khartoum where he was killed in 1885.

Loss and Reconquest of the Sudan

Their occupation of Egypt had quickly involved the British in the Sudan, that unknown, undefined, and largely waste land south of Egypt. Never a part of the old historic Egypt, it had been conquered sixty years earlier by Egypt, which founded Khartoum at the junction of the Blue and White Niles. Ismail, who fondly believed that if he ended slavery there he would be acclaimed in Europe as an advance agent of civilization, established garrisons all the way from the Second Cataract of the Nile southward to the great lakes of central Africa, and east and west from Ethiopia to the Sahara. British officers were appointed to the high command there. As anarchy came to an end in Egypt it broke out in the Sudan. A prophet known as the Mahdi headed an insurrection which grew steadily through 1882 to 1884. His fierce "fuzzy-wuzzy" followers threatened the Egyptian garrisons.

Since England for the time being was responsible for the government of Egypt, she felt obliged to rescue the remaining garrisons and to evacuate the Sudan. The task fell to "Chinese" Gordon (see page 456), who had served there as governor-general under the Khedive and had made himself unpopular with the influential slave-traders by his rigorous measures against their traffic. Now the English newspapers demanded that he be sent to Khartoum, capital of the Sudan. He was temperamentally unfitted for a task which consisted of withdrawing and retreating. The British officials in Egypt would have preferred someone more diplomatic and less audacious for this delicate situation. Nevertheless, Gordon was sent there in February, 1884. He probably could have carried out his mission of withdrawal had he begun at once, but he did not intend to withdraw. He planned to stay and save the city. Within two months he was cut off from Cairo by the Mahdi's dervishes and began to call for a relief expedition. But, hoping against hope, the anti-imperialistic Gladstone delayed sending it until autumn. The Mahdi in the meantime pressed hard on Khartoum, where, with food supplies dwindling, Gordon was withstanding the siege in magnificent fashion. The commander of the relief column, at last realizing that the slow hauling of boats around the Nile rapids involved too much delay, and awakening to Gordon's peril, sent part of his troops hurrying overland. Late in January, 1885, the vanguard came in sight of Khartoum—just too late. Over the Sudan capital flew the green flag of the Mahdi, whose dervishes only two days before had captured the city and murdered Gordon.

The Sudan was given over to ten years of frightful anarchy. It was a hornet's nest ever threatening Egypt, and Cromer determined upon its recovery. This time the British, resolving to undertake the task scientifically, left the campaign in Kitchener's hands. He pushed on slowly southward by railway, steamboat, and camel corps. In 1898 his army annihilated the dervishes of the new Mahdi in a great battle at Omdurman across the river from Khartoum, and then, with a number of gunboats and several hundred men, sailed up the Nile five hundred miles to Fashoda. Here the British expansion from north to south met the French expansion across northern Africa. Kitchener was in a hurry; for the French, under Captain Marchand, having come in a northeasterly direction from the French Congo, were already flying the tricolor at Fashoda. Another French expedition which was to come westward from French Somaliland never arrived. Kitchener was determined to oust Marchand. The French could claim priority; the British, that they were acting for Egypt, to which the Sudan belonged in theory. Kitchener's force, moreover, was overwhelmingly superior. The French did not attempt to support their claims, and Marchand lowered the tricolor. This dramatic clash of imperial ambitions produced excitement at Paris and London, and it might have had serious consequences had not the French backed down.

Kitchener returned to Khartoum and completed the annexation of the entire Sudan conjointly to England and to Egypt. The flags of these two nations were to fly side by side at equal elevation. This seemed necessary, for although the reconquest had been planned by Britain, the Egyptian troops had been British-led, with the Egyptian treasury paying the bill. In this condominium (joint rule), a governor-general would administer this Anglo-Egyptian Sudan in the name of both countries. Although there was little money to spend, a vast region to govern, and many problems to handle, the joint rule was succeeding to a remarkable degree by 1914 principally through the agency of young British residents scattered through the Sudan and armed with independent administrative powers.

Diamonds and Gold in South Africa

A major turning point came in South Africa in 1869 (see page 524). Just as the opening of the Suez Canal was robbing Cape Town of its old importance as the "Tavern of the Seas," precious metals were suddenly beginning to stir up the slumbering animosity of the Boers for the Britons. Two years earlier a visitor at a Boer farm on the edge of the Orange Free State noticed a child playing with an unusual sort of stone: it was a diamond worth £500. Adventurous fortune seekers were soon crowding into that remote back country to which the Boers had trekked to get away from outside contacts. And the diamonds at Kimberley were only a beginning; by 1886 gold would lure even greater hordes into the Transvaal (South African Republic).

The Boers, particularly in the Transvaal, were already restive from other problems. They were running into all kinds of difficulties with the natives and with the British missionaries, who sponsored actively and not always wisely the cause of the Negro. The Transvaal seemed powerless to control even its own citizens, who did as they wanted, paid taxes or not as they chose, and on the slightest provocation either resisted their own authorities or, driving their cattle before them, sought homes even more remote. As for the inhabitants of the Orange Free State, they likewise were unhappy. The Kimberley diamond mines, they thought, lay within their boundaries, but Cape Colony disputed this. The question was arbitrated; and the Cape was given the mines. The Free Staters felt a further grievance.

Thus lay the situation when Disraeli's Colonial Secretary, Lord Carnarvon, eager to federate all South Africa on the Canadian model, sent out the historian Froude to persuade the Boers and British. Although public opinion was definitely unfavorable, Carnarvon tried to force the issue. His commissioner, Shepstone, in 1877 suddenly annexed the Transvaal, basing his action on the anarchy which was apparent and on a petition signed by a number of its citizens requesting annexation. This hasty performance ended what little chance there had been for voluntary federation. The Boers in the Cape still outnumbered the British there, and to them, as well as to the Boers in the Transvaal, this annexation seemed an act of tyranny. The new British governor was unpopular, and so was his tiny army. Loud and vociferous in their complaints, the Boers refused to co-operate, nor would they pay taxes.

Among those who listened was Gladstone; consequently upon his return to office in 1880 the Boers expected immediately to recover their liberty. His time, however, was much occupied. His missionary supporters were opposed to such independence for the Negro-hating Boers; and so he delayed action. Not so the Boers, who attacked the British garrisons and who terribly mauled the British army at Majuba Hill in 1881.

Gladstone knew that, although possible, it would be expensive and unjust to subdue the Transvaal. He therefore made a convention with the rebels by which their independence was restored, with a string attached. They were to manage their own affairs, but suzerainty was reserved for Britain—a vague word that caused trouble later.

While the British guns boomed at Alexandria, young Cecil Rhodes was busily at work in South Africa laying the foundations of a colossal fortune. Something of a dreamer and idealist, he was both a son of Oxford and a son of the frontier. Rough in manner and in action, he sought money first in the Kimberly diamond mines, which he organized into a syndicate, and then through the Consolidated Goldfields, Ltd., the most important of the corporations exploiting the newly discovered Transvaal gold deposits. But his end in view was neither paltry nor selfish. What he wanted was to extend north and south through Africa all the way from the Cape to Cairo a broad empire of self-governing, liberty-loving states, bound to one another and the motherland by ties of language, religion, blood, and common political institutions.

As a member of the legislature of Cape Colony he tried first to interest the Cape in Bechuanaland, that indeterminate region, unoccupied except for its scattered Negro tribes, between German Southwest Africa and the Transvaal. If the Boers, the Germans, or the Portuguese were to spread into this territory, any all-red line from Cairo to the Cape would be blocked. When the Cape government refused to take over Bechuanaland, he shifted his efforts to London. Largely through his persuasion, Britain did annex part of Bechuanaland as a crown colony and the rest as a protectorate. To accomplish this much took many years, and the impetuous and dictatorial Rhodes sought for quicker ways to his end. One of them was to fill his purse to overflowing through Kimberley diamonds and Transvaal gold.

Rhodesia

Rhodes turned his attention next to the vast undulating plateau of grassy pasture and woodland in south-central Africa, a no-man's land stretching hundreds of miles through which flowed the Zembezi. Much of this had sufficient altitude to be good "white man's country." He set his money to work this time; his agents, well supplied with champagne, rifles, and other inducements, cajoled Lobengula, king of the Matabele, a fierce fighting branch of the Zulus, into signing away his land. Then Rhodes shifted his operations to London to fight for a charter. He was a suspicious character to many of the orthodox imperialists, but again his money stood him in good stead. He subscribed handsomely to the cause of the Irish Nationalists and to various philanthropies; and in 1889 he secured a charter for his British South African Company which granted full political and economic rights in the new region, the future Rhodesia. Like the Royal Niger Company and the Imperial British East African Company, it followed the old pattern of the East India Company, with the government granting generous powers to private interests ready to invest capital and take risks. The next year his well-selected "pioneer force" hewed their way northward the whole length of Bechuanaland along the old missionary trail, through swamp, forest, and desert. By another year Salisbury, the capital tactfully named for the Conservative prime minister, already "showed the beginnings of a busy little town," with some four hundred European inhabitants whose food and supplies had been sent overland 1700 miles by the company. Time and again there were fights with the fierce Matabele who resented the intrusion; Lobengula, like native chieftains in many other regions, had not realized all that he was signing away.

Meanwhile new tensions were developing in the Transvaal gold fields, which ulti-mately produced about one-third of the world's supply. In the center of the Witwatersrand (Ridge of the White Waters), a "golden arc" sixty miles long, lay Johannesburg, one of the world's fastest growing cities. Only nine years after its site was open fields, it had some hundred thousand inhabitants, many of them *Uitlanders,* as the Boers called the outsiders who had swarmed to the mines. The Boers were unwilling to admit them to citizenship. Yet they taxed them unmercifully, and then spent little tax money for the customary urban facilities in which Johannesburg was deficient, such as water supply, lighting, schools, and fire protection. The distressed miners turned to their friend, Rhodes, now premier of Cape Colony. Determined to help them and impatient as always, he fomented a bold and thoroughly wrong-minded scheme to seize power in the Transvaal by stirring up a rebellion of the miners and having them ask for the protection of his South African Company's armed patrols. His plot exploded prematurely in 1895. His lieutenant, Dr. Leander Jameson, in charge of his armed police on the border, drove at Johannesburg as planned but the miners did not rise, and the raiders were captured by the Boers. Rhodes had disgraced himself and also his country.

This affair ended virtually all hope of reconciliation between Boer and Briton. European public opinion was anti-British. The German emperor, Victoria's grandson, William II, went so far as to send a message of sympathy to the president of the Transvaal, old "Oom Paul" Kruger. Even if the British government had put Rhodes in prison for the raid, instead of merely depriving him of his privy councilorship, it is doubtful if the suspicious Boers would have forgiven that attempted coup d'état. Besides, the furious Boers remembered that they had beaten the British at Majuba Hill in 1881 and were confident that they could do it again. They bought arms and ammunition on a large scale, paying for them

Boer sharpshooters behind a wall, with their usual informality of costume.

with money made from the Uitlanders; and as they did this the British government made the cause of the latter its own.

The Boer War

The British Colonial Secretary, Joseph Chamberlain (see page 488), determined to force the issue. The Boers gave way somewhat. They promised larger appropriations for local government, and agreed to lower their franchise requirement from a ten years' residence to one of seven; they would lower it even to five if England would relinquish all claim to sovereignty over their republic. This Chamberlain would not grant, and by the summer of 1899 a deadlock was reached. Lord Milner, sent down to handle the situation, was as inflexible as old Kruger. British troops came pouring into South Africa, and the Boers decided that it was now or never. They gave an ultimatum to the British, received no answer,

waited a certain time, and then declared war.

The Boer War (1899-1902) shook the empire to its foundations. It found Britain without a friend in Europe and with Britons themselves divided as to the justice of their cause. The British army was shown to be in a pitiful plight as far as military technique was concerned. British prestige was to suffer grievously from the fact that less than a hundred thousand Boers—the total manpower of the two republics—could stand off the mighty resources of the British Empire for three years, including several thousand troops from Canada, Australia, and New Zealand.

During the autumn of 1899 the Boers, invading Natal, defeated the main British army at Colenso. Then they bottled up the British garrisons at Ladysmith and at Mafeking. The next year the British, with Lord Roberts in command and Kitchener as chief of staff, swept through the Transvaal and its ally the Free State. He relieved the garrisons; and captured both capitals, Bloemfontein of the Free State, and Pretoria of the Transvaal. Apparently the war was over. Roberts returned to England, leaving Kitchener to complete any necessary "mopping-up" operations.

But the war was not over. The Boers were ably led by General Louis Botha, in command of the Transvaalers, and by General Christian De Wet, heading the men of the Free State. For nearly a year and a half more they kept up the fight against the quarter of a million British. South Africa was a huge region which the Boers knew. Guerrilla warfare, the most difficult type of opposition for regular troops to overcome, was suited to the psychology and equipment of the Boer farmers, who were excellent horsemen and dead shots. Such informal fighting reduced military discipline to a minimum and permitted frequent if dangerous visits home. Rapid mobility, surprise attacks, and quick escapes left the British wondering from what direction the next blow would descend. A few years later it could have been a different story with automobiles and airplanes available to the British. Thus the Boers fought on, month after month, a losing war; and all the while their ranks were thinning fast by death and capture. They could not even afford to win victories if they lost many men in the process.

Meanwhile Kitchener decided to make the entire country one gigantic net, burn down Boer farmhouses, ruin crops, herd women and children in refugee camps, build blockhouses but a thousand paces apart, lace barbed wire and trenches between them, and by a number of swift, sharp drives redeem more and more land from the Boers until, either captured or exhausted, they gave over the fight. These methods won out. By the summer of 1902 only six thousand soldiers were left to the Free State and ten thousand to the Transvaal. The British were agreeable to a negotiated peace, promising a degree of self-government within the empire. For a time, however, it looked as though the Boers would not accept. De Wet was for continuing the war; but Botha pointed out to the soldier delegates that further resistance was madness, and to his pleas were added those of young General Smuts (see page 543).

By the peace terms, the Boers were to recognize the sovereignty of the British crown. They were not to be deprived of their personal liberty or property. Military government was to be succeeded at the earliest date by civil, and, as soon after as it was feasible, representative institutions were to be introduced. The Afrikaans language, based on Dutch, was placed on a parity with English in the schools and courts. No indemnities were to be levied to pay the cost of the war; on the contrary, the British government granted £3,000,000 to assist the people back to their farms.

Lord Milner, who had gone to South Africa as High Commissioner before the war, became governor of the two new crown colonies, the Transvaal and the Orange River. He quickly and wisely spent this £3,000,000 for food, livestock, and rehabilitating a ravaged land. He borrowed ten times that sum on the surety of the British government. He then tried to entice the Boer leaders into accepting nominations to a legislative council; but warily they refused, wanting Milner solely responsible. His importation of Chinese coolies to work in the gold mines created an uproar in England, and was one of the main causes which led to the ousting of the Conservative party there in 1905 (see page 491). This political turnover resulted in the speedy triumph of self-government in the two conquered colonies.

Milner had approved a new constitution for the Transvaal with a popularly elected legislature, but appointed governor and executive officials. One of the first acts of the triumphant Liberals in London was to suspend this and confer responsible government, long enjoyed by the Cape, upon both the Transvaal and the Orange River Colony. This was a brave act inasmuch as Britain's late enemies were likely to triumph at the polls; for many of the miners had scattered during the war, and a Boer majority was inevitable. In this generosity to their late enemies, moreover, Britain was abandoning the huge Negro population of South Africa to a group who had never been sympathetic to them (see pages 543, 710 ff.).

Post-Mutiny India

Nearly two decades after the Mutiny, Disraeli in 1876 persuaded Parliament to give Victoria the additional title of Empress of India. He knew this would please her and it might do something to soften her grief and loneliness as a widow. He planned also to please India by giving the Indian princes and the people, accustomed to imperial magnificence, an empress, and likewise to impress them with Britain's majesty and power. The proclamation of the new title at a superb Indian durbar, he thought, would gratify India, the queen, and himself. To many this seemed melodramatic and absurd. "Queen of England" was a sufficiently glorious title for any woman, so the Liberals said. The title of "Empress" seemed to suggest an aggressive imperialism which might endanger world peace. The queen, as well as Disraeli, however, was not to be thwarted; and consequently it came about that Victoria wrote after her name "Regina et Imperatrix."

Despite that proclamation the control of India did not center in London. Theoretically it was a direct imperial charge. A member of the British cabinet held the portfolio of Indian affairs, and a council exclusively British assisted him. To this great dependency, however, Parliament paid slight attention; it remained a place apart. A peculiar sanctity was attached, seemingly, to the India Office in London. It was not so much above criticism as beyond it;

and Indian policies were seldom debated in the House of Commons.

Nor could one say with fairness that the real government of India centered in the viceregal office. Though the viceroy, appointed for five years, and his executive council comprised its government, even they did not pretend to administer India. Policies they did determine; but the real administration depended on the three thousand district officers and the subordinate officials of the Indian civil service (see pages 451, 508). In their charge were the administration of justice, the collection of taxes, and the enforcement of the laws. They alone came into direct contact with the native population, the practical government being in their hands. Others served as "residents" at the capitals of the native princes. Their esprit de corps was excellent, they worked hard and efficiently, the salaries were high, their accomplishments noteworthy, corruption was unknown among them, and they had triumphantly upheld justice, peace, and order for several decades. Yet there were some who criticized the system, because of its almost wholly British make-up. Indians might receive appointment to it, but the examinations, held in London and restricted to men under twenty-four, were of a type that virtually limited success in them to graduates of the "public schools" and universities. The occasional Indian who passed them almost never rose to the higher ranks. To this exclusive and also expensive government by foreigners Indian nationalists were already taking exception in the nineteenth century. They complained too about the size of the Indian army, although there were in 1890 only about 5000 white officers and 70,000 white enlisted men to guard a country of 200,000,000. They did not talk of democracy; what they wanted was India for the Indians.

Before Lord Curzon became viceroy in 1899, however, these critics of the British *raj* were not particularly vociferous, compared to those in the twentieth century.

Lord Curzon, Viceroy of India, riding in state at celebration of accession of Edward VII.

From many points of view the appointment was excellent. The Indian post had been the constant dream of Curzon's youth, and he had early begun to train for it. He not only knew India thoroughly but all Asia as well; the geography of northwest India was as familiar to him as his own English county. Furthermore, he had served as Undersecretary of State for Foreign Affairs, and the complexity of British world policy had been his daily concern. Now governing India from 1899 to 1905, he safeguarded and extended the frontiers, and overhauled the educational, economic, and sanitary administrations. But he repressed also every Indian impulse toward self-government, quarreling the while with his own British colleagues. This course of action compelled him eventually to retire, a defeated man, the chosen target for radical criticism throughout the British world.

In frontier policy Curzon was aggressive.

On the northwestern frontier, the situation in Afghanistan had continued to be disturbing, with Russia slowly but surely absorbing the oases to the north of it, Bokhara, Samarkand, and other remote places with romantic pasts. The tragic story of 1839-1840 had been repeated in part in 1878 (see page 452). Two years earlier the amir at Kabul had become displeased with what he termed "the dry friendship of the English," as he wanted an alliance to guarantee to him his shaky throne; and in consequence he had veered toward the Russians. Thereupon, the Viceroy had suggested that the amir receive a British mission; but he declined. But when the Russians were greeted at Kabul, in 1878, the Viceroy sent a British envoy; a recent family death made his visit inopportune anyway, and he was stopped at the frontier. The second Afghan war followed. Once more the British-Indian army marched toward Kabul; once more Afghanistan agreed to accept British advice. England was to control Afghanistan's foreign relations as well as to patrol various Afghan passes. A resident was to be located permanently at Kabul and a subsidy paid the amir. But that resident and all his staff were promptly murdered by the Afghans shortly after their arrival. The British reoccupied the country, but with the triumph of the anti-imperialists in Gladstone's victory in 1880, the troops were withdrawn. Afghanistan was a bone of contention between Britain and Russia until, in the middle nineties, British and Russian troops stood facing one another on a bleak plateau in central Asia on the verge of war. But diplomacy intervened, England yielded slightly, and the Russians soon shifted their activities farther eastward toward China.

A few years later, Curzon created near the Afghan border a new Indian province, the Northwest Frontier Province, which lay in the semi-no-man's-land on the borders of the Punjab, over which Britain claimed suzerainty. This plan was to entice, cajole, and bribe the tribesmen to friendship with Britain.

To the south and west of the new province lay Baluchistan, and beyond that Persia. European access to India was possible from this direction by land and by sea. In that area, the French, the Germans, and the Russians were all busily engaged in intrigue; and, one after another, Curzon checkmated them. Turning then to the north and the east, he cast his eye on Tibet, a strange, isolated state ruled by a religious order of unusual characteristics. To forestall the Russians he dispatched an expedition which forced its way to Lhasa, the capital, and made the monastic head of the state sign a treaty that no foreign agency might be stationed there without British approval.

Curzon meanwhile devoted much care to combating famine, malaria, and bubonic plague. He fought famine by spending large sums on irrigation projects, so effectively that Britain could claim credit for over forty thousand miles of canals, which irrigated some 23,000,000 acres. He fought malaria by establishing schools, the graduates of which were sent all over India urging the people to kill mosquitoes and eat quinine. He fought the plague by publicly submitting himself and his entire staff to vaccination, and by starting a campaign against rats, the fleas of which were carriers of the dreaded disease. Few men ever interested themselves more in the poor of India than did this British aristocrat.

Despite these achievements the British disliked his cold disdain, and objected to his disciplining English soldiers in India. The Hindus became his bitter enemies, primarily because of his partition of Bengal, the huge nucleus of British India, won by Clive in 1757. Its highly centralized government under a lieutenant governor had become top-heavy. Curzon divided Bengal into two separate provinces. But to the patriotically inclined Bengalis, essentially one race and speaking one language, the old Bengal had been a sacred motherland.

Curzon's reforming zeal resulted in his recall in 1905. He was succeeded by Lord Minto. The Secretary of State for India in the new Liberal cabinet, John Morley (soon Lord Morley), a distinguished author, took a more active part in Indian affairs than was usual in his office. A series of so-called Morley-Minto reforms were moderate steps toward self-government. Indians were placed on the legislative council, and one was even nominated to the viceroy's executive council. In provincial councils they were given a majority of seats, and were enabled there to pass resolutions condemning the government. These reforms, however, did not satisfy the nationalists, who were growing steadily in number. The British sternly suppressed popular demonstrations; but they rescinded the partition of Bengal, and tried to flatter Indian opinion by making Delhi instead of Calcutta the capital of British India.

But the rise of Indian nationalism proved inevitable. The victory of the Japanese army over a great European power in the Russo-Japanese War of 1904-1905 was one cause. The spread of British education, with its emphasis on English history and literature, was another cause, carrying with it as it did a passionate devotion to political liberty. The Indians were quick to draw analogies between the India of their own day and England in Cromwell's time. In addition, there was the general wave of unrest in many semidependent countries against European control—nationalism was beginning to make headway fast.

Imperialism in China

The break-up of the Chinese Empire was retarded throughout this time by the political astuteness of its leading statesman, Li Hung Chang. By yielding here and there to the British, French, and Japanese in Burma, Indo-China, and Korea, by playing off one faction against another, and by announcing reforms which generally existed on paper only, he staved off disaster for many years. One reform, at least, went beyond the paper stage; for he was instrumental in the appointment of an Englishman, Robert Hart, as chief of the Chinese customs service. Hart, later Sir Robert, organized a unique force of customs inspectors. Englishmen, well paid, with assured tenure, and appointed in accordance with strict civil-service regulations, administered under his direction the collection of all customs duties at Chinese ports, a fact which added greatly to Britain's prestige in the Orient.

In the last years of the century the Far East became the scene of an imperialistic scramble which for the moment eclipsed the partition of Africa. It was occasioned by the short, decisive war in 1894-1895 when Japan, who had "gone Western" with remarkable speed and thoroughness, soundly whipped backward China. That Sino-Japanese War opened Europe's eyes to two new factors which were to make the Far Eastern situation a matter of increasing concern: the rising power of Japan and, even more important, China's tempting weakness. That she had lost to Britain in the middle of the century had not been surprising, but this decisive defeat by another Oriental nation, only a tenth of her size, was a different matter.

The ensuing rapid scramble of the nations for China's wealth revealed some of the new devices of economic imperialism. She was not formally partitioned among the powers; her nominal sovereignty, like that of Egypt, was preserved. Instead the powers secured "spheres of interest," concessions, and leased ports. A sphere of interest was a particular region in which a foreign power had been granted prior rights to furnish capital for the development of railways and mines. A concession was similar in nature, but was usually limited to a specified railway or mining property rather than extended over a whole district. Whereas "treaty ports" had been opened to the commerce of various outside nations, a leased port became for a period (ninety-nine years was the common period) the private preserve of a particular power which might, if it desired, fortify it as a naval base. The spring and summer of 1898 saw the scramble at its height. France leased Kwangchowan, and secured a sphere of influence in the far south, adjacent to her possessions in Indo-China. The center of the scramble, however, was in north China, around the waters of the Yellow Sea, just east of Peking. Two peninsulas jut into those waters: Liaotung from the north and Shantung from the south. Russia secured a considerable sphere of interest in Manchuria, and leased Port Arthur and another port at the tip of the adjacent Liaotung peninsula. Germany's sphere of interest was the Shantung peninsula, with a lease of Kiaochow.

The whole situation was distasteful to Britain. Having enjoyed some three-fourths of China's trade for many years, she resented having some of it staked off for the exclusive use of her rivals. She was not anxious to obtain more actual territory than Hong Kong; but, to prevent the Russians and Germans from controlling all north China, she apologetically joined in the scramble and leased Weihaiwei, at the tip of the Shantung peninsula, a port which she never fortified but which she considered might come in handy as a naval station. Once started, she went on to secure additional territory near Hong Kong, as well as a sphere of interest in the Yangtze valley and further concessions. Her heavy investments in China were to give her a vital interest in the Far Eastern situation. The United States, meanwhile, was becoming interested through her acquisition of the Hawaiian Islands and, as a result of her victorious war with Spain in 1898, the Philippines. She took no direct part in the Chinese scramble, advocating instead, as most favorable to her own interests an "open door" policy. This was directly opposed to any partition of China and was designed to give all nations equal rights in her economic exploitation.

Canada, The First Dominion

In the meantime, the colonies of settlement were achieving "dominion" status, which meant a gradual shift from the position of possessions of the mother country to partnership with her. Canada was once again the pioneer. The granting of responsible government through Durham's recommendations had been a first step (see page 460), but this new principle, flexible and never very closely defined, went farther in developing the concept of nationhood. Dominion status came next to Australia, New Zealand, and South Africa, also peopled primarily by Britons and other Europeans, and much later would spread to some other parts of the empire with largely native populations.

In 1867, Parliament passed the British North America Act, creating the "Dominion of Canada." The Canadian leaders had wanted to call it the "Kingdom of Canada" to imply full national status. Out of deference to the anti-monarchical feelings in the United States, however, the word "Dominion" was substituted, even though it carried the implication of British domination. It became the general term for the new relationship even though none of the other dominions were to include it in their formal titles.

That Canadian consideration for United States' feelings was not surprising. The *Trent* affair had caused some alarm early in the Civil War (see page 423). There was even more at the war's end when some of the Irish Fenians in the Northern army talked of punishing Britain by capturing Canada, and even made a few border threats. That helped unite the various provinces in self defense. Then, too, the twelve-year Reciprocity Treaty of 1854, allowing relatively free trade across the American border had just expired, and the Canadians, who had found it advantageous, were hoping to have it renewed. Already, they were becoming aware of a duality in their relationship with Britain and the "States," so close to them. Though they were bound by tradition, loyalty, and political ties to the mother country, geographical propinquity and common interests were bringing them into increasing contacts with their fellow North Americans south of the border. The Canadians would succeed in making the best of both valuable ties with a minimum of friction. But always they would be Canadians first and foremost in their allegiance to their own fast-growing nation.

"The Dominion," writes one Canadian, "was not the outgrowth of a popular movement, but the work of a small group of political leaders supported by important economic interests, and the final scheme was never submitted to popular ratification."[2] The impetus came chiefly from populous "Canada West," the later Ontario, and was primarily the work of two of its rival statesmen, John A. Macdonald and George Brown. The French Canadians were suspicious, and in fact, most sections had to be promised railroad construction or assumption of provincial debts to join. The bait for the Maritime Provinces was an "intercolonial" railroad to link them with Montreal; its desirability had been demonstrated during the *Trent* affair when, with the St. Lawrence frozen, some troops from Britain had to be transported overland by sleigh. Even at that, many Nova Scotians tried to get out of the "confederation." Prince Edward Island only came in six years later when its debts were assumed. British Columbia on the Pacific coast held out not only for assumption of its debts but also for the promise of a transcontinental railroad. Newfoundland refused to

[2] Edgar McInnis, *Canada: Political and Social History*, Revised ed. (Rinehart and Company, Inc., 1958), p. 305.

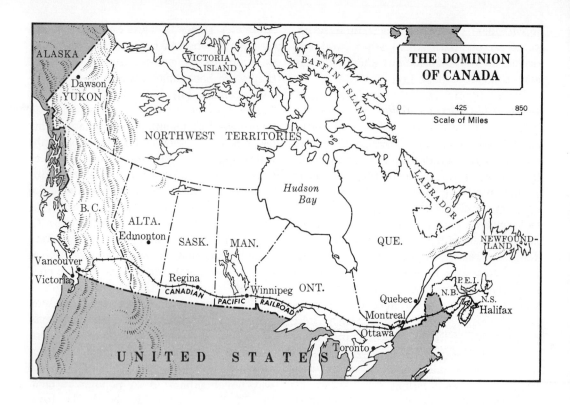

THE DOMINION
OF CANADA

Scale of Miles

come in at all and was later rated as a separate dominion. Despite all that, a conference at Quebec late in 1866 worked out a 72-point program which formed the basis for the act upon which the Canadas (Ontario and Quebec), Nova Scotia, and New Brunswick agreed. There was apparently some apathy in Britain, too; the measure passed the Commons "with hardly more than formal attention . . . compared to the eagerness with which members plunged into the debate on a new dog tax immediately afterward."[3] Some prominent "Little Englanders" are said to have even expressed regret that Canada had not gone the whole way to independence!

By this 1867 landmark in British imperial history, the dominion government became a blend of the "responsible" procedures of the British cabinet system, already familiar to the Canadians, continuing in use, and of a federation like the United States in the

[3] *Ibid.*, p. 299.

relationship of the central government with the provinces. The governor-general, still appointed by the crown which he represented, was like it a figurehead. The real power, as at home, lay with the premier or prime minister. Because the Civil War had shown the dangers of "states rights" in her neighbor's constitution, Canada's central government was given all the powers not specifically delegated to the provinces. At Ottawa, the dominion parliament was to consist of two houses: a Senate, nominated for life by the governor-general (acting, naturally, on his ministers' advice), and a House of Commons chosen by popular vote. Corresponding to the United States setup, each province had its own legislature. Instead of having an elected governor like the American states, however, the provinces followed the British system with a provincial premier, responsible to the legislature as its real authority, and a lieutenant governor as nominal representative of the crown.

As with later dominions, high commissioners at London and at the other dominion capitals would look out for Canadian interests.

During the formative years, leadership was long in the hands of John A. Macdonald, later Sir John, who now headed the Conservative party. Something of an opportunist like Disraeli, he had a sound vision of Canada's needs and the political skill to achieve much. Except for a five-year Liberal period under Alexander Mackenzie, another of the Scots so prominent in Canadian life, Macdonald was premier until 1891. Like the fifteen years' tenure of Wilfrid Laurier and the twenty-two years of Mackenzie King later, this represented a unique Canadian trend toward long premierships—Gladstone's four terms totalled only fourteen years.

Two bold imaginative acts during the Dominion's first years made possible the expansion from sea to sea. An objective of Macdonald and the others in promoting confederation had been expansion through the thousands of miles of untouched fertile prairies between the provinces of Ontario and British Columbia on the Pacific, to which the old Hudson's Bay Company held title. The Dominion parliament was worried lest the United States might move northward into this unoccupied land, or that the Hudson's Bay Company, which was accustomed to bring in its supplies by way of St. Paul, Minnesota, might sell some of the land to the United States. British Columbia would then be forever separated from Canada. Consequently the Dominion in 1869 bought out the rights of the Hudson's Bay Company for £300,000, and in 1870 admitted the only settled part as the province of Manitoba. Territorial government was provided for the rest. To keep order in that wild region, which stretched up into the Arctic, the Dominion established the Royal Northwest Mounted Police, the celebrated redcoated "mounties," who were reputed always to "get their man."

Twice the French-Indian "halfbreeds," resenting the encroachments of the new settlers, revolted; on the second occasion, the hanging of their leader, Louis Riel, greatly angered the French Canadians of Quebec.

Following close upon the acquisition of the prairie regions came the Canadian Pacific Railway, the second step, which would bring about their development. The immediate initiative came from remote British Columbia which made the road the price of its admission as a province in 1871. The project was pushed to completion, thanks to the vigorous and determined premier Sir John Macdonald and the financial genius of Donald Smith, later Lord Strathcona. The first such transcontinental line had been opened in the United States in 1869; but Canada was far less wealthy and the final spike of the Canadian Pacific Railway was not driven in, at a lonely spot in British Columbia, until late in 1885. This famous corporation, although privately controlled and operated, became virtually a semipublic enterprise. It built hotels, sold farms, established transpacific and transatlantic steamship lines, and advertised extensively in Europe for emigrants. It became perhaps the greatest single agent of Canadian nationalism. An excess of enthusiasm later carried the movement too far. Two more transcontinental lines, the Grand Trunk Pacific and Canadian Northern, were not really needed and, unlike the "C. P. R." did not pay.

In 1870, there had been barely 12,000 people in Manitoba, and only a handful in the remainder of the vast territory from which the provinces of Alberta and Saskatchewan were to be carved in 1905. By 1901 the total population of the prairie regions had risen to 419,000; then came a tremendous influx which brought the number by 1911 to 1,327,000, about a third of the total population of Canada. Some of the newcomers were from the old Canadian provinces, some from the British Isles, some

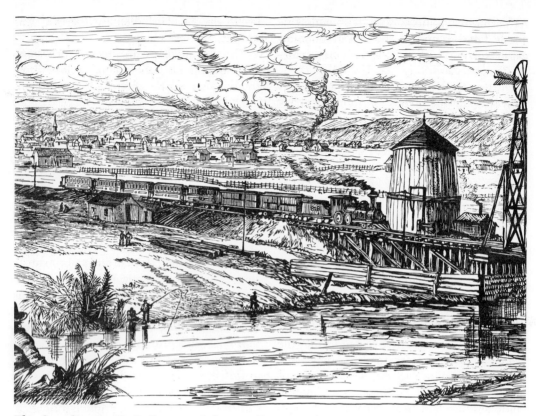

The Canadian Pacific Railway at Calgary, Alberta, shortly after both the town and the railway came into being in 1883.

from the Continent, and many from the United States. Manitoba, Alberta, and Saskatchewan still offered virgin fields to the pioneers who flocked to this last frontier. As in the Dakotas and other states to the south, they devoted themselves principally to the raising of wheat, which became Canada's chief source of wealth. In 1867 Canada had furnished less than 3 per cent of the British grain imports; by 1914 she had overtaken seven other grain-producing regions and furnished more than 30 per cent, standing in second place, just behind the United States. Without railway communication the grain at least, and perhaps the provinces too, would have gone to the United States.

Friction rose rapidly between those of British and French descent when the lat-

ter, increasing in numbers, spilled over from their original province, Quebec, into Ontario and the prairie provinces. The French Canadians refused to adopt the English language and in their Roman Catholic schools insisted upon French as the language of instruction. Clannish and exclusive, they kept themselves apart from their neighbors in many ways.

Fortunately for the Dominion, these racial difficulties were held in check through the wisdom and adroitness of a famous Canadian himself of French extraction, Sir Wilfrid Laurier, who headed the government from 1896 to 1911. Gracious and learned, speaking with equal facility in French or English, this competent statesman succeeded in making the French and the British work together for Canada.

So popular, indeed, was Laurier that he might have continued indefinitely as prime minister had he not sought a reciprocity tariff agreement with the United States in 1911. For twelve years just before the confederation of 1867 the two countries had drastically lowered the duties on each other's wares; but since then the tariff walls had grown higher and higher, particularly in the United States. In 1911 the Congress at Washington proposed free trade in many Canadian and American products, with low duties on the rest. Twenty years earlier, Canada might have welcomed such reciprocity, but now she had become actively interested in protecting her own growing industries. Her manufacturers contributed heavily to the campaign funds of the Conservatives, who staged a bitter fight when Laurier appealed to the country in a general election. Patriotism became mixed with economics in the campaign. The Conservatives argued that reciprocity might be the first step toward annexation by the United States, and injudicious remarks by some high officials at Washington increased prejudice on that joint. The Conservatives carried the day, bringing Sir Robert Borden into office as prime minister and ending the fifteen-year Liberal government of Laurier.

Australia and New Zealand

Next to become a federated dominion was the Commonwealth of Australia; various complications delayed this until 1901. Commercially it was absurd for six different colonies, with separate railway systems and separate tariffs, to hold aloof from one another in this isolated all-British continent. Politically both Germany and the United States were extending their sway in Pacific waters, and though perhaps there was not much to be feared, the Australians had no intention of permitting swarms of Japanese, whose power also was growing, to dig in upon Australia's northern shores. Standing shoulder to shoulder in a firm union seemed to them the best defense against this danger.

The making of a constitution was a long-drawn-out affair, lasting many years; for there were more complicated problems than those which confronted the United States in 1787. Like her, Australia had widely scattered large and small states but besides, Australian railways had already been constructed on different gauges, and intricate economic problems had appeared. None the less, the form of government drawn up more closely resembled the American prototype than any other British constitution. It provided for a strong upper house, the Senate, to represent the Australian states rather than the Australian population, and a supreme court, the permission of which was necessary before appeals could be made to the Privy Council in England on cases arising from purely Australian disputes. As in the United States, and unlike Canada, certain specified powers were granted to the federal government, with all the rest belonging to the individual states. In one major respect, responsible government, however, it followed British precedent; the separate colonies had long enjoyed this (see page 447). There was to be a premier, who must be supported by a majority vote in the Australian parliament. According to the standard dominion pattern, a governor general represented the crown at Canberra, a new city soon created as the capital. Like the Canadian province, each Australian state had its own premier, responsible government, and a representative of the crown called governor (instead of lieutenant governor as in Canada). The constitution once adopted, Australian nationalism grew apace, and Australians for the first time began seriously to consider the extent to which they were prepared to stand alone and the extent to which they would unify their national policy with that of the British.

While New Zealand had been a single political entity from the beginning and did

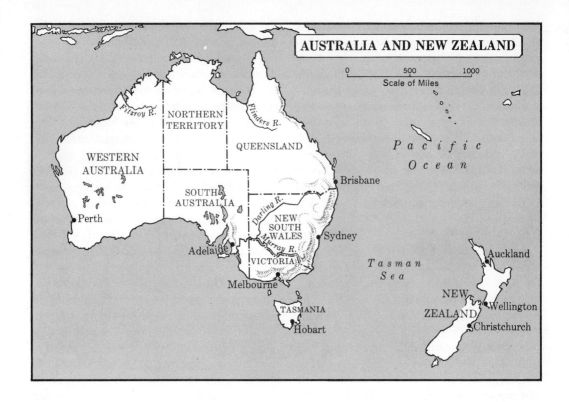

AUSTRALIA AND NEW ZEALAND

not require a federation like Canada and Australia, it was not formally created a dominion until 1907. Dominion status was a matter of external relationship to Britain, rather than any special form of internal government. New Zealand had made a distinctive name for herself in the 1890's. She was called "the most radical state in the world," a laboratory for political and social experiments.

At a time when Britain and America were still mulling over the socialistic ideas of John Stuart Mill, the Fabians, Henry George, and the rest (see page 487), the New Zealanders were actually putting some of those ideas into practice, under the leadership of William P. Reeves, John Ballance, and Richard J. Seddon. Taxes were readjusted to influence big landowners to subdivide their property; easy loans were made possible for small proprietors to purchase land. The graduated income tax, with increased rates for higher incomes, was introduced. In the field of labor, machinery for conciliation and compulsory arbitration was set up. In the political field, the introduction in 1869 of the secret ballot first adopted thirteen years before in Australia (see page 447), and manhood suffrage in 1879 were followed in 1893 by the granting of the vote to women, the first time in the world except for the American state of Wyoming.

The Union of South Africa

The Union of South Africa, the fourth of the major dominions, was inaugurated in 1910 only eight years after the Boer War (see page 532) with Louis Botha, late commander in chief of the Boer army, as first premier. It resembled Canada in containing a large non-British European population, but there was an important difference that went back to the big migrations from Britain earlier in the century. Enough Britons had swarmed over to Canada to outnumber the French Canadians then and later. But the British migration to South Africa still left the Boers with a continuing advantage, at least three to two. Full imperial participation would depend upon a fair number of moderate Boers co-operating with the British, a situation achieved for a considerable period under General Botha and then under General Smuts. South Africa also differed radically from the other three major dominions in that its European population was heavily outnumbered by the Negroes, whereas the Indians and Eskimos in Canada, the Maoris in New Zealand, and the aborigines in Australia were relatively few. The continuing friction between Boers, Britons, and Bantus would become a major problem.

The four provinces—the Transvaal, the Orange River Colony (soon to revert to its old name, Orange Free State), Natal, and Cape Province—retained their political identity and certain local administrative powers; but almost all important matters were left to the Union Parliament at Cape Town. The only real concessions to local feeling were the constitutional retention of the right to vote by the colored men in the Cape (mulattoes, Malays, and so forth, not full Negro), and the location of the government's executive offices at Pretoria and of the judiciary at Bloemfontein, the capitals of the Transvaal and the Free State respectively.

Botha, already having been the first premier of the new colony of the Transvaal, was trusted by Boer and Briton alike. During the war, as Boer commander, he had proved an excellent fighter; at the same time his moderation, good sense, strong character, and wise judgment had been demonstrated again and again. Various problems promptly put his political tact and acumen to the test.

Unlike some in his South African party, Botha was for letting bygones be bygones and for working in harmony with the British, but this proved difficult. Many of his old soldiers resented his favoring immigration from England, and thought it wrong for their old commander to attend imperial conferences in London, and accept an honorary generalship in the British army. Under General Hertzog some of the Boers repudiated Botha's leadership. The Free Staters had been bitter-enders in a war which was none of their choosing, and now they forced the issue. The South African party endorsed Botha, and Hertzog, discomfited, withdrew the minority of the Boers, organizing the National party.

There was much more unanimity of opinion in regard to the Negro. The blacks outnumbered the whites in every province of the Union, the ratio being two to one in the Free State, three to one in the Transvaal, nearly four to one in the Cape Colony, and almost ten to one in Natal. Both Boer and Briton considered this a threat to white supremacy, and Botha's determination to segregate the races met with the approval of his parliament. Land was given the Negroes, and provision was made to prevent its alienation. A special form of government was adopted for these allotted tracts, somewhat paternalistic in character, putting them partly under that of white inspectors.

The large number of Hindus, imported to work on the sugar plantations, were British subjects; but a special head tax was levied against them, free movement within the country was checked, and free immigration was prohibited. The Indian Nationalists in India complained bitterly of the ill-treatment of their brothers in South Africa, and Gandhi (see page 613), then a young lawyer, intervened on their behalf. Botha soothed troubled feelings by passing an immigration law which did not mention Indians by name but which excluded them none the less. When Gandhi, seeking the removal of other restrictions, led a pilgrimage of Indians from Natal to Pretoria, he was imprisoned and then released. He suddenly ceased from agitation when new labor difficulties confronted Botha. A strike broke out which involved both miners and railway employees. Revolutionary socialism was behind it, and the red flag flew over Johannesburg. Botha struck at that city with a hastily organized force, seized the ringleaders, and put them on a ship bound for England. This act presumably was illegal; and British opinion, both Liberal and Conservative, denounced it heartily, but the South African party stood united behind him; and there was nothing England could do, inasmuch as the Union was a self-governing dominion.

In addition to South Africa, Australia, Canada, and New Zealand, there was the self-governing colony of Newfoundland, which had refused to join the Dominion of Canada. It was not until 1917, however, that she was formally recognized as a dominion; that status did not last long (see page 617).

Imperial Conferences and Co-operation

In 1897 Victoria's diamond jubilee was celebrated at London; and although it was primarily a tribute to the Queen, it was also a graphic portrayal of the magnitude of her empire and of the triumphant progress of Greater Britain. The jubilee parade was led by a thousand men from beyond the seven seas in uniform: Dyak police from North Borneo, Maoris from New Zealand, Hausas from West Africa, mounted riflemen from the Cape Colony, armed men from Hong Kong (some of them European, some Sikh, some Chinese), black fighters in the employ of the Royal Niger Company, mounted Zaptiehs from Cyprus, a contingent of Rhodesian horse, men of Australia clad in brown, and Canadians in the varied uniforms of thirty military organizations. The colonial premiers in sober black were, however, perhaps the most significant feature, symbolizing as they did the spread of British liberty beyond the sea. To them, Joseph Chamberlain made definite overtures on the question of imperial federation, which had been discussed academically in one way or another earlier in the century; but he was rebuffed. The premiers had no power to negotiate with the British government; and if they had, they probably would not have utilized it, for any change in the status quo presumably would have meant a sharing of the burden of defense, and therefore an increase in taxation.

Chamberlain, being a determined man, summoned a new conference in 1902, immediately after the Boer War, during which Canada, Australia, New Zealand, and Newfoundland had all sent troops. This time he tried for federation in the field of economics; and the conference did commit itself in favor of imperial preferential tariffs. The colonies had long been used to tariffs, and it was quite to their way of thinking that the empire should become more united commercially, but this ran counter to England's free-trade tradition. In the election of 1906 Chamberlain's Conservative party went down to defeat on the Liberal slogan "Your food will cost you more."

At the next imperial conference (1907) the idea was aired again. The more doubtful the British at home felt about Chamberlain's idea, the more acceptable did imperial tariffs become overseas. Once again they were defeated, owing to lack of support in England, with the Liberals in power now.

In 1911 at the most important of these conferences before World War I, New Zealand's plan to have the entire constitutional machinery of the empire reorganized through the creation of a super-Parliament was rejected. For the first time, formal consultation began on foreign affairs when Sir Edward Grey took the dominion premiers into his confidence on recent foreign policy and promised to continue the practice. The conference saw also the beginning of a determined drive for military and naval preparedness that was to continue until 1914. In this, New Zealand, as the most isolated, was the most enthusiastic of the dominions. She had hoped to have the Pacific patrolled by an all-dominion fleet of New Zealand, Australian, Canadian, and South African ships. When the Admiralty disapproved of this, she cheerfully offered to contribute a battleship to be used as the Admiralty directed. The Union of South Africa was the least interested in dominion naval affairs, since the memories of the Boer War still rankled, although pro-British Cape Colony had given the royal navy a big cruiser, the *Good Hope,* in that war. But now Premier Botha was unwilling to endorse anything more than a small subsidy.

Meanwhile the Australian flag made its debut on the high seas; for Australia proudly demanded her own fleet. She insisted that naval vessels for which she paid must be stationed in Australian waters and that although they might be built in Britain and manned by officers and crews trained in the royal navy, their control and direction must be determined by her parliament. Her aroused interest in naval and military preparedness at this time was caused by Asiatic rather than by European complications. Europe was far distant, but Japan was near. In consequence she adopted universal, compulsory military service—the first Anglo-Saxon nation to take that step—but limited it to home defense (see page 578). The battleship *Malaya* was given to the royal navy by that rich colony, even though it was not a dominion.

Canada began naval activity by following Australian precedent, and then shifted to a different policy. The Canadian Liberal party, which was in power, was dubious about building warships at all; and if Canada were to build them, it preferred that they should form a Canadian fleet, under Canadian control, rather than be a mere contribution to the royal navy. Many Liberals dreaded that Canada would be drawn, willy-nilly, into the dangerous maelstrom of European rivalries. Consequently the Canadian government bought two small cruisers for the Dominion, stationing one on the Pacific and the other on the Atlantic. Then, in the same year as the conference, came the defeat of Laurier's Liberal ministry, and the Conservatives came into power, waving the Union Jack.

London was jubilant at this change in parties. The new Canadian premier, Sir Robert Borden, was immediately informed that a naval crisis confronted the empire, because of German competition. Borden instantly promised three large battleships for the royal navy, a promise he was to have difficulty in fulfilling. The proposal was bitterly fought by the Canadian Liberals, who maintained that the scheme menaced Canadian autonomy. The French Canadians were particularly recalcitrant. The Conservative majority in the House of Commons at Ottawa finally approved the bill, only to have it rejected by the Liberal majority still surviving in the Senate. Borden did not choose to hold a new election on this issue, and World War I began before anything effective was done.

Chamberlain's proposals thus were rejected, one after another. Neither in armament nor in political co-operation nor in economic policy were the dominions and the mother country to be drawn really closer at this time. His efforts had not been wasted for the sentimental influence for unity was strong on both sides. Each had been given an opportunity to see the others' point of view and to appreciate the spirit of the empire as a whole. These preliminary endeavors were no doubt partly responsible for the magnificent and very tangible co-operation, which the dominions were soon to demonstrate in World War I, when the achievements of the Anzacs at Gallipoli, the Canadians at Ypres, and the South Africans in handling their local troubles disproved for the time being the German contention that the British Empire was simply a "rope of sand" which would crumble away under the first strain.

Overseas Capital Investment

From the financial standpoint, Britain was finally appreciating the value of the dominions, which had been scorned by the Little Englanders because of their meager trade. By 1913, they accounted for nearly a third of the British overseas investments of capital which had been increasing steadily (see pages 390, 424) until they finally reached £4 billion ($20 billion). The loans were generally of mutual value both to the British lenders and the overseas borrowers. To the British, who were investing half their savings beyond the seas, their five and a half per cent yield was considerably more than the usual rate at home. The interest and dividends amounted to nearly a tenth of the total national income and helped Britain to pay for the imports she needed. At the same time, those loans enabled the overseas regions to develop their potential resources much more rapidly than they could have done with only their own capital. Almost half the British loans went to railroads which were rapidly opening up the interior in all continents; considerable went into mining; and substantial amounts into such utilities as street railways, telephone and telegraph companies, and plants for water, gas, and electricity. Some was invested in rubber, tea, and coffee plantations, but only a relatively small amount in oil, later so important. As for geographical distribution, relatively little went to Continental Europe. There was some investment in Japan; in Britain's sphere of interest in China; and in Egypt, where loans had caused such a stir; but those were small compared with what went to the United States, the largest single borrower; to Latin America; and to the Empire.

The importance of the dominions in this field is indicated by this table showing the 1913 situation in respect to the £3,763 millions loaned through the "money market" in addition to some £300 millions in less formal private loans:

BRITISH OVERSEAS INVESTMENTS, 1913

(Million £)

Within the Empire	
Total	1,780
Total Dominions	1,300
Canada-Newfoundland	514
Australia-New Zealand	416
South Africa	370
India-Ceylon	378
West Africa	37
Straits Settlements	27

Foreign	
Total	1,983
United States	754
Latin America	756
Argentina	319
Brazil	148
Europe	218
Russia	110
Japan	62
Egypt	44
China	43

Comprising, as it did in 1913, roughly a quarter of the earth's land surface and a quarter of the world's population, the British Empire was impressive indeed from the quantitive standpoint. On every continent portions of the world map were colored in British red, and some 400,000,000 subjects at home and overseas owed allegiance to George V. The dominions had some two thirds of the land, while the rest of the empire had nine tenths of the people. The distribution of the white population in the overseas possessions is particularly significant. Fourteen million lived in the dominions; one million upheld British power and prestige among the third of a billion brown, yellow, and black peoples. To many Englishmen customs statistics meant more than figures for area and population. In respect to foreign trade the self-governing and the dependent portions of the empire were

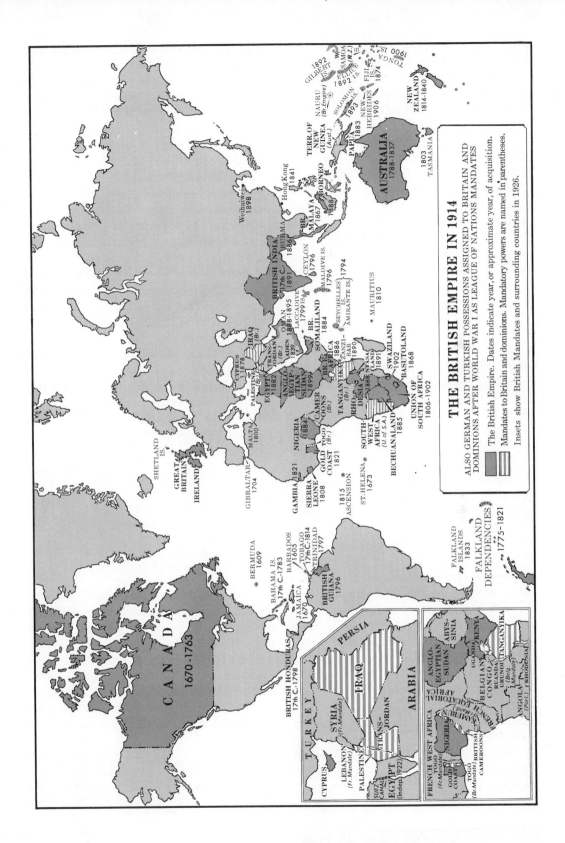

THE BRITISH EMPIRE IN 1914

ALSO GERMAN AND TURKISH POSSESSIONS ASSIGNED TO BRITAIN AND DOMINIONS AFTER WORLD WAR I AS LEAGUE OF NATIONS MANDATES

The British Empire. Dates indicate year, or approximate year, of acquisition.

Mandates to Britain and dominions. Mandatory powers are named in parentheses.

Insets show British Mandates and surrounding countries in 1926.

SHETLAND IS.

GREAT BRITAIN

IRELAND

GIBRALTAR 1704

MALTA 1800

CYPRUS 1878

PALESTINE (Br. Mandate)

IRAQ (Br.)

TRANS-JORDAN (Br.)

EGYPT 1882

ANGLO-EGYP-TIAN SUDAN 1899

ADEN 1839

OMAN 1888-1891

BRITISH INDIA 17th C.

BURMA 1886

CEYLON 1796

MALDIVE IS. 1796

LACCADIVE

MALAYA 1867

BR. BORNEO 1888

Hong Kong 1841

Weihaiwei 1898

GILBERT 1892 IS.

NAURU (Br. Empire)

ELLICE IS. 1892

SOLOMON IS. 1893 IS.

SAMOA (N.Z.)

TONGA IS. 1900

FIJI 1874

NEW HEBRIDES 1906

NEW ZEALAND 1814-1840

TERR. OF NEW GUINEA (Aust.)

PAPUA 1883

AUSTRALIA 1788-1837

TASMANIA 1803

BR. SOMALILAND 1884

SOMALILAND 1884

SEYCHELLES IS. 1794

AMIRANTE IS.

MAURITIUS 1810

NIGERIA 1884

GOLD COAST 1821

TOGO (Br.)

CAMER-OONS (Br.)

BR. EAST AFRICA 1886

UGANDA 1894

ZANZI-BAR 1890

TANGANYIKA (Br.)

NYASA-LAND 1891

RHO-DESIA

SOUTH-WEST AFRICA (U. of S.A.)

BECHUANALAND 1885

SWAZILAND 1902

BASUTOLAND 1868

UNION OF SOUTH AFRICA 1806-1902

GAMBIA 1821

SIERRA LEONE 1808

ST. HELENA 1673

ASCENSION 1815

CANADA 1670-1763

BRITISH HONDURAS 17th C.-1798

BERMUDA 1609

BAHAMA IS. 17th C.

JAMAICA 1670

BARBADOS 1605

TOBAGO 17th C.-1783

TRINIDAD 1797

BRITISH GUIANA 1796

FALKLAND ISLANDS 1833

FALKLAND DEPENDENCIES 1775-1821

Inset (left)

TURKEY

SYRIA (Fr. Mandate)

LEBANON (Fr. Mandate)

CYPRUS

PALESTINE

SUEZ CANAL

EGYPT (Indep.) 1922

TRANS-JORDAN

IRAQ

PERSIA

ARABIA

Inset (right)

ANGLO-EGYPTIAN SUDAN

ABYS-SINIA

FRENCH WEST AFRICA (Fr. Mandate)

NIGERIA

GOLD COAST

TOGO (Br. Mandate)

BRITISH CAMEROONS

CAMERUON (Fr. Mandate)

FRENCH EQUATORIAL AFRICA

BELGIAN CONGO

RUANDA-URUNDI (Belg. Mandate)

UGANDA

KENYA

TANGANYIKA

RHODESIA

ANGOLA (Port.)

about equal. The importance of Raffles's act in establishing Singapore is evident from the substantial exports and imports of the Straits Settlements with their scant population and scantier area; their trade was over seven times as much as that of Nigeria's whose inhabitants outnumbered all the white men of the dominions. The decline of the West Indies which in the eighteenth century had overshadowed all colonial rivals (see page 320) was still marked. Every year the British published statistics of their population, trade, and much else in vast quantities, with the calm assurance that Germans, Frenchmen, Italians, and Russians could not produce such evidence of imperial success.

But there were other aspects of empire which were less tangible. Canada, India, Nigeria, and St. Helena might all be in the empire, but there the resemblance ceased. Unity and homogeneity, both in structure and in spirit, were completely lacking among the scores of separate units involved in Britain's "dominion over palm and pine." It has been contrary to English nature to attempt to jam everything into a rigid mold, and the empire was a reflection of that. The picture is confused, with the governments of the dependencies like Sarawak, Kenya, India, the Sudan, Hong Kong, Jamaica, Sierra Leone, Fiji, Gibraltar, and a score of other places varying from rather strict, semidespotic paternalism to indirect supervision; but the major developments were along the overall division between settlement and exploitation. The dominions were the logical fruition of the initial settlements in Virginia and Massachusetts. From the first Virginia legislature and the Mayflower Compact there has been a steady development in self-government by men who have carried with them a strong sense of the basic rights of Englishmen; before long the dominions would be emerging as full partners rather than as possessions of the mother country. But while some Englishmen had been setting out for Jamestown and Plymouth, others had been sailing eastward to carve out fortunes in India. Exploitation had spread into other distant lands, where, for better or for worse, millions became subject to British rule, with practically nothing to say about the manner in which they were governed. On its good side this rule of the white minority meant order, efficiency, discipline, and comparative peace for a long period. Some of the ruling caste, as usually happens, exhibited a tendency, to a greater or less extent, toward harshness, brutality, arrogance, and exploitation naturally resented by those subjected to it. The native African, forced to gather palm oil or work in mines in order to pay a hut tax for the benefits conferred by British civilization, did not appreciate the latter; nor did most of the Indians warm to those aliens from overseas under whose arbitrary rule they lived. In "The White Man's Burden," Rudyard Kipling, imperialism's poet, stressed the self-sacrificing altruism of the empire-builders, with their civilizing mission.

> Take up the White Man's burden—
>   Send forth the best ye breed—
> Go bind your sons to exile
>   To serve your captives' need;
> To wait in heavy harness,
>   On fluttered folk and wild—
> Your new-caught, sullen peoples,
>   Half-devil and half-child.[4]

But increasingly such an attitude was denounced; and a cartoon of the time, under the same caption showing John Bull and Uncle Sam, shaking bloody hands over the bodies of dead Boers and dead Filipinos, indicated a rising bitterness towards "colonialism." What the World Wars would do to this magnificent but utterly illogical structure of empire remained to be seen.

[4] Rudyard Kipling, "The White Man's Burden," from *The Five Nations* (1903). By permission of Doubleday, Doran and Company, The Macmillan Company of Canada, Limited, Methuen & Co., Ltd., and Mrs. Rudyard Kipling.

Chapter Twenty-nine · 1878-1914

From Isolation to Alliance

The great powers of Europe between 1879 and 1907 aligned themselves in two rival groups. Germany, Austria, and Italy quickly formed the Triple Alliance, while France, Russia, and Britain later joined forces in the Triple Entente. Britain was the last of the six powers to take sides; for the others had all formed definite alliances long before the British put an end to the "splendid isolation" which had characterized their foreign relations since the days of Canning. The growth of the two alliances had tremendous historical consequences, for this international rivalry led in 1914 to the greatest war the world had yet seen.

The story goes back to the international congress at Berlin in 1878, whence Beaconsfield returned with Cyprus in his pocket, with Russia blocked in her expansion toward the Straits, and with German relations exceedingly cordial (see page 474). Britain's position in Europe seemed safe and preeminent. Her interventions in the Near East, where her eyes were upon India and the Suez Canal rather than upon the Continental consequences of Turkey's decline, had scarcely impaired her general policy of isolation; and her triumph at Berlin had been complete.

For more than half a century, the Foreign Office on Downing Street under Can-

ning, Palmerston, and other foreign ministers, had kept Britain aloof from intimate, longstanding contact with any of the Continental powers. She perhaps flattered herself that she could act as the "balance wheel of Europe" by interfering only when the equilibrium seemed threatened or when her own particular interests seemed involved. Although she cherished no such permanent enmities as the Franco-German or the Russo-Turkish, she had no permanent allies, save little Portugal. Between 1800 and 1918 Britain was engaged in war with practically every important country, at one time as ally and at another time as enemy. This insular policy gave her constant freedom of action, and the strength of the royal navy enabled her to speak with authority.

Of the five Continental powers, Russia came nearest to being regarded as her constant enemy. The most populous of them, Russia's potential strength seemed tremendous. The economic, social, and political changes which were transforming Western Europe, however, had left her relatively untouched in her agricultural economy. Her population consisted almost exclusively of the two medieval classes: a small, wealthy aristocracy and a vast, ignorant peasantry. The Czar, an absolute autocrat, without constitutional checks, was engaged in harsh repression after a brief reform period. In her continual efforts to add to her already vast area, she particularly sought an ice-free port on the open sea. The Russians had the unique advantage of being able to reach most of their objectives by land; this made it the more difficult for England to oppose them in the Near East, the Middle East, and, shortly, in the Far East.

Friction with France, Britain's traditional foe, still existed. Smarting from the loss in 1871 of Alsace and Lorraine, a revengeful France feared further German aggression. Yet she realized that for every two Frenchmen there were three Germans. France was the most democratic of the Continental powers, with responsible government, but the Third Republic lacked prestige. More than once France had been prevented from taking a strong hand because of a cabinet crisis in her short-lived ministries. Her commercial and industrial development was moderate, but she was still predominantly agricultural. Her colonial ambitions were centered in North Africa, where Algeria, taken in 1830, was her principal colony. Her other colonial interests were scattered in Indo-China, India, the South Seas, and the Caribbean.

Germany was forging ahead more rapidly than any other power. Under the presiding genius of her "Iron Chancellor," Prince Otto von Bismarck, Prussia had whipped Denmark, Austria, and France in rapid succession, and the king of Prussia had become head of the new German Empire, proclaimed at Versailles in 1871. Then Bismarck dropped his blood-and-iron policy and sought to dominate the Continent by shrewd diplomacy, backed by the best army in the world. Until his forced retirement in 1890, he was the most influential man in Europe. Germany's government was autocratic, for a chancellor's tenure of office depended solely on the emperor, who not only appointed him but controlled, as king

of Prussia, either by influence or by appointment, the upper house of the legislature. On the democratic side, the consent of the lower house, popularly elected, was necessary for new expenditures, such as naval construction. About 1878 Britain was more favorably disposed to Germany than to any other power; for the two peoples had much in common, and Victoria's prejudices were strongly pro-German. But with remarkable energy and thoroughness the Germans were making rapid strides in industry and commerce, which, in conjunction with their later colonial and naval ambitions, would conflict with British interests.

Britain's path frequently crossed those of Russia, France, and Germany in various parts of the world, but with Austria and Italy, she was much less concerned. Austria—or, more properly, since 1867, the Dual Monarchy of Austria-Hungary—as an illogical, heterogeneous assortment of lands and races under Hapsburg rule, lacked national unity. She was troubled by the mutterings of her discontented minorities, and by the rising tide of nationalism in the Balkans, where, like Russia, she too had ambitions. Italy, after her unification about 1860, considered herself a first-rate power, but was scarcely accepted at par by the others, whose resources and prestige she lacked. Her foreign policy was dubious and tricky, and her imperialistic ventures were to yield little more than sandy wastes which no one else desired. The diplomacy of the period, in its major aspects, was largely the concern of the great powers, with the lesser nations of Europe in minor roles. Across the seas the United States and Japan were to be accepted as world powers by the turn of the century.

The two great alliances, whose later aggressive rivalry would lead to war began as strictly defensive. Seeking to remove as many sources of international friction as possible, Bismarck told Austria that her future lay not in Germany but in the Balkans. Disturbed by French animosity, he sought to isolate France and encouraged her expansion in North Africa, hoping that thus she might forget Alsace and Lorraine. This policy, being more successful at Vienna than at Paris, Bismarck turned more and more toward Austria. Fearful lest France make an alliance with either Russia or Austria against Germany, he organized the "League of the Three Emperors" (Germany, Austria, Russia), thus linking together the three eastern autocratic powers in a common agreement to preserve the status quo. Ever since the days of Castlereagh and Canning, they had tended to act in concert; but the events of 1877-1878 had demonstrated that the conflicting ambitions of Russia and Austria in the Balkans made it almost impossible for any country to be on intimate terms with both. At Berlin, Bismarck had seemingly tried to act the "honest broker" between the two; but the results had been far more favorable to Austria than to Russia who felt aggrieved and blamed Bismarck. Thus, he now felt that Austria was the safer ally.

The Triple Alliance

In the first step of the Triple Alliance, in 1879, Bismarck drew Austria into closer relationship. He wanted an ally who would come to his aid against France; what he got was a pledge that if Russia should attack either Germany or Austria, the other would come at once to the aid of her ally, but if either should be attacked by a power other than Russia (which obviously meant France), the other need give only "benevolent neutrality" unless Russia should come into the conflict. At first only a five-year agreement, subject to renewal, it was to be kept secret unless its announcement might seem threat enough to prevent war. Three years later Italy rounded out this Triple Alliance. It was formerly believed that Bismarck deliberately drew Italy into the alliance by encouraging France to seize Tunis. It is true that the Italians were furious about that but it seems that Italy herself

sought admission to the alliance and that Bismarck agreed only reluctantly. He knew that Italy wanted support for her colonial ambitions, and he foresaw that "her promise will have no value if it is not in her interest to keep it." This triangular alliance had Germany at its principal angle, and the Austro-Italian its weak side, for in addition to their traditional enmity, Austrian holdings north of the Adriatic stood in the way of Italian expansion. This alliance had the advantageous position, in war, of occupying a central strip in Europe from the Baltic to the middle of the Mediterranean. As long as Bismarck was in power, he kept this a purely defensive alliance, which had been his objective in bringing Germany and Austria together. He prevented the alliance from being used by Austria to extend her Balkan influence and by Italy to further her African ambitions.

Although he chose Austria rather than Russia for close partnership, he did his best to keep on friendly terms with St. Petersburg. The old "League of the Three Emperors"—of Germany, Austria, and Russia —was kept alive for a while, and he drew up a "reinsurance" treaty with Russia in his desire to prevent a Franco-Russian alliance which would catch Germany with potential foes on two sides. But in 1890, the new German "Kaiser," the energetic and erratic William II, "dropped the pilot" and took matters into his own less steady hands. Almost immediately the "wire to St. Petersburg" was pulled down.

Bismarck's fears quickly came true; between 1891 and 1894, the French and Russians arrived at a defensive alliance. France had felt completely isolated and was now comforted by the prospect that if German troops should start for Paris, the Russians would start for Berlin. The terms of the 1894 agreement stipulated that France or Russia would support her ally with all available forces in case either were attacked by Germany or if Germany supported an attack by Italy or Austria. This alliance was

"Dropping the Pilot," famous *Punch* cartoon of dismissal of Bimarck by young William II.

Isles themselves might be from Continental aggression, England's far-flung colonial possessions presented numerous points vulnerable to the imperialistic ambitions of Russia, France, and Germany. The sudden outburst of imperialism in the last quarter of the century had led to a feverish scramble in Africa, at its height about 1885, and in China, beginning ten years later (see pages 522, 535). At every turn she had already encountered the advances of one of her three Continental rivals. Her vast empire, commercial success, and sea power excited envy, while her calm assumption of superiority exasperated those who were less sure of themselves. If Russia, France, and Germany should all join forces against her, her position would indeed be serious, but Alsace-Lorraine so far stood in the way of that.

Africa, north, central, and south, was presenting numerous causes of imperialistic friction. Britain and France had disputes over Madagascar, but these paled into insignificance in comparison with hard feeling over Egypt until the crisis in 1898 at Fashoda cleared the air (see page 528). Bismarck had refrained for a while from colonial activity, but he finally yielded to pressure and, once involved, played an energetic part. In 1884-1885 Germany became an African power almost overnight (see page 520). Later events in South Africa would strain Anglo-German relations nearly to the breaking point when the Kaiser sent his telegram of congratulation to President Kruger of the Transvaal, and the Boer War, which followed shortly, rendered England's international position even more acute (see page 531).

Russia was not involved in the African scramble, but she gave Britain grave concern in Asia, all the way from Turkey to China (see page 473). From about 1878 to 1895 the storm center was central Asia, north of India, where Russia was steadily pressing southward into the desert regions of Turkestan and pushing on toward Af-

cemented by huge French loans which Russia used for railways, particularly the Trans-Siberian, and for industrial development, as well as for purely military and naval purposes. This was the first step in what was to become, with the subsequent inclusion of Britain, the Triple Entente.

Isolation No Longer "Splendid"

Meanwhile it seemed highly improbable that within fifteen years Britain would unite with France and Russia, her most active colonial rivals and her former enemies, against Germany, a power with whom she had long been on friendly terms. In the 1890's, however, she was no longer in the relatively powerful position of the days of Palmerston.

Gradually she began to realize that while she was certainly isolated, there was considerable doubt about the "splendor" of that isolation. However secure the British

ghanistan. There was a time, in the middle nineties, when British and Russian forces faced one another on a bleak plateau in that remote region, and the nations seemed on the verge of war; but diplomacy intervened, England yielded slightly, and the Russians soon shifted their activities farther eastward toward China. Britain had minor imperialistic encounters with France for influence in the independent kingdom of Siam (Thailand), which lies between British Burma and French Indo-China, and with Germany and France in the South Seas islands; but these were completely overshadowed by the sudden emergence of the Far Eastern question, which became acute with the surprising victory of Japan over China in 1894-1895. By revealing China's weakness this whetted the appetites of England's three imperialistic rivals, particularly Russia, and their concerted action pointed out more clearly than ever the danger of her isolation (see page 535).

The year 1898 saw a combination of events significant in England's foreign and colonial relations. In the course of those twelve months the Chinese ports were distributed among the powers; Kitchener reconquered the Sudan and met the French at Fashoda; the United States fought Spain and thereby became a Caribbean and Pacific power; and Germany passed her first important law for a strong navy.

Britain was worried. Ever since 1886, except for the brief period of Liberal government (1892-1895), the control of her foreign policy had rested in the competent hands of Lord Salisbury (see page 489), who had shown the same shrewd skill in preserving "splendid isolation" that had enabled his Cecil ancestor to steer England through the problems of Elizabeth's reign. A keen realist, able to size up men and motives, he had been cautious in commitments, and all ideas of a general alliance had found him very skeptical. Nevertheless, he was open to conviction; and some men in his own cabinet, especially Joseph Cham-

berlain, his colonial secretary, thought that the time had come to cast about for an ally, Russia, Germany, and the United States being their first three choices. Now in January, 1898, Salisbury approached Russia, not with the slightest idea of an alliance but with the suggestion of merely a friendly understanding about "spheres of preponderance" in Turkey and China. A few weeks later his proposal was sharply rebuffed with the leasing of Port Arthur by Russia. Then Joseph Chamberlain proposed an alliance with the Germans, but they quickly passed their naval law, an act which did not set well with the British.

Britain's only real friend during that troubled time was the United States. The two had a common interest in resisting the Russian, French, and German advances in China. The former thirteen colonies had a population more than double that of the mother country. For many years they had been so busy pushing westward to the Pacific that they had turned their backs on outside affairs; but now that task was completed. The army was fighting its last Indian battle, and the frontier, by official statement, no longer existed. The United States was ready to play her part in the outside world. Britain welcomed her appearance, though as late as 1895 the Americans had "twisted the British lion's tail" by invoking the Monroe Doctrine in a border dispute between Venezuela and British Guiana. For several years to come, however, England performed constant favors for the United States and asked little that was definite in return. During the brief war of 1898, in which the United States took away most of Spain's remaining colonial possessions, Continental opinion was bitter against the United States; but England favored the American cause. England hoped that if the Americans gained the Philippines as a definite foothold in the Far East, they would give stronger support to England's desire for equal trading rights in China. After the Americans had defeated the

Spanish naval forces in Manila Bay, a German squadron of superior force arrived on the scene and behaved in a threatening manner. The British naval commander thereupon made it clear that if trouble developed he would stand by the Americans. Back in England, Chamberlain was advocating an alliance with the United States as well as with Germany. The Anglo-American understanding soon bore fruit; the American Secretary of State, John Hay, secured general, but rather half-hearted, international agreement to the "open door" policy of equal trading rights in China, which England had been trying to maintain singlehanded against the Russians, French, and Germans in 1898. In gratitude, Britain virtually recognized the Caribbean as an "American lake," withdrawing most of her naval force and modifying an old treaty of 1850, so that the Americans might have the exclusive right to construct the Panama Canal. There was no alliance between Britain and the United States; but in the Pacific, at least, they were united for common action.

Still further to strengthen her hand in the Far East, Britain in 1902 formed an alliance with Japan. In case of an attack upon either of them in China or Korea by two powers (which implied Russia supported by France), the ally would give support. The alliance was to be renewed more than once, with the terms extended in 1905 to India, and the stipulation made for mutual support if either of the two signatories were attacked by even a single power. The alliance did much to increase the prestige of Japan, whose potential strength was not yet realized, and it added to Britain's security in Asiatic waters.

But Britain remained worried about her European isolation. Humiliated by the Boer War and universally unpopular on the Continent, she foresaw that after its difficulty in subduing that small force of farmers, her army would be outclassed by a major European opponent. With the need of a Continental ally increasingly apparent, several semi-official overtures were made to Germany between 1898 and 1901, chiefly by Joseph Chamberlain. He was enthusiastic and persistent, although not all the cabinet were behind him. He approached the German ambassador at London, discussed the matter with the Kaiser when he came to England, and in a speech at Leicester said "I think any far-seeing Englishman must long have desired . . . that we should not remain primarily isolated on the continent . . . the natural alliance is between ourselves and the great German nation."

But this diplomatic kite was not welcomed in Germany. On the practical merits of the proposal Germany felt that she would gain less than Britain; for the royal navy would be of little help if the Russians should invade East Prussia. The British, however, kept on making informal offers, which were not directly rejected. Germany might have been more willing if England had suggested joining the Triple Alliance, along perhaps with Japan. It did not help matters to have his nephew the Kaiser write to Edward VII that the British ministers were "unmitigated noodles." Eventually Chamberlain began to lose hope. Even his intimation that England would turn to France made no impression on the German Foreign Office, which was confident that British rivalry with France and Russia was too deep-rooted for such a partnership, and that Britain needed an ally so much that she would ultimately come on Germany's terms. This refusal of the proffered alliance was one of the significant steps in the approach to the war.

Prominent among several factors which tended to promote ill-feeling between the two nations was a mutual popular antipathy, as well as commercial competition and the beginning of naval rivalry. German feeling was probably more anti-English than English feeling was anti-German. Part of the German dislike was based on jealousy; Britain was already well entrenched in the colonial, naval, and commercial fields, where the Germans had ambitions of their own. The German newspapers, to prepare the people for the naval measures of 1898 and 1900, often deliberately stirred up anti-British feeling. The Boer War intensified this; a speaker in the Reichstag, called to order for referring to Chamberlain as "the most accursed scoundrel on God's earth," received hundreds of congratulatory telegrams. Counterattacks by the British press and public naturally followed. Kipling, about this time, was referring to "the Goth and the shameless Hun." In such an atmosphere neither nation was in a mood to welcome an alliance.

Britain, moreover, was increasingly aware that out on the fringes of the empire, Germany's growing commercial and naval activity seemed to jeopardize things far more vital than France in the Sudan or Russia in Manchuria. Ever since Trafalgar, England had been virtually undisputed "mistress of the seas" and for more than a century the "workshop of the world" thanks to her early start with the Industrial Revolution. Wherever British traders or warships had gone, they had been masters of the situation. And now Germany was challenging England, in both these fields that had been so distinctively her own. Germany's colonial activity was no particular cause for British concern, but her increasing exports, her merchant marine, and, above all, her navy were a different matter.

German Commercial Competition

The German commercial rivalry, which began to be serious about 1880, the contemporary activity of the United States, and the later activity of Japan were triple blows at British industry and commerce. With high protective tariffs the newcomers shielded infant industries against British goods and began to supply their own domestic needs. They then challenged British supremacy in markets of the outside world, and finally managed to flood the markets of free-trade Britain herself with their goods. Although American exports were almost equal to the German, they were less of a threat to British manufacturers, since some two thirds of them were grain, meat, and raw cotton.

In industrial and commercial matters Britain had had the field to herself for so long that she had fallen behind in methods of production and sale. With pride in the traditions of their firms and the quality of their products, the British felt it undignified to push their wares too vigorously. The Germans, with their remarkable capacity for thoroughness and detail, co-ordinated factories, railways, steamships, and finance to challenge Britain in one world market after another. By cutting production costs and deliberately sacrificing quality, they could turn out articles more cheaply. Their experts carefully analyzed the needs and desires of particular markets and reported, for instance, that cheap knives with colored handles and poor blades would sell better than the conventional British knives, with their somber black handles and excellent blades. That was typical of a thousand experiments, and the Germans were ever ready to introduce new articles and create new tastes. They sent out traveling salesmen, persistent, aggressive, and able to speak the language of the region. German banks offered liberal credit terms to overseas buyers, and German consuls actively aided the nation's commercial interests. The Hamburg-American, North German Lloyd, and other steamship lines radiated from Hamburg and Bremen in every direction, offering excellent service with freight rates often much lower than the British.

From 1875 on, while British export totals remained fairly static, the Germans forged rapidly ahead. In many Continental nations Germany actually began to sell more goods than Britain. With the advantage of direct rail communication, which eliminated the cost of loading and unloading ships, she began to outsell Britain; in Russia, by 1913, she was selling four times as much. Outside Europe, in the United States, Latin America, and elsewhere, the Germans were steadily creeping up on the British total. As foreign markets fell off, Britain increased her proportion of trade with her own possessions, where the German inroads were less marked, although the United States ran far ahead of England in trade with Canada. Even at home the "workshop of the world" discovered that it was being flooded with a wide range of articles marked "Made in Germany," even to that most English of objects, the cricket bat. Britain, in fact, was Germany's best customer. In order to check the German forging of British trade-marks, Parliament required that all imports should be stamped with the country of origin. In 1870, Britain's exports of domestic products at £256,000,000 were more than double Germany's at £124,000,000; but by 1913 Germany's £509,000,000 were almost up to the British at £525,000,000. In their sales to the United States, Britain led Germany in 1872 at £50,000,000 to £9,000,000; in 1913, they stood at £59,000,000 to £34,-000,000.

On the eve of Chamberlain's alliance proposals, an English writer's *Made in Germany* aroused popular apprehensions by declaring that Germany was "battling with might and main for the extinction of her [England's] supremacy"; and another, shortly afterward, stated that "if Germany were extinguished tomorrow, the day after tomorrow there is not an Englishman in the world who would not be the richer." Some Germans were charging that Britain desired to crush their commercial development by force, as they had the Dutch (see page 265). Those, however, were irresponsible opinions and diplomatic historians are inclined to discount the commercial friction; for the foreign office archives indicate that the ministers, perhaps too proud to soil their hands with anything so prosaic as exports, rather neglected the subject.

German Naval Competition

Next from Germany came what appeared to be a threat to the security of Britain herself and her empire. In 1890 Captain Mahan, an American naval officer, coined the phrase "sea power" and, in a brilliant study, demonstrated its influence in the spread of England's power on the seas and in the lands beyond the seas. Sea power, which provided the means of going where one pleased in wartime while preventing one's enemy from doing likewise, was suddenly made to seem very desirable. At the time Britain's sea power was fully taken for granted. She had long maintained her navy on a "two-power" basis, large enough to handle any two rivals that might combine. As long as France and Russia remained the runners-up, she believed that hers was decidedly the superior navy in quality. Suddenly the Germans appeared as ardent disciples of Mahan's teachings; a well-organized and aggressive Navy League, financed at first by the Krupp munitions concern, which saw prospects of huge orders, stirred up propaganda. The Kaiser, who "liked tall ships as an earlier Hohenzollern had liked tall soldiers," supported the idea. The guiding force was the old sea dog Admiral von Tirpitz. In 1898, the Reichstag voted to construct, over a period of years, nineteen battleships and numerous cruisers. In 1900, while the proposals for alliance were still under way, a more ambitious naval law was passed. Its preamble declared that "Germany must have a battle fleet so strong that, even for the adversary with the greatest sea power, a war against us would involve such dangers as to imperil his position in the world." It provided for thirty-four battleships in sixteen years, together with a large number of cruisers and lesser craft. Before this naval spurt she had only fourteen battleships to England's fifty-four. To protect her supremacy, Britain would have to lay down keels at an even faster rate.

Edward VII in the royal box at the Longchamps races in 1903, part of his successful cultivation of Anglo-French relations leading to the 1904 Entente.

Failing to secure an alliance with Germany, Britain turned to strengthening the royal navy and making approaches to Germany's rivals. In 1903 she began building a new base on the east coast of Scotland, at Rosyth, and commenced a new building program calling for four capital ships every year. She next began to concentrate the fleet in home waters. Tirpitz found a doughty rival in Sir John Fisher, another tough old sailor, and the two persistently pushed their plans toward a "naval race."

The "Entente Cordiale" with France

After her unsuccessful approaches to Russia and Germany, Britain turned toward France to end her "splendid isolation." Delcassé, the French minister of foreign affairs, was even more anxious than England to bring about a friendly understanding, although the French had many grievances against Britain, particularly in Africa, where the memory of Fashoda was still fresh (see page 528). Furthermore, Edward VII did not like the pushing ways of his nephew the Kaiser, who was reported to have called his uncle an old peacock. Edward was pro-French, in marked contrast to Victoria's prejudices in favor of everything German, and Paris knew this. Utilized by his cabinet as a harbinger of good will, Edward did much to reconcile the French to the strange notion of an understanding with Britain, while the French president was cheered in London. Thus was a new friendship finally consummated.

What Britain wanted was a friend on the Continent and a free hand in Egypt. France wanted many things, particularly Morocco, the westernmost of the old Barbary States. She had had Algeria since 1830, had made Tunis a protectorate in 1881, and Morocco would round out her colonial empire there well.

In 1904 Britain aligned herself definitely with France in an "Entente Cordiale" or friendly understanding. A bargain was made in this second stage of the Triple Entente as in the others. Lord Lansdowne, who succeeded Salisbury as Foreign Secretary agreed to accept the then-existing political status of Egypt, and France promised not to interfere in anything that England might do in that country. In return, France stated that she recognized the existing status in Morocco, and Britain agreed to give her a free hand there. The lesser agreements ended the centuries-old disputes relative to the Newfoundland fisheries, drew new boundaries between British and French colonies in Africa, led Britain to withdraw certain claims over Madagascar, arranged spheres of influence in the hinterland of Siam, and provided for joint rule over the New Hebrides, in the Pacific. Wherever the Union Jack and the tricolor flew throughout the world, understanding and friendship were now to take the place of suspicion and hostility. All that was made public, but not the secret agreements by which mutual promises of diplomatic support were given in case England or France sought to extend her power in Egypt or Morocco.

This Entente Cordiale was to become a momentous landmark in British history. A prominent member of the British cabinet of 1914 once declared that George III began the destruction of the British Empire and that Edward VII consummated it when he tied his country to the chariot wheels of Franco-Russian imperialism. Whether this was a false conclusion or not, the Entente ultimately did far more than end colonial friction and reverse the course of Anglo-French relations. By her "diplomatic revolution" Britain became aligned with the Continental system and thereby lost much of her old freedom of action. She was not a member of the Dual Alliance between France and Russia. While, unlike the other nations, she did not make (except in her alliance with Japan) formal agreements as to what she would do in case of war, her "friendly understandings" were to prove more binding when the crisis came in 1914 than Italy's pledged word. When this new English entente with France was shortly extended to Russia, the new triangular arrangement was to surpass in wealth and population the rival Triple Alliance, and so would upset the delicate balance between Europe's armed camps.

Within a year France took action in Morocco, offering money to the sultan for needed reforms, and sending a mission to his capital, Fez, to arrange for spending it. Thereupon the Kaiser landed at Tangier, publicly congratulated the sultan upon his independence, and warned him to be on his guard lest he lose it. The question of Morocco, Germany declared, concerned Europe as a whole, and she insisted that an international conference be held to determine its status. Delcassé now lost his head; for he preferred war to the projected conference, which, he feared, might retard French projects in Morocco. He intimated that Britain was ready to fight, which the British Foreign Office denied, and Delcassé resigned. Germany won a temporary victory; for early in 1906 a conference assembled in Spanish town of Algeciras, near Gibraltar, to discuss Moroccan affairs.

Just before the conference met, the coming of the Liberals into power brought Sir Edward Grey to the Foreign Office, where he was to remain for more than ten years. Lean, aloof, and dignified, Grey belonged to one of the foremost families of the English aristocracy, with a prominent career of public service. He had been a champion tennis-player and was an enthusiastic fisherman and birdwatcher. Though the Germans later called him "Liar Grey," his integrity was apparently above reproach. Yet he had his shortcomings. Lacking Salisbury's knowledge of the Continental point of view, he was apt to rely on the permanent Foreign Office officials and was too prone to consider others as honorable as himself—an unfortunate trait considering certain allies of the near future. Like many previous secretaries he tended to compromise rather than to formulate a far-reaching policy. He accepted fully Lansdowne's Anglo-French agreement.

The calling of the Algeciras Conference was a diplomatic victory for Germany; its results were a sharp defeat. France got what she wanted by prior bargaining. Secretly, Italy agreed not to obstruct France in Morocco if the French would consent to Italian absorption of Tripoli. Thereafter Italy was to keep a foot in both armed camps; for although she still remained publicly a member of the Triple Alliance, she flirted secretly with France. Spain also was bought off by France with prospects of a share of Morocco. Russia, from her position in the Dual Alliance, and Britain, from hers in the Entente Cordiale, sided with France. Only Austria supported the isolated Germans. The independence of Morocco was acknowledged, but France was given control over the policing of its ports, and a predominant position in its finances.

The Triple Entente, Including Russia

The next year Britain and Russia drew closer together to round out the Triple Entente. Behind them was that long record of hostility and rivalry in the Near East, Middle East, and Far East (see pages 534 ff.). Russia had rebuffed Salisbury's proposal for an understanding in 1898, and England had allied herself with Japan to offset Russian influence in the Far East. With Russia's defeat by Japan in 1904-1905, Britain, and Germany too, now had less to fear from Russia; Britain seems to have taken the initiative in 1907, in fear of a Russo-German alliance. Russia, repulsed in the Far East, was glad to compound her disputes with Britain in the Middle East in order to have a free hand in the Near East. The Anglo-Russian agreement, like the Dual Alliance of Russia and France and the Entente

THE HARMLESS NECESSARY CAT.

British lion to Russian bear, 1907: "*You* can play with his head and *I* can play with his tail and we can both stroke the small of his back." Persian cat complains he was not consulted.

Cordiale of France and Britain, was sealed with a bargain. The British and Russians both agreed to stay out of Tibet. Afghanistan was recognized as a British sphere of influence. Persia was virtually partitioned between the two. Aside from these matters, the agreement was not specific: there were no military or naval commitments, and the opening of the Straits at Constantinople, the project closest to the heart of the Russian foreign minister, was hinted at vaguely and indirectly. It boded ill for the future that that foreign minister was Isvolski, one of the men who probably did most to bring on World War I.

The most important part of the bargain was the offering up of Persia as a sacrificial lamb. Although her independence was recognized as a matter of form, Russia and Britain divided the country into three zones without consulting the Persians. Russia received the most valuable zone—including the capital, Teheran—as a sphere of influence for economic exploitation. There was a neutral zone between this and Britain's share in the south and east, protecting the approaches to India. Theoretically, there was to be an "open door" policy. Actually the door was closed in the face of Germany. Following hard upon this agreement came the strangling of Persian independence by Russia, with Britain somewhat sorrowfully sacrificing Persia for the exigencies of European politics. The Persians did not take their strangling quietly. They stirred up a revolution, exiled their pro-Russian Shah, and attempted to rule themselves, bringing in an American, W. Morgan Shuster, as financial adviser. He was finally driven out by a Russian ultimatum to Persia, backed by England. His vehement public protest caused Grey considerable embarrassment in Parliament. Grey expostulated with Russia in private, but in public defended her good faith. Russia, feeling that England needed her alliance, exploited that to the limit; she punished Persia for employing Shuster by blowing up the citadel at Tabriz, and by a general massacre.

This showed Britain how far she had gone from her "spendid isolation." She soon found she was tied up to two dangerously ambitious nations. If a member of one alliance gained something anywhere in the world, the other one felt it necessary to secure compensation. In those tense years there were a series of incidents any one of which might have plunged Europe into war.

In Morocco, where French influence had grown apace, there was the "Agadir affair." In 1911, because of a palace revolution at Fez, the French dispatched a military force, alleging that the Europeans there were in danger. As the situation was like the one that gave Britain control of Egypt in 1882, the Germans felt that such an occupying force might lead to Morocco becoming a French protectorate. After hinting in vain that they might accept compensation elsewhere, they sent a gunboat to Agadir, an obscure Moroccan port on the Atlantic. If France was going to tear up the Treaty of Algeciras, Germany was determined to have something for herself, either in Morocco or elsewhere.

That brought in Britain. She wanted no German naval base there, lying athwart her sea lanes. While Grey awaited the assurance he had demanded that Germany did not intend to occupy Agadir, Lloyd George, then Chancellor of the Exchequer, declared with official approval in a speech: "Britain should at all hazards maintain her prestige amongst the great powers of the world" and if treated "as if she were of no account," peace at such a price would be an intolerable humiliation. German public opinion was inflamed. The British cabinet ordered the fleet to make ready, and France and Germany also started war preparations. Cooler heads prevailed; what Germany wanted was not Agadir, it seemed, but a large though rather worthless portion of the French Congo, to add to Kamerun. With this, she was bought off, and the Triple Alliance saved its face.

Britain had now drifted far into the Franco-Russian camp, conniving with them in their inroads on Persian and Moroccan independence. From the German point of view, this meant that Britain was actively participating in the encirclement of Germany by a ring of enemies. From her own point of view, she was only compounding her differences with France and Russia while taking out insurance policies against a restless and militant neighbor who threatened her peace.

The Dreadnought and the Naval Race

The main cause of Britain's hostility lay in the continued naval rivalry. She had given Germany an excellent chance to catch up in the naval race by laying the keel of the *Dreadnought* in 1905. Ever since the old wooden ship of the line had given way to the ironclad, about 1860 (see page 427), warships had been undergoing constant

The "all-big-gun" *Dreadnought,* hastily completed in 1906, rendering obsolescent the existing "predreadnoughts" with only four big guns.

evolution toward increased size, fire power, defensive strength, speed, and cost. At the turn of the century, when the naval race began, the British battleships carried four twelve-inch guns and twelve six-inch guns, with armor plate from seven to nine inches thick. The race for "bigger and better" ships had already made some progress in tons, guns, plates, and knots when the British began work on the *Dreadnought,* with her seventeen thousand tons and twenty-one knot speed. She was not only larger and faster than the other battleships of that day; her real distinction, which made her a landmark in naval construction, was that she was an "all-big-gun" ship. She had ten twelve-inch guns, whereas the others had only four, with some smaller ones. Consequently, in an action, she could stay out of range of the smaller guns and had a tremendous advantage in hitting power. So important was she that battleships came to

be designated as "predreadnoughts," "dreadnoughts," and "superdreadnoughts." By rendering all earlier battleships obsolete, however, she wiped out Britain's heavy advantage and gave her rivals a fresh start. Aware that the idea of an "all-big-gun" ship was in the air, the British secretly rushed her to completion in a year and four days. It was nearly four years later before Germany had her first two dreadnoughts at sea; and by that time England had five, as well as three battle cruisers which had the size and gun power of dreadnoughts but sacrificed some armor protection for extra speed.

Britain's fear of the German navy was in part fanciful, in part justified. Although this challenge to her naval supremacy was resented, the costs of a naval race collided head on with the Liberal party's social reform program. The party, in control since 1905, was historically pledged to peace, retrenchment, and reform. The reforms made retrenchment impossible, but they might still be had without too great a strain unless money had to go for the fleet. Public opinion would not permit Britain to lose control of the seas; for, pride apart, her dependence upon an overseas supply of food and other essentials made it imperative. Germany, as she soon was to demonstrate, could fight four years with her fleet completely cooped up; Britain could not last four months. If rising German naval expenditure were not countered by Britain, she obviously would no longer be mistress of the seas. This, more than anything else, had driven the peaceful Grey into the arms of France and Russia.

There was truculence on both sides. Fisher secretly proposed to the king in 1908 that he "Copenhagen" the German fleet; in other words, seize or sink it without a declaration of war (see pages 374, 379). The Germans, so far as is known, did not go that far, but steadily augmenting their striking force, they began, apparently, to anticipate their program for 1909-1910, whereupon the British laid down superdreadnoughts, which implied guns of 13.5 inches or more. England, though forced to beg ships from the dominions, managed to keep a safe lead at the heavy cost of a nearly doubled naval budget.

Both governments meanwhile started negotiations to end or at least slow down this race. The British gave up their time-honored two-power standard and insisted only on a 3-2 ratio over any given nation. The Germans refused to answer the suggestion of Winston Churchill, First Lord of the Admiralty, for a "naval holiday" by both sides; but they offered to slow down their building if Britain would stay neutral in a Continental war. The British shied away from that proposal, being already too far involved with France to risk such a pledge. By 1914, Britain was ahead 18 to 13 in new battleships and 9 to 4 in battle cruisers.

In 1912, these efforts at compromise ended. The British felt the Germans were trying to browbeat them into a political agreement and were using as a club their projected naval increase. Those figures horrified the Admiralty, for they would bring the German navy close to equality in a few years. Britain, therefore, increased her own appropriations again and drew closer to France. The latter was seeking to make the Entente Cordiale a more definite alliance, like hers with Russia, but Britain wanted to retain freedom of action. It was agreed, at least, that their military and naval experts were to continue to consult together. They had been doing this secretly for six years, but now for the first time, the whole British cabinet learned of it and were divided on its advisability. The particular point at issue was the proposed transfer of part of the British Mediterranean ships to the North Sea to increase the force opposed to Germany, while the French would move their Atlantic fleet from the Channel to the Mediterranean, thus leaving their western coast unprotected unless the British were to guard it. This, to the opponents of the policy, seemed to mean that Britain would be in honor bound to protect the French coast in case of a Franco-German war.

Great Continental Armies

The British navy was still the strongest in the world; but the army was another story. Britain and the United States, alone of the great nations, still clung to small professional armies. The others had adopted the conscription of all able-bodied men of certain ages which had been inaugurated in Revolutionary France and then had been made into a system by Prussia after her defeat by Napoleon. Limited by him to an army of 42,000, Prussia used the clever ruse of training that number intensively for a few months and then conscripting another batch until, while still keeping their standing army small, they had built up a large reserve of trained men. The revival of this sytem had helped Prussia defeat Austria and France in 1866 and 1870. This compulsory, universal military training, adopted by France, Austria, Russia, Italy, and most other Continental nations, accounts for the vast armies of trained men instantly mobilized in World War I. Every officer and soldier knew exactly where to report, when mobilization was declared. In 1911, Germany had in standing army and trained reserves 4.8 million men; France, 3.1 million; Austria, 1.9; and Italy, 1.5. Russia, theoretically with 5.0 million, lacked adequate equipment for that many.

The professionals of Britain's regular army were of excellent quality, but they were only about 250,000 strong, one half stationed in the British Isles and the other in India or elsewhere beyond the seas. She also had some 130,000 reserves. The size of the army was debated in thousands of British homes at this time, for it was recognized that if Germany invaded France, an expeditionary force might have to be sent. Lord Haldane, the War Secretary, announced the creation of "territorials" or trained militia, more than 200,000 strong. These, with the reserves, he felt were enough to keep an expeditionary force of 160,000 at full strength, as well as provide a framework for a new army. Foremost among those who demanded instead continental conscription was the aged Lord Roberts, hero of the Afghan and Boer Wars (see page 531). So vehement was his voice and great his popularity, that to the government's dismay, an army scare also spread through the country. Later some felt that had his advice been taken, Germany might have hesitated long before invading Belgium. As it was, Germany did not take Britain's army seriously. Bismarck was reputed to have said earlier he would ask the police to arrest a British expedition, were one sent over.

Meanwhile, Balkan events were fast moving toward a crisis which did not primarily concern Germany or France or Britain except as they involved Austria and Russia. Britain's sole interest was the control of Constantinople, and her anti-Russian tradition was still too strong to permit support of Russian policy in any Balkan quarrel. But, as tension increased, every country became more and more convinced that it could not be safe without allies, and to keep its allies it felt forced to support their interests even in quarters where its own were not at stake.

Russia, Austria, and the Balkans

Unfortunately, the foreign policies of Russia and Austria now fell into the hands of men more reckless than capable. Their intrigues produced a series of crises between 1908 and 1914, when they finally dragged their more cautious allies into war. Particularly conspicuous was the Russian foreign minister Isvolski, a tireless intriguer whose one great aim was the opening of the Straits to Russian warships. Toward that end he bargained with one nation after another and planned for the war as soon as Russia recovered from her Japanese defeat. He had helped to arrange the Anglo-Russian agreement of 1907, and later, as ambassador at Paris, he did much to turn the Franco-Russian alliance from a defensive into an aggressive one.

When the Young Turk revolution drove old Abdul-Hamid from his throne in 1908, Isvolski hoped to take advantage of Turkey's temporary weakness. He was furious when Austria annexed the Balkan provinces of Bosnia-Herzegovina, while he failed to make progress at the Straits. Determined on revenge, he went to London for British support, but was treated coldly. The utmost crumb of comfort he received was that sometime the British might consider it desirable to change the status of the Straits, provided Turkey consented. Russia reviving a pan-Slavic policy in the Balkans, a new version of the old religious excuse for interference, backed Serbia in her intrigues to join to herself the South Slavs in Austria-Hungary. Austria felt compelled to take strong measures to protect herself against disintegration. Out of this situation the war would come, and Isvolski would say, "It is *my* war!"

The two fierce Balkan wars of 1912 and 1913 likewise affected Britain only indirectly. The first, in which Serbia, Bulgaria, Greece, and Montenegro decisively defeated Turkey, nearly brought Russia and Austria to blows. Britain joined hands with Germany to preserve international peace. In the second war, with Bulgaria in a hopeless fight against her former allies, joined by Rumania and Turkey, London and Berlin again tried to restrain their turbulent friends. The peace negotiations, in which the powers participated, were held in London.

There had been some heartburning in England over the Berlin-Baghdad railway which was being built under German auspices. Britain feared a loss of trade in Turkey and Mesopotamia, a particular British preserve, and a possible threat to India. Britain secured a protectorate over a little state on the Persian Gulf to block a railway terminus there. Russia and France also opposed the project. But between 1912 and 1914, the three allies finally agreed that although Britain would monopolize the river trade from Basra to the Gulf, Germany might build the railway as far as Baghdad.

But despite that mutually satisfactory settlement, the general international situation in early 1914 was dangerous. In the successive crises in Morocco and the Near East the powers had shown more and more readiness to run risks in order to hold their allies and to maintain the prestige of their group. Britain's allies were being drawn into a more aggressive alliance by Isvolski and Poincaré, the French president, and any remote incident might drag all Europe into conflict.

The Alliances Fall into Line

Thus things stood in June, 1914, when Francis Ferdinand, heir to the Austrian throne, and his morganatic wife were murdered by a young Serb at Sarajevo, in Bosnia. This produced a conflict between Austria and Serbia, which was backed by Russia. Grey insisted it was no concern of Britain's. The British government would not under any circumstances threaten armed intervention on either side, but would gladly act as mediator in the interest of peace.

Only through indirect causes did Britain become involved in World War I and the same holds true, to a somewhat less degree, for Germany and France. The main cause of the war was the long-standing quarrel between Russia and Austria over the control of the Balkans. Serbia was a pawn in the game. Whether Serbia started the war by conniving at the plot which ended in the death of the Archduke, or whether Austria started it by her untimely ultimatum to Serbia, or whether Russia started it by commencing mobilization on such a scale as to impel Germany into the conflict are mooted points of European rather than of British history. As far as England is concerned, Sir Edward Grey tried to keep the war from beginning and then from spreading.

Matters were moving fast the week before England declared war on August 4. Although Serbia had accepted most of the exacting demands in the sharp Austrian ultimatum, Austria declared war on July 28. Thereupon the two systems of alliances began to fall into line. Russia, interfering on behalf of the Serbs, commenced the mobilization of her immense army. Because of the alliance situation the Russian general staff had made a double mobilization plan whereby troops were to gather on the German frontier as well as on the Austrian. Germany, aware of this, took no chances. As soon as she was certain of Russian mobilization she gave Russia twelve hours to stop it on July 31. Russia continued; so on August 1 Germany declared war. The Germans, like the Russians, had a double mobilization plan. When troops headed for the Russian frontier, others went toward the French border; and at this crisis such an involved plan was very difficult to change. By August 3 France too was in the war.

In those hectic days, Grey had made one suggestion after another to the various powers—direct conversations, neutral mediation, or a conference of neutral ambassadors, but each attempt met with objections. France would not agree, lest it appear that she was not supporting Russia; Germany had a similar attitude concerning Austria; for she had taken the grave responsibility of assuring her that she would stand behind her in any action she might take. Also she feared that Italy was too undependable and that Russia would gain too much time with her mobilization. Finally, Grey told the German ambassador at London, on July 29 "as long as the conflict remained confined to Austria and Russia, England could stand aside; but if Germany and France should be involved, then the British government would be forced to rapid decisions."

That was the first indication of anything like a threat from Grey. He might have told Germany that unless she called off Austria, Britain would stand by Russia. He might have told France to warn Russia to cease mobilizing, or Britain would refuse to be drawn into any resultant war. He might have appealed to Austria directly to accept the Serbian reply or at least to refrain from an overt act. He took none of these steps, which might have averted the war. He lacked authority to act without cabinet approval, which might have been refused. A more daring and less scrupulous Secretary might have taken a chance for such high odds.

With France in the war, the next question was whether England was bound to follow her. The public had not been told about those ambiguous military and naval arrangements made in 1912, but there were rumors about them. Asquith, challenged on the subject in 1913, declared, "This country is not under any obligation, not public and known to Parliament which compels it to take part in a war." But now with a war on,

France was pleading for definite support. All the morning of August 2, the cabinet debated whether Britain was morally bound to keep the 1912 agreement to protect her undefended Atlantic coast. When a message arrived from the Conservative leaders that "It would be fatal to the honor and security of the United Kingdom to hesitate in supporting France and Russia," the cabinet came to a decision. It assured the French ambassador that "if the German fleet comes into the Channel or through the North Sea to undertake hostile operations against the French coasts or shipping the British fleet will give all the protection in its power." This pledge was made before Britain heard of the German ultimatum to Belgium.

But Britain was not yet at war; it is barely possible that she might never have been if the Germans had kept out of Belgium. Through neutral Belgium, however, lay the road to the least fortified French border, and Germany's trump card was speed. Palmerston had done what he could to guarantee Belgian neutrality in his treaty of 1839 (see page 421) but at the time he called it only parchment that might be broken. Now a German statesman referred to it as a scrap of paper. An ultimatum went to Belgium requesting that German troops be allowed to enter France by that route. The same ultimatum went to the adjacent little neutral duchy of Luxemburg, which merely protested against the German advance and did not fight. But Belgium, bound up with French interests, rejected the ultimatum and stubbornly resisted.

Britain Enters World War I

Germany had sought previous information about England's attitude toward Belgian neutrality but had received evasive replies. A prompt and militant intimation to Germany on August 1 that if she invaded Belgium Britain would fight might possibly have stopped her. Grey did not want war, but if war came he wanted England to enter it on the French side. This invasion gave him a popular and moral reason for fighting. The threat to Belgium, wrote Lloyd George, "set the nation on fire from sea to sea. . . . Before then the cabinet was hopelessly divided. After the German ultimatum to Belgium the cabinet was almost unanimous." On August 4, the German troops were already invading Belgium when Germany received Britain's ultimatum that an invasion must not be attempted. At midnight, Britain declared war.

Britain gave the violation of the Palmerston treaty as her reason for plunging into war and asserted that she was in honor bound to do so. But as far as a strictly legal interpretation of the treaty went, she was pledged simply not to violate Belgium's neutrality. She had been a guarantor of Luxemburg's neutrality too, but she had not prepared to fight over its violation because her own interests were not involved there as they were in Belgium. Britain dared not stand by when a great power menaced the Low Countries in the twentieth century any more than when she opposed Spain in the sixteenth, or France in

the days of Louis XIV and of Napoleon. Now she was ready to fight Germany.

Thus, after what seemed an almost unbelievably sudden crisis, a stunned and astonished world found the two great alliance systems aligned against each other in the greatest war history had yet seen. Italy alone had held aloof and would later join England, France, and Russia, along with Serbia, Belgium, and other nations. Turkey and Bulgaria, both disgruntled by the Balkan situation, joined Germany and Austria. In the course of the four devastating years, the United States, Japan, and many other overseas nations came in on the Entente's side. As for the question of responsibility for starting the war, it is generally conceded on the basis of postwar revelations that one cannot draw the line between black and white. Austria's and Russia's shares seem greatest, however, with Germany and France somewhat less. Britain made sincere efforts for peace; but they had been neither vigorous nor clear. Yet a quarter century later it was by making just such a definite threat that she would become entangled in World War II.

Chapter Thirty

Britain in the First World War

England and her empire were taxed to what seemed the limit of human and material resources in the First World War, which surpassed all previous conflicts in its magnitude and in its direct influence upon the people of almost the entire world. Lasting from midsummer of 1914 to the late autumn of 1918, the fighting centered in Europe but spread to Asia, to Africa, and to distant seas. Altogether, some sixty-five million men were mobilized, including more than six million from the British Isles and an additional three million from the empire. At least ten million men were killed, including nearly a million from Britain and the empire. Ammunition and supplies were expended with unheard-of lavishness. The bravery and dogged determination of the British on land and sea played a major part in the ultimate victory of the Allies.

The war was fought in several separate theaters of operations, called "fronts." The most important was the western front, where the British, the French, the Belgians, and later the Americans faced the Germans in Belgium and northern France. Britain's sector lay in and around her old fighting ground, Flanders, the region she was vitally interested in defending and to which men and munitions could easily be shipped. On the eastern front, Russians opposed Germans and Austrians on their common frontiers. Later, the Italian front saw the fighting of the Italians and Austrians between the Alps and the Adriatic. Other theaters included the Balkans and what was later to be called the Middle East. England conducted three separate campaigns against the Turks: at the Straits, in Mesopotamia, and in Palestine. Russia also fought the Turks far out in the Caucasus. In Africa, the Far East, and the South Seas most of the German colonies were quickly seized although some troops in German East Africa held out until the end of the war. Finally, there was the sea. So far as Britain was concerned, interest centered in the western front, the Turkish operations, and the sea.

The two sides were so evenly matched that almost until the end the outcome was in doubt. The Central Powers (Germany and Austria) occupied the strip through middle Europe from the Baltic to the Adriatic and, after Turkey and Bulgaria joined them, across Europe from the Rhine into western Asia. They thus had the help of "interior lines," whereby they could operate as a single unit against enemies who had to operate from different directions. They could, for instance, quickly shuttle troops and munitions from the French to the Russian front, while Russia was almost completely cut off from her allies. To offset this, the Allies controlled the seas, thanks to Britain's mighty Navy. They were able to draw men, munitions, and supplies from beyond the seas and at the same time to shut off the Central Powers from similar aid. The Allies had more men; but the great Russian hordes were largely untrained and unequipped, while the British, with their little regular army, needed considerable time to whip a larger one into shape.

This was literally a war of nations. Not merely did armies fight armies, but peoples opposed peoples, whether in front-line trenches or at home. The older men, women, and the children remaining behind had to take up tasks hitherto performed by able-bodied men. Women toiled even in the munitions factories and on transportation systems. All the countries were flooded with propaganda designed to bolster the morale of their own "home front" or to undermine the enemy's. The terrific stress of the four years strained the morale of most of the leading belligerents almost to the breaking point. When a country collapsed, as several did, the home front generally cracked before the army went to pieces. Thus Russia was to go out, followed by Turkey, Bulgaria, Austria, and finally Germany. In such an endurance contest the grim doggedness of the British character was no small element in the final Allied victory.

Grey and his Foreign Office had been unable to prevent the conflict; the burden was now shifted to the Admiralty and the War Office. The First Lord of the Admiralty was Winston Churchill, a kinsman of the Duke of Marlborough, brilliant, versatile, and, at that time, by some considered unpredictable. Associated with him as professional First Sea Lord was Admiral Fisher, while Admiral Jellicoe at the last moment was placed in command of the Grand Fleet. The Secretary of State for War was, contrary to peacetime custom, not a politician

but one of Britain's most celebrated soldiers, Lord Kitchener. Despite his reputation, based on his record in the Sudan and South Africa, many soon felt that he was too rigid to adapt himself to the new large scale warfare. The first commander in chief in France, Sir John French, proving inadequate, soon gave way to Sir Douglas Haig. Finally, David Lloyd George, Chancellor of the Exchequer, was to grow steadily more influential.

The gray-steel fighting ships of the royal navy went quietly to their posts even before Britain entered the war on August 4, and quickly began to exercise their superiority in an effective if unspectacular manner. They formed one of the two most powerful fighting machines in the world; but for the moment all eyes were centered upon the other—the German army, whose gray-clad regiments were steadily advancing toward Paris.

Prewar Staff Planning

All the various general staffs had drawn up elaborate plans during the preceding years. The late Count von Schlieffen, largely responsible for the German plan, realized that if the Germans marched toward Paris, the Russians would start for Berlin. He knew that Germany's trump card was speed, as she could mobilize faster and maneuver more rapidly than her neighbors. At the same time, France was quicker at mobilization than Russia, with the creaking, corrupt machinery of the Czar's vast empire. Consequently Von Schlieffen planned to put France out of the fight in a quick campaign before Russia was ready. The Central Powers throughout the war could take advantage of their interior lines and could concentrate their efforts on one front at a time.

Von Schlieffen had been responsible for the decision to attack through Belgium which helped to bring England into the war. The Germans might have crossed the frontier directly into eastern France without violating neutrality, but there powerful modern French fortresses would have slowed them down. He therefore planned to hold that eastern end of the French line lightly and to drive through Belgium with an irresistibly strong right wing, so as to encircle the French and to crush them from the rear. Economy had kept the French from replacing their antiquated fortresses behind the frontier of neutral Belgium. Ignoring Von Schlieffen's dying injunction to "keep the right wing strong," his successor, in order to bolster up less essential parts of the line, foolishly weakened it—just enough to cause failure.

The great German military machine went crashing into Belgium according to its fast schedule, which called for arrival at Paris within six weeks. The Belgians put up a brave resistance; but their forts at Liége and Namur were battered to pieces, and the invasion schedule was scarcely delayed. The French rushed troops to the threatened area where they were joined by the British Expeditionary Force.

The Retreat From Mons

The Kaiser is reported to have sneered at Britain's "contemptible little army." Calling themselves the "old contemptibles," the British fell in on the French left. There were barely 100,000 of them in a war in which other nations were mobilizing by the millions; but they were the flower of the old regular army. Around the Belgian mining town of Mons they stubbornly made a stand near the French frontier on August 23 and then retreated more than a hundred miles to the southeast of Paris. Having lost some fifteen thousand men, Sir John French felt that his exhausted troops needed rest and reorganization. Instead they were to have a crucial position in one of the decisive battles of world history.

Early in September, the Germans had overrun France's richest industrial section. Then their plans went wrong, for the High Command lost adequate contact with the armies in the field. Thanks to that weakening of the right wing, the commander of their First Army believed that he lacked sufficient force to swing west of Paris as he was supposed to do in order to roll up the Allied left flank, so he headed southeast of Paris. By September 5 some of his units were barely twenty miles from that city. This exposed his own flank to the enemy and left a gap of twenty miles between his forces and the Second Army.

The Battle of the Marne

Joffre, the French commander, gave the word for a firm stand near the river Marne. It happened that the British were directly opposite the gap between the two German armies. It was not certain that Sir John French would throw in his tired men, so Joffre hurried to British headquarters to plead for co-operation: "I intend to throw my last company into the balance to save France. It is in her name that I come to you to ask for British aid . . . the honor of England is at stake." There was a pause before Sir John, in a low voice, said, "I will do all I possibly can." The fierce fighting of the next four days, in this first battle of the Marne, wrecked the German hopes of speedy victory. The British threw themselves into the gap, while the French on either side fought desperately. Finally the Germans fell back to a strong position thirty miles in the rear. By a close shave the initial advantage of Germany's speed was destroyed, part of northern France regained, and Allied morale restored.

Both sides began to extend their lines toward the north to get around each other's flanks in a "race to the sea." If the Germans could have reached the Channel ports first, they might still have rolled up the French left flank and have threatened England. At Ypres the old British regular army was nearly wiped out, but the Allied line held. This place, which the "Tommies" called "Wipers," would see year after year some of Britain's most desperate fighting.

Typical Western Front trench scene, showing Lancashire Fusileers fixing bayonets prior to assault on German lines, July 1916.

Trench Warfare

"Open warfare," with maneuvering from place to place, was now over for a long time on the western front. There were no more flanks left to turn on either side since the rival armies stretched nearly five hundred miles from the North Sea to Switzerland. As winter set in, the enemies dug in and faced each other in two solid lines of trenches. As the armies could no longer get around each other, the next four years saw rival attempts to break through the opposing lines. At times, after terrific losses, the lines bent a few miles; but they were never to break decisively until 1918.

A new and unaccustomed type of fighting resulted, as most of the military efforts were to be spent holding or attacking such trench lines. The war on the western front, in fact, became a gigantic siege with elaborate trench systems behind barbed-wire entanglements. Thus the foes rested, a few hundred yards apart, week after week and month after month, with frequent lesser raids and occasional major efforts to break through. Artillery, heavy and light, increased in importance. The heaviest burden in work and in casualties, however, fell on the infantry, who, when not soaking or freezing in the mud, were exposed to the deadly effectiveness of the new weapons. The conventional plan for a "break-through" called for a preliminary effort to blast out the enemy lines with heavy artillery. Then the quick-firing field artillery would lay down a "rolling-barrage," providing a curtain of shells just ahead of the infantry, who would go "over the top" to attack the enemy lines at the "zero hour," frequently just before dawn. Then such of the enemy as managed to survive the bombardment would cut loose with machine guns, which too often mowed down the advancing infantry. It was planned that after the infantry had captured the enemy positions, cavalry would be let loose to exploit the success. Ammunition and men were spent lavishly to gain a few square miles of shell-torn waste; but the cavalry stage never came.

The new weapons made fighting less individual and personal. In the older days one saw at close quarters the foe, into whose stomach one pushed a pike or a bayonet. Even with the Brown Bess musket, fire was withheld until one saw the whites of the enemy's eyes. Now the artillery fired their high explosives and their shrapnel on distant objectives, while machine gunners sprayed a whole line of advancing infantry. Even at close grips it was more common to hurl an explosive hand grenade than use a bayonet. Millions of soldiers were to go through year after year of that muddy and bloody hell. The most spectacular novelty in fighting methods was the development of aviation, which though still in its infancy took over the old scouting functions of cavalry and made possible the bombing of positions far in the enemy's rear. Later poison gas and tanks would be used.

On the eastern front the Russians drove a deep wedge into Austrian territory, but farther north in East Prussia brilliant German strategy led to the routing of two great Russian armies by small German forces. Serbia repulsed an Austrian attack. Japan came with the Allies and quickly took Kiauchow, while Turkey joined the Central Powers.

The War at Sea: 1914

The royal navy meanwhile had taken up its tremendous task: to guard Britain, to patrol all oceans, to sweep the German merchant marine from the seas, to protect British shipping from German cruisers, and, above all else, to blockade the German High-Seas Fleet. In the North Sea the British, by long, patient watchful waiting, sought to keep the enemy cooped up just as they had done to the French in Nelson's day (see page 326). The British Grand Fleet still held its 3-to-2 advantage over

THE WAR IN THE NORTH SEA 1914-1918

the German High-Seas Fleet. The diplomacy that had persuaded Japan to police the Pacific and France the Mediterranean had been designed to enable England to concentrate her battle strength in the North Sea. The German ships, to reach the high seas, had to go either to the southward, through the twenty-one mile wide Strait of Dover, or, to the northward, the one-hundred-and-ninety-mile passage between Norway and the isles off Scotland. The British were concentrated, to guard this latter opening, at Scapa Flow, in the Orkneys, just off the northern tip of Scotland, a new rendezvous where, after the first few months, the battleships were well protected by land batteries and by steel nets to baffle submarines. To the southward, near Edinburgh, was placed a squadron of large, fast battle cruisers under Beatty, and near the Channel was a third force of smaller and older craft. To the eastward, safe behind its mine fields, lay the German High-Seas

THE WESTERN FRONT

Territory of German occupation
1914-1918

0   50   100
Scale of Miles

Fleet; also, the Germans had converted the island of Heligoland (see page 523), into an impregnable base. Jellicoe had secured Admiralty consent to the passive strategy of making the defense of England first consideration and was later to be bitterly criticized for not risking his ships in an attack. But his responsibility was enormous—as Churchill said, no one else was in a position to lose the war in a single afternoon. The Germans knew that in a general encounter they would be badly outnumbered. Each side therefore watched the other warily, waiting for a misstep, for month after month until 1916.

Out on the high seas there was more activity. Before August, 1914, was over, the German flag had all but disappeared from the surface of the high seas. A few fast ships raced into neutral ports, and a few cruisers escaped; but the remainder felt the full force of British sea power. Of ten regular German cruisers at large, two raced to safety at Constantinople, where they later flew the Turkish flag. The others were in distant waters, where they could not only snap up merchantmen but also overpower many of Britain's small older warships, which were patrolling remote stations and trade routes. One raised havoc in the Indian Ocean until sunk by an Australian cruiser. One was soon chased into an

African river, where she was later sunk. Another blew up mysteriously in the West Indies. The major threat came from the five in Admiral von Spee's strong Asiatic squadron which had disappeared in the Pacific. Two cruisers, sent out to catch him, encountered the squadron off Coronel in Chile. The British, silhouetted against the setting sun, were helpless targets. In an hour both ships and 1650 men were at the bottom of the sea; only two Germans were even wounded. Revenge came quickly. Coming around into the South Atlantic at the Falkland Islands, all but one of the squadron were destroyed by the powerful guns of two battle cruisers from Jellicoe's Grand Fleet.

Each side had successes and failures in 1914. Germany had shoved the Russian "steam roller" out of East Prussia and had almost taken Paris. She held northern France, Belgium, and part of Poland. Turkey, by joining the Central Powers, cut off Russia from easy communication through the Mediterranean with her Allies. But the Battle of the Marne had stopped Germany from a quick, decisive victory. Austria had been badly beaten by both Serbia and Russia. Japan had joined the Allies. The sea was dominated by the British, and the German High-Seas Fleet was bottled up.

In 1915 the Germans successfully concentrated on the Russians in the east. The British and French launched several drives on the western front, where their heavy casualties were out of all proportion to their meager gains of a few miles. At Neuve-Chapelle, a major attack in conjunction with the French failed to take the industrial and rail center of Lille. In the second battle of Ypres, with the artillery reduced to two shells a day, the bombardment was unable to smash the enemy trenches and barbed wire, making casualties unnecessarily high.

The Shell Shortage

This latter battle shook British political and military circles to their foundations that spring when the *Times* military correspondent, somehow escaping censorship, wrote, "The attacks were well-planned and valiantly conducted, the infantry did splendidly . . . want of an unlimited supply of high explosive shells was a fatal bar to our success." He had just seen his old battalion of 29 officers and 1090 men come out of action with one officer and 245 men. The French had pounded the German lines for four hours to the British forty minutes; and their losses were slight. Kitchener, still thinking in terms of his old campaigns, had been deaf to the pleas for more shells, although in two weeks that spring more ammunition had been used than in the whole Boer War.

Those words in the *Times* proved highly explosive, leading to an amazing increase in ammunition output and also ending the decade of Liberal control. Britain's vast industrial potentialities needed arousing and co-ordinating. That task fell to Lloyd George, who gave up the Exchequer to be the first Minister of Munitions. He drew big industrialists to his side as assistants and made hurried trips to France to find what was needed while arousing labor and the rest of the populace to a high pitch of enthusiasm for the production of war materials. Factories were converted from peacetime tasks and women by the thousands went into this important but often dangerous work.

Orders were sent for further munitions to the United States which began her role as the "Arsenal of Democracy." Within a year, the supply of shells had risen from 75,000 to more than 19,000,000 and that same correspondent could now write, "I was very much surprised to find that our artillery had all the fun to itself . . . I cannot swear that a single German shell came over us." Large quantities of heavy guns, rifles, small-arms ammunition, grenades, and much else were produced also.

Just before the second battle of Ypres in 1915, Allied troops were suddenly beset by a cloud of poisonous chlorine gas. Hundreds writhed in agony, giving the Germans almost a clear field into Ypres for a moment, but they were not ready to follow up their advantage; and again the line held. The Allies soon had crude masks for protection, and before long used gas themselves. It put many men out of action, but killed relatively few.

The Dardanelles-Gallipoli Operations

The British in 1915 also launched a major attack against Turkey in an effort to open the Straits between the Mediterranean and Black Seas, to capture Constantinople, and in particular to open up communication with Russia. With her meager industrial development, she was unable to turn out sufficient munitions for her huge armies. With Turkey at Constantinople, these could reach Russia only through the White Sea, frozen most of the year, or by way of North America and the Pacific to Vladivostok, and the Trans-Siberian Railway. With free access to the Black Sea, England and France could furnish Russia with manufactures and receive Russian wheat. These Dardanelles-Gallipoli operations were vigorously promoted by Churchill as First Lord of the Admiralty. Like the other "Easterners," who included Lloyd George, he felt the war could be won more quickly and for less cost by attacking Germany through her back door. This ran counter to the prevailing view of the "Westerners," the majority of the military who had been persuaded by France that "Every man not employed in killing Germans in France and Flanders is wasted." Kitchener, however, won over to the Easterners' view, swung the cabinet in favor of Churchill's proposed attack on the Straits. It was arranged that old British and French warships should be used for the forcing of the Dardanelles; a British army would then occupy the Gallipoli peninsula, and a joint military and naval advance would secure Constantinople.

The whole affair, both military and naval, proved a tragic failure. Yet several times

victory was missed by the narrowest of margins. A chance event in connection with the main naval attack in mid-March may have changed the course of the war. The warships had already cleared six miles of the Straits. The Gallipoli peninsula at this time was so lightly held that a moderate landing force could have captured it easily. The forts on the inner straits were so low in ammunition that Constantinople was generally expected to fall. Daily minesweeping had supposedly cleared a safe channel for the battleships but had missed one row of twenty mines near the Asiatic shore. While the attack was going well, three battleships were sunk by those mines. That virtually ended the naval attempt to force the Straits, for the cautious admiral held back despite the urgings of his chief of staff.

It was now the army's turn, but that was to mean a grave loss of momentum, for Kitchener had not even appointed a commander-in-chief until the week before that attack. Then the supply ships were so stupidly packed that weeks were wasted in Egypt rearranging the cargo. The Turks under able German leadership utilized this delay to fortify the Gallipoli Peninsula strongly and bring in many more troops. When the attack came in April, the landings were difficult, with no harbors and precipitous terrain, and in some places the slaughter was terrific. In others, the troops landed successfully, only to waste the clear opportunity to seize the main objective— the high land that commanded the forts.

This bogging down of the attack caused serious repercussions in London, including the resignation of Fisher and the dismissal of Churchill as head of the Admiralty. In August, a triple attack was initiated with the arrival of ample reinforcements. There were high hopes for one, a surprise landing at Suvla Bay, which was virtually undefended. For two days, the all-important heights were there for the taking, but green troops had been used, while the veterans

Scene at "V" Beach at tip of Gallipoli peninsula, showing Turkish shell bursting near the *River Clyde* which had been beached for the deadly initial British landing there on April 25, 1915.

were being wasted on the two well-defended Turkish beachheads, and the woefully inadequate general did not press an advance. Then Mustafa Kemal, ablest of the Turks, counterattacked heavily. For the third time, the British threw away victory. "Then, as the pitiless sun beat down on the Anzacs [Australians and New Zealanders] in their narrow bit of conquered territory, disease stalked abroad. The trenches of the foe were but a few feet distant; . . . and myriads of flies, attacking dead and living alike, brought with them dysentery, typhoid, and other fevers. Thirst was added to their sufferings, since drinking water there was none, except the precarious supply brought up by donkeys from the launches."

The government was satiated with Gallipoli, and in the last days of 1915 the bloody peninsula was abandoned to the Turks. The withdrawal was expected to cost a third of the troops but in the one well-executed part of the whole campaign, the Navy took the whole army off without losing a man. Altogether the Allies and the Turks each used about a half million men and each lost about a half of them in casualties.

The Allies had had great hopes when Italy joined them in the spring of 1915. Though she had been in the Triple Alliance more than thirty years, most of the land she wanted belonged to Austria. The Allies could make generous promises of such territory, so after sharp bargaining, the Italians deserted their former allies. It was hoped that by attacking Austria from the rear the Italians could relieve the pressure on Russia, but the mountainous frontier made it extremely difficult.

Meanwhile, in the Balkans, the Gallipoli failure helped to throw Bulgaria into the arms of Germany and Austria. Serbia was overrun and put out of the fight. The Cen-

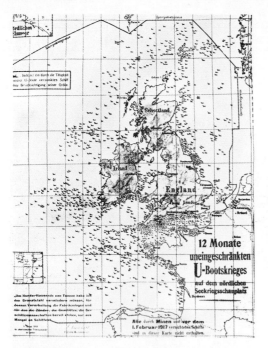

German diagram showing vessels sunk in British waters in the first year of unrestricted U-boat warfare, starting February 1, 1917.

to cause intense suffering and deaths among the German noncombatants, especially the old and very young.

In February 1915, the Germans answered this British blockade by announcing that their submarines would sink every hostile merchant ship approaching the British Isles. These "undersea boats" or "U-boats" were still in their infancy—the United States Navy had acquired the first one in 1900 and no nation had more than a few. Originally they were expected to be used to sink surface warships—one U-boat early in the war sent three British cruisers to the bottom in rapid succession. Some junior German officers, realizing that their surface ships were being swept from the open seas, suggested using the submarines for commerce destruction. That idea would have a profound effect on maritime warfare. With Britain far more dependent than Germany upon outside supplies, raising in a whole year only enough to feed her millions for a few weeks, the Germans hoped to starve her into submission fairly quickly. According to Admiral Von Tirpitz, the tough, bewhiskered naval chief, "England wants to starve us. . . . We can bottle her up and torpedo every English or Allied ship which nears any harbor in Great Britain, thereby cutting off large food supplies." With merchantmen, however, a serious problem arose. An ordinary surface warship could take the crew aboard before destroying a merchantman or sending it into port with a prize crew. The U-boat had no room for extra passengers; and frequently it dared not wait for the merchant crew to take to the lifeboats, for a single shot from the victim might sink the submarine.

In February, 1915, the Germans, declaring all approaches to the British Isles a war zone, announced that they would "seek to destroy every hostile merchant ship which enters the War Zone, and it will not always be possible to obviate the dangers with which the persons and goods on board will be threatened. Neutrals are therefore

tral Powers now had direct communication from Berlin and Vienna to Constantinople and the eastern Mediterranean. The British and French tried to remedy this by an expedition to Salonika, but for three years it accomplished nothing.

The British blockade was already depriving Germany of many essential overseas supplies. The royal navy, patrolling relentlessly the two entrances to the North Sea, sent neutral vessels into British ports, to be searched for materials which might find their way to Germany. Against lively protests from the United States and other neutrals, the British steadily extended the old conventional list of contraband materials liable to seizure, adding oil, copper, and rubber, the loss of which would severely handicap the Germans in the war. Late in 1914, they added foodstuffs. This caused a bitter outcry in Germany, which raised only part of the food she needed, and was

The ill-fated White Star liner *Lusitania* leaving the Port of New York.

warned not to risk crews, passengers, and goods on such ships." They even published a special notice in the New York newspapers giving warning as the Cunard liner, the *Lusitania*, was about to sail. She was not armed, but she was heavily loaded with munitions though that was denied at the time. Off the southern Irish coast, her captain, contrary to orders, slowed down in the fog to get his bearings; and by chance along came the "U-20," homeward bound with only two torpedoes left. Struck by them, the big ship went down in eighteen minutes with 1195 of her passengers and crew, including 124 Americans. That wholesale slaughter of noncombatants undid months of zealous German propaganda; and was more responsible than anything else in starting the United States on the road to war. For almost two years thereafter, the Germans eased up on their sinkings.

Altogether, the position of the Central Powers was further improved in 1915. The British attack on the Straits had failed. For want of munitions, the drives on the western front had been ineffectual. Russia had suffered a terrific defeat, though her line was still intact. The Balkans had come more thoroughly under the control of the Central Powers, who now had a clear route across Europe into Asia. Italy had accomplished little.

War of Attrition:
Verdun and the Somme

"Warfare of attrition," or the wearing down of manpower, seemed the only recourse left on the western front. Brilliant maneuvering was giving way to wholesale slaughter, in the hope that one's own human reserves would last longer than the enemy's. Huge forces were shattered against strong positions by both sides with terrific losses. The names of Verdun and the Somme remain associated with this brutal policy. Though casualties in those huge 1916 drives were reckoned by hundreds of thousands, the western front remained virtually the same.

Britain next faced a manpower shortage. Many had expected that she would, as in past wars, simply guard the seas, furnish money and supplies to her allies, and maintain only a small, efficient army. Kitchener in this had had the foresight or the luck to predict that Britain must think of military forces in terms of millions. His great contribution to her military success was his organizing of the nation's manpower in time. The initial call for volunteers had met with an amazing response; and by the time the old regular army was melting away, late in 1914, in the "race to the sea," the first hundred thousand of Kitchener's new army was ready to take its place. By the summer of 1916 he had expanded six divisions into seventy. The last one sailed for France on the very day on which the cruiser *Hampshire*, bearing Kitchener to Russia, struck a mine and went down off the Orkneys.

A volunteer system in a protracted war, however, tends to draw off the best elements in the population while the least desirable hold back. The lengthening casualty lists in 1915 led to a widespread demand that the latter be forced to bear their share. A final effort was made to swell the numbers through a volunteer system, but more than a million bachelors held back. Thereupon, not without violent protests, Parliament, early in 1916, passed a conscription act drafting all able-bodied men between the ages of eighteen and forty-one. Though all free Englishmen had been regarded as liable for militia service in time of danger, since the days of the Saxon fyrd and the Assize of Arms, England had been until now able to raise her armies by the volunteer system, though the old naval press gangs were a rude sort of conscription. Canada, New Zealand, and New-

foundland followed England's example. Australia would not conscript for overseas duty, but maintained a splendid volunteer record. At times conscription seemed inadvisable: in Ireland, among the French Canadians of Quebec, and in South Africa, where the loyal Boers had been busy keeping the rebellious ones in check.

The Germans started wholesale attrition early in 1916. Concentrating on the western front, they surprised the French by a terrific bombardment of Verdun, hoping to blast their way to a "break-through." The French somehow managed to weather the initial storm, rallied to the cry of "They shall not pass!" and mowed down the Germans, who kept pushing into the fight long after reasonable prospects of victory had gone. Each side lost about 350,000 men in five months.

Even heavier were to be the casualties at the Somme, where the Allies attacked near Amiens in early summer after months of preparation. This time the British bore the main Allied burden, as they were opposite one of the strongest positions in the German line. Haig, now in command, had provided, seemingly, for everything: new roads for trucks, causeways across swamps, miles upon miles of communication trenches, hundreds of thousands of fresh troops, plenty of artillery and shells, and railway lines to feed the artillery. Unfortunately, there were no new ideas of attack. "Ingenuity of execution was sacrificed to the immensity and elaboration of the preparation." The Germans knew what the British were doing and had dug line after line of trenches on the ridges which the British would have to ascend. Bombproofs, deep cellars, pits, and quarries were linked together by underground passages. Behind mines, machine guns, and concrete emplacements and redoubts, they awaited the attack.

It came after a seven-day torrent of artillery fire, using nearly two million shells produced by Lloyd George's feverish munitions programs. The British in close lines advanced slowly, to be mowed down by German machine-gunners: whole rows of khaki-clad corpses were later found. On that first day more than half of the officers and nearly half of the men were casualties. That was the heaviest single day's loss in British military history; whole wars, such as the American Revolution, had been fought with fewer total casualties. Yet the British fought on; by the end of a month, they had gained two and a half miles. In the autumn came heavy rains, which turned the low-lying terrain into a sea of mud, in which hundreds of thousands of men floundered. To carry on was impossible. The Germans had been thrust back only a few miles by Britain's greatest effort. The battle had demonstrated that "bravery was more common than brains." Attrition at Verdun and the Somme, therefore, had used up about 850,000 Germans and 950,-000 of the Allies, including 410,000 British. France was so thoroughly exhausted that thereafter the British took over increased responsibilities.

Toward the end of the Somme attack the British introduced a novel instrument, the tank, an armored car, moving by caterpillar tractor, armed with machine guns or light artillery, and able to waddle over trenches and crush out machine-gun nests. It was designed to assist infantry's unequal struggle against machine guns and barbed wire. A plan submitted to the War Office in 1912 was pigeonholed with the comment "This man's mad"; when a general proposed it in 1914, the army would do nothing, and Churchill had some tanks built from Admiralty funds. There were not enough at the Somme to be effective; but the Germans, finding no sure defense from them, blamed them in part for Germany's defeat. They were labeled "tanks" in transit to keep their preparation secret; and tanks they remained.

In May 1916, Britain's greatest sea battle, Jutland, was fought off the Danish coast, the only time the navies clashed in full force during the watchful waiting in the North Sea. The Germans had put to sea, hoping to fall with their whole strength upon a part of the British. In addition to the well-armored dreadnoughts of Jellicoe's Grand Fleet and Hipper's High-Seas Fleet, each side had a squadron of fast but lightly armed battle cruisers under Beatty and Scheer respectively. Of the 151 British and 101 German ships, more than half were small destroyers; the capital ships were fewer than at Trafalgar. There was not enough breeze late that May afternoon to sweep away the heavy mist. The farthest units were over a hundred miles apart when the first shots were fired. The action started with a running fight of the battle-cruiser squadrons, speeding at twenty-five knots and exchanging heavy blows which their weak armor could not withstand. Flotillas of little thirty-knot destroyers darted between the lines to launch torpedoes. Hipper knew that he was leading Beatty into a trap, for he was heading southward to join Scheer's battleships. Finding themselves thus outnumbered, the British turned northward in retreat until at dusk their own dreadnoughts reached them to turn the tide. After brief, furious, confused encounters in the mist and smoke, the Germans cleverly turned in their tracks toward home, eluding by a narrow margin the pursuing British during a long night chase. The British suffered the heavier material damage with three battle cruisers sunk, one in seventeen minutes by German shells from eight to ten miles away.

Admiralty censorship made the news of Jutland sound worse than it was, and Britain was dumfounded that the navy had come out of a major encounter with a suspicion of defeat. It has been fought over and over by critics ever since then. Tactically, the Germans had maneuvered brilliantly and inflicted heavier damage, but strategically, the honors went to the royal navy, for the Germans never emerged again

German battle cruisers leading the High Seas Fleet to surrender at Scapa Flow. Those veterans of Jutland were later scuttled there by their crews.

from their home base. Many Britons kept complaining that Jellicoe had not pursued and annihilated the enemy in Nelson fashion. But the losses in a night action in mine-infested waters could have been disastrous to his prime mission of keeping the North Sea and the high seas clear.

Surrender in Mesopotamia

But there was no question about Britain's defeat a few weeks before at Kut-el-Amara in Mesopotamia by the Turks—for the first time since the American Revolution a British army formally surrendered. Early in the war, the Indian government had sent a force to occupy Basra, the seaport of Mesopotamia, to protect the royal navy's Anglo-Persian oil supply nearby. Late in 1915, although London repeatedly vetoed the idea, the authorities in India decided to send General Townshend with those troops up the Euphrates to capture Baghdad from the Turks. It was a risky undertaking, for communications were difficult, the distances long, and the climate abominable. From start to finish, the Indian authorities mismanaged everything. Following the retreating Turks, Townshend kept stretching out his communication line until at ancient Ctesiphon near Baghdad the Turks counterattacked. Something went wrong in the dark, and he retreated down river until finally cooped up at Kut-el-Amara, where he held out almost five months before surrendering. Britain lost prestige heavily throughout the Moslem world for this ill-starred adventure.

On the eastern front, in 1916, in spite of their munitions lack, the Russians, in a last magnificent spurt of energy, were pushing the Austrians hard when German troops were sent to the rescue. Those same troops quickly put out of the fight Rumania, who had just joined the Allies.

At home, the British civilian was at last awakening to the fact that the war was not being won. The temporary shock of the long retreat from Mons had been dispelled by the "miracle of the Marne." There was great faith in the rumors that Russian troops were being hurried through England to the western front; some had seen them shaking the snow from their boots on station platforms and jamming slot machines with kopeks. "Business as usual" was the optimistic slogan, while rigid press censorship withheld much. With 1915 deliberate efforts were made on both sides to develop hatred of the enemy. Exaggerated reports of German murder, mutilation, and rape of defenseless civilians in Belgium were circulated along with accurate accounts of the destruction of priceless historical structures. Late in 1914 a German naval force had bombarded two east-coast towns, with heavy loss of civilian lives, a foretaste of later air raids which were more successful in killing noncombatants than in destroying munition plants. There was poison gas, the *Lusitania,* and the shooting, on charges of espionage, of the English nurse Edith Cavell in Belgium. Gradually as casualty lists lengthened, hatred grew, making life miserable for those of German extraction. But over in the trenches "Tommy" was often more irritated by his allies than he was by "Fritz." By spring of 1916, the home front had at last buckled down to the war in dead earnest. Women were taking over more and more of the jobs formerly monopolized by men, not only in munitions plants but in transportation, in offices, and in many other fields.

The Irish Revolt

Then came Ireland. Home rule, like other domestic problems, had been set aside for the duration of the war. England's treatment of the Catholic Irish in the early part of the war had not been tactful. Kitchener placed Irish Unionists, rather than Irish Nationalists, in charge of recruiting. Of the officers appointed to an Irish division less than one in five were Catholics. Meanwhile, Ulstermen had been permitted to keep their prewar organization intact and, like the Welsh and Scots, to wear distinctive insignia. The commander of the Ulster Volunteers announced, without reprimand, that, when the war was over, his force would be ready to "relegate home rule to the devil." Under such circumstances Sinn Fein (literally, "We Ourselves") made fast headway. This movement aimed at the withdrawal of Irish members from the House of Commons, the boycotting of the English government, and complete self-government for Ireland.

Once more, as in the days of Philip II, Louis XIV, and the French Revolution, the Irish looked to England's enemies for deliverance. This active Sinn Fein minority planned a general uprising throughout Ireland and the seizure of Dublin, while the Germans were to provide arms and ammunition and raid the east coast of England. British vigilance nipped the plans in the bud. On Good Friday in 1916 a German submarine landed on the Irish coast Sir Roger Casement, who had won knighthood for excellent work in Africa. He and a companion were immediately caught. A German tramp steamer with munitions was stopped by the British and blown up by her own crew. The raid on the east coast amounted to little. The most serious trouble came in Dublin, where on Easter Monday a week of Sinn Fein revolt broke out. The insurgents seized the greater part of the city and also proclaimed a republic. Dublin Castle, however, was not captured, nor was there a general uprising. Instead the British army came. The fight was fiercely waged. The rebels surrendered at discretion. The people of Ireland, most of whom had taken no part in the revolts, made no resistance to the imprisonment of nearly two thousand men. Despite taut war nerves, strained further by what they considered a treacherous stab in the back, the British executed only fifteen rebels, including Casement. The military trials and executions were, however, carried out in an unfortunate manner with executions at intervals over nine days, and with the announcement of the trial simultaneous with that of the execution. No one knew how many more victims were to follow. This produced a wave of fear and rage among the volatile Irish. Prisoners, hissed in the streets at the beginning of May, were heroes by the end of the month. Sinn Fein, which had been almost dead, was revived by the manner of the English reprisals.

Lloyd George's Coalition Ministry

English politics also felt the impact of the war. The Liberal party had been in the saddle since 1905, with the fair-minded and scholarly, but slow-moving, Asquith as prime minister since 1908. In August, 1914, the Conservatives had announced that disputed domestic issues would be set aside to ensure a united front for the war. In the spring of 1915, however, the munitions situation, coupled with an Admiralty dispute between Churchill and Fisher, ended Liberal ascendancy. Asquith formed a coalition government including numerous Conservatives. By the end of 1916, the terrible casualty lists increased the clamor for change. The British were nobly doing their best to win the war, but many questioned whether all their sacrifices were producing the proper results. Asquith lacked the quick power of decision and the popular appeal essential for a war leader; with all his other faults, Lloyd George had, as his munitions experience showed, the ability to inspire co-operation. With his agile if not profound mind, he seemed closer to an "organizer of victory," such as Pitt had been in the Seven Years' War, than anyone else. By some clever and perhaps unscrupulous maneuvering, he replaced Asquith as prime minister in December, 1916, in another coalition ministry, with an even stronger Conservative element.

Along with this came an important, though temporary, constitutional change, with the formation of the War Cabinet. The regular cabinet, which had doubled in size since Walpole's day, was unsuited for original and decisive action on the wartime problems arising constantly (see page 294). Most of the two dozen members were heads of executive departments; the First Lord of the Admiralty and the War Secretary could ill spare the time for cabinet meetings or for sitting through debates in the Lords or the Commons. Consequently, for the time being the normal workings of the cabinet system were set aside. The answer was the creation of the War Cabinet, a little group of five men including the prime minister. Parliament and the rest of the old cabinet virtually handed over to them the major policy decisions. They became a policy-making body, all but one being relieved of departmental and Parliamentary duties. Though still theoretically responsible to Parliament, the War Cabinet had a free hand and used it. Parliament lapsed into a subordinate role, enacting what the War Cabinet advised, with only minor changes and few protests. From the party standpoint, three of its members were Conservatives, one a Liberal, and one a Laborite. Bonar Law, Conservative leader and opponent of home rule, the rather colorless, but politically adroit son of a poor New Brunswick parson, as Chancellor of the Exchequer, was the only one to hold a departmental portfolio, and to represent the War Cabinet in Commons. The other members were the proud, cold, and brilliant Lord Curzon, former viceroy of India; Lord Milner, who had handled the civil end of affairs in South Africa before and during the Boer War and was called the most capable administrator in England; and, in strange company with those peers, Arthur Henderson, son of a Scottish workingman, and once one himself until he became a trade-union leader. Finally, Lloyd George's compelling personality contributed much to the speeding up of the conduct of the war. Quick, facile, buoyant, he began each day as though all problems were new and fresh. Not bound by tradition he could change his mind instantly. He knew how to grip the imagination of the people and for three years was to be England's hero.

The years of prewar propaganda for imperial co-operation bore sudden fruit in the Imperial War Cabinet, a temporary enlargement of the regular War Cabinet through the addition of the representatives from the dominions and India. Twice this body gathered for several months during the war and once just after its close. General Smuts, the former Boer leader, was particularly active, being sent on delicate diplomatic missions and holding a responsible air post as well. Prime Minister Hughes of Australia toured up and down Great Britain with his vigorous message "It is a battle to the death. . . . And we shall win." While the policy-making part of the old cabinet was being compressed into the small War Cabinet, new departments, such as food control, were formed until the ministry numbered about a hundred department heads, many of them businessmen serving without salary. An unofficial element, journalism, was becoming more powerful in political circles, because of the growing importance of the voting population, whose views were largely based upon the newspapers. This gave immense political weight to men like Lord Northcliffe, who owned and controlled many papers, including the venerable and authoritative *Times,* and the future Lord Beaverbrook, another New Brunswick minister's son like Bonar Law, who took part in Asquith's fall. Their support or opposition could do much to mold public opinion.

Another wartime break with tradition was the Defense of the Realm Acts, the "Doras," which were a mass of regulations that became law through royal proclamation and Orders-in-Council. By the first of these, suspected spies could be arrested, tried before a secret court-martial, and executed without habeas corpus or jury trial. From spy-hunting the "Doras" extended into almost every activity: industry, commerce, and transportation were minutely regulated; mail and news were censored; food, drinks, amusements, lights, sounds and much else came within the wide embrace of these administrative laws, which set up a jurisdiction outside the regular courts, and which, beyond their general broad authorization, were not Parliamentary statutes. Some protested that the government was acting in excess of its authority, but the House of Lords, the highest court of appeal, upheld the "Doras," though one law baron's dissenting report said much about Star Chamber and certain clauses of Magna Carta. As in the French Revolutionary period, the government swung to a drastic curtailment of the traditional freedom of the subject. France and the United States, however, went fully as far during the war.

The drag of war had set in by the end of 1916. The Germans and French were badly exhausted by the terrific attrition at Verdun and the Somme. Germany, fresh from her conquest of Rumania, made guarded proposals for a peace conference. Lloyd George spurned them. "To enter," he said, ". . . without any knowledge of the proposals she has to make, into a conference is to put our heads into a noose. . . . we ought to know that she is prepared to accede to the only terms on which it is possible for peace to be obtained and maintained—complete restitution, full reparation, effectual guarantee."

That note of confidence heartened the "home front" in Britain and the dominions. The latter, contrary to German expectations, were a comfort to the motherland. The Union of South Africa not only had helped conquer the adjacent "German Southwest" but had suppressed a Boer revolt at home and was sending troops to German East Africa and to France. The

Britons in Canada responded in magnificent fashion and performed many prodigies of valor at Ypres. The Anzacs fought valiantly at the Dardanelles and in France. Newfoundland, the only dominion represented at the opening of the Somme, had most of its small force wiped out. India and other parts of the empire also shared in the difficult imperial task.

Unrestricted Submarine Warfare

For the Allies 1917 proved the blackest year of the war. The Germans, with no desire for another Verdun, rested on the defensive on land, hoping to win the war by the cheaper and easier method of unrestricted submarine warfare. Their U-boats, active since 1915 (see page 576), hitherto had shown some respect for neutral rights. Now they began to sink at sight every ship inside a danger zone surrounding the British Isles. It was a clever plan that nearly succeeded. With Britain thoroughly dependent upon outside regions, there was a reasonable prospect that she would quickly be brought to her knees; for Allied shipping was being sunk at the rate of fifty vessels a week. The ocean floor just south of Ireland was strewn with the sunken hulks of torpedoed tramp steamers. Britain met this black crisis resolutely, and "seamen torpedoed again and again were ready to sign on as usual." Gradually, she built up a defense against the U-boats: destroyers accompanied the convoys of merchantmen, ever alert for the telltale periscopes. By summer the rate of sinkings had begun to fall off.

The United States Enters the War

Just as the German advance through Belgium in 1914 had brought Britain into the war, so now the unrestricted submarine warfare added the United States to Germany's enemies. The Germans had foreseen both those possibilities, but had considered the immediate advantages worth the risk. They had laughed at the "contemptible" little British army; they scorned even more the Americans. They felt that the United States could not train enough soldiers to make any difference and could not get them overseas anyway. Consequently they had not been worried by the frequent notes of protest from President Woodrow Wilson, who was re-elected in 1916 on the slogan "He kept us out of war." But American ships, cargoes, and lives were lost, and early in April, 1917, the United States declared war. At first her participation was expected to be limited pretty much to munitions and financial assistance. Her navy co-operated with the British against the submarines, and her shipyards began to turn out steamships faster than the U-boats were sinking them. It was a full year, however, before the United States army was in condition to take an active part; and in the meantime the Allies were desperate for men, as Russia had collapsed.

The Russian Revolution

In March, just before the United States entered the war, a revolution in Russia overthrew the Czar's government. The Russian soldiers had been fighting bravely; but they finally became tired of trying to pull down barbed-wire entanglements with their bare hands. Moreover, they rightly suspected treachery in high places. The revolution, under liberal auspices, was so orderly at first that the Allies felt that Russia might make even greater efforts. But the army discipline went completely to pieces when the death penalty for insubordination was abolished and soldiers debated whether or not to obey orders. In a final flare-up of energy the Russians did advance once more against Austria in the summer, but once again the Germans pushed them back.

Then in November came a far more radical revolution. The most extreme group, the Bolshevists, or majority wing of the Marxian socialists, seized control of the government and began at once to achieve by force a "dictatorship of the proletariat." At last the economic doctrines preached by Karl Marx's followers since the middle of the last century, and feared for years by the conservatives of Europe, were to be put into practice. So radical in their methods were these Bolshevists that many socialists in other countries disowned them, and popularly they have since been known as "Communists" or "Reds." A reign of terror now developed in which members of the middle, "capitalistic," class were hunted as well as the aristocrats. The Bolshevists believed in class war—workingmen of all lands against the owners of capital—but in the present war they were ready to stop fighting at once. In December they agreed to an armistice, and later, at Brest-Litovsk, ceded considerable territory to Germany. The Central Powers now had a vast new region from which to draw supplies, and, still more important, Germany was free to move some 600,000 men from the eastern front for a concentrated effort on the western front the next year.

Continued Allied Reverses

The British on the western front in 1917 had assembled once more a vast quantity of munitions and men, but their blow fell on empty air. Hindenburg and Ludendorff, now in command, had their troops withdraw quietly to a shorter, more powerful line, leaving behind a skeleton force. The British swept through almost unopposed until they suddenly came up against the concrete defenses, or "pill boxes," of the new "Hindenburg Line." There, after a month of fighting, Haig realized the futility of further effort. Later in the year the British blew up Messines Ridge with a million pounds of high explosive, and then staged a successful surprise attack with tanks at Cambrai; but these made only local gains.

Not only was Russia out, but France and Italy came close to defeat. The French launched an ambitious "drive to end the war." The Germans, forewarned, repulsed it with terrific losses. Serious mutinies broke out along the French front, and defeatism reared its head in Paris until stamped out by "the Tiger," old Georges Clemenceau, the new premier. To prevent the Germans from striking a fatal blow at the demoralized French, the British throughout the summer kept up a series of attacks in Flanders, fighting much of the time in a sea of liquid mud. A combined German and Austrian force struck the Italians, who within three weeks lost all they had gained in two and a half years and had to be bolstered up by their Allies.

Only from Asia could the Allies draw any comfort. There the British invaded Mesopotamia, where Townshend had been captured in 1916, took Baghdad, and continued onward toward the valuable Mosul oil fields. In another action against the Turks, a British force under Allenby advanced from Egypt across the Suez Canal in a "last Crusade" to Palestine. They found valuable allies in the Arabs, who had been roused against their Turkish masters, with promises of independence, by T. E. Lawrence, a young archaeologist. Allenby, an old cavalryman, waged a brilliant campaign amid scenes where Old Testament kings and medieval Crusaders had fought. In December, Jerusalem fell to the British. These campaigns, which pried the Arab lands away from Turkey and added them to the sphere of European imperialism, would eventually lead to anti-western Arab nationalism (see pages 591, 609).

The Allied situation grew even more desperate in the early months of 1918. The troops from the Russian front gave the Germans a tremendous advantage over the tired French and British. Ludendorff assembled "by far the most formidable fighting force the world had ever seen." It was a case of now or never, for the American troops were landing fast.

In March, the German blow fell upon a weak British army near the Somme battle-

General Allenby arriving at the Citadel of Jerusalem at the culmination of his successful Palestine campaign.

field. If the Germans could once break through here and reach the main railway line at Amiens, the two allies would be separated and the British thrown back on the Channel. Within two weeks the Germans had pushed forward forty miles, the biggest gain since trench warfare began. The French rushed to the aid of the British, and, although the Allied line bent ominously, it did not break. In the crisis the various Allied nations accepted a Frenchman, Ferdinand Foch, as Allied generalissimo. Ludendorff next struck at the British left, near the coast, in a vain attempt to gain the Channel ports. Then he outwitted Foch by a surprise blow at the middle of the western front. It caved in, and within three days the Germans had advanced thirty miles to the Marne and were only fifty miles from Paris.

In June, the Allied premiers reported, ". . . there is great danger of the war's be-

ing lost unless the numerical inferiority of the Allies can be remedied by the advent of American troops." About 600,000 troops from the United States were then in France, and they kept coming at the rate of about a quarter million a month. The Allies, as well as the Germans, had been skeptical about these hastily trained soldiers. But, while the Germans were smashing through to the Marne, the Americans demonstrated that they too could fight; and discouragement gradually settled upon the Germans. With fresh millions of fighters available to the Allies, they knew they must hurry or lose all chance of winning.

The Allies Seize the Offensive

Twice more Ludendorff strove to break through. The Germans struck without effect at the western corner of the Marne salient, the pocket in which the Germans found themselves. Finally, they drove at its eastern side in their last desperate offensive, the second battle of the Marne. As they did so, Foch launched a counterattack from the opposite side of the salient. The Americans and French hurled the Germans back. There, around Soissons, the tide of war turned. The German chancellor later wrote: "We expected momentous events in Paris for the end of July. That was the fifteenth. On the eighteenth even the most optimistic among us understood that all was lost. The history of the world was played out in those three days." Once having seized the offensive, Foch gave the Germans no respite. All along the line the French, British, and Americans hammered relentlessly.

When a force, largely British, Canadian, and Australian, preceded by 450 tanks, smashed the Amiens salient, Ludendorff called it "the black day of the German army." With the old salients flattened, the Allies drove on against the main lines of the German defenses—the British in the west, the French in the center, and the Americans in the east.

Meanwhile Germany's allies, one by one, gave up the fight: first Bulgaria, then Turkey, where Allenby had continued his smashing, and Austria a week later. The German army as a whole did not collapse. In most cases it fought stubbornly and heroically in its long retreat. But behind the army the people revolted. They had been promised victory in the spring, but only longer casualty lists resulted. The privations caused by the Allied blockade had sapped their morale. They were disillusioned, and President Wilson's "Fourteen Points" made them more ready to give in. Early in November the German High-Seas Fleet received orders to go out and battle the British; the sailors mutinied, and revolt spread through Germany. The Kaiser, William II, abdicated and fled the country. The Germans immediately signed an armistice, and on November 11, 1918, the fighting ended—only to be resumed twenty-one years later.

Of the six great powers which had formed the alliances in prewar days, only Britain maintained her morale unimpaired throughout. Russia had collapsed completely; Austria had been ready to give up long before the war was over; Germany had finally caved in; and in 1917 both France and Italy had shown dangerous signs of cracking. The British, though sometimes badly disturbed, had kept their chins up from beginning to end, not only in the trenches but at home and out on the fringes of empire. The old Saxon heritage of infinite capacity to take punishment had stood them in good stead.

Armistice Terms and Fourteen Points

The terms of the armistice put Germany at the mercy of the Allies on land and sea pending the settlement of peace terms. Military equipment and supplies were handed over to the victors, and regiments were disbanded. The Allies stationed armies of occupation along the Rhine and continued their relentless blockade of starving Germany. The German High-Seas Fleet, which had not seen action since Jutland, steamed abjectly to Scapa Flow, where some time later it disappeared beneath the waves, scuttled by its own crews.

The Germans had not made an unconditional surrender. Though clearly defeated, they were counting on the terms given them when they laid down their arms, which were based on President Wilson's Fourteen Points. They included open diplomacy, freedom of the seas, reduction of military and naval armaments, removal of economic barriers, fair settlement of colonial claims, evacuation of Russian territory invaded during the war, a restored and compensated Belgium, restoration of Alsace-Lorraine to France, a readjustment of the Italian frontiers, self-determination for the peoples of Austria-Hungary, the Balkans, and Turkey, an independent Poland with an outlet to the sea, and the creation of a League of Nations. Wilson's allies accepted these as a basis for the peace settlement with two qualifications. The point about the freedom of the seas must be omitted, and German reparations must be defined more sharply. Consequently compensation to be made by Germany for the restoration of invaded territories must also include all damage done to the "civilian population of the Allies and their property by land, by sea, and from the air." This was deemed essential so that Britain might obtain compensation for the damage done by the U-boats and by German air raids.

Peace Conference and Versailles Treaty

In January, 1919, the Allied representatives assembled at the old palace at Versailles, just as the representatives of the powers had gathered at Vienna a century earlier. They had the double and somewhat contradictory purpose of making a lasting settlement along with meeting the particular desires of the victors. The name "Versailles" is often incorrectly applied to the whole work of the conference, instead of to just the treaty with Germany. Practically all the negotiations were carried on in Paris, and the treaties with the other defeated nations—Austria, Hungary, Bulgaria, Turkey—were signed in other Paris suburbs. It was a departure from precedent that the defeated nations were excluded from the Conference. At Vienna, Talleyrand had played an active role for defeated France, but the representatives of the Central Powers were only called in to sign the terms.

Of the five great powers, England, France, Austria, Russia, and Prussia in 1814, the last three empires had crumbled in ruins. In place of them there were now the United States, Italy, and Japan. Before long, Japan, realizing that she could have relatively little to say in such a conference, dropped out, and then Italy withdrew when some of her Adriatic ambitions were thwarted. That left Clemenceau, Lloyd George, and Wilson. When disputed mat-

The "Big Three" of the Paris peace conference: Lloyd George, Clemenceau, and Wilson.

ters came up, they listened to the spokesmen for both sides, consulted their staffs of experts, and then made their decisions. Like Metternich at Vienna, Clemenceau represented the victorious nation which had borne the heaviest brunt of the fighting; for the Germans had been on French soil from beginning to end. He was a realist, who sought definite measures to prevent a recurrence of another such war. To him that meant a Germany too weak to be dangerous. Wilson, in contrast, was an idealist, who wanted practically nothing for his own country and was intent upon a peace settlement that would not provoke another war. His particular desire was for a League of Nations in which the various peoples might work together for the preservation of peace. Lloyd George, a clever opportunist, got all that he could for Britain by siding sometimes with Clemenceau and sometimes with Wilson. This "Big Three" were in no small measure the authors of the final settlement. As far as words went, it was a peace treaty; but it did not make for peace.

Regarding the Fourteen Points, the Allies kept their word only where it suited their own interests. Wilson's idea of the "self-determination of nations," the keynote of the conference, meant that conquered peoples and minority nationalities were to have the right to decide by what country they should be governed. But it was carried out only where it would weaken the defeated nations or reward one of the victors; otherwise the pleas of the nationalists were not heeded. The same treatment held for the other Fourteen Points. Lloyd George was inclined to bargain, and Wilson was outmaneuvered, while Clemenceau fought single-mindedly for a stronger France at the expense of as weak a Germany as possible. His steel will secured some of the harshest terms for the defeated nations. None of the German allies had bargained before their armistices, so only Germany could claim the protection of the Fourteen Points, although their generalities applied to half of Europe.

In territory Germany lost two small sections of land to Belgium; Alsace-Lorraine to France; the northern part of Schleswig to Denmark; considerable territory to Poland; and the cities of Danzig and Memel. In some cases, but by no means in all, plebiscites were held in accordance with the principle of self-determination. In the Fourteen Points the Allies had promised Poland, which had disappeared from the map in 1795 (see pages 370, 387), that she should be an independent country, with an outlet to the sea. The outlet to the sea might be interpreted to mean either an extension of Polish territory through a "corridor" which would bisect Prussia or else merely Polish docks and warehouses in a German seaport; the conference accepted the former definition. Danzig, one of the important German seaports, was at the end of this "corridor" to the sea. It was taken from Germany but, instead of being given to Poland, was placed under the League of Nations as a "free city." Several other districts in dispute between Germany and the new Poland were granted plebiscites. The placing of Memel under the League of Nations, to serve as a seaport for the new republic of Lithuania, was a breach of the Allies' word. Other treaty terms included the opening of the Kiel Canal to all nations; the demilitarization of the left bank of the Rhine, where Germany was forbidden to have fortifications or to station military forces; and the placing of the rich industrial Saar Valley under the League of Nations, with its coal going to France for fifteen years, at the end of which a plebiscite was to decide whether the valley should belong to France or to Germany (see page 609).

Yet, with all those various nibblings at her frontiers, Germany escaped lightly compared with Austria-Hungary. If the latter had been primarily guilty in starting the war, she was now severely punished. Her former territory found itself under seven different flags, split up in the name of self-determination, which proved a very convenient formula for this purpose. Austria and Hungary became separate little countries only a fraction of their former size; the new republic of Czechoslovakia was carved out in the north; Serbia, doubled in size by a grant of former Hapsburg land and the inclusion of Montenegro, became the kingdom of Yugoslavia; Rumania likewise was greatly increased by new Danubian lands; Galicia became part of the new Polish republic; and considerable territory around the Adriatic went to Italy.

The Italians had bargained sharply before they threw in their lot with the Allies, and were insistent upon payment in full. They had stipulated a large amount of Austrian territory as *Italia Irredenta,* or "Unredeemed Italy," and secured the northern shore of the Adriatic, including the seaport of Trieste. They also demanded the

EUROPE IN 1922

0   250   500
Scale of Miles

Trentino, although some 250,000 Germans lived there. Italy's claims to Fiume, on the east shore of the Adriatic, were disputed by Yugoslavia. Over this point the Italian delegate angrily left the conference. Later Italy seized Fiume by force.

The Turkish Empire was to be broken up almost as thoroughly as the Austrian in the name of self-determination. The Arab states were taken away, to be set up separately (see page 609); Greece was rewarded by large grants in Thrace and Asia Minor; but this "porcelain treaty" of Sèvres was to prove short-lived (see page 600); for the Turks were to settle matters differently. Bulgaria, which had lost territory in the Balkan wars, now lost a little more. The Straits (the Bosporus and the Dardanelles) were neutralized; Turkey was not to fortify

them, and they were to be open to ships of all nations. Out of the former Russian Empire were carved the new Baltic states of Lithuania, Latvia, and Estonia, while Finland likewise escaped from Russian rule to become an independent republic.

Mandates

As for the German empire overseas, the Fourteen Points made only one pledge— that the settlement of colonial questions should be fair, impartial, and to the best interests of the native peoples. The British seem from the outset to have intended to parcel out the German colonies among the Allies, since, by a treaty made during the war, the Pacific colonies north of the equator were to fall to Japan, and those south to the British; while, by an even earlier agreement, the African colonies were to be divided between the French and British. Lloyd George tried to rush through the colonial settlement. He suggested that, since the dominions were all democracies and had all fought manfully throughout the war, they should have the German colonies that they had captured, but this was vetoed by Wilson. So the principle of the mandate was invoked. It was originally suggested by the British Labor party as a way to detach certain sections of the Turkish Empire. Instead of the direct annexation by the victor nations, the colonies would be placed under the League of Nations. Then the League was to entrust them to certain of the victor nations to administer as trustees for the League. The League, retaining the title, would require annual reports with the authority to call the mandatory power to account if conditions warranted such action. There were three categories: "A," headed for independence; "B," with no trade restrictions; and "C," to all intents and purposes regular colonies except that the League had the right of inspection and supervision. In accordance with this mandate principle, Great Britain received most of German East Africa (Tanganyika), sections of Togoland and Kamerun, and the island of Nauru (important for its potash). The Union of South Africa was made the mandatory power over German Southwest Africa; Australia, over the Bismarck archipelago and the German Solomon Islands; and New Zealand, over Samoa. Belgium got a small part of German East Africa, adjacent to her Congo. The remaining German colonial regions in Africa went to France and those in the Pacific to Japan as mandates.

Likewise in the region formerly known as the Near East but soon to be called the Middle East, four mandates would be formed in the Arab lands wrested by the British from Turkey with some Arab aid. Britain received mandates for Iraq (Mesopotamia), Palestine, and Transjordania (later Jordan), while the French were granted one for Syria and Lebanon. The Arabs had hoped, from their 1916 agreement with Britain, that they would get one big Arab state, but the British had already recognized France's claims to Syria, and in 1917 had promised the Jews a homeland in Palestine. Both of those arrangements would lead to years of friction. Egypt, a British protectorate since 1914, became a Class A mandate (see page 611).

Reparations

The economic clauses of the Treaty of Versailles proved not only cruel but impossible to enforce. The Germans could not have complied with them even if they had tried to do so. Lloyd George, principally to blame, had pledged himself to two contradictory proposals. Having signed the agreement with the Germans, limiting their liability for damages to that done the civilian population of the Allies from the air, on land, and on sea, he afterward promised the British that the enemy should pay for the whole cost of the war. When the full severity of the terms had become obvious, he made, to be sure, a real effort to alleviate them. He seems to have infuriated the French by this stand, and apparently was not supported by Wilson. A junior member of the British delegation wrote at the time: "Cannot understand Wilson. Here is a chance of improving the thing, and he won't take it. Lloyd George, however, is fighting like a little terrier all by himself."

Lloyd George's difficulties in this matter were largely the result of the British Parliamentary election of 1918. The Coalition War Cabinet had done wonders during the conflict, and it thought that it could depend upon a grateful people to return it enthusiastically to office. The mild and conservative addresses of Lloyd George and Bonar Law, however, evoked little interest. Then Northcliffe, owner of the London *Times,* and Hughes, the Australian premier, stirred up trouble by suggesting that Lloyd George planned to let the Germans off with an easy peace. Thereupon, Lloyd George began to threaten the Germans as he violently denied this charge. The more he did so, the more he was applauded. He declared they should pay heavily, even up to the whole cost of the war. How Germany was to do this nobody knew, but that did not matter to the war-weary man in the street, who was shouting for revenge. A politician who spoke of generosity to the defeated would have been pushed from power on the instant. "Hang the Kaiser!" became the popular slogan.

At Paris Lloyd George was caught between the electorate's demands and Wilson's insistence upon the terms offered Germany before surrender that the amount be limited to the actual damage caused by the German land, sea, and air forces. Germany, according to one British expert, could probably have paid such a relatively reasonable amount in a few years. Abetted by dominion leaders, Lloyd George had military allowances and pensions to Allied soldiers included; once the latter were added, the bill could be made out for any figure. Yet even Wilson finally signed the revised terms. As the amount of the reparations had not been decided, the Germans had to sign what amounted to a blank check. They also had to accept a "war guilt" clause by which they acknowledged for themselves and their allies full responsibility for beginning the war. But all this they had to accept along with the other harsh terms; for the Allied blockade continued, and the defeated nations were starving.

The final amount set for reparations in 1921 was some $32 billion—a reduction from the original $56 billion, but still an impossible figure. The Germans, moreover, were left with almost no resources with which to pay. The treaty had stripped them of their overseas investments; all their larger ships and part of their smaller ones; their rich Lorraine iron deposits; their coal from the Saar Valley and Upper Silesia; and much of their railway rolling stock. Also, they had to deliver without compensation thousands of tons of coal to the Allies. All that plus new high tariff barriers made it impossible for Germany to fulfill these terms.

The League of Nations

The one ray of hope, and that none too bright, was the League of Nations; Wilson had yielded on other of his Fourteen Points to secure this regular machinery for future international co-operation. Its member nations were to be banded together to remove the menace of war by means of joint action. Its Covenant, or constitution, stipulated three bodies: the Council, the Assembly, and the Secretariat. The Council, the executive body, was to consist of five permanent members, representing the leading powers, together with four (later nine) non-permanent members chosen by the Assembly. It was to meet regularly four times a year, and might be summoned in special session. The Assembly, composed of the representatives of all the member states, each having one vote, was to be the "instrument by means of which the nations of the League" were to "confer, advise and deliberate" in annual session. The Secretariat was to consist of a Secretary-General and a staff of assistants for administrative tasks. Headquarters were to be at Geneva, Switzerland. Membership was to be open to all nations specified in the Covenant, which originally excluded the defeated countries, and to any other nation whose admission should be approved by two thirds of the Assembly. Any member might withdraw upon two years' notice.

The League's particular significance lay in the provisions for preventing war. Article Ten of the Covenant stipulated that the League undertook "to respect and preserve as against external aggression the territorial integrity and existing political independence of all members." All international disputes likely to cause war were to be submitted to arbitration or to judicial investigation through the Permanent Court of International Justice, the World Court, at the Hague. Those refusing to abide by its decision or unlawfully resorting to war would be punished by the League by "sanctions" involving the severance of trade, financial, or diplomatic relations. The Council might also recommend to the member states collective military or naval action to be taken against an offending nation. The League was, moreover, to work for the limitation of armaments "to the lowest point consistent with national safety," the restriction of private manufacture of munitions, the abrogation of all earlier treaties incompatible with the Covenant, the publication of all future treaties, and the rigid enforcement of international obligations. Upon its effectiveness in upholding those provisions depended the League's prestige and usefulness.

It was also entrusted with supervision of the mandates, of plebiscites in disputed regions, of free cities like Danzig, and of the Saar Valley. It was to undertake, in addition, through its various commissions and bureaus, numerous nonpolitical humanitarian functions, such as the promotion of labor legislation, child welfare, and health, together with the suppression of slavery and the traffic in "white slaves" and narcotics.

Though Britain and each dominion received a vote in the Assembly, they were occasionally to be divided on disputed questions. Britain, too, had a permanent seat on the Council, and an Englishman was the League's first Secretary-General. Although General Smuts, the former Boer leader, drew up much of the Covenant, the League was generally recognized as Wilson's creation. His political opponents in the Senate, however, kept the United States from membership. The opportunity for all the smaller nations to voice their opinions freely in an international gathering was something new in history. But the actual domination of the League tended to rest with the Council, where the great powers—France and Britain in particular—were apt to use it as an instrument for enforcing the Treaty of Versailles in their own interests, just as Metternich had utilized the Quadruple Alliance a century before.

Altogether this postwar period would bear numerous resemblances to that which had followed the Napoleonic struggle. In the bitter dissatisfaction of the vanquished with the peace settlement were dangerous seeds of future revolt. Many saw the need of stronger safeguards than the League if this new map of Europe was to be kept intact. Others felt that such a crazy patchwork could not last and that any League of Nations entrusted with its defense would eventually collapse. The Vienna settlement had stabilized Europe sufficiently so that there was no world conflict for a century, but that of Versailles lasted only twenty-one years.

Between the Wars

The war was over, with England and her allies victorious. Once more an enemy lay crushed, with her sea power broken and her colonial empire at Britain's mercy. The price had been high and had imposed a cruel strain on Britain's resources and morale. She faced hard years ahead, which in many ways resembled the aftermath of her struggle with Napoleon. Lloyd George talked bravely of making England a land fit for heroes; but in 1919, as in 1815, there were not enough jobs for her returning soldiers.

Economically Britain was to find herself in serious straits. The national debt had increased more than twelvefold in five years, and the interest burden was staggering. Every one of the immense key industries was badly shaken. Foreign trade, always the foundation of Britain's prosperity, was diminished, complicated by the financial clauses of the peace settlement. Many of her former Continental customers were no longer able to buy British goods. Russia, in particular, was in the throes of revolution, and Germany, while temporarily eliminated as a trade rival, was out of the picture as a purchaser. New rivalry came from the United States and Japan which had taken advantage of England's wartime distractions to invade some of her old markets.

For the British coal trade the general postwar shift to oil-burning ships was a calamity. Furthermore, with France and Italy able to get free German coal by the peace treaties, they bought less from England. In addition, American coal began to compete seriously. The war, moreover, had overstimulated the British mining industry, new mines had been opened, and the government had granted the striking miners a seven-hour day. Now it seemed either that many mines must be closed or that miners must work longer hours at lower wages.

British shipping felt keenly this slump in the coal trade for it had furnished bulky cargoes which kept many ships busy (see page 425). The merchant marine was larger than ever before; not only had feverish building offset the heavy submarine losses, but also many former German ships had been handed over to England. This increase in ships, however, was soon to prove a boomerang, for other nations, too, had increased their merchant marines, particularly the United States. For a postwar year or so, all ships were busy carrying troops home and replenishing war-starved markets, but then came a severe slump with too many rival bottoms competing for the diminishing cargoes. As ship after ship was tied up in dock or anchored permanently in harbor, silence inevitably descended upon the great shipyards at Belfast, at Glasgow, and on the Tyne.

Industrial Competition and Unemployment

The cotton mills of Lancashire, stronghold of the greatest industry, had not faced such a crisis since the American Civil War. Half of England's cotton spindles became idle soon after the peace, and remained so, largely because of Asiatic competition. While the British were fighting, the Japanese began to turn out vast quantities of cheap cotton goods to capture old British markets. Always good imitators, they had ferreted out most British textile secrets. Above all, they had a supply of good workers for only a fraction of British wages. That was what made their competition so much more deadly than that of the Germans before the war. Cheap labor meant goods so cheap that the British were undersold in market after market. Particularly grave was the situation in India, which before the war bought more British wares, chiefly cotton goods, than any other two regions combined. During the war, Japanese exports to India jumped ninefold and continued to gain, whereas British cotton goods fell off four-fifths in twenty years. Japan by that time, 1934, had overtaken England in the production of cotton cloth and rayon. In India and China, moreover, British capital had erected new textile factories which did not help British unemployment. India, soon to become self-governing in fiscal matters, made conditions worse by clapping a high tariff upon all imported cotton goods.

Some economists criticized Britain's refusal to follow Germany and France in depreciating her currency. Instead after a few years she returned to the gold standard. While tending to keep prices and wages down, this benefited the investing class and those living on fixed incomes, since their financial returns remained static while their purchasing power increased with lower prices. But it made the industrial situation worse by hampering competition against foreigners for such little trade as remained; for British gold-standard prices were high in comparison with the depreciated currencies. On the other hand, inflation has usually been accompanied by worse penalties.

Unemployment was a particularly difficult problem for Britain. Having adjusted herself to being the "workshop of the world," she had a larger proportion of her population engaged in industry than the other nations, so that when the demand for her products fell off, she was in a more vulnerable position than a country like France, which was still half agricultural. There were a million unemployed at the beginning of 1921, and two million a year later. Then, after a brief improvement, came the world depression beginning in 1929; and unemployment jumped to a peak of nearly three million at the beginning of 1933. Population increasing annually at the rate of 3 per cent, foreign trade well under the 1914 standards, a poverty-stricken working class, and a drastically taxed middle class and aristocracy characterized Britain for many years thereafter.

To remedy this situation, the insurance laws concerning unemployment were expanded, and repeatedly modified (see page 495). Specified sums a week were paid to the unemployed. At first regarded as a temporary palliative, this practice soon became so habitual that the "dole" eventually ceased to be insurance and had a demoralizing effect. Many gradually lost the will to work, as well as the old readiness to migrate overseas when things went wrong at home. Other proposals to relieve unemployment involved large outlays for housing projects, road-building, and further naval construction; but the tangible results seemed inconclusive, and the cost meant more taxation.

The financial burden which fell upon those who still had money was terrific. Austen Chamberlain, one of the two capable sons of Joseph Chamberlain, and Chancellor of the Exchequer, put into practice his theory that Britain should pay as she went along, without further burdening future generations. The 1920 budget called for a total national revenue of £1,425,000,000, nearly nine times the Lloyd George Budget (see page 496); and the nation was no longer as rich as in 1909. The interest on the war debt alone came to more than double the whole 1909 budget. Now with a drastic rise in the income-tax rate, persons with even moderate incomes had to pay a tax running up to 25 per cent. Supertaxes on the larger incomes made the proportion even greater. The local taxes or "rates," as well as the "death duties," out of which the poor funds were drawn, were so heavy that scores of old landed estates in the possession of one family for generations were being sold by their owners, who could no longer afford to keep them.

Altogether, it was evident that Britain must recover her foreign trade or cease to be a world power. A general economic revival in Europe seemed essential, so British statesmen worked to straighten out the economic tangle left by the peace settlement. In conference after conference Lloyd George tried to undo his own work at Paris and to persuade France to lessen the claims upon Germany. France, however, was torn between the desire to have reparations paid and the fear of a Germany that would be sufficiently prosperous to pay them. Lloyd George succeeded in having a world economic conference meet at Genoa in 1922, but the French refused to have the reparation question considered.

Meanwhile, Lloyd George's coalition government, re-elected in 1918 (see page 591), was becoming increasingly unpopular. Ostensibly there were three political parties. The Conservatives, commonly known by their old name of Tories, were divided into the "die-hards" and the moderates. The old Liberal party likewise was split. One sec-

tion, the followers of Asquith, who was not in the coalition government, had no use for the adherents of Lloyd George. The Labor party too had its moderate and radical wings, which were to divide in 1929. Outside the coalition, the Asquith Liberals kept up a running fire of criticism of the peace treaty, which was becoming rather generally recognized as unjust to Germany and as injurious to England's interests. These Asquith Liberals, together with the Laborites, who were growing constantly in numbers as the economic clouds darkened, began to win some of the by-elections (held in individual constituencies to fill vacancies occurring between general elections). The Conservatives, who comprised the bulk of the ministerial forces, becoming restive under the Liberal Lloyd George, wanted to return to regular party rule.

Fourth and Fifth Reform Bills

This coalition, of which everyone now seemed to be wearying, had been re-elected in 1918 by more voters than any preceding government because, in the closing year of the war, the fourth Reform Bill had been passed. Not only had the bill given the suffrage to all male citizens over twenty-one who had been resident in a Parliamentary division for at least six months, by including the small group which had been left without the vote in the third Reform Bill of 1884, but the franchise was extended also to women. This came almost simultaneously with the granting of woman suffrage in the United States, Germany, Russia, and elsewhere. There was, however, a joker in the British act. With about two million more women than men, partly as a result of war casualties, some alarmists foresaw a danger of "petticoat rule," and the minimum age for women voters was set at thirty years.

All elections were to be held on a single day, instead of being spread out over a longer period. "Plural voting," whereby an individual might be entitled to as many as a dozen votes, was restricted to a maximum

Virginia-born Lady Astor, elected at Plymouth in 1919 as first woman member of the House of Commons; her husband was in House of Lords.

of two. A university graduate might still, for example, have a second vote as the holder of a degree.

In 1928, the Fifth Reform Bill or "Flapper Franchise Act" reduced the voting age for women to twenty-one years, the same as for men. With universal manhood suffrage achieved in 1918, and with this now, both the suffrage movement begun in 1832 and the fifth of the six Chartist demands were realized. Women were now eligible also to membership in the House of Commons, but they were not admitted to the House of Lords until 1958.

In 1919, with the end of the War Cabinet, the old system returned. Lloyd George had wanted to retain the efficient little group (see page 582), but the House of Commons objected strongly, and a cabinet of some twenty members, most of them heads of departments and participating in Parliamentary debates, was resumed.

Sinn Fein and the Irish Free State

The perennial Irish question once more flared up. Easter week of 1916 still lived in Irish memories, and, outside of Ulster, Sinn Fein was carrying practically every parliamentary seat. It would have nothing to do with England, even refusing to permit its representatives to attend Parliament or to allow taxes to be paid in Ireland. It boycotted British law courts, setting up its own judicial bodies, and enforcing their decisions. Coercion met with bloody resistance. Between Irish and British actual war arose. The officials of the crown and of the Irish republican (Sinn Fein) army were both guilty of the orgy of cruelty and bloodshed in 1920-21. The British introduced an auxiliary police force, the "Black and Tans," wearing the old army khaki with black hats, who were venomously hated by the republicans. To wear their uniform soon became foolhardy, and to wear it after dark without friends at hand was to invite death. On a recruiting poster inscribed "Join the Royal Air Force and see the world," someone scrawled, "Join the Royal Irish Constabulary and see the next world." The government vowed that it would never yield to the "murder gang"; but British liberal opinion was demanding conciliation.

Suddenly Lloyd George asked for a conference with the rebels. He agreed to give Ireland dominion status, with entire control of her own finances, police, and law. In return, he demanded among other things that free trade continue, that Ireland assume a proportion of debt, and that Ulster receive permission to make separate arrangements. The Sinn Fein representatives, scorning the substance of self-government, held out for the symbols of complete independence. The British then whittled down their own terms, including free trade, and a treaty was signed late in 1921. It was ratified by an Irish election. Thus the Irish Free State came into being, Ulster remaining outside. The turmoil, however, was not over. War continued bitter and murderous but now between the Irishmen who accepted the treaty and those "Irreconcilables," led by Eamon de Valera, who refused to do so. By 1924 the moderate party had won a decided victory and was able to turn to civil organization in the new state, which was carried out with complete success under President Cosgrave, a very fortunate choice for the position.

The Irish Free State (Eire) now emerged from chaos. The army was greatly reduced; old-age pensions were cut down; arrears of back taxes were ruthlessly collected; and a protective tariff was instituted. Cosgrave, in 1932, finally gave place to De Valera, who adopted a bitter anti-British policy. The economic dependence of Ireland upon Britain, however, made it necessary for even this fierce republican to be somewhat conciliatory, and Ireland continued for a while longer within the empire. Britain, on the whole, was glad to be thus largely rid of the vexing problem.

In the meantime Ulster was going its separate course as "Northern Ireland." Though it had a parliament of its own for domestic business, it continued to send members to the House of Commons of the "United Kingdom of Great Britain and Northern Ireland."

The Washington Naval Conference

With Germany's fleet scuttled by its own crews, Britain, to relieve the crushing taxation, had suspended most of her naval construction. Then she realized that the two Pacific rivals, the United States and Japan, already her commercial competitors, were building navies of maximum size. In 1916 the United States had suddenly decided on a navy "second to none." Their new program called for battle strength considerably superior to Britain's. Japan, likewise spared the financial exhaustion of Europe, was also building up a large fleet, presumably to sustain her aggressions in China. England resented and regretted what she considered their artificial and unreasonable desire for navies approaching her own size. With her eighty thousand miles of sea lanes to guard and her dependence upon overseas regions for many necessities, she could not afford to let command of the seas pass into other hands, but she was to co-operate to make the competition less costly.

The Washington Naval Conference in 1921-1922 was a landmark in naval history because of Britain's acceptance of the United States as a potential equal. The ratio of 5-5-3 was established for the battleship strength of Britain, the United States, and Japan, respectively, with 1.75 for France and Italy. Britain, abandoning her time-honored supremacy, at least secured in return an agreement that the United States would not carry through her program to outbuild her. The United States, on her side, was pleased to see a limit placed upon the battleship strength of Japan. The Japanese, for their part, gained security through the agreement that neither British nor Americans would build or strengthen any naval bases within striking distance of Japan. The United States was further gratified by the abrogation at Canada's suggestion of the 1902 Anglo-Japanese alliance, with its naval stipulations (see page 554). In its place, Britain, France, Japan, and the United States signed a four-power pact to preserve the status quo in the western Pacific. Thus the Washington Conference checked the most expensive form of rivalry, but it left opportunity for unlimited building of cruisers, submarines, and other craft.

Changes on the Continent

France, meanwhile, as distrustful of Germany as ever, was acquiring allies for herself in such a successful manner that some have called the postwar decade the "ascendancy of France." Belgium, no longer neutral by international treaty, and Poland, into which France poured money for the equipment of an army that might be used against Germany or Russia as occasion demanded,

U.S.S. *West Virginia*, whose nearly-completed sister ship *Washington* was sunk at sea as part of the Washington Conference agreement.

were her close allies. Also decidedly pro-French was the "Little Entente," Czechoslovakia, Rumania, and Yugoslavia, which had profited with the splitting of the ramshackle Austro-Hungarian Empire seven ways in the name of self-determination. The once-proud Austria was prostrate, having been stripped down to "a capital and its suburbs." Hungary, surrounded by the watchful, hostile Little Entente, was in as serious a plight. The League of Nations was supposed to be Europe's guarantee of peace, but alliances were springing up anew. England, as under Castlereagh, recognized the need for a united front, but with France aspiring to such influence, the principle of the balance of power inclined Britain to a more lenient attitude toward the defeated enemy.

This changed attitude toward the German side of the war was already evident in the work of scholars on both sides of the Atlantic. It had, in fact, begun to undermine the foundations upon which the Versailles settlement had rested. As early as 1920, the British economist, John Maynard Keynes, in his *Economic Consequences of the Peace* had attacked the reparation terms as unrealistic and damaging. Germany had been forced to admit in the peace treaty that she had started the war, but the American historian, Sidney B. Fay, demonstrated a few years later that Austria, Russia, and France were at least equally responsible (see page 592). Conversion to both these "revisionist" points of view was gaining ground.

There was a growing tendency toward autocratic reaction as in Metternich's day. Before the war, nation after nation had been copying England's democratic form of limited monarchy. After the war republics with similar responsible governments had been set up in Germany and Austria, and some of the new countries such as Poland, Czechoslovakia, Estonia, Latvia, Lithuania, and Finland; but the latter were unimportant in the general situation, while the German republic lacked prestige and strength. In Italy, where the cabinet and parliament had proved themselves unable to cope effectively with a threatened communist revolt, Benito Mussolini had formed a "Fascist" party, and with his "Black Shirts" was making his famous "March on Rome" in 1922. Although Italy remained a monarchy, he was soon dictator, thanks to vigorous methods and to the general fear of communist disorder. Once this forceful, bull-like man was in the saddle, Europe saw the beginning of the repressive, strongly state-regulated, rabidly nationalistic and antisocialistic movements in support of law, order, and the continuation of capitalistic society that characterized the postwar years, when the economic situation and the fear of the spread of Russian radical doctrines continued to harass Europe. Mussolini gave Italy certain increased efficiency; but, as in the other Fascist regimes of this sort, liberalism and liberty were lost in the complete subordination of the individual to the state.

In Russia revolution ran a bloody course. The radical Marxian group—the Bolshevists, Communists, or "Reds," as they were called —maintained the control which they had seized in November, 1917. They had triumphed over the counterrevolutionary "White" armies, which had received more than moral support from England and her former allies. One small Anglo-American military force, for example, had operated in frozen futility around Archangel. The Bolshevists under Lenin were building up a state on the basis (supposedly) of Marx's doctrines. The old autocracy of the Czars was giving way to an equally rigid dictatorship of the proletariat, which amounted, actually, to a dictatorship of the well-organized Communist party. The new masters of Russia, like the leaders of the French Revolution, sought to spread their doctrines to other lands and to supplant capitalism with communism.

Elsewhere in one region after another, both within the far-flung British Empire and all about its boundaries, that same spirit of nationalism was fast germinating. This was particularly true in the new Arab states just pried loose from Turkey (see page 591). China, a republic since 1911, was torn with constant civil strife, while Japan, with her expanding population and avowed need for territory, and Russia, with her communism, were dangerous neighbors for that weak, divided country with her tempting resources. Iran (Persia) was growing more nationalistic, and in 1921 overthrew her government, which was thought too pro-British.

The republic of Turkey had a dictator in her president, Mustafa Kemal, the vigorous leader of the Turkish nationalists, who had ousted the Sultan. This change freed Britain from the old embarrassing fact that Turkey's ruler had been spiritual head of all Moslems, of whom there were more than Christians among British subjects. Also a strong rejuvenated Turkey seemed a solution of the "Eastern Question." But Kemal was busily tearing to pieces the humiliating terms of the Treaty of Sèvres in the Paris peace settlement. His ousting of the Greeks from Asia Minor regions given them as a reward for their tardy support of the Allies reached a cruel climax in a terrible massacre at Smyrna in the summer of 1922. Kemal then started northward for Constantinople and Lloyd George intervened. The French and Italians, rather than fight, withdrew speedily; but Lloyd George, feeling that Britain's vital interests were endangered, sent troops to Çanakkale (Chanak), on the Asiatic side of the Dardanelles. Neither the war-weary British public nor the dominions, to whom he appealed for support, relished the thought of another Gallipoli; and the Turk, unopposed, had his own way.

The Conservatives Oust Lloyd George

This "Chanak affair" helped to terminate the six-year coalition ministry of Lloyd George in the autumn of 1922. The spell of the little "Welsh wizard" was weakening, and the Conservatives, who formed the bulk of his support, grew restive at his autocratic actions. A five-year general election would be due the following year. Consequently, the majority of the Conservatives determined to operate thereafter as a separate party. Lloyd George resigned at once. The king requested Bonar Law to form a Conservative ministry, and the general election shortly afterward established the Conservatives in power with a moderate majority. The Liberal party went to pieces; Asquith's and Lloyd George's followers were not on speaking terms. The electorate swung largely either to the Conservatives or to the Laborites, so that for the first time His Majesty's Opposition was the Labor party.

The remainder of George V's reign saw frequent ministerial changes. Bonar Law after eight months was followed by another Conservative, Stanley Baldwin, who after another eight months, gave way, early in 1924, to the Laborites under MacDonald. After nine months Baldwin returned to power, from November, 1924 to June, 1929. Then Labor, under MacDonald, was again in the saddle until August, 1931, when, under his leadership, a "National" coalition government, principally Conservative, was formed. In the summer of 1935 Baldwin succeeded him, becoming prime minister for the third time, until in 1937, under George VI, he was followed by another Conservative, Neville Chamberlain.

Between the wars the Conservatives were thus definitely the predominant party, with three separate ministries under their own name in addition to four coalitions, which relied principally upon their support. Along with this went the eclipse of the Liberals and the steady rise of Labor. Not once were the Liberals the majority party, and usually

THE WAIT-AND-SEESAW.

Cartoon showing situation after 1923 election, with Asquith's Liberals holding balance between Baldwin's Conservatives and MacDonald's Laborites, whom they finally joined.

even their place as the official opposition was taken by Labor. In their two ministries the Laborites, lacking a majority in the Commons, had to depend upon the Liberals as allies.

Bonar Law, of the War Cabinet and a Versailles delegate, was the first dominion native to be prime minister (see page 582). Already mortally ill, he died shortly. Three important candidates were in line as his successor. Austen Chamberlain's solid rather than showy qualities had been useful at the Exchequer, as Secretary of State for India, and in the War Cabinet, but he was passed by as punishment for his loyalty to the Lloyd George coalition. Lord Curzon, the proud ex-viceroy of India, also in the War Cabinet and more recently Foreign Secretary, "fully expected the post but his arrogance had antagonized too many and he was passed over." No peer, moreover, had been prime minister since Salisbury's resignation in 1902, and, in the new democratic age, leadership in the Commons seemed necessary. Thus the choice fell upon the less conspicuous Stanley Baldwin, Chancellor of the Exchequer and formerly president of the Board of Trade. Exceedingly shrewd, unassuming in manner, and possessed of an even temper and common sense, Baldwin had behind him years of practical business experience through his inherited position as head of one of the large iron, steel, and coal combinations. He was a country gentleman as well, an excellent judge of livestock, and a local magistrate. Sound rather than brilliant, he answered the country's desire for strength and security in that troubled period. Austen Chamberlain was out of office, but his brother Neville served at the Exchequer.

The Conservative prime ministers were to find the foreign situation as difficult to manage as had Lloyd George. In 1923 Turkey, securing at Lausanne a revision of the 1919 Sèvres treaty, was permitted to reoccupy the lands granted to the Greeks. Britain accepted this to preserve what she could of her vital interests in the Mosul oil fields on the upper Tigris, for she had to look to outside lands for oil, now a strategic economic factor in colonial and foreign policy as naval masts and ship timber had earlier been. Not only was it essential for general commercial needs, but for the navy and the air force. With their capital moved inland, far beyond the reach of British naval guns, which more than once had bullied Constantinople, the Turks by 1936 had gotten rid of the Lausanne treaty too and would secure international permission to fortify the de-militarized Straits. A reason for Britain's acquiescence in Turkish demands in 1923 was that early in that year the French sent military forces to occupy the valuable Ruhr mining region, alleging minor defaults in Germany's reparation payments. The British protested strongly, but in vain, at this French action.

At home Baldwin, baffled by the con-tinued increase in unemployment, favored Chamberlain's plan of protective tarrifs. Bonar Law, however, had promised not to bring up this question and apparently feeling bound by this unless given a mandate by the voters, Baldwin risked his ministry to request a general election late in 1923. With protection the issue, the Conservatives won the largest number of seats but not a majority. The Laborites and Liberals combined had about ninety more than the Conservative total. The Labor party could thus form the ministry with Liberal support. Had the Liberals combined with the Conservatives, they might still have kept Labor from office. However, they were too proud to play second fiddle to the Tory interests and were inclined to feel that if Labor were given its chance they might return to power on its heels.

The First Labor Ministry

Consequently, the socialist Ramsay MacDonald became prime minister in the first Labor Ministry. This seemed revolutionary, with the Labor party pledged as it was to a capital levy and to the nationalization of industry on socialistic lines; but MacDonald proved "safe." Although his goal was socialism, he moved toward it at a walking pace. The bulk of his following were the only very mildly socialistic trade unionists, and his majority, being dependent upon the Liberals, was, of course, uncertain. He set out to prove that a Labor government was respectable and not too radical. No exodus of capital occurred. The first Labor budget won general praise, and businessmen breathed more easily. The only tax lowered was that on cheap cinema tickets; but it was generally admitted that no government could have reduced taxes more at the time.

The Labor leaders were of two types. Some had long furnished intellectual guidance to the movement, while others had risen from the ranks of labor itself to influential trade-union leadership. MacDonald, nearly sixty, and known for his personal charm, was the son of a laborer in a Scottish fishing village. He had made his own way through diligent self-education as a clerk, teacher, journalist, and writer on socialism. Active in building up the Independent Labor party since 1894, he had been for some years before the war prominent in the Commons. He gave up his party leadership after opposing the declaration of war. He refused to serve in the armed forces, was widely denounced, and lost his seat in the 1918 election. Four years later he returned to Parliament and to the leadership of his party there. Philip Snowden, the Chancellor of the Exchequer, lean, frail, and a brilliant orator, had been another pioneer of the Independent Labor party thirty years before; likewise, Sidney Webb, later Lord Passfield, president of the Board of Trade, was an early leader of the Fabian Society and former member of the War Cabinet. On the other hand, Arthur Henderson, the new Home Secretary, and member of the War Cabinet, son of Glasgow working parents, had been an apprentice molder at Newcastle and later a power in north-country labor circles. John Henry Thomas, another cabinet member, a Welshman, had once cleaned locomotives and had risen to leadership of the great railway union. He was the first cabinet minister in British history to lose his office charged with divulging official secrets. There were also a few peers in the new cabinet for duties in the Lords, including a former viceroy of India and a one-time governor of Jamaica.

MacDonald, who was also Foreign Secretary, won general approval by winning over the French to a new plan for clearing the reparation muddle. This so-called "Dawes Plan," named after one of its framers, an American, was a temporary solution which facilitated the withdrawal of the French army from the Ruhr Valley. MacDonald also suspended work on the great naval base at Singapore to avoid antagonizing Japan. At the meeting of the League of Nations in

Baldwin and MacDonald at a press conference during their 1931 National Government; this early "candid" picture was said to be the first ever taken at the Foreign Office.

1924 he signed the Geneva protocol by which the signatory nations agreed to accept as compulsory the jurisdiction of the World Court on any questions that seemed to be leading to war; but the action was not sustained. Otherwise, his pacifism was not especially in evidence; he slightly increased the navy (which, however, was much smaller than it had been in 1914) and refused to yield to either Indian or Egyptian Nationalists.

His attempt to draw Russia (the Union of Soviet Socialist Republics) into the circle of friendly powers led to the downfall of his ministry. To increase the sale of British goods abroad, he was ready to aid Britain's potential customers. He wanted to arrange by treaty the floating of a Russian loan in the British market, the interest and repayment of the bonds to be guaranteed by the British, in return for the Soviet government's pledging, among other things, to abstain from revolutionary propaganda in England. Sharp and shrill was the outcry from all sides, Conservatives, Liberals, even some Laborites. Many Englishmen had no desire for relations with Russia because, for one thing, the Bolshevists looked forward to a world revolution against all capitalistic powers.

The treaty never came up for ratification in Parliament because of the appearance in an English communist newspaper of the following: "Form committees in every barracks, aerodrome and ship. Let this be the nucleus of an organization which will prepare the whole of the soldiers, sailors and airmen not merely to refuse to go to war or to refuse to shoot strikers during industrial conflicts but will make it possible for the workers, peasants and soldiers, sailors and airmen to go forward in a common attack upon capitalism." The editor was arrested, but the case was dismissed by the attorney general, whose reasons failed to satisfy an incensed Parliament. Not only the Conservatives, but also the Liberals, whose friendship with Labor was wearing thin, voted against MacDonald, and this ended the first Labor ministry within its first year.

In the 1924 general election the Conservatives triumphantly returned to power with a big majority. During the campaign they had advocated a protective tariff. Such a position had less to do with their victory, however, than various weak spots in their opponents' armor. Although MacDonald's term had been short, and his majority uncertain, more had been expected of Labor. It had not filled mouths, housed people, nor lessened the number on unemployment dole. But his defeat was caused chiefly by a mysterious letter which was sprung upon the people a few days before election. Supposedly written by Zinoviev, the Russian president of the Third International (the communist revolutionary organization), it advocated preparation for revolution in England. This so alarmed the Liberals that they flocked to support Conservative can-

didates, almost killing their own party. Their seats were reduced to 40, while Labor retained about 150, and the Conservatives increased their total to over 400.

The Second Baldwin Ministry and Efforts for Peace

Thus the genial Stanley Baldwin began his second ministry (1924-1929). Winston Churchill, once a famous Liberal and then a coalitionist, now, surprisingly enough, went over to the Conservatives, serving at the Exchequer. The versatile Churchill had previously held six other Cabinet posts— Board of Trade, Home Office, Admiralty, Munitions, War and Air, and Colonies—besides finding time to write several valuable books on the war and the postwar period.

Austen Chamberlain, as Secretary for Foreign Affairs, successfully opposed the Geneva protocol because, in his opinion, it made the League of Nations into a superstate, thus endangering the British Empire's freedom of action. Parliament's rejection of it rather lessened England's influence in the League. Nevertheless, Chamberlain consistently strove for peace, as MacDonald had done—particularly for a more friendly feeling between France and Germany.

In this Chamberlain achieved his most notable work. He was fortunate to have as allies with the same goal two ministers, Briand in France and Stresemann in Germany. At Locarno in 1925, at a conference of the powers, France and Germany mutually guaranteed their frontiers in the Rhine region. By this they pledged themselves not to invade each other's territories, and to keep the boundaries as established at Versailles, with the left bank of the Rhine as a demilitarized zone in Germany. Belgium and Germany signed similar pledges. Britain and Italy guaranteed the pledges to the extent of promising aid in case of violation of the agreements. Other pacts signed at Locarno provided for the arbitration of disputes in other areas; but Britain did not share in the arrangements about Germany's eastern boundaries. A significant result was the paving of the way for Germany's entrance into the League of Nations the following year.

Strikes and Trade Union Curbs

At home the crippled mining industry became the focus of discontent. In 1925, when the operators announced a wage cut in the less profitable mines, the desperate miners appealed to their fellow trade-unionists. Baldwin, to stave off trouble, consented to a temporary subsidy in order to continue hour and wage terms pending the report on the industry by a royal commission. This merely postponed the storm that burst upon England in 1926 when that report recommended a closing down of some mines, which would eliminate thousands of jobs, or else a reduction of costs, involving longer hours or lower pay, or both. Thereupon the government refused to continue the subsidy; the miners insisted upon "not a penny off the pay, not an hour on the day"; and the trade unions declared a general "sympathetic strike."

All railway men, all those in iron, steel, and building trades, and all printers stopped work. Baldwin, denouncing the strike as an attempt to "set up an alternative government," summoned the country to resist. The middle class responded almost to a man, running the railways after a fashion, distributing food, and so on, with determination and vim. In eight days the strike was broken with virtually no violence on either side.

The embittered miners kept up the struggle within their own industry for seven months. Slowly they drifted back to work. Their hours were uniformly increased to seven and a half, while their wages were lowered in some localities. Many mines, particularly in South Wales, were now abandoned altogether.

In 1927 the Conservatives succeeded in passing the Trade Disputes and Trade Union Act—the first setback the influen-

tial trade-union movement had received in many years. It made the general strike illegal, forbade the intimidation of strikebreakers, excluded government employees from membership, and otherwise limited union activities. Henceforth, a worker would be breaking the law if he threw down his tools to remedy difficulties in any line of work other than his own. Many felt that this prohibition of the general strike would be hard to enforce.

In other domestic matters Baldwin, showing that he was far from a "die-hard" Tory, kept the extreme Conservatives in check (as, for instance, in their desire to strengthen the House of Lords) and also made friendly gestures to Labor, in particular, with a new pension law for widows. Although he was unable to do much about the economic crisis, the budget of 1928 was a determined effort toward improving conditions. One thing in the way was the impasse caused by the insistence of businessmen that lower wages were essential for competition in the world market and by the refusal of the trade unions to consider them. A slight improvement in trade persuaded Baldwin and his followers that all Britain needed to do was to sit tight and wait for better times.

Consequently, when a Parliamentary election again came due in 1929, the Conservatives' slogans were: "Safety First!" and "Trust Baldwin!" Little difference was apparent in the platforms of the Liberals and Laborites, with the former promising to abolish unemployment in a year by a huge loan for public works. The liberals won less than one tenth of the seats; the Conservatives acquired about 260 seats; but Labor outnumbered them, with over 285.

The Second Labor Ministry

Again in his second ministry (1929-1931) MacDonald's insecure majority made it necessary to have the support of the Liberal "rump" and to continue a cautious course, accomplishing more in foreign affairs than at home. At an international conference at the Hague in 1929, a commission under another American, Owen D. Young, evolved a second plan for the reparation payments, since the Dawes Plan had proved inadequate in some ways. At the Hague, also, MacDonald, with the co-operation of Briand and Stresemann, effected a compromise to facilitate the removal of the Allied troops from the Rhine region. MacDonald also reestablished relations with Russia, which since Lenin's death had been under the virtual dictatorship of Stalin. Britain had had no official connection with Russia for three years, because of alleged communist agitation.

At the London naval conference in 1930, only partial success attended the effort to extend the principle of the 5-5-3 ratio, established for battleships at the Washington Conference, to other categories. In regard to cruisers, the British and American admirals differed radically and only reached a compromise of sorts. The British wanted many small ones to guard their far-flung responsibilities, while the Americans, with few overseas bases, wanted a few large ones with wider cruising radius. Arrangements were made for another conference in 1935.

These various efforts for better international understanding did not materially change the ominous world situation. The spread of Russian communism was still actively feared, while its antithesis, Fascist dictatorships on the Italian model, were soon to spread with increased momentum. Revolution had been rearing its head in this postwar decade from South America to Greece. In 1931, Spain revolted against her monarchy; but the new republic found difficulty in retaining control between the opposing forces of communism and Fascism. Meanwhile Japan's aggressive and successful moves against China defied the protests of the League and the powers.

Unemployment presented an insuperable problem. Snowden believed that the only way to balance the budget was by sound

finances with increased taxation. Furthermore, he made it clear that the government had no surplus for additional social legislation. Friction rapidly increased within the Labor party, the more conservative elements, including MacDonald, supporting Snowden, while the more radical threatened revolt.

Financial Crisis and Coalition Cabinet

By 1931, too, Britain was feeling the effects of the world-wide "economic blizzard" which had spread rapidly after the crash of securities in the United States in the autumn of 1929. The world was so closely linked together economically that the depression was contagious. As revenues in England continued to decline, Snowden admitted that the budget for 1931 could not be balanced, and the deficit would be enormous by 1932. Snowden and MacDonald were prepared to insist upon immediate drastic economies, but the storm broke first with a crisis of the first magnitude in August, 1931. The Bank of England was in danger of failure, in spite of hurried loans from New York and Paris bankers, because of heavy withdrawals of gold in exchange for currency.

MacDonald and Snowden, agreeing that the Bank of England and the pound sterling must be saved, prepared to cut unemployment insurance drastically. At this juncture there came word from the bankers that the further essential financial aid of some eight million pounds would not be forthcoming unless the cabinet could reduce expenditures to meet prospective income. The majority of the cabinet refused to sacrifice the dole. The trade unions, too, opposed such a measure, as did the majority of the Labor members of the Commons. Obviously, MacDonald could not continue in office with most of his party against him.

Time pressed. MacDonald parleyed with Liberal and Conservative leaders to find some way out of the impasse. An unusual solution was found. MacDonald resigned as

Labor's prime minister, only to be immediately recommissioned by George V to deal with the emergency as prime minister of a so-called "National government." Thus, MacDonald, although deposed by his party, remained as prime minister, but king or no king, he could not have done so had he not retained a majority in the Commons. In the new cabinet, virtually a coalition, were four, including MacDonald, from the previous ministry; four Conservatives, including Baldwin; and two Liberals.

When Parliament reconvened, it gave the ministry a vote of confidence of 311 against 251. The bulk of the support was Conservative; thus MacDonald kept his position "on the strength of his enemies" rather than on that of his erstwhile friends. A 10 per cent cut in unemployment insurance was effected; drastic cuts were made in the salaries of all servants of the crown, from cabinet ministers, to policemen and bluejackets. By October the budget was balanced. Yet day by day the ominous depression of the pound sterling in foreign exchange continued. Finally, to prevent bankruptcy, the government "went off the gold standard," by suspending the customary regulation that the Bank of England must redeem, upon demand, its paper money with gold. In order to secure approval for this drastic step, the government appealed to the country.

In one of the most exciting campaigns in British annals, MacDonald, with a few loyal followers from the Labor party, together with the Conservatives under Baldwin, urged tariffs as the remedy. Some Liberals, moreover, under Sir John Simon, head of the 1926 commission to India and a cabinet member, were prepared to swallow the prospective tariffs. Other Liberals, under Sir Herbert Samuel, another cabinet member, and chairman in 1925 of the commission on the mining industry, likewise supported the National government, but vehemently opposed protection. MacDonald, a lifelong socialist, was thus appealing to the electorate, as the head of a coalition of which the Tories were the mainstay. Against the government was the rump of the Liberals, under Lloyd George, and, more important, Labor itself, under its new leader Arthur Henderson. The panic that had swept over England in 1924 was as nothing to the financial fear which now gripped the heart of nearly every English man and woman who had saved a pound or two ahead. This time, the scare succeeded, for the coalition was given an overwhelming vote of confidence. The Conservatives triumphed with 470 seats, more than three quarters of the total number. The National Liberals (the followers of Simon and Samuel) and MacDonald's group of National Laborites added another seventy-odd government seats, while in opposition were left only 52 Laborites and four Liberal members of Lloyd George's own family. Thus it looked as if the Labor party had collapsed.

Whether MacDonald had proved a traitor to his cause remained a debatable point. Yet if he had done otherwise, the economic ills of England would probably have been intensified, with commercial credit shattered, and banks and factories closing their doors. MacDonald continued as prime minister, with a coalition cabinet including Neville Chamberlain, Baldwin, Simon, and Samuel.

The End of Free Trade

At last the insistent Conservative clamor for protective tariffs was to succeed. MacDonald had no choice; for evidently the majority felt that England must abandon free trade if she was to remain a capitalistic nation. Within one year the work of Huskisson, Peel, Cobden, and Bright was reversed by a low tariff wall. At first it did not affect most foodstuffs; but the Conservatives, traditionally the spokesmen of the agricultural interests, and the Imperial Economic Conference at Ottawa (see page 616) saw that it did so. This change was, on the whole, popular, but it further split the Liberal party and the Samuelites resigned in protest from the Cabinet.

The End of Reparations

Britain and the United States differed over the relationship of the German reparations (see page 592) and the war debts that the Allies owed to the United States. If Germany could not pay what she owed them, Britain and her allies felt, it was understandable if they did not pay the United States. Because of the world-wide depression, President Hoover declared a year's moratorium, or suspension, on reparation and war-debt payments, and a conference of the powers met at Lausanne. This meeting resulted in the virtual cancellation of reparations, upon certain lump-sum payments from Germany. The Allies now optimistically expected the United States to cancel the war debts. If they were to pay, they presumably would have to ship more goods to the United States than they would take in return; and this was extremely difficult unless the latter lowered her tariffs or the Allies decreased their purchases of American goods, both of which measures would be injurious to the United States trade. The American viewpoint had once been expressed by the previous president, Coolidge: "They hired the money, didn't they?" When this attitude became obvious, the British, with pride in their financial past, paid the usual installment, but not as interest; they called it a reduction of the principal. The French had already ceased to make payments. Britain twice paid a relatively small sum, purely as an acknowledgement that she recognized the debt. Thereafter she ceased payments altogether, like all the other foreign debtors except Finland.

Little headway was made in naval and military disarmament. The chief naval question concerned England, the United States, and Japan in the Pacific, where Japan now insisted on the abrogation of the 5-5-3 ratio as determined at Washington (see pages 598, 606). Neither the United States nor Japan was willing to compromise. Japan soon denounced the Washington treaty, which she considered humiliating to her national dignity. In the next naval conference in 1935 at London, she refused to budge in her demand for equality, while the United States was equally insistent in her desire for larger ships. The Japanese abandoned the conference in disgust. England, France, and the United States signed a treaty of a sort, which left them free to build as many battleships or submarines as seemed desirable.

Hitler's Rise to Power

No progress was made in disarmament on land. Germany weathered the postwar chaos with a republic, with steady old General Hindenburg as president after its first years. In 1933 she came under the dictatorship of Adolf Hitler. An Austrian by birth but an ex-corporal in the German army, he headed the National Socialist German Labor party, called Nazi for short, which won the election that year. In many respects they resembled Mussolini's followers, since in both Italy and Germany new dictatorships, both violently nationalistic, represented an avowed determination on the one hand to hold in check the great capitalists and on the other to blot out revolutionary socialism. The Nazis focused popular interest against Marxian socialists, Jews, and the Versailles treaty. Germany was increasingly incensed at the limitations imposed upon her, while her former enemies, who had indicated at Versailles an intention to disarm, had not done so. Consequently she withdrew from the League of Nations and proceeded toward rearmament. Hitler's proposed air program and the rumors of his plan for general rearmament grew increasingly ominous. Also disturbing were his apparent designs upon the independence of Austria, whose political troubles came to a climax in 1934 with the assassination of the anti-Nazi Austrian chancellor. In 1935,

Hitler, probably encouraged by the return of the Saar region to Germany as the result of a plebiscite, openly repudiated the Versailles treaty by announcing the rearmament of his country.

Ten days before, the British government called for a defense increase of about 40 per cent. The air force, in particular, was to be greatly enlarged; for England was visualizing more and more the dangers from the air, which threatened her formerly secure insular position. She had been doing more, probably, than any other European power for disarmament and had kept her own forces relatively low; this was the sequel. Baldwin already had referred significantly to the Rhine, rather than the Channel or the North Sea, as her first line of defense.

England, however, was not definitely hostile toward Germany, although she protested against Hitler's arms proclamation. In mid-1935, apparently without consulting France, she entered into a naval understanding with Germany, who was to be free to build ships as she chose, provided that she did not go over 35 per cent of British strength. Such a percentage would virtually put Germany on an equality with France.

Meanwhile the prestige of the National government, now in its fourth year, was somewhat diminished. It had stimulated business to a certain extent by fiscal reform and had brightened the prospects of agriculture by direct governmental intervention and subsidy. Nevertheless, the "depressed areas" remained: shipping, shipbuilding, steel, coal, and cotton showed little improvement. To aid these industries, the government was planning to spend two million pounds; but little could be accomplished by a sum of that size. With another election soon, the Labor party began to show signs of life. Its more radical members sought to commit it to a frontal attack upon the House of Lords. The more conservative majority voted that down, but

pledged the party to a policy of the government's taking over or nationalizing banking, transportation, and certain key industries.

The silver jubilee of King George in 1935, celebrated throughout the British world, together with a slight decline in unemployment and a general improvement in the economic situation, created an atmosphere so favorable to the National government that it considered calling the general election. This was not done; but MacDonald, exhausted and ill, resigned to take a less exacting post, and Baldwin for the third time became prime minister.

Changes in Empire

The year 1920 might be taken as the high water mark in area of the British Empire. The League of Nations, by giving Britain mandates for the former German colonies in Africa and Oceania and for former Turkish territories in the Middle East, added over a million square miles, increasing the empire by a tenth. In population, the total would continue to grow in the next decades, as the people in many of her lands beyond the seas multiplied rapidly. During that same period, however, imperial bonds were steadily loosening. The doctrine of self-determination preached so loudly at the peace conference soon came home to roost when Ottawa, Sydney, and Pretoria, as well as Delhi, began to show signs of nationalism. Before even the first decade was out, Britain was recognizing the dominions as partners rather than possessions, and was making concessions of sorts to the stirrings in India and Egypt.

Britain was instrumental in freeing most of the Arab lands in the Middle East from their four centuries of political and economic stagnation under the Turks, her military successes in World War I being largely responsible. Her acceptance of Class A mandates for Iraq, Jordan, and Palestine brought her the responsibility of preparing them for ultimate independence. The aroused Arab nationalism throughout the area was complicated by the French in Syria and Lebanon and the Jews in Palestine blocking Pan-Arab aspirations. The great desert area of Arabia proper went its own independent way under a tough desert ruler, Ibn Saud; he soon took over Hejaz from King Hussein, the original aspirant for all-Arab leadership.

One of Hussein's sons, Abdullah, was set up by the British as king of Transjordania (Jordan). Ninety-five per cent desert, this was a rather artificial creation between Palestine and Arabia with meager resources and few natural boundaries (see page 591).

In Iraq, Britain installed another son of Hussein, Feisal, who had fought along with Lawrence (see page 585) and had just been ousted by France from a brief rule in Syria, as king in a constitutional setup. Under the mandate, his advisers were British and British garrisons were maintained because of Britain's overland communications with India. In 1932, Britain relinquished her mandate and Iraq became independent, but only after Britain had seen to it that she had further rights. She could have air bases, move troops across Iraq, and in case of war have further facilities. Also, only British experts were to be used in the Iraq army and government, and Britain was to have diplomatic precedence over all other countries. Though the government was English in form, the power lay between the king and a small privileged ruling class; twenty-one changes of ministry occurred in the first four years.

Oil was what made Iraq worthwhile to Britain, who since 1908 had been drawing upon the rich petroleum deposits of adjacent Iran (Persia). Her military occupation of the Mosul area helped her to gain it for Iraq despite the claims of Turkey and France. Oil began to gush out in 1927, and two pipelines were built across the desert to the Mediterranean. The further fantastic discovery and exploitation of Middle East oil in southern Arabia and along the Persian Gulf by the British and Americans would be even more profitable.

As early as the eighteen fifties, Palmerston had recommended giving "just encouragement to the Jews of Europe to return to Palestine." At the turn of the century, a Zionist organization was formed to gain support for such a homeland. In 1903, Joseph Chamberlain offered them a generous tract of land in the "white highlands" of Kenya for an autonomous Jewish state, but the Jews of central and eastern Europe had their hearts set upon Palestine. During World War I, Zionism found a most effective advocate in a distinguished scientist, Chaim (or Hayyim) Weizmann, who built up strong support in America and in Britain. In November 1917, just before Allenby's forces captured Jerusalem, Balfour, now Foreign Secretary, issued the fateful declaration that had come from the pen of his fellow-cabinet member, Lord Milner: "His Majesty's Government view with favor the establishment in Palestine of a national home for the Jewish people, and will use their best endeavors to facilitate the achievement of this object, it being clearly understood that nothing shall be done which may prejudice the civil and religious rights of other non-Jewish communities in Palestine."

When Palestine became a class A mandate the British tried their best to make those terms work, but they were hopelessly contradictory. The Jews wanted still more —a full-fledged political state of their own, and not simply a home. The Arabs, far outnumbering them, did not want the Jews there at all in what they considered their own land. There was friction from the outset. The British High Commissioner, who was a very able Jew himself, was unable to please all the factions, nor were his successors any more successful in steering an even course between these racial hatreds. Although the country prospered, self-governing institutions were not established because Arab and Jewish leaders refused to co-operate. England tried more than once but was rebuffed; the Arabs wanted representation on the basis of population, and the Jews, as a decided minority, held out for racial equality. When opportunity offered, as occasionally it did, for a massacre of their enemies, the Arabs were quick to take advantage of it. When punished by British soldiers or the police, they complained bitterly to the League of Nations of British tyranny, while the Jews loudly lamented the failure to give them better protection. Yet in all the glare of publicity thrown upon Palestine by the Jewish press and by the Jews of all countries, no major mistake could be laid at the door of the British save the unworkable original promise to make a Jewish home on what had become Moslem land. But had the British withdrawn, the Arabs would have driven the Jews into the sea. Jerusalem was holy ground to Arabs as well as to Jews and Christians, and it was Arab efforts, in part at least, which had wrested it from the Turks during the war; on that account the Arabs felt all the more strongly that the land was theirs.

At first the flow of Jewish immigration was restricted. With Hitler's brutal anti-Jewish policy, the bars were temporarily let down and in the ensuing flood of those seeking admission, the Jews doubled between 1929 and 1935, coming mostly from Poland and Germany. At the same time, the Jews of the United States began to contribute generously, facilitating the remarkable economic development of the once-neglected land. Jerusalem prospered as never before in its history. Tel Aviv, a Jewish city, grew up near Haifa, on the Mediterranean; orange groves dotted the landscape; a university was opened; huge electric works in the Jordan valley supplied light and power; and oil was pumped through the desert.

The more Jews that came, the more aroused were the Arabs. And when the Arabs protested loudly, Jewish pressure on Parliament secured new Zionist advantages. By 1936, the Arabs called a general strike and, reinforced by armed bands from neighboring states, engaged in sharp fighting. A royal commission declared in 1937 that "the promises made to Jews and Arabs were irreconcilable, and the Mandate in its existing form unworkable." It recommended that Palestine be divided into separate Jewish and Arab states, with the numerous Arabs in the Jewish region to be "resettled, either voluntarily or compulsorily." The Arabs refused this absolutely; and fighting broke out still more violently, nearly a hundred British being killed in addition to many Jews and Arabs. Thus matters stood when World War II broke out.

In Egypt nationalism was creating still further grave problems. With Turkey's entrance into the war on the German side late in 1914, Britain did away with the old farce of nominal Turkish sovereignty, carried on under Cromer and his successors (see page 526), and declared Egypt a protectorate. With it at last a formal part of the British Empire, the khedive was deposed and a "sultan," of the same family, set up. British authority was administered by a high commissioner instead of a consul general. The British continued to keep a garrison in Cairo and a naval base at Alexandria, while a British general served as "sirdar" of the Anglo-Egyptian Sudan. Primarily to guard the Suez Canal, Britain kept large numbers of troops in Egypt during the war, and many peasants were virtually forced into a labor corps for the Palestine campaign.

By the end of the war, the old 1882 cry of "Egypt for the Egyptians" was heard again and a powerful nationalist party, the "Wafd" was growing rapidly. It found a shrewd but quite unsavory leader, Zaghlul Pasha, who was, despite his powers of organization, "vain, timid, and irresponsible, always ready to run away from the consequences of his own action. While his diplomatic efforts won concession after concession, his appeals to the mob produced a series of bloody outrages."[1] He hastened to Versailles in 1919; but the "Big Three" paid no more attention to his pleas than to those of the other disregarded nationalists in Persia, Ireland, or Korea. He returned home such a bitter enemy of England that he was exiled. Thereupon trains were derailed and rioting broke out. A royal commission was sent to Egypt under Lord Milner, a Conservative member of the War Cabinet and Versailles delegate (see pages 532, 582), whose stiff manner had earlier irritated South Africa. The commission's reception was similar to that given the Simon Commission in India but Milner got in touch with Zaghlul and drew up a treaty draft. Although the terms were unpopular in both countries, they were virtually the same as the 1922 settlement. Zaghlul, inducing their rejection, again went into exile amid renewed rioting.

Britain, in 1922, finally declared Egypt "independent." Sultan Fuad was promoted to be king, "the first sovereign ruler of Egypt since Cleopatra." England clung to qualifying reservations, however, similar in their general nature to those later imposed upon Iraq. These were: (1) the security of imperial communications; (2) the defense of Egypt against all foreign aggression or interference; (3) the protection of foreign residents and minorities; and (4) the continued joint control of the Sudan, where Britain would not agree to abandon either the British capital invested in irrigation projects or the natives under her protection. Those terms remained highly distasteful to Zaghlul, who returned as prime minister, and to his Wafd nationalists, strongly entrenched in the Egyptian Parliament.

Thus matters stood when Sir Lee Stack, Sirdar of the Sudan, was assassinated in Cairo in 1924. Thereupon General Allenby, the High Commissioner, delivered a drastic ultimatum. Not only must a heavy fine be paid and all Egyptian troops withdrawn from the Sudan, but in case of noncompliance Britain threatened to cut off Egypt's water supply from the Upper Nile. That marked the end of Zaghlul's power.

During the next dozen years there was a tedious but trying series of negotiations, demands, and outrages; three times British warships were rushed to Alexandria to exert pressure or protect foreigners. The Wafd extremists held out for thorough elimination of British influence, but the conservatives refused to yield any further in that vital Suez area. MacDonald's government was ready to offer more concessions.

Not until 1936, when the Italian invasion of nearby Ethiopia caused alarm, (see page 617) was an Anglo-Egyptian treaty, promising eventual real independence, achieved. In the meantime, there were still some strings attached. Each country was to aid the other in case of war, and the British could even impose martial law in an emergency. Recognizing British interest in the Suez Canal, Egypt for the time being permitted Britain to retain troops and other personnel in the Suez Canal Zone; but she would withdraw from her Alexandria naval base in eight years, and also, eventually, from Cairo. The Sudan was to be administered in the primary interest of the Sudanese. Egypt would henceforth be responsible for the protection of foreigners, but they would now be subject to Egyptian law. As at Baghdad, the British were to enjoy diplomatic precedence over other foreign representatives. Although the Italian–Ethiopian crisis had led to those compromise concessions, there was reason to expect that, once it was over, the nationalists would seek "complete independence by obtaining the evacuation of the British forces, freedom to follow a foreign policy untrammelled by the alliance with Britain, and the reassertion in fact of Egypt's sovereignty over the Sudan."[2]

[1] C. E. Carrington, *The British Overseas* (1950), p. 960. By permission of Cambridge University Press.

[2] G. E. Kirk, *A Short History of the Middle East* (Praeger, 1959), p. 173.

Gandhi and Unrest in India

During the war the British had promised India self-governing institutions and the Government of India Act of 1919 was the very limited answer. In a legislature for all British India, the lower house had fairly high financial requirements for electors, while the upper house, carefully hand-picked, had even higher requirements, with the Viceroy left with much power. The protected native states were excluded. Another feature was the "dyarchy," (double government) whereby in the provinces of British India alone certain functions such as education, sanitation, and forestry were under officials who held offices at the will of the elected legislators; while others, such as the judiciary and finance, were left under the control of members of the civil service responsible only to the British officials. After ten years, the British promised to consider further self-government.

To many, Mohandas Gandhi, the "Mahatma" (or Holy One), was a saint, but for years he was a thorn in the flesh of the perplexed rulers of British India. A high-caste Hindu, he had studied law in England and practiced in South Africa (see page 543), where he tried to aid his badly treated fellow Indians. During the Boer War he organized a Red Cross unit, and in World War I, returning to India, he helped to raise recruits for the British army. Although a Nationalist, he was then friendly to the British *raj* but became antagonized by the harsh treatment of his fellow Nationalists. In 1920 he put himself at the head of the movement for "swaraj," or home rule, advocating a policy of passive resistance to combat British authority—the same method he had tried in South Africa. He urged his followers never to engage in violence under any circumstances, but to show their disapproval of British control by boycotting British schools, law courts, and goods, besides having nothing to do with the British themselves. In particular, Gandhi encour-

Gandhi, in his usual scant garb, with a group of Indian political leaders at Bombay, 1931.

aged "swadeshi," a movement which urged the use of handmade goods, as a protest against the manufactures of the British. He taught the Indians to resurrect their spinning wheels and to make their own cloth. If he had succeeded in uniting the Indians in this non-co-operation, Britain would indeed have been hurt in a vulnerable spot, the Indian market.

Gandhi taught nonviolence; but his disciples made bonfires of British cloth, and he was put in jail. As this happened, insurrections broke out at Delhi and at Amritsar, where a British general ordered shot down, without warning, several hundred persons in a mob which had gathered in defiance of prohibitions. Thus was the growth of Indian nationalism accelerated. Gandhi, released, became practically dictator of the Indian Nationalist Congress; but his followers continued to find difficulty in living up to his precepts, and they beat a number of policemen to death. The Mahatma, in humiliation, suspended the non-co-operative campaign, but he was sentenced anew to jail.

For a short time it seemed as though the ten-year experimental period might pass without further outbreaks. The Moslems, nearly one quarter of the entire population, did not take kindly to swaraj, and the Hindus were not altogether disinclined to co-operate in the British reforms program. The first elections returned a majority of moderates, but those in 1924 showed increasing radical strength. The Swarajists who rejected Gandhi's advice to refrain from voting had a plurality in the lower house, and demanded immediate home rule, except in military and foreign affairs. The British refused and in revenge the assembly threw out the budget. Thereupon the viceroy, in accordance with his right under the 1919 act, certified a state of danger; and so put the budget into effect without legislative approval.

With increasing unrest in 1926-1928 a Parliamentary commission was sent out under Sir John Simon to report upon conditions. Wherever it went it was greeted by cries of "Go back, Simon!" because the Indians were affronted at not being represented on it; and its findings were delayed. In 1929 the viceroy, Lord Irwin, asserted that regardless of the Simon report, Britain was pledged ultimately to grant dominion status to India. Gandhi thereupon offered to cease civil disobedience and non-co-operation if the salt tax were halved, political prisoners released, and the salaries of British civil servants slashed. When these conditions were refused, he made a "march to the sea," a religious pilgrimage to break the law publicly by obtaining salt, a government monopoly, without paying for it. The sea was at last reached; the salt scooped up; the law defied. The Mahatma then advocated the seizure of the salt works; and his followers, rushing upon the salt, were struck down by the police.

The Simon report favored making India a federation of states except for Burma and the North West Frontier Province. Responsible government was to be granted the separate provinces, but not to the All-India legislature at Delhi. The federation was to be open to the native states. This did not go far enough for the Nationalists. Riots and cloth-burning began again. Gandhi, once more freed (he was always being sent to prison or released), had a futile conference with the viceroy.

Next, round-table conferences were held at London in 1930 and 1931 at which native princes, Hindus, Moslems, and Englishmen sat together to iron out their differences. Gandhi, in his loincloth, and accompanied by goats for his milk, attended one reluctantly. Nothing was accomplished, although the British offered further compromises. The Hindus stood fast for electoral districts on the basis of population, and the Moslems, unexpectedly joined by the lowest-caste Hindus, some five million "untouchables," demanded they be based on religion. With this impasse, the British assumed responsibility themselves for the new constitution.

Meanwhile, a "Red Shirt" movement among Moslems for the nonpayment of taxes was quelled by force. In the Central Provinces the Indian Nationalist Congress assumed the right to say what, if any, rent should be paid to landlords. Further imprisonments followed. In Bengal two young girls murdered a British official, and all legal rights there were suspended. On his return Gandhi sought an interview with the viceroy, the Earl of Willingdon, who refused because of Gandhi's leadership of a nonconstitutional body, the Indian Nationalist Congress. Thereupon, he renewed his civil-disobedience campaign, and was once more clapped in jail. The government's firmness cowed the agitators, and the violence diminished under Willingdon.

The British now proceeded to draw up a plan with a legislature based on representation according to religious belief. Gandhi called this an insult to the untouchables, since it perpetuated caste lines; and to show his disapproval he began a fast to death. The leaner he grew, the more worried grew public opinion. In an effort to prevent his death, a hurried compromise accepted representation by population in modified form. The Government of India Act of 1935 provided for an Indian federation with responsible government in both central and provincial legislatures but with Britain retaining in large measure the substance of power—control of finance, the army, and international relations. Although this was quite different from dominion status, it seemed a long step forward. It enlarged the provincial electorate, gave really responsible government to the provinces (except for certain emergency police powers left to the governors), opened the door for the native states to enter the federation, and increased decidedly the power of the central legislature at the viceroy's expense.

Yet the majority of Indians denounced it bitterly, as they would probably have received any British-made constitution. The British Labor party also was against it for not approaching Irwin's promise of eventual dominion status. On the other hand, the Conservatives felt that even as it was, it granted too much; the autonomous powers implied in dominion status were proving risky enough in Ireland and South Africa where the white man was in control; what such self-government might mean if granted to the ignorant and divided masses of India was not pleasant to imagine. Baldwin had to use all his prestige and personal popularity and to warn, "We shall lose India within two generations unless these reforms are passed," to secure its passage by Parliament. The responsibility of initiating the constitution was given to the Marquess of Linlithgow, a distinguished and experienced authority on India, who had been on the commission responsible for it.

The Dominions and The Commonwealth

The self-governing dominions had sent their own soldiers to the war, paid for their maintenance, signed the peace treaty, and joined the League of Nations as individual states. After 1919, except for less nationally-minded New Zealand, they tended to be somewhat aloof from British foreign policy. The two islands of small and completely isolated New Zealand at the Imperial Conference of 1921 alone pleaded for closer constitutional unity. In the Chanak crisis of 1922, when Lloyd George cabled the dominions for support, New Zealand alone offered immediate assistance, whereas Canada and South Africa were both noncommittal and Australia qualified her support with "if circumstances permit" (see page 600). Canada, moreover, established a new imperial precedent in exchanging ministers with the United States. This was more convenient than dealing through the Foreign Office at London, and the practice spread. Canada next exchanged diplomats with France and Japan, and the other dominions followed suit. The premier of Canada publicly affirmed that it was not bound by the Treaty of Lausanne with Turkey in 1923, because it was not represented at the conference. So great an impression did this make in London that Britain expressly stated in 1925 that the Locarno pacts did not obligate any of the dominions unless they so chose.

Although Canada retained genuine loyalty to the crown, South Africa reacted to the British tie in a different spirit. In South Africa's first postwar election the Boer irreconcilables, headed by General Hertzog, who was still bitter toward England, won a plurality of seats in its legislature, but he was kept out of office because the ultra-British Unionist party submerged itself in the South African party of moderate Boers friendly to England. Hertzog, however, successfully won these Boers to his Nationalist party. He also made an agreement with the dominion Labor party to form a joint ministry, if successful in the next election. In 1924 Hertzog thus became prime minister, a post which he was to hold for many years. The ultimate secession of the Union seemed a possibility. Shortly, it adopted its own flag and only after terrific protests did it consent to permit therein a tiny Union Jack, one twenty-seventh of the whole flag. In other ways South Africa stressed its aloofness; it chose its own seal, and amended its constitution to term itself "a sovereign independent state." In 1935 came a hot dispute with Britain over the three native protectorates of Basutoland, Bechuanaland, and Swaziland. Originally England had planned to let the Union control them; but Hertzog's anti-Negro policy led her to retain her trusteeship. The Union was already drawing the color line sharply, with special discrimination against the Negroes in the mining industry, even establishing separate post offices for white persons and Negroes. In 1936, when the Ethiopian crisis threatened Suez, and Britain turned her attention to the longer but safer route around the Cape, the Union government offered her naval facilities only if she would transfer those protectorates to the dominion.

A landmark of first importance in British imperial history was established by the 1926 Imperial Conference in its declaration that the dominions were Britain's partners and not her possessions. Chamberlain's earlier efforts to bring closer co-operation with the dominions had come to little, but in World War I the premiers had several times participated in an imperial War Cabinet (see page 583). Before the 1926 conference a Secretaryship of State for the Dominions had been set up creating a Dominion Office apart from the Colonial. The conference "refused to lay down a constitution for the empire," but for the first time the relations of the dominions and Britain were clearly defined. The dominions were, it asserted, together with the mother country, "autonomous communities within the British Empire, equal in status, in no way subordinate one to another in any aspect of their domestic or external affairs, though united by a common allegiance to the Crown, and freely associated as members of the British Commonwealth of Nations." This formal acknowledgment of complete equality cleared the air of any possible suspicion of British domination. Treaties in the future might be signed by all the dominions, by several of them or by one. All were to be signed in the name of the king, but none were to be negotiated save by the governments concerned. In the dominions the governors-general were to be considered as the personal representatives of the crown rather than of the British government. No longer were official communications from Britain to pass through the governors-general to the dominion governments, New Zealand alone excepted. Instead, the governments would communicate through recognized semi-diplomatic channels provided by the appointment of dominion high commissioners to London and British high commissioners to the dominion capitals. Before this absolute equality between the dominions and Britain, in status if not always in function, was achieved, Parliament had to repeal the Colonial Laws Validity Act of 1865. This had proclaimed invalid any law passed by a colony that conflicted with a law passed by Parliament. In 1931 the Statute of Westminster did this, stating that "no act of the British Parliament shall apply to any dominion unless the latter requests it."

The Imperial Economic Conference of 1932, at Ottawa, was intended to be the British answer to the world depression. The more enthusiastic participants, looking forward to free trade within the Empire-Commonwealth, sought reciprocal agreements to lower tariffs therein while retaining or raising those against the non-British world. Since most of their industries had been built up by protective tariffs, the dominions were unwilling to jeopardize them; but some intra-imperial trade pacts were concluded. Preferential rates given to British goods were automatically increased by raising dominion tariffs against outside countries. Britain in turn placed a tariff against foreign wheat and other agricultural products.

These advantages were refused to the Irish Free State, which immediately upon her formation in 1922 had registered her treaty with Britain with the League of Nations, thereby implying that the treaty was a pact concluded between independent countries. Membership in the League gave the Free State a chance which she sometimes seized to act against British interests. Nevertheless, there was little real friction until 1932 with the defeat of Cosgraves's moderate government. The extremist De Valera became president and attacked the oath of allegiance to the king, as stipulated in the Anglo-Irish treaty. Temporarily thwarted by the Irish senate in this, he did succeed in virtually abolishing the office of governor-general. After completely ignoring the latter he nominated an obscure workingman for the post. In finances it had been agreed that the Free State (now Eire), although not assuming any part of the British national debt was obligated to pay the land annuities due for money advanced in the past by the British treasury for the purchase of small homesteads (see page 480). It now refused to do so; nor would De Valera arbitrate as Britain suggested, if the arbitrator were chosen from within the Commonwealth. Instead he stopped payments and Britain raised the money by increasing the tariff against Ireland, to the distress of the agricultural interests, much of whose income had come from selling dairy products to her. The Irish electorate, however, continued to support De Valera. In 1935 a law defining citizenship was so drawn as to make it appear that a citizen of Eire was no longer, ipso facto, a British subject. In 1938, Britain agreed to give up her naval bases in Irish ports. By 1939 the Irish republican army was engaging in bombing outrages, both at home and in England. And so it went; Eire was the weakest link in the Commonwealth chain, though an essential one since the island lies athwart England's lines of communication.

One other nominal dominion also dropped out of the postwar sextet. In 1933 Newfoundland fell upon evil days; for the world depression proved a last straw to this island, long a prey to political dissension and to economic hardship. It asked to be reduced to the status of a crown colony. Britain generously advanced the much-needed money and assumed responsibility. In 1949 by a narrow margin Newfoundland voted to join Canada as the tenth Canadian province.

Italian Aggression in Ethiopia

Meanwhile in 1935, with German conditions near a dangerous pass and Japan, too, in defiant mood, Mussolini took what was widely believed to be the first step toward controlling the Mediterranean. Italy wanted the old native kingdom of Ethiopia (Abyssinia), a League of Nations member, to round out her colonies, Eritrea and Italian Somaliland; her excuse was border raids by Ethiopia. She relied upon Anglo-French need of her friendship because of German designs on Austria. The League, having already lost prestige by not taking action in Japanese aggression against China in Manchuria in 1931, and by the withdrawal from membership of Japan and Germany, had to do something to stop Mussolini if it expected to continue to function. As for Britain, Ethiopia bordered upon the Anglo-Egyptian Sudan, and Lake Tana there was essential for its irrigation.

Baldwin's cabinet decided to support Ethiopia through the League. The League met, and exhausted every means of reconciling Italy and Ethiopia. With the cessation of the summer rains, Italy began the invasion. The British garrisons at Malta and in Egypt were strengthened, and the

Admiralty brought into the Mediterranean a fleet overwhelmingly superior in tonnage, if not in speed, to the entire Italian navy. Then the League, acting under British advice, voted for economic sanctions, which meant virtually an economic boycott of Italy. Mussolini was furious; for Italy depended on other nations for many war materials, particularly petroleum.

In England people as a whole apparently approved this policy. The war scare gave Baldwin a superb opportunity to hold in November, 1935, the Parliamentary election which must legally have come by 1936 at the latest. The result was a foregone conclusion: Liberals, Laborites, and Conservatives all were agreed in favor of sanctions, and the government received approval of rearmament. The election resulted in 431 supporters for Baldwin, almost all Conservatives, with 185 in opposition. Labor managed to increase its membership by a large percentage, but the Liberals shrank further. England seemed to be returning to the old two-party system, with the Conservatives opposed by Laborites instead of by Liberals.

Soon afterward Sir Samuel Hoare, the Foreign Secretary, came to an understanding with the French government whereby Italy might be permitted a free hand in a considerable part of Ethiopia. A cry of shame went up in press and Parliament. Hoare resigned and was succeeded by Anthony Eden. Nevertheless Baldwin was unwilling to press the Italians hard without French support, and this was not noticeably forthcoming. The League applied sanctions, but not very stiff ones, the Italians continuing to import the all-important petroleum. The British fleet stayed ready for action off the coast of Egypt. The triumphant Italians, entering the Ethiopian capital, made it obvious that Italy could not be dislodged without war. Hoare seemed vindicated; and he returned to the cabinet as First Lord of the Admiralty. Shortly afterward England reluctantly gave up her policy of sanctions against Italy, thus tacitly recognizing the latter's conquest of Ethiopia.

With Britain and Italy at swords' points, Hitler quickly moved German troops into the demilitarized Rhine valley. France, demanding the support which England had promised at Locarno, found her lukewarm. Hitler was apparently not hostile to Britain; but he might soon seek the return of Germany's colonies; and he might possibly combine with Mussolini, and even perhaps with Japan.

The Axis "Have-Not" Threats

Whereas the twenties had witnessed a constant series of efforts toward peace, the thirties brought a recurrence of crises. The seven major powers seemed to fall into three groups: the troublemaking "have-nots," Germany, Italy, and Japan; the peace-desiring "haves," eager to maintain the status quo, which suited them, Britain, France, and, less closely involved, the United States; and in a mysterious class by itself, the Union of Socialist Soviet Republics. During 1936 the "have-nots" drew together in an Anti-Comintern Pact, allegedly aimed against communism. Germany and Italy first formed the so-called "Rome-Berlin Axis," to which Japan adhered a few weeks later. Britain and France, aware that they had everything to lose by wars, were drawn closer together by the repeated crises until they made a regular alliance in 1938. As for Russia, the enigma, the widespread distrust of her government and her economic setup made her still not quite respectable internationally.

Britain and France, in a cruel dilemma, had the choice of trying to nip these aggressive acts in the bud by force or threats of force or of trying to preserve the peace by "appeasement." Collective security by the united action of all the powers through the League of Nations was daily becoming less likely. The small nations were afraid of the covetous eye of Axis neighbors, and the larger ones never seemed to be ready to stand firm at the same time. In 1931 the United States sought to check the Japanese in Manchuria, but the others would not follow her; in Ethiopia France was not ready to support Britain on sanctions against Italy; and Britain held back when France might have stamped down reviving German armament. In the savage civil war begun in Spain in 1936 all three were inclined to a hands-off-policy even when they saw active aid from Italy and Germany ensuring victory to the reactionary rebels, while Russia helped the radical Loyalists. The Axis powers took full advantage of this hesitant attitude by never pushing their aggression far enough at any one time to force war. In England Anthony Eden was among those who demanded action before too much was lost, but was overruled by the so-called "appeasers."

Under the circumstances it seemed best to rearm, rapidly, extensively, and expensively. Particularly, the Royal Air Force was to be expanded, with thousands of fast fighter planes, for as Hoare warned, the threat of aerial bombing made the island kingdom vulnerable. Altogether, in the budget for 1936-1937, Parliament voted an increase of 30 per cent for national defense over the large appropriation of the year before and of some 400 per cent over that of 1911; yet this was far below the next year's budget and those thereafter.

King George V, who had given dependable leadership during these critical days, died in 1936. His eldest son and successor, Edward VIII, had long been popular throughout the world as the informal, charming, and sports-loving Prince of Wales, who nevertheless had taken his duties conscientiously and, in his almost constant travels, had made himself familiar with the lives and problems of his future subjects in all walks of life. Although the tremendous expenditures for armaments left the depressed classes in a subordinate place in the government's plans, they were not forgotten by their new king. At the launching of the new superliner named for his mother, for instance, Edward asked, "How do you reconcile a world that has produced this mighty ship with the slums we have just visited?" And again, on a visit to the forlorn region of abandoned mines in south Wales, he declared that something must be done. Altogether, in spite of economic ills and threats of war, it seemed to be a reign of unusual promise, with a popular king determined to improve the conditions under which his half-billion subjects lived.

Yet before ten months had passed, swift developments resulted in the first voluntary abdication in English history. According to Prime Minister Baldwin, no constitutional crisis (although many called it that) caused this decision, but rather it was Edward's wish to marry the woman of his choice, an American, twice divorced and therefore, in the cabinet's opinion, unacceptable to the British peoples. Forthwith his brother ascended the throne as George VI.

In the spring of 1937, Baldwin voluntarily relinquished the prime ministership to Neville Chamberlain, the Chancellor of the Exchequer. Tall, gaunt, and somber, Chamberlain had shown ability in finance, but he lacked the dynamic vigor of his father and even more the adroit diplomatic skill of his brother. The government still went under the name of "National," although, like the two preceding ministries, it was essentially Conservative.

About this time Japan suddenly intensified her drive against China. Without a declaration of war, she launched a determined attack into China proper, which brought her closer to British holdings than her earlier invasion of Manchuria. Britain's interests around Shanghai alone suffered a billion-dollar loss, and her prestige was dealt a severe blow, but again she took no decisive action.

Bloodshed in China and in the continuing bitter struggle in Spain was soon overshadowed by Hitler's intention to join to

Germany all contiguous areas occupied by German people. Many in predominantly German Austria, first on his list, had since 1919 preferred such a union to being merely "a capital and its suburbs." Italy had prevented this in 1934 (see pages 589, 608); but now, in the spring of 1938, no one lifted a hand to stop Germany from occupying Austria.

Democratic Czechoslovakia came next on Hitler's program. She had been an example of the self-determination of peoples, except for the Germans in the Sudeten Mountains, who had been included to form a strategic barrier between Germany and the Danube valley. France had promised to protect the Czechs, and Russia had agreed to help. Thus matters lay when Hitler proposed to annex the Sudeten region in September, 1938.

Munich and World War II

Three times within two weeks Chamberlain flew to Germany to reason with Hitler. On the third trip, war was averted by a conference at Munich of Hitler, Chamberlain, the French premier, and the Italian foreign minister; but the Russians and the intimately concerned Czechs were not invited. The result was humiliating acquiescence in Hitler's annexation of the Sudetenland. His statement that this was the end of his territorial desires was the one encouraging note. Chamberlain returned to England, announcing that he had achieved "peace in our time." The House of Commons upheld him by a vote of 266 to 144; but many were shocked at his failure to resist the Hitler terms. Eden had already resigned in anger over appeasement.

German aggression did not stop but took a new and infinitely graver turn. In the spring of 1939 German troops marched into non-German Prague, Czechoslovakia's capital. No longer could any nation feel safe from German ambition; Poland, in particular, was aware of her peril in view of the bitter German resentment concerning the

Leaders at the fateful Munich Conference, September 29, 1938: at the left, Chamberlain and Daladier, who backed down; at right, the Fascist leaders, Hitler and Mussolini.

corridor to Danzig, which cut East Prussia from the rest of Germany.

The unjustifiable attack upon the Czechs ended appeasement in Britain. Sir Edward Grey had been criticized for not taking a vigorous stand in 1914 (see pages 565 ff.). Heavy pressure from labor, from Eden, from Churchill, from Lloyd George, and from many others now pushed Chamberlain into declaring before the Commons that if Poland's independence was threatened and her "government accordingly felt it vital to resist with their national forces, the Government would feel themselves bound at once to lend to the Polish government all support in their power." These fighting words were to be put to the proof before the year was out.

But after his Munich victory, they apparently did not worry Hitler. Within the month he denounced his 1934 non-aggression pact with Poland and his 1935 naval agreement with Britain. His Axis partner, Italy, meanwhile invaded Albania across the Adriatic.

Britain pursued a new vigorous course of developing a peace front. To Rumania, to Greece, and to other anxious nations, she extended guarantees similar to that given to Poland. France stood with her in this, and together they began to integrate plans for a possible war. During that troubled spring England decided upon compulsory military service, despite some labor opposition. George VI and his queen, who had already visited France, now went to Canada and the United States to build up good will.

Russia shocked the peace front in August by making a commercial agreement with Germany, followed it four days later by a nonaggression pact. This startling reversal of policy ended British and French expectations that they could rely again, as in 1914, upon Russia's help. Russia had some cause for this action: she had not been invited to Munich; Poland had refused to let Russian troops defend the Polish-German frontier; and France and Britain had been dilatory in sending a military mission to Russia to discuss co-operation.

Hitler, now free to deal with Poland, wasted no time. After a hasty ultimatum, which Poland did not have time to act upon, his troops attacked early in the morning of September 1; and the Second World War was under way.

England sent a note saying that either hostilities must be stopped at once or she would carry out her pledge to Poland. When no answer had come by September 3, Chamberlain broadcast to the nation that Hitler could be stopped only by force; that the situation had become intolerable; and that England was resolved to stand by her pledged word. At noon Parliament received the formal announcement of the state of war. The French declaration followed a few hours later.

Chapter Thirty-two

"Blood, Toil, Tears, and Sweat"

The superlatives used to describe the first World War are inadequate for the magnitude of the second. For the British it was a tragedy from which even "total victory" did not bring back the prestige and power that had long been theirs. A new and stronger mistress of the seas and air, the United States, emerged from the holocaust; while in Europe, the balance of power recently endangered by Nazi Germany now tended to be even more out of alignment with the growing dominance of Soviet Russia.

The conflict lasted from September 1, 1939, to September 1, 1945, a year and nine months longer than the first war, which had seemed to tax human endurance to the limit. This time Britain and her Commonwealth stood almost alone during one terrible year, with France collapsed and neither Russia nor the United States yet allies. The German air force rained destruction upon old and young, women and children, homes and factories. Little short of miraculous did it seem to those beyond the seas, who watched this dread assault, that Britain escaped invasion.

Yet with all the accelerated horror of the new warfare, Britain's dead were fewer than those in World War I, even with some 60,000 civilian victims of air power, of whom there had been but a few before.

Winston Churchill vowed that this time Britain would not let war wipe out a whole generation of her young men; and that did not happen again. But capital, built up over the generations, was blasted into rubble. Not only was property destroyed at home, but England's Victorian heritage of invested wealth across the seas was dissipated in the desperate rush for armament credits.

This was, geographically, truly a world war. Whereas the bulk of Britain's fighting in World War I had been along the trench line of the western front in Europe, this time the whole long middle years of the contest found major fronts in the sandy wastes of North Africa or in the distant jungle terrain of Malaya, Burma, and New Guinea. For three years, England was unable to attain a foothold in western Europe; only at the beginning and at the end were British armies fighting on their centuries-old battleground (see page 277).

Technologically, the unheard-of and the fantastic in 1939 were commonplace by 1945. Whereas the forms of ships and weapons changed relatively little during the first war; in this one, soldiers and sailors were having to try out one strange gadget after another, and never knew, from day to day, whether the enemy had found something better. Fighter planes of amazing speed and bombers of ever-increasing range and capacity made aviation constantly more effective. Carriers at sea brought air power close to enemy shores and into every phase of naval fighting. On land, tanks, coupled with motorized infantry and artillery units and used in conjunction with planes, enabled ground forces to hit harder and faster. Whole air-borne divisions of parachute troops radically increased the mobility of armies. Amphibious warfare, with newly devised landing craft, enabled navies to put men and equipment ashore even in shallow water. Rockets greatly extended fire power, both afloat and ashore. Radar became an almost human "seeing eye" for both offense and defense in sea and air warfare. And finally to a stunned world came the atomic bomb, frightful in its original destructive form and carrying threats of infinitely far worse to come.

Actually, there were two fairly distinct contests in World War II: one with Germany and one with Japan. Although many nations came in on the Allied side at one time or another, a large part were belligerents in name only. The main burden of the fighting, as before, was carried by a few countries. Britain alone was in the war from start to finish, and with her stood most of her empire. Probably their greatest contribution was the firm stand during that terrible year in which they fought alone. Russia wore down German manpower in a bloody war of attrition at appalling cost to herself, as well as to the Germans. The Americans with their tremendous offerings of men, ships, and material sustained most of the Pacific war and also contributed heavily to the blows in Europe. But France collapsed in the first year, and China was able to do no more than drag through, under crushing handicaps. On the axis side Germany took the worst punishment, Italy lasted only three years, and Japan surrendered before her home islands were invaded.

Blitzkrieg

World War II represented another turning point in military annals. According to the American military attaché at Berlin, who witnessed Hitler's invasion of Poland in its first weeks, a revolution had occurred in military science. The last war had degenerated into a gigantic siege because the weapons of defense were developed beyond the power of those of attack. At the same time, so close was the balance that men died by tens of thousands, both charging and defending the trench systems of that day. The French and the Germans had drawn opposite strategic conclusions from that deadly but inconclusive warfare, where it took four years to get a real breakthrough. The French, deciding the defense had not been strong enough, put their faith in the costly, supposedly impregnable Maginot Line. Thus they hoped to sit out the next war safely in its shelter while the enemy did the dying under its defensive fire. The Germans, on the other hand, felt the attack had not been strong enough, so they developed fast offensive methods, to be known as *Blitzkrieg* or lightning war. Now, for the first time, motorized, armored equipment and aviation were synchronized with the old infantry and artillery to return warfare to a mobile and offensive status. In this development of new techniques and weapons the Germans, stripped of major armament at Versailles, were not handicapped, like their rivals, by having usable, too-good-to-scrap, yet obsolescent material on hand. The new strategy, more reminiscent of the days of Marlborough and the Napoleonic Wars than of the last war, could catch the Allies napping from Poland to France in that first year.

German Invasion of Poland

This new Blitzkrieg struck Poland before dawn on September 1, when swarms of German planes swept over the border to smash the Polish air force, still grounded at its airfields. The Polish troops, drawn up along the frontiers to fight the conventional defensive action, were pierced at one place after another by the Panzer mechanized forces, which then dashed behind the lines to disrupt headquarters and communications. Droves of planes constantly bombed the jammed roads, bridges, and railroad centers to isolate reserves. The Poles fought bravely but were helpless in the destruction wrought by this new type of warfare.

Sixteen days later a new enemy, Russia, moved in from the east. Warsaw, the besieged capital, surrendered before the month was out and Poland was divided between her conquerors. An almost complete news black-out closed down but later terrible tales leaked out of the fate meted out to the Poles, particularly the Jews.

About all Britain and France could do for Poland was to drop a few bombs around the Kiel Canal, and attack German outposts. Consequently, Hitler, declaring that he had "no war aims against Great Britain," suggested that since the purpose in declaring war had not been accomplished, hostilities might well cease. England rebuffed this peace feeler and others which followed.

For the next six months it was pretty much a war in name only. Daily the Basel express ran between the near-by bristling guns of the French Maginot Line and the German West Wall. The guns were fired only occasionally, inflicting slight damage. German loud-speakers worried the French command by their uncanny knowledge of troop movements and of the intimate home affairs of individual soldiers, whom they taunted by name. The Royal Air Force flew sometimes far over Germany to let loose showers of pamphlets warning the Germans that they did not have a chance. Such was the "phony war," or Sitzkrieg.

The War at Sea, 1939

At sea, again Britain's prime concern, each side picked up its maritime offensive about where it had dropped it in 1918.

Once again the royal navy swept most of the German merchant marine off the seas, as superliners rushed to safety. A rigid blockade was resumed to strangle German imports and exports (see page 576). Both sides laid mines freely, with Germany's new magnetic mine causing concern until the British found ways to neutralize its effects. This time the British lost no time in establishing convoys to safeguard their merchantmen (see page 584). The U-boats were back with improvements which rather nullified the effectiveness of the new submarine detectors and other devices of the royal navy. Larger and with a wider cruising range, they used detectors, too, and no longer had to keep their periscopes in sight. Enemy surface raiders were at large. The airplane brought many new complications, even menacing merchantmen in port. Also the sea lanes were threatened more extensively than before as the war engulfed the Mediterranean and the Pacific. Through March, 1940, the losses from U-boats was moderate compared with past and future sinkings.

Enemy surface raiding was a different story that year. Germany, stripped of her fleet and forbidden at Versailles to build any warships over ten thousand tons, lacked enough capital ships for another Jutland (see pages 579, 587), so she no longer had to conserve battle strength but could scatter her units to break up convoys. Particularly threatening were her three so-called "pocket battleships," a type of super-cruiser with guns which could outrange those of any ordinary cruiser and with speed enough to run away from any battleship. This same combination had made American superfrigates so effective in the War of 1812 (see page 381), and then, too, had forced some of the royal navy's most powerful capital ships to be on convoy patrol and lesser warships to cruise in groups. The *Graf Spee* had only nine freighters to her credit when she was crippled by three British cruisers, hunting as a pack off South

America in December, 1939. Her eleven-inch guns should have been able to sink all three of them, but they boldly slid in close enough to use their guns of shorter range. She sought neutral refuge in Montevideo, but Uruguay, in accordance with international law, ordered her to leave within the brief prescribed period or be interned. After calling Hitler by transatlantic telephone, her captain ordered her scuttled. Except for the distant war between Russia and little Finland, that was the principal dramatic event of the six strange months of Sitzkrieg.

The Commonwealth War Effort

Beyond the seas the British Commonwealth of Nations quickly joined the war, although there were some marked differences in the reaction toward this step. In 1914, dominions and crown colonies had been regarded as automatically at war after England's declaration. In 1939 that held true only for the scattered units of the dependent empire, such as Jamaica, St. Helena, Hong Kong. The independent status of the dominions had been made definitely clear by their signing the peace treaties in 1919 and by the Statute of Westminster (see pages 593, 616). Yet now they all had various ideas about the technicalities of their status.

In Australia war was declared by executive action an hour after Chamberlain's announcement of war by radio. The dominion prime minister boadcast that "Great Britain has declared war and, as a result, Australia is also at war." New Zealand also was at England's side within a few hours.

Canada and South Africa, on the other hand, waited for action by their dominion parliaments. In a two-day debate at Ottawa a few radicals and French Canadians railed against being dragged into an imperialistic struggle, but it was another French Canadian who made the most spirited plea for war. The decision was never in doubt; war was voted by an overwhelming chorus.

South Africa's decision had come a few days sooner, but only after sharp dissension. The motion of neutrality made by the anti-British prime minister, Hertzog, was voted down, 80 to 67, and by a similar vote, a motion for participation by the pro-British Smuts was passed. Hertzog asked for an appeal to the country, but the governor-general refused, and accepted Hertzog's resignation. Smuts, called in as prime minister, at once proclaimed a state of war.

This rapid adherence of those four dominions had great importance, for they contained nearly one third of the white population of the British Commonwealth, as compared with barely one fourth in the previous war. Leaving out Southern Ireland and the dark-skinned people of South Africa, the United Kingdom had numbered some 41 million in 1914 and the four dominions barely 14 million (see page 546). Now, as against the United Kingdom's 47 million, the dominions totaled nearly 22 million. Although the question arose as to whether their forces should be used overseas, the spring of 1940 found Australian and New Zealand troops in the Middle East, and Canadians in England. Canada, whose navy heretofore had been negligible, began to build one to patrol the North Atlantic. She undertook also a tremendous program of training her own airmen, along with some from Britain and the other dominions. A small New Zealand cruiser already had helped to defeat the *Graf Spee,* and several Australian cruisers were patrolling the western Pacific.

Despite Nationalist opposition, India was in the war the very first day by action of the viceroy. The Nationalist protests continued vehemently, coupled with a demand for independence, but to no avail. Indian troops were quickly dispatched to various danger spots from North Africa and Aden around to Singapore and Hong Kong. Troubled days lay ahead with the chronic friction, ever growing worse, between India and the British *raj* (see page 650).

Eire, still somewhat legally within the perimeter of the British Commonwealth, stuck to neutrality from first to last. Northern Ireland (Ulster) was, of course, automatically in the war as part of the United Kingdom. President De Valera had already announced, early in 1939, that Eire had decided to be neutral in case of war, adding later, "We know, of course, that should the attack come from a power other than Great Britain, Great Britain, in her own interests, must help us repel it." This would handicap England severely in combating the submarine menace. Her abandonment in 1938 of her south-coast naval bases (see page 617), centers of antisubmarine activity in the last war, would be keenly felt, for the "Southwest Approaches," off the Irish coast, were again to be one of the U-boats' happiest hunting grounds. Air bases likewise were denied to the British.

Civilian Defense

At home, the nightmare of air attack that had hung over the nation for at least six years now came close. The whole nation went feverishly to work on detailed plans for defense against the expected fury. Planes were designed and constructed; rings of airfields were built to protect the cities; and the fliers of the Royal Air Force underwent the rigorous training that was to pay dividends. Some two million civilian volunteers, men and women of all ages and of all social strata, commenced tedious, and often arduous, training as air-raid wardens, plane-spotters, fire-fighters, demolition corpsmen, extra policemen, motor-transport drivers, first-aid assistants, stretcher-bearers, and hospital and rescue workers of every sort: all the vast army needed to warn of air attack and to help a city dig itself out after one. Parliament authorized more than two million steel air raid shelters for use in courts and gardens, and thousands of homemade ones were built, while the London subway tunnels were to prove a haven for countless sleeping families year after year.

Powerfully protected underground quarters, deep under Whitehall, served as an impregnable "nerve center" for the War Cabinet and the heads of vital services. Precious historical documents and art treasures were hidden in distant regions. Through some two thousand nights the British lived in darkness, in a rigid black-out to make night bombings more difficult. Whole families later evacuated London and the industrial centers; but at first chiefly children were sent to remote villages. Some went to America, but the U-boat sinking of a westbound ship with child refugees aboard caused postponement of large-scale migration overseas.

The civilian volunteers most closely connected with the military were some thirty thousand men and women who day and night manned the posts of the aircraft warning system. By telephone, their warnings of approaching enemy planes went to secret filter stations, which plotted the route from the successive reports; notified the nearest airfield and antiaircraft batteries and the probable target area. Every minute, almost every second, counted in sounding the alarm. Earlier warning even before planes came into sight came later from radar, an electronic device, long kept secret. Spotters were still needed to report whether a plane was friend or foe.

The British had not forgotten their hunger in the last war, and with U-boats already at work, food-rationing went into effect in January, 1940. Grain was no longer the acute need, with a huge reserve and extra acreage; but for a balanced diet much other food had to be imported. Also at this time, the need for foreign credits was another reason for rationing. As Winston Churchill, again back as First Lord of the Admiralty, explained it: ". . . we wish to save every ton of imports, to increase our output of munitions . . . to maintain and extend our export trade, thus gaining the foreign credits wherewith to bring more munitions of war. We mean to regulate every ton . . . carried across the sea and make sure . . . it is carried solely for . . . victory."

German Invasion of Norway and Denmark

That first winter of the war passed without the dreaded raids. But suddenly with the spring the Blitzkrieg was let loose on Western Europe, seven months after its tryout in Poland. In a single day, April 9, 1940, the Germans seized Denmark and invaded Norway, both neutrals in the last war. Denmark was occupied in a matter of hours; except for the palace guard in Copenhagen, the stunned people did not resist. Norway was a different story, for the sea lay between. The simultaneous invasions had been planned with amazing detail. Naval forces, which eluded the British, seized six of Norway's chief ports at one stroke, and were instantly reinforced by troops hidden in the holds of innocent-looking freighters. Quickly airfields were seized, and more troops, planes, and some mechanized equipment came over from Germany. The Norwegian army, such as it was, put up what fight it could.

It looked at first glance as if the royal navy should have been able to save Norway. Its attention was focused there, against Norway's protests it had entered her territorial waters on the day before the invasion to mine them. The port of Narvik, in the far north, was captured, and a few confused encounters were fought; but with air control, the Germans were not wholly dependent on the sea for the conquest of this sparsely populated and weakly prepared land. Within a week a British expeditionary force, without proper air coverage or anti-aircraft guns, landed near Trondheim; but German planes and armored equipment made short work of their attempt to struggle inland. By May 1 they were homeward bound, in failure. Fortunately most of Norway's excellent merchant marine escaped, a godsend to England in her coming dependence on shipping.

Dunkirk and the Fall of France

Nine days later, the *Blitzkrieg* was launched with tremendous force toward France. The Netherlands, Belgium, and Luxembourg were the first victims of that campaign, which Hitler promised his armies would "decide the fate of the German nation for the next thousand years."

The Netherlands, overrun, surrendered in four days; Rotterdam was leveled in a merciless bombing. A supposedly impregnable Belgian fortress fell to paratroopers and engineers who had practiced its capture on a carefully made duplicate. This opened the way for an advantageous attack by the Germans on the Allied armies in Belgium. The British and French had hurried there to prevent the Germans from concentrating their striking force against France in the powerful right-wing movement which they had used in 1914; but the Germans had new plans (see page 568).

The various Allied armies, deficient in planes and tanks, did not have a chance against this efficient war machine. Britain had about a quarter-million troops across the Channel. Belgium was much better prepared than the Netherlands, but that was not saying much. Great hopes were placed in the large French army—generally called, not so long before, the best in the world. But even with her faith in the Maginot Line, France had failed to continue, on the same scale, that powerful series of defenses, northward from Sedan into the flat country to the sea, relying over-much on Belgium's new defense line. Even in staff work the Allies were deficient. Belgium had refused this time to compromise her neutrality by any prewar conferences, and so, too, had the Netherlands; but even the British and French had left their own staff work in a state of uncertainty and flux.

Now came the German master stroke with the main thrust around Sedan, where the west end of the Maginot Line joined the weaker defenses. Through the Forest of

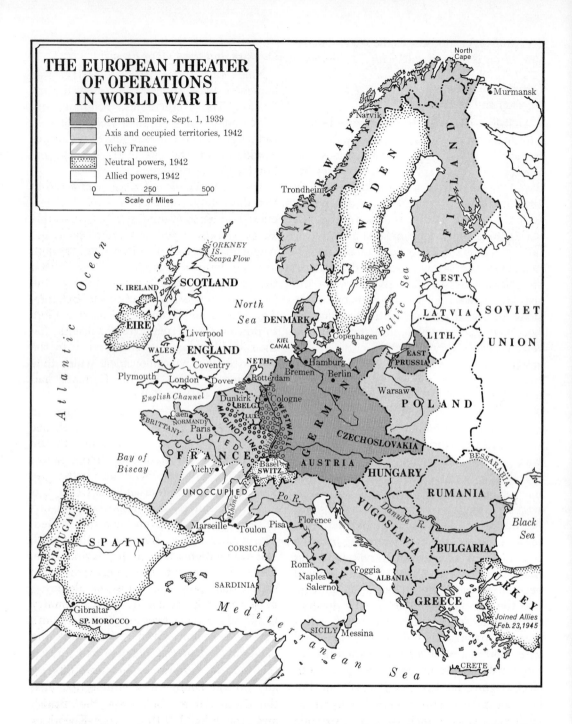

THE EUROPEAN THEATER OF OPERATIONS IN WORLD WAR II

German Empire, Sept. 1, 1939

Axis and occupied territories, 1942

Vichy France

Neutral powers, 1942

Allied powers, 1942

0   250   500
Scale of Miles

North Cape

Murmansk

Narvik

Trondheim

N O R W A Y

S W E D E N

F I N L A N D

ORKNEY IS.
Scapa Flow

SCOTLAND

N. IRELAND

EIRE

Liverpool

WALES   ENGLAND
Coventry

Plymouth   London   Dover

English Channel

Atlantic Ocean

North Sea   DENMARK

Copenhagen

Baltic Sea

EST.

LATVIA   SOVIET

LITH.   UNION

EAST PRUSSIA

KIEL CANAL

NETH.   Hamburg
Bremen   Berlin

Warsaw

Dunkirk
BELG.   Cologne
Caen   LUX.
NORMANDY   WESTWALL
BRITTANY   Paris
MAGINOT LINE

P O L A N D

Rotterdam

G E R M A N Y

CZECHOSLOVAKIA

BESSARABIA

Bay of Biscay

O C C U P I E D   F R A N C E

Vichy

Basel
SWITZ.

AUSTRIA

HUNGARY

RUMANIA

UNOCCUPIED

Rhône R.

Po R.

Danube R.

Black Sea

Marseille   Toulon

Pisa   Florence

Y U G O S L A V I A

BULGARIA

P O R T U G A L

S P A I N

CORSICA

Rome
Naples
Salerno

ALBANIA

Foggia

T U R K E Y

SARDINIA

Joined Allies
Feb. 23, 1945

Gibraltar
SP. MOROCCO

I T A L Y

GREECE

M e d i t e r r a n e a n

SICILY   Messina

CRETE

S e a

Ardennes, weakly defended because the French thought it impassible for major troop movements, hurried two German mechanized columns to Sedan. From there they began to disrupt everything behind the main Allied lines.

Another race to the sea was on; and this time the Germans won (see page 569). With unsurpassed speed their Panzer divisions, preceded by clouds of Stuka bombers, swept in a great arc. Disregarding Paris they were intent on separating the French divisions

The Dunkirk evacuation: long lines of allied soldiers waiting on the sands to be taken off by the rescuing vessels.

from their Belgian and British allies. Reaching the Somme the Germans followed its course almost to the Channel. Turning north they rushed on Calais and continued up the coast, thus drawing an iron ring around the Belgian and British armies. In the "Battle of the Pockets," the British and Belgians, with some French, were trapped in one large pocket; the rest of the French, in a number of smaller ones. The Belgians surrendered, exposing the British flank; it seemed as though the British must do likewise, since the French commander was powerless to break through to their aid. With fresh German forces pressing on them from east, west, and south into an hourly constricting pocket around the coastal town of Dunkirk, escape was apparently impossible.

The "miracle of Dunkirk" it was called, that astonishing evacuation of 338,000 troops from a seemingly hopeless trap on exposed beaches. Never had the royal navy

saved the British army from more certain annihilation. But the navy could not have done it had not Britain's outnumbered Royal Air Force been concentrated here to provide an "umbrella" against the mighty Luftwaffe. The whole amazing nine-day operation was under the direction of the navy, whose vessels rescued most of that force. Just about everything that floated, a strange mongrel assortment of some six hundred vessels were rushed across the Channel to ferry the soldiers home. With German bombs and shells falling around them, the interminable queue of waiting soldiers waded out shoulder-deep to be hauled into the rescue craft, which came and went, time and again, through enemy-infested waters while air battles raged overhead. Of these third of a million soldiers, nearly a third were "lifted" by destroyers and torpedo boats, a quarter by liners serving as transports, and nearly another quarter by minesweepers and fishing boats. But most dramatic were the civilian amateurs whom the navy had mustered for the all-out effort. In their own small motor boats—203 of them —they carried at least five thousand across to England and they ferried countless others from shore to the larger ships, while twenty-seven private yachts, some manned by the navy, rescued another five thousand. All but thirty thousand of those troops were saved. Without a breathing spell came the generally overlooked sequel to Dunkirk, down the French coast, where the navy took off 200,000 more British and Allies.

The defeat to British arms was none the less a stunning one. Only the men returned from Dunkirk: all their tanks, artillery, and even many rifles were left behind. And precious little of such ordnance was there at home. England would have been almost helpless had the Germans managed to land, but they chose to attack France. The British had no foothold left in the whole of Western Europe, save for isolated Gibraltar, at the mercy of the uncertain Spaniards. For three years to come no British troops were able to land for more than hit-and-run raids.

Within three weeks France surrendered to the Germans. This swift collapse astounded the world in 1940, as had the valiant French rally at the Marne in 1914 (see page 569). In Hitler's renewed drive into France herself, the Maginot line was enveloped and attacked from the rear; and Paris, declared an open city, fell undamaged to the enemy. The disorganized French forces fled southward, disputing the roads with hordes of frantic civilians under the machine-gun fire of low-flying German planes.

Meanwhile, in the week after Dunkirk, Mussolini threw Italy into the war. As in 1915, Italy had waited until she thought she had picked the winning side. Confident that France was falling and that England would soon follow, Mussolini hoped by this "stab in the back" to annex some French territory with a minimum of effort and danger.

Winston Churchill, Prime Minister

In those dark days of May and June began the ministry of Winston Churchill which lasted until the German surrender. The Norway fiasco caused England "to change horses in the middle of the stream." Chamberlain's government, although called "National," was essentially Conservative, for the Laborites and Liberals had declined to join his reorganized ministry on the first day of war. Now the discontent with what even some Conservatives considered inept leadership was unleashed. In the Commons, a Conservative quoted Cromwell's dismissal speech to the Long Parliament: "You have sat too long here for any good you have been doing. Depart, I say, and let us have done with you." By the narrow margin of 281 to 200, Chamberlain escaped a formal vote of censure, but he resigned a few days later.

In Churchill, Britain had a superlative war leader without whom she might never have weathered the storm. He had already sampled eight cabinet posts and more than one political party in his colorful but far from tranquil political past (see page 604). He had been Edward VIII's only champion of consequence. "Brilliant, versatile, and by some considered unstable" had been the earlier verdict; the brilliance and versatility remained, but "tough, forceful, dogged," were now better words for this vigorous and undaunted leader of forlorn hopes. In his late sixties he still had the fresh vision which had caused him to cut military red tape to have tanks built from Admiralty funds in 1914, and his old flair for the dramatic in strategy (see page 574). His mastery of "the arrogance and splendor of Elizabethan language," which had made him a writer of high distinction, had long enlivened Commons debate. Now he warned the Commons: "I have nothing to offer but blood, toil, tears, and sweat."

Under him the Laborites and Liberals consented to join in a real coalition government. He retained the small War Cabinet of 1916, revived by Chamberlain (see page 582). It eventually numbered nine including the Laborites: Clement Attlee, Lord Privy Seal and the leader of Commons until he became deputy prime minister; and Ernest Bevin, Minister of Labor and National Service. Churchill, with his old desire to have his say in high strategic councils, kept the role of Minister of Defense himself and was also inclined to take over many of the functions of Foreign Secretary.

The week before France collapsed, Churchill flew to Tours, the temporary capital, to discuss the French request for release from the agreement not to make a separate peace. After this conference came the amazing proposal from England that the two nations link themselves in a Franco-British union. But France sued for peace; old Marshal Pétain, the defender of Verdun in 1916, became premier. Most threatening to England of the severe terms was the German occupation of three fifths of France, including Paris, the industrial north, and the whole west coast. As for the unoccupied two fifths of France, Pétain set up his government at Vichy, and Pierre Laval, an unscrupulous former premier, saw to it that the co-operation with the Germans was close. Yet in the French colonial empire and on the seas were elements far from Vichy's control.

Britain quickly raised a standard to which might rally those Frenchmen who wanted to keep on fighting. Furthermore she recognized the new "Free French" government, an exile group headed by General Charles de Gaulle, whose prewar writings on mechanized warfare had been neglected by all save German readers. Thus every general, admiral, or colonial governor in Africa, Syria, Indo-China, and the Caribbean could follow his conscience or his interests, and still pride himself upon being a loyal Frenchman. Some stood apart, however, and joined neither Vichy nor the new Cross of Lorraine.

Britain felt she must take a rather high hand with the French navy with its powerful units, in view of its threat to her precarious situation on the seas. The armistice terms stipulated that they should not be used by the Germans or Italians, but such a stipulation was not to be trusted. Some French warships accepted her invitation to come over to British ports; others refused, particularly a strong squadron at Oran in Algeria. When its admiral ignored an ultimatum from a British fleet, British gunfire then sank or crippled most of his ships. The Vichy government broke diplomatic relations at once, but within the week another French squadron, at Alexandria, agreed to demilitarize itself to avoid a similar fate. At Dakar, on the western tip of Africa, however, the pro-Vichy governor beat off a British naval force accompanied by Free French troops, but not until a daring boat crew had immobilized the great battleship *Richelieu* by blowing out her stern.

Although at Toulon a goodly number of French warships were safe from British interference, the German occupation of the French coast was the real worry. Germany's navy could no longer be cooped up in the North Sea; submarines and surface vessels had many new bases, often very close to England. Worst of all, enemy planes could take off from just across the Channel to threaten the sea approaches and Britain herself. Guns from that French coast could throw shells into Dover; and in this dreadful year other grave complications were multiplying in North Africa and other distant regions.

To most outsiders it seemed next to impossible that Britain could long survive. Churchill, however, refused to be dismayed; he told his fellow countrymen:

We shall go on to the end . . . we shall defend our Island, whatever the cost may be, we shall fight on the beaches, we shall fight on the landing grounds, we shall fight in the fields and in the streets, we shall fight in the hills; we shall never surrender, and even if, which I do not for a moment believe, this Island or a large part of it were subjugated and starving, then our Empire beyond the seas, armed and guarded by the British Fleet, would carry on the struggle.

And in another speech, he urged:

Let us therefore brace ourselves to our duties, and so bear ourselves that, if the British Empire and Commonwealth last for a thousand years, men will say, "This was their finest hour."

"Operation Sea Lion"

Once again England was keyed to meet destruction; but the summer days came and went after Dunkirk, and still the Germans paused. Some scattered raids had followed but they were mild. Not until many years later was the full story of that escape from invasion made public. Had Germany sent a few divisions across the narrow strait directly after Dunkirk, while the British were still dazed, invasion might have succeeded. But she had no plans for such an immediate follow-up. Not until six weeks after Dunkirk, did Hitler announce: "As England, in spite of the hopelessness of her military position, has so far shown herself unwilling to come to any compromise, I have decided to begin to prepare for, and if necessary to carry out an invasion of England."[1] His projected "Operation Sea Lion" called for close inter-service cooperation. The army was to provide some 200,000 men as the invading force. The Navy assembled some 3500 barges, towboats, and other small vessels in the "invasion ports." The planes of the Luftwaffe were to provide the essential preliminary bombing. But the three services were scarcely on speaking terms, and the naval chief was more and more convinced that the idea was impracticable. The royal navy had dozens of destroyers and other vessels on constant watch, a much more

[1] Peter Fleming, *Operation Sea Lion*, (Simon & Shuster, 1957), p. 15.

effective deterrent than the English home guards who were organizing as they had been when the Armada and Napoleon's Grand Army threatened. British bombers sank some of the invasion flotilla in their crowded ports, but the main reason why the rest never sailed was that the aerial "Battle of Britain" failed to secure control of the Channel and the southeast coast.

The "Battle of Britain"

The storm struck on August 8, 1940. Hundreds of German planes launched a terrific, all-out attack on shipping and ports and airfields along the southeast coast. Thus began three months of a fiery trial that defies description; after that came seven months of intensive night bombings to wear down still further the heroic survivors.

Yet the enemy found no easy victory. Adequately warned and superbly manned, the Royal Air Force took a tremendous toll. One day, for instance, out of more than a thousand German planes, 158 were shot down by the defending fighters and 17 more by antiaircraft fire; the R.A.F. lost only 34 planes, and half the fliers were saved. Not only did the Germans fail to obtain air mastery to safeguard an invasion, but they also did not smash enough of the well-scattered airfields to halt the angry swarms of fighters, which rose day after day to meet the oncoming Luftwaffe.

In this crucial test of the R.A.F., the quality of its pilots and fighter planes made up for its being seriously outnumbered. Britain's defensive hopes were pinned on their two types of single seater monoplanes, easily maneuverable and well armed, with speeds of some 350 miles an hour. They were more than a match not only for the slow and lightly armored enemy bombers, but even for their fast fighters. The Germans had concentrated on a tactical air force, designed to co-operate with the tanks and other ground forces. Their dive bombers were less well adapted for the work ahead over Britain.

The London "Blitz": buildings in Ludgate Street near St. Paul's Cathedral.

After a month of pounding the southeast coast, the Germans made their first great daylight raid on London itself; thereafter the capital sustained thirty-eight such attacks throughout September into October. The bombs themselves and the fires which followed destroyed docks, factories, railroads, and electric and gas installations, together with thousands of homes. If the Germans hoped to break British morale, they failed. From the wreckage and debris, volunteers pulled out the dead, rushed the wounded to such hospitals as survived, and tried to fight the fires amid broken water mains, while millions kept up their daily routine at office or store, all with amazing fortitude. In the first three months of the battle of Britain the Luftwaffe lost 2375 planes and their crews; the R.A.F., only 375 pilots and a somewhat larger number of planes. The Germans could not keep up this rate of loss, and by the end of October they

had abandoned daylight raids, which meant also the abandonment of immediate invasion. The R.A.F. had saved Britain; "never in the field of human conflict was so much owed by so many to so few," Churchill declared.

The Luftwaffe turned to night bombing, which the British fighters could not intercept as efficiently. Throughout that winter and the following spring, night after night was made hideous with the sirens, the anti-aircraft fire, the falling of bombs, and fire. The City, London's financial district, was almost wiped out by a terrible shower of incendiary bombs, with St. Paul's Cathedral spared almost miraculously. Birmingham and the ports from Southampton to Plymouth and Bristol and Liverpool were visited and revisited. Coventry was devastated by the first of the so-called saturation raids, eleven hours of bombing by successive trips of four hundred planes. Finally, when Germany turned to new attacks in Crete and Russia, the raids died down. German bombs killed 23,767 civilians in 1940 and 20,881 in 1941; thereafter the score fell off to 3236 in 1942 and 2367 in 1943. Many more were seriously injured, and the casualty list from accidents in the black-out was appalling.

Meanwhile, in the battle of the Atlantic, the bright outlook of March, 1940, had turned black by mid June. With the whole western coast of Europe from the North Cape to Spain in German hands, the Mediterranean too had become another perilous sea lane. The enemy U-boats now had their choice of harbors from Norway to the Bay of Biscay, including ports just across the Channel. Planes were also utilizing those same bases to blast shipping in British ports and even to menace it several hundred miles at sea. After Dunkirk, England had less than 150 available destroyers in contrast to the 781 in Allied use towards the end of the first war. Without this valuable escort vessel the convoy system deteriorated; and the use of seaplanes instead was helpful only comparatively near shore. Antisubmarine defense was further badly handicapped by Eire's neutrality.

From the toll of 98,000 tons sunk in March, there was a rapid rise to 538,000 tons in June. Yet, as in 1917, a steady flow of oil, food, munitions, and other essentials must pour into Britain, or she was finished. And to the rescue, once again, came the United States, not only to be the arsenal of democracy, but also to see that those precious cargoes reached their destination however distant.

American Assistance

Churchill had closed his speech after Dunkirk with the hope "until, in God's good time, the New World, with all its power and might, steps forth to the rescue and the liberation of the old." He was cultivating close community of interest with President Franklin Delano Roosevelt, who was to prove England's most useful supporter

beyond the seas. Much earlier than Wilson, in the first war, Roosevelt began to place abundant resources at England's disposal in spite of the determination of a large portion of the American public not to be drawn into another war "to save the British Empire." Most Americans, however, were prepared to go a good way in that direction so long as they did not become involved in a "shooting war." The amazing events of May and June made them fear the elimination of the royal navy, and the possibility of Germans in Bermuda and Newfoundland. Congress authorized a tremendous "Two-Ocean Navy," which was soon followed by compulsory military service. By then, the nation had gone far enough on the road to war to accept the presidential announcement that fifty overage American destroyers had been given Britain in exchange for long-term leases of eight western-Atlantic colonial bases. These stretched from Newfoundland to British Guiana, with sites in Bermuda, the Bahamas, Jamaica, Antigua, St. Lucia, and Trinidad.

The fifty destroyers helped somewhat. During the winter months the sinkings dropped to roughly two ships a day; but with the spring of 1941 they rose again. The situation was fully as gloomy as the higher toll of 1917 because the longer duration of this crisis meant a greater total drain on shipping. The home waters were gradually made comparatively secure by the planes of the Coastal Command and the swarms of hastily built corvettes; but the German answer was to move out into mid-Atlantic, beyond the range of the shorebased planes. New tactics caused the U-boats to hunt in "wolf packs," which tore into shipping with devasting effect.

The mighty battleship *Bismarck*, suspected of being the most powerful warship afloat and reputedly unsinkable, was missing from her Norwegian base and apparently bent on commerce-raiding or worse. Spotting her at last between Greenland and Iceland, the royal navy gave immediate chase. Its greatest ship, the *Hood*, went down in the ensuing battle, and its new *Prince of Wales* withdrew badly mauled. Later, however, the *Bismarck* was cornered by the determined British, who called in everything they had for the pursuit, and she was sunk by the combined pommeling of naval guns and torpedoes, four hundred miles from the French coast.

In August, 1941, Churchill met with Roosevelt on warships off the coast of Newfoundland. They laid down general principles, reminiscent of the Fourteen Points, as the basis for peace. This Atlantic Charter emphasized to the world the growing unity of Britain and the United States.

With Britain's stormy North Atlantic life line in such peril, the United States quietly and gradually stretched neutrality to and beyond the limit. It was war, except in name. More and more of the Atlantic patrolling was taken over by the United States navy. British warships were allowed to seek haven for repairs in American navy yards. American forces occupied Greenland, at first secretly, and relieved the British in Iceland, where the British had sent troops earlier to circumvent a possible German seizure. In the autumn American destroyers were being fired upon south of Iceland. In return, orders were sent American naval vessels to "shoot at sight." All in all, tonnage losses decreased, thanks to this cooperation, until the spread of the war to the Pacific in December forced a relaxation of the convoy precautions.

When the war broke out, it looked as if this time the United States might be going to avoid the pitfalls that had brought her into war in 1812 and 1917. Her new neutrality acts, of 1935 and later, passed in the hope of keeping out of future wars and in disillusion over past war profits and unpaid foreign loans, were reminiscent of the days of Embargo and Nonintercourse (see page 381). Not only was the sale of war supplies, either directly or indirectly, to belligerents prohibited, but loans also were barred, and American vessels were forbidden to enter any war zone. Four years later, with the outbreak of war, the sale of munitions to belligerents again was allowed, but the belligerent must pay for them without aid of loans, must take possession of them in the United States, and must transport them in non-American vessels. This was blatantly aid to Britain alone, since Germany could never get by the British navy to take advantage of it. By 1941 not even this cash-and-carry arrangement served Britain's needs, for she was running short of cash. Try as she would to ship tweeds, heirlooms, and Scotch whisky westward to pay for the planes, guns, and munitions that she had ordered, they were not enough. Then she took a step which was to be one of the heaviest prices she would have to pay in the war. For a century she had been investing her surplus capital beyond the seas; when the war began, this Victorian inheritance amounted to some fourteen billion dollars, the dividends and interest from which were a vital part of the British economy. The war was to see all that spent; and England would actually be owing several billions to her former overseas debtors.

By this time the United States was too far committed to her old role of being England's arsenal to refuse aid in this new financial crisis. More quickly than before she assumed the old British role of "Paymaster of the Allies." She did not repeat her heavy loans, still unpaid, of the first war, but took the more realistic attitude that if a friend needed money which was unlikely to be repaid, it was better to get credit at the outset for generosity than to whistle vainly for repayment at the end (see page 608). This policy also might give the donor more control than he would have if the recipient felt that he was spending his own money. "Lend-lease" empowered United States government agencies "to manufacture in arsenals, factories, and shipyards under their jurisdiction ... any defense article the President deems vital to the defense of the United

States," and "so sell, transfer title to, exchange, lease, lend or otherwise dispose of, to any such government any defense article." This made outright gifts possible not only to Britain, but to the other belligerents. Out of the 42 billion dollars of lend-lease supplies and services furnished by the United States by July 1, 1945, to the various recipients, about two thirds went to Britain and her empire and one quarter to the Russians.

Lend-lease was not altogether a one-way affair. England, Australia, New Zealand, and India, for example, furnished munitions and supplies to American forces quartered there. This "reverse lend-lease" from the British amounted to over five billion dollars' worth; Australia and New Zealand returned almost as much as they received; Canada had a direct arrangement not included in lend-lease.

Italy and North Africa

In the Mediterranean and North Africa in 1940-1941, a third threat was Italy, lying athwart the usual trade route to the East by Suez. The old pre-Suez detour around Good Hope was available, but its added length cut the number of round trips a year that the all-too-scarce ships could make (see page 616). Yet Britain had to use it to supply her forces in Egypt and other parts of the Middle East as well as the Far East. Later many supplies to Russia had to go around Africa to the Persian Gulf ports. The bulk of this armament came increasingly from the United States; it was 14,000 miles from New York around the Cape to the Persian Gulf or to Suez, in contrast to the 3000 of the North Atlantic shuttle and even to the 9000 via Panama across the Pacific to Australia.

Italy's fleet was not much by British or American standards, but it had enough fast, well-built ships to bother the already burdened British. Much of the time it was a "fleet in being," which meant lying safely in port, but this strategy kept a corresponding number of British ships standing by on watch. In an attempt to lure them out, British torpedo planes attacked and crippled severely one force at its base in Taranto in November, 1940.

Britain's island base of Malta (see page 376) was terribly pounded by enemy air attacks; yet she clung to it, for it was her only foothold in the mid-Mediterranean. In some of the hottest naval encounters of the war, convoys, guarded by carriers and other warships, fought their way through to the beleaguered island time and again from Gibraltar or Alexandria to replenish its munitions and food. They were about the only Allied shipping that dared venture into the Mediterranean.

The British army was chiefly occupied for three years with a constant series of campaigns across the deserts of North Africa. It was a fantastic sort of fighting, the very antithesis of that of the old, static western front. The tides of fortune shifted often as first one side and then the other advanced long distances across the sands. The British had more to lose than their Italian or German opponents, for the capture of Suez would jeopardize their wide imperial holdings.

It was a grave gamble on Britain's part to send every man, gun, and tank that could be spared to this theater at the very moment when invasion threatened at home. Even at that, the Italian forces alone outnumbered the British five to one. General Wavell had barely 100,000 men to protect the widely separated British interests in Egypt, East Africa, Palestine, Syria, Iraq, Iran, Turkey, and the Balkans. There was imminent danger that Italian troops, divided between Libya and Ethiopia, might close in on them at the very time that the Luftwaffe was giving England her heaviest punishment. In mid-August, 1940, Italian troops from Ethiopia occupied British Somaliland, but were pushed out of both places in the following spring.

The North African fighting proper began

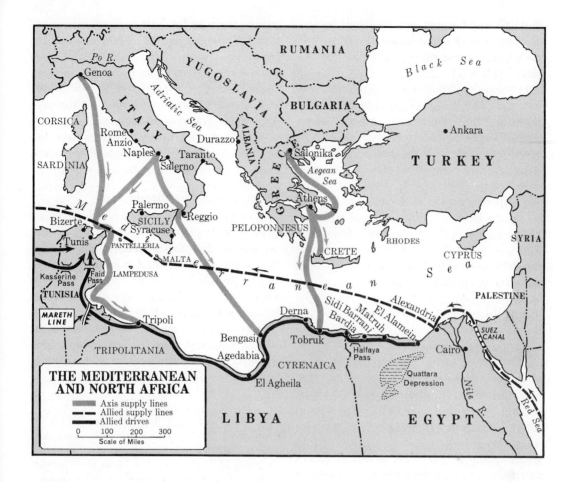

THE MEDITERRANEAN
AND NORTH AFRICA

━━━ Axis supply lines
- - - Allied supply lines
━━━ Allied drives

0   100   200   300
Scale of Miles

when Italy's Libyan army crossed the frontier into Egypt in September, 1940. After penetrating fifty miles, they stopped to dig in; three months later the British fell upon them in a surprise attack.

This precipitated the first of the great North African chases. The demoralized Italians fled westward along the coast road, trying to hold town after town with the British tanks in a hot pursuit. The great northward bulge of the coast at Bengasi gave the British their chance. Cutting across the base of that bulge through nearly two hundred miles of almost trackless desert, while the Italians went along its northern edge, they headed off the fleeing enemy in February, 1941, with barely two hours to spare. With only 30,000 men, the British bagged some 135,000 Italian prisoners and

themselves lost only 604 men; and eastern Libya was theirs!

Rommel in North Africa

Then, as happened often for both sides in this disheartening desert fighting, the North African picture suddenly turned black for the British. Crises in the Balkans and elsewhere to the eastward drew off troops that the British could ill spare; and the Italians were replaced by crack German troops. The lightning winter desert campaign was undone before summer. Eastern Libya, so quickly gained, was lost even more quickly in a counterdrive by the German Afrika Korps and some Italians under the brilliant Rommel, a master of mobile warfare. He had been able to get a considerable force to Africa while the royal navy was busy with the Balkan situation; but he failed to capture the port of Tobruk, where an Australian division withstood an eight months' siege.

Meanwhile, Hitler's move to the eastward had made the Balkans a trouble-spot of the first order. Italy had already staged an invasion of Greece, in the preceding fall, only to be badly mauled by the heroic Greek defense. At the same time, the British had moved into Crete. Some weeks later the way was cleared for Hitler's eastward projects when Hungary, Slovakia, and Rumania joined the Axis, with Bulgaria following. Then, in April, 1941, Hitler sprang a sudden offensive, with Yugoslavia and Greece the victims. Yugoslavia put up one of the bitterest fights the Germans had met, though to no avail; but Greece added to Britain's troubles.

Britain had promised to defend Greece, as she had promised Poland; but she was in no state to keep this pledge either. Yet political considerations prevailed against the hopeless military outlook. One reason for the concurrent defeat in North Africa was that Wavell was ordered to send to Greece some 76,000 of his troops. A recent smashing naval victory over the Italians at Cape Matapan, enabled them to be transported across the Mediterranean, but on land inevitable defeat waited them at the hands of the Germans. The British lost 30,000 soldiers, and Greece succumbed quickly. Late in May came another German demonstration of new military ideas. With the British in Crete 180 miles from Greece and with the royal navy in control of the intervening waters, German air-borne troops, arriving by parachute, glider, and transport, descended upon the island and wrested it from the British despite bitter fighting. Some 13,000 more men were lost as well as several more vessels, which Britain could ill spare.

The unfortunate scattering of Wavell's forces did not end here, however, for it began to look as though German intrigue were

paving the way for further jumps into western Asia. In late spring, while some of his troops were clearing the Italians from Ethiopia, a revolt had to be put down in Iraq. In early summer Wavell's forces joined with Free French forces in clearing out the pro-Axis Vichy government in Syria. Later they co-operated with the Russians to save the situation in Iran. By that time Wavell had gone to India, where he became viceroy.

Hitler's Invasion of Russia

A most providential stroke of luck befell Britain in June, 1941, when Hitler turned on Russia. The British finally had an ally. Hitler, on the other hand, now had the two-front war that he had always feared. With his invasion of Russia, the Luftwaffe soon eased its bombing of Britain to seek new targets. In the long run the Russian campaigns were still more helpful through their attrition of German manpower. Three years later Churchill declared:

It is the Russian Army that has done the main work of tearing the guts out of the German Army. In the air and on the ocean and seas we can maintain ourselves, but there was no force . . . to maul and break the German Army and subject it to such terrible slaughter and manhandling as has fallen upon the Germans by the Russian Soviet Armies.

The lightning campaigns up to that invasion of Russia in 1941 had killed and wounded few men compared with the toll of World War I; the casualties had been largely prisoners.

The Russians "traded space for time" and did not check the Germans until they were almost at Moscow and Leningrad and had overrun most of the Crimea. Then winter set in, and the Germans were not prepared for that. Blizkrieg gave way to months of grim slaughter. At terrific cost to themselves, the Russians performed the grim task of eliminating millions of Germans.

Russia had been doing her share of annexing territory since 1939. Her pact with the Germans on the eve of the war had given her eastern Poland (see page 621). That fall of 1939 she had attacked her small neighbor Finland, which put up a gallant resistance. The following spring Russia had quietly annexed Lithuania, Latvia, and Estonia, her former Baltic provinces. A month later she had moved into two Rumanian provinces.

In retrospect Hitler's attack on Russia, like Napoleon's long before, stands out as his most ghastly military blunder. Up to then, his campaigns had easily made him master of western and central Europe. His "intuition" has been credited with the success of many of the brilliant moves at which his professional soldiers had shaken their heads. This time it led him too far; but it must be recalled that military experts in many lands had expected another swift victory for him.

By the time snow and cold had bogged down the Germans in Russia, the United States had changed from an informal to a formal ally. On December 7, 1941, Japan struck simultaneously at the British and the Americans in various parts of the Pacific and eastern Asia; in the next few days the United States was at war with Germany and Italy also.

The Japanese, allies in the first World War, had been working aggressively to spread their power in the Far East. They had begun to wrest Manchuria from China in 1931, without serious protest from the Western powers. In 1937 they launched a strong attack on China proper, after withdrawing from their agreements for naval disarmament. When the war in Europe began, they occupied the China coast and temporarily forced England to close the Burma Road, the only remaining route of any importance by which British and American supplies could reach China. In mid-September, 1940, they secured permission from Vichy France to send troops, ships, and planes to strategically located Indo-China. A week later Japan formally joined

Germany and Italy in an Axis military alliance.

Japan in the War: Pearl Harbor and Malaya

As had been their wont, the Japanese struck first and declared war afterward. Early on the Sunday morning of December 7 their planes from a carrier force swooped down upon the great American naval base at Pearl Harbor in Hawaii. They wiped out most of the American planes before the latter could rise to meet the attack, and sank or crippled the battleships of the Pacific fleet, to say nothing of other ships and installations. Within a few hours they had achieved their purpose: the United States navy would not interfere with their plans elsewhere for some time to come. That same day they attacked also the Philippines and the little crown colony of Hong Kong.

Three days later two mighty British warships, the battle cruiser *Renown* and the battleship *Prince of Wales*, which had fought the *Bismarck* in the spring, went to the bottom under the blows of bombs and torpedoes from Japanese planes. These great ships had been hurried to the British naval base of Singapore, which was supposedly impregnable to attack, with the royal navy to brush off any approach from the sea and with the supposedly impassable Malay jungles behind it. But the admiral in command had failed to secure air protection; and this second naval disaster within a week further expedited the Japanese progress southward.

To the further consternation of the British and Americans, the impossible kept happening. On the day after Pearl Harbor, Japanese soldiers headed for Singapore were already approaching the upper neck of the long Malay Peninsula; and the thick tangle ahead did not stop such well-trained jungle fighters. Whenever the British defenders tried to form a defense line, the Japanese simply cut in behind them and forced their retreat. Unlike the Americans in the Philippines, who were receiving valuable aid from native soldiers whom they had trained, the British had scorned, until the last minute, to rely on the Malay natives, so they naturally received no support. Without air coverage they found themselves helplessly exposed to Japanese reconnaissance and bombs. In a few weeks only Singapore island was left. In contrast to the antiquated efforts of the army, the royal navy had equipped its base with big guns and the most modern of fortifications; but all that bristling armament pointed seaward—and the enemy came from the defenseless rear. Singapore fell in February. An army of some 100,000 British, Australian, and Indian troops, which had previously sustained relatively few casualties, was captured by only 30,000 Japanese.

Well could Churchill call it "the greatest disaster to British arms which history records." For centuries it had been understood that if the British army was in a jam, the royal navy would extricate it. Except for Yorktown it had performed this service regularly, even to Norway and Dunkirk in this war. It was understandable that nothing could save the diminutive Hong Kong garrison, whose surrender on Christmas Day had been followed by the bayoneting of prisoners and the raping of English-women. But for a city world-famed as a naval base to surrender with an army three times the size of the enemy's quite intact was indeed something new in British annals. The psychological effect of that sorry surrender would do much to undermine white prestige.

All this served merely to clear the way for the prime objectives of the enemy; what the Japanese really wanted were the rich British and Dutch possessions at the southeast corner of Asia—Malaya, Java, Sumatra, Borneo, and the rest. With the American fleet at Pearl Harbor immobilized for the moment and the British base at Singapore in her hands, Japan had practically within her grasp vast reserves of oil, which she had lacked, together with the lion's share of the world's rubber and tin supply and much other rich plunder. While the getting was good, the Japanese would pick up whatever else they could, to protect the approaches against counterattack; they might even threaten Australia and India. Their propaganda told the sullen native subjects in those regions how much more fortunate they would be as partners in Japan's "Greater East Asia Co-Prosperity Sphere" than under the heel of the arrogant white man.

Java, the next great prize, was already ripe to fall. During late winter of 1942, a small force of British, American, and Dutch cruisers and destroyers in those waters fought a desperate delaying action in the Strait of Macassar and the Java Sea, but were overwhelmed. Japanese air superiority continued; and Port Darwin, at the northeast tip of Australia, toward which refugees from Java were heading, was almost demolished. Not only Java, but Sumatra, Borneo, and many others were overrun by the swarming Japanese advance.

In Australia the people were both alarmed and disgruntled. They felt that England was letting them down and demanded the return of their troops sent up to Suez two years before. This was done; and by the time these troops reached home in the spring, American forces, under the American general, MacArthur, the Allied commander of the Southwest Pacific Area, were already there to defend the dominion. Danger was closer, with the Japanese already in New Guinea.

The seemingly irresistible onward march of the Japanese was not only island-jumping. They were spreading westward into Burma, with India just beyond, even before they were halfway down the Malay Peninsula. If the Malays were apathetic, the Burmese showed definite hostility to the British rule. By early spring, Rangoon was gone; the British were out of southern Burma; and Mandalay was to be next. With Singapore theirs, the Japanese navy now moved

Areas occupied by
the Japanese

0   200 400 600 800
Scale of Miles

SOVIET   UNION   SAKHALIN
                                  I.

MONGOLIA   MANCHURIA

                        Vladivostok
              Hsinking

         Peiping   KOREA
         Tientsin

                                  Tokyo
                              JAPANESE EMPIRE

         Nanking   Nagasaki
    Hankow   Shanghai
Chungking   C H I N A
         Yangtze R.
BURMA ROAD   Wenchow   VOLCANO
    Amoy Foochow OKINAWA   ISLANDS
Kunming Swatow
         Canton   IWO JIMA
              FORMOSA
BURMA Hanoi
(Br.)   HONG KONG
              (British)
         HAINAN   WAKE I.
THAI- FRENCH
LAND   INDO-   MARIANAS
Rangoon Bangkok CHINA Manila PHILIPPINE ISLANDS
         Saigon   ISLANDS   (Jap.)
                               GUAM I.
         BRITISH
         NORTH
         BORNEO
BRITISH   CAROLINE ISLANDS
MALAYA SARAWAK   (Jap.)
Singapore (Br.)
  (Br.)
         BORNEO
         CELEBES
         Strait of Macassar
NETHERLANDS INDIES (Neth.) NEW
Batavia JAVA Surabaya   GUINEA SOLOMON IS.
                               (British)
              TIMOR I.   Port Moresby GUADAL-
                                         CANAL I.

out into the Gulf of Bengal to threaten the shipping lanes to Calcutta and Madras. Ceylon was raided, and two British cruisers and a carrier were sunk. There seemed no limit to the distances the Japanese victors might travel. Fearing the worst, the British quickly seized the French island of Madagascar, off Africa's east coast.

The Pacific war became, by the spring of 1942, primarily the responsibility of the United States navy, together with her air forces and to a lesser degree her army, in co-operation with the Australian and New Zealand forces. Gradually the Japanese were slowed down. Having broken the Japanese naval code, the Americans were able to anticipate their moves. A drive toward Australia was smashed early in May in the battle of the Coral Sea, a carrier fight in which the ships never came within a hundred miles of one another. Soon after, the Japanese navy was further severely crippled in the battle of Midway. The Japanese occupation of the Solomon Islands, however, still endangered the southern supply route between the United States and Australia.

In August the Americans moved in there with a desperate minimum of force; but the Solomons fight went on, with the enemy sending repeated expeditions to recover them. Beaten back or smashed in constant minor and occasional major engagements, they gave up the attempt in November. From that point their fleet showed that it was past its peak.

Meanwhile, from Australian bases, the Australians and Americans were fighting bitter battles in New Guinea jungles to check the enemy approach there. Finally the time came for counterdrives toward Japan.

Anglo-American Military Coordination

Two weeks after Pearl Harbor, Churchill arrived in Washington. With Germany and Italy at war with the United States, he wanted to be sure that the present emphasis on the Pacific would not slacken American support of the fighting in Europe. His visit began a formal integration of British and American war-planning, already on an informal basis. There followed a series of policy conferences by the two leaders, sometimes with others present, such as Stalin of Russia and Chiang Kai-shek of China. A permanent mechanism for translating those policies into action also was to be evolved. Less immediately tangible, but important for the future was the signing of a military alliance by the United Nations, on January 1, 1942. These twenty-six included Britain, the United States, Russia, China, the British dominions, many of the governments in exile from Holland to Yugoslavia, many of the Latin-American republics, and various other nations. Britain was obviously no longer the dominant power. Yet Churchill seldom came from such gatherings without getting a good deal of what Britain wanted. He persuaded the United States to give priority to Europe in their war plans; he kept lend-lease supplies flowing freely; and his adamant refusal to commit British forces to a repetition of the "sombre mass slaughters" of the first war made good his promise that Britain should not have another "lost generation." Both he and Roosevelt, after consultation with their professional advisers, felt themselves competent to make the final military and naval decisions. Stalin generally played a lone hand, and the other nations carried little weight.

Out of such conferences came the general approval of major operations to be launched months later. To preserve secrecy, these were always referred to by nicknames, such as "Torch" (North African landings), and "Overlord" (invasion of Normandy). The details of what, when, and where were worked out by the Combined Chiefs of Staff, consisting of the American Joint Chiefs of Staff sitting with their British counterparts. Their decisions were binding on the armed forces of both nations, whose appropriate staffs then developed the overwhelming amount of necessary detailed planning.

The British and Americans set up an over-all combined command in each major theater of war to avoid the difficulties which would arise when more than one nation participated, as Marlborough, Wellington, and Haig had learned to their cost. One man was now given command over all land, sea, and air forces of both nations in a particular theater or area, a control more tangible than Foch had had in 1918 (see page 586). Thus ultimately an American admiral (Nimitz), commanded the Pacific Areas; an American general (MacArthur), the Southwest Pacific Area; a British admiral (Mountbatten), the Southeast Asia Command; and a British general (Wilson), the Mediterranean area, relieving an American general (Eisenhower), who eventually was promoted to command the European Theater of Operations. If the top layer was British, the next layer would contain some Americans, and vice versa. This integration was essentially an Anglo-American arrangement; some of the smaller nations came under this leadership, but the Russians and Chinese were linked simply by Allied missions. Outside the purely military field, other joint groups controlled shipping, economic resources, and other essentials. Altogether, this unique venture in integration was an important cause of final victory.

The Turning of the Tide

The summer of 1942 marked the low ebb of Allied fortunes; and it followed months of seeing their enemies victorious east and west, on Russian plains and African deserts, in the jungles and swamps of southeastern Asia, and among the clustered islands of the South Seas. September 1, 1942, the middle day of the six-year war, found the conquering Germans far across Russia at the Volga and far across North Africa into Egypt; the Japanese navy was pounding at the Solomons, and their army was at the gates of India; the precious supplies for those hard-pressed fronts faced worse jeopardy than ever before on sea lanes near and far. Had the two German drives joined, as looked all too possible at this grim moment, they would have forced the British out of the Middle East, and presumably could have swept on toward India to meet the Japanese swarming toward them. In these weeks Britain and the United States were faced with possible loss of the war, and Russia seemed on the verge of surrender. Churchill flew to Moscow to plan with Stalin a way out of the desperate plight.

Yet that fall of 1942 marks the turning point toward total victory for the sorepressed Allies. In the Solomons, the Japanese navy already was losing its offensive power; while in Russia and Egypt the turning point was thorough and dramatic. In Northwest Africa the United States and Britain staged their first major invasion. Only in southeastern Asia did the tide fail to turn in favor of the Allies. Henceforth, Britain's part in the war was overshadowed by that of Russia and the United States,

in contrast to the previous years, when she carried the bulk of the burden.

In Russia the Germans were on the march again, headed toward the oil of the Caucasus, which they needed badly. In August, 1942, after a victorious sweep, they reached the distant industrial city of Stalingrad on the Volga. If that fell, all Asia seemed before them, as well as the Middle East, with the chance to unite with Rommel. Week after week, they stormed and pounded until little was left of Stalingrad but a mass of rubble. Yet the Russians doggedly held their ground; finally a relieving army doomed the German attackers, but Hitler ordered them to stand to the last man. Blasted by Russia's crack artillery, they had lost a third of a million men when their pitiful remnant surrendered in February, 1943. The Stalingrad stand gave the war on that front to the Russians, who were now able to push steadily westward to recover their devastated lands.

In North Africa the German reverses were as complete, but for the time being were less deadly. In the spring of 1941 Rommel had rapidly recovered eastern Libya, which the British had wrested from the Italians. For a whole year the fortunes of war had shifted back and forth in Libya, with some of the coastal towns being taken and retaken time and again. Late in the spring of 1942, Rommel started a major drive, which quickly assumed dangerous proportions. In one surprise action he nearly wiped out the whole British tank force with his heavy guns. Tobruk, which had withstood an eight months' siege at the time of his previous attack, now was taken with surprising ease. Crossing the Egyptian frontier, he pushed on to the little railroad station of El Alamein, only seventy-five miles from Alexandria. A state of near panic developed, secret papers were burned at British headquarters lest they fall into enemy hands, and hasty plans were made to evacuate the whole Suez area. All through midsummer Rommel's tanks

British tanks in the North African desert campaigning against Rommel's potent Afrika Corps.

seemed poised to bring disaster. The royal navy, during those tense weeks, had been strengthening the army's tight supply situation; now it was able to threaten Rommel's shorter supply run across the Mediterranean from Germany via Italy. At the same time, a steady stream of tanks, trucks, guns, and troops for the British were reaching the Red Sea by the long run around Good Hope from America or Britain. A change in command may have played its part also. At sea British admirals had been handling the Mediterranean naval situation with masterly skill; but on land North Africa, like Norway, Flanders, and Malaya, had been a graveyard for British military reputations. One commander after another had been tried, and the general who had routed the Italians in 1941 had been killed in action. Now General Sir Harold Alexander was given the over-all Middle East Command and General, later Field Marshal, Sir Ber-

nard Montgomery, became field commander in charge of the Eighth Army.

In October the British were able at last to smash at Rommel. Their planes gained mastery of the air; their sappers cleared paths through the deadly fields of land mines; and then, with a great assemblage of artillery and tanks, carefully camouflaged against aerial detection, they hit the German lines in full force. After a few days of furious fighting, in which many of his tanks were destroyed, Rommel started westward, with the British pounding steadily at his heels. But they did not catch the "desert fox" as they had trapped the Italians; he kept ahead of them in the 1400-mile pursuit.

The North African Landings

As this retreat was under way, the Americans and British made their highly spectacular and "top secret" landings in force on the northwestern coasts of Africa. Simultaneously, and with complete surprise, a tremendous armada of 700 warships and transports landed a mighty army in French North Africa: British forces at Algiers, Americans at near-by Oran inside the Mediterranean, and other Americans at Casablanca on the Atlantic coast of Morocco. Much depended upon the very uncertain attitude of the French leaders in Africa. After much melodramatic negotiation, Algeria did not resist, but fighting was necessary at Casablanca. Some of the ships came from Britain, others directly from American ports; yet the secret of the enormous preparations for this gigantic undertaking had been perfectly kept. It came as a stunning surprise to the world; more important, it caught the enemy unawares.

These North African landings were the best that the United States and Britain could do at the moment in answer to Stalin's clamor for a "second front" to relieve the pressure on Russia. Adequate forces were not available for direct crossing from England into France, which Stalin most desired. According to Churchill, this new stroke would expose "the soft underbelly of the Axis" to Allied attack.

The Allies did not consider themselves strong enough to occupy Tunisia at once, when the taking would have been easy. With Rommel steadily racing toward that goal, other German forces slipped across the Mediterranean to occupy it. The advancing Allies still hoped to trap Rommel between themselves and his British pursuers; but early in 1943 he turned on them and was able to join the other German forces. Complicated operations ended in the surrender of Tunis and near-by Bizerte, and more than a quarter-million crack German and Italian troops were captured. Thus, at long last, the three years of North African fighting came to an end.

Shortly before this surrender Churchill and Roosevelt had held another meeting,

The allied triumvirate at their 1945 "summit" conference at Yalta in Russia: Churchill, Roosevelt and Stalin. Roosevelt died two months later. The same group had met at Teheran in Iran in 1943.

at Casablanca, near the battle fronts. Churchill at last accepted the plan for a second front in France, but saw to it that the Americans agreed to furnish most of the troops. It was at this conference that the drastic words *unconditional surrender* and *no negotiated peace* were hurled at the enemies of the United Nations.

Sinkings and Shipbuilding

Although the battle of the Atlantic had been going better at the time of Pearl Harbor, the months thereafter were among the grimmest for the Allies. The United States found herself confronted with a two-ocean war without a two-ocean navy. Five weeks after she entered the war, the Germans launched a terrific, all-out U-boat attack on shipping in general and on oil tankers in particular. Boldly they did much of this sinking in American coastal waters within sight of the shore. The United States was caught without adequate small patrol vessels for this sort of inshore warfare and had to borrow some from the British. As the antisubmarine patrols were improved in that region, the Germans moved down into the Caribbean, and the old Spanish Main was ablaze with burning vessels.

Naturally these sinkings reduced still further the number of cargo vessels. Already the lengthening of the sea lanes with the spread of the war to the Far East had cut that tonnage. Such long hauls inevitably meant fewer trips: a vessel could make only about one third as many round trips to Australia via Panama from New York, for instance, as it could across the North Atlantic, and less than one quarter as many to the Persian Gulf. Congested ports in these out-of-the-way places and inadequate facilities further tied up tonnage.

Into this emergency stepped the tremendous shipbuilding program of the United States; Britain was already building to capacity. In contrast to the first war, these new American cargo ships were to be at work on the seas long before peace came. Welding and preassembling made it possible to build more ships faster. Instead of the ten to twelve months in the first war for building a steel freighter, it took only weeks and even days. Despite war losses, this unprecedented shipbuilding gave the United States, at the end of the war, the world's largest merchant marine, 5529 seagoing merchant ships against 1401 in 1939. Britain too had built many freighters, and, in spite of her far severer losses, was in second place with 2347 ships, only 545 fewer than she had had in 1939, when she occupied first place. And during hostilities these rapidly built ships kept the supplies reaching the distant fronts, despite all the enemy could do by undersea, surface, and air attack.

Not until the fall of 1942 was the latest U-boat offensive checked to any extent but by the following spring the end was in sight. In this war, when things became too hot, the U-boats shifted their hunting grounds; thus, from the waters just west of Britain, they had moved into the Greenland-Iceland region, then from the coastal waters of Canada and the United States to the Caribbean and beyond. By May 1943, the toll of U-boats sunk by the Allies began to mount, as the merchant sinkings fell off. The use of little escort carriers, which could give air protection even on the hitherto bad Iceland stretch, drastically reduced losses. Danger still lurked on the icy run from the United States to Murmansk, beyond the North Cape on the open Arctic. This shortest way for supplies to the Russian front was so perilous that altogether about one fourth of the vessels that risked it were lost. Some of its danger was eliminated when superior forces of the royal navy trapped and sank the German battleship *Scharnhorst* as she was trying to raid a convoy in the last days of 1943. Later the giant *Tirpitz*, formidable sister ship of the *Bismarck*, which had long lain sheltered in a Norwegian fiord, was sunk by British bombers.

The "Home Front"

The first half of 1943 brought rumblings of restlessness in Britain. Compared with the first war, this second had been packed with dramatic action all around the world. Now came a lull in the fighting as the Allies shifted from the defensive to the offensive. Britain's series of dangerous crises had reached a climax the preceding fall. The North African landings had aroused high hopes of a speedy major counter offensive, which the stubborn German stand in Tunisia delayed for six months. All this contributed to a general sense of letdown. While the feeling of acute danger had declined as the air raids grew less frequent, most wartime discomforts continued unabated. The black-out was still just as black, but the novelty had worn off.

The nation too was becoming heartily tired of "Woolton pie," a nourishing but unexciting concoction of potatoes, cauliflower, turnips, carrots, and oatmeal, with a pastry top and gravy. It was named for the peer who had been doing a most effective job of adjusting Britain's diet to her food supply. The nation had become infinitely more self-supporting in foodstuffs than it had been in 1917. Four million grassy acres, including parks and golf courses, had come under the plow; the new Women's Land Army, eventually a half-million strong, was producing huge quantities of potatoes, barley, Brussels sprouts, and other crops which nutrition experts had recommended. England did not go hungry, but there were nostalgic yearnings for eggs, fish, tomatoes, oranges, and onions as well as steaks and chops. Sugar and tea were scarce. Clothing too was severely rationed, alike for a duke and a docker, the queen and a charwoman.

A large portion of the population, moreover, had been uprooted from its familiar surroundings. More than a quarter of London's millions had abandoned the city by mid-1941, while the exposed southeastern counties and the great industrial centers likewise had fallen off. Remote and quiet communities like York, Oxford, and Salisbury were struggling to accommodate swarms of newcomers. Some, including the evacuated children, began to return after the aerial Blitz had subsided, but the millions of damaged or demolished homes checked that process. Also, the policy of scattering industries around the country anchored large numbers of workers to new communities. These readjustments of population, with their attendant friction, were complicated by the increasing presence of overseas troops all over Britain—Canadians from the start and, by 1943, the advance guard of a million and a half Americans, who would use England as a staging area for the next year's assault on the Continent.

Along with black-out, rationing, and transplanting went a concentration of governmental power which made the "Doras"

of the last war seem tame in comparison (see page 583). The Emergency Powers Act, passed a week before the war began, had re-enacted that former permission to govern by decree, rather than by legislation, during the emergency. The new feature was the Emergency Powers Defense Act, introduced by Attlee in May, 1940, while the British army was retreating toward Dunkirk. It gave the government "complete control over persons and property, not just some persons in some particular class of the community, but all persons, rich or poor, employer or employed, man or woman." The Minister of Labor was empowered to direct anyone to perform any service required and to prescribe wages, hours, and conditions of labor. Employers could be told what to produce, and excess profits were eliminated. Even banks and finance in general came under this sweeping control. Conscription for the armed services had been introduced before the war; now every adult civilian of working age was placed at the government's disposal. Ernest Bevin, as Minister of Labor and National Service, administered both military conscription and these new powers. The inclusion of women in the compulsory category was a complete novelty. By the end of the war a large proportion of them were engaged either in the armed services as "Wrens" (navy), "Waafs" (air force), or "Ats" (army); in full-time civilian defense; in agriculture or in industry.

Industrial unrest became evident in 1943, with the first strikes since 1939. The trade unions had pledged themselves not to strike, and legislation forbade the practice. Nevertheless, scores of unofficial strikes sprang up, primarily among the coalminers, but also among aircraft workers, bus-drivers, shipyard workers, and others. Some of the Conservatives felt that Bevin, who had organized a great trade-union himself, was not sufficiently severe in handling the strikes. On the other hand, government refusal to let the postal workers unionize caused acrimonious debate in Parliament.

Lloyd George, during the first war, had promised the nation that it would be "a land fit for heroes," but it had proved anything but that; this time, even with the war in full swing, people in general, particularly labor, began to give thought to the future (see page 594). In mid-February, 1943, the Commons took up a sweeping report on social insurance made public ten weeks before by Sir William Beveridge, who proposed to "abolish want . . . from the cradle to the grave." When the government wanted to postpone definite action, the Labor party mustered 119 votes against 335 in a demand for immediate action. Churchill, a month later, tried to calm labor with a "Four-Year Plan" for reconstruction, but widespread dissatisfaction at the delay continued. In November, 1943, this feeling produced a new post; Lord Woolton, who had administered the food problem, was created Minister of Reconstruction, with a seat in the war cabinet. Labor, in the meantime, had decided to remain in the coalition while the war with Germany lasted.

Dominion Problems and Achievements

That question of discussing postwar reconstruction raised distant echoes in some of the dominions, where the Beveridge report had been read with keen interest. In Australia, where the political balance between the Labor party and the two anti-Labor parties was very close, a constitutional convention at Canberra discussed the continuation of the wartime emergency powers of the federal government into peacetime in order to carry through a reconstruction program. The proposal was defeated by a narrow margin in a referendum. The question arose also in Canada and New Zealand, where the right-wing parties considered it inappropriate to devote much time to social reform in wartime.

Linked with that were questions involving the nature and extent of the war effort. Except for the die-hard Afrikaner element in South Africa, there was no question but that the people supported the war as such. The Australian Labor party, however, was opposed to sending the dominion's armed forces, even the volunteers, outside the Southwest Pacific and had drawn back the Australians from the Middle East when the Japanese menace grew acute. New Zealand, with its tradition of ultraloyalty, which some have termed a "mother complex," toward Britain, allowed its division to proceed from North Africa on up into Italy, despite occasional mutterings. Canada, which had refrained from conscripting the French Canadians in the first war, put through a modified conscription for home service, with only volunteers to go overseas (see page 577). Later, after a referendum permitted foreign service for conscripts, some of the drafted "Zombies" rioted in protest. In South Africa, with its ticklish political situation, the original limitations of its troops to African service was finally relaxed.

Despite their loyalty to the mother country, the dominions seemed to be growing more aware of their nationhood during the war. More and more they took external relations into their own hands, made their own combinations among themselves and with outsiders, and, except for South Africa, tightened their links with the United States. An outward symbol of this was the rapid growth of the various dominion diplomatic corps, which had begun just after the first war, when ministers were exchanged between Ottawa and Washington (see page 615). Canada, by 1944, had missions to twenty-four different countries, and its envoys to the United States, Russia, China, and Brazil had been elevated to the rank of ambassador. The Pacific dominions had had no direct foreign representation before the war, but in 1940 Australia decided to find out for itself what was going on, and consequently exchanged envoys with Washington, Tokyo, and Ottawa. Two years later New Zealand sent its first diplomat to Washington.

Australia, particularly jealous of its international status, clamored unsuccessfully for direct representation on the Combined Chiefs of Staff, while Canada kept a military mission at Washington to consult with them. Canada entered into a joint defense agreement with the United States and arranged its own substitute for lend-lease. Australia and New Zealand, early in 1944, drew up at Canberra an agreement for cooperation in regional defense. Later, when the United Nations began to take form, Prime Minister Curtin of Australia was the outstanding exponent of the rights of the smaller nations, as opposed to domination by the great powers. It was also significant that a Canadian, tired perhaps of hearing that England fought alone between the fall of France and the entry of Russia, referred to his dominion as "Great Britain's strongest ally" during that period. Not until the spring of 1944 did England finally summon a conference of the dominion prime ministers—Mackenzie King of Canada, Curtin of Australia, Smuts of South Africa, and Fraser of New Zealand. Curtin's proposal of an Empire Secretariat was rejected.

There was an implied practical threat to England's postwar prosperity in the rapid development of the dominions' war industries. Previously they had drawn a considerable part of their manufactured needs from Britain, but during the war all four developed industrially. This, of course, was of immediate valuable assistance to the imperial war effort, but England, already beginning to think in terms of "export or die," might suffer if those war plants were to be converted to the peacetime manufacture of planes, automobiles, and other products of her own industry. Canada already had a moderate industrial development, and Australia, starting almost from nothing, built plants to equip an armored division, yards to turn out warships and merchantmen, and much

else. The industrial efforts of New Zealand and South Africa were more modest, yet far beyond any they had made before.

The military efforts of the dominions were magnificent and contributed mightily to the final victory. It is out of the question to recount all their accomplishments here. The North African desert campaigns and other fighting in the Middle East depended to no small extent upon the Australians, New Zealanders, and South Africans, along with Indian troops. The South Africans were the mainstay of the operations which cleared the Italians out of Ethiopia and Somaliland. The Australians, finally called home, contributed a major part of the ground forces which fought the Japanese in the jungles of New Guinea, but the New Zealanders continued into Italy. The Canadians, after long training in England, also had an important role in Italy and in the final great drive against Germany; they had already made a bloody raid on Dieppe and were represented in the defense of Hong Kong. The dominion navies likewise had relieved the royal navy of some of its burden. Canadian warships ultimately took over half the escort duty in the North Atlantic. Of Australia's little navy, three cruisers were sunk in action. The surviving vessels, with the New Zealand navy, carried on in the Pacific fighting. Fliers from all the dominions were constantly active, operating either from England or from other bases throughout the world. Tens of thousands of them had been trained in Canada in the Commonwealth Air Training Program; still others at home. Preliminary casualty totals showed that 77,710 soldiers, sailors, and airmen from the four dominions were killed in the war (Canada, 37,476; Australia, 23,365; New Zealand, 10,028; and South Africa, 6840).

India in Wartime

India also made a heavy contribution. Indian troops not only fought well in North Africa and in Italy, but helped to make possible the daring exploits of General Wingate in North Burma in 1943, the defeat of the vicious Japanese thrust at the life line through the upper Brahmaputra valley to China in 1944, and the reconquest of Burma in 1945. India's economic contribution to the war effort, meanwhile, was, like that of the dominions, so extensive that even before the end of hostilities the financial ledger, for the first time in history, showed Britain in debt to India.

This did not mean that the majority of Indians approved of the war; quite the contrary. So densely populated was India, so illiterate and isolated were many of its people, that millions did not even know there was a war. Millions more, however, did know; and many of them either belonged to or sympathized with the Indian National Congress, that extra-legal organization, not recognized by the Indian constitution, which claimed, under the leadership of Gandhi and Nehru, to speak for India, and which opposed the war. Nevertheless, since the viceroy's cabinet was exclusively appointed by him without prior approval of the Indian legislature, the people had no option but to submit to war. Such control of local affairs as did remain in their hands in this far from democratic government did not affect the war one way or another.

The Indian National Congress agreed to co-operate in the war, but at a price: immediate and complete independence for India. Gandhi, however, was a pacifist, who openly stated that he would not oppose the Japanese by force, and many Moslems, among them India's best fighting men, rejected independence under the domination of the Congress. The Moslem League demanded not only independence, but the separation of the predominantly Moslem provinces from the rest of India. So Britain compromised, by sending out Sir Stafford Cripps with the promise of dominion status after the war and, for the time being, further representation in the viceroy's cabinet, even

their own minister of defense. The war itself continued to be waged, of course, by a British commander in chief, untrammeled by political control. The Congress and the Moslem League both refused this offer.

Then in mid-summer of 1942 the Congress summoned all Indians to revolt. The British promptly threw the leaders into jail. This proved to be something more than a sit-down strike, something less than civil war. There were only a few thousand British troops in India, but they had machine guns and planes; with them they soon restored order. Luckily the Japanese were too busy elsewhere to take advantage of this.

The inability of the British in India to recognize their danger and incompetence tided them over this crisis, as it had over so many others in the past. As things stood, all of near-by Burma but its northern tip was lost; Japanese planes skimmed over the Bay of Bengal; disaffection was rife; the Nationalist Congress was in revolt. But this did not ruffle Wavell, sent from his North African command to be the new viceroy. He reorganized the Indian army, prepared to invade Burma, and actually did so on a small scale in 1943.

Wingate's Burma Campaign

This British counterthrust into Burma was led by General Wingate who introduced something new in warfare. He planned a campaign in which commissariat and munitions for several thousand air-borne infantry were transported entirely by plane. So closely did he articulate the planes with the offense that they replaced railroads, motor trucks, and bullock trains to make movement rapid, despite rain, forest, and jungle. His long-protracted hardening of recruits into tough, resilient units and the minute drill in geographic lore produced a new type of British soldier, better trained than the Japanese in jungle tactics.

The immediate task in this counterattack was to sever enemy communication lines. His men had to drive west-east, over high mountains, down through deep valleys, roughing it over bridle paths or no paths at all. They succeeded in demolishing the Mandalay railroad in seventy-five places and in dynamiting three steel bridges. They ambushed munition trains and captured supply dumps. Scattering to right and left, they always escaped capture. They were fed and supplied throughout by aerial transport, the R.A.F. flying some 50,000 air miles in their support. By the time that they returned to India they had disrupted communications over an important strategic area of 10,000 square miles in North Burma. Their feats proved that a small army could be fed, clothed, and armed by air, even in the tropics.

The British had all they could do in 1944 to repel a Japanese attack directed against Imphal, capital of a tiny Indian state, tucked away amid the hills on the borders of North Burma and India. If they were successful, the allied forces in the upper tip of Burma would be isolated; and then the Japanese, assisted, they hoped, by revolting Indians, could swing down the Brahmaputra valley into Bengal, perhaps to stage another Singapore at Calcutta. Against Imphal the Japanese hurled 80,000 picked troops and besieged it for over two months. Surging on north, they surrounded for eighteen days a British force at Kohima.

Then the tide of battle turned with dramatic swiftness. The British drove the adversary into headlong flight, like thistledown before the wind, counting more than 50,000 Japanese dead. Many more of that original 80,000 doubtless perished in the jungle of sickness or by the knives of irate tribesmen. Before the year was out, General Slim was back on the frontier of India. Thereafter it would be the British Empire that would take the offensive in Burma.

Allied Invasion of Italy

The British and Americans, by the middle of 1943, were ready to advance against the Continent. Three full years had gone since Dunkirk, and no British army had stood on European soil, except for the brief fiasco in Greece and occasional commando raids at Dieppe and elsewhere on the French coast. With American industry getting into its stride and with the enemy cleared from North Africa, Italy was next on the list. This was by no means what Stalin wanted as a second front, but it was the most the British and Americans dared now attempt; and it would be something to put Italy out of the war.

Early in July, some three thousand strange-looking vessels, under heavy naval escort, crossed the Mediterranean from North Africa to Sicily. Crowded aboard were 160,000 men, half British, half American, ready to be disgorged by these new landing craft directly upon the beaches ahead. A terrific gale struck this unwieldly armada, but the wind subsided in time for the seasick armies to land safely under the protection of naval guns. From these amphibious landings on the southeast corner of Sicily, they overran the whole island in thirty-eight days, and took 100,000 Italian and German prisoners. The rest of the German troops seemed trapped at Messina, but they staged a Dunkirk escape across the strait to Italy.

On the very day in early September that the first British troops crossed to the toe of Italy, that nation surrendered. Mussolini had fallen from power in July. But bitterly disappointing were the results; the worst fighting of the Italian front lay ahead. While the Allies were delaying in Sicily, the Germans took over in Italy. They were to persist in a stubborn rear-guard action northward to the very last days of the war.

The southeastern part of Italy fell quickly to British air-borne troops. By fall the great air base at Foggia was in British hands, laying Austria and southern Germany open to bombing raids for the first time. A bloody amphibious landing, chiefly by Americans, had been made at Salerno, just below Naples, which was soon taken. Meanwhile, most of the Italian navy (some ships were seized by the Germans) came into Allied hands, releasing Allied warships from the Mediterranean and helping to save cargo vessels the delaying detour around Africa.

Some think that the Allies would have been better off if they had been content with such useful gains. Instead, they doggedly kept on in a painful progress up the peninsula, a British army under Montgomery on the right, and an American on the left, under the over-all British command of Alexander. It took months and heavy casualties to dislodge the Germans from their perfect defense positions in the jagged Apennines and behind swift rivers. To pass Cassino, where Saint Benedict had begun Western monasticism in the sixth century, was costly and long-drawn-out. Rome was not entered until mid-1944, only two days before the invasion of France.

The slow push northward was not abandoned. Allied forces in this theater, called a "demonstration of the solidarity of the United Nations," comprised "Americans, British, Canadians, French, New Zealanders, South Africans, Poles, Indians, Brazilians, Italians, Greeks, Moroccans, Algerians, Goums, Senegalese, and a brigade of Jewish soldiers." There were even American-born Japanese. Florence and Pisa fell; but the Germans stood firm behind their powerful "Gothic line," guarding the Po valley. Not until spring, 1945, with Germany about to collapse, were the Allied troops able to sweep into that valley. But in spite of its disheartening aspects, this campaign kept a quarter-million of the best German soldiers too busily engaged to aid in the defense of the fatherland.

Strategic Bombing

Britain had not been idle during those years when she had no armies in the European theater; her air force was dealing out increasing punishment ever closer to the heart of Germany. Early in the war Marshal Göring had promised the German people that no bomb would fall on Berlin; but even before the end of 1941 hundreds of bombers from Britain were proving him a false prophet. The destruction wrought by the Luftwaffe in London, Coventry, and Bristol seemed mild, indeed, as the Allies constantly stepped up their raids upon German cities and military targets. Such strategic bombing was the airmen's own private show. Enemy cities hundreds of miles from the nearest British regiment or warship were laid in ruins by the planes of the R.A.F. Experts carefully studied the industrial and transportation systems of Germany in order to make every bomb do the maximum damage in softening up the enemy. Some air enthusiasts predicted that these attacks alone would be enough to bring Germany to her knees. That did not happen, but continuous bombing left the Germans greatly handicapped when the Allied ground forces finally came to grips with them.

Whereas British efforts had been concentrated on the production of fighter planes, now as the battle of Britain slackened in mid-1941, emphasis was shifted to bombers for the aerial counterattack. That fall, four hundred planes raided Berlin; but the Germans had their first real taste of the horrors to come when, late in the spring of 1942, a thousand planes in ninety minutes dropped three thousand tons of bombs on Cologne. The casualties of that single night of horror were about equal to the total in England during the whole year of 1940. Such night saturation attacks became the conventional R.A.F. formula.

American bombers based in England soon joined the offensive with a different technique. Their giant, multimotored, well-armored planes, with their excellent bomb-sights, went in for daylight precision bombing of specific factories or other key targets. By mid-1943 a round-the-clock schedule gave the Germans little respite: by night the R.A.F. would leave a saturated city in a sea of flames; the next day the Americans would single out specific objectives for destruction. With the clearing of North Africa and the landings in Italy, Axis installations beyond the range of British-based bombers came into the danger zone.

From time to time target priorities changed. Attention at first was concentrated upon submarines and planes, together with the plants that built them. Germany's synthetic oil production next was systematically cut down to about a fifth of its capacity; and the great steel works of the Ruhr were laid waste. Pilots hunted out locomotives, railroad yards, and other key links in the transportation system until it was frequently and badly disrupted. Plants where secret weapons were in production or in blueprint suddenly disappeared. And so it went, month after month. Many Allied bombers did not return from their flights over Germany, for the German antiaircraft flak was effective and the enemy fighter planes, sometimes firing rockets, took their toll. To defend the homeland, Germany weakened her air force on the Russian front. In one wild week the Luftwaffe went all out in a desperate defense against the incessant terror from the skies, and lost far more planes than it could afford. But the never-ceasing punishment went on. As Churchill put it, "He who sows the wind shall reap the whirlwind."

Early in 1944, as the invasion date grew closer, the bombings by the R.A.F. and the American air forces took on an even intenser fury. Hamburg almost disappeared; the heart of Berlin was gutted. Preparatory bombing wiped out bridges and disrupted all routes by which the Germans could bring reinforcements to the threatened invasion areas.

The Normandy Landings

During these months other tireless preparations were completed for the invasion. Landing on the exceedingly well-fortified coast of France presented problems of the gravest sort; and failure could not be risked. American troops had been pouring overseas at the rate of 150,000 a month to join in training with the British and Canadians. American industry, now in high gear, was making amazing production records. Huge concrete and steel caissons were assembled to be towed across the Channel to make artificial ports. Engineers were building underwater oil pipe lines to France. All this —and infinitely much else planned in the minutest detail—was guarded with the utmost secrecy as the ground, air, and sea forces rehearsed again and again. The landing site was not singled out for special softening until the very last hours. Meanwhile, all along the invasion coast from Calais to Brittany, worried Germans waited anxiously behind their mined beaches, artillery-protected cliffs, and elaborate concrete defenses for this new war machine to select its point of attack.

June 6, 1944, was D-Day; the British and Americans landed in force upon the shores of Normandy. The final drive to victory and Berlin was under way. The establishment of beachheads was of unsurpassed difficulty. A storm delayed the invasion flotilla, but at last, in the dark hours long before daylight, the terrific bombing of the German defenses began, as paratroopers and other air-borne troops were dropped in the rear of the fortifications. The surprise was complete. Some eleven thousand Allied aircraft of every sort crowded the skies over the Channel. The main armies filled some four thousand landing craft, and were convoyed across by eight hundred warships. As this immense fleet neared France, the battleships and cruisers stood in to give the shore defenses further punishment by their devastating big guns. The soldiers stormed ashore with guns and tanks under the protective screen of fire from bombing planes and naval guns. Yet there was bloody fighting on the beaches, and the casualties were heavy. But the invaders won a foothold. Slowly, the enemy were pushed back from the shore, and the beachheads were joined. Reinforcements were brought in on an average of

Assault troops going ashore in the initial Normandy landings on "D-Day," June 6, 1944. Along the shore are amphibious vehicles which assisted in the landings; the smoke in background is from the naval supporting gunfire.

nearly 40,000 a day to reach a million within the first twenty days, even though the worst June gales in forty years wrecked half of the artificial port installations.

The British and Americans had shared the initial attack in almost equal numbers, but ultimately almost three quarters of the total forces were from the United States, with part of the remainder from Canada. An American general, Eisenhower, was the Supreme Allied Commander.

Nine days after D-Day, Germany struck back with a new and highly destructive air assault against Britain. Small robot bombs without pilots, jet-propelled from bases on the French coast, descended upon southeast England in general and on London in particular. Each carried a ton of high explosive, causing extensive damage, especially to buildings. They came without warning at any hour, day or night, and with such speed that they were not heard until

they had passed by. Fighter planes, barrage balloons, and antiaircraft fire brought down many, but some 2300 of them landed. It was a fresh nerve-shattering ordeal for the weary people; more than four thousand were killed, and a million homes were damaged before September when the advancing armies captured the major robot bases. These bombs were forerunners of the later important missile development.

Through June and well into July the fighting was stubborn and savage in the battle of Normandy; it ended with the spectacular break-through of American armored divisions. They tore through France, separating two German armies and forcing their retreat to their own borders, much as the Germans had split the Allies in their onrush in France in 1940. Paris was freed late in August, and by mid-September two American armies had crossed the German border. On their right another American army, which had been landed in southern France, was moving steadily up toward the Rhine, having met its chief resistance at Marseilles and Toulon, where the French fleet had long before been scuttled by its crews. Meanwhile, the British and Canadians, advancing up the Channel coast, were capturing the robot bomb emplacements. Moving into Belgium they took Antwerp with its docks intact. The greatest air-borne operation of the war landed British and American troops in Holland, by a plan to turn the enemy right flank in order to advance over easy level country into Germany.

It looked as though final victory were coming before snowfall; then various misfortunes bogged down the onrushing offensive. The lightning advance of the American armored divisions had to be halted until supplies caught up with them. An adequate port was needed; Antwerp was useless until the lower Scheldt was cleared, and there was stubborn fighting there. And at Arnhem the Germans successfully checked the air-borne offensive. The Siegfried line, or West Wall, and the broad Rhine still guarded much of their front. Suddenly, just before Christmas, the Germans counterattacked with fury against a thinly held American sector in the Ardennes. For a few desperate days a break-through threatened. The American losses were heavy. Forces from the north and from the south rushed to the rescue, and relentlessly pushed the enemy back and out of the salient. This "Battle of the Bulge" gave the Germans a six weeks' respite, but it cost them most of their remaining armored force.

By late winter the Allied forces were ready to cross the Rhine. On the extreme left in Holland were the Canadian First Army and the British Second Army; on the extreme right, toward the Swiss border, was the French First Army. In the center, comprising nearly three quarters of the total strength, stood the Americans. Early in the opening of 1945 by a lucky stroke an American armored patrol successfully rushed the bridge at Remagen before the Germans could blow it up. In great force the American First Army poured across; the Germans had to hurry troops from all directions in an effort to stop them, thus dislocating their carefully planned defense behind their river. Meanwhile, the Canadians were mopping up the rest of the Netherlands, while the British sped ahead to take Bremen and Hamburg. The main objective lay in the vital industrial region of the Ruhr, where the British co-operated with the Americans to trap a huge German force.

It had become pretty much a rout in the west by the first of April; and in the east the Russians were pushing German forces steadily ahead of them into Germany. The gap between the two fronts narrowed daily, until later that month Russian and American patrols met. To the Russians was granted the costly but ultimately profitable honor of the assault on Berlin.

The German Surrender

The end came during the first week of May; the Germans in Italy surrendered first and next those in northwest Germany, Holland, and Denmark; finally the Germans made their complete and unconditional surrender at Reims. The two men who had led their nations to disaster disappeared in those last days. Hitler, in the final Russian assault on Berlin, apparently married his mistress, and together they committed suicide. The fleeing Mussolini and his mistress were captured by fellow countrymen and shot on the spot, and their battered bodies were hung by the heels in a public square of Milan.

The United States took V-E (Victory-in-Europe) Day in her stride; her mind was still on the war with Japan. London and the rest of Britain, however, went wild at the surrender, for the imminent menace of years at last was gone. The distant fighting on Pacific islands was almost forgotten in their sense of overwhelming relief.

Churchill Defeated by Labor

Churchill soon suffered as the victim of that attitude. Labor had agreed to co-operate in his coalition government while the war lasted, but had not specified which war. Churchill had promised that Britain would throw her full resources against Japan, but the Labor party was unwilling to wait for the outcome of that contest. They had recognized his unique value as a war leader, but felt that he was not sufficiently sympathetic toward their ideas of social reform to give them the reconstruction which they had long had in mind.

In view of the growing opposition, Churchill secured a dissolution of Parliament late in May. Until the appeal to the country could be made and its results known, he set up a provisional "caretaker" government in place of the wartime coalition. After the general election, the first in ten years, weeks elapsed before the votes of distant soldiers and sailors could be counted.

Labor won a smashing victory, jumping from only 163 seats to 390 out of the total of 640 in Commons. With this clear majority, it would not this time be dependent upon Liberal support. Churchill kept his own seat and headed the Opposition. Only time would tell what this would mean to the British way of life. In addition to its long-range social reconstruction, the Labor party's immediate plans called for such socialistic measures as the nationalization of mines, utilities, and the Bank of England. Such other projects as the stimulus of export trade and the mass building of homes in the bomb-ravaged nation would probably have found a place on the program of any ministry at this time, however conservative in viewpoint.

The Labor leaders were still a mixture of old-school-tie intellectuals and former workmen who had come up the hard way (see page 602). Like Ramsay MacDonald, Clement Attlee, the prime minister, represented the former, and so did the head of the Board of Trade, Sir Stafford Cripps, the brilliant lawyer of the 1942 mission to India. Attlee, as leader of the Opposition for five years before he joined the coalition cabinet in 1940, as Lord Privy Seal and later as Deputy Prime Minister, was the obvious choice as Churchill's successor. Son of a London lawyer, he had won honors in history at Oxford, and keenly interested in social work, had lived among the poor in East London, at times working at the docks. "An enthusiastic convert to socialism," he joined the Fabian Society and the Independent Labor party (see pages 488, 492). He taught at the London School of Economics for nine years, interrupted by his service in France, Gallipoli, and Mesopotamia in World War I, in which he rose to major. Four years after the war, he was beginning to hold a series of junior political posts, and by 1935 headed the Opposition. Though lacking the Churchillian color and oratory, he was at sixty-two well versed in government and thoroughly respected for his sincerity and integrity.

From the ranks of labor itself came his Foreign Secretary, Ernest Bevin, big, ruddy-faced, and vigorous Minister of Labor and National Service of the War Cabinet. Son of a West Country farmer, an orphaned farm hand at ten and later a truck-driver in Bristol, he showed in the Dockers Union that he was a born labor organizer. His master stroke in 1922 was the merging of thirty-two unions into the powerful Transport and General Workers Union. In 1936 he became head of the central council of the trade unions, the highest position in British organized labor. Lord President of the Council and leader of Commons was another self-made man in the new ministry, Herbert Stanley Morrison, son of a London policeman. He had started as errand boy, become an authority on local government, served in the second MacDonald ministry, organized London's air-raid precautions, and been Home Secretary in the coalition

War Cabinet. Nine of the new ministry had been miners; one of the new Lords of the Admiralty was a former stoker in the royal navy.

Potsdam and the United Nations

As this change of government took place, another conference of the leaders of the Big Three was going on at Potsdam on the edge of ruined Berlin. But only Stalin was left of the old triumvirate. President Truman was there instead of Roosevelt, who had died in April, and Churchill, in the midst of the negotiation, had to relinquish his place to Attlee. The plans for the control of Germany drawn up at this meeting were harsh in the extreme and made the severe terms of 1919 seem mild indeed (see page 591). Germany was to be permitted no government of her own for the time being; she was to be divided into four zones to be occupied and ruled separately by Britain, Russia, the United States, and France; her industries were to be stripped to a bare subsistence minimum to give her a standard of living far lower than she had had; and her war-making potential was to be completely destroyed. An innovation in international relations was the plan to put her leaders on trial for their lives as war criminals, her army and navy commanders, even her diplomats, and perhaps even her industrialists. The world had been particularly angered and shocked by the deliberate and efficient murder in concentration camps of millions, especially Jews of many nationalities, and of Poles, but also Russians, Frenchmen, anti-Nazi Germans, and others.

Neither this conference nor the San Francisco gathering of representatives from more than fifty United Nations during the late spring pretended to deal with the final peace settlement. That was left to the future. In the meantime, the United Nations tried hard to draw up a workable organization to keep the peace and to settle international disputes without war. It was much on the order of the old League of Nations, but every effort was made to avoid the pitfalls which had wrecked that earlier international organization for peace.

A somber realization came over Englishmen during these months: London was now overshadowed in influence by both Washington and Moscow. It was one thing that the United States, grown from Britain's former transatlantic colonies, now was hailed as mistress of the seas and air, outstripping her in population, wealth, and much else besides. At least, the two nations still spoke the same language in more senses than one and had behind them over a century and a quarter of peaceful settlement of disputes. But Russia exploiting her hard-earned gains was a different matter. It was ironic that she was now accomplishing the very thing which Britain had gone to war to prevent Germany from doing: the domination of Poland and of most of central and eastern Europe. In Greece, the one Balkan state not yet under her sway, British troops were intervening, and Churchill had spent the previous Christmas Day in Athens in efforts to check the spread of Russian influence. Elsewhere too the Lion and the Bear were already growling; future prospects were not pleasant.

The Defeat of Japan

Through all this the distant war with Japan was heading fast toward victory. Britain's contribution to it was to be mainly on land and in Burma, while the Americans were making their spectacular advances across the Pacific. Of the ground troops in Burma in 1945, only about 25,000 were Americans, whereas about 250,000 came from Britain, some 470,000 were Indian, with some 30,000 each from British West Africa and British East Africa. Chinese forces engaged were approximately 125,000. With 40,000 casualties and no fewer than 237,000 cases of illness, the fighting there in 1944 had proved costly to the British both from enemy action and from the execrable climate. But the next year the fighting reached its climax with the capture of Japan's main base, Mandalay, in a brilliant campaign under General Slim. He then raced south and took Rangoon, just before the monsoon rains put an end to the campaign. "Slim had beaten the enemy and the monsoon" in Japan's severest defeat on the Asiatic continent. Burma, approximately the size of Germany, was thus rewon.

The real threat to Japan, however, was coming by sea. Being an island kingdom, like England, she was very vulnerable. Cutting an island off from its essential supplies means surrender sooner or later. Germany had known, in both world wars, that if she won the battle of the Atlantic, victory might well be hers. What the U-boats failed to accomplish against England, the United States navy, with modest help from other Allied warships, succeeded in doing to Japan.

This essentially American effort, like the Russian victories, needs but brief mention. The desperate days of 1942 had long since passed in the Pacific, where the tremendous industrial output of the United States was furnishing an overwhelming superiority in ships, planes, rocket guns, and all sorts of other tools for victory; and skilled leadership was making the most of these material assets.

Two separate drives were placing the Mikado's home islands in deadly peril. American and Australian forces, land, sea, and air, were "climbing the ladder" of the coast of New Guinea and adjacent islands. The American Pacific Fleet, with air and ground forces, was slashing across the Central Pacific. Some islands were captured and others by-passed, with their garrisons left to "wither on the vine." Once Saipan and the other Marianas were taken in mid-1944, the giant B-29 bombers were based only seven hours from Tokyo, Yokohama, and other inflammable targets; and they began to pound them regularly.

The autumn of 1944 saw the two drives joined with landings in the Philippines. Japan's communications with her stolen riches in Malaya, Java, Borneo, and the rest were now in serious jeopardy. In March, 1945, the costly capture of tiny Iwo Jima, only 775 miles from Japan proper, enabled fighter planes to accompany the bombers on their raids of the home islands. By that time some capital ships from the royal navy had joined the American fleet. The bloody assault on Okinawa, still closer to Japan, came as Germany surrendered.

In the secret councils of the combined command tremendous forces were being assembled for the "Olympic" invasion of the southern island of Japan proper, planned for the fall of 1945, and to be followed by the "Coronet" attack on the main island early in 1946. After the desperate resistance on Iwo Jima and Okinawa, these final drives, it was feared, might take a million lives, but they never came.

The Atomic Bomb

Instead, the first atomic bomb put Japan immediately out of the war. B-29's and carrier-based planes had been inflicting terrible destruction upon Japan's cities and the remnants of her fleet, but that was nothing compared with what happened to the populous industrial city of Hiroshima in August. Its heart was wiped out by a single bomb of a new and revolutionary nature. That one bomb, flattening a wide area, killed more people than the entire total of civilian victims of air power in England during the whole war. Scientists had known for some time of the tremendous force which might be released by splitting the atom; and during the war both sides had been racing to translate that power into a practicable weapon. With utmost secrecy the combined efforts of hundreds of scientists, chiefly American and British, finally produced a workable atom bomb. Some of these bombs were rushed by fast cruiser to the Marianas; and Hiroshima was selected as the unlucky target. Three days later a second such bomb wrought similar annihilation in the port of Nagasaki. Between those two bombs Russia declared war upon Japan and launched an attack upon Manchuria.

Thus came the end of the Second World War less than a week later as peace negotiations culminated in a cessation of hostilities. The formal signing of unconditional surrender by the Japanese took place on September 1 in dramatic ceremonies on the deck of the American battleship *Missouri* in Tokyo Bay. Nine of the United Nations, among them the three Dominions of Australia, Canada, and New Zealand, signed the document that ended this second catastrophe of the twentieth century.

Britain had weathered another world war, but grave problems of peace clouded the hour of triumph. The terrible potentialities of the atom bomb sobered the whole world in that moment of victory. At home her economic future looked grim. Along with labor's plans for social reconstruction went the realization that the nation must "export or die" and tighten its belt with even shorter food rations. With all that, Britain's millions faced the uncertain future with the same undaunted fortitude which had carried them through the battle of Britain and earlier crises of their history.

Austerity and Cold War

Once again, victory was to bring stress and strain to Britain. The years after the defeat of Napoleon in 1815 and of the Germans in 1918 were, at their worst, but mild previews of the sheer dreariness that had to be endured after World War II (see pages 390, 594). Behind much of the trouble lay Britain's inability to pay for what she needed from beyond the seas.

Always before, much of the outside world had owed money to Britain; now, roles were reversed, and Britain was the debtor. Largely because of that, the fifty million Britons were forced to forego, year after year, many of the things that make life more pleasant. For the same reason, it was necessary to cut down the size of the once-great royal navy and the other armed forces. And, partly because of that, the British Empire-Commonwealth began to disintegrate. Those difficulties would probably have beset Britain whether Conservatives, Liberals, Labor, or even a divine-right king had been in power. But, further to complicate the picture, the British government for the first six postwar years was in the hands of the Labor party, which was determined to carry out its socializing, nationalizing, leveling policies, come hell or high water.

Some of these postwar problems had their roots back in the mid-Victorian pe-riod. In 1850 Britain still had what the Mercantilists had termed a "favorable balance of trade," with exports exceeding imports. Ten years later, British exports no longer paid for the imports, and the gap between them grew wider as the "workshop of the world" drew more and more of its food from beyond the seas (see pages 425 ff.). There was no cause for alarm then, however, because Britain had ample "invisible" means of paying for the surplus imports. Part of those consisted of the earnings of shipping, of banking, and of insurance; and in later days the spending of foreign tourists. Behind those special sources of revenue, moreover, lay rich resources from money invested beyond the seas—the so-called "Victorian heritage" (see page 546). That in itself was enough to pay Britain's heavy bill for food imports.

The situation was not to be that good again. During World War I, Britain, hard pressed to pay for American munitions liquidated a quarter of that total. Despite that heavy cut, the "Victorian heritage" by 1939 had climbed back to £3,600,000,000 ($14,-400,000,000). By that time, however, with exports shrinking, the interest and dividends from those overseas investments could pay for only half the food imports.

Then, during World War II, Britain's account with the outside world went "into the red." By 1945 she owed outsiders more than they owed her. Once again in this war she was forced to liquidate another heavy share of the "Victorian heritage." The government required private investors to turn over, in exchange for government securities, their marketable stocks and bonds to be sold in New York to build up the needed "dollar exchange." A substantial part of these assets were sold this time. In addition to this, Britain ran deeply into debt, not only within the Commonwealth, but with some foreign nations as well. This debt, coupled with the sale of the securities, meant a total "disinvestment" of some £4,200,000,000 ($16,000,000,000). Britain now owed some £112,000,000 ($448,000,000) a year in interest alone to outside regions, outweighing four to one the income from the meager remnant of her once-great overseas investments. Now and then during the postwar years, it again became necessary to dispose of more of those distant holdings. When Britain sacrificed her Argentine rail holdings to pay for meat, a London newspaper cartoon showed a butcher telling his customer: "In the future, Mrs. Jones, every time you eat a sausage say to yourself 'Wallop! There goes another British-owned railway in Buenos Aires.'"

Further complications were caused by the new wide gap between the American dollar and the British pound sterling. Before 1914, most nations were on the gold standard, with no artificial barriers to prevent them from using the London money market as a sort of clearing house to keep their accounts straight. If they wound up owing more than was coming to them, they could ship gold to make up the difference. The relationships of the various currencies to gold and to each other remained virtually unchanged year after year. Everyone knew that in terms of American dollars the pound sterling was worth about $4.87, the German mark about 24 cents, the French franc and the Italian lira about 19 cents, and so on. After World War I, things were never the

same again. One nation after another went off the gold standard; even Britain did so in 1931. This meant that no longer must paper money be redeemed on demand, in gold (see page 607). New strange patterns, even including barter, took the place of the old free exchange of the London money market.

Gradually the American dollar began to achieve a unique commanding position in the world of international finance, even though it, too, was no longer redeemable in gold. The United States had a great many assets that made her dollar desirable, including a large share of the world's gold supply buried at Fort Knox in Kentucky. Her vast natural resources and tremendous industrial plant gave her a surplus of materials which other nations wanted and needed; but there was comparatively little which the United States needed from them. Unlike Britain, she had ample meat, wheat, oil, and much else within her spacious borders. To complicate matters further, her tariff walls protected many of her industries, which made it difficult, of course, for other nations to repay their debts in manufactures. Consequently, there arose around the world a clamor for "dollar exchange," which was very hard to come by. The world's currencies were divided into the "hard," which meant principally United States and Canadian dollars, and the "soft," which included the pound sterling and almost everything else.

Back around 1930, when she went off the gold standard, Britain had organized the so-called "sterling area," consisting chiefly of herself, most of her Empire-Commonwealth except Canada, and a few other nations. To avoid running into debt to outsiders, trade was encouraged within this group as far as possible. Could Britain have developed as completely a "self-sufficient empire" as the Mercantilists had sought in the seventeenth century, perhaps all might have been well; but things were required from the United States that neither Australia, South Africa, India, Malaya, nor the

As an example of the "export or die" campaign, a case of British clocks is shown being hoisted aboard the Cunard liner, *Queen Mary*, for the American market.

other sterling regions could produce. To make this "sterling area" more effective in the postwar situation, Britain established a "dollar pool," with herself acting as the banker. In this the various members would deposit what they received from sales to the Americans, and from it they might draw what they needed for purchases from the United States and Canada. It was rather like a joint bank account, in which sometimes one party does most of the depositing and the other most of the withdrawing.

Britain tried three ways to solve this severe dollar exchange shortage. The first, called "earning dollars," necessitated a drastic increase in the nation's exports, particularly to dollar areas. In the second, "saving dollars," purchases from America were reduced, and from this came the grim years of austerity for the average Briton. The third step consisted of getting loans or gifts of dollars from the United States or Canada.

The most satisfactory solution naturally would have been the stimulating of exports, a field in which England had so long led the world (see pages 424 ff.). It was estimated in 1945 that she would have to export at 175 per cent of the 1938 rate in order to pay for her imports, now that not enough was left of the "Victorian heritage" to close the export-import gap. During these postwar years there was constant exhortation to meet that goal, with varying success in different industries.

Britain had long exported coal, that mainstay of her Industrial Revolution, in large quantities to Italy, Brazil, and other countries that had lacked their own supply, and had maintained bunkerage depots in seaports all around the world to keep ships moving. These steady outward cargoes had been one of the things that had made British tramp shipping so profitable. In 1913 she had produced 287,000,000 tons of coal, of which 94,000,000 tons were exported. This amounted to 55 per cent of all world exports. By 1938 production had dropped to 227,000,000 tons, with only 46,000,000 exported; in 1945, with World War II still dislocating industry, production was down to 182,000,000 tons, with a mere 8,000,000 exported. Difficulties lay in the way of reviving that once lucrative trade. The general shift to oil-burning ships and the competition from American coal mines had seriously damaged the profitable returns from the British mines. The crippled industry became the center of labor unrest in the mid-twenties, as the hard-pressed operators tried to cut costs (see pages 594, 605). It had continued to be a troublesome sore spot. Some mines had been abandoned; others having been worked for a century or more now had to be dug very deep; and machinery and equipment were too often obsolete. Young workers in the thirties had avoided such an obviously "sick industry." Those still in it were inclined to be recalcitrant with little fear of discharge or wage cuts. The trade unions had opposed a proposal to bring over 100,000 displaced Polish miners. To complicate matters further, the unions demanded the same pay for a five-day week as they had been getting for six days' work. Their new employer under the Labor government, the National Coal Board, allowed this, although it brought higher coal prices. In spite of better pay, the curse of absenteeism continued to lie heavy over the mines. Early in 1947 a bad coal shortage paralyzed industry for several weeks. Later that year, 40,000 miners in Yorkshire staged a thirty-five-day strike that cost some 570,000 tons of coal. The effort to "earn dollars" from coal was, consequently, hardly a success.

At the opposite extreme, the manufacture and export of automobiles and trucks began what was to become a remarkable boom (see page 690). In steel, a more typically British field, Britain produced in 1950, just before the industry was nationalized, 16,-200,000 tons, which was an all-time record.

Textiles responded more slowly. Labor had been dislocated, and wages had not been attractive enough to lure large numbers back to the spindles and looms.

The difficulties of the export-import race were that while the export totals might climb in a most encouraging manner, the imports kept well ahead of them. The "invisible services," such as banking, shipping, and insurance, might make up some of the export deficit, but there was still indebtedness left, especially to the dollar area. One factor was that the general trend of postwar international trade was unfavorable to Britain, since the prices of some raw materials that she had to import increased much more rapidly than the prices which could be obtained for manufactured exports. Another dilemma was that while the United States and Canada furnished nearly 20 per cent of the imports, they took only 7.6 per cent of Britain's exports in return. Her best customers—Australia, South Africa, India, and Ireland—were within the sterling area; and that, of course, was no help in the crucial dollar situation.

In September, 1949, the government took a drastic step to improve the export situation. The pound sterling, once rated at about $4.87, had been stabilized at $4.08 for the past ten years. Now it was suddenly devalued to $2.80. This move cut the price of British exports in America 30 per cent, which it was hoped would increase their sale. Devaluation, however, was a two-edged weapon. The British themselves would now have to pay more of their devalued pounds to purchase needed American goods. Within a month after Britain reduced the value of the pound, twenty-eight other countries, including most of her Commonwealth, had followed her example in adjusting their currencies downward.

Hand in hand with "earning dollars" by exportation had to go the unpleasant task of "saving dollars" by reducing imports from the hard money countries. One way of doing this—and the least painful—was to grow as

A scene all too familiar to Britons during the austerity years: a queue of women at a shop selling jellied eels at the Elephant and Castle; London, 1949.

much food as possible at home. England's agriculture slump of the 1870's made her so dependent upon overseas foodstuffs that in World War I what she grew in a year provided food enough for only a few weeks (see pages 425 ff.). During World War II she had extended her agricultural acreage to produce a much larger proportion of her necessary food (see page 647). This process was further extended in the postwar years. By 1950 she was raising 40 per cent of her food, which was excellent progress in view of past performance.

This left still 60 per cent of the food supply, along with a host of other imported goods, to be kept in check by the hard road of austerity. The consumption of meat, bread, gasoline, tobacco, and much else had to be low. Newspapers, too, felt the pinch when they were cut to four pages to save newsprint imports. Even amusements were curtailed in the form of American movies,

another item on which dollars could be saved. Likewise clothing and liquor—both in demand overseas as popular British products—had to be conserved for export to "earn dollars." Crushing taxes intensified the depressing impact of all this.

The first postwar years brought relatively scant relief from wartime deprivations. The first disheartening shock was the Labor government's request for five more years of much of the wartime rationing of many commodities (see page 626). When submarine-infested seas caused the shortages, the people had been buoyed up by the expectation that the war was not going to last forever. "The Briton's life is still an interminable sequence of eating dull food, standing in queues and going home to a shabby house or apartment," as one writer put it in 1946. The meager supplies for home consumption, the high taxes, and the exorbitant cost of average comforts made for an inexpressible weariness among the people as a whole.

As far as food was concerned, the government subsidies kept prices down, so that few went hungry. In fact, for much of the period, more was spent on food subsidies than on the Navy and the Air Force. In theory, all economic groups felt equally the impact of the national struggle to keep food imports as low as possible. Opinions differed over the official claim that the national health was better than in prewar days, but no one disputed the poor quality, lack of variety, and general drabness of the fare. Housewives, struggling under such handicaps, could scarcely have been pleased when the Economic Secretary of the Treasury referred to them as "not to be trusted to buy the right things. . . . In the case of health and nutrition, just as in the case of education, the gentleman in Whitehall really does know better what is good for people than the people know themselves." Fresh fruit, canned goods, meat, and butter were among the strictly rationed goods. Then in 1947, bread, the staple of restricted diets, was added to the list. After that black year, there was some gradual relaxation; but even at the end of 1952, when the meat ration was to be raised a bit, it still was not quite enough to buy a pound of ground beef a week.

With the vexatious restrictions on clothing, morale was not helped by shop windows well stocked with clothes marked "For Export Only." The forty-two clothing coupons a year covered also such household equipment as sheets and towels. Already shabby from the lean war years, the public became increasingly tired of an allowance far too short to meet bare replacement needs.

Soaring prices were counted upon to curb demand for the so-called luxury items when, in one year's analysis of dollar expenditures, it was found that 12 per cent had gone abroad for tobacco and 4 per cent for movie films, the tobacco supply was thereupon drastically curtailed, with the result that by the end of 1947, a package of twenty cigarettes cost more than three times the American price. There was a rush for preparations to make it easier to stop smoking. A 75 per cent levy was laid upon the profits from American movie films. In the matter of gasoline (petrol), an increase in the allowance for so-called pleasure driving at the end of the war was withdrawn by 1947. The price of poor quality beer increased to the equivalent of twenty-three cents a glass. Scotch whiskey, an export item of importance, brought fantastic prices or was diluted in content. The long-standing British passion for travel was rudely curtailed by the rigid restriction on the amount of cash which could be taken out of the country and the necessity of buying exchange for each particular currency.

It began to look as though there never might be an end to going without, as the situation grew gradually worse into 1947. In a Christmas broadcast that winter of 1946-1947 General Slim, the hero of Burma, declared, "We are dissatisfied, restless, uncertain. We were more at peace inside ourselves when we were at war." A few days later, one newspaper referred to the weariness from "forever making do and mending in a way of life that is drab, grubby, undersoaped, and starved of color." And this was now pretty much the lot of everyone, as it had always been for the poverty-stricken. Storms, then, gave England the worst winter since 1894; for weeks on end the sun did not shine. The Minister of Fuel had gambled on mild weather with the coal supply. It was necessary to shut off electric power for several weeks; mills closed down; two million were unemployed; the export goals suffered a heavy setback; and in homes throughout the land the lack of facilities for lighting and heating accentuated the long-accumulating discontent. "England is bitterly cold and coldly bitter," snapped one commentator. Slowly, in 1948, conditions began to improve somewhat; and by coronation year, 1953, most controls had been relaxed.

The third possibility for solving the dollar problem was to seek financial relief from beyond the seas. This meant from the United States in particular, of which the British, who had borne the heavier wartime burden, were somewhat resentful. Yet, those former colonies were the one real source of hope; and they had come to Britain's aid even before entering the war. Altogether, the British had received more than two thirds of the billions spent by the United States on lend lease (see page 635). Scarcely was the war over, however, when Washington's announcement that lend-lease was to terminate immediately created consternation in London, which then began to look for a substitute form of financial aid. Consequently, an Anglo-American agreement, made in December, 1945, and approved by Congress the following summer, provided for a $3,750,000,000 loan at low interest. This was expected to be enough to enable Britain to meet her dollar obligations. At about the same time, Canada loaned an additional $1,250,000,000. Even this total of five billions proved insufficient; the United States' funds were virtually gone by mid-1947, and once more it was necessary to go to Washington, hat in hand.

At this point the American Secretary of State, General Marshall, proposed in June, 1947, that the United States contribute financially to the democratic nations of Western Europe to put them on their feet. The purpose was to keep them from economic and social distress, which might turn them toward Communism. By the next year Britain was the principal beneficiary of this "Marshall Plan," as she had been of lend-lease. By the end of 1950 affairs in Britain had taken a turn for the better, and the government announced that it could get along without further Marshall Plan help. The estimate was premature, however, and Britain once more turned hopefully to Washington.

During these dismal postwar years the Labor party was going right ahead with its plans to change the British way of life. This was the first time the party had a clear majority in Commons to push through its program (see page 656). Neither the dislocations, the wreckage, and the dilapidated condition of war-torn Britain, nor the staggering losses in manpower and economic resources were to stop the Labor government from attempting much and achieving a fair amount. And all this added tremendously to the already smothering financial load on the nation. Through the increased taxes and subsidies, moreover, the leveling theories of the Laborites could be carried out, making the rich ever poorer and the very poor better off, with the full weight crushing the middle, white-collar classes.

In its manifesto of 1945, the Labor party proclaimed itself "a socialist party and proud of it. Its ultimate purpose at home is the establishment of the Socialist Commonwealth of Great Britain—free, democratic, efficient, progressive, public spirited, its material resources organized in the service of the British people." Such a socialistic state implies "the collective common ownership and collective control of the means of production and exchange." This was one of the beliefs of Marxian socialism (originally called communism). It was on its tenets that the Socialist Soviet Republics of Russia had been founded, although the Russian Communists later tended to diverge from the gospel both of Marx and of their own Lenin (see pages 434, 584). The more radical Labor theorists hoped that some day all the fruits of privately owned capital investment (the economic rent from land and mines, the interest on bonds, stocks, etc., and profits from business enterprises) might be altogether discarded as relics of a defunct nineteenth century laissez-faire economy. And when that day arrived all individual income would be on either a salary or a wage basis.

In the meantime the government began to take over industries—to nationalize them—as a major step in ending the private ownership of capital. Simultaneously controls were stiffened over such rents, interest, and profits as remained in private hands. Imports of many sorts were put under close regulation, and overseas agricultural experiments were attempted. Various projects for social betterment included free medical service, the extension of the required school age, and state-built houses with regulated rent.

Nationalization was instituted in finance, in certain key industries, in the overseas communication field, and in transportation. Actually this was not as revolutionary as it seemed. There was already government ownership of the telephone and telegraph, operated by the post-office officials. The British Overseas Airways Corporation and British European Airways were financed by the state with a virtual monopoly of air transportation. The British Broadcasting Corporation, with control of all domestic radio communication, was a government operation. Many docks and harbors, along with most public utilities, were owned by public trusts, while the supplying of electric voltage in bulk was under similar ownership and operation.

First to be nationalized, in 1946, was the Bank of England. That hardy "Old Lady of Threadneedle Street," dating back to 1694, would seem the last stronghold that Labor would dare approach, but its nationalization was accomplished without much hue and cry. Actually, it had long been accustomed to submit to the dictates of the Treasury. Here, as in other fields, the stock holders received three per cent government bonds in exchange for their shares.

Coal in its time did not make the hoped-for comeback, nor did hoisting the Union Jack over the pits make that disagreeable occupation more popular with the rank and file of workers. Overseas cables and radio communications were also taken over at this time. Then came the nationalization of transportation facilities, including railways, long-distance trucking, London buses, and the like.

The experiment with coal cast something of a shadow over the pledge to nationalize the steel industry. Unlike coal, it had been highly successful under private ownership. Also, the technical problems in steel were extremely complicated. Yet the Labor government could scarcely claim Britain socialistic while such a basic industry flourished in private hands.

The bill for its nationalizing led to a constitutional change; Labor utilized its majority to amend the 1911 Parliament Act. The Lords' right to hold up non-money bills was reduced to one year. Again in 1958, the Lords were modified, when women were first admitted and the creation of non-hereditary members was extended to others than bishops and law lords.

With that new one-year restriction on the Lords, Labor was able to push through its steel nationalizing law a year before the election, due in 1950. Attlee's government promised to postpone nationalization until after the election, so the Conservatives agreed to its passage, planning to repeal it if returned to office.

The need to curb imports led to a series of special controls devices between 1945 and 1950. A Raw Cotton Commission was authorized to buy all cotton imported into England. The wartime Ministry of Food was continued to buy all imported meats, livestock, cereals, eggs, sugar, and tea. The Board of Trade was put in charge of all imports of chemicals, flax, hides, molasses, paper, plastics, timber, wool, sulphuric acid, and, for a short time, rubber. A Ministry of Supply supervised all imports of iron, steel, manganese, aluminum, and radioactive substances.

The Overseas Development Act carried experimentation into the colonial field. In Africa the state undertook to utilize waste land to grow ground nuts (peanuts) on a mammoth scale, to be crushed into vegetable oil. This bright scheme was sponsored by John Strachey, Minister of Food, who persuaded the government to set aside some 3,250,000 acres of bush land in East Africa. By 1952, it was confidently expected, 609,834 tons of peanuts would be harvested annually. For 1948, the estimate was 56,920 tons; for 1949, 227,676 tons. Some £23,000,000 had been spent for the experiment by 1949; but the harvest in 1948 was only 1,566 tons and by 1949 merely 7,150. Everything had gone wrong: the land proved poor for peanuts, proper machinery was not available, the native laborers misused what there was, and so it went.

The government's attempt to go into the poultry business in West Africa was another, though smaller, fiasco. In this £825,000 was spent; theoretically, the state-owned chickens were to produce 20,000,000 eggs a year. Instead only 38,000 eggs were laid, which were imported for the home market at a total cost to Britain of £20 per egg!

Nationalization of industry continued to remain a labor ideal, but as time passed, less and less stress was put upon it. The key place in the Labor program went instead to the social welfare services, whereby Labor planned to end poverty and unemployment. The National Health Services Act in 1948 was the pride of Aneurin Bevan's heart. That fiery miner—not to be confused with Ernest Bevin, the Foreign Secretary—had fought vigorously for unadulterated and immediate socialism; and now, as Minister of Health, he was doing all he could to achieve that end. Free medical and dental services were made available to everyone living in Britain. Doctors who joined the national service were paid by the state. People could still go to the doctor of their choice if he was able to take on that number of patients. Those who still wanted to pay for medical treatment were allowed to continue to do so. Some doctors were critical, claiming that the quality of service was lowered, because of the larger number of patients, and the required paper work. Apparently dentists objected less, perhaps because so many of them were making a better living than before. Almost a mania for teeth extractions, now free, seemed to seize a large section of the population.

It did not help Britain's financial woes that free prescriptions, spectacles, and dentures proved so popular. Many were said to be going to the doctor for written prescriptions for such remedies as aspirin. The state thus had the apothecary as well as the doctor to pay. Even wigs were provided for the bald; and since one only had to be in Britain to be eligible, Frenchmen were said to be crossing the Channel to obtain theirs from John Bull.

The National Insurance Act, in effect the same day as the National Health Act, rounded out what Attlee called "the most comprehensive system of social security ever introduced in any country." It was by no means the first attempt to safeguard people against the causes of insecurity—sickness, accident, unemployment, and old age. Bismarck had tried to "kill" the German Socialists "with kindness" by the first such major program in the 1880's. Britain had made further advances in the proposals that led to the Lloyd George Budget of 1909; and the United States in the 1930's had followed a similar path with its "New Deal" legislation. Sir William Beveridge, under Churchill's ministry in 1943, had gone still further with his plan to insure the populace against life's hazards "from the cradle to the grave" (see page 648). And now the Labor government was putting his ideas into effect.

Everyone above school age was required to make a single weekly payment that made one eligible for all the benefits, as circumstances might arise. For men, at the outset it was the equivalent of $1.00 matched by 85 cents from the employer; for women, the respective figures were the equivalent of 85 and 66 cents. There were seven general benefits: (1) the equivalent of $5.30 a week while unemployed, with extra for dependents; (2) the same amount when ill; (3) a maternity benefit at the birth of each child, plus a weekly allowance for thirteen weeks for working mothers; (4) a widow's benefit beginning at the equivalent of $7.34 a week plus $6.83 a week for each child in school; (5) a small "guardian's allowance" for any family with an orphan in it, one of whose parents had been insured; (6) retirement pensions of $5.30 a week for men over 65 and $3.26 for women over 60, if actually retired from work; and (7) a "death grant." This last, coupled with the maternity benefit, literally fulfilled the promise of insurance "from the cradle to the grave." A special setup in the act for Industrial Injuries Insurance took the place of the old Workmen's Compensation Acts. Men made an additional payment of about 7 cents and women about 5 cents; this was matched by the employers in equal amounts. These payments made them eligible for injury, disablement, and death benefits.

The weekly premiums paid barely 30 per cent of the cost of the insurance program at the outset and 9 per cent came from local "rates." The remaining cost of some £825 million ($3.3 billion), was one more drain on the overstrained national Exchequer. But however expensive all this new social legislation might be, the people liked it too well for any political party to dare attack it in principle.

The improvements in the educational system were likewise costly. The so-called "school-leaving age" was raised from fourteen to fifteen years; it was hoped eventually to extend this to sixteen. More money was granted for the building of new schools, the training of new teachers, and for free school lunches and milk, as well as for increased adult education. The universities received financial grants and scholarships for unusually promising students.

Some action had to be taken in connection with housing, with 460,000 houses completely destroyed by bombing or fire and 3,500,000 damaged during the war. Public housing, along with town planning, were old issues in British politics (see pages 472, 494). But now Bevan was in the driver's seat, and new houses were needed in almost astronomical numbers. A board was established to dictate what new buildings would be built and how land would be used. Reluctant landlords found themselves forced to sell at a low valuation. If a landowner wanted to keep his property for future development value, he was allowed to do so, but he was then faced with a development tax whether or not he built on his land or otherwise developed it. And if his decision was to build, he ran into restrictions on speculative building and on houses for individual ownership. Houses for rent were given priority over those for sale, because Bevan felt they served the interests of the poor better. A low ceiling price was put on the cost of private housing when allowed. Local authorities had to certify, moreover, that there was a surplus of labor and materials before granting such a permit. Those local boards were under orders to build quantities of low-cost rental units, with the government bearing three fourths or more of the construction costs as well as subsidizing the future rents. It was inevitably a bitter pill for many a citizen to swallow, when he was, perhaps, paying interest on his own mortgaged home, taxes on that home, and then had to help with further taxes to subsidize state-built houses occupied by those who had never saved, as he had.

Yet the number of housing units still was insufficient, although Bevan pointed with pride in 1950 to the new housing completed since 1945 that had more than replaced in numbers those destroyed by war. But, as his political opponents quickly showed, only a little more than half of the new units could be classified as permanent dwellings. Meanwhile the population had so multiplied that these were not nearly enough.

These social and economic changes would have been costly experiments even for a government operating well "in the black," but to the overstrained finances of postwar Britain they meant more taxes for an already overburdened people. Government bonds had largely paid for what was taken over. Also, the ever-widening mesh of controls necessitated an army of inspectors and officials. All this added up to an ever greater indebtedness. The drastic income taxes from the war, kept without much change, were just about as high already as the traffic could bear, with a normal tax of 45 per cent and with surtaxes running up to 98 per cent on the few incomes of £100,000 or more. Death duties were increased; they became so high that they could not normally be paid out of income, and capital assets had to be sold to meet them. Taxes on profits rose to an unprecedented height. The tax on dividends went up from 5 per cent in 1945 to 12½ per cent in 1946, and to 25 per cent the next year. The purchase (excise) tax on all luxury or near luxury goods was also increased, often running from 20 to 70 per cent. And on top of all this the government imposed a "once-in-a-lifetime" sort of "capital levy." Many taxpayers had to sell capital assets to pay this also. It was no wonder that peers and landed gentry were selling their estates or turning them over to the state.

And with all this the over-all picture of British life was changing. In the Civil Wars in the seventeenth century a radical sect, the "Levelers," had proposed to make the "lowest" men in England equal with the "greatest" (see page 242); now these postwar years saw rapid progress toward that goal. Politics has sometimes been described as a means of transferring money from the pockets of one group into those of another; and something of that sort was happening. A graphic example was the drop in the number of Britons with net incomes of £6,000: from 7,000 in 1938-1939 to 79 in 1945-1946. While the condition of the laboring classes improved, with a 20 per cent increase in the purchasing power of their wages, the salaries of white-collar workers and executives fell off 17 per cent. Profits from investments went down 27 per cent. Taxes were so heavy on the people of the so-called middle class that they were in danger of being liquidated as a group. Postwar costs of their standard of living were prohibitive, pushing them down toward a grubby sort of existence. On the surface, this was not always apparent, with Britishers traveling in Europe still, and with the famous and expensive public schools crowded as never before. But, in reality, many of the upper-middle-class group were living on capital, spending what they had while they still had some to spend. And that was hardly a good augury for the future stability of the nation.

Postwar Foreign Relations

Along with her economic ills and the disintegration of her empire (see pages 696 ff.), Britain was caught in the tangled, seething aftermath of the war in her foreign relations. Peace treaties had not yet been negotiated with the defeated nations, and British troops had to help make up armies of occupation, particularly in Germany. Throughout the world, within and without the empire, the rising surge of nationalism was becoming an irresistible force. The ever-threatening hostility of the Union of Socialist Soviet Republics, coupled before long with that of Communist China, and the ever-present fear of a nuclear "World War III" dominated international relations.

All seven of the world's former great powers found themselves in different relative positions from what these had been in 1939. The United States and Soviet Russia emerged from the war as the two most powerful nations on earth, respective leaders of the democratic West and the Communist East in the years of contest ahead. Germany and Japan were under the occupation of the victorious nations, the former by four powers and the latter by the United States alone. France had not recovered from the loss of prestige following her sudden collapse in 1940 and the later collaboration with the enemy; at this time, her Fourth Republic was becoming increasingly unstable. Italy's position was similar, with Communist elements stronger than in France.

As for Britain, long accustomed to being one of the top world powers, she now had to reconcile herself to a lower position as junior member of the "big three." With her drastically lessened armaments, due to her straitened finances, she could no longer speak with all her old authority. Yet foreign affairs made numerous demands upon her attention and her resources; the disintegration of her empire would blend into foreign relations in this disturbing period. In particular there was her heavy share in the occupation of Germany and the bitter hatred of much of the Moslem world with the relaxing of her imperial influence. Leadership had definitely passed to the United States, for she alone had the wealth and power to face Russia on something like equal terms. During the war Lord Halifax, then ambassador at Washington, warned, "What really matters for the future is to remember that after victory for the next hundred or two hundred years, the American people will be running the world. What matters even more is that they should begin to study how they are going to discharge that responsibility." That was not easy for the British to accept. Of particular concern to them and to many in Western Europe was the immediate peril that they would all be in if a wrong decision by the United States should cause the Russians to roll westward. Consequently, time and again, London would try to tone down some of the more drastic moves planned in Washington.

Even in the weeks before V-E Day, in 1945, Britain and the United States became aware of an attitude in their ally, Russia, that boded ill for the future. As time went on, it grew increasingly apparent that Stalin had driven some extremely sharp bargains both at Yalta, that spring, at the conference with Churchill and the dying Roosevelt, and at Berlin, that summer, when he met Attlee and Roosevelt's successor, Harry Truman. Despite her already tremendous area and population, and the need of repairing war damages, Russia seemed bent on obtaining all possible new territory and population with the apparent aim of ultimate world conquest at the expense of the "capitalistic, imperialistic democracies." In the Far East, her reward for belated and unneeded aid against Japan was privileges in Manchuria and some island territory. In Europe she shared the rule of Germany and Austria. But that was not enough for the Communists; they gained control in one helpless "satellite" after another: Poland, Rumania, Bulgaria, Hungary, Czechoslovakia, Albania, and, for a while, Yugoslavia.

Out of that situation came two new phrases signifying new experiences in international relations. The "iron curtain" denoted the barriers which the Russians raised to shut off themselves and their satellites from contact with the western world. The master minds of the dominant Politburo in the Kremlin at Moscow were aware that a full realization of what life was like in the democratic countries would be apt to cause serious discontent among the peoples in the sphere, whose meager economic existence made British austerity seem mild inconvenience. And under that Soviet domination was the constant terror of surveillance by a police state—the threat of the concentration camp. The "iron curtain" frontiers had to be guarded not only to keep out knowledge of western conditions, but also to keep in those distressed wretches who might long to escape to the democracies.

The phrase "cold war" was applied to the never-ending manifestations of hostility which the Russians for many years were to apply with keen ingenuity in one area after another, and also to the countermeasures taken by the democracies, in their turn, against such aggression. Behind it all was an ever-present apprehension that the cold war might turn into a major shooting war. Whether or not the Russians were at that time actually planning "World War III," the democracies had to strain themselves to try to be ready.

The terrible possibilities of the atomic bomb, to say nothing of the still more devastating hydrogen bomb, meant that a nuclear war might well be the end of civilization. The democracies had hoped that their head start with the atomic bomb might give them some years of relative security. Traitors passed on some of the Anglo-American secrets to the Russians, however, and enabled the latter to develop their own atomic weapons much more speedily than had been anticipated.

The United Nations

Russia's attitude was to limit severely the effectiveness of the United Nations as an organization. It had come into being in the summer of 1945, just as World War II was ending in the Pacific (see page 657). Both in its purposes and in its organization it resembled its late predecessor, the League of Nations. Its two principal bodies, the General Assembly and the Security Council, were in general similar to the Assembly and Council of the old League. The General Assembly consisted of representatives of all the member nations—fifty-one in number at the outset. It met once a year. The real direction, however, lay in the smaller Security Council, which had five permanent members in the United States, Britain, Russia, France, and China, along with six short-term representatives from the rest of the membership. Four lesser groups were the Economic and Social Council, the Trusteeship Council, the International Court of Justice, and the Secretariat. Affiliated with the United Nations were a number of specialized agencies, such as the United Nations Educational, Scientific, and Cultural

Organization (UNESCO), the World Health Organization, the International Monetary Fund, the International Labor Organization, and so on. The United Nations eventually selected New York City as its base.

Fundamentally, the United Nations was one more effort to achieve "collective security" through the curbing of aggression, an aim in which the League of Nations had proved ineffectual in the 1930's. It was hoped this time that by giving authority to the Security Council to call upon members of the United Nations for armed forces to oppose disturbances of the peace, aggression might be arrested. But there was a fatal weakness in the Security Council; it had been agreed that any majority decision of the Council in matters of a "substantive," as opposed to a "procedural," nature should include the votes of all the five permanent members. The veto of any one permanent member consequently would be enough to prevent any positive action by the Council. Quickly, Russia began to abuse this power, vetoing all sorts of measures.

With Russia thus in a position to nullify effective action by the United Nations, the democracies began to draw together in various other international organizations which were not handicapped by the veto. Some of these were military, some economic. Their major purpose was to unite the nations of Western Europe so that they might be able to check an attack by Russia's huge armed forces.

The most important of the organizations proved to be the North Atlantic Treaty Organization (NATO). In February 1948, Czechoslovakia's government came under internal Communist control and thus became part of the circle of Soviet satellite states. Like her seizure by Germany ten years earlier, this sounded a grave warning to the western nations; again none of them knew who might be next (see page 620). Within a month, Britain, France, and the "Benelux" countries (Belgium, Netherlands, and Luxembourg) signed a fifty-year treaty "for collaboration in economic, social, and cultural matters and for collective self-defense." The United Nations' charter permitted such a regional alliance for mutual security. The United States and Canada hailed this "Brussels Treaty Organization," which soon was to extend across the Atlantic. That June, the United States Senate recommended "the association of the United States with such regional and other collective agreements as are based on continuous self-help and mutual aid, and as affect its national security." The mighty armed forces and the deep pocket of the United States naturally would increase the effectiveness of any "collective security" group. The following year the North Atlantic Treaty Organization came into being in Washington, an unprecedented alliance, involving in peacetime both sides of the north Atlantic. Its twelve original members were the United States, Britain, France, Italy, Canada, Norway, Denmark, Iceland, Portugal, and the three Benelux nations. Greece and Turkey were admitted within two years; though distant from the Atlantic, they were like Scandinavia particularly vulnerable to Russian aggression. In 1954, West Germany, also vulnerable and beginning to possess strong military possibilities, was admitted. NATO policy was in the hands of a Council, composed of the foreign or defense ministers of the members; it met two or three times a year.

The treaty's primary objective was clearly stated in Article Five: "The parties agree that an armed attack against one or more of them in Europe or North America shall be considered an attack against them all and consequently they agree that, if such an armed attack occurs, each of them . . . will assist the party or parties so attacked by taking forthwith individually and in concert with the other parties, such action as it deems necessary, including the use of armed forces . . ." This was where Article Ten of the League of Nations had failed (see pages 592, 618) and wherein action by the United Nations Security Council could be nullified by one nation's veto. The "teeth" of NATO consisted of the forces allotted to its use by its members; each was assigned a quota, which did not always materialize. Late in 1950, an integrated command for the Western European defense forces was set up at a chateau near Paris, with General Eisenhower (see page 654) as the first Supreme Allied Commander, Europe. His effective persuasiveness did much to move the somewhat reluctant nations to agree to the burdens involved in building forces strong enough to meet the Russians. His Deputy was British, the colorful Marshall Montgomery (see page 644). Later another American became Supreme Allied Commander, Atlantic, with headquarters at the Norfolk, Virginia, naval base. There had been no strong objection to an American as supreme military commander; but the British loudly protested at having another American in over-all command where their royal navy had so long been dominant. The United States Navy, on the other hand, opposed a British admiral for supreme command partly because in its opinion, the British had not sufficiently developed naval aviation and amphibious warfare to utilize them fully. In deference to Britain's attitude, a separate over-all Channel Command was set up under a British admiral and air vice-marshal for the waters most vital to her. Even in the Mediterranean the British also, and later the French, kept their naval forces pretty much in their own hands. Frequent maneuvers of the various NATO land, sea, and air forces were held to overcome the handicaps of different languages and methods.

There would be times when some of the members lost their enthusiasm and the organization would seem to be in danger of bogging down. On its tenth anniversary, however, it could still point proudly to the fact that since its formation, not a single additional nation had lost its freedom to the Communists in Europe.

Economic Co-operation

From the first, a prime essential in these efforts to contain Communism had been to help Western Europe achieve a more satisfactory economic condition, not only to support such military expenses as might be necessary, but also to prevent such distress among the people as might throw them into the hands of the Communists. The number of Frenchmen and Italians already favoring Communism were too numerous for comfort. The United States took the initiative in many of these moves, frequently paying a considerable part of the costs and sometimes assuming the leadership, as she took over Britain's old role as "paymaster of the allies." Year after year Congress granted billions to other nations for both military and economic purposes; and this aid was to go to free nations all over the world. One of the first steps in economic co-operation was the setting up of the Organization for European Economic Co-operation (OEEC) in 1947. In this the sixteen recipients of United States Marshall Plan aid could discuss how such aid might be distributed to the best advantage. OEEC proved so useful in developing economic co-operation between its member countries that it continued after the Marshall Plan program had come to an end. In successive years, it centered its efforts on the increase of production, on internal financial stability, on European co-operation in the liberalization of trade and payments, in dealing with raw material shortages, and with continuing deficits with the dollar area.

In contrast to her participation in NATO and OEEC, Britain held back from some further steps in economic matters undertaken by France, Germany, Italy, and the "Benelux" countries. The first of these, the European Coal and Steel Community was set up in 1951 at the suggestion of Robert Schuman, French foreign minister, with the purpose of doing away with the sharp rivalry between those nations. A common market was established for coal, iron ore, and scrap, and frontier barriers of customs duties, quantitative restrictions, discriminatory freight rates, and currency restrictions were abolished. This was to be a precedent for the later more comprehensive "common market" which would be of considerable concern to Britain (see page 692).

Divided Germany

By the Potsdam agreement Germany had been divided into zones, with the country as a whole under an Allied Control Council, made up of the commanders in chief of the four armies of occupation (see page 657). Britain's portion in northwestern Germany included the industrial regions of the lower Rhine valley, the great port of Hamburg, and the state of Hanover, whence had come England's royal line. Although potentially the richest section, with the largest population and the most factories, it had suffered great ruin from Allied bombs. Consequently, its population, for whose sustenance Britain was responsible, was impoverished. Russia had eastern Germany, with about a quarter of her population. The United States' share was a generous section of southwest Germany, while the French were reluctantly granted a small area adjacent to France. Berlin, the former capital, lay well within the boundaries of the Russian portion, but the city itself was divided among the four powers, each with its own sector.

Such a four-nation setup would have been a drag upon the effective handling of the chaotic German problem under any circumstances. The situation in Japan was very different, with a single American general empowered to manage the whole show without having to defer to other points of view. In Germany, from the very first, Russia refused to co-operate in any reasonable manner. No sooner was the Potsdam agreement signed than the Russians drew a veil of silence over their zone. Neither British, French, nor Americans were allowed there.

In Berlin, some eighty miles inside the Russian zone, a constant succession of petty annoyances made it obvious that Moscow proposed to force the evacuation of that city by the three western powers.

Russia pressed hard for the dismantling of the factories still standing in the British zone, and for an equal voice in the control of the Ruhr steel mills, also in that section. Britain went slowly in the dismantling so that her sector would not be a continued drag on her slender resources. Her policy of denazification, also, was too mild to suit the Russians or, to some extent, the French and Americans, but she realized that German production would be hamstrung if all former Nazis, both big and little, were excluded from positions of responsibility in industry. Altogether, Britain was soon being accused by Russia of favoring her former enemies at the expense of her allies.

The Berlin Airlift

Early in 1948 the Russians walked out of the Allied Control Council. Shortly afterwards they produced one of the spectacular incidents of the cold war. In the agreement for the four-power garrisoning of Berlin nothing had been stipulated about the transmission of supplies to the troops there. The British, Americans, and French assumed naturally that the right to station troops included the right to feed them. Suddenly the Russians prohibited all rail and motor travel into Berlin through their surrounding zone, confident that this would force the evacuation of the city by the other three powers. To circumvent this, the Americans and British used aviation to supply the isolated parts of the city. This "Berlin airlift," which was primarily American, with the British assuming about a quarter of the huge task, proved successful after a most trying winter and at tremendous cost. For 15 months, some 300 planes made about 275,000 individual flights; they carried some 2,000,000 tons of supplies, including even coal, for the troops and the residents of the block-aded zones. At the same time, the western powers retaliated with a counter blockade, depriving Russia's eastern Germany of much-needed industrial supplies. Russia at last lifted the ban on surface travel, as the airlift continued to prove its effectiveness as a surprisingly adequate substitute.

As far as Britain was concerned, the expense of the airlift was one more serious drain on the fast-emptying Exchequer. A further heavy outpouring of her money was buying the necessities of life for the fast-growing population in her zone in the northwest of Germany. A constant stream of refugees poured in there from eastern Germany, the Baltic states, and Communist Czechoslovakia. Britain was burdened with probably the most restive and overcrowded part of a war-torn land, within whose shrunken boundaries were crammed several million more people than in 1939.

By the time the Berlin blockade was lifted in 1949, two separate Germanies had emerged. It had become evident that Russia had no intention of agreeing to any German peace treaty unless the western powers abandoned Berlin, ceased to demand a plebiscite in which they would share the supervision, and allowed Russian participation in the management of the Ruhr; and none of these proposals would the other allies accept. In the meantime, the British and Americans had long since united their two zones economically. Those two, with the French region, were joined formally in 1949 into a new German Federal Republic. The Allied military government gave way to an Allied High Commission, under civilian high commissioners of Britain, the United States, and France, with sovereign powers. A month afterwards, Russia set up a German Democratic Republic in its eastern zone; this new state had only 17 million inhabitants, as compared with 47 million under the western "Bonn" government and 3 million in Berlin, still divided among the four powers. Under Allied guidance and with a shrewd Chancellor, Konrad Adenauer, the German Federal Republic assumed more and more of the status of a normal, independent state. But the tension remained, as Germany continued under the control of the victors.

The same general situation that prevailed in Germany was duplicated in Austria, where detachments of the British army also formed part of the occupation forces. The Russians, on one pretext or another, kept refusing to agree to peace terms, and conditions remained unsettled. Italy, after long wrangling, fared better and received a peace treaty. It left much to be determined later, however, particularly in regard to Libya and the port of Trieste. Italy agreed to pay Russia $100 million and, at Russian insistence, also some $125 million to Yugoslavia. British detachments, however, still remained in the former Italian colonies for a while; eventually Eritria was given to Ethiopia while Libya and Somaliland became independent. Also, a small Anglo-American force garrisoned Trieste until it was finally divided between Italy and Yugoslavia.

The Far East

In the Far East, the unsettled conditions in China were, from the Western point of view, suddenly to take a turn for the worse. During the war, China, one of the Allies (see page 639), had been the scene of a bewildering three-cornered conflict. The Japanese in a continuation of their prewar invasions were overrunning much of China. Opposing them were the so-called Nationalist Chinese of the regular government forces, headed by Generalissimo Chiang Kai-shek, and Communist Chinese insurgents under the very able leadership of Moscow-trained Mao Tse-tung; at times, the two co-operated against the invaders. The United States, although troubled by the widespread corruption in Chiang's government, a dictatorship, did all she could to build up his resistance against the Japanese; the British were not interested in seeing a strong China develop. After the war the Nationalist-

Communist rivalry continued. Although not at all happy about the situation, the United States kept on backing Chiang, who held his own for a while. Then, in 1949, Nationalist efforts collapsed. Thereupon, the Communists quickly took over the whole of China's mainland. Inevitably this was to align that huge land with her hundreds of millions of people, not only ideologically but politically with Russia. At the end of that year Chiang's government and forces had taken refuge on the island of Formosa (Taiwan), under the protection of the United States Navy.

As for Britain in this ominous turn of events, her small frigate *Amethyst* had barely escaped in a brutal Communist attack far up the Yangtse. Far more serious to her was the capture of Shanghai with its rich international settlement, the center of her wide commercial holdings in the Yangtse Valley. Yet she was to be more tolerant toward Communist China than the United States, and this led to one of their few sharp differences in policy. With Shanghai gone, Britain's island of Hong Kong had more commercial possibilities than ever as an entrepôt for China trade, but the island and its adjacent mainland were constantly vulnerable to capture by China. Consequently Britain lost no time in recognizing the new government; and she kept on reaping profits from Hong Kong.

The United States, on the other hand, continued to recognize Chiang's Nationalists as China's legitimate government, though their Formosa "rump" was only a fraction of the total population. By the Charter of the United Nations, the Republic of China was one of the five permanent members of the Security Council, and the United States managed to keep that post in the hands of the Formosa government, illogical as it would seem to many. Strategic considerations to a large extent dictated her insistence upon this. In this effort to hold strategic control in the Far East, where land forces could be mustered in the millions, she arranged for naval and air bases on a string of offshore islands. At the north end of this was Japan, currently under American occupation and later allied; then the hard-won Okinawa, a trust territory; next the Philippines, independent since 1946; and at the southmost end, Formosa. All these were protected by the powerful American Seventh Fleet and Air Force installations.

Despite those conflicting policies regarding China, Britain unhesitatingly backed United States resistance, under the aegis of the United Nations, against an invasion of South Korea in 1950. This was something new in international relations and was hoped to be an augury of peaceful settlement of international disputes in a foreseeable future. It seemed to indicate possible success for the United Nations, in an area where the League of Nations had so badly failed in the 'thirties by not implementing its charter provisions for stopping aggression against Japan, Italy, and Germany (see pages 592, 617 ff.). Korea, a strategic, oft-disputed peninsula on Asia's Pacific coast, had been definitely annexed by Japan in 1910. As a Japanese possession at the close of World War II, its administration had been taken from Japan, and it had been divided into two parts at the arbitrary line of the thirty-eighth parallel, with a Russian sphere of influence in the north and an American one in the south. In the latter zone a Republic of Korea was soon set up, but the Russians refused to allow the country to be united under it. In June, 1950, prompted probably by the Russians, an army from Communist North Korea crossed the border and invaded South Korea. The United States led the move in the United Nations for immediate action to deal with this flagrant aggression against a neighbor. Normally, in such a case, Russia could have killed any such move by the use of its veto in the Security Council. It so happened at this crucial moment that the Russian representative was deliberately boycotting the

Council sessions over another matter. As a result, the Security Council, when hastily summoned, authorized immediate armed opposition to the invasion of South Korea. The United States rushed ships, planes, and troops to the scene; and the North Koreans were temporarily stopped, as they swept down the peninsula, by American soldiers from nearby Japan. Britain, which had supported the United States in the Security Council, made the next heaviest contribution, with some fourteen thousand ground troops and some ten thousand men in her naval forces in those waters. These troops were to be the nucleus of what was to be known, by 1952, as the Commonwealth Division—with Canada, Australia, and New Zealand joining Britain in this United Nations action. The bulk of the troops and the supreme commander, however, were American.

This deployment of British forces was the source of no little friction within Attlee's own ranks. Many were inclined to feel that the nation had become too prone to follow along with the United States, especially in the Far East. Britain had so much more at stake there, with her investments in China, and the very existence of Hong Kong depending on trade with the Chinese mainland. The British feared that the Americans were trigger-happy, and might drag them into an Asiatic war which might become worldwide.

The United States was to continue to bear the brunt of the Korean task, suffering more than 125,000 casualties in the next three years. By the late fall of 1950 success seemed in sight; the United Nations forces had pushed the North Koreans up to the Yalu River, which marked the boundary of Communist China. Then suddenly the Chinese Communists joined the fight, and it was the Allies' turn to retreat. Eventually the front became stabilized approximately at the thirty-eighth parallel, while localized fighting and armistice negotiations dragged on and on in a sort of stalemate. Fearful of provoking Russia into "World War III," although she was already the main supply source for the North Koreans, or even of goading Communist China into such a major war, the United Nations refrained from bombing the Communist airfields and supply bases beyond the Yalu River in Chinese territory. When the United States contemplated such action the British sought strenuously to prevent them from doing anything drastic, for fear of reprisals.

The Balkans and Middle East

During the last months of World War II, with the Russians overrunning the Balkans, Britain became concerned over the eastern Mediterranean. Had Russia obtained a hold upon Greece, as she did over Rumania, Bulgaria, and Yugoslavia, she would have had air and submarine bases for the future, penetrating far into the Mediterranean and threatening British interests throughout that region. Ally though Russia was, Churchill rushed British troops to Greece and went to Athens himself at Christmas, 1944, to counteract Russian influence. As a result, Britain was in Greece when peace came that spring (see page 657). The anti-Soviet government of the Greek king was inefficient and weak, but it was approved by a plebiscite carefully executed under Allied supervision. Communist guerrillas were active in Greece, and such bands were also constantly crossing the border from Yugoslavia and Bulgaria. These were kept at bay by the British troops garrisoned there. Britain also had a strong personal interest in protecting Turkey against any threats of Russian aggression, as she had so often in the past.

Gradually these responsibilities became more than Britain could afford. The United States took them over in 1947, thus releasing British troops from duty in Greece. At the same time, the powerful Sixth Fleet of the United States Navy was stationed in Mediterranean waters. The British were grateful for that, but American support, for

political reasons, of Jewish ambitions in Palestine was to be a different matter. The reaction of that American policy upon the Moslems of the Middle East seriously threatened British interests.

Far more persistent and puzzling were developments in the mandates in the Middle East, which had been in the British imperial sphere since World War I (see pages 585, 609). For a good many years, this area was to be on the borderline between empire and foreign relations. Arab Iraq passed into the foreign field with the ending of the British mandate and her admission to the League of Nations in 1932; Jordan (Transjordania), too, became independent in 1946. Egypt is included in foreign relations here, even though there were holdovers of the old British occupation in Cairo and the Suez Canal Zone. The Anglo-Egyptian Sudan is classified as an imperial problem, as it remained in that category until the later fifties, and so, also, is Palestine before 1948, when it was divided between Jordan and the new Jewish nation, Israel (see pages 610 ff.).

As early as 1945, the "Arab League" had been organized. It was, of course, the phenomenal development of the new oil fields in Arabia and the Persain Gulf region that gave added significance to every aspect of that tangled situation and made what happened there of vital interest to the western world, with its insatiable need for oil. Russia, too, was too close for comfort, with the ever-present possibility that it might grasp the chance to fish in troubled waters. A fanatic, with the title of Grand Mufti of Jerusalem, was tireless and fairly successful in his efforts to stir up anti-British feeling throughout the Moslem world. Several pro-British statesmen in the Middle East were assassinated. One of these had been perhaps Britain's staunchest ally, King Abdullah of Jordan with his effective British-trained military force (see page 610).

Aside from the very hectic Palestine situation, the first serious British problem with the Moslem world arose in Iran (formerly Persia). This country, which was non-Arab though Moslem, had long been divided between Russian and British spheres of influence (see page 559), and its people lived in constant fear of Russian aggression. The outbreak in 1951, however, was a direct conflict between Iran and Britain over the rich oilfields in the south. In 1914, when the navies of the world were changing from coal to oil, Winston Churchill, then First Lord of the Admiralty, had arranged for the Admiralty to purchase a controlling interest in the wealthy Anglo-Persian (later Anglo-Iranian) Oil Company. Ultimately it developed the greatest refineries in the world at the port of Abadan. The Iranians, however, became dissatisfied because their government was not getting as generous royalties in their contract with the Anglo-Iranian company as the 50 per cent royalties that American companies were paying for the operation of oilfields in Saudi Arabia.

In March, 1951, the pro-British, "strong man" premier of Iran was assassinated, and shortly afterward the Iranian Parliament passed an act taking over all the oil properties of the Anglo-Iranian Oil Company. Britain's efforts at negotiation, as well as those of the United States as mediator, proved fruitless in view of the excited attitude of the Iranians. Early that fall Iran ordered the last British technicians out of the country, and a British cruiser bore them away from Abadan. The Iranians did not know how to refine the oil; they owned no tankers in which to deliver it to customers overseas; mountains made it difficult to pipe the oil to Russia; but that made no difference, the oil business henceforth must be an Iranian industry. Gradually, however, they began to realize that they had cut off the nation's main source of revenue. Eventually, after the emotional premier who had caused the trouble was disposed of, oil production was resumed by an international group of eight oil companies, American, Dutch, and French in addition to the British Anglo-Iranian (later British Petroleum Company). That British company, moreover, was to receive compensation for its losses from the Iranian government and from the other companies.

In Egypt the trouble that erupted after the war was not a new story but the continuation of anti-British feeling that went back a good many years. The need to have troops concentrated in that strategic area during both world wars had tended to deepen this nationalistic attitude. Egypt had not been a part of the empire, of course, since 1922, when Britain ended her protectorate there and acknowledged the independence of the Egyptian kingdom (see page 612). The adjacent Suez Canal and the Sudan, however, were still very much the concern of Britain, as well as of Egypt. The canal was, as always, a vital link in Britain's overseas communications, and the Sudan had been under a nominal joint control by Britain and Egypt, but mostly the former, since 1899. Serious anti-British riots early in 1946 jeopardized the Anglo-Egyptian Treaty of 1936, which had continued some few of Britain's military privileges (see page 612). Britain now had to relinquish most of those; she abandoned the Cairo citadel, where she had had a garrison stationed, and the naval dockyard at Alexandria. She withdrew her forces to the canal zone. There they were involved in fighting in 1951, after Egypt tried to interfere with British commerce. Five years later, this Suez situation would erupt in a dramatic crisis. Such were the major foreign problems which had plagued the Labor government during their six years and would continue to plague the Conservatives after they took over.

Like her neighbors in Western Europe, Britain was having to wrestle with the constant problem of whether to spend her limited funds for "guns or butter." For a while, the Labor government hoped to achieve its socialistic goals by economizing on the armed forces. In the grim days of 1947 the Home Fleet, which in earlier days had numbered scores of vessels, was now for a while reduced to one cruiser and four destroyers! Not a single battleship was available for active service; there was nothing larger than light aircraft carriers in both the Mediterranean and the Pacific. Early in 1948 Churchill stormed in the House of Commons, "Britain has always floated upon her Navy. Well, the great Indian Empire has gone down one drain and now the Admiralty proclaim that the Royal Navy has gone down another. . . . Can you wonder that . . . we are checked by Chile and abused by Argentina—and fired at by Guatemala?" In this emergency, galling though it was to British pride, the United States Navy was strong enough to take over those tasks in which the two nations had a common interest.

But on land no other friendly nation had an army big enough to underwrite Britain; it was, therefore, not so easy to cut down the Army budget. Several divisions had to be maintained as occupation troops in Germany. Some forty thousand British soldiers were eventually needed to fight in Malaya. Although heavy forces had been withdrawn from Palestine, as well as those troops formerly needed in India, Egypt, Greece, and other regions, considerable forces were still stationed in Austria, Trieste, the Suez Canal Zone, Iraq, Gibraltar, Malta, Cyprus, Libya, and Hong Kong.

With the Korean crisis in 1950 and the North Atlantic Treaty Organization drive for armament, further economizing on the military budget was out of the question (see pages 677, 673). Resentfully the Laborites had to allow the military program to overshadow social welfare.

In the 1948 budget, the Army was allotted £347,000,000, equal to the Navy and Air Force combined. But the social services ran up to a total of £850,000,000 to £753,000,-000 for defense. By 1950, the score was £1,280,000,000 to £780,000,000 in favor of the social needs. By 1952 defense was in the lead at £1,480,000,000 to £836,000,000.

The "cold war" was cutting down on the "butter" to provide the "guns," but even at that the British had far more of the pleasant things of life than did most of those beyond the "Iron Curtain." Above all, they lived where the rights of the individual were still respected and safeguarded. It was in the hope of preserving such a way of life that the expenditures for the armed forces were allowed to creep up each year.

The Election of 1950

The election campaign in 1950 was unusually quiet. Foreign affairs played little part in it, and even regarding controversial domestic issues, neither side was particularly aggressive. Attlee's strategy was to point to the recent accomplishments of his party and to stress the grim unemployment of the thirties as the nation's fate, should his party lose. The tory-baiting "Nye" Bevan was kept as much as possible in the background. Further nationalization was softpedaled, although the sugar and cement industries were mentioned as next on the list, with shipbuilding, chemical production, and life insurance to come later. Labor, with two alluring slogans "Fair Shares for All" and "Full Employment," constantly reiterated that the poor had better food, higher wages, steadier jobs, and a higher standard of living than before the war. The popularity of the social-welfare measures kept the Conservative party leaders cautious, too. Their strategy had to be to accept, in general, what Labor had done, and then to argue that they could do it more effectively and cheaply. They promised to appeal the nationalization of steel, but otherwise only urged more decentralization and more elastic controls. They blamed the continuing housing shortage on the way private builders had been hamstrung by Bevan's restrictions on building materials. Their frontal attack against Labor's financial policy claimed it was leading straight to economic collapse, which had only been postponed by the American loan of 1946 and Marshall Plan aid soon due to run dry. They declared the desperate efforts to sell widely in the world market had been stymied by the mounting production costs under Labor; and pointing to the rapid rise in the price of nationalized coal, warned that taxes were having to make good the deficits in coal, in railways, and much else. Labor won the election in February, 1950, but their victory was a slim one. Instead of the 390 seats of the past five years, they won only 315; this meant such a small majority that it would take little to turn them out of office. The Conservatives found cold comfort in their increase to 294 seats. The old Liberal party seemed, at long last, ready to give up the ghost, with but nine seats left, while the Communists lost even the two seats they already had.

It was obvious that Attlee's second ministry would probably be brief. If the political skies should become overcast, his hold on Commons was too slender to save him from having to resign or dissolve Parliament for a new election. The latter proved to be the case for both international and domestic reasons. These were the months when Britain's most prosperous overseas investment, oil, met disaster in Iran; when Egyptian hostility threatened Suez and the Sudan; when Malaya and its rubber plantations were aflame; and when open fighting "to stop aggression" was undertaken by the United Nations in Korea (see pages 703, 678). To people with the horror of the German bombs so fresh in their memory, the Korean war was particularly disquieting as a possible prelude to World War III. At home, for one thing, the nationalization of steel was running into snags. Within the Labor party itself there was growing dissension. It had lost two of its ablest leaders: Ernest Bevin, who had been conservative enough to please even the tory-minded, was dead, and Sir Stafford Cripps, Chancellor of the Exchequer and generally admitted to be a financial wizard, was dying in Switzerland.

Into this vacuum in the party's leadership rushed Aneurin Bevan, recognized for some time as the head of the left-wing Laborites. For two decades there had been enmity between Bevan and Bevin, both of whom had risen from the ranks of labor (see pages 656 ff.). Compromise with capitalism, or with any conservative ideas whatsoever, was not in Bevan. His hates were many, from Bevin to Churchill. During the war, he had called the latter "turgid, wordy, dull, and prosaic"—a "bloated bladder of lies." Now he charged that his precious National Health Act was menaced in the new budget; for one thing, henceforth the recipient would have to pay for half the cost of dentures and spectacles. He was violently opposed to any cuts in social welfare in the search for additional funds for stepped-up rearmament. He resigned his post within a week of the announcement of the budget, and a handful of Labor members of the Commons sided with him.

Feeling that this split between the radical and the moderate wings of the party was more than his narrow majority in Commons could stand, Attlee dissolved Parliament after a ministry of only twenty months. The election was held in the fall of 1951. Trying to steer a middle course in his party's disunity, Attlee promised little that was new with the result that his campaign was colorless and conciliatory. He shied away from the issue of nationalization for fear of alienating the Liberal vote, which both parties were wooing. A clear-cut issue was lacking until Churchill brought in foreign policy. That gave Labor its slogan, "Keep the Peace with Attlee." Both parties had acted pretty much as one in support of the United Nations, in continuing rearmament and conscription, and in the defense of British interests overseas; but this anti-war cry appealed to many, especially to the Liberals.

In the Conservative campaign Churchill

blamed the Laborites for the difficulties in the Middle East, stating the Iranian oil seizures laid Britain "flat on the face as though she was a booby and a coward." He was outspoken on the necessity for Britain and the United States to stay together in mutual interest. The Conservatives were inclined to be somewhat overconfident for, beyond the good employment situation and certain social services, little else gave comfort to those who had been on short rations for over a decade. Yet they dared not repudiate the welfare state. Once again they promised to stay the advance of socialism and to put both domestic and foreign affairs on a firmer foundation. When Laborites argued that if the nation was as near economic collapse as was claimed, rearmament must be curtailed, Churchill pointed to the increased danger from Russia and the impairment of Anglo-American unity invited by such a course. This question tended to overshadow domestic issues.

The Conservative Return in 1951

The Conservatives won in October, 1951, but it was not a clear-cut victory; they won 321 seats to Labor's 294, with only 6 Liberals left. The Conservatives thus had only 6 more votes to bolster their small majority than Labor had had. The schism in the Labor party was threatening to grow worse, for in spite of the party's defeat, Bevan and his left wing group had personally triumphed: they were all re-elected by increased majorities.

Churchill at seventy-seven undertook his second ministry with his accustomed courage. Anthony Eden was again Foreign Secretary. The task ahead was formidable and about all that Churchill could do was to play for time, as he took office in the face of almost insoluble situations at home and abroad. With the fighting going on in Korea, in Malaya, and at Suez; the unsettled disputes with Iran and Egypt; the seething undercurrents elsewhere in Asia and Africa; and the ever-present shadow of a hostile Russia, international skies had seldom, if ever, been darker for Britain. On the Continent, plans for a European army were still in the blueprint stage, with neither Churchill nor British public opinion indicating any intention of doing more than support its creation by words—a fact that irked France and annoyed the United States.

Churchill postponed the opening of Parliament until the end of January to give himself time for a trip to Washington. He attended to a few stop-gap measures in the bad home situation. Gold reserves were declining again, so he clamped tighter controls on its leakage. Imports were further restricted, and the food ration cut. In Washington he had to make some concessions to the United States but achieved his main objective—steel for British rearmament. He also eased the dollar situation by persuading the United States to agree to take some of Britain's stores of tin and rubber.

Elizabeth II

Early in 1952, the death of King George VI brought to the throne his daughter, England's second Queen Elizabeth, the fifth queen regnant. Her marriage in 1947 to Philip Mountbatten, lieutenant in the royal navy and related to the German royal house of Greece, had been almost the sole bright spot in that dreary year. Elizabeth had won the hearts of the Britons with her unusual charm. Because of King George's failing health, the young couple had already taken on a fair share of the ceremonial duties that have become the chief function of royalty; and they were on the way to Australia, in the king's place, when the news of his death brought them home from Kenya. The very fact of having a queen again seemed to bring cheer to the people, for, except for Mary Tudor, England had prospered under her queens. Two of her greatest eras had been symbolized in the reigns of the first Elizabeth and

Philip, Duke of Edinburgh, kneels to pay homage to his wife, Elizabeth II, at her coronation in Westminster Abbey; she is wearing the St. Edward's crown.

Victoria. The pageantry of the coronation in June, 1953, seemed to dramatize the link between the glorious past and the ever-changing present. In the midst of medieval ritual was proclaimed the new royal title, which reflected the latest weakening of Britain's ties with her old "dominion over palm and pine": "Elizabeth the Second, by the Grace of God of the United Kingdom, Canada, Australia, New Zealand, South Africa, Pakistan, Ceylon, and her other realms and territories, Head of the Commonwealth, Defender of the Faith."

Relaxation of Controls

It so happened that the new reign of the young queen seemed to mark the end of the dreary lean years for the British populace. Gradually, as the nation's financial position became more favorable, the grim postwar austerity was relaxed. No small part of the credit belongs to the Conservative Churchill ministry, which had come into office four months before Elizabeth succeeded to the throne. Taking over a nation in desperate financial straits, they handled the situation with skill; for a brief time, they had to impose even more rigid controls. The people themselves, however, were in no small measure responsible for the final upturn, because of their patience in submitting with only moderate grumbling to the myriad regulations and restrictions which were necessary. As the decade progressed, the oppresive wartime controls were one by one relaxed.

Industry was being relieved by the end of 1952 of some of the restrictions that had been hampering production; for the first time in years, there was a favorable trade balance and the nation's dollar reserve had increased. The next two years saw further progress along those same lines as manufactures became more plentiful. In 1953, the Conservatives kept their campaign promise to denationalize the steel industry and take steps for its return to private ownership; road transport was also denationalized. No effort was made to do likewise with coal, railways or the other industries nationalized by the Labor party; unlike steel, most of them were operating at a loss and the former stockholders preferred their three per-cent bonds. By the end of the fifties, the railways would have piled up a billion-dollar deficit. Of all the government-operated activities, only electricity and the post office were breaking even.

One of the better days of the postwar decade for the average Briton came in July 1954 when food rationing ended, with meat finally taken off the list; coupons and queues disappeared and the roast beef of old England was no longer only a nostalgic memory. By the end of the year, with the revival of industry and increased incomes, the public soon began a "buying spree" for automobiles, television sets, refrigerators, washing machines, and other long-scarce consumer goods. Much of this was bought on the installment plan—"hire purchase" or the "never-never plan," as the British called it.

Naturally it began to look to the Conservatives like a good time for a general election, although one was not due for another year. With the election in mind, the able Chancellor of the Exchequer, Butler, announced in the budget for 1955 another reduction in the income tax, the removal of the purchase tax on textiles, and increased old age pensions. The Conservatives went into the election confidently with their slogan of "peace and prosperity"; but the Laborites were rent with dissension. Aneurin Bevan, in addition to opposing armaments and hating the United States, wanted still more nationalization and social benefits. The party's moderates, vigorously opposed to those views, eventually ejected him from its parliamentary organization.

The Trade Unions Congress, as distinct from the party, had expressed its opposition to further nationalization. It was not an exciting campaign and the victory for "Tory democracy" was no great surprise. The Conservatives won 334 seats; Labor 277; Liberals 6; and others 2; the Conservative margin rose to 67 from 27. Nearly a third of the Trade Unionists voted against Labor.

Churchill, now eighty, resigned before the election. For two years he had been Sir Winston as a member of the Order of the Garter. To him that unique honor meant more than a peerage which would have taken him out of the House of Commons, where his incomparable oratory was so effective. His rival, Attlee, soon retired as head of the Labor opposition, going to the House of Lords as a peer, and was succeeded by an able, reasonable moderate, Hugh Gaitskill.

Eden Prime Minister

The new prime minister was the shrewd and charming aristocrat, Anthony Eden, long regarded as Churchill's logical successor. Foreign secretary three times—once under Chamberlain, twice under Churchill—he had been an energetic supporter of the League of Nations and international cooperation in general and always a bitter foe of appeasement (see pages 618 ff., 682). He had gone directly from Eton at eighteen to serve as an officer in the infantry on the Western Front, where the casualties were so enormous; two brothers and an appalling number of his school friends had been killed.

With the improved economic situation, foreign affairs had become the government's prime concern. Both in the Middle and in the Far East, signs of trouble were appearing. And from the standpoint of the Foreign Office, there was growing annoyance at the dominant role in western diplomacy of the American Secretary of State, John Foster Dulles, who had come to that post in Eisenhower's cabinet better equipped than most of his recent predecessors. What irked the British was his insistence on running much of his department's business himself and his constant travels to handle matters personally in all parts of the world. In the cold war, he dismayed them in more than one crisis by seeming to bring the world to the brink of war by being less ready than they to make concessions: this policy was derisively dubbed "brinkmanship".

The Far East situation deteriorated sharply in 1954 when, after a long frustrating fight and a final surrender, the French at last had to withdraw from Indo-China. That quickly led to an anti-Communist regional organization on the NATO model, the Southeast Asia Treaty Organization (SEATO). This was a collective defense pact, including Britain, the United States, Australia, New Zealand, Pakistan, the Philippines, and Thailand (Siam). Britain and the United States continued their widely separated policies toward Communist China. Not only did the United States still insist that the Nationalists on Taiwan (Formosa) retain China's Council seat in the United Nations but she also still blocked Communist China from joining that organization. War seemed threatened more than once, when Communist China's guns deliberately shelled the small nearby Nationalist-held islands, Quemoy and Matsu.

If the Far East was primarily an American concern, the troublesome Middle East was still a traditional British sphere of influence. Another regional treaty organization, the "Baghdad Pact," which Britain helped create shortly after SEATO, built up a protective Moslem "northern tier" of Turkey, Iran, Iraq, and Pakistan against possible Russian aggression in that area. Britain was a full member, while the United States participated in some of the pact's functions. When revolt-torn Iraq withdrew from it in 1958, it was renamed the Central Treaty Organization (CENTRO).

Nasser and the Suez Crisis

Britain's immediate trouble in the Middle East came not from Russia but from Egypt, where in 1952 a group of colonels had deposed the playboy King Farouk. A year later, Egypt became a republic, and the power soon became concentrated in the hands of the dynamic Colonel Gamal Abdel Nasser, who quickly extended his influence to other parts of the Arab world. Late in 1954, Britain was forced to make a further withdrawal from the Egyptian area (see page 679); now she had to evacuate the Suez Canal Zone.

Two years later Britain was to be embroiled in a far more humiliating situation. Egypt's heart had been set upon a new great dam at Aswan, the site of the original one built in Cromer's day (see page 526) to regulate the waters of the Nile, thereby increasing fertility of the land. Funds seemed to be available through a loan from the World Bank, financed largely by the United States. Nasser, like Nehru at first, did not want to commit himself completely to either side in the cold war; and he had been making several deals with the Communists also. Thereupon in July 1956, Dulles and the World Bank withdrew the offer of the Aswan loan. A furious Nasser announced that Egypt was seizing the Suez Canal from the French-based international corporation, in which Britain, thanks to Disraeli, held the controlling interest (see page 524). By its charter stipulations, Egypt was to get it anyway in a few years, but Nasser was not waiting. Britain, the United States, and other canal users held several hurried protest meetings; and then sent an international committee, headed by Premier Menzies of Australia, to Cairo to discuss matters with Nasser, but it got nowhere with him.

Britain was caught in a bad dilemma. Besides her traditional concern for her Suez "lifeline" to the East, she was faced with the threat of lost prestige in the Middle

Aftermath of the 1956 Suez Crisis; salvage operations to clear the canal of the twenty-odd vessels sunk by the Egyptians after the attack on Port Said.

East. She decided that once more she would let the lion roar in the old Palmerstonian way. France was more than ready to co-operate in a show of force. The chance came in the last days of October when the new Jewish state of Israel (see page 702) suddenly threw her excellent army against Egypt, invading the Sinai region in the direction of Suez. Again, as in 1948, the Israelis made rapid advances (see page 702). The next day Britain and France delivered a twelve-hour ultimatum to both Israel and Egypt to draw back from the canal zone; Israel agreed conditionally, but Nasser refused. Thereupon, the British and French began bombing the Egyptian airfields in preparation for an airborne paratroop attack on the canal zone. Within three days, on November 2, the United Nations passed a United States resolution calling for a cease fire; nevertheless, the paratroopers landed as planned and continued

their attack until Britain and the others grudgingly agreed to the cease fire on November 7. Their whole operation had been well-executed and successful from the purely military standpoint, but their intervention was to have more damaging results in their foreign relations than they had apparently anticipated.

This use of force was disturbing to much of the world. Its effect was particularly unfortunate coming as it did at the time of Russia's shockingly brutal suppression of a revolt in her satellite, Hungary. Labor had attacked the Suez project in the Commons. Formal protests were made, with the United States, Canada, and India prominent among them. The Moslems were infuriated even in countries hitherto friendly to Britain. Russia selfrighteously added her voice to the widespread disapproval. There were, to be sure, some who shared the Eden ministry's view that a stand must be taken before it was too late and that appeasement was not the answer; some went so far as to regret that the victorious Israeli army had not been allowed to sweep further into Egypt and thus damage Nasser's prestige. Perhaps the most serious result was that Anglo-American relations were strained almost to the breaking point. The American presidential campaign somewhat complicated matters, for peace was a prime issue, and many Jewish voters were naturally inclined to sympathize with Israel. To Britain, it was especially galling that the United States led the United Nations opposition that had forced her to halt. Eden, in his later bitter memoirs, claimed that Dulles had originally approved taking strong measures, but then had not backed the Anglo-French efforts to impose economic pressure upon Nasser. When Britain and France saw how strongly the United States and much of the Commonwealth disapproved of armed force, they had kept their final plans secret.

The Suez affair had effects in other fields. For months world shipping had to resort to the old lengthy route around Africa, because the Suez Canal was blocked by the dozens of vessels sunk therein by the Egyptians. As for Egypt herself, she was eventually advanced the funds for the Aswan dam, but by the Soviet Union, which furnished the materials and the technical direction.

Macmillan Prime Minister

Eden, whose health had been steadily failing, resigned a few weeks after the Suez fiasco. It had been quite generally expected that his successor would be Richard A. Butler, whose excellent years at the Exchequer had contributed much to Britain's economic revival. Instead, the Queen, consulting Churchill and Lord Salisbury, selected Harold Macmillan, scion of the well-known publishing house. A product of Eton and Oxford, like Eden, he had likewise served on the Western Front, where he had been

thrice wounded. After marrying the daughter of a duke, he had alternated between the family business and public service in various diplomatic and ministerial capacities. Within the last three years, he had been successively Minister of Defense, Foreign Secretary, and Chancellor of the Exchequer. An asset in favor of his appointment in the current disagreement with the United States was his long-standing friendship with Eisenhower, who had just been re-elected President. The two had been in close wartime contact after the North African landings of 1942, when Eisenhower was commander in chief and Macmillan, British minister-resident for politico-military liaison. Selwyn Lloyd continued as Foreign Secretary, but Macmillan, like Eden, would take an active role himself in foreign affairs.

There was ample need for such guidance. The Middle East in 1958 produced a whole crop of definitely serious crises, though none were as damaging to Britain as the Suez affair. Already the previous year, Jordan had terminated its twenty-year treaty with Britain, which still had twelve years to run; and had dismissed the British brigadier, "Glubb Pasha" (see pages 678, 701). Early in 1958, Nasser created the so-called United Arab Republic by joining Egypt and Syria, a rather uneven merger since Syria had but one-sixth the population of Egypt and soon became a sort of satellite. They shared a common legislature, army, diplomatic corps, and flag. If Nasser hoped, as many thought, to make this the nucleus of a great pan-Arab state he did not get far at this time; the only other volunteer was remote and amazingly backward Yemen, far down in Arabia. Instead, a counter merger was immediately announced by two young royal cousins, Feisal II of Iraq and Hussein of Jordan, who had been schoolmates at Harrow in England not long before. It ended in five months with the brutal murder of Feisal, others of the royal family, and Nuri-el as Said, Iraq's strong pro-western premier, by a group of army officers at Baghdad. Abdel Karim Kassem, a general, seized power. Five other Afro-Asian states—Lebanon, Sudan, Pakistan, Burma, and Thailand—had their democratic form of government supplanted that year by army officers, while Syria's merger had the same result.

The Baghdad murders were a particular shock to the British, who had regarded Iraq as the dependable cornerstone of their Middle Eastern defense; Kassem soon withdrew from the "Baghdad Pact." During the coming turbulent months, no one was sure whether he was pro-Communist, pro-Nasser, or simply pro-Kassem. That overturn triggered other emergencies in the region. Young Hussein, faced with grave plots and threatened invasion by his neighbors, called for British troops, which were to remain in Jordan until the crisis passed. At almost the same moment, American marines and soldiers were landed in Lebanon at the call of her pro-western president. In the Sudan, however, a Communist coup was prevented when a tough general took over in the nick of time.

Trouble came from Moscow directly that year as well in a Soviet threat to end the Allied occupation of Berlin. In the ruthless scramble for power after Stalin's death, the victor was burly Nikita S. Khrushchev, clever, crude, and cruel. Often as brutally grim as Stalin, he was nonetheless a man of many moods; he could change in an instant from genial buffoonery or pious platitudes on peaceful "coexistence" to coarse personal insults or savage threats. He now declared that he would give control of the communications into Berlin to East Germany, the unlucky Soviet satellite, which the West would not recognize as a nation, unless Berlin were thoroughly safeguarded from any Communist domination.

Defense Problems

The cocky Russian mood came in part from their recent scientific achievement in launching a successful earth-circling satellite; the first of several such Russian and American creations for outer space in the next few years. They had not only produced atomic and hydrogen bombs far sooner than had been deemed likely, but they were also racing with the Western powers in developing long-range ballistic missiles as a substitute for manned bombers for delivering distant blows. This led Parliament in 1957, soon after Macmillan became prime minister, to approve a drastic five-year reorganization of the armed forces. As a "deterrent," in the hope of making the threat of reprisal too grim for an enemy to risk an atomic attack, it was decided to concentrate on nuclear weapons and rocket missiles, instead of further development of manned aircraft. At the same time, the troops stationed abroad in large numbers (see page 680) were to be cut almost in half. Instead, a strong mobile reserve was to be maintained in the United Kingdom, which could be rushed by transport airlift to the scene of any little "brushfire" wars. The Navy's reorganization emphasized anti-submarine warfare, a very vital concern in view of Russia's huge submarine fleet. Early in 1959, an Anglo-American agreement provided that intermediate range ballistic missiles (IRBM), capable of reaching Russia from Britain, would be supplied by the Americans, who had long had air bases in Britain. The United States also furnished the designs and propulsion machinery for a British atomic submarine, which was launched in 1960 with the famous old name *Dreadnought*.

The new defense policy brought strong political repercussions from the more extreme elements of Labor. Besides general annoyance at the United States and her bases in Britain, these Laborites argued that the nuclear policy was perilous because it exposed the country to devastating attack. With the general international disarmament negotiations at Geneva getting nowhere, Labor extremists demanded a "neutralist" role, with withdrawal from

NATO and "unilateral" British disarmament, whatever the other nations might do. They were particularly insistent about getting rid of the American-manned bases, and staged angry demonstrations against the government's agreement to give the United States a base at Holy Loch near Glasgow for her atomic submarines carrying "Polaris" ballistic missiles which could be launched from hidden underwater locations.

This issue split the already-battered Labor party wide open in the fall of 1960. "I am not prepared to see my loved ones go up in radioactive dust so that we should act as a lightning conductor . . . to draw enemy fire on our heads to divert it from New York and Chicago," shouted one left-wing Laborite at the party convention. Hugh Gaitskill retorted "Would these people follow the cowardly, hypocritical course of saying 'We don't want nuclear bombs, but for God's sake, America, protect us'"?. And he continued that if Britain did get out of NATO, "the United States might wash its hands of Europe." Despite an initial vote favoring neutralism, Gaitskill maintained his moderate leadership of the party.

The forward strides in the field of nuclear power led to other problems, both in its military and nonmilitary uses. Britain took a lead in the latter, opening in 1956 at Calder Hill the first atomic power station, which produced part of the nation's electricity needs. Other nations showing interest in the matter, an international organization was formed to encourage and supervise such peaceful uses of nuclear power. But along with that went the determination to keep nuclear military power with its terrifying potentials in as few hands as possible. For a while, the exclusive "Atomic Club" was restricted to the United States, Britain, and Russia, but in 1960 the French, feeling that national pride demanded their participation, had reached the point in their nuclear experiments of

testing their bombs in the Sahara Desert. Angry repercussions came from all sides, especially from the new African nations. But the danger to civilization if Communist China or some of the less stable smaller nations also acquired this most terrible of threats was intensely alarming for the future of mankind.

Prosperity and Another Conservative Victory

"This has been one of the most prosperous years in their history" came a report from London late in December 1959. Just two centuries before, the British had hailed 1759, when it "rained victories" in Canada, in India, and at sea as the *annus mirabilis;* and now, relieved of the grim austerity of the late 1940's, they were in a mood to call 1959 another wonderful year. The persistent postwar struggle to increase exports was at last paying off. They are the real test of economic success; imports require only the ability to pay for them or the seller's belief that he will be paid eventually. The total customs figures for 1959, compared with 1946 and of 1951, when the tide turned with the Conservative victory, have a broad historical significance; they showed that Britain was in a better position to defend herself and that the well-being of her people was greatly enhanced. So far as the official records in pounds sterling go, Britain's export total had nearly trebled between 1946 and 1959. The devaluation of the pound from $4.08 to $2.80 in 1949, however, makes the dollar equivalent a more accurate basis for comparison. By that standard, the total United Kingdom exports had risen from $4.6 billions in 1946 to $7.2 in 1951 and $9.3 in 1959.

Almost a third of the big 1959 export total came from machinery, which rose in value from $609 millions in 1946 to $2,878 millions in 1959. Chemicals, at a somewhat lower level, increased almost fourfold. The most spectacular gain was in the small automobile, that had for some years been

UNITED KINGDOM EXPORTS AND IMPORTS, 1946-1959

Million $ (£ at $4.08, 1946; $2.80, 1951, 1956)

EXPORTS	1946	1951	1959	IMPORTS	1946	1951	1959
PRINCIPAL COMMODITIES							
Total	4638	7221	9312	Total	5308	10,959	11,172
Machinery	609	1285	2878	Petroleum	326	840	1307
Vehicles	469	1344	1462	Meat	567	596	930
Chemicals	269	366	982	Fruit & Vegetables	204	299	658
Textiles	632	1198	834	Cotton, Wool, &c	408	1568	763
Iron & Steel	326	445	641	Grain, Flour &c	367	686	645
PRINCIPAL COUNTRIES							
Commonwealth-Empire				*Commonwealth-Empire*			
Australia	224	904	624	Canada	795	728	873
Canada	130	383	579	Australia	273	705	564
Union of So. Africa	306	462	414	New Zealand	301	459	512
India-Pakistan	359	448	579	India-Pakistan	281	516	471
New Zealand	110	308	271	Kuwait	–	–	372
Malaya-Singapore	81	224	158	Union of So. Africa	61	173	246
Nigeria	44	123	201	Nigeria	102	263	243
Rhodesia &c	36	100	137	Rhodesia &c	65	170	252
Foreign				*Foreign*			
United States	142	380	1008	United States	934	1061	1038
West Germany	69	144	386	Netherlands	44	361	450
Sweden	85	263	310	West Germany	24	207	403
Netherlands	122	198	313	Sweden	130	383	358
France	138	151	212	Argentina	269	240	295
Italy	24	86	201	France	57	378	291
Norway	73	182	178	Italy	77	232	260
Belgium	106	156	160	Venezuela	16	53	212

growing increasingly important as an export asset. The American car builders had been caught napping in what seemed a safe supremacy both at home and abroad; a sudden world-wide demand snowballed for cars cheaper in price and upkeep and easier to park. Britain produced over a million cars in a year for the first time in 1959. Many were bought at home, to cause grave congestion on her picturesque roads, now too winding and narrow for the influx of motorists. Also, in hot competition with Germany, the little cars helped swell the export total to various lands beyond the seas. In South Africa, for example, which had been an excellent automobile market for American makes, these were almost crowded out of the field by British and German small cars. In a sort of "coals to Newcastle" movement, British cars invaded the United States to the tune of more than a quarter million dollars a year. A few of those were luxury items, selling as high as $25,000, but the bulk were the little ones at prices well below the standard American makes.

Textiles, however, were dropping yet farther from their old primacy (see page 425).

From 46 per cent in 1820 to 29 per cent in 1910 and to 13 per cent in 1946, they were now barely 9 per cent, outranked by machinery, vehicles and chemicals. Cloth was one of the easiest articles for the new industrial nations around the world to make; and with their infinitely lower wages, Japan, India, and many other nations were cutting more heavily than ever into the demand for the products of Lancashire and Yorkshire.

In the worldwide distribution of those exports, 40 per cent went to the Sterling Area (see page 661), which included most of the Commonwealth except Canada, as well as the Irish Republic and a few other areas; while 27 per cent went to Western Europe. The most gratifying aspect in British eyes was the sale of 17 per cent of their offerings to the "hard dollar" United States and Canada, where previously they had been able to pay for only a fraction of what they needed. In 1946, for instance, the exports thither, at $272,000,000, had been less than one-sixth of the imports at $1,729,000,-000; now, the $1,640,000,000 million export total was almost equal to the $1,924,000,000 in imports. In the case of the United States, exports and imports were almost equal at the billion dollar level so far as actual exchange of commodities went; the "invisible items" gave Britain a good favorable balance. Particularly important was what some call "tourism." During the course of 1958, it was estimated that American tourists spent $90,000,000 in Britain in addition to what British steamship and air lines earned for their transportation.

Those export figures did not tell the whole story of Anglo-American commercial intercourse; about two-fifths of the automobile production and a sizeable share of other "British" offerings were produced by subsidiaries of American concerns. In full reversal of the former all-pervasive spread of British capital around the world (see page 546), American overseas investments had doubled since the war. They had invaded not only Canada and other parts of the Commonwealth but also Britain herself. Loud protests came when the Ford Motor Company planned to increase its ownership of its British subsidiary from 54 to 100 percent; General Motors already owned outright the huge Vauxhall works. Yet the arrangement benefitted both nations. The Americans could cut their labor costs drastically, with British manufacturing wages only about $.77 an hour instead of $2.68. Thanks to "imperial preference," moreover, wares produced in Britain could enter other Commonwealth countries more cheaply than those from the United States. The British profited from the increased employment and from not having to import so much. Eventually the return flow of dividends and interest could be expected to give the Americans a counterpart of the old "Victorian heritage." But the initial investment abroad of so many billions on top of those other billions in the heavy American military and economic grants to nations around the world and the support of American forces and bases overseas caused an alarming drain on the American gold supply.

The corresponding increase in imports was a natural corollary of the mounting exports; for the British could now indulge themselves in some of the products they had not been able to afford. The increase in meat, fruit, and vegetables was one indication of this. Britain could almost pay for its $117,000,000 worth of tobacco imports from America by the $98,000,000 worth of Scotch whiskey, the largest amount yet, sent in return. The sharp increase in petroleum imports reflected the newly increased use of automobiles; Britain had effected an economy in that by setting up refineries so that she could import the cheap crude oil.

The Conservatives decided they had better hold a general election at once while affairs remained in this happy state, although their five-year term was not up. Again they were to take advantage of the excellent financial status to please the voters by bringing the income tax to a new low level. During the war, the "standard rate" before exemptions had reached 50 per cent or "ten shillings in the pound"; now it was reduced from 42½ to 38¾ per cent. This meant that a Briton, married with two children, who was paid £2,000 ($5,600) a year, paid $843 a year instead of $896. This was still roughly $368 more than an American in equivalent circumstances, of whom there were many more at this level income than in Britain, paid in federal income taxes.

In the general election in October 1959, Macmillan "led his party to its third straight victory and doubled its majority in the House of Commons, a feat without parallel in the annals of British politics." Prosperity and lower taxes had paid off, as indicated in the increase of Conservative seats from 345 to 365, and a margin over Labor increased from 68 to 107 votes. The Laborites had had relatively little to offer as a positive program, and the party was left in a despondent mood.

The public as a whole, however, was anything but despondent, for as Christmas approached they went on "a spending spree unequalled in the nation's history." The stock market, on the news of the Conservative victory, enjoyed an exceptional boom. Installment buying hit a new high though it was still far below the American and Australian. The new feeling of well-being was still running strong in the spring of 1960 despite the renewed fulminations of Khrushchev and the dropping away of African colonies. For the first time in years, currency restrictions were relaxed so that plenty of money could be taken out of the country for travel. Automobiles and appliances of all sorts were now easily available. The number of cars on the roads had jumped in twenty years from two to eight million; Britain began to appreciate some of the traffic control problems with which other nations had been wrestling. Great numbers were taking advantage of the new mobility. "Families are avoiding the old vacation stand-bys like Blackpool and Margate," according to a June 1960 news item, "to try resorts hitherto confined to the well-to-do . . . they leave London by the thousand in sport shirts and summer frocks to drive into darkest Wales and Cornwall."

The Common Market and Outer Seven

But by then some dark clouds were rising on the horizon—how rapidly was not easy to foresee. There was the nightmare of the "Common Market," a combination of economics and foreign relations which threatened to cut off Britain's exports to some of her best Continental customers. Since World War II, there had been a succession of efforts at integration among the democracies of Western Europe: the Organization for European Economic Co-operation, the Western European Union, the Council of Europe, the European Coal and Steel Community, and, more recent, the European Atomic Energy Community in particular. Some were primarily economic; others also aimed at closer political and military unity (see page 672). The membership varied, but there was one common denominator—the hard core of six Continental neighbors, France, West Germany, Italy, and the three "Benelux" countries.

When, in 1958, those six signed at Rome a treaty forming the European Economic Community, or Common Market, Britain was inclined to dismiss it as one more loose, well-meaning affair, and for various reasons, once again did not try to become a member. Gradually, however, she found that the new organization, with its headquarters at Brussels, really meant business. After first ending tariff barriers for coal and steel among the six members, it undertook a gradual reduction and final elimination of all tariffs among them. Along with that, there was to be a wall of increased tariff rates against commodities from outside countries. Their announcement that they were planning to lower custom duties among themselves by twenty per cent in

1960 was to bring a rival organization into being in July 1959 at a Swedish seaside resort. Britain, long and naturally opposed to such regional impediments to trade, first proposed a general 17-nation free trade arrangement; the "Inner Six" rejected this. Thereupon, the "Outer Seven," Britain, Norway, Sweden, Denmark, Austria, Switzerland, and Portugal, formed the European Free Trade Association and declared a similar twenty per cent tariff reduction among themselves. This "Outer Seven," even including the British Isles, had little more than half the population of the "Inner Six," far less industrial development, and far less geographic unity. As customers for British products they absorbed only three-fourths as much as the Common Market. Well into 1961, Britain sought some way out of the problem. She had certain good reasons for not joining the Common Market—it ran afoul of her preferential arrangements with the Commonwealth and of her general reluctance to losing any freedom of action; by this time, moreover, there was the possibility of being rebuffed by the "Inner Six." At the same time, of course, she hated the prospect of losing such valuable customers.

In addition to the continued concern over that problem, the economic picture at home was beginning toward the end of 1960 to dim from its 1959 climax. The Conservatives were fortunate to have held the election at a time when things were going so well, for declining markets were once again reviving the old "export or die" slogan. The automobile plants in particular were feeling the pinch; with the Americans finally manufacturing "compact" cars of their own, their purchases from abroad fell off sharply.

The Summit Fiasco

Even more serious in possible consequences were failures in high-level contacts with the Soviets in the cold war. Macmillan believed that the best chance for peace lay in getting the heads of the principal powers together for a "summit" conference where they might exchange views freely. This "personal diplomacy" as a substitute for the normal dealings of ambassadors had worked very successfully for Britain in the frequent wartime meetings between Churchill and Roosevelt, but when Stalin joined in such talks, the results were quite different; he usually came away with far more than he had conceded (see page 671). In 1955, a summit meeting at Geneva yielded scant results. That experience strengthened the opposition of Secretary Dulles to such affairs, but his energetic world negotiations were soon cut short by death. Macmillan worked persistently for another such meeting. He visited Moscow, only to face rude treatment from Khrushchev. Not deterred by that, he consulted earnestly with Eisenhower and De Gaulle in preparation for what would prove an abortive meeting at Paris in the spring of 1960. Using as an obvious excuse the discovery of American aerial "spying" over Russia, which he later said he had known about for four years, Khrushchev coarsely insulted Eisenhower to his face at Paris. Whatever his real reasons, one, often attributed to him, was to undermine Eisenhower's world popularity. Khrushchev scuttled the conference before it really began, despite Macmillan's tactful efforts.

By that time, Khrushchev had a troublesome rival in the Communist camp in the person of Mao Tse-tung, the shrewd and ruthless head of Communist China, which had come far since it ran out the Nationalists in 1949. At home, the new regime had made the populace more miserable but the country more powerful; it tried herding everyone into a communal agricultural or industrial way of life. As for her Asiatic neighbors, China had overrun remote Tibet and then ruthlessly suppressed a revolt there. The Chinese were also threatening some borderlands of India, thoroughly disillusioning India's Nehru and other Asians who had hoped to play a neutral role in the east-west rivalry but who were realizing that Asiatic "colonialism" might be even more dangerous than the European variety. Khrushchev had a dual concern in this new truculent expansion of long-dormant China. For one thing, he could see the threat to the vast sparsely-settled areas of Central Asia which Russia claimed but which China might covet for her overcrowded population. Then, too, Mao and his right-hand-man Chou-en-lai were still imbued with the pure Marxist-Leninist doctrine of the inevitable struggle with capitalism which they had once imbibed in Moscow, whereas Moscow itself was taking at times a more sophisticated attitude toward possible coexistence with the capitalist west. Consequently, fresh from Paris, Khrushchev went out to China to try to calm his wild colleagues. But China remained a threat to all about her.

But the climax to the amazing international events of 1960 came with the United Nations General Assembly's fifteenth annual session at New York in September. For one thing, its structure underwent a transformation, which, in Western eyes, was definitely not for the better. The scramble for independence in Africa was reflected in the sudden influx of new nations, which completely upset the old balance. When the United Nations was created in 1945, there were 51 members; when it met for this session, it had 82; within three weeks there were 99, with all but three of the new ones admitted in a single day. That was the year that Britain and France each freed about 35 million Africans (see page 708). Two new votes came with the former British states, Nigeria and Somalia. The former French regions, through a fantastic splintering of sovereignty, added fifteen. That led to a regular "rotten borough" system in the Assembly (see page 296). Many of the new states were primitive and economically weak. The capacity for nationhood of a few of the earlier members, such as Haiti and Yemen, had been questionable, and several of these new ones were in a similar category. Little Gabon, just above the Congo, for example, had only 400,000 inhabitants—there were nine cities in the United Kingdom and thirty-three in the United States with larger populations than that. Yet its vote in the General Assembly counted as much as that of Britain or the United States. There was obviously a question as to how intelligently some of these new states would vote on major questions, and also how susceptible they might be to outside pressures. The value of the Security Council had long been crippled by the highly concentrated negative power represented in the Soviet veto, but heretofore, the General Assembly had been fairly dependable, with the bulk of its votes from Western Europe and the Americas. Now, with a very vocal, anticolonialist bloc of Asian and African states, totalling almost half of the membership, anything could happen.

The African situation provided a further grave complication when Belgium's sudden withdrawal from the rich Belgian Congo led quickly to such chaos that the United Nations was asked by its new government for a force to preserve law and order (see page 708). The old League of Nations had failed to respond adequately to three successive international crises (see page 618). The United Nations, profiting by that experience, had already intervened in Korea, and was still preserving peace on the Israeli-Egyptian frontier (see pages 677, 717). Now the United Nations rose to this new challenge, magnificent in its inception but continually frustrating in action. The Security Council voted to send in an international force. That delicate operation was the primary responsibility of Secretary General Dag Hammarskjöld, an able Swede.

With the United Nations session already influenced by that dual African impact, Khrushchev arrived in New York to fish in troubled waters. Normally, nations were represented by their special ambassadors at such sessions, but Khrushchev personally suggested to a large number of like-minded heads of state that they come to New York for a sort of summit session. This resulted in the gathering of the largest number of top statesmen ever assembled, for many Westerners also came. Khrushchev hoped to win over the new African states by posing as the champion of anti-colonialism—a stand that was punctured by frequent reminders from the Assembly members of Russia's own subject satellites. He also launched a vicious attack on the post of Secretary General, angered because Hammarskjöld's forces were checking the Soviet penetration of the Congo. Khrushchev proposed that the single powerful Secretary General be replaced by a tripartite group representing the West, the East, and the neutrals, each with a veto. That measure, which would have wrecked the United Nations, was voted down; so, too, was Khrushchev's demand for the resignation of Hammarskjöld. Khrushchev, used to having his own undisputed way at home, made a crude spectacle of himself. Twice when Macmillan was speaking, he interrupted loudly, to Nehru's obvious contempt. Angered when the Philippines delegate referred to Russia's cruel "colonialism" in Europe, he used his shoe to pound louder. A fairly definite development was that of a "neutralist bloc," which refused to identify itself with either side in the cold war. It included Nehru, Tito, and Nasser. That longest and stormiest session of the General Assembly did not close until late in April, 1961. The United Nations was left severely strained; but it had weathered the storm for the time being.

Tension continued to tighten that spring. The most explosive situations seemed concentrated, however, in the areas from the China Sea to the Caribbean where Com-munists were working overtime to infiltrate and pervert the new nationalistic groups and from Algeria to Cape Town, where die-hard Europeans kept trying to stem the on-rushing tide of native domination.

Macmillan had plenty to worry him. The uncertainties surrounding the new, inexperienced administration in Washington loomed larger with a blundering anti-Communist effort in Cuba. The problems of the Common Market were still unsolved. A Berlin crisis remained an ever-present menace. De Gaulle was striving for full equality in NATO and had refused along with Russia to share in the huge Congo costs of the United Nations. French troops in Algiers staged a brief revolt. Western and Russian negotiators, approaching their three hundredth futile session at Geneva, were deadlocked over nuclear tests. Communist aggression in the strategic but somewhat apathetic kingdom of Laos threatened all South East Asia. SEATO, including four Commonwealth members, conferred at Bangkok, uncertain how far to go in Laos's defense. And Russia announced she had the first man in space.

Throughout those hectic months, Macmillan encountered occasional setbacks, but so far his deft diplomacy spared him Eden's fate. With his "languid air of Edwardian elegance," he was said to possess "an acute sense of the location of power," and to be able "to group it to his purposes." With Labor impotent for the time being, his party seemed secure, but within its ranks was some rumbling over policy. It seemed to be discarding the name "Conservative," associated with the "big business" emphasis of the Baldwin period, in favor of "Tory," claiming kinship with Disraeli's social reforms.

The Commonwealth and Independence

In the Empire-Commonwealth, as at home, the postwar years were difficult for the mother country and disheartening to a people who had long been able to boast of an "empire upon which the sun never sets." The Britons most personally affected were those living in the regions that were breaking loose. In Asia and Africa, there was an irresistible trend toward self-government and more and more toward even independence. Since the relinquishing of many of the old imperial powers was to prove unavoidable, it was perhaps fortunate that the initial liquidation was in the hands of the Labor government. Winston Churchill had once angrily announced that he had not become prime minister to preside over the dissolution of the empire. Had he been in office at this time instead of Attlee, British resources might have been unduly strained if he had attempted to hold some of the reluctant regions, which probably would have been lost in any event.

This sharp diminution of the Empire-Commonwealth, that had covered a quarter of the earth's surface and included a quarter of the earth's population, did not show on the map the extent of the actual loss of British control. Palestine, Jordan, Burma, and Ireland were to be completely separated. Britain's hold upon the vast Indian Empire

became only a faint shadow of the old *raj;* Ceylon secured a similar status. Elsewhere in Asia many difficulties, some large and others small, kept cropping up to plague the path of empire. In Africa, trouble developed all the way from "the Cape to Cairo" in increasing crescendo.

For all that, Britain for the time being weathered the "rising tide of color" more successfully than did most of the other colonial powers. The Dutch were to lose their rich empire in Indonesia; and the desperate fight of the French in Indo-China was at one time killing off officers faster than the military schools could produce them. Then France faced long, bitter, and costly fighting in Algeria, in addition to losing much territory elsewhere in Africa. The rich Belgian Congo was unexpectedly to gain independence for which it had had no preparation whatsoever. The United States had long since voluntarily and quickly relinquished the Philippines at the end of the war. And so it went around the world.

There were various reasons behind this upheaval in long-standing colonialism. Since the turn of the century there had appeared signs of growing nationalism both among the self-governing dominions and also in India and other subject lands. Some concessions were made to meet the situation, particularly between the two World Wars. The Japanese had been among the pioneers in the growing reaction against European imperialism. Then during World War II came their attack on Pearl Harbor, their seizure of Singapore, and their swift, spectacular conquest of Southeast Asia and the Pacific islands. They showed to all the yellow, black, and brown peoples of the world not only that the white men were vulnerable to defeat in battle, but they too could be forced to sweat away the years as starving slave laborers. Before the powerful Allies could gather their resources to stop the onrushing tide of triumphal Japanese occupation of one colonial possession after another, white prestige had suffered an almost fatal blow. With the defeat of Japan in 1945, there was a widespread determination in Southeast Asia to resist the return of the white masters. Another reason for the disintegration of the empire was the hard fact that postwar Britain simply could not afford the sort of armed forces that would have been able to keep her overseas regions in hand against their will.

The Independence of India and Pakistan

The largest rebel against the old order was the Indian Empire, with eight times the population of the British Isles, where the unrest long fostered by Gandhi and others had grown more serious during the war. Dominion status had then been promised, only to be rejected by the Indian National Congress and by the Moslem League. The ensuing revolt, called by the Congress, was quickly put down by force (see pages 649 ff.). With the war over, Britain could no longer postpone the issue; by the beginning of 1946 small units of the Royal Indian Navy were already in mutiny. Three cabinet ministers were hurried out to study the situation and to recommend proper action for the crisis. The decision was to let India go its own way. This time there were no "ifs" and "buts"; the date was set, June,

1948, after which Britain refused to accept any responsibility to India whatsoever.

In the mid-nineteenth century the "Little Englanders" had been ready to let Canada, Australia, and New Zealand go because they cost more than they seemed worth to the mother country; but in those days India was far too valuable an outlet for the textiles of Manchester and the iron of Birmingham to risk losing. In 1946, however, India no longer "paid"; in fact, quite the reverse, for it had become the creditor of Britain to the tune of heavy sums. No longer were there profits to offset the responsibilities, inseparable from that enormous stretch of territory with its bitterly divided peoples.

A certain sense of responsibility still lingered nonetheless—a tradition so ingrained and long-standing as the "white man's burden" did not die instantly. It had been predicted—and by an Indian—that, if the British ever withdrew, such chaos would ensue that "within a year, there would not be a virgin or a rupee in all India from Cape Comorin to the Himalayas." And now, with that day at hand, a particular reminder of responsibility existed in the fears of the minority Moslems of being subjected to Hindu control. The situation was somewhat like that in Ireland, where the Protestants in Ulster in the northern part stubbornly and successfully resisted inclusion in the Irish Free State, with its Catholic majority (see page 485). The Moslems in northern India, only about a fifth of the whole population, were equally determined not to participate in an Indian government that had a Hindu majority. In this stand they had an able and insistent leader, Mohammed Ali Jinnah, tall, lean, and ascetic, and, like Nehru, the Hindu leader, English — educated.

Britain offered to assist the Indian National Congress and the Moslem League in drawing up a constitution for a united India, but no agreement could be reached. The Moslem stand was adamant against inclusion in a Hindu-controlled India. There

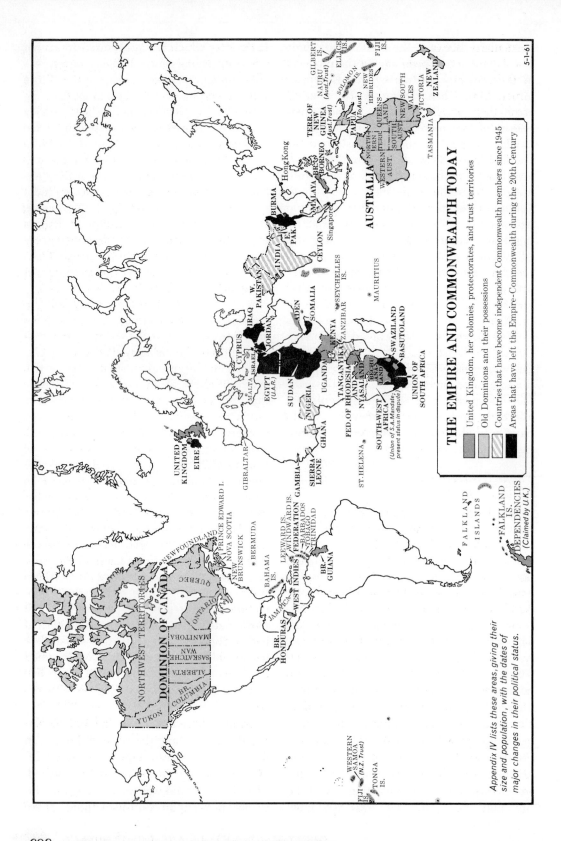

THE EMPIRE AND COMMONWEALTH TODAY

United Kingdom, her colonies, protectorates, and trust territories

Old Dominions and their possessions

Countries that have become independent Commonwealth members since 1945

Areas that have left the Empire-Commonwealth during the 20th Century

Appendix IV lists these areas, giving their size and population, with the dates of major changes in their political status.

5-1-61

was rioting with many lives lost. Gandhi reluctantly agreed, rather than witness further bloodshed, to the division of India into two countries, India and Pakistan. The British, finding no compromise possible, moved up the date of their departure one year, to 1947.

Boundary commissions made the division, while Parliament hastily passed the Indian Independence Bill. The new India, composing most of the subcontinent, had an area of some 1,246,880 miles with a population of approximately 325,000,000. New Delhi was its capital. The scattered location of the Moslem population resulted in a strange arrangement for Pakistan in the north. West Pakistan included the old region of the Northwest Province out as far as the Khyber Pass. East Pakistan, with a thousand miles of Hindu territory intervening between the two sections, was carved out of eastern Bengal, but did not include the great city of Calcutta. The minor port of Karachi, at the head of the Arabian Sea, was made the capital of the new state. Altogether, Pakistan was granted some 337,524 square miles for its population of approximately 75,000,000. The state was handicapped by its geographical separation, which made administration very complicated, and by its lopsided economy. It was primarily agricultural, with ample production of grain, cotton, and a major part of the world's jute supply, but it had little industry or mineral resources, such as India had in abundance.

By the Indian Independence Act of 1947 Britain renounced all control, and both India and Pakistan became, for the time being, self-governing dominions. The several hundred independent native states, in which 25 per cent of the total population of old India lived on approximately 45 per cent of its land area, were allowed by this act to adhere to either Pakistan or India. The Earl of Mountbatten, the last Viceroy of India, became the Governor General in each of the new dominions. The words

British troops on July 4, 1946, lowering flag on leaving the Cairo Citadel, occupied since 1882.

"Emperor of India" were dropped from the title of King George VI, while the traditional "India Office" became a bureau in the "Commonwealth Relations Office."

In August, 1947, the old British *raj* thus came to an end, just one hundred and ninety years after Clive's victory at Plassey had opened the way for the spread of English rule over the huge country. Some of the British officials and soldiers—the "pukka sahibs" of whom Kipling wrote—remained on under the new regimes. This was particularly true in Pakistan, which lacked trained personnel for its more responsible governmental and business positions, since in the old Indian empire such jobs, when not held by the British, had usually gone to Hindus. The other Britons sadly returned home, preferring a lean existence on pensions rather than service under the new leaders of another race.

Relations between the two states were

far from happy during the following years, although the British withdrawal did not on the whole produce quite the dire conditions that had been feared. In the Punjab, which was divided between the two states, however, there was a ghastly readjustment for months. In Pakistan's section, Moslems massacred Hindus and Sikhs by the thousands, while across the line in India's territory, local Moslems in their turn were murdered by Hindus and Sikhs. Such slaughters caused a mass migration of millions of Moslems from the Indian section into Pakistan and of Hindus and Sikhs in the opposite direction. Each fleeing horde of desperate, homeless families left a grim trail of corpses in its wake—men, women, and children dead from violence, hunger, or exhaustion. Likewise in Bengal, to the eastward, Hindus trying to escape to Calcutta from the countryside that was now eastern Pakistan were slain by Moslems. And in that big city, largely Hindu in population, Moslems were killed in retaliation. Years later there was still trouble between Sikhs and Hindus.

Gandhi struggled to calm the bitterness in Calcutta, and in January, 1948, entered his last fast in protest against the slayings. He ended it five days later, when the leaders of both sides pledged to keep the peace. His efforts to bring about better understanding with the Moslems and his desire to abolish untouchability in the old Hindu caste system had made him hated by some of the orthodox aristocratic Hindus. Shortly thereafter he was killed by a nationalistic fanatic of high caste.

The assassination of Gandhi centered the direction of India more than ever in the hands of Jawaharlal Nehru, the first prime minister of India. Cultured, polished, a graduate of Harrow and Cambridge, Nehru was a gifted writer and historian. Like Gandhi, he had frequently been imprisoned by the British, particularly during World War II's civil disturbances.

Another bone of contention between the new states was the distribution of the native states. For the most part, the choice between Pakistan and India was undisputed, but in some cases, the Hindu-Moslem line was not clearcut. The native rulers, seeing the handwriting on the wall, generally preferred to accept the good pensions offered them rather than resist. Of the larger states, only in Hyderabad did the Moslem ruler, with some 16,000,000 Hindu subjects, threaten to fight. One of the world's richest men, he had an ancient treaty in which Britain guaranteed his throne; but his defiance was short-lived when India sent an army against him.

More serious was the case of Kashmir, the border state that controlled mountain passes into Afghanistan, Tibet, and China. In this Hindu-Moslem impasse the Hindu ruler wanted to join India, but his Hindu subjects were only a small aristocracy, the population at large being some 80 per cent Moslem and mostly illiterate. To prevent the ruler from having his way, Moslem tribesmen from the wilds of Pakistan invaded Kashmir, massacring, looting, and abducting women. Nehru, upon an appeal from the ruler, countered by sending in an army, 15,000 strong. Only heavy pressure from the United Nations prevented this incident from expanding into war between the two states; but the efforts of various intermediaries to achieve a permanent settlement met with almost no success.

In the meantime, in Ceylon, south of India, Parliamentary government was introduced in December, 1947, by the Ceylon Independence Act, which provided that the island would have full dominion status by February, 1948. Burma, over across the Bay of Bengal, established itself as an independent nation in January of that same year. The opposition to the British was strong, and the country was torn by internal strife. Consequently, it was allowed to go with no particular objection. Actually, like India, it did not "pay" enough to be worth an attempt to hold it.

The arrangement for "dominion" status for India, Pakistan, Ceylon, and later Ghana, Malaya, and others, was a master stroke of mutual benefit to all parties. In contrast to the violent rupture of imperial ties in French Indo-China and Dutch Indonesia, these new nations remained nominally within the British sphere, even though managing their own foreign relations and defense in addition to internal affairs. The original dominions, outgrowths of colonies of settlement, had been represented at the imperial conferences by premiers of European descent; from now on, the Asians and eventually Africans would meet with them.

British flexibility was to stretch even further with some members of the Commonwealth remaining within it even when they became republics. India, the first of these, became in 1950 a "sovereign democratic republic" with a native president. The conference of Commonwealth premiers at London had agreed unanimously that the Republic of India should remain a full member of the Commonwealth, accepting the king as "the symbol of the free association of its independent member nations and, as such, the head of the Commonwealth." Pakistan followed the same course in 1956. Just how much such membership meant in the Commonwealth was, in characteristic British fashion, never very clearly defined. The new "multiracial commonwealth" at least had the common heritage of contact with British law, forms of government, and tradition.

Meanwhile, one former member of the Commonwealth was leaving it. The Irish Republic had obviously been no more than a nominal dominion. In 1921, when the republic was set up, in order to avoid the necessity of defining things too closely at that tense time, it was simply stated that relations to Britain would be the same as those of Canada (see page 597). Eire severed her last remaining ties with the crown and the Commonwealth in 1949. Her dominion status had long been wearing thin. She had

pretty much conducted herself as an independent nation, even to remaining neutral in World War II. Now her Parliament repealed the External Relations Act, effective in 1949, whereby she had been represented by the British Foreign Office in those nations where she did not send her own ambassadors or ministers. At the same time, she took a lone stand in refusing even to join the other nations of the west in the North Atlantic Pact. Nonetheless, the following year Britain unilaterally defined British citizenship as falling into three categories: United Kingdom citizens, Commonwealth citizens, and Irish citizens!

British imperial holdings were also receding in the Middle East. Of the former mandates in Arab lands, Iraq and Egypt had already left the empire (see pages 609 ff.). Now Britain relinquished the other two: Transjordania very amicably in 1946 and Palestine two years later after considerable violence.

Transjordania became an independent state under the Emir Abdullah, who was soon promoted to king of the "Hashimite Kingdom of Jordan," as the region came to be known. British influence remained strong in the region; Jordan received an annual subsidy from London, and a British brigadier, soon known as Glubb Pasha, created Jordan's Arab Legion, the only really effective fighting force among all the Arab states.

In Palestine, the thirty years of British rule were fast running out. The British were not sorry to relinquish it. Responsibility for it had conflicted with their much wider concerns with the Arab world; for the Arabs still persistently and bitterly resented the intrusion of the Jews into what had been their lands for centuries. The presence of the British garrisons alone had kept Arab and Jew from flying at one another's throats; and small thanks was Britain to get for trying to keep the peace. At first, it was the Jewish colonists the British had protected from Arab outbreaks, but now the British found themselves faced by hostile Jews, determined to be rid of British control (see pages 610 ff.).

The main postwar troubles revolved about Jewish immigration policies, which had long been one of the chief problems of the administrators of the mandate. The traditionally pro-Arab attitude of the Colonial Office was strengthened by Britain's need for Arabian oil. Britain contended that she had kept her promise to admit Jewish immigrants up to the absorptive capacity of the land, but that to go beyond it would be unfair to the Arabs. By 1944, the Jewish minority had risen to nearly one third of the population. The Jews, however, pointed to the progress their coming had meant for Palestine: their city of Tel Aviv, their flourishing orange groves, the hydroelectric possibilities of the Jordan Valley, and the potentialities of the desert lands south of Jerusalem, inhabited by only a few wandering Arab tribes. In most postwar situations Bevin found himself in close agreement with the successive American secretaries of state, but a wide rift opened between the two nations over Palestine. There was widespread sympathy for the Jewish stand in the United States, with its substantial Jewish population, and little realization of the Arab side of the matter.

With the defeat of Germany came a rush toward Palestine of Central European Jews who had survived Hitler's gas chambers. No other country wanted them and most of them wanted no other country. This new pressure against immigration restrictions brought the whole Palestine problem to a head. Aided by the Jewish underground, wholesale smuggling of these refugees was organized. The British intercepted most of the ships headed for Palestine with the European Jews, whom they then placed behind wire fences on Cyprus. The Jews began a campaign of increasing violence and terror within Palestine, directed mainly against the British. There were three main categories of armed Jewish extremists, differing in their degree of radicalism and in the violence of their tactics. Bridges and trains were dynamited; the bombing of a hotel killed numerous British officers; British personnel were ambused and killed; others were kidnapped and held as hostages.

As the terror accelerated, the British officials worked hard, during the last months of 1946, to find some compromise by which Jew and Arab might achieve a peaceful solution. Failing in this attempt, Britain referred Palestine to the United Nations. There an independent Jewish state was recommended, but then no agreement could be reached on the terms of partition. Just six weeks after giving up India, Britain washed her hands of this trouble spot by announcing in September, 1947, her intention of withdrawing from Palestine. The outbreaks of violence persisted as the British prepared to leave. Two months later, the Council of the United Nations, which had taken over the League of Nation's mandates as trusteeships, voted to divide Palestine into three parts. The Jews were to get the portion near the coast for their homeland; the Arabs would have the inland area, ultimately going to Jordan; and Jerusalem was to be an international area administered by the United Nations. The British quickly began to pull out of the region.

In May, 1948, as soon as the British terminated the mandate, the independent state of Israel came into being. The quickness of the United States in recognizing the new government annoyed the British. Israel soon became a member of the United Nations; but peace did not come to it. The Israelis started to move into the supposedly international Jerusalem area, whereupon Jordan's crack Arab Legion raced in there also and took over the "Old City" with the holy places, leaving the Jews the "New City," an arrangement that became permanent. The other Arab states also attacked Israel which beat them off, with particular success against the Egyptians. Border disputes and raids became common during the ensuing years. The partition of Palestine involved cruel hardship for the Arabs, almost a million in number, who had lived in the part allotted to the Jews. Most of them moved into adjacent Arab states where a dozen years later they were still an unhappy displaced populace, living on United Nations bounty. The continuing Israeli-Arab friction would more than once threaten peace in the Middle East (see page 686). Most Britons breathed a sigh of relief to be no longer embroiled there; they felt well rid of a place that had cost them more than 300 lives and £100,000,000.

However ready Britain might be to let those various troublesome and unprofitable regions go, trade considerations made her feel differently about three Asiatic possessions that had been in the hands of the Japanese during the war—Hong Kong, Singapore (formerly in the Straits Settlement), and the Federation of Malaya. In the broadest sense, Malaya includes Singapore as well as the native states of the peninsula. With the financial stringency at home, which made it difficult to pay for essential imports, these "dollar earners" were very important members of the sterling block (see page 661).

Hong Kong and Singapore were valuable as busy entrepôts for much of the Far East and Southeast Asia, and also had much else in common. Long crown colonies, they were both small islands, very close to the mainland with relatively few Europeans in their populations of more than a million Chinese each. The value of their trade with Britain was almost identical. In the postwar era, Hong Kong became more important than ever to Britain after the Chinese Communists captured the rival commercial port of Shanghai and overran the whole mainland of China by 1949. The United States wanted to curb drastically all commerce with Red China, but the British felt otherwise; Hong Kong continued to trade with the Communists and Britain quickly recognized them. The little colony, of course, so near China was vulnerable to easy capture

whenever the Communists might see fit. It became a shelter for swarms of destitute refugees from the mainland. It remained a crown colony while Singapore followed the trend toward nationalism.

Malaya's value as a "dollar earner" came from its production of a considerable share of the world's rubber and tin. Like some of the other colonies with raw materials, it had not been altogether happy at that role in the sterling bloc where all sales to the American "hard money" countries were pooled. If, say, Malaya earned a million dollars for tin, or Gold Coast for cocoa, the British themselves, or possibly the Australians or New Zealanders, were apt to use that credit from the common pool to meet their own needs from America. The colony would be given the equivalent amount in sterling which had to be spent within the sterling bloc; rigid import controls prevented their spending much of it in the United States or Canada. Because Malaya "paid" so well, Britain spared no pains in protecting it vigorously against years of Communist attacks. That was no simple task; the Chinese had invaded its jungles and rubber plantations so successfully that the rubber supply was threatened. Their "hit and run" guerrilla tactics were hard to combat in the jungles, but the British this time, unlike 1942, enlisted the co-operation of large forces of Malay police and special constables. They eventually succeeded in restoring order.

In 1957, Malaya went the way of India and Pakistan in becoming an independent state within the Commonwealth. A federation of native states, most of them ruled by rajahs, it developed the unique arrangement of its own royal "supreme head of state," a post designed to rotate every five years among those rajahs.

Financial Aid and Self-Government

Britain had become so liberal to her overseas possessions, aside from the pooling of sales in the sterling bloc, that the old phrase colonies of exploitation" was no longer applicable. In colony after colony, millions of pounds were granted each year to enable underdeveloped areas to improve their standard of living. At the same time, many colonies were given increasing amounts of self-government. Both of these movements, begun in the years between the World Wars, were carried far after the second. Recognizing that many colonies were too poor to raise the capital for essential public development programs, Parliament passed in 1929 the first of several Colonial Development and Welfare Acts. These provided loans and outright grants from the British treasury, amounting to almost £ 140,000,-000 between 1946 and 1959, with a further £ 140,000,000 planned for the next five years. None of that money went to the "old dominions," but there were some loans or grants to all of the new independent Commonwealth countries. The bulk of the funds went to the still-dependent colonies. Of the total £ 56,000,000, in "grants and technical aid" in the 1959-1960 estimates, Africa received nearly one third and Asia a quarter, while Jamaica and the other old sugar islands, now fallen on difficult times, received about one tenth. Besides those "handouts," the government loans came to an additional £ 61,000,000 more than half of which went to India. Britain also participated in several co-operative programs, including the World Bank and the "Colombo Plan" of 1955 for mutual Commonwealth assistance in Southeast Asia, while private loans also went to colonial regions. Those amounts, to be sure, were only about one-seventh of what the United States was giving to the underdeveloped regions of the world. Such grants were in part a product of the cold war, for it was realized that the Soviets might otherwise extend their influence through similar assistance.

The stimulation of colonial education, one of Britain's principal objectives, became increasingly imperative as the impetus for independence or increased self-govern-ment gained momentum. In the earlier days, the missionaries had conducted most of such education as there was, but with the gradual development of government-supported schools, the heavy illiteracy was reduced. Universities in Malaya, Nigeria, the West Indies, and elsewhere eventually resulted. Related to that educational growth was an ambitious program of technical assistance in many spheres, including civil service, communications, medical research, and much else. In the nineteen fifties came the emergency necessity for more and more education as fast as possible. "We are running a race against time to produce a few Africans capable of occupying the key posts they are demanding," declared the head of a British college in Uganda. "Education," said one government report, "is essential not only for material prosperity through technological changes, but for the training of leaders and led in government, industry, the professions and other aspects of a nation's life. In this sphere, even more important than money is . . . the supply of teachers . . . from the United Kingdom and the provision here of facilities for training teachers and others from overseas."

Side by side with that educational assistance came the gradual, increased colonial participation in government. Whereas that had existed in the colonies of settlement from the first, reaching its culmination in the "old dominions," it had come more slowly to the yellow, brown, and black peoples. This had begun in India (see page 535) and in the practice of "indirect rule" through tribal chiefs or other local potentates. During the nineteen twenties, Britain had admitted elected natives to the colonial legislatures in several colonies of West and East Africa. After World War II, this practice was extended to many distant regions, with fully or partly elected legislative assemblies or legislative councils. At the same time, natives were given an increasing share in many functions of governmental operation.

As a result of all this, when the British possessions began to break loose, they had a nucleus of trained leaders and officials with at least some understanding of how governments operated. The other colonial powers were very remiss in such preparation. France had poured even more money than Britain into her colonies, but relatively little of it had gone for education. Colonial natives could sit as senators or deputies at Paris, but few had any training in colonial administration. In the vast, fabulously rich Congo, one of its distracted Belgian officials a few weeks before Independence Day shuddered at its unreadiness. "When Ghana [Gold Coast], with just over a third of our population became independent, it had 1,500 blacks already in top jobs of the civil service. We in the Congo have fewer than a dozen now at work in such jobs." Less than sixteen natives, moreover, even held college degrees. The situation in Portugal's large colonies was even worse; but controlled with an iron hand, they were about the last to be affected. Not until 1961 did vicious revolt strike Angola.

Anti-Colonialism

The initial independence drive of the forties right after the war had freed India, Pakistan, Ceylon, Burma, Jordan, and Palestine by 1948; then the movement slowed down for the next six years. The serious unrest in Asia was no great surprise, but the sudden explosive upheaval in Africa, both north and south of the Sahara, had scarcely been expected as early as the fifties. Accelerated undoubtedly by the French defeat in Indo-China and Nasser's rise in Egypt (see pages 685, 696), some leaders made efforts to unite the Asian and African peoples in an all-out attack on what they denounced as colonialism. This was to lead in 1955 to a gathering of representatives of various regions in those two continents at Bandung in Indonesia, whose new head voiced the idea that they "should reject everything from the West except its money." The next step was the formation of a rather loose "Afro-Asian bloc" in the General Assembly of the United Nations whose membership was being steadily swelled by the admission of ex-colonial nations.

The Mau Mau

Although the British felt the bitter hatred spreading quite literally from "Cape to Cairo," the worst shock came even before Bandung from the violence of native attacks in tropical Africa, where the Negroes had been heretofore among the most docile people of her overseas lands. By the end of 1952, Kenya (British East Africa), with a good climate for its many white settlers, was the setting for ugly native uprisings. A Negro sect, known as the Mau-Maus, suddenly began a reign of terror, swooping down upon one British farm after another to torture and slaughter any whites they might find. The extreme secrecy of its membership not only made it difficult to suppress but added to its terror; the gentle cook of many years' devoted service was as likely as not to be the one who unlocked the door to the murderers and helped them destroy the family. This appalling uprising took on a still grimmer aspect with the possibility that it might spread through the whole of central Africa. There in the possessions of Britain, France, Belgium, and Portugal lived a quarter of a million white Europeans in the midst of 150,000,000 blacks. Before the Mau-Maus were crushed in 1956, almost a hundred white men, women, and children, along with twenty-nine Asians, had been killed, often with vicious savagery. Particularly tragic was this sect's additional slaughter of more than twelve thousand Negro tribesmen who refused to co-operate against the British.

The British were reluctant to abandon the thousands of settlers in the Kenya "white highlands" to the tender mercies of a Negro-dominated state, but the alternative seemed even worse. Hopeful signs in adjacent Tanganyika, moreover, seemed to indicate that under intelligent, moderate leadership, resident whites might have little to fear even with the majority control African (see page 719). The grant of partial self-government was starting well with the current African leader, Julius K. Nyerere. By 1961, talk was increasing of a possible East African federation, including Kenya, Tanganyika, Uganda, and perhaps the adjacent island of Zanzibar.

In steaming West Africa freedom could be granted more easily, for there the white settlers had no rights to lose, not even being allowed to acquire property. The British, moreover, wanted no more of the difficult and expensive guerrilla fighting of which they had had plenty in Kenya and Malaya, if it could be avoided. Among the Africans, in their new spirit of nationalism, many felt: "We would rather go to hell on our own than to heaven with the British." But others did not forget the danger of civil disorder and tribal warfare when British power was removed. One Negro leader, when asked his plans if the British pulled out, replied "I'd take the next steamer for England." And that is what the leader of the opposition party in Ghana did; incidentally, he barely made the boat.

Ghana and Nigeria

Already in 1948, the old crown colony of Gold Coast (Ghana) on the Guinea coast, became under British auspices the first laboratory of Negro self-government. It had become prosperous through the successful cultivation of cocoa. By the close of the war a United Gold Coast Convention was clamoring for home rule; and, by 1948, disputes over cocoa prices led to some fairly severe rioting in the colonial capital. A parliamentary commission hurried down from London, with the result that the Gold Coast was given a new constitution with popular elections. Then there entered upon the scene a flamboyant youth just back from college in the United States and England. This young Negro, Kwame Nkrumah, loudly

demanded immediate self-government and spread about his half-digested ideas about Marxian socialism until the British jailed him. Proclaiming him a "martyr," his improvised party swept to victory in the general election. The British governor of the Gold Coast, known as "a wise old Africa hand," then appointed Nkrumah a virtual prime minister.

That example was not lost upon either the blacks or the whites throughout Africa. Nigeria, in starting out on the same path, had a leader who predicted that within a century Black Africa would have crushed the armies of Europe and brought the United States to the verge of extinction, while black missionaries would be preaching the gospel of peace in "darkest Europe." Down in South Africa, Malan, the prime minister voiced the apprehension of many whites: "If other African native territories demand with the same success what the Negroes in the Gold Coast have gained, it means the expulsion of the white man from everywhere between South Africa and the Sahara."

Nkrumah's success did not stop there. Early in 1957, the colony of Gold Coast became the independent "dominion" of Ghana, as the tenth member of the Commonwealth, with Nkrumah as premier. He at once sought to build up a position as leader of African independence, before the other regions achieved their freedom. When Nasser began to talk of leading the pan-African movement, Nkrumah told him that he was an Arab, with the Middle East his proper sphere. Altogether, Ghana began as a nation with more advantages than most of the others: her wealth from cocoa, her own university, and her long experience with British law and principles of government. Even at that, it was a risky proposition to organize an opposition party. In 1960 Nkrumah ended the dominion relationship and made Ghana an independent republic with himself as president. His face replaced that of Queen Elizabeth on coins and stamps; he

Princess Alexandra of Kent, representing Queen Elizabeth II, opening Federal Parliament of newly independent Nigeria, October 3, 1960.

had statues erected to himself as "Founder of the Nation" and was even pictured as the "Savior." He tightened his autocratic rule. Though always denying any Communist leanings, he began to align Ghana with Guinea, which was openly flirting with Russia, and some of the other more vocally "anti-colonial" new African states.

One reason for Nkrumah's haste in his quest for African leadership was Nigeria's approaching independence. That great colony had some 35 million inhabitants to Ghana's five million. Nigeria had, in fact, a larger population than that of the fifteen new former French states south of Sahara. Britain had prepared the Nigerians well for their new role. In 1954, she had created a federation in Nigeria, with the three separate parts, Northern, Eastern, and Southern, each having internal self-government. In 1960, Nigeria became an independent do-

minion, the twelfth member of the Commonwealth. Northern Nigeria, conservative, Moslem, and the most populous, furnished the first premier, the reserved and unassuming Abubakar Balewa, who had already held that role under partial self-government. In him, Nigeria now had a leader who has been called "an astute and impressive statesman." He had studied in London, had made the pilgrimage to Mecca, and, visiting New York, had decided that if diversified Americans could achieve political unity, there might be hope for Nigeria's widely varied tribes and regions. Realizing the necessity for education, he sent a mission to the United States to recruit teachers. "Nigeria's sober voice, urging the steady, cautious way to prosperity and national greatness," it was remarked late in 1960, "seems destined to exert ever-rising influence in emergent Africa."

The Scramble for Independence

To the eastward, the jointly-controlled Anglo-Egyptian Sudan, long coveted by Egypt, voted instead to become an independent republic. This was established in 1956. In that same general sandy area, Britain lost yet another African possession in 1960, when primitive British Somaliland was joined with the former Italian Somaliland to form the independent republic of Somalia. Neither of them wanted, or rated, membership in the Commonwealth.

France, bogged down with her frustrating and costly troubles in Algeria, suddenly released her hold on the rest of her African empire. Tunisia and Morocco had gone quickly. After General de Gaulle was called in to handle the difficult situation, he gave the remaining colonies the choice of autonomy or complete separation. Only Guinea at the time chose the latter and turned toward the Communists. But very soon Madagascar and the various provinces of French West Africa and French Equatorial Africa shifted to independence in 1960 with only a vestige of connection with France in a hazy counterpart of the Commonwealth. The fact that the twelve regions within French West Africa and French Equatorial Africa thus became separate nations, each with its own vote, was the main cause for the distortion of voting power in the United Nations General Assembly (see page 694). The former French mandates of Togo and Cameroons were granted their independence by the United Nations, thus adding two more African votes.

The year 1960 saw the creation of more new states than any previous year in history. That startling phenomenon, which was changing the map of Africa, would have seemed incredible less than ten years before. The European colonizing powers were moving out as suddenly and much faster than they had moved in during the great "scramble" three-quarters of a century before. From every quarter of that vast continent, whether from primitive tribes scarcely removed from cannibalism or modern congested cities, came louder and more impatient demands for freedom from the white man. By whole squads, little splinter states were taking on the trappings of sovereignty, their own flags, diplomatic corps, and membership in the United Nations (see page 694). Most of them were far less prepared than Ghana and Nigeria for their new responsibilities; some were desperately unprepared, particularly the Belgian Congo.

The shocking aftermath of Belgium's sudden release of her tautly organized and tremendously profitable Belgian Congo, after she had failed to train the natives for their new responsibilities, was chaos for the Congo and intensified forebodings in the cold war. Almost at once, the army, without its Belgian officers, went on a rampage, raping white women en masse and also black. The vast region began to split up along tribal and regional lines. The cocky new premier, Patrice Lumumba, a postal clerk who had served a sentence for embezzlement, was a successful rabble rouser, and many blamed him for the terror. He began to intrigue openly with the Russians after he had asked the United Nations to help restore law and order. It sent a police force, that lacked authority to take control. Kasavubu, the more stable president, dismissed Lumumba, who was soon arrested. He was later killed; Communists made it an issue and tribal war threatened. The Western world had breathed more freely when the United Nations stepped in with its police force, wisely containing no troops from any of the big powers. Its troops came from various Asian and African nations and also from Sweden and Ireland, both of the latter being innocent of "colonialism." Among these contingents were several from the Commonwealth—India, Pakistan, Malaya, Ghana, and, as soon as it became independent,

Nigeria; for a while, an Indian and an Irishman were respective political and military United Nations heads in the Congo. In one fantastic encounter, natives armed only with bows and arrows killed several Irish soldiers and reportedly ate one of them. But, blasted by Russian criticism and frustrated by the warring Congo factions, these forces were unequal to the task, until Kasavubu, now co-operating, gave hope of a non-Communist central government.

To the southward of those regions, the "Central African Federation of Rhodesia and Nyasaland" was a unique racial and political mixture. An "almost-dominion," it was formed in 1953 of Southern Rhodesia, Northern Rhodesia, and the Nyasaland Protectorate. Though lying entirely in the tropics, its high elevation, averaging from three thousand to five thousand feet, made much of its territory, like Kenya's, good "white man's country." Each of the three regions had around two million Negroes with the Europeans very unevenly distributed. In Southern Rhodesia, promoted by Rhodes in 1889 (see page 530), they numbered at the end of 1957 about 200,000; in Northern Rhodesia, some 74,000; and in Nyasaland, only 7,900. Politically, that was reflected in the fact that Southern Rhodesia had had responsible government ever since the British South Africa Company gave it up in 1923. Northern Rhodesia at that time became a sort of crown colony, while Nyasaland was a protectorate. Those separate forms continued for local government under the Federation. Economically, too, there was a difference; Northern Rhodesia shared huge copper deposits with the Belgian Congo's Katanga region. Southern Rhodesia in addition to considerable mining and agriculture had developed great hydroelectric power from its huge Kariba Dam in the Zambesi below Victoria Falls. Nyasaland's economic resources were very much less, which was an argument for joining it with these richer neighbors. But that was unpopular with its almost all-native population which resented the idea of being dominated by the white controlled Rhodesias. The Federation had many dominion features: a governor general, high commissioners, and its own consuls, while its premier often attended the meetings of the Commonwealth premiers. The British government, however, remained "generally responsible for its international relations." The increasing tensions between the whites and the Africans produced rioting, first in Nyasaland and then in Southern Rhodesia. By 1961, some of the African leaders took the problems to London, and the Federation's future status was discussed with the government authorities.

Nearer home, in the Mediterranean, strategic considerations precipitated a thorny problem in the island colony of Cyprus, Disraeli's prize, secured from Turkey in 1878 (see page 474). Britain felt she could not afford to let this go, for it was her last chance for a naval, military, and air base in the strategically critical eastern Mediterranean, now that her former bases in Egypt and Palestine were gone. This was a complicated crisis. The population consisted of Greeks and Turks in a proportion of about four to one. The former, under Makarios, a Greek Orthodox archbishop, resorted to terrorism to secure autonomy and a union of sorts with Greece. Both Greece and Turkey, Britain's fellow allies in NATO, supported their respective groups. Britain exiled Makarios, but the bitter fighting continued. Finally, in 1960, Cyprus became independent under an ingenious compromise, which guaranteed British retention of bases, but left the government in the hands of the islanders with stipulated protection for the Turkish minority.

Halfway round the world, some of Britain's oldest colonies were likewise being welded into a federation with prospective dominion status. In 1958, she formed the Federation of the West Indies, composed of her old, and once fabulously profitable sugar islands. In later days, their economy had dwindled and the oldtime white planter class had virtually disappeared. Jamaica was 95 per cent Negro and many of the other "islands in the sun" had a similar ratio, which involved both economic, social, and political problems. In the year of federation, for example, the British treasury had to pay out some £4,500,000 to keep their depleted economies going. The members of the Federation included Jamaica, the former Leeward Islands federation, the Windward Islands, Barbados, Tobago, and Trinidad, where the new capital was located. It was expected that the Federation would soon become a dominion within the Commonwealth.

Late in 1960, the United States, which still held bases in the British islands acquired during World War II, released some of her holdings on Trinidad. She stated her intention of retaining the rest of them as well as those on the other islands until 1977.

The British took decisive action in one colony in this Caribbean area in 1953, because like Cyprus it was a sensitive strategic location. A cruiser was rushed to British Guiana and its colonial constitution was suspended for four years, when a left wing party headed by an Indian won control of the assembly and disorder threatened.

Old Dominions: South Africa

Although the ties with the four old dominions had been loosening long before her colonies began to drop off, Britain could take real pride in the achievements of three —Canada, Australia, and New Zealand. South Africa was quite the reverse with her recurrently hostile attitude and increasingly with her dangerous racial policies. There was no problem for Britain with her trade and economy, which were both good, but politically, she was a worry.

Her relation with the Crown was becoming constantly more strained; in some ways this resembled Ireland's strange record as a dominion. In each case, there were bitter memories—the Afrikaners had not forgotten the Boer War. One of the most arrogantly anti-British Nationalists had been forced on Queen Elizabeth as her governor general. No longer did the South Africans sing "God Save the Queen," and they were replacing the traditional pounds, shillings, and pence with a new currency. They were continuing their long standing offishness in much else (see page 616). Matters came to a climax in 1960, when the government held a referendum to decide whether or not South Africa should break with the crown altogether and become a republic. The British element in the Union, outnumbered about three to two, worked strenuously in opposition and were supported by some of the more liberal South Africans. The vote was very close; out of the three million whites (the eleven million non-whites had no say in the matter) the republic won by a margin of only 52 per cent. The republic was scheduled to come into being in May, 1961. There was a question, however, as to whether or not it would be permitted to remain in the Commonwealth (see page 719). At the meeting of the Commonwealth premiers in the spring of 1960, Macmillan had to exercise all his tact and influence to keep India and Ghana from pushing South Africa's expulsion from Commonwealth membership.

Afrikaners and Apartheid

Expulsion might have come then, for a crisis at the time in her racial situation had been handled in a way to alienate world opinion. Racial tensions had been approaching the explosive point since the defeat of General Smuts' party in the general election of 1948. Britain had good cause to regret that he was no longer premier of the Union, for he had long kept the dominion loyal to her. He was succeeded by Dr. Daniel Malan of the Afrikaner Nationalist Party. A dour Calvinist, Malan hated the British only a little less

MMONWEALTH CLUB

"Boy! Chuck that fellow out!"

Cartoon satirizing the pressure of Nkrumah and others to expel South Africa from the British Commonwealth. This appeared in 1960, a year before the final South African withdrawal.

than he hated the Negroes. Immediately the strange racial situation was subjected to new stresses. Among the white minority there were more Boers, or Afrikaners, than Britons; Smuts had managed to hold power by a coalition of the more moderate Boers with the British (see page 615). Malan, like Hertzog before him, was able to win with the slogan "British hands are still red with Boer blood." He then proceeded to utilize his premiership to foster racial discrimination, a matter in which Boers and Britons had long disagreed. This race question involved the treatment, not only of the Negroes and mulattoes, but also of the numerous Indians. The British in the Cape and Natal had been less illiberal than the Afrikaners in the Transvaal and Orange Free State. As early as 1858, the Boers of the then independent Transvaal had written into their fundamental law that "the people will not tolerate equality between the colored and white peoples either in church or state."

Malan was representing the feeling of a large proportion of those Boers when he launched a campaign to enforce a policy of *apartheid* (literally, apartness). This carried to much greater extremes the spirit of "segregation" and the old "Jim Crow" laws in the southern United States. The South African constitution was altered in high-handed fashion to disenfranchise the "colored" people in the Cape province, who had long been able to vote. Malan's party also passed a new nationalization law, which discriminated against not only the Indians living in the Union but against British immigrants, who might be inclined to vote against them. Despite loud outcries against such irregularities, the Nationalists pushed their harsh policies further and further. Yet the 1953 election continued them in power, with Malan still premier.

Behind much of the trouble was the maladjustment of the Negro population between their old tribal existence and the life of the cities where their labor was needed not only in factories but in most other activities. Nearly one-sixth of South Africa's native population lived in the ten largest cities; Johannesburg, the tense, hectic metropolis had a half million of them; Cape Town and Durban each a third of a million; only Pretoria, with its government office workers, had more white than "non-white" residents. No one could make in a few years a shift in living conditions that normally has taken centuries of slow evolution and not find the new ways vastly disturbing, but for the Africans, government harassment made it almost insurmountable. The huge numbers for the Transvaal mines were brought in on six- or nine-month contracts; then they were forced to go back to their tribes. Others had fairly permanent jobs in the cities but the government sought to curb the crowd of unemployed who, lured by the city's life and excitement, crowded into squalid slums. Consequently, every

Ghanian troops arriving by United States plane to join the United Nations forces in the Congo, July, 1960.

Negro had to carry a pass book, indicating his tribe, his job if any, and much else—those without jobs were herded back to the country. That general situation was now intensified by the application of a new basic Nationalist policy. All Negroes, except those needed regularly as workers around the cities, were to be moved willy-nilly out to remote "Bantu reserves," where they would have to develop their own economy. This meant that should the swelling wave for independence penetrate this white paradise, the back country could go its own way, leaving the whites in control of the valuable and settled parts of the Union.

Along with such strategy went needlessly irritating and sometimes brutal tactics. Every Bantu was required to carry his pass book at all times; he could be jailed if he just stepped outdoors a minute without his book. After Malan's death, the next two premiers, Johannes Strijdom and Hendrik Verwoerd, carried on these policies with ever-increasing harshness.

This unrelenting pressure coupled with the accelerating native independence movement elsewhere in Africa inevitably brought Bantu restlessness to the edge of defiance. This culminated early in 1960 in a sort of "Peterloo" (see page 392) at Sharpesville near Johannesburg. In an effort to be rid of the hated passbooks, a large group of Negroes, deliberately not carrying them, swarmed to the local police station and asked to be arrested. The police fired into the crowd, killing 69 men and women and wounding 178. The repercussions from this spread around the world. The United States formally deplored the action; South African products were boycotted in some countries; foreign investments fell off sharply; and an irate wealthy Briton shot and wounded Premier Verwoerd. Arrests were said to have been in the thousands, including a good many opponents to the Afrikaner ideas, even whites of prominence. The government's propaganda that they acted only for the welfare of the Bantu did not alleviate the hostile world reaction.

The Other Old Dominions

In contrast, Canada, Australia, and New Zealand, like Britain's still earlier colony of settlement, the United States, were among the best-governed democracies of the world. They had early gained experience in the political and legal methods and principles of the mother country, and this persisted even after some of them began to absorb non-British elements. In this, their record of stability and progress stood in marked contrast to that of the Spanish-American lands which had not had self-governing tutelage.

Reminiscent of a century earlier was the stream of emigration from the United Kingdom to the Anglo-Saxon regions beyond the seas, which rose almost eightfold between 1938 and 1956. Canada's immigrants increased from 3,300 a year to 41,500; Australia's from 5,400 to 32,100; and New Zealand's from 2,400 to 11,500. The United States shared in this movement, rising from 1,900 to 13,900. Only to Afrikaner-dominated South Africa was the gain less marked, 6,000 to 8,900.

These old colonies of settlement that the "Little Englanders" had wanted to give away because they did not "pay," now ranked among the world's most prosperous nations. In the matter of annual per capita production Canada was in second place at $1,350, following the United States at $1,870 as an average for the years 1952 to 1958. Switzerland was in third place at $1,010, New Zealand in fourth at $1,000, while Australia and Sweden were tied at $950. In a single year, 1956, New Zealand had been in first place. South Africa's figures were not comparable, with her small white population. The extreme poverty in Asia and Africa was indicated by Pakistan with an average of $70, India with $60, Burma and Uganda each with $50, and Libya with $25.

In addition to NATO and other organizations, a strong, albeit informal community of interest had been developing since the beginning of World War II among the peoples of Britain, the United States, Canada, Australia, and New Zealand; each of those in the Commonwealth had an intimate relationship to the United States, as well as to one another. Australia and New Zealand might be said to be committing a sort of imperial bigamy. While still loyal to Britain, they were also growing closer and closer to the United States, Britain's "best friend." In older days, the royal navy had been able to protect the distant dominions, while the London money market could furnish ample loans for their economic expansion. In the depleted state of Britain's postwar finances, however, she could no longer support them in the style to which they had become accustomed. The Americans could, and did.

Whereas the United States and Canada with their three thousand miles of unfortified border had long had much in common, this relationship was growing still closer (see page 389). Australia and New Zealand had had slight contact with the United States until early in World War II, when they realized that embattled Britain could not spare forces for their defense. "Without any inhibitions of any kind," declared the Australian premier early in 1941, "I make it quite clear that Australia looks to America, free of any pangs as to our traditional links or kinship with the United Kingdom." After Pearl Harbor, American ships, planes, and troops based in Australia and New Zealand protected them from the Japanese. In 1952, the three nations formed ANZUS, the Australian–New Zealand–United States defense pact for that Pacific area. There were some heartburnings in Britain, when she was not invited to join this. The new transpacific relationship was appreciated more than ever by 1960 when American investments in Australian industry had reached nearly a billion dollars, while the United States Seventh Fleet was still offering protection in those waters.

Normally, Ottawa, Canberra, and Wellington had little difficulty in keeping their relations with London and Washington on an even keel, but occasionally one or another of them was caught by a hard decision between loyalty, self-interest, or principle. In the Suez crisis, Australia and New Zealand, alone of the Commonwealth, stood by Britain in supporting Eden's invasion, albeit without enthusiasm. Canada joined with the United States as leading opponents (see page 686).

Australia: Industrial Growth

In the middle years of the century, Australia was transformed into an industrial nation. Her traditional wool and mutton still remained her chief exports, but manufactures in 1956, for example, had become 60 per cent of the value of her economic production. This rapid development of industry had been suddenly stimulated during World War II when she had to produce war materials in a hurry (see page 649). Without even machine-tool production before the war, she was turning out by 1960 "not only planes, ships, and diesel locomotives but such sophisticated products of modern technology as guided missiles, transistor radios, and radioactive isotopes". She had the third largest steel company in the Commonwealth and her General Motors subsidiary was making over 100,000 motor vehicles a year.

Much of Australia's population and economic activities were still concentrated in the narrow "fertile crescent" in the southeast, with a third of the people in the two big cities of Sydney and Melbourne. Sydney's two millions made it larger than any other "white" Commonwealth city except London, while Melbourne with over a million and a half residents was tied for next place with Montreal, well ahead of the other big cities of Great Britain. The continent's population jumped from seven to ten millions between 1940 and 1960, partly from deliberately stimulating immigration. Australia never lost sight of the fact that she was too small to stave off possible invasion from what the rest of the world knew as the "Far East" but which she called the "Near North." Also she was well aware that a large part of her area was uninhabited and susceptible to easy conquest. Her minister of immigration in the postwar years warned that she had only "perhaps twenty-five years to justify" having a continent for herself alone, and revived the slogan "Populate or Perish". His program was to bring in over 100,000 immigrants a year, nearly half from Britain and the rest from other "white" countries.

Back in 1904, despite the small industrial development, an aggressive Labor party achieved its first ministry almost twenty years before Britain's. Thereafter Labor was to share power about evenly with the more conservative city and country elements. From 1941 to 1949, it was in office under "earnest, colorless" John Curtin; next, as in Britain two years later, the voters decided on a change from experimentation and controls. Then, for more than a decade, there was a Liberal-Country coalition under Robert Gordon Menzies, a Melbourne lawyer of Scottish descent. His success in attracting foreign investments resulted in increasing prosperity, which, as in Britain, weakened the appeal of the Labor party. By 1960, import restrictions were greatly relaxed and the Australians were able to buy American articles once more.

New Zealand

New Zealand's situation was generally similar but she had neither undergone such drastic industrial expansion nor had she encouraged such wholesale migration. With the almost universal feeling among nations, old and new, that prosperity depended upon industrial expansion, she nevertheless achieved one of the world's highest levels of per capita production, even the highest in 1956, with an economy largely based on four basic pastoral offerings: wool, meat, butter, and cheese. These came from her 42,000,000 sheep and 5,000,000 cattle. Also like Australia, political power was fairly evenly divided between Labor and a coalition of conservative farmers and urban business interests, with the latter coming into office also in 1949. But unlike Labor's experience in Australia and Britain, here it was returned to power in 1957. William Nash became premier.

With Labor in control, the "welfare state" trend, in which New Zealand had been a world pioneer in the eighteen nineties (see page 542), was accentuated. She now went further toward state socialism than almost any place in the world except Canada's sparsely settled province of Saskatchewan. Nearly half the population received government benefits in one form or another; one fifth of the nation's workers were in government jobs. Britain's "cradle to the grave" social security was almost niggardly in comparison. In New Zealand, almost two-thirds of the government's revenue went to social security. The corollary of that ultra-generous policy was a terrific tax rate. No one, it was said, was really rich, and no one was really poor as the result of this levelling combination of social benefits and high progressive tax rates. Everyone, so some grumbled, was being crowded into a lower middle class level. After three years of the Nash Labor government, it was reported in mid-1960 that workers were losing incentive with so little "difference between the take-home pay of a skilled and unskilled worker. . . . A department head in the Government is earning, after taxes, only twice as much as his stenographer." For all that, New Zealanders boasted that they ate more meat and had a higher caloric intake than anyone else in the world.

Then, by the end of 1960, Labor was ousted, with a new ministry coming into power under Keith J. Holyoake. This made the move toward the right unanimous in the "white" Commonwealth: Labor or Liberal parties had been supplanted in Australia in 1949, Great Britain in 1950, and Canada in 1957; South Africa, of course, had retained its own unique party of ultra-conservatism since 1948. The Holyoake ministry made no immediate attempt to soften the extreme socialization, but concerned itself with reducing the compulsory union membership and with encouraging immigration, which Labor opposed raising above the existing limit of ten thousand a year. Newcomers from many lands were welcomed into the previously homogeneous country, although according to Holyoake, "we just don't give entry permits to Asians." There was talk of aluminum smelting and other new industries, but the economy still rested primarily on the export of wool and butter, which was supporting the population on a higher per capita income than that of most other regions in the world.

Canada

At the beginning of the sixties, Canada, with the most impressive dominion record of all, was steadily growing in stature as a nation. In the two centuries since Wolfe's victory at Quebec, she had profited by one British innovation in colonial policy after another: the Quebec Act, Durham's responsible government, the inauguration of dominion status, and the Commonwealth principle of partnership. The Canadians themselves had gone much further in developing their unique nation, and were duly proud of their achievements. Though still relatively small, with a population only one third the size of Britain and a tenth that of the United States, she stood among the leaders in prosperity and good government at home and in an active and enlightened role in international affairs.

Of her 17,500,000 people, nearly half were British with about 24 per cent of the total of English descent, 14 per cent Scottish, and 10 per cent Irish. These maintained a long-standing numerical advantage over the French descendants, who numbered 31 per cent. For the rest of the population, her fairly liberal immigration policies had made Canada something of a melting pot by this time. There were considerable numbers of Germans, Russians, Dutch, Poles, and more than a dozen other nationalities.

On the whole Canada was free from the Anglo-French tensions of her earlier days. In the province of Quebec in the nineteen fifties, to be sure, the provincial automobile licenses around Montreal read "Quèbec," with the French accent, and carried the old royal French lilies, while the provincial blue and white flag, with its cross, was generally flown instead of the red union jack with its Canadian symbol in the corner. But the Union Nationale party, with anti-British feelings, was in power then; it was decisively defeated at the polls in 1960 after the death of the ultra-French premier, Maurice L. Duplessis.

Whereas Australia and New Zealand worried about being thousands of miles from the nearest "white" region, Canada was becoming concerned over the propinquity along three thousand miles of common frontier with the United States. In the postwar years, Canada's booming economy was beginning to make the two neighbors competitors. In addition to wheat, long Canada's most valuable product, and pulpwood that furnished a generous part of the world's newsprint, the threefold discoveries of rich deposits of oil, iron ore, and uranium suddenly pointed the way to an almost limitless economic potential. The first oil strike in the neighborhood of Edmonton, Alberta, was followed by others in that area, until more than 9,000 wells were in operation. Pipelines soon carried some of it out to Vancouver and the American North-

west and some east to Ontario, with Montreal a possible later terminal. Additional lines took natural gas south to the United States. The big boom in the mining of uranium ore fell off with the promotion of outside sources; and the flourishing centers became deserted ghost towns. Canada also did much to develop hydro-electric power, used in one case to process bauxite for aluminum. The most spectacular development came from the discovery of vast deposits of excellent iron ore, stretching from the lower St. Lawrence River up along the disputed frigid frontier between Quebec and Labrador to the arctic wastes explored centuries earlier in the quest for the Northwest Passage. American steel makers took a major financial part in developing the new region, for their own Great Lakes deposits of first-rate ore were running low. Rail lines over the frozen tundra were built to link the ore deposits with new ports at Seven Islands and Port Cartier on the lower St. Lawrence.

There, as elsewhere, heavy capital outlay was needed, and most of it came from the United States. Hundreds of American firms, moreover, were developing subsidiaries in Canada, just as they were doing on a large scale in Britain and more modestly in Australia and South Africa (see page 691). Altogether, it was estimated in 1960 that total foreign investments in Canada came to some $20,000,000,000, three-quarters of which was American. Most of these stimulated activities employed numerous Canadians, but almost $1,000,000,000 a year had to be paid out in interest and dividends, the major share to investors south of the border. Times had changed since the days when Britain's "Victorian heritage" was expanding and most of Canada's debt was owed to the British and not to her American economic rival.

One important Canadian-American joint activity was the construction of the St. Lawrence Seaway, opened in 1959. This ambitious project enabled ocean shipping to reach the Great Lakes and also produced much hydroelectric power. The matter had been under negotiation for years; Washington was finally prodded into action only after Canada threatened to go ahead with it herself.

In the field of defense and preparedness, the two nations were, in the meantime, making remarkable progress in pooling their efforts. Early in 1940, they had made a formal joint agreement, that was of great service during the war. Then the movement tended to lapse until Canada suddenly realized that she lay right in the path of any bombing operations over the top of the world between Russia and the United States. That led to the establishing of three radar warning lines, the most ambitious of which, the Distant Early Warning ("Dewline") system consisted of a string of lonesome Arctic posts, partly in Alaska, partly in Canada, but all manned by United States troops. Even closer coordination came with the creation of a joint air defense command under an American general, with a Canadian as his deputy. Much else in the military field was also coordinated. Like ANZUS, Britain was not included in this; it was an American liaison with a member of the Commonwealth.

In the general field of foreign affairs, Canada became active directly after the war. Just as she had been the first dominion to set up her own diplomatic force (see page 615), she now established a "minister of external affairs," the dominion equivalent of a foreign secretary. Particularly effective in that role was Lester Pearson, one of the first presidents of the United Nations General Assembly. Feeling that the "great powers" took too great a share of the authority there, Canada began to preach that the "Middle Powers" like herself deserved more recognition of their capabilities and responsibilities instead of simply being herded in with all the smaller members. In the United Nations, at least, she was to have her full share of recognition. Twice

she was one of the elected members of the Security Council and was a permanent member of the Subcommittee of the Disarmament Commission. She also participated in several social and economic activities. It was in the United Nations also that she made one of her most distinctive contributions in international matters. After the cease fire in the Suez crisis, of which she strongly disapproved, she helped the British and the other invading forces to save face to a fair extent. She was instrumental in having a United Nations international force set up to police the disputed areas. A Canadian general commanded this successful innovation.

According to some Canadians, Canada was particularly glad to have contact with various outside nations in the Commonwealth conferences and in NATO: they were a welcome counterweight to the traditional influence of Britain and the increasingly close association with the United States, which threatened to "smother" her. NATO conferences were especially opportune as they helped her combine her North American and European interests. In fact, St. Laurent did much to bring about the extension of that alliance system to the North American side of the Atlantic.

In her domestic political situation, Canada differed from Australia, New Zealand, and Britain herself in not having a dominion-wide Labor party at this period. The prairie provinces, to be sure, had their radical organizations, the Social Credit Party in Alberta and the Co-operative Commonwealth Federation, based chiefly in Saskatchewan; the province of Quebec had its Union Nationale. From 1921 to 1957 the Liberal Party was in control except for the five-year Conservative interlude from 1930 to 1935. William Lyon Mackenzie King, the solid "middle-of-the-road" grandson and namesake of the Toronto Scot who had led the 1837 revolt, was premier a record-breaking twenty-two years. The Liberals remained in power another nine years after

The Tenth Commonwealth Conference, London, March, 1961, at which South Africa withdrew. Nkrumah of Ghana, Diefenbaker of Canada, Verwoerd of South Africa, Nehru of India, Khan of Pakistan, Queen Elizabeth II, Welensky of Rhodesia, Mrs. Bandaranaike of Ceylon, Macmillan of Britain, Menzies of Australia, Archbishop Makarios of Cyprus, and Holyoake of New Zealand. Rahman of Malaya and Balewa of Nigeria are not shown.

he turned over the premiership in 1948 to the charming and able Louis St. Laurent of French descent.

In 1957, Laurent went out of office under similar circumstances to Laurier in 1911. The Conservatives then had ended the long Liberal sway, partly in order to register their disapproval of the United States. Now it was the same; the fear of too much American control of Canada's economic life was one of the factors that brought the Conservatives back after twenty years, under John Diefenbaker, a Saskatchewan lawyer, attractive and eloquent. He promised to divert some of Canada's business from the United States to Britain, a move in which he was not particularly successful. At the beginning of 1961, the Diefenbaker government announced an extra 15 percent tax on dividends from American subsidiaries in Canada. A welcome boom for the farmers came with a huge order for grain from Communist China, suffering from the worst famine in years.

As they had been for years, the Canadians were still naturally first and foremost for Canada. Since 1946, they had formally taken on the status of "Canadian citizens" in addition to the traditional status of "British subjects." That dualism was evident at the end of every Canadian Broadcasting Corporation program when, over the air first came "O, Canada" and then "God Save the Queen."

Commonwealth Conferences

During this period the meetings of the prime ministers of Britain and the Commonwealth had been continuing much as usual, sometimes in London and sometimes at some other Commonwealth capital; but their membership had been increasing as more colonies became dominions or independent republics within that framework.

At the tenth meeting of the Commonwealth heads at London in the spring of 1961, the four leaders from Asia—India, Pakistan, Ceylon, and Malaya—and the two from West Africa—Ghana and Nigeria —outnumbered the original homogeneous all-white group from the United Kingdom and the four "old dominions." The latter would be joined during the session by Archbishop Makarios of Cyprus, just five years to a day after a British destroyer carried him off to exile in the Indian Ocean. The premier from Ceylon, Mrs. Bandaranaike, was the first woman member, aside from the Queen. Her husband had been assassinated while holding the same post. Before the year's end, the Afro-Asian bloc was scheduled to have a majority, with two new Negro states, Sierra Leone and Tanganyika, added and one old dominion out.

The premier of the Federation of the Rhodesias and Nyasaland, Sir Roy Welensky, attended as an observer. He was determined to stem the rising tide of color and had expressed the hope that the Commonwealth would not take in every little colony.

The Colonial Secretary, Ian MacLeod, took an opposite stand. Some of the Conservatives at home, as well as the white settlers, thought that he was going too fast in granting independence, especially in Kenya. As he stated his position, "It is our aim to see that freedom is realized in conditions where it can mean something in terms of individual fulfilment; and where it will not be a mere mockery; and where anarchy in which productive life comes to a standstill, and the downward slope to poverty, famine, and every form of degradation, can be avoided."

The world was watching this meeting with keen interest, for at the previous one in 1960, the apartheid question had produced a rift between South Africa and the Afro-Asian members (see page 710). Now since South Africa had voted to become a republic in May, her continued membership would have to come before this meeting.

Further fuel was added by the Union's refusal to exchange diplomatic representatives with non-white states. As in 1960, Macmillan tried to smooth things over, but the ever-vocal Nkrumah launched a bitter attack on the Union, in which India, Malaya, and others joined. Tanganyika had already announced that it would not join, if South Africa was still a member. Diefenbaker of Canada finally supported the mounting condemnation of the Union's practices as counter to the principles of the Commonwealth.

Matters came to a dramatic climax. Verwoerd, who had left the room with Macmillan for a private talk, returned to read this announcement: "In the circumstances, I wish formally to withdraw my request for South Africa to remain a member of the Commonwealth." Menzies of Australia murmured an anguished "My God." Verwoerd went on to charge that this "vindictive attack" had come primarily from "Prime Ministers in whose countries oppression and discrimination are openly practiced. . . . I refer particularly to Ghana, India, Malaya, and Ceylon." With that he left the room. The question of interference in members' internal affairs caused Menzies to declare "There will not be any Commonwealth if it becomes a court with people on trial, because we shall all expel each other." Macmillan, on the other hand, bitterly termed South Africa's refusal to modify apartheid as "abhorrent to the ideals with which mankind is struggling in this century." At home, Verwoerd was cheered by his fellow Afrikaners only. Otherwise, there was grave concern over the continued outflow of invested capital and deep worry over what might happen in the explosive racial situation on the coming independence day, when ties with Britain would be completely severed.

Not content with that Commonwealth victory, Nkrumah sought to have the United Nations impose extreme sanctions on South Africa, cutting off all trade, communications, and other outside connections. The General Assembly did not go that far, but it called upon all its members to take "separate and collective action" against the ex-dominion.

The Commonwealth, like other Anglo-Saxon institutions down through the centuries, had a loose flexibility and little in the way of rigid definitions of powers and practices. In fact, that traditional vagueness was particularly marked therein, and fortunately so. Now, more than ever, questions arose as to just what the Commonwealth amounted to; and the answers too were vague. One of the few tangible aspects of membership concerned imperial preference, with its lower custom duties. Yet even there, Ireland after withdrawing from the Commonwealth was allowed to continue enjoying it. Basically, one of the chief advantages was psychological. From Britain's standpoint, her former possessions were not completely lost in the eyes of the world. From the members' angle, independence did not make them merely little second- or third-rate nations; they were still part of one of the greatest political combinations on earth. They all shared exposure in varying degree to those principles of law and government that had produced some of the best-governed and most prosperous nations of the day in Canada, Australia, New Zealand, and the long-independent United States. The future would show whether some of these other former products of British "colonialism" in less temperate regions might not also prove the better equipped for that association. At any rate, these new nations were moving bravely, along with Britain, into what one of Macmillan's ministers called "the most desperate and exciting adventure in human history."

Appendix I SOVEREIGNS OF ENGLAND

Sovereigns	Basis of Title
Important Before Conquest	
871–899 ALFRED	Wessex line
1017–1035 CANUTE	Conquest
1042–1066 EDWARD (Confessor)	Return to Wessex line
1066 HAROLD	Son of Earl Godwin; elected by witan
Normans	
1066–1087 WILLIAM I	Conquest
1087–1100 WILLIAM II (Rufus)	2d son of William I
1100–1135 HENRY I	3d son of William I
1135–1154 STEPHEN	Son of daughter of William I
Angevins—Plantagenets	
1154–1189 HENRY II	Son of daughter of Henry I
1189–1199 RICHARD I	Eldest surviving son of Henry II
1199–1216 JOHN	Next surviving son of Henry II
1216–1272 HENRY III	Son of John
1272–1307 EDWARD I	Son of Henry III
1307–1327 EDWARD II	Son of Edward I
1327–1377 EDWARD III	Son of Edward II
1377–1399 RICHARD II	Son of eldest son of Edward III
Lancastrians	
1399–1413 HENRY IV	Son of 4th (3d surviving) son of Edward III
1413–1422 HENRY V	Son of Henry IV
1422–1461 HENRY VI	Son of Henry V
Yorkists	
1461–1483 EDWARD IV	From Edward III through his 3d and 5th sons
1483 EDWARD V	Son of Edward IV
1483–1485 RICHARD III	Younger brother of Edward IV
Tudors	
1485–1509 HENRY VII	From 4th son of Edward III through Beaufort line
1509–1547 HENRY VIII	Son of Henry VII
1547–1553 EDWARD VI	Son of Henry VIII
1553–1558 MARY (I)	Elder daughter of Henry VIII
1558–1603 ELIZABETH I	Younger daughter of Henry VIII
Stuarts	
1603–1625 JAMES I	From daughter of Henry VII through Scottish line
1625–1649 CHARLES I	Son of James I
1649–1660 INTERREGNUM	(Commonwealth and Protectorate)
1660–1685 CHARLES II	Elder son of Charles I
1685–1688 JAMES II	Younger son of Charles I
1688–1702 WILLIAM III AND MARY (II)	Mary, elder daughter of James II
1702–1714 ANNE	Younger daughter of James II
Hanoverians	
1714–1727 GEORGE I	From James I through Hanoverian line
1727–1760 GEORGE II	Son of George I
1760–1820 GEORGE III	Son of eldest son of George II
1820–1830 GEORGE IV	Eldest son of George III
1830–1837 WILLIAM IV	2d son of George III
1837–1901 VICTORIA	Daughter of 4th son of George III
1901–1910 EDWARD VII	Son of Victoria
1910–1936 GEORGE V	Son of Edward VII
1936 EDWARD VIII	Eldest son of George V
1936–1952 GEORGE VI	2d son of George V
1952– ELIZABETH II	Daughter of George VI

A = First Lord of the Admiralty; BT = President of the Board of Trade; C = Colonial Secretary; D = Minister of Defense; DPM = Deputy Prime Minister; E = Chancellor of the Exchequer; F = Foreign Secretary; H = Home Secretary; Ind = Secretary for India; Ire = Secretary for Ireland; L = Minister of Labor; PC = Lord President of the Council; PMG = Postmaster General; PS = Lord Privy Seal; S = Secretary of State (eighteenth century); Scot = Secretary for Scotland; T = Minister of Transport; W = War Secretary

"Prime Minister"		*Other Prominent Cabinet Members*
1721	WALPOLE	TOWNSHEND (S), STANHOPE (S), NEWCASTLE (S)
1742	WILMINGTON	CARTERET (S), NEWCASTLE (S)
1744	PELHAM	NEWCASTLE (S)
1754	NEWCASTLE I	
1756	DEVONSHIRE	PITT (S)
1757	NEWCASTLE II	PITT (S)
1761	BUTE	G. GRENVILLE (S)
1763	G. GRENVILLE (also E)	
1765	ROCKINGHAM I	GRAFTON (S)
1766	CHATHAM (PITT)	TOWNSHEND (E), SHELBURNE (S)
1767	GRAFTON	NORTH (E), SHELBURNE (S)
1770	NORTH	SANDWICH (A), GERMAIN (C)
1782	ROCKINGHAM II	FOX (S), SHELBURNE (S)
1782	SHELBURNE	PITT (E)
1783	PORTLAND I	FOX (S), NORTH (S)
1783	PITT I (also E)	W. GRENVILLE (F), DUNDAS (Ind, W)
1801	ADDINGTON	
1803	PITT II (also E)	CASTLEREAGH (W)
1806	W. GRENVILLE	FOX (F)
1807	PORTLAND II	CANNING (F), CASTLEREAGH (W), LIVERPOOL (H)
1809	PERCEVAL (also E)	CASTLEREAGH (F), LIVERPOOL (W)
1812	LIVERPOOL	CASTLEREAGH (F), CANNING (Ind, F), PEEL (H), HUSKISSON (BT), ROBINSON-GODERICH (E)
1827	CANNING (also E)	HUSKISSON (BT)
1827	GODERICH	HUSKISSON (W)
1828	WELLINGTON	PEEL (H)
1830	GREY	PALMERSTON (F), MELBOURNE (H), DURHAM (PS)
1834	MELBOURNE I	PALMERSTON (F)
1834	PEEL I	WELLINGTON (F)
1835	MELBOURNE II	PALMERSTON (F), RUSSELL (H)
1841	PEEL II	ABERDEEN (F), DERBY (W), GLADSTONE (W)
1846	RUSSELL I	PALMERSTON (F)
1852	DERBY I	DISRAELI (E)
1852	ABERDEEN	PALMERSTON (H), CLARENDON (F), GLADSTONE (E)
1855	PALMERSTON I	CLARENDON (F), GLADSTONE (E)
1858	DERBY II	DISRAELI (E)
1859	PALMERSTON II	RUSSELL (F), GLADSTONE (E)
1865	RUSSELL II	CLARENDON (F), GLADSTONE (E)
1866	DERBY III	DISRAELI (E)
1868	DISRAELI I	
1868	GLADSTONE I (also E)	BRIGHT (BT)
1874	DISRAELI II	DERBY (F), SALISBURY (Ind, F), CARNARVON (C)
1880	GLADSTONE II (also E)	J. CHAMBERLAIN (BT)
1885	SALISBURY I (also F)	R. CHURCHILL (Ind)
1885	GLADSTONE III (also H)	ROSEBERY (F), MORLEY (Ire)
1886	SALISBURY II (also F)	R. CHURCHILL (E), BALFOUR (Scot, Ire)
1892	GLADSTONE IV (also PS)	ROSEBERY (F), ASQUITH (H)
1894	ROSEBERY (also PC)	ASQUITH (H)
1895	SALISBURY III (also F to 1900)	LANSDOWNE (F), J. CHAMBERLAIN (C)
1902	BALFOUR	LANSDOWNE (F),
1905	CAMPBELL-BANNERMAN	GREY (F), LLOYD GEORGE (E)
1908	ASQUITH	GREY (F), LLOYD GEORGE (E), W. CHURCHILL (A)
1916	LLOYD GEORGE	BALFOUR (F), BONAR LAW (E)
1922	BONAR LAW	BALDWIN (E)
1923	BALDWIN I	N. CHAMBERLAIN (E)
1924	MACDONALD I (also F)	SNOWDEN (E), HENDERSON (H)
1924	BALDWIN II	A. CHAMBERLAIN (F), W. CHURCHILL (E)
1929	MACDONALD II	SNOWDEN (E), HENDERSON (F), MORRISON (T)
1931	MACDONALD III	BALDWIN (PC), SIMON (F), N. CHAMBERLAIN (E), ATTLEE (PMG)
1935	BALDWIN III	MACDONALD (PC), HOARE (F, A), N. CHAMBERLAIN (E), EDEN (F)
1937	N. CHAMBERLAIN	SIMON (E), EDEN (F), HALIFAX (F), HOARE (H)
1940	CHURCHILL I (also D)	ATTLEE (DPM, PS), HALIFAX (F), EDEN (F), BEVIN (L), MORRISON (H)
1945	ATTLEE (also D)	BEVIN (F), MORRISON (PC), CRIPPS (BT, E)
1952	CHURCHILL II	EDEN (F), BUTLER (E)
1955	EDEN	MACMILLAN (F, E), BUTLER (E, H, PS) LLOYD (D, F)
1957	MACMILLAN	BUTLER (H, PS), LLOYD (F, E), AMORY (E), HOME (F).

DOMINION-COMMONWEALTH PREMIERS
AND PRIME MINISTERS

A. The Old Dominions

Canada (1867)

1867	JOHN A. MACDONALD
1873	ALEXANDER MACKENZIE
1878	JOHN A. MACDONALD, II
1891	JOHN J. C. ABBOTT
1892	JOHN S. D. THOMPSON
1894	MACKENZIE BOWELL
1896	CHARLES TUPPER
1896	WILFRID LAURIER
1911	ROBERT BORDEN
1920	ARTHUR MEIGHEN
1921	WILLIAM LYON MACKENZIE KING
1926	ARTHUR MEIGHEN, II
1926	W. L. MACKENZIE KING, II
1930	RICHARD B. BENNETT
1935	W. L. MACKENZIE KING, III
1948	LOUIS S. ST. LAURENT
1957	JOHN G. DIEFENBAKER

Australia (1901)

1901	EDMUND BARTON
1903	ALFRED DEAKIN
1904	JOHN G. WATSON
1905	ALFRED DEAKIN, II
1908	ANDREW FISHER
1909	ALFRED DEAKIN, III
1910	ANDREW FISHER, II
1913	JOSEPH COOK
1914	ANDREW FISHER, III
1915	WILLIAM M. HUGHES

1923	STANLEY BRUCE
1929	JAMES H. SCULLIN
1931	JOSEPH A. LYONS
1939	EARLE PAGE
1939	ROBERT G. MENZIES
1941	JOHN CURTIN
1945	JOSEPH B. CHIFLEY
1949	ROBERT G. MENZIES, II

New Zealand (1907)

1906	JOSEPH WARD
1912	WILLIAM F. MASSEY
1925	JOSEPH G. COATES
1928	JOSEPH WARD, II
1930	GEORGE W. FORBES
1935	M. JOSEPH SAVAGE
1940	PETER FRASER
1949	SIDNEY G. HOLLAND
1957	WALTER NASH
1960	KEITH J. HOLYOAKE

South Africa (1910)

1910	LOUIS BOTHA
1919	JAN C. SMUTS
1924	JAMES B. M. HERTZOG
1939	JAN C. SMUTS, II
1948	DANIEL F. MALAN
1956	JOHANNES G. STRIJDOM
1959	HENDRIK F. VERWOERD
	(Severed last ties, May, 1961)

B. The New Dominions

India (1947)

1947	JAWAHARLAL NEHRU

Pakistan (1947)

1947	LIAQUAT ALI KHAN
1952	KHAWAJA NAZIMUDDIN
1953	MOHAMAD ALI
1957	H. S. SUHRAWARDY
1958	MALIK F. NOON
1958	MOHAMMED AYUB KHAN (PRES.)

Ceylon (1948)

1948	D. S. SENANAYAKE
1954	JOHN KOTELAWALA
1956	S. W. R. D. BANDARANAIKE
1959	W. DAHANAYAKE
1960	D. S. SENANAYAKE, II
1960	MRS. SIRIMAVO BANDARANAIKE

Ghana (1957)

1957	KWAME NKRUMAH (PRES. '60).

Malaya (1957)

1957	TENGKU ABDUL RAHMAN PUTRA

Nigeria (1960)

1960	ABUBAKAR A. T. BALEWA

Cyprus (1960)

1960	ARCHBISHOP MAKARIOS (PRES.)

Sierra Leone (1961)

1961	MILTON MARGAI

Tanganyika (December, 1961)

1961	JULIUS K. NYERERE

C. Prospective Dominions

Central African Federation (1953)

1953	GODFREY HUGGINS (LORD MALVERN)
1956	ROY WELENSKY

West Indies Federation (1958)

1958	GRANTLEY ADAMS

	Area Sq. Miles	Population	Political Status
United Kingdom	94,275	51,984,000	
England-Wales	58,343	45,386,000	
Scotland	29,796	5,191,000	
Northern Ireland	5,241	1,407,000	
Old Dominions			
Canada	**3,560,000**	**16,080,000**	Federal dominion created in 1867
Quebec	523,860	4,628,000	Joined dominion, 1867
Ontario	344,092	5,404,000	Joined dominion, 1867
Nova Scotia	20,402	694,000	Joined dominion, 1867
New Brunswick	27,835	554,000	Joined dominion, 1867
Manitoba	211,775	850,000	Joined dominion, 1870
British Columbia	359,279	1,398,000	Joined dominion, 1871
Prince Edward Island	2,184	99,000	Joined dominion, 1873
Alberta	248,800	1,123,000	Joined dominion, 1905
Saskatchewan	220,182	880,000	Joined dominion, 1905
Newfoundland	143,045	415,000	Joined dominion, 1949
Australia	**2,971,081**	**10,008,000**	Federal "Commonwealth," 1901
New South Wales	309,433	3,745,000	
Victoria	87,884	2,796,000	
Queensland	667,000	1,428,000	
South Australia	380,070	914,000	
Western Australia	975,920	715,000	
Tasmania	26,215	343,000	
New Zealand	**103,736**	**2,174,000**	Recognized as dominion, 1907
South Africa	**472,359**	**12,671,000**	Federal "Union" created, 1910; republic, 1961;
Cape Province	278,465	4,426,000	severed last ties, May, 1961
Natal	33,578	2,415,000	
Transvaal	110,450	4,812,000	Former Boer republic
Orange Free State	49,866	1,016,000	Former Boer republic
New Dominions			
India	1,269,640	356,891,000	Dominion status, 1947; republic, 1950
Pakistan	364,737	75,842,000	Dominion status, 1947; republic, 1956
Ceylon	25,332	8,929,000	Dominion status, 1948
Ghana	92,100	4,911,000	Dominion status, 1957; republic, 1960
Malaya	50,690	6,278,000	Independent federal state, 1957, with rotating native "supreme ruler."
Nigeria	373,250	35,300,000	Federal dominion status, 1960
Cyprus	3,572	549,000	Independent republic, 1960, with British bases; Commonwealth, 1961
Sierra Leone	27,925	2,500,000	Dominion status, 1961
Tanganyika	361,000	8,762,000	Dominion status, December, 1961
Prospective Dominions			
Central African Federation	**486,722**	**7,846,000**	Internal self-governing federation, 1953
Southern Rhodesia	150,333	2,820,000	Internal self-governing federation, 1923

* Statistics are applicable for the late 1950's.

	Area Sq. Miles	Population	Political Status
Central African Federation (Cont.)			
Northern Rhodesia	290,323	2,330,000	Crown colony
Nyasaland	46,066	2,740,000	Protectorate
West Indies Federation	**8,028**	**3,152,000**	Federal union, 1958
Jamaica	4,613	1,237,000	
Trinidad-Tobago	1,980	557,000	
Barbados	166	236,000	
Leeward Islands	422	137,000	Formerly a federation to 1956
Windward Islands	133	91,000	

Other Possessions (Colonies, unless otherwise noted; many with varying degrees of self-government)

America

Bermuda	20	43,000	
Bahamas	4,404	136,000	
British Honduras	8,867	88,000	
British Guiana	83,000	539,000	Constitution suspended, 1953-56
Falkland Islands	4,618	2,000	Also has Antarctic "dependencies"

Mediterranean

Gibraltar	2	25,000	
Malta	94	320,000	

Africa

Gambia	3,977	268,000	Colony and protectorate
Southwest Africa	317,887	458,000	Former mandate; administered by Union; present status in dispute
British South Africa	293,420	1,174,000	Bechuanaland, Basutoland, Swaziland protectorates
Kenya	224,960	6,150,000	Colony and protectorate
Uganda	93,981	5,678,000	Protectorate
Zanzibar	1,020	278,000	Protectorate
Mauritius	720	613,000	Island, Indian Ocean
Seychelles	156	43,000	Islands, Indian Ocean
St. Helena	47	4,000	Island, South Atlantic

Asia

Aden	112,075	938,000	Colony and protectorate
Singapore	224	1,445,000	Internal self-government, 1958
Hong Kong	391	2,677,000	
British Borneo	78,618	1,106,000	North Borneo, Brunei, Sarawak

Oceania

Fiji	7,036	374,000	
Papua-New Guinea	183,000	1,828,000	Trusteeship, Australia, 1949
Other Islands	18,000	367,000	Solomons, Gilbert and Ellice, Tonga, West Samoa, Nauru, New Hebrides

Completely Separated in 20th Century

Egypt	386,198	8,362,000	Independent kingdom, 1922; republic, 1953; part of United Arab Republic, 1958
Iraq	168,040	6,538,000	Mandate ended, 1932
Transjordania	30,000	1,600,000	Mandate ended, 1946; became "Jordan"
Palestine	7,993	2,032,000	Mandate ended, 1948; partitioned, chiefly between Israel and Jordan
Burma	261,789	19,242,000	Independent republic, 1947
Ireland (Eire)	26,600	2,898,000	Last tie severed, 1949
Anglo-Egyptian Sudan	967,500	262,000	Independent republic, "Sudan," 1956
British Somaliland	68,000	640,000	In independent republic, Somalia, 1960, with former Italian Somaliland.
Union of South Africa	472,359	12,671,000	Complete separation, 1961

Suggested Books for Further Reading

For the student who desires to follow up particular subjects in British history, the following suggestions contain the titles of some of the books most likely to prove useful. Many excellent works have been omitted deliberately because their detailed or controversial treatment seems to adapt them to the needs of the advanced scholar rather than to those of the college undergraduate. There is, moreover, no space here for a detailed bibliography, nor is one necessary since several very comprehensive critical bibliographical aids are available in most college libraries.

Particularly useful and up-to-date is the sixty-eight-page bibliography in W. E. LUNT, *History of England* (4th ed., 1956), with its special emphasis on the earlier period. For still more comprehensive coverage, consult C. GROSS, *The Sources and Literature of English History* (2d ed., 1915), for the period to 1485; and the bibliographies of C. READ for the Tudor period (2d ed., 1959); G. DAVIES for the Stuart period (1928); and S. PARGELLIS and D. J. MEDLEY (1951) for 1714-1789; also C. L. GROSE, *A Select Bibliography of British History, 1660-1760* (1939). Select bibliographies covering the whole span of British history will be found in the successive volumes of the *Oxford History of England* and, less detailed, in the *Pelican History of England*. Many of the more specialized works cited below contain ample bibliographies, and there are brief lists of the most appropriate works attached to many of the articles in the *Dictionary of National Biography*, *Encyclopedia Americana*, and *Encyclopaedia Britannica*, and also throughout the annual volumes of the *Statesman's Year Book* in connection with various aspects of Britain, her empire, and all foreign countries.

I · General Works

This section is devoted to works which cover more or less the whole period of English history. Books more limited in their time scope are listed under the subsequent sections for particular periods: to 1066; 1066-1485; Tudor period; Stuart period; 1714-1815; 1815-1914; and since 1914). These general works, of course, should be consulted in connection with the studies of the limited periods.

The best single-volume by a British author is G. M. TREVELYAN, *History of England* (1926), condensed as a Pelican paperbound edition under the title *Shorter History of England* (6th ed., 1960). Also very readable is W. S. CHURCHILL, *A History of the English-Speaking Peoples* (4 vols., 1956-1958). Several co-operative series, with each volume by a different author, and sometimes uneven in quality, give more detailed treatment. The old *Political History of England* (12 vols., 1905-1910), and the "Oman Series" (8 vols., 1904-1934) have been generally superseded by the *Oxford History of England* (ed. G. N. CLARK, 14 vols., 1934-1959) and the briefer, paperbound *Pelican*

History of England (ed. J. E. MORPURGO, 8 vols., 1950-1955). Two volumes have also appeared in a projected "Longmans-Medlicott" series, succeeding the old *Political History*. Another co-operative series is *Social England* (ed. H. R. TRAILL and J. S. MANN, 6 vols. in 12, new ed., 1912), with separate sections in each period on political, religious, social, economic, cultural, military, and other aspects. Certain chapters or sections are devoted to British history in the *Cambridge Medieval History* (8 vols., 1911-1936) and the *Cambridge Modern History* (14 vols., 1902-1912, and new series, 1958-   ). The earlier period is well covered in H. CAM, *England Before Elizabeth* (1961).

General Works in Special Topics

CONSTITUTIONAL AND LEGAL. Useful for the whole period are G. B. ADAMS, *Constitutional History of England* (new ed., with additional chapters by R. L. SCHUYLER, 1935); G. SMITH, *A Constitutional and Legal History of England* (1955); F. G. MARCHAM, *A Constitutional History of Modern England, 1485 to the Present* (1960); M. M. KNAPPEN, *Constitutional and Legal History of England* (1942); and M. AMOS, *The English Constitution* (1930). More detailed are F. W. MAITLAND, *Constitutional History of England* (1926); A. B. KEITH, *The Constitution of England* (2 vols., 1940); W. R. ANSON, *The Law and Custom of the Constitution* (2 vols., 1935). For the modern period, see D. L. KEIR, *Constitutional History of Modern Britain since 1485* (6th ed., 1960). A valuable collection of constitutional documents is C. STEPHENSON and F. G. MARCHAM, *Sources of English Constitutional History* (1937). The most comprehensive legal study is W. S. HOLDSWORTH, *History of English Law* (9 vols., 1903-26); briefer are E. JENKS, *A Short History of English Law* (1912) and T. F. T. PLUCKNETT, *A Concise History of the Common Law* (4th ed., 1948).

ECONOMIC AND SOCIAL. The best single volume is G. M. TREVELYAN, *English Social History* (1942); more strictly economic are A. P. USHER, *Introduction to the Industrial History of England*, and the *Cambridge Economic History* (ed. J. H. CLAPHAM and E. POWER, 1941). For the period to the end of the eighteenth century, the standard authority is E. LIPSON, *Economic History of England* (3 vols., 1915-1931); the subsequent period is covered by J. H. CLAPHAM, *Economic History of Modern Britain* (3 vols., 1930-1938); and G. D. H. COLE and R. POSTGATE, *The British Common People, 1746-1946* (1947). For agriculture, see R. E. PROTHERO (LORD ERNLE), *English Farming, Past and Present* (4th ed., 1927) and N. S. B. and E. C. GRAS, *Economic and Social History of an English Village, A. D. 900-1928* (1930).

RELIGION. The best brief study is H. O. WAKEMAN, *Introduction to the History of the Church of England* (rev. ed., 1920). For greater detail consult the co-operative work, *History of* the *English Church* (ed. W. R. W. STEPHENS and W. HUNT, 9 vols., 1899-1910), and H. GEE and W. J. HARDY, *Documents Illustrative of English Church History* (1914). For particular subjects or individuals see the *Encyclopedia of Religion and Ethics,* ed. J. HASTINGS, et al. (13 vols., 1908-1927), and the *Catholic Encyclopedia,* ed. C. G. HERBERMAN et al. (16 vols., 1907-1914). See also M. D. KNOWLES, *The Religious Orders in England* (3 vols., 1948-1959).

LITERATURE, ETC. Two useful brief surveys are A. C. BAUGH, *A Literary History of England* (1948), and I. EVANS, *A Short History of English Literature* (1940). Longer co-operative works, sometimes uneven in quality, are the *Cambridge History of English Literature,* ed. A. W. WARD and A. R. WALTER (15 vols., new ed. 1933); the *Oxford History of English Literature,* ed. F. P. WILSON and BONAMY DOBRÉE (5 vols. as of 1960); and the *Pelican Guide to English Literature,* ed. B. FORD (6 vols., 1954-1958). For particular fields of literature, see W. ALLEN, *The English Novel: A Short Critical History* (1955); the longer, more uneven E. A. BAKER, *The History of the English Novel* (10 vols., 1924); *The Pelican Book of English Prose,* ed. K. ALLOTT (6 vols., 1956); H. J. C. GRIERSON and J. C. SMITH, *A Critical History of English Poetry* (1946); and J. A. R. MARRIOTT, *English History in English Fiction* (1941). The early period to 1509 is covered in W. L. RENWICK and H. ORTON, *The Beginnings of English Literature* (1939). For architecture, the most useful brief accounts are P. L. DICKINSON, *History of Architecture of the British Isles* (1926), and H. B. GARDNER, *Outline of English Architecture* (1946). For science, see *Studies in the History and Methods of Science,* ed. C. J. SINGER (2 vols., 1917-1921), and L. THORNDIKE, *A History of Magic and Experimental Science* (2 vols., 1929).

SCOTLAND, IRELAND, AND WALES. For Scottish history, see P. H. A. BROWN, *A Short History of Scotland* (1920), and his longer *History of Scotland* (3 vols., 1902-1909). A livelier account is A. LANG, *A History of Scotland* (4 vols., 1900-1907). For relative objectivity in Irish history, a difficult achievement, see E. A. CURTIS, *A History of Ireland* (1937), and P. W. JOYCE, *A Short History of Ireland* (1911), and *A Social History of Ireland* (2 vols., 1920). The most satisfactory Welsh accounts are J. E. LLOYD, *History of Wales* (2d ed. 1912), and D. A. WILLIAMS, *A History of Wales, 1485-1931* (1934).

FOREIGN POLICY. There is no good overall study for an extended period. J. R. SEELEY, *Growth of British Policy* (2 vols., 1897), analyzes the evolution in the sixteenth and seventeenth centuries. The *Cambridge History of British Foreign Policy,* ed. A. W. WARD and G. P. GOOCH (3 vols., 1922-1923), covers only the period 1783-1919. Also useful are ADMIRAL H. W. RICHMOND, *Statesmen and Sea Power* (1946), and *The Navy as an Instrument of Policy, 1558-1727* (1953). For the rest, see separate sections.

GEOGRAPHY. H. J. MACKINDER, *Britain and the British Seas* (1902) was a pioneer work in "geopolitics." Useful in their respective spheres are H. C. DARBY, *A Historical Geography of England before A. D. 1800* (1936); L. A. BROWN, *The Story of Maps* (1949); A. C. HARDY, *Seaways and Sea Trade, being a Maritime Geography* (1927); A. V. T. WAKELY, *Some Aspects of Imperial Communications* (1924); and J. F. HORRABIN, *An Atlas of Empire* (1937). Pertinent maps for various periods will be found in W. R. SHEPHERD, *Historical Atlas* (8th ed., 1956); R. R. PALMER, *Atlas of World History* (1957); and E. W. FOX, *Atlas of European History* (1957).

MARITIME. England's activity in this field did not become important until after 1500, but thereafter grew increasingly significant. Useful surveys are J. A. WILLIAMSON, *The Ocean in English History* (1941); C. E. FAYLE, *A Short History of the World's Shipping Industry;* W. ABELL, *The Shipwright's Trade* (1948) and, with emphasis principally upon the recent period, A. W. KIRKALDY, *British Shipping: its History, Organization, and Importance* (1914), and R. H. THORNTON, *British Shipping* (1939). An interesting survey of Britain's relation to adjacent waters is R. HARGREAVES, *The Narrow Seas* (1959).

COLONIZATION AND EMPIRE. This was likewise late in getting under way. The most useful comprehensive survey is C. E. CARRINGTON, *The British Overseas: Exploits of a Nation of Shopkeepers* (1950); more detailed and generally less critical is J. A. WILLIAMSON, *Short History of British Expansion* (2 vols., 3d ed., 1945). Co-operative coverage, still more detailed, is in the *Cambridge History of the British Empire,* ed. J. H. ROSE et al. (8 vols., 1929-1959), with the first volume covering the whole "Old Empire" to 1783 and the later ones, specific major regions; and C. P. LUCAS et al., *Historical Geography of the British Empire* (8 vols., 1887-1923), arranged regionally. Excellent studies for the earlier period are J. H. PARRY, *Europe and a Wider World, 1415-1715* (1950), and A. P. NEWTON, *The British Empire to 1783* (1941), followed, for the later period, by P. KNAPLUND, *The British Empire, 1815-1939* (1942).

NAVAL AND MILITARY. Two of the best brief general accounts of the Royal Navy are M. A. LEWIS (of the Royal Naval College), *The Navy of Britain: An Historical Portrait* (1948), a topical account, analyzing the development of ships, officers, men, administration, and tactics; and *History of the British Navy* (1957), a narrative of its activities. A comprehensive co-operative work is W. L. CLOWES, ed., *The Royal Navy: A History from the Earliest Times to the Present Day* (7 vols., 1897-1903). The most useful comprehensive naval history, devoting much attention to the British experience, is E. B. POTTER and C. W. NIMITZ, eds., *Sea Power: A Naval History* (1960, prepared by the History faculty at Annapolis). See also R. G. ALBION, *Maritime and Naval History: An Annotated Bibliography* (rev. ed., 1955). The standard military work is J. W. FORTESCUE, *History of the British Army* (13 vols., 1899-1930); see also R. G. ALBION, *Introduction to Military History* (1929);

and T. Ropp, *War in the Modern World* (2 vols., 1959).

REFERENCE WORKS. An extremely useful outline of dates and events is W. E. Langer, ed., *An Encyclopedia of World History . . . Chronologically Arranged* (2d ed., 1948), the successor to the old *Ploetz's Manual of Universal History*. The standard work for British biography is the *Dictionary of National Biography* (63 vols., 1885-1900), with six supplements covering prominent Britons who died up to 1950; there is also a brief single volume epitome (1914). For later years, the issues of *Who's Who* and *Who Was Who* can be consulted. A mine of useful statistical and other factual data for Britain, her empire, and other countries is *The Statesman's Year Book: Statistical and Historical Annual of the World* (annual since 1864). Finally, as one old professor remarked, "I don't know which man is more of a fool—the one who never uses an encyclopedia or the one who never uses anything else."

II • Works Listed by Periods

1. To 1066

NARRATIVE AND GENERAL. This is covered in the *Oxford History* by Vol. 1, R. G. Collingwood and J. N. L. Myres, *Roman Britain and the English Settlements* (1936); and Vol. 2, Sir F. M. Stenton, *Anglo-Saxon England* (2d ed., 1947), which is considered by far the best account of that subject. In the *Pelican History*, the corresponding works are Vol. 1, I. A. Richmond (1955), and Vol. 2, D. Whitelock (1952).

The hazy problems of prehistory and racial backgrounds are treated in J. and C. Hawkes, *Prehistoric Britain* (1953); V. G. Childe, *Prehistoric Communities of the British Isles* (1940); M. C. Burkitt, *Prehistory* (1921), and *Old Stone Age* (rev. ed., 1955); S. Piggott, *The Neolithic Cultures of the British Isles* (1954); and H. J. Fleure, *Races of England and Wales* (1923).

For Roman Britain, two works of F. J. Haverfield, *Roman Britain* (4th ed., 1923), and *The Romanization of Roman Britain* (1924), are important. Accounts of the archaeology on which findings have been based are J. N. L. Myres, *Archaeology of Roman Britain* (1930), and accounts by Sir G. Macdonald, by T. D. Kendrick and C. F. C. Hawkes, and by G. Ashe, *Caesar to Arthur* (1960).

In addition to Stenton's volume in the *Oxford History*, modern views on Anglo-Saxon England are embodied in R. H. Hodgkin, *A History of the Anglo-Saxons* (3d ed., 1952), and A. P. H. Blair, *An Introduction to Anglo-Saxon England* (1956). The Germanic migrations are well described in H. M. Chadwick, *The Heroic Age* (1912); for the later Viking raids, see T. D. Kendrick, *A History of the Vikings* (1930); M. W. Williams, *Social Scandinavia in the Viking Age* (1920); A. R. Lewis, *The Northern Seas: Shipping and Commerce in Northern Europe, A. D. 300-1100* (1958); and L. M. Larson, *Canute the Great* (1912). For the outstanding figure of the period, see C.

Plummer, *Life and Times of Alfred the Great* (1902), and B. A. Lees, *Alfred the Great* (1915).

CONSTITUTIONAL AND LEGAL. Good relatively brief studies which also cover at least part of the next period are B. A. Lyon, *A Constitutional and Legal History of Medieval England* (1960); W. A. Morris, *Constitutional History of England to 1216* (1930); and J. E. A. Jolliffe, *The Constitutional History of Medieval England* (1937). See also the latter's *Pre-Feudal England: The Jutes* (1933).

ECONOMIC AND SOCIAL. On the disputed nature of the early manor and town, earlier discussed by F. Seebohm and P. G. Vinogradoff, see H. L. Gray, *English Field Systems* (1915); C. S. Orwin, *The Open Fields* (1938); C. Stephenson, *Borough and Town* (1933) and J. Tait, *The Medieval English Borough* (1936).

RELIGION. On the relations with the outside world, see S. J. Crawford, *Anglo-Saxon Influence on Western Christendom* (1933), and W. Levison, *England and the Continent in the Eighth Century* (1946). The numerous biographies include J. A. Robinson, *The Times of St. Dunstan* (1923); J. B. Bury, *The Life of St. Patrick* (1905); and C. E. S. Duckett, *Alcuin, Friend of Charlemagne* (1951), and *Saint Dunstan of Canterbury* (1955), in addition to her very readable account of Aldhelm, Wilfrid, Bede, and Boniface in *Anglo-Saxon Saints and Scholars* (1947).

LITERATURE, ETC. For literature, in addition to the erudite saints above, see M. L. W. Laistner, *Thought and Letters in Western Europe, A. D. 500 to 900* (1931); E. Dale, *National Life and Character in the Mirror of Early English Literature* (1907); W. W. Lawrence, *Beowulf and the Epic Tradition* (1928); and C. W. Kennedy, *The Earliest English Poetry* (1943). Most useful on art are E. T. Leeds, *Early Anglo-Saxon Art and Archaeology* (1930), and T. D. Kendrick, *Anglo-Saxon Art to A. D. 900* (1938).

2. 1066-1485

NARRATIVE AND GENERAL. *Oxford History:* Vol. 3, A. L. Poole, *From Domesday Book to Magna Carta, 1087-1216* (1951); Vol. 4, F. M. Powicke, *The Thirteenth Century, 1216-1307,* (1953); Vol. 5, M. McKisack, *The Fourteenth Century, 1307-1399;* Vol. 6, on the fifteenth century, in preparation. *Pelican History:* Vol. 3, D. M. Stenton, *English Society in the Early Middle Ages, 1066-1307* (1951); Vol. 4, A. P. Myers, *England in the Later Middle Ages, 1307-1536* (1952). Other good general works are F. M. Powicke, *Medieval England, 1066-1485* (1931); K. Norgate, *England under the Angevins* (2 vols., 1887); V. H. H. Green, *The Later Plantagenets, A Survey of English History between 1307 and 1485* (1955); and G. M. Trevelyan's delightful *England in the Age of Wyckliffe* (1909).

A valuable and very readable account of the Normans in England and on the Continent is C. H. Haskins, *The Normans in European History* (1915). For the Crusades, see D. C. Munro, *The Kingdom of the Crusaders,* and S. Runciman, *A*

History of the Crusades, (3 vols., 1953-1954). Other accounts of particular general aspects are E. PERROY, The Hundred Years War (1951); C. W. C. OMAN, The Great Revolt of 1381 (1906); and C. L. KINGSFORD, Prejudice and Promise in Fifteenth-Century England (1925). A first-hand picture of the earlier part of the Hundred Years' War is found in J. FROISSART, Chronicles (of England, France, etc.).

Among the more useful biographies for the period are the following: those of William the Conqueror by F. M. STENTON (1908) and G. E. SLOCOMBE (1959); A. S. GREEN, Henry the Second (1888); L. F. SALZMAN, Henry II (1914); C. H. WALKER, Eleanor of Aquitaine (1950); K. NORGATE, Richard the Lion Heart (1924); S. PAINTER, William Marshal (1933), and The Reign of King John (1950); C. BEMONT, Simon de Montfort (new ed., 1930); T. F. TOUT, Edward the First (1893); A. M. MACKENZIE, Robert Bruce, King of Scots (1934); R. P. DUNN-PATTISON, The Black Prince (1910); J. H. WYLIE, The Reign of Henry the Fifth (3 vols., 1914-1929); C. L. SCOFIELD, Life and Reign of Edward the Fourth (2 vols., 1923).

CONSTITUTIONAL AND LEGAL. LYON, MORRIS, and JOLIFFE are useful for this period as well as for the preceding one; see also B. WILKINSON, Constitutional History of Medieval England, 1216-1399 (3 vols., 1948-1958). Some of the best studies on the feudal system are C. H. HASKINS, Norman Institutions (1918); J. H. ROUND, Feudal England (1895); F. M. STENTON, The First Century of English Feudalism (1932); N. DENHOLM-YOUNG, Seigneural Administration in England (1937); and R. S. HOYT, The Royal Demesne in English Constitutional History, 1066-1272 (1950). The standard work on its subject is W. S. McKECHNIE, Magna Carta (rev. ed., 1914).

Important for the beginnings of Parliament are C. H. McILWAIN, The High Court of Parliament and its Supremacy (1910); A. F. POLLARD, The Evolution of Parliament (1920); F. THOMPSON, A Short History of Parliament, 1295-1642 (1953); T. F. T. PLUCKNETT, The Legislation of Edward I (1949); and G. L. HASKINS, The Growth of English Representative Government (1948).

A basic work in administrative history is T. F. TOUT, Chapters in the Administrative History of Mediaeval England (6 vols., 1920-1933). Other useful studies in that field are J. F. BALDWIN, The King's Council in England during the Middle Ages (1913); The King's Secretary and the Signet Office in the XVth Century, (1939); J. H. RAMSAY, History of the Revenues of the Kings of England, 1066-1399 (2 vols., 1926); R. L. POOLE, The Exchequer in the Twelfth Century (1912); and S. K. MITCHELL, Taxation in Medieval England (1951). In the legal field, see M. HASTINGS, The Court of Common Pleas in the Fifteenth Century (1947), and B. H. PUTNAM, Proceedings Before the Justices of the Peace in the Fourteenth and Fifteenth Centuries (1938).

ECONOMIC AND SOCIAL. Good general surveys include E. POWER, Medieval People (1924);

L. F. SALZMAN, English Life in the Middle Ages (1926); G. BARRACLOUGH, ed., Social Life in Early England (1960); and B. D. TAYLOR, Chaucer's England (1959). For the manor and agriculture, in addition to GRAY and ORWIN mentioned for the preceding period, see G. G. COULTON, The Medieval Village (1925); N. J. HONE, The Manor and Manorial Records (1906); N. NEILSON, Medieval Agrarian Economy (1936); H. S. BENNETT, Life on the English Manor: A Study of Peasant Conditions, 1150-1400 (1938); M. CAMPBELL, The English Yeoman (1947); and A. L. POOLE, Obligations of Society in the Twelfth and Thirteenth Centuries (1946). Additional works on the towns and industry include C. GROSS, The Gild Merchant (2 vols., 1890); S. KRAMER, English Craft Gilds (1927); L. F. SALZMAN, English Industries of the Middle Ages (new ed., 1923); H. E. SALTER, Medieval Oxford (1948); and W. F. HILL, Medieval London (1948). An intimate picture of life in the late middle ages is H. S. BENNETT, The Pastons and their England (1922); the original Paston Letters are available in various editions.

For medieval trade, the most useful works are G. UNWIN, Finance and Trade under Edward III (1918); E. POWER, The Wool Trade in Medieval England (1941); E. POWER and M. M. POSTAN, Studies in English Trade in the Fifteenth Century (1933); E. M. CARUS-WILSON, Medieval Merchant Venturers (1954); S. L. THRUPP, The Merchant Class of Medieval London (1948); and N. S. B. GRAS, The Early English Customs System (1918).

RELIGION. For the Church in England in general, see Z. N. BROOKE, The English Church and the Papacy from the Conquest to the Reign of John (1931); F. A. GASQUET, Henry III and the Church (1905); J. R. H. MOORMAN, Church Life in England in the Thirteenth Century (1946); W. A. PANTIN, The English Church in the Fourteenth Century (1955); A. H. THOMPSON, The English Clergy and their Organization in the Later Middle Ages (1947); and H. M. SMITH, Pre-Reformation England (1938).

For monasticism, in addition to the works of D. D. KNOWLES already noted, see F. A. GASQUET, English Monastic Life (6th ed., 1924); A. H. THOMPSON, English Monasteries (1913); E. POWER, English Nunneries (1922); A. JESSOPP, The Coming of the Friars (7th ed., 1895); and A. SAVINE, English Monasteries on the Eve of the Dissolution (1909). A delightful first-hand account of the inner workings of a great monastery is Jocelin of Brakelond, in various editions.

The outstanding religious biographies for the period are A. J. MACDONALD, Lanfranc (1926); R. W. CHURCH, Saint Anselm (1888); S. DARK, St. Thomas of Canterbury (1927); F. M. POWICKE, Stephen Langton (1928); F. S. STEVENSON, Robert Grosseteste (1899); and H. B. WORKMAN, John Wyclif (1926).

LITERATURE, ETC. Two general surveys are C. S. BALDWIN, Three Medieval Centuries of Literature in England, 1100-1400 (1932); and W. H. SCHOFIELD, English Literature from the Norman Conquest to Chaucer (1906). Stimulating and important volumes by an eminent medievalist are C. H. Haskins, *The Renaissance of the Twelfth Century* (1927); *The Rise of the Universities* (1923); and *Studies in the History of Medieval Science* (2d ed., 1927). Also important for the education of the period are A. F. Leach, *The Schools of Medieval England* (1915), and H. Rashdall, *Universities of Europe in the Middle Ages* (new ed., 3 vols., 1936). A valuable analysis of the general intellectual background is H. O. Taylor, *The Medieval Mind* (2 vols., 4th ed., 1930).

Among the principal works on Chaucer are H. S. Bennett, *Chaucer and the Fifteenth Century* (1947); R. K. Root, *The Poetry of Chaucer* (1922); G. G. Coulton, *Chaucer and his England* (1921); and W. A. Neilson and K. G. T. Webster, *Chief British Poets of the Fourteenth and Fifteenth Centuries* (1916).

The architectual development is well treated in J. Harvey, *Gothic England* (1947); F. Bond, *Gothic Architecture in England* (1905); C. H. Moore, *Mediaeval Church Architecture in England* (1912); F. N. Crossley, *The English Abbey* (1943); H. Brown, *The English Castle* (1943); and F. Salzman, *Building in England down to 1540* (1952). For other special fields see J. Evans, *English Art, 1307-1461* (1949); G. Reese, *Music in the Middle Ages* (1941); and C. W. C. Oman, *History of the Art of War in the Middle Ages* (2 vols., 2d ed., 1924).

3. Tudor Period, 1485-1603

NARRATIVE AND GENERAL. Oxford History: Vol. 7, J. D. Mackie, *The Earlier Tudors, 1485-1558* (1952); J. B. Black, *The Reign of Elizabeth* (1936). Pelican History: S. T. Bindoff, *Tudor England* (1950). Other valuable brief surveys are C. Read, *The Tudors* (1936); J. A. Williamson, *The Tudor Age* (1953); and G. R. Elton, *England Under the Tudors* (1955). For the early Tudors, the reign of Henry VII is covered by A. F. Pollard (1914); J. Gairdner (1899); and G. Temperley (1914). The best life of his son is still A. F. Pollard, *Henry VIII* (new ed., 1905); see also C. W. Ferguson, *Naked to Mine Enemies: The Life of Cardinal Wolsey* (1958). Pollard continued his account with *England under Protector Somerset* (1900). "Bloody Mary" is the subject of two good studies: H. F. M. Prescott, *Mary Tudor* (1952) first appeared under the title *A Spanish Tudor* (1940); also, B. White, *Mary Tudor* (1936).

The history of Elizabeth's reign has been enriched by some of the best British and American recent scholarship. For the Queen herself, the best works are J. E. Neale, *Queen Elizabeth* (1934), and E. Jenkins, *Elizabeth the Great* (1958). A. L. Rowse, *The England of Elizabeth* (2 vols., 1951-1955), has the respective subtitles of "The Structure of Society" and "The Expansion of Elizabethan England." The role of the great secretaries is ably analyzed in three studies by C. Read: *Mr. Secretary Walsingham and the Policy of Queen Elizabeth* (3 vols., 1925); *Mr. Secretary Cecil and Queen Elizabeth* (1955); and, for Cecil's later years, *Lord Burghley and Queen Elizabeth* (1960). A valuable older account of the later part of the reign is E. P. Cheyney, *History of England from the Defeat of the Spanish Armada to the Death of Elizabeth* (2 vols., 1914-1926). Mary Stuart has been a difficult subject for impartial treatment; possibly the most satisfactory life is T. F. Henderson, *Mary Queen of Scots* (2 vols., 1905).

CONSTITUTIONAL AND LEGAL. New views on the early reigns are included in G. R. Elton, *The Tudor Revolution in Government: Administrative Changes in the Reign of Henry VIII* (1953), and K. M. Pickthorn, *Early Tudor Government* (2 vols., 1934). Particularly valuable new analysis is in J. E. Neale, *The Elizabethan House of Commons* (1950), and *Elizabeth and her Parliaments* (1953). See also W. C. Richardson, *Tudor Chamber Administration* (1952); J. R. Tanner, *Tudor Constitutional Documents* (1922); and C. Morris, *Political Thought in England—Tyndale to Hooper* (1953).

ECONOMIC AND SOCIAL. Perhaps the best overall picture is the first volume of A. L. Rowse, *The England of Elizabeth,* noted above, dealing with "The Structure of Society." A valuable cooperative work, containing chapters on many aspects of Tudor life is *Shakespeare's England* (ed. C. T. Onions et al., 2 vols., 1917); see also L. F. Salzman, *England in Tudor Times: an Account of its Social Life and Industry* (1926); R. H. Tawney, *The Agrarian Problem in the Sixteenth Century* (1912), and *Religion and the Rise of Capitalism* (1926); G. Unwin, *Industrial Organization in the Sixteenth and Seventeenth Centuries* (1904); H. Bradley, *The Enclosures in England* (1918); H. B. Trevor-Roper, *The Gentry, 1540-1640* (1953); and W. K. Jordan, *Philanthropy in England, 1480-1660: A Study in the Changing Patterns of English Social Aspirations* (1959). Several works dealing with the maritime activity of the period are listed in the Maritime section.

MARITIME (NAVAL, COLONIAL, COMMERCIAL). The most useful overall studies are J. A. Williamson, *Maritime Enterprise, 1485-1558* (1913); C. P. Lucas, *The Beginnings of English Overseas Enterprise* (1917); and the second volume of A. L. Rowse, *The England of Elizabeth,* dealing with "The Expansion of Elizabethan England" (1955), and his *The Elizabethans and America* (1959). For the "sea dogs," the old standard works of J. S. Corbett, *Drake and the Tudor Navy* (2 vols., 1898) and *Successors of Drake,* should be supplemented with R. Unwin, *The Defeat of John Hawkins* (1960), M. A. Lewis, *The Spanish Armada* (1960), and G. Mattingly, *The Armada* (1959), a classic which also analyzes the religious and diplomatic situation in 1588. See also C. R. Beazley, *John and Sebastian Cabot* (1898). Important contemporary collections of maritime narratives are R. Hakluyt, *The Principall Navigations . . . of the English Nation,* and S. Purchas, *Purchas his Pilgrimes,* both of which have appeared in various multi-volume editions.

For commercial development, see T. S. Willan, *Studies in Elizabethan Foreign Trade* (1960),

and *The Early History of the Russia Company,
1553-1603* (1956); W. E. LINGELBACH, *Merchant
Adventurers of England* (1902); A. J. GERSON et al,
Studies in the History of English Commerce
(1912); W. FOSTER, *England's Quest of Eastern
Trade* (1933); A. C. WOOD, *History of the Levant
Company* (1935); and D. BURWASH, *English Mer-
chant Shipping, 1460-1540* (1948).

RELIGION. The briefest adequate summary is
T. M. PARKES, *The English Reformation to 1558*
(1950), in the Home University Library. See also
F. M. POWICKE, *The Reformation in England*
(1941); and H. M. SMITH, *Henry VIII and the
Reformation* (1948), a sequel to his *Pre-Reformation England* (1938), already noted. The Catholic
viewpoint is given by a future cardinal in F. A.
GASQUET, *The Eve of the Reformation* (new ed.,
1905), and *Henry VIII and the English Monasteries* (new ed., 1906), and in P. HUGHES, *The
Reformation in England* (1941). The Protestant
side is presented in E. G. RUPP, *The English
Protestant Tradition* (1947). See also C. H. SMYTH,
Cranmer and the Reformation under Edward VI
(1926); G. BASKERVILLE, *English Monks and the
Suppression of the Monasteries* (1937); L. B.
SMITH, *Tudor Prelates and Politics, 1536-1558*
(1953); and W. K. JORDAN, *The Development of
Religious Toleration in England, 1558-1660* (4
vols., 1932-1940).

LITERATURE, ETC. *Shakespeare's England*,
already mentioned, has valuable chapters in this
field. Some of the foremost writers are described
in S. LEE, *Great Englishmen of the Sixteenth
Century* (1904). Useful summaries are F. E.
SCHELLING, *English Literature during the Lifetime of Shakespeare* (1910); L. D. EINSTEIN, *The
Italian Renaissance in England* (1902) and *Tudor
Ideals* (1921); and F. SEEBOHM, *The Oxford Re-
formers* (1914). There are excellent lives of Eras-
mus by E. EMERTON (1899), J. HUIZINGA (1924),
and P. SMITH (1923). For More, there are R. W.
CHAMBERS, *Thomas More* (1935), and E. M. G.
ROUTH, *Sir Thomas More and his Friends* (1934).
The best life of Shakespeare is E. CHAMBERS,
Shakespeare (1930). For science, including navi-
gation, see E. G. R. TAYLOR, *The Mathematical
Practitioners of Tudor and Stuart England* (1954).

4. Stuart Period, 1603-1714

NARRATIVE AND GENERAL. *Oxford His-
tory*, G. DAVIES, *The Early Stuarts, 1603-1660*
(1937), and G. N. CLARK, *The Later Stuarts, 1660-
1714* (1940). *Pelican History:* M. ASHLEY, *England in the Seventeenth Century, 1603-1714*
(1952). G. M. TREVELYAN, *England under the
Stuarts* (6th ed., 1914) in the old "Oman Series"
is readable and still useful. The period has been
covered also by a succession of detailed, multi-
volume works. The most ambitious of these is S.
GARDINER, *History of England* (with various subtitles) covering the years 1603 to 1656 (18 vols.,
new ed., 1901-1903); it is continued by C. H.
FIRTH, *Last Years of the Protectorate, 1656-1658*
(2 vols., 1909). One of the classics of English
history is T. B. MACAULAY, *History of England*

from the Accession of James II, for the period
1685-1697. Originally published between 1849
and 1861, it has gone through numerous editions,
usually in five volumes. It is written in the grand
manner, and despite its strong Whig prejudices,
it has been called "one of the most brilliant and
popular pieces of writing in any language." A
decidedly worthy continuation, by Macaulay's
grand-nephew, G. M. TREVELYAN, is *England
under Queen Anne* (3 vols., 1930-1934).

For the early Stuart period, in addition to the
constitutional works noted below, there are biographies of James I by D. H. WILSON (1955),
Charles I by F. M. G. HIGHAM (1932), Buckingham by H. R. WILLIAMSON (1940), Stafford by
C. V. WEDGEWOOD (1935), Eliot by H. HULME
(1957), and Pym by J. H. HEXTER (1941).

An excellent account of the civil war is C. V.
WEDGEWOOD, *The Great Rebellion* (2 vols., 1955-
1959). Two of the best accounts of Cromwell
are by J. BUCHAN (LORD TWEEDSMUIR) (1934) and
M. ASHLEY (1957), in addition to the earlier ex-
cellent works by C. H. FIRTH (1900) and J.
MORLEY (1900). Also useful is H. G. WORMALD,
*Clarendon: Politics, History and Religion, 1640-
1660* (1951). For the Roundheads, see L. SOLT,
Saints in Arms (1959).

The once-neglected Restoration period finally
received very adequate coverage in D. OGG, *England in the Reign of Charles II* (2 vols., 1934),
continued in his *England in the Reign of James
II and William III* (1955). Other important studies
include G. DAVIES, *The Restoration of Charles
II, 1658-1660* (1955); A. BRYANT, *King Charles
II* (1932); F. C. TURNER, *James II* (1948); H. D.
TRAILL, *Shaftesbury* (1888), and K. FEILING, *History of the Tory Party, 1640-1714* (1924). An invaluable and delightful source for the period is
the diary of SAMUEL PEPYS, naval official and
man-about-town, published in various editions,
particularly that by H. B. WHEATLEY (9 vols.,
1893-1899). Also valuable is A. BRYANT, *Samuel
Pepys* (3 vols., 1933-1939).

For the reign of Queen Anne, in addition to the
Trevelyan trilogy noted above, there is W. S.
CHURCHILL, *Marlborough: his Life and Times* (4
vols., 1933-1938), in part an effort to whitewash
his illustrious ancestor. On the political side there
are W. M. MORGAN, *English Political Parties and
Leaders in the Reign of Queen Anne* (1920), and
biographies of Bolingbroke by W. S. SICHEL (2
vols., 1901-1902) and Godolphin by T. LEVER
(1952).

CONSTITUTIONAL AND LEGAL. Good summaries of the period are J. R. TANNER, *English
Constitutional Conflicts of the Seventeenth Century* (1928), M. THOMPSON, *A Constitutional History of England, 1642-1801* (1938), and M. A.
JUDSON, *The Crisis of the Constitution* (1949). For
political theory, consult B. ZAGORIN, *A History of
Political Thought in the English Revolution* (1954),
and J. W. ALLEN, *English Political Theory, 1603-
1640* (1938), in addition to the older standard
works: J. N. FIGGIS, *The Theory of the Divine
Right of Kings* (new ed., 1914), and G. P. GOOCH,

Political Thought in England from Bacon to Halifax (new ed., 1923) and English Democratic Ideas in the Seventeenth Century (2d ed., 1927). Important for more limited aspects are C. H. McILWAIN, ed., The Political Works of James I (1918); W. NOTESTEIN, Winning of Initiative by the House of Commons (1925); F. D. WORMUTH, The Royal Prerogative, 1603-1649 (1939); D. H. WILSON, The Privy Councillors in the House of Commons, 1604-1629; M. F. KEELER, The Long Parliament, 1640-41: A Biographical Sketch of its Members (1954); and M. CRANSTON, John Locke (1957). An interesting and valuable legal study is C. F. BOWEN, The Lion and the Throne (1959), an account of Chief Justice Coke.

ECONOMIC AND SOCIAL. Excellent surveys of the various aspects of English life will be found in MACAULAY's third chapter, in the opening chapters of TREVELYAN's Stuarts and Queen Anne; in W. NOTESTEIN, The English People on the Eve of Colonization, 1603-1630 (1954), and A. BRYANT, The England of Charles II (1935). Also useful are W. C. SCHENCK, The Concern for Social Justice in the English Revolution (1948); M. CAMPBELL, The English Yeoman under Elizabeth and the Early Stuarts (1947); E. TROTTER, Seventeenth Century Life in the Country Parish (1919); A. M. ANDRÉADÈS, History of the Bank of England (1909); and W. H. B. COURT, The Rise of the Midland Industries, 1600-1838 (1938).

RELIGION. W. K. JORDAN's volumes on toleration continue useful for this period. Also pertinent are W. HALLER, The Rise of Puritanism, 1570-1643 (1938), H. W. SCHNEIDER, The Puritan Mind (1930), and biographies of Archbishop Laud by A. S. O. JONES (1927) and H. R. TREVOR-ROPER (1940).

LITERATURE, ETC. A helpful introduction is B. WILLEY, The Seventeenth Century Background (1934); see also B. WENDELL, The Temper of the Seventeenth Century in English Literature (1904), and C. V. WEDGEWOOD, Poetry and Politics under the Stuarts (1960). More specialized are B. DOBRÉE, Restoration Comedy (1924) and Restoration Tragedy (1929); T. S. ELIOT, John Dryden (1932); W. RALEIGH, Milton (1900); A. E. TAYLOR, Francis Bacon (1926); G. N. CLARK, Science and Social Welfare in the Age of Newton (1937); and J. A. SCHOLES, The Puritans and Music in England and New England (1934).

MARITIME (COMMERCIAL, NAVAL, COLONIAL). Contemporary commercial theories are well expressed in J. CHILD, A New Discourse of Trade (1693), and T. MUN, England's Treasure by Foreign Trade (new ed., 1895). Minute details of regulation are in L. A. HARPER, The English Navigation Laws (1939).

Broad naval studies are A. T. MAHAN, The Influence of Sea Power upon History, 1660-1783; H. RICHMOND, Statesmen and Sea Power (1946) and The Navy as an Instrument of Policy, 1558-1727 (1953); and J. CORBETT, England in the Mediterranean (2 vols., 1904). Also useful are G. S. GRAHAM, Empire of the North Atlantic: The Maritime Struggle for North America (1951); R.

BEADON, Robert Blake (1935); G. N. CLARK, The Dutch Alliance and the War against French Trade (1923); R. G. ALBION, Forests and Sea Power: The Timber Problem of the Royal Navy, 1652-1862 (1926); and J. EHRMAN, The Navy in the War of William III, 1689-1697 (1953).

See also B. E. SUPPLE, Commercial Crises and Change in England, 1600-1642 (1960); and C. W. WILSON, Profit and Power: a Study of England and the Dutch Wars (1957).

One of the best analyses of the colonial system in America is C. M. ANDREWS, The Colonial Period of American History (4 vols., 1934-1938), especially Vol. IV, "England's Economic and Colonial Policy." Also valuable are A. P. NEWTON, The European Nations in the West Indies, 1493-1688 (1933) and M. G. HALL, Edward Randolph and the American Colonies, 1676-1703 (1960). There are also very numerous works dealing with the individual colonies.

MILITARY. The make-up of the civil war forces, as distinct from their operations, is ably handled in C. H. FIRTH, Cromwell's Army (1902); consult also C. V. WEDGEWOOD, The Great Rebellion (2 vols., 1955-1959). Marlborough's military career is well treated in C. T. ATKINSON, Marlborough and the Rise of the British Army (1921), and F. TAYLOR, The Wars of Marlborough (2 vols., 1921) as well as in J. W. FORTESCUE, History of the British Army (Vol. I, 1910), and CHURCHILL's Marlborough already noted.

FOREIGN RELATIONS. SEELEY's Growth of British Policy, noted for the Tudor period, continues useful, as do the works of ADMIRAL RICHMOND mentioned above. See also K. FEILING, British Foreign Policy, 1660-1672 (1930), for the intricate Restoration developments.

SCOTLAND AND IRELAND. There is an excellent general picture of Scotland about 1700 in the second volume of TREVELYAN's Queen Anne. The romantic side of Scotland in the civil war period is well portrayed by J. BUCHAN (LORD TWEEDSMUIR), Montrose, a History (1928). Also useful are A. V. DICEY and R. S. RAIT, Thoughts on the Union between England and Scotland (1920), and W. L. MATHIESON, Politics and Religion in Scotland, 1550-1695 (2 vols., 1902) and Scotland and the Union, 1695-1747 (2 vols., 1905). The principal works on Ireland are R. BAGWELL, Ireland under the Stuarts (3 vols., 1909-1916), and R. DUNLOP, Ireland under the Commonwealth (1913).

5. Eighteenth Century, 1714-1815

NARRATIVE AND GENERAL. Oxford History: B. WILLIAMS, The Establishment of the Hanoverians, 1714-1760 (1929); and J. S. WATSON, The Reign of George III, 1760-1815 (1960). Pelican History: J. H. PLUMB, England in the Eighteenth Century, 1714-1815 (1954). A comprehensive work, on the scale of GARDINER and MACAULAY, is W. E. H. LECKY, History of England in the Eighteenth Century (new ed., 7 vols., 1913); originally written between 1878 and 1890, it gives particular emphasis to social, economic, philosophical, Irish, and American aspects. See also L. KRONENBERGER, *Kings and Desperate Men: Life in the Eighteenth Century* (1942; paperback, 1959). The latter part of the period is well handled in G. M. TREVELYAN, *British History in the Nineteenth Century, 1782-1901* (1922), and in A. BRIGGS, *The Age of Improvement* (1959), covering the years 1783-1867 in the projected Longmans-Medlicott series.

Among the best works on the early period are R. WALCOTT, JR., *English Politics in the Early Eighteenth Century* (1956); biographies of Walpole by J. MORLEY (1889), G. K. TAYLOR (1931), and J. H. PLUMB (1956); J. B. OWEN, *The Rise of the Pelhams* (1957); B. WILLIAMS, *Carteret and Newcastle* (1943); and C. PETRIE, *The Stuart Pretenders* (1933).

Some important revaluation of mid-century political developments followed the appearance of L. B. NAMIER, *The Structure of Politics at the Accession of George III* (2 vols., 1929) and *England in the Age of the American Revolution* (1930). The new views are well summed up in R. PARES, *George III and the Politicians* (1953). The elder Pitt has been the subject of new biographies by O. A. SHERRARD (2 vols., 1952-1955); J. H. PLUMB, (1953); and B. TUNSTALL (1938) in addition to the older works by A. VON RUVILLE (3 vols., 1907) and B. WILLIAMS (2 vols., 1913). See also E. EYCK, *Pitt versus Fox: Father and Son 1735-1806.* (1952); J. BROKE, *The Chatham Administration, 1766-1768;* H. BUTTERFIELD, *George III, Lord North, and the People, 1779-1780* (1949); and K. FEILING, *The Second Tory Party, 1714-1832* (1951). G. O. TREVELYAN, *The Early Life of Charles James Fox* (new ed., 1908), is a delightful picture of social and political conditions.

For the later part of the period, one of the foremost works is J. H. ROSE, *Life of William Pitt* (2 vols., 1924), originally published in 1911 as *William Pitt and the National Revival* and *William Pitt and the Great War.* See also D. G. BARNES, *George III and William Pitt, 1783-1806* (1939); J. W. FORTESCUE, *British Statesmen of the Great War* (1911); W. P. HALL, *British Radicalism, 1791-1797* (1912); R. COUPLAND, *Wilberforce, a Narrative* (1923); P. MAGNUS, *Edmund Burke* (1939); and H. FURBER, *Dundas* (1931).

CONSTITUTIONAL AND LEGAL. The THOMPSON study continues useful for this period. E. and A. G. PORRITT, *The Unreformed House of Commons* (2 vols., 2d ed., 1909), is a valuable study of the subject. See also W. T. LAPRADE, *Public Opinion and Politics in Eighteenth Century to the Fall of Walpole;* the NAMIER works cited above; H. J. LASKI, *Political Thought in England from Locke to Bentham* (1920); E. A. HOON, *The Organization of the English Customs System, 1698-1786* (1938); and L. RADZINOWICZ, *A History of English Criminal Law and its Administration,* (3 vols., 1948-1956), covering the period 1750-1830.

ECONOMIC AND SOCIAL. One of the best general works is T. S. ASHTON, *An Economic History of England: the Eighteenth Century* (1955), which may be continued into later periods. Also important are J. L. and B. HAMMOND, *The Rise of Modern Industry* (1926); P. MANTOUX, *The Industrial Revolution in the Eighteenth Century* (1929); A. P. USHER, *Introduction to the Industrial History of England* (1920) and *History of Mechanical Inventions* (1929); and C. R. FAY, *Great Britain from Adam Smith to the Present Day* (3d ed., 1933).

The social impact of the changes is described in J. L. and B. HAMMOND, *The Town Labourer, 1760-1832* (1917), *The Village Labourer* (new ed., 1920), and *The Skilled Labourer* (1919); M. C. BUER, *Health, Wealth and Population in the Early Days of the Industrial Revolution* (1926); and W. BOWDEN, *Industrial Society in England towards the End of the Eighteenth Century* (1925). For general social surveys, apart from the purely economic, the foremost works are D. MARSHALL, *English People in the Eighteenth Century* (1956); *Johnson's England: An Account of the Life and Manners of his Age* (2 vols., 1933), ed. A. S. TURBERVILLE, who also wrote *English Men and Manners in the Eighteenth Century* (1926); F. J. F. JACKSON, *Social Life in England, 1750-1850* (1916); and J. B. BOTSFORD, *English Society in the Eighteenth Century as Influenced from Oversea* (1924).

For particular industries, see T. S. ASHTON, *Iron and Steel in the Industrial Revolution* (1924); H. HEATON, *The Yorkshire Woollen and Worsted Industries* (1921); E. LIPSON, *The History of the Woollen and Worsted Industries* (1921); S. J. CHAPMAN, *The Lancashire Cotton Industry* (1904); G. W. DANIELS, *The Early English Cotton Industry* (1920); H. HAMILTON, *The Cotton Trade and Industrial Lancashire* (1931); and J. U. NEF, *The Rise of the British Coal Industry* (2 vols., 1932). A valuable contribution to the history of invention is L. T. C. ROLT, *George and Robert Stephenson: The Railway Revolution* (1960), in addition to his recent biographies of Thomas Telford, the roadbuilder, and Isambard K. Brunel, versatile designer of steamships and much else.

RELIGION. See H. SYKES, *Church and State in England in the XVIIIth Century* (1934); the *Journal of John Wesley* (ed., N. CURNOCK et al., 8 vols., 1909-1916); and biographies of Wesley by R. GREEN (1935) and C. T. WINCHESTER (1906).

LITERATURE, ETC. Among the best general works are B. WILLEY, *The Eighteenth Century Background* (1946); L. STEPHEN, *English Literature and Society in the Eighteenth Century* (1904) and *History of English Thought in the Eighteenth Century* (3 vols., 3d ed., 1902). For particular aspects see J. B. BLACK, *The Art of History, a Study of Four Great Historians of the Eighteenth Century* (1926); C. B. TINKER, *The Salon and English Letters* (1915) and *Nature's Simple Plan* (1922); H. N. BRAILSFORD, *Shelley, Godwin and their Circle* (1913); and E. DOWDEN, *The French Revolution and English Literature* (1897). Among the best biographies or analyses are those of Johnson by J. BOSWELL (various editions); Sterne by W. CROSS (1925); Pope by R. K. ROOT (1938); Swift by C. VAN DOREN (1930); Defoe by W. P. TRENT (1916); and Chesterfield by S. A. SHELLA-

BARGER (1935). Useful works in the field of art are R. FRY et al., *Georgian Art, 1760-1820* (1929); B. GRAY, *The English Print* (1937); E. NEWTON, *British Painting* (1943); J. STEGMAN, *Sir Joshua Reynolds* (1938); and A. E. RICHARDSON, *An Introduction to Georgian Architecture* (1949).

SCOTLAND AND IRELAND. See A. M. MACKENZIE, *Scotland in Modern Times, 1720-1939* (1941); C. A. PETRIE, *The Jacobite Movement* (3d ed., 1959); T. H. D. MAHONEY, *Edmund Burke and Ireland* (1960); and F. MACDERMOT, *Theobald Wolf Tone* (1939).

THE DUEL FOR EMPIRE. An ambitious and valuable American contribution is L. A. GIPSON, *The British Empire before the American Revolution* (9 vols., 1936-1956), concentrating on the period about 1740-1770, with detailed description of the various colonies and of the Anglo-French rivalry. The works of MAHAN and GRAHAM, already cited, continue valuable for this period; see also J. S. CORBETT, *England in the Seven Years' War* (2 vols., 1907); F. PARKMAN, *A Half Century of Conflict* and *Montcalm and Wolfe* (each 2 vols., various editions); C. P. STACEY, *Quebec, 1759* (1960); and R. PARES, *War and Trade in the West Indies, 1739-1763* (1936).

THE AMERICAN REVOLUTION. On the background causes, see, in addition to GIPSON, O. M. DICKERSON, *The Navigation Acts and the American Revolution* (1951); E. S. and H. M. MORGAN, *The Stamp Act Crisis* (1953); C. UBBELOHDE, *The Vice Admiralty Courts and the American Revolution* (1960); C. H. McILWAIN, *The American Revolution* (1923); C. L. BECKER, *The Eve of the Revolution* (1918); C. R. RITCHESON, *British Politics and the American Revolution* (1954); G. H. GUTTRIDGE, *English Whiggism and the American Revolution* (1942); and D. M. CLARK, *British Opinion and the American Revolution* (1930). For the naval and military aspects of the war, consult, in addition to MAHAN and FORTESCUE, T. S. ANDERSON, *The Command of the Howe Brothers during the American Revolution* (1936); W. M. JAMES, *The British Navy in Adversity* (1926); and R. G. ALBION, *Introduction to Military History* (1929). The postwar imperial readjustments are treated in H. T. MANNING, *British Colonial Government after the American Revolution, 1782-1820* (1933); R. L. SCHUYLER, *The Fall of the Old Colonial System: A Study in Free Trade* (1945); C. H. VAN TYNE, *The Loyalists in the American Revolution* (1902); and V. T. HARLOW, *The Founding of the Second British Empire, 1763-1793* (Vol. I, 1952).

OTHER COLONIAL ASPECTS. For the Caribbean, see J. H. PARRY & D. M. SHERLOCK, *A Short History of the West Indies* (1956), and R. PARES, *Yankees and Creoles* (1956), a study of the trade between the sugar islands and mainland colonies. For India, A. LYALL, *Rise and Expansion of British Dominion in India* (5th ed., 1910); G. FORREST, *Life of Lord Clive* (2 vols., 1918); K. FEILING, *Warren Hastings* (1954); P. MOON, *Warren Hastings and British India* (1947); C. N. PARKINSON, *Trade in the Eastern Seas, 1793-1813*

(1937); and H. FURBER, *John Company at Work* (1948). For the Pacific, J. C. BEAGLEHOLE, *The Exploration of the Pacific* (1934); J. A. WILLIAMSON, *Cook and the Opening of the Pacific* (1946); and COOK's *Journals*, edited by BEAGLEHOLE for the Hakluyt Society (Vol. I, 1955).

WAR WITH FRANCE, 1793-1815. The period is well covered by A. BRYANT, *The Years of Endurance, 1793-1802* (1946), and *The Years of Victory, 1802-1812* (1944). Valuable on the naval side are A. T. MAHAN, *The Influence of Sea Power upon the French Revolution and Empire* (2 vols., 10th ed., 1898) and *Sea Power in its Relation to the War of 1812* (2 vols., 1905). The best life of Nelson is by C. OMAN (LENANTON) (1947). General naval conditions in the period are treated in J. MASEFIELD, *Sea Life in Nelson's Time* (1905); M. LEWIS, *A Social History of the Navy, 1793-1815* (1960); L. H. C. KENNEDY, *Nelson's Captains* (1951); and A. MOORE, *Sailing Ships of War, 1800-1860* (1926). Special subjects include C. N. PARKINSON, *The Trade Winds: A Study of British Overseas Trade during the French Wars* (1948) and *War in the Eastern Seas, 1793-1815* (1954); E. F. HECKSCHER, *The Continental System* (1922); F. E. MELVIN, *Napoleon's Navigation System* (1919); P. GUEDALLA, *Wellington* (1931), entitled *The Duke* in British editions; and C. OMAN (LENANTON), *Sir John Moore* (1953). Relations with America are treated in H. ADAMS, *History of the United States* (3 vols., new ed., 1929); R. G. ALBION and J. B. POPE, *Sea Lanes in Wartime: The American Experience* (1942), and C. S. FORRESTER, *The Age of Fighting Sail* (1956), in addition to his excellent Hornblower fiction.

FOREIGN RELATIONS. The most useful work for the period after 1783 is the *Cambridge History of British Foreign Policy, 1783-1919*, ed. A. W. WARD and G. P. GOOCH (3 vols., 1922-1923). In the earlier period one of the best studies is B. WILLIAMS, *Stanhope: A Study in Eighteenth Century War and Diplomacy* (1932). For the Vienna peace settlement see W. A. PHILLIPS, *The Confederation of Europe* (2d ed., 1919); A. W. WARD, *The Period of Congresses* (1919); and C. K. WEBSTER, *The Congress of Vienna, 1814-1815* (new ed., 1934), and *The Foreign Policy of Castlereagh, 1812-1815*.

6. The Nineteenth Century, 1815-1914

NARRATIVE AND GENERAL. Oxford History: E. L. WOODWARD, *The Age of Reform, 1815-1870* (1939); and R. C. K. ENSOR, *England, 1870-1914* (1936). Pelican History: D. THOMSON, *England in the Nineteenth Century* (1950). Also excellent are G. M. TREVELYAN, *British History in the Nineteenth Century, 1782-1901* (1922), already mentioned, and E. HALEVY, *History of the English People* (6 vols., 1924-1952), covering the years 1815-1914. For briefer portions of the century, see G. M. YOUNG, *Portrait of an Age* (1936); A. BRIGGS, *Victorian People: Some Reassessing of People, Institutions, Ideas and Events, 1851-1867* (1956); C. A. PETRIE, *Victorians* (1960); and A. BRYANT, *English Saga, 1840-1940* (1953).

Useful studies in the earlier part of the century are H. W. C. Davis, *The Age of Grey and Peel* (1929); A. Aspinwall, *Lord Brougham and the Whig Party* (1927); G. K. Clark, *Peel and the Conservative Party* (1929); S. Macoby, *English Radicalism, 1832-1852* (1935), with a similar volume for 1886-1914, and biographies of Canning by H. W. V. Temperley (1905); Cobbett by G. D. H. Cole (3d ed., 1947); Grey by G. M. Trevelyan (1920); Shaftesbury by J. L. and B. Hammond (1923); Francis Place by G. Wallas (4th ed., 1925); Godwin by F. K. Brown (1926); Palmerston by H. C. F. Bell (2 vols., 1936) and P. Guedalla (1927); Bright by G. M. Trevelyan (1925); Melbourne by D. Cecil; and Cobden by J. Morley (10th ed., 1903) and J. A. Hobson (1919).

For the middle period of the century, J. Morley's biography of Gladstone (new ed., 1921) is an old classic, with later studies by W. P. Hall (1931) and P. Magnus (1954). The fullest account of Disraeli is by W. F. Monypenny and G. E. Buckle (6 vols., 1910-1920); there is a shorter one by A. Maurois (1928). See also D. C. Somervell, *Disraeli and Gladstone* (1929) and W. E. Houghton, *The Victorian Frame of Mind, 1830-1870* (1957). There are biographies of Queen Victoria by G. L. Strachey (1921); E. Sitwell (1936); and E. L. Benson (1935).

For the later part of the period, the good biographies include those of Salisbury by G. Cecil (4 vols., 1921-1932); Randolph Churchill by R. R. James (1960); Chamberlain by J. L. Garvin and J. Amery (4 vols., 1932-1934); Edward VII by S. Lee (2 vols., 1925-1927); Balfour by B. E. C. Dugdale (2 vols., 1937); Asquith by J. Spender and C. Asquith (2 vols., 1932); and Curzon by Lord Ronaldshay (3 vols., 1928) and by L. O. Mosley (1960); in addition to Haldane, Autobiography (1929). Also useful for this later period are H. Pelling, *The Origins of the Labour Party, 1880-1900* (1954); H. S. Reid, *The Origins of the British Labour Party* (1955), carrying the story to 1914; and H. Slesser, *History of the Liberal Party* (1944).

CONSTITUTIONAL, LEGAL, ETC. Two useful surveys are R. L. Schuyler and C. C. Weston, *British Constitutional History since 1832* (1957), and G. K. B. Smellie, *A Hundred Years of English Government* (1937). Three older analyses of contemporary government are W. Bagehot, *The English Constitution* (new ed., 1872); S. J. M. Low, *Governance of England* (new ed., 1915); and A. L. Lowell, *Government of England* (2 vols., new ed., 1912). Important in their particular spheres are G. L. Dickinson, *The Development of Parliament during the Nineteenth Century* (1895), and S. and B. Webb, *English Local Government* (4 vols., 1906-1922). Leading works on political theory include E. Barker, *Political Thought in England from Herbert Spencer to the Present Day* (1915); W. L. Davidson, *Political Thought in England . . . Bentham to J. S. Mill* (1915); C. C. Brinton, *English Political Thought in the Nineteenth Century* (1933); and H. J. Laski, *Liberty in the Modern State* (1930).

ECONOMIC AND SOCIAL. In addition to several of the works already noted for the preceding century, J. H. Clapham, *An Economic History of Modern Britain* (3 vols., 1926-1938), is valuable, as are C. R. Fay, *Life and Labour in the Nineteenth Century* (1933); G. D. H. Cole, *Short History of the British Working Class Movement, 1789-1947* (new ed., 1952), and *The British Common People, 1746-1938* (1947); S. and B. Webb, *English Poor Law History* (3 vols., 1927-1929) and *History of Trade Unionism* (new ed., 1920); J. L. and B. Hammond, *The Age of the Chartists, 1832-1854* (1930); and C. J. H. Hayes, *British Social Politics* (1913), which analyzes the 1906-1911 legislation. Useful in their special spheres are L. H. Jenks, *The Migration of British Capital to 1875* (1927); H. Feis, *Europe, the World's Banker, 1870-1914* (1930); R. W. Hidy, *The House of Baring in American Trade and Finance, 1768-1861* (1949); J. B. Condliffe, *The Commerce of Nations* (1950); W. T. Jackman, *The Development of Transportation in Modern England* (2 vols., 1916); and R. H. Thornton, *British Shipping* (1939). The works of Court and Redford continue useful.

RELIGION. A good general survey of modern developments is W. L. Mathieson, *English Church Reform* (1923). See also C. S. Carpenter, *Church People* (1933); R. F. Wearing, *Methodism and the Working Class Movement of England, 1800-1850* (1937); B. N. Ward, *The Dawn of Catholic Emancipation* (3 vols., 1911-1912); S. L. Ollard, *Short History of the Oxford Movement* (1915); biographies of Cardinal Newman by C. Sarole (1908); and C. F. Harrold (1945); and of General William Booth of the Salvation Army by St. J. G. Ervine (2 vols., 1934).

LITERATURE, ETC. In addition to the appropriate portion of A. C. Baugh, ed., *A Literary History of England* (1948), W. Allen, *The English Novel: A Short Critical History* (1955) is more useful than the longer, uneven E. A. Baker, *The History of the English Novel* (10 vols., 1924). For general poetic analysis, see D. Bush, *Mythology and the Romantic Tradition in English Poetry* (1937) and J. W. Beach, *The Concept of Nature in Nineteenth-Century English Poetry* (1936). For specific aspects see E. Bernbaum, *Guide through the Romantic Movement* (1931); D. Cecil, *Early Victorian Novelists* (1935); H. Walker, *Literature of the Victorian Era* (1921); and G. K. Chesterton, *The Victorian Age in Literature* (1932). For the later movements in poetry see A. Symons, *The Symbolist Movement in Literature* (1911); G. Hough, *The Last Romantics* (1949), and M. Praz, *The Romantic Agony* (2d ed., 1954).

FOREIGN RELATIONS. The whole period is ably covered in the *Cambridge History of British Foreign Policy*, already mentioned. Two very useful summaries are G. P. Gooch and J. H. B. Masterman, *Century of British Foreign Policy* (1917), and R. W. Seton-Watson, *Britain in Europe, 1789-1914* (1937). Excellent studies for the beginning of the period are C. K. Webster,

Foreign Policy of Castlereagh, 1815-1822 (1925), a continuation of his 1812-1815 study; and H. W. V. TEMPERLEY, Foreign Policy of Canning, 1822-1827 (1925). The middle period is well covered by C. K. WEBSTER, Foreign Policy of Palmerston, 1830-1841 (2 vols., 1951), and for a longer span by H. C. F. BELL's biography of Palmerston (2 vols., 1936). Relations with the United States are analyzed in H. C. ALLEN, Anglo-American Relations since 1783 (1860); E. D. ADAMS, Great Britain and the American Civil War (2 vols., 1925); M. B. DUBERMAN, Charles Francis Adams, 1807-1886 (1961); D. JORDAN and E. J. PRATT, Europe and the American Civil War (1931); G. SMITH, The Treaty of Washington, 1871 (1941); and C. S. CAMPBELL, Anglo-American Understanding, 1898-1903 (1957). Also for the middle period see P. KNAPLUND, Gladstone's Foreign Policy (1935); and A. H. IMLAH, Economic Elements in the Pax Britannica (1958).

The diplomatic background of World War I is ably covered in its broadest aspects by S. B. FAY, Origins of the World War (2 vols., 1928), which had a significant influence on the question of responsibility for the outbreak of the war. Also important are W. L. LANGER, European Alliances and Alignments, 1871-1890 (1931), and The Diplomacy of Imperialism, 1890-1902 (2 vols., 1935); and G. L. DICKINSON, The International Anarchy, 1904-1914 (1926). See also EARL GREY, Twenty-five Years (2 vols., 1925); G. M. TREVELYAN, Grey of Falloden (1937); and R. J. S. HOFFMAN, Great Britain and the German Trade Rivalry, 1875-1914 (1933); in addition to some of the naval works listed below.

NAVAL AND MILITARY. A particularly penetrating analysis is A. J. MARDER, The Anatomy of British Sea Power; a History of Naval Policy in the Pre-Dreadnought Era, 1880-1905 (1940); MARDER has also edited the letters of Admiral Fisher, under the title Fear God and Dread Nought (3 vols., 1952-1956). Also important are E. L. WOODWARD, Great Britain and the German Navy (1935); O. PARKS, British Battleships (1958), analyzing their evolution step by step; and C. LLOYD, The Navy and the Slave Trade: The Suppression of the African Slave Trade in the Nineteenth Century (1949). On the military side, there are two good works on the Crimean War by C. WOODHAM-SMITH: The Reason Why (1953), an amazing picture of stupidity in command; and Florence Nightingale, 1820-1910 (1951), pioneer in military nursing. There are also two good biographies: P. MAGNUS, Kitchener, Portrait of an Imperialist (1958), and G. E. ELTON, Gordon of Khartum (1955).

IRELAND. Among the more objective accounts are N. MANSERGH, Ireland in the Age of Reform and Revolution, 1840-1921 (1941); E. BARKER, Ireland in the Last Fifty Years, 1866-1916 (new ed., 1919); J. O'CONNOR, History of Ireland, 1798-1924 (2 vols., 1925); ST. J. G. ERVINE, Parnell (1925); J. L. HAMMOND, Gladstone and the Irish Question (1938); W. A. PHILLIPS, Revolution in Ireland, 1909-1923 (1923); and J. E. POMFRET,

The Struggle for Land in Ireland, 1800-1923 (1930).

EMPIRE. Most comprehensive is the Cambridge History of the British Empire, ed. J. H. ROSE et al., (8 vols., 1929-1940). Vols. I-III cover the Empire as a whole; IV-V, India (identical with V-VI of the Cambridge History of India); VI, Canada-Newfoundland; VII, Australia-New Zealand; and VIII, South Africa. For a briefer survey, in addition to CARRINGTON, see P. KNAPLUND, The British Empire, 1815-1939 (1941); A. P. NEWTON, A Century of Empire (1940); and A. L. BURT, The Evolution of the British Empire and Commonwealth from the American Revolution (1956). For briefer periods, see P. KNAPLUND, James Stephen and the British Colonial System, 1813-1847 (1953), and Gladstone and Britain's Imperial Policy (1927); W. P. MORRELL, British Colonial Policy in the Age of Peel and Russell (1930); J. A. HOBSON, Imperialism, a Study (1905); P. T. MOON, Imperialism and World Politics (new ed., 1932); W. L. LANGER, The Diplomacy of Imperialism, 1890-1902 (2 vols., 1935), already cited; and W. P. HALL, Empire to Commonwealth: Thirty Years of British Imperial History (1928), for the years 1897-1927. For African exploration, see A. MOOREHEAD, The White Nile (1961), and J. E. FLINT, Sir George Goldie and the Making of Nigeria (1960).

For Canada, perhaps the most useful surveys are E. W. McINNIS, Canada (new ed., 1959); C. F. WITTKE, History of Canada (rev. ed., 1933); and G. M. WRONG, The Canadians: The Story of a People (1938). Also important in more restricted spheres are A. R. M. LOWER, Canadians in the Making (1958); J. B. BREBNER, North Atlantic Triangle (1945); R. G. TROTTER, Canadian Federation, Its Origin and Achievement (1934); A. SIEGFRIED, The Race Question in Canada (1907); D. G. CREIGHTON, The Commercial Empire of the St. Lawrence, 1760-1850 (1937); C. P. STACEY, Canada and the British Army, 1846-1871 (1936); M. W. CAMPBELL, The North West Company (1957); M. L. HANSEN, The Mingling of the Canadian and American Peoples (1940); P. C. CORBETT, The Settlement of Canadian-American Disputes (1937); and J. K. HOWARD, Strange Empire: A Narrative of the Northwest (1952). There are good biographies of Durham by C. NEW (1929); Macdonald by J. POPE (2 vols., 1895); and Laurier by O. D. SKELTON (2 vols., 1921).

The declining years of the British West Indies are recounted in L. J. RAGATZ, The Fall of the Planter Class in the British Caribbean (1928); P. D. CURTIN, Two Jamaicas (1955); and M. AYEARST, The British West Indies: The Search for Self-Government (1961).

One of the most useful histories of Australia is G. GREENWOOD, ed., Australia: A Social and Political History (1955); see also E. SCOTT, Short History of Australia (5th ed., 1927); R. C. MILLS, The Colonization of Australia, 1829-1842 (1915); T. A. COGHLAN, Labor and Industry in Australia (4 vols., 1918); and G. NADEL, Australia's Colonial Culture (1957).

7. Since 1914

NARRATIVE AND GENERAL. Most of the multi-volume series originally carried the story only to 1914. One of the few comprehensive sketches for the later period is C. L. Mowat, *Britain Between the Wars, 1918-1940* (1955). Two ambitious works, in which the distinguished author is also one of the heroes, are W. S. Churchill, *The World Crisis* (6 vols., 1923-1931), covering World War I and its "aftermath" to 1930; and *Second World War* (6 vols., 1948-1953) and a single-volume abridgement (1959), with an epilogue covering 1945-1957 (1959). A valuable survey not confined to Britain alone is G. Bruun, *The World in the Twentieth Century* (1948). See also W. P. Hall, *Iron out of Calvary* (1946).

The first Labor governments received considerable attention, including R. W. Lyman, *The First Labour Government, 1924* (1957); A. A. Rozow and P. Shore, *The Labour Government and British Industry, 1945-1951* (1956); G. D. H. Cole, *A History of the Labour Party from 1914* (1948); R. B. McCallum and A. Readman, *The British General Election of 1945* (1946); H. G. Nicholas, *The British General Election of 1950* (1951); and the views of four prominent members of the Labor government: C. R. Attlee, *The Labour Party in Perspective—and Twelve Years Later* (1949); S. Cripps, *Democracy Alive* (1946); H. S. Morrison, *The Peaceful Revolution* (1949); and A. Bevan, *In Place of Fear* (1952).

Biographies include those of King George V by H. Nicolson (1953), J. Buchan (Lord Tweedsmuir) (1935), and D. C. Somervell (1935); Keynes by G. R. Harrod (1951); Churchill by L. Broad (new ed., 1956); MacDonald by M. A. Hamilton (1929); Baldwin by G. M. Young (1952); Austen Chamberlain by C. Petrie (2 vols., 1939-1940); Neville Chamberlain by K. Feiling (1946); Lloyd George by T. Jones (1951); and Ernest Bevin by A. Bullock (1960); in addition to the memoirs of Lloyd George, Eden and others.

CONSTITUTIONAL AND LEGAL. See K. Mackenzie, *The English Parliament* (1950); I. Bulmer-Thomas, *The Party System in Great Britain* (1953); C. H. Gibson, *The Spirit of British Administration* (1959); P. A. Broomhead, *The House of Lords and Contemporary Politics, 1911-1957* (1958).

ECONOMIC AND SOCIAL. Two important economic surveys are K. Hutchison, *The Decline and Fall of British Capitalism* (1950); and G. D. N. Worswick, and P. H. Ady, eds., *The British Economy, 1945-1950* (1953). The economic impact of the two wars is analyzed in J. M. Keynes, *The Economic Consequences of the Peace* (1920); F. W. Hirst, *The Consequences of the War to Great Britain* (1934); A. E. Kahn, *Great Britain in the World Economy* (1946); and G. D. H. Cole, *The Post-War Condition of Britain* (1957). Special aspects are treated in E. W. Cohen, *English Social Services* (1949); E. M. Hubback, *The Population of Britain* (1947); F. Zweig, *The British Worker* (1952); T. H. O'Brien, *British Experiments in Public Ownership and Control* (1937);

L. F. Easterbrook, *British Agriculture* (1938); and R. H. Thornton, *British Shipping* (1939).

FOREIGN RELATIONS. Useful surveys of the whole between-war period include F. H. Soward, *Twenty-five Troubled Years, 1918-1943* (1944); G. M. Gathorne-Hardy, *A Short History of International Affairs, 1920-1939* (1950); W. N. Medlicott, *British Foreign Policy since Versailles* (1940); C. Petrie, *Twenty Years Armistice and After* (1940); W. M. Jordan, *Great Britain, France and the German Problem, 1918-1939* (1943); and A. Wolfers, *Britain and France between Two Wars* (1940).

Among the best works on the 1919 peace settlement are H. Nicolson, *Peacemaking, 1919* (new ed., 1945); H. W. V. Temperley, ed., *A History of the Peace Conference of Paris* (6 vols., 1920-1924); D. Lloyd George, *Memoirs of the Peace Conference* (2 vols., 1939); J. M. Keynes, *A Revision of the Treaty* (1922); A. J. Toynbee, *The World after the Peace Conference* (1925); and P. Birdsall, *Versailles Treaty Twenty Years After* (1941).

On disarmament, see A. J. Jacobs, *World Peace and Armaments* (1931); G. Engeley, *The Politics of Naval Disarmament* (1932); R. L. Buell, *The Washington Conference* (1922); and G. R. Crosby, *Disarmament and Peace in British Politics, 1914-1919* (1957).

Other aspects of general foreign relations include A. J. Mayer, *Political Origins of the New Diplomacy, 1917-1919* (1959); H. Nicolson, *Curzon, the Last Phase, 1919-1925, a Study in Postwar Diplomacy* (1934); E. Windrich, *British Labour's Foreign Policy* (1952); M. A. Fitzsimons, *Foreign Policy and the British Labour Governments, 1945-1951* (1953); E. S. Meehan, *The British Left Wing and Foreign Policy, A Study of the Influence of Ideology* (1961); C. K. Webster and S. Herbert, *The League of Nations in Theory and Practice* (1933); C. M. Frasure, *British Policy on War Debts and Reparations* (1940); and L. M. Goodrich and F. Hambro, *The Charter of the United Nations* (1947).

Accounts of relations with particular regions include F. W. Forester, *Europe and the German Question* (1940); S. R. Graubard, *British Labor and the Russian Revolution, 1917-1924* (1950); H. C. Wood, *Communism and the British Intellectuals* (1959); E. W. Newman, *Great Britain in Egypt* (1928); C. M. Woodhouse, *Britain and the Middle East* (1959); G. E. Kirk, *A Short History of the Middle East* (1959) and *Contemporary Arab Politics* (1961); G. L. Hudson, *The Far East in World Politics* (1937); H. Shearman, *Anglo-Irish Relations* (1948) and M. J. McManus, *Eamon de Valera* (1946).

On the approach to World War II, see D. E. Lee, *Ten Years: The World on its Way to War, 1930-1940* (1940); N. Henderson, *Failure of a Mission* (1940); W. S. Churchill, *While England Slept* (1938); and N. Chamberlain, *In Search of Peace* (1939). For the postwar period see H. Feis, *Between War and Peace: The Potsdam Conference* (1960) and A. Eden, *Full Circle* (1960), the highly subjective memoirs of that veteran expert in foreign affairs.

WORLD WAR I. Very useful background for both World Wars will be found in T. Ropp, *War in the Modern World* (2 vols., 1959). For compact surveys of World War I, particularly for the British aspects, see C. B. Falls, *First World War* (1960), and C. R. M. F. Cruttwell, *A History of the Great War, 1914-1918* (1934). The most complete accounts, both on the military and civil aspects, are the numerous volumes of the *History of the Great War, based on Official Documents*. Two of England's foremost statesmen of the war wrote full and interesting, but not unbiased accounts: Churchill's *World Crisis*, already mentioned, and the *War Memoirs of David Lloyd George* (5 vols., 1933-1936). For the Western Front, see the biographies of Haig by J. Charteris (1929) and A. D. Cooper (1935); also S. L. Sassoon, *Memoirs of an Infantry Officer* (1930), and F. B. Maurice, *The Last Four Months* (1919). Earlier writings on the Gallipoli-Dardanelles operations have been generally superseded by A. Moorehead's excellent *Gallipoli* (1956). The naval aspects of both World Wars are well covered with excellent maps and diagrams, in E. B. Potter and C. W. Nimitz, eds., *Sea Power: A Naval History* (1960). For the huge 1916 fleet encounter, the best studies are L. Gibson and J. E. T. Harper, *The Riddle of Jutland* (1934), and D. G. F. W. Macintyre, *Jutland* (1958); the dramatic raid to close the submarine bases is well treated in B. Pitt, *Zeebrugge* (1958). The writings of Lord Jellicoe, the British commander-in-chief, and of Admiral R. J. B. Keyes are valuable. The campaigns in the Middle East are told in T. E. Lawrence, *Revolt in the Desert* (1927) and *The Seven Pillars of Wisdom* (new ed., 1935). For the "home front" see H. L. Gray, *War Time Control of Industry: The Experience of England* (1918).

WORLD WAR II. The better overall accounts include C. B. Falls, *The Second World War, a Short History* (1948); J. F. C. Fuller, *The Second World War, 1939-1945, a Strategical and Tactical History* (1949); and L. L. Synder, *The War: A Concise History, 1939-1945* (1960). The most ambitious work is W. S. Churchill, *The Second World War* (6 vols., 1948-1953), which contains many of the wartime prime minister's official papers; each volume has its special title, such as *The Gathering Storm* and *Their Finest Hour*. The series was later compressed into a single volume, *Memoirs of the Second World War* (1959).

Again, the government sponsored an ambitious and well-executed multi-volume *History of the Second World War*, with a military series, edited by J. R. M. Butler, and a civil series, edited by W. K. Hancock. The former, in addition to volumes on the separate fronts and areas, has two valuable comprehensive analyses, *Grand Strategy* and *The War at Sea*, each in several volumes. Studies in the civil series include *The British War Economy, British War Production, Civil Industry and Trade, Control of Raw Materials, Manpower,*

Coal, Food, Agriculture, North American Supply, Merchant Shipping, Economic Blockade, Inland Transportation, and Civil Defense. Canada, Australia, New Zealand, and India each also had its official series.

The initial invasion threat is covered in P. Fleming, *Operation Sea Lion* (1957) and W. Ansel, *Hitler Confronts England* (1960). The naval side, in addition to S. W. Roskill's official *The War at Sea* and the E. B. Potter and C. W. Nimitz *Sea Power*, already noted, is treated in S. W. Roskill, *White Ensign, The British Navy at War, 1939-1945* (1960); and P. K. Kemp, *Victory at Sea, 1939-1945* (1958); there are several works on individual ships. The Normandy landings are the subject of O. Ryan, *The Longest Day, June 6, 1944* (1959) and the fall of Singapore in K. Atwill, *Fortress* (1960). Several high commanders, including Marshal Montgomery, Lord Ismay, and Admiral Cunningham have written memoirs, while the diaries of Lord Allenbrook have been presented by A. Bryant.

COMMONWEALTH AND EMPIRE. In addition to the works previously cited, some of the most useful general studies are N. Mansergh, *The Multi-Racial Commonwealth* (1955) and *Survey of British Commonwealth Affairs* (1960); J. Strachey, former member of the Labor government, *The End of Empire* (1960); R. Emerson, *From Empire to Nation: The Rise to Self-Assertion of Asian and African Peoples* (1960); A. Brady, *Democracy in the Dominions*, (3rd ed., 1958); K. Hancock, *Survey of Commonwealth Affairs* (2 vols., 1937-1942); and R. M. Dawson, *Development of Dominion Status* (1937).

For Canada, see E. A. Stovel, *Canada in the World Economy* (1959); C. Martin, *Foundations of Canadian Nationhood* (1955); and the R. M. Dawson biography of Mackenzie-King (Vol. I, 1959). An interesting linking of the Canadian and United States relation to Britain is B. Thomas, *Migration and Economic Growth: A Study of Great Britain and the Atlantic Economy* (1954).

There has been a wealth of material, of widely varying value, on recent developments in Asia and Africa. A useful brief, paperbound guide to the situation in India is T. W. Wallbank, *A Short History of India and Pakistan* (1958), an abridgment of his *India in the New Era* (1951). Other useful works are A. R. Desal, *The Social Background of Indian Nationalism* (1948); K. M. Pannikar, *Asia and Western Dominance* (1953); J. Nehru, *The Discovery of India* (1946) and the biographies of Gandhi by B. R. Nanda (1959) and Nehru by M. Brecher (1959). For Africa see Lord Haile, *African Survey: A Study of Problems Arising in Africa South of the Sahara* (rev. ed., 1957); J. Gunther, *Inside Africa* (1955); and F. M. Bourret, *Ghana: The Road to Independence, 1919-1957* (1960) with earlier editions entitled *Gold Coast*. For the serious color problems of South Africa, see G. M. Carter, *Problems of Equality* (1958), and S. Patterson, *The Last Trek* (1957).

Index

Where an individual's name was changed upon his receiving a title of nobility, he will be listed under the name by which he is best known to history, with suitable cross-reference. Thus the title will be used for Marlborough (Churchill), Wellington (Wellesley), and Cromer (Baring), but the "maiden name" for Walpole (Orford), Pitt (Chatham), and Disraeli (Beaconsfield).

Augustine, Saint, 11
Austerlitz, battle of, 377
Australia: and Captain Cook, 444; convicts, 444ff., other settlers, 440f., 446f., 714; separate divisions of, 445f.; responsible government in, 447, 462; imperial defense, 463, 545, 649; dominion status, 541; investments in, 546; and World War I, 575, 578, 591f.; between wars, 609; and World War II, 625, 640, 648f., 659; postwar, 677, 685, 713f.
Austria: in 16th and 17th centuries, 176, 264, 277; in 18th century, 283f., 289f., 306ff., 368ff.; Congress of Vienna and Metternich era, 385f., 389, 416, 421; and alliance systems, 550ff., 564; and World War I, 567f., 575, 588f; between wars, 599f., 620; postwar, 676
Austrian Netherlands, see Low Countries
Austrian Succession, War of, 306ff.
Automobiles, 663, 689ff., 692f.
Aviation: beginnings, 346; in World War I, 571, 581; between wars, 609, 619; in World War II, 623, 626, 632f., 638, 651, 652ff.; postwar, 667, 675, 688
Axis, 618f., 621, 623, 639, 645, 653, 678

Babington plot, 204
Babylonian Captivity, 133f., 178
Bacon, Francis, 95, 166, 211, 219
Bacon, Roger, 95, 219
Baghdad, 564, 580, 585, 688; Pact, 685, 688
Bahamas, 634
Baker, Sir Samuel, 519
Bakewell, Robert, 331f.
Baldwin, Stanley, later Earl Baldwin, 509, 601; first ministry, 601f.; second ministry, 601, 604f.; in National Cabinet, 607; third ministry, 609, 617ff.
Balewa, Abubakar, 707
Balfour, Arthur, later Earl, 482f., 489ff., 610
Balfour Declaration, 610
Balkan problem, see Turkey
Ball, John, 129, 135
Ballance, John, 542
Balliol, John, 112f.
Ballot, secret, 447, 470, 480, 542
Bandaranaike, Mrs. S., 719
Bandung conference, 705
Bank of England, 280f., 292, 607, 667

Bannockburn, battle of, 117, 285
Barbados, 231, 248, 458. See also West Indies.
Barbary pirates, 233
Barebones Parliament, 248f.
Baring, see Cromer
Barnet, battle of, 149
Barré, Isaac, 318f.
Battle of Britain, 632ff., 652
Bayeux Tapestry, 34, 36, 41, 51
Beachy Head, battle of, 279
Beaconsfield, see Disraeli
Beatty, Adm. David, later Earl, 571, 579
Beaufort, Cardinal, 143
Beaufort, Edmund, Duke of Somerset, 145f.
Beaverbrook, W. M. Aitken, 1st Baron, 583
Bec, Compromise of, 61
Bechuanaland, 529, 616
Becket, Archbishop Thomas, 76ff., 184
Bede, 7, 17, 22
Bedford, John Plantagenet, Duke of, 143f.
Bedford, John Russell, 4th Duke of, 317
Belgium: independent and neutral, 420f., 471, 565; and Congo, 519f., 523, 694f., 705; in World War I, 568f.; between wars, 598; in World War II, 627, 629, 655. See also Low Countries.
Bellême, Robert of, 52, 61
Benefit of Clergy, 77f.
"Benelux" countries, 672ff.
Benevolences, 150, 218f.
Bengal, 313ff., 320f., 448ff., 535. See also India.
Bennett, Arnold, 411, 512ff.
Bentham, Jeremy, 413f., 428
Bentinck, Lord William, 451
Beowulf, 11
Berlin: decree, 379; Congress of (1878), 474f., 549, 551; colonial conference (1884-1885), 522; Potsdam conference (1945), 657; airlift (1948), 675
Berlin-Baghdad Railway, 564
Bermuda, 229, 458, 634
Bessemer, Henry, 335, 425
Bevan, Aneurin, 668f., 680f., 684
Beveridge, Sir William, 648, 668
Bevin, Ernest, 631, 647, 656, 668, 681
Bibles: Wycliffe's translation, 134; Coverdale's and Tyndale's translations, 184; King James version, 215
Bill of Rights, 90, 274
Birmingham, 257, 336f., 399, 415, 488

Bishops' War, first, 235; second, 236
Bismarck, Count Otto von, 474, 525, 550ff., 668
Bismarck, 634f., 639, 646
"Black Country," 335f.
Black Death, 125f., 127, 170
Black Prince, Edward, 124, 126, 145
Black Sea neutralized, 423, 471
Blackstone, Sir William, 73
Blake, Adm. Robert, 248
Blake, William, 361
Blenheim, battle of, 285, 377
Blitzkrieg, 623, 627ff.
Boer War, 422, 531ff., 554
Boleyn, Anne, 181, 183f., 187
Bolingbroke, Henry St. John, Viscount, 288ff., 292, 316
Bombay, 262, 309, 449
Bonaparte, Napoelon, see Napoleon I
Boniface VIII, Pope, 113
Book of Common Prayer, 191
Bordeaux, 125, 131
Borden, Sir Robert, 541, 545
Boston, Lincolnshire, 230
Boston, Massachusetts, 230, 321f.
Boswell, James, 354, 356
Bosworth Field, battle of, 148, 151, 173
Botany Bay, 444f.
Botha, Gen. Louis, 532, 542ff.
Bothwell, James Hepburn, 4th Earl of, 200
Boudicca (Boadicia), Queen, 3, 4
Boulogne, 188f., 376
Bouvines, battle of, 87, 277
Boyne, battle of the, 276, 279
Bracton, Henry de, 73f.
Braddock, Gen. Edward, 310
Bradford, 337
Braganza, Catherine of, 262
Breakspear, Nicholas (Pope Adrian IV), 77, 79
Breda, Declaration of, 260
Bretigny, Treaty of, 124, 126
Brian Boru, 78
Bridgewater, Francis Egerton, 3d Duke of, 346
Bright, John, 417f., 423, 464ff., 488
Bristol, 25, 160, 163, 172, 239f., 257, 633, 652
British Columbia, 539
British Commonwealth of Nations, 616f. See also Colonies and Dominions.
British East Africa, see Kenya
British Guiana, 387, 634, 710
Brittany, 36, 62, 66, 83
Brougham, Henry, 404

postwar withdrawal, 691, 696, 701, 708f.
"Iron Curtain," 671
Iron and steel, 335, 425, 690, 716
Irwin, Lord, *see* Halifax
Isabella, wife of Edward II, 117, 119, 120
Israel, 686, 694, 702. *See also* Palestine.
Italian Penisula (before unification): in English commerce and finance, 104, 110, 131f., 163; revival of learning, 153ff.; trade with East, 159; struggle for unification, 421
Italy, kingdom of: 550, 617; colonies, 523, 550, 559; and alliance system, 551, 559; in World War I, 567ff., 575f., 585; peace settlement, 589f.; fascism between the wars, 600, 617f.; in World War II, 630, 636ff., 649, 651f.; postwar, 690, 692

Jacobites, 281, 285, 291, 327; uprisings, 292, 307
Jamaica, 249, 458, 634, 710. *See also* West Indies.
James I, 212ff.
James II: as Duke of York, 258, 262f., 266; characteristics, 269f., reign, 269ff.; efforts to regain throne, 276, 283
James, Prince, the Old Pretender, 275, 281, 283, 287, 290, 292
James, Henry, 506, 511
Jameson Raid, 530
Jamestown, 229f.
Japan: westernization of, 535, 553; Sino-Japanese War, 535; and Russia, 536, 559; alliance with England, 554, 598; in World War I, 571; peace settlement, 591; naval conferences, 598, 606, 608; attacks China, 619, 639; in World War II, 639ff., 650f., 655f., 657f., 670, 697; postwar, 675ff.
Java, 456, 640, 658
Jeanne d'Arc, *see* Joan of Arc
Jeffreys, George, 1st Baron, Lord Chief Justice, 270, 273
Jellicoe, Adm. John R., Earl, 568, 572, 579f.
Jenkins's Ear, War of, 306, 393
Jenner, Edward, 357
Jerusalem, 82, 585, 702. *See also* Palestine.
Jesuits (Society of Jesus), 198, 270, 442
Jews: in England, 58, 85, 92, 104, 163; permitted to enter

Parliament, 414; and Kenya, 523; and Palestine, 523, 608, 610f., 652, 667; and Israel, 686, 695, 702
Jinnah, Mohammed Ali, 697
Joan of Arc, 143f., 164
John, 83ff.
John of Gaunt, Duke of Lancaster, 126ff., 129, 134, 136, 138, 143, 146, 151, 158
Johnson, Samuel, 354f., 358, 499
Jordan, Kingdom of, 678, 687, 710f. *See also* Transjordania.
Jumièges, Robert of, 38
Jury system, 69ff.; and Magna Carta, 89
Justices of the peace, 171, 252, 269, 299, 340, 400, 490
Justiciar, 57, 68
Jutes, 7
Jutland, battle of, 579f., 624

Karachi, 699
Kashmir, 700
Kay, John, 334
Kenya, 522f., 705f.
Keynes, John Maynard, 599
Khartoum, 527f.
Khrushchev, Nikita S., 688, 693ff.
Killiecrankie, battle of, 276
King, W. L. Mackenzie, 539, 649, 717f.
King James Bible, 215
King's Bench, Court of, 69, 104, 138, 217, 500
"King's Friends," 317ff., 362, 364
Kingsley, Charles, 428, 431f., 494
Kipling, Rudyard, 507ff., 517, 548, 555, 699
Kitchener, Gen. Horatio H., 1st Earl, 526f., 530f., 553, 568, 573f., 578, 581
Knighthood, distraint of, 104, 232f., 237
Knights, *see* Social classes
Knox, John, 180, 198, 200, 234, 276
Korea, 677f., 695
Krak des Chevaliers, 82
Kruger, Paul, 530, 552
Kut-el-Amara, 580
Kuwait, 690

La Hogue, battle of, 279
La Rochelle, 224
Labor, *see* Industrial Revolution, Labor party, Trade Unionism
Labor Exchanges Act, 494
Labor legislation, *see* Factory legislation
Labor party, 492, 500, 601; first ministry, 602f.; second minis-

try, 605f.; opposition to National Government, 606f.; in World War II, 630f., 647; third ministry, 656f.; postwar program, 660, 666ff., 680, 688f.; defeat, 682
Laborers, Statute of, 128, 172, 494
Lafontaine, Louis, 461
Laissez faire, 337, 357, 396, 419, 472. *See also* Commerce and Trade.
Lancaster, Duke of, *see* John of Gaunt
Lancaster, Thomas, Earl of, 119
Lancastrian line, 138, 149, 166
Land League, 479ff.
Landholding: free-holders vs. tenant farmers, 252f., 327f., 332; landowning instead of landholding, 260; ownership of land, 327; and free trade, 396f.; in Ireland, 246, 468, 477ff., 480, 483; and Lloyd George budget, 496. *See also* Feudal system, Law, Manorial system, Social classes.
Lanfranc, Archbishop, 51, 53f.
Langland, William, 135
Langton, Stephen, Archbishop, 84, 88f., 90
Languages: Celtic, 8; Old English, 8; Norman French, 51; use of various, 73; Middle English, 135; Bible translations, 134, 184, 215; Renaissance influences, 155
Lansdowne, 1st Marquess, *see* Shelburne
Laos, 695
Latimer, Bishop Hugh, 186, 190
Latin America, 161, 290, 306, 393, 426, 546
Laud, Archbishop William, 226, 233ff., 236
Lauderdale, John Maitland, Duke of, 263
Laurier, Sir Wilfrid, 539ff., 545, 718
Lausanne Conference, 602, 615
Law, Andrew Bonar, 582, 591, 601
Law: dooms, 30; Anglo-Saxon principles and methods, 30ff.; shire courts, 31ff., 49f., 68, 71, 252; hundred courts, 31, 50, 67; church courts and canon law, 30, 68, 76ff.; ordeals, 31f., 70; the sheriff, 49f.; feudal courts, 50, 67f., 103; Curia Regis, 57, 59, 68, 195, 295; reforms of Henry I and II, 57, 67ff., 88; itinerant justices and circuit courts, 59, 68ff., 102f., 138,

New England, 230f.
New Guinea, 640f., 649, 658
New Lanark, 390f.
New Netherland, see New York
New Orleans, 301, 315, 381
New York, 247, 263, 322, 324f., 424, 426, 606
New Zealand: early conditions, 442, 447; Captain Cook, 441; migration to, 440, 447f., 714f.; colonial government, 448, 462; dominion status, 542; and imperial defense, 463, 544f., 648f.; radical socialist development, 542, 715; World War I, 575, 578; between wars, 591, 615; World War II, 625, 636, 648f., 652, 659; postwar, 685, 707, 713ff.
Newbury, battle of, 239
Newcastle, Thomas Pelham Holles, Duke of, 298, 311f.
Newcastle-on-Tyne, 335, 337
Newcomen, Thomas, 335
Newfoundland, 160, 289, 301, 459, 462f., 537, 544, 558, 578, 584, 617, 634
Newman, Cardinal John Henry, 415, 432
Newton, Sir Isaac, 349f., 359
Nigeria, 441, 458, 521f., 548, 690, 694, 707, 709, 719
Nightingale, Florence, 423
Nile, battle of, 374
Nkrumah, Kwame, 706f., 719
Nonconformists, see Dissenters
Nootka Sound, 370
Norfolk, Thomas Howard, 3d Duke of, 189; 4th Duke of, 201
Norman Conquest, 40ff., 43, 51f.
Normandy, 35ff., 61f., 65f., 84, 142, 144, 653f.
Norsemen, see Danes
North, Frederick, Lord, later 2d Earl of Guilford, 317, 321, 362
North Africa, campaigns in, 636ff., 643ff., 649, 651
North Atlantic Treaty Organization, see NATO
Northcliffe, Alfred C. W. Harmsworth, Viscount, 583, 591
Northampton, Assize of, 168
Northampton, battle of, 148
Northern Ireland, 598, 697. See also Ulster.
Northumberland, John Dudley, Viscount Lisle, Earl of Warwick, Duke of, 189ff.
Northumberland, Henry Percy, 1st Earl of, 141
Northumbria, 9, 11ff., 18f., 21, 32
Norway, 34, 304, 627, 690, 693

Norwich, 257
Nottingham, 239
Nova Scotia, 289, 301, 308, 310, 315, 459, 461, 537f. See also Acadia, Canada.
Nuclear energy: weapons, 658, 672, 688f.; ships, 688f.; non-military power, 689, 692
Nyasaland, 709
Nyerere, Julius K., 706

Oastler, Richard, 408
Oates, Titus, 266, 268
"Occasional conformity," 275, 288, 398
O'Connell, Daniel, 398, 404
O'Connor, Feargus, 416f.
Odo, Bishop of Bayeux, 54
Oil, 602, 610, 640, 678, 690f., 716
Old-age pension act, 493
"Old Pretender," 275, 281, 283, 287, 290, 292
Old Sarum, 297, 311
Omdurman, battle of, 528
"Operation Sea Lion," 632
"Opium War," 455
Oran, actions at, 631, 645
Orange Free State, see South Africa
Ordeals, 31f., 70
Orders in Council (1807), 379, 381
Ordinances, 102, 218
Ordinances of London, 118
Organization for European Economic Co-operation (OEEC), 674, 692
Orleans, siege of, 143f.
"Osborne Judgment," 500
Oswald, 13
Oswy, 13
Ottawa, 538, 607, 616, 648
"Outer Seven," 693
Overseas Development Act, 667f.
Owen, Robert, 390f., 408, 415, 433
Oxford (town), 239, 269, 647
Oxford, Provisions of, 100
Oxford, Robert de Vere, Earl of, 137. See also Harley, Robert.
Oxford Movement, 414f.
Oxford University, 75, 95, 134, 154, 172 ,176, 233, 257, 271, 329, 414, 431, 464f.

Paine, Thomas, 360, 367
Pakistan, 685, 688, 690, 699ff., 708, 713, 719. See also India.
Pale (Ireland), 79
Palestine, 523, 567, 585, 591, 610ff., 696, 701ff. See also Israel.
Palmerston, Henry J. Temple, 3d

Viscount, 412, 419ff., 464f., 565, 610
Pankhurst, Mrs. Emmeline, 501
Papineau, Louis, 460
Paris, treaties of: (1763) 315; (1783) 322, 325f.; (1856) 423, 471, 473
Paris, Matthew, 96
Parliament: Saxon and Norman origins, 28, 49, 56; under Henry III and Montfort, 100ff.; Model Parliament, 105ff.; financial powers, 105, 139, 149f., 166, 217f.; withdrawal of lower clergy, 107; division into two houses, 107f., 139; petitions, bills, and statutes, 139, 294, 499; changes royal line, 139, 273f.; strengthened by Hundred Years' War, 139f.; impeachment and attainder, 140, 219, 236; co-operates with Lancastrians, 140, 216; less influential with Yorkists and Tudors, 140, 148, 165f., 216; utilization by Tudors, 181, 183f., 196, 208; beginning of contest with Stuarts, 212, 215ff.; and foreign affairs, 220, 225; Petition of Right, 225; eleven years without Parliament, 226, 232ff.; Long Parliament, 236ff., 243, 248, 250; in Civil War and Interregnum, 246ff.; during Restoration, 254, 259f., 261ff., 265ff.; beginning of parties, 267f.; permanent victory over king, 273ff.; Bill of Rights and Revolution Settlement, 274f.; duration of, 275, 499f.; and Union with Scotland, 287; and responsible government, 293ff.; corruption and manipulation of, 295f., 364; relations between the houses, 295, 298, 499; reform acts, 364, 403ff., 466ff., 488ff., 596f.; Parliament Act of 1911, 499ff.; War Cabinet, 582f., 597, 631; postwar changes, 667. See also Commons, House of; Lords, House of; Parties.
Parnell, Charles Stewart, 478ff., 483
Parr, Catherine, 188
Parties: beginnings of, 237, 266; under William III and Anne, 281, 287f.; and responsible government, 293ff.; after 1760, 316ff., 362ff., 392f.; after 1832, 407, 419, 480, 489; during and after World War I, 582, 591, 596, 601, 604, 607, 609, 618; during World War II, 630f.,

Rockingham, Charles W. Went-worth, 2d Marquess of, 317, 363

Rodney, Adm. George B., Baron, 325

Roger, Bishop of Salisbury, 57

Roger of Wendover, 96

Rollo (Hrolf), 35

Roman Britain, 1ff.

Roman Catholic Church, *see* Church

Romilly, Sir Samuel, 397

Rommel, Gen. Erwin, 637f., 643ff.

Romney, George, 329

Roosevelt, Franklin Delano, 634f., 657, 671

Rosebery, Archibald P. Primrose, 5th Earl of, 489f., 498

Roses, Wars of the, 146ff., 151

Rossetti, Dante Gabriel, 433, 504

Rothschild family, 346, 395, 524

"Rotten boroughs," *see* Electoral system

Roundheads, 238ff.

Royal Air Force, *see* Aviation

Royal assent or veto, 139f., 294, 376, 399

Royal power: in Anglo-Saxon period, 27f., 32; increased under early Norman kings, 42, 49, 53, 62; weakened by Stephen-Matilda anarchy, 62; strengthened by Henry II and Edward I, 67, 76; baronial ef-forts to curb, 53, 56, 87, 88ff., 100, 108; deposition of Rich-ard II, 139; decline under Lan-castrians, 139f.; increased un-der Yorkists and Tudors, 140, 148, 165f., 216; centralized royal governments, 173; divine right of kings, 214; opposition under early Stuarts, 214ff.; pre-rogatives, 215f., 232; struggle between king and Parliament, 212, 232ff.; execution of Charles I, 244; restoration of king with power reduced, 259; definite subordination to Parlia-ment in 1688, 273ff.; last royal veto, 294, 376, 399; influence, rather than power, henceforth, 294ff.; George III, 316ff.; Vic-toria, 412f.

Royal Society, 257

Royal warrant, 470

Rufus, *see* William II

Rump Parliament, 243ff., 248

Runnymede, 88

Rupert, Prince, 239f., 248, 291

Rush-Bagot agreement, 389

Russell, Lord John, Earl, 400, 404, 418, 421, 423, 463, 466

Russia: Chancellor at Archangel, 193; French Revolution and Napoleon, 370f., 379, 383; Congress of Vienna and Met-ternich period, 386f., 393; Balkan friction with Turkey, 394f., 421f., 474f.; Anglo-Russian relations, 471f., 549f.; expansion in Asia, 452, 523, 534, 552, 536; and alliance systems, 551, 559f.; World War I, 563f., 567ff.; Revolu-tion of 1917, 584f.; Soviet re-gime, 600, 603f., 618, 666; World War II, 621, 624, 638f., 643, 655, 659; postwar, 657, 670ff., 677, 686, 688

Ruthwell Cross, 18

Ryswick, Peace of, 279

Saar, 589, 592, 609

Sacheverell sermon, 288

Sadler, Michael, 408f.

Said, Khedive, 524

St. Albans, battle of, 148

St. Helena, 384, 439

St. John, Henry, *see* Bolingbroke

St. Laurent, Louis, 717f.

St. Lawrence Seaway, 716f.

St. Vincent, battle of, 373

Saladin tithe, 81, 105

Salamanca, battle of, 383

Salic Law, 121

Salisbury (Rhodesia), 530

Salisbury, Robert Cecil, 1st Earl of, 213f., 221

Salisbury, Robert Cecil, 3d Mar-quess of, 475f., 480f., 489, 522

Salisbury Cathedral, 95

Salisbury Oath, 46

Samuel, Sir Herbert, 607

Sanctions, 593, 618f.

Sandwich, John Montagu, 4th Earl of, 323, 325

Saratoga, battle of, 324

Saskatchewan, 539, 715, 717

Satellites, *see* Space exploration

Saxons, *see* Anglo-Saxons

Scapa Flow, 571, 587

Schism Act, 290

Science, 95f., 257, 349, 357, 434f.

"Scotch-Irish," 277. *See also* Ulster.

Scotland: in pre-Norman period, 7, 9, 21, 32, 39; early Norman period, 54, 64, 112; and Eng-lish suzerainty, 32, 66, 78, 113; Highlands and Lowlands, 112, 285f. 307f.; Edward I, Ed-ward II, Wallace, and Bruce, 112ff., 115ff.; later middle ages, 112ff., 117, 124; marriage of Margaret Tudor and James IV, 167; other Tudor contacts,

175, 188f., 198ff.; Presbyterian-ism, 180, 198, 200, 215, 234, 262, 276, 286; Mary Stuart, 188f., 196, 199f., 204, 213; per-sonal union, James VI-I, 212, 221; National Covenant, 234; Bishops' Wars, 235f.; West-minster Assembly, 239; and the Civil War, 239ff., 243; and Cromwell, 246f.; and William III, 275f.; Darien colony, 286; Act of Union, 286, 375; High-land regiments, 287; Jacobite uprisings, 292, 307

Scott, Sir Walter, 51, 286, 400

Scutage, 76, 87, 89

Sea Dogs, 201ff.

SEATO (Southeast Asia Treaty Organization), 685, 695

Sebastopol, siege of, 422

"Second British Empire," 439ff.

"Second Hundred Years' War," 277ff., 301ff.

Seddon, Richard J., 542

Sedgemoor, battle of, 270

Self-Denying Ordinance, 240

Senegal, 315

Sepoy Mutiny, 452f.

Serfs, 25, 47f., 52, 89, 128. See *also* Manorial system, Social classes.

Settlement, Act of, 275, 290

Seven Years' War, 311ff.

Seymour, Edward, Lord Beau-champ, 213

Seymour, Jane, 187f.

Seymour, Lord Thomas, of Sude-ley, 189

Seymour family, 189. *See also* Somerset.

Shaftesbury, Anthony Ashley Cooper, 1st Earl of, 263, 266, 409

Shaftesbury, Anthony Ashley Cooper, 7th Earl of, 409ff.

Shakespeare, William, 90, 209ff.

Sharpesville massacre, 712

Shaw, George Bernard, 434, 488, 506, 514, 515f.

Sheffield, 335ff.

Shelburne, William P. Fitzmaur-ice, 2d Earl of, later 1st Mar-quess of Lansdowne, 325, 362ff.

"Shell shortage" (1915), 573

Shelley, Percy Bysshe, 360, 401

Sheriff: shire reeve, 20, 29; im-portance under Normans, 49f., 58, 68, 89; power reduced, 89, 171

Sheriffs, Inquest of, 68

Ship money, 233, 237

Shipping and seafaring: pre-Nor-man, 4, 7, 20, 22; medieval,

EFGHIJKL 7069876

PRINTED IN THE UNITED STATES OF AMERICA

Picture Credits

EUROPE

55°N

50°N

45°N

40°N

35°N

20°W 15°W 10°W 5°W 0° 5°E

Atlantic Ocean

MERIDIAN OF GREENWICH

Hebrides

Orkney Islands

• Edinburgh
Glasgow

North Sea

UNITED KINGDOM

• Belfast

REPUBLIC OF IRELAND

• Dublin

• Leeds

Liverpool • Manchester
• Sheffield

Birmingham

Amsterdam
The Hague

NETHERLANDS No

Rotterdam

Essen

Antwerp **Brussels** Col
BELGIUM THE RUHR
Lille Bonn

London
Bristol
Portsmouth

LUX.

Channel
Le Havre

English

Brest

Strasbourg

Paris

Seine R.

Loire R.
Nantes

Bern
SW

F R A N C E

Geneva

Bay of Biscay

Bordeaux

Lyon Mt. Blanc
15,737 FT

Rhône R.

Turin

Bilbao

Vigo

Toulouse

Pyrenees
AND

Nice

Porto

Zaragoza

Ebro R.

Marseille

CORSICA
(FR.)

Barcelona

Madrid

S P A I N

P O R T U G A L

Lisbon
Tagus R.

SARDINIA
(ITALY)

Valencia

Seville

Balearic Islands
(SPAIN)

M e d i t e r

Málaga
Strait of Gibraltar GIBRALTAR
Tangier (BR.)

5°W

Algiers

5°E

Oran

0°

10°W